Rumi

PAST AND PRESENT,
EAST AND WEST

R u m i

PAST AND PRESENT,
EAST AND WEST

The Life, Teaching and Poetry of Jalâl al–Din Rumi

FRANKLIN D. LEWIS

ONEWORLD

OXFORD

RUMI – PAST AND PRESENT, EAST AND WEST

Oneworld Publications
(Sales and Editorial)
185 Banbury Road
Oxford OX2 7AR
England
http://www.oneworld-publications.com

Oneworld Publications
(US Marketing Office)
160 N Washington St.
4th Floor, Boston
MA 02114

ISBN 1–85168–214–7

Cover design by Design Deluxe
Typeset by LaserScript, Mitcham, UK
Printed and bound in the United Kingdom by Bell & Bain Ltd, Glasgow

Contents

PART IV RUMI AND THE MEVLEVIS IN
THE MUSLIM WORLD

PART V RUMI IN THE WEST,
RUMI AROUND THE WORLD

CONTENTS

Figures and Maps

Foreword

"Speech that rises from the soul, veils the soul." In this opening line of one of his ghazals Rumi voices the paradox which lies at the heart of his poetry: the inability of words, of language, to convey reality. Words interpose themselves between the soul and reality like the veil that conceals the beloved's face from the long-suffering lover; or (in another image from the same poem), like the shell which conceals the pith of meaning. "Split the shell, so that you may arrive at meaning's pith," counsels the poet; "cleave through the flotsam and jetsam that floats, along with the foam, on the surface of the sea, to arrive at the purity of the sea's depths." For Rumi, all of creation is a veil between the questing human being and the truth:

> This transient world is a sign of the miracle of Truth;
> but this same sign is a veil which hides the eternal Verities.

What are we to make of a poet who, while confessing to the impotence of language, and while constantly reiterating his reluctance to write poetry, is among the most prolific of the Persian poets: producing thousands of lyric ghazals, tens of thousands of narrative-didactic *masnavi* verses? The long history of discussion and scholarship on the poet – both Eastern and Western – has created many Rumis: the ecstatic mystic; the theosophist; the teacher and preacher; the Mevlevi dervish, lost in the whirling of the dance. Hagiographers (like Aflâki, for example) have told of his miraculous acts; more sober writers have endeavored to make of the ideas expressed in his poems a theosophic system.

Who was Rumi? What was Rumi? Frank Lewis's study tries to reconstruct both the man and the poet, and does both, I think, highly successfully. Rumi was, first of all, an exile from his native land of Khorasan. He had travelled much in search of learning (which was, at the time, the common practice amongst Muslim scholars), and in search of teachers. At one point, he encountered the mysterious figure of Shams-e Tabrizi. Lewis, to his great credit, does much to untangle the mystery, and the myths, that surround Rumi's relationship with this, his greatest teacher, and the name that – instead of Rumi's own, as might have been expected – informs the closing lines of many of his ghazals.

Although existence is but a fragment of Shams-e Tabrizi,
it is a fragment which veils the soul from its source
Shams-e Tabrizi, you are the sun behind the cloud of words;
when your sun shows its face, the words become effaced.

Rumi was a teacher, with many disciples. He succeeded his father Bahâ Valad as head of what later became the Mevlevi order, and founded its ritual turning dance, for which many of his ghazals were composed. He was no ascetic, renouncing the world and its trappings to devote himself to pious observance in some remote and quiet corner; on the contrary, he was a frequenter of courts, of princes and high officials, to whom he offered spiritual advice. (Moreover, as Aflâki tells it, on discovering he had been replaced as one prince's spiritual advisor, Rumi went off in a huff and predicted a dire fate for the prince in question – which, predictably, happened, although the account is, it seems, totally anachronistic).

In short, Rumi was many things – as we might expect from a real person, rather than from a hagiographical saint-cum-hero or from more recent constructions of "Rumi the mystic," "Rumi the poet," and so on. He was, for one thing, a highly learned man, whose poetry – even the lyric ghazals – is not the rapturous outpourings of the ecstatic mystic, but can be highly complex. Thus it is that, when singing of the "drunken camels" who have been so entranced by the voice of the camel-driver that they have begun dancing, he relies on his audience to make the connection between these "camels of God" – the whirling mystics – with the miraculous camel sent (so says the Koran) to the Arabian prophet Sâleh, and which was hamstrung by Sâleh's people, who could not (or refused to) recognize this divine sign of his prophetic mission. Even so (we may interpret) do many people to recognize the divine nature of the mystic's calling.

It is this complex and many-sided figure that Lewis attempts – successfully, in my view – to reconstruct in the present book. He appears to have read everything, in every relevant language, both by and about Rumi, and much related material besides (for example, the *Maqâlât* of Shams-e Tabrizi himself, which gives at least verbal shape and form to this otherwise shadowy personage). He disentangles and debunks myths, misreadings and misrepresentations; not least, he gives due voice to Rumi the poet. For this is what remains to us (for most of us, who will not dig and delve into Rumi's correspondence, or Shams's *Maqâlât*, or other of the conflicting and contradictory source material): that vast outpouring of poetry which, despite Rumi's own insistence on the impotence of language, shows his own constant engagement with it, his own attempt, if not to express, at least to point to the ineffable – to what lies, as he so often puts it, on "that side," the side which puts words into the mouth of the reed which sings its tales of separation from its source in the opening section of the Masnavi.

At a time when "Rumi" has become a growth industry (especially in the United States – a phenomenon which Lewis duly takes on board; readers may like to check out the Rumi and Rumi-related websites, CDs, videos and so on), this book is especially welcome. It will without doubt become an indispensable source both for students of Rumi (of whatever inclination) and for scholars wishing to do further research on the poet. For though words may be a veil, they are also (as Rumi knew well) signs that can point us in the right direction.

Julie Scott Meisami
University of Oxford

Acknowledgments

I would first of all like to thank my friend and mentor Professor Heshmat Moayyad of the University of Chicago, for his many years of conversation about and instruction in the ways of Persian poetry and Rumi. Not only has he read over portions of the text and helped with a number of difficult readings, saving me from many errors; his unfailing encouragement over the years has kept me going. To him this book is dedicated.

I am also grateful to Sunil Sharma, Persian bibliographer at Harvard, and Hasan Javadi of Jahan Books, for their bibliographic expertise, help in obtaining books, and comments on chapter 11. I am especially obliged to Sunil for his help in locating verses in the *Masnavi*. Devin Stewart of Emory University and Todd Lawson have read over various chapters and provided helpful suggestions and corrections. Rhett Diessner has kindly read over and commented on portions of the text, as has Gordon Newby of Emory University. I remain responsible, of course, for all errors, infelicities and malapropisms.

This work, by its nature, required access to a great number of books; most of the research was completed at the Regenstein Library at the University of Chicago and at the Woodruff and Pitt's Theological Libraries at Emory University. My thanks go to Middle East librarian Bruce Craig at Chicago and Middle East bibliographer Hikmat Faraj at Emory, as well as the interlibrary loan staff at both institutions. I am very grateful to Mrs. Marjory Luther who made a gracious gift of the Persian studies library of the late Professor K. Allin Luther to Emory University. Thanks are also due to Mikâil Bayram of the Seljuk University for sharing his thoughts on Rumi's social relations in Konya; Alan Godlas of the University of Georgia for valuable leads about the history of Sufism and the Mevlevi order in the United States; Shantanu Phukan of the University of Chicago for information on Afghan and Indian vocalists; Julij Ioanessjan of the Russian Academy of Sciences in St. Petersburg for background on Russian translations; and Geoff Lewis for newspaper articles in California. Judith Pfeiffer of the Orient Institut helped navigate the streets, bookstores and historical sites of Istanbul, as did Sara Yildiz of the University of Chicago. I am also grateful to Hayrettin Yucesoy of the University of Chicago for help in navigating Turkish names and titles.

I am also grateful to a number of people who kindly provided information and answered questions I put to them: Abdol Karim Soroush, Nader Khalili of CalEarth, Kabir Helminski of the Threshold Foundation, Mariam Baker and Jeri Anne Hampton of the Mevlevi Order of America. On the Internet, the discussions on the Tariqas lists have often provided valuable information about Sufism in America.

Versions of the poems have been read at the Persian Community Center in Atlanta, the Middle East Center at the University of Utah and the Friends of Persian Culture Conference in Chicago, Illinois, and in my classes at Emory. I'd like to thank Jaroslav Stetkevych, Robert Dankoff, John Perry, Paul Losensky and Dick Davis for their suggestions and critiques over the years as I have grappled to find a personally satisfying idiom for translating classical Persian poetry.

Finally, I am indebted to the wonderful folks at Oneworld Publications – Novin Doostdar, Juliet Mabey, Helen Coward, Victoria Warner and Rebecca Clare – who provided encouragement, graciously put up with delays and helped imagine the texture of the text. I am greatly obliged to Judith Willson, whose caring and careful attention in copy-editing the text saved me from many inconsistencies and infelicities. Thanks are also due to Mary Starkey for proofreading, and especially for creating the indispensable index. I would also like to thank Jillian Luff, the cartographer who produced the maps. The book would never have been possible without the cooperation of my lovely wife, Foruzan, who has shared my appreciation of Rumi; of my daughters, Sahar and Ava, who had to put up for three years with a distracted dad; of my father, Robert, who gave sage advice about enjoying life and keeping work and deadlines in proper perspective; and of my mother, who provided encouragement, help, and the inspiration for the search that led me to Rumi.

Notes on Transliteration

The Arabic script is used to write not only Arabic, but also Persian, Urdu and, prior to Atatürk's adoption of the Latin alphabet, Ottoman Turkish. Unfortunately (speaking now from the point of view of transliteration), these various languages do not all pronounce Arabic letters in the same way. Since Rumi was a native speaker of Persian but knew Arabic fluently and lived the greater part of his life in an area where Turkish, and to a lesser extent, Greek, were the major spoken languages, the question of how to represent names, book titles, technical terms and so forth in a study of this nature is extremely problematic. Should one write the title of a Persian work as if it were Arabic? Should one write a Turkish name as if it were Persian?

We are confronted with the dilemma of either accurately reflecting the pronunciation of each individual language, which would require a number of different systems of transliteration and perhaps even cause confusion about the identity of individuals discussed, or using one transliteration system that treats all the languages generically, but may not accurately reflect the spelling or pronunciation of a word or name in the language it comes from.

For example, we have the Persian/Arabic name transliterated as Jalâl, now written in Turkish as Celâl; or modern Turkish Çelebi, written in Arabic transliteration as Chilibî, sometimes voweled as Chalabi, but common in Persianate pronunciation and transliteration as Chelebi. In Persian one pronounces as Mohammad what is transliterated and pronounced as Muhammad in Arabic, though the same name becomes Mehmet in Turkish. Originally an Arabic word, "şulṭân" would Romanize as soltân in conformity with modern Persian transliteration systems, but since the word has been native to English-speakers for some time now, we may dispense with accent marks all together and just write "sultan."

It is virtually impossible to find a solution to this problem that will suit the dictates of logic, aesthetics and clarity for all readers. I have generally opted to transliterate names and titles from the medieval period in conformity with the phonetic values of modern Persian, using a simplified version of transliteration which employs a minimum of diacritical markings. The vowels are:

"a" as in "bat"
"â" as in "law"
"e" as in "bed"
"i" as in "machine"
"u" as in "tutu"
"o" as in "toe"
"ow" as in "glowing"
"ay" as in "pay"

Consonantal values are more or less as in English, with these clarifications:

"kh" as in Scottish "loch"
"zh" as in the second "g" of "garage"
"gh" and "q" represent sounds not found in English, a hard velarized "g" pronounced higher up in the mouth
"h" is aspirated and notably pronounced in all positions

The ʿayn (ʿ) and the hamza (ʾ) do not carry a separate phonetic value of their own, but are included to help those familiar with the Arabic script reconstruct the spelling of the original. I have not, however, added the usual diacritical marks to distinguish the various homophone letters in Persian ("z" renders four separate letters – zâl, ze, zâd, zâ; "s" renders three separate letters – sin, se and sâd; "t" renders both te and tâ; and "h" renders both he-jimi and he-havvaz). I believe this will make the text easier on the eye and will not unduly inconvenience those wishing to reconstruct the spelling in the original language.

An exemption from these rules of transliteration has been made for words accepted in English (e.g., ulama for ʿolamâ); for Turkish proper names and book titles after the conversion to the Latin alphabet in 1928; and for Arabic names and titles more generally known in a certain form (e.g., Ibn, al-Mutanabbî, etc.). These generally appear in their more familiar forms.

Also, let readers beware: names they read in works about the Islamic world may be spelled quite differently in various books, depending upon whether the author is French, English or German and whether their principal familiarity with a given historical figure comes through Arabic, Persian or Turkish sources. An example of the variety of spellings readers may encounter is given below, first as the name appears in this book, and then as it may appear in other works from other countries and other centuries:

Bahâ al-Din:	Bahâeddin, Bahâʾuʾd-Dîn, Bahâʾ-i Walad, Bahâ-e Valad
Jalâl al-Din:	Dschelaleddin, Jalâluʾd-Dîn, Jelâl al-Din, Djalâl al-Din, Celâl al-Din, Celaleddin, Geláleddin, etc.
Rumi:	Rûmî, Rúmí, al-Rûmî, Roumi
Shams al-Din:	Shamseddin, Shemsoddin, Shamsuʾd-Din, Shems
Sultan Valad:	Soltân Valad, Veled, Sultân Walad

Introduction

RUMI-MANIA

Jalâl al-Din Rumi, as the *Christian Science Monitor* recently proclaimed (cover article by Alexandra Marks, November 25, 1997), has become the best-selling poet in the United States. Audiences at poetry readings enthusiastically respond to Rumi's poems, often recited to the accompaniment of live music by Coleman Barks, who, more than any other single individual, is responsible for Rumi's current fame; his *The Illuminated Rumi* (New York: Broadway Books, 1997), a coffee-table collection of translations and inspirational illustrations, is enthusiastically recommended by the most widely read newspaper in America (Deirdre Schwiesow, *USA Today*, November 3, 1997, D8). Devotees of Sufism, adepts of New Age spirituality and those with a mystical orientation toward religion all revere Rumi as one of the world's great spiritual teachers. Beyond that, Rumi has entered American popular culture, so that along with such self-help and personal-improvement material as Stephen Covey's *Seven Habits of Highly Effective People*, spiritually driven commuters now unwind to audiobooks of Rumi's poetry as they sit in traffic jams on their way home from a hard day's work (William Davis, *Boston Globe*, March 30, 1998, C1).

On Lafayette Street in New York City, a clientele of about four hundred people a day at the Jivamukti Yoga Center, including such celebrities as Mary Stuart Masterson and Sarah Jessica Parker, do spiritual aerobics to a background beat that sometimes mixes rock music and readings of Rumi (Penelope Green, *New York Times*, March 15, 1998 Sec. 9,1). Meanwhile, Robin Becker and her dance company, inspired by the whirling dervish tradition, have performed two vignettes – "Night" for solo dancer and "Doorways" for five dancers – as part of a program called "Dances From Rumi" to favorable reviews at Playhouse 91 (Jack Anderson, *New York Times*, December 12, 1994, C18). In December 1994 Pir Publications and Sufi Books gathered Coleman Barks, Robert Bly and the dancer Zulaika with musicians from the Paul Winter Consort in Manhattan's Symphony Space for a concert/recitation to observe the 750th anniversary of Rumi's meeting with Shams. The acoustic band Three Fish, which features vocalist Robbi Rob of Tribe After Tribe, drummer Richard Stuverud and bassist

Jeff Ament of the heavy metal rock band Pearl Jam, derives its name from an allegory in Rumi's *Masnavi*. With lyrics from Rilke, Lorca and Rumi, Three Fish produced an eponymous CD in June of 1996 thematically organized around three songs taken from this Rumi tale: "The Intelligent Fish," "The Half Intelligent Fish," and "Stupidfish" (Mark Jenkins, *Washington Post*, July 14, 1996 and http://www.sonymusic.com/artists/PearlJamchords/framex.html, the Pearl Jam website, under "Other Projects").

Anthologies aimed at unchurched Westerners hungry for some form of non-institutional religion or non-traditional spirituality often include Rumi in the company of other visionaries, poets and seers. The poet David Halpern sets poems by Rumi next to those of other spiritual poets like Blake and Rilke in his anthology *Holy Fire: Nine Visionary Poets and the Quest for Enlightenment* (New York: HarperPerennial, 1994). Robert Barzan brought the case of Rumi to the attention of the gay community in an article entitled "Homoeroticism and Spirituality: Rumi and the Sufis," which, as editor, he included in *Sex and Spirit: Exploring Gay Men's Spirituality* (San Francisco: White Crane Press, 1995). Barry Walters claims in *The Advocate*, a gay liberation paper published in Los Angeles, that Islamic scholars have tried to ignore or cover up "the probable homosexual relationship" between Rumi and Shams al-Din of Tabriz ("Music Heart Beats," *The Advocate*, September 1, 1998, 54). Rumi translations also make an appearance in Sam Hamill's anthology *The Erotic Spirit: Poems of Sensuality, Love and Longing* (Boston: Shambala, 1996).

While Rumi seems slightly out of place in company with Yeats and Ginsberg, and seriously misunderstood as a poet of sexual love (whether gay or straight), it simply defies credulity to find Rumi in the realm of haute couture. But models draped in Donna Karan's new black, charcoal and platinum fall fashions actually flounced down the runway to health guru Deepak Chopra's recent musical versions of Rumi, with Madonna and Demi Moore looking on all the while (Robin Givhan, *Washington Post*, April 6, 1998, D1). It should, however, come as small surprise that the American minimalist composer and Buddhist activist Philip Glass, who has devoted previous operas to Einstein, Gandhi and the Hebrew Bible, now offers with Robert Wilson a massive multimedia piece called *Monsters of Grace* (version 1.0), complete with 3-D glasses and featuring a libretto of 114 poems of Rumi in the translations of Coleman Barks. Though the score begins with a soft solo voice singing "Don't worry about saving these songs," this mega-monster event effectively memorializes Rumi in the most modern and technological of media.

Meanwhile, in Turkey, the so-called Whirling Dervishes, descendants and disciples of the spiritual fraternity Rumi founded, billed as folk dancers since the government of Atatürk proclaimed the dervish orders illegal in 1925, attract the interest of tourists from all over the world and provide a symbolic link between modern secular Turkey and the religious heritage of its Ottoman past. In 1999 ubiquitous red banners commemorating the seventy-fifth anniversary of the founding of the Turkish Republic hung from government buildings and tourist attractions, including the front of the shrine of Rumi.

International film crews have traveled to Turkey to make documentaries about the Mevlevi ensemble of dancers and musicians for broadcast on French and British television. The ensemble itself has traveled through Europe and the United States on several tours over the last ten years, making several visits to the recording studio along the way. More recent visits include Australia in 1996, where tickets sold for between $20 and $30 to see the ceremonies of meditative turning (*samâ^c*) and/or the performance of the Turkish State Mystical Music Ensemble. In 1994, when the Mevlevi dervishes came through Atlanta, the two prominent American translators of Rumi's work, Coleman Barks and Robert Bly, turned out for the event (Helen Smith, *Atlanta Journal-Constitution*, November 6, 1994, N5).

The British actress Vanessa Redgrave, in collaboration with the Mevlevi ensemble, provided the narration for a recent film directed by Fehmi Gerceker about "the idea of acceptance, urging human beings to respect each other's faiths, orientations, and religious ideals," entitled *Tolerance: Dedicated to Mawlana Jalal al-Din* (Falls Church, VA: Landmark Films, Prima Productions, 1995). Richard Brookhiser, a senior editor of the *National Review*, an important American journal of conservative thought, visited Rumi's shrine in Konya a few years ago and, impressed with Rumi's ecumenical and understanding spirit, cautioned American politicians that it would be wrong to consider Islam as a monolithic fundamentalist danger ("Islamic Fundamentalism Revisited," *National Review* 45 [November 15, 1993]: 62–3). Indeed, any objective western reader who takes the time to compare the *Divina Commedia* with the *Masnavi*, which is about twice as long as the former, will have to acknowledge that Rumi, who wrote a half century before Dante, reflects a much more ecumenical spirit and a far broader and deeper religious sensibility.

In the nearby Islamic Republic of Iran, Rumi has reached new heights of popularity among the modern heirs of his language and culture. New commentaries, studies, and editions of his works, but especially recitations and musical performances of his poetry, have captured the imagination of intellectuals and the general public in Iran. Not just for scholars and literature-lovers, Rumi is championed by proponents of civil society, such as the Shiite philosopher Abdol Karim Soroush, as a precedent for and exemplar of a more expansive and tolerant Islam. Although Rumi societies have not yet reached the erstwhile popularity of the Omar Khayyâm clubs once found in major British and American cities, small groups of non-Muslim Americans, like "the lovers of Rumi" in Kirkland, Washington, meet every few weeks in a prayerful attitude for readings of Rumi's poems followed by dervish dancing to Turkish music, much to the surprise of Iranians in America (^{c}Abd al-Hosayn Âzarang, "Va bâz hamchonân shab-e Rumi," *Kelk* 89–93 [1997]: 629–35). Iranians who visit Rumi's shrine in Konya are also surprised and amused by the Turks and Europeans who come there on pilgrimage (Mehdi Nafisi, "Dar jostoju-ye jâ-ye pâ-ye Mowlânâ dar Qonyâ," *Iran Nameh* 15, 4 [Fall 1997]: 647–8).

Memorialized by his poems, Rumi has remained very much alive for over seven hundred years in the hearts of readers of Persian from Bosnia to India. Soon after his death in 1273, a legendary haze obscured the actual circumstances of his life, however, and the hagiographical tradition transformed Rumi from a remarkable man into a mythical, even archetypal figure. Although Iranian, Turkish and European scholars have attempted over the last half century to recover a more historically factual account of Rumi the man, no one has as yet undertaken a rigorous investigation of all the published information available on Rumi. We therefore remain some way off from reconstructing an exhaustive biography detailing all that can be known about him.

My personal encounter with Rumi began as a teenager in southern California in the mid-1970s, where I first learned of him through devotional and religious texts, especially the *Seven Valleys* by Bahá'u'lláh (1817–92), the founder of the Bahá'í Faith, who quotes many lines from Rumi in his own writings. In college I read the scholarly works of Nicholson, Browne and Arberry, and after making enough progress in Persian, also became acquainted with Rumi's poems in the original. A cassette recording of the modern Persian poet Ahmad Shâmlu reciting Rumi's poems has been a constant companion of mine since the early 1980s. I watched with delight as Rumi won a growing following in North America. I watch now with concern as pop culture dilutes and distorts his message, with a foreboding sense that modern secular culture will inevitably reduce the sacral into the banal through its relentless commercialism and consumerism. Meanwhile, I continue to read and reread Rumi with a deepening appreciation of his insight, which is continually enhanced by the efforts of scholars to understand and explain him.

The proliferation in English of works about Rumi and translations of his poems and sermons over the past several decades has presented the interested reader browsing shelves of libraries, bookstores and web sites with a bewildering array of materials – some popular, some devotional and some scholarly. Since much of this literature approaches Rumi from a limited or particular perspective, it is easy to come away with an incomplete or even distorted picture of Rumi, the teacher, the preacher, the poet, the humanist, the pious Muslim and mystic visionary. In his magnum opus, "The Spiritual Couplets," or *Masnavi-ye ma'navi*, Rumi retells a tale told by an earlier Persian mystic poet, Sanâ'i (d. 1131), whose "Garden of Truth," the *Hadiqat al-haqiqat* (69–70), provided a model for Rumi's own *Masnavi*. This little parable, which originated in Buddhist scripture[1] and retains its association with India in the version of Rumi, illustrates the woolly and mammoth nature of truth, humorously reminding us that no one person from his or her necessarily limited human perspective can wholly comprehend the nature of reality (M3:1259–78):

> In a darkened room stands an elephant
> brought by Hindus promoting spectacle
> throngs enter the pitch black to see it
> but eye-blind, they grope with palms to sense it
>> Each in turn describes aloud
>> what he feels he sees, as follows:
> (Touching the trunk)　It's shaped like a drainpipe
> (Reaching the ear)　It appears to be a fan
> (Feeling the leg)　An elephant's a pillar
> (Petting the back)　Feels I'm touching a plank!
>> And so it goes: each knows the beast
>> by the part where he feels it
> Their words seem to outward eye in discord
> one calling P what the other called Q
> But give them a candle to hold up to it
>> and discord departs from what they intuit!

ROOM ON THE SHELF FOR ANOTHER RUMI?

The book you now have in your hands attempts to hold up a candle to the growing body of publications on Rumi, casting some light on the historical Rumi, the myths and traditions that developed around him, the history of his reception in the Islamic world and in the West, and especially the phenomenon of his recent popularity. It hopes to give a bird's-eye view of the elephant, providing a primer to a serious contemplation of Rumi's life and writings, including a summary of the current state of knowledge about Rumi, a bibliographical guide to works about him and translations of his writings, a historical overview of his life and influence, and suggestions for future avenues of research and investigation. As such, *Rumi – Past and Present, East and West* should prove a helpful companion to scholars and serious students of Rumi, as well as to lovers of his poetry, those inspired by Rumi's spiritual vision, or those simply curious about what all the ruckus over Rumi is about. My hope is that these pages will guide readers working or wading through either the original Persian or the available translations of Rumi's work, and enhance their understanding of his message, his appeal and his relevance for Western culture.

This book also presents a great deal of new information about Rumi's life and circle, based on a careful and critical evaluation of the original Persian sources. The general outline of Rumi's life has been recounted in many books, but rarely with any detail to the historical and social context. Many books about Rumi have uncritically accepted or even deliberately perpetuated a legendary image of Rumi. I have tried to rectify this by providing direct access to the pivotal sources in translation, thus making the reader privy to the cruxes around which debates and controversies over the life of Rumi revolve.

Medieval works recounting the lives of saints must be used judiciously, for the hagiographical tradition does not concern itself with historical accuracy and biographical facts. *Rumi – Past and Present, East and West* makes a concerted effort to distinguish the factually accurate and plausible from the legendary and mythical aspects in the biographical tradition of Rumi, so that we may get a closer glimpse of the historical personage of Rumi. Rumi himself gives us precious little in the way of autobiography. The sources which give us the bulk of our information about the life of Rumi were written down, like the Gospels, some time after his death and they take as their subject, not the mundane historical details of his life, but the panorama of his spiritual influence. Throughout the chapters of part I (Rumi's Fathers in Spirit) and part II (Rumi's Children and Brethren in Spirit), we will evaluate the nature and accuracy of our three principal sources, whose authors wrote between twenty and seventy-five years after Rumi's death, compare and contrast their accounts, and lay out their discrepancies. Readers can therefore make their own judgments, though I will offer a number of new solutions and conclusions about how to evaluate and understand the mass of hagiographical detail.

Perhaps more importantly, *Rumi – Past and Present, East and West* provides a wealth of contextual detail about the intellectual, religious and mystical circle in which Rumi grew up, studied and matured (part I). Though the name of Shams al-Din of Tabriz is well known to us as the source of Rumi's inspiration, precious little of substance has been written about the life and writings of Shams in English or any other Western language. Most of what we read about Shams derives from the hagiographical sources and has little if any basis in fact. Yet we can learn a good deal about Shams through his own writings and sayings, and through Shams, we learn much more about Rumi. I therefore draw heavily upon the writings of Shams and make the latest Persian scholarship about him available (chapter 4).

Likewise, Rumi's father, Bahâ al-Din, and Rumi's mentor, Borhân al-Din, both exercised a major influence over Rumi's life and thought. Here, for the first time in English, the lives and works of these teachers and companions are discussed at length, reconstructing the specifically Islamic context of religious law, spiritual discipline, and metaphysical yearning, as well as the system of patronage in which Rumi functioned and flourished. A translation of one of Rumi's sermons also appears here in English for the first time (chapters 1 through 3). With this understanding of the intellectual and spiritual influences that shaped Rumi's thought, we can then turn our attention to his later life and writings (chapters 5 and 7). Our insight into his poetry and his devotional life then becomes much keener and the essence of what he taught and stood for comes into sharper relief (chapter 9).

The reader will also learn in these pages about how Rumi has been received by later readers in both the East and the West (parts IV and V). Chapter 6 describes the hagiographical tradition that grew up around Rumi's memory and chapter 10 provides the longest and most detailed account available in English of the history of the Mevlevi order, the spiritual fraternity founded in Konya by Rumi's son, Sultan Valad, and now operating in America. Rumi has had a greater impact on Persian, Turkish and Urdu literature than perhaps any other single author, and commentaries on his thought and theosophy have been written by Muslim thinkers from Bosnia to Bengal. An overview of his influence and reception in the Muslim world is therefore given in chapter 11. Readers in the West began to discover Rumi about two hundred years ago; he not only left his impression on nineteenth-century metaphysical thought in the West, influencing a number of the pioneers of the study of comparative religion, but more recently he has become an integral part of the spiritual beliefs and practices of many Americans and Britons.

Although Rumi's influence and popularity in the Occident will never rival his importance in the Middle East and India, he has nevertheless touched the lives of authors and thinkers from Hans Christian Andersen to Hegel and of Eastern gurus transplanted to the West, from Gurdjieff to Meher Baba. A history of his reception in the West is sketched out in chapter 12. Not surprisingly, academic interest in Rumi has steadily intensified in all corners of the globe; several professors and scholars have devoted much of their careers to the study of Rumi (chapter 13). Of course, a legion of translators from Rückert to Bly to Barks, and a host of others in between, have tackled the poems of Rumi. Chapter 14 details the translation history of Rumi into European languages and analyzes the strengths and weaknesses of the English translations currently available. In the last few decades Rumi has jumped off the page and into multimedia formats, inspiring musicians, choreographers, film-makers, video artists and others, even establishing a presence in cyberspace (chapter 15), making Rumi fun and sometimes funny. The discussion and evaluation of this wide variety of presentations of Rumi will, I hope, prove a helpful guide to both beginning and advanced readers of Rumi.

THE POEMS

Scattered throughout the text of this book, I have quoted lines and even entire poems where relevant to the narrative. The quality of his poems is the reason most of us are interested in Rumi in the first place, so rather than providing prose paraphrases or straightforward explications of the meaning, I have tried everywhere to translate Rumi's poetry as poetry, in a modern poetic idiom. Likewise, I have also translated extended passages from the verse of Sultan Valad, Sanâ°i and others, where relevant to the discussion. I have tried to render those poems consisting primarily of narrative couplets (designated by the generic Persian term *masnavi*) into blank verse for the most part. However, I felt the more lyrical poems (primarily ghazals) generally better suited to free verse and non-traditional structures and patterns.

Most contemporary English "translators" of Rumi work from scholarly English or Turkish translations, and not directly from the original words of Rumi, which are in Persian. Many of these "translators," for better or for worse, have taken liberties with the text of Rumi's poems. Those in the West who take spiritual inspiration from Rumi likewise tend to wrench him from his Islamic context; their representation of his teachings consequently appears blurred or blanched. Therefore, chapter 8, after describing the main features of Persian prosody, offers a selection of fifty new translations, done directly from the Persian with an eye toward replicating something of their poetic qualities, while at the same time accurately relaying the original content. I hope that some of these translations will suit the taste of some readers and find their place among the many other versions already available in English.

HOW TO USE THIS BOOK

This book was conceived as a narrative, but the various sections can be read independently, as some readers may find it more useful as a reference work. Specific topics of interest can be found in the index, and the names of historical figures, authors, translators or scholars discussed at length in the body of the text are printed in boldface on their first occurrence for ease of reference. The sources of information are clearly and copiously spelled out for those wishing to follow up on various points. Most of the citations are given in abbreviated form in parentheses in the body of the text so that readers will not need to refer constantly to endnotes. These are keyed to a table of abbreviations which give the full citations for each text. Because of the extensive range of sources utilized, and the fact that much of the narrative of the book is devoted to a detailed description of the various books available on Rumi, a separate bibliography has not been provided. A companion website to the book, with images and links to other Rumi-related sites (see chapter 15) can be accessed at www.oneworld-publications.com/Rumi.

This is not the final and definitive biography of Rumi, but I have tried to map the terrain that such a book should cover. Likewise, it is not an exhaustive study of all that has been said about Rumi and all that he has meant to different people in different ages, but it does chart in some depth the reception history of his poetry and ideas, both in the Muslim world and in the West, tracing Rumi's impact on literature, music, the arts and contemporary spirituality. If nothing else, the sections on scholarship and translation should help the reader situate her favorite English renditions of Rumi among all the other available versions and discover their relative strengths and weaknesses.

Rumi – Past and Present, East and West is intended, then, as a kind of Rumi bible, a manual for anyone interested in the life, poetry, teachings and influence of Jalâl al-Din Rumi, who has been called the greatest mystic poet of mankind. The whirling dervishes plant one foot on the floor with their toes fixed around a wooden peg and turn in Rumi's memory. In like manner, I hope this book will help ground all the lovers of Rumi as they circle, moth-like, around the flame of his works.

A RUMI BACKGROUND

A hagiographical tradition grew up around Rumi rather quickly after his death. The devotion and veneration of these hagiographers (Sultan Valad, Sepahsâlâr and Aflâki – about whom much will be said later) for Rumi led them to write about him in a way that obscures our view of the historical person. Despite several centuries of celebrating Rumi's memory, only during the last half century have scholars begun to penetrate to the man behind the legend. But even though we may reject the accounts of miracles supposedly performed by Rumi, no academic enterprise will ever be able to dull the wonder we feel when reading his poetry or to unravel the essential mystery at the core of his life. How is it that a Persian boy born almost eight hundred years ago in Khorasan, the northeastern province of greater Iran, in a region that we identify today as Central Asia, but was considered in those days as part of the greater Persian cultural sphere, wound up in central Anatolia on the receding edge of the Byzantine cultural sphere, in what is now Turkey, some 1,500 miles to the west? How is it that after training as a Muslim preacher and jurist, Rumi developed into an ecumenical teacher of poetic bent, now recognized as one of the most profound mystical teachers and poets in human history, and revered as a saint by people of many faiths, such that Muslims and Westerners alike make pilgrimage to his resting place in Konya, Turkey?

RUMI AS NAME

The full complement of names and titles pertaining to Mowlânâ Khwodâ-vandgâr Jalâl al-Din Mohammad b. Mohammad al-Balkhi al-Rumi would require a small caravan to carry it. Rumi, as he is known in the West, is a toponym and refers to the fact that he lived in Anatolia, what is now Turkey, but was then considered, from the Islamic point of view, Rome. The Anatolian peninsula, which had belonged to the Byzantine, or eastern Roman empire, had only relatively recently been conquered by Muslims and even when it came to be controlled by Turkish Muslim rulers, it was still known to Arabs, Persians and Turks as the geographical area of *Rum*. As such, there are a number of historical personages born in or associated with Anatolia known as Rumi, literally "from Rome." In Muslim countries, therefore, Jalâl al-Din is not generally known as "Rumi."

His given name at birth was Mohammad, like his father and, of course, like the Prophet of Islam. From an early age, however, his father apparently called him Jalâl al-Din, a title meaning "The Splendor of the Faith." Such titles were common for religious scholars, men of letters and politicians in the medieval Islamic world, and Rumi's was rather similar in meaning to his father's title, Bahâ al-Din, "The Glory of the Faith." Many of Rumi's Persian-speaking disciples called him *khwodâvandgar*, meaning "lord" or "master." However, the earliest Persian sources, such as Sultan Valad's *Ebtedâ nâme* (*Valad nâme*), Sepahsâlar and Aflâki, usually refer to Rumi by the Arabic title Mowlânâ, "Our Master," which was his father's title before him. Two early non-Mevlevi sources, Semnâni's *Resâle-ye eqbâlie* and Mostowfi's *Târikh-e gozide* both refer to him as Our Master of Rum (*Mowlânâ Rumi*, ME 1:xiv). Rumi himself appears to allude to this title (D 1493) and it therefore must have already gained currency during his lifetime. In later Persian sources, we find a variation on this title: Mowlavi, "My Master," first attested in the poetry of Qâsem-e Anvâr, who died in 1434, or the work of Anvâr's contemporary, Kamâl al-Din Hosayn-e Khwârazmi (Mei 423 n. 2).

Because *Mowlavi* (Indo-Pakistani "Maulvi") and *Mowlânâ* are applied as honorific titles to refer to literally dozens of other Islamic figures, particularly in the subcontinent, encyclopedia entries and the indexes of Persian books will sometimes refer to the subject of our book as Mowlavi, Jalâl al-Din al-Balkhi, with Balkhi specifying the family's origins in Balkh (situated in what is now Afghanistan), though as we shall see, Rumi probably did not come from Balkh itself, but from a smaller town in what is now Tajikistan. But our Rumi is the master par excellence, and Mowlânâ or Mowlavi serve to identify him immediately for most Persians, who do not perceive Mowlavi or Mowlânâ as Arabic titles, but as the pen name of the poet. We are told that the title Mowlânâ had already taken on the quality of a proper name, meaning Rumi to the exclusion of other masters within a few generations of his death (Af 597). In Turkey, he is known by the Turkish pronunciation of this title: Mevlânâ. In the West, of course, he is known primarily as Jalâl al-Din Rumi.

How did Rumi introduce himself? In the prose preface to the *Masnavi*, he writes: "This meek servant, dependent on the mercy of the Almighty God, Mohammad, the son of Mohammad, the son of al-Hosayn al-Balkhi."

RUMI AS MUSLIM

It will simply not do to extract quotations out of context and present Rumi as a prophet of the presumptions of an unchurched and syncretic spirituality. While Rumi does indeed demonstrate a tolerant and inclusive understanding of religion, he also, we must remember, trained as a preacher, like his father before him, and as a scholar of Islamic law. Rumi did not come to his theology of tolerance and inclusive spirituality by turning away from traditional Islam or organized religion, but through an immersion in it; his spiritual yearning stemmed from a radical desire to follow the example of the Prophet Mohammad and actualize his potential as a perfect Muslim.

Islam itself was an ecumenical religion, teaching that Mohammad, Jesus, Moses, Abraham and the lesser prophets of the Hebrew Bible were all sent by the one true God as successive messengers to mankind. God sent Mohammad as a messenger (*rasul*) to the Arab peoples, just as Sâleh and Hud had been sent before him, but the message, the Koran, had a wider relevance for the whole world. The voice of God in the Koran speaks of having revealed or sent down (*nazzalnâ*) to Mohammad from the Mother Book (*Omm al-ketâb*) a tablet preserved (*lowh mahfuz*) in the realm of God. Throughout history, God has sent down successive chapters of this pre-eternal book to mankind through various men – such as Jesus, Moses and Abraham – chosen to be His prophets (*nabi*) or messengers. The Koran brought by Mohammad was the most recent reading from the divine scriptures, the heavenly prototype of God's message to man. Indeed, the Arabic word *qurʾân*, from which the English word "Koran" derives, means "recitation," for it was that portion of the heavenly scriptures which God revealed to Mohammad through the angel Gabriel and entrusted him to recite to his fellow man.

Orthodox Muslim theology views Mohammad as a human being, and not as the son of God or some other kind of divinity whose essential nature is distinct from ordinary mortals. Nevertheless, the fact that God singled him out and selected him from among all other men (one of Mohammad's epithets is Mostafâ, the Chosen One) to bear the revelation of the Koran, testifies to God's special favor toward Mohammad and Mohammad's closeness to God. As such, Mohammad's morality, his actions and his pronouncements all point out the path, or Sunna, to piety. By the third and fourth centuries after the advent of the Prophet Mohammad, a highly elaborate system of law and theology had been worked out on the basis of the Koran and the body of traditions, or Hadith, about how the Prophet acted and what he said. Discussions about the law (*feqh*) and the theory of law (*osul al-feqh*), as well as the theosophy and praxis of the mystical life, were carried on mostly in Arabic, though Persian had increasingly become a medium for such discussions from the twelfth century of our era onward.

To understand Rumi one must obviously understand something of the beliefs and assumptions he held as a Muslim. Rumi's beliefs derived from the Koran, the Hadith, Islamic theology and the works of Sunni mystics like Sanâʾi, ʿAttâr and his own father, Bahâ al-Din Valad. A preacher by profession, Bahâ al-Din chose to settle down in Konya in part because a good deal of the nearby populace was either not yet fully committed to or educated in Islamic doctrines and/or was not observing Islamic laws, and in part because he had been unsuccessful in securing a professorship of law elsewhere. Anatolia was a frontier area only recently Islamicized. The populace of Asia Minor had been mostly Greek for centuries, but beginning in the late eleventh century, it was conquered and populated by Turkmen tribesmen and urbanized Turkish Muslims. It still needed to be conquered by the civilizing forces of religion and the Persian culture that dominated the courts of the Turkish Seljuk governors and sultans. Bahâ al-Din hoped he, or his son Jalâl al-Din Rumi, could reach these people and teach them the rites, beliefs and theology of Islam.

As a Muslim, Rumi acknowledged Mohammad's prophethood and professed himself submissive to God. Rumi himself states in one of his letters (Mak 227) what should be obvious to any careful reader of his poems: he performed the five obligatory prayers that constitute one of the central tenets and requirements of an observant Muslim. Other sources indicate that Rumi performed the pilgrimage to Mecca with his father and not only observed the obligatory period of fasting during the month of Ramadan, but also pursued ascetic exercises and voluntary fasting at other times of the year, as well. We also know from our sources and from Rumi's own letters that he acted charitably with his disciples and their dependents, helping to distribute alms and needed assistance. Rumi thus conscientiously upheld the five principal "pillars" of Islam and encouraged others to do so, both in word and deed. However, Rumi held the spirit behind the observance of these laws of Islam far dearer than the outward performance of any rite.

RUMI AS SUNNI

Though there were Shiite communities scattered throughout Iran, Iranians were predominantly Sunni in the time of Rumi. Shiism was more popular among Iraqis near the shrines of Imam ʿAli and Imam Hosayn, and among Egyptians, where the Fatimid dynasty had maintained Ismaili Shiism as the state religion until its collapse a generation or so before Rumi's birth. The intersection of Shiism and Sufism in Azerbayjan, in the northwest of Iran, would eventually lead to the establishment of the Safavid order, which imposed Shiism as the state religion of Iran in the sixteenth century. But prior to this, the Shiites had left their mark on Iranian politics primarily through the terrorism of an Ismaili splinter group, the Assassins, who had attacked the heads of state of the Sunni Seljuk government during the eleventh and twelfth centuries, emerging from their mountain fortresses for occasional sorties against towns. The Ismailis were therefore greatly feared and despised, and the majority Sunni population in Iran commonly described them as infidels (*molhed*).

Because the Mevlevi order in later centuries has accepted many Shiite influences, some Shiites have attempted to claim Rumi as a sympathizer. Though Rumi's heart was generous and his mind quite open when it came to differences of creed, we should not be deceived by his tolerance into imagining that all beliefs were equal to him. In one passage of the *Masnavi* (M6:777–805), Rumi expresses his impatience with the Shiites of Aleppo and their mourning rituals during Ashura for Hosayn, the grandson of the Prophet Mohammad who was killed at the Battle of Karbalâ in 680. These may have been the only Shiites

Rumi had the opportunity to see practicing their creed in public, and he upbraids them through his poetic persona, incredulous that people could put on such a display of lamentation for someone who had been dead almost six hundred years. He tells the Shiites to mourn instead for the corruption of their beliefs (M6:802a): "Loudly lament over your own ruined heart and creed!"

It is true that Rumi, like most Sufis, holds a special place in his heart for ʿAli, above and beyond the other so-called "rightly guided" caliphs, the reason being that many Sufi orders consider ʿAli the first recipient of the Prophet Mohammad's esoteric knowledge. In addition, ʿAli's intense moral concerns make him a more likely subject of devotional attention among ethically minded Sunnis and Sufis, than say the third caliph, ʿOsmân (ʿUthmân). Rumi refers to ʿAli as the pride of every prophet and every saint (M1:3723).

Note, however, that when Rumi gives a historical list of the spiritual *axis mundi*s, the godly men by whom the spiritual world was sustained, he does not noticeably place ʿAli above ʿOsmân or Bâyazid, Maʿruf-e Karkhi or Ebrâhim b. Adham (M2:922–31). Just as Moses was in need of the guidance of Khezr (about whom, see below), so ʿAli must not rely upon his bravery, but should seek out the shade of the wise sage (ʿâqel) whose spirit circles over the primordial mountain of Qâf like the mythical bird of divinity, the Simorgh. Only through such submission to the spiritual guidance of the *pir* (wise elder) will ʿAli, and all other Muslims, find spiritual salvation. Though this *pir* may do incomprehensible things, just as Khezr did with Moses, he is the Hand of God (M1:2959–80). In the following lines, Rumi explicitly denies that the spiritual universe revolves exclusively about the descendants of ʿAli. Rather, it revolves around the spiritual *axis mundi*, that saint (*vali*) who, though concealed from the eyes of most men, guides the people in every age, and assumes the role that Shiites assign to the Hidden Imam or the Mahdi (M2:815–19):

> So, in every age, a saint arises –
> testing continues till the Resurrection
> All those of goodly character are saved
> all those who have a heart like glass will break
> The "living established Imam" is that saint,
>   whether descended from ʿOmar or ʿAli.
> He, O seeker, is the Mahdi and the Guide
> Whether hid or seated right before you.
> He is like light and wisdom is his Gabriel.

The followers of the Prophet must accept the truth of the message without giving it an esoteric interpretation (*taʾvil*), as the Shiites do with some Hadith or with some verses of the Koran, in Rumi's view (M1:3741–2). It seems to me that Rumi considered each of the first four so-called "rightly guided" caliphs as the spiritual axis of the age. Rumi tells many positive stories about Abu Bakr and ʿOmar (ʿUmar) in the *Masnavi*, as well as one very long passage in which

Mu'âwiya (the Syrian governor who opposed 'Ali by force of arms and usurped the caliphate from him, thus winning the eternal enmity of Shiites), whose name is followed by the honorific "may God be pleased with him," features as a spiritual hero in combating the temptations of Iblis, or Satan (M2:2603–740). As Rumi himself points out, you would never talk like this if you were a Shiite (M3:3201):

> When will a Shiite let you talk of 'Omar?
> What good is playing music for the deaf?

RUMI AS HANAFI

Academic institutions in the medieval Islamic world focused primarily on the sciences of religion, as in medieval Christendom. Though Islam lacks a precise parallel to the institution of the clergy in Christendom, it was to the class of men considered scholars of religion and theology, the ulama ('olamâ), literally the men of knowledge or science, that the populace generally looked for instruction in matters of law, ritual and belief. To be recognized as one of the ulama, one had to have knowledge of Arabic grammar, Koran, Hadith and a variety of other disciplines. The pride of place among the religious sciences belonged to the study of law, feqh, which elucidated the Shari'a, the prescriptions for proper and divinely sanctioned behavior. Islamic law did not encompass political matters per se, but it addressed a wider range of questions than Christian canon law, including not only prescriptions about matters of ritual and worship, but also contracts (including marriage, which Islamic law views as a contract rather than a sacrament) and inheritance. Knowledge of the basic laws of fasting, prayer, alms and pilgrimage was incumbent upon every believing Muslim, as well as the laws pertaining to their particular profession. Abu Hanifa describes feqh as an individual's "knowledge of his rights and duties" (Zar 24). As Abu Hanifa's student al-Shaybâni put it, knowledge of feqh "is the best guide to piety and fear of God." It protected the believers from tribulation, such that a pious man versed in feqh was able to combat Satan with a thousand times the strength of an ordinary believer (Zar 21–2).

By the eleventh century, legal and ritual practice within Sunni Islam congealed around four canonically recognized schools, or mazhabs: Hanafi, Mâleki, Shâfe'i and Hanbali. In Rumi's time, Iranian Sunnis mostly followed either the Hanafi or the Shâfe'i school. Though both were considered canonical rites, in practice, the two creeds were often at odds on the local level. The rationalist theology of the Mutazilites (Mu'tazilî), with its affinity for Greek logic and philosophy, was in decline and Asharite (Ash'arî) scholasticism, which the Shâfe'ite school favored, was officially sanctioned by the Nezâmiye colleges. The Hanafis' legal principles were more liberal than those of the other schools. In addition to Koran and Hadith, Hanafi teachings allowed for considered opinion (*ra²y*) and juridical preference (*estehsân*) to serve as a basis in Islamic legal rulings. Hanafi judges also frequently took the common law praxis (*ʿorf*) of the areas conquered by Islam into consideration, whereas the other schools often did not, at least in theory, recognize these as legitimate sources of authority. The thrust of the teachings of Mohammad al-Shâfeʿi (d. 820) was to base legal principles and decisions on traditions that reflect the praxis of the Prophet, and to eliminate human reasoning as much as possible, though not to the radical extent on which the fourth canonical school, the Hanbali, insisted.

The teachings of **Abu Hanifa** (d. 767), the eponymous founder of the Hanafi school in Kufa in Iraq, were presented in the works of his pupils Abu Yusof (d. 795) and Mohammad al-Shaybâni (fl. c. 800). Though considered a single school, the Hanafi teachings represent diverse influences and preserve internal differences of opinion much more than the other three schools, which reflect the conscious efforts of a specific founding authority at codification and consistency. Favored by the early Abbasid caliphs (most judges appointed by the Abbasids were Hanafis, including, for example, the famous Hanafi theorist al-Khassâf [d. 874] at the court of the caliph al-Mohtadi), the Hanafi school spread to Khorasan (where special laws of irrigation were developed), Transoxania and into Turkish Central Asia. As a result, it became the favored school of the Seljuk rulers, who carried the Hanafi doctrines into Anatolia as that area was conquered.

The Hanafi school continued to take shape throughout the tenth century with the compilation of a number of summaries and handbooks of its teachings. In the work of Shams al-Aʾemma al-Sarakhsi (d. c. 1090), who wrote a systematic book on the application of Islamic law and another book on the theoretical principles of jurisprudence, Hanafi teachings assumed a more cogent, uniform, and therefore somewhat more rigid character, a tendency which continued in the work of al-Kâsâni (d. 1191), writing a generation before the birth of Rumi. However, the Hanafi school was still producing important new theoretical works during the lifetime of Bahâ al-Din, such as the "Guide to the Branches of Feqh," *al-Hedâyat fi foruʿ al-feqh*, by ʿAli b. Abu Bakr al-Marghinâni (d. 1196), about which commentaries continued to be written through the sixteenth century. Likewise at this time, the Hanafi ulama were compiling collections of fatwas, legal briefs or responsa about specific questions, by famous Hanafi authorities like Borhân al-Din b. Mâza (d. c. 1174) and Serâj al-Din Sajâvandi.

Rumi's thinking, especially his attitude toward logic and reason, would have been strongly shaped by the teachings of another Hanafi jurist and theologian, **al-Mâtoridi**, who lived in the area of Samarqand. Mâtoridi, who died sometime in the 940s, wrote a Koran commentary, a work on theology and several other works, many of which have been lost, including refutations of the teachings of the Ismailis, the Twelver Shiites and the Mutazilites. Mâtoridi elaborated a

Hanafi theology opposed to the radical traditionalism reflected in the scholastic theology of the Asharites, whose views the Shâfeᶜite school by and large adopted. At the same time, Mâtoridi rejected many of the Mutazilite doctrines, but retained a greater respect for the faculty of reason than did the Asharites, acknowledging that man could come to know God through reason without recourse to divine revelation. Likewise, his views on the question of predestination versus free will moderated between the extremes of the Asharite and Mutazilite views.

Mâtoridi's views were especially influential in the eastern Islamic world, specifically in Transoxania, the area where Rumi was born. The Seljuks promoted Mâtoridi's doctrines and even ordered that al-Ashᶜari be cursed from the pulpits in the mid-eleventh century, a fact which explains the animosity and occasional violence between the Shâfeᶜi and Hanafi schools. By the mid-twelfth century, the Hanafis in Syria and Damascus were teaching this eastern doctrine, so that in Rumi's lifetime the Mâtoridi doctrine of his homeland prevailed even in Anatolia.

Another influence on some Hanafis in Khorasan were the Karramites (Karrâmi), often treated as a separate sect of Islam. Relatively little is known about the Karramite doctrines, though the movement seems to have appealed to a number of mystically minded people. Whether or not Bahâ al-Din was attracted to the Karramites, his strong mystical preoccupations may have left him somewhat outside the inner circle of Hanafi theologians and legal theorists. This, or perhaps political frictions with the Khwârazmshâh, may in part account for his relative obscurity and his failure to secure a legal professorship in Khorasan (see chapter 1).[2]

Despite the fact that Sufism and mysticism permeated Persian and Turkish religious culture after the fourteenth and fifteenth centuries, the Hanafis, along with other schools of Islamic law, continued to produce compendiums of law and theoretical works, through which they exercised an important and sometimes stifling influence over religious praxis in cities and towns throughout the Islamic world. The rigidity of thought and spirituality often reflected in the concerns and works of Islamic law and its practitioners is precisely the sort of religiosity that Rumi often rejects in his poetry.

The Study of the Law

Classes on the religious sciences began originally as regularized gatherings (*majles, halqe*) at a mosque around a particular learned speaker. This speaker might preach proper Islamic behavior and ethics, interpret the Koran, or relate traditions about the Prophet. Eventually, during the Seljuk period, the transmission of Islamic law (*feqh*) became semi-professionalized in the *madrase* system, though religious scholars might still emerge from the milieu of the mosque or the Sufi lodge. The *madrase* was a private sectarian institution, usually teaching one particular school of law – mostly either Hanafi or Shâfeᶜi in the case of eastern Iran – with different legal texts for each school. Following the example of the Seljuk vizier Nezâm al-Molk (d. 1092), after whom the exemplary Nezâmiye college in Baghdad was named, private citizens wishing to do a pious deed – in this case, the furtherance of religious knowledge – would establish a college of law by legal endowment (*vaqf*), often in a bequest, with a charter stipulating the purposes of the college. By the end of the reign of Saladin (Salâh al-Din), who encouraged the establishment of *madrases* in Syria and Egypt, the institution had become firmly entrenched in the Levant.

The *madrase* building typically included a lecture hall and small apartments for students, usually around twenty students per school, though the number was less in the colleges of Anatolia. It also provided a stipend for the students and a salary for the professor (*modarres*), there being usually one professor per college, except in the very large *madrases* of major cultural centers such as Baghdad and Damascus, where some schools taught all four schools of law with a different professor for each. The optimal ratio of students per professor appears to have numbered around twenty, and the students would typically pursue an initial four-year curriculum of study, though those wishing to obtain a professoriate of their own would often study for a decade or more with one or various professors. The favorite student at the beginning level might be made a teacher's aid (*mofid*), though it does not appear to have been a paid position. The endowment would usually include provision for a drill assistant, or repetitor (*moᶜid*). Although writing was considered more accurate than memory (Zar 62), medieval Islamic culture thrived on oral transmission of knowledge. Study of a text consisted in large part in memorizing it – students were recommended to memorize at least one law book in its entirety (Zar 54). One Hanafi student manual recommends repeating yesterday's lesson five times, the lesson of the preceding day four times, the lesson of the day prior to that thrice, and so on, all of them aloud (Zar 53–4). Advanced students who knew a text or a given professor's lectures by heart could take on the role of *moᶜid*, a paid position, and help new students memorize their lessons.

After completing his studies, the successful student, now known as a *faqih*, often translated as jurisconsult, would defend his knowledge in an examination (*monâzere*) and then obtain a document of permission (*ejâze*) to teach from his professor. Recognized henceforth as a legal scholar, the *faqih* would typically attempt to secure his own position as a professor of law, *modarres*, in a *madrase*. Other functions associated with the *madrase* and often funded by pious endowments included preachers, a Koran reciter (*qâriᵓ*), a librarian, occasionally a professor of Hadith (*mohaddes*, though this position tended to be associated with another institution, the Dâr al-Hadith), a muezzin to call to prayer (though this is more properly associated with a mosque), and a number of janitorial positions, as well as a director to oversee the finances and approve appointments.[3]

The anonymous author of "The Acts of **Owhad al-Din Kermâni**" (*Mânâqeb-e Owhad al-Din Kermâni*) gives us further details about the social and scholastic hierarchy of the medieval *madrase*. Owhad al-Din (c. 1164– c. 1238), a famous Sufi and a contemporary of Rumi's father, Bahâ al-Din Valad, left home at the age of sixteen, fearful for his life as a result of the conquest of his hometown, Kerman, and journeyed alone and on foot to Baghdad. He had no trade or skill and was not able to perform the hard labor of construction (*mashshâqi*),[4] but he had gone to primary school and acquired a basic education (*siâh o sepidi âmukhte-am*). He determined to enter a *madrase*, where he could be a student (*tâleb-e ʿelm*) and learn the sciences (*taʿlim-e ʿolum*), from which he might make ends meet.

He proceeded to an unnamed *madrase* and went to see the professor (*modarres*), announcing himself as a seeker of knowledge. The professor set him to the study of Islamic law (*feqâhat*) and appointed a room for him in the dormitory of the college. This professor had Owhad study the *Meftâh*, one of the principal books of Shâfeʿi law, which he learned in a short period of time. Having thus proved himself a quick study, Owhad soon moved on to read several other books and was eventually appointed as a repetitor, or *moʿid*, for which he received a stipend, clothes and a ʿmount. He began to win a reputation about town and when the teacher of the Hakkâkie Madrase in Baghdad died, the position of professor of law (*modarres*) at this college was given to "Shaykh" Owhad. After this, Owhad supposedly won great fame, though this did not mean he stopped studying and acquiring knowledge (Owh 2).

Though the historical sources make no mention of a Hakkâkie college in Baghdad, educational prestige in the Islamic world was associated not primarily with individual colleges or institutions, but with particular professors, who might hold simultaneous posts in more than one college. The absence of written testimony about this Hakkâkie college need not therefore provoke undue consternation, although Sufi hagiographers are not known for understatement or accuracy. However, since the hagiographer does not tell us who Owhad al-Din's professor had been, we may conclude that Owhad and his teacher were not among the best-known or even intermediate professors of their day.

Even though the standard medieval works do not mention Owhad al-Din's Hakkâkie Madrase, the position of professor must at least have provided him with a steady income. It would appear that Rumi, by the 1240s, held a similar professorship in just such a school in Konya, with the exception that colleges had been introduced to the city only relatively recently; there were far fewer institutions of learning than in Baghdad, Damascus, or Aleppo, and the professors who taught there would probably not have been among the most famous professors or jurisconsults. Aflâki tells us that Rumi was engaged in teaching the religious sciences (*tadris-e ʿolum-e dini*) at the professorial rank (*modarresi mikard*) in four different institutions, all of them respected (Af 618).

One of these was the Cotton Sellers' Madrase, a college most probably endowed by the guild of cotton merchants/growers, or at least located on their street.

The Practice and Abuse of the Law

Owhad al-Din of Kerman lays out the scholarly and social hierarchy of the legal profession for us. At the bottom of the academic ladder stood the rank or condition of *feqâhat*, apparently designating both students of the law and those who held minor or irregular positions in a college. The next stage of the profession was teaching the law (*tadris*, Owh 3), normally undertaken by the *modarres*, or professor of a college. The best legal scholars received permission from their teachers not only to teach the law (*tadris*) but also to render opinions on matters of law or doctrine (*eftâ*⁾), allowing them to perform the function not only of professor, but also of *mofti*, issuing legal or doctrinal opinions – fatwas – in response to various questions put to them. A fatwa had no authority behind it other than the reputation for learning of the jurisconsult or *faqih* who issued it; other equally qualified *faqih*s might issue contrary fatwas. But the highest rank among the ulama, beyond which there was no higher position (*mansab*), belonged to those who rendered binding legal verdicts (*qazâ*) in the capacity of judge, or *qâzi* (Owh 3).

While many professors could also act as *mofti*s, this did not give them the right actually to enforce or try legal cases. This right was reserved for the *qâzi*, a position usually appointed by the ruling political authority. Although a *qâzi* might also hold a professorship at a college, not many professors of law could aspire to this position; there was usually only one *qâzi* in town, except in larger cities, where the Shâfeᶜi and Hanafi schools might each have their own judge. In major metropoli, such as Baghdad and Cairo, more than one judge per school was needed, in which case one individual was usually appointed chief judge, or Qâzi al-qozât. By virtue of his learning and his reputation for piety, a judge would command respect and, by virtue of his office, he could wield considerable influence. Since a judge could make tremendous profit from his office, it was not unknown for an aspiring judge to bribe his way into the position. Rashid al-Din Fazl Allâh (1247–1318) complains in his history of the Mongols that

> some *qâzi*s go so far as to take securities before reaching a decision. A judge must rule constructively and sympathetically, and must not take anything from anyone. When judgements are rendered by securities and bargaining, one can imagine what the situation is! (cited in Mov 28–9)

A century earlier **Sanâ⁾i** (d. 1131) had denounced the behavior of such worldly judges and men of religion in an ethico-religious poem which created the prototype for the long mystical–didactic *masnavi*, of which genre Rumi's own *Masnavi* is the premier example. In this poem of Sanâ⁾i, "The Garden of

Truth" (*Hadiqat al-haqiqat* 670–71), we read the following description of a *qâzi*:

> Good-for-nothing, two-faced, full of nonsense!
> A tyrant, grief-mongering, life-sapping!
> He threatens you with prison or with pain
> and treats you like no dog would treat a man.
> He is bad, bad, though he knows what is good;
> He's a dog, dog, though he heads up the flock.
> He sits there coldly poring over books,
> you shiver, fearful of his sophist tricks . . .

Likewise, Sanâ'i castigated the ambitious men of religion who seek gold while pretending to be dervishes (*Hadiqat* 676–9):

> Estate-mongers, heart-set on the heartlands
> can't keep the heart of reason, law and faith . . .
> The very founts of friction, lacking knowledge,
> their tongues are greased, their piety starved
> Full of vim and leisure, all void of light,
> Now all woe and loss, now all full of lies . . .
> Writing fatwas calling for all men's blood
> moved by malice, ignorance and by greed . . .
> All of them full of words and thin on facts
> All of them ghouls, monstrous shapes in barren sands
> In speech, stampeding like unbridled camels
> Like the ostrich, all consumers of the fire . . .
> In enmity, treachery, deception
> More deep in hell's depths than the devil
> Holding orphans' property as lawful
> living on the wealth of kids and widows,
> Breathing of piety's scent not one whiff
> Bone dry as potsherds empty of water . . .
> All taking bribes and writing up rules,
> All lowly and load-burdened, like the ass

The last line alludes to the Koran (K62:5), which indicates that those who carried the Torah but failed to observe it benefited from it no better than an ass that bears a load of books; God will not guide those who oppress people and distort the meaning of his scripture.

Corruption and temptation, then, might seduce a judge from the path of righteousness. Furthermore, the position of judge was also fraught with political dangers, since either the local prince, the sultan or the caliph might try to impose certain doctrines or decisions, or otherwise involve the office of *qâzi* in partisan matters. A number of pious and holy scholars were known to refuse judgeships on these grounds, fearing the application of the law would entangle them in politics or tempt them into the lap of luxury. This moral austerity certainly fit with the idea of spiritual poverty and humility which the Sufis championed. Shams al-Din says (Maq 178):

> By God, to God and for God!! Those people studying in the *madrases* do so in order to become repetitors (*mo'id*), to get their own *madrase* and to win place and position. They say, "We have to make a good impression, this is what should be said in these gatherings in order to get such and such position."

> Why do you acquire knowledge for the purpose of a worldly morsel? The purpose of this rope is to lift yourselves out of the pit, not so that you can climb out of this pit and into deeper pits. Fix your sight on knowing who you are, what your essence is, why you have come here, where you are going, and what the source of your being is. What are you doing at this very moment? Where are you headed?

RUMI AS SUFI

The movement we know as Sufism began as a confluence of ascetic exercises (*zohd*), sharing much in common with Christian monasticism in Syria and gnostic attitudes toward the material world, and of mystical speculation (*'erfân*), fed probably by Zoroastrian, Manichaean, Buddhist and Hindu theosophical teachings. Sufism entails a pious orientation toward religion, privileging the spiritual over the material, self-renunciation exercises and other forms of discipline (in addition, of course, to the ritual prayers and obligatory fasting required of all Muslims) as a means to approach God. In some individuals it might also include a predilection for divine visions, including lights, glimpses of heaven, angels, or even God. As such it involved an individual and personal orientation toward God, often at odds with the communal and legalistic definition of piety expounded by the legal scholars (*foqahâ*) and other men of religious learning, collectively known as the ulama. The ulama concerned themselves with the domain of acquired knowledge (*'elm*) – knowledge of the Koran and knowledge of the praxis, or Sunna, of the Prophet, as reconstructed from traditions, or Hadith, handed down about Mohammad. Religious scholars might specialize in the study of history and genealogy as a means of verifying the authenticity of the chains of transmission (*esnâd*) of prophetic tradition, or Hadith; in interpretation of the Koran (*tafsir*); in the jurisprudential principles (*osul al-feqh*) by which religious law (Shari'a) was ascertained; in dialectical argumentation about specific matters of law (*qil o qâl*), or in speculative theology (*kalâm*).

Practitioners of a personal devotional approach to God were called at different times and places *zâhed* (ascete), *darvish* (poor man), *sâlek* (sojourner [on the spiritual path]), *'âref* (gnostic) and Sufi. The word "Sufi" has been explained variously as a borrowing from Greek *sophia* (wisdom); a derivative of the word *soffe*, or stone bench outside the mosque at Medina, where certain ascetic-minded companions of the Prophet used to sit (*soffe* is also the source of the English word "sofa"); or as a reference to the wearing of shirts or cloaks of wool (*suf*) by early Islamic ascetics. This latter explanation seems the most likely source of the word, as Sufism was early on associated with the self-renunciation practiced in the hermitages of the Syrian desert.

Many Sufis came from the class of the ulama, religious scholars by training who had developed a mystical or interior spirituality. They concentrated on a person's inner attitude and orientation, in contradistinction to the conventional, piety-minded, who seemed to the Sufis preoccupied with legalistic and ritual matters, content to tally their good versus bad deeds as indices of spiritual advancement (similar in some respects to Calvinists in Europe). A judge (*qâzi*) respected for his devotion, piety and political independence might be considered a Sufi, as in the case of Hasan al-Basri (d. 728). A religious scholar such as ʿAbd Allâh Ansâri (d. 1089) might also attain the status of saint through learning, insight, piety and devotion. In the early years of Sufism many acquired saintly reputations by virtue of their acts of asceticism and self-renunciation; likewise preachers or holy men with reputations for working miracles might attain the status of saint among the local populace. From the twelfth century onward, many Sufis would study the religious sciences in a Sufi lodge or cloister (*khâneqâh, rebât, zâvie*). Here they might also learn the law (*feqh*), but the Sufi orientation toward the law reflected a divergence from the professionalism of the legal colleges and their orientation toward the law. The members of a Sufi lodge did not, generally speaking, follow as rigorous a course of study as in the legal colleges, and were sometimes criticized (as in the *Talbis-e Eblis* of Ibn al-Jowzi) for their laziness and false claims to religious knowledge. Not every Sufi, therefore, came from the ranks of the learned, though often times the subsequent hagiographical tradition exaggerated the extent of a saint's learning or power.

While most Sufis did not advocate an antinomian rejection or suspension of religious law – the Shariʿa – they did privilege the meaning (*maʿni*) of deeds and the intentions (*niyat*) motivating them above the actual deeds, since one's inward orientation could not be measured simply on the basis of outward compliance with religious law. A person's observance of religious law, his acts of worship and charity, might proceed in varying degrees from the prideful desire to appear pious. Even worse, the ambitious or greedy might pretend hypocritically or deceitfully to piety; in the words of the beloved Persian poet, Hâfez:

> *vâʿezân k-in jelve dar mehrâb o manbar mikonand*
> *chon be khalvat miravand ân kâr-e digar mikonand*

> Preachers give glorious talks in the pulpit;
> But, oh, what they won't do when in private!

Owhad al-Din of Kerman, whose career in the *madrases* of Baghdad we have noted above, determined not to pursue a judgeship and the more worldly ways of religious knowledge, preferring instead to teach and deepen his knowledge of the religious sciences by following the spiritual path (*soluk*) that leads to apprehension of the divine mysteries (*asrār-e elâhi*), like the Sufis before him (Owh 2–3). His hagiographer tells us that Owhad eventually quit his position at the college and set out to purify himself by acts of asceticism. These included fasting, in which exercise he would eat only once in seven days; continual devotions, during which he prayed throughout the night and denied his body sleep; and undertaking the pilgrimage to Mecca, in preparation for which he sold all his belongings, manumitted his household slaves, and set out on foot through the desert (Owh 3–4).

The locus classicus for this abandonment of academe and the life of knowledge in favor of the life of the soul is, of course, **Abu Hâmed Mohammad al-Ghazzâli** (1058–1111). His autobiographical work "Deliverance from Error" (*al-Monqez men al-zalâl*) poignantly illustrates the dilemma felt by some medieval Muslim scholars in relation to the status, wealth and power conferred upon them by society as men of religion, and the desire for authenticity, integrity and purity in worship of God. Ghazzâli chose to leave his teaching position and rededicate himself to enlivening Islamic spirituality, which he did by straddling the world of Sufism and orthodoxy (his brother Ahmad al-Ghazzâli was a more thorough-going mystic). Ghazzâli's magnum opus, the "Vivification of the Religious Sciences" (*Ehyâ ʿolum al-din*), written circa 1106, constitutes one of the important sources for later Sufis in the Iranian cultural sphere, as well as for the more conventional ulama. The *Masnavi*'s paraphrase of passages or stories from Ghazzâli's "Vivification" testifies to Rumi's familiarity with this work.

Some Sufis, such as the Malâmati and the Qalandars, addressed the spiritual dangers of a pious reputation by intentionally acting in apparent contradiction to religious law or social standards. In order not to succumb to the temptations of sham piety, they might drink wine in public (or feign to), and shear themselves of all outward signs of social respect, such as the hair and beard, respectable clothes (which even more than now indicated rank and standing), and so forth. Most Sufis did not go this far, choosing instead to concentrate with minute attention on the states (*hâl*, plural *ahvâl*) which the soul experienced and the stages (*maqâmât*) of development through which it progressed. Hârith al-Muhâsibî of Basra in Iraq (d. 857) composed a treatise on this method of interior compliance with the will of God. By following a *via purgativa* and subduing his concupiscent soul (*nafs-e ammâre*), the Sufi could so purify his immortal spirit (*ruh*) from the pollution of worldly desires that his own personality could be effaced or absorbed in the spirit of God. Western scholars have commonly described this state, *fanâ*, as annihilation of the self, but the term refers not so much to an annihilation of the individual consciousness, as in the Buddhist concept of nirvana, as to the effacement or dissolution of the concupiscent or selfish self in the ocean of God's attributes. Sufis considered this spiritual struggle to conquer the self the greater jihad (*jehâd-e akbar*), as opposed to the lesser and far easier jihad of defending and spreading the temporal dominion of the faith of Islam.

Above and beyond acquired knowledge (*'elm*), the Sufis therefore concerned themselves with an intuitive and experiential knowing of God, or *ma'refat*, a term used, if not coined, by Dhu al-Nun of Egypt in the 800s. *Ma'refat*, or gnosis, is achieved not by studying the law, but by loving God. As Rumi explains (D 395):

> Love resides
>> not in learning
>> not in knowledge
>> not in pages and pamphlets
> Wherever the debates of men may lead
>> that is not the lovers' path
>
> Love's branches arch over pre-eternity
>> its roots, you see, delve in Forever
>> a tree resting not on soil
>>> nor trunk
>>> nor even Heaven's throne
>
> We deposed reason,
>> punished passion with the lash:
>>> For such reason and such morals
>>> were degrading to such glory
> You see,
>> So long as you long
>>> you idolize longing;
>>> but become the beloved
>>>> and then no being longs
>>>>> The incessant hopes and fears
>>>>> of the sea-faring man
>>>>> float upon planks;
>>>>>> but obliterate
>>>>>>> both planks and seaman
>>>>>>> and only submersion remains
>
>>>>> Shams of Tabriz! the sea is you,
>>>>> the pearl, too,
>>>> because your being
>>>> head to toe
>>>>> is nothing
>>>>> but the mystery
>>>>> of the Maker

A Sufi did not necessarily experience progress along the spiritual path (*tariqe*) as a constant intensification of illumination or gnostic understanding. His soul might be subject to alternating periods of divine grace (*bast*), during which visions and intimations might come upon him, and of spiritual contraction (*qabz*), periods of frustration or despair during which he could not feel God's presence. However, having advanced far enough along the journey to God, a Sufi might attain the ecstatic state of *fanâ*. In the throes of *fanâ* a Sufi would perceive himself and his self effaced in God. Feeling thus submerged in the divine, a worshiper might give voice to this sensation in expressions which appeared to the orthodox as *sherk* (joining partners with God) or *kofr* (utter blasphemy). Such ecstatic outbursts, known by the technical term *shathiyât*, included "Glory be to me" (*sobhâni*), shouted out by Bâyazid Bestâmi in eastern Iran (d. 874) and "I am the Truth" (*anâ al-Haqq*), spoken by Mansur al-Hallâj, executed in Baghdad in 922 for the likes of this and other statements. Most Sufis, such as Hallâj's contemporary Jonayd (d. 910), argued that even if a mystic did experience states of God-intoxication (*sokr*), he must not share such mysteries with the uninitiated, but should instead maintain a sober demeanor that did not offend those who had not reached this plane of enlightenment. Rumi and other Persian Sufis admired Hallâj for his honesty in sharing his vision of the *mysterium tremendum* and championing the mystical mode of worship, despite the knowledge that this would lead to martyrdom. Hallâj was thus rightfully executed for speaking the mystery which must not be revealed. Most later Sufis, like Rumi, while revering Hallâj as a martyr of divine love, refrain from outwardly blasphemous or "drunken" exclamations of mystical bliss.

Though Sufism oriented the spiritual quest toward experience (*zowq* or "tasting") and gnosis (*ma'refat*) rather than book learning (*'elm*), by the eleventh century several manuals about the theory and praxis of Sufism were available. These include Kalâbâdi's "Introduction to the School of Sufism" (*Ketâb al-ta'ârrof le mazhab al-tasavvof*, tenth century), the "Book of Flashes" (*Ketâb al-loma'*) of Abu Nasr al-Sarrâj (d. 988), the "Provisions for the Heart" (*Qut al-qolub*) of Abu Tâleb al-Makki (d. 996), the "Treatise" (*Resâle*) of Qoshayri (986–1072), all in Arabic, and the Persian "Lifting of the Veil" (*Kashf al-mahjub*) by Hojviri (d. 1072). Likewise, *vitae* of the Sufis were first compiled by al-Solami (d. 1021) in his "Biography of the Sufis" (*Tabaqât al-sufiye*) and in the "Adornment of the Saints" (*Helyat al-owliâ*) of Abu No'aym Esfahâni (d. 1038).[5] For a deeper understanding of the sources and assumptions of Rumi's mysticism, a thorough study of such works is necessary. Space does not permit us to go into such matters here, but the interested reader may refer to a number of widely available works.[6]

Some later Sufis espoused quasi-pantheistic doctrines, with **Ibn ᶜArabi** (1165–1240) usually singled out as the outstanding exponent of this idea. Ibn ᶜArabi argued that while the Koranic doctrine of unity (*towhid*) means that the believer should seek union with God, cosmologically it signifies that the created universe, as a manifestation or effulgence of God, is in some respect also a continuation of God's being. Those who helped spread Ibn ʿArabi's ideas, either by espousing them, like Sadr al-Din of Konya in his *Meftâh al-ghayb*, or by opposing them in various degrees, like ʿAlâ al-Dowle Semnâni and Ibn Taymiya, formulated this as a doctrine of the unity of being, *vahdat al-vojud*, a term which, though not used by Ibn ʿArabi, became forever associated with his name. Nicholson ascribes this pantheistic trend in large part to the tide of Neoplatonism that eventually swept away the essentially dualist mysticism of al-Ghazzâli (NiM, 222–4). This speculative and esoteric theosophizing would come to dominate Sufism in later centuries and divert it from its original ascetic and pietistic roots (NiM 229):

> The typical saint is no longer one who has sought God with prayer and aspiration and found Him, after sore travail, in the transfiguration of dying to self through an inexplicable act of grace depending on nothing but the personal will of the Creator; he is rather the complete theosophist and hierophant from whom no mystery is hidden, the perfect man who identifies himself with God or the Logos.

Though this transformation was already underway during Rumi's lifetime, his own course to sainthood more closely resembles the conventional one of sore travail and self-transfiguration, though many have seen in Rumi's theosophy the influence of Ibn ʿArabi (see chapter 9, below).

Shaykhs, Saints, Spiritual Confraternities and the Sufi Orders

As far as the praxis of Sufism is concerned, a system of discipleship to spiritual guides and teachers began to develop in which the aspirant (*morid*) would train and discipline his spiritual powers under the supervision of a guide (*morshed*), usually known as Shaykh or Pir, the Arabic and Persian words, respectively, for elder or sage. Once a shaykh or *pir* attained a saintly reputation, he was numbered among the friends of God, or *owliâ Allâh*, *owliâ* being the plural form for *vali*, "one befriended by God." Depending upon the spiritual station attained and the particular school to which he belonged, a *vali*, through his powers and mystical dominion (*velâyat*), might also be viewed as a *qotb* (an *axis mundi*, or pole of the spiritual world) or as a perfect man, *al-ensân al-kâmel*, a concept elaborated by Ibn ʿArabi and ʿAbd al-Karim al-Jili (1366–1403).[7] Whether generally recognized by the people or not, the world must always be graced with and sustained by the living presence of a *qotb*, who acts as a conduit for the release of spiritual energies.

In the course of the eleventh and twelfth centuries, the disciples of various pious scholars of religion and mystical teachers began to construct hospices or centers in which to gather, hold devotions, discuss the meaning of the Koran, the spirituality of the Prophet, and so forth. Although religious discussions typically took place in the mosques, the scholars, theologians, judges and jurists of the conventional religious sciences, whose mode of discourse dominated at most mosques, did not particularly encourage or create a conducive atmosphere for the non-traditional modes of spiritual knowledge. Circles of the spiritually and gnostically minded would therefore convene in alternate venues, variously called **khâneqâh** (among eastern Iranians), *zâvie* (cloister or shrine), *rebât* (mostly in the Arabic-speaking world; originally meaning a fortress), or *takye* (a support for the poor, or religious institution; a Persian word mostly used however among Turks, where it is pronounced *tekke*). A *khâneqâh* might typically include lodging for travelers or disciples who wished to live in a cloister-like atmosphere, a library for religious and mystical literature, as well as a place for lectures, worship, devotions, and the gnostic approach to God. A mosque or saint's shrine might develop into a *khâneqâh* if the founder, director or an important later donor had Sufi proclivities. Like the *madrases*, however, Sufi centers could be established in perpetuity by the pious endowment of a wealthy benefactor. Many *khâneqâh*s were expressly built for and dedicated to the modes of Sufi worship, often in the name of a particular spiritual teacher.

We have a description of one such *khâneqâh* in Sarakhs, in Khorasan, not too far from where Rumi was born. Sanâ'i, writing in about 1120, composed the following dedicatory verse for this *khâneqâh*, built by or for the chief Qâzi in Sarakhs, Sayf al-Din Mohammad b. Mansur, who, like Rumi, was a mystically minded Hanafi scholar:

> Is this the breath of God,
>   this *khâneqâh*
> of Mohammad Mansur,
> or has the hornblast ushered in the Resurrection?!
> for from three directions,
> with its classes, books and medicines,
> it lays a festal board
> for creed and soul and body
> In this building three things
>   are preserved from two:
>   body, heart and soul
>   from grave and languor
> Each and every corner resounds with beauty:
>   the melodies of David and the singing of the Psalms.
> The ornamentation of this edifice
> obscures the glow of Mercury's orb
> and from its glorious effulgence
> Sinai's shattered stones are put to shame
> Any ailment afflicts your body?
>   ask here for lozenges, concoctions
>   that will wet and warm your humors

27

Any doubts plague your heart?
   read here the Sealed Tablet and the Hidden Scroll
There are books here for the heart of the seeker
There are medicines here for the suffering flesh
Jesus is here to dispel the foul air
Khezr is here to dispel the mirage of pride

From now on, this pillar will uphold
fortune and mercy and palaces of learned men [?]
   When you take it in
   it exceeds in appearance
   the sound of spirit
   the sight of houris
   Even with two good eyes you cannot comprehend it
   so there's no need to wish:
      "May the evil eye be far from you."
In the face of such grandeur
how can one sing praises
equal to your radiance?
   For this, Sanâ'i must be excused.

To this same patron, Mohammad-e Mansur, Sanâ'i dedicated his allegory of the soul's ascent to its creator, the *Sayr al-ʿebâd elâ al-maʿâd*, along with a few other odes. These suggest that sermons (*majles-e vaʿz*), classes on Koran interpretation, *zekr* sessions and even *samâʿ* ceremonies took place in this *khâneqâh*.[8]

One of the disciplines or modes of worship that spiritual masters would prescribe for their students was the meditative repetition or chanting of certain formulas or mantras – *zekr*. Though specific meditations might be handed out to disciples according to their particular personality or level of development, each teacher or order might have a particular *zekr*, or mantra, which he taught to all of his disciples. This would effectively constitute the motto of the order and was performed congregationally, accompanied by rhythmic breathing and sometimes movement, usually in the Sufi lodge.

The ***samâʿ*** ceremony, of which not all Sufis and certainly not all jurisconsults approved, consisted in listening to music or even dancing, once again a congregational activity held usually in the lodge. Since music and dancing were associated with royal courts, slave girls, wine drinking and debauchery, Islamic law generally did not encourage it, though it did not necessarily forbid it outright, as has often been claimed. Sultan Valad, Rumi's son, defended the practice against the objection that it contravened the Shariʿa. The Sufi undertakes *samâʿ*, a kind of instrumental and motive orison, only after years of spiritual poverty, fasting and retreats, when he has attained a certain state of mystic development. In *samâʿ*, this mystic state intensifies, for the goal is a closer approach to God. If one can attain this state through the ritual prayers, so much the better, but if not, the goal of the Shari^c a is to bring everyone closer to God. Since *samâ^c* helps the spiritually disciplined to achieve that goal it cannot be contrary to the Shari^c a.

Prior to joining these congregational forms of worship, novices would be assigned exercises of self-discipline such as fasting, hermitic retreats, etc. Formal acceptance as a pupil or disciple of a master might also require the shaving off of one's hair and the swearing of an oath to follow his directives and any tasks or disciplines he might assign. In the Mevlevi order, for example, a disciple must first serve in the kitchen of the *khâneqâh* for 1,001 days before being accepted as a novice. For some dervishes, initiation required not only shaving of the head, but also of the face, including the eyebrows. After heeding his master for some time and demonstrating his spiritual susceptibilities and his devotion, a disciple might be admitted into the inner circle of his master's followers (*khavâss*). A teacher might convey authority on one or more of these close, hand-trained disciples to initiate others on his behalf. A master might typically deputize such disciples by bestowing upon them a ceremonial dervish cloak, or *kherqe*, and perhaps giving them authority to represent the master's teachings in another city. It was usually through the efforts of such disciples, rather than the direct efforts of the shaykhs and saints themselves, that the disciplines and teachings of the master were codified and systematized into the rules of an order. The founding figures of these larger orders traced (or their followers traced for them) a spiritual lineage stretching back in a chain (*selsele*) through various well-known Sufis, all the way back to the Prophet. In this manner, the Sufi teacher could claim to possess the esoteric knowledge of the scripture in addition to the conventional outward knowledge of the Koran.

Eventually, certain mystically oriented teachers gained a wider reputation as their followers spread their fame and teachings during visits to other lodges. The local centers in other areas began to affiliate with these teachers and the spiritual disciplines they practiced. Many of the itinerant promoters and organizers of Sufi centers were Iranian; as Ibn Battûta tells us, even in Cairo, as late as 1326, most of the members of Sufi *zâvies* were cultured Persian men, who even used the Persian word *khâneqâh* to describe their lodges (Bat 37–8), suggesting that the practices of Khorasan had made an impact on the structure and organization of mystical confraternities as far west as Egypt.

The twelfth and thirteenth centuries saw the formalization of many such spiritual confraternities or Sufi orders. For example, the Sohravardi order formed around the example of Abu Najib Sohravardi (1097–1168), who followed Ghazzâli's example and left the Nezâmiye Madrase for the mystical life, initiating disciples like Ruzbehân Baqli from Shirâz (d. 1209) and others who exercised their influence, in turn, upon Najm al-Din Kobrâ. However, Abu Najib's nephew, **Shehâb al-Din ^c Omar Sohravardi** (1145–1234), actually shaped the Sohravardi order under the patronage of Caliph al-Nâser in

Baghdad, who encouraged the formation and structuring of the youth guilds (*fotovvat*) in Baghdad. Sent by the caliph on various embassies, Shehâb al-Din Sohravardi spread this model to Konya, Aleppo and Damascus (TrS 34–6). The Yasavi order, active among Turkish-speaking tribes in Central Asia, traces its lineage to an eponymous founder, Ahmad al-Yasavi (d. 1166), whose practice of spiritual retreats also inspired the Khalvati order and the Bektâshis (TrS: 58–60), both of which would later prove rivals to the Mevlevi order in the Ottoman lands. The Naqshbandis, though named after Bahâ al-Din Naqshband (d. 1389), trace their lineage back to Abu Yusof Hamadâni (d. 1140), but were shaped into an order with codified rules by ʿAbd al-Khâleq Ghodjvâni (d. 1220). The Naqshbandis were centered in Central Asia, but also proved popular in Ottoman Turkey and the Caucasus. In India the Cheshtiye, promoted by Bâbâ Farid Ganj-e Shakar (1175?–1265), a follower of Moʿin al-Din Cheshti (d. 1236), began to spread at about the same time Rumi came under the influence of Shams.

Rumi as Kobravi?

It has often been suggested that Rumi's father, Bahâ al-Din Valad, and Bahâ al-Din's disciple, Borhân al-Din, were both members of the Kobravi order or somehow associated with **Najm al-Din Kobrâ** (1158–1221) and his followers. Najm al-Din Kobrâ was initiated in Egypt to the teachings of Abu Najib Sohravardi and then devoted himself to the Sufi path of Bâbâ Faraj of Tabriz. He returned to his native Khwârazm where he built a *khâneqâh* (TrS 55–6) and produced so many disciples that he earned the epithet *vali-tarâsh*, "the sculptor of saints" (JNO 419). Hamd Allâh Mostowfi, writing in 1330, reports in the *Târikh-e gozide* (ed. E.G. Browne, Gibb Memorial Series facsimile edition [Leiden: Brill, 1910], 1:789) that Najm al-Din accepted twelve people as disciples in his day, all of them great shaykhs. Mostowfi names only seven of these: Majd al-Din Baghdâdi, Saʿd al-Din Hamuye, Razi al-Din ʿAli Lâlâ, Sayf al-Din Bâkharzi, Jamâl al-Din Kili and, finally, "Mowlânâ Jalâl al-Din Bahâ al-Dowle." Of course, it is chronologically impossible for Rumi to have been a member of the Kobravi order and a successor to Najm al-Din Kobrâ; Rumi left eastern Iran when still a boy of about nine, or twelve at the very most, and would not become a great shaykh until circa 1240, some twenty years after the death of Najm al-Din. Some have tried to resolve the discrepancy by assuming that Mostowfi or one of the scribes who copied his history confused Mowlânâ Rumi with his father, Mowlânâ Bahâ al-Din (indeed, the text appears rather confused on this score). Similar reports of Kobravi affiliation may also be found in the introduction of the *Javâher al-asrâr* of Kamâl al-Din Hosayn Khwârazmi (written c. 1432) and the *Nafahât al-ons* of Jâmi (1414–92), though Jâmi himself seems reluctant to give this claim full credit (JNO 457). We may assume both of these authors had access to Mostowfi, who may therefore constitute the primary authority for this claim.

Early scholarship on Rumi (e.g., BLH 2:493) tended to take these reports at face value and to assert the influence of the Kobravi teachings on Rumi and his father. Even Foruzânfar credited these reports in his early work on Rumi (FB 9). However, a closer examination of the writings of Bahâ al-Din and Borhân al-Din eventually led Foruzânfar to rule out the possibility of any direct relationship between them and the founders and followers of the Kobravi order (FA 69–70 and Bor yw–yt). As a result, Persian and Turkish scholars no longer generally credit the claim of Kobravi influence (e.g., GB 395; ZrJ 278; ZrP 23; ME 1:xv). Meier is aware of this (Mei 74), but other Western scholars still cling to the theory of Kobravi influence: Annemarie Schimmel tends to believe the circumstantial reports (ScT 13) as does Muhammad Isa Waley (IS 89), at least as regards Bahâ al-Din.

The reasons for rejecting the notion of direct Kobravi influence on Bahâ al-Din are manifold and compelling. First of all, there is no mention of Najm al-Din Kobrâ, **Majd al-Din Baghdâdi** (killed 1219) or **Najm al-Din Râzi** (also known as Dâye, 1177–1256), the principal promoters of the Kobravi order, in the extensive writings of Bahâ al-Din, Borhân al-Din or Jalâl al-Din Rumi. Shams al-Din Tabrizi does mention Najm-e Kobrâ once (perhaps, however, intending Najm-e Râzi), though not in favorable terms (Maq 183, 495). On the other hand, Shams al-Din Tabrizi speaks highly of the Shâfeᶜi scholar Abu Mansur Mohammad of Nayshâpur, known as Imam Hafade (d. 1175 in Tabriz), reputedly one of the teachers of Najm al-Din Kobrâ. However, Shams-e Tabrizi explicitly tells us that Rumi revealed things in his sermons that the great Imam Hafade had never mentioned (Maq 284–5).

The rules of etiquette among Sufis required disciples to acknowledge the debt to their mentors and to mention the names of their teachers. The Kobravi disciple Najm al-Din Râzi mentions the name of his teacher, Majd al-Din Baghdâdi. Borhân al-Din and Rumi both mention the names of their spiritual mentors, but make no mention of any Kobravis. Shams-e Tabrizi talks freely about a wide variety of the famous people whom he had met or whose works he had read, yet he makes only one passing comment about a known Kobravi, and that not complimentary.

Rumi does quote a quatrain from Najm al-Din Râzi (Dâye) in his Discourses (Fih 76, 290), and two quatrains also appear in Shams al-Din Tabrizi's *Maqâlât* (Maq 138, 463 and 234, 530), but in all cases without attribution. Likewise unattributed is Shams al-Din's quotation of a quatrain from Sayf al-Din Bâkharzi (1190–1261), a close disciple of Najm al-Din Kobrâ based in Bokhara (Maq 247, 537). Rumi and Shams quite possibly quoted these quatrains without knowing their source, as such poems circulated extensively in oral form; Abu Nasr al-Sarrâj notes that Sufis would sing such quatrains during musical *samâᶜ* sessions.[9]

Indeed, the manuscript tradition attributes the first of the quatrains of Najm al-Din quoted by Shams to the pen of Rumi and even Foruzânfar's critical edition of the *Divân-e Shams* includes this poem, probably erroneously, as a composition of Rumi's (D R620 or R738)! Najm al-Din Râzi's *Mersâd al-ᶜebâd* ("Provision for the Servants of God") itself includes a line apparently borrowed from a poem of the little-known thirteenth-century poet Rafiᶜ al-Din Lonbâni (Maq 282–3). So, the quotation of a quatrain in a manuscript does not necessarily mean that the composer was known to the author or scribe.

Even so, it is not implausible that either Shams al-Din or Rumi had read Najm al-Din Râzi's *Mersâd*. In the event that they did, the extent of their indebtedness would appear to be a couple of poems which they did not even remember to attribute to Najm al-Din Râzi, whereas Rumi frequently acknowledged his indebtedness to Sanâᵓi and ᶜAttâr, attributing poems to them by name. We may also note that Najm al-Din Râzi dedicated an edition of his *Mersâd al-ᶜebâd* to the Seljuk sultan ᶜAlâ al-Din Kay Qobâd in 1223 in hopes of gaining Kay Qobâd's patronage (Mei 41–2). ᶜAlâ al-Din Kay Qobâd was apparently not impressed enough to retain Najm al-Din, though within a few years (no more than six), ᶜAlâ al-Din did establish Bahâ al-Din Valad in a college in Konya, apparently under princely patronage.

Sepahsâlâr (Sep 25) indicates that while in Damascus, Rumi spoke with several famous Sufis, including Saᶜd al-Din Hamuye (d. 1252), a noted successor of Najm al-Din Kobrâ. It is not clear that Rumi and Saᶜd al-Din were both in Damascus at the same time, but in any case, Rumi does not speak of any of the individuals with whom he supposedly met in Damascus as major influences on him. On the contrary, we know that either Rumi or Shams al-Din Tabrizi formed critical opinions of several of these individuals (see chapter 4, below). And while Jâmi noncommittally relates one report linking Bahâ al-Din with Najm al-Din Kobrâ (JNO 457), he also relates an anecdote suggestive of antipathy between Najm al-Din Râzi (Dâye) and Rumi. Though probably untrue, the anecdote nevertheless reveals early Mevlevi perceptions about Najm al-Din and his relationship to Rumi, and is therefore worth retelling. When Najm al-Din Râzi came to Konya, he met with both Rumi and Sadr al-Din of Konya, the son-in-law of Ibn ᶜArabi. Asked to lead the evening prayers, Najm al-Din selected a Koranic verse for recitation during the two prostrations of the prayer which included the phrase "O you infidels." When the prayers were finished, Rumi turned to Sadr al-Din and jokingly told him, "He pronounced it the first time on me and the second time on you" (JNO 435).

Bahâ al-Din, as we learn from his own writings, used to repeat "Allâh, Allâh" (God, God) as his *zekr*, and Aflâki (Af 250–51) tells us that Rumi adopted "Allâh, Allâh, Allâh" as the Mevlevi *zekr*, "because we are the Allâhis – we come from Allâh and we return unto Him." In contrast, the *zekr* of the early Kobravi order, as Majd al-Din Baghdâdi indicates, was *Lâ elâha ellâ Allâh* – "There is no god but God" (Bor yh). This leaves only the importance of light and color in Bahâ al-Din's visions in common with the Kobravi heritage of Majd al-Din

Baghdâdi and Najm al-Din Râzi. But the visionary imagery of divine colors and lights also appears in the writings of other Iranian mystics (e.g., Ghazzâli's important treatise "The Niche of Lights," *Meskhât al-anwâr*) and does not necessarily point to Kobravi influence. Since Najm al-Din Kobrâ and Majd al-Din Baghdâdi were about the same age as Bahâ al-Din, and since Najm al-Din Râzi was actually a generation younger than he, if further research does establish a direct link between the chromatic and photic symbolism (such as shared terminology or phrasing) in the writings of Bahâ al-Din and those of the Kobravi founders, it might derive from earlier common sources in the Iranian Sufi tradition, and not directly from one another.

When Aflâki traces the Mevlevi order's spiritual heritage or *selsele*, he does not link it to any of the Kobravi teachers, but has Jonayd pass on his knowledge to Abu Bakr Shebli (d. 946), who transmits it to Mohammad Zojjâj (d. 1091), and then through Abu Bakr Nassâj (d. 1094) to Ahmad Ghazzâli (d. 1123, younger brother of the famous Abu Hâmed Mohammad Ghazzâli), Ahmad Khatibi (d. 1123?, the grandfather of Bahâ al-Din), Shams al-Aʾemme Sarakhsi (d. 1090), Bahâ al-Din Valad, then Borhân al-Din Termezi, and finally to Rumi, who passes it to Shams al-Din, who passes it to Sultan Valad, Rumi's son. Though the chronology of this spiritual lineage seems extremely doubtful, it is significant that no mention is made of Najm al-Din Kobrâ or his disciples, only of Ahmad Ghazzâli. Aflâki (Af 143–4) relates a tale that shows the son of Sayf al-Din Bâkharzi, the Kobravi Shaykh of Bokhara, upstaged by Rumi while visiting Konya. We may dismiss this as an exaggerated or misremembered anecdote, but Aflâki probably had first-hand knowledge of the following report. Aflâki tells us (Af 933) that a copy of Najm al-Din Dâye's Koran commentary (*Tafsir*) was given as a gift to Chelebi Amir ʿÂref (Ulu ʿÂref Chelebi), the head of the Mevlevi order after the death of Rumi's son, Sultan Valad. Apparently Ulu ʿÂref Chelebi had no interest in this precious book, no copy of which was at that time available in Anatolia, as he simply gave it away.

All this clearly shows that the early Mevlevis did not recognize any influence from the founders of the Kobravi order or place any special importance in their teachings. It is only in a source which was not close to the Mevlevis, the "Selected History" of Mostowfi, who probably did not know the details of the origins of the various orders, that such a rumor begins sixty years after the death of Rumi.

Sufi Bohemians: Ovaysis, Khezr and the Qalandars

Everything we know about Bahâ al-Din, Shams al-Din and Rumi indicates that they were not attached to any of the famous spiritual teachers or Sufis of their day. They believed in the praxis of mysticism more than its theory, in what the Sufis called "tasting" (*zowq*) or experiencing for oneself. Bahâ al-Din himself experienced frequent mystical visions, for which he was not indebted to the theosophical doctrines of a particular mystical teacher. Rather, the path chosen by Rumi and his predecessors was to "follow the Prophet" by disciplining and training one's soul, watching over one's heart and concentrating the mind on God. Shams, as revealed in his *Maqâlât*, was an eclectic person who listened to many thinkers and Sufis without being particularly attached to any of them. Shams was not the type to fit in easily and formally join an order.

Some gnostics laid claim to esoteric insight derived not from one of the established teachers, but from their own efforts, effectively placing themselves outside the conventional Sufi orders and their spiritual lineage. Such Sufis were often referred to as Ovaysis, taught by the mysterious figure Ovays al-Qarani, who supposedly had his inspiration directly from Khezr. **Khezr** is a mythical figure, sometimes associated with the Biblical Elijah, believed to have initiated Moses into the ways of esoteric knowledge and guided Alexander through the realms of darkness to the fount of life. Since Rumi's own son, Sultan Valad, explicitly compared the relationship of Shams and Rumi to that of Khezr and Moses (SVE 41–2), we would do well to recall the basic outlines of the Koranic basis for the story of Khezr and Moses.

The Koran does not mention Khezr by name, but commentators identify him with the man described as "one of God's servants" in a parable from the Sura of the Cave (*Surat al-kahf*, K18:65–82). God has, however, endowed this particular servant (as the deity's voice, which narrates the passage, confirms) with a special divine wisdom. Though the Koran reveres Moses as a prophet sent by God, just like the Prophet Mohammad, nevertheless, in this particular vignette, Moses proves lacking in the patience and supernatural insight of Khezr. When Moses sets out to find the junction of the two seas, he walks a long way through the desert with his servant. Eventually they come upon Khezr (K18:65–82), and recognizing that he possesses the wisdom of the Lord, Moses asks if he may follow Khezr in the hope of learning this special divine guidance. Khezr demurs, explaining that Moses would never be able to keep patience with him, insofar as he would encounter things beyond the compass of his experience and would fail to comprehend them. Moses persists: "God willing, you will find me patient and I will not rebel against your command." Khezr relents, warning Moses not to question him about anything unless Khezr were to first broach the subject.

Along their journey, they embark in a boat. Khezr pierces a hole in the hull and Moses, incredulous, reprimands him, demanding to know if Khezr would have all the passengers drown. Khezr reminds Moses, "Did I not tell you that you will never keep patience with me?" Moses apologizes for his heedlessness and they go on.

Khezr comes next upon a youth and kills him. Moses, wondering aloud why he would kill an innocent soul, chastises Khezr. Khezr again reminds Moses of his vow to remain silently patient. Once again, Moses apologizes: "If I ask you about anything else again, cut me off from your company and I will not blame you in the slightest."

Next they come upon a village and ask for food, but the people there refuse them hospitality. Khezr nevertheless repairs a wall in the vicinity that was about to cave in. Moses blurts out in his impatience that Khezr could have at least asked the townspeople to pay him for his labor.

Here Khezr parts company with Moses, but not before revealing the reasoning behind his inscrutable behavior. In the case of the boat, it belonged to poor working people. A certain king in those parts was expropriating every vessel he came upon, and he was about to overtake this particular boat. Khezr, by rendering it temporarily unseaworthy, wished to save it for its rightful owners. As for the young man, Khezr feared that he would rebel against God and commit blasphemy, bringing great anguish to his parents. Khezr intended that in his stead, God would grant them a more compassionate and pious son. Finally, in the case of the wall, a treasure lay buried beneath it, the legacy of a righteous man. He had died, leaving behind two orphaned boys, who knew nothing about their inheritance. God wished for these boys to prosper, and so caused Khezr to uncover their treasure as he rebuilt the wall.

Moses' impatience, as Khezr had predicted, kept him from seeing the wisdom in all these acts, which Khezr explains he committed not by his own volition, but by the command of God (K18:82). Many Sufis concluded from this passage that certain saints might receive inspiration directly from God; such direct knowledge from God could complement or even surpass the knowledge revealed to humanity by the messengers chosen by God to reveal His will to all mankind.

Another type of unaffiliated Sufi was the **Qalandar**. Qalandars were typically mendicant Ṣufis who signaled their withdrawal from all social conventions by shaving their faces and heads and traveling from town to town in little bands, sometimes flaunting antinomian behavior. Many poems describe the arrival of a Qalandar-like figure in the bazaar as a disruption of the social order; like a beautiful beloved, his overpowering charisma creates chaos, causing the merchants and townsmen to forget religious law and piety in their desire to please him and do his bidding. This motif of the Qalandar appears in the eleventh-century poems of Abu Saʿid Abi al-Khayr (967–1049) and recurs throughout the work of Sanâʾi, ʿAttâr and others, though the relationship of this literary motif to the actual practice of Qalandar Sufism is not well established.[10]

It would appear that **Hâji Bektâsh** (d. 1271?) came from just such a Qalandar milieu in Khorasan, only to settle down in Anatolia sometime before 1240 (Hamid Algar, "Bektâş," *EIr*). His spiritual lineage is traced to two Turkish saints, Ahmad al-Yasavi and to a certain Bâbâ Rasul, executed in Amasya in 1240. Although the order now associated with the name of Hâji Bektâsh did not assume its current structure until later, certain remarks by the

Mevlevi disciple Ahmad Aflâki indicate that Bektâsh had a sizeable circle of disciples around him, and that the Mevlevis considered him a rival. Aflâki (Af 381) critiques Hâji Bektâsh as one who, though an illuminated gnostic at heart, failed to follow the ways of the Prophet (*dar motâbaʿat nabud*), which, as we shall see (in chapter 4, below) was the animating spirit of Rumi and his teachers. Aflâki recounts an anecdote, probably greatly embellished, in which Hâji Bektâsh sends his deputy, Shaykh Eshâq, to sniff out the secrets of Rumi's popularity and success as a spiritual teacher. Rumi discerns the adulterated motives of Eshâq and composes a poem for him (D 3061), beginning:

> If you don't have somebody to love,
>   why don't you seek somebody?
> and if you've found that someone to love,
>   why don't you sing out for joy?

Upon Eshâq's return to Hâji Bektâsh, he learns that Bektâsh has had a dream in which he is forced to admit the inferiority of his own spiritual attainments and to submit to the greatness of Rumi's station (Af 382–3). The point of the anecdote, of course, is to reassure Mevlevi disciples that they have nothing to learn from Bektâsh and his followers which cannot be learned more fully from complete devotion to their own master, Mowlânâ Jalâl al-Din Rumi, and the disciplines taught in his Mevlevi order.

A phenomenon perhaps not unrelated to the Qalandars is the **Malâmati** strain of Sufism, "the blamers." Since a Sufi could win a public reputation as a saint for remarkable acts of piety and asceticism, he might be tempted to work miracles or parade his powers for social gain. In order to avoid such worldly distractions from the spiritual path, Malâmati Sufis might purposely discredit themselves by acting in an impious manner, or at least seeming to, by appearing drunk in public, for example. Of course, in the long run this might also have the converse effect of making debauchery appear religiously permissible in the pursuit of mystical insight.

Although the early Sufis generally tended toward asceticism and the reclusive lifestyle, refusing affiliation with political authority, many of the orders eventually developed relations with the princely courts and governors, many of whom had a genuine interest in the spiritual life. Besides, the patronage of pious persons could be politically provident, helping to create good impressions with the ulama and the artisan classes. From about 1126 to his death in 1131, Sanâʾi, though not a member of a formal order, became the personal poet and spiritual adviser to Bahrâmshâh (r. 1118–52), the Ghaznavid ruler. Jâmi (d. 1492), a member of the Naqshbandi order, developed close relations with his disciple ʿAli Shir Navâʾi (1441–1501), poet and vizier to the Timurid ruler of Khorasan, Hosayn Bâyqarâ (1468–1506). Rumi's father, Bahâ al-Din, accepted the patronage of ʿAlâ al-Din Kay Qobâd, and Rumi himself advised Moʿin al-Din

Parvâne on political relations with the Mongols (e.g., Discourse 1, Fih 4–5). In later centuries, the Mevlevi order became integrally involved with the ceremonials of the Ottoman state (see chapter 10).

A RUMI VIEW

ISLAM, THE LAW, THE SPIRIT

In the prose introduction to the fifth book of the *Masnavi*, Rumi tells us exactly where he stands within the Muslim tradition of law (*shari'at*), the way of the Sufis (*tariqat*), and gnosis or the attainment of truth (*haqiqat*). He tells us that the law of religion is like a candle that shows us the way; without that candle we cannot even set foot on the spiritual path. Once the way is lit with the light of the law, the wayfarer begins his spiritual quest, which takes place on the Sufi path. At the end of the journey, one arrives at truth.

Rumi uses alchemy as an analogy. The theories behind the transmutation of metal as learned from a teacher or a book are like the laws of religion. One needs to know these before one can begin walking down the path, but one only comes to see how the theory applies to real life as one walks the Sufi path. It is in the experience of the spiritual path that we actually apply the chemical agents to the metal, as it were. Only by following the path to the end can we turn the actual copper into gold and attain the truth.

At any given moment we all stand at different points on this spiritual path and, as humans, we tend to rejoice in and champion the particular stage we happen to occupy at the moment. Those who know the theory of alchemy boast of their attainments. Those who actually perform alchemy rejoice in their transformative magic. But those transmuted into gold have left behind the preoccupations of either knowing or applying the theory.

Rumi next compares the three stages of religion to the field of medicine. Religious law is like learning the science of medicine. Actually taking the appropriate medicine and observing a proper diet is what the Sufi path is all about. But true health consists in dying to the passions of the world, and when we die both the law and the path fade into nothingness; only the face of God remains in our field of vision (K28:88). Therefore, those who wish to meet their Lord should do good works and keep their hearts and minds focused on the worship of the one true God, allowing nothing and no one else to adulterate their aspirations, as the Koran demands (K18:110).

Though Rumi had a wealth of approaches and manuals to draw upon for his Sufi practice, his theosophy and mysticism, we should look directly to his immediate formative influences – his father, his teacher Borhân al-Din, and his spiritual master, Shams al-Din – to learn more about how and what he learned and taught. The following chapters in part I of this book therefore focus in depth on the influence of Rumi's fathers of the blood and of the spirit.

PART I

RUMI'S FATHERS IN SPIRIT

Bahâ al-Din Valad:
The King of Clerics

I obliterated myself, stripping myself of all forms so that I could see God. I told myself I would obliterate God and strip God of all forms to see God and attain His blessings more immediately. I chanted "God" and my consciousness joined to God and I saw God, in the guise of His Godhead and the attributes of perfection. I saw that as regards His essence and attributes, how and why are inadmissible questions. The world of God is something other than this, I reflected, for His realm is not the realm of phenomena and perishability. No, when I see His meta-propositional [*bi-chun*, literally "howless"] essence and attributes, I see that forms and modes and dimensions all dangle from His holiness like leaves and blossoms, and I know that God and His attributes are something other than these, which they merely bring into existence but do not resemble. When my consciousness is busied with God, I move beyond the world of existence and decomposition and have my being not in space or in a place, but I wander through the world beyond modality (*bi-chun*) and look. (Bah 1:169)

I was saying: "O God, I am in love with You and seeking for You. Wherever will I see You? In the world, beyond the world?"

God moved me with the thought that the four walls of your body and the space that contains you are aware of you and live through you, but do not *see* you. Though they do not see you, neither from within nor from without, yet every atom of you is filled with the evidences of you. Likewise, you will not see Me within or without the world, but the atoms of the world all have something of Me – change, transformation, heat, cold. Your atoms thrive through Me and find joy in Me. How could you not see Me?

So I thought, "O God, then all creatures see you to the extent that your evidences flow through them." (Bah 1:212–13)

These entries from Bahâ al-Din's spiritual diaries reveal the mystical concerns which preoccupied him. They also show how much Rumi's thinking owes to his father, born in about 1152 in Khorasan, the homeland of classical Iranian Sufism, probably in the area around Balkh and Termez, near the modern border of Afghanistan and Tajikistan.

THE FACTS OF LIFE

In an informal sermon or discussion with his disciples, Mohammad Bahâ al-Din-e Valad mentions that on the first day of the month of fasting, Ramadan, about six hundred some years after the Prophet Mohammad's migration to Medina, he was about to turn fifty-five years-old (Bah 1:354). He would have measured this in lunar years, according to the Islamic calendar; if we subtract fifty-five lunar years from 1 Ramadan 600, corresponding to May 3, 1204 in the Julian calendar, this would take us to 1 Ramadan 545, corresponding to December 22, 1150. The passage in question seems susceptible of two different interpretations, depending on which manuscript one reads. At least one manuscript reads "in the year 600 I reflected that ..." (... *senne-ye settame'a va andishidam*). Other manuscripts, however, are less precise about the date and say that "six hundred and a few odd years after the Hegira of Mohammad I heard ..." (*senne-ye settame'a va and shenidam*). Assuming this latter reading is correct, we cannot place Bahâ al-Din's birth in late December 1150 or early January 1151, but a few years later, probably around November of 1152 or 1153.

What was it that Bahâ al-Din had heard or was thinking about at this time? That he would live only ten more years, more or less, to the age of sixty-five, if he were fortunate, since this was a lifespan only the strong and hearty (*mardomân-e qavi va jasim tan*) could expect (Bah 1:354), whereas Bahâ al-Din suffered from various ailments (Bah 2:1, 44, etc.). Bahâ al-Din became preoccupied with how best to occupy the ten remaining years, or as he calculates, 3,600 days which he estimated might round out his natural span of life. He concludes, as one might expect of a preacher, that his time – which he should count a blessing – would best be spent in the mention of God and obedience to His commands (Bah 1:354–5).

As it happens, Bahâ al-Din survived for about another quarter century, with the final twenty years or so of his life proving far more eventful than the first sixty. When Bahâ al-Din recalled the meditation on mortality which preoccupied him on the eve of his fifty-fifth birthday, his wife was perhaps pregnant with or already suckling his second son. This son, Mohammad Jalâl al-Din, born on September 30, 1207, was to become one of the greatest mystical poets in human history (so thought his translator, R.A. Nicholson, and Bausani, among others). When little Jalâl al-Din was born, Bahâ al-Din must have been just shy of sixty. And when this boy had not yet reached his teen years, Bahâ al-Din pulled up roots and moved his family all the way from Central Asia to Central Anatolia. By 1231, when Bahâ-e Valad finally passed away, he had managed to attract a circle of disciples around him in a seminary in Konya, in the land of Rum (the name which the Muslims gave to Asia Minor, and which today we know as Turkey), where he groomed the young man Jalâl al-Din Rumi to take his place as teacher and preacher at the head of this circle.

SOURCES FOR AND STUDIES OF BAHÂ AL-DIN'S LIFE

A good deal of factual and anecdotal information about the life of Bahâ al-Din-e Valad can be gleaned from his own journal, entitled *Ma'âref*, meaning mystical "Intimations". Jalâl al-Din Rumi, Bahâ al-Din's son, provides a meager detail or two in his Discourses, collected in *Ketâb-e fihe mâ fih*, literally "the book which contains what it contains," an odd title suggestive of a hodge-podge, connoting something like "For what it's worth." Bahâ al-Din's grandson, Sultan Valad, gives us a soft-focus portrait in his verse history of the family, known both as *Ebtedâ nâme*, "The Book of Beginnings," and as the *Valad nâme*, or *Masnavi-ye Valadi*, which conveys the dual meaning "The Filial Book" and "The Book of the Valads." Though it claims to relate factual information, it appears incorrect on some points of fact and concerns itself more with events transpiring on the spiritual plane than on the historico-physical plane. Two separate chronicles written at a greater remove by Sepahsâlâr and Aflâki, disciples of the mystical order which formed around the family and its shrine, give us much more detail. These chronicles – Sepahsâlâr's *Resâle* ("Treatise") and Aflâki's *Manâqeb al-'ârefin* ("Acts of the Gnostics") – reflect the legendary anecdotes circulating about one hundred years after Bahâ al-Din's death and must be digested with a healthy dose of salt.

Scholarly treatments of the life of Bahâ al-Din began with an article by Hellmut Ritter which introduced manuscripts of a work by Bahâ al-Din entitled *Ma'âref* that had been uncovered in collections in Turkey by the time of the Second World War.[1] Badi' al-Zamân Foruzânfar subsequently located several further manuscripts, on the basis of which he published an edition of the *Ma'âref* in 1955. In 1959 Foruzânfar added a second volume to this after coming across yet another manuscript of the *Ma'âref* which contained a hitherto unknown portion of the text. Working from this, A.J. Arberry provided an English translation of twenty of the several hundred discourses of Bahâ al-Din's *Ma'âref*.[2] Hellmut Ritter provided a brief synopsis of Bahâ al-Din's life in an article for the *Encyclopaedia of Islam*, and these details were summarized once again in 1989 in the *Encyclopaedia Iranica*.[3] Carefully analyzing a wide variety of sources, principally Bahâ al-Din's own work, the Swiss scholar Fritz Meier produced a superb study of the life and teachings in his 1989 book *Bahâ'-i Walad: Grundzüge seines Lebens und seiner Mystik*, the definitive statement on Bahâ al-Din. The account of Bahâ al-Din given here relies heavily upon Meier.

BAHÂ AL-DIN'S PARENTAGE

Bahâ al-Din's father was Hosayn Khatibi, a Muslim preacher and scholar traditionally believed to have lived in Balkh. Balkh is today a small town just west of Mazâr-e Sharif in Afghanistan, but from the tenth through the twelfth centuries it was a flourishing center of Islamic culture under first Samanid, then Ghaznavid, and finally Seljuk rule. The prosperous city, protected by a wall, supported several bazaars, including a garden and the "Lovers' Market" (Bâzâr-e ʿâsheqân), built by the famous Sultan Mahmud of Ghazna. As in most Persian and Central Asian cities, the houses in Balkh were built of clay. An ancient settlement whose populace had been Zoroastrian and then Buddhist before the city was destroyed in the Arab invasions, Balkh also harbored a centuries-old Jewish quarter which persisted into the Islamic period alongside the dominant Muslims.

A century before the birth of Bahâ al-Din the Seljuks wrested control of Balkh and its environs from the Ghaznavids, and a great college (the Nezâmiye) was built there with the encouragement of the famous vizier Nezâm al-Molk (assassinated 1092). About the time of Bahâ al-Din's birth, however, the Seljuks lost control of the area and during the subsequent century the city went into decline. First came the occupation of 1152 by the Ghurid conqueror ʿAlâ al-Din Hosayn (nicknamed Jahânsuz, the World-Burner), then the sacking of the city by Oghuz tribesmen. In 1198 rule of Balkh transferred from the Qarakhitây back to the Ghurid prince of Bâmiân, Bahâ al-Din Sâm. Seven years later, the Shah of Khwârazm, ʿAlâ al-Din Mohammad b. Takesh (r. 1200–1220), seized the city, and it was during his reign that Bahâ al-Din eventually fled from Khorasan. The great Mongol hordes of Genghis Khan destroyed Balkh in the spring of 1221, a blow from which it never really recovered. It is said that the Mongols massacred thousands of the 200,000 some inhabitants who lived in Balkh at this time.[4]

Bahâ al-Din's father, Hosayn, had been a religious scholar with a bent for asceticism, occupied like his own father before him, Ahmad, with the family profession of preacher (*khatib*). Of the four canonical schools of Sunni Islam, the family adhered to the relatively liberal Hanafi rite. Hosayn-e Khatibi enjoyed such renown in his youth – so says Aflâki with characteristic exaggeration – that Razi al-Din Nayshâpuri and other famous scholars came to study with him (Af 9; for the legends about Bahâ al-Din, see below, "The Mythical Bahâ al-Din"). Another report indicates that Bahâ al-Din's grandfather, Ahmad al-Khatibi, was born to Ferdows Khâtun, a daughter of the reputed Hanafite jurist and author Shams al-Aʾemma Abu Bakr of Sarakhs, who died circa 1088 (Af 75; FB 6 n. 4; Mei 74 n. 17). This is far from implausible and, if true, would tend to suggest that Ahmad al-Khatibi had studied under Shams al-Aʾemma. Prior to that the family could supposedly trace its roots back to Isfahan.

We do not learn the name of Bahâ al-Din's mother in the sources, only that he referred to her as "Mama" (*Mâmi*), and that she lived in to the 1200s. Bahâ al-Din also confirms that he answered to the nickname Valad (son), which may suggest that he was an only son, especially since we have no other information about siblings (Bah 2:45). Bahâ al-Din does not give a full portrait of his mother, but she appears on several occasions in a nagging role, disturbing his concentration or his writing, causing him grief (e.g., Bah 1:30, 317; 2:107), or even throwing temper tantrums and cursing in front of others, such that Bahâ al-Din felt mildly anxious about his reputation (Bah 2:62). However, to some degree Bahâ al-Din and his mother must have shared philosophical or religious conversation (Bah 1:177ff.).

BAHÂ AL-DIN'S WIVES AND CHILDREN

Islamic law permits marriage to as many as four wives at a time. We do not know how many marriages Bahâ al-Din contracted simultaneously, but he does name several women, paramount among them for our purposes, Mo'mene Khâtun, the mother of Rumi, who accompanied him on the journey westward, but died in Lârende (modern Karaman), before reaching Konya. The *Ma'âref* speaks of a certain Bibi 'Alavi, which Zarrinkub (ZrP 61) identifies as a nickname for Mo'mene Khâtun, but whom Meier (Mei 427) takes for a separate wife. Bahâ al-Din elsewhere speaks unabashedly of his sexual desire for the daughter of the Qâzi Sharaf (Bah 1:327–8), whom we may assume to be another wife. He also speaks frankly about his desire for coitus with a certain Tarkân (Bah 2:175), which may be the name of a fourth wife or perhaps a title or nickname for one of the previously mentioned wives. Though Bahâ al-Din was an ascetic by temperament and tried to control his passions (e.g. Bah 1:352), he did not share the Christian and Manichaean loathing for the physical world. Instead, Bahâ al-Din's view reflected an Islamic attitude toward sexuality, one that acknowledges the power of our sexual appetites and seeks to appease them within a strictly regulated framework that preserves social stability. Bahâ relates that one morning when staring into the oven in a spiritual meditation on the qualities of fire, a dog barked and disturbed his concentration. Bibi 'Alavi got up and came to him, at which point a powerful lust seized him. He tried to combat passion's goading, but then sensed God had inspired him with this desire. As such, his promptings could not be evil (Bah 1:381):

> This is incited by God, so why should it have been a cause of torment (*'oqubat*) and distraction? God inspired me with the thought: "My business and My incitement is abasement and elevation. Now I incite to greatness and again to degradation." Now, whenever a realization comes over our spirit, first remember God, for it is God who incites you, and reflect whether or not the incitement will lead to punishment and degradation and suffering; in which case pray to God that he not incite you so. And if it is the cause of grandeur and fortune, praise

God so that He may always keep you in that state. Whenever your spirit gives you one of these two sensations, know that you are favored by the light of Prophethood.

While Bahâ al-Din certainly experienced a tension between his spiritual nature and his physical desires, this tension arises from the question why lust for a wife to whom he was lawfully married should seize upon him and break his concentration when he was attempting to pray. It does not mean that Bahâ al-Din would have tolerated adultery or promiscuity. We learn elsewhere of Bahâ al-Din's astonishment on seeing the carnival-like atmosphere prevailing after a circumcision ceremony, possibly influenced by Chinese (Khotanese) practice, during which the women wore no headcover, held hands with the men in public, drank wine (*seyaki*), danced and even bared their breasts (Bah 2:17).

According to Aflâki (Af 994), Bahâ al-Din had a daughter by the name of Fâteme Khâtun, who married in Khorasan and remained behind with her husband when the Valad family migrated westward. He also had a wet-nurse in the household, called Nosob Khâtun, who some say was Bahâ al-Din's sister; in any case, she was married (Af 15–16), and likewise probably remained behind with her husband. The *Ma'âref* (Bah 2:45, 142) mentions a son who was called Hosayn, the namesake of Bahâ al-Din's own father, and probably therefore Bahâ al-Din's first-born. Since neither Aflâki nor Sepahsâlâr mention him, Hosayn likely remained behind with Bahâ al-Din's mother in Khorasan or perhaps died before the family's relocation to Anatolia (Mei 50). All the sources agree, however, that 'Alâ al-Din Mohammad was Rumi's older brother by two years, which places his birth in the year 1205 (A.H. 602), since Rumi was born in 1207 (A.H. 604). Both 'Alâ al-Din and his younger brother, Jalâl al-Din Mohammad (Rumi), accompanied their father on his peregrinations, though the *Ma'âref* mentions neither of them by name.

BAHÂ AL-DIN VALAD'S OCCUPATION AND STATUS IN LIFE

Bahâ al-Din used the title *Sultan al-'olamâ*, the Sultan of the Ulama, or as I shall render it here, the "King of Clerics," suggesting that he was the most pious or spiritual of the religious scholars. Based on this title, and on the hyperbolic claims we read in the hagiographical accounts written by Sultan Valad, Sepahsâlâr and Aflâki about the fame of Bahâ al-Din and the huge crowds that came out to greet him and hear him lecture wherever he went, most scholars have assumed that Bahâ al-Din was among the most renowned Hanafi jurists of his day. This is not, however, the picture which emerges from Bahâ al-Din's own writings or from the historical dictionaries written in the medieval period about the famous scholars of Islam. As yet no sources dating from the lifetime of Bahâ al-Din have been found which make mention of him, and we must therefore assume that he was not widely known (Mei 423). Had the ulama widely recognized him as their "sultan," particularly with respect to Islamic law, he would certainly have been offered a professorial position in one of the important colleges where he lived or in the cities through which he passed. And, had he been a professor in an important college, his name would almost surely have been recorded by the biographers.

The name of Bahâ al-Din is remembered, however, solely on account of his son, Rumi. The first biographical dictionary of specifically Hanafi jurists which has come down to us, *al-Javâher al-mozi²e fi tabaqât al-hanafiye* by ʿAbd al-Qâder Ibn Abi al-Vafâ (1297–1373), devotes separate (though quite inaccurate) entries to Rumi and his son, Sultan Valad, but nothing to Bahâ al-Din. Ibn Abi al-Vafâ compiled this information within 150 years of Bahâ al-Din's death and presumably used earlier sources which are no longer available to us.

The profession of preacher (*vâ²ez*) and jurisconsult (*faqih*) adapted itself to a mobile lifestyle, providing Bahâ al-Din and his forebears with the opportunity to relocate in search of a following. Bahâ al-Din may have been born in Balkh, but at least between June 1204 and 1210 (Shavvâl 600 and 607), during which time Rumi was born, Bahâ al-Din resided in a house in Vakhsh (Bah 2:143). Vakhsh, rather than Balkh, was the permanent base of Bahâ al-Din and his family until Rumi was around five years old (Mei 16–35). At that time, in about the year 1212 (A.H. 608–9), the Valads moved to Samarqand (Fih 333; Mei 29–30, 36), leaving behind Bahâ al-Din's mother, who must have been at least seventy-five years old.[5]

VAKHSH

Vakhsh, which has tentatively been identified with the medieval town of Lēwkand (or Lâvakand) or Sangtude, falls within the borders of modern-day Tajikistan, about 65 kilometers southeast of Dushanbe, 35 kilometers northeast of Kurgan-Tyube, and within 500 kilometers of the Chinese border. It is situated just north of the 38th parallel on the east bank of the Vakhshâb river, a major tributary flowing into the Amu Daryâ river, known in those days as the Jayhun, but which the Greeks had named the Oxus in antiquity. Indeed, the Greek word "Oxus" perhaps derives from the word Vakhsh, the Vakhshâb being the water that feeds or "swells" into the Oxus proper. Geographers from the central Islamic lands regarded the Oxus as the historical boundary between the land of the Persians and the Turks. What lay beyond the river (*Mâ varâ al-nahr*), or more properly the two rivers – the Oxus and the Jaxartes – constituted the imaginary pale between civilization and the steppes. The area between these two rivers had a flourishing urban life, however, and featured two of the more glorious Islamic cities of the early middle ages – Bokhara and Samarqand.

In terms of culture or population, Vakhsh did not rate as one of the important centers of Transoxania. By extension, the name Vakhsh also referred to the region between the Akhshavâ and Vakhshâb rivers in the vicinity of the ancient stone bridge[6] over the Vakhshâb, about 45 kilometers north of Vakhsh. In the tenth century, according to Estakhri, the area of Vakhsh was fertile and fruitful, enjoyed a reputation for its horses and pack animals, and supported a goodly number of towns on the banks of its rivers and streams. The region to the south, closer to the Oxus, was known as Khottal, the provincial seat of which was Holbok, large enough during this period (about two hundred years before the lifetime of Bahâ al-Din) to support a Friday mosque. Monk and Halâvard were, however, the larger and finer cities of the region. We may infer from the early medieval geographers that the town of Vakhsh or Lēwkand was smaller than these mid-sized provincial towns, though the demographics may have changed somewhat by the time Bahâ al-Din lived there.

Though a number of intermediate towns lay nearby, such as Qobâdiân and Vâshgerd, the closest large city was Termez (Termed or Terme<u>dh</u>), situated in the Chaghâniân region on the northern bank of the Oxus at its confluence with the Zâmel river, 175 kilometers to the southwest of Vakhsh as the crow flies, and a few days' journey along the main road. Termez, the hometown of Bahâ al-Din's disciple Borhân al-Din Mohaqqeq, was a trade entrepôt for goods going to Khorasan from Transoxania. Surrounded by two walls and an outlying suburb, Termez was the seat of the district governor in the tenth century. At that time the city streets were paved with burnt brick, materials also used in the building of the market, though the Friday mosque, from an earlier period, was built with unbaked brick. Genghis Khan (Changiz Khân, 1162–1227) destroyed Termez after the Valad family had moved to Asia Minor, but the city was completely rebuilt. Ibn Battûta, who visited it probably some time around 1330, describes it as large and prosperous, with canals, gardens, a variety of foodstuffs, and beautiful architecture.

Ibn Battûta recalls that it took a day and a half's march from Termez through sandy wilderness to reach Balkh, which he found run down and uninhabited, thanks to Genghis Khan's deliberate depopulation of the city. Even so, the many mosques and law colleges of Balkh made an enduring impression on Ibn Battûta; as he puts it, there were four historically great cities in Khorasan, two of which – Herat and Nayshâpur – remained inhabited when he passed through, and two of which – Marv and Balkh – had been destroyed by the Mongols (Bat 382).

Balkh is situated about 250 kilometers from Vakhsh. When Bahâ al-Din and Jalâl al-Din spoke with other emigres from Khorasan, they perhaps specified the city of their origin more precisely, at least indicating they came from the region of Vakhsh. But they apparently allowed the people of Anatolia to believe that they came from Balkh, one of the major cultural centers of the day, before it was sacked by the Mongols. While this provided a known point of reference (suburbanites the world over still introduce themselves when away from home as living in the major metropolis nearest them), it also enhanced their prestige, since to be from Balkh suggested a more cosmopolitan and sophisticated background than did Vakhsh. In any case, Bahâ al-Din, his father or his grandfather probably did at some time live in Balkh.

Samarqand, where the Valad family had moved by the year 1212 or so, lay about 250 kilometers to the northwest of Vakhsh, in what today is Uzbekistan. Samarqand was a major urban center, perhaps the major economic center of Transoxania. The geographer Yâqût, writing within about a decade of the departure of the Valad family from Samarqand, describes the city as encompassing about 750 acres. The fortified citadel was protected by a wall and a deep moat. The gardens and orchards of Samarqand were famous and water was delivered in lead pipes via aqueducts to homes from the canals outside the city wall. Unfortunately, the city was laid ruin by the Mongols in 1219, but the Valads had probably left town at least three years before this tragic event (LeS; Bat; and Mei 14–16).

BAHÂ AL-DIN'S PROFESSION

According to Sepahsâlâr, Bahâ al-Din wore the attire of scholars and lived in Balkh, where he received a fixed stipend (*marsum*) from public funds (*bayt al-mâl*). He lived modestly, in accordance with the Shari‘a, and never siphoned off or diverted to some other purpose any funds from the charitable trust (*vaqf*) which supported him (to divert funds from a charitable endowment was an immoral, even illegal, though not apparently uncommon practice). Scholars flocked here from all parts of Khorasan to ask Bahâ al-Din for his fatwas on various abstruse matters. He would teach classes open to the public, presumably on Islamic law (*khalâyeq râ dars farmudi*), until the time between the two prayers (*bayn al-salâtayn*), probably an allusion to the noon and afternoon prayers, with their four prostrations each (the prayer times being dawn, noon, late afternoon, sunset and evening). After the late afternoon prayer (*namâz-e digar*), he would lecture to his disciples (*ashâb va molâzemân*) on spiritual and gnostic matters (*ma‘âref va haqâyeq gofti*). On Mondays and Fridays – Fridays being the day of the official, state-sponsored, congregational prayer and sermon – Bahâ al-Din would give public sermons (*mow‘eze*) with Jalâl al-Din-e Mohammad, the Khwârazmshâh, frequently in attendance, though the Khwârazmshâh was under the sway of another theologian, Fakhr al-Din Râzi (Sep 10).

Since Bahâ al-Din was not in Balkh when Jalâl al-Din-e Mohammad was Khwârazmshâh (also called Mingburnu, r. 1220–31), we may choose to dismiss this report in its entirety, or we may assume that Sepahsâlâr has simply mistaken Jalâl al-Din the Khwârazmshâh for his father, ‘Alâ al-Din Mohammad (r. 1200–1220). However, Sepahsâlâr oddly refers to the Friday prayer here as *mow‘eze*, perhaps signifying a sermon given after the *khotbe* or one given in a small mosque (i.e., not the congregational mosque). But if the sultan or Shah attended

Friday worship services, he almost certainly attend the *khotbe*, the official Friday prayer in the congregational mosque; whether he would attend any other sermons is another question. In any case, the particulars of Sepahsâlâr's report (i.e., locating it in Balkh, making Jalâl al-Din Khwârazmshâh contemporary with Fakhr-e Râzi, having the ruler attend a *mow'eze* on Friday, but not the official *khotbe*, etc.) cast considerable suspicion on the accuracy of his account. We can, of course, choose to accept the generalities and reject some of the particulars.

Perhaps the general outlines of the story accurately reflect Bahâ al-Din's activities in Vakhsh, with the exception of the Khwârazmshâh's attendance. The life described sounds consonant with the activity of a preacher (*khatib* or *vâ'ez*), though when Bahâ al-Din refers to his own preaching, he uses the word *tazkir*, roughly an admonition, a genre of sermon that originally must have called to mind the commandments and exhortations of God and recited the promised rewards of heaven for the righteous and the punishments destined for the sinners. Bahâ al-Din does reflect on these matters, but when he presents them to his disciples – and he does specify that he had some disciples (*moridân-am*, Bah 1:374) – he does so not in a fire-and-brimstone manner, but as a spiritual counselor concerned with the intrinsic value of righteous works. Bahâ al-Din writes that he enjoyed the profession of pious oratory (*va'z*, Bah 2:60). He also taught classes on the religious sciences, including exegesis of the Koran (Bah 2:56, 60). He was capable of teaching these in Arabic (Bah 2:159), though he usually chose to do so in Persian. He strictly observed the law and the doctrines of religion, and expected others to do the same, expressing disgust for those who did not (Bah 2:60, 97).

Aflâki (Af 11, 33) makes mention of a certain "Qâzi of Vakhsh," confirming that Vakhsh was a town of some size, in any case, not a mere village. We cannot conclude from this alone that the town was large enough to support its own *madrase*/law college. If it did, Bahâ al-Din does not mention having studied or held a professorship there. Of course, Bahâ al-Din could have studied Islamic law (*feqh*) earlier, somewhere outside of Vakhsh, in Termez or Balkh, for example, where the professors of law would have been well known. If he obtained a certificate of permission (*ejâze*) to teach or to give legal opinions, or fatwas, he would have been entitled to teach students of his own.

Bahâ al-Din at some point taught Islamic law and preached five days a week, from Saturday through Wednesday, leaving Thursday and Friday free for him to contemplate his mortality and to take spiritual account of his actions (Mei 427). This would mean he did not deliver the Friday sermon, or *khotbe*. He does not seem to have cared greatly for disputation or debate, but did lecture on theological topics. He was not trained in the science of Hadith source-criticism, but appears to have known something of medicine and astronomy, thinking for a while that he might even make a study of medicine with the physician 'Emâd al-Din (Bah 2:30). We may note that among Hanafi jurisconsults, a modicum of medical knowledge – specifically the study of Abu al-ᶜAbbâs al-Mostaghferi's medical text, *Tebb al-nabi* – was recommended, while study of astronomy was discouraged, except insofar as it was needed to ascertain the direction to face when praying – the *qeble* – and the times of prayer (Zar 23–4, 74). Bahâ al-Din perhaps supervised the worship practices of a small circle of disciples (Mei 428).

Even if Vakhsh housed no *madrase*, the mosque may have provided funds for a professor, but if any students came to study with Bahâ al-Din in a mosque or even in his home, the number is unlikely to have been large. Endowed colleges, the *madrases*, usually made provisions to lodge and feed a fixed number of students, but Bahâ al-Din would not have been able to provide stipends to support any students on his own. Furthermore, Vakhsh would have attracted students only from the surrounding villages; more ambitious students would have gone to the larger cities. Nevertheless, Bahâ al-Din did undertake the ascetic and spiritual training of at least one disciple, Borhân al-Din Mohaqqeq, from nearby Termez.

Bahâ al-Din's grandfather, Ahmad al-Khatibi, seems to have held the position of preacher, *khatib*, as his name suggests. According to Hanafi law, the *khatib* must lead the Friday prayers and give the *khotbe* – the official sermon delivered in the congregational mosque (*jâmeᶜ*) on Fridays, at the beginning of which the caliph and the current ruler of the city or country were invoked and praised. In theory, as sanctioned by a hadith, each town would have just one congregational mosque (MRC 21), designated by the caliph or local ruler. In large cities, though, the entire populace could never fit into a single mosque, so the number of Friday mosques proliferated. In mid-eleventh-century Baghdad there were six congregational Friday mosques, in contrast to hundreds, perhaps as many as three thousand, smaller mosques; in Cairo the practice was for a much larger number of mosques to function congregationally (MRC 13–14). Shâfeᶜi and Mâleki law call for only one *khatib* per town, whereas Hanafi law allows for more. Cities like Balkh and Baghdad therefore employed a handful of *khatibs*, and Cairo even more. A place like Vakhsh, however, probably had no more than one.

If Bahâ al-Din delivered the *khotbe* in Vakhsh, this would have embroiled him in political affairs, particularly when the ruler changed. If he called the Khwârazmshâh a deviant (*mobtadeᶜ*, see below) in the *khotbe*, the official Friday sermon, this may have caused serious problems for him when the Khwârazmshâh took over Vakhsh, and could account for why Bahâ al-Din eventually left the city and the area. However, if he spent Fridays in contemplation, as we are told, he could not have delivered the *khotbe*, and if there is any truth in his alleged dislike of seeking out princes or kings, we would not expect Bahâ al-Din to praise the rulers and their virtues as part of his official duties. We might furthermore expect to find the title *Khatib* among Bahâ al-Din's honorifics had he actually held this position in Khorasan.

51

Instead, Bahâ al-Din probably made his living as an occasional preacher (*vâ'ez*), perhaps with a position in a mosque. The *vâ'ez*, usually a jurisconsult in his own right, preached learned homilies at various times, usually to gatherings in a mosque, *madrase* or Sufi lodge. He exhorted the populace to moral behavior and reminded them of their religious and spiritual obligations; aside from the obvious requirement of speaking ability, a preacher had to be erudite and very pious himself in order to inspire the people to heed his admonitions (*tazkir*). In contradistinction to the learned preaching of the *vâ'ez*, the revivalist/raconteur (*qâss*) stood in the streets and recited from memory popular hadith, stories of the Koran, and saints' lives.[7]

Bahâ al-Din did not pursue this task with a completely tranquil or rigidly convinced mind. He himself tells us that the writings of Abu al-Moʿin Nasafi (al-Makhuli, d. 1115), a Hanafi jurist and follower of Mâtoridi in theological matters, set him to thinking about the utility of preaching and exhorting to good deeds (*khayrât, vaʿz, nasihat*). The command of God is not to compel obedience (*itmâr*) and prohibition (*nahy*) cannot prevent acts in the end (*entehâ*), for God already knows what His servants will do. He forgives disobedience and pardons sin. He does not grant paradise for good deeds, but only on account of His grace (*fazl*). When Bahâ al-Din reflected on these matters, his homiletic resolve wavered and he withdrew (*motaqâʿed shodam*) from preaching, thinking that it was all in vain. However, further reflection made him lean toward the views of the Mutazilis, and their belief that man is a free agent and chooses to act as he does (Bah 2:137). This convinced him once again that there was indeed a purpose in enjoining the good and forbidding the bad, in preaching, counseling and calling the people to their higher conscience (*mashvarat-hâ*). He concluded that one had to act in consort with the principles of whichever school of thought (*mazhab*) seemed most agreeable and true to him. In his own case, Bahâ al-Din came down upon the side of the fence that believed one gains benefit through obedience and by avoiding what is wrong. Furthermore, one ought to counsel others to observe what is ethical and legal (Bah 2:138), and Bahâ al-Din therefore continued in this profession.

Though it seems Bahâ al-Din was able to support his family from the income he received for preaching, he did not hold a powerful position among the ulama. On the one hand, he felt that his lack of access to power kept him untainted by politics and worldly concerns; on the other hand, he sometimes yearned for the attention and social respect that come with higher positions. As he tells us (Bah 1:374):

> Sometimes my heart fills with the thought that I am a king with no dominion, a judge (*qâzi*) with no authority (*qazâ*), a man of standing (*sâheb-e sadr*) with no position (*bi-sadr*), and a wealthy man with no money. Such thoughts betray love of wealth and position, covetousness and envy. By concerning yourself with such things, you only make yourself depressed (*sowdâ-hâ midahi*). You must unify

your spirit with the attributes of God such that nothing of these [thoughts]
remains within you. People strive in the worldly markets after rank and wealth.
Ambitions are just like a ladder, long and very high. They go up rung by rung,
but I know for certain that they will fall off the middle of the ladder.

DREAMING OF THE KING OF CLERICS

Sepahsâlâr (Sep 12) tells us that the kings and shaykhs and learned men from all
around heeded Bahâ al-Din and attended his sermons (*majles-e vaʿz*), placing
the number of his disciples, students and those who believed in him at three
hundred (Sep 13). This might theoretically be possible if Bahâ al-Din had had a
position traveling from mosque to mosque giving sermons or series of classes on
Islamic law and the Koran, indicating that he had appointments in two or more
institutions to lecture or preach. Much more likely, however, this number
represents the hagiographer's attempt to match Bahâ al-Din disciple-per-disciple
in importance with Fakhr al-Din Râzi. Whatever public following Bahâ al-Din
did command, it must have consisted primarily of those who attended his
sermons, although it also appears that he wrote juridical opinions, or fatwas.

The hagiographers claim, with typical exaggeration, that three hundred
pious and licensed jurisconsults (*mofti*) and scholars in the area of Balkh all had
a dream one night in which the Prophet came to them and told them to call
Bahâ al-Din the Sultan of the Ulama, "King of the Clerics." Of course, as a
result of describing their similar dreams to one another, these people became his
disciples in great numbers (Sep 11–12; Af 10). Both hagiographers have taken
this story from Bahâ al-Din himself, whose actual dream was remarkable
enough, though not quite as grandiose as the hagiographers have made it in the
retelling.

Bahâ al-Din tells us that just one person, albeit a very spiritual person, one of
God's elect (*ʿazizi az ʿazizân va gozidegân-e Haqq*), had a dream. This person did
not explicitly specify that the Prophet told him to call Bahâ al-Din "Sultan al-
ulama," but he did say that an illuminated elder (*piri nurâni*), one of those nigh
unto God, stood upon a great elevation and addressed Bahâ al-Din as follows:
"O Sultan al-ulama, come out so that the world may be filled with light and the
darkness of heedlessness may be set to flight." Bahâ al-Din told a certain
nobleman (*khwâje*) from Marv, who had served kings or other aristocrats, about
this dream and this man revealed to Bahâ al-Din that he, too, had seen God's
servants testifying that the Prophet had designated Bahâ al-Din as Sultan al-
ulama. This nobleman from Marv sympathized with Bahâ al-Din, expressing
surprise that when he was thus designated in the other world, anyone would
dare to erase his title in this world. The man from Marv further indicated to
Bahâ al-Din that he had dreamed or seen a group of people calling out loudly,
"Mercy upon the friends of Sultan al-ulama." From this, Bahâ al-Din drew the
conclusion that his enemies were cursed, and his prayer had been answered

(Bah 1:188–9). Possibly this nobleman from Marv is the same Razi Mahmud ʿAbd al-Razzâq who, Bahâ al-Din elsewhere tells us, prayed to see a dream of the Prophet and saw Bahâ al-Din instead (Bah 1:283). Or it may be the ʿAbd Allâh-e Hendi who dreamed that Bahâ al-Din was seated on a throne in front of the Sultan of Vakhsh with his retinue and army, while all the people came forward to kiss the foot of Bahâ al-Din (Bah 1:283, 303).

By actually signing his fatwas as *Sultan al-ʿolamâ*, Bahâ al-Din explicitly reserved the place at the top of the hierarchy of jurisconsults and religious scholars for himself. This did not, unfortunately, impress other people in authority. Bahâ al-Din tells us that the *qâzi* used to erase his title "Sultan of the Ulama" out of enmity. Though Bahâ al-Din does not wish to question the hand of God in the affairs of the world, he prays that God will change this state of affairs, since it is an injustice. The *qâzi* does this only out of a desire to increase his own reputation and to appease his own desires (Bah 1:188–9). Aflâki further pinpoints this individual: it was the Qâzi of Vakhsh, a respectable religious scholar (*mardi bud moʿtabar va az ʿolamâ-ye in ʿâlam*), who tried to erase the title "King of the Clerics" from Bahâ al-Din's fatwas and from the introduction to his *Maʿâref* (Af 33). It seems unlikely that the *Maʿâref* circulated in book form for this *qâzi* to read – probably Aflâki had seen a copy of the manuscript with the title "King of the Clerics" written on it and assumed that the Qâzi of Vakhsh had also seen the same manuscript.

However, it was a practice among legal scholars to take their opinions to other jurisconsults and try to gain a signature of assent from them. Quite likely, if Bahâ al-Din's juridical opinions were sent before the judge in Vakhsh with the signature "King of the Clerics," the judge would have had the impertinent title erased to signify Bahâ al-Din's lower rank in the hierarchy of ulama. Obviously, if one had the respect of all of the religious scholars on grounds of reputation or one's teachers' reputation, no dream would be necessary to convince others of one's rank. This tells us that only among the spiritually awake was Bahâ al-Din's true worth and rank perceived, the type of man revered by Sufis for divine susceptibility and temperament, rather than worldly and scholarly accomplishments.

This shows us that even in Vakhsh, Bahâ al-Din could not lay claim to great fame or standing among the ulama. Even Rumi does not refer to his father in the *Divân* or in the *Masnavi*, though we may attribute this in part to modesty and a desire not to boast (after all, everyone in Rumi's circle would have known very well who his father was). Rumi does mention Bahâ al-Din by name in the Discourses (Fih 12–13 and 177), notes of lectures meant for his immediate disciples, to whom Bahâ al-Din would have been known either personally or through oral tradition. From this we might infer that his father was not well known enough to warrant mention in works meant for wider publication. All this, along with the relative obscurity which a mid- or lower-level position as preacher in Vakhsh would have guaranteed among the ulama, and the absence of entries about Bahâ al-Din in biographical dictionaries or in other sources contemporary to him, forces us to conclude that the title "King of Clerics" could not have been widely applied to Bahâ al-Din in Khorasan. Of course, close association with a prince or ruler would be one of the primary means of gaining wider fame as a juriconsult or preacher and Bahâ al-Din's distaste for the Khwârazmshâh may indeed have consigned him to relative oblivion. Ironically, however, by refusing to become a royalist jurisconsult, Bahâ al-Din evidently gained the reputation, at least among the limited circle who preserved his memory, as the king of religious scholars.

Bahâ al-Din challenged the Qâzi of Vakhsh for rejecting him as insufficiently learned to preside over the religious affairs of Vakhsh (Bah 1:345). The Qâzi refused to stand in Bahâ al-Din's presence and attempted to intimidate the people who were inclined to follow him (Bah 1:425). Bahâ al-Din elsewhere reveals his displeasure over the fact that Qâzi Ebrâhim (perhaps this very same Qâzi of Vakhsh) did not use any title of respect when addressing Bahâ al-Din's son, whereas Bahâ al-Din's son referred to the judge by his title (Bah 2:45). Among those opposed to him, Bahâ al-Din also lists a certain Hâji Saddiq and his son, Nâseh. Their feud with Bahâ al-Din apparently began with a dispute (monâzere, perhaps signifying a formal disputation over a legal question) after the Friday prayer one day in 1208 (A.H. 605), when Rumi was an infant. Within the same week, a woman by the name of Omm Sho'ayb also became embroiled in this dispute (Bah 2:73). It does not seem they were especially high-ranking members of the ulama in Vakhsh (Bah 2:190), but Bahâ al-Din challenged them to a dispute (Bah 2:77).

Besides the Qâzi of Vakhsh, Aflâki mentions the names of several other members of the ulama, such as Fakhr-e Râzi, Qâzi Zayn-e Farâzi, Jamâl al-Din Hasiri, 'Amid-e Marvzi, Ibn Qâzi-ye Saddiq, Shams al-Din Khâni and Rashid-e Qobbâ'i, all of whom were veiled by their great knowledge from recognizing Bahâ al-Din. After Bahâ al-Din gained a reputation, they upbraided him out of jealousy and attempted to humiliate and offend him, "as is the wont of the ulama of the age, may God forgive them." Aflâki dates all this to the year 1208 (Af 11), but Bahâ al-Din apparently continued his activities in Vakhsh for a couple more years after this.

THE VALAD FAMILY UPROOTED

Bahâ was still in Vakhsh in September of 1210 (Bah 2:181–2), but came to Samarqand sometime between 1210 and 1212, when the Khwârazmshâh seized it. It would appear that the Valads remained in Khorasan for several years after this, but then left the area, never to return. Towards the end of his life, in the late 1260s, Rumi had a momentary flashback to his childhood in Vakhsh while contemplating the question of mortality in his *Masnavi* (M4:3319–20):

Limited reason's like a lightning flash:
We can't go in a flash from here to Vakhsh
The flash of lightning's not to guide your way
but comes instead commanding clouds to cry.

The notes and discourses contained in Bahâ al-Din's *Ma'âref* come to an end just after the move to Samarqand sometime around the year 1212, at which time Rumi would have been only five. Rumi speaks little of the family's history, nor does Sultan Valad give us much detail. Besides, Sultan Valad was too young when his grandfather died to have heard and accurately remembered first-hand from Bahâ al-Din the story of his life, which in any case appears in Sultan Valad's *Ebtedâ nâme* embellished in the form of verse. Sepahsâlâr and Aflâki both describe the Valads' peregrinations in greater detail than Sultan Valad, but draw upon legendary oral accounts circulating among the Mevlevis almost one hundred years after the clan had ended their meanderings. Aflâki's *Manâqeb* provides the most specific itinerary of the family's peregrinations, which continued for perhaps ten years before they finally settled down in Konya.

However, we cannot credit everything we read in these three sources as factually or even generally accurate. They are interested in the typological and morally instructive more than the mundane facts of the matter. All the hagiographers, including Sultan Valad, associated Bahâ al-Din and Rumi with Balkh, either because it was the family's ancestral home, or simply because it was the largest and most famous city in the region, whereas their actual home, Vakhsh, would have been relatively unheard of to the people living in Anatolia. We must likewise regard with skepticism the reasons Sultan Valad, Sepahsâlâr and Aflâki provide for Bahâ al-Din's pulling up roots. The motivations ascribed to Bahâ al-Din by the hagiographers include flight from the approaching Mongol hordes and/or a dispute with the Khwârazmshâh and Fakhr al-Din Râzi. In fact we cannot know for certain why or even when the Valad family left Samarqand and Khorasan. Our sources do all agree that the Valads left Khorasan before the conquest of Balkh at the hands of Genghis Khan in 1221. Although Aflâki relates contradictory reports, the weight of the information he provides places the family's departure at least four or five years before this. Let us, then, consider the circumstances more closely.

We do know that Bahâ al-Din Valad was residing in Samarqand under the rule of the Qarakhânid 'Osmân (r. 1204–11?) when the Khwârazmshâh besieged the city. Rumi himself mentions the siege of the city at the hands of the Khwârazmshâh in Discourse 45 (Fih 173), and describes how the most gorgeous noblewoman in their neighborhood kept praying to God and committing herself to his protection so that she would not fall into the hands of the attackers (fearing, of course, that she would be raped or taken captive and made into a slave girl). When the conquerors plundered the city, they carried off all her servants, but left her completely untouched ("Despite her surpassing beauty, no one so much as looked at her"), a fact which Rumi submits as evidence for the efficacy of prayer and reliance upon God. According to Ibn al-Athîr the Khwârazmshâh's siege of Samarqand took place somewhere around 1211 (A.H. 607), but the *Târikh-e jahângoshâ* of Jovayni dates the siege to 1212 or 1213 (A.H. 609), which is likely more accurate. The incident obviously made an impression on Rumi, who would have been a small boy at the time. It seems he speaks of the beauty of this woman from personal knowledge – elsewhere in the Discourses (Fih 159) Rumi alludes to the women (*shâhedân*) of Khwârazm and their famed beauty, some of whom he perhaps saw in Samarqand. At the time of the siege, he would have been a young boy between the ages of four and six, young enough to remain in the women's quarters with his mother and other unveiled females.

FAKHR-E RÂZI

As for Fakhr al-Din Râzi (1148–1209), he was the son of a *khatib* and himself an excellent preacher. He was a jurisconsult, but is perhaps best remembered as a theologian and philosopher. An Asharite in matters of theology, he quarreled with the Mutazilites in Khwârazm and was eventually compelled to leave the area. ʿAlâ al-Din Mohammad Khwârazmshâh (r. 1200–1220) built a *madrase* for him in Herat, where he spent most of his life and converted many Karrâmis to Sunni orthodoxy. Râzi was perhaps the most famous man of religion in his age in Khorasan (*EI²*). Râzi had been taught by the same teacher, Majd al-Din Gilâni in Marâghe, who taught the famous illuminationst philosopher Shehâb al-Din Sohravardi (Mov 87). Like Sohravardi, Râzi rejected the peripatetic philosophy of Aristotle and Avicenna (Ibn Sinâ). Râzi had been accused of apostasy when he fell in with Ibn al-Qodwa, the leader of the Karrâmis, and his life was in danger (Mov 90).

Fakhr al-Din Râzi was a dignified man of medium height, stocky, well dressed, with a full beard and a strong voice. When he was traveling, about three hundred students followed him around (Mov 93), primarily because of the fame which the royal patronage of the Khwârazmshâh conferred upon him, effectively making him the theologian and religious authority par excellence of Khorasan.

Râzi died in Herat in the year A.H. 606, dictating his will and testament on 21 Muharram 606, corresponding to July 26, 1209, and dying within the year (i.e., before July 1210, but probably some time in the summer or fall of 1209).

Râzi was renowned for his conceit. Perhaps this was projected on to him out of jealousy, but Shehâb al-Din Moqaddasi in *Tarâjim rejâl al-qarnayn* and Sebt Ibn Jowzi in *Merʿât al-zamân* both report that Fakhr-e Râzi would play upon the similarity of his own name to that of the Prophet. Râzi's given name was Mohammad, just like the Prophet's. He came from Rayy (near modern Tehran), and since a resident of that city would be known as Râzi (Rayyan), he was

Mohammad-e Râzi, preceded by the honorific title Fakhr al-Din (Pride of the Faith). The Prophet Mohammad, on the other hand, was known as Mohammad-e Tâzi, meaning "Mohammad the Arabian." Fakhr al-Din used to say, "Mohammad-e Tâzi said such and such, whereas Mohammad-e Râzi says such and such ..." This struck many listeners as the height of impiety – mentioning one's own name in the same breath with the Prophet and flippantly seeming to trump what the Prophet had said.

Rumi's future spiritual guide, Shams-e Tabrizi, alludes to this saying of Râzi in the following terms:

> What gall Fakhr-e Râzi had to say, "Mohammad-e Tâzi says thus and Mohâmmad-e Râzi says thus"! Doesn't this make him the apostate of the age? Was [sic] he not an absolute infidel? Unless he repents. Why does he wrong himself so, striking himself with a sword as sharp as this? And what a sword! The servant of God deals with him with compassion, for he has no compassion on himself. (Maq 288)

Rumi also spoke of this saying, according to Aflâki (Af 676). Elsewhere Shams al-Din-e Tabrizi ridicules the suggestion that Fakhr-e Râzi was superior to Jonayd or Bâyazid, or that he can even be mentioned in the same breath with these forerunners of Sufism, even if Râzi had composed five hundred pages or even a thousand pages of exegesis on the Koran (Maq 128). Shams rather considers him a "philosopher or something of this ilk" who met with the Khwârazmshâh and toadied up to him in order to receive a robe of honor (Maq 658). Shams depicts Râzi boasting of his books and his unsurpassed prowess in every field of knowledge, particularly philosophy, in which he claims to have read every book from the time of Aristotle onward (Maq 658–9). This at least shows us that Râzi was as famous in the west of Iran, even after his death, as he had been in Khorasan during his life, but did not enjoy a positive reputation among the piety-minded jurists and Sufis.

Fakhr-e Râzi did repent, however, as Shams suggested. In his will, dictated on 21 Muharram 606 (July 26, 1209) to his student, Ebrâhim Abi Bakr Esfahâni, Râzi asked forgiveness for the theology (*kalâm*) and philosophy (*falsafe*) which had occupied the better part of his life. He confided that all his critiques of famous people's sayings had merely been intended to sharpen the mind of the intellectuals. Otherwise, these disciplines merely made a great noise, but like a big drum, were hollow inside (Mov 92; *EI²*). Râzi also wrote an Arabic *qaside* which shows him thinking along these same lines before he wrote his will (Maq 933):

> Lifelong debate brought no profit to us
> For we gathered from it only words, words

Shams quotes one of the lines of this poem in his *Maqâlât* and says that Fakhr-e Râzi was reciting it at the time of his death (Maq 730):

The scope of all our reason's tied; in vain
the greatest efforts of the ulama

One passage of Rumi's *Masnavi* alludes directly to this poem of Râzi and the repentance expressed in his will. The tone of this passage hovers somewhere between affirming that the man had been too proud in his life and extending forgiveness to him on account of his late-found wisdom (M4:3354–7):

Then strive, and you too, in the end, fatigued
will recognize yourself "our reason's tied"
Like that philosopher the day he died,
who saw reason stripped of flight and power.
With nothing left to prove, he then admitted:
   We charged our mental steed too hard and fast
   In pride we raised our head above all men
   and swam in vain imagination's sea
But nothing here, in the vast sea of soul,
can swim; Noah's ship's the only savior.

A second passage perhaps alludes to Râzi, as well; it sums up the situation of the lion who had been the pride of religion (*Fakhr-e din*), but was caught in a trap by a hare because of his foolish pride (M1:1350). Rumi does explicitly invoke Fakhr-e Râzi once by name, describing him as one who walked solely in the ways of the intellect (M5:4144–5):

If reason clearly saw its way along,
then on faith's truth had Râzi zeroed in!
But "he who has not tasted does not know,"
and so his fancy reason just confused him

Neither did Bahâ al-Din hold Râzi in high esteem. Bahâ al-Din Valad found Fakhr-e Râzi's worldliness and his friendliness with various rulers unsavory (Bah 1:82). He quotes with disapproval the following statement about Râzi from Zayn-e Zaruye:

The gathering of Fakhr-e Râzi doesn't fit in the Friday mosque of Herat. Every night they come, candles in hand, to take their place and he is the Shaykh al-Islam of Herat. The Khwârazmshâh has appointed a member of his own retinue – with his gold belt and hat stitched with silver thread – to sit at the foot of his [Râzi's] pulpit wherever he may be and to whatsoever province he may go. (Bah 1: 245)

Bahâ al-Din even referred to Fakhr-e Râzi and the Khwârazmshâh as theologically suspect "deviants" (*mobtade*ᶜ) from established religious practice (Bah 1:82, 245–6), though he did not call them this to their face. Bahâ al-Din does tell us, though, that he did once deliver a sermon in the presence of the Khwârazmshâh, Zayn-e Kishi, Fakhr-e Râzi and "several other deviants" (Bah 1:82). Though a preacher and man of religion might be permitted certain leeway within the format of a sermon to admonish the ruler, perhaps Bahâ al-Din on this occasion said something that went beyond the proper bounds and angered them. If so, however, it was not a significant event in Fakhr-e Râzi's life, as he apparently does not mention Bahâ al-Din either in his *Monâzerât*, a book detailing his legal disputations with Shâfeʿis, Hanafis, Asharites and Mâtoridis, or in his *Mohassel afkâr al-motaqaddemin va al-motaʾakhkherin*, a work on religious and philosophical thought of the ancients and moderns (*EI²*).

The Valad family's move from Vakhsh to Samarqand did not take place until a couple of years after the death of Râzi (or the year of his death at the earliest) and their exodus from Khorasan not until a few years after that. Therefore, whatever enmity may have existed between Bahâ-e Din and Fakhr-e Râzi, it could not have been the proximate cause of Bahâ al-Din's departure. Our sources are therefore mistaken on this score, with the exception of Sultan Valad, who implies that Fakhr-e Râzi had never met Bahâ al-Din. Had Fakhr-e Râzi (or, for that matter, Avicenna or Abu Hanifa) ever met Bahâ al-Din, they would have appeared like schoolchildren in comparison, at least according to Sultan Valad (SVE 188).

THE KHWÂRAZMSHÂH

Khwârazm, the kingdom on the southeastern shores of the Caspian sea, grew quite powerful in the last quarter of the twelfth century under the rule of ʿAlâ al-Din Takesh (r. 1172–1200), who ousted the Seljuks from eastern Iran. His son and successor, ʿAlâ al-Din Mohammad b. Takesh, came to the throne in 1200 (A.H. 596) and drove the Ghurid ruler Moʿezz al-Din from Khorasan in 1204 (A.H. 601). Therefore Bahâ al-Din's remark about the "deviance" of the Khwârazmshâh must refer to ʿAlâ al-Din Mohammad b. Takesh; he must have said this sometime after 1200, probably after ʿAlâ al-Din's conquest of Khorasan in 1204, but before his siege of Samarqand in 1211 or 1213, since Bahâ al-Din's comments seem to suggest that Fakhr-e Râzi (d. 1209) was still alive at the time. Incidentally, from the point of view of Sunni orthodoxy, Bahâ al-Din was absolutely correct about the Khwârazmshâh ʿAlâ al-Din Mohammad being a "deviant"; in about 1217 or 1218, probably after the Valads were already in Anatolia, the Khwârazmshâh declared the caliph unfit to rule, proclaimed a member of the Alid family as the anti-caliph and marched on Baghdad, though unsuccessfully (*EI²*).

Sepahsâlâr (Sep 12–13) and Aflâki (Af 11–13) both attribute Bahâ al-Din's departure from Khorasan to a conflict with the Khwârazmshâh (wrongly calling him Jalâl al-Din Khwârazmshâh). Sultan Valad alludes to Bahâ al-Din's displeasure with the Khwârazmshâh, but places the blame for Bahâ al-Din's departure more on the shoulders of the people of Balkh, who had harassed Bahâ al-Din. In retribution, God scourged the inhabitants of Balkh after inspiring Bahâ al-Din to leave (SVE 189–91). However, Sultan Valad's view of his grandfather as the spiritual *axis mundi* (*qotb*) of the age leads inexorably to the need for a visitation of divine punishment on his tormentors, for this had been God's *modus operandi* with those who reject His prophets in the Koran (and ever since the time of Lot). Nature abhors a vacuum and Sepahsâlâr, who had access to Bahâ's *Ma'âref,* most likely concluded from the passage about the Khwârazmshâh and Fakhr-e Râzi being deviants that this must have been related to the troubles suffered by Bahâ al-Din at the hands of the people of Balkh. The myth then assumed the tropological form of the encounter between spiritual and worldly king, a myth which we will find repeated several times in Bahâ's encounters with other kings in the West.

OTHER MOTIVATIONS

The hagiographers portray Bahâ al-Din as hypersensitive about the propriety of associating with or accepting favors from kings and princes who behaved in an illicit or religiously suspect manner, and what we read in the *Ma'âref* tends to confirm this. Perhaps Bahâ al-Din felt it impious or impolitic to remain in the realm of the Khwârazmshâh after having condemned him. Perhaps he realized that he would never win a wider audience for his ideas in the Khwârazmshâh's dominions, where Râzi's ideas had reigned supreme. Bahâ al-Din may have set out from Vakhsh in search of a pious patron who could afford him the circumstances to expand his preaching activities, for Bahâ was discontented with his lot in out-of-the-way Vakhsh, and dreamed of a more cosmopolitan home (Bah 2:138):

> My heart began to wonder, why Vakhsh? Others are in Samarqand or Baghdad or Balkh, in majestic cities. I'm stuck in this bare, boring and forgotten corner! [Then] God inspired me with this thought:
> "If you are with Me and I am your companion, you will not be in any place – not Vakhsh, not Baghdad or Samarqand. Nor will you be with any one, nor will you be outwardly adorned, or possessed of virtues and arts. But if you are not with Me, wherever you are your heart will feel constricted and you will be abased and wayward. None who come to know My companionship can bear the abasement of companionship with anyone but Me."

The decision to embark upon a journey seems to have been taken in advance, as we see Bahâ al-Din, who conceived of his physical condition as rather fragile, gradually preparing himself for the hardships of the road ahead (Bah 1:360).

At the same time, changes or instability in the local political circumstances of Vakhsh perhaps gave Bahâ al-Din cause to fear expulsion or arrest (Mei 432). By 1213 (A.H. 609), but perhaps even as early as 1210 (A.H. 607), the family had moved to a larger city, Samarqand, one controlled by the Qarakhânid vassals, the non-Muslim Qarakhitây (Mei 35, 432), from whose empire the old word for China, Cathay, derives. Within four years of the siege of Samarqand, Bahâ al-Din left Khorasan for good, though he perhaps at first returned for a while to

Balkh. It is true that Küchlüg Khan, a fugitive vassal of the Mongols, began encroaching on the area of Khorasan in 1211, and this may have caused some early apprehension about Mongol power. But the Khwârazmshâh's real problems with the Mongols did not begin until 1218, when he ordered the execution of some Mongol traders acting as envoys of Genghis Khan, a situation to which Rumi apparently alludes in Discourse 15 (Fih 65). Even before the Mongol attacks, though, the Khwârazmshâh's declaration of war on the caliph had probably created a climate which pious scholars of religion like Bahâ al-Din found highly objectionable.

In any case, we may suppose that the regional political situation, with borders shifting back and forth between the Qarakhânids, Ghurids and the Khwârazmshâh, made the region seem unstable before the Mongols ever arrived. The Ghurid ruler from Bâmiân, Bahâ al-Din Sâm, occupied Balkh in 1198 after the death of its Turkish governor, who had ruled as a vassal of the Qarakhitây. Perhaps Bahâ al-Din originally lived in Balkh but left at this time for Vakhsh, or perhaps in 1200 when the Ghurid Ghiâs al-Din took over most of Khorasan. When Ghiâs al-Din died in 1203, his brother Mo'ezz al-Din took control, only to lose Khorasan, with the exception of Herat, to the Khwârazmshâh 'Alâ al-Din Mohammad b. Takesh in 1204 (A.H. 601, *EI²*). Vakhsh was ruled in 1203 (A.H. 600) by a certain Chap Khân, apparently a vassal of the Ghurids, and probably the "Sultan of Vakhsh" referred to elsewhere by Bahâ al-Din (Bah 1:283, 303). When the King of Ghur (*Malek-e Ghur*, probably Bahâ al-Din Sâm) came to Vakhsh in June of 1204 (Shavvâl 600), wresting the town from Chap Khân, the latter's vizier, 'Emâd al-Din, went to intercede with him on behalf of the inhabitants. (Is Rumi's story in the *Masnavi* about a certain 'Emâd al-Molk [M4:2934ff.] who plays the role of intercessor with an angry king when no one else dared to do so, a memory of this passage from Bahâ al-Din's *Ma'âref*?) Bahâ al-Din did not speak with the Ghurid king, arguing that to speak about peace with rulers is useless, since one wins the right to be king only through might and the weak lose all right to rule. Some supported Chap Khân as the rightful ruler, and others the Ghurid king, but Bahâ al-Din professed neutrality since he could not be certain of the will of God (Bah 1:355).

Just as one could not always be sure about the truth of the varying theological and doctrinal claims of the contending schools or sects of Islam (*mazâheb-e mokhtalefe*), likewise, Bahâ al-Din tells us we cannot judge the legitimacy of a given ruler. Bahâ al-Din compares the multiplicity of doctrinal positions to the various armies and servants of a king. One faction might plot or rise up against another faction, cursing them and claiming they had acted disrespectfully or treacherously toward the king. This is as it should be, for if they had perceived disrespect and treachery but passed over it in silence, the king would be greatly displeased. In the end, the sincerity of one's servitude to God, the monarch on high, determines the truth and rightfulness of his claims (Bah 1:355–6).

Bahâ al-Din recalls how at this time he had reflected on the shifting politics of the region, aware that he might perish in the maelstrom, doubtful that he would live ten more years (Bah 1:354–5). He muses that when one has something to lose, such as wealth, books or children, he fears death, but if one can obliterate his own selfhood (*hasti*) and achieve detachment from all these, he will not be afraid. Thus we may conclude that Bahâ al-Din tried to resign himself to the fate of God's decree in matters of politics, recognizing that life was, in any event, precarious. Even so, he must have been shocked and devastated when he learned, several years later, of the destruction wreaked by the Mongols on his compatriots. If Bahâ al-Din prophesied the downfall of the area as a retribution for the wickedness of the Khwârazmshâh, as the hagiographers delight in telling us, we need not postulate, as they do, that Bahâ al-Din had any foreknowledge of the impending Mongol invasion.

The Mongol Invasion?

Two other historical figures – the geographer Yâqût al-Rumi and the mystic Najm-e Râzi – left Khorasan about the same time as Bahâ al-Din, also motivated, according to tradition, by fear of the approaching Mongols (Mei 36), which in the case of Yâqût is fairly certain. But unless we accept the very latest date for the Valad family departure, it seems extremely unlikely that Bahâ could have been fleeing the Mongol onslaught. Sultan Valad (SVE 192) dates the family's arrival in Konya to 1229 (A.H. 626), two years before the death of Bahâ al-Din, though Jalâl al-Din Homâ'i, the editor of Sultan Valad's verse chronicle, points out (SVE 44) that if instead of two (*do*) we read ten (*dah*), it would place the Valad family's departure from Balkh just after the first conquest of Balkh by the Mongols in 1221 (A.H. 618), thus permitting us to join the hagiographers in blaming the Mongols for Bahâ al-Din's departure. Foruzânfar (FB 16; Fih 333), and following him, Movahhed (Mov 91), incline toward the Mongol theory, placing the Valad family exodus in the year 1219 (A.H. 616), when the Mongols first breach the eastern borders of the Khwârazmshâh's territory, or even as late as 1220 (A.H. 617), when the Mongols take Termez.

While the absolute latest date for the Valad family to have packed up and set out from Khorasan is thus the Mongol conquest of Balkh in 1221, all the speculation about the Mongol invasions provoking their departure seems rather farfetched. Doubtless it owes its existence to a Biblical and Koranic trope – the divine punishment that befalls a wicked ruler who refused to listen to a holy man. As we have seen, the hagiographers do not deserve our faith on matters of chronology or historical detail, but Aflâki, who is most elaborate in this regard, does give a number of dates and locations for the course of the Valad family's migration, and the dates he gives us place their departure years before the Mongol invasion.

First of all, before it actually occurred, it would have been hard to predict the extent of devastation the Mongols wreaked on Balkh. In hindsight, the sack and depopulation of Balkh is a watershed event in the history of Khorasan, but that does not mean the inhabitants, who were periodically terrorized by various marauding princes and their armies, knew that the Mongols would rupture the fabric of their society. Furthermore, if Bahâ al-Din did flee an imminent Mongol attack, why would he leave his daughter and other parts of his family behind, as we are told he did (see above), defenseless before this threat to life and limb? Up until two or three years before the invasions, the relations between the Khwârazmshâh and the Mongols in Peking remained cordial enough; ᶜAlâ al-Din received ambassadors in 1218 from Genghis Khan and a policy favoring trade relations was in force, with several successful commercial delegations exchanged. This situation fell apart after an incident involving a governor and relative of ᶜAlâ al-Din, Enaljek, who robbed and killed some of the Mongol traders, giving the pretext for the invasions (Tür 3–4).

We have, in any case, seen how the political circumstances in the region were unstable before the Mongols arrived, and how Bahâ himself was longing to find a position in a more cosmopolitan urban center. It seems likely that he left Khorasan well before the Mongols threatened to attack the area.

FROM KHORASAN TO KONYA

THE MYTHICAL MEETING WITH ᶜATTÂR

Dowlatshâh's *Tazkerat al-shoᶜarâ* (Dow 214) tells a famous anecdote about Bahâ al-Din stopping in Nayshâpur, where the young Rumi, about ten years of age, encountered the famous mystic poet Farid al-Din ᶜAttâr (d. c. 1220). ᶜAttâr supposedly presented the boy with a copy of his *Asrâr nâme* and predicted the child's future greatness. A number of scholars have accepted or repeated this story (e.g., GB 97; ZrP 50; ME 1:xvi–xvii), but as I shall argue below, this must be dismissed as a legend.

Nayshâpur, near modern-day Mashhad in northeast Iran, where ᶜAttâr did in fact live, was one of the four most famous cities of Khorasan, situated to the west of Samarqand and Balkh. None of the hagiographers of Rumi, including Aflâki, who gives the most details, mention the route taken by Bahâ al-Din Valad from Balkh to Baghdad. Hellmut Ritter (*EI²*) has argued that Bahâ al-Din returned from Samarqand to Balkh before quitting Khorasan for good. If the Valad entourage left in fear of the approaching Mongols, it seems likely that they would have traveled through Marv al-Rud and then south to Herat and from there westward to Baghdad, staying as far away as possible from the aggressors. This southerly route might also have proved more attractive if Bahâ al-Din was worried by the encroachments of the Khwârazmshâh. But it seems more likely that Bahâ al-Din and his family, having left well before the Mongols threatened the area, were not fleeing any immediate physical danger. The conventional route from eastern Khorasan to Baghdad would have passed through Nayshâpur, so we cannot rule out that Bahâ al-Din did indeed pass through the city.

The circumstances of time and place therefore make a meeting between Rumi and ʿAttâr theoretically possible, but Rumi himself never hints that such a meeting took place. Considering Rumi's obvious affinity for ʿAttâr's poetry, we would expect to find some allusion to this exciting and important event in young Rumi's life, connecting him with the great Sufis of the past. If Rumi remembered this supposed encounter, or if his father, Bahâ al-Din, had told him about it, he would certainly have passed on the story to his own son, Sultan Valad, as part of the family lore. Sultan Valad, however, makes no mention of any such encounter with ʿAttâr in his account of the family's journey westward. Let us assume for a moment that Sultan Valad somehow forgot to mention this anecdote. Had it enjoyed any currency among the Mevlevis half a century after Rumi's death, the hagiographers Sepahsâlâr and Aflâki, who delight in just such stories, would never have overlooked it.

The fact is that no one intimately connected with Rumi and his family ever mentions such a meeting – not Bahâ al-Din, not Rumi, not Shams al-Din, not Sultan Valad, not Sepahsâlâr, not Aflâki. The first mention of this mythical meeting makes its appearance only two centuries after Rumi's death in a book on the lives of the poets written by someone who displays no first-hand knowledge of the Mevlevis. Later readers of Rumi noted the many quotations of ʿAttâr's poetry and observed that, by weaving the text of his *Masnavi* on the pattern of the *Elâhi nâme*, Rumi had donned ʿAttâr's mantle as the leading exponent of narrative Sufi poetry. These later readers simply imagined this meeting from whole cloth to fit the trope of how the mystical torch is passed on from generation to generation. There is not a shred of credible evidence to suggest that Rumi met with ʿAttâr, only a tale told in the fifteenth century by Dowlatshâh – not known for his historical accuracy. There is, however, a small mountain of circumstantial evidence against it, to wit the silence of Bahâ al-Din, Borhân al-Din, Rumi, Shams al-Din, Sultan Valad, Sepahsâlâr and Aflâki, at least one of whom we would have expected to share this important bit of bio/hagio-graphical detail.

ON TO BAGHDAD

Aflâki (Af 16–17) describes the Valad family's itinerary through Khorasan without mentioning the names of the places where they stopped before arriving in Baghdad. We are told that Bahâ al-Din traveled in a camel litter at the head of a huge retinue of scholars (Af 17). As they approached the imperial Abbasid city of Baghdad, the caliph supposedly summoned his spiritual adviser, Shehâb al-Din ʿOmar Sohravardi (d. 1234), to explain who these new arrivals were. Sohravardi immediately deduced from the caliph's description that it was Bahâ al-Din, and proceeded with all the notables of the city to greet him. Aflâki

(Af 18–19) goes on to report that though Bahâ al-Din gravely insulted the caliph, the caliph nevertheless invited him to preach a sermon (*va͑z* is specified, not the *khotbe*) on Friday in the Congregational Mosque (*masjed-e jâme͑* is specified, though there was more than one congregational mosque in Baghdad). In the course of this sermon Bahâ al-Din upbraided the caliph once again for corruption and failing to follow the law, and tropologically threatened him with the impending Mongol invasions.

Sepahsâlâr (Sep 14) tells a slightly less colorful story about the Valads' arrival in Baghdad, with all the viziers, deputies, judges and notables of this great imperial capital coming out to greet Bahâ al-Din. They subsequently attended his lectures every day, the likes of which had never been heard before. The accounts of both Aflâki and Sepahsâlâr are equally ludicrous; if they reflect any kernel of truth, it may be that Bahâ al-Din approached the noted Sohravardi or some other *faqih*, and was welcomed or favorably received by some of the Hanafi scholars in Baghdad. Somewhat more plausibly, Sepahsâlâr (Sep 14) indicates that an emissary from ͑Alâ al-Din Kay Qobâd, the Seljuk sultan of Rum, happened to be in Baghdad at this time and heard Bahâ al-Din speak; upon returning to Anatolia, the Seljuk sultan heard glowing reports of Bahâ al-Din.

Sepahsâlâr (Sep 14) implies that the Valad family stayed about one month in Baghdad. The family is said to have lodged at the Mostanseriye college in Baghdad (Af 18), but as this institution, probably built on the ruins of the previous palace, was not dedicated until 1234, a few years after the death of Bahâ al-Din, we may dismiss the report. For this reason, if no other, we may also dismiss the report that Rumi would go out in his pajamas at night to fetch water for his father from the Tigris and would miraculously reenter the locked gates of the school without a key (Af 24).

However, the famous Nezâmiye college was at this time still in good repair. If he remained for a month in Baghdad, Bahâ al-Din probably would have paid a visit there with young Rumi in tow. A Hanafi scholar visiting Baghdad would almost certainly have made a pilgrimage of sorts to the shrine/college of Abu Hanifa, circumstances permitting. But if his arrival in Baghdad did in fact take place in 1217 (A.H. 614), as I suggest below, the Tigris had flooded in this year, causing great damage in the city. If this did not hamper their movement across town, they quite likely also visited the shrine of Ma͑ruf al-Karkhi, the famous Sufi, which had been rebuilt in 1214 when the youngest son of Caliph Nâser died and was buried nearby.[8]

THE PILGRIMAGE TO MECCA: A POSSIBLE CHRONOLOGY

Aflâki insinuates that Bahâ al-Din had originally planned to stay in Baghdad, but determined to undertake the pilgrimage to Mecca (Af 18), evidently with the entire family accompanying him. Sepahsâlâr tells us only that they returned from the pilgrimage via Syria to Erzincan. Aflâki gives a somewhat more detailed itinerary (Af 22): from Arabia, they proceeded to Damascus, and from there to Malatya, where Aflâki places the family in the year A.H. 614. If correct, this would mean that they passed through Damascus sometime between the spring of 1217 and the spring of 1218 (A.H. 615).

Malatya was then under the control of the Seljuks, whereas Syria was a collection of loosely allied princedoms under the Ayyubids. Aflâki tells us that when the family reached Damascus, it was during the rule of Ashraf (Af 22), referring to the Ayyubid al-Malek al-Ashraf Musâ (d. 1237). Al-Ashraf's father, the Ayyubid sultan al-cÂdel I in Damascus, appointed his sons to rule as princes on his behalf in various parts of the Ayyubid domains. He had made al-Ashraf prince of the area around Edessa and Harran in 1201, to which territories al-Ashraf added Ahlat (Akhlât) and Van in 1211. Al-cÂdel died in 615/1218 while fighting off the Frankish troops of the Fifth Crusade in Egypt (the Crusaders were also advancing from Acre in Palestine up through the Lebanon). Al-cÂdel had already ceded much of the day-to-day control of Damascus to one of his sons, al-Mocazzam cIsâ, as inscriptions on public monuments of the period testify (Hum 150ff.). When word of al-cÂdel's death got out in the fall of 1218, al-Mocazzam assumed power in Damascus, ruling over central Syria, Jordan and Palestine, even though his brother based in Egypt, al-Kâmel, was recognized as the Ayyubid sultan (Hum 160–61).

Meanwhile, as al-cÂdel fought off the Crusaders in Palestine and Egypt with the help of al-Mocazzam and al-Kâmel, the Seljuk sultan Kay Kâvus had made an alliance with one of Saladin's sons, al-Afzal, to attack Aleppo (Hum 159). Al-Zâher Ghâzi, another son of Saladin, had ruled Aleppo from 1186 until his death in the early autumn of 1216 (A.H. 613). At this point Aleppo had come under Ayyubid control, with the Atabeg Shehâb al-Din Toghrol ruling the city in the name of al-cÂdel's infant grandson, al-cAziz (Hum 155). The Seljuk attack came in June of 1218 (A.H. 615), but al-cÂdel had dispatched his son, al-Ashraf, to the city's defense. Ashraf soundly defeated the Seljuk forces and was pursuing them back into Anatolia when he learned of his father, the sultan's, death. Under these circumstances, the Atabeg of Aleppo was compelled to recognize Ashraf as the military protector, if not the formal ruler, of Aleppo (Hum 160, 166–7).

It would therefore have been possible to speak of Ashraf as the ruler of *Aleppo* after 1218 (A.H. 615), though not of Damascus, and not in 614, as Aflâki would have it. Al-Ashraf eventually did come to live and rule in Damascus, from 1229 to 1237, but this only after the Valads were already well established in Konya. It may be that Rumi studied in Damascus during al-Ashraf's reign, but when the Valads first came through the city on their way to Anatolia, al-Mocazzam was certainly the ruler. And, if we suppose that Aflâki has confused Damascus with Aleppo, the date of 614 he gives is still a year too early to match with Ashraf's control of that city.

Incidentally, al-Mo^cazzam ʿIsâ, the de facto governor in Damascus, was a man of letters. He had been educated by Hanafi teachers, to whom he showed great deference and respect, eventually switching allegiance from the family's hereditary Shâfeʿi rite to the Hanafis. Al-Mo^cazzam commissioned a huge compendium of Hanafi *feqh* and in 1209 endowed a Hanafi college in Jerusalem, which was completed in 1217. In the Sâlehiye district of Damascus, he had a large Hanafi mosque built in 1224. In 1227 he restored the *zâvie* of al-Kindî in the Umayyad Mosque in the citadel of Damascus, an important center of Hanafi law. He had also undertaken to improve the facilities along the pilgrimage route from Damascus to Mecca, including better roads, baths and lodgings (Hum 189–91). Al-Mo^cazzam was furthermore acquainted with Shehâb al-Din Sohravardi, who had come to Damascus as the caliph's deputy in 1207 to invest al-ʿÂdel with Abbasid authority; both al-Mo^cazzam and al-Ashraf had been present and participated in the ceremonies with this famous Sufi ambassador. Interestingly, when al-ʿÂdel sent an embassy to Baghdad in 1217, he chose Sadr al-Din b. Hamuye, the chief shaykh representing the Sufi orders in Syria, as his representative (Hum 139–41).

All this patronage of Hanafi institutions of learning would doubtless have appealed to the Valad family (though al-Mo^cazzam also allowed the Hanbalis in Damascus to flourish). It might even lend some credence to Aflâki's statement that the people in Syria (by which he evidently intends Damascus) desired Bahâ al-Din to stay there (Af 22). Damascus had been heavily damaged in an earthquake in 1201, but al-Mo^cazzam's restoration project had restored the city to its former splendor by the time Bahâ al-Din arrived. During the Ayyubid period, Damascus would have been one of the three most important religious centers west of Iran, along with Baghdad and Cairo, so it seems somewhat difficult to believe that Bahâ al-Din would have refused the offer of a position to preach or teach there. Aflâki explains this apparent enigma by saying that Bahâ al-Din had already decided upon Anatolia as his destination (Af 22). It was a good thing, too, for al-Mo^cazzam would later contract an alliance with the Khwârazmshâh Jalâl al-Din in 1226 (Hum 177ff.), a turn of events that Bahâ al-Din would not have appreciated.

Aflâki (Af 22) tells us that the Khwârazmshâh Jalâl al-Din laid siege to Ahlat in the year 1219 (A.H. 616), only to be defeated and killed by the combined forces of Ashraf and ʿAlâ al-Din the Seljuk. However, the Khwârazmshâh's two attacks on Ahlat took place in 1226 and 1230; it is this latter battle of 1230 that Aflâki anachronistically places in 1219.

Though Aflâki does not exactly inspire confidence in his historical accuracy, we have very little else to go on and can only attempt to reconstruct a chronology for the Valad family's peregrinations on the basis of the 614/1217 date which Aflâki gives for their arrival in Malatya. On this basis, Ritter (*EI²*) dated the family's emigration from Balkh to 1216 or 1217 (A.H. 613–14), though Meier (Mei 34) pointed out that in order for Aflâki's chronology to work out, the family must have departed Khorasan no later than 1216. We must side with Meier in this case. A possible chronology is outlined below, though it depends upon so many unknown factors and untrustworthy "facts" that we should consider it merely hypothetical.

The Islamic year 614 began on April 10, 1217. It is likely that Bahâ al-Din, in compliance with his religious obligations as a Muslim, performed the full pilgrimage ritual (*hajj*), rather than a minor pilgrimage (*ʿomra*). The full *hajj* is performed each year in the final month of the Islamic calendar, Dhu al-hijja, which in the year A.H. 613 began on March 11, 1217. By the twentieth of Dhu al-hijja, or March 30, 1217, the pilgrimage rites would have been completed and the pilgrims' caravan for Syria would have shortly thereafter set out heading northward. It took Ibn Battûta, who set out on the pilgrimage caravan from Damascus in September 1326, almost two months to reach Mecca, stopping for several days in many locations. The pilgrimage caravan perhaps tarried less on its return journey, so the Valads may have arrived in Damascus before the end of May 1217. Unless they lingered in Damascus for several months, they could have then reached Malatya in the early summer of 1217, about three or four months into the Islamic year 614.

If the Valads did indeed set out to make the pilgrimage of Dhu al-hijja 613/ March 1217, they must have left Baghdad sometime in January (February at the latest) and proceeded to Kufa, whence it took the pilgrimage caravan about a month or more to reach Mecca. If, as Sepahsâlâr indicates, the family stayed in the caliphal city for a month or more, this places their arrival in Baghdad sometime in November or December of 1216. The trek from Samarqand or Balkh across Khorasan, into central Iran and finally to Iraq would have taken several months, even if they did not stay for an extended period in any location. This would mean they departed from Khorasan by the summertime of 1216 or perhaps even earlier.

BAHÂ AL-DIN IN ÂQSHAHR

In any case, Aflâki puts Bahâ al-Din in Malatya in 1217. He does not tell us how long the family tarried there, but does describe a period of four years during which Bahâ al-Din stayed at Âqshahr near Erzincan under the patronage of ʿEsmati Khâtun (Af 24–5). Sepahsâlâr (Sep 14) refers to this princess as Tâj Malek Khâtun, a paternal aunt of ʿAlâ al-Din Kay Qobâd, while Aflâki knows her as the wife of Fakhr al-Din Bahrâmshâh (r. 1155?–1218?), the Manguchak prince of Erzincan and the patron of the *Makhzan al-asrâr*, by the famous poet Nezâmi (c. 1141–1209). According to Aflâki, first the wife and then the husband became disciples of Bahâ al-Din.

Erzincan (Arzangân) was then the capital of the Muslim Manguchaks, but the geographer Yâqût describes Erzincan at about this time as inhabited mostly by

Armenians, who scandalized Muslims by publicly drinking wine (LeS 118). Aflâki (Af 24) tells us that despite the urging of his disciples, Bahâ al-Din refused to visit the city because of the large number of bad people living there. ʿEsmati Khâtun nevertheless discovered Bahâ al-Din near Âqshahr and had her husband, the prince Bahrâmshâh, come to meet him. Bahrâmshâh begged him to settle in Erzincan, but Bahâ al-Din instead requested a college (*madrase*) be built for him in Âqshahr, where for four years Bahâ al-Din taught general classes (*dars-e ʿâm*, probably signifying that the regular law curriculum was not offered) with the princess in attendance (Af 25). Sepahsâlâr (Sep 15), on the other hand, while confirming that the princess built a structure called the ʿEsmatiye for Bahâ al-Din, calls it a *khâneqâh* (a Sufi retreat or center) rather than a *madrase*, and says that the Valad entourage lived there for a year, more or less, with the princess providing all their needs. Note that the features which distinguish a *madrase* from a *khâneqâh* in Anatolia during this period seem somewhat flexible; Ibn Battûta sometimes seems to use these two terms interchangeably with *zâvie* (Saf 3/1:184).

Sepahsâlâr (Sep 15) places Bahâ al-Din's arrival in Âqshahr to the winter, and we may venture to guess, following the hypothetical chronology worked out above, that this would have been between November 1217 and March 1218. The Âqshahr where Bahâ al-Din taught was near Erzincan, in eastern Anatolia. Though no such toponym exists today (Mei 37 n. 7, 433), in the fourteenth century Mostowfi mentions a town of this name, some 120 kilometers east-northeast of Sivas, two stages east of Zâre and three stages west of Erzincan (LeS 147). This, and not the more famous city known today as Akşehir, north of Antakiya, is the location in question.

Bahâ al-Din spent four years teaching in this *madrase/khâneqâh* until Fakhr al-Din Bahrâmshâh and ʿEsmati Khâtun died (Af 25), which would bring us to about the year 1221, reckoning from the dates reported in Aflâki. The date of death for Fakhr al-Din is elsewhere given as 1225/A.H. 622 (Mei 37 n. 9), but this seems unlikely, as Fakhr al-Din's son, Dâvudshâh, had acceded by 1218 (Dâvudshâh was to hand over Erzincan to Sultan Kay Qobâd the Seljuk in about 1228 [Akh clx, 142ff.]). We may surmise that Bahâ al-Din's appointment to the college or Sufi center in Âqshahr was not endowed in perpetuity by a charitable trust (*vaqf*); at some point the funds dried up, perhaps because the princess changed her mind about supporting Bahâ al-Din, or after her death another member of the family did. On the other hand, perhaps a better offer from a more central city enticed Bahâ al-Din to leave. According to Ibn Bibi's history of the Seljuks (written c. 1285), the daughter of Fakhr al-Din Bahrâmshâh, Saljuqi Khâtun, was married to ʿEzz al-Din Kay Kâus I (r. 1211–19) in Konya (Akh 70). Perhaps it was she who introduced or mentioned Bahâ al-Din to members of the ruling Seljuk family in Konya.

From this point Aflâki (Af 25–7), but not Sepahsâlâr (Sep 15), follows Bahâ al-Din to Lârende, known in modern times as Karaman, to the southeast of

Konya. Lârende was ruled by Christians in 1210 but reconquered by the Seljuks in 1216 under ᶜEzz al-Din, who settled Turkmen tribes and refugees from Khorasan there in order to Islamicize this hill-top town. Lârende/Karaman still had a large Greek population who wrote Turkish in the Greek alphabet (Tür 11–12). Amir Musâ, the local Seljuk governor (*subâshi*) in Lârende, who ruled in the name of Sultan ᶜAlâ al-Din Kay Qobâd, invited Bahâ al-Din to his home. Bahâ al-Din instead asked that a college be built for him, and Amir Musâ complied, erecting a building in the middle of the town (Af 26). Allusions to the delicious fruits of Lârende have been found in Rumi's poetry (ScW 13). We do not know much else about the Valad family's experiences in Lârende/Karaman, though they stayed here for a further seven years or more (Af 26), until about 1228 by our reconstruction.

RUMI STARTS A FAMILY OF HIS OWN

Rumi attained the age of maturity in Lârende (Af 26), and in his seventeenth year (Af 48), corresponding to 1224 (A.H. 621), he married Gowhar Khâtun, the daughter of Sharaf al-Din-e Lâlâ of Samarqand (Af 26), who knew or had heard of the Valad family in Samarqand and accompanied them on their journey westward. Gowhar Khâtun's mother had been a leading female disciple of Bahâ al-Din (Af 681), so the match between Rumi and Gowhar Khâtun may have been prearranged. By the time they arrived in Konya five years later, Rumi and Gowhar Khâtun had two sons, Sultan Valad and ᶜAlâ al-Din. Aflâki (Af 26) conflates the birth of both sons to the year 1226 (A.H. 623), but ᶜAlâ al-Din appears elsewhere (Af 303) to be a year older. There is some suggestion that Rumi's older brother, also named ᶜAlâ al-Din, died around this time and that Rumi named his own son in remembrance of this brother (ScW 13). In an oral report transmitted by Aflâki (Af 303), Sultan Valad names Lârende as his birthplace. This places the birth of both boys somewhere between 1225 and 1228; we may conjecture that ᶜAlâ al-Din was born first in 1225 with little Sultan Valad arriving the following year, in 1226. The grave of Moᵓmene Khâtun, wife of Bahâ al-Din and mother of Rumi, called Mâdar Sultan by the Mevlevis (GB 95), has been discovered in Karaman/Lârende, so she must have died sometime between 1222 and 1229.[9]

KONYA: THE KING OF CLERICS MEETS THE KING OF SELJUKS

Conflicting stories and dates are given for Bahâ al-Din Valad's meeting with Sultan ᶜAlâ al-Din Kay Qobâd. Sepahsâlâr (Sep 15) has the sultan invite Bahâ al-Din to Konya with great respect and fanfare, giving him a house (*manzel*) to live in. At this time Rumi was fourteen years of age according to Sepahsâlâr. Rumi turned fourteen in 1221 and although this would conform with Aflâki's date for the departure of the family from Âqshahr, it completely ignores the period spent in Lârende. Sepahsâlâr shows Bahâ al-Din in a very cozy

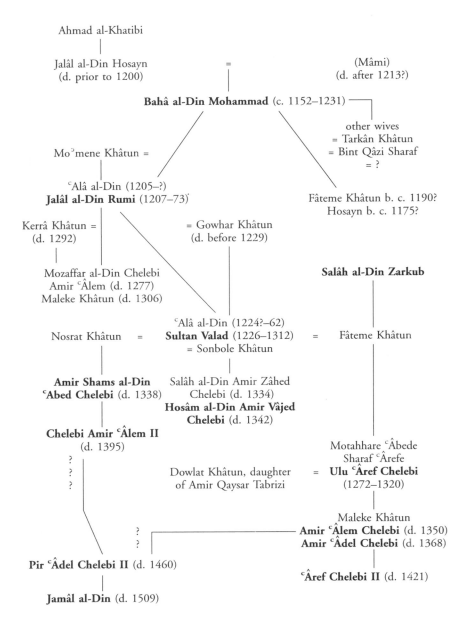

The Valad Family Tree

Note: According to the dates above, which are culled from various sources, some of the descendants of Sultan Valad outlived their fathers by fifty to sixty years. This would suggest that these fathers (Amir Shams al-Din, Amir ʿÂlem II, etc.) had their children quite late in life, around sixty years of age. This is not beyond the realm of possibility, but it does not seem likely that Amir ʿÂlem Chelebi, son of Ulu ʿÂref Chelebi, could have fathered Pir ʿÂdel Chelebi II, who died 110 years after him.

relationship with the sultan; the sultan would visit him constantly and also invite him to come sit upon his throne. Bahâ al-Din addressed the sultan as *Malek* (King) and once told him, "We are both sultans, but your sovereignty endures so long as your eyes are open, and mine will begin once my eyes close forever" (Sep 15). If we suppose that Sepahsâlâr has confused or conflated Bahrâmshâh in Erzincan with the Seljuk sultan in Konya, we might then square his chronology with Aflâki's. But others question the account of the four-year stay in Erzincan (ME 1:xix). We may opt as an alternative to abandon the attempt to reconcile the conflicting chronologies of Sepahsâlâr and Aflâki. If Sepahsâlâr is correct, then Bahâ al-Din and Rumi were living in Konya from 1221, which would mean they moved to Lârende at some later date.

Sultan Valad, Rumi's son, gives a very telescoped account of the family's passage to Konya, which, however, depicts the people of Konya becoming enamored of Bahâ al-Din before ʿAlâ al-Din ever heard of him. As Sultan Valad tells it, Bahâ al-Din came from the Kaaba in Mecca to the land of Rum to shower mercy upon the people of Anatolia. From all of Anatolia he chose Konya and made it his home. All the people in town heard that the wonder of the age, one peerless in knowledge and apprised of the mysteries of mystic love, had arrived. They turned to him, men, women and children, old and young, witnessed his miracles and pronounced themselves his disciples. Finally Sultan ʿAlâ al-Din, too, came with his commanders, heard his sermons and became his true and loving disciple (SVE 191). The sultan supposedly told his commanders and the inner circle of the court (*khavvâss*) that:

> When I see this man my faith and sincerity grow stronger. My heart trembles before his majesty, I am afraid when I see him. The whole world trembles in fear of me, what is it about this man for me, Lord? A fear overtakes me in his presence which causes my body to tremble. I am certain he is a regent (*vali*) of God; he is rare and unique in the world. (SVE 192)

Aflâki, on the other hand, portrays Bahâ al-Din as reluctant to meet the sultan (Af 27). Amir Musâ obligingly concealed Bahâ al-Din's presence from the sultan, but when the sultan learned through the hostile reports of Amir Musâ's enemies that he had detained Bahâ al-Din in Lârende (Af 26–7), he grew angry and determined to punish Amir Musâ. Bahâ al-Din explained that he could not look upon the face of a man who drank wine and listened to singing girls (Af 27–8), but when Amir Musâ bravely reported this to the sultan, the sultan supposedly wept and renounced listening to music for the rest of his life (Af 28).

We will probably never know for certain exactly how it came about, but Aflâki, Sepahsâlâr and Sultan Valad all agree that the Seljuk prince ʿAlâ al-Din Kay Qobâd (r. 1219–37) invited Bahâ al-Din to settle in Konya, the local capital, warmly welcoming him as a spiritual leader. Aflâki (Af 28–9) says that Bahâ al-Din gathered his children and his entourage of disciples and headed for

Konya in response to this invitation. The sultan went to receive them, accompanied by the men of letters and the standard bearers of the army (*ashâb-e ᶜalam*), and indeed all the people of Konya. The sultan dismounted from his horse and, in a show of respect, kissed Bahâ al-Din's knee. ᶜAlâ al-Din wanted to have Bahâ al-Din stay in the palace lounge (*tasht khâne*), but Bahâ al-Din refused, indicating that the *madrase* was the proper place for religious scholars (*aᵓemme*) to stay, just as the *khâneqâh* was proper for Sufi shaykhs, the palace for army commanders or princes (*omarâ*), the inn (*khân*) for merchants, and the lodge (*zâvie*) for members of the young men's groups (*ronud*, probably the Akhis).

So Bahâ al-Din lodged in the Altunpâ Madrase (or Altun Apâ), the only one then existing in Konya, or so we are told (Af 29). Ibn Bibi repeatedly mentions a commander during the reign of ᶜAlâ al-Din Kay Qobâd called Shams al-Din Altunbey; perhaps he founded this *madrase*. In any case, if Bahâ al-Din did indeed take a position there, it would tend to indicate that he considered himself a member of the ulama and not a Sufi shaykh, though his attitudes in religious matters certainly tended to the mystical. This structure, on the site behind the Iplikçi mosque in Konya, was demolished in the eighteenth century, but one room remains standing, which legend claims to have been the room of Rumi's father (Tür 12). One should note that during the Ottoman period, a structure originally established as a Sufi center (*tekke*) might often be transformed into a *madrase* at a later date, or vice versa, depending upon who controlled the facility and its endowment (Klaus Kreiser, in LDL, 51). The exact nature of the facility in which Bahâ al-Din taught or preached therefore remains somewhat obscure.

As to the date, Sultan Valad tells us that Bahâ al-Din died two years after ᶜAlâ al-Din installed him in Konya. This means the *terminus ad quem* for the family's arrival in Konya is 1229 (A.H. 626), and this agrees with the chronology derived from Aflâki. Meier (Mei 39–40) argues, however, that the family must first have come to Konya in 1221 (A.H. 618), and from this base, made several extended junkets to other nearby cities in Anatolia before gaining influence in Konya itself. This would mean that Bahâ al-Din did not immediately catch the attention of ᶜAlâ al-Din, but had to spend several years in nearby Lârende building a following.

PIOUS PATRONAGE

Although the early sources approach their subject with hagiographical rather than historical intentions, depicting Bahâ al-Din as famous throughout the Islamic world, hailed, honored and feted wherever he went, the reality appears much bleaker. Bahâ al-Din – a man just shy of eighty years of age when ᶜAlâ al-Din Kay Qobâd recognized him and installed the Valad family in Konya – until then commanded little if any authority outside of his home base in Vakhsh and Balkh (see Mei 39–40). We know that Bahâ al-Din passed through Baghdad,

Damascus and Aleppo on his way to Anatolia. According to Rumi's contemporary Ibn Shaddâd (1216–85), Aleppo featured twenty-one Hanafi madrases. In the larger city of Damascus, there were thirty-four Hanafi colleges.[10] In addition to the madrases, a large number of mosques and Hadith or Koran institutes also had endowed teaching positions, not to mention the Sufi lodges or centers (rebât, zâvie), many of which taught the law alongside the more mystical approaches (Zia 155, 248; MRC 10).

The institution of the madrase had come to Syria from Khorasan, where the movement to patronize the teaching of Islamic law by founding colleges began, and consequently professors from eastern Iran enjoyed a certain prestige. Most of the madrases in Aleppo and Damascus were founded in the century between the death of Saladin and the invasion of the Mongols, exactly during the time that Bahâ al-Din came in search of a position. Yet none of these institutions, nor the ones in Baghdad, saw fit to give Bahâ al-Din a position as professor or deputy professor. We must therefore dismiss the hagiographers' claim of wider fame for Bahâ al-Din as mofti or jurisconsult. Incidentally, in Syria Bahâ al-Din had at least one rival for the title sultan al-ᶜolamâ, namely his younger contemporary ᶜEzz al-Din b. ᶜAbd al-Salâm (1181–1262), a Shâfeᶜi faqih and author of the Targhib ahl al-Eslâm fi sokna al-Shâm (Zia 175, 255 n. 24). Neither did Bahâ al-Din secure a position as khatib or vâᶜez anywhere along the way to Anatolia, though in Iraq and Syria he may have been at some disadvantage in the preaching profession because his native language was not Arabic. Bahâ al-Din of course had a thorough command of Arabic as a reading language, could compose in it and could probably also converse readily in formal Arabic, but competing with native speakers of Arabic in oratory and homily may have been another matter. After his pilgrimage, Bahâ al-Din could have returned to Iran – if not to Khorasan, then somewhere like Tabriz or Shiraz. Instead, something induced him to try his luck in Asia Minor, perhaps the prospect of a professorship for himself or his sons, perhaps the promise of greater political stability, or perhaps the desire to promulgate the teachings of Islam on the frontier, where the Christian Greeks and Armenians and the Turkmen tribes did not yet accept or observe the practices of Islam.

Far from a triumphal tour, then, Bahâ al-Din traveled from town to town in search of an optimal situation for a mystically minded preacher, such as the one Sanâᵓi enjoyed a century earlier at the court of Bahrâmshâh the Ghaznavid. While the search for knowledge from cradle to grave sometimes led even men of advanced years to travel to distant lands in hopes of visiting and listening to the great scholars of the day, Bahâ al-Din did not tarry long in Baghdad, Damascus, or even Aleppo, where the most noted scholars lived. He must, therefore, have been in search of a position for himself and his sons, a position more easily gained in the Persian-speaking lands of the Seljuks of Rum.

In a guidebook for *madrase* students, the *Ta'lim al-mota'allem* ("Instruction of the Student"), written in 1203 by a Persian-speaking Hanafi jurisconsult of Khorasan (whose work Bahâ al-Din would therefore almost certainly have known), Borhân al-Din al-Zarnuji quotes Abu Hanifa to the effect that the use of knowledge for egotistical purposes or to gain social advantage is sinful. However, he does consider it permissible to seek a position for the purpose of establishing the truth, enjoining what is proper and forbidding what is rejected by religion (Zar 26). Bahâ al-Din Valad believed that to accept gifts or stipends of an illicit nature would cut off God's blessings (Af 20). One of the stories told by Aflâki, though it is a complete myth, nevertheless illustrates the ambivalence felt by pious men of the law and learning when offered positions by temporal rulers, who often resorted to illegal and immoral means to fill the coffers of the treasury. According to Aflâki (Af 18), the caliph in Baghdad (Aflâki does not name him, but it would have been Nâser, r. 1180–1225) had offered 3,000 Egyptian dinârs to Bahâ al-Din, who refused on the grounds that his money was illicit (*harâm*). The caliph not only acquired his money in doubtful manner, he listened to musical instruments and singing, and drank constantly (*modmen-e modâm*). For Bahâ al-Din, the ideal situation would undoubtedly have included a ruler predisposed to heed and foster his teachings, to abstain from wine and other impieties, and to uphold and spread piety and religious learning, preferably of the Hanafi school and preferably in a Persian-speaking area. He would have had few if any qualms of conscience in accepting princely patronage or cultivating influence for pious purposes under such ideal circumstances.

However, to find such a comfortable match between prince and preacher was no easy task. For the early thirteenth century, Shehâb al-Din 'Omar al-Sohravardi (d. 1234), with his role as spiritual and theological adviser to Caliph al-Nâser in Baghdad, provided a practical model for the relationship of ruler and Sufi, as well as a theoretical justification for the relation between the caliphate, the urban youth associations (*fotovvat*) and the Sufis. On behalf of the caliph, Sohravardi traveled to Konya to confirm 'Alâ al-Din Kay Qobâd as sultan of the Seljuks of Rum sometime in 1220. This proved a grand ceremonial occasion, with all the notables, commanders, *qâzis*, ulama and Sufis going out to meet Sohravardi and usher him into Konya (Akh 94–6). On his return to Baghdad, Sohravardi met with Najm al-Din Dâye Râzi (1177–1256) in Malatya. Though Sufis did not usually seek out the company of kings, Sohravardi provided a letter of introduction to Najm al-Din and encouraged him to seek out Sultan 'Alâ al-Din, who impressed him as a patron of religious scholars and mystics.

We do not know if, in fact, Najm al-Din, a refugee from the Mongol invasion of Iran, proceeded to Konya to meet with the sultan and with Sadr al-Din of Konya and Rumi, as Jâmi claims (JNO 435; the seventeen-year-old Rumi was presumably living with his father in Lârende at this time, not in Konya). Najm al-Din does tell us, however, that he began writing his mystical work "The Provision for God's Servants" (*Merşâd al-ʿebâd*) in Kayseri in the autumn of 1221. He completed the book in Sivas on July 31, 1223 and dedicated it to ʿAlâ al-Din Kay Qobâd. Najm al-Din, however, failed to achieve the recognition or arrangement he expected, and went on to Erzincan in 1224. Here he tried to gain the attention of the Manguchak ruler Dâvudshâh (r. 1218?–27?), son of the same Fakhr al-Din Bahrâmshâh whose wife had earlier patronized Bahâ al-Din in Âqshahr. This he did by editing his *Merşâd*, adding quite a bit of information about Iranian kingship (mostly taken from the *Nasihat al-moluk* attributed to Ghazzâli) and rededicating it to Dâvudshâh (d. 1228?) under a different title. He also denounced the irreligious domain of the Seljuks of Anatolia, where the market for religious law (*shariʿat*) and the Sufi path (*tariqat*) was bearish, and the people boorish, unable to distinguish the sincere from the charlatan. Najm al-Din called the people of the area ignorant and godless, though he of course praised Dâvudshâh. However, either because of political or professional instability, Najm al-Din found no contentment here either and returned to Baghdad in about 1225, where he translated his *Merşâd* into Arabic before he died.[11] Meier speculates that because Najm al-Din had written books in Arabic, it was easier for him to find a position or a patron in Syria and Iraq than it was for Bahâ al-Din, who had published no book (Mei 43).

Sepahsâlâr (Sep 15) puts the Valad family in Konya when Rumi was fourteen years old, as early, then, as 1221. However, this does not mesh with Aflâki's claim that Bahâ al-Din died two years after his arrival in Konya. An account related on the authority of Sultan Valad by Aflâki (Af 303) states that one year after being invited to Konya, Bahâ al-Din was asked back to Lârende by Amir Musâ, and it was then that Rumi married Gowhar Khâtun and fathered Sultan Valad. This could account for this discrepancy – perhaps Bahâ al-Din first came to Konya in 1221, but returned in 1222 to Lârende for a further seven years. However, it seems somewhat unlikely that Bahâ al-Din would have left Konya for the more provincial town of Lârende after having been invited to Konya by the sultan. If we assume that Bahâ al-Din went to Konya in search of a position, rather than in response to an offer, we might surmise that he initially failed to attract the attention of the sultan and obtain a position in the capital in 1221. He did, however, find a patron in Lârende, Amir Musâ.

In any case, Bahâ al-Din attained the favor of ʿAlâ al-Din Kay Qobâd and was installed in the one *madrase* of Konya by 1229. At this time his sons would still have been young men, aged twenty-four and twenty-two respectively, too young to hold professorships or preacherships on their own. It seems unnecessary to assume with Meier (Mei 40) that Bahâ al-Din had ceased to function as the head of the household or of the teaching activities at this time. Zarnuji tells us that students should choose as their teacher the man "most learned, the most pious and *the most advanced in years*" (my emphasis; Zar 28).

Of course, we may also assume that the prospects for his sons' future success figured prominently in Bahâ al-Din's decision to settle in Konya.

It has been estimated that a family of five in nearby Syria had essential expenses of around 30 dirhams a month for foodstuffs, exclusive of clothes and lodging. Salaries would vary from college to college, depending upon the particulars of the institution's endowment. The value of currency fluctuated, of course, from period to period, reign to reign and region to region. But the following figures, mentioned by Ibn Kathîr in the fourteenth century, probably fall within an average range: a *modarres* received 80 dirhams per month; a muezzin, 30; a shaykh of Hadith, 30; a *moᶜid*, 20; a Koran reader, 20; a student, 10 (Zia 101–2, 233). The mosques in Syria typically had a *nâzer* or director, a *khatib* to preach the Friday sermon and teach, and an imam to lead the prayer (Zia 114). In the late fifteenth century, the imam (and presumably also the director) of the al-Dolâmiye mosque in Damascus received 100 dirhams per month (Zia 233 n. 285). Some of these positions came with a room, and some of them included board as well.

In the fourteenth century, Ibn Kathîr describes many colleges with endowments that included baths, markets and several villages as sources of income. A Hanafi college founded by Jamâl al-Dowle Eqbâl in 1206 was endowed with half of a village, a third of two separate farms and a portion of the proceeds from a salt mine. The al-Shâmiye al-Jovvâniye Madrase was endowed in 1230 with a house, a village, and percentages of two further villages. The professor's salary was stipulated as 130 dirhams per month and the director of the college was to receive ten percent of all incomes. An indication of the value of the total income may be gauged by the fact that the endowment specified the expenditure of 800 dirhams for fruits and sweets for the celebrations of the 15th of Shaᶜbân. If the endowment's value increased, the charter allowed the director of this school to increase the number of faculty and other positions. The initial endowments of the colleges in Aleppo and Damascus were sufficient in many cases to build large and impressive structures, as Ibn Jobayr testifies in the late twelfth century (Zia 156). If Kay Qobâd was indeed personally involved in establishing the Altunpâ school for Bahâ al-Din, we may surmise that, as he was the sultan of the Seljuk lands of Rum, it was quite well endowed.

ᶜALÂ AL-DIN AND THE SPIRITUAL FRONTIER

We do not know as much about the political history of pre-Ottoman Turkey as we do about many other places and periods of the Islamic world, and more precise information about the interrelations between the various Turkish princedoms which helped Islamize Asia Minor would be useful.[12] The decisive defeat of the Byzantine army at Manzikert in 1071 led to the populating of Asia Minor by Turkish tribesmen. Qelij Arslân shaped these tribesmen into a loosely organized state during his nearly forty-year rule, corresponding to the time of the Crusades and Saladin's rule in Syria. When he died in 1192, his sons fell to fighting amongst themselves, but Kay Khosrow I eventually consolidated power in his own hands and took control of Konya in 1205. His regnal name, and those of his successors, all harked back to the glories of the pre-Islamic Iranian kings, an indication that though Turkish in origin, the Seljuks of Anatolia consciously modeled themselves on Persian culture and royal traditions. Having replaced the Persophilic Samanid and Ghaznavid empires in eastern Iran, the Seljuk Turks consciously set about acquiring the Iranian habits of kingship, assisted by their Iranian viziers. It was to instruct the early Turkish Seljuk rulers in the ways of the pre-Islamic Iranian court traditions that Nezâm al-Molk wrote his famous book on royal politics, *Siâsat nâme* (also known as the *Seyar al-moluk*, "The Manners of the Monarchs"), so that they might convincingly wear the Iranian crown. As the Turkmen tribes spread westward conquering new lands, at least nominally to the glory of the Seljuks, they brought the language, culture and administration of the Persians in their wake. The populace they conquered in the former countryside of Byzantium was, however, primarily Armenian and Greek by ethnicity, Christian by religion and agricultural by occupation. The towns and cities, however, consisted of Turkish tribesmen, urbanized Turks and Iranians, many of whom had fled from the Mongols.

After Kay Khosrow died in May 1211, his eldest son, ᶜEzz al-Din Kay Kâus I (r. 1211–19) assumed the throne. He managed to extend Seljuk power northward to Sinop on the Black Sea while pursuing a policy of peace with the Greeks. He maintained good relations with Bahrâmshâh, the Manguchak ruler of Erzincan, but foolishly attacked al-Zâher in Aleppo and was squarely defeated in 1218, about the time that Bahâ al-Din and the Valads arrived in Âqshahr.

When Kay Kâus I died in 1219, his brother ᶜAlâ al-Din Kay Qobâd I took over. ᶜAlâ al-Din Kay Qobâd (r. 1219–37), so Ibn Bibi tells us, was versed in all branches of knowledge; perhaps a little haughty, but generous and a good politician (Akh 91–4). He read Nezâm al-Molk's manual on statecraft and took as role models two famous patrons of architecture, literature and the arts, Mahmud of Ghazna and Qâbus b. Voshmgir. Exemplary not only in political matters, ᶜAlâ al-Din Kay Qobâd read Ghazzâli's ethico-mystical treatise *Kimiâ-ye saᶜâdat*, "The Alchemy of Happiness" (Akh 94), and, according to one of his commanders, Jalâl al-Din Qarâtây, slept but little, following the pious maxim, "stay up throughout the night, except for a little," to which Kay Qobâd attributed his good fortune. He considered it obligatory to follow the Hanafi rites, except in the matter of the morning prayer, which he followed according to the Shâfeᶜi rite (Akh 93).

His ethical and religious inclinations did not, however, prevent him from pursuing a bold campaign of battle and conquest. Between 1221 and 1225 he conquered the southern coast of Anatolia all the way up to Syria, after which he turned his attention northward, where the Seljuks took the Crimea, an area they held until 1239. To facilitate trade, he established dozens of fortified stage towns with caravanserais along the roads to Europe and to Iran. He settled Turkmen tribes in Cilician Taurus, married a Georgian heiress after wresting some castles from Georgian possession, annexed the territory of Dâvudshâh, the Manguchak ruler of Erzincan, and the territory of Erzurum.

As ʿAlâ al-Din Kay Qobâd expanded eastward into the realms of the Manguchaks and Artuqids, he came face to face with Jalâl al-Din the Khwârazmshâh, son of Bahâ al-Din's old nemesis from Khorasan. Chased out of Khorasan by the Mongol invaders, Jalâl al-Din the Khwârazmshâh arrived in Azerbayjan in 1225, took Georgia in 1226, and on November 7, 1226 laid siege to Ahlat in eastern Turkey, though he did not succeed in snatching it from Ayyubid control until April of 1230. This caused the Ayyubid al-Ashraf in Syria to join forces with ʿAlâ al-Din Kay Qobâd in Anatolia, and together they defeated the Khwârazmshâh near Erzincan on August 10, 1230. ʿAlâ al-Din Kay Qobâd used this as an occasion to remove the Seljuk prince of Erzurum and extend his borders to the east. But this marriage of convenience with the Ayyubids eventually soured, and al-Kâmel invaded the Seljuk domains in 1233. Kay Qobâd successfully repulsed him, but within a few years the Mongols had begun to encroach on Seljuk Anatolia, sometimes with the connivance of later Seljuk sultans or ministers. Indeed, Rumi would make an issue of Moʿin al-Din Parvâne's dealings with the Mongols (see Discourse 1 in Fih 4–5).

With the wealth generated from the sale of luxury items to Europe, the Seljuks were able to build impressive cities and to patronize Persian and Turkish poets, architects and religious and mystical teachers. ʿAlâ al-Din constructed a great many buildings, including a palace in Kayseri – the Kayqobâdiye (c. 1224–6) – where he held the reviews of the army and where he often stayed, dying there in 1237. The Seljuks of Anatolia founded a great many *madrases*, mosques and funerary monuments, proving their piety by supporting the ulama and providing them the opportunity to preach to and convert the subject populations of Greek and Armenian Christians, as well as the incompletely Islamized Turkmen. For example, in Sivas a Friday mosque was built in 1196 and in 1217 Kay Kâus I built a hospital, college and tomb complex there, called the Shafâʾiye Madrase (Şifaiye). ʿAlâ al-Din built a mosque and *madrase* in Sinop soon after its capture, as well as a mosque in Antalya. His daughter, Khodâvand Khâtun, built the Çifte Mınareli Madrese in Erzurum in 1253. The subsequent Seljuk sultans, and especially their ministers, continued the practice of building mosques and *madrases*, often including a family mausoleum.

The practice of building *madrases* had initiated in Khorasan, as we have seen, and became systematized under the early Seljuk vizier Nezâm al-Molk. The Ayyubids had recently started to build *madrases*, hundreds being founded in the twelfth century in Syria. The practice of establishing a family mausoleum within a *madrase* ensured that one would always be remembered in the prayers of the students and professors who taught in the college one had endowed. The most appealing form of Islam to the subject peoples in Anatolia (as in India and elsewhere) proved to be Sufism; in addition to the *khâneqâhs*, the *madrases* often supported mystically minded preachers. The Altunpâ Madrase of Bahâ al-Din's appointment in Konya was probably just such a place, though we do not know precisely what position Bahâ al-Din held there or the courses he taught. Since the Seljuks favored such mystical poets and thinkers as Rumi, Ibn ʿArabi, Sadr al-Din of Konya, ʿErâqi and Yunus Emre, it would not be surprising if Bahâ al-Din taught a combination of mystical Islam, ethics and the law in Konya.[13]

DEATH OF BAHÂ AL-DIN

According to Aflâki (Af 32, 56), Bahâ al-Din died late in the morning of February 23, 1231 (18 Rabiʿ II 628), probably just shy of eighty years of age (or eighty-two according to the Islamic lunar calendar). Note that Aflâki gives Friday as the day of the week, whereas February 23, 1231 fell on a Sunday. Aflâki also relates an imprecise statement by Sultan Valad indicating that his grandfather, Bahâ al-Din, was eighty-five when he died (Af 41). Hasan Özönder indicates that Bahâ al-Din was buried in the rose garden of Sultan ʿAlâ al-Din Kay Qobâd, who had Bahâ al-Din's tombstone inscribed with phrases describing him as the guide of Islamic praxis and reviver of the Sunna, the King of the Clerics and Mufti of East and West (Tür 13).

Sultan Valad describes the last days of Bahâ al-Din in this manner:

> After two years, God decreed that Bahâ al-Din lay his head on the pillow of affliction. The king was saddened by his suffering; he came and sat down by him, crying, saying, "If God is inclined to me, this suffering will decline. If he gets better, from now on he'll be sultan and I'll gladly be his slave" ... Every time the sultan saw him, he reaffirmed this vow. When the king went off toward his house, he [Bahâ al-Din] would say to those present, "If this man is telling the truth, my time has come to go; I'll go from this mortal world, for if I become the king also in outward appearance, then this world will be as nothing and all the people will grow drunk with God, and all will go about distracted like me. The works of the world will go undone, all will be amazed in the love of Him and no food or clothing could be found, as none would work ... [193] I must surely go so that the physical world not be destroyed."
>
> This befell soon after – he moved on from this world to the next. When Bahâ-e Valad made the final journey, men and women attended his corpse like the Day of Resurrection, shedding tears of blood. A conflagration befell the city of Konya, lords and servants were burned in their grief for him. The ulama and amirs, bareheaded, all went before the corpse with the sultan. No one in Konya was left – man, woman, noble or commoner – who did not attend the procession ... The sultan, in grief, did not hold court for seven days; his heart, like glass,

shattered in pain. For one week he laid a spread in the mosque so that all, whether gluttonous or content, ate. He granted bounties to the poor on account of the "marriage feast" (*ors*) of that exalted king. Day and night he wailed in separation from him, he shed tears and blood from both eyes. After the mourning (*ta'zie*) was complete, all the people gathered, young and old, and turned to his son [Jalâl al-Din Rumi], saying, "You are like him in beauty; from now on we hold to your hem ... from now on you will be our king, for we seek wealth and gain from you." (SVE 192–3)

THE SPIRITUAL LIFE OF BAHÂ AL-DIN VALAD

Bahâ al-Din's preoccupation with the presence of God and with divine intimations and promptings cannot escape the notice of even a casual reader of the *Ma'âref*. Even more striking is Bahâ al-Din's predisposition to mystical visions of an almost surreal, synaesthetic or even psychedelic quality. He describes visions in which he hovers in the air, predicts the life span of individuals, sees colors, fluids and matter flowing within and without himself and other objects, and sometimes talks with God as one would with a friend. According to what the hagiographers would have us believe, Rumi did not know of his father's mystical proclivities until Borhân al-Din introduced them to him. Given his near obsession with purity of heart, the divine presence, and his frequent visions, it seems extremely implausible that Rumi knew nothing of his father's mysticism. Part of the reason for the family's departure from Khorasan and its pilgrimage to Mecca may indeed have been the process of cleansing the soul from worldly attachments and rededicating oneself to the perfection of the spirit, as Owhad al-Din Kermâni set out to do before becoming a disciple of Rokn al-Din Sajjâsi (Owh 3–5).

Bahâ al-Din believed that his understanding, and that of all mankind, came from God (Bah 1:127). As a child Rumi often saw his father standing and repeating "Allâh, Allâh." As Aflâki (311) tells it, when Bahâ al-Din would tire of chanting this name of the Lord, his mouth would fall open, and the sound "Allâh, Allâh" could still be heard issuing from his breast. Bahâ al-Din would attribute the events that happened around him to the acts and deeds of God (Allâh), focusing on the Koranic word "Allâh," as opposed to other words in Arabic and Persian often used for God. Bahâ al-Din understood the human spirit (*ruh, nafs*) to be the breath of Allâh (as the etymology of the words in Arabic and Hebrew suggest), but also conceived of it, in the old Irano-Manichaean fashion, as the light of God captured in our fleshy frames. He therefore pictured our spirits escaping the material world to join with God (*ruh-hâ hamchonin be Allâh payvandand*) (Bah 1:321).

In Discourse 3 (Fih 12) Rumi relates how one day Bahâ al-Din's companions found him engrossed in contemplation when the time for prayers arrived. Some of his disciples called out to Mowlânâ, "Time for prayer!," but Mowlânâ did not acknowledge them. So they went to pray and turned toward the *qeble* (the direction one faces during prayer – toward the Kaaba in Mecca), with their backs to Mowlânâ. But two of the disciples preferred to remain with their shaykh, Bahâ al-Din, and so did not stand to perform the prayers. During the prayer, God intimated to one of the disciples who had gone to pray that all the companions had turned their backs on the true *qeble*, except for the two disciples who had remained by Shaykh Bahâ al-Din. It was these two who had their faces toward the true *qeble*, since the Shaykh had passed beyond we and I and his selfness had been obliterated and erased in the light of truth, as in the hadith, "Die before you die." Rumi tells us that whoever turns away from the light of Truth to face a stone wall has assuredly turned his back on the *qeble*, for such a shaykh is himself the spirit of the *qeble*.

This anecdote gives us an opportunity to hear Rumi talking about his own father, whom he indirectly describes as the light of God and the true *qeble*. When Rumi directly invokes his father's name in this anecdote, he refers to him, according to one manuscript of *Fihe mâ fih*, as "Our Master, the King of Scholars, the (spiritual) axis of the world, Bahâ al-Haqq va al-Din, may God sanctify his magnificent spirit." It is not at all unusual for such honorific formulas to appear in conjunction with the mention of Sufis in the medieval period, and these are even tame in comparison with the epithets Rumi gives to Shams. But another manuscript has Rumi describe Bahâ al-Din even more modestly and unceremoniously as simply "Bahâ al-Din Valad, God sanctify his spirit."

THE *MA^CÂREF* OF BAHÂ AL-DIN

Like many of the imams and Hadith scholars who taught in mosques and *madrases*, Bahâ al-Din never "published" any books (Zia 173). Although the descendants and disciples of Rumi in Konya preserved a miscellany of Mowlânâ Bahâ al-Din of Balkh's journals and teachings, most of the mystical thinkers and Sufis of Iran were ignorant of it (Bah 1:b). Jalâl al-Din Rumi was certainly aware of it, as he sometimes paraphrases his father in the *Masnavi* (FB 33; Bah 1:y/d–k/t). Aflâki relates anecdotes which depict Rumi reading from (Af 93, 652) or copying out the text (FB 32) of his father's spiritual journals. Sepahsâlâr (Sep 119) indicates that Borhân al-Din first introduced Rumi to the spiritual teachings (*ma^câref*) of Bahâ al-Din, going over them with Rumi a thousand times; Shams al-Din later forbade Rumi from studying his father's book (Af 623).

The followers of Bahâ al-Din would write down his public comments, according to Sepahsâlâr (20–21), who quotes by way of example an extended passage that likewise appears in Bahâ's *Ma^câref* (Bah 1:1–2). Aflâki (12, 33, 93) confirms that such a book existed in his day and thrice refers to the *Ma^câref* by name. A manuscript of the first section of this work, copied out by a certain

Khodâdâd al-Mowlavi of Konya in March 1549 (Safar A.H. 956), was first brought to scholarly attention in the mid-1920s. Further manuscript copies soon turned up, including a version of 278 folios containing a second and third section of the work; this copy, discovered in the University Library of Istanbul, was written out in the spring of 1586 (A.H. 994). A manuscript from the Hagia Sophia library, written out in the fall of 1346 (A.H. 747), proved to be the oldest and most reliable (though not the most complete) copy (Bah 1:a–j, lt, m, ma).

An edition of the Persian text of the *Ma'âref* was finally published in February 1955, but a second volume was added to this in 1959 after the discovery of another manuscript, preserved in the Konya Mevlânâ Museum (no. 2116), which included previously unknown portions of the text:

> Bahâ-e Valad, *Ma'âref: majmu'e-ye mavâ'ez va sokhanân-e Soltân al-'olamâ Bahâ al-Din*, ed. Badi' al-Zamân Foruzânfar (Tehran: Edâre-ye koll-e Vezârat-e Farhang, 1333/1955 and 1338/1959; reprinted Tehran: Tahuri, 1352/1973).

This edition is not definitive, insofar as the Hagia Sophia manuscript was discovered too late to be collated and properly integrated into the critical edition. Foruzânfar thought that the second volume (part 4) of his edition contained a recension or an earlier portion of the text, but he did not attempt to edit the various recensions into a single work. Furthermore, Foruzânfar subsequently turned up another manuscript dating from 1597 (in the possession of Feridun Nafiz Uzluk) which contains further portions of Bahâ al-Din's text along with the text of Sayyed Borhân al-Din's *Ma'âref*. This manuscript also supplies previously unknown information about Bahâ al-Din (Bor k–ka). A new, fully collated edition of Bahâ al-Din's *Ma'âref* is therefore a desideratum.

One of the surviving manuscripts dates to the lifetime of Bahâ al-Din and from the corrections and marginal notes one might infer that the author himself wrote out the text, though Sepahsâlâr implies it was collected by his disciples (Sep 20–21). Meier suggests that Rumi may have read this very manuscript, though a passage (corresponding to Bah 1:219) quoted by Sayyed Borhân al-Din Mohaqqeq in his own work (also called *Ma'âref*, Bor 67–8) does not come from this Konya manuscript (Mei 2–3, 5, 426). It would appear then that the various manuscripts of the *Ma'âref* reflect different stages of the work, including notes or diary entries written down by Bahâ al-Din himself, along with further recensions which draw upon those notes, but also contain supplementary material (perhaps the notes of his disciples) from one or more other sources. Despite the convoluted transmission history of the text, the essence of the work, if not the redacted form, almost certainly reflects the thoughts and words of Bahâ al-Din (FB 33; Mei 5).

Bahâ al-Din's miscellany is designated *Ma'âref*, meaning mystical intimations or insights, though this is more a description than a title (see Af 33); it constitutes the most important source for understanding not only Bahâ al-Din's thought, but also the history of the Valad family and the early influences on Rumi's thought. It provides a record of Bahâ al-Din's devotional life and spiritual praxis, including meditations, confessions, visions and realizations. It also includes accounts of some lectures or sermons, but it retains a personal and even intimate flavor. Bahâ al-Din did not intend the work for general publication; instead it provides a personal record of his spiritual development, reflecting a genre of confessional writing practiced by many Sufis – a kind of spiritual journal. Some Sufis kept daily journals of what they said, wrote and felt and would review this journal at the end of the evening to keep a running account of their deeds and spiritual development. Shaykh Sayf al-Din Bâkharzi (d. 1231) kept such a daybook (*ruz-nâme*) in which he secretly wrote down his every move. But such spiritual diaries were private and not meant for public consumption. Many Sufis felt antipathy to writing things down, as the secrets of the path could not be learned from books (Mov 103–4). The subtitle which Foruzânfar gave the work, "Bahâ al-Din's Spiritual Intimations: A Collection of the Sermons and Speeches of the King of Clerics," is therefore somewhat misleading.

Historical events mentioned in the text allow us to date portions of Bahâ's *Ma'âref* to the years 1200–1211, though some sections may indeed be earlier, even as early as about 1190, when the author turned forty (Bah 1:40). Mahbub-e Serâj concluded that parts of the *Ma'âref* were composed after the family's westward migration,[14] but Meier does not find the evidence for this compelling (Mei 6). The Konya manuscript which provides the basis for volume 2 of Foruzânfar's edition seems restricted to the years 1208–10 (Bah 2:y). Bahâ al-Din gives an explicit date in some portions, such as in passage 227, written sometime after June 1204 (Bah 1: 354–5).

Foruzânfar (FB 33) was much taken by the "elegance of expression" found in Bahâ al-Din's *Ma'âref* and considered it "one of the best examples of poetic prose" in Persian; Serâj (51, cited Mei 8 n. 43) compared Bahâ's delicacy of style with Hâfez, Sa'di and Rumi. Some of this may be dismissed as the editor and specialist's partiality to his own particular subject of study, yet the sincerity, spontaneity and unfiltered immediacy of Bahâ al-Din's narrative truly do charm and endear, while the psychedelic visions he describes sound awe inspiring.

BAHÂ AL-DIN'S TEACHINGS

Though Bahâ al-Din did not subscribe to any formal Sufi praxis or order, his spiritual preoccupation, we may even say his obsession, centered on acquiring divine attributes and approaching God. For Bahâ al-Din this meant reading and meditating on the Koran, for through reading the Koran one might steel the soul against all manner of frailty and sickness (Bah 1:365–6).

Foruzânfar (Bah 1:yd–kt) has given a list of almost twenty pages demonstrating similarities between Rumi's *Masnavi* and the *Ma'âref* of Bahâ al-Din. Indeed, there are few subjects in the *Ma'âref* which Rumi does not also treat in his poetry or prose (ZrJ 274), but Jalâl al-Din Rumi did not simply borrow his father's teachings lock, stock and barrel; as Meier (5) puts it, the two are quite different personalities. Rumi must be seen as by far the greater teacher, not only because of his conscious effort to dictate and publish his ideas in edited form, but because he chose the medium of poetry and parable to convey them. Nevertheless, familiarizing ourselves with some of the concepts of Bahâ al-Din will enhance our understanding of Rumi's teachings. A brief sketch follows of some of the views reflected in Bahâ al-Din's *Ma'âref.*

Attitude Toward Poetry

Though Bahâ al-Din did not leave behind any body of poetry, his *Ma'âref* contains scattered quotations of about thirty lines of verse, some in Arabic and some in Persian, some of them by known poets. Other verses would appear to be either of his own composing or popular lines he had heard recited orally. We presume the former, since Bahâ al-Din at various points alludes to having composed numerous lines of verse (*bayt-hâ-ye besyâr*) in praise of God (Bah 1:392) or compares himself in praising God to a lover composing countless verses (*sad hezâr bayt*) for his beloved (Bah 1:16); indeed, he argues that all praise of beauty, of the beloved's face, eyes and eyebrows, is in effect praise of God.

Detachment

Bahâ al-Din urges people not to allow the dross of the world (which includes the learned, and the cities, and the armies and the rulers of the world) to cover their hearts and hinder them from knowledge of God and meditation on the other world (Bah 2:133). In one vision, Bahâ al-Din makes an analogy between the fire in a brick oven and how it first turns things black, then red and finally white in its flames, and the process of spiritual purification. In the fire of God's love man's impurities are burned away; this fire will at first make him sad and black-faced, then it will move him to ecstasy and make him glow crimson like a coal until finally it illumines him and turns him forever white, white as the light of Moses, Mohammad and the other prophets (Bah 1:381).

Piety and Worship

The Koran promises that God's presence permeates our moral universe: "We are closer to him than his jugular vein" (K50:16) and "He is with you wherever you are" (K57:4, 58:7). Muslim theologians and mystics had frequently discussed the meaning and implication of these statements of God's immanence prior to Bahâ al-Din. Bahâ al-Din sided with those mystics who addressed the question more from the standpoint of ethics and piety and strove to discover phenomenologically how one might better sense and discern this divine proximity (e.g., Bah 1:372). We may approach God by lifting the veils from our sight, at which point we may experience the paradise of seeing Him present all around us (Bah 1:163–4). Our soul purified and our spiritual insight sharpened, we too may see God on Sinai like Moses (Bah 1:140). All the atoms of existence indeed respond to the divine and universal charge of God's permeating presence and answer His call. Bahâ al-Din feels directed by God to busy himself with the Koran and its meaning: "Always busy yourself with the word of the Koran and know that the meaning of the whole world is in that one word of the Koran" (Bah 1: 33).

Ritter has described Bahâ al-Din's piety and mysticism as quietist, aesthetic and narcissistic,[15] but Meier (Mei 11) feels that this mischaracterizes Bahâ's approach to the religious life. Meier has himself schematized Bahâ al-Din's views on God's presence in great depth, with quotations from earlier works of theology and Sufism, all of which greatly assist us in contextualizing Bahâ al-Din's views.

Bahâ al-Din Valad most often describes his experience of God with the emotions of awe, love and fear, reflected predominantly in three modes of worship – magnification of God, contemplation of God and self-purification. His love of God and his visions often raise him into a state of bliss. He talks often of "taste" (*maze*), a Persian word corresponding to the more common Arabic term found in Sufi manuals (*zowq*), signifying direct experience of the spiritual world, as opposed to ratiocination about it. By "taste" Bahâ al-Din also implies a feeling of delight or a capacity to be moved by, sensitive to and receptive of life and the wonders of God's creation.

Bahâ al-Din, like many Sufis before him, approaches God from a variety of motives or promptings, especially love, fear and hope. Each of these attitudes leads man to worship, to magnify (*ta'zim*) and to glorify (*ejlâl*) God (see Mei 185–91). He urges himself to "magnify God in suchwise that God will refresh your every doing," so that your body will appear verdant and luxurious like gardens of subtle meaning in the springtime (Bah 1:163). Man may accomplish such magnification through contemplation of God and through the *via purgativa*, purging the soul of the baser self. Bahâ al-Din's preferred technique for doing this seems to have been by reading the Koran and meditating upon its passages. He summarizes its essential meaning as follows:

> I have followed the entire Koran and found the gist of every verse and story to be this:
>
> > O servant, cut yourself off from all but Me, for that which you attain through others, you will attain through Me, without obligation to anyone else. And that which you will attain through Me, you will attain through no one else. You who follow Me, follow Me more closely!
>
> "Prayer is joining with God and alms are joining with God and fasting is joining with God." These are the means of joining with God, and every joining brings

with it joy (*maze*), just as sitting next to a beloved brings joy and resting your head on her shoulder brings joy. Whether you read from the beginning of the Koran or from the end of the Koran, the Koran is this:

> O you who are sundered from Me, join Me, for "He who is separated from the Living One is of the dead." (Bah 1: 219)

We will later see how following the Prophet became the principal focus of the quest of Rumi and Shams to join with God.

The previous manuals and discussions of Sufism surely colored Bahâ al-Din's reading of scripture, but like many other Sufis from Khorasan, he was far more concerned with praxis. Achieving an experiential, individual and even visionary understanding takes precedence over expounding one's intimations in any systematic fashion or in terms of any pre-existing discourse, whether it be that of scriptural exegesis, philosophy, the law, or whatever else. In addition to prayer and reading of the Koran, Bahâ of course counseled observance of the law, but the law does not seem to have concerned him as a subject in its own right, only as an ethical foundation for an intelligent and ardent approach to God.

Family Life and Children

Bahâ al-Din sometimes felt that attachment to, responsibility for and love of his wives and children hindered him from the Herculean labors of spirit he wished to undertake. He tells himself that the Khwârazmshâh leaves behind his house and home and children in order to rule the land, as do all the merchants and prophets (Bah 2:156). On the other hand, very much like a modern father, he worries that while engaged in his work he is neglecting his children – yet he also worries that the children will perpetually distract him from achieving anything (Bah 2:109):

> Every moment I would hear a cry from one of the children I would sigh, thinking "What calamity has befallen my child now?" I would think to myself, "If I spend my life worrying over them, I'll be ruined and if I keep to myself, they will be ruined!"

But Bahâ al-Din does seem to carry on theological and spiritual discourses with women and to allow them to sit in on his lectures, thus perhaps finding some way to combine his home life and his work.

Knowledge

There are two kinds of knowledge. We acquire conventional or customary knowledge (*'elm-e rasmi*) for the purpose of preaching, sermonizing, judging questions of law and so forth. However, this conventional knowledge conveys us only halfway down our path, whereas the knowledge of true realities (*'elm-e haqâ'eq*) looks to the end of the quest and strives to attain the goal. This true knowledge comes to a person through the grace of God and divine election.

88

Those enthused with this knowledge are blessed, and those devoid of this knowledge lack inspiration (Bah 1:381).

Free Will

Bahâ-e Valad apparently held a middle position on this hotly contested issue in Islamic theology and political theory, reflecting the Mâtoridi school of Hanafi thought on the question of free will. Man should attempt to act and to achieve results in this world as though possessing free will. Nevertheless, he must submit to his fate and powerlessness before God.

Mystical Cosmology

Bahâ al-Din and his son were not pantheists, but often they describe the world in terms that circumvent scholastic theism.[16] Instead of positing a personal and anthropomorphic Godhead above and beyond the world yet in communion with His creatures, the Valads instead portray God's presence as suffusing the world. Meier (Mei 436) sums up Bahâ al-Din's notion of God's relation to his creation as a placeless and indescribable presence (*ma'iyat*, "withness") or nearness to all spiritual, mental and physical beings. God is always with man, ontologically, as creator and in our thoughts and perceptions.

This does not contradict or ignore the personhood of God as historical actor depicted in the Koran, but concentrates attention on God's presence in the handiwork of creation, thus focusing the believer's attention on God no matter where he may turn. One should not, however, make the mistake of assuming that God therefore exists within the physical world; God remains "beyond every created being" (Bah 1:179). As Bahâ al-Din says (Bah 1:360), the distance from my soul and God's creative work within my soul, to God's being, is very far indeed.

For Bahâ al-Din, God is a placeless entity. In one passage (1:245), Bahâ al-Din describes an argument with a materialist who asks where God resides. The question is invalid, Bahâ explains, like asking "How is white black?" The importance of God's role as creator resides not in the physical creation, but in the spiritual inspiration and sustenance of that physical creation (Bah 1:380):

> It is as if bodies, mountains, the lands and heavens, the clouds and rains, winds and waters, the fruits and flesh of animals, all are like a chain linked together, whereas spirits descend into another world beyond these created things. From beyond these created things, God blows into these created things, inspiring them with spiritual realities and joy and sorrow and grief and humility and wrath, just as one blows into horns and trumpets.

Bahâ al-Din goes on to explain that every image of a beautiful face or the sound of music or other such forms exist within the world of created beings, but point beyond this to a spiritual reality. All creation came into being through a chain set into motion by "Here I am, my servant," God's reply to man's prayers in the spiritual realm. God, then, continuously speaks to man through spiritual realities as a means of training His servants. The saints are aware of this divine intervention, whereas common folk are not. The prophets can see through the veils of this great chain of being to the spiritual realities beyond.

Elsewhere Bahâ al-Din compares the structure of earthly forms to syntactic and grammatical structures. All creation came into being with God's command, "Be," so that the universe is speech, created by a single world. If God's speech is so glorious in the beautiful forms it manifests in this world, imagine what God must be like in His essence (Bah 1:25). This thought, once again, can be traced to the Koran: "The seven heavens and the earth and whatsoever they contain, all praise Him; there is no thing that does not sing His praise, only you cannot discern their mode of praise" (K17: 44).

Bahâ al-Din therefore inclines his ear every day to the speech of God and looks at the forms of speech He has created, for man's essential ego, or "I-ness" (*mani*) lies in his powers of discernment and apprehension, his pleasures and experiences. These do not arise from his physical being, but from God's continuous speech, such that human consciousness emanates in reality from God (Bah 1:25): "And if we ask who is God, He is the creator of these meanings, and we should therefore occupy all our thoughts with Him."

In essence Bahâ al-Din adopts, along with the Asharites, an atomist theology in which God constantly recreates each particle (*jozv*) of existence. In his visionary states, Bahâ al-Din sometimes describes the atoms of his body, themselves like little microcosms panpsychically endowed with anima (*hayât*) and consciousness (*ʿaql*), calling out to the other atoms of existence, all obedient unto God's command, intoxicated and delirious, submerged in the love of God (Bah 1:29).

THE MYTHICAL BAHÂ AL-DIN

The persistence of a community of individuals residing physically in the shrine of a saint and the schools and hospices that sometimes grew up around them, as well as the spread of an order promulgating esoteric teachings and a reverential attitude towards its founding fathers, naturally tends to create a legendary and even miraculous *vita* for them. Sultan Valad himself already contributed to this supernaturalizing tendency in his "Book of Beginnings" (*Ebtedâ nâme*), in which he compares Bahâ al-Din to the famous Sufis of the past. This naturally leads him to describe his grandfather's life according to the expectations of the hagiographical genre.[17]

Because his pupil, Borhân al-Din, and his son, Jalâl al-Din Rumi, provide precious little information about Bahâ al-Din, the brief account by Sultan Valad (SVE 187–93) offers the earliest coherent portrait of him. The halo of holiness which already obscures Bahâ al-Din the man in his grandson's account shines even more blindingly in the chronicle of Sepahsâlâr (Sep 10–21) and in the

"Acts of the Gnostics" by Ahmad Aflâki (Af 7–55). Later writers, such as Jâmi, Dowlatshâh and Amin Ahmad Râzi, whether committed or not to the perpetuation of a mythic image of Bahâ al-Din and Jalâl al-Din, effectively reinforced or enhanced the popular and miraculous reputation of their subjects by repeating the tales of the earlier "biographers." For decades scholars, relying rather too credulously on these accounts, have likewise repeated these legends, lending them an air of respectability.

The outstanding feature in the hagiographer's mythical portrait of Bahâ al-Din is his fame as a theologian and scholar of religious law. Though Bahâ al-Din may indeed have achieved some reputation in Vakhsh or even in Balkh or Samarqand, he did not enjoy wider renown as a religious scholar or public figure, as I have been at pains to show. No mention of Bahâ al-Din Valad has turned up in sources contemporary to him, such as biographical dictionaries or the works of other religious scholars such as Fakhr al-Din Râzi. Much later sources describe him only in relation to his famous son, not as an independent figure. Bahâ al-Din's own writings, Ma'âref, were never disseminated to a wider audience in the medieval period and he could not, therefore, have been famous as an author.

Bahâ al-Din's disciples also traced his family lineage to the first caliph, Abu Bakr (Sep 9; Af 7; JNO 457; Dow 213). This probably stems from willful confusion over his paternal great grandmother, who was the daughter of Abu Bakr of Sarakhs, a noted jurist (d. 1090). The most complete genealogy offered for the family only stretches back six or seven generations and cannot possibly reach to Abu Bakr, the companion and first caliph of the Prophet, who died two years after the Prophet, in A.D. 634 (FB 5–6 n. 3). One would furthermore expect descent from Abu Bakr, were it part of the family lore during the lifetime of Bahâ al-Din, to be a source of pride and professional authority, yet there is no mention of this in the writings of Bahâ al-Din or Jalâl al-Din Rumi, nor do the inscriptions on their sarcophagi mention it. Mention of this supposed lineage does turn up in some manuscripts of our earliest biographical source, Sultan Valad's Ebtedâ nâme (SVE 187), but Gölpınarlı speculated that a later copyist interpolated these remarks on the basis of Aflâki (Af 8) or Sepahsâlâr (Sep 9).[18] Whether or not this is so, we have seen how Sultan Valad errs or ignores a great many facts about his grandfather.

Ahmad Aflâki (Af 7–9) makes the claim that Bahâ al-Din's mother was the daughter of 'Alâ al-Din Mohammad Khwârazmshâh (r. 1200–1220), described as "the paternal uncle" of Jalâl al-Din Khwârazmshâh. Jâmi repeats this (JNO 458), but the chronology is impossible (FB 7), and in any case, the portrait of her that emerges from Bahâ al-Din's comments does not square with a royal lineage (Mei 45). Furthermore, the association of religious figures with royalty in the Iranian hagiographical tradition (e.g., the intermarriage of the last Sasanian princess with the 'Alid family) is typological and must therefore be viewed with extreme skepticism.

The hagiographers likewise assert spiritual descent from famous Sufis for Bahâ al-Din. Aflâki (998) and Sepahsâlâr (9) link him, through his grandfather, with Ahmad Ghazzâli (d. 1126), younger brother of the more famous Abu Hâmed Ghazzâli, and Jâmi (JNO 457) relays the suggestion that Bahâ al-Din may have been a disciple of the great Najm al-Din Kobrâ (d. 1220). Neither attribution is corroborated, explicitly or implicitly, in the writings of Bahâ al-Din, Rumi, or Sultan Valad; this fact, in itself, almost certainly negates the possibility. The meeting with ʿAttâr has been dealt with above, along with the miraculous dream about the title "Sultan al-ulama." Though the main contours of this legendary image of Bahâ al-Din dissolve like a mirage under closer scrutiny, the picture which emerges from the *Maʿâref,* of a visionary, God-intoxicated mystic who achieved wider recognition only in his seventies, is no less remarkable.

RUMI TAKES OVER

Rumi was born on 6 Rabiʿ I in 604, corresponding to September 30, 1207. We do not know for certain if his mother and the womenfolk of the family lived with Bahâ al-Din in Vakhsh, but since Bahâ al-Din resided there in a house for some years, it seems likely that they did, and that Rumi was therefore born in Vakhsh. By 1213, however, the family had moved to Samarqand, possibly because of the political disturbances of the region and the Khwârazmshâh's conquest of the regions around Balkh. Aflâki (Af 16, 994) relays one report to the effect that Rumi was five and his brother ʿAlâ al-Din seven years old at the time of their exodus from Khorasan. This would suggest an earlier date of 1212 or 1213 (A.H. 609). However, this probably refers to the family's departure from Vakhsh for Samarqand, not the migration from Khorasan westward. On the basis of Aflâki's date of 1217 for the family's arrival in Malatya (a date which is not necessarily firm itself), I have estimated that the Valads left Khorasan in the spring or summer of 1216, when Rumi was eight.

Little Jalâl al-Din (not yet called Rumi) would have turned nine along the way, before reaching Baghdad, and his tenth birthday would have come in Anatolia, after completing the pilgrimage to Mecca. By age fourteen or fifteen, after his father had taught for a while in Âqshahr, the family moved to Lârende, where Rumi spent the rest of his teen years, and where his mother passed away. Here Rumi married in the year 1224 at the age of seventeen (Af 48) to Gowhar Khâtun, a girl whose father had traveled with them or at least knew them from Samarqand (it is not impossible that she and Rumi were betrothed as children). Most likely, Rumi attended his father's lectures and sat by his side. By the time the family was invited to settle in Konya in 1229, Rumi had two boys, Sultan Valad and ʿAlâ al-Din, one of whom was born in 1226 (there is no mention of their having been twins, so we will assume that they were not both born in that year). When Bahâ al-Din died in 1231 after two years teaching in Konya, Rumi was twenty-four years of age (Af 48) and had been married seven years.

Sultan Valad tells us (SVE 193) that "the monarch" Jalâl al-Din Rumi assumed his father's place at the request of the disciples, young and old, who considered Rumi the heir of his father's spiritual beauty. According to the *Haft eqlim*, however, it was the wish of Sultan ʿAlâ al-Din that Rumi assume his father's position (IqL 65). Browne speculates that it had been Bahâ al-Din's wish that Rumi take his place (BLH 2:438).

Like his father, Rumi was a scholar and an ascetic, distinguishing himself as the head and king of the men of religion. Like his father, he wrote legal opinions, dispelling ignorance with his knowledge, such that he became the Mofti of East and West (SVE 194). Apparently, then, Bahâ al-Din had taught his son Islamic law (*feqh*), or had someone else teach him (perhaps the *qâzi* of Konya?). Sultan Valad was about sixteen when Shams al-Din came to town; Aflâki tells us that Sultan Valad used to sit by his father's side and people would mistake them for brothers (Af 26; Rumi was thirty-seven at this time). It is likely, therefore, that Sultan Valad's knowledge about Rumi's activities during this time came first-hand. Though we may discount as hyperbole Sultan Valad's claims about the worldwide fame of his father as a jurisconsult, if Rumi wrote even one fatwa, he had to have had an *ejâze* to teach (*tadris*) and to opine (*eftâ*) on questions of law. Rumi was more than old enough to have studied the law with his father and mastered the primary texts of legal study, in addition to the Koran.

The law curriculum varied widely from *madrase* to *madrase*, depending upon the wishes of the donor who endowed it, as well as on the particular interests of the professor who occupied its chair at any given time (MRC 84). Typically, however, the primary subject of instruction in the *madrases* of Rumi's period revolved around the canonical law manuals of the particular *mazhab*, as specified by the charter of endowment (usually Shâfeʿi or Hanafi in Iran, Syria and Asia Minor). The curriculum in some *madrases* was more diverse, including grammar, Koranic exegesis, and Hadith, though some knowledge of these was usually a prerequisite for study of the law (*feqh*). Usually one would not go on to study theology (*kalâm*) until after completing law and the *osul al-feqh*, or principles of jurisprudence (see MRC 80ff.). As an example of a given institution's offerings, in the mid-tenth century the Madrase al-Bayhaqi in Nayshâpur held three different sessions at different times of day: a class for law, a class for Hadith and a plenary lecture for preaching. Some *madrases* were devoted primarily to the study of Prophetic Traditions, but such institutions were usually styled as Dâr al-Sunna or Dâr al-Hadith, and since hadiths were not taught according to a specific rite, the Hadith seminary attracted a more ecumenical student body than a law college.

We cannot know Bahâ al-Din's precise function at the Altunpâ Madrase during the two years he spent there. Though the professor at a *madrase* would normally teach Islamic law, Bahâ al-Din perhaps taught a more mystically oriented curriculum. Perhaps he did not hold the post of a *modarres*, but rather of a *khatib* or *vâ'ez*. On the Anatolian frontier, where colleges were being newly founded, the position of *modarres* may not have corresponded exactly to the classical concept of law professor. For example, the wandering ascetic Shaykh al-Haravi al-Mowseli (d. 1215) won his fame in Baghdad and Aleppo as a preacher, mystic and miracle worker. Shaykh al-Haravi may not have been well versed in law, but the Ayyubid prince of Aleppo, al-Malek al-Zâher Ghâzi, nevertheless built a Shâfe'i *madrase* for him, in which the shaykh was eventually buried. Shaykh al-Haravi primarily practiced *va'z* there, acting also as a kind of spiritual counselor and adviser on matters of war to the Ayyubids, even traveling to Anatolia during the reign of Saladin.[19]

If Bahâ al-Din did indeed teach law here, we may speculate that Rumi was designated as a deputy professor (*nâyeb modarres*) or a repetitor (*mo'id*) in this *madrase* under the supervision of his father. More likely, however, Bahâ al-Din taught general classes on religion and not courses leading to the equivalent of a degree in law. Still, Rumi may have functioned as his father's deputy in teaching duties. From a remark in Discourse 42 (Fih 156), we may conclude that once Rumi had become a famous teacher in his own right, those engaged in a traditional course of religious education (*tahsil-hâ*) hesitated to join his classes for fear that they might get sidetracked from their profession (*târek shavand*) and forget their discipline ('*elm râ farâmush konand*). Rumi indicates that on the contrary, their scholarship would come alive, as the traditional religious sciences are just the body of knowledge, whereas Rumi teaches the spirit that brings them to life. This seems a clear indication that the curriculum taught by Rumi at the height of his fame did not lead to a professional degree (*ejâze*) in law, and we may assume that the same held true for his father.

Whatever Bahâ al-Din's teaching duties, he doubtless continued to preach, and Rumi must have learned how to deliver a fine sermon. As young as he was, there was no inherent reason why Rumi could not keep the position of his father. Zarnuji tells us that students were supposed to honor the children and other family members of their teacher, standing up when they entered (Zar 33). Since the students were not supposed to sit close to their teachers during lectures, but in a semi-circle at a respectful distance (Zar 36–7), Bahâ al-Din's seating Rumi at his side would be seen as significant, a kind of visual sign of Rumi's status as successor. A professor usually made (or attempted to make) arrangements to transfer his position to a son or hand-picked student upon his death. Oftentimes the endowments of the college were written such that the professorship or rectorship became virtually hereditary. Rumi could therefore have retained the position of his father at the *madrase* in Konya even if he was not yet widely recognized as a *faqih* or accomplished scholar in his own right. Perhaps 'Alâ al-Din Kay Qobâd had established a charitable trust making Bahâ al-Din and his progeny hereditary teachers or preachers of the Altunpâ school.

In fact, there was ample precedent for a school to pass down to minor children. The *madrase* of the Sufi Abu ʿAli al-Daqqâq, built in Nayshâpur in 1001, passed to the control of his young daughter until she married the famous Abu al-Qâsem al-Qoshayri (d. 1073), after which the facility became known as the Qoshayri Madrase, having apparently transferred to her husband's control. This *madrase* seems to have functioned more as a Sufi lodge than a college of law, with sermons and Sufi activities taking place there; no specific mention of law classes or legal disputations is made, though Qoshayri was schooled in law and well versed in Asharite *kalâm*, in addition to Sufism (about which he wrote a famous manual). Even in a quasi-official institution such as the Nezâmiye of Nayshâpur, when the first director, Imam al-Haramayn al-Jovayni, died in 1085, the rectorship of the college passed on to his son, Abu al-Qâsem Mozaffar, though he was only eighteen. When Abu al-Qâsem was killed in 1093, one of Imam al-Haramayn's pupils became the rector.[20]

There are other cases, however, in which disciples acceded to the professorship if the deceased professors' sons were under age, at least until such time as they graduated from their course of study (MRC 170–71). Maybe Rumi did not retain his father's post; perhaps it went to one of the older disciples. Even if Rumi earned a certificate of permission to teach Islamic law in Konya, his father, Bahâ al-Din, had not been – all the claims of the hagiographers to the contrary – one of the most respected jurists of his day. In any case, confirmation of your academic competence from a member of the ulama in Konya would not have carried with it the same cachet as a diploma from one of the ulama in the established centers of Aleppo, Damascus, Baghdad or Iran. A diploma from a non-relative known outside the borders of Seljuk Anatolia would enhance the prestige and authority of Rumi and of his family's school. So it should not come as a surprise that Sayyed Borhân al-Din Mohaqqeq, Rumi's next mentor, sent him to study with the recognized authorities of the day in Syria.

2

Sayyed Borhân al-Din Mohaqqeq
of Termez

It's easy to flee from everything, but so difficult to flee from the self. The source of your woes is the self. Unless you become as naught and slay your self and your desire, you will not find release from your tribulations. Die before death and bury your self in the grave of desirelessness and be happy. (Bor 69–70)

Aflâki (Af 56) and Sepahsâlâr list the given name of Borhân al-Din as Hosayn, but it seems from his own *Ma'âref* (Bor 28, 41, 42) that Borhân al-Din referred to himself or was commonly known to others by his pen name, Mohaqqeq, meaning "the Perfecter" or "one who Attains to Truth." His title, Borhân al-Din, means the Proof of God, a not uncommon title for scholars or pious men in eleventh- through thirteenth-century Iran. Both hagiographers also call him the Knower of Secrets (*Sayyed-e Serrdân*), suggesting an ability to read the hearts of men. Rumi calls him Borhân-e Mohaqqeq Termezi, but the name sometimes acquires the Arabic definite article in later works, so we find Borhân al-Din al-Hosayn al-Termezi, just as Bahâ al-Din-e Valad becomes Bahâ al-Din al-Valad. In earlier texts, the city of Termez is spelled with a "z" (<u>dh</u>), but in later eras it has often been written with a "d" as Termed.

BORHÂN'S WRITINGS

The teachings of Borhân al-Din Mohaqqeq, like those of Bahâ al-Din, remained unpublished, probably in the form of notes taken down by his disciples, perhaps including Rumi. If these were ever collected and presented to Borhân al-Din for his approval, it does not appear that he had them widely disseminated or published. No reference to the existence of a "published" book by Borhân al-Din is to be found in Rumi, Sultan Valad, Sepahsâlâr or Aflâki. Aflâki does relate anecdotes or attribute teachings to Borhân al-Din, the kernel of which can be traced to the *Ma'âref*; it often appears, however, as if Aflâki's quotes come from oral lore circulating among the Mevlevi disciples rather than from the manuscripts of Borhân's *Ma'âref* that have survived down to our day. Although as yet little studied, Borhân al-Din's teachings have been published by Badi^c al-Zamân Foruzânfar along with a commentary on two suras of the Koran, the attribution of which to Borhân is not entirely certain:

> Sayyed Borhân al-Din Mohaqqeq, *Ma'âref: majmu'e-ye mavâ'ez va kalemât-e Sayyed Borhân al-Din Mohaqqeq-e Termedi; be-hamrâh-e tafsir-e sure-ye Mohammad va Fath*, ed. Badi^c al-Zamân Foruzânfar ([Tehran]: Enteshârât-e Edâre-ye Koll-e Negâresh-e Vezârat-e Farhang [1340/1961], xxvi + 234p).

Foruzânfar first encountered a partial copy of the work in a manuscript (no. 567 in the Selim Aghâ library in Istanbul) containing an anthology of the writings of the founders of the Mevlevi order, including the *Ma'âref* of Bahâ-e Valad, the so-called "Seven Discourses" of Rumi and his *Fihe mâ fihe*, the *Ma'âref* of Sultan Valad, the *Maqâlât* of Borhân al-Din (folios 302–15) and the *Maqâlât* of Shams-e Tabrizi. This collection was neither well known nor widely distributed, but was obviously intended for the study of advanced disciples. Since the text of Borhân's *Ma'âref* as contained in this manuscript was obviously deficient, Foruzânfar sought further exemplars and Mojtabâ Minovi soon turned up a copy in the Mevlana Museum in Konya. This copy, completed on February 10, 1288 (A.H. 687) by the hand of a certain Erghun b. Aydmer b. 'Abd Allâh al-Mowlavi, a disciple of the Mevlevi order, dates to just a half century after the death of Borhân al-Din. The notation on the cover includes the title "*Ma'âref* of our master ... Shaykh Borhân al-Din al-Mohaqqeq," with a long series of honorifics, identifying him as the spiritual heir of Bâyazid and Jonayd, the essence of all the saints, and so forth.

A further manuscript of 256 folios copied by a Darvish Jazbi Mowlavi in February 1597 (Rajab 1005), and now belonging to the library of F.N. Uzluk, contains two versions of the *Ma'âref* of Bahâ-e Valad, two short treatises attributed to Bahâ al-Din Valad, and the *Ma'âref* of Borhân al-Din (13 folios). Unfortunately, Foruzânfar did not have time to incorporate this into his published edition of Borhân's *Ma'âref*. Another manuscript (no. 145 in Konya) containing the *Ma'âref* of Borhân al-Din and dating from 1353 (A.H. 754) also exists, and Foruzânfar expressed the desire to re-edit the text of Borhân's *Ma'âref* using these two latter manuscripts.

Also included in Foruzânfar's edition of Borhân al-Din's *Ma'âref* are two commentaries on suras of the Koran, Sura Mohammad and Sura Fath. These follow in the main the Arabic commentary of Solami (d. 1021), *Haqâ'eq al-tafsir*. Though lacking documentary proof of authorship, Foruzânfar feels (Bor kj) that stylistic evidence points to Borhân al-Din Mohaqqeq as author.

The material in the *Ma'âref* of Borhân al-Din dates to the period during which he acted as Rumi's spiritual guide: from his arrival in Anatolia circa 1232, about one year after the death of Bahâ al-Din Valad, until his own death in about 1241. It confirms that Borhân considered himself a disciple of Bahâ al-Din (Bor 21):

> I see the prophets and saints in the sealed tablet; I know each one of them. From Mohammad the Messenger onward there have been many saints. None have had the station of Our Master Bahâ al-Din, and that is no exaggeration.

It also confirms that Rumi was already called Mowlânâ (our Master) during the lifetime of Borhân al-Din, by virtue of the fact that Borhân refers to Bahâ al-Din as *Mowlânâ-ye Bozorg*, the Elder Mowlânâ, to distinguish the two. It furthermore shows Bahâ al-Din as a teacher concerned with cultivating an exclusive relationship with his close disciples (Bor 67–8):

> The Elder Mowlânâ, May God be pleased with him, has said: I have followed the entire Koran. I've attained the meaning of every verse and story in it, so cut your ties to all but me, for that which you gain from others you will gain from me without help of others, and that which you gain from me you will gain from no other person. You who follow me, follow me more closely!

In the *Ma'âref,* Borhân, apparently addressing Rumi (who must therefore have been present at the sermon), prays that Rumi will attain to the station of his father (Bor 24):

> God, the Exalted, elevate you to the rank of your father. No one has a higher rank, otherwise I would have prayed, "God make him surpass it." But that is the ultimate, there is no going beyond it.

Rumi attributes to Borhân al-Din the ability to argue fine points well, this as a result of his study of the books of spiritual teachers, their mysteries and discourses (Fih 111). Foruzânfar concurs that Borhân offered lucid arguments, often more felicitously expressed than what we find in the prose works of other better-known Sufis (Bor yd).

BORHÂN'S TEACHINGS

> The world is the roof of hell. You see all these roses and lights and delights and desires, while inside are a million torments. What if someone tells you in the end this roof will cave in and "anguish will be piled on anguish" [K75:29]? Beware lest you wax proud up on the roof among the tulips and sweet herbs. (Bor 48)

If a servant resists the path of hell, strewn with its many enticements and temptations, God will make him worthy of a station close to Him, cloak him in a robe of eternal grace and purify his outward and interior aspect of all hypocrisy. After this "No room will remain within him for the love of any others ... his sustenance will be the mention of the beloved" (Bor 19).

This, then, provides the rationale for Borhân's insistence on slaying the self (Bor 50, 54):

> Whatever is opposed to the self brings us near and whatever agrees with the self makes us more distant.

> When you act contrary to the concupiscent soul, Almighty God is at peace with you; when you make peace with the self, you are at war with God.

Like the mystics before him, Borhân taught that "the mortal body dies but the spirit is immortal and does not pass away," for (Bor 17):

> In a world where reason and faith exist
> death of the body is birth of the soul

We therefore find Borhân, like his pupil Rumi, urging "death before death" (Bor 19, 57, 69):

> The kernel of worship is melting away the self and the rest of worship is merely the husk.

> Until you pass away from this plane of being, you will not receive being from His being.

> Die before death and bury your self in the grave of desirelessness and rejoice.

Pride, covetousness, anger, jealousy, all these qualities inherent in human nature obstruct our spiritual progress. Borhân calls jealousy a quality of the "dog" of self as it feeds on the corpse of the world (Bor 31), alluding to a hadith popular among Sufis: "The world is a corpse and those who desire it are dogs." For this reason we need to sharpen our spiritual inclinations through the exercise of self-abnegation, just as we cut and trim the reed pen before it becomes worthy of the fingers of the All-Merciful and can record the words of God (Bor 34).

Borhân urges fasting as the best of spiritual exercises, asserting that even if an aspirant fails in other spiritual disciplines, proper observation of fasting by itself will assure that he achieves something in life. All other types of ascetic exercises, in comparison with fasting, seem but trifles (*bâziche*, Bor 20). Although Borhân teaches that one cannot starve the body, since our corporeal form has been given to us as an instrument for contemplation and remembrance of God (Bor 11), nevertheless, the praxis of self-mortification makes us more godly (Bor 14–15):

> The lamp of the light of faith is lit within the glass of the body of the believer. The body of the gnostic through self-abnegation becomes just like a glass through which the light of faith shines ... A light has been placed in the human frame and that light does not appear but by self-abnegation (*mojâhede*, self-struggle). The thicker the skin, the weaker and more hidden is the meat. The more the skin is stretched and thinned by self-abnegation, so in turn, the brighter the light becomes, just as, the thinner the shell of a walnut, the fuller is its nut, and likewise for the almond and pistachio, the thicker the shell, the weaker the nut.

Basically an abstention from food and drink practiced by all Muslims during the daylight hours of Ramadan and by Sufis at many other times as well, Borhân further understands fasting in a broader sense as detachment from worldly things (as did Ghazzâli before him). Borhân even alludes to the Sufis' division of fasting into three levels, urging believers to go beyond fasting from food and women, beyond "special fasting" from the commission of sins by any members of the body, and to strive for the "fasting of the elite," which consists in forsaking all but God (Bor 20).

Indeed, the imagery of fasting, eating and digesting appear frequently as a metaphor of the human situation in the world (e.g., Bor 13–14, 18, 23, etc.). At one point, Borhân compares words motivated by anger to eating oven-hot bread that will burn the mouth. We must therefore cool off before speaking, which Borhân illustrates through an anecdote in which ʿAli, the Sword of Truth, was attacked by an infidel who spat in his face, provoking ʿAli's anger. ʿAli did not strike back, however, and when approached by his followers to find out why, ʿAli explained that his anger had polluted his intentions: had he struck, it would no longer have been with the sword of Truth, but the sword of self (Bor 2–3). Rumi learned this story from his teacher, Borhân, and later elaborated upon it in the *Masnavi* (M1:3721ff.).

Borhân emerges as a figure of ascetic bent and a learned but practical preacher, very like Bahâ al-Din Valad in many ways, and very much an inspiration to Rumi in his didactic methods. Borhân's aspirations, though, were not confined merely to the achievement of piety through the praxis of self-abnegation; he also shared the mystical goal of uniting with the beloved, for which the subjugation of the self is but a prerequisite. One must long for truth as a fish longs for water, and not just for a brook or a stream, but for the ocean, so that the fish can become a leviathan (Bor 21).

Borhân makes this statement in connection with a discussion of the shaykh or Sufi saint, specifically Bahâ al-Din Valad, and asserts that only the Sufi saint fathoms the true meaning of Islam, substantiating the claim with this quotation from the Koran: "On their hearts it is that He inscribes faith" (K58:22). In one famous hadith, much quoted by Shiites, Mohammad says toward the end of his life that he leaves behind him two weighty matters, the Book and his family. In an allusion to this hadith, Borhân identifies the Sufi spiritual teacher or saint as the metaphorical book and family of the Prophet (Bor 22):

> The book of God is within the shaykh ... by the Book is meant that which has been hidden in him, and the family is the body of the shaykh. Since you do not have the familiarity to read the book, the family will tell you the secret of it.

As such, one must follow the saints of God, whose bodies may die, but whose hearts live eternally and constitute our vantage point for the vision of truth (Bor 24). Through emulation of these saints of God, we can train our concupiscent souls by weeding out their mortal qualities and nurturing the eternal and noble nature of the soul, the soul of certitude, the *nafs-e motma'enne* isolated by Ghazzâli and other mystical thinkers (Bor 24). The saint stands like a great tree of faith, with roots in God and branches sheltering mankind (Bor 22, 25); the disciple ought to seek out the shade of the shaykh as refuge from the blazing sun of the world (Bor 41).

The saints, such as the famous Sufi Mansur al-Hallâj, express a knowledge of God which would constitute blasphemy in the mouths of others (Bor 26):

> Pharaoh, God's curse upon him, said, "I am your Lord." His use of the word "I" was God's curse upon him. Mansur said "I am God" and his use of the word "I" was a mercy from God.

Rumi would later allude in the *Masnavi* to this paradox, pointed out by Borhân, in the vast difference between the claim of Pharaoh and of Mansur al-Hallâj (M2:305):

> "I am the Truth" shone from Mansur's lips like light
> "I am the Lord" fell from Pharaoh's lips by force

In Discourse 52 (Fih 193), Rumi explains that the insistence on duality of subject and object disappears when one has submerged his self in the divine, and this phrase, "I am the Truth," in this state actually reflects the extreme humility (*ghâyat tavâzoʿ*) of the speaker, whereas to speak of oneself as servant and God as an exterior "thou" merely insists upon one's own existence, and therefore on duality.

The spiritual teacher or shaykh is described by Borhân as having completely white hair without a single black strand (Bor 35), a physical characteristic which Rumi elaborates in the *Masnavi*. Borhân's teachings about the nature of the disciple's relationship with his shaykh would appear influential in shaping Rumi's later relationship with Shams. Borhân says that the disciple should look only to his shaykh so that the shaykh's regard for the disciple may increase (Bor 36), for the shaykh is like a mirror and looks to you as much as you look to it (Bor 47). By shaykh, Borhân does not apparently intend any ordinary shaykh, but the spiritual *axis mundi*, whom the disciple should consider as present at all times (Bor 36).

Borhân al-Din states, as noted above, that Bahâ al-Din was the most perfect saint he had seen. Nevertheless, Borhân also claims an extremely advanced station for himself; in a subtle play on words between his own title, *Mohaqqeq*, which derives from the same root as *Haqq*, or Truth (the Sufis' term for the divine essence beyond Godhead and attributes), Borhân says: "Between Truth (*Haqq*) and the attainer of truth (*Mohaqqeq*) not a hair's breadth remains" (Bor 28). He compares the saints or friends of God to the bright full moon, neither of the East nor of the West (an allusion to the famous Koranic verse of the light, K24:35) and says of himself that he has become a source of light (Bor 28), his heart illumined with the light of God's gnosis (30).

101

Religious study may be the key to progress, but one cannot acquire such a station through book-learning, since outward knowledge is ephemeral and functions only as a medium to approach God. Borhân explains: "In the perfection of knowledge I became as naught; having reached the Known, what use have I for knowledge? ... The remembrance of God becomes perfect when one forgets all else but Him" (Bor 26). Echoing a hadith, he warns that many who interpret the Koran do so in error or in stupidity (Bor 48–9). Most people interpret the passage "Remember your Lord when you forget" (from K18:24) to mean that one must call God to mind in those moments when He has not been foremost in our consciousness. According to Borhân, those with understanding (*ahl-e ma'ni*) say that, since it is impossible for the lover ever to forget the beloved, this verse rather means that the lover will reach a state when he has forgotten all but God. It is only then that the verse "Remember your Lord when you have forgotten" all besides Him applies (Bor 26).

Borhân argues then that the spiritual quest, guided by these friends of God, must take us through an inward journey of discovery, an uncovering of the dross of self from the divine gem of the soul (Bor 56):

> We have two souls (*nafs*), a soul dark as night and one bright as the sun. If we decrease the former soul by spiritual exercises and burnishments it will decrease, and the other spirit becomes manifest and day takes the place of night.

Self-knowledge and self-awareness, then, are the root of all understanding (Bor 18):

> Knowledge is the knowledge of gnosis. If you know nothing, but know and understand your self, you are a scholar and a gnostic, and if you do not know yourself, what good is all of that knowledge of yours?

This idea appears, of course, in the writings of earlier Sufis and still earlier in the Greek wisdom tradition, which encapsulated the essence of wisdom in the phrase "know thyself" (*gnóthi seautón*), inscribed over the temple of Apollo in Delphi. Borhân expresses the essential divinity of the human soul in terms that prefigure a passage from the *Masnavi* of Rumi (Bor 10):

> Your pearl is you yourself, for if it *belonged* to you, it would be other than you. The jewel is at one and the same time *in* the treasury of the king, and also the king himself ...
>
> > You, you; and I, I? This can never be!
> > You, me; and me, you – this is union!

Should man progress on the spiritual path, he attains perfection and joins with the divinity (*be hazrat-e oluhiyat payvandad*), exceeding even the angels in station (Bor 11). And yet our quest does not end here, for even having attained this station, still "there is no end to the path," for the Sufis talk of two journeys, the journey to God and the journey in God. As Borhân tells us (Bor 11, 14):

There are stages on the path, which is to say, when you reach the city of reunion, there is no end to progress within that city.

... the path of reunion has no end, God is the goal and destination, as it is said, "Verily, in your Lord is the destination [K53:42]."

This particular teaching about the two journeys to God and in God made a special impression on his disciples and was subsequently quoted by Rumi's hagiographers.

Having achieved this station of union with God, one must not demand, like Moses, to see God (Bor 40), but must wait patiently and observe what God ordains for him. As on many other occasions Borhân al-Din quotes Sanâʾi: "Whatever you see but God is an idol; shatter it!" (Bor 63). In the closing pages Borhân exhorts his readers (Bor 72–3):

Busy yourselves with reading the Koran and speaking the words of God and do not lose hope ... when you free yourself from both worlds you will be free and will see things which are Truth.

BORHÂN'S INFLUENCE ON RUMI'S POETRY

Rumi urges the reader of his *Masnavi* (M2:1319) to follow the example of Borhân al-Din and unite with light. Indeed, Rumi is often following Borhân's example in the choice of stories and poems he includes in the *Masnavi*, many of which he quotes or paraphrases from Borhân al-Din. Many of the Koran verses upon which Rumi later dwells in the *Masnavi* already appear of special importance to Borhân al-Din, such as "vision did not falter" (*mâ zâgha al-basar*, K53:17).

Borhân al-Din was quite fond of poetry, much more so than Bahâ al-Din, and he often epitomizes or punctuates his points with a poetic proof-text. Here, for example, we see Borhân composing or quoting a verse which sounds very much like what Rumi would later write (Bor 17):

All are both "are" and "are not"
All are both wine and are drunk

The hagiographers say that Borhân taught the poetry of Sanâʾi and even some Arabic verse to Rumi (Af 272–3) and Borhân's *Maʿâref* provides ample confirmation of this fact. Rumi had evidently taken note of Borhân's fondness for Sanâʾi, as Rumi reveals in the following anecdote from his Discourses (Fih 207):

They said that Sayyed Borhân al-Din speaks well but he quotes the poetry of Sanâʾi a lot. The Sayyed replied, "It is as if they say, the sun is good but it gives light, for quoting the words of Sanâʾi reveals the point one makes, putting things in the sun, for in the light of the sun, one can see."

In addition to repeated quotations from Sanâʾi, scattered throughout the *Maʿâref* of Borhân al-Din we also come across verses from Khâqâni (Bor 6),

ʿAttâr (10), Nezâmi (53), Saʿd al-Din Kâfi of Bokhara (18) and Asir al-Din Akhsikati (46). There are also references to the heroes of classical Sufism, such as Jonayd (Bor 12), Hallâj (26) and Hasan al-Basri (70).

BORHÂN AND THE SUFI TRADITION

Borhân does not generally attribute the poems he quotes nor does he point the reader to specific expositions of the Sufi path. He does speak at one point of the "manners of the disciples" (Bor 55), a phrase reminiscent of (but not necessarily alluding to) the *Âdâb al-moridin* of Abu al-Najib ʿAbd al-Qâher Sohravardi (1096–1167), a manual of Sufi manners. When Borhân refers to the Sufis, however, he does not typically use the term "Sufi" (except Bor 63) or "Sufism" (*tasavvof*). Instead, he speaks of "the people of understanding" (*ahl-e maʿni*), or "the gnostics" (*ʿârefân*), or the *darvish* (the poor in God). However, he does allude to "the companions of the bench" (*ashâb-e soffe*, Bor 18), indicating familiarity with the classical manuals of Sufism, where the origins of the Sufis and the etymology of the word "Sufi" are traced to those ascetic-minded companions of Mohammad who would sit on the stone bench (*soffe*) in front of the mosque of the Prophet in Medina.

Towards the end of Borhân al-Din's *Maʿâref* we also encounter many Arabic quotations or allusions to Sufi traditions and expressions found in the classical manuals, like Qoshayri's "Treatise." Yet Borhân al-Din seems wholly unconcerned with systematic expositions of the path or with spiritual genealogies, except to describe the lofty spiritual station attained by Bahâ al-Din and himself. He rejects Râbiʿa and Hallâj as worthy models for emulation (Bor 60). We may take all this as a likely indication that Borhân al-Din had no affiliation to any order or any other shaykh besides Bahâ al-Din.

Likewise, Borhân al-Din, though obviously traveling in a class of religious scholars, holds no special regard for the rules of jurisprudential reasoning and Hadith criticism, or other kinds of knowledge upon which the ulama pride themselves. Borhân acknowledges that Fakhr-e Râzi possessed the knowledge of the twelve sciences, but chastises him for not *forgetting* them (Bor 11). That is to say that one must go beyond the twelve sciences acquired by worldly reason, since worldly reason is not attuned to the Koran, nor to God, nor to the light of God. True knowledge consists in knowing God, and one bereft of this remains veiled from truth and can never be a gnostic. The spirit of the true gnostic is infused with the divine mystery and becomes the source of the knowledge of God (Bor 70). Mocking the science of transmission that evaluates the chain of authority for any given prophetic tradition, Borhân says, "'My heart related to me from my Lord' is a pleasing school" (63). This formula (which may ultimately stem from Bâyazid Bestâmi) was attributed to the Sufis in Abu al-Faraj b. al-Jowzi's critique of religious scholarship and scholars, *Talbis-e Eblis*.

Borhân writes clearly and, like Bahâ al-Din, provides us with an elegant example of early twelfth-century Persian religious prose. In addition to its philological and literary interest, the *Ma'âref* of Borhân al-Din is equally important for theological reasons and the background of Rumi's own thought. Borhân's facility with Arabic is evident, with abundant quotations from the Koran and Hadith translated, explicated or otherwise seamlessly integrated into the narrative throughout. This fact probably indicates he wrote or spoke with a non-specialist audience in mind, non-scholars who might not have been comfortable with Arabic. Rumi, too, would later address his works to just such an audience.

THE LEGEND OF BORHÂN AL-DIN

Rumi cites Borhân al-Din once in Discourse 4 of *Fihe mâ fih* (Fih 16–17), so he must have had access to one of his manuscripts. Aflâki (Af 70), quoting Sultan Valad (who mentions this in his *Ebtedâ nâme*, SVE 237), attributes to Borhân al-Din a comment about the nature of the spiritual journey:

> The path itself comes to an end but the stations along the way are without end, for the journey is twofold: one to God and one in God. The one to God has an end because it passes beyond being, the world and self, all of which come to an end and terminus, but when you reach Truth, after that the journey continues in knowledge and the mysteries of knowing God, all of which is without end.

Though this saying does not occur word for word in the *Ma'âref* of Borhân al-Din, it does paraphrase the gist of one passage (Bor 11–14), as we have seen. Likewise, according to Aflâki (Af 60, 63–4, etc.) and Sepahsâlâr (Sep 120), Shams al-Din Mohammad-e Esfahâni (executed 1249), a vizier of Ghiâs al-Din Kay Khosrow II (r. 1237–46) and one of his successors, 'Ezz al-Din Kay Kâus II (r. 1246–60, east of the Kizil river), attended the lectures of Borhân al-Din and would sometimes question statements he made. Some confirmation of this may be found in the *Ma'âref* (Bor 38), as well. We may conclude that Sepahsâlâr and Aflâki, or at the very least one of their sources, had access to the writings of Borhân al-Din.

Nevertheless, we cannot credit everything that the hagiographers say about Borhân. First of all, their accounts differ substantially on some rather important questions. According to Sultan Valad (SVE 193–7), for example, Rumi assumed his father's teaching position immediately after his death. Already the equal of Bahâ al-Din as scholar and ascetic, Rumi's judicial opinions, or fatwas, were sought throughout east and west.

Borhân, meanwhile, had supposedly lost track of Bahâ al-Din. But upon receiving word that his master was in Anatolia, Borhân came to join him there, only to find on arrival that Bahâ had died the year before (SVE 194). Borhân al-Din, who referred to Bahâ al-Din as "Shaykh" or Master, declared

105

that the Shaykh remained among them, like oil saturating yoghurt (SVE 195). Borhân, in fact, claimed to be the Shaykh and invited the people to accept him. The whole town did so, recognizing in Borhân the same light that had shone through Bahâ al-Din Valad.

Rumi had inherited only one part of his father's legacy – the shell, or worldly knowledge – whereas Borhân had inherited the pith – his spiritual powers. Borhân explained that Bahâ al-Din, in addition to acquired knowledge, had also experienced mystical states and possessed gnostic knowledge. According to Sultan Valad (SVE 195), Borhân told Rumi:

> Attain your father's legacy full-share
> and sun-like you'll scatter light worldwide

These mystical states were not anything that could be learned; they had to be deserved. Borhân explained that he himself had achieved such states under Bahâ al-Din's guidance; under Borhân's guidance, Rumi, too, could attain them.

Rumi became a devoted disciple to Borhân al-Din and for nine years remained in his company until Borhân died, whereupon Rumi undertook another five years of fasting and self-mortification. After all this, Rumi achieved shaykh-hood, and ascended unto the spiritual heavens like an angel (this would, however, bring us to 1246, two years after Rumi's encounter with Shams, though Sultan Valad implies that all this took place before they met). Rumi became the spiritual axis (*qotb*) of the age, such that those who had attained the goal of the mystic path, and beyond them even the spiritual axes of previous ages, all received grace through Rumi's bestowals.

Rumi's miraculous powers now attracted disciples in the thousands and even the great *moftis* – jurists sought out for their juridical opinions, or fatwas – and other people of capacity considered him the successor to the Prophet. Rumi replicated the Prophet's heart-warming sermons from the pulpit, revivifying human psyches (SVE 197). Thus does Sultan Valad, who would have been fifteen years of age when Borhân al-Din died, recount the matter.

SEPAHSÂLÂR'S ACCOUNT

Sepahsâlâr (Sep 119–22), on the other hand, gives a more sober account, suggesting that Bahâ al-Din had designated Borhân al-Din as the spiritual guide or godfather of Rumi (*be-atâbeki-ye hazrat-e Khodâvandgâr-e mâ mansub*). When word of Bahâ al-Din's death reached Borhân, he was incapacitated with grief for a full year. One night Borhân had a dream of Bahâ al-Din, who chided him for not looking after his spiritual charge; immediately afterwards Borhân made his way to Konya.

When Rumi had finished his official course of study, Borhân told him (Sep 119):

"Light of my heart and eyes, though you have labored in the ways of knowledge and distinguished yourself, know that there is a knowledge beyond this, which is merely the husk. Your father has favored me with the key to that knowledge and now it is desirable that you acquire it."

Thenceforth, his holiness, our lord, inclined to the attainment of inner knowledge (*ʿolum-e yaqini*), following the path and example of the shaykhs.

For nine years Borhân taught him the truths he had realized through Bahâ al-Din, having Rumi read his father's *Maʿâref* one thousand times until, eventually, Rumi achieved a station the likes of which no eye had ever seen (Sep 119–20). Once Rumi had achieved perfection and sainthood, Borhân sought his permission to move to Kayseri, but Rumi refused, not wishing to be parted from the Sayyed's company. Borhân went anyway, but had an accident with his mount which forced him to return. Borhân then explained that, in view of Rumi's greatness, the town was too small for both of them. At that point, according to Sepahsâlâr, Rumi finally agreed for him to go (Sep 121–2).

Shams al-Din Sâheb-e Esfahâni, who governed over Kayseri at this time, supposedly became a disciple of Borhân al-Din (Sep 120; Af 60). Another story tells of a meeting arranged by Shams al-Din Sâheb between Borhân al-Din and Shehâb al-Din ʿOmar Sohravardi, when the latter came to the Seljuks on a mission from the caliph. The two men met but did not speak, carrying on a great telepathic conversation between themselves (Sep 120–21; Af 72; normal speech was apparently beneath the dignity of accomplished mind-reading mystics!). Politically, Kayseri was as important as, if not more so than, than the city of Konya, for ʿAlâ al-Din spent a great deal of time in Kayseri and had built his Qobâdiye palace here. With Borhân's withdrawal to Kayseri, Bahâ al-Din's teachings were being promoted in the two most important centers of Seljuk power in Anatolia.

AFLÂKI'S ACCOUNT

Aflâki tells yet a third version of Borhân al-Din's reunion with Rumi (Af 56–8). When Bahâ al-Din left Balkh, Borhân had gone to Termez and Bokhara, where he became known as "The Master of Mysteries" (*Sayyed-e serr dân*) for revealing hidden realities (mind-reading, *zamâyer-e darun*) and unseen truths of the spiritual and physical world (foretelling events, *moghayyebât-e soflâ va ʿolvi*). On a certain day at a certain hour Borhân, in the midst of a talk, let out a great cry and began lamenting that his honored Shaykh had sloughed off his mortal coil and journeyed to the great beyond. He ordered that the prayer for the dead should be said and that the ceremonies of mourning be observed; all the notables of the town grieved for forty days. Those present wrote down the date, and when Borhân reached Anatolia, it was found to correspond precisely to the time that Bahâ al-Din had died.

After the forty days of mourning, Borhân determined to go find and attend to Jalâl al-Din Mohammad (Rumi), who was left alone and would be looking to Borhân. Borhân felt obliged to go to Anatolia and "turn over to him the mission which my Shaykh has entrusted to me" (Af 57). This story, if a kernel of truth can be abstracted from it, suggests that Borhân had been deputized by Bahâ al-Din to propagate his doctrines in Termez. Upon learning of his master's death, however, Borhân determined to abandon his appointed post in Termez (which, of course, caused great sorrow among the notables there) and act as young Rumi's guide to the spiritual galaxy. Sayyed Borhân had a dream one night in which Bahâ al-Din appeared to him and urged him to seek out Rumi. The spirit of Bahâ al-Din reprimanded him: "This is no way to be a godfather and spiritual guide!" (lâlâ, atâbek; Af 71). Borhân now had to ensure that Rumi would be able to pass on his father's teachings and praxis.

One year after Bahâ-e Valad's death, Borhân arrived in Konya, where he stayed in the Senjâri mosque, sending word to Rumi, who was then living in Lârende (modern Karaman), and urging him to return to the burial place of his father. Rumi, overjoyed, kissed the letter with his lips and eyes, exclaiming (Af 57):

> Fortune's bower bears a gifted rose like you
> but once each thousand years; not every age,
> not each celestial house, brings forth a You.
> Time bears a You to set the world in motion

After Rumi returned, Borhân examined him on all manner of academic questions, each of which Rumi answered in detail. Borhân kissed the soles of Rumi's feet and confessed that Rumi had surpassed his father a hundred leagues in worldly and religious knowledge (ʿelm-e dini va yaqini), but told him that in addition to acquired knowledge (ʿelm-e qâl), Bahâ al-Din had also possessed inspired knowledge (ʿelm-e hâl). This is the same divinely intimated knowledge that the prophets and saints derive from God and which Borhân had inherited from "his holiness, my Shaykh" (Bahâ al-Din), and which he now desired to pass on to Rumi. Rumi obeyed all that Borhân said, brought Borhân to his college and served him for nine years (Af 58).

If Aflâki (Af 57) is correct, Rumi did not immediately assume his father's position in Konya, but had gone to Lârende for an extended stay. If anyone lectured in Bahâ al-Din's stead in Konya, Aflâki does not tell us the name. However, Sultan Valad does tell us (and Aflâki leaves us to infer) that after arriving in Konya, Borhân al-Din assumed the role of shaykh to the late Bahâ al-Din's circle of disciples. Because spiritual understanding was conventionally associated with the middle years of a man's life, specifically the age of forty, Rumi might have seemed rather young to preach to the notables and elders of Konya. As an experienced older disciple, Borhân would have been experienced in the practical application of Bahâ al-Din's spiritual guidance.

RUMI IN SYRIA

As part of Rumi's further education, Borhân al-Din apparently sent him to Syria. According to what Aflâki had heard, Rumi's first trip to Syria would have taken place in the second year after his father's death (Af 77), though a manuscript variant extends this to the second or third year after Bahâ al-Din's death (Af 1015). Bahâ al-Din died in February 1231. Borhân al-Din arrived in Konya about one year later, according to all the sources.

We may assume that Borhân and Rumi spent some months together after his arrival in Konya, getting reacquainted. It had been some fifteen years since Borhân al-Din had seen the Valads, and Rumi would have been a young boy of about ten at their last meeting. It was customary among the community of ascetics and mystics to appoint a godfather (*lâlâ, atâbek*), or spiritual guide, for a young boy, and in this capacity, Borhân al-Din used to carry Rumi about on his shoulders (Af 58). Borhân had been a close family friend, then, in addition to being a disciple of Bahâ al-Din. It would appear that when he arrived in Konya, he stayed for a while in Rumi's room (*hojre*) in his father's *madrase* (Af 63). After grieving, reminiscing, and sizing up the situation, Borhân and Rumi began to make plans for the future of their father's community of disciples.

This entailed an education for Rumi at the most prestigious schools. A student in a college of Islamic law usually lived alone in a cell at the school, receiving room and board. Rumi must have left his sons, Sultan Valad and ʿAlâ al-Din, who would have been young boys of about six to eight, with Gowhar Khâtun and the other womenfolk, including Gowhar Khâtun's mother, who had been a disciple of Bahâ al-Din, and whom Bahâ al-Din had praised as possessing a station equivalent to his own (Af 681). If still alive at this time, the mother and wife of Bahâ al-Din would probably also have lived with them. Borhân al-Din is recorded as the source for certain things said by the young Sultan Valad, which suggests that he helped look after the family during Rumi's absence, probably in conjunction with other followers of Bahâ al-Din (ZrP 84–8).

Aflâki tells us that for Rumi's first trip to Syria, Borhân accompanied him all the way to Kayseri. Borhân remained in Kayseri as the guest of Sâheb-e Esfahâni (Af 81), while Rumi proceeded on to Aleppo, attended by a few of his father's disciples (Af 77). We may estimate on this basis that Rumi arrived in Aleppo in the summer of 1232 at the earliest, though perhaps as late as 1233, at which time he would have been about twenty-five years old. Aleppo was a flourishing intellectual center in those days, with its wood-roofed bazaar, the Friday mosque with its beautiful pool, the large plaza and impressive buildings, including many colleges.[1]

In Aleppo, we are told that Rumi studied the conventional disciplines at the Halâviye mosque with **Kamâl al-Din Ibn al-ʿAdim** (1192–1262), a famous Hanafi scholar whose family held the office of *qâzi* for five generations (Af 77).

This Ibn al-ʿAdim is better remembered now as a historian of Aleppo, but he was one of the most famous jurisconsults of his day. He had studied in Aleppo, Damascus and Mecca and became the professor of the Shâdbakht college in Aleppo in 1220 and was subsequently appointed Qâzi of Aleppo, while simultaneously holding a visiting lectureship in Damascus. He was among the foremost experts of his day in law, jurisprudence and Hadith, but he also was an accomplished stylist and poet and his calligraphy was especially prized (S. Nafisi, in Sep, 216–19). Ibn al-ʿAdim also kept very busy as an emissary, repeatedly traveling to Cairo, Damascus and other capitals, negotiating on behalf of Aleppo's rulers. Indeed, he would later come to Konya in June of 1237 as part of al-Malek al-Ashraf's mission to the Seljuks, seeking military assistance against the incursions of his brother, al-Kâmel, based in Egypt (Hum 231). When the Mongols finally sacked Aleppo in 1260, Ibn al-ʿAdim fled to Cairo and though the Mongol Khan, Hulegu, invited him back to Aleppo as *qâzi*, the sight of his beloved city in ruins was too much for him to bear, and he died in exile in Egypt in 1262 (*EI²*).

In addition to being an outstanding man of letters and religion, Kamâl al-Din Ibn al-ʿAdim obviously wielded a great deal of influence within the elite structures in Aleppo and, indeed, throughout Ayyubid Syria and Egypt. Aflâki (Af 77–9) even describes him as the Prince of Aleppo (*Malek-e molk-e Halab*), perhaps confusing this Kamâl al-Din with the Ayyubid sultan al-Kâmel. From all around the Levant and even the entire Islamic world, Kamâl al-Din Ibn al-ʿAdim would have been sought out as a teacher.

Aflâki specifies that Rumi first stayed at the Halâviye Madrase in Aleppo. The Halâviye college had been built in 1145 on the site of the cathedral of St. Helen (Constantine's mother) and took its name from an endowment of 3,000 dinars that provided for a feast of pastries (*halvâ*) for all the religious scholars during Ramadan every year (IqL 70 citing *Târikh-e Halab*). It still stands today, half a kilometer to the west of the city citadel of Aleppo, south of Jamia al-Ayyoubi Street, near the Great Mosque. The Halâviye was a famous college in its era, except that by the time Rumi arrived (c. 1232–3), it was run down and almost abandoned. It was still maintained by charitable endowments, though, and could therefore support residential students. At the time, this could not have been Kamâl al-Din Ibn al-ʿAdim's principal teaching appointment, which was rather at the Shâdbakht Madrase. Ibn al-ʿAdim had it restored in 1245 and then moved his classes from the Shâdbakht school to the Halâviye school, but this was not until several years after Rumi had returned to Konya (ZrP 86–9). Perhaps Rumi was never one of the principal students of Ibn al-ʿAdim, insofar as he seems to have spent most of his student years in Damascus. It is also possible that Aflâki names the Halâviye school in error, anachronistically assuming that it had always been the center of Ibn al-ʿAdim's classes. Sepahsâlâr (Sep 30–31), in contrast, indicates that Rumi studied with Ibn al-ʿAdim in various *madrases* in

Aleppo and obtained advanced degrees in several different subjects (*dar hame-ye fonun ejâzât-e ʿâli hâsel farmud*).

Even if Rumi was not one of Kamâl al-Din Ibn al-ʿAdim's close personal students, he certainly would have attended Kamâl al-Din's public lectures and would likely have been familiar with his works. Kamâl al-Din Ibn al-ʿAdim wrote many histories and works of belles-lettres, and one might conceivably discover in them further information about the formal curriculum Rumi studied and the books he would have read in Arabic while in Aleppo. Zarrinkub (ZrP 86) observes that since Hanafis were favorably disposed toward the use of the intellect and analogical reasoning (*raʾy, qiâs*) in reaching legal decisions, it was especially important for Rumi to know the fine points of the Koran. He therefore must have read many of the classical Koran commentaries.

Rumi supposedly distinguished himself among his fellow students and proposed novel solutions to certain intractable problems, answers which could not be found in any book (Sep 31). Anecdotes like this appear often in biographical dictionaries of legal scholars and should be seen as a typical way of stressing the precocity or originality of the subject. Of course, this does not necessarily exclude the possibility that such incidents actually did happen. Nor is it impossible that Ibn al-ʿAdim found Rumi exceptionally intelligent and favored him with additional private lessons, as Aflâki tells us (Af 77).

From here, however, Aflâki (Af 77–9) proceeds to relate a completely unbelievable yarn about Ibn al-ʿAdim being teletransported out of the city after glimpsing the miraculous spiritual powers of Rumi. As a result of this incident, of course, Ibn al-ʿAdim became a disciple of his student, as did the entire population of Aleppo, male and female alike! Rumi's ensuing popularity was such that he found it impossible to remain in Aleppo, and so set off for Damascus. Shortly afterwards, an emissary arrived in Aleppo from Sultan ʿAlâ al-Din in Konya; Kamâl al-Din Ibn al-ʿAdim related the miracle, which was in due course conveyed to the Seljuk sultan, thereby increasing Rumi's stature at home (Af 77–9). Syria is, of course, famous as the land of Christian monasticism, and Rumi's disciples had to imagine their saint's powers in comparison with those of the desert fathers. On his way to Damascus, Rumi therefore encounters a band of forty monks in a cave, all of them able to read minds, predict the future and to levitate. To impress their powers on Rumi, they instruct a child to levitate himself, but Rumi retaliates by causing the child to remain suspended in mid-air, unable to bring himself down until he pronounces himself a Muslim (Af 80–81)!

Rumi must have been in Aleppo at least once in the month of Muharram, for he describes with disapproval how he saw the "entire populace of Aleppo," "man and woman alike," gather together at the Antioch Gate of Aleppo to observe Ashura (*ʿâshurâ*), the Shiite mourning ceremony for Hosayn (M6:777–8). We do not know how long Rumi remained in Aleppo, but he reportedly spent a period of either four or seven years in Damascus (Aflâki had heard two conflicting accounts, Af 81). The confusion may be due in part to Rumi staying in Damascus at different times; Sepahsâlâr conveys one report about how Rumi once stayed in Damascus for a period of one year (Sep 123). At some time during his stay in Damascus, Rumi supposedly stayed in the Moqaddamiye Madrase, where he devoted himself wholeheartedly to the study of the religious sciences (Af 81). Sepahsâlâr (Sep 24) tells us, on the other hand, that Rumi stayed in the Barrâniye Madrase.

The Moqaddamiye Madrase, built by Shams al-Din Mohammad b. al-Moqaddam (d. 1187), stood inside the Bâb al-Farâdis, in the north-central part of Damascus. The Barrâniye was another name for the Madrase al-Shâmiye, situated outside the city walls of Damascus in the Sovaqat Sârujâ district a little to the north of the Bâb al-Farâdis.[2] Zarrinkub proposes instead that Barrâniye refers to the outer dormitory of the college, from which one could freely come and go, as opposed to the inner lodgings in the Javâniye, where strict rules of order would keep students from leaving the premises at night or attending classes in other colleges (ZrP 90). On the other hand, Foruzânfar explains "Barrâniye" as a generic name for a type of college, in which case this could refer to any one of a number of different Hanafi colleges (FB 198).

Sepahsâlâr relates a story to the effect that the holy figure of Khezr was frequently observed in the cell (hojre) where Rumi lodged in the Barrâniye college, such that this room became a place of pilgrimage after he left (Sep 24). Sepahsâlâr (Sep 24–5) also informs us that while in Damascus, Rumi spent some time in the company of great men like Ibn ʿArabi, Saʿd al-Din Hamuye, ʿOsmân al-Rumi, Owhad al-Din Kermâni and Sadr al-Din of Konya, and exchanged views with them. Zarrinkub observes that Rumi would probably also have visited the Nuriye college to attend the classes of Jamâl al-Din Mahmud Hasiri (d. 636/1238), a scholar from Bokhara (ZrP 90). Rumi speaks of Damascus and Samarqand together as pleasant cities (M4:3289) and he apparently liked to look at the panorama of the city from the hilltop village of Rebve (M3:3753).

THE RELIABILITY OF OUR SOURCES CONCERNING RUMI'S STAY IN SYRIA

The only conclusive inference to be drawn from the conflicting information given by Rumi's hagiographers and literary biographers is that legendary tales about Rumi and his family proliferated early on. We may assume Sultan Valad less likely to commit utterly implausible mistakes about his father's life than some of the later writers working at third and fourth hand. Even so, Sultan Valad was not witness to the events occurring before the family's arrival in Anatolia and was a small boy at the time of his grandfather's death. Furthermore, the motivation behind the verse history of his father and family was as much to illustrate the powers unleashed in the spiritual plane as to present worldly facts and historical events. And, as the head of the fledgling Mevlevi order, Sultan Valad's authorial agenda included magnifying the importance of his family's celestial powers and terrestrial influence.

In Sultan Valad's view, this apparently included passing silently over Rumi's student days in Aleppo and Damascus. Despite the miraculous nature of many of their stories, it seems impossible that both Aflâki and Sepahsâlâr could manufacture this period of Rumi's tutelage out of thin air. Furthermore, Shams al-Din Tabrizi alludes in his *Maqâlât* to having seen Rumi fifteen or sixteen years earlier in Damascus or Aleppo, a meeting to which Aflâki also briefly alludes in archetypical fashion (Af 82; for the details, see "The Meeting Before the First Meeting" in chapter 4, below).

We may attempt to mesh the accounts of Sultan Valad, Sepahsâlâr and Aflâki together and sketch the following hypothetical outline of Rumi's further education under Borhân. Rumi did not necessarily complete his studies in Syria all at once. The sources allude to a period of one year here, four years or seven years there, and give a variety of names for the *madrases* at which Rumi supposedly studied. We do not find any firm dates, only approximate ranges. Shams al-Din mentions having seen Rumi fifteen or sixteen years before their first meeting in Konya. If his memory on this score was accurate, it would place Rumi in Syria sometime between 1228 and 1233.

Aflâki, however, dates the period of Rumi's study in Syria to the second year after the death of Bahâ al-Din, which would be sometime in 1232 or 1233. If Rumi went first to Aleppo in 1233, he may have soon thereafter proceeded to Damascus. It is possible that Shams met Rumi at this time in Damascus, though we cannot rule out the possibility that Rumi had made an earlier trip to Syria while his father was still alive.

In the previous chapter we saw how Aflâki dated Bahâ al-Din and family's arrival from Mecca to Damascus on their way to Anatolia to A.H. 614 (A.D. 1217). Aflâki erroneously refers to this period as the reign of al-Malek al-Ashraf in Damascus. Perhaps Aflâki associates Damascus with Ashraf because Rumi studied there during Ashraf's reign. Ashraf died at the end of August 1237 and Damascus subsequently went through a rather tumultuous period. In December of that year the city was besieged, and by January of 1238 several of the suburbs outside the walls had been destroyed. The political situation remained somewhat unstable there and the city was once again stormed in September 1239 (Hum 235ff., 257ff.). From September of 1240 and for a few years thereafter, a marauding band of Jalâl al-Din Khwârazmshâh's former troops terrorized the countryside in Syria and Palestine (Hum 269ff.).

It seems unlikely that Rumi would have remained in Damascus during all this commotion, though Aleppo seems to have enjoyed greater stability at this time under the rule of its queen, Zayfa Khâtun. Although both Sepahsâlâr and Aflâki do indicate that Rumi studied for a while in Aleppo under Ibn al-ʿAdim, they concentrate on Damascus as the site of Rumi's education in Syria. More important, however, for Rumi's future was the situation in Konya itself. His father's patron, ʿAlâ al-Din Kay Qobâd, the Seljuk sultan, died on May 31, 1237 and was succeeded by Ghiâs al-Din Kay Khosrow II. If Rumi were not already in Konya at that time, he would probably have felt anxious to return. Whatever patronage arrangement had existed with his father might be nullified if he did not pay his respects to the new sultan and claim the right to his father's position as professor or shaykh at the *madrase* where he had taught.

The oral report preserved by Aflâki that Rumi stayed for a period of four years in Syria, from 1233 to 1237, therefore seems quite plausible. Of course, one might also validate the seven-year figure by assuming that Rumi had already spent some years on and off in Syria before his father's death. There may have been two separate sojourns: one to Aleppo, perhaps during his father's lifetime, after Rumi's sons were born, as early as 1227 or 1228; and a second to Damascus after the arrival of Borhân al-Din. All of this must remain in the realm of speculation.

BORHÂN PASSES THE MANTLE TO MOWLÂNÂ

When Rumi returned from Syria to Kayseri and met Borhân al-Din, the local prince, Sâheb-e Esfahâni, invited Rumi to his estate, but Borhân al-Din instructed Rumi to refuse, as Bahâ al-Din's practice had been always to lodge in a *madrase*, never in a palace. So began Rumi's spiritual, as opposed to merely religious, education; the way Aflâki tells it, only after Rumi had returned from his studies in Syria did Borhân al-Din encourage him to study his father's mystical teachings. Borhân al-Din displays what may almost pass for an obsession with fasting in his *Maʿâref*, a work probably reflecting his lectures and writings during this period in Konya and Kayseri. Certain anecdotes in the hagiographies suggest he neglected his personal hygiene (Sep 120). He did not wash his clothes for twelve years (Af 71) and may have damaged his teeth (Af 61) and digestive system by excessive fasting (Af 64). But Borhân supposedly knew something of medicine and herbal healing, and recommend raw turnips for improving the eyesight and as a digestive aid (Af 63); indeed, boiled turnip still serves as a herbal folk remedy for colds among Iranians and Turks.

Insofar as they are grist for the hagiographer's mill, we must be prepared to swallow tales of excessive asceticism with a grain of salt, but Borhân al-Din's own comments in his *Maʿâref* tend to corroborate the picture Aflâki portrays of Borhân as consumed by fasting. Nevertheless, though Borhân had lived the life of a hermit for many years (Af 61), and scrupulously practiced prayer and fasting, in his later years he apparently stopped fasting and missed most of the prayers. A shaykh of advanced years would usually not practice fasting and retreats any longer, as these were generally exercises of youth and middle age

(Saf 3/1:196). Nevertheless, a female disciple once teased Borhân about no longer fasting, to which Borhân replied that he was like an old worn-out pack camel, bald and emaciated. He had now put himself out to pasture, so that he could fatten up and become a fitting sacrifice for the table of the Divine Sultan (Af 65).

Not surprisingly, then, Borhân recommended that Rumi sit in seclusion (*khalvat*), which entailed being literally sealed up alone in a room and fasting for a week. Rumi, who had already followed a frugal and abstemious regimen as a student (Sep 123–4), thought this period too short and volunteered to sit in seclusion for the more stringent forty-day period, with only a pitcher of water and a few loaves of barley bread, according to a report Aflâki transmits (Af 82).

Rumi certainly did practice fasting, following the example of his father and Borhân al-Din. One passage from the *Masnavi* plays on the etymological similarity of the words for soul (*ruh*) and sweet basil (*rayhân*) and urges that we graze on the herbs of spirit and not the cud of beasts (M5:2472–9):

> Do you, novice, wish to turn dung to musk?
> Then graze the garden many years – you must!
> Don't chomp on hay and barley like an ass
> like musk deer graze the redbud in Khotan
> Graze jasmine or on clove or rose alone
> Into the plains of Khotan, go with him
> Get your gut accustomed: Sweet basil, rose
> you'll taste sagacity, prophetic might
> wean your stomach juices off of barley, straw
> Your regimen is rose, sweet basil; start!
> The body's stomach calls us to the hay trough,
> The belly of the heart to basil sweet.
> He who eats hay and barley goes for slaughter
> He who eats the light of Truth becomes Koran
> Half of you is musk and half is dung; watch out:
> Amass that Chinese musk, don't fill with dung!

Beyond this metaphorical fasting, however, Rumi clearly did participate in physical fasting, during Ramadan and at other times. There are several poems in Rumi's *Divân* completely dedicated to the celebration of the fast of Ramadan and of fasting to purify the spirit (see Poems 34 and 35 in chapter 8). The following lines from a ghazal (D 1602) with the refrain "fasting" (*siâm*), recommends fasting as the human vehicle for following Mohammad on his ascent into the heavens (*me'râj*):

> If you're melancholic and long to make
> a *me'râj* high above the wheel of life
> the Arabian steed to take you there
> stands awaiting in the field of fasting
>   ❧ ❧ ❧

Better the body of the striving man
along the path of heart's desire be filled
not by loads of vital spirit, but fasting

❧ ❧ ❧

Ever seen a beast bright with learning's light?
Your body's a beast; don't let it stop fasting!

Nevertheless, when Sufis tell stories about the ascetic feats of their masters, they enter into the realm of the archetype. We need to remember this as we return to the tale Aflâki tells about the miraculous powers of Rumi's self-renunciation. As we have seen, Rumi volunteered to undergo the demanding forty-day period of seclusion with but a few pieces of bread and a drop of water. Aflâki continues (Af 82–3): When the forty days had gone by, Borhân al-Din opened the door and found Rumi deep in meditation, having experienced a mystical vision of the spiritual world. Borhân waited for an hour, but Rumi took no notice of him, so he withdrew and sealed the door again. Forty days later, Borhân returned and found Rumi standing there fervently engrossed in prayer. Again he waited a while, but Rumi did not acknowledge him, so he withdrew once again. Finally, after a third period of forty days, an anxious Borhân tore down the door and found Rumi smiling.

At this point, Borhân pronounced Rumi's spiritual education complete and acknowledged his joy at having attained to the presence of such a saint. He sent Rumi back to Konya, where Rumi donned a scholar's turban and wide-sleeved cloak (redâ-ye farâkh âstin), assumed the role of teaching the conventional religious sciences (ʿolum-e zâher), preaching and sermonizing (mavâʿez va nasâyeh va tazkir). Rumi perhaps returned to Kayseri to visit Sayyed Borhân al-Din, but in due course, Borhân passed away (Af 84).

Sultan Valad indicates that Rumi spent five years in fasting and renunciation after the death of Borhân al-Din. This may refer to the time between Borhân al-Din's death and the arrival of Shams in Konya in 1244, but Aflâki indicates that Rumi at this time was living a very public life as a scholar. Let us, then, assume that the five years of asceticism mentioned by Sultan Valad took place during Borhân al-Din's lifetime and at his instruction, rather than after his death. This would then constitute part of the nine years of Rumi's discipleship to Borhân. We might imagine, then, a period of four years of exoteric studies in Syria, from 1233 to 1237, and a further four or five years of esoteric study under Borhân. This would have included, in addition to fasting and seclusion, reading from the Maʿâref of Bahâ al-Din.

Borhân, as the spiritual coach of Rumi, certainly wanted him to assume the seat of learning and teaching that had been his father's before him. Out of devotion to his teacher, Rumi would likely have refused to accept the role of shaykh so long as Borhân were present in town, and thus Borhân may have felt it necessary to move to Kayseri. Did Rumi retain the right to his father's position during this time, or did Borhân al-Din withdraw to Kayseri because Bahâ al-Din's post had been occupied by someone else? Kayseri (Roman Caesaria) perhaps rivaled Konya in political importance at the time, insofar as 'Alâ al-Din built his Qobâdiye palace here. An elaborate hospital named after a Seljuk princess, Gevher Nisibe, had been built here in 1206 and a grand mosque also dates from the period. A fine mosque, *madrase* and shrine complex had also been built at Hunat Hatun in Kayseri.

However, on the basis of what Aflâki relates, it is Shams al-Din Esfahâni, and not the sultan, who provided patronage for Borhân in Kayseri (Bay 151–2). This Shams al-Din Sâheb built another *madrase* in Kayseri in 1268, which still stands. He also composed poems himself in both Persian and Arabic, and wrote his correspondence in fine epistolary style (FB 190–91), so he undoubtedly appreciated Rumi's poetry. Borhân was grooming Rumi to succeed his father in Konya. Perhaps one of the disciples of Bahâ al-Din had retained his former position in Konya, or perhaps patronage of the Valad family had been cut off with his death. Either way, Borhân's activities in Kayseri effectively disseminated Bahâ al-Din's teachings and reputation more widely throughout Anatolia. This was surely a goal close to the heart of Borhân al-Din Mohaqqeq, Bahâ al-Din's first disciple.

A century and a half after Aflâki, Dowlatshâh of Samarqand (not exactly famous for his precision about names, dates and places), asserts that Borhân al-Din was the teacher of not only Rumi, but also of Bahâ al-Din. Dowlatshâh (Dow 214), based upon what authority we do not know, claims that Borhân al-Din accompanied the Valad family on pilgrimage and afterwards as far as Syria, where he passed away, but not before encouraging the Valads to go to Anatolia and seek out Sultan 'Alâ al-Din Kay Qobâd.

Dowlatshâh surely errs here, not only about Borhân's whereabouts, but also about the nature of the relationship between Borhân al-Din and Bahâ al-Din. Judging from the evidence of the writings of both Borhân and Bahâ, the former looked to the latter as a spiritual guide, whereas Bahâ al-Din looked upon Borhân al-Din as a friend and confidant. Bahâ al-Din saw Borhân al-Din in the role of spiritual mentor only to his son, Jalâl al-Din, not to himself. Dowlatshâh's work, though, proved very influential and contributed to the spreading of further myths and obfuscations about the historical circumstances of the family Valad.

THE DEATH OF BORHÂN

Sultan Valad puts Borhân's arrival in Anatolia one year after the death of Bahâ al-Din and says that Rumi spent nine years under his tutelage, which would place his death in 1240 or 1241. He died in Kayseri. Aflâki tells us that Sâheb-e Esfahâni twice raised a memorial arch or dome (*tâq*) above Borhân's grave, but that both collapsed within a few days of construction. Borhân then appeared to

Sâheb-e Esfahâni in a dream, asking that no structure be erected over his grave (Af 68–9). This miraculous story about Borhân's powerful posthumous humility toppling his own funerary tower perhaps developed among the Mevlevis to explain what seemed to them an anomaly. Great saints should have great tombs (like Rumi's), but perhaps Borhân al-Din's resting place was not marked by an elaborate tomb at the time Aflâki wrote.

There is, however, a tomb associated with him today in Kayseri, known as Seyyid Burhaneddin Türbesi, about a half kilometer southeast of Hunat Hatun Kulleyesi. A grave marker was eventually erected, though probably not by his own disciples. A follower of Ibn ʿArabi composed the three verses inscribed here; we know this because they claim that Borhân was second to Ibn ʿArabi, whereas it was not customary to mention the names of other shaykhs in a Sufi saint's epitaph. The verses do contain helpful chronograms, indicating the date of birth for Borhân al-Din as A.H. 561 (A.D. 1166) and the date of death as A.H. 637, sometime between August 1239 and August 1240 (GB 102). Since it seems the inscription was done later, we cannot assume these dates to be authentic (it was not usual, in any case, to include the date of birth on the funerary inscription, either). Nevertheless, the dates 1166 to 1240 agree quite reasonably with the rest of the information we have about Borhân from other sources.

Recently Mikâil Bayram (Bay 149–50) has taken issue with Gölpınarlı and Foruzânfar's reading of Sultan Valad, and has argued that Borhân al-Din did not die nine years after Bahâ al-Din, in 1240 or 1241. Bayram instead understands Sultan Valad to say that Borhân lived in Konya for nine years after the death of Bahâ and then moved on (*naql kardan*) to Kayseri, where he lived for five more years before passing away in 1245 (SVE 48). This interpretation would help make more sense of the anecdote about Rumi objecting to Borhân's decision to move away from Konya. It requires, however, a somewhat far-fetched reading of Sultan Valad. *Naql* in this context usually refers not simply to "moving on" from one town to another, but from "the dominion of this world to the heavenly realm"; indeed, Aflâki (Af 84) uses the word *naql* to describe the death of Borhân al-Din.

When Borhân died, his powerful disciple Shams al-Din Sâheb-e Esfahâni held an elaborate funeral for him and, after the customary forty days of mourning, sent a letter to Rumi in Konya, notifying him of Borhân's death. Rumi came with a number of disciples to pay his respects at the grave of Borhân. Sâheb-e Esfahâni afterwards offered them their pick of Borhân's books and notebooks (*ajzâ*). Rumi and his disciples took what they wanted, leaving some of the notebooks as a memento and a blessing for the Sâheb, and then returned to Konya (Af 68–9).

Rumi on his Own

Rumi, who would have been twenty-four years of age when his father died, could not have remained wholly ignorant of his father's mystical inclination until Borhân al-Din initiated him in the 1230s. Though Rumi probably established a separate household after he married, he must have kept close company with his father. He would have spent much time with his father in private, and, as we have seen, he sat at the side of Bahâ al-Din during the latter's public gatherings. If Jalâl al-Din was known as Mowlânâ the Younger among the circles who attended Bahâ al-Din's lectures and sermons, his father must have anticipated and groomed Rumi to become his successor, an indication that Bahâ al-Din had confidence in his son's abilities and spiritual proclivities. In view of the preoccupation with ascetic exercises, visionary ecstasies and personal intimacy with God ("Allâh") reflected in Bahâ al-Din's *Ma'âref,* it stretches credulity to think he could have completely hidden this side of his nature from Rumi. Rather, it seems that ascetic and mystical inclinations constitute the bedrock of Bahâ al-Din's spirituality, with study of the law itself providing a means to enable the believers to follow the example of the Prophet, rather than constituting a goal and end in itself.

What, exactly, then, did Borhân al-Din teach him? Perhaps Bahâ al-Din had waited to introduce his most esoteric and advanced beliefs until Rumi completed his conventional education in the religious sciences. If so, then Borhân al-Din would certainly have felt himself, as the direct disciple of Bahâ al-Din, more qualified than anyone else to initiate Rumi, his spiritual charge, in the esoteric doctrines of Bahâ al-Din and the inner mysteries of the Koran.

It seems extremely unlikely that Borhân al-Din would have entrusted Rumi's spiritual discipline and the training of his soul to anyone else. Rumi most assuredly had already learned much about the Sufi path from his father, and from books, during his studies in Syria. But it would seem that he did not begin actively to pursue the mystical path until his return. Borhân al-Din explicitly states that Bahâ al-Din was the greatest saint he had ever seen and no other disciple had been as close to Bahâ al-Din as Borhân al-Din. He surely could not have intended, then, for Rumi to receive his spiritual and esoteric training in Damascus.

It may be that while in Damascus Rumi did encounter mystical doctrines and theosophical teachers such as Ibn ꜥArabi. However, Rumi does not describe the influence of any spiritual or mystical teachers from this period in his subsequent works (even though he may have first met Shams in Damascus). It seems clear from Rumi's own writings that Bahâ al-Din and Borhân al-Din, and the masters they recommended – ꜥAttâr and Sanâ꜄i – constitute the primary spiritual, mystical and doctrinal heritage of Rumi. Various mystical orders were active in Damascus – the Sohravardis, for example, and the biographical sources suggest some connection between Bahâ al-Din and Shehâb al-Din ꜥOmar Sohravardi. But other mystical orders active in Anatolia – the Bektâshi and Kobravi – would have been more involved with the eastern Iranian and Central Asian traditions of Sufism. Were Rumi seeking out deeper mystical knowledge or experience, the latter two orders would have been likely to appeal to him more.

Damascus, as an older, established intellectual center, primarily Arabic- and not Persian-speaking, would have been a place for traditional religious and legal learning. We may surmise on the above circumstantial evidence that the intellectual program of study recommended by Borhân for Rumi did not involve the esoteric doctrines so much as the conventional Islamic sciences, which Borhân felt Rumi should learn from the reputable authorities in the fields of theology, prophetic traditions, canon law, math, astronomy, philosophy, etc. While Rumi may have already enjoyed a reputation among his father's circle for piety and spiritual insight, as well as homiletic eloquence and intelligence, he would likely have perceived his prospects for achieving greater recognition to be in scholarly and legal pursuits (i.e., a professional career), and not in poetry and mysticism (the equivalent of pursuing a career as artist or actor). The more his fame as a Koran commentator, traditionist and legal scholar spread, the more likely it was that Rumi would attract students from other locales to study with him and attend his sermons.

Bahâ al-Din, despite the hagiographers' claims, had not been particularly famous as a juridical scholar beyond the area of Vakhsh and perhaps Balkh. He had been trained in law, however, and after gaining the attention and support of the Seljuk rulers, his stature in Konya as a learned man and spiritual teacher appears to have been substantial. Borhân al-Din must have enjoyed some prestige as a spiritual teacher by this time if the powerful Shams al-Din Sâheb-e

Esfahâni favored him in Kayseri with his patronage (Af 60, 62). Aflâki describes this Sâheb, the ruler of Kayseri, as a disciple of Sayyed Borhân al-Din, who came to visit him and attend his lectures. The Sâheb gave much money to the poor on his account (Af 63–4) and appointed Borhân al-Din as an imam in one of the mosques in Kayseri (Af 61).

This same Sâheb-e Esfahâni later on became a vizier of the Seljuk sultan ʿEzz al-Din Kay Kâus II from 1246 to 1249. Borhân had undoubtedly introduced the Sâheb to Rumi, and Aflâki insinuates that after Borhân's death the Sâheb eventually became a disciple of Rumi. He was so attracted to Rumi, in fact, that he did not frequent the lectures of anyone else. The sultan noticed this and criticized Sâheb-e Esfahâni for it, asking what Rumi had that other holy men lacked. Sâheb-e Esfahâni launched into an eloquent defense of Rumi and his qualities, making ʿEzz al-Din Kay Kâus want to meet with Rumi and test his powers. Of course, Rumi and Salâh al-Din managed to impress and win over the sultan (Af 706–9).

FAMILY LIFE

When Rumi returned to Konya from Syria sometime between 1237 and 1241, he would have been in his early thirties, now educated, distinguished and old enough to assume the mantle of his father and the leadership of his circle of disciples. Not long afterwards, Gowhar Khâtun, Rumi's first wife, passed away, perhaps in 1242 or 1243 (A.H. 640 is the date offered by ZrP 100). From Gowhar Khâtun, ʿAlâ al-Din and Sultan Valad had been born, apparently in 1225 and 1226 respectively, since one account in Aflâki describes their circumcision as taking place when they were eight and seven years old respectively (Af 302–3).

Sometime during the years 1240 to 1245, Rumi's teenage sons quite likely went to Damascus to acquire an education like their father's (Af 681). Rumi wrote a joint letter to both boys sometime during this period charging them to mind Sharaf al-Din as they would their own father. Sharaf al-Din, the boys' maternal grandfather, must have acted as their guardian in Syria, but they apparently chafed under his rule and had openly quarreled with him. Rumi asks the boys to handle their anger by going for a walk or going to sleep, and promises that he will pray for them to return successful and happy from their studies (Mak 142). They did return, probably before Shams-e Tabrizi arrived, as Aflâki tells us that Rumi would sometimes seat Sultan Valad next to him during his lectures and people would mistake them for brothers rather than father and son (Af 26), on account of the relatively small difference in their ages (less than twenty years, whereas the difference in age between Rumi and his own father was about sixty years).

Gölpınarlı, who does not specify his sources but appears to draw the information from the funerary inscriptions on the cenotaphs in Rumi's shrine in

Konya, places the death of Gowhar Khâtun prior to Rumi's marriage with his second wife, called **Kerrâ Khâtun**. *Kerrâ* may be either a name or a title, as it is used to refer to Gowhar Khâtun's mother (Af 681) and to Fâteme Khâtun, the daughter of Salâh al-Din, so it would not appear to be of Greek or Anatolian origin, as has sometimes been claimed (GB 237, summarizing Yazıcı's argument in his introduction to *Ariflerin Menkibeleri* 2:vi–xxii). According to Kerrâ Khâtun's funerary inscription, she had been previously married to a Mohammad Shâh (GM 429). Rumi, himself a widower, therefore married a widow. From the anecdotes relayed by Aflâki, we may infer that she was somewhat superstitious (e.g., Af 251). On one occasion she supposedly complained that there were jinn (genies) living in their house and these genies had complained about her husband's habit of standing throughout the night until dawn reading the *Ma'âref* of Bahâ al-Din. The light from all the candles greatly annoyed the jinn and they hinted that some evil might befall the inhabitants of the house on account of their vexation. Worried, she approached Rumi with this tale, but he gave no answer and merely smiled. After three days had gone by, he told her, "Do not worry anymore, for the jinn have come to believe in me and are my disciples. They will not harm any of the children or our companions" (Af 92–3).

From the union of Rumi and Kerrâ Khâtun issued a son and a daughter, Mozaffar al-Din Amir 'Âlem Chelebi and Maleke Khâtun. **Mozaffar al-Din Amir 'Âlem Chelebi** must have been born in the 1240s. According to a story related by Aflâki (Af 488–9), Rumi composed a ghazal on the occasion of his birth beginning "Hail, O Lovers! The beloved of splendid orb has come" (D 580). This seems rather unlikely, however, in view of the poem's explicit dedication to Shams al-Din of Tabriz. Mozaffar al-Din sought a career in the Seljuk government ministry and apparently worked in the treasury, but was unsuccessful in gaining regular and constant employment. Rumi wrote several letters to government officials asking them to assist in Mozaffar al-Din's career. In one letter to the vizier Mo'in al-Din Parvâne, Rumi praises the Parvâne for his assistance to the poor and needy (*darvishân va mohtâjân*) and apologizes for troubling him in this regard, but asks him to help Mozaffar al-Din Amir 'Âlem Chelebi (Mak 100–101).

Rumi also wrote to the family physician, Akmal al-Din Tabib of Nakhjavân, himself one of Rumi's disciples (Discourse 57, Fih 209), asking that he intervene with the Parvâne to secure a better salary for Mozaffar al-Din Amir 'Âlem (Mak 214–15). Rumi also asked Amir Bahâ al-Din, entitled the Governor of the Coasts (Amir al-Savâhel), who had once before received Mozaffar al-Din Amir 'Âlem and provided some assistance to him, for help with his difficult circumstances (Mak 202–3). In the end, Amir 'Âlem, who had apparently received training as a religious scholar before embarking on a civil service career, apparently washed his hands of worldly affairs, gave up politics, donned a Sufi cloak (*kherqe*) and assumed the life of a dervish. A letter written on behalf of

Rumi to a certain Majd al-Din expresses a sense of pride and relief about this decision (Mak 129–31). Mozaffar al-Din died, according to the inscription on his cenotaph, on October 5, 1277 (GM 429) and is buried to the front of Rumi.

Maleke Khâtun, the daughter of Rumi and Kerrâ, married **Shehâb al-Din Qonyavi**, a merchant from Konya. Rumi's letters indicate that this son-in-law went for some time to Sivas on business, but had to pay such high tolls and taxes along the way that he nearly went broke. Rumi wrote to the Parvâne again on behalf of this son-in-law, asking that he be exempted from these tolls (Mak 95–6). This perhaps did not sit well with the other family members or disciples, because Aflâki recounts a story suggesting that Shehâb al-Din was perceived as something of a miser (Af 323).

Maleke Khâtun died between 1303 and 1306 (Gölpınarlı, GB 238 and GM 430, reads her funerary inscription variously as A.H. 703 or 705), and is buried near her brother (GB 238). Kerrâ Khâtun's funerary inscription indicates that she outlived Rumi by nineteen years, passing away on Thursday 13 Ramadan A.H. 691, or Thursday August 28, 1292 (GM 429).

RUMI'S ACTIVITY AND STATUS IN KONYA BEFORE SHAMS

Rumi, illumined by the halo of his father, perhaps enjoyed a local reputation even when a young adolescent; Zarrinkub thinks that one of the preserved sermons of Rumi may date from before the family's arrival in Konya (ZrP 60). However, when Borhân arrived in Konya, we are told that Rumi had been in Lârende/Karaman, apparently for many months and therefore not just on a temporary visit. Borhân stayed in the Senjâri mosque in Konya, presumably rallying the former disciples of Bahâ al-Din, for it is said that Salâh al-Din made Borhân al-Din his shaykh (Af 65). Borhân had a servant carry a letter from Konya to Rumi in Lârende, cajoling him to return to Konya (Af 57). If we can rely upon these accounts, Rumi clearly did not assume his father's position immediately. Perhaps he withdrew to the family's former patron in Lârende, Amir Musâ, or sought out another dignitary there who knew him.

Though Aflâki and Sultan Valad portray Rumi as a legal expert famed throughout the world at this point, he was not the only or even the most famous and respected legal scholar in Konya. In the *Mosâmerât al-akhbâr va mosâyerat al-akhyâr*, a history by Mahmud b. Mohammad Karim al-Âqsarâ'i written in the fourteenth century, we learn the names of a number of the *qâzi*s of the Seljuk dominions in Anatolia during the reign of Sultan Ghiâs al-Din Kay Khosrow II (1237–46) and his vizier, Mo'in al-Din Parvâne. Âqsarâ'i claims that the *qâzi*s of this period were far superior in knowledge to those of the later period. Among the names listed (Akh 419), we find in first place the Qâzi of Konya, Serâj al-Din Mahmud al-Ormovi, also mentioned eight times in Aflâki, who is described as second only to al-Shâfe'i, the founder of one of the four legal schools in Islam.

123

Qâzi Serâj al-Din was favorably disposed to Rumi, if we can believe Aflâki. Aflâki describes how a group of people approached the *qâzi*, attempting to get him to condemn Rumi's practice of *samâ^c*. Qâzi Serâj al-Din refused to do so, calling Rumi a true man, confirmed by God and unmatched in all the outward sciences, to boot (Af 165–6). In another account, a certain ^cAlâ al-Din Seryânus (Therionous?) was hauled before Qâzi Serâj al-Din accused of heresy for calling Rumi God. He managed to extricate himself from punishment by explaining that Rumi made gods of men and had inspired him to convert to Islam from Christianity (*gebri*) and make him a seeker of the divine. After his speech, the ulama felt ashamed for having accused him (Af 274–6), but Aflâki, in his epilogue to the anecdote, suggests the charge was true after all: "In the way of the people of truth [the Sufis], whatever a sincere disciple may say about his shaykh is considered permissible. He cannot be taken to task for it" (Af 276).

Also mentioned in the *Mosâmerât* is Qâzi ^cEzz al-Din of Sivas, whom Aflâki describes as initially opposed to *samâ^c* (Af 104) and proud of his knowledge (Af 422), until Rumi showed him his superior spirituality. These anecdotes from Aflâki presumably relate to the period after Rumi's encounter with Shams, when Rumi's fame was well established; they reveal, however, that even after he had become famous, Rumi was not the only or even the principal legal authority in town.

The *Mosâmerât*, written in the century after Rumi, still recalls a number of famous spiritual authorities besides Rumi. Included in a list of the famous Sufis of the period, the companions of the path (*ashâb-e tariqat*), are Shaykh Sa^cid-e Farghâni. Aflâki describes him in passing (Af 360) as having been, along with other mystics, among the special disciples of Rumi, but this would seem to be wishful thinking, insofar as the *Mosâmerât* lists him as a separate master. The *Mosâmerât* also lists Fakhr al-Din ^cErâqi, whom Aflâki mentions four times (Af 360, 399, 400, 563) and likewise portrays as a partisan, though not necessarily a follower, of Rumi. The vizier Mo^cin al-Din Parvâne built a *khâneqâh* for ^cErâqi in Tokat, and according to the Mevlevis, he followed the practice of *samâ^c* there and made favorable mention of Rumi (Af 399–400). Though Aflâki portrays the relations between them as cordial, the assertion that Rumi and ^cErâqi were close friends cannot be substantiated on this basis. Though the likelihood that the two met seems high, Rumi makes no mention of him, which may actually indicate a kind of rivalry.

The *Mosâmerât* says that just as the *qâzis* during the reign of Ghiâs al-Din Kay Khosrow were superior to those of the present day, likewise the teachers (*ahl-e tadris*) of the days of Ghiâs al-Din, including the Shaykh al-Islam Sadr al-Din (of Konya), to whose famed circle people flocked from around the world, make the teachers of the present appear like hypocrites in comparison (Akh 419). Among those great teachers of the past, he numbers Sadr al-Din, said to have been an expert in Hadith, as well as a mystic teacher (Akh 432).

Among this group of teachers, the *Mosâmerât* (Akh 419) does devote special attention to the "divine lover and Spiritual Axis of the age," Mowlânâ Jalâl al-Din Mohammad of Balkh, whose fame and the effect of whose speeches cannot be described. It corroborates the testimony of Rumi's hagiographers and Rumi's own statements that Rumi enjoyed access to the highest officials of the Seljuk state. When the *Mosâmerât* (Akh 432) describes the deaths of the great men of the era, it mentions Tâj al-Din al-Moʿtazz b. Tâher among them (Akh 433), whom Aflâki describes as one of the special disciples of Rumi, a reliable commander who did good deeds like founding colleges, Sufi lodges, hospitals and cloisters (*rebât*). Among all the commanders of the sultan, Rumi liked this man the most. Since he was also from Khorasan, Rumi used to address him as my "compatriot" (Af 239).

The hagiographies mention a wide variety of Seljuk officials and sultans with whom Rumi had contact, but predictably do not concern themselves with a systematic or factual description of Rumi's relationship with them. We have already seen how Aflâki portrays Sâheb-e Esfahâni as a disciple first of Borhân al-Din and then of Rumi, introducing the latter to Sultan ʿEzz al-Din Kay Kâus (r. 1246–60). We may surmise, however, that Rumi did not have particularly close relations with the Seljuk royal family during the nine-year reign of Ghiâs al-Din Kay Khosrow II (r. 1237–46), corresponding to the period of Rumi's career after his return from Syria up through the arrival of Shams in Konya. This may mean that Rumi was not yet famous enough to attract the attention of a sultan, or that he did not attract this particular sultan, or even that Rumi did not find this particular sultan worthy.

Ghiâs al-Din was the eldest son of ʿAlâ al-Din Kay Qobâd, but in order to secure his place on the throne, he had two half-brothers killed, along with their mother, an Ayyubid. He also purged the military and the ruling elite. His tenure saw the rebellion of the Turkmen tribes in the southeast and central part of his domains in 1239. Led by a folk preacher called Bâbâ Eshâq (see A. Karamustafa in LCP, 179–83), this insurrection lasted for three years and quite likely made Ghiâs al-Din suspicious of popular preachers like Rumi. The arrival of the Mongols in the area, however, proved a more long-term threat. They took Erzurum in 1242 and soundly defeated Kay Khosrow II at Köse Dag in 1243, at which point Kay Khosrow II fled to Antalya. The minister Moʿin al-Din Parvâne negotiated a treaty in which the Seljuks effectively became a tributary state of the Mongols.[1]

Ghiâs al-Din Kay Khosrow II was married to a Georgian princess, Tamar, the daughter of Queen Rosudan of Georgia (1223–47). This Tamar, referred to as "the Georgian Lady," Gorji Khâtun, by Aflâki, bore Kay Qobâd II, who ruled as sultan in part of the Seljuk territories east of the Kizil river from 1249 to 1257 (though power was concentrated in the hands of his ministers). The Georgian Lady was thus a wife and mother to Seljuk sultans. After the death of Ghiâs al-Din, she remarried, this time to the powerful minister Moʿin al-Din Parvâne, and became a follower of Rumi (Tür 26).

From this we may infer something about Rumi's position and his appeal. On the one hand, he attracted powerful followers from a Christian background, like this Gorji Khâtun, and on the other, he appealed to Muslim merchants like Salâh al-Din Zarkub, who had been a disciple of Borhân al-Din. He also appealed to men from the *fotovvat* or Akhi orders, like Hosâm al-Din. None of these people were religious scholars of a legalist bent; quite the opposite, they were lay people, probably not especially attracted to the kind of Islam propagated by the *qâzi*s and theologians. Sultans and men of state found it useful to support religious scholars and pious men of various bents for political reasons. By founding law colleges, patronizing religious scholars, associating with popular preachers and saints, they could gain the respect of various classes of society and earn some kind of religious or spiritual legitimation for their rule.

Beyond this, of course, many of these individuals were pious believers. Even though as politicians they engaged in a rather ruthless and often brutal business, men of state usually had a good education in literature and statecraft and often wished to know more about the fine points of theology, doctrine, Islamic history and spirituality. Sometimes the sultan would even consider himself a disciple of a particular holy man, as in the case of Bahrâmshâh of Ghazna and Sanâʾi. For example, it would appear that Ghiâs al-Din's successor, ʿEzz al-Din Kay Kâus II (r. 1246–60), held a particularly high regard and even love for Rumi (see the apocryphal story in Af 254). At some point Sultan ʿEzz al-Din invited Rumi as his guest to Antalya, but Rumi hid from the messengers the sultan had sent to escort him there (Af 1020–21). It seems the story is based on some real historical circumstance, as Rumi himself alludes to his reasons for not going to Antalya in Discourse 23 of his *Fihe mâ fih* (Fih 97):

> One should go to Tokat, for it is a warm place. Antalya is warm, too, but the people are mostly Greek (*Rumiân*) there. They do not understand our language, though there are some even among the Greeks who understand us!

Sometime between 1257 and 1260, Rumi dictated to Hosâm al-Din a letter addressed to this ʿEzz al-Din Kay Kâus II, thanking the sultan for appointing a certain Najm al-Din b. Khorram (on whom see Mak 300) to a government position. In this letter, Rumi refers to himself as "father," suggesting that he stood in relation to this sultan as a father to a son or a shaykh to a disciple. Rumi calls the sultan a sea of justice and righteousness and commiserates with him on his exile, giving him words of consolation and advice from the Koran (Mak 59–61). According to Aflâki, Sultan ʿEzz al-Din would seek out Rumi's counsel and on one occasion Rumi even upbraided him (Af 443–4):

> One day the sultan ʿEzz al-Din Kay Kâus, may God make him a shining proof, came to visit his holiness, Mowlânâ. He did not pay befitting attention

to him and did not engage in any discourse or sermon. The Sultan of Islam humbled himself like a servant and said, "May his holiness Mowlânâ advise me."

Rumi replied, "What advice should I give? They have made you a shepherd and you act like a wolf. They have made you a watchman and you act like a thief. The Merciful made you sultan, but you follow the teachings of Satan."

Thereupon the Sultan came outside crying and with bared head stood at the door of the *madrase* repenting profusely. He said, "O God, though his holiness Mowlânâ has spoken to me harshly, he did so for Your sake. I, Your helpless servant, likewise humble myself and importune You by Your sovereignty. By virtue of these two purely sincere acts have mercy upon me." And he recited these verses:

> Have mercy on me for these moistened eyes,
> and mercy for this burning sorrowed breast.
> You whose mercy exceeds every excess
> Have mercy on me, who am less than less.

Thereupon his holiness Mowlânâ came striding out and showed great concern for him, saying, "Go, for the Lord on high has shown you mercy and forgiven you."

Sultan Valad (SVE 197) claims that before the arrival of Shams in Konya, Rumi performed miracles left and right before young and old alike, and had attracted to himself more than ten thousand disciples. A historian will naturally have to balk at this number, which would represent a significant proportion of the population, but Sultan Valad goes on to explain that many of these disciples were as yet not so very sincere (*gar che avval ze sedq dur bodand*). We may infer that Rumi enjoyed support from a considerable number of merchants and artisans, and was able to attract and convert Greek and Armenian Christians. Rumi refers to this ability of his in Discourse 23 (Fih 97):

> One day I was speaking to a large crowd among whom there were a number of unbelievers (*kâferân*, non-Muslims). As I spoke, they were weeping and extremely emotional, overcome by ecstasy (*hâlat*). [You] ask, "What can they understand and what do they know about it? Even among Moslems only one chosen among a thousand understands this kind of talk. What did they understand of it that they were weeping so?" [I] reply that it is not necessary for a soul to understand the words, he can understand the spirit behind them.

Such conversions would have won Rumi great popular support as a teacher of Islam and garnered the support of members of the ruling elite. Sultan Valad tells us that nobles and commoners alike became his disciples and servants, vivified by his teachings like newly blossomed plants in spring. As Sultan Valad poetically puts it, Rumi would, in his magnanimity, preach sermons from the pulpit in the warm and heart-winning way of the Prophet. Rumi spoke hidden mysteries, words glittering like pearls on a beatific necklace; Rumi made the world his prey, he brought to life the psyche of man. He revealed such mysteries that every single one of his disciples surpassed the station of the famous Sufi, Ma'ruf al-Karkhi.

Sultan Valad even claims (SVE 197):

> moftiân-e bozorg o ahl-e honar
> dide u râ be-jâ-ye payghambar

> Great *mofti*s and people of capacity
> saw him standing in the Prophet's place

Though we may not wish to take Sultan Valad at his word, the *qâzi*s and conventional religious scholars could not raise strenuous objections against a man well trained in the Islamic sciences with a popular following and institutional support, who also managed to win converts to the faith. If we dismiss Sultan Valad's claim that Rumi had 10,000 disciples, it does not seem so implausible that Rumi held professorial positions at four separate reputable colleges (*dar chahâr madrase-ye mo'tabare modarresi mikard*), where he was occupied with the teaching of classes on the religious sciences (*be-tadris-e 'olum-e dini mashghul bud*). It does not, however, seem quite likely that, as Aflâki (Af 618) goes on to tell us, a retinue of the most important ulama in town followed Rumi about from place to place.

A meticulous study of Rumi's letters in conjunction with historical sources and biographical dictionaries should reveal a great deal more about his relations with state officials, judges and other religious scholars, and with his own disciples, particularly for the period of the 1250s to 1270s. Towfiq Sobhâni's excellent annotated edition of Rumi's letters (*Maktubât*) has done much in this regard; used in conjunction with Foruzânfar's annotations to the Persian text of Rumi's "Discourses", *Fihe mâ fih*, or, in English, with Thackston's annotations in his *Signs of the Unseen* (see chapter 9), we may yet be able to tease out further reliable information about Rumi's position and the extent of his reputation during the period before Shams arrived in Konya.

RUMI THE REVIVALIST

A SERMON BY RUMI

Here follows the text of one of Rumi's sermons as recorded in the *Majâles-e sab'e* ("The Seven Sermons"). There is little indication when the seven sermons preserved by the manuscript tradition were delivered. Foruzânfar believed that one of them dated to the lifetime of his father, and so before 1231 (FB 216), but we cannot know for certain whether they represent Rumi's style before or after his encounter with Shams al-Din of Tabriz. Aside from illustrating the genre expectations of medieval Persian preaching and the shared assumptions of a Sunni audience, this will give us an idea of the public use to which Rumi put his formal education. Sermons were performed in an essentially oral environment, in a mosque or college, with the speaker in a pulpit or seat of honor. Usually following prayers or recitation of the Koran, the preacher stood at the head of a congregation some of whom were fervently attentive, and some who came out of social convention. Most of them would be familiar with at least a smattering of Arabic and vaguely aware of most of the Hadith and Koranic verses which they heard. Only a man of acknowledged piety and learning would be given the pulpit to deliver a sermon, by virtue of which he would hold some sway of authority over much of the audience. An effective sermon would nevertheless employ all the theatrical devices of intonation, gesture, modulation of the voice, and so forth, which a good speaker commands.

In his Persian sermons Rumi delivered the opening benediction in Arabic, the liturgical language, along with quotations from the Koran and passages from the Hadith. He also recited the verse of poets, most of them in Persian, and told a few stories to illustrate his point (some of these appear in the *Masnavi*). In the Arabic benediction Rumi employs rhymed prose (*saj*^c), a stylistic device derived from the Koran, in accordance with the fashion of his day. In the particular sermon rendered below,[2] a single rhyme is observed throughout the entire length of the benediction, requiring Rumi to use some rare words along with some common words in their more obscure forms. The benediction begins with a kind of doxology about God's transcendence and the need for man to accept his decrees. It concludes with a more or less ritual evocation and praise of the first four orthodox caliphs recognized by the Sunnis.

Rumi does not translate the Arabic benediction for his audience, but he follows the Arabic prayer for Mohammad and the companions which concludes the benediction with a much longer prayer in metaphorical Persian prose, a habit Rumi apparently always observed. The remainder of the sermon is delivered in Persian – the language spoken at court and by the educated public in Seljuk Anatolia – except for the quotation of a long hadith, which is then given in colorful and interpretive Persian translation. Brief phrases from a variety of prophetic traditions are also evoked in Arabic.

Towards the end, Rumi plays upon the wording of the Muslim confession of faith: *lâ elâha ellâ Allâh*, "No god is there but God." To convert to Islam, one would utter this formula in front of witnesses. It was also called out from the minarets five times a day at the times of the ritual prayers; it was furthermore a common everyday expression, still used by Iranians in frustration or anger. Sufis had contemplated the deeper meaning and sacrality of the phrase, noting that it begins with the principle of negation (*lâ*) sweeping away the idolatry of false gods (*elâha*), before leading to the affirmation of God. The Sufis took this as confirmation of their belief that a worshiper must first pursue the *via negativa*, obliterating all trace of idolatry and disciplining the concupiscent self until it achieves self-effacement (*fanâ*) in the divine. After sweeping away these obstacles, one could then set out on the *via positiva*, leading to the meeting with God, who stands at the end of the journey.

> Praised be God, who is sacrosanct above compare and contrast, sanctified from all peer and likeness, exalted above death and decomposition; the Ancient of Days, who exists eternally, the transformer of hearts, the motive force behind fate and events, He who brings about revolutions in our circumstances, of whom it cannot be asked when or how long, for the imputation of such concepts to the Ancient of Days is impossible! He began the world without exemplar or precedent, created Adam and his progeny from clods of clay [K55:14, etc.], some of them destined for bliss, some for hellfire, some for remoteness, some for reunion. Among them some are given to drink of defeat while others are clothed with the raiment of acceptance. Should any tongue object, it is dumbfounded by this saying of the Almighty: "He shall not be asked of His doing, but they will be questioned" [K21:23]. Exalted is our lord above contention and disputation! Where does creation derive the right to question and contend? It was non-existent, then came into being and will decompose once again, going as the mountains go: "You see the mountains and suppose them firm, but they will pass away as clouds do. Such is God's handiwork, who brings all things to perfection" [K27:88]. "There is no God but Him" [K2:163], "the Great, the Exalted" [K13:9].
>
> He raised up our Prophet, Mohammad (God's peace and blessings upon him) when ignorance appeared and blasphemy and waywardness reigned, and he counseled his community through words and deeds, making clear to them which paths were forbidden and which permissible. He exerted himself in the path of God under all conditions until the sea of negation evaporated like a mirage and the Truth was established straight and tall by his effort.
>
> God's peace and blessings upon him and his family – the best of families – and upon his companions: upon Abu Bakr, the righteous, who liberally supported him with his wealth; upon ᶜOmar, distinguisher of truth from error, whose obedience to him intensified even in terrifying floods of tribulation; upon ᶜOsmân, possessor of the twin lights, who held fast to recitation of the Remembrance [i.e., the Koran] every morn and every eve; and upon ᶜAli b. Abu Tâleb, the smasher of idols and slayer of champions. So long as the gazelle cubs graze in the meadows and the darkness is lit up and the wicks blaze, our fervent and humble supplications [for them] will not cease.
>
> [PRAYER IN PERSIAN] O Lord, O God, O Sustainer! Wrap us in that light with which you envelop your chosen servants, that we may meet the Friend. Nurture us not in the pastures of lust where you nurture the enemies, as the cows and stable goats are nurtured for their meat and pelts. Nurture the birds of our senses with the grains of knowledge and wisdom that we may fly in the heavens, and not with the seeds of lust, that our throats may be slit.
>
> The fickle firmament brings forth its little dramas, just as shadow players manipulate imaginary stars and planetary puppets from behind a screen. We crowd around awhile engrossed by this spectacle, whiling away our night of life.

In the morning death will arrive and this throng from the firmament's shadow play will grow cold and the night of our life will have blown by us.

O Lord, before the morn of death dawns, make our hearts cold to this play so that we might escape from the throng in time and not fall behind those who travel through the night. When morning dawns, let it find us in the precincts of your approval.

O Lord! The ears of all souls have heard your call of life, all souls are set in motion through this long desert, thirsting for the water of life. This world loomed up and all flailed about in it, though the guides and those who divine water call out: "Though it resembles the water of life, it is not the water of life. The water of life lies ahead, pass on by this."

The water of life is such a thing that whoever drinks from it will never die. Any tree branch turned green by it will never yellow and wither; any flower blossoming by virtue of that water of life will never wilt. But this is not the water of vitality, this is the water of mortality. He who drinks deepest from this mortal water of life will die soonest. Do you not see how the princes and kings have a shorter span of life than their servants? The branch which soaks up this water most will yellow soonest. See this rose – the one most saturated with this water now blooming most fully – it will of necessity wilt before all the other brides of the garden.

Rare is the body whose ear hears this cry and counsel, and rarer still the somebody who leaves this murky water to the nobodies. O God! O Monarch! Make us one of those somebodies and grant us deliverance from this black and brackish water, that we may not die like those others with swollen face and bloated belly at the fount of this spring and may not be held back from the quest for the water of life.

[HADITH IN ARABIC] It is related by Abu Dharr from the Prophet, peace upon him: I asked the Messenger of God, God's peace and blessings upon him, what is in the scroll of Moses? [He answered]: "I am amazed by those who have certain knowledge of death, how can they be joyful? And I am amazed by those who have certain knowledge of the Fire, how can they make light? And I am amazed by those who have certain knowledge of the Reckoning, how can they do wicked deeds? And I am amazed by those who have certain knowledge of the decay of the world and the vicissitudes which afflict its denizens, how can they amass worldly things and rely upon them?"

[PERSIAN] Among the servants of his holiness the Messenger and those blessed at the threshold of Prophecy, was Abu Dharr, one of the true chamberlains to chivalry, and this is what he said:

One day the head of the army of the people of religion, the refuge and support of the people of the world, the compass point of the earth, the fruit of the tree of Adam, the royal insignia of "Soon will your Lord bestow upon you and you will be content" [K93:5]; He who is the trainer of the Borâq[3] of "Praised be He who made his servant to ascend at night" [K17:1], he who passes beyond the heights of "then he approached and came nearer" [K53:8] he climbed above both this world and the next, alluding to the verse "He came within two bow lengths or closer" [K53:9].

So Abu Dharr said: This great one [Mohammad] emerged one day from the Sacred Mosque and the place of prayer from which he called his Lord. He said, "Supplications after the obligatory are always answered." He mounted the throne of "I am the chief of the sons of Adam but take no pride in this." He spread the carpet of "Poverty is my pride," and set out the cushions of "Adam and the other prophets are under my banner," reclining upon the support of "the first thing God created was my light." Those who accompanied him from Mecca and those who supported him in Medina and all those "who seek forgiveness at dawn" [K3:17], those who in gratitude "stay up through the night and fast during the day," drew around him in a circle. There was the Righteous Abu Bakr, who like a jeweler, set forth pearly words of divine mystery in fine array. There was the Discriminating ʿOmar, divining the distinction between truth and falsehood. There was ʿOsmân of the Twin Lights, preparing light for the darkness of the tomb. There was ʿAli the Acquiescent, forging bonds of contentment. There was Belâl, singing like a bulbul. "Rejoice us [with the call to prayer], O Belâl!" Sohayb was there, quaffing the chalice of the wine of faithfulness. Salmân was there pacing in the path of peace.

And I, Abu Dharr, was there, reduced to a mote of dust before his majesty. I brazenly opened my mouth and asked our great leader [in Arabic], "What is in the scroll of Moses?" [Meaning in Persian] What is in the scroll of Moses, that consolation of the soul of lovers and the confidant of yearning hearts?

Our leader, at the command of the One Who lives and never dies, removed the seal of silence from the treasure chest of truth and said: [Arabic] "I am amazed," [meaning in Persian] I am amazed by the servant of God who has set foot in the field of faith, has believed in Hades and the all the levels of hell, has heard the call of the King and His aides; how can he, in this thicket of calamity and prison of catastrophe, laugh lightheartedly?"

What else, our leader?

He said, "I am amazed by the servant who has lived his precious life to the end, believes in death but has not made provision for it, admits he will be questioned in the grave, but has prepared no reply! How can he be happy?"

A third time he said, "I am amazed by the servant who has believed that he will be called to account for each of his tiniest words and deeds – as it is said, 'And whoso does a gram's weight of good will see his reward' [K99:7] and the scales of justice are set out – how can he act so rashly?"

And the fourth: "I am amazed by that servant who sees how unfaithful the world is, who lays his dear ones to rest in the earth and hears the Koran reciters chanting 'Every soul shall taste of death' [K3:185]! How can he amass worldly things with such eagerness, desire, covetousness, and anticipation and fix his heart on them? And he sees the grave and the winding sheet and the dead and tastes the sting of bereavement?! But he has not known even for one night the bitterness his departed friends have tasted, so how can he know the value of union? How can one who has felt no pain appreciate the balm?"

No, no, my brother! Try to escape from this prison, set foot on the path of repentance so that you may have both the here and hereafter in this world. But what good is this? Rather you should set your sights even higher and spur on the steed of religion even faster until you pass beyond all regard for the world and even close your eyes to the next world. In this way you will see the beauty of the *mysterium tremendum.*

Sweep all away with the broom of "No"! Every king or prince has a herald for every ceremony. The herald which sweeps aside both worlds from before the face of the Courtiers and Kings of Holiness is the phrase: THERE IS NO GOD BUT GOD.

> Everything keeps you distant from your quest
> whether words of blasphemy or of belief
> everything holds you back from the Friend
> whether images of beauty or of beast
> You'll clean no thorn and thistle from this path
> unless the creedal NO serves as your herald
> When NO casts you from fame into confusion
> Then follow Godhead's light through BUT to GOD

Look on nothing but God's beauty, hear nothing but God's word, that you may be among the closest confidants of the King.

> I passed through a rosebed with my belle
> My inadvertent gaze fell on a rose
> My idol, seeing this, reproved: For shame!
> Here is my cheek and you look there at the rose?

And God is the All-Knowing.

4

Shams al-Din Tabrizi

Shams means "sun" in Arabic. The full title of the dervish who wholly transformed Rumi's life and thought, Shams al-Din Tabrizi, means "the Sun of Faith from Tabriz," and Rumi plays upon this repeatedly in his lyric poems. Aflâki (614) gives his full name as Shams al-Din Mohammad b. ᶜAli b. Malek-e Dâd, but grandiloquent titles and honorific addresses were obligatory in polite society in the medieval period, and Shams is accorded his share. Sepahsâlâr (Sep 122) gives him the following caravan of honorific titles: King of the Saints (*Soltân al-owliâ*⁾) and those who have attained unto God (*al-vâselin*), the Spiritual Axis of the Gnostics (*Qotb al-ᶜârefin*), God's Proof for the Faithful and the Heir (*Vâres*) of the Prophets and Messengers. Rumi evokes Shams by many other less cliched and therefore more impressive titles, among them Sea of Mercy (*Bahr-e rahmat*), Sun of Grace (*Khworshid-e lotf*), the Mighty Monarch (*Khosrov-e aᶜzam*), the Lord of the Lords of Mysteries (*Khodâvand-e khodâvandân-e asrâr*), The King of Kings of the Spirit (*Soltân-e soltânân-e jân*) and Pure Light (*Nur-e motlaq*).

Shams al-Din might have remained an obscure footnote in works on the history of Sufism had Rumi not made of him a virtual god and bruited his name about. Though Rumi turned Shams into a picture of apotheosis in the *Divân*, he does not tell us many factual particulars about Shams al-Din the man. We can glean some information from the discourses of Rumi in *Fihe mâ fih* and a tiny amount from the *Masnavi*, but Shams has been known mostly through the hagiographical accounts given by Sultan Valad, Sepahsâlâr, and especially Aflâki. Although these sources do give biographical anecdotes and details about his personal characteristics, they present a mythologized picture of Shams which later authors blew up into even larger than life proportions.

Legend portrayed Shams as an untutored charismatic, an ordinary Qalandar or wandering dervish possessed of miraculous powers, whose name Rumi chose as the focus of his devotion in order to test his disciples and provide a literary persona for his ghazals. This view is reflected in Jâmi, Dowlatshâh and to a certain extent in Aflâki. Early Western scholarship reflected this later mythical view of Shams. Browne (BLH 2:516–17) thought that Shams was the son of Jalâl al-Din Now Mosalmân, who dissolved the Assassin sect. Redhouse (*The Mesnevi* x) referred to Shams' "exceedingly aggressive and domineering manner." Sprenger calls him "a most disgusting cynic,"[1] whereas Nicholson (NiD xx) calls him "comparatively illiterate, but his tremendous spiritual enthusiasm, based on the conviction that he was a chosen organ and mouthpiece of Deity, cast a spell over all who entered the enchanted circle of his power." For Nicholson in 1898, Shams "curiously resembles Socrates" in his "strong passions, his poverty, and his violent death."

At one time it may even have been possible to suppose that Shams was an imaginary persona created by Rumi as a foil to convey his ideas, just as Socrates was suspected in some circles to be a literary fiction created by the mind of Plato. But the romantic and legendary view of Shams, based upon medieval authorities like Jâmi and Dowlatshâh, was challenged by the publication in 1937 of Sultan Valad's verse history of the Valad family, which details Rumi's relationship with Shams. Sultan Valad, who knew Shams personally, calls him a man of "knowledge and learning, an eloquent author" (SVE 71). The subsequent publication in 1959 of a critical edition of Aflâki's "Acts of the Adepts" added to this a statement attributed to Rumi that Shams was fully apprised of the learning of his day, had studied Islamic law, met with the learned men of his age and even possessed knowledge of mathematics and astronomy (Af 625–6).

Fortunately, Shams did leave behind a body of writings or, more precisely, notes taken down by his own or Rumi's disciples from the lectures of Shams. These, like the *Ma'âref* of Bahâ al-Din and Borhân al-Din, were never widely disseminated, in part because they were never read back to and approved by Shams for publication (Mov 218). Rumi repeatedly refers to the *asrâr*, or "secrets," of Shams (Maq 39), which may of course refer to his oral teachings, but may also designate a written text. If the latter, it represents the name which Rumi gave to the collection of Shams' writings. Some manuscripts of these discourses of Shams are entitled the *Kalemât* ("Sayings") or *Ma'âref* ("Gnostic Wisdom") of Shams. By scholarly convention, however, these notes are now generally referred to as the *Maqâlât*, or "Discourses," of Shams. This is the title given to them in one partial manuscript of the work, a copy in all likelihood written out in the hand of Rumi's son, Sultan Valad; if so, the copy may date to the lifetime of Shams. About a century after the death of Sultan Valad, this copy passed into the possession of Shams al-Din Mohammad al-Fannâri (d. 1431),

himself a well-known author of mystical works, and is now housed in the library
of Velieddin Effendi (MS no. 1865). Another manuscript was copied out by
Jalâl al-Din Mohammad Monajjem, the son of Hosâm al-Din Hosayn, one of
Sultan Valad's successors. Aflâki had a copy or copies of these collected notes of
Shams, and he quotes a selection of them in his "Acts of the Gnostics."

Altogether a score or so of manuscripts of the text have survived, all of them
more or less haphazard, unedited collections, proving that the book was never
published in a formal way. The existence of such a collection was apparently
unknown beyond a relatively small circle of Mevlevis, among whom it was
known as "The Mantle of Shams" (*Kherqe-ye Shams*). Shams was himself
uninterested in bestowing ceremonial cloaks or mantles upon his disciples to
designate his successors, as other Sufis did. Instead, Shams pointed to his words
and their effect upon the listener as his mantle of investiture (Maq 41);
elsewhere, Shams expresses the opinion that it is not the writings, but the
personage and the kerygma of a spiritual teacher that work upon the soul of the
disciple: "that which will free you is the servant of God, not abstract writings.
He who follows words on a page is lost" (Maq 18). Shams applies this rule of
thumb even to the person of the Prophet over and above the Koran, which
though not strange in the context of Protestant theology, sounds rather
heterodox in an Islamic context: "The meaning of the Book of God is not the
text [*moshaf* = scroll or codex], it is the man who guides. He is the Book of God,
he is its verses, he is scripture" (Maq 18).

Perhaps this notion explains the failure of the Mevlevis to edit and publish in
book form the sermons and sayings of the first heads of the order – Bahâ al-Din,
Borhân al-Din and Shams al-Din. These were collections of notes, not books
authored according to some plan, and more importantly, the words of these
teachers were perceived as secondary to the spirit which they infused into their
disciples through personal contact and interaction. Fortunately, scholars like
Hellmut Ritter, Abdülbâki Gölpınarlı and Badiᶜ al-Zamân Foruzânfar
uncovered some manuscripts of the works of these founding fathers of the
Mevlevi order in Turkish archives in the 1940s, and, immediately recognizing
their surpassing importance for the study of Rumi and the Mevlevis, called them
to the attention of the scholarly community.

Selections of Shams' *Maqâlât* have been available in Persian for some time
now, first in an edition by Ahmad Khwoshnevis (Tehran: ᶜAtâᵓi, 1970), followed
by Nâser al-Din Sâheb al-Zamâni's *Khatt-e sevvom: darbâre-ye shakhsiat,
sokhanân va andishe-ye Shams-e Tabrizi* (Tehran: ᶜAtâᵓi, 1972), and then the first
edition of Mohammad-ᶜAli Movahhed's *Maqâlât* (Tehran: Dâneshgâh-e Sanᶜ
ati-ye Aryâmehr [Aryâmehr Polytechnic University], 2536/1977). In the last ten
years, interest in Shams has increased dramatically. A critical edition of Shams'
lectures with copious annotation and indices running to slightly over 1,000
pages was published by Mohammad-ᶜAli Movahhed in 1990 as *Maqâlât-e*

136

Shams-e Tabrizi (Tehran: Khwârazmi). All citations of the *Maqâlât* in this work refer to Movahhed's 1990 edition, based upon a careful collation of six antique manuscripts, supplemented by a dozen other more recent manuscripts and lithographs. Collating the partial, scattered and varied material preserved by the manuscript tradition into a unified text made for a herculean task.

From Shams' sayings and lectures Movahhed has since teased out a short but extremely useful biography, *Shams-e Tabrizi* (Tehran: Tarh-e Now, 1996). In addition to these two scholarly works, Movahhed produced a selection of Shams' writings for the general reader, *Khomi az sharâb-e rabbâni*, "A Jug of Divine Wine" (Tehran: Sokhan, 1994). In the same year, Ja'far Modarres-e Sadiqi's edition of the *Maqâlât* (Tehran: Nashr-e Markaz, 1994) appeared. The words and life-story of Shams had already inspired an original volume of poetry by 'Abd al-Hosayn Jalâliân called "The First Flutist," *Naynavâz-e avval: ahvâl-e Shams-e Tabrizi va sokhanân-e u be she'r*, which he self-published in Tehran in 1992.

A reading of the *Maqâlât* of Shams will go much further to dispel the myths about the man. Shams' writings reveal him to have been a man well versed in the philosophical and theological discourse of his day, though something of an iconoclast. The *Maqâlât* reveals Shams as an engaging speaker who expressed himself in a Persian both simple and profoundly moving. Foruzânfar considered Shams' *Maqâlât* one of the true treasures of Persian literature, with a depth that required several contemplative rereadings (Mov 217–18). In addition to its own intrinsic value, Shams' *Maqâlât* constitutes the single most important primary source (aside from Rumi's own writings, of course) for understanding Rumi's spiritual transformation and his teachings.

Inexplicably, however, works about Rumi in European languages have yet to make use of the writings of Shams. The closest thing to a biography of Rumi in English, Schimmel's *Triumphal Sun* (ScT 1978, 1993), only knows Shams' writings through second-hand sources like Gölpınarlı; it was not until Chittick's 1991 article "Rumi and the Mawlawiyyah" (IS) that the first few quotations directly from the *Maqâlât* were incorporated into biographical sketches of Rumi. As Movahhed notes (Maq 17), though thousands of pages have been written about Rumi, there has been virtually nothing about Shams, even though Rumi explicitly indicates that Shams is the voice speaking through his poems (D 2056):

> *mafkhar-e tabriziân, Shams-e Haq va Din, begu*
> *balke sedâ-ye to ast in hame goftâr-e man*

> Speak, Sun of Truth and Faith, pride of Tabriz!
> but it is your voice that mouths all my words

Movahhed's biography and his edition of the *Maqâlât*, to which the following account is heavily indebted, allow us for the first time to peer directly at the Sun of Faith, Shams-e Tabriz.

TABRIZ: THE FIRST HOUSE OF THE SUN

THE POLITICAL SITUATION IN AZERBAYJAN

According to Mevlevi tradition, Shams al-Din of Tabriz was sixty years of age when he came to Konya, which would put his birth in the 1180s. At about this time the boy Toghrol b. Arslân ruled over the Seljuk dominions with the Atabeg Nosrat al-Din Mohammad Pahlavân, son of Shams al-Din Ildeguz, governing in central and western Iran, including Tabriz, in the boy-sultan's name. According to Ibn al-Athîr, Mohammad Pahlavân was a "just" ruler, wise, patient and skillful in politics, as a result of which the people of Azerbayjan, Rayy, Arrân and Isfahan lived in "peace and security." When the Atabeg died in 1186 this security came to an end as the Shâfeᶜis and Hanafis fell into dispute in Isfahan and burned the city, while in Rayy communal strife between the Sunnis and Shiites led to ruin (Mov 29–32).

After gaining ascendancy over the political infighting that surrounded him, Sultan Toghrol came through Tabriz and proceeded from there to Hamadan, only to be killed in battle with the Khwârazmshâh. Atabeg Abu Bakr subsequently ruled over Tabriz until his death in about 1210. Shams al-Din of Tabriz describes this Atabeg (Maq 369) as a head taller than everyone else, forever surrounded by armed guards a whole arrows' range around. Unfortunately, both Atabeg Abu Bakr and his brother, Atabeg Uzbek, who succeeded him, proved to be drunkards and wastrels (Mov 31–2).

In 1220 the Mongol hordes swept through Tabriz and Atabeg Uzbek surrendered the city to save it from plunder. Instead, one of Atabeg Uzbek's generals took the men under his command, joined forces with the Mongols, and together they went off to plunder Georgia. When the second wave of Mongols attacked, Atabeg Uzbek was in Nakhjavân and Shams al-Din Toghrâ'i had control of Tabriz. Toghrâ'i ordered that the city resist, but fortunately the Mongols did not sack Tabriz, contenting themselves instead with some tribute, after which they rode off to plunder the Caucasus, where they remained until 1223.

In the meanwhile, Jalâl al-Din Khwârazmshâh rode on Azerbayjan and laid siege to Tabriz. The city resisted for five days but surrendered in the end to Jalâl al-Din, who demanded to know why his Muslim soldiers had been killed and their heads sent to the Mongols. The Tabrizis blamed Atabeg Uzbek and threw themselves at the mercy of the Khwârzmshâh. The wife of the Atabeg, who was a daughter of Sultan Toghrol and therefore a princess, sweetened the deal with a kiss. She married the Khwârazmshâh after the judge, ᶜEzz al-Din Qazvini, allowed himself to be persuaded by some witnesses that the Atabeg had divorced her in absentia. Although the Khwârazmshâh promised security to Tabriz, he fled as soon as the Mongols returned.

In these tumultuous circumstances, where power forcefully and repeatedly changed hands in Tabriz, it was best to stay aloof from politics. Shams-e

Toghrâ'i had apparently attempted to do so, while standing up for Tabriz against the non-Muslim Mongol invaders. For this Shams-e Toghrâ'i's townsman and namesake Shams-e Tabriz praises him in his *Maqâlât* as the wisest counselor of the age (Maq 822).

SUFISM IN TABRIZ

But what of the religious and spiritual life of Tabriz? Persian poetry and Sufism developed first in Khorasan, in the east of Iran, and western Iran was not felt to be particularly fertile ground for the mystical way of life. By the sixteenth century, however, there was more than enough mystical history to devote a whole book exclusively to the Sufis of Tabriz, and Hâfez Hosayn Karbalâ'i of Tabriz did just that in his *Rowzât al-jenân*. This Hâfez Hosayn Karbalâ'i of Tabriz relates that when Shaykh Abu Eshâq Ebrâhim-e Jovaynâni, a Sufi from the east of Iran, found it necessary to undertake a trip to Tabriz, his mentor, Bâyazid Bestâmi, warned him not to mix with the people of Tabriz, who were apt to follow fools and reject the wise (RaJ 1:275–6). To the contrary, Shaykh Abu Eshâq apparently found the people there quite congenial, for he remained in Tabriz until he died in 888, becoming the pioneer Sufi there.

A horrible earthquake destroyed Tabriz in 1032, but the Rawwadid ruler, Vahsudân Mohammad, had the city rebuilt. A certain Bâle Khalil Sufiâni represented the Sufis in the reconstruction (RaJ 1:17), in recognition of which an area of the town was named after him. Many gravestones in Tabriz include the titles *dâdâ* or *dede*, which usually designate a spiritual teacher. A poet of the fourteenth century living in Tabriz, Kamâl-e Khojandi (d. c. 1400), refers to an area in Tabriz called Valiânkuh, or Saints' Mountain, apparently a *khâneqâh* or shrine near which 480 Muslim saints were reputedly buried (according to Mohammad Amin Hashari, *Rowze-ye athâr*, 63; cited in Mov 13). There were two quarters in Tabriz, Sorkhâb and Charandâb, from where, as legend has it, the souls of saints would arise at night, form two groups of red and green doves, and fly to Mecca to circle round the Kaaba (Mov 13). The Sorkhâb district to the north of the city featured a cemetery with a number of pleasant tombs at the foot of Mount Sorkh (RaJ 47), probably identical to Khojandi's aforementioned "Saint's Mountain." The Charandâb district, to the south of the city, also featured a cemetery where a number of Sufis lay buried.

At the time when Shams was a young man, it is said that a group of seventy saints were living in Tabriz (RaJ 1:49–50). The leader of these seventy saintly elders, or Bâbâs, who must have been populist teachers relying more upon inner experience, spiritual discovery and charismatic holiness than a reputation for conventional knowledge and learning, was Bâbâ Hasan-e Vali (d. 1214), who built a *khâneqâh* in 1198 (Mov 15). 'Ayn al-Qozât-e Hamadâni (executed 1131) describes his own shaykh, Berke of Hamadân, as just such a Sufi guide (JNO 416):

Berke only knows the Fâtehe (the opening verses of the Koran) and a couple of suras by heart and cannot even recite them on demand. He has no idea what debate (*qâl yaqul*) is and if you want to know the truth, he cannot even make verse in Hamadâni dialect, but I know that he knows the truth of the Koran and I do not, except for parts of it, and those parts of it I know, I have learned not from commentaries and so forth, but from serving him.

Khwâje ʿAbd al-Rahim Azhâbâdi (d. 1257), another Tabrizi saint who was contemporary with Shams al-Din, is described as follows (RaJ 1:117–18):

He was apparently unlettered, informed by the inspiration of the Mother Book. He had not frequented any teacher and had read nothing, but when he opened the portal of speech, fine and elegant Arabic words came out which even the learned ulama and the knowledgeable ones of the world had difficulty understanding.

Shams-e Tabriz himself relates a story (Maq 321) about a certain Ahmad Ghazzâli (evidently not the famous mystical author by that name) who had not studied the conventional learning of the day. A messenger came to him with some books, and Ahmad, being unlettered, asked the man to read some parts of the book to him. Ahmad then said:

Now write down on the introduction of the book these lines I will dictate:
> In search of treasure
>> ruined is the body of me
> On the fire of love
>> charred is the heart of me
> Of the Treasure Chest and Kernel
>> what's the point for me?
> A concoction from the friend's lip
>> is the wine for me

This favorable attitude toward experiential Sufism distinguishes Rumi from his more theoretical contemporaries in the school of Ibn ʿArabi. But Rumi did not learn this first from Shams al-Din; Bahâ al-Din and Borhân al-Din, though both learned men, share the experiential, rather than the theoretical, approach to mysticism. This perhaps accounts, at least in part, for Rumi's attraction to Shams. As Rumi says:

> The Sufis' book is filled not with ink and words
> it holds but a heart white as driven snow

(M2:159)

❧ ❧ ❧

> Would anyone write over writing
> or plant a sapling in a forest?
> O brother, be earth in a spot unsown
> become white paper, unwritten upon

(M5:1961–3)

This is not to suggest that the Sufism of Tabriz or of Shams was exclusively an unlettered Sufism. Many learned Sufis had spent time in Tabriz, including Ahmad Ghazzâli, Najm al-Din Kobrâ and Abu Najib, the latter two as students of Bâbâ Faraj Tabrizi (d. 1172). Owhad al-Din Kermâni also went to Tabriz sometime between the years 1191 and 1196. About a generation after Shams, Shaykh Hasan Bolghâri describes his spiritual transformation in Tabriz and lists twenty-eight people among the ranks of "those who have truly attained and intimately know, upon whose sincere and loving breasts the rays of the sun of divine gnosis shine" (for citations and details of the above, see Mov 11–19).

Of Tabriz, Rumi writes that it is a shrine, from whose graves the folk of love inhale revivifying breezes (Mov 14). Shams had wished that Rumi could come to Tabriz and see its spiritual sights: "We would have traveled together to Mosul – you haven't seen those parts – and up to Tabriz. You could have given sermons at such-and-such pulpit and seen their society and their retreats" (Maq 353). That Tabriz was a city much concerned with mysticism and the saintly life is reflected in another statement of Shams: "There are people there in comparison to whom I am nothing, as if the sea cast me up, just as a sea casts out driftwood. My state being thus, imagine what they are like!" (Maq 641). It was in such an atmosphere that Shams grew up.

THE DAWN OF SHAMS

The oldest and most reliable sources about the life of Shams, Sultan Valad and Sepahsâlâr, are not concerned with the life of Shams before he came to Konya. Aflâki gives more information, including the name of Shams, his father and his grandfather, and a number of biographical tidbits, though one cannot necessarily trust Aflâki on such matters. Fortunately, Shams' *Maqâlât* confirms some of Aflâki's statements, such as that Shams lived obscurely and did not support himself from colleges of law or Sufi lodges, but made his living from tutoring and primary-school teaching, and we now have as much or more biographical information about Shams at our disposal as we do about most other figures from that period of history.

Shams claims that he was gifted with special spiritual abilities from childhood which his parents could not fathom. His father was "a good man of generous nature," easily moved to tears (Mov 41), though he was not a "lover," or gnostic. To be a good man is one thing, but to be a lover of God is quite another story, so Shams was unable to reveal his mystic visions (*tatavvo'ât*) to his father, though he wanted to (Maq 119).

> I fault my mother and father for having coddled me. If the cat knocked over a bowl and broke it, father didn't hit it in front of me and didn't get upset. He would laughingly say, "What have you done now? It's just as well, fate has decreed this, or else something would have happened to you or me or mother." (Maq 625–6)

Shams was a strange child, displaying unusual spiritual sensibilities from before puberty. This resulted in a sense of otherworldly estrangement which he could not explain to those around him (Maq 740):

> It was said that at a young age my appetite would leave me and I would not eat for three to four days, on account of something which, not the people, but God had said.
>
> Father would say, "Alas for my son, he says he will eat nothing."
>
> I said, "But I'm not weak; I'm so strong that if you want I'll fly out of that window like a bird." Every four days a little lethargy would overtake me for a while and leave. During this time no morsel of food would go down.
>
> "What's wrong with you?"
>
> "Nothing's wrong. Am I crazy? Did I tear anyone's clothes? Did I fall on you, did I rip your clothes?!"
>
> "Aren't you going to eat?"
>
> "I'm not eating today."
>
> "Tomorrow, the day after, the next!?"

Elsewhere he says (Maq 677) that for a period of about thirty or forty days just before he reached puberty, his mystical love made him indisposed to food, which he would hide in his sleeve whenever it was offered to him.

Shams felt estranged from his father; Shams describes himself as a duck egg under a common hen. Shams' home was the sea and if the father could not follow him into it, that was because he was of different mettle and should return to his birdhouse. Reduced to tears, the father would ask, "If you act thus with friends, how will you treat your enemies?" (Maq 741).

> My father didn't understand me at all. I was a stranger in my own town. My father was a stranger to me and my heart recoiled from him. I thought he might fall upon me. He'd speak kindly to me, but I thought he'd beat me and expel me from the house. (Maq 740)

When his father would ask him, "What's wrong? I know you're not crazy, but I don't understand your ways" (Maq 77), Shams would answer by telling him that they were not cut of the same cloth.

RELIGIOUS TRAINING

Shams was a Shâfeᶜi (Maq 182) and he studied *feqh*, reading extensively in the standard legal textbooks. He specifically mentions one of the five major Shâfeᶜi legal texts, *al-Tanbih fi foruᶜ al-shâfiᶜiye* (Maq 676) of Abu Eshâq Shirâzi (d. 1083), who had been one of the first teachers in the famous Baghdad Nezâmiye college. Meanwhile, Rumi was a Hanafi and had studied the *Hedâyat*, the principal work of Borhân al-Din ᶜAli b. Abu Bakr-e Marghinâni. Aflâki (301) quotes Rumi as saying: "In my youth in Damascus I had a friend who was my partner in studying the *Hedâyat*." Rumi presumably also taught this work to his son, Sultan Valad.

Though Rumi does voice a rebuke to the Shiites over the ritual mourning for Hosayn (M6:777ff.), the other Sunni schools, particularly the Shâfeᶜi, seem to have held his respect. Given his ecumenical views, Rumi did not consider affiliation with a different legal school as an obstacle to association with someone. One anecdote related by Aflâki shows Rumi discouraging Hosâm al-Din from changing his affiliation from Shâfeᶜi to Hanafi (see "The Succession" in chapter 5, below). Nor was Shams fanatical about his denominational affiliation. Shams specifically says he would not allow it to stand in the way of his accepting useful things in the works of Abu Hanifa (Maq 183).

Because of the variations prescribed in ritual matters by the two schools and the different legal texts they had read, at some point Rumi and Shams probably discussed the relative virtues of Shâfeᶜi versus Hanafi affiliation. Their theosophy, however, transcended such affiliations. Shams seems far less concerned with ritual and jurisprudence than with his mystical intimations. He says (Maq 178):

> Your preoccupation should be to know "Who am I, what is my essence? And to what end have I come here and where am I headed and what are my roots and what am I doing this very hour and what is my focus?"

But he never completely rejected the scholarly study of religion, for he did not like the pretense of many who prided themselves on their spiritual questing (Maq 249):

> At first I wouldn't mix with jurists, only with the dervishes. I'd say that the jurists are ignorant of dervish-hood. Now that I have realized what dervish-hood is and where they are, I find myself more eager for the company of jurists than dervishes, because the jurists have struggled to attain something. These others boast that we are dervishes. But where is the true dervish?

Shams was thus very educated, contrary to what the accounts of a common man turned mystic suggest. However, he cloaked his nature from religious scholars as well as from practicing pietists, such that his contemporaries were confused about whether he considered himself a scholar of law (*faqih*) or a fakir (*faqir*), a Sufi practicing spiritual poverty (Maq 326):

> Someone asked my friend about me, "Is he a *faqih* or a *faqir*?"
> "Both faqih and faqir," he replied.
> He asked, "Then why do all speak of his *feqh*?"
> He answered, "For his poverty is of such a nature that it cannot be spoken about with that group ... he speaks beyond the boundaries of knowledge and speaks of mysteries in a knowledgeable way in the cloak of knowledge."

Sultan Valad describes Shams as "a man of learning and wisdom and eloquence and composition" (SVE 71), while Aflâki has Rumi describing him as peerless in his knowledge of alchemy, astronomy, astrology, logic, theology and philosophy, "but when he kept the company of the men of God, he kept these hidden" (Af 626).

THE EDUCATION OF SHAMS-E TABRIZI

Among the legal scholars favorably mentioned by Shams is **Shams-e Khoᵓi of Azerbayjan** (d. 1239 or 1240 at the age of fifty-four, from tuberculosis), also a Shâfeᶜi, who is mentioned in the *Tabaqât al-Shâfeᶜiye*, a biographical dictionary of Shâfeᶜi scholars by Jamâl al-Din ᶜAbd al-Rahim al-Esnavi (1305–70), as an accomplished scholar in scholastic theology (*kalâm*), philosophy (*hekme*, also possibly herbal healing), and medicine (*tebb*). He had studied in Khorasan with a student of Fakhr-e Râzi before returning to Syria, where he became a *qâzi*.[2] Quite possibly this Shams al-Din Khoᵓi is the Shâfeᶜi Qâzi al-qozât (Chief Judge) of Damascus, appointed by al-Moᶜazzam in 1226 after the death of the ineffective Hanafi *qâzi*, Jamâl al-Din Yunos al-Mesri. Shams al-Din Khoᵓi had frequented al-Moᶜazzam's study circle (*majles*) prior to his appointment, but apparently did not like to interfere in political matters, according to the historians. Nevertheless, he did briefly travel to Konya in 1237 with Kamâl al-Din b. al-ᶜAdim as al-Malek al-Ashraf's emissary to the Seljuks (Hum 187, 231). Zahabi identifies Shams-e Khoᵓi as a student of Fakhr-e Râzi and the editor of Râzi's unfinished Koran commentary, calling Khoᵓi the Qâzi al-qozât. According to Movahhed (Mov 50–51), this Shams-e Khoᵓi was also very close to Ibn ᶜArabi, quite unusual for a jurist, but unlike many teachers, Khoᵓi favored those students who were innovative and did something new with what they learned over those who simply memorized and repeated what was in the books.

There is some discrepancy in the manuscripts of the *Maqâlât*, such that we cannot be absolutely certain that Shams-e Khoᵓi or an otherwise unknown figure, Shams-e Khonji, is the intended object of discussion (Mov 54). Nevertheless, the *Maqâlât* does refer to him as the Qâzi of Damascus, which (unless it is a later interpolation) would seem to fix his identity as the Shâfeᶜi Chief Judge in Damascus from 1226 to 1239.

Shams-e Tabrizi appears to have been present at his public meetings in Damascus (Maq 607). Teachers in mosques or Sufi lodges would typically distinguish between subjects discussed in general public lectures and the subjects discussed with close disciples. Qotb al-Din Abhari, called "the Mofti, chief and leader of Baghdad," taught two classes, "one in private and one in public, in accordance with everyone's various aptitudes, both in private and in public" (Owh 56). Apparently Shams-e Khoᵓi did not accept Shams-e Tabriz as one of his close disciples. This meant not only that Shams-e Tabriz was not invited to attend his private classes, but also that he did not receive a regular student stipend.

Movahhed (Mov 53) speculates that Khoᵓi did not want to take on someone with Shams-e Tabrizi's unpredictable nature as a close disciple. Perhaps Shams realized his character was too iconoclastic to make a living as a jurist, but perhaps he nevertheless expected something more than ordinary public lectures on Islamic law. Shams pressed Khoʾi to find out why he was not teaching him much (Maq 221):

> I separated from Qâzi Shams al-Din because he wasn't teaching me. He said, "I can't be ashamed before God. God has created you good just as you are and I can't make the creatures of God ugly. I see a jewel most noble and I can't write upon that jewel."

Of course, this may simply have been a way of letting Shams down lightly, for another comment by Shams-e Tabriz seems to indicate that Khoʾi did not want him as a pupil (Maq 831):

> That Qâzi of Damascus, Shams al-Din Khoʾi, if I had given myself to him, his career would have been good to the end of his life, but I dissimulated and he was fooled by it. Beware the day when I begin to dissimulate!

Failing to gain entry to the inner circle of Khoʾi's private disciples, Shams-e Tabriz decided to go to work. When Shams announced his decision, Khoʾi asked him (Maq 241):

> "But is this what I have taught you?" I said, "No, I'll do some little job." He said, "My son, do you know how to work with all your contemplation and delicate disposition?" He would point me out to the legal scholars saying, "Look at him! With such spiritual attainment and majesty, he works."

THE MYSTICAL TEACHERS OF SHAMS

While still a boy, Shams kept company with a passionately spiritual master (*yâr-e garm-hâl*), who would twirl him around in meditative dance (*samâ*). In the hands of this master, he felt like a captive bird or like a piece of bread being torn up and devoured by the hands of a stout youth who had not eaten for two or three days, his eyes two bowls of blood in anticipation of the meal. But Shams was still raw. "Put him off to the side until he catches fire himself" (Maq 677).

Sepahsâlâr says nothing of Shams' mystical mentors. Aflâki only mentions a **Shaykh Abu Bakr Sallebâf of Tabriz**, to whom Shams was "in the beginning" a disciple. After training with him for some time, Shams wished to gain greater perfection and so went on a journey to "visit several saints and holy men" (*abdâl va aqtâb*, Af 615). For this information, Aflâki apparently relied upon the *Maqâlât*, which describes this *pir*, or "wise elder" – Pir-e Sallebâf – as one who spent his time with the dispossessed. Movahhed (Mov 62) feels that Sallebâf's students must have belonged primarily to the urban working class, which often formed youth gangs with their own code of honor (*fotovvat*). Whenever a government official came to visit Sallebâf, his followers exaggerated a hundredfold the customary deference shown toward their master, effectively thumbing their noses at the government official, who would in other circles have been accorded a respect equal to that of the shaykh. In any case, it does not seem as if Sallebâf indulged in the ceremonial rituals of many Sufi orders; Shams indicates (Maq 756) that Sallebâf was not in the habit of bestowing honorary cloaks (*kherqe*) on his disciples.

Pir-e Sallebâf is not mentioned much in other sources. The sixteenth-century text *Rowzat al-jenân* begins by telling us that Sallebâf mentored Shams-e Tabriz, at which point the usual late and suspect legends about the teachers of Shams and Rumi are trotted out (RaJ 1:291). This leads to a brief discourse on the meaning of mentor and disciple (*morid o morâd*), followed by a quotation from the *Bustân* of Sa'di about a precious saint of Tabriz, which, so we are told, refers to Abu Bakr-e Sallebâf (RaJ 1:293). The author tries to disguise the fact that he has no further information on Sallebâf by giving general anecdotes from the Prophet and various unnamed Sufis (RaJ 1:294–6). Pir-e Sallebâf would have been contemporary with the "seventy saints" of Tabriz, but he is not included among them in the list given by Hosayn-e Karbalâʾi (RaJ 1:49–50). Pir-e Sallebâf apparently headed his own Sufi lodge in the Charandâb district of Tabriz, to the west of the shrine of Imam Hafade (d. 1175), whereas the seventy elders of Tabriz were attached to Bâbâ Hasan Vali, whose shrine and lodge were in the Sorkhâb district.

THE WESTWARD COURSE OF SHAMS

Aflâki's accounts indicate that after leaving Tabriz Shams traveled through Baghdad, Damascus, Aleppo, Kayseri, Aqsaray, Sivas, Erzerum and Erzincan. Sepahsâlâr gives no such specifics, but confirms that Shams traveled hidden from the people, not claiming a station for himself (Sep 123):

> Before the time of his holiness our lord [Rumi], no creature was apprised of his [Shams'] state and even now no one will ever comprehend the truths of his mysteries. He constantly hid his miracles and cloaked himself from the people. He acted and dressed like merchants. Everywhere he visited, he stayed in the caravanserais and put a huge lock on his door, though on the inside there was nothing but a straw mat.

In those days, one's choice of lodging was determined by occupation and social class. The caravanserais were largely for merchants, whereas scholars would be put up at a legal college (*madrase*), judges would be invited to stay in the home of a judge, and Sufis would stay in a dervish lodge. Dervish lodges generally provided free hospitality, but in the caravanserais Shams would have had to pay for room and board (Mov 68). Even though he ate little (Af 629, 689) and would often go without food for several days (Maq 626, 776), Shams needed a source of income. He would teach children to read the Koran (Maq 291, 729) and had even developed a method for teaching the whole Koran in three months (Maq 340, 343). But when he did not plan to stay very long in a place, he would weave trouser ties to make his expenses (Sep 123; Af 690). Aflâki and Sepahsâlâr (Sep 125) both indicate that in his youth Shams would go incognito to do construction work (*mashshâqi*, Mov 69). Shams says that in Erzincan he tried to do construction work (*fâ'eli*), but owing to his excessively frugal eating habits, he appeared too frail for hard labor and no one would hire him (Maq 278).

Many Sufis came from working-class, artisan or merchant families, as confirmed by their names: Khayr-e Nassâj (the Weaver), Bu Bakr-e Kattâni (the Flax Weaver), Mohammad 'Ali-ye Qassâb (the Butcher), Farid al-Din 'Attâr (the Apothecary) or, as in the case of Shams' teacher, Abu Bakr-e Sallebâf (the Wicker-Worker). As such, they opposed the practice of begging, and probably felt manual labor more honest than administrative jobs and government posts. Then as now, primary education was an unheralded profession, and Shams at one point tells Shaykh Ebrâhim, one of the early followers of Bahâ al-Din and Rumi: "You used to come to the middle school (*kottâb*) and saw me as [a mere] teacher (*mo'allemi*). But how often an unknown person does us a service" (Maq 729).

SHAMS' ENCOUNTERS

Shams probably spent much of his life wandering from place to place and sitting in on the lectures of famous teachers, most of whom he found disappointing in one respect or another. Jâmi, who does not specify any source and seems rather noncommittal about the information, relates that according to some reports, **Abu al-Ghanâ'em Mohammad Rokn al-Din Sajjâsi** (d. after 1209) had been a teacher of Shams-e Tabrizi (JNO 464). Sajjâsi (and not Sanjâbi, as Dowlatshâh [Dow 217] erroneously records his name) directed a Sufi lodge called Rebât-e Daraje on the western bank of the Tigris river in Baghdad. This lodge had been built by Sharaf al-Dowle 'Ali b. Hasan, whose father was the vizier of the Abbasid caliph al-Mostarshed be Allâh (r. 1118–35). Rokn al-Din was in Mecca in 1193 (Owh 16–18), but the young Shams, who, Aflâki and Sepahsâlâr (Sep 123) tell us, spent time in Baghdad, could have met him there sometime after his return, when Shams would probably have been in his teens or twenties.

Shams does not mention Rokn al-Din Sajjâsi in his *Maqâlât*, but he does mention one of Rokn al-Din's disciples (Owhad al-Din Kermâni) and one of his teachers, Abu Najib 'Abd al-Qâher Sohravardi (1097–c. 1168), the founder of the Sohravardi order. Shams tells two anecdotes he heard about this Abu Najib Sohravardi (Maq 178, 367). As his successor at the head of the Sohravardiye movement Abu Najib Sohravardi designated Qotb al-Din Abhari (1107–81), who, in turn, designated his principal disciple, Rokn al-Din Sajjâsi, to succeed him at the Daraje lodge in Baghdad. Qotb al-Din died in Baghdad well before Shams could have arrived there, but he came from the village of Abhar in Azerbaijan and may therefore have enjoyed a reputation in Tabriz, in which case Shams may have deliberately set out to find his disciples. Since Shams did know Sajjâsi's pupil and successor Owhad al-Din Kermâni, we cannot rule out that Shams also frequented Sajjâsi's circle at some point.

Jâmi (JNO 464) also dutifully reports having heard or read claims naming Bâbâ Kamâl Jondi, a disciple of Najm al-Din Kobrâ and Bâbâ Faraj-e Tabrizi, as a teacher of Shams. It seems quite likely, however, that Shams would have mentioned Jondi or Bâbâ Faraj in his *Maqâlât* if he had spent any time with them or if they had left any lasting impression upon him. As we have already seen, Shams makes a disparaging remark about Najm al-Din (see "Rumi as Kobravi?" in the introduction for a discussion of this question).

Shams himself confirms an encounter with a scholastic theologian, **Asad al-Din Motakallem**, who resided, according to Aflâki (673), in Sivas in Anatolia (Maq 294–5):

> One day Asad-e Motakallem was commenting on the verse "And He is with you wherever you are." Despite his learning, he'd get all out of sorts when I would ask something in public. I asked him, "When you say 'And He is with you' – in what way is God with you?"
>
> He said, "You pipsqueak, what do you mean by asking this question?" As he was in forbearance, so he was in anger and would explode.
>
> I replied, "You're a tongue-tied dog with a bad habit of harassing people. How do you explain the meaning of 'He is with you?' How is God with a servant?"
>
> He said, "God is, indeed, with a servant in knowledge."
>
> I said, "Knowledge is not separate from God's essence; no attribute is separate from His essence."
>
> He said, "You are asking old questions."
>
> I said, "What do you mean, 'old.' It's dying of newness. This is what people call a scholastic these days?!"

Shams also calls Asad "unjust" in his denunciations of **Shehâb al-Din Sohravardi** (Maq 297), the great Illuminationist philosopher. Elsewhere he defends Sohravardi from the "dogs" who accused him of blasphemy (Maq 275). Shams probably did not meet Sohravardi, who was executed in Aleppo in 1191, but his teachings obviously created a great deal of discussion and controversy in Shams' day. Shams (Maq 296) says that Sohravardi had wanted to remove gold and silver as a means of commercial exchange, as they were the root of all evil. This idea must have appealed to Shams, who considers this Shehâb al-Din Sohravardi, the philosopher, superior to his townsman, Abu Najib Sohravardi, the Sufi (Maq 297, Mov 90), though Shams does confirm the judgment shared by many others[3] that the philosopher's knowledge was greater than his reason (Maq 297).

Shams also tells of his encounters with another philosopher, "the sage" **Shehâb-e Harive**, who strongly believed reason to be an unerring guide, whereas revelation, miracles and the Resurrection were irrational, useful only to the common folk (Maq 82, 118). As such, this Shehâb-e Harive was a materialist (*dahri*) and an unbeliever (*kâfer*), but this did not get in they way of their mutual affection, perhaps because Shams admired his retiring and ascetic behavior (Maq 271). Shehâb saw death as release from suffering (Maq 286, 678) and eschewed companionship with most people as burdensome, but he enjoyed the company of Shams (Maq 271), who had a similar temperament. The followers of Shehâb-e Harive believed in him as a "philosopher" who knew everything; while Shams denies this, he does allow that Shehâb was a philosopher knowledgeable about many things (Maq 658). Shams always remembered him in amiable terms, saying of him "he was a pleasant little infidel, Shehâb" (Maq 697) and "that Shehâb, though he spoke blasphemy, was pure and spiritual" (Maq 225). Shehâb-e Harive's family came from Herat, but he himself had lived in Nayshâpur, in eastern Iran, before coming to Damascus, where Shams met him (Mov 84–7).

The *Maqâlât-e Shams* refers to a certain **Shaykh Mohammad**, an astonishing man (*shegarf mardi*) with an amazing personality, a great rope in comparison with whom the other famous people of the age were but individual strands. He was simpatico (*niku hamdard*) and wonderfully on the same wavelength (*niku mo᾿nes*) with Shams, whom he addressed as "brother" or "son" (Maq 299). This Shaykh Mohammad was also a friend of Shehâb-e Harive, whose death he foretold in a dream. Shams does not identify this individual by occupation, nor does he specify that Shaykh Mohammad had authored any books. The popularity of the name Mohammad makes it nearly impossible to know with certainty to whom it refers. It could refer to the Mohammad Rokn al-Din Sajjâsi we have already met. However, some manuscripts of Aflâki's *Manâqeb al-ârefin* quote brief portions from the *Maqâlât*, including one of the quotations ascribed in the *Maqâlât* to this Shaykh Mohammad (Maq 299). In recounting this conversation between Shams and Shaykh Mohammad, Aflâki (Af 676) specifically identifies him as "Shaykh Mohammad b. ᶜArabi in Damascus." Of course, the memory or suppositions of Aflâki and the Mevlevi disciples on matters such as this are not always accurate, but it does seem quite likely that Shams sought out the famous men of his age. In Damascus, few could have been more famous than Ibn ᶜArabi. For these reasons we would like to believe, along with Movahhed (Mov 100–103), that this Shaykh Mohammad is the famous mystical theosophist **Mohyi al-Din Ibn ᶜArabi** (d. 1240), author of the *Fotuhât-e makkiye* ("Meccan Revelations").[4]

Ibn ᶜArabi was born in Spain in 1165, probably about twenty years before the birth of Shams. Between 1202 and 1204, Ibn ᶜArabi was in Mecca, where he met Majd al-Din Eshâq, an Iranian associate of the Seljuk ruler of Konya, Ghiâs al-Din Kay Khosrow I. In 1210 Ibn ᶜArabi visited Konya, and when his friend Majd al-Din died, he married his widow, the mother of Sadr al-Din Qonyavi. This Sadr al-Din of Konya, a contemporary of Rumi, became Ibn ᶜArabi's greatest disciple, though Ibn ᶜArabi himself moved on to Damascus. Ibn ᶜArabi taught quite heterodox views and several times came under suspicion of heresy.

Shams learned much from this Shaykh Mohammad, though not as much as he learned from Rumi, primarily because Shams was not convinced of his sincerity (Maq 304–5):

> Many times Shaykh Mohammad would bow and prostrate in prayer and say, "I am the servant of the Shari'a-minded." But he did not follow [the Prophet]. I gained a great deal from him, but not as much as from you. How different the pearl from the pebble! Except that the disciples (*farzandân*) have not recognized you at all and this is very strange! But perhaps in the end they'll realize. You are not out to show yourself off to disciples or other. Some people try a thousand ways to show off something of themselves and some try a hundred subterfuges to conceal themselves.

Shams upbraids Shaykh Mohammad in one conversation for laying implicit claim to a station higher than the Prophet Mohammad. Shaykh Mohammad says that the Prophet was just his chamberlain (*parde-dâr*, one who controls access usually to a king or other royal figure seated behind a curtain) except that in this case the allusion of the veil or curtain also suggests that the Prophet Mohammad merely gave us a glimpse into the realm of divine secrets which Shaykh Mohammad occupies (Maq 299):

> As Shaykh Mohammad [b. 'Arabi in Damascus] would say, "Mohammad is our chamberlain!" I would say, "Why don't you see in Mohammad that which you see in yourself? Everyone is his own chamberlain." He said, "Where gnostic truth is concerned, what room is there for laying claims, or for saying do this and don't do that?" I said, "But that is true [only] for him [the Prophet], and these other qualities are secondary. Denying this to him and appropriating it [for yourself], is this not itself a claim? When you call me brother and son, is this not a kind of claim? So you lay claims for yourself while saying that one must not make claims!"
>
> He was very simpatico and a great companion. He was an astonishing man, Shaykh Mohammad, but he did not follow [the Prophet]. Someone said, "He was the essence of following" (*motâba'at*). I said, "No, he did not follow."

Shaykh Mohammad would often accuse other scholars or thinkers of mistakes, and so Shams would sometimes point out when Shaykh Mohammad erred himself (Maq 240; Af 677). On one occasion Shams mildly rebuked him with a rhetorical question about Hadith. When Shaykh Mohammad realized what Shams was up to, he said, "You're giving me a real lashing!" At the end of this exchange, Shaykh Mohammad addressed Shams as "my son," but began to laugh at the incongruity of addressing Shams as a shaykh would address a young man or a submissive disciple (Maq 240). Obviously Shams had something to teach him, too. Sometimes Shaykh Mohammad would give in to Shams' arguments, though this did not please Shams, as it was through this dialectical method that he learned (Maq 120).

Thus, though Shams shared the deep interest of the great shaykh in mystical speculation, and called him "a mountain [of a man], a mountain" (Maq 239), he faulted him for his failure to follow in the way of the Prophet and observe the law. That is why, though "Shaykh Mohammad was a seeker of truth," and desired for Shams to become his confidant, Shams did not accede, desiring instead to have this kind of relationship with Rumi. "Do you see, then, how high your station is?" Shams would later ask Rumi (Maq 144).

OWHAD AL-DIN KERMÂNI

The *Maqâlât* twice mentions **Owhad al-Din Kermâni** (d. c. 1238), a Turkish Sufi whose wondrous acts are described in *Manâqeb-e Owhad al-Din Kermâni*, a collection of tales collected by his disciples a generation or two after his death, probably between 1250 and 1300. As we have seen, Kermâni was a disciple of Rokn al-Din Sajjâsi and was therefore affiliated with the Sohravardi order. Kermâni, however, had a reputation for loving young boys. As Jâmi explains, "They say he relied upon outward forms to witness truth and used to gaze upon the beauty of the Absolute in contingent forms." His own followers describe (Owh 194) how on one occasion the shaykh was enjoying himself in *samâ* with a number of beautiful boys and, overwhelmed by ecstasy, they removed their turbans. A number of non-initiates were present on this occasion and they chid and denounced the shaykh for his proclivities. Other anecdotes show him overtly ogling handsome boys he came across in public (Owh 193, 212). According to some histories, Jâmi records that "when immersed in *samâ* he would tear open the shirts of pre-pubescent boys and put his chest up against theirs" (JNO 590). As a result of such behavior, we are told that Abu Najib Sohravardi did not allow Owhad al-Din into his gatherings, calling him a "deviant" (*mobtade*, JNO 589). This makes a nice story for Jâmi, but since Sohravardi died some seventy years prior to Owhad al-Din, if the incident described did indeed take place, it must have been someone else (Abu Hafs ʿOmar Sohravardi?) who called Owhad a deviant.

Iran was a country thoroughly Hellenized after the conquest by Alexander the Great and the contemplation of God through the visage of a beautiful boy (*shâhed*) can be seen as a survival of, or parallel to, the cult of the ephebe. We know that Sufis sometimes used the dervish cloak to hide antinomian behavior and libertine excess, for authors sympathetic to Sufism, such as Saʿdi, Owhadi of Marâghe and Ibn Jowzi all condemn it. Shams counsels the young Sultan Valad to avoid hashish and sodomy, two great vices apparently widespread among the Sufis (Af 633). Sepahsâlâr (Sep 25) reports that Rumi met Owhad al-Din Kermâni in Damascus. Rumi apparently formed an unfavorable opinion, if we can believe Aflâki (Af 439–40; cf. JNO 590), who reports that Rumi rejected the notion that Owhad loved the boys around him chastely and once said, "Shaykh Owhad al-Din left a bad legacy in the world."

A famous anecdote about Shams and Owhad is related in a number of sources (e.g., JNO 590). Aflâki (Af 616) describes it thus: in Baghdad Shams came up to Owhad, who was bent over a wash basin. Shams asked him what he was trying to do, and Owhad explained that he was looking at the moon in a tub of water. Shams famously retorted that "Unless you have a crick in your neck, why don't you look at it in the sky? Go get hold of a doctor to treat you." Jâmi gives a verse rendition of the same story, with the exception that it transpires in Damascus and involves the sun, not the moon (cited in Mov 97–8):

> Shams-e Tabriz saw that Owhad al-Din
> made gazing on idols his ritual creed
> (The passion to flirt stirred up circling clouds
> of seditious dust in Damascus)
> Shams brought his head down near the shaykh's and asked:
> Shaykh, in what state or vision are you now?
> He said: I gaze into the sun's center
> > only I see it in a tub of water.
> Shams said: Reflect, dear Shaykh, how blind you are
> > Look straight up, why do you avert your gaze?
> > Raise up your downcast head and heavenward
> > cast up your open eyes unto the sun.

Apart from these legendary anecdotes, the *Manâqeb* of Owhad (191, 265) records that Owhad al-Din had an exchange in the Battâl Mosque in Kayseri with a certain Kâmel-e Tabrizi ("the Complete Man from Tabriz"), a title which Aflâki (615, 634) tells us was sometimes applied to Shams. It has been argued by Ebrâhim Hakki Konyavi (Bay 151–2) that a pious endowment dated 1232 proves that Shams al-Din of Tabriz was residing in Kayseri in that year. Shams says that Owhad completed the first stage of spiritual development, the level of the drunkenness of passion, which is (ironically) similar to a Christian monk's aversion for the world (Maq 700). While the fancies of Owhad soared above the stages of ignorance and knowledge, they did not reach the heights of the unveiling of the eyes (Maq 217).

Several folks mentioned as successors of Owhad are also mentioned by Shams in the *Maqâlât*, from which it appears that Owhad was older than Shams. Shams did not, however, consider Owhad a fitting mentor (Maq 294, 218):

> Owhad al-Din told me, "How about if you come and stay with me?"
> I said "I'll bring a wine glass, one for me, one for you, and we'll circulate them round when everyone is gathered for *samâ*'!
> He said, "I can't do it."
> I said, "Then you are no match for my company. You must give up your disciples and the whole world for a chalice."

This anecdote illustrates how Shams must have acted with Rumi and why he found Rumi so congenial – because Rumi was willing to throw away his reputation for the spiritual companionship Shams provided.

But Owhad al-Din Kermâni and his circle did not impress Shams. Two of Owhad's disciples, Zayn al-Din Sadaqe and Shaykh ʿEmâd al-Din, were in Konya, where Zayn Sadaqe had attracted an unsophisticated group of female disciples to himself (Owh 184). Shams says, apparently referring to these two (Maq 82–3):

> The sweetness of faith is not such that it comes and then goes again. I saw Zayn Sadaqe had become foolish. If you let a racehorse loose into the fields it will get lost. As for ʿEmâd, he is better . . .

ʿEmâd may have been better, but other comments in the *Maqâlât* nevertheless belittle him; it would appear that ʿEmâd, for his own part, did not think much of Shams (Maq 331).

SHAMS' QUEST

Usually a Sufi *pir* would not let a neophyte travel far away, but once a disciple had completed his spiritual development (became *kâmel*), his repentance and ascetic exercises, absence from the presence of the shaykh was not harmful (Maq 144–5). The motivation for Shams' wanderings and his seeking out of the remarkable men of the age stems from his desire to find the companionship of a true saint (Maq 759–60):

> I implored God to allow me to mix with and be a companion with His friends (= saints, *owliâ-ye khwod*). I had a dream and was told, "We will make you a companion of a saint." I asked, "Where is this saint?" The next night I was told in a dream, "He is in Anatolia (Rum)." After some while I had another dream and was told, "It's not yet time. All things come in the fullness of time."

Shams claims for himself the status of an Ovaysi Sufi, one whose spiritual illumination comes not through a teacher, but directly from God (Maq 133–4):

> Everyone talks of his own shaykh. In a dream the Prophet, peace upon him, gave me a ceremonial cloak (*kherqe*), not the kind that will wear out and rip after a few days and fall in the bath house and be washed of dirt, but a cloak of converse (*sohbat*), not a converse that can be comprehended, but a converse that is not of yesterday, today or tomorrow.

As a result of this innate spiritual intuition, Shams does not easily submit to the authority of spiritual teachers (Maq 784):

> I've seen many special dervishes and spent time in their company; through what they say and through their behavior, the true ones are distinguishable from the impostors. My meek heart will not incline to them unless they are extremely praiseworthy and special, nor will this bird peck at every seed.

Instead, he tests those companions and friends in whom he perceives some spiritual gifts (Maq 219):

Whomever I love, I oppress. If he accepts it, I roll up like a ball in his lap. Faithfulness is something that you practice with a five-year-old child, so he will believe in and like you. But the real thing is oppression.

By this, Shams apparently intends that he refuses to act hypocritically, even for the sake of social convention (Maq 778):

If you live without hypocrisy (*nefâq*) for an instant, Muslims will no longer greet you with *salâm*. From the beginning to the end I tried to practice truthfulness without hypocrisy with the followers of the path.

This required someone with a similar commitment and disposition, and Shams therefore set out in search of someone after his own nature to be his spiritual companion (Maq 99, 219–20):

I can talk to myself. I can talk with anyone in whom I see myself . . .

I wanted someone of my own type to make into my *qeble* [the direction one faces in prayer] and turn to, for I had grown tired of myself. Do you understand what I mean by having grown tired of myself? Then, having turned into a *qeble*, he would understand and comprehend what I am saying.

Shams never found exactly the shaykh he was looking for, but he did come close to finding in Rumi the kind of spiritual companionship he desired (Maq 756):

Since leaving my hometown, I have not seen a single shaykh. Mowlânâ is a fitting shaykh, if he would agree, but he doesn't give out ceremonial cloaks (*kherqe*). If they come up to him and oblige him, saying, "Give me a *kherqe*, shave off my hair," he does so under duress. This is quite different from someone who says, "Come, be my disciple."

Shaykh Abu Bakr [Sallebâf] does not have the habit of giving *kherqe*s. I haven't found my shaykh. There is one for me, but I left my hometown in search of this and haven't found him. However, the world is never empty of a shaykh. He says that [true] shaykh bestows a *kherqe* without the recipient being aware, and grants dominion and then died [sic]. I didn't find my shaykh, not even a person who would not take offense when something is said about him . . . Even when someone has this quality, it is still a hundred-thousand-year-road to shaykh-hood.

I haven't found this either, except for Mowlânâ, whom I found possessed of this quality. It was on account of this quality that I returned from Aleppo to be in his company. Whereas, suppose they had told me, "Your father has risen from the grave in the desire to see you and is come to Tel Bâsher [30 kilometers outside Aleppo] to see you. Come see him before he dies again." I would have said, "Tell him, die, what can I do?" And I wouldn't have left Aleppo. But I came [to Konya, over 400 kilometers away] for that [quality of Rumi].

SHAMS IN THE ZENITH OF KONYA

Aflâki (Af 618) tells us the exact date of the arrival of Shams in Konya, which he probably copied from one of the manuscripts of the *Maqâlât-e Shams*, the earliest of which appear to have been written down while Shams was still alive. These manuscripts all agree that Shams arrived in Konya on a Saturday morning, the 26th of the month of Jumâdi II in the year A.H. 642. This date corresponds to November 29, 1244 in the Julian calendar, but that was a Tuesday according to universal calendar conversion charts. The 26th of Jumâdi II fell on a Saturday the following year, in 1245. Of course, the year (1244) or the day of the week (Saturday) may have been incorrectly remembered decades later when the "facts" were recorded, but owing to local variations in sighting the first quarter moon and marking the beginning of the calendar month, the date in Konya may not have been precisely aligned with universal calendars. In any case, as Movahhed notes (Mov 107), just as the Muslim era begins not with the birth or death or even initial preaching of the Prophet, but rather with his entrance to Medina, so, too, the era of Shams, whose year of birth and death are not known, begins with his entry to Konya.

In the *Maqâlât*, which seem to date primarily from the time when he was in Konya, Shams speaks of himself as an old man (Maq 734), and this accords with a tradition preserved by the Mevlevis that Shams was over sixty when he came to Konya (Mov 124). Upon arriving in town, Shams set up at the inn of the rice sellers according to Sepahsâlâr (Sep 126, who says Shams arrived in Konya at night), or, according to Aflâki (Af 86), at the inn of the sugar sellers, a discrepancy which Movahhed (Mov 107–8) resolves by suggesting that this inn had changed hands or names sometime in the interval between 1244 and the writing down of the accounts. Sepahsâlâr says they met at a little shop or pavilion (*dakke*) outside the inn, where the notables of the city would meet. Gölpınarlı says that there is no longer any sign of the location of this inn or the pavilion, but that in the past the place was known as Marj al-bahrayn (the plain wherein two seas surge together), an allusion to the Koran (K25:53 and 55:19) and the meeting of these two unfathomable sources of spiritual power. The followers of Rumi used to bring candles from his tomb at night and leave them at this location to commemorate their meeting (Mov 108).

SHAMS ILLUMINATES RUMI

Though most of the *Maqâlât* is in Persian, Shams describes his first meeting with Rumi and the words they exchanged in Arabic (Maq 685):

> The first thing I spoke about with him was this: How is it that Abâyazid did not need to follow [the example of the Prophet], and did not say "Glory be to Thee" or "We worship Thee?"
> And Rumi completely understood the full implications of the problem and where it came from and where it was leading to. It made him inebriated on account of his purity of spirit, for his spirit was pure and cleansed and it shone within him. I realized the sweetness of this question from his inebriation, though I had been previously unaware of its sweetness.

Just before this part in the narrative, Shams talks about his own gift for receiving divine promptings and praises Rumi as someone worthy of worship. Despite their mystical prowess, however, both Shams and Rumi follow the Prophet, unlike Bâyazid Bestâmi (d. 848 or 875). Shams returns again and again to this question of following (*motâba'at*) the Prophet, and the case of Bâyazid apparently provided a touchstone by which Shams could gauge the inner orientation of others and test whether a fancy for mystical speculation or indulgence in antinomian behavior outweighed a person's love and respect for the spiritual attainments of the Prophet.

According to one hadith, the Prophet Mohammad had cried out to God, "We have not worshiped Thee as it befits Thee, nor have we known Thee as it befits Thee," and also, "My heart is clouded over and I ask forgiveness of God seventy times every day." According to Sufi lore, on the other hand, Bâyazid in the throes of a state of mystical union with God had cried out "Glory be to Me," identifying himself with the Godhead in a way most Muslims felt to be blasphemous. Of course, Sufis had explained and understood this and similar statements as a genre of momentary and involuntary exclamation (*shathiât*) that might overtake a mystic at a particular transient moment of divine rapture. As such they were not to be construed as beliefs or claims, in which context they would have been blasphemous.

This type of apologetic was so commonplace among Sufis that we might be tempted to dismiss the question Shams posed to Rumi as simplistic. Indeed, scholars (FB 60) have objected that even the greenest Sufi recruit would have been able to answer such a question, and there is nothing spectacular in the answer which Aflâki reports Rumi to have given Shams (Zarrinkub, *Serr-e nay*, 1:100). But the question is indeed more complex. Not only did the conventional religious scholars brand such speech as heretical, but many Sufis could not so easily forgive the excesses of Bâyazid. Ibn Sâlem Basri, for example, accused Bâyazid of heresy and reportedly said, according to Abu Nasr Sarrâj's *Ketâb al-lomaᶜ* (Mov 115):

> What Bâyazid said, Pharaoh never said. If Pharaoh had said, "I am your lord on high," he meant lord to his people, as they say, lord of the house or lord of the land, whereas Bâyazid was saying "Glory to me" and glory is one of the special names of God on high that cannot be applied to anyone else.

When Hallâj was tried and executed in 922 for his statement "I am the Truth" (*anâ al-Haqq*), the outcry included a denunciation of the blasphemies of Bâyazid. Shebli and Jonayd both distanced themselves from Hallâj, claiming commitment to the principles of faith and reliance upon the Koran and the example of the Prophet (Sunna), even as they attempted to explain the statement away as the product of spiritual inebriation (*sokr*). Just as a drunken man is not responsible for what he may say, so a man intoxicated with God should not be held to account for his flights of fancy.

156

Yes, but one cannot follow God in drunkenness, Shams objected (Maq 690). Of the title "Emperor of Mystics" (*Soltân al-ʿârefin*) applied to Bâyazid, Shams poses the following questions (Maq 738–9):

> How can I call him "The Emperor of Mystics"? He's not even a prince! What about following Mohammad? What about following in form and in meaning? I mean, the same light and brightness of the eye of Mohammad should become the light of his eyes, Mohammad's eyes should become his eyes, and take on all his qualities.

Shams elsewhere states (Maq 690):

> He said, "We need a *zekr*" [a phrase, often one of the names of God, uttered repeatedly to focus meditative concentration] and he instructed that "It must be a *zekr* that does not hold one back from the one mentioned, and that is the *zekr* of the heart. The *zekr* of the tongue is of little account." Abâyazid wanted to express the *zekr* that was in his heart through his tongue. As he was drunk, he said, "Glory be to me." One cannot follow the Chosen One [Mohammad] in drunkenness. He is beyond drunkenness. In drunkenness one cannot follow with awareness. "Glory be to me" is fatalism (*jabr*). Everyone has sunk into fatalism.

From the mild manner of Shams' criticisms of various figures, it is evident that he did not like to denounce anyone as a heretic. On the other hand, it seems clear enough that he felt Sufis who were insufficiently committed to the law – and for Shams this would include Bâyazid, Owhad al-Din Kermâni and Ibn ʿArabi, among others – were not worthy of emulation as spiritual leaders. "It is not fitting to follow them" (Maq 131).

The concept of following (*motâbaʿat*) and obeying (*tâʿat*) can be traced back to the Koran, where it is often repeated; the very act of becoming a Muslim etymologically signifies one's submission (*taslim*) to the decrees or commands of God. In K2:38, for example, the verb "to follow" (*tabiʿa*) derives from the same root as *motâbaʿat*. "And when guidance comes to you from Me – the ones who follow My guidance will not be plagued by fear nor shall they grieve." Shams, however, did not understand by this a simple obedience or rote repetition. By following Mohammad, Shams meant following him on the mystic path, following in Mohammad's footsteps all the way on his ascent through the heavens (*meʿrâj*), past the previous prophets and into the sacred precincts of divinity. Shams is explicit about this: "Following Mohammad is this: he went on the *meʿrâj*, you too must follow in his footsteps" (Maq 645).

It is not that Shams wants us to follow a mundane, narrow and legalistic interpretation of the significance of Mohammad's message. Shams' own vision and temperament are those of the mystic and gnostic. Alluding to a hadith in which the Prophet says that his own hair turned gray with worry over complying with God's exhortation in the Koran to be steadfast in His commands (K11:111 and 42:15), Shams says (Maq 119):

Lovers [i.e., mystic lovers] know what a lover feels, especially those lovers who follow in his footsteps. If I show what real following is, it will make great men despair. Following means that one does not complain at [His] command, and [even] if he should complain, that he not abandon following. As the Messenger said, "The Sura of Hud has turned my hair gray." If you can say "the Sura of Hud turned my hair gray," then we will seat you next to him. One does not say "it turned my hair gray" except for a weighty matter. See how the Righteous Messenger cried out when "Be steadfast as you have been commanded" was revealed? Let's talk about what that cry meant.

So, when Shams detected an attitude of superiority to the law or to the Prophet, he could no longer trust that teacher as a spiritual guide, however gifted, intelligent or insightful this teacher might otherwise have been. This attitude was apparently epitomized for him in the person of Bâyazid of Bestâm, whom Shams repeatedly mentions in a negative light. Bâyazid reportedly was so concerned to follow the example of the Prophet that he refrained from eating melons because he never found any report describing how the Prophet had eaten melons. Despite this, Shams reserves for Bâyazid one of the most caustic things he has to say about anyone (Maq 741):

They say that (A)bâyazid did not eat melons. He explained, "I have never found out in what manner the Prophet, peace upon him, ate melon." But following [of the Prophet] is both superficial and meaningful. You have observed the superficial aspect of following, but how is it that you failed to observe the truth and meaning of following?

As the Chosen One [Mohammad], God's blessings upon him, says: "Glory to Thee, we have not worshiped Thee as it befits Thee." As he [Bâyazid] says, "Glory to me, how great is my station." If someone supposed his station to be greater than the station of the Chosen One, he is a real idiot and ignoramus.

Shams mentions Bâyazid in several other places in the *Maqâlât*, usually to show him as insufficiently humble, as in the story about a woman who unveils in front of him while he lectures and chides him when he objects to her behavior (Maq 702). Elsewhere he says that a hundred thousand Bâyazids would not reach the sandals of Moses (Maq 761), though he also quotes a positive anecdote in which Bâyazid plays down the importance of the miracles attributed to him (Maq 795).

All these negative comments about Bâyazid suggest that Rumi may have been favorably disposed to him. Apparently Shams' initial question about Bâyazid and the way that he posed it struck a chord with Rumi, perhaps even convinced Rumi of his own advantage over Bâyazid by virtue of his commitment to Mohammad. Shams searched long and hard and found none but Rumi who could tolerate his unhypocritical and unconventional pursuit of truth. None of the great men Shams had met had possessed a gnostic understanding of religion combined in equal measure with an intense love for the Prophet. Shams tells Rumi (Maq 723), "Abâyazid could not stand to converse with me, not for five days, not even for one day, not at all! Only one to whom my heart and affections are inclined [can stand this]!"

THE MAKING OF A MYTHICAL ENCOUNTER: LOVE AT FIRST SIGHT

Until the discovery and publication of the *Maqâlât* of Shams, we could only rely upon second- and third-hand accounts to reconstruct the first momentous meeting between Shams and Rumi. Let us compare the account of Shams in the *Maqâlât* with those of later sources. Sultan Valad may or may not have been present when Rumi and Shams first met, but in any case, he is not interested in worldly specifics, only in the transformation that takes place on the spiritual plane. Sultan Valad describes the meeting of Shams in the language of love poetry, with Rumi glimpsing the face of Shams when the veil was lifted, falling in love (by which he intends the Platonic love of a disciple for his teacher), and taking him home where they lived happily for a year or two before the disciples of Rumi began to act on their jealousy (SVE 42).

Sepahsâlâr (Sep 127) says that Shams and Rumi sat staring at one another for some time before Shams spoke to him. Shams asks Rumi about two contradictory reports about Bâyazid. On the one hand, Bâyazid was so insistent on following the example of the Holy Messenger that he refused to eat melons because there was no record in any of the biographical information about the Prophet indicating if or how he had eaten them. On the other hand, Bâyazid says "Glory to me, how great is my station" and "Within my cloak there is naught but God," whereas the Prophet, despite the grandeur of his station, said "Seventy times every day I ask forgiveness at the threshold of the Lord."

Aflâki (Af 619), apparently following the oral accounts current among the Mevlevi disciples in his day, comes up with a more embellished version:

> It is related by the great companions that one day his holiness Mowlânâ had come out of the Cotton Sellers School in the company of a group of learned men and was passing by the Shekar-rizân (Sugar Sprinklers') Inn. His holiness Mowlânâ Shams al-Din got up and came forward and took the reins of Mowlânâ's mount, saying, "O leader of the Muslims! Was Abâyazid greater or Mohammad?"
>
> Mowlânâ indicated that: "At the awesomeness of that question it seemed that the seven heavens split apart from one another and fell to the earth and a great conflagration rose within me and engulfed my skull and I saw smoke rising up to the throne." Rumi replied, "His holiness Mohammad, the Messenger of God, was the greatest of all creatures. Bâyazid is not in the same category."
>
> He [Shams] replied, "Then how do you explain that with all his grandeur, he would say 'We have not known the truth of Thee,' whereas Abâyazid says, 'Glory to me, how great is my station and I am the kings of kings?'"

Aflâki (Af 619–20) has Rumi reply that Bâyazid journeyed to a point where he lost control of himself and stared dumfounded at the grandeur of it all, whereas the

Prophet never stopped progressing, climbing seventy rungs of the ladder of perfection every day, looking down at the previous one and asking forgiveness. After hearing this reply, "Shams shouted out and fell down. His holiness Mowlânâ ... directed that he should be picked up and carried to the school of Mowlânâ."

The famous traveler Ibn Battûta (1304–69) came to Konya in 1323 – about sixty years after the death of Rumi and twenty years after the death of Sultan Valad. He speaks of the Mevlevis and the shrine of Rumi, and relates the following story of the "Poet–Shaykh" (Bat 294):

> It is said that in the beginning he [Rumi] was a legal professor (*faqih^an modarres^an*). Seminary students would gather around him in his college in Konya. One day a man selling halva, carrying a tray of it on his head, entered the college. The halva was cut into pieces and he would sell each piece for a penny. When he came upon the class (*majles al-tadris*), the Shaykh [Rumi] told him, "Bring your tray here." The confectioner picked up a piece of it and gave it to the Shaykh, which the Shaykh took in his hand and ate. The confectioner fed no halva to anyone else and left the college. The Shaykh, too, went following after him and left off teaching. A long time passed and when the students could wait no longer they went in search of him, but could not find him anywhere.
>
> Then, after a few years, he returned to them, but he wouldn't speak except to utter incomprehensible Persian poetry in couplet form. His students followed him around writing down his poems and collected them into a book called the *Masnavi*. The people in these parts hold this book in great respect, revere its words and teach it. They recite it aloud in their Sufi lodges on Friday nights.

A short while later, in *al-Javâher al-mozi'e* of Ibn Abi al-Vafâ (1297–1373),[5] the story has reached truly miraculous proportions. Rumi was sitting in his library with some books and his pupils gathered around him. Shams came along, greeted them, sat down and gesturing toward the books, asked: "What are these?" Rumi replied, "You wouldn't know." Before Rumi finished speaking, the books and the library caught on fire. "What's this?" cried Rumi. Shams retorted, "You wouldn't know either," and got up and left. Rumi got up, leaving his position and family behind, and followed after him, captivated and extemporizing poems, from city to city, but never caught up with him again (FB 57).

Jâmi, Amin Ahmad Râzi and Âzar all tell a version of this mythical encounter, but substitute water for fire. Rumi was sitting near a garden pool with a few books when Shams arrived and asked, "What's this?" Rumi replied, "These are called debates, but you needn't bother with them." Shams touched them and threw them in the water. Rumi got upset at the ruin of these rare and precious books. Shams reached in the water and retrieved them one by one. Rumi saw that there was no trace of water damage on them. "What secret is this?" he asked. Shams replied, "This is spiritual inclination and entrancement, what would you know of it?" (see, e.g., JNO 467).

Dowlatshâh (Dow 217–18) says that Rumi was riding on a donkey when Shams suddenly jumped up and seized the reins to pose the question, "What is the purpose of self-abnegation and exercises of renunciation and the transmission and acquisition of knowledge?" Rumi replies, "It is the path of the Sunna and the custom of the Shariᶜa." Shams said, "That's only the outer semblance." Rumi asked, "What is beyond that?" Shams said, "Knowledge is for attaining the Known" and he quoted from Sanâ'i's *Divân*:

> Knowledge that takes you not beyond yourself –
> such knowledge is far worse than ignorance.

Rumi was amazed by this and fell before the great man and ceased his teaching.

THE MEETING BEFORE THE FIRST MEETING

In at least four places in the *Maqâlât*, Shams alludes to an interval of fifteen or sixteen years between the present and his first meeting with Rumi. He says in one place that his mission was to release Rumi: "They have sent me because that precious servant is caught in the company of crude people; it's a pity that they should squander him" (Maq 622). Shams alludes to fifteen years spent waiting in another place (Af 734), a period of separation he attributes to his own reclusiveness (Maq 290):

> I don't mix much with anyone. Even with one so great [*sadr*] that though you sift the whole world you won't find another like him, sixteen years passed during which I said only "hello" and he left.

Shams apparently heard Rumi lecture or at least discuss problems with other students at that period, for he tells us (Maq 690):

> The outward aspects vary, but the reality is one. I remember about Mowlânâ from sixteen years ago – he would say that creatures are just like clusters of grapes. The individual numbers are the outward aspect. When you squeeze them in a bowl, are there individual grapes?

It may have been in one of the joint Hanafi–Shâfeᶜi *madrases* of Damascus that Shams heard Rumi lecture or debate (Zia 248 n. 11).

Shams already perceived a special quality in Rumi, but felt he had not yet attained the level of spiritual maturity which would make him receptive to Shams. He tells Rumi (Maq 618–19):

> I was strongly inclined to you from the beginning, but I saw in the opening of your speech that at that time you were not ready for this secret. Even if I had told you, it would not have been destined at that time, and we would never have attained this present moment together, for at that time you didn't have this spiritual state.

During this time, however, Rumi had apparently not taken notice of Shams (Maq 763):

The quality of the one sought-after is that there is no sign of him in the world. All signs point to the seeker, not to the one sought-after . . . The one sought-after looks upon the face of the Friend for sixteen years so that the seeker, after fifteen years, will find him worthy of attention (ahl-e sokhan).

Sepahsâlâr and Sultan Valad make no mention of the earlier acquaintance of Shams and Rumi, but Aflâki does mention a brief encounter in the square of Damascus (Af 82, 618) at the time when Rumi was a student there. If so, this could have been a few years after the death of Bahâ al-Din, in about 1233 or so, after Borhân al-Din sent him to further his education. Fifteen or sixteen years prior to the first meeting in 1244 would however place this event as early as 1229. Movahhed (Mov 139) speculates that Shams even knew Bahâ al-Din and Sayyed Borhân from a distance, but that they were not aware of him, because he never spoke to them. Shams tells us, "I've talked with no one except Mowlânâ" (Maq 739).

THE RELATIONSHIP BETWEEN SHAMS AND RUMI

That Shams brought about a spiritual metamorphosis in Rumi we cannot begin to doubt, but the nature of their relationship transcended the traditional roles of master and disciple. If Rumi submitted to much of Shams' guidance, he was nevertheless an accomplished scholar and teacher in his own right, with a following of his own. Shams saw his own spirit reflected in Rumi, the most gifted and spiritualized scholar he had ever met. Had Rumi been a young man, he might have assumed the conventional role of disciple, but Shams, by his chiding and his praises, reveals the unique nature of their relationship. Shams complains of Rumi that "at times his extensive knowledge would come before him and get in the way" (Maq 361), or that he would continue to read the works of others for guidance and inspiration.

> This multi-talented scholar, well-versed in feqh and the principles and details of the law! These have no relationship to the path of God and the path of the Prophets. Rather, they cloak him from it. First he must become sick of these, though you wag your finger, saying "There is no God but God." He has achieved a detachment from that knowledge and has become like that little Russian [The Russians in Konya were poor and reduced to peddling, according to Mov 142] – he wears a pelt and puts a cone hat on his head and sells matches for a while, just like a slap in the face, so that a bit of his ego is lost and the path of being a Muslim becomes evident to him.
>
> One cannot say this to him, so one must dissemble. He is just right for mastership and discipleship, though there are a hundred thousand such Mowlânâs, whereas there is a path beyond master and discipleship. (Maq 778–9)
>
> I go everywhere alone, by myself and sit at every shop. I cannot bring him – a man who travels in the circle of the Mofti of the City – with me everywhere or into every shop. I stop in at every bath house. You know I have never acted

shaykh-like, unmindful of your station, and said "I'm going here whether you like it or not and if you are mine, you'll come with me." No, I do not demand whatever is difficult for you. (Maq 761)

I first came to Mowlânâ with the understanding that I would not be his shaykh. God has not yet brought into being on this earth one who could be Mowlânâ's shaykh; he would not be a mortal. But nor am I one to be a disciple. It's no longer in me. Now I come for friendship, relief. It must be such that I do not need to dissimulate (nefâq). Most of the prophets have dissimulated. Dissimulation is expressing something contrary to what is in your heart. (Maq 777)

In my presence, as he listens to me, he considers himself – I am ashamed to even say it – like a two-year-old child or like a new convert to Islam who knows nothing about it. Amazing submissiveness! (Maq 730)

I need it to be apparent how our life together is going to be. Is it brotherhood and friendship or shaykh-hood and discipleship? I don't like this. Teacher to pupil? (Maq 686)

As we have seen Rumi remarried after the death of Gowhar Khâtun, the mother of Sultan Valad and ʿAlâ al-Din. Of his second wife, the still young Kerrâ Khâtun, Shams says (Maq 661):

Do you not consider my entrance into this household? He even permitted his own wife in my company! Though he was jealous even of the Angel Gabriel looking upon her, she would sit before me just as a son sits at his father's foot until you give him a bit of bread.

Shams was himself a jealous companion (Maq 74):

The person who enters my company is distinguished by the fact that he loses his appetite for company with others and finds it bitter. Not such that he loses his appetite and yet continues to keep company with them, but in such wise that he cannot keep their company.

Shams tells Rumi that he must learn to practice mysticism, not just read about it: "You want to discover through learning; but it requires going and doing" (Maq 128). Shams boasts that his compelling answers to various conundrums eventually turned Rumi away from his book learning (Maq 186):

Whatever problem the people of this quarter pose, they find me with a ready answer for every one of their difficulties. My words provide answer upon compelling answer. For each one of their questions are ten answers and proofs, graceful and sweet, not recorded in any book. Mowlânâ says: "Since I have become acquainted with you these books have become lifeless in my eyes."

Shams engaged Rumi in debate so that together they could arrive at the truth. Sometimes Shams could be relentless and Rumi would tire of it or have to get on with other business, but Shams would persist (Maq 119–20).

It seems Shams abandoned Rumi as a deliberate part of guiding him to the next stage of spiritual development. Shams explains that his enforced separation from Rumi did not stem from disappointment, anger or a cooling of affection:

> I did not behave with you as I did with my own shaykh. I abandoned him in anger and I left. But he was saying, "I'm a shaykh." Mowlânâ was saying something else. (Maq 221–2)

> Well, how could I offend you? I am even fearful to kiss your feet, lest my lashes scratch them. (Maq 99–100)

> Union with you is most precious. Alas that life will not last. I wish I had a world full of gold to bestow upon union with you. (Maq 665)

Shams apparently saw in Rumi's intemperate kindness a fault or deficiency of sorts:

> Mowlânâ has a drunkenness in kindness but no soberness in kindness. But I have both drunkenness in kindness and soberness in kindness (*mahabbat*). I'm not subject to forgetting in drunkenness. (Maq 79)

> This Mowlânâ has said many times that he is more compassionate than me. He is truly drunk. If a person falls in dark water or in fire or in hell, he [Rumi] sits watching with his chin in his hand. He neither jumps in the water nor into the fire after this person, but just watches. I watch, too, but grab him by the tail, saying "O Brother, you too are falling in. Come out here with us, look on with us." It is such talk that pulls him out by the tail. (Maq 774)

Movahhed (Mov 145–51) sees three consecutive stages of development in Rumi based upon what Shams says about him at different times. The first is a raw Rumi, not yet empty of pride for his learning. At this point, according to Movahhed, Rumi is not sure to give in to everything Shams says, and continues to read the works of others. In the next stage of their relationship, Rumi becomes totally absorbed in Shams, but Shams tries to guide him out of this absorption back into the real world. This stage includes at least the initial separation from Rumi, but upon his return to Konya after his first disappearance, Shams sees Rumi as a perfect man in the making. In the first stage of this attainment of perfection, Rumi reflects the teachings and achievements of Shams to others, just as the moon reflects the light of the sun. This corresponds, in Movahhed's view, to the period of composition of the *Divân*. In the second stage, reflected in the *Masnavi*, Rumi attains a degree beyond even the ken of Shams, one which makes prophets and saints long to be in his company.

While Shams' comments about Rumi do reflect the entire range of attitudes outlined by Movahhed, we do not know that these statements were, in fact, made sequentially. Although it appears that the *Maqâlât* dates mostly from the time Shams spent in Konya, it is not possible, at least not yet, to periodize specific statements on the basis of internal evidence. Therefore, we have little way of knowing if they represent three stages of chronological development or merely reflect changes in mood or behavior from day to day and circumstance to circumstance, or perhaps the difference between public and private utterances.

Whatever the case may be, it is clear that Rumi was more than a simple disciple of Shams; at the same time he was a teacher, one in whom were combined virtues or achievements that Shams himself did not perhaps possess, like the gift of explaining mystical truths in common language to ordinary people: "I said openly to Mowlânâ in front of them that my words will not make them understand. 'You explain. I have not been charged by God on high to speak in such vulgar terms'" (Maq 732). But if Rumi can illumine the common people, that is only because he reflects the light which Shams shines upon him:

> Shall I speak without any hypocrisy or not? This Mowlânâ is like moonlight. The eye cannot take in the sun of my being, but it can take in the moon. The extreme brightness of the rays make the eye unable to tolerate the sun. The moon cannot reach the sun, unless the sun reaches out to the moon. (Maq 115)

> The sun faces Mowlânâ because Mowlânâ faces the sun. (Maq 720)

Rumi himself affirms and alludes to this reflection: "Shams-e Tabriz, through your sun we shine just like the moon" (D 1579); "Shams-e Tabriz is more famous than the sun – I who am Shams' neighbor am as famous as the moon" (D 1629). Elsewhere, Rumi compares himself to the shadows cast across all horizons by the light of Shams (D 1637).

Although Rumi sees himself as a reflection of Shams, Shams himself sees something even greater in Rumi, who is on a par with the saints and even the prophets:

> He has two ways of talking (sokhan): one public [nafâq, or possibly nefâq, cautious, dissimulation] and one heartfelt (râsti). As for the public one, the souls of all the saints and their collective spirit long to have found Mowlânâ and sat with him. And as for the heartfelt one, devoid of hypocrisy (nefâq), the spirit of the prophets long for it: "If only we had been in his time and been his companions and heard his words!" So don't you miss out now. Don't look to the first, but to this other thing, to which the spirit of the prophets looks with longing and regret. (Maq 104–5)

> The prophets rue not attaining his presence. (Maq 684)

> Seeing your face, by God, is a blessing! Anyone wishing to see the Prophet sent by God should look on Mowlânâ when he is at ease (bi-takallof), true to himself (bar raste), and not when he is standing on ceremony ... Happy the one who finds Mowlânâ! Who am I? One who found him. Happy am I! (Maq 749)

By God, I am deficient in knowing Mowlânâ. There is no hypocrisy or politesse or interpretation in these words; I am deficient in knowing him! Every day I realize something about his state and his deeds which I didn't know yesterday. Discover Mowlânâ better, so you do not later grow confused. "That is the Day of Disillusion" [(K64:9) *Yowm al-taghâbon* – the day of mutual disillusion, or Resurrection, because those who fancy themselves righteous will be punished and those who have been fearful of hell will attain paradise]. This handsome appearance and this fine speech he makes, don't be content with these, for beyond them there is something. Seek that out. (Maq 104)

I speak well and fine from a bright and illuminated mind. I was water boiling within myself and twisting and taking on qualities (*bu*), until the existence of Mowlânâ worked on me, and it began to flow. And now it flows pleasant, fresh and abundant. (Maq 142)

Shams describes Rumi as having attained the second of the four stages of development (Maq 700–701), the stage of drunkenness of the spirit. Although Sayyed Borhân al-Din had a greater sense for this stage, the most spiritually realized of all those Shams had known was Shaykh Abu Bakr (Sallebâf), who attained the drunkenness of God, but not the awareness that comes after it.

GAZING INTO THE SUN: RUMI'S VIEW OF SHAMS

Surprisingly, Rumi does not narrate many specifics about Shams either in the Discourses or the *Masnavi*, distilling everything instead into symbolic poetry. But Aflâki (Af 652) relates a report that Rumi had once said that he used to carry around a copy of his father's writings with him and frequently peruse it, but that Shams al-Din forbid him from doing so, and for some time Rumi minded him in this matter. One night Rumi dreamed that he was reading his father's *Ma'âref* and upon awaking, Shams came into the room to chastise him. Rumi protested that he had not looked at the book for some time, whereupon Shams began to relate Rumi's entire dream to him, and to point out that dreams are the expression of our waking thoughts. "Afterwards, so long as Shams al-Din was alive, I did not touch that book" (see also Af 623).

We have already seen some of the titles by which Sepahsâlâr and Rumi invoked Shams al-Din, the Sun of Faith. Titles with the suffix "al-Din" were often elaborated in encomiums or in the address of a letter, such that we find Shams al-Haqq va al-Din, the Sun of Truth and Faith. In the *Masnavi* and *Fihe mâ fih*, however, Rumi refers soberly to Shams al-Din Tabrizi or Shams-e Tabrizi, and once in the *Masnavi* to *Shaykh-e Din* (The Shaykh of the Faith). In one of his letters, Rumi calls Shams "Sultan of the poor, God magnify his strength." In one poem (D 898) Rumi asks Shams if he is a sorcerer. Shams laughs lightly and replies, "What would witchcraft accomplish? The mention of God works well enough."

Referring to the heroes of Sufism, Rumi once tells Shams, "You are my Zu al-Nun, Jonayd and Bâyazid" (D 1507); he is also the Pride of the Saints (*Fakhr-e owliâ*). Rumi variously invokes him as the Sun of the Age, the Pride of all Tribes, King of Truths and Mysteries, the Essence of the Essence of Faith, the Special Elite Mystery of God, a Divine Manifestation, Messenger of the Placeless, the Point of Eternal Spirit, the Light of Mohammad, the Verse of Insight, Absolute Spirit, and the Epitome of Existence ... (Mov 163, 176). In many poems Rumi also calls him *khodâvand,* or lord, even when it does not quite fit the meter.

Shams is "the Lord of the lord of the lords of truth" and "the Chief of the lord of lords." As in English, the Persian word for lord, *khodâvand,* means a temporal master, but also God. And indeed, in the poems from the *Divân,* Rumi depicts Shams as a divinity. In one place, Rumi calls Shams the point toward which he prays (D 1687). Readers familiar with classical Persian poetry know that such hyperbolic language is hardly unprecedented in courtly literature, but the repeated use of such phrases distinguishes Rumi's attitude toward Shams from all temporal objects of encomium. There was probably no precedent for addressing any person, other than the Prophets, in the following terms (D 1526):

> You are that light which told Moses:
> "I am God I am God I am God I am"

Shams is the Moses of the age (D 245), beyond the comprehension of Gabriel (D 117), the sanctified angel who revealed the Koran to Mohammad. Let us hear Rumi invoke Shams at length (D 1310):

> O mouthpiece of God
> Eye of truth
> Salvation of creatures from this seething ocean of fire!
>> How pre-eternal your mastery
>> How peerless your royalty!
>> deliverer of the soul
>> from attachment's travails
>
>> You swoop upon souls
>> walking the ways of sacrifice
>>> all of them dying to know
>>> whose soul is worthy to be game
>>>> For what creature can claim your love
>>>> when the Creator's glorious light
>>>> is in love with your beauty?
>
> What remedy can you recommend
> for me who am hunted down by love?
> I'm racked in love's convulsions,
>> my physician with power to heal

Your grace says approach
your wrath says withdraw
   let me know which of the two to obey

O Sun of souls
O Day-star of truth from Tabriz
   in each beam you radiate
  emanates a spirit,
      subtle
       eloquent

Rumi calls Shams to the Friday pulpit to recount his own attributes, but concludes that were he to do so, the pulpit would sprout wings and flutter in the air like Rumi's heart (D 2078). Even Rumi himself has been catapulted to a realm above the cherubim; by virtue of the love which Shams-e Tabrizi has lavished upon him, the holy spirit has became manifest within Rumi (D 1747). But whatever Rumi possesses, he has received from Shams (D 1754).

Shams and the spiritual revolution he brings about in Rumi produce a gushing torrent of words that pour forth from him as poetry. Rumi describes himself as impregnated by the spirit of Shams:

The lady of my thoughts gives constant birth
she's pregnant but with the light of your glory

                                       (D 2234)

Shams al-Haqq of Tabriz, my belly's pregnant with you
when will I see a child born by your fortune

                                       (D 2331)

You are my sky, I am the earth, dumbfounded:
what things you sprout from my heart each moment!
I'm parched earth, rain down on me drops of grace,
for your water makes the earth grow rosy
   What does the earth know what you sow in it?
   you made it pregnant, you know what it bears
   every atom pregnant with your mysteries –
   you make it writhe a while in pangs of birth
What marvels writhe to birth through the world-womb:
An *I am God*, the call *Glory to me*

                                       (D 3048)

My thoughts and reflections inspired by you,
as though I were your phrases and expression

                                       (D 1683)

In the following poem, Rumi describes the strange and wondrous transformation wrought by Shams (D 2789):

Before the candle
    that lights   the soul
                      the heart
              is like a moth
      In the flickering
      flame
of the beloved   the heart
           makes itself a home
A towering figure
      lion-taming
      drunk on love
      a revolution
           in the beloved's presence,
    sober,   on his own
      a madman
the shape of anger
the soul of peace
a bitter face of sugar
I've never seen in all the world such a sanguine stranger
A reservoir of rational insight
when he watches the candle
his feathers shrivel to his feet
he staggers like a drunkard
The crops in flames
on the outstretched plains of love
fiery: his wheat
a goblet: his soul.

Light would soak the world entire
    as once it did on Sinai's Mount
      if I reveal the ecstasy
      of my heart's fabliaux:
      Shall I call him candle,
            picture of love,
            heart-stealer,
            life-sustainer,
            pure spirit,
            tall statured,
            infidel,
            soul's beloved?
An old man stomping before his dais like a drunk –
but a sea of knowledge, a philosopher and sage
holding to the hem of knowledge with his teeth
but the smith's tongs of love
    having left him not a single tooth . . .
There I am, transfixed by this sage's light,

the old man completely absorbed in the beloved
He like a mirror's face, pure reflection
                        I, two-headed, like a comb
I grew old in that subtile old man's beauteous glory
I like a moth in him, he having in me a moth

I finally called out:
                Master of all beings in knowledge
                and of all the climes in art
                grant us of your grace an abode
He said:
                You who are farsighted
                    but closed of eye,
                I'll tell you. Heed this, the sure and
                august counsel of my heart:
                            My knowledge and knowing,
                            sagesse and wisdom and culture
            see how all of it is drowned
in the beauty
of one rosy-cheeked
    and priceless pearl

When I looked, what did I see
    but the ruin of the heart and soul?
                    O Muslims!
                        have mercy, a little aid and succor!

    You cloak your words in mystery; say it plain!
    Do not fear the jealous, tell true and manly who it was!
    That Tabrizi Sun of Truth and Faith, that Lord
    who turned this laggard by his love into a leader!

Rumi wants Shams to absolve him for his pride, as he depicts in this poem (D 2449):

    Before I wanted an audience to buy what I said
    Now I only want you to ransom me from my words
    I carved many an idol to deceive the folk
    Now I am drunk on the Abrahamic friend
    and am sick of the carver of idols [reading *âzarî*]
    A colorless imperceptible idol
    distracted my handiwork
        Go find another master
        for the gallery of idols
        I've sold the studio
        put aside suppositions
        learned the value of madness
        purified myself of speculations

> When some form comes before my eyes
> I yell at my heart: Get out, deceiver!
> and if it hesitates at all,
> I raze its foundations

The diametrically opposed emotions that Shams evokes in Rumi remind one of a Zen master both beckoning his disciple and shooing him away. Rumi describes the oxymoronic effects as being brought to life to be slain:

> Enemy of my prayers and fasting,
> my long life and happiness . . .
> hunted down, how can I fly
> slaughtered by you, what have I left to lose?

(D 1565)

> He said with a smile, go and give thanks
> I'll offer you up
> to celebrate the festival
> I asked for whom I am the sacrifice?
> and the friend said:
> you're mine, you're mine, all mine

(D 2114)

TO DANCE BENEATH A DIAMOND SKY, SILHOUETTED BY THE SUN

The encounter with Shams triggered the completion of a paradigm shift in Rumi's approach to piety and spirituality; he discovered that beyond the safe, dry and socially approved forms of obedience (prayer, sermonizing, discovering and applying the principles of law) and renunciation (fasting, controlling the passions and the ego), there is a meta-spirituality of love, which consists in joyously and creatively celebrating our relationship with God. Herein lay the difference between the monkish and the mystic Rumi; as Sultan Valad explains (SVE 53–5), the eyes of the mystic (*ʿâref*) are fixed upon God while the eyes of the ascete (*zâhed*) are fixed upon his own deeds. The man practicing spiritual poverty wonders what he should do; the gnostic waits to see what God will do. The gnostic has forgotten himself, or more properly, his self has been dissolved in God, for he combines both knowing (*ʿâref*) God and forsaking (*zâhed*) his self.

> Whether I go east or west
> or climb the sky,
> there is no sign of life
> until I see sign of you
>
> ❧ ❧ ❧
>
> I was the ascete of a country
> I held the pulpit
> Fate made my heart

171

fall in love and
follow after you

(from D 2152)

Sepahsâlâr (Sep 64) reports that Rumi followed the example of his father in preaching and practicing ascesis. Any act of worship or discipline which the Prophet Mohammad was reported to have accomplished, Rumi followed and imitated. He had, however, never practiced samâ^c before he met Shams, who directed him to participate in this form of physical and auditory meditation, for "whatever you are striving for will find increase in samâ^c." Shams, according to Sepahsâlâr (Sep 65), explained that samâ^c was forbidden in religious law because it increased the passions and lust of most people, but for the seekers and lovers of God, it only increased their focus of attention on the divinity and was therefore permissible to them.

Surely this is one of the things Rumi meant when he said that Shams set him on fire and burned away his books, his careful piety and his acts of propriety? We have already seen how Owhad al-Din Kermâni's practice of samâ^c implicated him in licentious acts. But once Shams taught Rumi the practice of samâ^c – moving the body in a meditative circular motion to the accompaniment of music and/or zekr (the chanting of a mantra) and/or poetry, Rumi followed his example and made samâ^c his own custom and practice. This paradigm shift allowed Rumi to participate in samâ^c, a method of ecstatic and therefore socially destabilizing worship which was considered morally suspect or even forbidden in many circles. Even when visitors of Rumi would rush up to and bump against him in samâ^c to express their devotion and receive blessings by kissing his hands or his hem, Rumi did not prevent them, although this behavior certainly exposed him to criticism (Fih 74):

> My disposition is such that I do not like a single heart to be offended by me. When a crowd of people brush up against me in samâ^c, some of my companions prevent them, but I don't like that. I have told them a hundred times, don't say anything to people on my account, it does not bother me.

Sultan Valad in the Entehâ nâme reiterates that before the arrival of Shams al-Din his father practiced the ways of obedience and renunciation. When Shams-e Din invited him to a samâ^c, Rumi came at his command (cited in GB 136–7):

> Samâ^c became his creed both true and straight
> from samâ^c a hundred flowers filled his heart

RUMI IN A WHIRL: A LYRICAL REVOLUTION

The hagiographical sources also link Rumi's career as poet to his practice of samâ^c. While he turned, he composed (Sep 65), and Aflâki gives the occasion of composition (perhaps more often than not purely imaginary) for many of his poems. But Rumi himself says:

> Since my heart amassed its store of love for you
> all that I owned but love for you is burnt
> My studied reason and my books he shelved;
> I now compose études of poetry

(D R606)

Sultan Valad, who would have been in his late teens in 1244, also attributes his father's composition of poetry to Shams, but seems to suggest that this happened only after Shams' final disappearance (SVE 53):

> The Shaykh grew mad in separation from him
> head- and heel-less in love, like Jonah in the whale.
> Through love, a fatwa-writing Shaykh turned poet
> though ascetic, he grew intoxicate
>   but not from a wine which is made of grapes –
>   a spirit of light drinks only wine of light

This is, however, an anachronism, for we find many poems evidently dating to the period of Shams' first disappearance, or to his return. But in telling an embellished story of his father twenty years after his death, Sultan Valad has obscured the minute facts for the sake of presenting the overall picture that Rumi took up poetry under the influence of Shams.

Foruzânfar accepted the traditions about Shams being the muse who first spurred Rumi to compose, but Movahhed (Mov 173) cannot quite believe that Rumi lacked all inclination for poetry before the advent of Shams. Rumi was well acquainted with al-Mutanabbî's Arabic verse (Af 623) and knew at least Sanâ'i and ʿAttâr through the writings and teachings of Borhân al-Din Mohaqqeq, if not through his own reading and study. But Rumi explains in one passage of the Discourses (Fih 74) that poetry was the most maligned of professions among his people and that had he remained in Khorasan, he would never have taken it up, remaining instead a conventional teacher, preacher, ascetic and author. He even claims that composing poetry was as disgusting to him as plunging one's hands into the guts of an animal. One does so not because he enjoys it, but because he knows his guests will enjoy the meal once the meat is cleaned and cooked:

> I compose poetry to entertain the friends who come to see me and save them from boredom. Otherwise what in God's name do I want with poetry? I am sick of poetry; nothing could be worse for me ... A man looks to see what goods the people of a given town need and will buy. That is what he buys and sells, even if it be the most despised of merchandise. I studied the learning of the day and took great pains to be able to offer precious, precise and wondrous things to the erudite, the clever and the seekers of truth who come before me. God Almighty willed thus. He gathered all that learning here and all the pains I took that I might be occupied with this task. What can I do?

173

We ought to take Rumi's explanation with a grain of salt, for one obviously must possess an inner disposition and inclination for poetry if one is to churn out more than fifty thousand lines of verse, much of it extemporaneously. Rumi no doubt possessed a gift for language and verse, but perhaps would not have pursued it had his scholarly prejudices against it not been burned away by Shams or had the social circumstances of preaching in Anatolia not warranted it. We may conclude that Shams freed Rumi from his conformity and his fear of opprobrium and opened up a way for him to reach the common people of Konya, who were not as yet fully schooled in Islam.

The Koran denounces the Arab poets as misled and immoral (K26:224–6) and emphasizes that the beautiful language of revelation was qualitatively different from the words of the poets (K36:69 and 69:41). Many of the piety-minded ulama of Islam therefore felt an aversion to poetry, particularly because the art of Arabic poetry flourished in the time of ignorance (*jâhiliye*) before the Prophet, and because the practice of poetry was associated with panegyrics for immoral kings and caliphs and the irreligious behavior (wine, women and song) prevalent at the royal courts. But the Prophet had been followed by a poet, Hassân b. Thâbit, who put his poetic talents at the service of Islam; to follow the Prophet, therefore, did not require a rejection of poetry altogether. This thought, combined with Rumi's growing detachment from the assumptions and prejudices of conventional Islamic piety and scholarship, and the psychic pain which the loss of Shams brought him, washed away his resistance to poetry and opened up a channel through which his creative talents could flow. As Sultan Valad (SVE 211–12) explains:

> A human being's essential characteristic is reflected in what he inclines toward or loves ... a person is known by what he eats, and there are two kinds of food: one physical, consisting of bread and meat and water and so forth, and the other mental, consisting of sciences and wisdom. Now some people incline to *feqh* and others to logic, some to scriptural exegesis and others to the poetry of ʿAttâr and Sanâʾi, God's mercy upon them, and still others to the poetry of Anvari and Zahir-e Fâryâbi and so forth. Anyone inclined to the poetry of Anvari or the other poets is a man of this world, ruled over by water and clay. Anyone inclined to the poetry of Sanâʾi and ʿAttâr and the bounties of Mowlânâ (God sanctify us through his precious spirit!), who was the pith of the pith, the best of the best and the cream of the thought of Sanâʾi and ʿAttâr, proves himself thereby a man of heart and one of the saints.

Sultan Valad also carefully distinguishes between the poetry of saints and worldly poetry, which suggests that even after Rumi's death the composition of poetry may have been looked down upon in certain circles of mystics and scholars. Sultan Valad (SVE 53) argues that the poetry of saints is nothing other than a gloss on the mysteries of the Koran, for the saints have effaced themselves and act only through God's inspiration, moving across the page like pens held in the hand of God. By way of contrast, the poetry of mere poets is a product of their own thoughts, fancies and distortions, composed for the purpose of drawing attention to their own skill and greatness. Worldly poets do not perceive the difference between poetry composed for the glorification of self and poetry composed for the glorification of God. The poetry of the saints is born of light in the world of joy; like Jesus, it can bring the dead to life (SVE 54).

Movahhed distinguishes two major stages in Rumi's composition, with the first decade devoted mostly to ghazals and quatrains and the subsequent years devoted to the *Masnavi*, which reflects a spiritual quietude which he attained only after achieving a catharsis over the loss of Shams (quoted Mov 173–4):

> At first when I began to compose poetry the motivation impelling me to do so was mighty. At that time it had its effects and now, when the motivation has slackened and faded, still it has its effects. It is the way of God on high to instill certain things as the sun rises, which shed much wisdom and bring about momentous effects. And during the setting of the sun, the things earlier instilled are still in place.

THE ECLIPSE OF SHAMS

THE GOSPEL ACCORDING TO SULTAN VALAD

In intense absorption, Rumi secluded himself with Shams and neglected his own disciples and students. Their jealousy, according to Sultan Valad, Aflâki and Sepahsâlâr, was the primary factor in Shams' departure. Sultan Valad (SVE 42) says that Rumi and Shams were together in peace for a year or two before the jealous began to spread rumors, asking why Rumi would ignore them for the like of Shams, who was not only inferior to Rumi, but even unequal to the least of themselves in standing. They did not know his origins or his lineage (SVE 43). His disciples, according to Sultan Valad's account, had seen Rumi perform miracles and regarded him as a "manifestation of God" (*mazhar-e Haqq*), on which account they had made him famous and won for him many disciples by bruiting about his deeds. Shams had come along and ruined their spiritual circle, blocking them from hearing Rumi's sermons.

> Who is this who stole our Shaykh from us
> just as a stream rushes off with straw?!
>   *   *   *
> Secluded him from all the folk such that
> we have seen neither hide nor hair of him?
> We see his face no more nor sit beside him
> He must be a sorcerer who's cast a spell
> with magic incantations on our Shaykh

> (SVE 43)

Here we come across the first hint of murderous intentions, with Sultan Valad describing their emotions toward him as bloodthirsty. Not only did some of these disciples curse Shams to his face, but they had sharpened their daggers and would have unsheathed them before his eyes. As Sultan Valad puts it in his poem: "All wondered when he would quit town or come to a wrathful end."

After Shams left town for Syria, Rumi was both grief stricken and doubtless furious with these disciples. Instead of resuming his teaching schedule or spending more time with his disciples, Rumi withdrew even further, according to Sultan Valad (SVE 46), who, however, is at poetic pains to mete out justice for the disciples' morally reprehensible behavior. Realizing the error of their ways, they repeatedly went before Rumi to repent (SVE 46–7) and finally assuaged his anger. Because of the special regard which Rumi had for his son, Sultan Valad, he entrusted him with a message for Shams in which he apologized profusely for the behavior of these disciples and promised that they had reformed their ways. And so Rumi sent Sultan Valad to Damascus to bring Shams back.

Sultan Valad convinced Shams to come back to Konya, and for the return journey, Shams invited Sultan Valad to ride on horseback. Sultan Valad refused, because, as he explains to us, he did not wish to claim equal station for himself, an exchange confirmed by Shams in references in the *Maqâlât*. Rumi was overjoyed at his arrival and all the doubters who had denied that Shams was the spiritual axis tearfully asked his forgiveness. Shams accepted their plea and all gathered around, with Rumi sitting at his side. They all held *samâ^c* and parties in celebration, and for some time all was well. Before long, however, most of them returned to their jealous ways (SVE 48–50).

When Shams discerned the coldness in their hearts, he told Sultan Valad that the disciples felt Shams unworthy of Rumi and wished to bar him from Rumi's presence (SVE 52):

> This time I'll disappear in such a way
> that none will know to where I've gone or am
> all will fail in their efforts to find me
> never will they detect the slightest clue
> many years will pass, me vanished in thin air
> as I draw out the time, someone will claim
> "Surely he was slain at some foe's hand."
> This he repeated several times for emphasis

THE GOSPEL ACCORDING TO SEPAHSÂLÂR

According to Sepahsâlâr (Sep 128), after Shams arrived in Konya, he and Rumi remained talking together in the room of Salâh al-Din Zarkub for six months, allowing in no one but Salâh al-Din. But we must have entered mythic time (*ille tempore*), as signaled by the emphatic assertion that during this extended period they took neither food nor drink nor responded to the call of nature! Finally, they emerged and Shams encouraged Rumi to participate in *samâ^c* ceremonies, by which means the truths and mysteries they had discussed would be expressed in the form of dance. After these sessions, Rumi would once again confine himself with Shams, and most of the students and companions of Rumi were therefore cut off from his presence, which they tolerated for some time in hopes that things would soon return to normal. As it became apparent that time would not heal this wound, they grew jealous and determined through the promptings of self to disobey their shaykh. They abused Shams (Sep 129), who tolerated the situation out of love for them, until things grew very drastic and he decided to sneak out of Konya when Rumi was not looking and head for Damascus.

For Shams' departure, Aflâki gives two different dates, which appear to reflect the corruption of a single traditional date. In one case (Af 88), he says that after the jealousy of the people of Konya – for whom Shams' origins and intentions remained unclear – had caused a rift and controversy, Shams disappeared on Thursday 21 Shavvâl 642. This would correspond to March 22, 1245, which, however, fell upon a Wednesday according to universal calendars. However, Aflâki elsewhere (Af 629–30) gives the year as A.H. 643, which he claims on the authority of Rumi, who dictated the information to Hosâm al-Din. Since it is given in Arabic, as though quoted precisely from a written source, we may presume this later date more accurate:

> The mighty master who calls us to what benefits us, the epitome of spirits, the mystery of the light and the glass of the lamp [K24:35], The Sun of Truth and Faith (Shams al-Haqq va al-Din), the hidden light of God in the beginning and in the end, may God lengthen his life and favor us with meeting him, departed on Thursday the 21st of the month of Shavvâl in the year 643.

This would correspond to March 11, 1246, which, however, is a Sunday according to calendar conversion programs, with the last quarter moon on the wane. The first phase of Shams' encounter with Rumi therefore began on November 29, 1244 and likely ended, after a stay of 468 days, or 15 months and 25 days, in Konya just before the arrival of spring and the Iranian New Year celebrations (Now Ruz) in the year 1246.

After Shams left, Rumi withdrew completely and secluded himself from his companions. This apparently caused a rift among them, with some of the disciples sorely grieved over the betrayal of their master and the pain it brought him (Sep 129). At some point Shams sent a letter to Rumi from Damascus, to which Rumi sent four replies in verse (Af 701–3), one of them the following poem (D 1760):

> By God, who was from pre-eternity
> living, knowing, powerful, self-subsisting;
> whose light set ablaze the candles of love
> revealing a myriad mysteries;
> who filled up the world by just one command
> with lovers and love, with ruler and ruled!

In the talismans of Shams-e Tabriz
the treasury of His wonders were concealed,
such that since the moment you departed
we've been stripped of sweetness and turned to wax –
consumed like candles, all night long we are
wedded to his flame, from his honey estranged;
In separation from his beauty, my
flesh is in ruins, my soul hoots like an owl
   Give those reins a shake in this direction
   lead joy's wild elephant here by its long trunk!
Without you present, *samâ*'s not lawful
like Satan, joy's pelted by piles of stones
Not a ghazal was composed in your absence
till your message arrived, ennobling me
The bliss of hearing your letter's music
parsed some five or six poems into verse
   May you end our darkness with your dawning,
   pride of Syria, Armence and Byzance!

Note that, if we take Rumi at his literal word here, the vast bulk of the poems mourning Shams' separation date from the period after his second disappearance.

It is also worth noting that Shams himself refers to Aleppo as the city of his exile, whereas Sultan Valad (and, doubtless following him, Aflâki and Sepahsâlâr) specify Damascus, a discrepancy which Gölpınarlı (GB 147) attempts to resolve with a manuscript variant from the *Maqâlât* of Shams. Gölpınarlı suggests that Shams may have come from Aleppo to meet Sultan Valad in Damascus, but if Shams were in Aleppo and Sultan Valad desired to bring him to Konya, it would have made far greater sense for Sultan Valad to come to Aleppo. For Shams to go to Damascus from Aleppo to meet Sultan Valad would have taken him 200 kilometers further away from Konya. Perhaps Shams withdrew from Konya to Aleppo but had planned to go to Damascus for a while, so that Sultan Valad set out to meet up with him there. On the other hand, Foruzânfar suggests there may have been two different trips of Shams to Syria, one to Damascus and one to Aleppo (FB 72 n. 3). In any case, the discrepancy between what Shams tells us and what we find in Sultan Valad, Aflâki and Sepahsâlâr reflects once again the impossibility of relying upon hagiographical sources for precise dates and facts.

In renewed bliss and expectation, Rumi once again took up musical meditation and showered his kindness on the group of disciples who had not taken part in the plot to uproot Shams while totally ignoring those involved in the machinations (Sep 129). Sepahsâlâr (129–30) appears to rely upon Sultan Valad for this part of the account, as he quotes the *Ebtedâ nâme*. In any case, finding themselves completely cut off, the plotters, too, eventually repented. All of Rumi's disciples then gathered together and appealed to Sultan Valad to head a delegation to Damascus to retrieve Shams. They provided him with expenses and a tribute of silver and gold coins for Shams, and Rumi himself added the poem quoted above. Sepahsâlâr (131) tells us that the search party arrived in Damascus and looked all around for a few days until they were able to find him, as he had once again hidden his spiritual station from the people. They bowed to him and kissed his hands and gave him the money and the letter from Rumi. Shams laughed sweetly and said: "Why do you try to bribe me with gold and silver? The request of our master, so like Mohammad in character, is enough. How could I transgress his word and suggestion?" (Sep 131–2).

Perhaps Rumi did try to bribe Shams to return, for he urges in one poem that his companions should go and drag back his friend: Bring me back that flighty idol by means of sweet songs, with golden excuses; drag that fair moon so sweet to see back to this house. If he promises to come in a while, all promises are tricks, he'll trick you (D 163).

For several days they held joyful *samâ'* and then headed back to Konya, with Sultan Valad walking alongside Shams' mount, because, as Sultan Valad explains, how could he, the servant, ride in the presence of such a king? When they arrived near Konya, Rumi and all the notables and dignitaries of the city came out to meet Shams. Shams praised Sultan Valad in the presence of Rumi for his selflessness and this greatly pleased Rumi (Sep 132), perhaps in part because the attitude of Sultan Valad and/or 'Alâ al-Din, Rumi's other son, toward the plot to exile Shams had been unclear.

KONYA FILLS AGAIN WITH THE WARMTH OF SHAMS

Gölpınarlı (GB 148), who gives no source, dates Shams' homecoming to Konya to May 8, 1247 (Muharram 645). Foruzânfar (FB 70 n. 3), however, estimates the date as sometime in April 1247 (Dhu al-hijja 644). On the other hand, Shams tells us that he took with him to Aleppo between 300 and 500 dirhams (he does not seem to recall exactly), and paid only 7 dirhams for the rent of his room. This sum was enough for him to live off of for about seven months (Maq 359). If Shams left Konya in March of 1246, and this passage from the *Maqâlât* indeed refers to Shams' first extended absence from Konya, seven or eight months later would bring us to October or November of 1246, though we cannot rule out that Shams then took up some kind of occupation to support himself for several additional months. In any case, whatever the exact date, parties were held in honor of Shams' return for several days (Sep 132), and it was probably at one of these occasions that Rumi recited lines like the following (D 633):

> My sun and moon has come, my ears and eyes have come
> those limbs of argent, that mine of gold has come!
> let ebriation fill my head and light my eyes –
> If there's anything else you like, that too has come!

179

That highwayman, breaker of repenting vows has come!
That Joseph with skin so fair, so sudden at my side!
Today beats yesterday, my friend of auld lang syne,
and yesterday I was drunk since news of you had come!
The one I sought for yesterday, lamp in hand
swept today like wildflowers straight into my hand! . . .

Sultan Valad in his *Entehâ nâme* explains that the notables of Konya and Rumi's disciples failed to discern Shams' greatness: We see nothing in him, how can he bring such a great one low? (GB 141–2). Rumi explains to his disciples in one lecture that there is no way for him to convince them of Shams' station or his worthiness of love (Fih 88):

> No lover can tell anyone the reason for the goodness of his beloved, nor can any sign be planted in the heart of the lover that would point towards the hatefulness of the beloved. So there is no place for proofs here; here one must be a seeker of love.

Shams, for his own part, realized that the displays of mirth and the disciples' protestations of love for him were motivated only by desperation (Maq 72):

> They felt jealous because they supposed, "If he were not here, Mowlânâ would be happy with us." Now [that I am back] he belongs to all. They gave it a try and things got worse, and they got no consolation from Mowlânâ. They lost even what they had, so that even the enmity (*havâ*, against Shams) that had swirled in their heads disappeared. And now they are happy and they show me honor and pray for me.

Movahhed (Mov 156) feels that Shams had disappeared as a calculated response to the companions' caviling, giving Rumi time to reflect and to decide between his love for Shams and his desire to please his disciples or preserve his reputation. We find Rumi (Fih 89) rather optimistically telling his disciples:

> This time you will find yourselves taking more pleasure in the words of Shams al-Din, for the sail of the ship of a man's being is his beliefs. When there is a sail, the wind will bear him to great places, but when there is no sail, talk is but wind.

Rumi had now chosen Shams over his disciples, and pledged his commitment come what may, steeling himself against their protestations (D 2179):

> Take love's chalice and on you go
> just choose this as your love and go
> Be limpid wine, pure as spirit
> unblurred by vinestalk scum, and flow
> One glance at him's worth scores of lives
> strike a bargain, sell your soul and go
> Such a body: argent, fluid, fine!
> pay the silver, close your purse, and go
> Let the whole world weep for you! So what?
> Look up at his smiling globe and go.

If they call you hypocrite, poseur,
Say "So I am, and ten times worse," and go
Thumb your nose at people, rub it in
suck the sugar of his lips and go –
    "The moon is mine, the rest is yours
    I need neither hearth nor home," you go
        Who is that moon?
            Lord of Tabriz, it's Shams, the Sun!
            Step into his regal shade
                                    let's go!

And if Sultan Valad had not himself gone to retrieve Shams, he most likely would not have returned (Maq 118):

> When I was in Aleppo, I was busy with prayers for Mowlânâ. I prayed a hundred prayers and brought things to mind that would increase my affection to the exclusion of things that would cool the affections, but I had no intention to come.

Rumi, like Shams, longed for frankness and freedom from conventional social formalities in his relations (Fih 89):

> How sweet it is when there are no formalities between lover and beloved. All these conventionalities are for strangers, [but for the lover and beloved], whatever is not love is forbidden to them.

WEANING: THE COST OF DISCIPLESHIP

It would appear that, though the advent of Shams caused major changes in Rumi's daily routine and in his relationship with his disciples, the state of hermetic seclusion that Sultan Valad and Sepahsâlâr depict is somewhat exaggerated. From an anecdote supplied by Aflâki (Af 121–2), it would appear that Rumi did not cease appearing in public altogether. At a meeting of the religious scholars of Konya held at the newly built *madrase* of Jalâl al-Din Qaratây, Shams al-Din sat all the way at the back of the crowd. Rumi, seated at the center of the gathering, was asked a philosophical question – "Where is the seat of honor?" Rumi replied that the seat of honor for the ulama was at the Sufis' bench, while the seat of honor for the gnostics was in a corner of the room, and the place of honor of the Sufis was beside the Sufis' bench; but in the school of lovers, the seat of honor was beside the beloved. And with this Rumi got up and went to sit beside Shams al-Din.

Another anecdote from Aflâki (683) has Shams seated outside the room of Rumi, controlling access to him. Shams would ask all the disciples requesting an audience with Rumi what they had brought in the way of tribute before deciding to admit them to his presence. One day a visitor demanded of Shams, "What tribute have you brought that you ask something of us?!" Shams replied that he had brought himself and sacrificed himself in the path of Rumi. This story has the ring of truth to it and certainly, if Shams acted as chamberlain or secretary to Rumi, such encounters would have been cause for great resentment.

Although the disciples caviled at Shams, both in private and in the open, it would appear that another factor also entered into his decision to leave. Aflâki (615) tells us that in Tabriz Shams was known as *Shams-e parande*, or Shams "the flier," by which Aflâki seems to understand that he traveled extensively or traveled by telekinesis (*tayy-e zamini ke dâshte*). Rather, we should understand by "flier," as Movahhed (81) points out, that Shams was considered a gnostic – *tayyâr* or bird – as opposed to an ascetic – *sayyâr* or traveler – a terminological distinction noted by Sarrâj in his *Ketâb al-lomaʿ* for the different kinds of wayfarers on the Sufi path. Sarrâj quotes Bâyazid Bestâmi as comparing the spiritual journey to the flight of the bird or soul, and ʿAttâr repeated this story in his "*Vitae* of the Saints," (*Tazkerat al-owliâ*). Rumi also seems to allude to this (M5:2189, 2191–2):

> The gnostic constant toward the King's throne arcs
> The ascete travels each month one day's road ...
> Love has a thousand feathers and each one
> soars over the throne beyond the Pleiades
> The fearful ascete charges on his feet
> Lovers fly lighter than lightning and air

Though Shams twice tells a story about a man suddenly seized by repentance who leaves his wife behind him to pursue a pilgrimage or spiritual quest (Maq 264, 228), we should not assume that Shams abandoned Rumi out of mere flightiness. Impromptu travel for travelers on the path of spiritual poverty was not uncommon, and cutting off from one's spiritual guide after a certain point was believed to bring one's potential and self-reliance to fruition. Shams seems to have wanted to separate from Rumi for similar reasons, but he could not send Rumi away, owing to Rumi's status as a teacher with a circle of disciples. Instead, Shams left Rumi. As Shams explained it after his initial return from Syria to Konya (Maq 163–4):

> It would be good if you can manage it so that I don't need to go away for the sake of your development, that this one journey I've made would suffice to reform you. I'm not in the position to order you to go on a journey, so it is I who will be obliged to go away for the sake of your development, for separation makes a person wise. In separation one asks himself, "Those exhortations and prohibitions were a small matter; why didn't I follow them? They were easy compared to the sufferings of separation"...
>
> I'd go away fifty times for your betterment. My going away is all for the sake of your development. Otherwise it makes no difference to me whether I'm in Anatolia or Syria, at the Kaaba or in Istanbul, except, of course, that separation matures and refines you.

Rumi also speaks of separation motivated by refinement in an Arabic ghazal (D 319):

I sleep and wake in love's afflictions
my heart turns on the spit of passion's fire
If you abandoned me to best refine me,
You are wise and I'm without you unrefined

     ❧   ❧   ❧

This absence would kill me the moment you left
if each day I did not expect to meet you.
I repent prayerfully, beseechingly
to my lord for my sins and shortcomings
   Tabriz radiates with my lord, Faith's Sun;
   I weep blood, choke on it, for what I've done.

FARE THEE WELL

If Rumi was beside himself with grief at Shams' departure, Shams apparently remained unfazed by their initial period of separation:

> If truly you cannot accompany me, I do not care. I was not bothered by separation from Mowlânâ, nor does union with him bring me pleasure. My pleasure comes from within me and my suffering comes from within me. Now, living with me is difficult. (Maq 757)

> When you [*shomâ* – Sultan Valad and others] came to Aleppo, did you see any change in my color? Even if it had been 100 years, it would have made no difference. (Mov 151, which incorrectly cites Maq 749)

Rumi's disciples, perhaps acting out of guilt for their role in separating their master from Shams and making him inconsolable, tried to cheer him with false hope of reported sightings of Shams. In the twentieth chapter of the Discourses (Fih 88), Rumi swears at those who claim to have seen Shams:

> These people say "We saw Shams al-Din Tabrizi. O Sir, we saw him!" You whore! Where did you see him? One who cannot see a camel on the roof says, "I saw the eye of a needle and I threaded it!"

The rebuke is repeated more elegantly in verse:

> He who claims to have seen Shams-e Din
> Ask him, where is the path to heaven?
> Don't go in that sea but by the sea's command!
> Aren't you afraid, where's your security?

>   (D 2186)

> Seeing Shams-e Din from afar?
>   the pride of Tabriz and envy of China!?
>   By God, not even Gabriel
>   the sacrosanct,
>   the trustworthy
> has heard word of him

>   (D 117)

After Shams' return, so Sepahsâlâr tells us (Sep 133), he and Rumi returned to their intense discussions. After some time Shams asked for the hand of Kimiâ, a pretty, demure girl who had been brought up in Rumi's household. Rumi accepted with delight and they were married in the winter (Sep 133), presumably then in November or December of 1247. Unfortunately, Kimiâ did not live long after the marriage. Apparently she went for a stroll in the garden without Shams' permission one day and upon returning fell ill and died (Af 641–2). Making Shams' entrance into the household even more difficult was the enmity of ʿAlâ al-Din, whose jealousy may have had any one of several causes: either because Shams had suggested that ʿAlâ al-Din might have something to learn from him, or because Sultan Valad received more praise and attention, or because ʿAlâ al-Din eventually hoped to take his father's place, but with Shams around, this proved impossible. Gölpınarlı suggests, on the basis of manuscripts of the *Maqâlât*, that Shams had threatened ʿAlâ al-Din (GB 149–50), quite possibly because the latter had never accepted Shams' presence. A group of Rumi's followers began to spread accusations that Shams had displaced ʿAlâ al-Din from his place of honor in his father's esteem and in his home. This situation was kept from Rumi, but Shams alluded to the situation in conversation with Sultan Valad and warned that this time he would disappear into thin air such that no one would find any trace of him (Sep 134; SVE 52).

Soon thereafter he did disappear; one morning Rumi came to the school and finding Shams' room empty, ran to wake up Sultan Valad, shouting for him to go look for his shaykh. Rumi composed many poems during the period of search that followed and cut off his association with all those who had plotted against Shams. Finally Rumi arranged to go with all of his close disciples to Damascus, where they remained for a while in search of Shams. Unsuccessful, they eventually returned (Sep 134).

Sultan Valad relates that Rumi undertook a second journey a few years later (SVE 61), apparently after he had already chosen Salâh al-Din as his successor (GB 163), and alludes to the period spent in Syria as lasting a few years and months (FB 87). The first journey in search of Shams must therefore have taken place sometime between his disappearance in late 1247 or early 1248, and the spring of 1249. Since Aflâki states that Rumi spent ten years with Salâh al-Din Zarkub, who died in 1258, even if Gölpınarlı is correct that the final journey in search of Shams took place after Rumi had already selected Salâh al-Din as his spiritual mirror, we may surmise that by 1250 or so, three years after Shams' disappearance, Rumi had given up on finding him again.

After this second search failed to turn up any sign of Shams, Rumi finally achieved a kind of catharsis. Sultan Valad tells us (SVE 61):

He said: Since I'm him, for what do I search?
I'm his mirror image and will speak myself

Alluding to a famous tradition of the Prophet, Rumi eventually found his mystic union not with Shams, but within himself:

Whoso has known himself has known God too
and knows all that the Prophets knew

Now it was time for Rumi to resume his role as teacher and author.

MURDER MOST FOUL?

As we have seen, Sultan Valad and Sepahsâlâr both report that Shams threatened to disappear forever from Konya. Both Sultan Valad, who wrote his account over a dozen years after the death of Rumi, and Sepahsâlâr, who wrote almost forty years after Rumi's passing, had been witnesses to the unfolding situation, yet neither of them mentions anything about murder. Rumi twice went looking for Shams in Syria, and contemplated going a third time, so he certainly could not have believed Shams had been murdered.

Nevertheless, the rumor of Shams' murder, started by Aflâki and perpetuated in other sources, has been gussied up in scholarly garb by Önder, Gölpınarlı and others relying upon the Turkish secondary sources, notably Schimmel (also Elias, in OxE, 77). Gölpınarlı (GB 155) places the "martyrdom" of Shams on December 5, 1247, but argues that Rumi did not discover the fact that Shams had been killed until many years later (GB 163–6; a tenuous argument based upon metaphorical allusions in the poems). According to this view, Rumi chose to keep this fact a secret. Sultan Valad and Sepahsâlâr, following Rumi's example, hushed the matter up, denying the "facts" to the end of their lives, even long after Rumi had died. What motive could they possibly have had to conceal this information?

Aflâki implicates Rumi's son, ʿAlâ al-Din (c. 1225–62), in the murder of Shams (Af 766) in the year 1247 (Af 686). At one point Aflâki quite implausibly relates that Rumi accepted Shams' murder with divine resignation (Af 684–5), quoting the Koran: He doeth what He willeth and commandeth as He pleaseth. Yet Aflâki (686, 766) also indicates that Rumi disowned ʿAlâ al-Din and that when the latter died after a fever and strange illness in 1262, Rumi neither attended his funeral nor performed the prayers for the dead. However, Aflâki's accounts reflect disagreement or confusion about this murder, as no one actually sees Shams die. Instead, after being wounded Shams miraculously disappears (Af 684), and so Aflâki reports on the disappearance (ghaybat) and concealment of Shams (estetâr), which he dates to "Thursday in the year A.H. 645," a date which might correspond to any time between May 9, 1247, the first Thursday of the year, and April 23, 1248.

Gölpınarlı derives his date for Shams' "martyrdom" (December 5, 1247/5 Shaʿbân 645) from a statement in Aflâki (641–2) to the effect that Shams once again set out for Damascus a week after the death of Kimiâ, in Shaᶜbân of 644. Though this would correspond to December 1246, Gölpınarlı (GB 155–6 n. 1) thinks that Aflâki, or a scribe who copied the text, has erred in writing the year, which should be 645, corresponding to December 1247. It is quite odd that Gölpınarlı finds no difficulty in Aflâki's explicit statement (which cannot be explained away as a scribal error) that Shams set out for Damascus at this date, that is, one week after the death of Kimiâ. Movahhed, on the other hand, takes Aflâki at his word and believes that Shams made a second trip to Damascus in Shaᶜbân 644, corresponding to sometime between mid-December 1246 and mid-January 1247.

Gölpınarlı suggests (GB 156) that ᶜAlâ al-Din may have blamed Shams for the death of Kimiâ, whom ᶜAlâ al-Din may have secretly loved, a theory which is, of course, extremely speculative. Gölpınarlı (GB 168) would like to submit Aflâki's testimony about Rumi's disownment of and non-appearance at ᶜAlâ al-Din's funeral as evidence that Rumi had by that time, fifteen years after the disappearance of Shams, learned of his murder. Though Rumi supposedly had a condemnatory verse from the *Masnavi* (2:335) inscribed on the gravestone of ᶜAlâ al-Din (Af 523), he felt that Shams had forgiven him in the other world. These stories have a typological flavor to them, and seem to be undercut by the fact that Sultan Valad wrote two quatrains in elegy over the death of his brother, ᶜAlâ al-Din (Mak 276). Furthermore, ᶜAlâ al-Din was buried (or at least a cenotaph was erected for him) in a spot of honor in the family plot in Rumi's shrine in Konya, near Bahâ al-Din and Salâh al-Din Zarkub (GB 237).

Beyond this, three of the surviving letters of Rumi (Mak 71–2; 92–4, 146) are addressed to ᶜAlâ al-Din, whom Rumi calls "My dear child," "Solace of the eyes," "Pride of the professors" (*modaressin*), "best of sons," and "beloved of those who turn to God" (*avvâbin*). This latter attribute does seem to hint at some family difficulty, for "those who turn to God" is used in the Koran in conjunction with the fidelity and patience exhibited by the Hebrew prophets, David, Solomon and Job (K38:17, 19, 30, 44), and those who "turn often unto God" receive God's forgiveness (K17:25). These letters most strongly urge ᶜAlâ al-Din to return to his house and his family from what appears to be a voluntary exile in response to accusations made against him. Rumi appears to have spoken to two government officials on behalf of ᶜAlâ al-Din, assures him of his love, prayers and concern, and seems quite pained by ᶜAlâ al-Din's absence. It would appear that they have a strained relationship, and that ᶜAlâ al-Din had indeed been involved in, or at least stood accused of some act, most likely a plot against Shams.

But what kind of a plot? Sepahsâlâr indicates clearly enough that ᶜAlâ al-Din plotted to get Shams to leave Konya, and such behavior against the wishes of his father would certainly give reason enough for estrangement. However, if Rumi had suspected his son of murdering Shams, it seems unlikely he would have forgiven him and asked him to return home, or that Sultan Valad would have elegized him in verse. Gölpınarlı (GB 168–9) agrees that the letters reveal a forgiving attitude toward ʿAlâ al-Din; if this is so, can we still credit Aflâki's claim that Rumi avoided ʿAlâ al-Din's funeral? That Rumi was at some point involved in the post-funeral arrangements is indicated by a letter written to Qâzi Serâj al-Din, who apparently acted as executor of ʿAlâ al-Din's will (Mak 101). This letter addresses itself only to generalities and a concern for Rumi's orphaned grandchildren, and provides little further information. But it seems far more likely that Rumi would forgive his son for a personality clash with Shams and for having tried to drive him out of town, than for killing him. Muslims in the medieval period did not look upon murder any more lightly than we do today, and we cannot assume that both Rumi and the legal authorities would blithely overlook a premeditated murder.[6]

NO WEAPON, NO BODY, NO MURDER

Let us, then, take a closer look at the reports Aflâki relates, which provide the basis for the accusation of murder. One must first note that Aflâki gives two contradictory versions. In the first, Shams and Rumi are sitting alone and there comes a knock at the door. Shams says, "They are calling me to my murder." He goes out and seven followers of Rumi all join together to stab him. Shams let out such a cry that all of them fell unconscious and when they came to, they saw only some drops of blood, but no sign of Shams (Af 684). Aflâki relates this on the authority of "the most accurate of accounts, that of Sultan Valad" (Af 683), though, as we have already seen, Sultan Valad makes no mention of this story nor does he state that Shams was murdered in his verse account of Rumi. Therefore, Aflâki is either relating something that Sultan Valad told him orally – in which case it is odd that he gives such a legendary and clearly miraculous account that contradicts his published version of the story in his *Ebtedâ nâme* – or Aflâki has received the information second-hand and is simply misinformed or deceived as to its source. I find this latter explanation far more believable. Indeed, when Aflâki later repeats the scenario in which Shams is wounded by attackers, he realizes that a murder cannot have taken place without a corpse, and so explains for us on rather dubious authority that "some of the companions are agreed that" Shams disappeared after he was wounded (Af 700). Jâmi, too, writing in 1478, repeats this story in his *Nafahât al-ons* (JNO 647).

Aflâki here (Af 700) goes on to explain that "some of the companions are agreed" that when Shams disappeared from amidst the conspirators who had wounded him, "some have related" that he was buried next to the elder Mowlânâ, Bahâ al-Din. This reflects substantial ignorance on the part of Aflâki's source(s), though, for any credible witness to the events which unfolded at the time of Shams' disappearance should have known very well who was buried next to Rumi's father, Bahâ al-Din. Gölpınarlı (GB 154–5), who has read the

187

inscriptions on the headstones in question in the Konya Mevlevi mausoleum, reports that Salâh al-Din Zarkub is buried to the left of Bahâ al-Din. The sarcophagus to the right has no inscription, but is reported to belong to Sepahsâlâr. Next to that is the grave of ʿAlâ al-Din Chelebi, the son of Rumi. The sarcophagus/cenotaph adjacent to this belongs to an Amir Shams al-Din Yahyâ b. Mohammad Shâh, who died on 7 Rabiʿ II 692, or March 17, 1293, according to the inscription. This Amir Shams al-Din Yahyâ was apparently the son of Rumi's second wife, Kerrâ Khâtun, by her previous marriage, and therefore the stepson of Rumi and half-brother to two of his children (GB 154–5 n. 2).

This confusion of Amir Shams al-Din, deceased in 1293, with the famous Shams al-Din Tabrizi, a dervish who disappeared in 1248, shows just how unreliable and uninformed were the rumors and legends circulating among the Mevlevis only a generation after the death of Rumi. Aflâki, who rarely exercises any critical acumen in evaluating the reliability of the anecdotes he relates, as usual refrains from passing judgment on this report. This Amir Shams al-Din had died only a generation or so before Aflâki began writing down his *Manâqeb al-ʿârefin*, and one would suppose that Aflâki should have known better, or that he might read the gravestone and refute this report. Perhaps Aflâki did not wish to offend the sources who reported this to him by debunking the idea, or perhaps he was himself unable to decipher the inscription. More likely, though, as a hagiographer he was simply not interested in verifying information as factual or legendary.

Although Aflâki does not explicitly reject this report, he does appear to favor a different one, which came to him from his own spiritual mentor, Ulu ʿÂref Chelebi. Ulu ʿÂref Chelebi heard from his mother, Fâteme Khâtun, the wife of Sultan Valad, that Shams was thrown in a well after he was killed. One night Shams came to Sultan Valad in a dream and told him "I am laid to rest in such and such a place." Sultan Valad "in the middle of the night gathered the close disciples and retrieved the blessed body" and washed it with rosewater and musk and then "buried him in the college of Mowlânâ next to the builder of the school, Amir Badr al-Din Gohartâsh." Though the account does not specify when Sultan Valad had this dream, we are left to infer that it was relatively soon after the supposed murder. Aflâki concludes this account by confiding in us that this is a secret of which not all are apprised (Af 700–701), an indication that he himself believes it.

While Fâteme Khâtun – the wife of Sultan Valad and mother of Ulu ʿÂref Chelebi – probably was present in Konya when Shams disappeared, by the time she told this account to Ulu ʿÂref Chelebi, born in 1272, at least thirty years had gone by. We may also ask ourselves why Sultan Valad does not say anything like this in his *Ebtedâ nâme*. Why does this oral anecdote about a dream that Sultan Valad supposedly had and an activity that he supposedly undertook – the proper burial of Shams – come not from Sultan Valad himself, but from his wife?

Sepahsâlâr does not mention such a dream at all. By the time Aflâki committed the account of this dream to paper, Fâteme Khâtun and Ulu ʿÂref had apparently already died, as the ritual benison "may God be pleased with the two of them" reveals. This places the written form of the anecdote to sometime after the year 1320, more than seventy years after Shams had disappeared.

Given Aflâki's taste for the miraculous and exaggerated, and given the elongated transmission history of this anecdote, a jury might already be inclined to dismiss it as tainted evidence. Furthermore, the account itself is internally inconsistent. Two Seljuk chronicles of this period, the *Saljuq nâme* of Ibn Bibi (written c. 1282) and the *Mosâmerat al-akhbâr* of Karim al-Din Âqsarâʾi (written c. 1320), indicate that Amir Badr al-Din Go(w)hartâsh was killed in or after 1261, over a dozen years after the disappearance of Shams (Akh 299; Mov 200–201; GB 152–3). Shams could not, therefore, have been buried next to Gowhartâsh and the whole fabric of this story begins to unravel. Either the anecdote has been garbled in Aflâki's retelling or in Ulu ʿÂref's memory, or it cannot have originated until some time after 1261, at least thirteen years after the disappearance of Shams. More likely, we are dealing with a baseless rumor dating to the period after Sultan Valad's death, fabricated to buttress the position held by some of the Mevlevis (perhaps including Ulu ʿÂref, the mentor of Aflâki), that Shams had been murdered.

Of course, anyone tenaciously determined to credit this anecdote might engage in some interpolative interpretation – perhaps Rumi's disciples recovered the bones of Shams from the well where they had supposedly dumped him some thirteen years or more prior and then reinterred them next to Badr al-Din Gowhartâsh. Gölpınarlı, though admitting that Aflâki errs in the majority of his accounts (GB 153), does believe the essence of Fâteme Khâtun's story as relayed by Ulu ʿÂref to Aflâki (GB 151). In offering his interpretation, however, Gölpınarlı takes a somewhat more rationalist tack (GB 151–6). He admits that Aflâki's anecdote has the chronology backwards – Badr al-Din was buried next to Shams, and not the other way around.

Since the chronicles tell us that Gowhartâsh was among a group of the supporters of ʿEzz al-Din Kay Kâus II arrested and sent from Konya to Istanbul, where they were killed, we must suppose that his body was returned to Konya for burial (GB 153), since Aflâki places his tomb "in the college of Rumi." Rumi's college was certainly a location known to the Mevlevis of Aflâki's day, and they apparently believed or knew that Gowhartâsh was laid to rest there. There can be no doubt that Gowhartâsh was a real person, well known to the disciples of Rumi. Aflâki and Sepahsâlâr mention him; Sultan Valad tells us in one poem that Gowhartâsh had established a certain village, Kara Arslân, as an endowment (*vaqf*) for the Mevlevis (GM 52); and two of Rumi's letters are apparently addressed to him (Mak 238, 241). Gowhartâsh must have been laid to rest somewhere.

One would not usually pose the question "who is buried in Gowhartâsh's tomb?" Yet Mehmet Önder, the director of the Mevlânâ Museum in Konya, has done precisely this (see chapter 13 below for examples of this Turkish patriot's polemical and uncritical evaluation of evidence). While repairs to the so-called "Shrine of Shams" (*torbat-e Shams*), a site in Konya, were underway, Önder summoned Gölpınarlı to the shrine. Önder had discovered a small wooden door raised up a few steps above the main structure. This trapdoor led to a stone staircase, at the bottom of which Önder found a small crypt housing a single plaster-inlaid sarcophagus along the edge of the left wall, directly under the decorative wooden sarcophagus/cenotaph on the floor above.

Though there was no inscription on this hidden sarcophagus, Önder won Gölpınarlı over to the opinion that it must be the grave of Shams. Across from this shrine traditionally associated with the name of Shams al-Din is a well, supposedly dug in the Seljuk era. Somewhere nearby this site, Önder claims to have found a stone inscription from the *madrase* of Gowhartâsh. Of course, this slab has been used in the rebuilding of a later minaret and therefore might not originally have been associated with this site. Far more troubling, however, is the fact that there is only one sarcophagus in the crypt of the mausoleum. Gölpınarlı assumes with Önder that the tomb belongs to Shams, leaving Gowhartâsh with no grave of his own (GB 151–2).

Naturally, we might just as well reach one of several other conclusions: (a) this is the grave of Gowhartâsh and Aflâki is wrong about Shams being buried next to him; (b) this is not the site mentioned in Aflâki's anecdote – Shams and Gowhartâsh are buried side by side at some other unknown location; or (c) the account of Aflâki is entirely baseless from beginning to end. Nevertheless, Schimmel has ratified the conclusions of Gölpınarlı and Önder, triumphantly concluding that "the truth of Aflâki's statement has been proved" (ScT 22). She even offers an imaginary reenactment of the crime. Professor Mikâil Bayram at the Seljuk University in Konya shares this opinion, even indicating that the bones of Shams have been found (personal interview with the author in Konya, May 15, 1999).

But there is simply no physical evidence of Shams' murder. No explicit statement from Rumi, from Sultan Valad or from Sepahsâlâr – the three sources closest to the situation – corroborates the murder theory. It seems unlikely that seven conspirators could plot to kill a famous person and have it kept a secret from Rumi for so long. Would Sultan Valad, who was apparently devoted to Shams and even looked upon him as his spiritual teacher, wake up all the disciples and bury Shams in the dead of the night in order to cover up the murder of a man he loved? Would the townspeople living near the school of Rumi not have found the sound of digging and plastering in the dead of night a trifle strange, if not alarming, and come to see what had happened? Would Sultan Valad suffer his father to make at least two trips to Syria in search of a dead man? How could the true disciples have remained silent over a period of years while Rumi searched for Shams (Mov 202)? How long did Rumi remain ignorant of the truth? Even if it were hidden from him all his life, how is it that his successors, Salâh al-Din Zarkub and Hosâm al-Din Chelebi, never visited the grave of Shams, whereas while Rumi was alive, Hosâm al-Din visited the graves of Bahâ al-Din and Salâh al-Din every day (Af 765)?

THE ANATOMY OF A MURDER LEGEND

After Aflâki, the suggestion of murder was also related by Ibn Abi al-Vafâ (1297–1373) in his *Javâher al-mozi²e* (cited in FB 57, 78): "Al-Tabrizi disappeared and his place was unknown. And it was said that the circle of Mowlânâ Jalâl al-Din set out to kill him and brought him low, but God is the most knowledgeable." Ibn Abi al-Vafâ clearly prefers the version that Shams disappeared to an unknown location. As Movahhed (Mov 199) points out, the author conveys his doubt about the supposed murder with the phrase, "God is the most knowledgeable." Movahhed (199), who knows of this source through Foruzânfar, assumes that it pre-dates Aflâki. Though Aflâki did not complete the final recension of his *Manâqeb* until 1353, he began compiling it in 1318. As we have seen, Aflâki's account of Shams' murder apparently dates to after 1320, but certainly before 1353 and perhaps decades before that. Ibn Abi al-Vafâ, on the other hand, probably undertook his encyclopedia of Hanafi jurists, the *Javâher al-mozi²e*, as a mature man, after completing his studies and obtaining a position of his own. We may estimate, therefore, that he did not write until sometime in the 1340s or even much later, probably continuing to compile information until well into the 1360s or even the early 1370s. The likelihood, therefore, is that Ibn Abi al-Vafâ's report – "it was said that the circle of Mowlânâ . . . set out to kill him" – comes from none other than Aflâki, and does not reflect independent corroboration of this report.

As already noted, Jâmi's *Nafahât al-ons*, written between 1476 and 1478, repeats Aflâki's story about the conspiracy against Shams, the knife attack, the fainting spell of the conspirators, the disappearance of the body and the three drops of blood. Jâmi, like Aflâki, names Rumi's son, ᶜAlâ al-Din, as one of the seven conspirators, indicating that Rumi disowned him and did not attend his funeral. Jâmi, following Aflâki, gives conflicting accounts about the location of Shams' grave (JNO 467).

Dowlatshâh of Samarqand, who wrote his "Biography of the Poets" (*Tazkerat al-shoᶜarâ*) in 1487, indicates that "some people say" that the people of Konya, having blamed Shams for distracting Rumi from his lectures and studies, incited one of Rumi's sons into killing Shams, which was accomplished by knocking a wall down on top of him. But Dowlatshâh goes on to point out that since he had only heard this from dervishes and travelers, and had not read it in any reputable book, he did not consider it creditable (Dow 222). Dowlatshâh does not refer directly to Aflâki's *Manâqeb* or to Sepahsâlâr's *Resâle*; he does, however, relate Jâmi's account of the murder of Shams from *Nafahât al-ons*. However, Dowlatshâh's quotation from Jâmi's account does not necessarily reflect agreement with it; he concludes his discussion of Shams with a statement that reflects a certain skepticism: "There is disagreement over the circumstances of his death; the truth of the matter is with God, the Most High" (Dow 222).

Sometime between 1481 and 1501, Uzun Ferdowsi Derâz collected the stories current amongst the followers of the Bektâshi dervishes about the miraculous acts of their founder, Hâji Bektâsh Vali. According to one report given in this hagiography, the *Velâyat nâme* (ed. A. Gölpınarlı, Istanbul: Inkilap Kitabevbevi, 1958), it was Sultan Valad who murdered Shams because he could no longer tolerate the bad things being said about his father on account of the dancing and singing in which Rumi engaged (including his wife and daughters in the ceremony) at the urging of Shams. Sultan Valad (given as Valid) cut off Shams' head, only to have Shams rise up in *samâᶜ* and dance off toward Tabriz with his own head in tow. Rumi followed after him and found him dancing in Tabriz at the top of a green minaret in Khâmush quarter, "the quarter of silence" (in many of his ghazals, Rumi brings his grief to an end in a call for "Silence!"). Rumi went and, having arrived at the top of the minaret, now saw that Shams was at the bottom. Coming back down again, he now saw Shams was up at the top. Seven times Rumi chases Shams up and down the minaret like this, until finally, exasperated, Rumi throws himself from the top. Shams catches him in mid-air and tells him, "Bury me here and then go see Hâji Bektâsh." Rumi buries Shams and then stays at the kitchen of Hâji Bektâsh for forty days, until the latter gives Rumi permission to return to Konya (GB 177–8).

The obvious point of this story is not to give the facts about Shams, but to make him part of Hâji Bektâsh's spiritual lineage. In this version, Shams is sent to Rumi by Bektâsh in response to Rumi's request for a spiritual guide. Then, in the end, after Shams is no more, Rumi, too, becomes a disciple of Bektâsh, thus asserting a claim for the superiority of the spiritual forces commanded by Hâji Bektâsh and his followers. Most of the fable can be safely dismissed as fantastic, but it is of interest that Shams returns to Tabriz to be buried (see below).

To sum up, Shams himself threatens to disappear without a trace in his *Maqâlât*, as he had done earlier. Rumi makes no mention of Shams' murder and, though apparently somewhat estranged from his son, ᶜAlâ al-Din, continued to seek out relations with him. Neither Sultan Valad in his family chronicle of 1291, nor Sepahsâlar, writing circa 1320 or earlier, make any mention of murder. Aflâki, sometime between 1320 and 1353, gives conflicting versions of the end of Shams, one in which he disappears and one in which he is killed and his body is thrown in a well, only to be discovered by Sultan Valad, to whom Shams had appeared in a dream. This account circulated orally among the Mevlevis and was written down by Aflâki sometime between 1320 and 1353. Sultan Valad, however, never spoke of this in his own writings. Subsequently, in the middle of the fourteenth century, Ibn Abi al-Vafâ doubtfully relates what seems to be a summary of Aflâki's account of the murder and cover-up. Over a hundred years later, Jâmi seems to credit the story of Shams' murder and the complicity of Rumi's son ʿAlâ al-Din. Dowlatshâh also relates this rumor and another, but seems somewhat skeptical. These are relatively scholarly accounts culled from mostly hagiographical materials. The mythical versions, unchecked by such sober scrutiny, actually have Sultan Valad himself slicing off the head of Shams, who, unperturbed, picks it up and heads off to Tabriz.

In modern times, some scholars, most notably Gölpınarlı, have subscribed to the thesis that ʿAlâ al-Din, Rumi's son, was responsible for arranging the murder and that Sultan Valad, though not one of the plotters, was involved in the cover-up. But this murder rumor arises late, circulates in an oral context, and is almost certainly groundless.

RUMI IN SEARCH OF SHAMS

Some of the poems in the *Divân-e Shams* seem to have been composed shortly after the departure of Shams, and they confirm that Rumi thought he had gone to Syria or Tabriz (D 677):

> Strange, where did that gorgeous heartbreaker go?
> Odd, where'd that tall supple cypress trunk go?
> He bathed us like a candle in his light;
> in thin air vanished, left us! Where'd he go?
> My heart, leaf-like, trembles all day long at this:
> where'd, at midnight, all alone, that heartthrob go?
>
> Run up to the road and ask the traveiers –
> That soul-quickening companion, where'd he go?
> Walk in the garden, ask the gardeners –
> That luscious bough of rosebuds, where'd it go?
> Clamber on the roof and ask the watchmen –
> Our one and only monarch, where'd he go?
>
> A man possessed, I wander in the plain
> crying, "Where in the world d'our gazelle go?"
> My tearful eyes outflow the mighty Oxus –
> That pearl's sunk in the sea, where did it go?
> All night through I beg the Moon and Venus –
> Where did, in heaven's name, that bright orb go?
>
> Since he's ours, how is it he's with others?
> Since here he's not, from here to where'd he go?
> And if he's left the world of clay and breath,
> his placeless soul to join with God did go.
> So tell me clear: Shams al-Din of Tabriz –
> who quotes "The Sun dieth not" – where'd he go?

One poem in the *Divân-e Shams* regales us with Rumi's loving recollection of the various places he had frequented in Damascus. This poem shows Rumi contemplating a third journey to Syria in search of Shams, though Aflâki claims it was composed on the way to Damascus (D 1493):

> I'm mad about, just crazy
> > for Damascus!
> My heart feels melancholic and
> > I left my spirit in Damascus!
> Blissful morn comes up in that direction
> Dawn and dusk, intoxicated
> > by Damascene bewitchments:
> Love bereft, we stand by Barid Gate
> Beyond the Lovers' Mosque
> > in the green field of Damascus
> Have you never sipped the spring of Bu Nuwâs?
> We love the quenching water
> > > of Damascus!
> Let me swear an oath on ʿOsmân's Scroll:
> > That heart-stealing pearl makes
> > > us sparkle in Damascus
> Far from the Gate of Release
> > and the Gate of Paradises
> > > you can't imagine what visions we see
> > > in Damascus
> Let's climb Rebva, and on Christ's Cradle
> we'll be like monks, drunk on the dark red wines
> > > of Damascus
> In regal Nayrab we saw a tree;
> > sitting in its shade, we're dizzied
> > > by Damascus
> We roll through her Verdant Field, struck
> > like polo balls by mallet curls of hair,
> > > on the quadrangle of Damascus
> > > We could never lack for Mezza, for we gain savor and delight
> > at the Eastern Gate of Damascus
> On Righteous Mountain is a mine of gems
> > > through which we swim in the jewels of Damascus
> Since Damascus is paradise of the world,
> > > we long for a vision of the fair angels of Damascus
> For a third time let's speed to Syria from Byzance
> For tresses dark as Syrian nights
> > > drench us in the fragrance of Damascus
> If that is where to practice servitude
> > > to Shams al-Haqq of Tabriz
> > > then my heart's mastered by Damascus,
> > > and mister, I'm Master of Damascus!

Here we find explicit mention of the Barid Gate on the western edge of the old city wall of Damascus and the Gate of Paradises (Bâb-e Farâdis, referring to the nearby gardens) on the north edge of the city wall, outside which there was a cemetery, thus amplifying the poem's allusion to being bereft of the beloved here (*az yâr boridim*). The Gate of Release (Bâb-e Faraj) stood just to the east of the new Sâlehiye ("Righteous") district, which had sprung up about two kilometers north of the city walls on the Yazid river at the foot of Mount Qâsiyun. Sâlehiye was founded by new immigrants to the city in the late 1100s. A Friday mosque was built there in 1202 and many Sufi hospices and centers (variously called *rebât*, *zâvie* and *khâneqâh*), many of them still standing, were located here.

Mount Qâsiyun overlooks the whole city from the northwest and is associated with prophets and saints. The "Verdant Field" (Maydân al-Akhzar) refers to a hippodrome to the west of town. Rebva is the name of a village three miles to the west of Damascus, though its association with the cradle of Christ in this poem perhaps points us to the so-called Church of Mary in the city center, just to the southeast of the Umayyad Mosque. The text also seems to make further allusions: the phrase "blissful morn" (*sobh-e sa'âdat*) may conjure up the governor's mansion, the Dâr al-Sa'âda ("Abode of Happiness"), located south of the city citadel; the phrase "the fair angels" (reading *hosnâ-ye*) may actually be a scribal corruption of Hasyâ, a station on the road from Damascus north to Homs; the spring of Bu Nuwâs may also be a scribal corruption for Bânâs or Bâniyâs, a river or underground aqueduct leading in to the city from the northwest; likewise Sovayd may have originally read Shovayka, a neighborhood to the southeast of Damascus.[7]

In any case, Rumi has clearly taken earlier Arabic poems in praise of Damascus as his model for this poem. In the last line Rumi apparently alludes to the title given him by his disciples, Mowlâ-ye Rum, the Master of Rome. But as he recounts all the sites of Damascus, such as the mountain of Rebve, a hill upon which were buried a number of holy men, and anticipates the possibility of finding Shams in Damascus and tending to him and hanging on his words, he shows that he is actually a servant (*mowlâ*) of Damascus, though if he were to move there permanently he would be called there Mowlâ of Damascus, the Master of Damascus.

A BREEZE FROM TABRIZ?

Rumi elsewhere expresses the desire to go to Tabriz. As we have already seen, Shams had longed to take Rumi to Tabriz, and perhaps Rumi heard or suspected that Shams had returned to his home town. Rumi wants to hear about Tabriz, though in the following lines from one of his ghazals (D 807), Tabriz may occur simply as a metonymy for Shams and does not necessarily pinpoint his location:

Tell for a while
the tale of Tabriz
tell for a while
the bloodthirsty tale
of an eye-fluttering flirt
How bitter to be
severed from such sugary lips –
spoon out the candy
of those godly sugars

However, one ghazal seems predicated on the premise that news of Shams has
been received from Tabriz. It casts Rumi in the Biblical and Koranic role of
Jacob discovering long-lost Joseph's coat, a sign that contrary to what Jacob had
been led to believe, Joseph was not dead. Perhaps Rumi received a letter from
Shams or heard from a traveler who had met with him in Tabriz; the poem
(D 997) suggests that Rumi expected Shams to return to Konya:

Here's Joseph's coat
        and the scent of him!
    He himself can't be
                far behind these two
        the must of ruby wine
        gives joyful tidings:
    After me, the goblet and the serving gourd!
        Your I-am-God soul ascends Hallâj-like
            its divine light shining ray upon ray
Stones can never harm the water
though stones can shatter jugs
Aqua Vitae
cannot be contained
within your mind;
dig a trough
for the water flows
and needs a channel
Douse with water
this jealous fire
whose winds blow
across this earth

The Love and Wisdom
of the house are
locked in strife
their screeching and screaming
echoes in the street outside
The wealth or clothes
that Love forgoes

come in the end
back to it again
    Though the groom pays
    great price to his bride
    her trousseau and herself
        both come to him
        in the end
You asked for a table from heaven
Rise up from your self and wash your hands,
            it descends!
            Glad tidings, love!
            a new sign has come
            from Shams-e Din in Tabriz

THE DARK NIGHT OF THE SOUL

All this suggests that Rumi believed Shams to be alive and well in Damascus or in Tabriz. At some point, however, it appears that Rumi received word of Shams' death. Movahhed (Mov 205) believes Shams probably died in the city of Khuy on his way to Tabriz, shortly after leaving Konya. Rumi probably did not receive word immediately, but it does not seem likely that Rumi would have continued to write poems to Shams for very long after learning of his death, insofar as Rumi believed that there must always be a living *axis mundi*, a spiritual pole or *qotb* upon which the spiritual welfare of human beings depends (M2:815–36). Salâh al-Din, who died in December 1258, is the dedicatee of about seventy poems in the *Divân-e Shams*, most of which must date to the period after Rumi knew Shams to be dead. The bulk of the poems for the absent Shams, on the other hand, probably date to the period between 1247 and the time Rumi internalized the teachings of Shams and achieved some kind of catharsis over the loss of his spiritual guide. It was only at this point that Rumi would have taken Salâh al-Din as the mirror in which to gaze upon his own, or Shams', spiritual achievements.

We can only guess at the date of some of the poems in the *Divân-e Shams*, but we do know the approximate dates of composition for the *Masnavi*. Salâh al-Din is mentioned only once in the *Masnavi* (M2:1321), which Rumi began several years after Salâh's death. Though we find allusions to the word Shams often, the *Masnavi* explicitly mentions the name of Shams-e Din of Tabriz only four times, three of them in Book 1 (M1:123, 142, 427). Perhaps the last mention Rumi makes of Shams is to be found in Book 2 of the *Masnavi*, in lines composed some time in 1264, which show Rumi now focused on Hosâm al-Din as the living substitute for Shams (M2:1122–3):

I am declawed by love of Shams-e Din
or else would I restore sight to the blind
So you, Truth's Light, Hosâm al-Din, cure him
and may it blind the evil envious eye!

197

Rumi therefore believed or at least spoke and acted for some time after the disappearance of Shams as if he were still alive. Eventually, however, he learned that Shams, who was already advanced in years when the two met, had died. One of Rumi's *robâ'is* would seem to suggest the arrival of such news (D R806):

> Who says the immortal man has died
> who says the sun of hope has set?
> A foe to the sun went up on the roof
> closed his eyes and said the sun is dead

A longish poem on weeping and mourning also evidently alludes to the news of Shams' death (D 2893):

> To dry full measure of their grief my eyes
> would weep nights and days, dark to dawn to dark ...
>
> * * *
>
> Death is deaf and hears no wailing,
> or it would weep with bloodied heart –
> The grim reaper's heartless; if he
> had a heart, he'd weep stony tears –
>
> * * *
>
> Shams-e Tabriz is gone and who
> will weep for the best among men?
> The world of meaning's gained in him a bride,
> but shorn of him the world of forms just weeps

THE GRAVEYARD OF THE SUN

Claims to harbor the remains of Shams have been made on behalf of a variety of locales, including Konya, Khuy and Tabriz. Local legend in Multan, Pakistan, even describes a saint's shrine there as the resting place of Shams al-Din of Tabriz, though it is in reality the shrine of Pir Shams al-Din, an Ismaili missionary from Alamut.[8] We have already seen how the legends surrounding the disappearance of Shams began to snowball as time passed. Sepahsâlâr, who ought to have known if Shams had died in Konya, gives no indication of the final resting place of Shams, but has Rumi last looking for him in Damascus. Aflâki gives conflicting accounts, but believes on rather dubious authority that Shams lay buried somewhere in Konya.

Mirzâ Mohammad Sâdeq b. Mohammad Sâleh Âzâdâni-Esfahâni, the author of *Shâhed-e Sâdeq*, written in India about 1646, gives the date of death of a number of the ulama from the beginning of Islam until 1632 (*fasl* 79, *bâb* 3; cited Mov 207–8). He places the death of Shams-e Tabrizi and of Shâhfur Ashhari of Nayshâpur in the year 1246 (A.H. 645), though likely as not, this date merely reflects the stories in Aflâki about the attack on and disappearance of Shams.

Fasih-e Khavâfi in his *Mojmal*, written about 1442, writes about the death of a Shaykh Hasan Bolghâri in Tabriz in 1299, in the course of which he states:

198

"He received his *kherqe* from the Perfect and Perfecting, fully attained shaykh, Shams al-Din al-Tabrizi, who is buried in Khuy, and in whose name the poems of Mowlânâ of Rum are written."[9] However, the same author also ascribes the death of Shams to the same year as the death of both Nasir al-Din Tusi and Rumi, 1273 (A.H. 672), which is surely wrong: "The death of Shaykh Shams al-Din al-Tabrizi, buried in Khuy, in whose name the poems of Mowlânâ Jalâl al-Din of Balkh, known as Mowlânâ of Rum, are written, took place in 672."[10]

Nevertheless, Movahhed credits the part about Shams being buried in Khuy, for there has been a grave with a minaret outside of Khuy known as "the minaret of Shams-e Tabriz," since the turn of the fifteenth century at the latest. Until recently it had two minarets, as mentioned by European travelers to Azerbayjan, but one has since collapsed due to the ravages of time. The minaret still standing has been described by Mohammad Amin-Riâhi as situated in "verdant gardens near a cluster of trees with an isolated atmosphere evoking the homesickness of travelers and the infirmity of the elderly."[11] The stones from the other minaret, which had only recently collapsed when Amin-Riâhi saw it, were used to rebuild a nearby mosque. Amin-Riâhi estimated that the tower dated from pre-Mongol times (cited by Mov 209).

We have seen how the *Velâyat nâme*, dating from approximately 1500, locates the grave of Shams in Tabriz, and not Konya. In his more recent book on the history of Khuy, Amin-Riâhi points to an account of a visit of the Ottoman sultan and grand vizier to Khuy in the end of August 1535, during which they went on horseback to visit the grave of Shams-e Tabriz.[12] This demonstrates that the Ottomans did not believe Aflâki's report about the location of Shams' grave in Konya, even though the modern tourist industry in Turkey now vigorously promotes this notion (Mov 211).

Iranian scholars have known for some time about local claims that Shams was buried in Tabriz or in Khuy. Foruzânfar discounted these for lack of evidence (FB 208). Tarbiyat, relying upon a history of the Dânbele dynasty written in 1844, had claimed that the site in Khuy known as the grave of Shams-e Tabrizi actually belonged to a patron of the poet Khâqâni (1121–99), called Shams al-Moluk Amir Ja'far of the Dânbele dynasty. Tarbiyat therefore dismissed the attribution of a grave in Khuy to Shams as local legend (*Dâneshmandân-e Âzarbâyjân*, 131; cited Mov 209). However, there is no such patron to be found in the modern editions of Khâqâni's *Divân*, so that the information attributing the grave to someone other than Shams is quite suspect (Mov 209–10).

Unfortunately we do not know the exact resting place for many figures of medieval Persian history and literature. In the case of Shams-e Tabriz, who traveled incognito and did not bring any followers with him, we should not be surprised to learn that he died obscurely with no spiritual heirs around him to commemorate his resting place and turn his grave into a place of pilgrimage. Since Aflâki's account of Shams' murder in Konya must be rejected, we must look elsewhere for his grave. We are unlikely ever to know for certain, but as Movahhed argues, there is a site in Khuy, on the road from Konya to Tabriz, associated with the name of Shams-e Tabrizi that dates back at least to 1400. Though there is nothing to prove it, there is no longer any evidence to dismiss it either. Since the minaret on the site would appear to be quite antique, in the absence of any contradictory evidence, Khuy may be considered the final resting place of Shams (Mov 210–11).

SOME OF THE TEACHINGS OF SHAMS

A commentary on a verse of the Koran (K62:10) states that after finishing the prayers the believers should "disperse throughout the land, longing for the blessing (*fazl*) of God, and make frequent mention of God, that haply you may prosper" Shams comments (Maq 231):

> Blessing is excess, so to speak, an excess of everything. Don't be content with being a *faqih*, say I want more – more than being a Sufi, more than being a mystic – more than each thing that comes before you.

On the meaning of the phrase *Allâhu akbar* (God is great[er]), which occurs repeatedly in the obligatory prayers of Islam every day:

> *Allâhu akbar* (God is great[er]) means that God is greater than that which you have imagined. It means don't stop there, come closer so that you see greatness. Seek so that you may find. (Maq 655)

> "God is great" expresses this: Raise your thoughts above the imaginings that come to you and your conceptions. Raise your sights higher, for He is greater than all those images. Though the image be of the Prophet and the Messenger and One Endowed with Constancy, He is greater than that. (Maq 648)

On the goal of the spiritual search:

> What is the pre-eternal world to you? Figure out your own pre-eternalness – are you pre-existent or contingent? Spend what life is given to you in investigation of your own state. Why spend it in figuring what in the world is pre-existent? The knowledge of God is deep. You fool, you are deep. If there is depth, it is in you. (Maq 221)

In condemnation of blind imitation (*taqlid*) of a spiritual or legal authority: "All the corruption in the world arises from this – someone believed in someone out of imitation or disbelieved in someone out of imitation" (Maq 161). The self gets in the way of the worshiper and should not be allowed to interfere in our relationship with God. This applies to everyone, for "There is no human who does not have some ego" (Maq 621), and there is no shaykh whose "hidden ego does not fetter him" (Maq 258). "If Bâyazid knew anything he would never have said 'I'" (Maq 728). "For when he says 'I,' where is God? And when God is there, what a naked and shameful word is 'I'!" (Maq 763).

On the self-renunciatory longing for death, Shams says:

Those sacrificial ones who long for death, searching it out just as poets search for rhyme, as the sick seek health, as prisoners their freedom and children Fridays. (Maq 159)

If you have the illumination and passion to desire death, congratulations and God's blessing upon you. Do not forget us in your prayers. And if you lack this light and passion, then strive and seek to attain it, for the Koran informs us that if you seek it out, you will attain such a state. So seek. "Desire death if you are faithful and righteous." Just as it is the righteous and faithful among men who seek out death, so it is the righteous and faithful among women. (Maq 87)

And yet Shams is himself happy in the world (and seems to have conveyed this contentment to Rumi):

I am amazed at this hadith: "The world is a prison to the believer." I have seen no prison! I have seen only pleasure, I have seen only precious things, I have seen only fortune. (Maq 317)

I was not troubled by any of the Prophet's sayings, except this, "The world is a prison to the believer." I see no prison and ask, where is this prison?! (Maq 610)

On joy and sorrow and their effects on the spirit: "Joy is like pure clear water; wherever it flows, wondrous blossoms grow ... Sorrow is like a black flood; wherever it flows it wilts the blossoms" (Maq 195). Of *samâ^c*, Shams says: "The dancing of the men of God is elegant and delicate. It's like a leaf flowing on the water's surface. Inside like a mountain, a whole range of mountains, and outside like straw" (Maq 623). On correct Islamic doctrine, Shams seems to reflect his Shâfe^ci upbringing and to reject the rationalism of the Mutazilites: "This creed of the Sunnis is closer to the matter than the creed of the Mutazilites. The latter is close to philosophy. He who digs a pit for his brother, falls in it himself" (Maq 740).

Shams has no time for complaining and criticizing:

A good man complains of no one; he does not look to faults. (Maq 91)

My character is such that I pray for Jews. I say, God guide them. I pray for those who curse me: O God, occupy him with a better and more pleasing pursuit than cursing. (Maq 121)

On the shaykh–disciple relationship:

What's a shaykh? Being. What's a disciple? Non-existence. Until a disciple ceases to exist, he is not a disciple. (Maq 739)

Though they may be possessed of learning, yet they change from state to state. You should know that all this learning bears no relationship to the interior, for the inner power makes this request: "No, let me see it!" It does not accept anyone's report. These words "gnosticism" and dervish are heard on everyone's tongue, but [the word] is all they understand when they hear it. (Maq 687)

I have no business with the common folk of the world; I have not come for their sake. Those people who are guides for the world unto God, I put my finger on their pulse. (Maq 82)

On the mystics' quest to identify with the prophets:

The claim of the prophets is this: "O outward stranger, you are part of me, why are you heedless of me? O Part, come! Do not be heedless of the whole. Become aware and come to know me". (Maq 162)

PART II

RUMI'S CHILDREN AND

BRETHREN IN SPIRIT

5

From Sun to Son

THE SUCCESSORS OF SHAMS

SALÂH AL-DIN ZARKUB: GOLDSMITH OF THE SPIRIT

Salâh al-Din Faridun (d. 1258) was born in one of the villages outside Konya, supposedly near a lake, though no trace of a village by the name Aflâki (Af 706) gives it – Kâmele – is to be found today (GB 187). Though his father was a fisherman, Salâh al-Din came to Konya and acquired the trade of goldsmith. He became a disciple of Borhân al-Din Mohaqqeq before he met Rumi, and we are told that Sayyed Borhân al-Din emphasized the practice of thwarting the passions by fasting, for there is no swifter steed than fasting for the wayfarer heading to the stage of union with God (Sep 169; Af 66). When Borhân went to Kayseri, Salâh al-Din returned to his village, married and fathered a son (Af 705). Several years later, sometime between the death of Borhân al-Din in 1241 and the arrival of Shams in 1244, Salâh al-Din returned to Konya and heard Rumi preaching the Friday sermon at the Bu al-Fazl mosque. Rumi was repeating many of the points that Borhân al-Din used to make and Salâh al-Din ran up to Rumi and kissed his feet (Af 706). After this they became fast friends, such that when Shams arrived in Konya, Rumi supposedly brought him to the house of Salâh al-Din, who apparently also owned a garden, to talk (GB 188).

Although Aflâki's version seems far more plausible, Sepahsâlâr, who relies heavily upon Sultan Valad for the rest of his account of Salâh al-Din, tells a more colorful anecdote (Sep 135–6). One day Rumi was walking past Salâh al-Din's shop in a particularly excited state and he heard the rhythmic tapping of the goldsmith's hammer, to which he began to dance in an ecstatic trance. Salâh al-Din saw this and kept up the beat even though it ruined the piece of gold he was working. Rumi eventually went over and led him out of the shop. After some discussion Salâh al-Din, convinced of Rumi's powers, became one of his closest disciples.

As we have seen, Rumi believed that God establishes a living saint in every age, around whom the spiritual energies of the universe revolve. First it was his father, then Borhân al-Din, and then Shams al-Din. When Rumi became convinced that Shams was no longer alive, he adopted Salâh al-Din as the new axis around which his metaphysical concentration and spiritual efforts would pivot (SVE 64):

> When that mystic Shaykh saw Salâh al-Din
> he chose him from among the ranks of saints
> turned his face towards him, put all else aside
> reckoned all others error, in the wrong ...
> "Axis of the seven climes and heavens"
> was the title given Salâh al-Din ...

According to Sultan Valad, Rumi explained his attitude toward Salâh al-Din as follows (SVE 64):

> That Shams-e Din of whom we always spoke
> has come back to us! Why do we slumber?
> Changed into new clothes, he has returned
> to flaunt and strut and show his beauty ...

In a poem which Sultan Valad seems to imply was occasioned by the changing of the guard from Shams to Salâh al-Din (GB 186–7), we find a quite similar idea expressed in Rumi's own words (D 650):

> That redcloak,
>   who rose over us last year
>   like the new moon
>   has appeared this year
>   in a rust-colored dervish coat
> The Turk you saw that year
>   busy with plunder
> is the same who came this year
>   like an Arab.
> It's the very same love,
>   though in different garb:
>   He changed clothes and appeared again
> It's the same wine, though the glass has changed
>   see how happy he comes in his tipsiness!
> The night's gone,
>   where are my partners in morning revel?
>   For the torch has appeared in the window of mysteries
>   The white Greek [Rumi] disappeared

when the black Ethiopic age began
today he appears with great hosts of battle
Proclaim:
    the Sun of Truth of Tabriz has arrived!
for this moon of many lights
    has climbed the wheeling skies of purity!

Does this mean that Rumi considered himself a disciple to Salâh al-Din? Though Rumi expresses himself in these terms, this seems unlikely. Rumi had first of all found the light of Shams within himself (Af 704; SVE 61) and stood in no further need of discipleship. But in the commotion and distress following the disappearance of Shams, one disciple had become the knight, prince and king of Rumi's house – Salâh al-Din. This probably involved controlling access to Rumi and helping him to manage his relationship with his disciples. Rumi himself felt disinclined to play the role of shaykh and therefore needed someone to play that role in his stead, and also to act as his successor (*khalife*), a position which Rumi confirms both he and Borhân al-Din had designated for Salâh al-Din (Mak 98). Sultan Valad calls him the deputy (*nâyeb*) and successor of Rumi (SVE 108).

In the mosque and *madrase*, this term *nâyeb* designates the individual, usually the student or intended successor of a professor, *khatib*, or even *qâzi*. Professors and preachers often held multiple positions and could not personally attend all the regular classes or sermons held in their name. In order to retain their position, the absentee professor or preacher would pay a substitute or deputy (*nâyeb*) to take his place. Although the deputy would receive only a portion of the professor's salary in compensation, the position helped fix his reputation and his chance of succeeding his master. Aflâki (Af 708) tells of one occasion on which, though Rumi had left off preaching and lecturing, Salâh al-Din was able to persuade him to speak to an assembled crowd. This suggests that Salâh al-Din, as Rumi's deputy, had taken on the public role of lecturing and preaching.

Rumi and his circle clearly no longer functioned in the manner of a typical law college, if they ever had. Beyond the functional and perhaps ceremonial role given to Salâh al-Din as deputy and successor, Rumi may also have seen Salâh al-Din as a mirror reflecting his own aspirations, thoughts and teachings. Part of the reason Rumi speaks highly of him is to confirm his status and authority as a teacher and preacher, and part of it perhaps reflects a genuine feeling that by acting as mutual wardens of one another's heart and conscience, they could hone their own spiritual powers. Nevertheless, their interpersonal relations seem rather formal, if the anecdote Rumi himself tells in *Fihe mâ fih* gives any indication. Discourse 21 (Fih 93) describes how Rumi once met Shaykh Salâh al-Din in the public bath, with both men displaying excessive humility and formality one to the other.

Primarily, though, Salâh al-Din interacted directly with the disciples in order to afford Rumi a measure of tranquility. At least this is how Sultan Valad presents it, when he has Rumi say (SVE 64):

> I'm in no mind for your company, go
> dedicate yourselves to Salâh al-Din
> I've no mind to be your head, your shaykh,
> for no bird can match flight with my wings
> I need no one – I'm happy all by myself
> When folks buzz about like flies, it bugs me.
> So from now on all of you seek him out –
> with heart and soul yearn to be with him, that
> you, like him, may walk the straight and narrow,
> be transformed through him to wheat from barley –
> not just wheat, but gems through him you will become ...
> Woe to anyone who would deny him!

Sayyed Borhân al-Din used to say (Af 705) that he had received two gifts from his master, Bahâ al-Din: eloquence in speech and fervor in mystical states. He explained that he bequeathed his eloquence to Rumi, since Rumi already possessed mystical susceptibilities, and he left his mystical fervor to Salâh al-Din, because he had little talent for debate and discussion (cf. Sep 169, who attributes a similar report to Salâh al-Din's daughter). Indeed, many objected to Salâh al-Din's station on the grounds that he was ignorant. Aflâki (Af 705) and Sepahsâlâr (Sep 138) relate anecdotes about Salâh al-Din mispronouncing words. Although they attribute this to Salâh al-Din not having formally studied or trained in the religious sciences, his pronunciation may also have reflected the accent of a Turk for whom Persian was a second language. No doubt Salâh al-Din could not match wits or knowledge with scholars like Rumi who had formal training in the religious sciences, but since he had studied with Borhân al-Din he could not have been completely uneducated or illiterate (*ommi*), as the hagiographical sources suggest.

Perhaps Rumi selected Salâh al-Din Zarkub as his successor in part to encourage the local populace – working-class and Turkic or Greek, as opposed to many of the more book-learned Persian and Arab emigres living among them – that they, too, could aspire to spiritual endeavors and mystical matters. In any case, the caviling at Salâh al-Din disturbed Rumi greatly and provoked him to angry retorts (Sep 138). Sultan Valad shows Rumi upbraiding the disciples for their doubt and stubbornness in this regard (SVE 65):

> Such a king has favored you, sought you out,
> but you are ruled by greed and passion.
> Greed and passion veil a man from God;
> Leave greed and passion behind like us:
> Feast your eyes upon his subtle beauty

unless defiled, misled by blasphemy.
You're an angel? Still, bow your head to him,
For if you doubt him, you are demonic!
Like the sun his light is obvious.
All who have heart are mad in love for him,
whereas the insincere and two-faced
will not bear away a penny from his treasure.

Rumi himself gives an example of the attacks on Salâh al-Din in Discourse 22 of *Fihe mâ fih*. Ibn Châvosh had apparently remarked that Salâh al-Din did not amount to much of anything, which brought Rumi rushing to Salâh al-Din's defense. Rumi reminds Ibn Châvosh how Salâh al-Din had always referred to Rumi's greatness and spoke submissively of himself (Fih 95), despite the fact that Rumi had effectively made Salâh al-Din his shaykh. Ibn Châvosh suspects that Salâh al-Din has some ulterior motive in the counsels he gives, but Rumi points out that Salâh al-Din will show his wrath when a disciple has deserved it, and that a disciple ought to accept the directives of his shaykh (Fih 96). Rumi refers to Salâh al-Din in this passage as "the Shaykh of shaykhs, the benefit of truth and religion (*Salâh al-Haqq va al-Din*), may God perpetuate his dominion."

Of course, just as Rumi's ecstatic accolades had not convinced all his disciples of the station of Shams al-Din, Rumi's public acclaim of Salâh al-Din was likewise unable permanently to deter jealous whispering against him. Rumi could relate to Salâh al-Din and he found peace in their companionship such that he excluded most others from his presence. This led some of the disciples to conspire against Salâh al-Din, in the hope of reestablishing direct access to Rumi and reaffirming his role as the object of the disciples' devotion. Sultan Valad directly compares the jealousy felt toward Shams al-Din and Salâh al-Din, when he has the disciples complain (SVE 70–71):

This one here's even worse than the first
The first was a light, this one's a spark
The first wrote books, was learned, well read ...
Wish the first was still here, to befriend the Shaykh –
He wasn't from Konya, but from Tabriz
He succored the soul and spilled no blood;
We all know this man – he's our countryman,
shares our table, grew up before our eyes;
That's all he is to us, though he's now big.
Not for knowledge, not for his script or speech
has he distinguished himself among us
He's ignorant, a simpleton, untrained
To him both good and bad appear the same
He was always in his shop banging gold ...
He can't recite the simplest sura right
When asked a question, he cannot reply

The plotters began to speak against him (SVE 72–4) and eventually pledged to murder him and bury him (notice that though Sultan Valad does not explicitly mention the disciples wanting to murder Shams, he clearly spells out a plot to kill Salâh al-Din). One disciple however came to Rumi and revealed the scheme. Salâh al-Din laughed at them and told them that no purpose could be achieved, no straw could move, unless God expressly willed it (SVE 75):

> How kill me, bring me down in blood and dust
> when God guards me, protecting flesh and soul ...
> It torments them to know that Mowlânâ
> singled me out above all the others
> They do not realize: I am a mirror
> a reflection, not a picture of myself
> When he sees his own face in me, how then
> could he do anything but choose me?

Rumi and Salâh reject the members of the cabal, shunning them completely. In the end, the schemers profess the error of their ways and throwing themselves at the threshold of Mowlânâ and Salâh al-Din, weep endlessly until Rumi relents and finally lets them in. They repent, pledge fealty to Salâh al-Din and Mowlânâ Rumi, the Shaykh, and are elated to be accepted back into the fold by the two "kings" (SVE 85).

Though the sources portray Salâh al-Din learning about the attempted coup against him with equanimity, this plotting nevertheless appears to have led him to take certain countermeasures. Sultan Valad, as the favored son of Rumi, would probably have been considered his father's most likely successor. When Rumi named Salâh al-Din as his successor shaykh, Sultan Valad was only in his early or mid-twenties, but already at age eighteen he had been entrusted by his father with the crucial mission to retrieve Shams from Damascus. The disciples who resented Salâh al-Din perhaps wished to replace him with Sultan Valad, who may have proved more impressionable and pliant in responding to importunate followers wishing to meet with Rumi. One sometimes feels that Sultan Valad himself betrays a hint of chagrin at not having been chosen by his father for this task.

Whatever the case may be, Rumi commended Sultan Valad to the spiritual discipleship of Salâh al-Din. Sultan Valad tells it thus (SVE 65):

> Mowlânâ, Our Master, summoned then Valad:
>   "Listen," he told him, "you're quite a smart lad."
> Bowing his head, Valad asked what to do.
>   "Look on Salâh al-Din and see his face,
>   what an essence, that God-discerning king!
>   Leader of the world of spirit, angel
>   of the realm beyond time and place; it's him."
> "Yes," I said, "but only in the eyes of one
>   like you, not to any worthless scum."
> He told me, "This is him, that Shams al-Din!"

Sultan Valad tells his father that he, likewise, sees only the sea of soul in Salâh al-Din. He pledges to obey Salâh al-Din and to do whatever Rumi tells him. Rumi says he must follow Salâh al-Din as his spiritual master, and Sultan Valad agrees.

This does not, however, completely assure Salâh al-Din. Despite this pledge, or perhaps to test it, Salâh al-Din demanded that Sultan Valad look to no other shaykh. "I am the true shaykh and companionship with other shaykhs is harmful." The shaykh affects his pupil like the sun affects a stone, transforming it only gradually into a ruby. The words of other shaykhs only cast shadows over the stone and block out the true shaykh's transformative powers (SVE 97). Salâh al-Din tells Sultan Valad, "God's mystery is contained within my essence" (SVE 98).

Sultan Valad gives Salâh al-Din his vow of fealty, but in a backhanded way suggests that Salâh al-Din may not be the equal of Shams (SVE 103):

> He told Valad, "Be my disciple
> if you accept me with your heart and soul."

To which Sultan Valad replies:

> O King, no one can match you in this age

Salâh al-Din then demands that Sultan Valad cease his public preaching, which suggests that he felt Sultan Valad may have been undermining his authority, whether consciously or not. Perhaps Sultan Valad's abilities as a speaker highlighted the supposed formal ignorance of Salâh al-Din and diverted attention away from Salâh al-Din to Sultan Valad. Quite possibly Sultan Valad also had a tendency to magnify Shams al-Din or his father, Rumi, to the neglect of Salâh al-Din. Salâh al-Din tells him, "My friend, stop preaching! From now on, only sing my praise" (SVE 103). Apparently, Salâh al-Din also asked that Sultan Valad hand over his sermons and speeches, as a sign of devotion, so that Salâh al-Din might deliver them instead (SVE 104):

> Let me be certain that you are all mine,
> you're in love, beyond all thought of me and you,
> that you've effaced your you within myself;
> For two can never fit within one place

Sultan Valad submits to Salâh al-Din's demand, as he does not wish to develop a rivalry between them. And in the end, Sultan Valad admits that this act of submission did, in fact, deepen his spiritual powers (SVE 104). Furthermore, Sultan Valad was the son-in-law of Salâh al-Din. Aflâki (Af 719) tells us that Rumi had taught Fâteme Khâtun, Salâh al-Din's daughter, how to write and to read the Koran. Rumi must therefore have known and admired her from when she was a small child; he thought more highly of Fâteme Khâtun than any of the other women who came to see him as disciples. Sepahsâlâr (Sep 169) refers to her as a female saint on earth (*valiyat Allâh fi al-arz*), and from the report he recounts, it is clear that Fâteme spent some time with her father in the presence of Sayyed Borhân al-Din. It is no surprise, then, that Rumi arranged for his favorite son, Sultan Valad, to marry her. The marriage is attested in a number of passages of Rumi's own writings, including two poems (D 31 and D 236) written around the occasion (Af 720). The date of the marriage remains obscure, but perhaps took place between 1249 and 1258 (FB 100). What follows, then, is Rumi's benediction either on the occasion of the marriage contract or the actual wedding celebration of his son, Sultan Valad, and Salâh al-Din's daughter, Fâteme Khâtun (D 236):

> May the blessings which flow in all weddings
> be gathered, God, together in our wedding!
> The blessings of the Night of Power,
>   the month of fasting
>   the festival to break the fast
>   the blessings of the meeting of Adam and Eve
>   the blessings of the meeting of Joseph and Jacob
>   the blessings of gazing on the paradise of all abodes
> and yet another blessing which cannot be put in words:
>   the fruitful scattering of joy
>   of the children of the Shaykh
>   and our eldest!
>
> In companionship and happiness
>   may you be like milk and honey
> in union and fidelity,
>   just like sugar and halva.
> May the blessings of those who toast
>   and the one who pours the wine
>   anoint the ones who said Amen and
>   the one who said the prayer.

Two of Rumi's letters also address the marriage. In one he writes to assure Fâteme that he will not allow Sultan Valad, his son, to slight her or offend her, for he realizes that she is guilty of nothing to warrant any insult (Mak 132–3). Rumi also delicately urges Sultan Valad to be solicitous of her, while at the same time assuring his son that neither he nor Fâteme wish to meddle in Sultan Valad's business (Mak 68–70).

Salâh al-Din had another daughter, Hedye Khâtun, who was raised in Rumi's extended household. We find Rumi, apparently after Salâh al-Din's death, writing to acquire a suitable trousseau for her to marry a certain Nezâm al-Din (Mak 98–9, 117–18). Aflâki (728) tells us that Rumi's efforts on her behalf were successful and that he composed a poem for their wedding, as well. Later on, however, according to Gölpınarlı's conjecture (GB 199 n. 2), Nezâm al-Din may have done something unseemly which upset Rumi, who in turn may have written a vulgar line of verse to rebuke him.

For a period of about ten years Salâh al-Din and Rumi lived happily amongst the disciples, imparting wisdom to them (SVE 109). Then Salâh al-Din fell ill. We can glean from one of Rumi's letters (Mak 97–8) that his illness was somewhat protracted and that it prevented Rumi from attending to daily business for a while. Sultan Valad (SVE 110) also confirms the extended and painful nature of the illness. Rumi prayed for Salâh al-Din during his illness, but to no avail (Mak 98). Finally, Salâh al-Din begged Rumi for permission to leave the world (SVE 110):

> He said to the Shaykh, "O potent king,
> Tear to shreds these garments of Existence;
> From afflictions freed, I will gain release,
> go towards the beyond, with joy and delight,
> I'll go towards that soul-vivifying sea
> and I'll go towards that heart-stirring palace
> that I might go beyond these dimensions,
> released from the world of why and wherefor."
> Rumi accepted, told him, "So be it."
> He rose from his pillow quick to his feet
> set off down the road toward his own house
> and busied himself with the balm for his pain.
> When for two or three days Rumi paid him
> no wonted visit, he turned his face to He.
> Salâh-e Din, that monarch, understood
> and said: "The soul will leave my body soon.
> I'm sure to go now from effacement's realm
> toward the towardless in absorption's abode.
> That he has not come is my sign to go,
> to the pious this command bids good-tide."

Salâh al-Din willed his well-wishers not to grieve with dirges and laments, but with joyous music and *samâ*, a last request that was more or less carried out (SVE 112):

> The Shaykh willed: "Over my dead body
> Bring the drum, tambourine, reed flute and snare
> And dancing a while, march on to my grave,
> joyous, with spright hands, happy and drunk
> that all may know the friends of God all go
> joyous and happy to meet with their God ..."
> All heeded his will with heart and with soul:
> the whole town came out, rending their garments,
> countless cries wailing over the body,
> both hands in their teeth to gesture regret,
> chagrin making them dazed, as if struck dumb,
> all admitting, we took him for granted

Salâh al-Din died on December 29, 1258 (1 Muharram A.H. 657) according to the date carved on his sarcophagus, and was buried to the left of Bahâ al-Din's sepulchre (GB 201–2). Some time after Salâh al-Din's death, Rumi attempted to obtain a loan from a government official to help his heirs pay off an overdue installment on the mortgage of a garden (Mak 165).

Salâh al-Din left no book behind, but a sizeable body of anecdotes can be found in Aflâki. Sepahsâlâr adds little in the way of detail (except to specify one of the words Salâh al-Din once mispronounced). But Sultan Valad had an extensive and close personal relationship with Salâh al-Din, which he details at some length in his *Ebtedâ nâme*. The relationship of Rumi with Salâh al-Din was also very close. Rumi wrote over seventy poems for Salâh al-Din and mentions him once in the *Masnavi* as well, placing him almost equal with Borhân al-Din Mohaqqeq (M2:1321). In one poem, Rumi says (D 1397), "the grace of the Salâh of our heart and faith shines within my heart; he is the candle of hearts in this world, I the basin where he drips." A careful study of these sources, along with the letters Rumi wrote for him and the supplementary details which we can cull from Aflâki, may one day provide us with a somewhat fuller portrayal of the man and Rumi's view of him. In the meantime, let the following poem suffice (D 1210):

> In the end of time
> there is no helper
> but Salâh al-Din,
> Salâh al-Din, that's it!
> If you know the secret of his secret
> Don't breathe a word
> so no one else finds out
>
> A lover's breast is sweetest water
> souls float on his surface
> like thorn and thistle
> When you see his face
> do not speak
> for breath obscures the mirror:
>> The sun rises
>>> from the hearts of lovers
>>>> the whole world shines
>>>>> fore and aft

Rumi wrote an elegy for Salâh al-Din that goes as follows (D 2364):

> Bereft of you both earth and sky shed tears!
> Heart adrift in blood, mind and soul in tears
> Because none in the world can take your place.
> For you space and meta-space mourn and weep:
> Gabriel, the angels, feathers blued,

the prophets and saints, eyes all ablur,
by lamentation choked, I cannot speak
to make you metaphors of how I cry.

As you left this house, fortune's roof collapsed
for Fortune grieves just like the sore-bereaved.
You proved not one man but a hundred worlds
Last night I dreamt the next world weeps for this.
All eyes fixed on you fading from our view;
Shorn of living light, these eyes wept bloody tears.
If not so proud for you, I too would burst
as my bloodied heart drips secret tears:
Cut off from you, each breath coughs blood.
Not tears, but sacks of fresh-cut musk are shed

Alas and alas and alas, alas
that doubtful hearts should weep for an eye so clear
   Salâh al-Din the king, fleet phoenix, flown,
an arrow upward sped, the bowstrings cried,
     Not just anyone can mourn Salâh al-Din,
but one who truly knows to mourn true men.

THE REIGN OF HOSÂM AL-DIN: THE SWORD OF FAITH

Rumi repeatedly refers to Hosâm al-Din as "The Light of Truth" (*Ziâ° al-haqq*) or the life of the heart, praising him in extraordinary terms in the introduction to the *Masnavi*. The *Divân* and the letters also echo this praise and magnification of Hosâm al-Din's spiritual attainments. Though Hosâm al-Din left behind no written record of his own, we may nevertheless infer something of his biography from the letters and poems of Rumi. Sepahsâlâr provides a number of details, which seem for the most part reliable. Sultan Valad tells little about Hosâm al-Din personally, but does give us some information about the process of succession from Salâh al-Din to Hosâm al-Din and the transformations brought about by the death of Rumi. Aflâki provides a great deal of interesting information, and though some of it seems rather dubious, without his "Acts of the Gnostics" we would have almost no details about the personal characteristics of the man.

Though given the name of his grandfather, Hasan, at birth, history knows him by his title Hosâm al-Din, the Sword of Faith. Chelebi Hosâm al-Din Hasan b. Mohammad b. al-Hasan, Ibn Akhi Tork, describes his full name and lineage. In the introduction to the *Masnavi*, as well as in his letters (e.g., Mak 102), Rumi invokes him with a litany of honorific titles and virtues, including but not limited to: the Bâyazid and Jonayd of the age, the charge of God entrusted to His creatures, the keys to the treasury of God's throne. Rumi traces Hosâm al-Din's descent through a famous but uneducated mystic, Abu al-Vafâ

Kordi (d. 1107). This would mean Hosâm al-Din had some Kurdish blood, which makes perfect sense, since Rumi describes his family as hailing from Urmia in northwestern Iran.

Sepahsâlâr (Sep 141) adds several more to Rumi's train of honorific titles for Hosâm al-Din, including "manifestation of divine light" and "the leader of all the spiritual axes" (*aqtâb*). Like his predecessors at the head of the Mevlevi community, and like virtually all Muslim saints, Hosâm al-Din is described as passionately abstemious by Sepahsâlâr. As flowery and grandiosely general as such ceremonial language may sound, one gets the sense from the titles used in reference to him by Sepahsâlâr that Hosâm al-Din was particularly kind and played an important role in helping to get the new disciples to follow Islamic law and practice spiritual discipline.

Hosâm al-Din apparently grew up in one of the urban youth guilds in Konya which promoted the values of chivalry and spirituality. These fraternal institutions, designated by the general terms *fotovvat* (young man's guild) or *akhavân* (brothers), exercised a good deal of influence in Anatolia, particularly among the merchant and artisan classes, as well as among soldiers. These brotherhoods, with their code of civic virtue and mercantile morality, but which also exhibited features of a militia or a mafia-like gang, constituted a kind of alternative to the Sufi orders and their focus on ascetic and gnostic spirituality. The members of these confraternities commonly addressed their shaykhs as "my brother" (Arabic *akhi*), though the term "Akhi" describing these orders in Anatolia actually derives from a Turkish word for generosity. The caliph al-Nâser had accepted membership in a *fotovvat* order in 1182 and promoted the institution throughout his dominions, perhaps with the intention of bringing them under centralized control. With the demise of the caliphate in 1258, the institution declined during the Mongol period, except in Egypt, where the Abbasid prince welcomed by the Mamluks transferred the special garb of the *fotovvat* to Baybars, which perhaps served as a sign of authority because of its association with the extinguished caliphate.[1]

Mikâil Bayram has written about the Anatolian Akhi orders, specifically the Akhi Evren brotherhood and the sorority of Fâteme Baji (the Bajiân-e Rum), detailing their relations with the political powers of the day and their rivalry with Rumi and the Mevlevi order. Indeed, Bayram believes that many of the stories of the *Masnavi* contain veiled allusions which portray Akhi Evren in a disparaging light.[2]

Hosâm al-Din's father, Akhi Tork, headed a branch of just such a fraternal order, so that Hosâm al-Din was known as Ibn-e Akhi Tork, the son of Brother Turk. But Akhi Tork died when Hosâm was an early teen, at which point leadership of the brotherhood apparently devolved upon Hosâm al-Din. As Aflâki (Af 738) tells it, the elder members of the association asked Hosâm al-Din to lead them, but Hosâm instead led them all to Rumi. He instructed his own servants and the youth of his order to go out and earn a living so they might turn over their income to Rumi (the members of the Akhi orders commonly turned over their daily income to the head of their lodge). When they complained that nothing of their property and possessions remained, Hosâm al-Din even instructed them to sell the furniture of his house, at which point he was finally satisfied that, at least outwardly, he had "followed the Prophet." As we have seen elsewhere, this desire to follow obediently in the way of the Prophet (*motâbaʿat-e rasul*) was an overriding concern of both Shams and Rumi. As a gesture of his love for Rumi, Hosâm al-Din thereupon released his followers from their vow of fealty to him and dedicated himself to the service of Rumi (Af 739).

Rumi, in turn, entrusted his financial affairs to Chelebi Hosâm al-Din, who acted as comptroller of the endowment for Rumi's school, by now developing into a kind of hermitage, with disciples and family members attached to or dependent upon it in various ways. Aflâki (Af 782–3) cites at least one report that has Hosâm al-Din fulfilling this function already during the time of Shams al-Din, exacting a tribute of 40,000 dirhams from Amin al-Din Mikâʾil, the sultan's deputy, before he would be admitted to the presence of Shams. The contributions received from princes and other donors included property and funds; if we are to believe Aflâki (751), the amir Tâj al-Din Moʿtazz once sent the sum of 7,000 royal dirhams from Aksaray for the purpose of hosting a feast, in return for which he requested the prayers of the assembled company. Hosâm al-Din would disburse these available funds and resources as he saw fit, with the complete confidence and backing of Rumi. On this particular occasion, after assuring himself that the money had been lawfully obtained (in this case from the *jizyah* tax levied on non-Muslim subjects, in lieu of military service), Hosâm al-Din gave 1,000 dirhams to Sultan Valad, 1,000 to Rumi's wife, Kerrâ Khâtun, and 500 to Chelebi Amir ʿÂlem, dividing up the rest among the companions and followers of Rumi (Af 752).

Sultan Valad (SVE 112–13) says that when Shaykh Salâh al-Din passed on, the office of deputy (*nâyeb*) and designated successor (*khelâfat*) of Rumi fell to Chelebi Hosâm al-Din. Rumi had showered much attention on Hosâm al-Din and in the darkness following the setting of the sun, he needed a light (SVE 113):

> When the moon's engulfed within the clouds
> what will light the way if not the stars?

Sultan Valad goes on to report that someone once asked Rumi who among these three deputies occupied the highest station. Rumi replied that Shams was like the sun, Salâh like the moon and Hosâm like the stars, for having joined the angels: "Know all as one, for each can show you God."

Rumi instructed the disciples (SVE 115–16) to obey Hosâm al-Din's command and consider him identical to Rumi. This time around, because the disciples had twice tasted the bitterness of disobedience to Rumi – once when he chose Shams and once when he chose Salâh al-Din as deputy – all the disciples accepted Hosâm al-Din and none had the inclination to rebel. Hosâm al-Din and Rumi lived and worked together in one household for the next ten years, the disciples happy and no longer jealous (SVE 120–21). They did not spend all their time together, though, as it would appear from Aflâki (Af 760) that Rumi would go for about forty or fifty days out of every year to the hot springs. Although many disciples supposedly accompanied him, dancing and composing poems on the way, Hosâm al-Din stayed behind in Konya, presumably attending to the daily business of the school and fledgling order, visiting the graves of Bahâ al-Din and Salâh al-Din every day to say prayers (Af 765). It was probably during such absences from Konya that Rumi penned the four surviving letters addressed to Hosâm al-Din. One of these complains of an illness that had stricken Rumi (Mak 224) and shares with Hosâm the machinations of some who wished to poison his followers' minds against Rumi (Mak 227).

Rumi publicly reinforced Hosâm al-Din's position by his behavior. Aflâki (Af 769) tells us of one occasion when Mo'in al-Din Parvâne invited a large group of nobles and grandees together to see Rumi, but neglected to invite Hosâm al-Din. Rumi declined to speak until Hosâm al-Din was also summoned. Rumi rushed to greet him upon his arrival, saying, "Welcome, my spirit, my faith, my Jonayd, my light . . ." Though perhaps embellished, at least a kernel of truth can be found in one of Rumi's own letters (Mak 224–5), where he tells of trying to postpone accepting a certain invitation to dine until such a time as Hosâm could be present. Elsewhere we find Rumi writing letters on behalf of Hosâm al-Din to secure him the position of shaykh at a given Sufi lodge (Mak 158), once specifically for the lodge of Ziâ al-Din (Mak 219). Aflâki (Af 100) shows Parvâne and Tâj al-Din initially uncertain about Hosâm al-Din's spiritual powers, suspecting that Rumi may have appointed him pro forma. One of the letters Rumi wrote to the Seljuk sultan (probably 'Ezz al-Din) suggests that the governor of Konya was harassing Hosâm al-Din's son-in-law and that Hosâm al-Din had considered leaving town because of it (Mak 162–3). Rumi asks that the sultan intervene and stay the governor's hand. Eventually, the worthiness of Hosâm al-Din, whether through the intervention of the sultan, or through his own behavior and the insistence of Rumi, became apparent to them. Tâj al-Din Mo'tazz had the Seljuk sultan appoint Hosâm al-Din as the shaykh of the Sufi lodge (khâneqâh) of Ziâ al-Din Vazir (Af 754–5). Rumi himself assures Hosâm (Mak 161):

> I have sworn a hundred times to the Creator and His creatures that whatever you
> – the one whom I serve – should think, is in every respect the same as my
> thoughts, and whatever [you] instruct or say is the epitome of what I say.

Composition of the Masnavi

Hosâm al-Din's reputation rests first and foremost on prodding or providing Rumi with the pretext for composing the *Masnavi*. Sepahsâlâr (Sep 142) says that the entirety of Rumi's *Masnavi* was composed at his request and reflects many of the spiritual states and discoveries of Hosâm al-Din. Hosâm al-Din would quickly write while Rumi composed, singing back what he had recorded in a pleasing voice for Rumi's confirmation and approval (Af 742). This would sometimes last all night through, as the *Masnavi* itself confirms (M1:1807):

> Pillar and haven of the morn, it's dawn!
> pardon me to my master, Hosâm al-Din!

Once the first book had been completed, Hosâm al-Din repeatedly reviewed the entire text line by line, correcting various words and emending the syntax (*qoyud*, Af 742), perhaps even adding new sections at the prompting of Rumi, who sometimes intrudes upon the narrative to say (M1:2934–8):

> O Light of Truth, Hosâm al-Din! Let's add
> a sheet or two, description of the *pir*.
> I know your subtle body has no strength
> and yet without your sun we have no light ...
> You hold our thread of thought within your hand
> your blessings string our heart with meaning's pearls.
> Write down the circumstances of the *pir*
> who knows the way. Choose this *pir* and let him guide!

During this period Hosâm al-Din's wife suddenly passed away, and a kind of mental and spiritual oblivion (*takâsol*) overtook him (Af 743). He withdrew from Rumi and the *Masnavi* for a while as his soul traversed the heavens, setting out as a nightingale and returning as a falcon (M2:1–8). Without Hosâm al-Din, Rumi felt no inclination to compose, but when Hosâm al-Din returned to his normal self, they resumed their sessions and Book 2 was produced. As the text of the *Masnavi* specifies (M2:7), work resumed in A.H. 662, which corresponds to some time between November of 1263 and October of 1264. One report in Aflâki reckons the preceding interval, during which nothing further was composed, as lasting two full years (Af 742). If correct, this would mean that Book 1 was completed sometime in A.H. 660, corresponding to the period between December 1261 and November 1262.

Rumi invokes Hosâm al-Din, the Light of Truth, as his muse in each of Books 2 through 6 of the *Masnavi*, and in the prose introduction to Book 1. It is Hosâm al-Din who asked Rumi to continue the book (M4:5–6) and tries to draw more and more out of him, though Rumi insists that Hosâm al-Din already knows the things that Rumi says (M4:2075–80). One verse (M6:4) at the beginning of Book 6 perhaps indicates a preconceived plan to furnish the *Masnavi* with as many books as there were directions in the physical plane (according to classical Islamic theory, six: up, down, right, left, backwards, forwards). Elsewhere, Rumi compares the *Masnavi* in its coverage of the roots (*osul*) and branches (*foru*) of the religious sciences to a tree which he commends to the care of Hosâm al-Din:

> My purpose in composing this, Hosâm –
> my *Masnavi* – was you, the light of truth.
> The *Masnavi*, with all its roots and branches
> belongs to you alone, for you accept it.
> The kings accept our gifts, both good and bad
> and in accepting, they declare them worthy
> It's you who's planted this, our sapling, so
> water it and as it grows unbind its ropes
> Your mysteries are the meaning of my phrases
> Your voice the reason of its composition:
> To me your voice sings with the voice of God
> Never parted be the lover from beloved!

Whatever metaphors Rumi may apply to the shape of the *Masnavi*, he could have continued the book in the same style, had leisure permitted or inclination prompted him, without disturbing or deforming the structural unity of the work. Rumi imagines the book eventually growing so large that forty camels would be needed to carry it (M4:740). Indeed, Rumi might have pointed to the seven heavens as an equally valid cosmological justification for a seventh book, had he or Hosâm al-Din wanted or managed to add one. In any case, Rumi tells us nothing more about the date of composition of this most influential poem in the history of the Islamic East. The only indication we have comes from Aflâki (744), who reports further delays, but a constant outpouring of Rumi's ideas, all taken down and then repeatedly reviewed by Hosâm al-Din. We do know that Rumi's disciples read or heard the *Masnavi* recited and would ask him to explain the deeper meaning behind certain lines during public gatherings. Discourse 53 (Fih 196) poses a question about one line in Book 2 of the *Masnavi* (M2:277), though it does not mention the source of the poem, which must have been obvious to all the listeners. Most of the discourses recorded in *Fihe mâ fih* seem to date from this period in the mid- to late 1260s.

Gölpınarlı (GB 214) points out that one line of the *Masnavi* (M1:2795) states that the caliphate of ʿAbbâs and his descendants will last forever until the Day of Resurrection. The Abbasid caliphate was toppled by the Mongols in 1258 and was not reestablished (however tenuously) in Egypt until 1261. Gölpınarlı concludes (GB 215) that Rumi must therefore have completed the text of Book 1 of the *Masnavi* before 1258, during the lifetime of Salâh al-Din. Schimmel adopts Gölpınarlı's argument, concluding that Book 1 "may have been dictated some time between 1256 and 1258" (ScT 34). She also points to another piece of evidence which might support Gölpınarlı's theory, directing our attention to a very interesting poem in Rumi's *Divân* which is dedicated to Hosâm al-Din (D 1839). This poem relates in verse a dream Rumi had had about the Mongol invaders and obligingly dates the dream (though not necessarily the poem) to a Saturday night, the 5th of the month of Qaᶜde, in the year 654, corresponding to November 24, 1256.

We should not be surprised if further study bears out that this or other poems addressed to Hosâm al-Din date to the lifetime of Salâh al-Din. Hosâm al-Din functioned as Rumi's secretary and took down the dictation for a letter Rumi wrote to Sultan ᶜEzz al-Din Kay Kâus II sometime between 1257 and 1260, as we have seen above ("Rumi's Activity and Status in Konya Before Shams," in chapter 2). We would assume that Rumi had at least contemplated the selection of Hosâm al-Din as the successor to Salâh al-Din during the latter's lifetime, at least during his lengthy illness. However, the existence of a ghazal or two for Hosâm dating from this period would not necessarily tell us anything about the composition of the *Masnavi*, which is a very different kind of poetry – narrative verse with an expressly didactic theme. Rumi may have composed exclusively lyrical poems for Hosâm al-Din, as he had done for Salâh al-Din, for quite some time before deciding to compose a larger and different type of poem. Schimmel's comments about the very early *Masnavi* (M1:125) portraying Hosâm al-Din as "still comparatively immature" likewise seem to me rather doubtful as evidence for the dating of the poem.

The Gölpınarlı–Schimmel thesis, however, does not easily harmonize with the rest of our admittedly sketchy information. First, Book 1 of the *Masnavi* makes no mention of Salâh al-Din, whereas Book 2, written five years after his death, does mention him once. If Salâh al-Din were still alive, why did Rumi neglect to mention him and why did he describe Hosâm al-Din in the prose introduction in terms that suggest he was already well known as the chosen successor of Rumi?

Schimmel suggests that Book 1 was completed by 1258 and that the subsequent death of Salâh al-Din plunged Rumi into despair, followed by the despair of Hosâm al-Din following the death of his wife. Work could therefore not continue on the *Masnavi* until about 1263, a year after Schimmel understands Hosâm al-Din to have been officially appointed Rumi's successor (ScT 34). If this is true, we must dismiss Aflâki's report that a period of two years elapsed between the completion of Book 1 and the beginning of Book 2. The Mongol advance on Baghdad began in the spring of 1257 from Qazvin, but was delayed until November 1257. Siege was laid to Baghdad in late mid-January of 1258 and the city surrendered on February 10. Plunder, devastation and massacre followed and the caliph al-Mostaᶜsem was put to death with his family on February 20, 1258.

If Book 1 were completed in 1257 before the siege or even during February 1258 as the city of Baghdad's defenses collapsed (it would have taken a couple of weeks for the news of the caliph's execution to reach Konya), this would mean that at least five full years, perhaps even more than six, elapsed before the composition of Book 2 began, sometime after November 1263. If we do credit Aflâki's report, related on the authority of Serâj al-Din the *Masnavi* reciter (see "The Formation of the Order", chapter 10, below), the passage at issue toward the end of Book 1 of the *Masnavi* about the Abbasid caliphs enduring forever could have been composed sometime during 1261 or 1262, perhaps after the Abbasid caliphate had already been reestablished in exile in Egypt, thus removing Gölpınarlı's objection in its entirety.

Even if we choose not to believe Aflâki's report and the chronology it establishes, we still have no compelling reason to take Rumi's statement about the caliphate enduring to the end of time as an expression of historical fact. It is made in passing, coming in the words of one of the characters in a story, a story which Rumi may even have borrowed from some earlier source. Even if we take this as a commentary by Rumi on political events, it could represent either a pious hope or pious fiction in the face of what was after all a theologically catastrophic event for the Islamic world – the extinction of the line of temporal succession to the Prophet Mohammad established some five hundred years before and the loss of control over the central lands of the realm of Islam to the hands of a pagan power. Given this disruption in the theological cosmos, one can easily argue that Rumi might have symbolically transformed the temporal caliphate into a spiritual one and allowed it to go on existing in the mind or in the spiritual plane in perpetuity, despite its physical extinction. He may also have meant to send a signal of encouragement to the caliph in exile in Egypt. On the other hand, neither Rumi nor his disciples mention the fall of the caliphate in the Discourses, so perhaps it was not an obsessive concern. By contrast, Sa°di wrote two poems on the fall of the caliphate, one in Arabic and one in Persian (Saf 3/1:125).

Gölpınarlı (GB 214–15) dismisses the report of Sayyed Sahih Ahmad Dede (d. 1898), the chief cook of the Yenikapı Mevlevi lodge in Istanbul, who says that the composition of the *Masnavi* began in 1261 (A.H. 659) and was brought to a conclusion in 1268 or 1269 (A.H. 667). Sahih Ahmad gives no source and writes at the remove of six hundred years, probably conjecturing from the date given in Book 2 and the information given in Aflâki to the effect that it took approximately one and a half years to write each book of the *Masnavi*. Though a guess, it is not a bad one. Yet the fact remains that we just do not know the details of the dates of composition of the *Masnavi*. Book 2 was begun sometime between the autumn of 1263 and the onset of autumn in 1264. Book 1 was probably composed a couple of years before that. Rumi's death in December of 1273 gives us our *terminus ad quem*, and although Book 6 has a rather inconclusive feel to it, this does not necessarily mean that it remained unfinished at Rumi's death. Gölpınarlı (GB 216) argues that a forty-five-line epilogue to the

Masnavi, added by Sultan Valad and contained in some manuscripts, suggests that Rumi could not have outlived the composition of the book by very long.

The Death of the Epiphany of Faith, Jalâl al-Din Rumi

Sultan Valad tells us in verse of the death of Rumi, specifying the date as 5 Jumâdi II 672, corresponding to December 17, 1273, which is also the date inscribed on Rumi's sarcophagus. Compare the account of heaven's cataclysmic response to the crucifixion of Christ and Sultan Valad's account of the celestial reaction to Rumi's death (SVE 121):

> From this foul, fulsome world, Rumi moved on
> After ten sweet years with Hosâm al-Din
> On a December's day, the seventeenth   [5 Jumâdi II]
> that proud monarch's moving on came to pass
> Seventy-two and six hundred of years   [A.H. 672 = A.D. 1273]
> since the Hijra of the Prophet had gone by
> The eye of mankind wept so sore that day
> its lightning struck and burned away the souls
> A quaking overtook the earth that moment
> in the heavens rose a wail of mourning
> The people of the town, both young and old
> wailed and wept and sighed in lamentation
> The villagers nearby, both Greeks and Turks
> in painful loss of him rent wide their collars
> all paid the corpse their last loving respects
> Folks from every faith proved faithful to him –
> in love with him the people of all nations

The Christians and Jews worshiped him, the Muslims called him the head and light of the Prophet. All rent their collars and poured dust on their heads. The collective mourning lasted for forty days and even then the fervor of distress did not die down, though everyone returned home.

Sepahsâlâr (Sep 109) explains that because our bodies are composed of four contrary elements, all of which seek to rejoin their essence, the body cannot endure forever in the world. The spirit, an emanation from the sanctified light of God, succeeds for a time in maintaining an equilibrium between these oppositely charged elements. However, since the soul has descended into the mortal plane from a higher realm, it too longs to rejoin its essence. If during its life on earth a soul has managed to acquire spiritual honor and perfections, it becomes a reflection of the divine and will immediately respond to the call to return to its Lord.

Rumi would not have felt a sense of foreboding; quite the contrary, he would have looked forward to the release of his soul from the prison of self. Sepahsâlâr (113) expresses amazement about the joyous and welcoming attitude toward death reflected in Rumi's poems and wonders if anyone before or after will ever rival his words in this regard. In several poems, some of them doubtless written on the occasion of the death of one of his close disciples or an important personage, Rumi meditates on the immortality of the soul. The following passages (from D 3172) sum up Rumi's view (see also chapter 9, below):

> You who fly from this narrow cage
> veering off beyond the heavens
> you'll see a new life after this;
>> how long will you bear this life's drear? . . .
>> This body wore a butler's garb
>> now sports more fashionable form.
>> Death means life and this life is death
>> though heathen eyes see negative
> All souls departed from this body
> live on, but hidden now, like angels . . .
> When body's bricks crumble, don't wail
> Sir, you've been only in a jail
> when you emerge from jail or pit,
> you stand regal, tall, like Joseph

Sepahsâlâr (Sep 113–14) tells us that Konya had been rocked by earthquakes for forty days before Rumi's death and the people came to him asking for his intercession to ward off any impending catastrophe: Rumi replied that they had no need to worry; the earth was hungering for a juicy morsel, but it would soon be satisfied and no harm would come to the town. However, the evidence Sepahsâlâr adduces for this is a poem that would seem to be related to Shams al-Din, not Rumi. Sepahsâlâr (114) also relates that Rumi composed a poem on his deathbed, to encourage Sultan Valad to go and get some sleep (Af 590), but judging from the contents of the poem (see Poem 11 in chapter 8, below), this seems quite speculative.

Sepahsâlâr relates (Sep 114–15) that two brilliant doctors attended Rumi for some days, constantly taking his pulse and then withdrawing to consult their medical books. Finally despairing of a diagnosis, they asked Rumi to inform them of his own condition, for they had concluded that he himself wished to die. Sepahsâlâr tells us with precision that the moment finally came on Sunday, December 17, 1273 at sunset. That evening the preparations for burial were arranged and the next day his body was lifted up on a bier and carried through the town, the streets of which overflowed with throngs of people from all walks of life (Sep 116). These included men, women and children, common folk and nobles, Christian, Jew, Greek, Arab, Turk and otherwise. All the religious communities joined in the procession, reading from the Psalms, the Torah and the Gospels, claiming that if Rumi was the Mohammad of the age for the Muslims, he was also the Moses and the Jesus of the age for them (Af 592). Of course, the Muslim community participated in the procession with Koran reciters, muezzins, poets who wrote down elegies, musicians with cymbals and horns, and so forth (Af 593).

Not long after Rumi's death a certain ʿAlam al-Din Qaysar approached Sultan Valad about erecting the Green Dome (Qobbat al-khazrâ), the building which houses the mausoleum of Rumi, for which he required the sum of 30,000 dirhams. The daughter of Ghiâs al-Din Kay Khosrow II and the wife of Moʿin al-Din Parvâne collected several times this amount (Af 792) and the construction of the shrine was begun under the supervision of Badr al-Din Tabrizi. An elaborately carved sarcophagus of walnut wood was prepared, probably by ʿAbd al-Vâhed b. Salim (GB 230–31), upon which was inscribed one of Rumi's poems (D 911), beginning:

> On the day I die
> as they bear aloft my bier
> do not suppose
> I'm consumed by cares of this world.
> Don't cry for me and do not lament

Several other poems of Rumi, along with verses from the Koran and at least three separate inscriptions, can be seen on the sarcophagus, one of them in the Kufic style which experts have been unable to decipher (GB 231–6).

THE SUCCESSION

HOSÂM AL-DIN THROUGH THE EYES OF RUMI AND SULTAN VALAD

Although the stewardship of Hosâm al-Din seems to have been a relatively unified and uneventful one, the sources nevertheless betray their particular allegiances when discussing him. Sultan Valad (SVE 113) relates that Rumi instructed the disciples to account Shams, Salâh al-Din and Hosâm al-Din as one, for they all led to the truth. In the same breath, however, Sultan Valad goes on to describe a relative hierarchy of light that places Hosâm al-Din in the dimmest position, for which he invokes Rumi's authority: Shams was the sun, Salâh the moon and Hosâm the stars. He also refers to Hosâm as the lamp brought out once the sun has set, a simile that would seem to stress the paleness of the comparison between the two.

Sepahsâlâr, on the other hand, explicitly states that Rumi loved none of the other successors (kholafâʿ) – and this would include Salâh al-Din and Sultan Valad – as much as Hosâm al-Din. So great was his love that it at times appeared Rumi was Hosâm al-Din's disciple (Sep 144). Rumi did indeed choose Salâh al-Din and Hosâm al-Din as his spiritual models. In the introduction to the *Masnavi*, Rumi calls Hosâm al-Din "My master, my stay and support, the spirit's place in my body, the treasury of my todays and tomorrows, the Shaykh, the exemplar of the gnostics, the Imam of the people of guidance and certitude." This should not however lead us to conclude that Rumi considered Hosâm al-Din his superior in mystic attainments. We have already seen that the relationship between Rumi and Shams could not be characterized as a traditional shaykh–disciple relationship. Recall also that Rumi himself speaks of how deferentially he and Salâh al-Din behaved toward one another one day in the public bath, rather like equals. That Rumi respected and cherished the companionship of these men, and showed them every honor, cannot be doubted.

Yet Sepahsâlâr soon tells us that Hosâm al-Din always knelt in front of Rumi in a posture of discipleship. We also learn that when Rumi began to compose the *Masnavi* Hosâm al-Din would fall unconscious for long periods on account of the dizzying vistas of spiritual insight which Rumi opened up to him. When he came to, he would bow his head at Rumi's feet and, weeping profusely, call blessings down on that pure soul (Sep 145–6). Aflâki (759) reports that Hosâm al-Din, like Shams of Tabriz, followed the rites of the Shâfeʿi school of Islamic law. One day Hosâm al-Din said that he wished to convert to the Hanafi creed, "because our master is of the Hanafi creed." Rumi told him that it would be better to keep his own creed and simply to follow the mystical teachings of Rumi and guide the people to his creed of love. This he did, for example, by defending Rumi's practice of listening to the rabâb and performing the *samâʿ*. After Rumi died, the Chief Qâzi Serâj al-Din summoned Hosâm al-Din to court to stop the practice of listening to the rabâb, but Hosâm al-Din refused (Af 761–2). All this leaves us in little doubt about who was the disciple and who the master.

Sepahsâlâr dutifully reports (Sep 146) that at the death of Rumi some of the disciples felt Sultan Valad should have replaced Hosâm al-Din as successor. Though Sepahsâlâr has already tipped his hand in favor of Hosâm al-Din by this point in the narrative, he treats the matter in a very dignified manner and carefully explains the case made on behalf of Sultan Valad. Sultan Valad is the flesh and blood of Rumi as well as his heir in knowledge, and he has attained an advanced stage on the mystic path. The supporters of Sultan Valad argued that he had been perfectly capable and worthy to run the community of disciples during the lifetime of his father, but that he dutifully kept his peace out of respect to his father's wishes. Aflâki (586) relates that all the important personages assembled around Rumi's deathbed and asked him about his successor. Three times the question was repeated and each time the answer came: Hosâm al-Din. On the fourth go round they asked, "What about Sultan Valad?" Rumi replied, "He is a hero and has no need of my will." So both Sepahsâlâr and Aflâki hint that Sultan Valad had partisans who preferred him to Hosâm al-Din.

Nonetheless, the claim put forth on behalf of Sultan Valad met with indirect resistance from another party of disciples, who said that we are all consumed by love and should not place any distinctions between love and the beloved (Sep 146–7). Doubtless, this party wished to avoid any dissension over the succession, so they suggested that the two leaders, Hosâm al-Din and Sultan

Valad, should get together and decide between themselves who should run the community, and all would pledge to follow their decision. The next day, according to Sepahsâlâr, all the family members, disciples, leaders and nobles gathered at the grave of Rumi ("the sanctified earth" – *torbat-e moqaddas*). There Hosâm al-Din professed his submission to Sultan Valad in the following terms (Sep 147):

> Light of my eyes and son of him I served! Now that the glorious sun of his holiness my Master has set on this lower plane and dawned over the horizon of the hereafter, he has entrusted this group of meek orphans to you. You should sit in the place of your great father and guide us all – high and low alike – in the ways of compassion and refinement.

The foregoing accounts suggest that Sultan Valad's expectations may have been somewhat disappointed by his father after Salâh al-Din's death in 1258. Sultan Valad would have been about thirty-two years old and just about of an age to assume a position of leadership. As we have seen, Sultan Valad tells us that his father compared Hosâm al-Din to the stars, whereas Salâh al-Din had been the moon and Shams the sun. Though Sultan Valad might point to one line from the *Masnavi* to support his celestial hierarchy (M5:1), another passage from it (M4:16–20) explicitly contradicts him, calling Hosâm the sun (*khworshid, shams*), whose light (*ziâ*) outshines the light (*nur*) of the moon.

We do not know Sultan Valad's place in the celestial sky, but Rumi has not praised his own son in writing in terms similar to those set aside for Hosâm al-Din in the *Masnavi*. Aflâki (Af 751) tells us that Sultan Valad once complained about the fact that all the monies contributed in the name of Rumi were put at the disposal of Hosâm al-Din. "We have nothing in our own house," complained Sultan Valad, "to pay our expenses, but every contribution (*fotuhi*) we receive his holiness our Master sends to Chelebi. What are we supposed to do?" Rumi replies that his trust in Hosâm al-Din as a man of God is so great that even if thousands of pious men were starving to death and he had only one loaf of bread, he would give it to Hosâm al-Din.

However much Sultan Valad may have felt slighted by his father's confidence in Hosâm, we know that he remained faithful to his father's will. Upon the death of Rumi, even though one party pushed forward a claim for Sultan Valad as successor, he chose to withdraw his name from consideration for the stewardship of the community, even over the protestations of Hosâm al-Din. In the account given by Sepahsâlâr, Sultan Valad humbly and eloquently replies to Hosâm al-Din as follows:

> During his lifetime, his holiness my Master and father, may God be pleased with him, chose you above all others and committed the leadership and direction of all the companions and descendants to you. Now that we are bereft of his resplendent beauty, the leadership remains as it was. (Sep 147–8)

With this Sultan Valad got up and led Hosâm al-Din to the seat of honor. As Sultan Valad himself explains it, he told Hosâm al-Din that the spirit of his father, Rumi, still hovered over them and there was no reason to change his arrangements. Hosâm al-Din nevertheless continued to insist that Sultan Valad should take over, relenting only when he saw Sultan Valad absolutely determined to refuse (SVE 122–3).

Sepahsâlâr (148) indicates that Hosâm al-Din remained at the helm of the Mevlevi community for the next twelve years until the end of his life. A manuscript of Sultan Valad's *Ebtedâ nâme* confirms the dozen years of Hosâm al-Din's ministry after the death of Rumi, though Jalâl al-Din Homâ°i has opted for a variant reading of ten years in his published edition of the text (SVE 123), a reading which Saᶜid Nafisi felt quite inferior (Sep 376). During this time he focused and purified the minds of the disciples and observed all the customs established by Rumi (Sep 148; Af 777). Aflâki reports (Af 777) that every Friday following the prayers and recitation of the Koran, Hosâm al-Din would hold readings of the *Masnavi* and a session of *samâᶜ*, attended by several hundred disciples, mystics, authors and so on. He also attended to the financial needs of Rumi's wife, Kerrâ Khâtun; his daughter, Maleke Khâtun; and his son, Sultan Valad.

When Hosâm al-Din felt he could no longer tolerate the pain of separation from Rumi he prayed for release from this life, and his prayer was granted (Sep 148). Aflâki (Af 779) gives the date of his death as November 4, 1284 (23 Shaᶜbân 683), whereas Sepahsâlâr (Sep 148) says he died sometime in 1285 (A.H. 684). Gölpınarlı (GM 39) describes the seven-line inscription on his grave, a brick sarcophagus inlaid with plaster located in the inner sanctum of the shrine of Rumi, facing his master's grave. The date of death reads October 24, 1284 (12 Shaᶜbân 683) according to Gölpınarlı, but Sobhâni deciphers it as October 30, 1284 (18 Shaᶜbân 683).

Approximately ten years elapsed from the time of Shams al-Din's disappearance, probably in early 1248, and the death of Salâh al-Din on December 29, 1258. Sultan Valad describes the reign of Salâh al-Din as lasting ten years, though we may wonder how long it took before Rumi accepted the disappearance of Shams and declared Salâh al-Din his successor. In any case, it seems likely that Salâh al-Din functioned as a kind of secretary and doorkeeper for Rumi from the very beginning of Shams' absence, guarding Rumi's privacy and guiding the crowd of disciples on his behalf.

Sultan Valad (SVE 112–13, 115–16) seems to imply that Hosâm al-Din Chelebi became the new deputy and designated successor for Rumi immediately upon the death of Salâh al-Din. He then goes on to state that Rumi and Hosâm al-Din shared close company for a period of ten years before the death of Rumi (SVE 120). Aflâki (Af 778) basically follows this, indicating that ten full years passed from the time of Hosâm al-Din's appointment until the death of Rumi, which occurred in the eleventh year. Sepahsâlâr at one point agrees with Sultan Valad that Hosâm al-Din acted as designated successor for ten years while Rumi was alive (Sep 145), but reckons at another point (Sep 142) that Hosâm al-Din spent nine years with Rumi between the time of Salâh al-Din's death and Rumi's death.

Even if we assume a full eleven years as the correct date this still leaves us with a puzzling chronological discrepancy. If Salâh al-Din served Rumi for ten years until the former's death in December 1258, how could Hosâm al-Din have spent only ten or eleven years with Rumi, assuming that he was appointed as his deputy sometime in 1259? Rumi died in December of 1273, about fifteen years, or 5,467 days, later to be precise. Although this period amounts to slightly less than fifteen years according to the solar calendar, according to the Islamic lunar calendar Rumi died exactly fifteen years, five months and five days after Salâh al-Din, if the dates handed down to us are correct. This leaves us with a period of between four to six years unaccounted for.

One might speculate that Rumi did not choose Hosâm al-Din immediately upon the death of Salâh al-Din, deciding upon him only about four years later. Our chronicles, however, do not give any indication of this, so we may consider this quite unlikely. On the other hand, perhaps the period of Hosâm al-Din's spiritual withdrawal, mentioned in Book 2 of the *Masnavi*, accounts for the missing years. In this case, we might speculate that after taking down Rumi's words in Book 1, Hosâm felt himself in need either of a deeper knowledge of the religious sciences or a period of spiritual retreat and contemplation. Perhaps Hosâm al-Din withdrew from Rumi's company during this period and traveled to another town.

A further, though extremely far-fetched explanation, is that we have the wrong date for the death of Salâh al-Din. Foruzânfar (FB 109 n. 4) mentions some accounts that place Salâh al-Din's death in 1264, which would square with the ten-year interval reckoned by Sultan Valad and Aflâki. Sepahsâlâr does not give a date, but Aflâki (Af 731) gives the same date for Salâh al-Din's death that appears on his tombstone, December 29, 1258.

Another solution, the one I find the most satisfying, is to attribute Sultan Valad's "ten years" to simple imprecision on his part. Sepahsâlâr and Aflâki, out of respect for Sultan Valad, and not out of faulty arithmetic, reckon the period of Hosâm al-Din's companionship with Rumi at ten years. Sultan Valad composed his verse account of the matter about nineteen years after the death of Rumi; Sepahsâlâr and Aflâki about fifty years after the fact. We may assume that during these events, as seminal and important as they now appear to us in hindsight, no journal or precise records were being kept. Therefore, when going back to reconstruct the history of the period, all three chroniclers seized on the two dates that they found in written records. Sultan Valad probably recalled the date of composition of Book 2 of the *Masnavi*, which Rumi specified in the seventh line for all to see as A.H. 662 (A.D. 1263–4). The date of Rumi's death, A.H. 672 (A.D. 1273), was likewise well known to the disciples, both because they commemorated it annually and because it was carved on his tomb, which they visited daily. In thinking back over the period, Sultan Valad probably seized upon these dates in his memory, rather than the date of Salâh al-Din's death, and calculated that Rumi and Hosâm al-Din were together for ten years. This led the other chroniclers to repeat the ten-year figure, though they also relay reports of just under or just over ten years. Aside from being a round number, this figure provides a nice parallel to the ten years that Salâh al-Din and Rumi are said to have spent together, making a decade the archetypal reign for both of the successors of Shams.

SULTAN VALAD, BAHÂ AL-DIN MOHAMMAD: SON AND SUCCESSOR TO RUMI

Aflâki (Af 784) and Sepahsâlâr (Sep 148) both refer to Rumi's son by the same title as his father and grandfather: Mowlânâ, Our Master. He was the last member of the family to be so designated. Among the other honorifics given him in these chronicles, we find sultan of the seekers, revealer of the secrets of certainty, God's friend (*vali*) on earth, God's proof to creation, the completion and seal of the circle of sainthood (*velâyat*), the lord and ruler of the climes of reality. According to Aflâki (785), Rumi used to say to Sultan Valad, "You resemble me more than anyone else, both physically and in disposition." Whenever Rumi went to any gathering to speak, he used to seat his son next to him. Just eighteen years apart, father and son were frequently mistaken for brothers (Af 26, 785). Rumi gave his own father's title and name to his little son, calling him Bahâ al-Din Mohammad Sultan Valad. Somewhat more difficult to believe is the following report from Aflâki, about the period before Sultan Valad was weaned of his mother's milk (784):

> He always slept in the arms of his holiness Mowlânâ and when he wanted to get up and perform the night prayer, Sultan Valad would scream and cry. In order to quiet him, his holiness Mowlânâ would interrupt his prayer and hug him. When he wanted his mother's milk, he would put his own breast in Sultan Valad's mouth. His paternal compassion was so great that, by the command of God – "pure milk, tasty to those who drink" [K16:66] – pure milk would flow until that babe had its fill of the milk of that lion of inner meaning and would sleep, just as clear water used to well up from the fingers of the Messenger of God.

Nezâm al-Din, the brother-in-law of Sultan Valad (the husband of Hedye Khâtun, sister to Sultan Valad's wife, Fâteme Khâtun), noted the date of Sultan

Valad's birth on his personal copy of the *Divân* of Sultan Valad. He gives the date as 25 Rabi^c II 623, corresponding to April 25, 1226 (GM 41 n. 1).[3] Sepahsâlâr (Sep 151), who also knew Sultan Valad and was probably present when he died, reports that he passed away on Saturday 10 Rajab 712, corresponding to November 11, 1312. If Sepahsâlâr is correct when he earlier states that Valad lived to be ninety-six years of age (Sep 149), this would place his birth, according to the Islamic lunar calendar, in the year A.H. 618, corresponding to A.D. 1221. However, Rumi did not marry Gowhar Khâtun, the mother of Sultan Valad, until he was eighteen, in about the year 1224 and the first of the sons, whether Sultan Valad or ^cAlâ al-Din, was not born until A.H. 623, or about 1226 (Af 26), so Sepahsâlâr surely errs when he says Sultan Valad lived to be ninety-six.

Given 1226 as the approximate year of birth for Sultan Valad, he would have been only about five when his grandfather Bahâ al-Din died in 1231. When twenty, Sultan Valad supposedly asked his father for permission to perform the traditional ascetic retreat or *chelle*, a forty-day period of seclusion practiced by many Sufis. Rumi told him that it was not necessary to afflict himself in this manner (it presumes a forty-day fast) as it was not something which Muslim law required but was an innovation introduced from Christian and Jewish practice. Sultan Valad determined to undertake it anyway, and when the time was up and they came to retrieve him, he was bathed in supernal light (Af 793). The mission entrusted to him by his father to retrieve Shams-e Tabriz from Damascus in about 1246, when Sultan Valad was only twenty, must have been another milestone in his life. When Salâh al-Din died, Sultan Valad would have been about thirty-two, and about forty-seven upon the death of own father in 1273. Nevertheless, he deferred to his father's wishes and followed the directives of Hosâm al-Din.

As we have seen, Sultan Valad and Sepahsâlâr both hint that the community initially disagreed over whether or not Hosâm al-Din should remain the leader of Rumi's community once Rumi was dead. Sultan Valad, or at least some of his friends, seem to think that the privilege should have fallen to him. However, just as the early Muslim community had thrice passed over Mohammad's own flesh and blood, ^cAli, preferring older more experienced men as the successors (*khalif*) to Mohammad, so the early Mevlevi community twice passed over Sultan Valad. Had Rumi and his followers been Shiites rather than Sunnis, perhaps the hereditary principle would have immediately prevailed.

THE FURTHER EDUCATION OF SULTAN VALAD

However, once Hosâm al-Din had passed away, twelve years after the death of Rumi, the disciples came back to Sultan Valad and asked him to assume the seat of the shaykh. Protesting that an army without a general is weak, they told him (SVE 129):

Until now, you declined on the pretext that his holiness, Mowlânâ, God sanctify his spirit, had designated Hosâm al-Din as his successor. Now that he has moved on, you must accept this and not make any further pretexts.

Even if Sultan Valad had felt slighted during the lifetime of Hosâm al-Din, Hosâm al-Din's death nevertheless brought him no sense of satisfaction or relief. Instead, Sultan Valad, then in his forty-seventh year, felt the weight of responsibility come crashing down upon him. He tells us he felt frightened and wretched, like an orphaned child (SVE 123). For some time he felt like beating his head against the wall and wailing over his situation. During this crisis, Hosâm al-Din revealed himself to Sultan Valad in a dream, comforting him with the thought that a spiritual support (*qotb*) is always present in the world, reflecting the divine light in human form. Hosâm al-Din's apparition reassured Sultan Valad that he would one day find his own saint (*vali*) in this world, and the spirit of Hosâm al-Din would work through that saint to fulfill the desires of Sultan Valad (SVE 127).

Valad indicates that he did indeed later meet this spiritual *axis mundi*, though in accordance with that teacher's wishes, Sultan Valad did not divulge his identity while he was still alive (SVE 130, 139–40). But when this "chosen saint" (*vali-ye gozin*) suddenly passed away, Sultan Valad felt free to reveal his name: **Shaykh Karim al-Din b. Baktamor** (SVE 325). When Sultan Valad does first mention the name of Karim al-Din, he enjoins everyone to visit him before he dies, so it would appear that Karim was still alive at this point in the narrative. Valad tells us that Karim al-Din is the (spiritual) remnant of Hosâm al-Din, who also used to praise Karim al-Din all the time. Sultan Valad tells the people that they will find no aid in the current age except through Karim al-Din (SVE 326):

> He is peerless in this world today
> there is none equal to him in this age ...
> They make mention of Jesus and Moses –
> know that their story is the same as his

On the basis of Baktamor's tombstone, located behind the graves of Ulu ˁÂref, Vâhed, and ˁÂbed Chelebi on the left side of the sanctuary, Gölpınarlı (GM 47) concludes that he died in November of 1292 (Dhu al-hijja A.H. 691). The inscription reads:

> This is the noble earth of the pride of the gnostic companions, the superior, the lover, the truthful Shaykh Karim al-Din b. al-Hâj Baktamor al-Mowlavi, God have mercy on him. In the month of Dhu al-hijja 691.

However, Sultan Valad's *Ebtedâ nâme*, composed between March and June of 1291, describes Karim al-Din at one point as alive and at another point as deceased. If Gölpınarlı is correct, then Sultan Valad's verses about Karim al-Din's death must have been interpolated about a year and a half after the poem had been completed. However, Sultan Valad speaks of a period of seven years from the death of Hosâm al-Din in October of 1284, during which time Karim al-Din functioned as leader (*rahbar*) of the Mevlevi order (SVE 230):

> For a while he was leader of this group
> his face like a candle in the dark night
> In the end the Mover of existence
> stole him away, this jewel, from our midst
> Karim al-Din sloughed off his mortal coil
> that chosen saint of righteous character
> No king could match his generosity
> He was a priceless pearl within this world
> He, after Hosâm al-Din, was leader,
> head for a period of seven years

This seems to take us only to 1291, though Sultan Valad may have assumed the mantle of leadership while Karim al-Din was still alive. It seems more likely, however, that the inscription on Karim al-Din's tombstone, which mentions only the month and not a specific day of death, reflects the date of the erection of the gravestone, rather than the actual date of Baktamor's death. We might conclude, then, that Karim al-Din passed away sometime in late May 1291, as Sultan Valad was nearing the completion of his verse chronicle.

Either way, when Karim al-Din died in 1291 or 1292, Sultan Valad became the undisputed head of the Mevlevi order. Sultan Valad tried to take heart in the knowledge that when a saint passes on, another always takes his place, because God has created the world not for its outward form but for its spiritual reality (SVE 330):

> Concerning the moving on of Shaykh Karim al-Din, the son of Baktamor, God have mercy upon him. When a saint (*vali*) travels on from this world, one should not lose hope, for so long as the earth shall stand, the saints of God will always be.

Curiously, the later Mevlevi tradition does not recognize Shaykh Karim al-Din Baktamor as one of the heads of the order. Aflâki mentions him but once (Af 176–7), calling him a man of spiritual attainments and insight. Sepahsâlâr (154) mentions him in passing as one of the close disciples. Both Aflâki and Sepahsâlâr had read Sultan Valad's chronicle, so their omission of the name of Karim al-Din Baktamor as a successor of the order is quite deliberate, probably motivated by a desire to magnify Sultan Valad and consolidate the authority of the Mevlevi order.

So just what was the role of Karim al-Din? Rumi had chosen Salâh al-Din and Hosâm al-Din as figureheads or foils, towards whom he could direct the attention and daily needs of his disciples. But since Sultan Valad did not reveal Karim al-Din's name until just before his death, Karim al-Din could not have been functioning as the titular head of the Mevlevi order, controlling access to Sultan Valad and dealing with dignitaries or other visitors in an official capacity.

Rumi also viewed Salâh and Hosâm al-Din as mirrors in and through which his spirituality could find reflection. Perhaps Sultan Valad (and Hosâm al-Din?) similarly saw himself in Karim al-Din and therefore chose to focus his spiritual energies upon him. It would appear from one quatrain written by Sultan Valad that Karim al-Din, like Salâh al-Din, was a man of spiritual powers rather than of impressive book-learning (GM 46–7).

SPREADING THE MESSAGE: SULTAN VALAD ORGANIZES RUMI'S FOLLOWING

Most of the Mevlevi disciples believed that Sultan Valad had agreed to become their shaykh after the death of Hosâm al-Din, and it appears that the people were happy with Sultan Valad's guidance (SVE 130). Whether or not Sultan privately considered Karim al-Din the spiritual heir of his father, he had been acting to outward eyes as the head of the disciples of his father. By 1291 when he composed his family chronicle, the "Book of Beginnings," Sultan Valad would have been teaching at the college of his father and grandfather for seven years. He tells us that he managed to dispel any lingering enmity among the disciples and lead them all to righteousness and piety. He began to acquire a reputation for himself, which he used to give structure to the order, and his glory soon surpassed that of other ages (SVE 130).

Sultan Valad tells us that during his tenure the wisdom and knowledge of the disciples increased, as did the number of both male and female initiates (SVE 155). In response to the growth and spread of the Mevlevi following, it became impossible to ask everyone to come to Konya and live in the shadow of Rumi's shrine. Some of those wishing to become formal disciples were constrained by family and children and would be faced with the prospect of either abandoning their dependents or pulling up roots and forsaking their livelihoods to move to Konya, which would make them dependents of the pious endowments of the shrine. Sultan Valad instead appointed a leader or successor (*khalife*), a term associated with Sufi orders, in every city where a sizeable number of disciples were living, so that the residents of those towns would not remain thirsty and parched for Rumi's teachings.

Cells of the order were set up throughout Anatolia and elsewhere, each with its own shaykh and leader (*moqtadâ, pishvâ*) acting as deputies (*nâyeb*) to Sultan Valad (SVE 155, 156), at the center of what came to be known as the Mevlevi movement (Mevlevi being the Turkish pronunciation of the Arabic-derived title, Mowlavi, by which Rumi's disciples addressed him). Sultan Valad praises the disciples in Âksaray for their spirituality, and also the town of Kütahya (GM 59). The center of the Mevlevi movement, of course, remained in Konya, which Sultan Valad praises in a couple of poems from his *Divân* as the king of cities; it is the city of spirit, because Rumi had chosen it and made it his Mecca and Kaaba (GM 58). Rumi had also called it, according to Aflâki (801), "a magnificently flourishing and blessed city."

According to a report transmitted by Aflâki (791), Rumi once told Sultan Valad that he, Rumi, had come into the world to bring Sultan Valad into being, telling him, "All of what I say are only my words, but you are the product of my deeds." If Rumi spent his life in words, expounding a set of teachings, Sultan Valad spent his life in deeds, assisting his father, helping strengthen the unity of the order and spreading it far and wide.

THE RANK OF SULTAN VALAD AMONG THE SUCCESSORS

Sultan Valad considers Shams al-Din of Tabriz as one of Rumi's deputies or successors (*kholafâ*), counting him as the first, followed by Salâh al-Din, then Hosâm al-Din, and then Sultan Valad himself (SVE 158). Before meeting Rumi, the first three were not famous in their own right for either learning, greatness or miraculous spiritual powers (*velâyat*), for although they were all great men possessed of spiritual powers, they were hidden from the eyes of men. It was only through the writings of Sultan Valad and Rumi that their repute shone bright as the noonday sun (SVE 158).

Rumi, in contradistinction, was not one of the hidden saints. He had many disciples dedicated to him heart and soul. During the tenure of Sultan Valad the number of these disciples increased, indicating that Sultan Valad, like his father, was not one of the hidden saints, a spiritual *axis mundi*, but a public saint. One might read this as an implicit claim to priority or superiority for Sultan Valad over the other successors to his father. None of them wrote any books, whereas Sultan Valad wrote a goodly number and was apparently an engaging speaker, like his father.

The Mevlevi order owes its existence to Sultan Valad; without him, the surviving disciples of Rumi would probably have dwindled and never maintained or achieved any formal structure outside Konya. Sultan Valad provided what every formal Sufi order requires: a proper *selsele*, or chain of teachers, which functions like a spiritual charter or statement of authority. Though Sultan Valad does not provide the complete chain, he includes Râbiᶜa, Hallâj and Bâyazid Bestâmi on one end, with Bahâ al-Din and Borhân al-Din Mohaqqeq being the direct founders prior to Rumi (SVE 179).

Sultan Valad spent a great deal of time shaping the community of his followers, counseling them and exhorting them not only in conversation, but also in verse. He tells us that on festival days the people of Konya dress in new clothes, crowd into the city squares or go out of town to picnic or visit tombs. But he reprimands those who fail to attend the Mevlevi *samâᶜ* ceremonies held on such occasions, or those who do not attend his lectures after the month of Ramadan has concluded; their absence deprives them of a great divine bounty. He tells one disciple who has recently come back from pilgrimage to Mecca that though performing the pilgrimage is a commendable act, it is wrong to leave for pilgrimage without the permission of one's shaykh. Some of his poems harshly condemn certain individuals, others counsel peacemaking and overlooking insults, yet others elegize Salâh al-Din and Hosâm al-Din at the time of their deaths (GM 78–9).

During the reign of Hosâm al-Din, but due primarily to the efforts of Sultan Valad, a shrine was erected on the spot of Rumi's father's resting place. Sultan Valad has left behind a number of poems which mention the architect of this project, ʿAlam al-Din Qaysar. These include two poems, a *tarjiʿ band* and a ghazal, which mention the restoration of the school in which Rumi had taught (GM 50). Unfortunately ʿAlam al-Din Qaysar was slain in 1284 (A.H. 683), an event which Sultan Valad elegizes (GM 51).

Sultan Valad also thanks a number of other patrons who provided financial donations or other assistance with panegyric poems. These include Moʿin al-Din Parvâne and his wife, Gorji Khâtun; the vizier Sâheb Fakhr al-Din ʿAtâ and his son, Sâheb Aʿzam Tâj al-Din Hosayn; and the Qâzi of Kayseri. The names of a number of Seljuk princes and other officials also appear in various poems, including Sharaf al-Din b. Khatir al-Din; Seljuk Khâtun and Fâteme Khâtun, the daughter and mother, respectively, of Sultan Rokn al-Din Qelij Arsalân IV (GM 51). Elsewhere, Sultan Valad wrote asking for the return of the village of Qara Arsalân, which Badr al-Din Gohartâsh had given as an endowment to the Mevlevis, but which had been usurped by a certain Najib (GM 52).

Sultan Valad actively sought to cultivate relationships with officials and attract their attention to the shrine of his father. One poem congratulates Sultan Rokn al-Din on the birth of a son. A versified letter to Akhi Ahmad invites him to come to Konya, and a poem for Sultan Ghiâs al-Din Masʿud celebrates his arrival in Konya on August 25, 1281 (25 Rabiʿ II 680). Sultan Valad also asks Sultan Ghiâs al-Din Masʿud for an even larger stipend than his father had been given and for a remission of taxes for fourteen Mevlevi disciples (GM 53). He counsels this sultan in his dealings with the Mongols, and praises him for reestablishing peace throughout the territory. At the same time, in one poem (GM 54), he extends a hand for friendly relations with Samâqar Nuyân, the chief amir of the Mongols in Anatolia. Aflâki (797–9) likewise relates a surely exaggerated report that one of the Mongol princes, Amir-e Kabir Iranjin Nuyân, paid a visit to Sultan Valad and, after a theological conversation, converted to Islam. Another of the reports relayed by Aflâki shows Sultan Valad once again conversing about Islam with another Mongol prince, Oposhghâ Nuyân, who declares himself a disciple of Sultan Valad (Af 818–19).

THE DEATH OF SULTAN VALAD

Even if the earth did not quake for seven full days and nights as Sultan Valad lay on his deathbed (Af 816), the passing of the son of Rumi marks a momentous event in the history of the Mevlevi order. Sultan Valad died at night on November 11, 1312 (10 Rajab 712) at the solar age of eighty-six and was buried on the right-hand side of his father's shrine. Aflâki (822) tells us that Sultan Valad composed this poem at the time of his death:

> Tonight's the night I'll meet with happiness
> I am freed from the selfness of my self!

If there was ever a separate stone marking his grave, it is no longer there, and the marble sepulchre of his father stands over both graves (GM 61).

By his first wife, Salâh al-Din's daughter, Fâteme, Sultan Valad had two girls, Motahhare Khâtun and Sharaf Khâtun, whom Rumi called respectively ʿÂbede and ʿÂrefe. These girls grew up to be spiritual leaders of women and worked saintly miracles, if we are to trust Aflâki (995), who says that most of the ladies of Anatolia became their disciples. One boy, Jalâl al-Din Ulu ʿÂref Chelebi, was also born of this union. It is said that Motahhare Khâtun was married to Solaymân Shâh Karmiâni (Germiâni?), and that she bore two boys, Khezr Pâshâ and Borhân al-Din Elyâs. Sharaf ʿÂrefe Khâtun also reportedly had two boys, Mozaffar Ahmad Pâshâ and Amir Shâh. None of these four male grandchildren of Sultan Valad were to become leaders of the order, however. The subsequent shaykhs of the Mevlevi order are descended for the most part through the line of Ulu ʿÂref Chelebi, and thus represent the union of the families of Salâh al-Din and Rumi.

After Fâteme Khâtun died, Sultan Valad married two other wives, both of them supposedly servant girls (Af 995). The first of these, Nosrat Khâtun, bore him one son, Amir Shams al-Din ʿÂbed. The second wife, Sonbole Khâtun, bore him two sons: Salâh al-Din Zâhed Chelebi and Hosâm al-Din Vâjed Chelebi (Af 996).

THE WRITINGS OF SULTAN VALAD

We have been relying quite heavily on Sultan Valad's verse chronicle of his family, the **Ebtedâ nâme**, or **Masnavi-ye Valadi**, about the history of the Mevlevi order, focusing primarily on Rumi but also on his immediate predecessors and successors. As mentioned earlier, his work provides a first-hand account by one who from an early age was very close to many of the events he describes. Of course, he writes in verse, not straightforward prose, and he writes at some remove from the events, in 1291, about eighteen years after his father's death and about thirty-five years after the disappearance of Shams. More importantly, Sultan Valad writes with a hagiographical motive, to call to attention the miraculous nature of the deeds of Rumi and Bahâ al-Din and promote an image of Rumi as a miracle-working saint. Apparently some of the disciples or Sufis from other orders had heretofore regarded Rumi as a great preacher and poet, but not necessarily as a holy man. Rumi had quoted the miraculous feats of his predecessors in the mystic path, and so Sultan Valad (SVE 2–4) felt it important that those who read Rumi's works should also know something of his saintly miracles.

Sultan Valad composed this work in response to a request that, since like his father he had composed a *Divân*, he should likewise compose a *masnavi* on his father's model (SVE 4). Sultan Valad did indeed accept, and penned this work, a historical *masnavi* of over nine thousand lines in the meter of the *Hadiqe* of Sanâʾi. The subject matter at hand is the formation of the Mevlevi order and the major personages associated with its history, from Bahâ al-Din to Borhân al-Din to Shams to Rumi, to Salâh al-Din to Hosâm al-Din and finally to Sultan Valad. Sultan Valad also writes with the intent of convincing the disciple of the importance of obeying his shaykh (SVE 3).

Jalâl al-Din Homâʾi produced a critical edition of this poem in 1937 with a very useful introduction and notes, as *Masnavi-ye Valadi*, known as the *Valad nâme* (Tehran: Eqbâl). Abdülbaki Gölpınarlı, however, chose to title the work *Ebtedânâme* ("The Book of the Beginning"), because the poem begins with this word *ebtedâ* and because this title creates a nice parallel with Sultan Valad's final *masnavi*, the *Entehâ nâme*, ("The Book of the End"). Gölpınarlı, who claims that Homâʾi's edition omitted a number of Turkish verses, translated the entire text into Turkish as *Ibtidâ-Nâme* (Ankara: Güven; and Konya: Turizm Dernegi, 1976), with an introduction. A French translation appeared in 1988 through the efforts of Djamchid Mortazavi and Eva de Vitray-Meyerovitch as *La Parole secrète: l'enseignement du maître soufi Rumi* (Monaco: Rocher).

Sultan Valad titled his second narrative poem the **Rabâb nâme**, a critical edition of which was prepared by ʿAli Soltâni Gordfarâmarzi in 1980 and published in Montreal as a collaborative effort between McGill University's Institute of Islamic Studies and the University of Tehran under the title *Rabâb nâme az Sultan Valad, farzand-e Mowlânâ Jalâl al-Din Mowlavi*. Sultan Valad composed the *Rabâb nâme* between April and August of 1301 at the request of a certain saint whom Sultan Valad repeatedly praises in the text. This "man of God" approached Sultan Valad with the suggestion that, since he had already produced a *masnavi* in the meter of Sanâʾi's *Elâhi nâme* (i.e., the *Hadiqat al-haqiqat*), he should now set to work on a *masnavi* in the same meter as the famous work of his father. Sultan Valad thus begins the work in imitation of the song of the reed flute at the beginning of Rumi's *Masnavi*, but instead has the rabâb strike this opening note:

> Hear in the cry and wail of the rabâb
> a hundred chapters on the depths of love

Rumi supposedly loved the rabâb, a kind of standing bowed string instrument, and incorporated it into the *samâʿ* ceremonies. Aflâki (Af 88) says that Rumi introduced an innovation into the construction of the rabâb, making its sound box hexagonal (rather than its former square shape), as a representation of the six directions.

Surviving exemplars of the poem include manuscripts dating from 1322, 1323 and 1345, but the oldest copy was written out in 1301 and supposedly given to the owner by Sultan Valad himself in 1304. Basically a commentary on mystical teachings which Sultan Valad presents in verse interspersed with prose passages, the work includes a number of tales based on the example set by his father's *Masnavi*. Sultan Valad sets forth his own views in prose prefaces and then justifies them with quotes from the Koran and Hadith, and frequently alludes to Rumi, Sanâ'i and al-Mutanabbî, but without citing the authors by name. At one point Sultan Valad refers to his father's works as having been "sent down" (*nazzalnâ*), suggesting he regarded Rumi's writings as quasi-divinely inspired. Sultan Valad's mysticism proposes a kind of activism, asserting that prayer without effort leads to nothing. One must always quest and never give up the spiritual search (*Rabâb nâme* 86, 380).

The *Rabâb nâme* contains 7,745 lines in Persian and 35 in Arabic. Surprisingly, the work includes 22 lines in Greek and 157 in Turkish, though Sultan Valad elsewhere admits (SVE 393) that he has little knowledge of Turkish. Nevertheless, according to E.J.W. Gibb, the work gives us "the earliest important specimen of West-Turkish poetry that we possess." Gibb gives many particulars about the poem and provides a verse translation of a considerable portion of it as "The Book of the Rebeck," as well as translations of a few ghazals.[4]

Sultan Valad wrote his final *masnavi*, the **Entehâ nâme**, to discourage his followers from treading the path of passion. It contains about 8,300 lines which for the most part lack the interest of his two earlier narrative poems, both from a poetic point of view and from the point of view of the historical usefulness of the information the work contains. The copy to which Gölpınarlı referred was written out in Aleppo in 1612 by Ghazanfar al-Mowlavi, a Mevlevi disciple (GM 68–9).

Sultan Valad also penned a respectably large collection of lyrical and occasional poems, collected together in a **Divân**. Sultan Valad describes this as his first literary effort (SVE 3), though he perhaps continued to add to it until his death. At least one manuscript, going by the title "The Poetic Contest between Rumi and Sultan Valad," *Monâzere-ye Mowlânâ bâ Soltân Valad* (Istanbul University Library, no. 1205) extracts at least 350 poems which directly imitate particular poems of his father. Altogether the *Divân* of Sultan Valad contains 925 ghazals and *qasides* along with 455 quatrains totaling some 12,500 lines. Sultan Valad used twenty-nine different meters and composed nine poems in Arabic, fifteen in Turkish and the rest in Persian. The two primary editions of this are:

Divani Sultan Veled (Ankara: Uzluk Basımevi, 1941) edited by F. Nafız Uzluk as number 3 in the series of Mevlevi works from the Seljuk era. This includes the Persian text of the poems, along with a hundred-page introduction in modern Turkish.

Divân-e Soltân Valad, ed. Saᶜid Nafisi (Tehran: Rudaki, 1959) Reprinted as *Mowlavi-ye digar: shâmel-e ghazaliyât, qasâyed, qeteᶜât, tarkibât, ashᶜâr-e Torki, ashᶜâr-e ᶜArabi, mosammât, robâᶜiyât* (Tehran: Sanâᵓi, 1984).

Sultan Valad does not always display technical control of the meter of his verse, but he is a generally competent Persian poet. In his introduction to the *Ebtedâ nâme*, Homâᵓi critiques Sultan Valad for a certain carelessness in composition, while praising his diction and particularly the prose headings for their pristine style of expression and clear lines of thought. Occasionally he turns out an arresting expression, though he lacks for the most part his father's innovative spontaneity, fervor and engaging storytelling style, relying for the most part on didactic and philosophical exposition rather than illustration and analogy. Sultan Valad speaks of Sanâᵓi and ᶜAttâr as the eyes of the heart and the spirit respectively, which he set before himself as an example (*Divân*, ed. Uzluk, 277; GM 80), and he considers those who read their poetry and the poetry of Rumi as people of heart and soul who follow in the ways of the saints (SVE 213–14).

However much he respects Sanâᵓi and ᶜAttâr, for the most part Sultan Valad follows the ideas of his father, Rumi, and often quotes phrases or entire lines from him (GM 74–7, 82–3). Also like his father, Sultan Valad in the course of some of his poems disclaims any interest in poetry for its own sake. In the case of Rumi, his fluid style and brilliant modes of expression belie this disavowal, but when Sultan Valad says it, we sense that he is indeed more committed to the ideas than to the art of poesy. Sultan Valad distinguishes between the poetry of poets, which is an effort of all their intellect and being, and the poetry of lovers and mystics, which flows from an excess of passionate intoxication (SVE 53–5). As the very first poem in his *Divân* tells us (*Divân*, ed. Uzluk, 4–5; GM 77–8):

> My poetry means nothing to me,
> why boast of verse, when I have greater art?
> Verse is a dark cloud, I the moon behind
> Don't read the black cloud, but the bright-faced moon.
> To see my face look past the clouds of ego
> Soar past the body's clouds to see the moon
> Metering speech is such a simple thing,
> you must look to take the measure of your self

Gölpınarlı concludes that had Sultan Valad not had before his eyes the poetic example of his father, he probably would not have inclined to the composition of poetry (GM 81).

Throughout his *Divân* and also in his *Ebtedâ* and *Entehâ nâmes*, Sultan Valad intersperses phrases, lines and passages of Turkish and even Greek. His *Divân* even includes ten poems entirely in Turkish (GM 84–5), though Sultan Valad himself did not feel confident about his command of Turkish (SVE 394). Because these poems represent some of the earliest recorded examples of Turkish poetry, much effort has gone into establishing the correct text and meaning of Sultan Valad's Turkish poems.[5]

Aside from his poems, Sultan Valad claims for himself no mean reputation as a speaker and preacher. A collection of fifty-six of his sermons and lectures demonstrates that he spoke from the pulpit in a straightforward and engaging prose, following the model of his father's *Fihe mâ fih*, though Sultan Valad names the collection after his grandfather's work – *Ma'âref* – and appears to have prepared the book for publication, in that the chapters give a coherent and edited feel. The written record of the *Ma'âref* shows us that, not surprisingly, Sultan Valad punctuated his discourses with lines of verse from the works of Sanâ'i, 'Attâr and his own father, Rumi. He also occasionally spoke about Shams al-Din (GM 70). The *Ma'âref* has been published in Turkish translation by Maliha Târıkâhya as *Maarif* (Ankara: Milli Eğitim Basımevi, 1949) and in Persian as *Ma'âref-e Bahâ al-Din Mohammad b. Jalâl al-Din Mohammad Balkhi, mashhur be Sultan Valad*, edited by Najib Mâyel Haravi (Tehran: Mowlâ, 1988). The book has not yet been translated into English, but a French version exists (see chapter 13 below).

In addition to these works, several others have been attributed to Sultan Valad throughout the centuries, including *'Eshq nâme*, *Tarâsh nâme* and *Resâle-ye e'teqâd*, along with a versified version of Nasir al-Din Abu al-Qâsem Samarqandi's (d. 1258) treatise on Hanafi law (GM 71). These we may dismiss with relative confidence as later forgeries, even though some of these falsely attributed texts have engendered their own commentary tradition, such as Halid's brief *Şerh-i aşkname-i hazret-i Bahaeddin Veled* (Istanbul: Mehran Matbaası, 1887). Another short work by Ahmet Remzi Akyürek (1872–1944) provides Turkish commentary on some of Sultan Valad's verse (Istanbul: Asır Matbaası, 1316/1898).

6

The Mythological Rumi

As we have seen, Rumi provides relatively little factual information about his personal life. From his discourses in *Fihe mâ fih*, his *Divân* and the *Masnavi*, we gain glimpses of his feelings about his father, about Borhân al-Din and about Shams al-Din. In these works Rumi also reveals a tiny amount about his relationship to Salâh al-Din Zarkub and Hosâm al-Din. The letters written by Rumi and contained in the *Maktubât* are somewhat more revealing, giving some idea of the kinds of assistance he gave to family members and his disciples.

But it is Sultan Valad who presents us with our first narrative picture of Rumi's life in his *Ebtedâ nâme*, alternatively called *Valad nâme*. Sultan Valad was a first-hand witness to many of the events he describes, and he composed his biographical poem within twenty years of Rumi's passing, all of which makes it a crucially important source. But Sultan Valad was the motivating force behind the organization of his father's disciples into a well-structured order, which Sultan Valad, of course, strove hard to promote. Furthermore, in composing his father's story, Sultan Valad had to conform to the expectations of the hagiographical genre of Sufi literature and the constraints of verse. To a large extent, Sultan Valad, as the son of Rumi and the revered head of the fledgling Mevlevi order, determined future expectations about how biographical information on Rumi should look. As we have noted, the genre of the spiritual biography of mystics was quite well established by this time in Persian letters, and these genre conventions greatly shaped the style and tenor of the works which provide us with what anecdotal details we possess about Rumi's life. These consist in part of personal experience, in part symbolic and tropological representations, and in part oral reports written down with little attention to their veracity.

FARIDUN B. AHMAD SEPAHSÂLÂR

Unfortunately, the nature of Faridun Sepahsâlâr's relationship with Rumi remains somewhat obscure. We know little about him, except that Sepahsâlâr was a title given to Seljuk military officials and several later followers of the Mevlevi order bear this title as a family name. Judging from the fact that Faridun Sepahsâlâr was laid to rest adjacent to the tomb of Bahâ al-Din Valad, he must have enjoyed special status among the inner Mevlevi circle at the time of his death. About a half century after Rumi's death, Sepahsâlâr wrote a "treatise," *Resâle-ye Sepahsâlâr*, which provides us with the second-oldest biographical source (after Sultan Valad's *Ebtedâ nâme*) that we possess for Rumi, his family and his successors. Sepahsâlâr, like Sultan Valad, wrote as a member of Rumi's inner circle and an eye-witness to many of the anecdotes he describes.

Sepahsâlâr's "Treatise" was evidently not widely known in the medieval period, having been eclipsed by the popularity of Aflâki's work, but a couple of sources show that at least some of the Mevlevis were familiar with Sepahsâlâr's name and work. These include a diploma issued in 1471 to a descendant of Sepahsâlâr which purports to give his family tree. This shows Sepahsâlâr to have been related to Akhi Tork, the father of Hosâm al-Din. Sâqeb Dede adds in his *Safine* that Sepahsâlâr married into the family (GM 169).

The Persian text of Sepahsâlâr's "Treatise" was printed for the first time by a Sayyed Mahmud ʿAli as *Resâle-ye Faridun b. Ahmad Sepahsâlâr* (Kanpur, India, 1319/1901). It was reprinted under the same title with the addition of extensive notes and a short introduction by Saʿid Nafisi (Tehran: Eqbâl, 1325/1947), though Nafisi's edition has been retitled in subsequent editions as *Zendegi-nâme-ye Mowlânâ Jalâl al-Din Mowlavi*. A Turkish translation was made available by Medhat Bahâri Hosâmi in 1913 and a second one by Ahmet ʿAvni Konuk appeared in 1938. A translation into Turkish verse was undertaken by Hosayn Fakhr al-Din Dede (d. 1911), but this was never published (GM 170). Tahsin Yazıcı has produced a new Turkish version as *Mevlânâ ve Etrafındakiler: Risale* (Istanbul: Tercüman, 1977). Sepahsâlâr has yet to be made available in English, though an annotated translation would be an excellent resource for all those interested in Rumi. Sepahsâlâr appears quite a bit more sober than Aflâki, but a critical comparison of the two, the sources they rely upon for their reports and the details they present, remains a desideratum.

Recently Bahrâm Behizâd published a study called *Resâle-ye manhul-e Sepahsâlâr: noskhe-ye gomshode-ye Masnavi* (Tehran: Moʾassese-ye Khadamât-e Farhangi-ye Rasâ, 1376/1997), which argues that this work was actually a recension of Aflâki's *Manâqeb* made perhaps sometime in the sixteenth century. Since the printed edition of Sepahsâlâr's text appears to follow the Bulâq edition of the *Masnavi* in quoting lines of Rumi's verse, it might therefore date from as late as the middle of the nineteenth century in its present form. Though

Behizâd's arguments merit further consideration, Foruzânfar, Gölpınarlı and other prior scholars did not cast any doubt on the authenticity of Sepahsâlâr's "Treatise." Since Behizâd's book reached my hands too late to evaluate and incorporate its arguments into the present study, the following discussion operates upon the premise, pending further investigation, that Sepahsâlâr's work is authentic, and not a later forgery.

Faridun Sepahsâlâr twice explains (Sep 6, 33) that he served as a disciple of Rumi for forty years, though this presents us with some difficulty in understanding the chronology of his life. It appears from internal evidence that Sepahsâlâr's "Treatise" was completed sometime between the years 1312 or 1320 (712 or 720) and 1338 (A.H. 739). It briefly describes the tenure of Ulu ᶜÂref Chelebi as successor to Sultan Valad, as well as the tenure of Amir Shams al-Din ᶜÂbed Chelebi, who assumed the role of head of the order after Ulu ᶜÂref's death in 1320 (A.H. 719). Sepahsâlâr's text speaks of ᶜÂbed Chelebi as if still alive and makes no mention of his successors. Nafisi (Sep 5) and Meier (Mei 424) both give 1329 (729) as the date of death of ᶜÂbed Chelebi and therefore the latest date of completion of the text. Gölpınarlı, however, places the death of ᶜÂbed Chelebi in 1338 (GM 132). If ᶜÂbed Chelebi died in 1338, Sepahsâlâr's "Treatise" must have been completed between these two dates.

If Sepahsâlâr, as he claims, spent forty years in the master's presence, this would place him in Rumi's inner circle a few years after the death of Bahâ al-Din Valad in 1231 (628). Though Sepahsâlâr tells us that he held the Valad family in great respect from his early boyhood, his remarks suggest that he was occupied with other matters for a time before destiny permitted him to join Rumi's circle in Konya. If this took place shortly after the death of Bahâ al-Din, and if Sepahsâlâr were about twenty years of age at that time, then he would have been about sixty when Rumi died, and well over a hundred years of age at the time his "Treatise" was completed, about a half century after Rumi's death in 1273. This appears improbable, but might be explained in at least two ways.

First, it is possible that Sepahsâlâr did not author the entire biography of the Valad family himself, and that the sections pertaining to Sultan Valad's sons, ᶜÂref Chelebi and/or ᶜÂbed Chelebi, were added by a later hand. Gölpınarlı believes (GM 170), on the basis of a history by Sâqeb Mostafâ Dede (d. 1735) called *Safine-ye nafis-e Mowlaviân* ("The Precious Ship of the Mevlevis"), that Sepahsâlâr passed away during the lifetime of Sultan Valad, in the early part of his tenure, and was buried in the shrine to the left of Rumi's son, ᶜAlâ al-Din. This would place his death between 1284 and 1312, but probably closer to 1295. This would of course mean that the last eight pages or so of his "Treatise," particularly the sections concerning the successors to Sultan Valad, were added as much as thirty years later. This later hand would probably have been that of his son, Jalâl al-Din, who Sâqeb Dede says was a disciple of Sultan Valad (GM 170; GB 79). Sobhâni argues that Sepahsâlâr completed his work in 1312 and the later sections on the Mevlevis after Sultan Valad were added by Sepahsâlâr's son between the years 1320 and 1338 (Mak 292).

Sâqeb Dede reports that in his youth Faridun Sepahsâlâr did indeed attend the gatherings of Bahâ al-Din Valad (GM 132, 169–70). Since Bahâ al-Din arrived in Konya in 1228 and passed away in 1231, this would place Sepahsâlâr in the company of Rumi for as many as forty-six lunar years (626–72), or forty-four solar years. However, Sâqeb Dede writes five hundred years after the fact and, as Gölpınarlı admits (GM 148–9), makes for a rather unreliable historian, at least insofar as dates are concerned.

As an alternative solution, we might suggest that Sepahsâlâr exaggerated the length of time he spent in Rumi's presence, or that he did not mean "forty years" as a precise calculation. After all, this number often appears as a topos in Persian literature, age forty suggesting middle age for a man, and forty years or forty days indicating a sacred or liminal span of time. If we assume that Sepahsâlâr rounds up from twenty-five or thirty to the magic number forty, and that he joined Rumi's circle in adolescence, this would still place his birth in 1230 at the latest, his admission into Mowlânâ's circle shortly after Rumi's encounter with Shams in the late 1240s, and his death as a nonagenarian in the 1320s.

Although Sepahsâlâr devotes a chapter each to Bahâ al-Din Valad and Borhân al-Din Mohaqqeq, he does not state that he met either one of them and most of the anecdotes he recounts about them are identified as second- or third-hand reports, without identifying a source, in this manner: "it is related that" (naql ast ke). Because Rumi spent much of the 1230s studying in Syria or under the tutelage of Borhân al-Din Mohaqqeq, who died about 1240, it seems unlikely that Sepahsâlâr kept company with Rumi during this time, and, indeed, in relating one miracle during Rumi's stay in Aleppo, Sepahsâlâr (79) uses the same phrase, "it is related that," whereas in most cases he begins accounts of Rumi's miracles either with the name of the person reporting them or with "once" (yek nowbat), implying Sepahsâlâr was personally present.

In his chapter on Shams al-Din Tabrizi, Sepahsâlâr once again employs the formula "it is related that" without naming sources, to introduce several anecdotes about Shams. Sepahsâlâr, who considered Sultan Valad a formal disciple of Shams al-Din (Sep 123), also quotes or summarizes extended passages (e.g., Sep 71, 124, 125, 130, etc.) about Shams and others from Sultan Valad's Masnavi-ye Valadi, the book now generally called Ebtedâ nâme, which Sultan Valad tells us in the excursus was written between March and June of 1291. Sepahsâlâr must have been alive, then, at least until the early 1290s, and could not have completed the sections of the book pertaining to Rumi and Shams until after the composition of Sultan Valad's Ebtedâ nâme in the spring of 1291.

Since Sepahsâlâr makes no explicit claim to have met Shams, and because he identifies many of the anecdotes he does relate as second-hand reports, one might surmise that he joined Rumi's circle some time after Shams' disappearance at the end of 1247 (A.H. 645). Sepahsâlâr does not explicitly state that he personally met Salâh al-Din Zarkub, Hosâm al-Din Chelebi, Sultan Valad, Ulu ʿÂref Chelebi or Shams al-Din ʿÂbed Chelebi either, but in speaking about them the "Treatise" does not use the formula "it is related that," suggesting that the information he provides about these individuals comes at first hand.

Sepahsâlâr tells us that he began his treatise at the request of an unnamed member of the inner Mevlevi circle, who pointed out that those who had seen Rumi in person were all aging and would soon take with themselves to the grave their memories of the works and miracles which they had witnessed from the master. Sepahsâlâr at first demurred, protesting that to describe Rumi was far beyond his meager powers. But his friend insisted, pointing out (Sep 8):

> Though none can drain the river Oxus dry
> One might taste enough to quench his thirst

Finally he persuaded Sepahsâlâr to put pen to paper. The following excerpt (Sep 4–6) provides a feel and flavor of Sepahsâlâr's purposes:

> Thus speaks the least and most humble of servants, Faridun b. Ahmad, known as Sepahsâlâr, who from early childhood harbored the greatest love and good wishes for this family (tâʾefe) in his heart and soul, until at last the winds of fortune directed this meek one's steps to the sacred court of his holiness my lord, our Shaykh and sire and support, pole of saints, king of the pious and godly, proof of God's unity, revealer of eternal mysteries, expounder of everlasting secrets, God's greatest mystery and His most resplendent proof, beloved of the Lord of Lords, pole of poles, exalted above all titles, our master, the glory of God, of the nation and of the faith (Jalâl al-Haqq va al-mellat va al-din), heir of the prophets and messengers, Mohammad, son of Mohammad, son of Hosayn Khatibi al-Bakri of Balkh, may God magnify their mention, sanctify their spirits through his perfections and sanctify the spirits of his disciples through the delectations of his words, to which the phrase "as a guidance and mercy unto the faithful" refers. I occupied my life with service to his holiness and inscribed the image of his love and affection upon the pages of my heart. I saw a beauty the likes of which "no eye hath seen" and heard words which "no ear hath heard," as his own blessed words describe his state:
>
> > What fires my breath will light in this world,
> > what forevers bubble up from my mortal words!
> > My outward words will overtake all ears
> > But none will hear within my soulful roars
>
> Since that blessed essence remains no more contained in human form, beware that any look to any other but him, as he said:
>
> > Know that the sage reflects Truth's attributes
> > Though the sage appears to habit human form
>
> At last I burned a thousand times in the affection of his love and my selfness was effaced until my outward and inward being consisted of nothing but his warmth . . .

For forty years this meek one, along with the other followers and lovers, each of whom were the outstanding leaders of the age, unequalled in the world in the exoteric and esoteric sciences as well as in their piety and abstemiousness, spending morning till evening and evening till morning in his presence, circling willy-nilly like the Bear constellation around the pole star ... until the unquestioned command "We are verily from God and unto Him do we return" of the Creator and the Lord of "Be and it Is" made that brilliant sun move from our imperfect view into the hidden paradise, rejoining that light of darkest night with its own source and origin, causing it to repose in the holy precincts at the right hand of the Powerful King.

Sepahsâlâr's work proceeds chronologically, relating information and anecdotes interspersed with poetry, mostly drawn from Rumi's own verse, with independent rubrics for the following topics:

1. The chain of mystical teachers leading from Mohammad to Bahâ al-Din Valad, including ᶜAli, Hasan al-Basri, Habib al-ᶜAjami, Dâvud al-Tâʾi, Maᶜruf al-Karkhi, Sari al-Saqati, Jonayd, Shebli, Mohammad Zojjâj, Abu Bakr Nassâj, Ahmad Ghazzâli and Bahâ al-Din's own father, Ahmad al-Khatibi (1 page).

2. The acts of Bahâ al-Din Valad (11 pages).

3. The birth of Rumi (1 page), the "best of hours and most joyful of occasions," occurring in A.H. 604 (A.D. 1207). We learn the date of his "return to the precincts of mercy of the caring Lord": 5 Jumâdi II 672 (December 17, 1273).

4. The chain of mystical teachers leading from the Prophet to Rumi (3 pages), which includes the same figures as in his father's chain with the addition of Sayyed Borhân al-Din Mohaqqeq, who taught Rumi the mystical teachings of Bahâ al-Din, not Bahâ al-Din himself. Sepahsâlâr's comments downplay, however, the importance of Borhân al-Din, emphasizing the importance of Khezr, who illumined Rumi with gnostic insight. While in Damascus at his room at the Barrâniye Madrase, Sepahsâlâr claims that Rumi was observed on several occasions in the company of Khezr, Moses' mystical guide in the Koran and beloved figure of Sufism. At the time he was writing his "Treatise," Sepahsâlâr indicates that Rumi's former room in that school had become a holy site and that supplicants praying there would have their wishes fulfilled.

Of course, Mowlânâ Shams al-Din Tabrizi, "His Holiness, King of the Saints and Poles, Diadem of the Desired, Beloved of His Holiness, the Lord of the Worlds," is not omitted, but is described as one from whom Rumi learned the ways of dance and joy and adopted his particular style of turban. Also mentioned in passing ("to write them here would take up much space") are conversations on mystical points in Damascus between Rumi and Mohyi al-Din ᶜArabi, Saᶜd al-Din Hamuye, ᶜOsmân al-Rumi, Owhad al-Din Kermâni and Sadr al-Din al-Qonyavi.

247

5. "The Acts of His Holiness, the Master, God Sanctify his Precious Soul" (92 pages), describing his ascetic habits of self-renunciation, fasting, prayer, piety, his spiritual states and mystical insight, his practice of *samâ^c* and poetry, his miracles and his death.
6. The companions and successors of Rumi, beginning with Borhân al-Din Mohaqqeq of Termez (4 pages).
7. Shams al-Din Tabrizi (13 pages).
8. Salâh al-Din Zarkub (7 pages).
9. Chelebi Hosâm al-Din (7 pages).
10. Sultan Valad (3 pages).
11. Chelebi ^cÂref (2 pages).
12. Chelebi Shams al-Din ^cÂbed (1 page).
13. The companions of Rumi and his prominent disciples (2 pages).

Sepahsâlâr believed in and relates several miracles performed by Rumi, carefully distinguishing between the categories of prophetic miracles (*mo^cjezât*), which Rumi did not perform, and saints' miracles (*karâmât*), which Rumi did perform. Though most Sufi writers maintained this theoretical distinction so as not to claim for the saints more spectacular miracles than the prophets, often times, for example in the "Spiritual Feats" of Shaykh Ahmad-e Jâm, there is little practical difference.[1] The *karâmât* that Sepahsâlâr attributes to Rumi seem subdued in contrast to the acts of teleportation, transmutation of elements and so forth reported for many earlier Sufi saints. Rumi's *karâmât*, according to Sepahsâlâr, chiefly include acts of remarkable kindness, demonstrations of power over the natural world and feats of precognition, such as the following:

> Once his holiness, the Master, was sitting at the edge of a pond, busy with the exposition of mystic truths. The frogs (*vazaghân*) on the water were making such a racket that the mystical explanations could not be heard. His holiness the Master, God sanctify his precious spirit, yelled at the frogs with utter majesty, "If you can explain better, go ahead and I will be silent, otherwise listen." They immediately fell silent and for some time afterwards the sound of the frogs was not heard in that area. (Sep 83)

Maleke Sa^cide Kumâch Khâtun, who was married to Sultan Rokn al-Din, relates that:

> Once we were sitting in a gathering of ladies in some buildings that had long ago belonged to the sultans. All of a sudden, his holiness the Master, God magnify his mention, came in the door and said, "Hurry, hurry, get out of the room." Immediately we rushed out of the room, barefoot. When everyone had come out, the stone arch caved in. We each and all fell at his blessed feet and gave thanks to God and alms to those who were needy. (Sep 91)

> Every time that his holiness the Master went to the public baths to shave his face most of the companions would attend and apportion out the trimmings amongst

themselves as a blessed keepsake. There was a weak dervish sitting in the corner of the bathhouse with no strength to move. The thought crossed his mind that it would be nice if those companions would give some of that blessed keepsake to him. Immediately the Master took a handful and sent it over to that person. The dear man prostrated himself at the beauty of this miraculous act and became a follower of his holiness. (Sep 104)

The genre of Sufi miracle tales often presents us with legendary and unbelievable feats of wizardry, mind reading and transmutation of elements, in contrast to which the above accounts of Sepahsâlâr seem quite restrained. Sepahsâlâr's life of Rumi presents us with a far more sober history than the contemporaneous account of Aflâki, who constantly lends his credence to incredible supernatural events associated with Rumi and Shams. As such, we may place a greater degree of faith in Sepahsâlâr, despite the uncertainty about the years of his companionship with Rumi and the date of composition of his "Treatise," and assume him, for the purpose of reconstructing the events of Rumi's life, to be generally more reliable than Aflâki.

SHAMS AL-DIN AHMAD AL-AFLÂKI

Far longer and even more detailed is the *Manâqeb al-ʿârefin* of Ahmad Aflâki (d. June 15, 1360). Shams al-Din Ahmad Aflâki al-ʿÂrefi began writing down his "Acts of the Gnostics" in the Mevlevi *khâneqâh*, or lodge, in Konya in the year 1318 (A.H. 718), as he tells us in the introduction (Af 4). He does not mention Sepahsâlâr's "Treatise," though his own work more or less follows the same organization and was written more or less contemporaneously. This is to say that Aflâki began writing while Sepahsâlâr was still completing his "Treatise," but continued to revise and expand his *Manâqeb*, which exists in more than one recension (Yazıcı's introduction, Af 9–18). Aflâki probably did not complete the final version of his *Manâqeb* until A.H. 754, corresponding to sometime between February 1353 and January 1354 (Yazıcı's introduction, Af 8–9), long after Sepahsâlâr must have been dead.

Oddly, however, Aflâki makes no mention of Sepahsâlâr's work, nor does Sepahsâlâr mention Aflâki, though certain individuals are quoted as sources in both works. Aflâki does mention a Jalâl al-Din b. Sepahsâlâr and/or a Jamâl al-Din b. Sepahsâlâr, as well as a Homâm al-Din b. Sepahsâlâr who owned a garden in Konya; they may be relatives of Faridun Sepahsâlâr, the author of the *Resâle*. The mutual silence is probably not accidental. Aflâki and Sepahsâlâr, though writing at the same time and covering the same events, reflect two different attitudes toward the life and sainthood of Rumi, and perhaps even two conflicting schools or tendencies among the Mevlevis two generations after Rumi's death.

Aflâki began work on the *Manâqeb* at the instruction of Ulu ʿAref Chelebi (Af 4), compiling reports from the individuals still living who had met with

Rumi and providing chains of transmission in the case of those reports that came to him third- and fourth-hand. It would appear that Aflâki reviewed the *Maʿâref* of Bahâ-e Valad and the *Maqâlât* of Shams, in addition to the *Ebtedâ nâme* of Sultan Valad, and, of course, the *Divân-e Shams* and *Masnavi* of Rumi. But the bulk of his material seems to have come from oral accounts, written down with no regard to weeding out the factual or the likely from the implausible.

Shams al-Din's pen-name, Aflâki, "the Heavenly," probably reflects his orientation to gnostic Sufism, rather than any interest in astrology. On the other hand, it may also allude to his association with Badr al-Din Tabrizi, who practiced alchemy and taught it to some of Rumi's disciples (Sep 39–40). Aflâki (272) also refers to Serâj al-Din Masnavi-khwân as his teacher, and to ʿAlâ al-Din of Âmasya as one of his fellow pupils (Af 880). Elsewhere, Aflâki tells of a threat against his life from a certain poet Hosâm al-Din b. Âyenedâr (Af 930).

Aflâki's devotion to Ulu ʿÂref Chelebi shows repeatedly in the first-hand accounts he relates, believing that Ulu ʿÂref cured him on one occasion (Af 253–4). Aflâki tells us that his father passed away in the home of Uzbek Khân in Sarây, leaving Aflâki some considerable possessions, including a number of books. Aflâki received word of his father's death while on the way from Kayseri to Sivas sometime during the tenure of Ulu ʿÂref Chelebi, that is between the years of 1312 and 1320. Greatly grieved, Aflâki determined to go and attend to the inheritance, but Ulu ʿÂref prevented him from doing so, saying that he needed to focus his attention on his shaykh, not on worldly possessions (Af 931–2). This shows, of course, that Aflâki was a disciple of Ulu ʿÂref Chelebi, who apparently honored Aflâki by referring to him as "Shaykh" (Af 932). The title "al-ʿÂrefi" appended to his pen name almost certainly derives from his discipleship to Ulu ʿÂref.

Sâqeb Dede unwinds a fancy yarn about Aflâki dying of grief forty days after Ulu ʿÂref Chelebi and being buried next to Sepahsâlâr (GM 170–71). Aflâki did not die, however, until the last day of Rajab in A.H. 761, which would correspond to the evening of Monday June 15, 1360, almost ninety years after Rumi. This information comes from the inscription on his tombstone, located in a plot in Konya adjacent to the shrine of Rumi in the yard of a certain Khwâje Tupbâsh. When his house was destroyed in 1929, the property was bought by the Mevlânâ Museum (GM 173). As for his birth, we have no information, but he appears to have met the wife of Sultan Valad, Salâh al-Din's daughter, as well as many others who had personal contact with Rumi.

Unlike Sepahsâlâr, Aflâki did not personally know Rumi, being born after his death, and this perhaps drove him to utilize more sources in order to provide a fuller range of biographical details than Sepahsâlâr. But Aflâki's picture of Rumi is unconstrained by any direct memories of Rumi, the human being, and this may account in part for his receptivity to the more fantastic and spectacular stories circulating about the object of his devotion. Aflâki reports supernatural events without batting an eye, alongside more mundane details about Rumi's family life which appear credible enough. And, writing much later, Aflâki provides far more information about the life of Ulu Chelebi and the later Mevlevis. If scholars have been disinclined to treat Aflâki's "Acts" more critically, it is because much of the biographical detail he provides cannot be found in any other source.

Parts of Aflâki's hagiography were first translated into English by Sir J.W. Redhouse and included as "Acts of the Adepts" in the introduction to his translation of parts of the *Masnavi* in 1881 (see chapter 14, below); this abridged translation has been separately published in paperback as *Legends of the Sufis* (Surrey, England: Coombes Spring Press, 1965; revised edition, Wheaton, Illinois: Theological Publishing House, 1976). There is also a French version in two volumes by Clément Huart (1854–1926), *Les Saints des derviches tourneurs* (Paris: E. Leroux, 1918–22; reprinted Paris: Sindbad, 1978), which, however, is not consistently reliable. Aflâki's text was widely known through the medieval period and was translated into Turkish numerous times over the centuries by devotees of Rumi and the Mevlevis, including Zâhed b. ʿÂref (1401), Gevrek Zâde Hasan (1795) and ʿAbd al-Bâqi b. al-Shaykh al-Sayyed Abu Bakr Dede Efendi (1797). In addition to these full translations, a number of abridged Turkish translations have been made over the years, including those by Kamâl Ahmad Dede (d. 1617), Darvish Khalil Sanâʾi (d. 1544) and Darvish Mahmud Masnavi-khwân (d. 1574). These frequently illustrated Turkish versions of Aflâki's *Manâqeb* circulated among the Mevlevi disciples themselves and played an important role in the transmission and preservation of the Rumi legend down to the present day.

More recently, Tahsin Yazıcı produced a scholarly translation into Turkish, *Âriflerin menkıbeleri* (Ankara: Millî Eğitim, 1953–4; reprinted Istanbul: Hürriyet, 1973) and subsequently published in two volumes the first critical edition of the Persian text, based on a comparison of a number of older manuscripts, as *Manâqeb al-Ârefin* (Ankara: Türk Tarih Kurumu, 1959 and 1961; 2nd ed., 1976–80). This edition, along with Yazıcı's very informative introduction in Turkish, was reprinted by offset in Iran, once again in two volumes, as *Manâqeb al-ʿârefin* (Tehran: Donyâ-ye Ketâb, 1983). A full English translation of Aflâki's work based upon Yazıcı's critical edition of the text would be most useful.

Like Sepahsâlâr's "Treatise," Aflâki's "Acts of the Gnostics" relates anecdotes and tales from the life of Rumi and his circle, with the exception that Aflâki's work runs to six or seven times the length. Aflâki's collection conforms to the expectations of the *"vitae* of the Sufi saints" genre which, like its medieval European "lives of the saints" corollary, tends to give highly stylized and hagiographical descriptions of its subjects. Earlier accounts of Sufi saints include

"The Character of Ibn-e Khafif of Shiraz" (*Sirat Ibn-e Khafif*), Mohammad b. al-Monavvar's "The Secrets of God's Mystical Oneness" (*Asrâr al-towhid*), Mohammad al-Ghaznavi's "Spiritual Feats of Shaykh Ahmad-e Jâm" (*Maqâmât-e Shaykh-e Zhandepil*) and ʿAttâr's "*Vitae* of the Saints" (*Tazkerat al-owliâ*), all of which ascribe miraculous deeds and supernatural powers to the Sufi saints they describe. We therefore cannot expect the author of such a Sufi *vita* to depict the founding saints of his own spiritual fraternity as ordinary mortals, and Aflâki does not disappoint.

The anecdotes Aflâki relates, expressed in prose tending toward the ornate, are hagiographical in character and punctuated with verses composed by Aflâki himself. He frequently provides the circumstances for the composition of various poems of Rumi, though these do not always convince us of their verisimilitude. Aflâki intended this work for an audience of initiates on the spiritual path; were it not so, he intimates that he would have included even more esoteric mysteries:

> Were it suitable to speak them,
> Many things had I to tell you.
> God has said it better than I:
> The reins of faith are held by you.

(Af 5)

In the introduction (Af 4), Aflâki tells us that his shaykh, the king of gnostics, Chelebi Jalâl al-Haqq va al-Din al-ʿÂref, directed him to write down the miraculous works of the great fathers and noble ancestors and successors of the Mevlevi order. Aflâki duteously began this task in 1318, writing down as a remembrance for the Mevlevi disciples all the accounts of the doings of the founders of the order that he could gather.

He arranged the lengthy compilation of anecdotes (covering 1,000 pages in the two-volume text of the critical edition) in ten chapters. Here follow the words of his own table of contents (Af. 5–6), with the pages devoted to each topic given in brackets, as an indication of the relative importance accorded each of these subjects by Aflâki, or perhaps also as a reflection of the extent of material about the various founding figures of the order that was still current among the Mevlevis a half century after Rumi's death:

Chapter 1: Concerning the Acts of His Holiness the King of jurisprudents in the world, the Divine Scholar Bahâ al-Haqq va al-Din al-Valad, May God be pleased with him. [7–58]

Chapter 2: Concerning the Acts of the Pride of the People of Yâ Sin, Borhân al-Haqq va al-Din al-Mohaqqeq al-Modaqqeq al-Termezi, May God be pleased with him. [56–72]

Chapter 3: An Explication of the Acts of His Holiness Mowlânâ, the great mystery of God, May God sanctify us through his mighty Spirit. [73–613]

252

Chapter 4: An Explanation of the Acts of the Sultan of the Poor, God's mercy to creation, Shams al-Haqq va al-Din al-Tabrizi, God sanctify his spirit. [614–703]

Chapter 5: Concerning the Acts of the Shaykh of Shaykhs in this world, Salâh al-Haqq va al-Din, known as Zarkub, May God vivify his precious soul. [704–36]

Chapter 6: Concerning the Acts of the Deputy of God amongst his creation, Hosâm al-Haqq va al-Din, known as Ibn Akhi Tork, May God sanctify his subtle essence. [737–83]

Chapter 7: Concerning the Acts of Our Leader, the son of Mowlânâ, Bahâ al-Haqq va al-Din al-Valad, God confirm us through his confirming light. [784–824]

Chapter 8: Concerning the Acts of His Holiness, the King of the mystics, the Glory of Truth and religion, Chelebi Amir Âref, may God exalt his position. [825–974]

Chapter 9: Concerning His Holiness the King of Kings of the Searchers, the Sun of the realm and religion, Chelebi Amir ʿÂbed, God magnify his mention. [975–93]

Chapter 10: Concerning the names of their children and descendants, along with a list of the chain of their teachers. I hope that by the blessings of God, the Exalted, each chapter will reach its full completion, and God is the Guide. [994–1000]

THE LEGENDARY BAHÂ AL-DIN

Among the legends that Aflâki tells about Rumi's family, and which had been more or less generally accepted until the researches of Foruzânfar, Gölpınarlı and Meier, are that his grandfather, Hosayn Khatibi, married the daughter of ʿAlâ al-Din Mohammad Khwârazmshâh (Af 7–8):

> He had a precious daughter who was peerless throughout all the inhabited climes in charm, proportion, perfection and beauty. None were found equal to her royal character that the king might give his daughter's hand and be quit of his responsibility to her, and the fortunate girl had already reached the age of maturity. Then, one evening the king was consulting in this regard with his minister. "Since no peer for our queen exists throughout the universe, what should be done and what arrangements made?"
>
> The minister, a wise and knowledgeable man, said: "The great and noble members of the ulama are the peers of the kings of Islam, for as it is said, 'The kings rule over the people and the ulama rule over the kings.'"
>
> The king asked, "Where might one find such a perfect and accomplished scholar?"
>
> He said, "Serving in the capital, Balkh. Jalâl al-Din Hosayn Khatibi, a descendant of the great righteous one [Abu Bakr], whose forebears were responsible, through their blessed striving and conquest, for the original entrance of Khorasan into the realm of Islam. In all the arts, he is the cynosure of the ulama of the world and of all the great men. At the age of thirty, he is still young and, having practiced much self-abnegation and renunciation, he has stolen the trophy of piety from the angels of the concourse on high."

Aflâki explains that so accomplished a scholar and thinker was Hosayn Khatibi that even in his early youth his disciples numbered three thousand jurisprudents and miracle-working ascetics, including several of the most prominent figures of his age. The story continues that on a single night Hosayn Khatibi, along with the aforementioned king, his daughter and his vizier, all separately saw the prophet in a dream instructing that the girl should be married to Hosayn Khatibi. These astonishing dreams naturally led to a wedding and nine months later Bahâ al-Din Valad emerged as a product of their union.

The story is pure myth and conforms to the stereotype of the spiritual and royal union; similarly, the third Shiite Imam, Hosayn, is said to have married the princess of the last Sasanian king. But it sets the following scenario: Presumably after the death of her royal father, Bahâ al-Din Valad's mother and her family members press a claim to the throne on behalf of her son. Being inclined to books and learning, however, he feels no yearning for power, and refuses the throne. Indeed, Aflâki relates that Sultan Mohammad Khwârazm-shâh, who acceded to the throne after ʿAlâ al-Din, at one point sent a messenger to Bahâ Valad, to test him by offering him the kingship of the domains of Balkh and control over the lands and armies therein, promising to go to another region "since it would be unseemly to have two kings in one domain." To this incredible proposition, Bahâ Valad replied that the possession of lands and armies and treasures and thrones and worldly fortune was fine for kings, but "we are *darvish*" and had no use for such things.

> The soul that leaps to hear
> "Poverty is my pride"
> will not look twice upon
> the crown and throne and flag.

"God be praised that his holiness was confirmed in two types of authority: authority in this world and authority in the hereafter" (Af 13). Bahâ is not destined for worldly kingship, but for the kingship of the religious scholars; three hundred juridical authorities in Balkh had independently dreamt on the very same night that all the juridical authorities of Islam were kneeling before Bahâ Valad, himself at the right hand of the Prophet, who was commanding them to call Bahâ Valad the King of Clerics (Sultan al-ulama). One can only imagine the kind of devotion such a mass dream might generate; we read only that "he was accepted by countless elite and common folk" (Af 11) and that this dream was responsible for Borhân al-Din Mohaqqeq's becoming a disciple of Bahâ al-Din (Af 34). Phenomenal dreams such as these, along with the ability to interpret them properly, constitute perhaps the most frequent type of miracle attributed to Bahâ al-Din in Aflâki's "Acts of the Gnostics."

Not surprisingly, the application of the title "King of the Scholars" also generated a fair amount of hostile jealousy. Aflâki names a number of religious scholars, officials and dignitaries of the age, including Fakhr al-Din Râzi and the Qâzi of Vakhsh, who began to cavil at Bahâ al-Din, "as is the wont of the ulama of the age, may God forgive them." Aflâki dates this opposition to the year 1208 (A.H. 605). But many of Bahâ al-Din's enemies, like the opponents of other legendary pious men, are made to taste divine retribution for their iniquity. For example, the Qâzi of Vakhsh ordered that the title "King of Clerics" be stricken from the legal documents signed by Bahâ al-Din and five days later passed away (Af 33). Bahâ al-Din confronted a certain Qâzi Tabari, who had spoken against him in the presence of Sultan ʿAlâ al-Din Kay Qobâd, and predicted that the qâzi and all his family would perish by divine command, whereas the progeny of the Valad clan would live on until the day of resurrection; several days later a plague descended and carried off the qâzi and his whole family (Af 31). On one occasion, it was not divine intervention, but Bahâ al-Din who took it upon himself to punish an evildoer:

> One day Bahâ al-Din came upon a watchman who was oppressing an innocent. On the authority of the verse "So Moses smote him and he died" [K28:15], Bahâ al-Din hit the watchman with his cane, who immediately gave up his soul to hell. They picked him up and carried him off to the grave. The Sultan of Islam was very troubled by this situation and asked, "Why did you kill him without good cause? What was your reason?" Our lord, so that the king might not remain in doubt, said, "No leaf falls from a tree except by the command of God ... in truth, I have killed a dog and freed an innocent from his oppression." The sultan ordered that the watchman be exhumed and a black dog was found lying in his grave. (Af 36)

Most of Bahâ al-Din's opponents, however, would become convinced disciples after witnessing his miraculous powers (Af 33).

As for the most famous opponent of Bahâ al-Din, Fakhr al-Din Râzi, we cannot attribute his hostility to simple jealousy; Bahâ al-Din gave him ample cause to take offense. Aflâki points out that in the middle of preaching from the pulpit, Bahâ Valad would constantly address both Mohammad Khwârazmshâh and Fakhr al-Din Râzi as "innovators" (mobtadeʿ), a word that connotes heretical deviation from accepted practice. This much is confirmed by the speeches of Bahâ al-Din in his Maʿâref, where he is recorded as saying in a public gathering that Râzi and the Khwârazmshâh were lost in darkness and vain imagination due to their concupiscent souls, as a result of which they sometimes committed bad actions (Bah 82; Af 11). According to Aflâki there were spies in the gatherings of Bahâ al-Din and it was reported to the Khwârazmshâh that Bahâ al-Din was planning to incite his followers against the state. Such reports led to the above-mentioned test of Bahâ al-Din's intentions. As Aflâki tells it, during this exchange with the king's agent Bahâ decided to leave with his followers as a means of assuring the king that they had no designs on political power (Af 13).

As the Prophet left Medina on account of the jealousy of the hypocrites, so Bahâ al-Din left Balkh. Forty juridical authorities and ascetics accompanied him out of the city with nearly three camels loaded with precious books and furniture and provision. Such an outcry and tumult arose among Bahâ al-Din's supporters in Balkh that the king and vizier went after the evening prayer to meet him and plead with him to abandon his journey. When they failed to dissuade him, the king begged him to abandon the area entirely, for if he were to stay in a nearby region, word would certainly reach his partisans, stirring up tumult and bringing ruin and destruction in the area of Balkh. Bahâ al-Din agreed, but in a final sermon in the area he warned the king that his dominion was only mortal, that soon an army of the Tatars would come to make Balkh taste the cup of death, and that the king himself would perish at the hands of the Sultan of Rum. In the course of this sermon, a loud cry arose, such that most of the audience fell unconscious and the pulpit moved from the alcove to the center of the mosque. Several people perished in awe of God.

On the way from Balkh to Baghdad, Aflâki tells us that the people in the cities and towns they passed by would see the Prophet in a dream telling them that the King of Clerics, Bahâ Valad of Balkh, was arriving and that they should go out to greet him and express their belief in him. People would come out one full day's journey from their homes to meet him and hold festivals in his honor. Indeed, as they neared Baghdad, the caliph sent an informant to find out who they were and summoned the famous shaykh Shehâb al-Din Sohravardi to the caliphal palace to inquire into the circumstances of these guests. Sohravardi was able to guess from the behavior and words ascribed to the traveler that it could be none other than Bahâ al-Din Valad. Sohravardi, along with all the other dignitaries of Baghdad, went out to greet Bahâ Valad. He kissed his knee in a sign of respect and invited Bahâ and his companions to stay in Sohravardi's own Sufi cloister. Bahâ, however, preferred to stay in the Mostanseriye school, indicating that it was more appropriate for religious teachers (imams) to stay in legal institutions (*madrases*) than in Sufi institutions (Af 17–18).

As a token of esteem the caliph then sent a golden tray with 3,000 Egyptian dinars on it to Bahâ Valad, who, however, refused the money on the ground that it was obtained by dubious means and was therefore religiously illicit, and that he did not wish to see the face of one who drank and listened to music and singing. Shaykh Sohravardi apologetically explained to the caliph that Bahâ Valad had not agreed to appear before him, and the caliph insisted that some arrangement must be made so that he could see the face of this unusual holy man. Sohravardi suggested that the caliph might see Bahâ Valad in the mosque on Friday and promptly went to plead with Bahâ Valad to give a sermon for the people of Baghdad, who longed to see him and were in need of his preaching. Bahâ agreed and that Friday all the people of Baghdad came to see the famous preacher of Balkh at the congregational mosque. The best Koran reciters chanted verses and Bahâ preached such a sermon that the audience were all transported and the caliph wept uncontrollably. At the end, Bahâ Valad removed his turban and turned to the caliph, calling him immoral and the worst caliph of the Abbasid dynasty (Af 19):

> Is this a fitting way to live? Is it fitting to act unlawfully with the divine laws? How strange! Have you found support for this in the Book of God or seen any legal opinion permitting this in the prophetic traditions? Is there any precedent for this in the sayings of the rightly guided caliphs or the leaders of religion? Have you seen any justification for this in the schools of the shaykhs of the Sufi path? Then will you not say on what basis you allow yourself to behave like this? ... Do you not fear the Lord on High and have you no shame before his holiness, Muhammad, Peace be upon him?

Bahâ continued his harangue, warning that the caliph would perish in the onslaught of the Mongols, whom God had raised up as an instrument of punishment. Despite this extremely public humiliation, however, the caliph felt repentant and tried to reward Bahâ al-Din with gifts of money and horses, which, of course, were refused. Aflâki closes this section with a description of the sacking of Balkh at the hands of the Mongol armies, elaborating upon the general destruction as vindication of the warning that Bahâ al-Din had given of divine retribution. In telling of the death of the Khwârazmshâh (wrongly dated to 1219 [A.H. 616]), Aflâki comes close to rejoicing, reflecting that the Mevlevis continued to blame the departure of the Valad family from Khorasan and that region's destruction by the Mongols, on the ungodliness of the Khwârazmshâh:

> The tyrant slain, the world revived
> All became anew God's subjects

(Af 23)

Aside from the unlikely events described in Aflâki's narrative, the above accounts must be largely discounted on the grounds that Bahâ al-Din Valad's fame is not reflected in other sources, nor were his sermons preserved among any group besides the Mevlevis, who themselves seem to have gradually forgotten them. Aflâki at one point does refer to them by name (Af 12) and quotes excerpts from a sermon delivered by Bahâ Valad (Af 11–12) and from his letters (Af 43), corresponding fairly closely to the versions found in the text of his *Ma'âref.* For the most part, however, Aflâki relies on anecdotal lore current amongst the Mevlevis a few generations after Rumi's death, including stories attributed to Rumi and Sultan Valad, among others. However, even Sultan Valad in his *Ebtedâ nâme* does not seem terribly well informed about his grandfather, and some of what he does report has already assumed legendary contours.

Nevertheless, portions of Aflâki's narrative reflect an essential kernel of truth. For example, it is true that religious scholars visiting other cities would often be warmly received, welcomed and asked to give lectures or sermons, and

Bahâ al-Din and his followers must have been welcomed and hailed as visiting pious scholars and dignitaries, particularly by adherents of the Hanafi rite. Likewise, that some sort of friendship or admiration developed between Bahâ al-Din and the renowned Sufi shaykh Sohravardi is generally accepted as a historical reality; Aflâki suggests that it was Sohravardi who introduced Bahâ al-Din to Sultan ʿAlâ al-Din in Konya. In any case, the portrait emerges of a stern and fearless preacher whose outspokenness may indeed have led to political problems for him in Balkh. Though we see a pious man whose destiny is shaped by the hand of God, Aflâki gives no indication of Bahâ al-Din's mystical visions and proclivities, which leads one to conclude that large parts of his *Maʿâref* were either unknown or downplayed by the time of Aflâki.

THE VALAD FAMILY FROM BAGHDAD TO KONYA ACCORDING TO AFLÂKI

Aflâki follows the Valad family from Baghdad to Kufa to pilgrimage in Mecca and Medina and thence to Damascus. Though the people of Syria plead with him to stay there, Bahâ al-Din has received divine intimations that his home will be in Konya. The family is said to have arrived in Malatya in the year of Genghis Khan's death, which however Aflâki erroneously dates ten years too early (he gives 1217 [A.H. 614]). In Erzincan a certain pious woman, ʿEsmati Khâtun, dreamed that the spiritual axis of the world was passing by her town and, after going out on horseback to greet him, she had a school built in Âqshahr for Bahâ al-Din to teach in, prevailing upon him to stay there for four years.

After her death, the family went to Lârende, where the local ruler, Amir Musâ, became Bahâ al-Din's disciple and had a school built for him (Af 24–6). It was during their seven-year stay there that Rumi, at the age of eighteen, married the elegant and beautiful daughter of Khwâje Sharaf al-Din Lâlâ of Samarqand, Gowhar Khâtun. Aflâki says that Sultan Valad and ʿAlâ al-Din were produced of their union, [both ?!] in the year 1226 (A.H. 623). Rumi, the young father, would sit in gatherings with Sultan Valad at his side, and most people mistook them for brothers (Af 26).

It would have been unusual for an official like Amir Musâ, who served at the behest of the sultan of the realm, ʿAlâ al-Din Kay Qobâd, to host such an illustrious guest and observe his following amongst the local populace grow without reporting the matter to the sultan. However, every time Amir Musâ had asked Bahâ al-Din to pay his respects to the sultan, Bahâ al-Din had indicated that he did not wish to see the face of one who drank and listened to the music of harps. When Bahâ al-Din's presence in Lârende was finally reported to the sultan, he became quite angry with Amir Musâ for concealing the matter from him. Amir Musâ went before the sultan and told him what Bahâ al-Din had said, whereupon the sultan wept and promised that if Bahâ al-Din would agree to come live with his sons in the city of Konya, he would become his disciple and would never again listen to songs and harps (Af 28) (notice that he does not, however, foreswear drink!).

Bahâ al-Din accepted and the sultan warmly welcomed him, humbling himself before the great teacher. Though the sultan offered him a place to stay, Bahâ al-Din once again affirmed that the place of a religious leader was in a school, whereas shaykhs ought to stay in Sufi cloisters, rulers in palaces, merchants in caravanserais and so on. Bahâ Valad and his clan therefore settled in the Altunpâ Madrase. As before, Bahâ al-Din refused all gifts from the sultan, explaining that the wealth of princes is of dubious origins, and that the Valad clan was content to live on the wealth passed down from their ancestors. Once again, the throne was offered to Bahâ al-Din, this time by Sultan ʿAlâ al-Din in a public gathering with all the religious scholars present. Bahâ al-Din blessed the sultan for the offer and said his sincerity had assured him dominion in both this and the next world, and the sultan became his disciple.

When the King of Scholars Bahâ al-Din died on February 23, 1231 (18 Rabiʿ II A.H. 628 [Af 32]), almost toothless at the age of eighty-five (Af 41), his son Jalâl al-Din Rumi was thirty-four and his grandson, Sultan Valad, sixteen (Af 48). The worldly sultan, ʿAlâ al-Din, was deeply grieved; he remained isolated in his palace for seven days, declined for forty days to ride a mount and sat on a reed mat rather than on the throne, as a sign of mourning. For forty days feasts and alms were given to the poor, and a shrine was erected around Bahâ al-Din's grave, itself marked by a stone inscribed with the date of his death. Following once again the genre of saints' lives, Aflâki recounts a number of miracles related to the grave site of Bahâ al-Din.

AFLÂKI'S MIRACULOUS LIFE OF RUMI

When the Valad family was living in the Mostanseriye seminary in Baghdad, Bahâ Valad would ask his son, Jalâl al-Din, to fetch water whenever thirst overcame him in the night. The young Jalâl al-Din would get out of the bedclothes and go through the locked doors of the seminary without using a key. (Af 24).

Sayyed Borhân al-Din, who sensed the death of Bahâ al-Din on the very day it happened, hurried from Termez to attend to Rumi in Konya. When Sayyed Borhân arrived, Rumi had gone to Lârende, where he tarried for some months, during which time Borhân stayed in the Senjâri mosque in Konya. He sent a messenger with a letter filled with counsels for Rumi, asking him to come back to his father's tomb to see Borhân. Rumi rejoiced upon reading this letter and hurried back to see him. Aflâki gives two conflicting accounts about the discipleship of Rumi to Sayyed Borhân; in the first Borhân al-Din remarked after some conversation that Rumi had far outstripped his father in outward knowledge, but that he lacked his father's mystical insight. Borhân al-Din proposed to teach this to Rumi and the latter acquiesced, holding

Borhân al-Din as his spiritual *magister* for nine years. In the second account, Bahâ al-Din had entrusted Rumi's spiritual development to Borhân al-Din before leaving Balkh. According to this, Rumi had become his disciple when still a child, when Borhân al-Din would carry him piggyback and spin him around (Af 58).

In a story Aflâki relates on the authority of "the noble companions" (Af 266–7), Sa'di of Shiraz, a contemporary of Rumi and an equally famous Persian poet, was asked by Malek Shams al-Din, a ruler in India, to write down a beautiful poem for him. Sa'di supposedly chose a poem by Rumi, referring to him as "a blessed king who has appeared in the regions of Greece" (Rum), and asserted that no one had or ever would best this verse. Sa'di was so taken with the poem that he even expressed the desire to visit Rumi in Konya. Sa'di appears to submit to Rumi's poetic mastery in this anecdote, whereas, in fact, Sa'di was widely known throughout the Persian-speaking world during his lifetime as a poet, and Rumi perhaps was not (though it should be noted that Sa'di was a professional poet with official court patronage, whereas Rumi wrote as an enthusiastic amateur for a less powerful audience). Actually, there is no evidence that either poet was aware of the other.

More miraculous still is the following story which Aflâki relates without blinking an eye. According to the "great companions" of Rumi, Khezr, the enigmatic prophet who teaches Moses the meaning of divine wisdom, used to converse regularly with Rumi and ask Rumi for guidance concerning the secret mysteries of truth which remain hidden from this plane of existence (Af 348)!

THE HALF-LIFE OF AFLÂKI

In 1540 the account of Aflâki was condensed and put into Persian verse as **Savâqeb al-manâqeb**, "The Luminary Passages of the Acts." A Mevlevi shaykh and *Masnavi* reciter in Konya, Mahmud Dede, subsequently translated the work to Turkish in 1590. About a year before it was finished, however, he went to Istanbul and presented two chapters to Sultan Morâd III, who commissioned the completion of the work and undoubtedly arranged for it to be illustrated. Numerous illuminated manuscript copies of the work survive (Morgan Library in New York, Topkapı Palace Museum in Istanbul, etc.), and they provide us with a number of beautiful miniatures, depicting various scenes, many of them miraculous in nature, such as two corpses rising from their graves as Bahâ al-Din preaches; Rumi rescuing a ship from a whirlpool; protecting Konya during a battle; speaking with a monster emerging from a pond; the murder of Shams al-Din. Some of the scenes are more realistic, such as Rumi giving a valuable piece of cloth to a beggar, keeping a vizier waiting, receiving a priest in humility, advising Sultan Valad, etc.[2]

THE *NAFAHÂT AL-ONS* OF ᶜABD AL-RAHMÂN JÂMI

In addition to his biography of the saints, which we will come to in a moment, Jâmi (1414–92) wrote a number of works of exegesis on the teachings of Sufis like Ibn ᶜArabi, ᶜErâqi and Ibn Fârid. He also wrote a narrative poem, "Salamân and Absâl" (which has been rendered to English by the same Edward FitzGerald who made ᶜOmar Khayyâm a household name in England and America), based upon the metrical model of Rumi's *Masnavi* and ᶜAttâr's *Manteq al-tayr*.

Born in Jâm in eastern Iran in 1414, Jâmi went to the Nezâmiye school in Herat and traveled to Samarqand with his father for further education in the conventional sciences. After a dream he realized the greater importance of gnostic modes of knowing and was initiated into the Naqshbandi order, eventually becoming its shaykh after the death of his teacher, Saᶜd al-Din Mohammad Kâshghari. In 1472 he set out for pilgrimage, stopping in Baghdad for a while and visiting the shrine of Imam ᶜAli in Najaf along the way. After completing the pilgrimage in April of 1473, he proceeded to Aleppo, whence he was invited to Tabriz, where he remained for one month as the guest of the Aq-Qoyunlu ruler Amir Hasan Beg. The Ottoman sultan, Mehmed the Conqueror, wished to bring him to Turkey, too, but Jâmi returned to Herat in January of 1474, where he lived until his death in 1492 (JNO, Towhidipur's introduction, 155–8).

A learned man familiar with princely courts as well as Sufi circles, and perhaps therefore more inclined, like court chroniclers, to dates and specific details, Jâmi seems slightly less credulous than Aflâki. Jâmi's *Nafahât al-ons* ("The Fragrances of Fellowship"), begun in 1476 and completed in 1478, four years after his return to Herat, provides biographical notices for more than six hundred shaykhs and mystics. For information on the early Sufis, it relies upon Solami's *Tabaqât al-sufiye* and ᶜAbd Allâh Ansâri's reworking and amplification of the same, to which Jâmi added information about the following four centuries up to his own day, gleaned and critically selected from a variety of "other reputable books" (JNO 3–4). Jâmi gives separate entries for Bahâ al-Din Valad, Borhân al-Din Mohaqqeq, Jalâl al-Din Rumi, Shams al-Din, Salâh al-Din, Hosâm al-Din and Sultan Valad, in that order, devoting almost 15 of 640 pages to the Mevlevi founders. Much of his information stems ultimately from Aflâki and Sepahsâlâr, and it seems quite likely that Jâmi was directly familiar with at least the former source.

Jâmi relates a report (probably taken from Hamd Allâh Mostowfi) that names Bahâ al-Din Valad as a successor of Najm al-Din Kobrâ, but does so without subscribing to this theory. As argued in the pages above (see "Rumi as Kobravi?" in the Introduction), this seems unlikely from a factual point of view. Jâmi also relays, probably from Aflâki, the legendary genealogy which traces Bahâ-e Valad's lineage to Abu Bakr on his father's side and claims that his mother was the daughter of ʿAlâ al-Din Mohammad, the son of the Khwârazmshâh (JNO 458).

Bahâ-e Valad's father died when he was two (which we also learn in Af 2). Jâmi subscribes to the stories which claim great fame for Bahâ al-Din, though he notes, like Aflâki (Af 10), that the title King of the Clerics came to him from the Prophet in a dream (i.e., the title was not granted because of the outward esteem in which other clerics held him). Owing to the accusations of some of the ulama like Fakhr al-Din Râzi, Bahâ al-Din was compelled to leave Balkh when Rumi was still a young boy. They went to Mecca via Baghdad, where they stayed in the Mostanseriye school for three days, during which time Shehâb al-Din Sohravardi showed Bahâ al-Din great honor (JNO 458, almost certainly following Af 7–18).

Jâmi puts the family in Azerbayjan for four years after the return from pilgrimage, followed by a seven-year sojourn in Lârende, where Rumi was made head of a household (kad khodâ) at the age of seventeen. Here Rumi sired Sultan Valad, born in 1226, who looked so much like Rumi that when he grew older people were always mistaking him for his father. Finally, the Valads were invited to Konya by the sultan, where Bahâ al-Din died (JNO 458). Again, Jâmi has added nothing we do not already know from Aflâki, and when it comes to Borhân al-Din, Jâmi basically repeats four of the two dozen anecdotes Aflâki gives us (JNO 458–9).

Jâmi continues to rely upon Aflâki for the information he gives on Rumi, but he also adds a story taken from some other source about Rumi's meeting with Farid al-Din ʿAttâr. Jâmi prefaces this anecdote with "they say," a phrase which, while not necessarily signifying disbelief, does show us that Jâmi may harbor doubts about the story. According to this account, the Valads stopped in Nayshâpur on the way to Mecca from Khorasan and had an audience with ʿAttâr, who gave a present of his Asrâr nâme to the young Rumi, who always thereafter carried it about with him. ʿAttâr also gives a little metaphysical lesson to Rumi which portends his future greatness (JNO 460).

Although ʿAttâr was still alive when (and if) the Valads came through Nayshâpur, modern scholars regard the purported meeting with suspicion (FB 17–18; FA 68–70; Mei 41). Rumi did hold ʿAttâr in high esteem, but he would have been quite young when passing through Nayshâpur and it is not entirely clear that Bahâ al-Din would have been predisposed to meet with a poet. Rumi himself makes no mention of such a meeting, though he does frequently refer to ʿAttâr. Since this pretty story does not appear in Sultan Valad, Sepahsâlâr or Aflâki, we may conclude that it does not derive from the early Mevlevi community, which makes it quite unlikely that Rumi ever mentioned this orally, either. The story may, instead, reflect a tradition told in Khorasan, since it is reported by both Jâmi of Herat and Dowlatshâh of Samarqand. Given the fact that it is reported two hundred years after Rumi's death, conforms to the archetypal imperative of Sufi hagiographies to link the transmission of spiritual (and poetic) insight from one generation to the next, we may dismiss this anecdote as unhistorical. In later works such as the *Rowzat al-jannât*, this legend takes on even larger proportions, making Rumi into a disciple of ʿAttâr and even of Sanâʾi, though the latter died well over a half century before Rumi was born (FB 18).

Jâmi continues with a number of anecdotes about Rumi and Shams, some of which derive nearly word for word from Aflâki, while others must come from a different source. The kernel of some of the sayings Jâmi attributes to Rumi may be found in the *Masnavi* or perhaps even in the *Maqâlât* of Shams. As for Shams, Jâmi seems to follow Aflâki in the main, but he does quote some reports extraneous to Aflâki, such as that some say Shams was a disciple of Bâbâ Kamâl-e Jondi (JNO 465).

We have already discussed the accounts Jâmi gives of Shams' first meeting with Rumi. We should note here, however, that Jâmi first relates the version of the story given by Aflâki (Af 619) almost word for word, with the ellipsis of a few sentences near the end (JNO 465–6). He then goes on (JNO 466) to report two further anecdotes from Aflâki (621–2 and 675), before reverting to the account of the first meeting of Shams and Rumi according to a different source. Jâmi does not name his source, telling us only that "some have said . . ." (JNO 466), but the basic archetype of the story that he then relates (JNO 467) may be found in the *Javâher al-moziʾe*, written sometime before 1373. Jâmi then returns to Aflâki for the account of the knife attack on Shams, as we have seen and seems to blame Rumi's son, ʿAlâ al-Din, as one of the seven conspirators against Shams. Jâmi also reflects Aflâki's confusion over the location of Shams' grave (JNO 467).

In his account of Salâh al-Din and Hosâm al-Din (JNO 468–9), Jâmi follows Aflâki (e.g., Af 705, 710ff., 740ff.). He also begins his account of Sultan Valad with information gleaned from Aflâki, but then specifically mentions that Sultan Valad wrote a *masnavi* "in the meter of Hakim Sanâʾi's *Hadiqe*, which contains many gnostic insights and secrets" (JNO 470). This certainly refers to Sultan Valad's *Ebtedâ nâme*, but while Jâmi may have seen this work at some point in time, it appears that he did not have a copy handy as he wrote his history of the Mevlevi founding fathers. If he had Sultan Valad's book in front of him, he most certainly would have quoted Sultan Valad's own version of his mission to bring Shams back to Konya. Instead, Jâmi (JNO 470–71) relies on Aflâki's *Manâqeb* (Af 695–6), which he follows word for word at first, with but a few omissions, for its account of Sultan Valad's journey to Damascus to retrieve Shams. Likewise, Jâmi simply retells Aflâki's version of the discussion between Hosâm al-Din and Sultan Valad over the question of succession (JNO 471–2; Af 786, 802, 822–3).

For the most part, then, Jâmi follows Aflâki. He does cite information from a few other sources, though not from Sultan Valad's *Ebtedâ nâme*. Further research might succeed in pinning down Jâmi's sources more precisely, which would help us evaluate the reliability of the supplementary information he gives. We may reasonably assume, however, that Jâmi's other sources are later and less reliable. Sultan Valad, Sepahsâlâr and Aflâki were all based in Konya and wrote the earliest "biographies" of Rumi, and therefore must have had greater access to first-hand information than other sources.

THE *TAZKERAT AL-SHO^CARÂ* OF DOWLATSHÂH

Early European scholars attempting to reconstruct the history of Persian literature relied heavily upon Dowlatshâh of Samarqand's *vita* of the poets, one of the more comprehensive medieval works providing information about the poets of Iran. Dowlatshâh completed his work on October 17, 1487, a little more than a decade after Jâmi's *Nafahât*. Dowlatshâh tells us he was around fifty years of age at this time (Dow 15, 610) and admits that in his youth he had not applied himself to the acquisition of knowledge. In hindsight, he felt that he had wasted his time in the royal courts and found it difficult to start research from scratch at an older age. Inspired by a quatrain of Jâmi and a line which the mystic muse (*hâtef-e ghayb*) brought to him, he nevertheless set to perusing the reputable histories and the *divâns* of the older as well as the more recent poets (Dow 14–17).

Unfortunately, at least from our point of view, Dowlatshâh was not a very exacting scholar and was interested in collecting entertaining and instructive legends as much as or more than he was interested in collecting factual information. Malek al-Sho^carâ Bahâr has pronounced a harsh sentence against Dowlatshâh in *Sabk shenâsi*, his study of the history of style in Persian.[3] Even those who look with a generous eye at Dowlatshâh's failings will realize that the material presented about Rumi in his *Tazkerat al-sho^carâ* cannot be considered authoritative, especially since it was written over two hundred years after the death of Rumi.

In any case, Dowlatshâh adds little of significance to our story. He repeats the claim that Rumi's lineage stretches back to Abu Bakr, that his family came from Balkh, that his father stood at the head of the herd of clerics in the days of Sultan Mohammad, the Khwârazmshâh (Dow 213). The enmity of the Khwârazmshâh offends Bahâ al-Din and forces him to leave Khorasan, swearing never to return so long as Mohammad was sultan.

Dowlatshâh of course relates the story about Rumi's meeting with Farid al-Din ^Attâr in Nayshâpur, indicating that ^Attâr came to meet Bahâ al-Din and gave young Rumi a copy of his work the *Asrâr nâme* as a gift. ^Attâr tells Bahâ al-Din that his son, Rumi, will soon set the heart of the world's mystics on fire. Dowlatshâh, relying upon a faulty memory or inaccurate sources, confuses matters by describing Rumi and his father as disciples of Borhân al-Din Mohaqqeq, who he says accompanied the Valads on their journey throughout

264

Syria and Mecca, dying finally in Syria (Dow 214). This, however, directly contradicts Aflâki and Sepahsâlâr, who based their statements on the oral history of the earlier Mevlevis. According to Dowlatshâh, Borhân al-Din designates "Mowlânâ" (ostensibly Bahâ al-Din) as his successor before dying, recommending that he settle in Anatolia. Bahâ al-Din did choose Konya and set up shop there as a preacher with the support of Sultan ʿAlâ al-Din.

Dowlatshâh names Sultan Valad's "verse epistle" (Dow 214–15), by which he means the Ebtedâ nâme, as one of his sources. Dowlatshâh tells us that in his day Sultan Valad's "Valad nâme" was well known (Dow 221), and he quotes from it more than once, but since some of what Dowlatshâh writes diverges from Sultan Valad's account, we may assume that Dowlatshâh either did not have access to a complete manuscript, or chose to credit other accounts which he does not name. In any case, Dowlatshâh records the death of Bahâ al-Din in the year A.H. 631 (A.D. 1233–4), three years later than the date given by Aflâki. Dowlatshâh tells us that Rumi had four hundred students at this time and that ʿAlâ al-Din was a great believer in him (Dow 215).

In Dowlatshâh's telling, Rumi went before Salâh al-Din Zarkub, who was an important shaykh of the Sohravardi order, to deepen in mystical matters. Rumi also sought out Ibn Abi Tork and finally Hosâm al-Din of Konya, becoming his disciple. Again, Dowlatshâh does not tell us precisely how he knows all this, but it does not come from Sultan Valad. It would appear that Dowlatshâh has surmised Rumi's discipleship to Hosâm al-Din from statements in the Masnavi, one of which he quotes (Dow 216).

The matter becomes even more confused, however, as Dowlatshâh tells us a number of stories about Shams al-Din that appear quite legendary, including that he was the son of Khâvand Jalâl al-Din Now Mosalmân, a man of Ismaili lineage who, however, burned all his forefather's heretical books and sent his son, Shams, to study in Tabriz. A little further on, however, Dowlatshâh records that Jâmi refutes this account, indicating that Shams was the son of a cloth dealer from Tabriz (which is more in line with what Aflâki tells). Dowlatshâh then goes on to quote yet other unnamed sources who explain that Shams' father was originally from Khorasan and had come to Tabriz to trade. Dowlatshâh affects lack of interest and says that it does not matter where he was from (Dow 216). Obviously, however, Dowlatshâh did not have Aflâki or Sepahsâlâr or Shams' own Maqâlât to consult, and simply cannot decide which of his sources to credit, since none of them are considered early authorities for this question.

According to Dowlatshâh, Shams al-Din had been such a beautiful boy that he was kept in the women's quarters of the house so that no man would see him and fall into homosexual desire for him (Dow 216). Here may be said to originate the claim which some modern homosexual authors and translators have made about the relationship between Rumi and Shams; though

Dowlatshâh does not specify that their relationship was physical, this passage is suggestive. Recall, however, that Shams al-Din himself in the *Maqâlât* condemns Owhad al-Din of Kerman for the physical nature of his relationship with the young male adepts around him.

In a passage further suggestive of effeminate tendencies on the part of Shams, Dowlatshâh tells us that he learned to embroider in gold from the ladies among whom he lived as a boy and become known as "the gold embroiderer"; this however is not a title very widely applied to Shams. Dowlatshâh does, however, rightly report that Shams al-Din was well trained in the conventional religious sciences (Dow 216), in contradistinction to some legends which view him as an untutored or even illiterate mystic.

The tale told by Dowlatshâh has Shams al-Din following the mystic path under the guidance of Shaykh Rokn al-Din al-Sanjâbi (probably an error on the part of Dowlatshâh or one of the copyists, as it appears from Jâmi that Rokn al-Din Sajjâsi is intended). This "Sanjâbi" in turn had sat at the feet of Abu Najib Sohravardi, and through Sohravardi Dowlatshâh traces the mystical lineage of Shams back to Ahmad Ghazzâli, Abu Bakr-e Nassâj and, eventually, to Jonayd. Through Jonayd his spiritual lineage supposedly reaches Maʿruf-e Karkhi, from which the mystical transmission branches back in two directions, one through the eighth Imam of the Shiites to the Prophet Mohammad, and the other through Hasan-e Basri to Imam ʿAli (Dow 217).

This Rokn al-Din Sanjâbi supposedly sent Shams to Anatolia (Rum) in search of a certain gnostic, whom Shams later recognized in the person of Rumi. We have already recounted Dowlatshâh's version of their first meeting, but it bears repetition here: Shams saw Rumi riding on a donkey from the school where he taught, with his disciples in tow, and posed a question about the purpose of practicing self-renunciation and acquiring knowledge. Rumi replied that this was the path of the Sunna and the etiquette of the Shariʿa. After Shams characterized these as superficial, Rumi asked, "What is above these?" (Dow 217). Shams replied that the purpose of knowledge is to arrive at the Evident (or the Known), and quoted a verse from Sanâʾi affirming that knowledge must take a person beyond himself.

This exchange left Rumi dumfounded and he fell at Shams' feet. He stopped teaching and spent all his time with Shams, talking only with him. All of this disturbed Rumi's disciples, of course, who could not believe that a bareheaded and barefoot man of suspect orthodoxy could have tempted such a great teacher of Islam from the straight path. These accusations led Shams to slip away to Tabriz, which only set the fire of longing ablaze in the heart of Rumi, who went to Tabriz in search of Shams and after finding him, brought him back to Anatolia. After another period of companionship, the caviling of the disciples once again led to the withdrawal of Shams, this time to Syria, where he stayed for two years. Note the discrepancy between Dowlatshâh, who has Shams withdraw first to Tabriz and then to Syria, and Aflâki and Sepahsâlâr, who make no mention of Shams' return to Tabriz (Dow 218).

As for the death of Shams, Dowlatshâh informs us that the accounts disagree and relates three separate versions. In the first account, at the instigation of Rumi's jealous disciples, one of the sons of Rumi knocked a wall over onto Shams al-Din to kill him. Dowlatshâh heard this from traveling Sufis but puts no faith in it, explaining that he has seen no such thing in any manuscript or reputable history. Dowlatshâh also repeats the story told by Jâmi, which derives in the main from Aflâki, that suggests the disciples of Rumi called Shams out of the house to kill him. However, Dowlatshâh opts for a different account, the authority for which he does not reveal, namely that Shams al-Din outlived Rumi (Dow 222).

Consumed with the thought of Shams, Rumi had singers compose poems and perform *samâ* day and night. As Dowlatshâh correctly observes, "Most of the poems recorded in the *Divân* of Mowlânâ were composed during Shams' absence." Dowlatshâh also describes a pillar in the home of Rumi which he used to grab on to with one hand, circling around and around and composing poems whenever the spirit moved him. The people around him would write the poems down, but Dowlatshâh recommends that, since the poems cannot truly convey the spirit of Rumi's mystical states, interested readers should turn instead to the epistle called *Valad nâme* (i.e., Sultan Valad's *Ebtedâ nâme*). Furthermore, Dowlatshâh finds the extensive corpus of Rumi's verse daunting; he has read or heard that there are 30,000 lines in the *Divân* and 48,000 in the *Masnavi*, though some say more and some less.

Since Dowlatshâh alludes to these various accounts about the number of lines of verse composed by Rumi, he evidently did not have complete copies of the *Divân* or *Masnavi* at his disposal. We may therefore conclude that Dowlatshâh had read Rumi only in anthologized form and probably did not even know of the existence of *Fihe mâ fih*. Indeed, the one ghazal that Dowlatshâh quotes from the works of Rumi (Dow 218–19), though a beautiful poem, is not considered an authentic composition of Rumi by Foruzânfar in his critical edition of the *Divân*.

Dowlatshâh does, however, refer to and quote from the *Ebtedâ nâme* of Sultan Valad, though he also alludes to a number of other sources, some apparently written and some oral. One of these sources is Jâmi, whose *Selselat al-zahab* (Dow 216) and *Nafahât al-ons* (Dow 222) Dowlatshâh mentions by name. Dowlatshâh does not name Aflâki as one of his sources and in fact he quotes the story of Shams' murder, which originates with Aflâki, only in the retelling of Jâmi. We may therefore infer that Dowlatshâh did not have access to, or at least chose not to use, Aflâki's *Manâqeb al-ʿârefin*. For the most part Dowlatshâh seems to have compiled his information from secondary sources, anthologies and even tertiary sources and oral reports. He does not tell us where he gets the information that Rumi died in the year A.H. 661 (Dow 221), but this date, corresponding to 1263, is certainly in error. Even so, Dowlatshâh reckons that Rumi was sixty-nine years of age at the time of death. This is only slightly incorrect; according to the lunar calendar, Rumi died at the age of sixty-eight years and three months.

Dowlatshâh is not as credulous as Aflâki and does not concentrate on the miraculous. He does not always stick to his principal written sources, Sultan Valad and Jâmi, which indicates a certain independence in evaluating information. Dowlatshâh may also have based some of his conclusions on personal conversations he had had with knowledgeable Mevlevis or manuscripts of which we are not aware. This is not to say that he has seen primary documentary evidence of any kind or has evaluated the sources at his disposal on the basis of philological or historical principles. Much of what he takes as factual must come from sources later than Sultan Valad, Sepahsâlâr and Aflâki. Since they apparently do not make use of Rumi's own works, they are not likely to be accurate. In the end Dowlatshâh adds no new information upon which we may rely. Although more sober than that of Aflâki, Dowlatshâh's account does not do much more than perpetuate the legends circulating a couple of centuries after Rumi's death, contributing a few other doubtful pieces of information.

PART III

THE TEXTS AND THE TEACHINGS

Toward a Biography of Rumi

A great deal more documentary evidence would be needed to write a modern biography of Rumi. A careful analysis of his letters, read in conjunction with medieval biographical dictionaries and historical texts, may help us better to pinpoint certain events in his life. We may also discover *vaqf* documents or further manuscript works which shed light on the outward aspects of his life. Further careful comparison and analysis of the details presented by Sultan Valad's "Book of Beginnings," Sepahsâlâr's "Treatise" and Aflâki's "Acts of the Gnostics," correlated with the lives of the religious scholars and theosophers of the day in Damascus and Baghdad will also, no doubt, turn up new details.

A solid basis for writing such a biography of Rumi is now mostly in place. Shebli No⁀mâni made the first attempt, in Urdu. In 1937 Foruzânfar's biography and Jalâl al-Din Homâ⁀i's introduction to his edition of Sultan Valad's *Ebtedâ nâme* set forth the parameters on which such a work must be based. The 1954 revision of Foruzânfar's biography remains an important work; Gölpınarlı's Turkish biography of 1951 adds further information and proposes several alternative theses. Afzal Iqbal tried to "reconstruct the atmosphere – political, economic, social and literary of the time in which Rumi lived" (IqL xi) with his 1956 biography in English. Hellmut Ritter, writing in the second edition of the *Encyclopaedia of Islam*, fixed the major dates in Rumi's life with further precision.

Since then, Annemarie Schimmel has created a vivid impression of how Rumi lived his life and what he was about, drawing from Aflâki and quotations from Rumi's poetry (ScT), as has Radii Fish in Russian. ⁀Abd al-Hosayn Zarrinkub has written a historical novel that gives a very full sense of Rum's life and supplies a fair amount of speculative psycho-biology (ZrP). Both

Zarrinkub, in his introduction to *Serr-e nay*, and Este'lâmi, in the introduction to his edition of the *Masnavi*, provide scholarly accounts of Rumi's life. Sobhâni gives us a good deal of background information on the political figures with whom Rumi corresponded (see chapter 13, below, for further details).

None of these, however, is definitive. A complete concordance to the life of Rumi as told by Sultan Valad, Sepahsâlâr and Aflâki is needed. These hagiographies should also be subjected to a bit more critical acumen, plotting and analyzing them in terms of genre conventions and historical facts. A detailed political history of the period is needed that would correlate historical sources and political events with the known facts of Rumi's biography. The sources Rumi drew upon for his ideas and the terms in which he expressed them require more thorough examination. All of this would make for a fuller picture of Rumi, and it is my hope that the present work will lay the groundwork for these tasks.

Even so, many of the details of Rumi's life will probably always remain unknown to us. No archives of the Seljuks survive and the medieval histories of the period provide far less detail than we would like. Most of what we know about Rumi comes to us clouded by a heavy mist of myth and legend. For this reason, focusing on Rumi's formative influences – Bahâ al-Din, Borhân al-Din and Shams al-Din – and what they actually wrote permits us to glimpse a much fuller and less distorted reflection of Rumi. The main thrust of part I of this book was to reconstruct the context in which Rumi's thought and life unfolded, but we will obviously come to know the man most directly in his own writings. For that reason, we turn now in part III to a detailed consideration of Rumi's works, followed by a selection of his poems in English and a summary of his teachings.

RECAPPING RUMI'S LIFE

At this point, it will be useful to review what we know about the life of Rumi up to the time of his intellectual maturity and spiritual metamorphosis. Born in the end of September 1207, Rumi probably lived with his father in Vakhsh as a toddler. His father, Bahâ al-Din, was a minor religious scholar, a preacher by profession. Bahâ al-Din's spiritual visions and ascetic inclinations, along with the dreams of some of his followers, made him feel destined for a more prominent role in the religious life of his community. These aspirations led to some unpleasant encounters with the *qâzi* and other religious scholars in Vakhsh, who denied Bahâ al-Din the rank and prestige he sought. Sometime between 1208 and 1212 Bahâ al-Din relocated to Samarqand, taking Rumi with him, perhaps also followed by some members of the small circle of disciples that had gathered around Bahâ al-Din.

A few years later, probably by 1216 (though some say as late as 1220), the Valad family emigrated from eastern Iran, heading first for the pilgrimage to

Mecca. Most likely they already had the intention to settle in one of the Persian-speaking princedoms of Anatolia, either that of the Seljuks or the Manguchaks. After some years at the court of the Manguchak ruler Bahrâmshâh, whose wife endowed a religious college or Sufi lodge and a pension for Bahâ al-Din, he eventually moved to Konya under the patronage of ʿAlâ al-Din Kay Qobâd and taught for two years at an institution that probably functioned as something in between a traditional *madrase* and a Sufi lodge. He remained there until his death in February 1231.

Before establishing themselves in Konya, however, the family spent some years in Lârende/Karaman under the patronage of Amir Musâ, a local governor. During their stay in Lârende, the seventeen-year-old Rumi wed Gowhar Khâtun and fathered two sons. His own mother passed away and was buried here. Bahâ al-Din evidently intended his son Rumi to succeed him as a preacher or *mofti*. He introduced Rumi to his congregation and students and gave Rumi the opportunity to preach and win the confidence of the townsfolk in Konya. When his father died, Rumi was probably not yet old enough or advanced enough in his studies to command the respect that his father had. He therefore asked for Borhân al-Din to come and step into the place of his mentor, Bahâ al-Din.

Sayyed Borhân temporarily agreed to this arrangement, but he evidently viewed this position in Konya as Rumi's by right. He therefore established himself in Kayseri under the patronage of the Seljuk minister Sâheb-e Esfahâni. During this time Bahâ al-Din's former position in Konya must either have been discontinued, taken over by one of his disciples, or held in trust for Rumi, on the condition that he pursue a formal education in the Islamic sciences and obtain a degree (*ejâze*) from one of the famous *madrases* in Syria.

Borhân soon sent young Rumi to be trained by the acknowledged legal and religious authorities of the day in Aleppo and Damascus. While there, Rumi pursued a traditional course of religious studies, including Hanafi law, Koran, Hadith and theology. He perhaps also listened to the public lectures of theosophers and Sufi theoreticians like Ibn ʿArabi while pursuing his course of studies. The mystical mentoring and maturation of Rumi, however, and perhaps his formal initiation into the Sufi path – though not his introduction to it, which, *pace* Schimmel (ScW 14–15), probably came at his father's knee – took place under the supervision of Borhân al-Din Mohaqqeq once Rumi had returned from Syria to Kayseri, perhaps sometime around the year 1237 (the same year that Ghiâs al-Din Kay Khosrow II succeeded ʿAlâ al-Din Kay Qobâd as sultan). Rumi undertook a period of hermitage and ascetic exercises. Rumi also read and contemplated his father's spiritual notebooks, with their polychromatic mystical visions, along with the spiritual notebooks and Koran commentaries of Borhân al-Din. Eventually Rumi's mastery over his concupiscent self and his progress along the gnostic path satisfied Borhân al-Din that he was no longer in need of a mentor, and the two resumed their teaching/preaching duties in Konya and Kayseri, respectively.

In Konya Rumi evidently resumed his father's old position or was awarded a new one, possibly as a professor of law, but more likely as the spiritual preceptor and preacher to a community of piety-minded and mystically oriented disciples. Our sources rather predictably tell us that Rumi attained great fame during this period, that he became a recognized expert in Islamic law whose juridical opinions were widely sought out. It seems rather more likely that he achieved a certain popularity as a speaker and representative of an authentic and accessible mode of Islamic spirituality, attracting a great many disciples among the class of merchants and artisans, and among the ruling class as well. His lectures were attended by women as well as men, and a number of women considered themselves disciples. Before Shams arrived in Konya, Rumi supposedly had professorial positions in four separate *madrases* (Af 618).

But Rumi, according to Sultan Valad, wanted to find a holy man like Khezr to be his guide. Rumi found Shams al-Din to be that guide, though his glory was veiled from most others, even from the saints near unto God. God blessed Rumi with the revelation of the glory of Shams because of Rumi's devotion and in order to rid him of all other attachments (SVE 41–2).

After Shams al-Din Tabrizi arrived in Konya on November 29, 1244 (26 Jumâdî II 642), a transformation occurred in the outward form of Rumi's spirituality. He became more ecstatic in his worship, expressing his love for God not only in a careful attitude of self-renunciation and control, but also through the joy of poetry, music and meditative dance (*samâ*ᶜ, see below).

> Love is but blessing and fortune
> nothing but guidance and a dilated heart
> Bu Hanifa never studied love
> Shâfeᶜi never related anything about it
> The law of permissible and impermissible
> pertains from now until the day of death
> The knowledge of lovers is eternal
>
>   * * *
>
> Whoever you see with sad and sour mien
> is not in love and has no part in that realm

(from D 499)

Though many Sufis promoted these practices, not all the ulama sanctioned such motile and celebratory forms of worship. Some members of Rumi's own circle, both family and disciples, objected to this behavior, feeling it beneath the dignity of a preacher and jurisconsult, to say nothing of a professor in a college of law. No doubt they also found Shams' domineering manner objectionable, feeling that Rumi's deference and devotion to Shams detracted from his own reputation and standing. At some point, complaints were made to the *qâzi* about the practice of *samâ^c* by Rumi's followers, though this would appear to date from the period after the final disappearance of Shams.

After a little more than a year, on March 11, 1246 (21 Shavvâl 643), Shams left town, hounded out by the hostility of some of Rumi's disciples. Distraught that this ecstatic and innovative exemplar of spiritual joy had left him, Rumi stopped composing poetry and performing the *samâ^c*. He searched frantically for Shams and after receiving word from Damascus, Rumi sent his son, Sultan Valad, to fetch Shams back to Konya. The disciples who had opposed Shams now understood that driving him away would not make things return to normal, and they reluctantly acquiesced to his reappearance in Konya in April of 1247 (Dhu al-hijja 644).

Shams married one of Rumi's disciples, Kimiâ Khâtun, who had been brought up in Rumi's household, but she died shortly thereafter. Perhaps Rumi's family and disciples blamed Shams for negligence in attending to her health. In any case, their hostility or jealousy toward Shams apparently led him to leave Konya for good that winter, in late 1247 or perhaps early 1248. A devastated Rumi went searching for him several times to Damascus, but never found him. From 1244, if not earlier, Rumi had begun composing the ghazals. During the time of his companionship with Shams, Rumi addressed many ghazals to him. When Shams disappeared the first time, Rumi's inspiration virtually dried up, but his joyous muse returned when Shams came back to Konya. With the final disappearance of Shams, the frenetic quest to recover the vision of this spiritual guide turned inward. Eventually, Rumi reached some kind of catharsis for his fervent longing and began to discover Shams within himself. He continued to compose poems in the persona of the seeker longing for guidance, but also began to assume the voice of Shams in his own poetry. Rumi appears in many of these poems as the survivor of spiritual crisis and a guide to the shores of inner enlightenment, which can be reached only through great suffering and burning away the self.

By the 1250s, Rumi was composing ghazals for Salâh al-Din, whom Rumi treated as Shams' successor. Gradually, the flood of composition of ghazals began to subside somewhat and, with Hosâm al-Din as his chosen disciple, he turned in the 1260s to the narrative, didactic and anecdotal poetry of the *Masnavi*. However, Sepahsâlâr and Aflâki both indicate that Rumi continued to compose lyrical poetry for *samâ^c* sessions and other occasions.

RUMI'S RELATIONS WITH THE SELJUK STATE

Throughout the rest of his career, and even before, Rumi came into frequent contact with the elite members of the Seljuk state and benefited from their patronage. Rumi provides us occasional glances into these relations in his Discourses and his letters. To supplement this, Aflâki provides a wealth of information about Rumi's contacts with such officials, though he often relates

A CHRONOLOGY OF THE VALAD FAMILY THROUGH THE DEATH OF RUMI

c.1152	Birth of Bahâ al-Din Valad
c.1200	Bahâ al-Din teaching in Vakhsh up until about 1210 writing his spiritual diaries, the *Ma'âref*
c.1205	ʿAlâ al-Din is born to Moʾmene Khâtun and Bahâ al-Din
1207	Rumi born to Moʾmene Khâtun and Bahâ al-Din
c.1208	Dispute with Qâzi of Vakhsh
c.1212	Valad family living in Samarqand; Khwârazmshâh lays siege to the city
c.1216	Valads leave Khorasan for Baghdad and Mecca (March)
c.1217	Brief stays in Damascus and Malatya (summer)
c.1218	Valads in Âqshahr near Erzincan for four years
1221	Mongols take Balkh
c.1222	Valads in Lârende (Karaman) for seven years
	Death of Moʾmene Khâtun, Rumi's mother (between 1222 and 1229)
1224	Marriage of Rumi to Gowhar Khâtun
1226	Birth of Sultan Valad (April 25?)
c.1229	Family settles permanently in Konya (perhaps first came to city as early as 1221–2)
1231	Death of Bahâ al-Din (February 23)
c.1232	Arrival of Borhân al-Din in Konya
	Borhân in Konya and Kayseri, composing *Ma'âref*?
	Rumi a student in Aleppo and Damascus (c.1232–7)
	Borhân directs Rumi's spiritual discipline, including seclusion, reading of Bahâ al-Din's *Ma'âref*
	Rumi returns to Konya as accomplished scholar
1241	Death of Borhân al-Din Mohaqqeq
1244	Arrival of Shams in Konya (November 29)
	During this period, Rumi takes up *samâ'* and composes lyrical poems
1246	Shams quits Konya for Syria (March 11)
	Rumi stops composing poetry. Resumes with five or six poems after receiving word from Shams
1247	Return of Shams to Konya (April). Joyful parties are held, Rumi composes new poems
1247	Shams marries Kimiâ (sometime between October and December)
c.1247–8	Shams disappears from Konya forever
	At least two trips to Syria or Damascus in search of Shams. Rumi chooses Salâh al-Din Zarkub as his successor. A conspiracy to remove Salâh al-Din is foiled. Ghazals composed for Salâh al-Din
1258	Death of Salâh al-Din Zarkub (December 29)
	The Abbasid caliphate falls to the Mongols
c.1262	ʿAlâ al-Din, Rumi's eldest son, dies (mid-September)
	Composition of the *Masnavi* begins
c.1264	Book 2 begins (A.H. 662, sometime between November 1263 and October 1264)
1272	Birth of Ulu ʿAref Chelebi, son of Sultan Valad by Fâteme Khâtun, daughter of Salâh al-Din
1273	Death of Rumi (December 17)

miracle stories and other unlikely anecdotes. Sepahsâlâr gives some further information, but does not focus in detail on this aspect of Rumi's life. Sultan Valad chooses not to deal with political specifics at all. Foruzânfar, Gölpınarlı, Sobhani and a few others have compiled biographies in outline of most of the important figures mentioned in these sources. Afzal Iqbal and, more recently, Erkan Türkmen have presented this information somewhat more systematically. A political historian of the Islamic dynasties in Asia Minor, Aydın Taneri, has written at great length on the relations between Rumi and the Seljuk state. His *Mevlâna ailesinde Türk milleti ve devleti fikri* (Ankara: Ocak, 1997; 1st ed. 1987) is a useful step in the right direction, though it relies somewhat too credulously on Aflâki and is not free of error. A careful examination and comparison of all these sources would allow us to draw much clearer conclusions about the social, political and economic conditions under which Rumi worked.

Rumi's career began with the Seljuk dynasty in Konya at its cultural and financial apogee. According to Mostowfi in *Nozhat al-qolub*, Sultan ʿAlâ al-Din Kay Qobâd had an annual revenue of 3,300,000 gold dinars. Fifty years later, owing to Mongol encroachment, disputes over control among members of the dynasty and its ministers and the diminution of Seljuk territory, this income had decreased to 135,000 (IqL 48–9).

Rumi had a particularly close relationship with Sultan **ʿEzz al-Din Kay Kâus II** (r. 1246 or 1248–60), who perhaps considered himself a disciple of sorts (Af 79; see also "Rumi's Activity and Status in Konya before Shams," in chapter 3, above). Rumi and this sultan used to see one another when the sultan was in Konya; after he left, Rumi maintained a regular correspondence with him. The text of as many as nine letters apparently addressed to him by Rumi survive, some of them evidently written in response to letters from the sultan (Mak 59–61, 107–9, 109–11, 133–4, 162–3, 177, 178–9, 187–8 and 189–92). Rumi addresses Sultan ʿEzz al-Din as "son" and refers to himself as "father" in the letters, and retells at length the story of Joseph's separation from Jacob, pointing out the similitude between the situation of Jacob and Joseph and the situation of Rumi and the sultan (Mak 107–8). Rumi also expresses the wish to see ʿEzz al-Din again as soon as possible (Mak 178).

Rumi's letters include lines of verse, a typical and almost obligatory feature of the medieval Persian epistolary form. At least one of Rumi's letters to ʿEzz al-Din dates from 1257 to 1261 and was written with Hosâm al-Din acting as Rumi's secretary (Mak 273). Another letter assures the sultan of the prayers of all Rumi's disciples on his behalf (Mak 188), and Rumi gives the sultan counsel about the unfaithful nature of the world and the impermanence of pomp and political power. Mowlânâ also warns that we cannot tell in this world who are the chosen ones among God's servants; he assures the sultan that his loss of political power does not necessarily indicate the withdrawal of God's blessings (Mak 108). In another letter, Rumi congratulates a sultan, apparently ʿEzz al-Din, on his marriage (Mak 178). Rumi, on his part, asks ʿEzz al-Din for assistance with respect to various individuals, including Hosâm al-Din.

After 1249 ʿEzz al-Din was compelled to divide his realm with his brothers Rokn al-Din Qelij Arslân and ʿAlâ al-Din Kay Qobâd III. Rumi consoles ʿEzz al-Din over his defeats and points to them as a proof of the unfaithfulness and impermanence of the material world. At one point ʿEzz al-Din was compelled to flee to Byzantium, though he succeeded, with Byzantine help, in regaining his throne in Konya in 1257. Rokn al-Din, with his vizier Moʿin al-Din Parvâne, nevertheless remained a powerful threat. Sometime in 1258 or 1259 ʿEzz al-Din went to Baghdad to see the Mongol commander Hulegu and secure his help, but this only resulted in the division of Anatolia between Rokn al-Din in the east and north and ʿEzz al-Din in Konya and the west. At this point, ʿEzz al-Din withdrew from Konya to Antalya.

We have seen (chapter 3) how Rumi declined to visit Antalya (Fih 97), probably at the invitation of Sultan ʿEzz al-Din (Af 1020), in about 1259. The Mongols were at that time moving on Anatolia once again and after some unsuccessful politicking, ʿEzz al-Din withdrew yet again to his Byzantine friends in 1260 or 1261 when the Mongols threw their support behind Rokn al-Din. Driven from the Seljuk throne, ʿEzz al-Din made a bid to claim the Byzantine throne instead, but was imprisoned in 1263 or 1264 for this effrontery (this at a time when Rumi was composing the *Masnavi*). The period of this sultan's visits to Rumi must therefore date to sometime between 1246 and 1250, or perhaps to the period 1257 to 1259. The story Aflâki relates of Rumi upbraiding Sultan ʿEzz al-Din (Af 443–4; see "Rumi's Status and Activity in Konya before Shams" in chapter 3, above), if it has any basis in fact, must also date to one of these two periods. Some of the letters written to ʿEzz al-Din, however, might well have been written in the 1260s.

Rumi also wrote to **Qâzi ʿEzz al-Din of Konya** (Mak 150–52), who became the vizier of Sultan ʿEzz al-Din in 1256 or 1257, but was killed a year or two later for having encouraged a Seljuk attack on the Mongols (Mak 271–2). Aflâki says that this figure admired Rumi's non-academic understanding of religious truth and built a congregational mosque in Konya for Rumi (Af 103–4).

Jalâl al-Din Qaratây (also Qaratâʾi or Karatay, d. 1256?), the Atabeg or regent from 1249 to 1254, was a Greek convert to Islam, a manumitted slave of ʿAlâ al-Din Kay Qobâd. Ghiâs al-Din Kay Khosrow II appointed him to the Palace Lounge (Tasht khâne) as treasurer and he later became a deputy of ʿEzz al-Din Kay Kâus II. Qaratây signed his edicts as *Vali Allâh fi al-arz* (Mak 257), meaning both "regent" and "friend" of God on earth. Aflâki (Af 218) relates an account by Chelebi Shams al-Din Valad-e Modarres describing Qaratây as a man of saintly character. It would appear that two of Rumi's letters are addressed to this Jalâl al-Din (though Rumi also wrote to an Amir Jalâl al-Din Mostowfi, so there is some uncertainty on this score). Rumi refers to him as one of the angels nigh unto God, a mine of charity and justice, a refuge to the weak, an aid to the oppressed and a friend of the dervishes. Rumi asked him to help Salâh al-Din Zarkub by making a payment of 500 dirhams on his behalf for a garden Salâh al-Din had purchased. Salâh al-Din was two weeks behind on making a payment and the lender would not give him an extension. Rumi indicates that he could think of no one more worthy to help the saintly Salâh al-Din with a loan than Qaratây.

Jalâl al-Din Qaratây built a college in 1251 not far from ʿAlâ al-Din's mosque on the central hill in Konya which Rumi visited on various occasions (Af 559), though we may infer that this *madrase* focused on the formal study of Islamic law (*feqh*), in contrast to Rumi's *madrase* (Af 510), and that sometimes the professors and *foqahâ* studying here tried to upstage Rumi with their conventional knowledge (Af 291–2). This may have to do with Rumi's metamorphosis under the influence of Shams; one passage in Aflâki (see Af 121–2) suggests Shams as a subject of contention, though the account related by Aflâki anachronistically places Shams in Konya after the building of the Qaratây Madrase. Rumi's practice of *samâ* may have prejudiced these ulama against Rumi, but it does not appear that their patron shared their sense of superiority, as one account has Qaratây sneaking in to watch Rumi pray (Af 228), and Rumi apparently had reason to hope for Qaratây's patronage. After Qaratây's death, Rumi and his companions passed by his *madrase* one day and Rumi remarked that Qaratây was calling to them from the other world saying how he longed for the companionship of Rumi's disciples. So they meditated for a while in his *madrase*, with Koran reciters chanting verses of scripture and Rumi's disciples reciting ghazals and passages from the *Masnavi* (Af 218). The Karatay Madrase, which also serves as Jalâl al-Din Qaratây's mausoleum, is still standing, with some of the original tilework on the dome intact (see Mak 256–7; *EI²*).

Rumi wrote two dozen letters to **Moʿin al-Din Parvâne**, one of the most powerful men in Anatolia during the middle decades of the thirteenth century. His father, Mohazzab al-Din (d. 1244), was from northern Iran and had been a vizier under Kay Khosrow II. Rumi once wrote to him (Mak 203–4) asking for his help in finding a position for one of his extended family members (*khwishân*). Moʿin al-Din came into prominence after the Mongol defeat of the Seljuks at Köse Dag, through the negotiation of a treaty which made the Seljuk dominions effectively a Mongol protectorate. Moʿin al-Din began his career as a commander in Tokat, but in 1256 the Mongol chieftain Bâyju directed that Moʿin al-Din should became the Amir Hâjeb and Parvâne, a kind of personal assistant to the sultan and the official responsible for apportioning fiefdoms to generals and others. Since Rokn al-Din Qelij Arslân IV was under age, the Parvâne acted as de facto ruler of his half of the Seljuk dominions. In August 1261, however, Rokn al-Din's forces under the Parvâne chased Sultan ʿEzz al-Din out of Konya. The Parvâne had the governors who remained loyal to ʿEzz al-Din killed (Mak 290); Badr al-Din Gowhartâsh, the patron of a *madrase* built for Rumi or perhaps even for Bahâ al-Din Valad, was among those delivered over to the Mongols for execution by the Parvâne (see "No Weapon, No Body, No Murder," in chapter 4). After this, the Parvâne effectively became the ruler of the Seljuk dominions in Anatolia, answerable only to the Mongols, whose confidence he enjoyed. When Sultan Rokn al-Din came of age and tried to have the Parvâne removed in 1265, Moʿin al-Din had him murdered at Aksaray and installed his small son, Ghiâs al-Din Kay Khosrow III, on the throne. Kay Khosrow III remained sultan until 1284, but all the power remained in the hands of the Parvâne, who married his daughter to the sultan to ensure good relations.

Eventually, however, the Parvâne came to doubt his policy of placating the Mongols and called upon the Mamluk Baybars to invade Anatolia, which he did in 1277, after Rumi's death. In the confusion of this invasion, a Turkmen tribal leader seized Konya, and made Turkish the language of administration. The Mongols struck back and drove the Mamluks out of the area, at which point Moʿin al-Din Parvâne was executed for betrayal in August 1277.[1]

Despite the dirty business of politics, the Parvâne funded the ʿAlâ al-Din Madrase in Sinope (1263) and another *madrase* in Merzifon (1265), an area his sons held for some while after his death. The Parvâne established a *khâneqâh* for Fakhr al-Din ʿErâqi in Tokat and also attended the lectures and *samâʿ* sessions of Rumi. The many reports Aflâki gives of the Parvâne's visits to Rumi (e.g., Af 255–6, 310, 417, etc.) and his attendance at *samâʿ* sessions (Af 181–2, 215–16) are corroborated by Sepahsâlâr. The Discourses and the letters also confirm an ongoing relationship between the two. Discourse 10 relates how Sultan Valad (Mowlânâ Bahâ al-Din) was apologizing to the Parvâne once when Rumi (Khodâvandgâr) was late for a particular gathering. As Sultan Valad explained, Rumi had said that the Parvâne (Amir) should not trouble himself by coming to visit him, since he, Rumi, was sometimes preoccupied with other matters, engrossed in meditation or mystical vision, etc., and Rumi did not want to offend him by refusing to see him. The Parvâne said that Rumi was trying to teach him a lesson by showing him what it was like for petitioners at the Seljuk court to have to wait for a reply. When Rumi arrived, he apologized himself by saying that he had kept the Parvâne waiting out of love for him, just as God sometimes delays responding to the prayers of His servants, out of love for the sweetness of their sincere supplications (Fih 37). Indeed, Aflâki recounts an anecdote from Sultan Valad that describes this same incident in further detail, indicating that the Parvâne bowed to Rumi and said that his own purpose in visiting the Master (Khodâvandgâr) was so that the whole world would know that Moʿin al-Din was one of the servants of Rumi's threshold. As Moʿin al-Din departed on this occasion, he gave 6,000 Sultani coins to Rumi's disciples to take to Hosâm al-Din (Af 299–300).

This incident perhaps dates to the late 1250s or early 1260s. Sepahsâlâr recalls what must be one of the earliest encounters between Mo'in al-Din and Rumi. Mo'in al-Din Parvâne called a large gathering of the nobles in Konya and invited Rumi. After the crowd had dispersed, Mo'in al-Din instructed his drink steward, a certain Mohammad, to ask Rumi to stay and perform the samâ' (Sep 83). The steward (khâdem-e ebriq) whom the Parvâne asked to convey this invitation/request was a disciple of Rumi and the Parvâne gave him 3,000 dirhams as reward for convincing Rumi to stay. He took the pitcher from the steward and humbly served Rumi himself (Sep 84). On a later occasion, the Parvâne explained to Sultan Rokn al-Din that Rumi had no care for anything but the samâ' (perhaps meaning that he did not ask for a lecture fee or a donation), so whenever they wish to have his presence, they need only bring musicians and arrange for samâ' and request Rumi to attend (Sep 85). Not all the ulama and officials who attended these gatherings were friends of Rumi. Sepahsâlâr recounts that at one samâ' ceremony, Sayyed Sharaf spoke critically of Rumi to the Parvâne and Rumi composed impromptu verses as he turned in reply. The Parvâne repented of having listened to Sayyed Sharaf's words (Sep 87).

Rumi criticized Mo'in al-Din for making common cause with the infidel Mongols (Fih 5) and for his superficial understanding of himself as a man of action (Fih 74). In Discourse 61 Rumi also plays upon Mo'in al-Din's title, Assister of the Faith, pointing out that without the first letter his name would read "Essence of the Faith" ('Ayn al-Din), and chastising him for aggrandizing himself by adding letters to perfection (Fih 219). Aflâki relates on the authority of Sultan Valad that the Parvâne came one day to Rumi begging for his counsel and advice. Rumi remained quiet for a while and then said that since the Parvâne had learned the Koran, and since he had read the collections of Hadith with Shaykh Sadr al-Din, but yet did not follow the advice of God and the Prophet, how could Rumi have an effect on him? (Af 165).

Such criticisms should be seen as permissible dialogue between an established holy man and a monarch, for the relations between Rumi and the Parvâne must have been cordial. Rumi frequently wrote to him, asking him for favors and the Parvâne evidently desired the presence of Rumi at various gatherings. Sultan Valad even composed a qaside and two quatrains in praise of Mo'in al-Din, which date either to the same period that Rumi made these criticisms, or perhaps to the years after Rumi's death, that is sometime between 1273 and the Parvâne's execution in 1277.

We have seen how one of the Parvâne's stewards was a disciple of Rumi, and in Discourse 40 (Fih 150), we meet with a certain Jowhar, a servant of the sultan, in attendance at Rumi's lectures and comfortable enough to pose questions of him. Perhaps through this servant the wife of **Sultan Rokn al-Din Qelij Arslân IV** and even the sultan himself became interested in Rumi.

According to Sepahsâlâr (Sep 86), the Parvâne once arranged for Sultan Rokn al-Din to see Rumi, probably their first meeting. Later on, when the sultan decided to visit another shaykh – a certain Bozâghu according to Sepahsâlâr, or Shaykh Marandi, according to Aflâki – Rumi said that if the sultan had found a new "father," Rumi, too, would find a new "son." To appease Rumi, Rokn al-Din invited him to a banquet, but Rumi began turning when the tablespread was laid out with gold and silver bowls (Islamic law discouraged or forbad eating from gold dishes); the servants had no choice but to clear the table settings for Rumi to dance. The sultan took this as an affront, to which fact Rumi alluded in the poem he extemporaneously composed on the occasion. Rumi and Hosâm al-Din danced their way right out of the assembly and back to Rumi's *madrase* (Sep 84–5; cf. Af 146–9).

On another occasion, Sultan Rokn al-Din and the Parvâne invited Rumi to deliver the Friday sermon (*va'z*) and Rumi accepted. However, on the appointed day, he withdrew to the wine taverns on the edge of the city (*kharâbât*), where he would go to escape the crowds of people always pressing upon him, and meditate (Sep 95). The rulers and his disciples would later build mosques on the spot of the taverns he visited (Sep 96), but pious Muslims would not set foot in these places (see "The Symbolism of Wine in Rumi's Poems," below). The sultan and all the notables had gathered in the mosque, waiting for Rumi to preach after the prayers. Rumi's disciples searched frantically for him and when it was reported that he was in the taverns, Hosâm al-Din determined to go fetch him. Hosâm did not like to set foot in the taverns, especially on a Friday, and so he closed his eyes until he was close enough to see nothing but Rumi's face. He reminded Rumi that the ulama and dignitaries awaited him, and so they set off for the mosque. Rumi took the pulpit and preached such a sermon that all wept profusely. The mythological proportions of this story are meant to illustrate that Rumi did not care for celebrity or power, nor for pious reputation, and that he felt as much affinity for the lowly and sinful as for the high and mighty.

The Parvâne's son-in-law, **Majd al-Din Atabeg** (d. 1277), was the finance minister of Rokn al-Din, and also a disciple of Rumi. Sepahsâlâr (Sep 100–101) indicates that Rumi pressed Majd al-Din to undertake a retreat of fasting (*chelle*), which he did for a few days until hunger overcame him and he snuck out of the school to a friend's house for a bite to eat. A few letters from Rumi and his circle are addressed to this figure, including one requesting financial help for Nezâm al-Din that dates from the last two years of Rumi's life (Mak 75–6, 288).

The Parvâne married **Gorji Khâtun**, a Georgian princess, who had earlier been the wife of Ghiâs al-Din Kay Khosrow II. Aflâki describes her as a disciple of Rumi (e.g., Af 263, 425, etc.), and Rumi once convinced her to return to her husband, the Parvâne, when she turned to Rumi for advice in a marital dispute (Af 432–3). According to Aflâki, when she had to accompany the sultan to

Kayseri, she could not bear to be separated from Rumi, so she had the painter ʿAyn al-Dowle-ye Rumi make a portrait, or rather several portraits, of Jalâl al-Din Rumi to take with her (Af 425–6). She also contributed a large amount of money, some 130,000 dirhams or more, to the building of Rumi's tomb (Af 792). One of Rumi's letters addressed to the Pride of All Ladies (Mak 118–19), congratulating her upon her recovery from illness, was apparently addressed either to her, or to **Gumâj Khâtun** of Tokat, the wife of Rokn al-Din Qelij Arslân IV. Rumi sometimes arranged *samâ ͨ* sessions for women, and Sultan Valad's daughter and other earlier Mevlevi women continued this tradition (Mak 279).

Rumi also invited the wife of **Amin al-Din Mikâʾil** to participate in the *samâ ͨ* of his disciples, at which she strewed roses over him (Af 490–91). A treasury official of ʿEzz al-Din and later a viceroy (*nâyeb*) in Konya from 1259 to 1277, Amin al-Din was tortured and killed in 1278 when Konya was captured. He attended Rumi's lectures (Af 133) and had met Shams al-Din Tabrizi (Af 782). Amin al-Din regretted the Seljuks' subservience to the infidel Mongols, as related in Discourse 17 (Fih 77); he also started the discussion in Discourse 11 (Fih 43). Rumi wrote three letters to him (Mak 252–3).

Rumi wrote several letters to **Tâj al-Din Moʿtazz** (d. 1272), who had been the chief judge of Jalâl al-Din Khwârazmshâh, asking him to assist Hosâm al-Din's son (Sadr al-Din) and son-in-law (Nezâm al-Din). He was therefore apparently a supporter of Hosâm al-Din, and Aflâki tells us that he attended the ceremony of investiture when Hosâm al-Din was made the shaykh of Ziâ al-Din's *khâneqâh* (Af 754). Tâj al-Din had come to Anatolia to collect tribute from the Seljuks, but Sultan ʿEzz al-Din rebuffed him and told him to go see Rokn al-Din. There he met the Parvâne and became friends with him, and when Rokn al-Din drove ʿEzz al-Din from Konya, Tâj al-Din was made head of the treasury in Kastamonu and Ankara (Mak 254–6). Aflâki tells us that Tâj al-Din used to come with the Parvâne to hear Rumi lecture (Af 100) and that he sent money to Rumi (Af 751). At the request of Sultan Valad, he had a few rooms built behind the *madrase* where Rumi taught (Af 241–2).

ʿAlam al-Din Qaysar was one of the governors of Ghiâs al-Din Kay Khosrow III (r. 1264–82). He was evidently devoted to Rumi and arranged for a *samâ ͨ* session at his home, to which he invited all the statesmen and ulama (Af 489). He also had a hand in the construction of Rumi's shrine (Af 792); Sultan Valad wrote several poems in praise of him (Mak 277). Rumi wrote two letters to him (Mak 278).

Rumi's attitude toward politics was one of studied indifference. While recognizing that he might have some influence over men of state, he did not set his hopes upon them. As he says in Discourse 15 (Fih 64–5), the Mongols were once lowly and powerless, but God befriended them and gave them might for a time. Eventually, though, God would destroy them. Indeed, this was an attitude deeply ingrained in Iranian ethical and Sufi literature. But Rumi also saw the advantage in having the elite attending his lectures or *samâ* ceremonies, as he describes in Discourse 62 (Fih 221). Princes were like bees who came to his garden, gathering wax and honey. They would then fly away to other gardens and pollinate the flowers there. This would spread Rumi's influence and attract more disciples.

RUMI'S RELATIONS WITH THE PEOPLE

Rumi, like most Iranians prior to the Shiite revolution of the Safavids in the sixteenth century, was a Sunni, and as we have seen, followed the Hanafi school in juridical and ritual matters. Though the majority of the Turks and Muslims in Anatolia followed the Hanafi rite, the Seljuks did not particularly favor the Hanafi school per se over the other three canonical schools. In fact, Nezâm al-Molk, the famous Iranian vizier who helped acculturate the early Seljuk rulers to Iranian forms of government and culture, adhered to the Shâfeʿi rite, and the Nezâmiye colleges founded in his name taught the Asharite doctrine, which opposed some of the rationalist premises of the Hanafis.

Neighborhoods in major cities tended to segregate along religious lines, with Jewish, Christian, Zoroastrian and Muslim quarters, and the Muslim population further tended to congregate along sectarian lines, with each mosque adhering primarily to a particular school. Although there was occasional sectarian tension or even violence (particularly between Sunnis and Shiites, the latter not recognized as a canonical school during the Seljuk period), the policy of the Seljuk administration was to moderate between the various schools and ensure stability and civil accord.

Rumi maintained cordial relations not only with Muslims from the various schools, but also with common people, and not just the ulama. Beyond that, he had friends among the Christians, including not only Gorji Khâtun, but also a monk. ʿAlam al-Din Qaysar alluded to this fact when Gorji Khâtun asked him what was the greatest miracle he had seen Rumi perform. Qaysar replied that a clan may follow a certain shaykh, and a whole faith community may love a prophet, but the greatest miracle (*karâmat*) of Rumi was that people from all faiths and all nations revered him and listened to his teachings (Af 519).

Once the Parvâne criticized Rumi, saying that he was an incomparable monarch, but that the people who became his disciples were of bad character. One of Rumi's disciples happened to be in the audience on this occasion and told his Master what had been said. Rumi wrote to the Parvâne saying that if his disciples had been of good character he, Rumi, would have followed them himself. However, he accepted them as disciples to help reform them. This answer both pleased and shamed Moʿin al-Din Parvâne, who apologized and made a sizeable contribution to the upkeep of the disciples (Af 129–30). No doubt this is why, as Sultan Valad describes (see "The Death of the Epiphany of Faith," chapter 5, above), people of all walks of life and various faiths came to pay their respects in the funeral cortege of Rumi, with the representatives of the sultan and other state officials carrying the bier (Sep 116).

INFLUENTIAL THINKERS IN RUMI'S NEIGHBORHOOD

In addition to men and women of state, Rumi must have met with other religious figures in Konya. As we have seen, Sepahsâlâr (Sep 24–5) claims that Rumi met a number of well-known mystics in Damascus, including the Kobravi Sufi Sa°d al-Din Hamuye (d. 1252), and the gifted poet Owhad al-Din Kermâni (d. 1238), whom Ibn °Arabi quoted in his *Fotuhât al-Makkiye*. Rumi and **Sadr al-Din al-Qonavi** (1210–73), the stepson and closest disciple of Ibn °Arabi, lived in Konya at the same time. Aflâki describes several encounters between them in which Sadr al-Din tends to appear as a social or spiritual inferior to Rumi, praising Rumi as the greater shaykh and guide, and indeed the greatest Sufi since Jonayd and Bâyazid (Af 359–60; cf. Sep 86–7, 92). Sadr al-Din had been born in Malatya, but came to Konya in 1254, where he prospered and eventually became Shaykh al-Islam, which would explain why Jâmi, in his *Nafahât al-ons*, describes Rumi following Sadr al-Din in prayer and showing him great respect. Whatever their relative social positions, we may infer that Rumi and Sadr al-Din met more than once. Aflâki and Sepahsâlâr relate (Af 353–4; Sep 116) that Sadr al-Din performed the prayers at Rumi's funeral (for the life of Sadr al-Din, see CBa).

Sadr al-Din helped spread Ibn °Arabi's doctrines (CBa 80), and the influence of the school of **Ibn °Arabi** on Rumi has long been assumed. As we have seen, Shams-e Tabrizi conversed with a Shaykh Mohammad – probably the very same Ibn °Arabi – and came away much impressed, though ultimately he distrusted Ibn °Arabi's spiritual claims and blamed him for not adhering to the example of the Prophet. Ibn °Arabi stayed for a while in Konya, but Sepahsâlâr and an early commentator on the *Masnavi*, Kamâl al-Din Khwârazmi (*Javâher al-asrâr*, 133), assert that Rumi met Ibn °Arabi in Damascus. This is entirely possible, as Ibn °Arabi resided there between 1229 and his death in 1241, during the time frame Rumi studied there. Rumi does recount the attractions of Damascus in one ghazal (D 1493) which alludes to various physical features of the city, including the Jabal-e Sâleh, a hill on which Ibn °Arabi and other Sufis are buried; while the ghazal mentions the Abbasid poet Abu Nuwâs, it does not mention Ibn °Arabi, focusing instead, as we might imagine, on the city's association with Shams-e Tabriz, and promising to go there in search of Shams for a third time (see chapter 4, above). Certainly Rumi was at least aware of Ibn °Arabi.

Rumi and Ibn °Arabi seem to have certain assumptions in common, including the unity of being (*vahdat al-vojud*), a notion generally attributed to Ibn °Arabi and sometimes described in Western works as a kind of pantheistic monism. Likewise, the two would seem to share a belief in the existence of an "imaginal world" (*âlam-e khayâl*) of thoughts and forms (see the excellent discussion in CSP 248–67). Of course, such ideas may well have been part of the wider zeitgeist among mystically minded Muslims, and Rumi may have imbibed them from a number of other sources. However, the great Shaykh Ibn ʿArabi's reputation as the fount for all such strains of thought in Islam, the fact that he expounded his theosophy more systematically than Rumi, the fact that Rumi was apparently in contact with Ibn ʿArabi and or some of his close disciples, and the fact that most of the major *Masnavi* commentaries of the pre-modern period approach Rumi's book informed by the assumptions of Ibn ʿArabi's school of thought, have created the impression that Ibn ʿArabi was an important influence on Rumi. Nicholson ventured the opinion in *Rumi, Poet and Mystic* (London: George Allen & Unwin, 1950) that even if later commentators exaggerated the extent, Rumi did borrow "some part of his terminology and ideas from his elder contemporary."

But Bausani has pointed out (BPR 267–9) that Ibn ʿArabi's influence, if any, must have been rather external, more philosophical than religious. Chittick (CSP 358 n. 14) noted that Rumi's concept of imagination is rather broader than Ibn ʿArabi's and that Rumi never uses the term *vahdat al-vojud* (CBa 91). Chittick concludes (CBa 92–4) that Ibn ʿArabi "exercised no perceptible influence on Rūmī," insofar as Rumi never uses the specific terms and ideas of Ibn ʿArabi as set forth in the writings of Sadr al-Din, or the poetry of ʿErâqi, Shabestari (d. 1320) and Maghrebi (d. 1407). Whatever points of similarity one detects, there remains a deep difference in the perspectives of Rumi and Ibn ʿArabi (CBa 95) and they addressed completely different audiences (CBa 96). The specific instances where Nicholson thought he had detected Ibn ʿArabi's influence on Rumi are dismissed one by one in Chittick's appendices to his article on the question (CBa 97–104).

We may hypothesize that Rumi did not consciously study or borrow from Ibn ʿArabi. Though Rumi may have imbibed some influence from Ibn ʿArabi indirectly, if so, this merely resonated with beliefs he already held, derived from his own teachers and from the tradition of ʿAttâr and Sanâʾi. Rumi does not mention Ibn ʿArabi, nor have any specific quotations from Ibn ʿArabi's works been detected in Rumi's writings. Though Rumi may have found some of Ibn ʿArabi's ideas congenial, like Shams-e Tabrizi, he likely faulted the great shaykh for insufficient commitment to following the example of the Prophet, which Shams and Rumi considered an essential prerequisite to proper spiritual praxis. The debate continues on this question,[2] but the burden of proof rests entirely on the plaintiffs – those partial to the idea of Ibn ʿArabi's influence. It is said that the title of Rumi's Discourses, *Fihe mâ fih*, derives from Ibn ʿArabi's *Fotuhât*, but the name could have come from anywhere and was not, in any case, chosen by Rumi, but by his later disciples. Unless paraphrases or quotations from Ibn ʿArabi's works can be demonstrated in Rumi's writings, any influence from his ideas must have been diffuse and quite secondary.

It is often said that Rumi and **Fakhr al-Din ʿErâqi** (d. 1289) were friends. The evidence for this is, however, circumstantial and ambiguous. ʿErâqi lived near Hamadan but came under the influence of certain Qalandars, wandering Sufis, whereupon he set out for India. In Multan he met Bahâ al-Din Zakariye, whom he left for a while, only to return for a twenty-five-year period of discipleship. Jealousy among the followers of Zakariye led ʿErâqi to leave; like Rumi, he came to Anatolia after performing the pilgrimage and settled in Konya, where he professed himself a disciple of Sadr al-Din of Konya. Having gained the favor of Moʿin al-Din Parvâne, ʿErâqi went to Tokat, where the Parvâne ostensibly endowed a Sufi lodge for him. Sometime before 1274 ʿErâqi wrote his famous *Lamaʿât* (available in English translation), and died in 1289 (*EI²*). If Rumi and ʿErâqi really did enjoy a friendship, neither considered himself a disciple to the other. The fact that ʿErâqi went to a *khâneqâh* in Tokat tends to suggest that Konya was not big enough for the both of them, or perhaps that the Parvâne felt it wiser to keep them apart.

Though Rumi never mentions Ibn ʿArabi or ʿErâqi, he does explicitly name a number of influences. These include, of course, Shams-e Din, Bahâ-e Din and Borhân-e Din, whom Rumi knew intimately through personal interaction as well as through their writings. Like his teachers, Rumi frequently mentions Sanâʾi and ʿAttâr and obviously saw himself as carrying on their tradition of didactic–mystical poetry (Sultan Valad explicitly states this in one of his poems).

RUMI'S READING

Rumi borrowed much in the *Masnavi* from other sources; a relatively small proportion of its stories originate with Rumi. However, Rumi does not simply borrow tales for the purpose of having something to tell. He alters the endings or highlights certain aspects of each story not emphasized in the original, tailoring the tales to point certain morals. We need to remember that Rumi took only the narrative outlines of his stories, mostly from prose sources in Arabic or Persian, and then versified them in his delightful way. Important as tracing the sources and influences of Rumi may be, as Nicholson pointed out in *Tales of Mystic Meaning*, he "borrows much but owes little; he makes his own everything that comes to hand."

Most of the time Rumi does not mention his sources, but this is hardly surprising. Authors in the medieval Persian tradition employed anecdotes, vignettes and lines of verse to strike a mood, support an argument, segue to the next theme, etc., with little or no anxiety over their origin. Indeed, such tales form a kind of pool of proverbial folk wisdom and, expressed in rhyme and meter, facilitate memorization. Rumi's contemporary, Saʿdi, followed much the same course in his *Golestân* (1256) and *Bustân* (1257).

In any case, Rumi was certainly not trying to hide his sources. In some places he reveals them explicitly and provides the rationale for retelling them, as for example in the story of the three fishes (M4:2202ff.). Rumi reminds the reader that he will probably already have read this story in *Kalile va Demne*, the Persian animal fables based upon a translation of the Panchatantra, known as the "Fables of Bidpai." But, he tells us, only the outer husk of the story is given in *Kalile*, whereas Rumi promises to give us the spiritual pith of the matter.

Other stories come from ethnic jokes about the stereotypical characteristics of individuals from various Iranian cities, or the trades or products for which they are particularly known. For example, Rumi associates Qazvin with its tattoo parlors (M1:2981ff.). Grammarians are thought to be pedantically conceited (M1:2835ff.). The qualities of gardener, jurist, Sufi, and *sayyed* (descendant of the Prophet) play against one another in one story (M2:2167ff.). Some stories are associated with legendary or historical events, such as "Sultan Mohammad Alp Ulugh Khwârazmshâh" and the conquest of Sabzavâr (this took place in 1186, according to Jovayni, during the reign of ʿAlâ al-Din Takesh [r. 1172–1200]). In this particular story the Khwârazmshâh, with whose son Mohammad b. Takesh (r. 1200–1220) Bahâ al-Din supposedly quarreled, appears in a favorable light, as the upholder of orthodoxy against the extremist Shiites (*râfezi*). In the moral of the story Rumi makes him a godly man, whereas Sabzavâr is associated with the heterodox Shiites, among whom a single righteous and orthodox man is scarce to be found (M5:845ff.). Likewise we find a story about the notorious and feared Turkmen fighters, the Ghuzz tribe (M2:3046).

As we might expect, a good number of the anecdotes and vignettes of the *Masnavi* come from the Koran, the Hadith, the biography of Mohammad, and the lore of the earlier prophets, the latter as preserved in a popular genre of Islamic literature (*Qesas al-anbiâ*) that drew upon rabbinic literature and Jewish folklore to embellish the Koranic and Biblical accounts of the Prophets. To this category belong the stories of Moses and the man who wanted, like Solomon, to speak the language of the birds (M3:3266ff.); Jesus and the fools (M3:2570ff.) and Pharaoh and his magicians (M3:1157ff.). Many other stories relate the legendary feats of various Sufis, like Bâyazid (M2:2231ff. and M4:2102ff.) or Ebrâhim b. Adham (M4:829ff.). Rumi not infrequently quotes a line from ʿAttâr (M1:1603) or Sanâʾi (M1:1763, 2035) and comments upon it, and occasionally even paraphrases an Arabic poet like Majnun Qays (M1:2691–4). Rumi seems particularly close to the parables and anecdotes of ʿAttâr and the points he raises; in Foruzânfar's reckoning (FA 70–71), as many as thirty-five passages of the *Masnavi* reflect borrowings or paraphrases from ʿAttâr (ZrJ 273, 409 n. 3).

Although such stories circulated orally, Rumi had studied widely and we might conclude something about the breadth of his reading by tracing the sources of the stories he retold in verse in the *Masnavi*. The partial list given below of possible sources for the stories from Book 1, as compiled by Foruzânfar (FMQ), reflects that Rumi read some or all of the following:

The king in love with the slave girl, M1:36ff.
Source: "The Four Discourses" (*Chahâr maqâle*) of Nezâmi ʿAruzi.

The Jewish king oppressing Christians, M1:324ff.
Source: Any of various Koran commentaries.

The master and the squinting pupil, M1:327–34
Source: ʿAttâr's *Elâhi nâme* (which takes the story, in turn, from the *Marzbân nâme*).

The caliph sees Layli, M1:407–8
Source: ʿAttâr's *Mosibat nâme*, taken from the *Nahj al-balâghe* or Zamakhshari's *Rabiʿ al-abrâr*.

The second Jewish king who oppressed the Christians, M1:739ff.
Source: As Rumi points out, this is from K85:4, as elaborated in the commentaries.

A man's mouth deformed from mocking the Prophet, M1:812–15
Source: Ghazzâli's "Vivification of the Religious Sciences."

Hud's tribe destroyed by the wind, M1:854–5
Source: Thaʿalabî's "Stories of the Prophets."

Shaybân the shepherd, M1:856–9
Source: *Helyat al-owliâ* of Hâfez Abu Noʿaym Esfahâni.

A lion harasses the animals of the valley, M1:900ff.
Source: *Kalile va Demne* ("The Fables of Bidpai" in the Persian version of Nasr Allâh Abu al-Maʿâli).

Solomon conveys a man to India to escape Azrael, M1:956–68
Source: ʿAttâr's *Elâhi nâme*, though several other prose sources all relate the same tale.

The fly's interpretation of his cosmos, M1:1082–9
Source: Ibn Qotayba's *ʿOyun al-akhbâr*.

Solomon and the hoopoe, M1:1202ff.
Source: Thaʿalabî's "Stories of the Prophets," though several other contemporary sources also relate a version of it.

Ambassador from Caesar of Rome to Caliph ʿOmar, M1:1390ff.
Source: Mohammad b. al-Monavvar's "Secrets of God's Mystical Oneness" (*Asrâr al-towhid*).

The merchant and the parrot, M1:1547ff.
Source: ʿAttâr's *Asrâr nâme*.

The musician and Caliph ʿOmar, M1:1913ff.
Source: Either from the "Secrets of God's Mystical Oneness" or ʿAttâr's *Mosibat nâme*.

The poor Arab, his wife and the generous caliph, M1:2244ff.
Source: ʿAttâr, *Mosibat nâme*.

The wolf and fox hunt with the lion, M1:3013ff.
Source: One of the literary compendiums, *Nasr al-dorr* of Abu Saʿd Âbi (d. 1030) or *Ketâb al-azkiâ* of Abu al-Faraj Ibn al-Jowzi.

The man who knocked and said "It's me," M1:3056ff.
Source: The original seems to be Jâhez' *Ketâb al-hayavân*, but Rumi probably took it from ʿAttâr's *Mosibat nâme*, Ansâri's *Resâle-ye ʿaql va ʿeshq* or Zamakhshari's *Rabiʿ al-abrâr*.

Joseph asks a visitor for a gift, M1:3157ff.
Source: Mohammad ʿOwfi's *Jâmeʿ al-hekâyât*.

The Greek and Chinese painters, M1:3467ff.
Source: Nezâmi and Anvari both give versions of this story in Persian verse. Ghazzâli gives it in Arabic prose in the "Vivification of the Religious Sciences."

The Prophet asks after Zayd's health, M1:3500ff.
Source: *al-Lomaʿ* of Abu Nasr Sarrâj, "Vivification of the Religious Sciences" of Ghazzâli, *Asad al-ghâbat* of Ibn al-Athîr and the Koran commentary of Abu al-Fotuh all give versions of this story, where, however, it is about the Khazrajite Hârese al-Ansâri, not Zayd.

Loqman stands accused, M1:3384
Source: "Stories of the Prophets" of Thaʿalabî or the commentary of Abu al-Fotuh.

Medina catches fire during the reign of ʿOmar, M1:3707ff.
Source: *Navâder al-osul* of Mohammad ʿAli Hakim Termezi or the *Dalâʾel al-nobovvat* ("Proofs of Prophethood") of Abu Noʿaym Esfahâni.

An opponent of ʿAli spits in his face, M1:3721
Source: There is a vaguely similar story about ʿOmar in Ghazzâli's "Vivification of the Religious Sciences," but if Rumi read the story here, he has introduced considerable innovation and elaboration.

The Prophet predicts ʿAli will be killed by his servant, M1:3844
Source: A combination of various hadiths and a passage from *Nahj al-balâghe,* a compendium of sayings attributed to ʿAli.

The Prophet's conquest of Mecca, M1:3948ff.
Source: A hadith appearing in Muslim's *Sahîh* and elaborated
upon in a number of works, including the commentary of Abu al-Fotuh,
Ghazzâli's "Vivification" (where it occurs repeatedly), *Helyat al-owliâ,*
Dalâʾel al-nobovvat of Esfahâni and *Fotuhât al-Makkiye* of Ibn ʿArabi.

We cannot of course be certain in any given case that Rumi actually read the
source or sources mentioned; a particular story may have been related in
multiple sources, and Rumi may have heard some stories told orally, etc. But we
can get a general notion of the breadth of his reading and the eclectic nature of
his thinking from this list. We know that the writings of Bahâ al-Din and
Borhân al-Din, and also the material contained in Shams' *Maqâlât,* constituted
the principal influences of Rumi, along with the poetry of Sanâʾi and ʿAttâr, and
to a lesser extent, al-Mutanabbî. He had also read the classical Koran
commentaries (especially Tabari and Abu al-Fotuh) and the "Stories of the
Prophets" *(Qesas al-anbiâ)* as compiled by Thaʿalabî. In addition to these, the
writings of Mohammad Ghazzâli, in particular his "Vivification of the Religious
Sciences," made a big impression on Rumi. "The Diadem of the Saints" by Abu
Noʿaym Esfahâni; a number of works of belles-lettres in Persian and Arabic that
contain stories, poems, etc., including ʿOwfi's "Compendium of Stories,"
Zamakhshari's *Rabiʿ al-abrâr,* Ibn Qotayba's "Sources of Reports"; also a variety
of works about Sufi saints and Sufism, including Mohammad b. al-Monavvar's
hagiography of Abu Saʿid b. Abi al-Khayr, "The Secrets of God's Mystical
Oneness" *(Asrâr al-towhid);* Abu Nasr-e Sarrâj's manual of Sufi doctrine, the
Ketâb al-lomaʿ; Qoshayri's treatise on Sufism; and Hojviri's *Kashf al-mahjub* were
all on his reading list. Chittick (LCP 339) has also detected the influence on
Rumi of the *Rowh al-arvâh fi sharh asmâ al-malek* by Ahmad Samʿâni (d. 1140).

All told, there are 275 stories mentioned in the headings of the *Masnavi,* and
Foruzânfar found sources for 264 of these. A little reflection on this list will help
us comprehend the facility with which Rumi drew upon, almost certainly from
memory, a wide variety of sources, to entertain and illustrate his points. Of
course, the main source and focus of Rumi's reading was the Koran and the
Hadith. As Foruzânfar put it in his talk at the Rumi UNESCO festival:

> In the *Masnavi* every subject and field of study known at the time was taken
> under consideration in one place or another – ethics, philosophy, *feqh, adab,*
> scholastic theology and the sciences – and Mowlavi raises a new point and
> innovative way of looking at it. For example, there are 745 different traditions of
> the Prophet interpreted and 528 verses of the Koran alluded to or quoted and
> then commented upon.[3]

RUMI'S WRITINGS

THE DISCOURSES

The Discourses of Rumi, or *Fihe mâ fih*, provide a record of seventy-one talks and lectures given by Rumi on various occasions, some of them formal and some of them rather informal. Probably compiled from the notes made by various disciples, they were put together in an effort to preserve his teachings, quite likely after his death. As such, Rumi did not "author" the work and probably did not intend for it to be widely distributed (compare the genesis of de Saussure's *Course in General Linguistics*). As Safâ points out (Saf 2:1206) the Discourses reflect the stylistics of oral speech and lack the sophisticated word plays, Arabic vocabulary and sound patterning that we would expect from a consciously literary text of this period. Once again, the style of Rumi as lecturer or orator in these discourses does not reflect an audience of great intellectual pretensions, but rather middle-class men and women, along with a number of statesmen and rulers.

The title *Fihe mâ fih*, meaning literally "what's in it is in it," signifies a miscellany or potpourri of disparate sources, topics, speech occasions and so forth. The notes probably reflect only a portion of what was said on any given occasion. Prayers, formal sermons and so forth have been left out and only the meaty instructions and elucidations that the disciples felt distinctive and worth noting were preserved. Some older manuscripts give the title *al-Asrâr al-jalâliye*, with the double meaning "the mysteries of Jalâl" and "the glorious mysteries." By whatever name, this work provides an indispensable source for both the thought of Rumi and his relations with the political figures of his day.

Early printings of the Persian text of Rumi's *Fihe mâ fih* appeared in Shiraz (Ketâbforushi-ye Jahân-namâ, 1318/1900), in Tehran (Matba‌ᶜe-ye Sayyed Mortazâ, 1333–4/1915–16), and in India (1928 or 1929). These were replaced by the critical and annotated edition of Badiᶜ al-Zamân Foruzânfar, *Fihe mâ fih* (Tehran: Majles, 1951), since reprinted several times (Amir Kabir, 1962, etc.). Citations in the present work follow the Foruzânfar edition, which remains the most frequently consulted text. However, Foruzânfar himself indicated that his edition was in need of revision, and the recent edition of Jaᶜfar Modarres-e Sadiqi, *Maqâlât-e Mowlânâ (Fihe mâ fih)* (Tehran: Nashr-e Markaz, 1994), may therefore be consulted as a complement to this.

English readers enjoy the advantage of two translations, the first by A.J. Arberry as *Discourses of Rumi* (New York: Samuel Weiser, 1972) and the second by Wheeler Thackston, *Signs of the Unseen* (Putney, VT: Threshold Books, 1994). The Thackston edition, with the benefit of hindsight, corrects a few of Arberry's mistakes and adds a fine critical introduction and some useful notes, but both English versions accurately convey the substance and flavor of Rumi's lectures. Turkish versions were done by Meliha Ülker Tarıkâhya (Istanbul: Maârif, 1954) and Gölpınarlı (Istanbul: Remzi, 1959). French and German translations were respectively published by Eva de Vitray-Meyerovitch (Paris: Sindbad, 1976) and Annemarie Schimmel (Munich: Diederichs, 1988).

"THE SEVEN SERMONS"

Majâles-e sabʿe, "The Seven Sermons," is, as its name suggests, a small compilation of seven sermons or formal lectures of a didactic nature (technically, "sittings" or *majles*) attributed to Rumi. Unlike the Discourses, Rumi delivered these homilies on questions of ethics and faith on ceremonial occasions, probably in a mosque, perhaps after Friday prayers. We cannot fix the date of most of these sermons, though one of them may have been delivered when Rumi's parents were still alive. Because the hagiographers say that Rumi left off teaching and preaching after the encounter with Shams, it has generally been assumed that the sermons date to the period between 1230 and 1245, but there is no compelling reason to believe that Rumi gave up preaching entirely. Indeed, the sermons contain many quotations of poetry and, if we are to believe the hagiographies, Rumi did not practice poetry before Shams. Some of the sermons could date from much later in his life.

Rumi's sermons typically began with an exordium in Arabic, followed by a prayer in Persian. The sermon itself gives a commentary on the deeper meaning of a Koran verse or a hadith. The style of the Persian is rather simple, but the quotation of Arabic and the knowledge of history and the Hadith display the preacher's firm grounding in the Islamic sciences. The sermons include quotations from poems of Sanâ'i, ʿAttâr and other poets, including many lines from Rumi himself. They also feature little stories or anecdotes, some of which also appear in the *Masnavi*. Rumi's approach must be rather typical of the genre of lectures given by Sufis and spiritual teachers of his age; a translation of the sixth sermon is given in chapter 3, above.

The "Seven Sermons" did not usually circulate as a separate book during the medieval period. They are preserved in various manuscript anthologies along with *Fihe mâ fih*, Rumi's letters, the *Maʿâref* of Bahâ al-Din and Borhân al-Din and the *Maqâlât* of Shams. The oldest and most accurate text of the "Seven Sermons" occurs in a manuscript (Konya Museum no. 79) written out in May 1352. The sermons were probably written down by Rumi's disciples, and though we do not know if it was Rumi who reviewed or approved them, it does appear that the sermons were edited by some hand. A poem of Sultan Valad has found its way into the manuscript tradition, and though it is not impossible that Rumi quoted from Sultan Valad, Sultan Valad or one of his followers probably added this poem as an afterthought when copying out the text.

F. Nafız Uzluk published Rumi's sermons in two different editions. The first appeared in Ankara in 1355/1936, edited by Ahmet Remzi Akyürek with Veled

Chelebi İzbudak, and included a Turkish translation and sixteen-page introduction. The following year Uzluk produced an expanded version with 108 pages of notes, edited by Ahmet Remzi Akyürek alone, with credit given to M. Hulusi for the Turkish translation: *Mevlânânın yedi Öğüdü* (Istanbul: Bozkurt, 1937). Mohammad-e Ramazâni produced an Iranian edition of the sermons as part of the *Masnavi* published by Kolâle-ye Khâvar in several volumes (Tehran, 1315–19/1936–40), but this text was fraught with error. It was replaced in Iran by an offprint of the Uzluk edition in 1984 (Tehran: Nashr-e Jâmi).

The text of choice was edited by Towfiq Sobhâni working from the oldest Konya manuscript as his copy text and published as *Majâles-e sab'e* (Tehran: Kayhân, 1986; reprint 1994). Gölpınarlı translated the text of the same Konya manuscript to Turkish with an introduction as *Mecalis-i Sab'a (Yedi Meclis)* (Konya: Yeni Kitap, 1965), but no English version as yet exists.

THE LETTERS

Maktubât, the collected letters of Rumi, have been published under the title *Maktubât-e Mowlânâ Jalâl al-Din*, once in Istanbul and twice in Tehran. The first edition was prepared with indices and an impressive introduction in Turkish by Ahmet Remzi Akyürek and a university-trained descendant of Rumi, M.F. Nafiz Uzluk, appearing as *Mevlânânın Mektupları* in the series Mevlevi Works from the Seljuk Period (Istanbul: Sebat, 1937). The book also has a brief introduction in Persian and in Turkish from the Grand Chelebi, Veled, who was deposed in 1919. Unfortunately, the use of an inferior manuscript, faulty editorial decisions and printing mistakes virtually nullify the usefulness of this edition. The seventeen pages of errata do include some manuscript variants, but primarily correct typographical errors; even so, Sharaf al-Din Yâlet Qâyâ added an additional five pages of mistakes to this (Mak 29)!

Ramazâni included seven of Rumi's letters as an appendix to the Kolâle-ye Khâvar edition of the *Masnavi* (Tehran, 1936–40). Twenty years later Yusof Jamshidipur and Gholâm-Hosayn Amin, unable to acquire any further manuscripts, published an edition of the letters based on Uzluk's faulty text, correcting some of the errors, but adding a few of their own, along with some biographical information about the individuals mentioned in the text (Tehran: Bongâh-e Matbu'âti-ye 'Atâ'i, 1335/1956). Hosayn Dânesh returned to the Uzluk edition for another offset edition of Rumi's letters in 1984 (Tehran: 'Elmi).

Towfiq Sobhâni has thankfully made these editions obsolete and readers should henceforth refer to his edition of *Maktubât-e Mowlânâ Jalâl al-Din Rumi* (Tehran: Markaz-e Nashr-e Dâneshgâhi, 1371/1992). Sobhâni bases his edition on a far more reliable copy text, and provides critical apparatus, extensive annotations, indices and a superb introduction. As copy text, Sobhâni has used the same Konya Museum manuscript (no. 79) from the early 1350s that provided the copy text for the *Majâles-e sab'e*. This manuscript anthology of

Mevlevi texts has the titles, Koranic verses and hadith written in red ink. It was donated to the shrine in Konya by a descendant of the Chelebis named Esmâ^cil ^cÂsem in 1739 and is inscribed with the name of Mohammad Sa^cid Hamdam, the Grand Chelebi of the Mevlevi order in the first half of the nineteenth century (Mak 3).

Rumi's letters reveal that an extended community of disciples and family members looked to Rumi as an intercessor, not only with God, but also with men of state and influence. He sought to help them in their economic and communal affairs, and wrote recommendation letters, introducing individuals to potential patrons and asking for assistance. The letters testify that Rumi kept very busy helping family members and administering a community of disciples that had grown up around him. It should dispel the notion foisted on us by Sultan Valad that he lived a reclusive life withdrawn from the affairs of the world after the disappearance of Shams. In contrast with the prose of his Discourses and sermons, the style of the letters is consciously sophisticated and epistolary, in conformity with the expectations of correspondence directed to nobles, statesmen and kings.

RUMI'S POEMS AND THEIR TRANSMISSION

Rumi's poems are, of course, what attract us most. They are collected into two books, the *Divân-e Shams*, a huge collection of shorter lyric poems, and the *Masnavi*, a sustained narrative poem presenting Rumi's Islamic theosophy in an entertaining, though didactic, mode.

MANUSCRIPT CULTURE AND THE HISTORY OF THE *DIVÂN*

Though the "publishing" tradition in the medieval Middle East dictated that a poet's poems be collected in a single volume, or *divân*, more often than not, this labor was undertaken at the direction of royal courts, booksellers, friends of the poet or later literary critics and rarely by the poet himself. A poet might present a patron with an album (*daftar*) of the poems dedicated to him, or circulate an album of poems on a particular theme (ascetic poems, wine odes, etc.), but the manual labor of editing and copying out manuscripts for the public seems to have fallen to professional scribes or disciples of the poet. If it was ever the practice for poets and other authors to make their own holograph copies of their works, precious few exemplars have survived. The effort to collect the various albums or partial collections of poems that circulated during a poet's lifetime was not usually made until after his death. By the sixteenth century, most editors arranged the poems in each poet's *divân* in alphabetical order according to the last letter of each line, without regard for topic or meter. This is the format in which Iranian editions present Rumi's lyrical poems today, though the Turkish manuscript tradition, reflecting the Mevlevis' own practice, groups them meter by meter.

The printing press was only introduced to the Muslim world two hundred years ago, and did not become the predominate mode of publication until the last quarter of the nineteenth century. In a pre-print culture, books must, of course, be copied out by hand, and this provides ample opportunity for scribal and editorial errors – misreadings of difficult words, deliberate "improvements" or interpolations added by scribes, erroneous or intentional misattribution of poems to other authors, etc. In some cases, the manuscript tradition has amplified the corpus of various authors' works by ten percent or more over the centuries. Ferdowsi's *Shâh nâme*, for example, probably consisted of about 50,000 lines originally, but before modern text editors began working from the oldest manuscripts and sifting out the lines which can with relative certainty be discarded as later accretions, the received text of Ferdowsi's poem contained about 60,0000 lines. Likewise, the *Masnavi* of Rumi contains 25,577 lines in Nicholson's critical edition (not 27,000 as Rypka says), but late pre-modern manuscripts and nineteenth-century printings contain anywhere from 27,700 to as many as 32,000 lines, an accretion of between two and seven thousand lines that do not come from the pen of Rumi.

Foruzânfar's critical edition of the *Divân-e Shams* contains over 35,000 lines, and though some scholars have questioned the attribution of a large part of the *Divân-e Shams* to Rumi (especially the *robâ*'is, many of which have been proven to be by other poets), radical skepticism seems unwarranted.

The corpus of Rumi's lyrical poems has gone by various names: *Divân-e Shams-e Tabrizi* ("The Collected Shams-e Tabrizi"), *Kolliyât-e Shams-e Tabrizi* ("The Complete Shams-e Tabrizi"), *Ghazaliyât-e Shams-e Tabrizi* ("The Shams-e Tabrizi Ghazals") and *Divân-e Kabir* ("The Grand Collection"). The various collections in circulation do not all contain the same poems. Obviously, to copy a collection of the size of the *Divân-e Shams* required an immense amount of time, and a great deal of writer's cramp. To pay a scribe to do this could be quite expensive. On the other hand, if an individual wanted to make a copy for himself, he had to get the permission of the owner and stay in the location where the manuscript was housed for the several months which it would take to copy out the entire manuscript. Consequently, individuals wishing to have their own copy of a particularly voluminous manuscript might, owing to limitations of time or money, copy only the first half or quarter of a book, or better, make a selection of the best poems.

Most medieval readers almost certainly encountered the lyrical poems of Rumi in literary anthologies or in abridged selections. This is one way in which spurious poems might become widely associated with a given author – an anthologist or editor wrongly attributed a poem he had heard or read somewhere to a given poet and, since most people did not have a copy of the *divân* of the poet in question, few people bothered to check the attribution. In the case of Rumi, for example, the anthologist Dowlatshâh already attributes the poem *ânânke be sar dar talab-e Ka'be davidand* to Rumi in the fifteenth century (Dow 218–19). Though this poem does sound similar to other poems of Rumi, it probably comes from a later Mevlevi author.

The libraries of most major Sufi hospices and princely courts would have contained a copy of Rumi's *Divân* and the private libraries of many men of letters and book collectors must also have included copies. A catalog of all known manuscripts of the *Masnavi* and the *Divân-e Shams*, giving such details as date, scribe, provenance, present location, etc., would tell us quite a bit about the reception history of Rumi's poems and would undoubtedly help in improving our ability critically to establish as nearly as possible the text of what Rumi actually composed. A sampling of the manuscripts which Nicholson, Gölpınarlı or Foruzânfar used in their editions of or selections from the *Divân* follows. Those who have never worked with a text preserved in manuscript exemplars may initially find the following details unnecessary, but attention to them will teach us a good deal about the reception history of the work. Though not enjoying quite the same degree of fame as the *Masnavi*, the *Divân* was nevertheless widely known throughout the Islamic world.

1. A copy in the Mevlânâ Museum in Konya (no. 2113) with 252 leaves (504 pages), each page averaging 22 lines of verse, for a total of 10,810 lines. It is undated but is very accurate and quite old, probably from within twenty-five years after the death of Rumi. Given its location and its accuracy, Foruzânfar speculates it may have been compiled from original copies authorized by Rumi and suggests that it follows Rumi's own example in using an archaic spelling of one particular word. The scribe for this manuscript notes variant readings and therefore must have used more than one existing manuscript as his source. The poems in this manuscript are organized by meter, as were the early copies of Sultan Valad's *Divân* (GM 64), establishing this arrangement as early Mevlevi practice. It was made for, or at one time belonged to, a certain Sultan Bâyazid b. Mohammad Khân and was bequeathed to the shrine of Rumi in Konya by 'Osmân Nuri al-Jelvati.

2. A copy purchased by Chester Beatty and placed in the library in Dublin that bears his name.[4] It contains 359 leaves, each page 27 lines long with four columns, for a total of 54 lines of verse per page, and 38,124 lines (3,229 separate ghazals and *qasides* in 34,662 lines, with the remaining 3,500 or so lines consisting of stanzaic poems and quatrains). The manuscript groups the poems by meter and then alphabetically within each different meter. Arberry (MPR1: 2–3) notes that the first line of each poem is written in red ink and the manuscript appears to have been used as a kind of hymn book, for ease of locating poems to perform to *samâ'*. We do not know the early history of this codex, but in May 1601 a certain Mohyi

donated it to a Mevlevi lodge in Egypt headed by Shaykh Ebrâhim Golshani.

Like the previous manuscript, this one bears no date but appears to have originated in the first couple of decades after the death of Rumi. Its scribe evidently had access to the authorized copies of Rumi and his disciples. In the case of one quatrain (no. 1022), the scribe has written that he had seen this particular poem in the handwriting of Rumi himself, but the bulk of the manuscript must have been copied from exemplars kept by the close disciples of Rumi. It was intelligently collated, making use of more than one existing copy. One poem of Sultan Valad is mistakenly included on page 155 and above it is written a correction in the hand of a later reader, "by his son, may God be pleased with him." The manuscript reflects the idiosyncrasies of Rumi's spelling; Rumi came from eastern Iran where the pronunciation and spelling of some words would have differed from what was common in Anatolia, the far west of the Persian-speaking world (akin to the differences, let us say, between American and English spelling). Rumi's close disciples preserved his spelling to reflect his pronunciation or to show their regard for the sanctity of his writing.

3. A copy of 348 leaves (696 pages), with 17 lines of verse per page, now in the Süleymaniye library in Istanbul (MS no. 2693). The last pages of the manuscript were added later, and thus the original colophon indicating the date of this copy is missing, but Foruzânfar estimates it was written out around 1300, give or take a quarter century. It arranges the poems alphabetically, by the rhyme letter.

4. A copy in the Konya Museum (no. 2112) dating to within fifty years of the death of Rumi and containing 524 leaves, each page of which contains 25 lines, with 30,535 lines in toto. In this copy we meet with 832 quatrains ascribed to Rumi.

5. An incomplete copy of 300 leaves now kept in the Baladiye library in Istanbul. It was organized by meter, but only the quatrains and the poems in two of the meters survive in this copy (depending on whether we count the possible permutations of a given meter as separate meters or as one meter with variants, there are as few as seven and as many as twenty-two meters used in Rumi's *Divân*). The copyist, who was a scribe of the Mevlevi order by the name of Ahmad b. Mohammad al-Mowlavi al-Ahadi, completed the quatrains in July and the ghazals in September of 1323. Judging from a pious expression – *madda Allâh zellaho*, equivalent to "long live Rumi" – that appears above some of the poems, Foruzânfar concludes that Ahmad apparently had access to a manuscript written out while Rumi was still alive. However, Ahmad uses a similar expression (*asbagha Allâh zellaho 'alâ kâfat al-'âsheqin*) in the colophon of another copy he made of the *Divân* a few years later in July 1327, well after Rumi's death, so these

pious expressions do not indicate that Rumi was still alive when the copy was made.

6. A copy completed November 28, 1372 (A.H. 774), now in the British Museum.
7. A partial, alphabetically arranged copy, containing the second half of the poems only (those rhyming from L to Y), dated to the autumn of 1421 (A.H. 824), now in the British Museum.
8. A copy completed May 25, 1441 (A.H. 845), now in Vienna.
9. A copy dated 1447 (A.H. 851) containing the *Masnavi* and the *Divân*, now in the Leiden University Library.
10. A copy in the Konya Museum compiled in 1855 from old manuscripts by Sar Tariq Hasan Fahmi Dede, organizing the poems by meter with a tally of the number of poems in each meter and the number of lines in each poem.

The shrine of Rumi, now the Konya Museum, did not always contain the manuscripts it now holds. Apparently a deliberate effort was made over the years to collect manuscripts, and many visitors to the shrine would donate them. One copy, written out by Mohammad b. Yusof al-Mowlavi in 1329, was donated on February 10, 1492 to the shrine of Rumi by a certain Qâsem b. Yunes. A two-volume copy of the *Divân-e Shams* comprising 649 pages was handwritten by a certain Hasan b. ʿOsmân al-Mowlavi, who began the task on June 1, 1367 and set down his pen in the end of the summer of 1368. The manuscript was not ready, however, until November 1368, by which time Hasan had completed comparing what he had written with his exemplar and correcting the errors. The governor who had commissioned the copy, Sharaf al-Din Abu al-Maʿâli Amir Sâti Beg, then had the pages brought from Damascus and gilded. Amir Sâti, who paid a total of 6,000 dirhams (?) for this copy, must have liked the work of ʿOsmân al-Mowlavi, for he had ʿOsmân make him a copy of the *Masnavi* a few years later in 1371. This Amir Sâti was the son of a certain Hosâm al-Din Hasan, perhaps the same Hosâm al-Din Hasan who died in 1349 in Konya and was grandson to the famous disciple of Rumi, Chelebi Hosâm al-Din. In any case, Amir Sâti bequeathed the two-volume *Divân* to his son, Mostanjed, who donated it in the spring of 1409 to the shrine of Rumi in Konya after noting that there was no complete copy of the *Divân-e Shams* on the precincts. The manuscript was later stolen from the shrine, but the Turkish government was finally able to recover it about fifty years ago and return it to the Konya Museum, where it is now kept under glass.

This particular copy of the *Divân-e Shams* is quite a bit larger than the other manuscripts mentioned above, containing 40,380 lines. Another manuscript of the *Divân* contained in the Moti Mahall in Lucknow contains approximately 41,000 lines of ghazals and nearly 4,000 quatrains, making for a total of somewhere around 60,000 lines of verse in its almost 1,500 pages. Elsewhere, in Turkey, Gölpınarlı mentions a manuscript in his possession containing 43,561 lines, not counting the 1,753 quatrains. Therefore, we know that with the passage of time the corpus of poems included in copies of the *Divân-e Shams* and attributed to Rumi began to grow, as was also the case in the corpus of several other medieval poets (Ferdowsi, Khayyâm, etc.).

As with many other poets' collected works (Hâfez and ʿErâqi, inter alia) the manuscript tradition reflects an amazing variety. A given poem will be longer or shorter in various manuscripts, with some lines omitted and others added. If two manuscripts agree on the number of lines in a given poem, they may present them in very different order. And, of course, not all the manuscripts include all the poems; some very delightful poems are attested only in a few manuscripts, and some poems which clearly cannot be from Rumi are included in many. For example, many editions mistakenly include poems by Sultan Valad, Shams-e Tabrizi, or Shams-e Maghrebi. The task of sorting out authentic compositions of Rumi from later accretions, establishing which lines of a given poem are Rumi's and which may have been added by scribes, as well as the likely order of the lines, is truly daunting. A hypertext variorum edition of manuscripts of the *Divân* and *Masnavi* would make a delightful tool.

PRINTED EDITIONS OF THE *DIVÂN*

The history of the printed editions of the *Divân* begins in Europe. Vincenz von Rosenzweig-Schwannau produced a not entirely reliable Persian text of seventy-five selected poems in 1838; R.A. Nicholson followed in 1898 with a much more exacting text of fifty selected ghazals, though the critical edition of Foruzânfar has since eliminated several of the poems included by Nicholson as not authentic Rumi compositions (see chapter 13). In the interim between the appearance of the small selections of Rosenzweig and Nicholson, two more ample abridgements of the work appeared in the Muslim world.

A well-known literary historian in Qajar Iran, Rezâ Qoli Khân Hedâyat, prepared a selected edition of the lyrical poems of Rumi which was lithographed in Tabriz in 1863 (A.H. 1280). This explains that the whole of the *Divân*, which Hedâyat estimated to contain roughly 50,000 lines, was unsuited to the needs of most readers (*Divân*, ed. Hedâyat, 4). Hedâyat therefore selected about 9,000 lines, reflecting the best poems of the collection in his estimation, dividing them into two sections, "The Divân-e Shams al-Haqâʾeq from the compositions of his lordship, the mystical Mowlavi," comprising just over 100 pages, and "The ghazals of Mowlânâ, may his soul be sanctified," comprising almost 250 pages, followed by 15 pages of quatrains. A larger edition, but inferior in terms of printing and accuracy, appeared in Lucknow in 1878 (A.H. 1295), with about 12,000 lines, representing perhaps a quarter of the poems found in the larger manuscripts. A second Lucknow edition appeared in 1885, but this contains many poems by other poets (some of them using the pen name "Shams").

Further selections of the ghazals continued to appear in Iran, one by Izad Goshasb published in Isfahan, and another by Fazl Allâh Gorgâni in photogravure. The one most widely circulated, however, was the selection by Mansur Moshfeq published by the Safi ʿAli-Shâh Press as *Ghazaliyât-e Shams-e Tabrizi* in May of 1956, which met with such commercial success that a second printing was undertaken in February of 1957, a third in 1960 and an eighth in 1989. This collection was fortified by an introduction of no less than 123 pages by three different authors, featuring an excerpt from Senator ʿAli Dashti's book on Rumi, and articles written especially for inclusion in Moshfeq's edition by Jalâl al-Din Homâ°i and Partov-e ʿAlavi. The 700 pages of text include roughly a thousand ghazals (not all of them Rumi's), but no *robâ°is*.

Noting the brisk market for the ghazals of Rumi, the publishing company Amir Kabir brought out its own *Kolliyât-e Shams* in 1957, a complete edition of the ghazals and *tarjiʿ band*s in Tehran, with a smattering of about two hundred *robâ°is*. This volume weighed in at 1,356 pages of text, with a 55-page index, featuring 3,209 ghazals and *qasides*. The anonymous editor explains that most of the available editions of the poem presented only a selection of the poems, whereas readers were clamoring for the complete text. Following the lead of Moshfeq, a multiple-author introduction was added to the text, featuring the same excerpt from Dashti's book, and an excerpt from Foruzânfar's biography of Rumi. Unfortunately, though the edition is linked with the name of Foruzânfar by virtue of this introduction, it does not incorporate the critical acumen which he had already begun training on the poems. This edition includes well over a dozen poems not actually by Rumi (several of them with a Shiite theme, whereas Rumi was clearly Sunni) and features many misleading and erroneous footnotes, though the glosses on difficult words make the text reader-friendly. Indeed, this remains one of the most widely disseminated texts of Rumi's poems.

That same year the magnificent editorial project of Badiʿ al-Zamân Foruzânfar, based upon nine manuscripts written within a hundred years of the death of Rumi, began to appear through the press of the University of Tehran, which published the ten volumes of the *Kolliyât-e Shams yâ Divân-e kabir* from 1957 to 1967 (1336–46 sh.). A second edition, in more compact dimensions, appeared through Amir Kabir in 1977 (2535 Shâhenshâhi), reprinted in 1984. Foruzânfar's edition includes the *robâ°is*, the ghazals, the *qasides* and *tarjiʿ band*s, as well as glossaries and other helpful material. It also has a critical apparatus that indicates significant manuscript variants. Foruzânfar's critical edition brings us closer than we have ever been to the corpus of what Rumi originally wrote, and all serious readers of Rumi's lyrical poems should rely upon it. However, the edition is not definitive; several spurious poems likely remain in the text and occasionally Foruzânfar chooses readings that could be improved upon.

A.J. Arberry, for example, collated Foruzânfar's edition with the Chester Beatty manuscript (which Foruzânfar had access to in a microfilm which Arberry had prepared for him) and felt that Foruzânfar had not fully taken it into consideration. Furthermore, we cannot rule out the possibility that a manuscript from the lifetime of Rumi, or even one in his own hand, may turn up somewhere among the 200,000 or so uncataloged manuscripts of Persian literature still extant in collections in Iran and Turkey. But for the time being at least, Foruzânfar's magnificent labor remains by far the best text of the *Divân* available.

With respect to the *robâ'is*, or quatrains, it is highly likely that many of the quatrains the manuscript tradition attributes to Rumi are not his. We have already seen how Rumi quotes a quatrain of Najm al-Din Dâye in his Discourses without mentioning the author's name. The *robâ'i* as a genre was early on associated with Sufi gatherings and music. Abu Nasr al-Sarrâj has specifically mentioned the singing of *robâ'iyât* during the *samâ'* ceremony of the Sufis, as well as at secular occasions by popular singers. At least forty-seven quatrains included by Foruzânfar are doubtfully attributed to Rumi, insofar as they appear attributed to other authors in the *Nozhat al-majâles* of Jamâl Khalil Shervâni, compiled sometime between 1250 and 1331.[5]

Despite the fact that Foruzânfar's edition far surpasses all others, the oversize volumes of the first edition and the multi-tome nature of the work kept this edition from gaining popularity. Many homes in Iran have copies of the *Divân-e Shams*, but usually one of the popular editions, some of which have more or less borrowed the editorial work of Foruzânfar. The most common of the popular editions is by M. Darvish, *Divân-e kâmel-e Shams-e Tabrizi* (Tehran: Jâvidân, 1973), buttressed by the apparently obligatory prefatory biographical essays of Foruzânfar and Homâ'i, and by partial indices of personal and place names prepared by Hasan 'Amid. The verse numbers of Koranic allusions are given in the footnotes at the bottom of the page, along with the meaning of more obscure words. This edition went through multiple printings: in 1992 the tenth printing was released in 4,000 copies, a sizeable print run for Iran. This edition is not a bad choice for those wishing to have an accessible and reasonably accurate copy of the *Divân* for their own reading, or to compare the original with translations. It contains 3,204 ghazals and *qasides*, fifty-six pages of *tarji' bands* and 436 *robâ'is*.

Supposedly prepared on the basis of the oldest manuscript, but certainly drawing heavily on Foruzânfar without giving him credit, the *Kolliyât-e Divân-e Shams-e Tabrizi* published in the mid-1970s (Tehran: Tolu', 2536/1978) is the next edition we encounter. In a cheap binding, edited by a certain Mohammad Levâ 'Abbâsi, who also provides the introduction, along with the lengthy glossary and the index of first lines, it contains 1,995 *robâ'is*, exactly as in Foruzânfar's second edition, but it presents 3,366 ghazals and *qasides*, more than in Foruzânfar. Since each individual stanza of the *tarji'* *band*s is through-numbered in the 'Abbâsi edition, we reach a total of 3,503 lyrical poems. Unfortunately, this edition contains almost 130 poems more than Foruzânfar, and every one of these extra poems is almost certainly spurious. An editor worth his salt should easily have detected most of these as misattributions, especially the three poems with the obviously Shiite refrain *Allâh Mowlânâ 'Ali*. Although the text of this edition follows Foruzânfar's text with some minor exceptions up to poem 3107, from this point on the problems begin to snowball.

The casual reader may not find this situation intolerable, but anyone wishing seriously to study Rumi's poems needs a reliable text, and will therefore want to have recourse to Foruzânfar, to the exclusion of inferior editions. Fortunately, Enteshârât-e Negâh in Tehran made this relatively affordable and convenient in 1995 with a two-volume version of Foruzânfar's edition, entitled *Kolliyât-e Divân-e Shams* and printed under the imprimatur of Nashr-e Rabi' in 4,000 copies. A further offset of 5,000 copies appeared through the auspices of Nashr-e Râd in 1996. These present the poems as Foruzânfar edited them, minus the critical notes, and will hopefully replace the earlier popular editions. A definitive edition of the poems awaits the skills of an enterprising and philologically grounded Persianist, but the task is a daunting one.

THE *ROBÂ'IYÂT*

The number of *robâ'i*s attributed to Rumi varies widely, even wildly, from one manuscript to another. Many of the larger collections contain quatrains attributed to earlier poets and can be discounted as false attributions to Rumi, but the short, pithy and essentially oral nature of the *robâ'i* genre has meant that many quatrains wander from poet to poet. The *robâ'i*s have appeared separate from the *Divân* in several publications. Valad Chelebi published an edition of the quatrains as *Robâ'iyât-e Hazrat-e Mowlânâ* in the journal *Akhtar* in Istanbul in 1894 (A.H. 1312) containing 1,642 quatrains, though some of these are spurious. A selection of 107 of these were translated to Turkish by Hasan Âli Yücel (?) and published in 1932 (Istanbul: Remzi). Another edition of 1,994 quatrains appeared in *Robâ'iyât-e Mowlânâ Jalâl al-Din* (Isfahan: Bahâr, 1941). Âsaf Hâlet Çelebi also prepared a volume of 276 of Rumi's *robâ'i*s in Persian along with Turkish translations, as *Mevlananın Rubaileri* (Istanbul: Kanaat, 1939; 2nd ed. 1944), before doing a French version. Next, Gölpınarlı prepared a selection of 210 quatrains as *Mevlâna' dan seçme Rubâiler* in the Turkish series Classic Works of the East ([Ankara]: Maarif Vekilligi, 1945), later replaced by *Rubâiler: Mevlâna Celâleddin* (Istanbul: Remzi, 1964).

THE *MASNAVI*

The **Masnavi-ye ma'navi** derives its name from the verse form Rumi adopted for it – rhyming couplets with the rhyme scheme following the pattern aabbccdd, etc. Poets generally employed the *masnavi* form for narrative verse; Ferdowsi used it in the epic *Shâh nâme*, whereas Fakhr-e Gorgâni and Nezâmi used it in the romances "Vis and Râmin" and "Layli and Majnun," respectively. Beginning with Sanâ'i, poets adapted this form to ethical–didactic and mystical poetry, and Rumi modeled his narrative couplets on the genre of such works, as exemplified in Sanâ'i and ʿAttâr. The adjective *maʿnavi* means "relating to the inner meaning," or for concision's sake, "spiritual." Hence in English one sometimes encounters the translation "Spiritual Couplets" for *Masnavi-ye maʿnavi*. Though many works prior to Rumi's *Masnavi* and a great many more after Rumi employed this verse form, Rumi's work is usually known as *the Masnavi*, par excellence. Already within a few generations after its composition, according to the testimony of Qâzi Najm al-Din-e Tashti as reported by Aflâki (Af 597), the book was commonly referred to simply as the *Masnavi*: "When they say the name *Masnavi*, reason naturally assumes the *Masnavi* of Mowlânâ is meant."

Rumi composed the *Masnavi* in his fifties and perhaps into his sixties. The poem was dictated to Hosâm al-Din and composed in his honor. We have a definite date only for Book 2, begun sometime between November 1263 and October 1264 (A.H. 662) after a hiatus which, according to a report in Aflâki, lasted about two years. Some have argued Rumi began composing the work as early as 1256 when Salâh al-Din was still alive and the caliphate had not been toppled. It seems more likely, however, that Rumi began writing the *Masnavi* sometime between 1258 and 1261, interrupted work until 1263 or 1264, and continued for several years after that. Gölpınarlı believes that Rumi did not finish composing until very near the end of his life, though Safâ (Saf 3/1:464) estimates that the sixth and final book was finished by 1267 or 1268 (A.H. 666).

The Persian text was printed for the first time in Egypt (Bulâq, 1835) in six volumes. Another edition appeared at Tabriz as *Masnavi-ye Rumi* in 1264/1847 and then in Bombay (1266–7/1850–51), followed by many other editions printed there throughout the nineteenth century, some of them including various commentaries. A lithograph was made in Lucknow in 1865 (Naval Kishor) and editions were also printed in Tehran (1273/1856) and in Istanbul (1289/1872). From then until the end of the century, some twenty editions or reprints were made in the Middle East and India, and selections began to appear in Europe as well (see chapters 13 and 14, below). The first text-critical edition was that by R.A. Nicholson (1925, 1929, 1933), a very solid piece of work which remains the most frequently cited. Recently, however, the editions of Mohammad Esteʿlâmi (ME), Gölpınarlı, Sobhâni and Soroush, all of which rely on older and more reliable manuscripts, have made improvements on Nicholson's text.

At some point, relatively late in the manuscript tradition, a forged seventh book of slightly over a hundred pages was added to Rumi's *Masnavi*. Mirzâ

Mohamed Shirâzi produced a lithograph edition of this 109-page book at his press in Bombay under the title *Daftar-e haftom-e Masnavi-ye ma'navi* (1280/ 1863). Aside from the fact that this seventh book appears only in more recent manuscripts, Nicholson considered it mere doggerel, though C.E. Wilson (see chapter 14, below) had thought it excellent. The so-called seventh book is no longer included in printed editions, but anyone working from a printed edition more than seventy-five years old should take care that Rumi composed only six books of the *Masnavi*.

WHAT'S SO CRITICAL ABOUT A CRITICAL EDITION?

Nicholson based the first volume of his edition of the *Masnavi*, containing Books 1 and 2 (1929), on five manuscripts, four of which date to within seventy years of Rumi's death, viz:

1. A MS of the *Masnavi* in 290 folios with 25 lines per page transcribed in 1319 (A.H. 718) by 'Ali b. Mohammad;
2. A MS of the *Masnavi* in 281 folios of 25 lines per page completed on 15 Dhu al-hijja 744 (April 29, 1344) by Mohammad b. al-Hâjj Dowlatshâh b. Yusof al-Shirâzi;
3. A MS of the *Masnavi* lacking the prose prefaces to each book, in 341 folios, also with 25 lines to the page, arranged in four columns, completed 7 Rabi II 843 (September 17, 1439). This manuscript contains many spurious interpolations;
4. A MS of Book 1 only in 114 folios with 18 lines to the page, estimated by Nicholson to date from the late thirteenth or early fourteenth century;
5. A MS of Book 2 only in 105 folios with 19 lines per page, in the hand of Musâ b. Yahyâ b. Hamza al-Mowlavi, completed on 4 Sha'bân 706 (February 8, 1307).

In the introduction to his own edition of the Persian text, Nicholson remarks on Rumi's laxness in prosody, in which he took metrical liberties that Sa'di or Hâfez would not have done, and sometimes bent the rhyme. The oldest manuscripts preserve more of such liberties, while the youngest manuscripts are the most prosodically correct, indicating that scribes ironed out prosodical problems over time. In Book 1, Nicholson counts sixty cases where the text has been altered "not capriciously,"[6] but with specific objectives in mind.

Nicholson also observes that the Persian copyists and commentators who interpolated verse gave technically excellent interpolations, while Turkish scribes often gave execrable interpolations as regards meter and form.[7] None of them, however, used off-rhymes as Rumi sometimes did. Scribes usually interpolated verses to make transitions in the narrative less abrupt, to explain incidents more fully, or to amplify the themes which Rumi treats only briefly. For example, in the story of the grocer and the parrot, scribal interpolations give a reason for the bird's fluttering about the shop – a cat startled it – though Rumi did not find it necessary to explain this detail.

The manuscript versions differ greatly in the size of the text and in the orthography. Nicholson's text has 25,577 lines, though the average medieval and early modern manuscript contained around 27,700 lines, meaning that scribes added two thousand lines or about eight percent more to the poem composed by Rumi. Some manuscripts give as many as 32,000 lines! The edition printed at Bulâq in 1268/1852 has 140 verses in Books 1 and 2 which are not found in the oldest manuscripts; there are 800 extra verses in the Tehran edition of 1307/1889, an edition that Nicholson acquired from E.G. Browne in 1890, while doing his Indian Language Tripos (an exam taken by those aspiring to positions in the Foreign Service or military office in British India; see chapter 13). Nicholson felt that existing Turkish editions were better than Indian or Persian ones,[8] because they did not include as many scribal emendations.

The Tehran edition of the *Masnavi*, which Nicholson consulted while collating the manuscripts, includes a concordance and follows in the main a version of the *Masnavi* prepared by ʿAbd al-Latif b. ʿAbd Allâh al-ʿAbbâsi of Gujurat (d. c. 1638) called *Noskhe-ye nâsekhe-ye masnaviyât-e saqime*. Though its name means "The Copy to Replace all Copies," Nicholson did not consider it very valuable. Latif, who also edited Sanâʾi's *Hadiqe*, wrote two commentaries on the *Masnavi* and compiled a glossary of rare words in the text. These were, respectively: *Latâʾef al-maʿnavi men haqâʾeq al-masnavi*, published at Lucknow (1292/1875); the *Merʾât al-Masnavi*, mentioned by Hermann Ethé; and *Lataʾef al-loghât* (Lucknow, 1877 and Kanpur, 1905). ʿAbd al-Latif had used eighty manuscripts, but seems to have added verses from all of them without removing any lines; rather than a proto-critical edition, then, this is a compendium of lines attributed to Rumi in a wide variety of faulty exemplars of the text. Books 1 and 2 in his "edition" contain eight hundred verses more than those chapters as they appear in Nicholson's text. The best old edition was by Ankaravi, who did the Persian text, Turkish translation and commentary (See chapter 11, below). Copies of this were rare in Nicholson's day.

For the second volume of his critical text, containing Books 3 and 4, Nicholson had obtained further manuscripts through the efforts of Hellmut Ritter. Beyond the five enumerated above, he now had several other early copies, one dating from 674/1275, one from 680/1281 (containing only Book 1), and one from 687/1288. Unfortunately, Nicholson did not have access to these for the first two books; readers should therefore note that the later books in Nicholson's *Masnavi* are derived from a sounder basis than Books 1 and 2. The manuscript dated 674/1275, now in Cairo, where it probably ended up during the Ottoman domination of Egypt, has a Turkish note at the end appended by Esmâʿil al-Hajj al-Mowlâ al-Mowlavi, explaining that the manuscript fell into the water and had to be repaired. This entailed rebinding and rearranging the pages, and running his pen over portions of the text that had been partially effaced (which, in Nicholson's opinion, only served to further mess up the MS).

The manuscripts tell a little story of their own. Ritter discovered one copy from Rajab 677 (December 1278) in the library of Rumi's shrine in Konya which had a colophon from a certain Mohammad b. ʿAbd Allâh al-Qonavi, indicating that he had copied the manuscript from an archetype that was corrected and emended by the author (Rumi) and by Hosâm al-Din. The preface page to each of the six books is highly ornamented in this copy. Another copy, transcribed by Hasan b. al-Hasan [Hosayn?] al-Mowlavi on Thursday 4 Shavvâl 687 (November 1, 1288), was supposedly collated with a copy that had been read to Rumi. A manuscript of Book 1 owned by Nafiz Pasha was written out by Esmâʿil b. Solaymân b. Mohammad al-Hâfez al-Qaysari on 15 Rabiʿ II 680 (July 4, 1281) in 130 folios with 17 lines per page. The title page has an inscription indicating that the copy was made:

> According to the practice of review by the magnificent Lord [i.e., Rumi], king of rulers and nobles, he who brings order to the realm, support of kingdoms, benefit to the world, protector of the weak, Friend of God on the earth, God and religion's victor, may God ever exalt him and cast down his enemies.

These colophons all show that very early on there was a concern for getting an approved and corrected text; there must have been many imperfect exemplars of the text circulated by disciples or occasional visitors who heard the text orally and noted down parts of it as they listened.

There was also an anxiety about the antiquity of manuscripts, for already it was recognized that copies dating to the time of the author were more authentic. A copy in the Egyptian Library in Cairo, transcribed by Mohammad b. ʿIsâ al-Hâfez al-Mowlavi al-Qonavi, notes that this manuscript was completed in Shaʿbân 768 (April 1367), but someone has tried to change the word "seven" into "six," which would have meant the text was written during Rumi's lifetime. This 511-page copy with 29 lines to the page was one of the first made in *nastaʿliq* handwriting. A note indicates that dervish ʿOsmân b. al-Hâjji ʿOmar, a Mevlevi shaykh of the Eskandar Pâshâ *zâvie*, purchased the text and left it as a bequest for his successor shaykh, indicating that if a copy needed to be made from this exemplar, it should be given only to a responsible person so that no damage would occur to it and no one outside the *khâneqâh* would get hold of it (and "forget" to give it back).

An old copy did not necessarily guarantee a correct copy, however. A manuscript of Book 6 in the Egyptian Library, dated by an anonymous scribe to 4 Safar 674 (July 30, 1275), only eighteen months after Rumi's death, has the order of the text confused and has been damaged and effaced to a great extent. As Nicholson explains, two separate recensions of the *Masnavi* existed, one of

307

them corrected and the other not.[9] Since Book 2 was not begun until 1263 or so, two years after Book 1 was completed, copies of Book 1 must have been in circulation well before the whole *Masnavi* was finished. The various books might have circulated in various drafts until a corrected copy of the entire text was made and propagated. If a manuscript used one of these pre-corrected drafts, it might contain many inaccuracies. But the standard corrected version of the *Masnavi* must have been in circulation soon after the author's death.[10]

Sometimes, we can get to know a little about the scribes themselves. One copy of the *Masnavi* was written out in the hand of ʿOsmân b. ʿAbd Allâh, a manumitted slave of Sultan Valad, in the year 723 (1323). This was the copy Gölpınarlı used for the basis of his Turkish translation. Gölpınarlı believes that the person who wrote out the two-volume copy of the *Divân* in the Mevlânâ Museum in Konya (no. 66), Hesâr b. ʿOsmân, was probably the son of this ʿOsmân b. ʿAbd Allâh. The same Hesâr, son of ʿOsmân, also made a copy of Sultan Valad's *Divân* (GM 62). The Persian scholar Mojtabâ Minovi believes that the manuscript of an anonymous Persian work written out in 1364 was copied (or authored) by one of the copyists hired by Sultan Valad and his family to make manuscripts of Rumi's works. The work in question, which survives in a unique manuscript in the Bibliothèque Nationale in Paris, provides the history of the Seljuks of Anatolia from their origins through the reign of ʿAlâ al-Din Kay Qobâd IV (Akh 341–2), and has been published in facsimile along with a Turkish translation as *Anadolu Selçukluları Devleti Tarihi* by Feridun Nâfiz Uzluk (Ankara: Kamâl-e Estambul, 1369/1952).

Nicholson's monumental work on the *Masnavi* was printed by the Cambridge University Press for the Trustees of the E.J.W. Gibb Memorial in the new series of the Gibb Memorial. It included not only his three volumes of the Persian text, but also three volumes of translation and two volumes of commentary.[11] A one-volume reprint of the Persian text established by Nicholson appeared in Tehran through Amir Kabir (1336/1977) and has been reprinted a dozen times or more. As he explains, Nicholson tried to restore the original or older readings, remove interpolations and add vocalization of the short vowels to aid in reading. However great his achievement, Nicholson realized: "My text does not claim to be a fixed, much less a final one. That is not yet in sight."[12]

Hellmut Ritter wrote reviews in the Austrian orientalist journal *Orientalische Literaturzeitung* as Nicholson's volumes appeared, and Nicholson incorporated his critiques. Recent editions take fully into account the two oldest known manuscripts, one dated 677/1278 which Ritter discovered only halfway through Nicholson's work, and possibly an even earlier one, copied in 1269 or 1270 (A.H. 668) in Konya during Rumi's lifetime and now in Cairo. Nicholson had discounted the 668 date as a later alteration from 768/1367, as we saw above; the colophon in question is reproduced in Esteʿlâmi's edition (ME1:4), so readers may judge for themselves. These two manuscripts do reflect some variant readings and some lines occur in a different order in one or the other. The 668 Cairo manuscript has a few more lines than the later one, and Este'lâmi speculates that in the final recension of the poem, which is reflected in the 1278 manuscript, Rumi struck these lines out (ME 1:xciii). Mohammad Este'lâmi's text of the *Masnavi* nevertheless restores these lines, using the manuscript of 668 as its copy text, and actually contains fifty-three lines more than Nicholson's edition. The six volumes of Este'lâmi's edition of the *Masnavi* (Tehran: Zavvâr, 1987?; 2nd printing, 1990 and several other reprints) come with an introductory essay on Rumi's life and works, along with notes and commentary appended at the end of each book, plus a seventh volume of indices.

A facsimile of the 677/1278 manuscript in Konya, the date of which has not been put in question, was prepared and published in Tehran (Markaz-e Nashr-e Dâneshgâhi) in 1371/1992. An introduction by Gölpınarlı in Turkish (with English translation) appears as the foreword to a facsimile reproduction of this same manuscript from the Mevlânâ Museum in Konya, a publication underwritten by the Turkish Republic (Ankara: T.C. Kültür Bakanlığı, 1993) and therefore quite affordable despite its bulk. Towfiq Sobhâni has prepared his edition of the text based on this manuscript, *Masnavi-ye ma'navi* (Tehran: Vezârat-e Farhang va Ershâd-e Eslâmi, 1373/1994; reprinted the following year), as has Abdol Karim Soroush (Tehran: 'Elmi va Farhangi, 1375/1996).

ORISONS IN MOTION: THE PRACTICE OF *SAMÂ*

Samâ is a difficult word to translate. It has usually been rendered as "audition," but this sounds like a musical try-out. "Spiritual concert" has also been tried, but in the usage of Rumi it is much more than listening. *Samâ* ideally involves the use of poems and music to focus the listener's concentration on God and perhaps even induce a trance-like state of contemplative ecstasy (*vajd, hâl*). When this happens, it often moves the listener to shake his arms or dance. It is therefore a kind of motile meditation or deliberative dancing, a mode of worship and contemplation. According to Mohammad b. al-Monavvar's *Asrâr al-towhid*, the *samâ* of Shaykh Abu Sa'id would include waving the hands (*dast-afshâni*) as well as circling about and stamping the feet (Tfz 27). Abu Sa'id had learned this practice as a child (MAS 218), which had been well known in eastern Iran for over two centuries before the birth of Rumi. *Samâ* was not, therefore, an incidental or chance hearing of music, but a liturgical and ritual use of music.

The manuals of Sufism had thoroughly covered the subject of *samâ* by the time of Rumi, giving it a theoretical justification. In the mid-eleventh century, Hojviri devotes the last chapter of his *Kashf al-mahjub* to it, first proving that the Prophet had encouraged the chanting of the Koran, and then proving that the Prophet had also listened to poetry. Hojviri goes on to show that the Prophet did allow singing and the playing of melodies. Of course, music can provoke a person's base passions or it can send him into transports of spiritual bliss. The act of listening to music was not, therefore, in itself wrong or evil, but it could became sinful if the listener responded improperly. Dancing was not approved by Hojviri, though he did not forbid it, explaining that the movements of the dervishes in *samâ^c* are not dancing but responding to mystical ecstasy. Hojviri gives rules for proper behavior in *samâ^c*, and these rule out looking upon beautiful boys (see below, "Rumi's Sexuality").

Sari Saqati had compared the *samâ^c* to rain on fertile ground. But it was a dangerous thing which needed a shaykh to guide and control it. As the *Owrâd al-ahbâb* describes *samâ^c*, it is a grace from God that attracts the hearts of His servants to him ... whoever listens with truth will reach the truth. Whoever listens with passion will become a heretic (Saf 3/1:200–201). Most of the Sufi orders practiced *samâ^c*, though not all; the Naqshbandis of Naqshband's own circle, for example, did not (Saf 3/1:203).

The theologians, however, were divided about whether or not poems should even be recited in the mosque. Mo^câd b. Jabal, a companion of the Prophet, had said not, but later jurisprudents tended to be less strict on the matter, with even the Hanbalis making some allowances. Ibn al-Jowzi held the recitation of ascetic-oriented verse in the mosque permissible; however, Ibn Jobayr even heard al-Jowzi recite love poetry (*ash^câr min al-nasîb*) in 1184 in the caliphal palace at Baghdad, where he preached twice a week (MAS 226). Abu Hafs ^cOmar Sohravardi, the caliphal envoy, also moved his hearers with poetry in the mosque once (MAS 227). Ibn Taymiya allowed preachers to recite verses of a religious/didactic nature in the mosque, if based upon the Koran, the Hadith, or exhortations to penance. The Hanafi legal handbooks held all of these permissible and eventually would add love poems for the Prophet as a licit genre for recitation in the mosque (MAS 226). The Shiites also allowed love poems for the Imams. However, the Shâfe^ci Zarkashi (d. 1392) held that reciting anything but religio-ethical verses in the mosque was forbidden (MAS 227). The preacher Mollâ Hosayn Vâ^cez-e Kâshefi (d. 1505) considered the singing of poems in the mosque impermissible, but he would allow them to be recited without music (MAS 228).

Abu Najib ^cAbd al-Qâher Sohravardi (1097–1168) in his "Manners for Disciples" (*Âdâb al-moridin*, written c. 1155) explains that all the authorities agree on the permissibility of listening to a beautiful and melodious voice reciting the Koran, as long as the chanting does not obscure the meaning of scripture. Having established that the act of chanting is not objectionable, he takes up the question of whether or not it is licit to chant poetry. One can only judge, Sohravardi says, by the content of the verse in question, and even then, poems which might be inappropriate for one person at a given level of development would not be objectionable for another person. Sohravardi explains that some people, as they listen to chanting and music, may weep out of sorrow, yearning or fear; others might clap or dance out of a sense of hope, joy or delight. Such movements and cries arise from the human spirit and are not, in and of themselves, forbidden, though those who have truly attained do not need to act in this manner.[13]

Among Rumi's contemporaries in Konya, Akhi Evren was opposed to *samâ* (Af 276–7), an attitude probably not atypical among the *fotovvat* orders. But Ahmad-e Faqih wrote a "whirling" poem,[14] and ʿErâqi praised the state of ecstasy brought about by listening to singers (*qavvâl*) tell of the beloved (Tfz 32).

One account which Aflâki (Af 680–81) attributes to Sultan Valad tells us that it was the grandmother of Sultan Valad (the mother of Gowhar Khâtun) who first encouraged Rumi to practice *samâ*. He did so, but at first simply shook his arms about. Only after Shams arrived in Konya did Rumi begin to practice the whirling dance.

On the other hand, Sepahsâlâr (Sep 64–5) says:

> His holiness, our lord – may God increase the light he shines upon us – from the beginning of his career followed the practice and procedure of his father – his holiness our lord, Bahâ al-Din Valad, may paradise be his – including teaching, preaching, renunciation and ascetic exercises. He [Rumi] followed whatever forms of worship and renunciation were attributed to his holiness the Messenger – God's peace and blessings upon him. In his prayers and fasting and exercises of self-renunciation, he [Rumi] would see epiphanies and spiritual stations to which no perfect man had ever attained, but he had never performed *samâ*. When his holiness, our lord and monarch of the beloved, looked upon our lord Shams of Tabriz, the Sun of Truth and Religion – God magnify his mention – with the eye of insight, recognizing him as the beloved and king of the saints who held a rank among the highest stations of the beloved ones, he fell in love with him and honored whatever he instructed. Shams then instructed him:

>> Enter into *samâ*, for you will find increase of that which you seek in it. *Samâ* was forbidden to the people because they are preoccupied with base passions. When they perform *samâ*, their reprehensible and hateful characteristics increase and they are moved by pride and pleasure. Of course *samâ* is forbidden to such people. On the other hand, those people who quest for and love truth, their characteristics intensify in *samâ* and none but God enter their field of vision at such times. So, *samâ* is permissible to such people.

> Rumi obeyed this instruction and attended *samâ* and observed with his own eyes in the state of *samâ* that which Shams had indicated, and he continued to practice and follow this custom until the end of his life.

Indeed, Rumi became quite enamored with the ritual of turning and singing verse. *Samâ* became Rumi's food of divine love, and he played it on and on. It brought on tranquility and made his imagination flow in thousands of lines of verse (M4:732–44):

> The wise men tell us that we take these tunes
> from the turning of celestial spheres
> These sounds are revolutions of the skies
> that man composes with his lyre and throat
>
> *　*　*
>
> We all were parts of Adam at one time
> In paradise we all have heard these tunes
> Though clay and water fill us up with doubts
> We still remember something of those songs
>
> *　*　*
>
> And so, like food, *samâ* sustains God's lovers
> within its harmonies the mind's composed
> imagination draws its inspiration
> takes its shape within this hue and cry

Samâ was an activity for the true men of God which liberated Rumi from the austere ways of self-renunciation and gave him a joyous vehicle for expressing his mystical rapture (M3:96–9):

> They dance, parade about the battlefield
> 　they dance in their own blood, all true men do.
> When they free themselves from their own clutches
> when they can leap right out of their own flaws:
> 　they clap their hands and then they do a dance
> Within their breasts a beat like minstrels' drums
> 　and all the oceans foam with their ferment
> You cannot see it with your outward eyes
> 　but even leaves on trees sprout hands for them
> the leaves keep clapping to their beat – but listen
> 　for it with your inner – not your body's – ear.

Adopting the practice of *samâ* transformed Rumi from a preacher and thinker inclined to mysticism and asceticism into a full-fledged Sufi, at least in the eyes of those around him. He was now no longer a popular preacher and learned, pious man, teaching in a *madrase*, but a shaykh and holy man, resembling other Sufi saints, at the head of a convent.

According to Aflâki, some folks in Konya attempted to get the *qâzi* of the city, Serâj al-Din Ormavi, to condemn the practice of *samâ*. He refused, and the opponents next resorted to sending Rumi excerpts from works of Islamic law about the impropriety of dance and music. Rumi, explaining that he had no care for the world and would willingly give up his position, gave convincing counter-arguments, with the result that the *qâzi* and all the other ulama in town, including the learned and the *mofti*-professors, expressed their submissiveness to

Rumi (Af 165–8) and ceased to harass him about *samâ᷾*. This *qâzi*, Serâj al-Din Mahmud Ormavi (1197–1283), came from Lake Urmia (Rezâ᷾iye) in northwestern Iran and settled in Konya in the latter part of his life. He authored a number of works, including a textbook on the principles of jurisprudence (*Tahsil dar osul al-feqh*, being an abridgement of Fakhr al-Din Râzi's *Mahsul*), a book on theology (*Mokhtasar al-arba᷾in*), and two others on logic (*Bayân al-haqq, Matâle᷾ al-anvâr*). But it seems he held Rumi and his spiritual praxis in respect.

POETRY: ANOTHER WAY TO PREACH AND PRAY

Hanafi jurisconsults in Khorasan did not frown upon poetry, per se; many of them composed their own lines of verse to punctuate the points they wished to make, or at least quoted lines from various Arab and Persian poets. For example, the Hanafi Zarnuji quotes many lines of verse in his treatise on education (see Zar) and Abu Hafs ᷾Omar Sohravardi, the caliphal ambassador and promoter of the young men's spiritual brotherhoods (*fotovvat*), though disinclined to *samâ᷾*, composed verses in both Arabic and Persian.[15] Rumi's own father, Bahâ al-Din Valad, quotes a number of lines of verse in his *Ma᷾âref*, mostly single lines of a popular or proverbial nature, and a few quatrains, or *robâ᷾is*, none of them attributed to an author.[16] Bahâ al-Din also quotes a few phrases or lines from Arabic poetry: part of a hemistich from Imru᷾ al-Qays (Bah 2:57, 262), part of a hemistich by al-Mutanabbî (Bah 2:68, 269), a hemistich that appears in Ghazzâli's "Vivification," *Ehyâ ᷾olum al-din* (Bah 2:94, 290), and one full line from an unidentified source (Bah 1:108).

Borhân al-Din quotes over a hundred lines of verse, most of the time without giving the source, but he is obviously fond of the mystical/ethical poets Sanâ᷾i, ᷾Attâr and Khâqâni, in that order, and even includes a line from Nezâmi (Bor 51, 139) and a hemistich from Fakhr al-Din Gorgâni (Bor 92, 234), though some lines – such as the hemistich from Sa᷾di (Bor 28) – have been interpolated by later copyists (Bor 127). Borhân also quotes five lines of verse and one hemistich in Arabic, including one line taken from Qoshayri's "Treatise" (Bor 71, 159), and one quoted from Qâzi Tannukhi (Bor 98), a tenth-century judge and author, probably by way of Khâqâni or Ibn Khallikân (Bor 176–7).

As a boy Rumi had certainly heard oral renditions of the poems of the tenth-century poet–minstrel Rudaki, which were still in vogue among the populace in the areas around Balkh and Samarqand. In his poem dedicated to Sanâ᷾i (for a translation, see NiD 87), Rumi quotes half a line from Rudaki's lament for Abu al-Hasan Morâdi, "the death of such a master is no little thing." It is clear, then, that Rumi and his teachers had no compunctions against poetry, per se. They read not only Sufi poetry, but also profane poetry. Composing poetry, however, may have been something Rumi and his father felt an undignified pastime for a preacher, at least while acting in his professional capacity, since the mosque and *madrase* had not been traditional venues for poetry recitation, and some jurisprudents felt poetry inappropriate in such settings.

The advent of Shams freed Rumi from any inhibitions of using poetry as a vehicle for teaching and preaching from the pulpit and podium. It seems Rumi even felt compelled to teach with poetry, using it in his sermons and getting his congregation to meditate with music, verse and dance. Pouring his thoughts into verse this way almost certainly got a better response among the general populace than more sedate and traditional forms of preaching.

POETIC OUTPUT

We have seen Rumi explain how reluctant he was to compose poetry, which he did only as a concession to his audience (see "Rumi in a Whirl," chapter 4). Foruzânfar's edition of the *Divân-e Shams* comprises 3,229 ghazals and *qasides* making a total of almost 35,000 lines, not including the several hundred lines of stanzaic poems and the nearly two thousand quatrains attributed to him. Add to this the 25,688 lines of the *Masnavi* (as per the Este^{c}lâmi edition), and we see that Rumi composed well in excess of 60,000 lines of verse. Should further textual scholarship eventually require that we eliminate many of the *robâ^{c}is* and even ghazals from the Rumi canon, his output will remain immense. Sixty thousand lines is more than Homer, Dante, Milton or Shakespeare produced. As we shall see in chapter 8 ("Metrics"), because of the number of syllables in the average Persian line of verse, the 60,000 lines of Rumi's Persian would actually equal about 120,000 lines of verse in English. The *Masnavi* measures out around 570,000 syllables, roughly the same number of syllables found in 57,000 lines of English pentameters, and therefore equivalent to approximately 4,000 sonnets. By way of comparison, Shakespeare's 154 sonnets contain only 2,156 lines, or 21,560 syllables.

Of course, bulk does not by any means determine merit, and a ranking of poets is not at issue here. But the sheer volume of Rumi's poetic output does confirm the stories about the extemporaneous and spontaneous nature of his composition methods, at least in the case of the ghazals. We see Rumi grappling with and chafing against the meter as he composes (from D 1367):

> My lover, my healer, fills the cup
> leave off then, iamb and anapest, trochee and dactyl

Schimmel suggests in connection with one such comment by Rumi that, like other Sufis, Rumi may have been subject to automatic writing (ScP 120). This interpretation seems somewhat overwrought, for we know that in the case of the *Masnavi*, Rumi heard his poems read back to him and edited them, making corrections and improvements as any craftsman would. Nevertheless, the rhythmic turning of *samâ^c* no doubt induced many an impromptu poem, and part of the reason that Rumi composed so many poems may have been to provide his followers with a suitable repertoire of librettos for the *samâ*. Many of the poems allude to or even address the musicians and singers who accompanied and enhanced the recitation of the poems.

Most of Rumi's poems seem to date from after his encounter with Shams, but if we assume that Rumi began composing poetry seriously the year before meeting Shams, this would give him a productive composing career of thirty years. On average, then, Rumi composed 2,000 lines per year for thirty years, over 5 lines per day. Of course, he did not compose methodically; like all poets, his oeuvre came out in spurts, and we may assume that the bulk of the poems of the *Divân* date from between the time of Rumi's meeting with Shams in 1244 and the year 1260, by which time the composition of the *Masnavi* was underway.

Aflâki and Sepahsâlâr give anecdotal information about the circumstances of composition of many of the ghazals, but information of this nature should not be taken too seriously, as biographers of poets made extracting this kind of "information" from poems a kind of hobby, and typically did not rely upon any documentary evidence, other than their imaginations and oral lore. What the hagiographers tell us should definitely be taken into account, but an effort should be made to periodize Rumi's ghazals on internal evidence. In addition to the information this would give us about his composition habits, such a study would help us to trace the development of Rumi's style.

MULTILINGUAL AND POPULIST POETRY

Rumi obviously had an excellent command of Arabic, not only as a reading language, but as a language in which he could compose poems, deliver sermons and so on. He appreciated the poetry of al-Mutanabbî, even though he represented the professional class of panegyrists. Aflâki (Af 623–4) has Rumi reading Mutanabbî at nights for pleasure, a practice which Shams al-Din condemned and tried to wean him of. Rumi quotes from Mutanabbî's poetry in *Fihe mâ fih* and also in the *Masnavi*, so Shams did not succeed in rooting this poet out of Rumi's memory. Quite likely, Rumi had come to appreciate al-Mutanabbî during his student days in Syria.

Once Nezâm al-Din Erzenjâni came before Rumi and began reading him a poem in Arabic. Evidently, Nezâm al-Din intended to impress or intimidate Rumi with his superior knowledge of Arabic, but Rumi, as it turned out, knew the *qaside* in question by heart, recited part of it and spoke extemporaneously about related issues of mystical truth, winning Nezâm al-Din over to him in the process (Af 1020).

Living amongst Turks, Rumi also picked up some colloquial Turkish. At least one poem from the *Divân* (D 200) begins on the pretext of Rumi teaching his Persian listeners a word or two in Turkish: What do you call a camel in

Turkish, and what do you call its kid? The poem then states that we are all born of fate and scatter like children before its decrees, to the east, to the west and even to heaven, as if alluding to his fate as a Persian emigre in Turkish Anatolia.

Another ghazal (D 1183) begins with two lines in Turkish, and then advises: Whether Totsen (Arab?) or Greek or Turk, learn to speak the tongue of silent communication. A few Turkish words appear in other poems (D 1949, D 1807). One three-line poem, evidently addressed to new disciples being initiated by Hosâm al-Din, is entirely in Turkish (D 1982):

> Come here, I have no designs on you, you understand?
> It's no good to stay over there, why be all alone?
> All life comes from the Chelebi (master) of the path;
>   find God, what are you following?
> The Chelebi wants his charges, what do you make of the Chelebi?

Other poems are macaronic, alternating lines in Turkish with lines in Persian (D 1362, 1363). These lines of Turkish, among the earliest surviving examples of quantitative verse in that language, have spurred the interest of Turkish linguistic and literary historians.[17]

Rumi also composed a thirteen-line poem (D 2542) with the refrain, "you are the Agapos," from the Greek word *agape*, meaning, "you are the beloved." Three poems have bits of demotic Greek; these have been identified and translated into French, along with some Greek verse of Sultan Valad.[18] Gölpınarlı (GB 416–17) indicates that, according to Mir Mirughli, the language of the inhabitants of Konya in the time of Rumi spoke a form of demotic Greek that Rumi represents in a handful of poems. However, Gölpınarlı jumps to an unwarranted and alogical conclusion when he says that, because Rumi knew classical Persian and classical Arabic well, but used a kind of colloquial Persian and Arabic in his poems, he may also have known classical Greek, including philosophy, but used colloquial Greek in his poems (GB 417).

We should also mention that preachers and mystics were not above vulgar and jocular use of language. In one poem included in Foruzânfar's edition (D 2137), obscene verse is used to condemn an enemy, a perfectly common and accepted use of poetry in the medieval period:

> That donkey's ass
> who in his jealousy
> even takes offense at Jesus
> – A hundred donkey dicks up his ass!
> – A hundred dog farts in his beard!
> How could an ass
> give chase to a gazelle
> or inhale the scent of musk?
> An ass smells an ass's piss
> or examines piles of shit

That ass-bitch pisses in every stream
she wades through
– true, no harm's done to the stream
but you've got to drink from it!
An ass feels shame at such deceit
hear it from the Book of Truth:
   "Rather are they strayed further from the path"   [K7:179]
How like a fag, all his flirtation!
How like whores, his scratching nails!
Shut me up!
– let God make him forever shamefaced
I'll fondle the Sâqi,
   since I'm drunk with her tickling

Rumi also swore, as we learn in the Discourses (Fih 88) and Aflâki (Af 151–2), saying *gharr khwâhar*, roughly "slut of a sister," a curse which would, addressed to a male, impugn his honor. Sanâ'i had also used this curse, as did Shams (Maq 83).

MODERN MYTHS AND MISUNDERSTANDINGS

RUMI'S AGE

We have seen that Sepahsâlâr gives Rumi's date of birth as 6 Rabi͑ I 604, corresponding to Sunday, September 30, 1207 in the Julian calendar. Later writers all depend on Sepahsâlâr for the date, which remained unquestioned for over six hundred years. Rezâ Qoli Khân Hedâyat (1800–1871), a historian, poet laureate and literary critic of the Qajar period, in addition to preparing a two-volume supplement to Mirkhwând's (1433–98) history, *Rowzat al-safâ*, and authoring a couple of biographical dictionaries of Persian poets, the *Majma͑ al-fosahâ* (1871) and the *Riâz al-͑ârefin* (posthumously in 1888), also edited several *divân* manuscripts for publication. In 1280/1863 Hedâyat produced an edition of the *Divân-e Shams* lithographed at Tabriz, to which he appended a three-page introduction. In this (*Divân*, ed. Hedâyat, 4) he implies that the *Divân* was written in memoriam, after the death of Shams. He also proposes that Rumi was sixty-two years of age at the time of his meeting with Shams, arguing this on the basis of one of the ghazals (244). Hedâyat kept the date of birth as given by Sepahsâlâr (604/1207), and therefore dates the meeting of Rumi and Shams to the year 666/1267, sixty-two lunar years later. As Nicholson points out, however, this conflicts with the evidence of the *Masnavi*: Shams is mentioned in Book 1 and we know that the composition of Book 2 was already underway by 662/1264.

In 1959 Abdülbâki Gölpınarlı, in the process of translating Rumi's ghazals to Turkish (apparently without reference to Hedâyat's prior argument), ran across the same line (D 1472), causing him to call into question the entire chronology of Rumi's birth and death. The line in question reads:

be andishe foru bord marâ ʿaql-e chehel sâl
be shasht o do shodam sayd o ze tadbir be-jastam

which means something like: "Reason of forty years submerged me deep in thought; at/in/by sixty-two I became prey and escaped that destiny." There were a couple of other verses that seemed to Gölpınarlı to cast doubt on the birth date of 604/1207 (cited in Mov 127–8):

> The elder has made me young again
> Therefore, I am both younger and elder

and:

> Shams of Tabriz made me young again
> so after sixty I see multi-form

There was also this account from Rumi's *Discourses* (Fih 173):

> We were in Samarqand and the Khwârazmshâh had besieged Samarqand and mustered the army for war. In that neighborhood there was an extremely pretty girl, more beautiful than any other in the city. I heard her say over and over: "O Lord, how could you permit Yourself to give me over into the hands of a tyrant? I know that You shall never permit such a thing; I have confidence in You." When the city was plundered, all its people were taken as captives, including the maidservants of that woman, but no harm befell her. Despite her extreme beauty, no one looked upon her. Know then, that he who entrusts himself to God is preserved from harm and remains safe.

The date of the siege of Samarqand is given in various histories as A.H. 604, 607, or 609. If he was born in 604 (1207), Rumi would have been at the most only five at the time of this siege, and, contended Gölpınarlı, he would have been too young to recall all this.

Taken together, Gölpınarlı felt this evidence indicated that Rumi must have been over sixty, sixty-two to be exact, upon meeting Shams.[19] On the other hand, Gölpınarlı accepted 1244 (A.H. 642), the date Sepahsâlâr gives for Shams-e Tabrizi's arrival in Konya, as correct. Operating on this assumption, Gölpınarlı then worked out that Rumi must have been born in about 1184 (A.H. 580) – twenty-four years earlier than the date traditionally believed. The date of death remains unchanged, making Rumi about ninety-two at the time of his death, about thirty-three upon the family's departure from Balkh, forty-two at the time of his marriage to Gowhar Khâtun and around forty-three upon the birth of Sultan Valad. This is not ipso facto impossible, as Bahâ al-Din was over eighty when he died and Sultan Valad (1226–1312) was almost ninety lunar years old at his death (A.H. 623–712). It would also mean that Bahâ al-Din was thirty rather than fifty-four when Rumi was born.

The revisionist dating of Gölpınarlı has not won general acceptance. Movahhed, in an article written in 1977, inclined to accept it (Mov 131), but

Schimmel treated the matter as unresolved in 1987, and Rypka professed himself skeptical about Gölpınarlı's interpretation of the ghazal in question in 1968.[20] M. Isa Waley argued in his dissertation and in one article[21] that the ghazal rendering sixty-two years seems to be echoed in a passage of Book 2 of the *Masnavi*, which was written not when Rumi first met Shams, but after the death of Hosâm al-Din's wife, which accounted for the two-year suspension of work on the great poem. According to Waley (using Gölpınarlı's dates for the *Masnavi*), Rumi began Book 1 of the *Masnavi* in 657 and completed it in A.H. 660. Therefore, Rumi began Book 2 in A.H. 662 and Waley thinks that the sixty-two years in the ghazal refers to this date, and not, as Gölpınarlı had thought, to Rumi's age. Rumi at this time (A.H. 662/A.D. 1264) would have been almost sixty years of age, and Waley reads another reference in the ghazals to "sixty" (cited by Gölpınarlı) as an allusion to Rumi's age (Mov 132–4).

Movahhed (Mov 135) finds the revisionist argument generally unconvincing, and we should reject it as well, for it creates many inconsistencies of its own. First, why was Sepahsâlâr so precise about the date of Rumi's birth? And if Rumi lived into his nineties, why did his followers, including his son, never refer to his longevity? Also, it seems incredible that Rumi could undergo such a great spiritual transformation past the age of sixty and compose such ecstatic youthful ghazals. This would make the *Masnavi* a product of his eighties. Furthermore, if Rumi had remained in Khorasan until his thirties, we would expect far more references than we have in his Discourses or his poetry to his experiences there. By 1231, when his father died, he would have been nearly fifty years old, and it is hard to imagine why he would have needed to go to Syria at this age to further his studies, or submit to the spiritual disciplines of retreat and seclusion under Borhân al-Din's tutelage, as these were generally the activities of young men in their teens, twenties and thirties.

Furthermore, the ages of forty and sixty often have a tropological function in Persian poetry. As Movahhed speculates (Mov 143) the topos of "youth in old age" alludes to Rumi's spiritual rejuvenation – that he became supple and verdant and grew out of a stiff religiosity – and not to his actual age. More precisely, the topos of forty and sixty refer to spiritual stages of life and not necessarily actual ages. Forty is generally midlife, the age of worldliness and career. Sixty is old age, the time of spiritual preoccupations and reflection on impending mortality. Furthermore, we do not need to assume that Rumi's ghazals addressed to Shams were necessarily addressed to his presence; indeed they were addressed to his memory and became a kind of signature of Rumi's quest. Furthermore, the one verse that began the whole confusion might also be interpreted differently. It could mean, as Gölpınarlı reads, that Rumi had to become the leader himself *at* age sixty-two. On the other hand, it could also mean that Rumi was forty and Shams was sixty-two: Rumi, the forty-year intellect, was hunted *by* Shams, an intellect of sixty-two.

Though we cannot be absolutely certain of the day of the week, the precise date, or the year given in our hagiographies, there is no reason radically to reject the traditional dates for Rumi's life as Gölpınarlı and Waley have done. We may assume that the traditional dates given for his life, from September 30, 1207 to December 17, 1273, are generally correct.

RUMI'S SEXUALITY

As we have seen ("Bahâ al-Din's Wives and Children" in chapter 1), Rumi's father admitted in his spiritual journals to powerful feelings of lust for his wives and, though resistant to these promptings on some level because they distracted him from contemplation on the divine, he ultimately accepted them as gifts from God. Rumi, too, married at a young age, about seventeen, and fathered two children from this marriage. When his wife Gowhar Khâtun died, Rumi took another wife, Kerrâ Khâtun, who bore him at least two children who survived to adulthood. The letters Rumi wrote show him playing the role of paterfamilias and trying to smooth out wrinkles in the lives of his children and their spouses.

In one passage of Aflâki's chronicle, we read an anecdote that testifies to Rumi's virility, in spite of his ascetic and abstemious behavior (Af 449). One of the female members of Rumi's household (ʿaffât-e mokhaddarât) related that Kerrâ Khâtun once complained that Rumi was obsessively occupied with fasting, performing samâʿ and lecturing on mystical subjects and theology. He took little food and practiced exercises of asceticism:

> For this reason, he does not even look in my direction and does not attach importance to physical beauty (gerd-e shâhed-bâzi nemigardad). I wonder if any traces of human quality and marital lust are left in him, or his appetites have left him entirely and he has abandoned them.

That very night, however, having read her mind, Rumi graced her with his presence and, like a wild roaring lion (shir-e gharrân-e mast), penetrated her seventy times (haftâd nowbat dokhul kard). In the end, she fled up on to the roof of the school from Mowlânâ (Af 450) and repented of her complaint, though Mowlânâ Rumi pursued, saying that he had not yet finished with her. Rumi explained that the men of God are capable of accomplishing whatever they want and insinuated that he could read what was in the heart and mind of other people. The men of God do not neglect the least detail of what troubles people. He further explained to her that his association with her had decreased only because he was immersed in the contemplation of God; in this, too, Rumi followed the example of the Prophet, Muhammad.

As we have seen, ("Owhad al-Din Kermâni" in chapter 4), Shams al-Din counseled the young Sultan Valad to avoid hashish and sodomy (Af 633), and condemned Owhad al-Din Kermâni for his practice of shâhed-bâzi, in this case his attention to beautiful boys, in the Hellenistic tradition of the ephebe. Shams and Rumi both condemned the excesses of Sufi behavior, as did other Sufis, and were opposed to libertinism. Rumi held a very unfavorable opinion of Owhad al-Din, believing that Owhad's relationship with the boys in his circle was not chaste: "Shaykh Owhad al-Din left a bad legacy in the world."

In the ecstatic abandon of *samâ'*, Sufis would often tear open their cloak or shirt; poets refer to this repeatedly, but it was more than just metaphor or hyperbole, as Sufi manuals like the *Kashf al-mahjub* and *Talbis-e Eblis* confirm it. It was undoubtedly in such a context that Owhad, as we have seen, would rub his bared chest against the chest of young boys. In the *Masnavi* (M5:354ff.) Rumi tells a story of how the open shirt (*faraji*) received its name – originally it was a closed-necked garment (*jobbe*) which a Sufi shaykh tore open. This shaykh tore the garment out of pure motives, but others who followed him had perverted the purpose. For Rumi, this act symbolized the rending of the body so that the soul could escape and ascend towards purity. It does not mean that one should remove conventions, ignore piety and the law and commit sodomy (*dabb, al-lavâte*):

> If you want spirit, son, then tear your cloak
> and head for purity, quickly wing your way
> A Sufi's one who quests for purity
> not for patches, woolen garb, and buggery!
> Vile folk have reduced Sufihood these days
> to nothing but patched cloaks and sodomy

(M5:362–4)

The passage goes on (M5:364–91) to explain that the transformative moisture of the divine wine created pearls, rubies, fruits and sweets as it sprinkled upon the earth. When this divine elixir fell upon clay, it created human beauty. We should not think of the physical form of the clay, but the divine intoxication within, for when the body dies, it becomes an ugly carcass, but the spirit within becomes even more beautiful. Only the pure, who do not become mired in the worship of the divine elixir as incarnated in human flesh, can attain to the exquisite beauty of transcendent truth.

Homoeroticism pervades medieval Persian poetry. The beloved in most ghazal poetry is androgynous, and often equated with the ruler, decked in armor and slaying those who approach him. We would be quite wrong to suppose that when a male poet describes a ruler in a panegyric as a beautiful young warrior, for whom the poet longs as a lover longs for the beloved, this implies physical love between the two. Sexuality, or at least the trope of male penetration, stands for a power relation in Persian poetry. The penetrator is the active partner (*fâ'el*) in a sexual liaison and holds the dominant position. The penetrated one (*maf'ul*) is objectified beauty or desire, and is equated with femininity and weakness, or with the weakness of pre-adolescent boys lacking facial hair. By penetration of the woman or boy, the active partner establishes his dominance in a sexual relationship. The woman or boy may arouse desire, but she or he occupies an inferior social status. Indeed, the collections of medieval Persian poetry are rife with boasting and insults which revolve around the issue of sexual penetration. A poet will boast of having humiliated his enemy by sodomizing him and/or penetrating his womenfolk. A stigma attached to being penetrated, and a self-respecting mature male would not allow this to happen to himself. Sodomy, though condemned by Islamic law, doubtless did take place among certain Sufi orders and the occasional legal case demonstrates that it was a real phenomenon.

Indeed, Aflâki (Af 188–90) recounts that Bahâ al-Din Bahri, one of Rumi's secretaries, once asked him what faults people commonly spoke of in Sufi shaykhs and whether such criticisms were accurate or arose from the misperceptions of outsiders. Rumi replied that he hoped the Sufi shaykhs would not fall prey to such faults. He warns, however, that some shaykhs, in the courage of their esoteric beliefs, disregard social conventions. For this they attract condemnation for their behavior and usually wind up guilty of what they are accused of, whether or not they begin that way. The example is given of a certain Shaykh Nâser al-Din in Konya, who cultivated a circle of sodomizers around him because of his unnatural inclination. His pupils eventually gave him medicine to cure him of this proclivity, but not before he achieved public infamy. Unscrupulous ruffians would take his money and possessions, such that people who knew the situation would whisper the Koranic verse "Those who follow false ways will encounter loss" (K40:78) as a pronouncement against him. As a result of his disgrace, people came to refer to "the disease of shaykhs." Rumi clearly condemns such behavior.

Elsewhere in the *Masnavi* (M6:3843ff.), Rumi tells the story of two brothers, one not yet pubescent and the other with four hairs and some peach fuzz on his chin. They come from a nearby village to a party in a young men's hostel (*'azab khâne*) in a certain town, where they stay carousing until late into the night. Having presumably imbibed a little, they do not want to return home, for fear that the night watchman will catch them and punish them for drunkenness and disorderly conduct. So, they stay the night in a young men's hostel. The older brother had a very handsome face. The younger boy was rather ugly, but since he did not yet have any facial hair, was androgynous-looking in appearance and therefore likely to be the object of homosexual advances. He therefore took the precaution of piling a few bricks to cover his behind before he went to sleep.

As he slept a certain fellow approached him lasciviously, knocking the bricks aside. The young boy awoke, startled by the stranger's touch, and cursed at him. The pederast, angered by ramming up against the bricks, shouted at him, "Why did you pile up these bricks?!" The boy retorted, "Why did you knock them over?" Of course, the boy knew very well why he had knocked the bricks over, but being smaller and younger, the boy was in no position to confront the pederast. The boy therefore concocted some story about being a sick and weakly child, whereupon the pederast, still smarting, told him he should have gone to a hospital or the house of a doctor for treatment instead of the hostel. The boy retorts that he can find no peace anywhere; wherever he goes some heretical, foul-minded pederast raises his beastly head to harass him.

> A better place for me's the Sufi lodge
> but even there I've not a moment's peace
> A crowd of porridge-guzzlers look me over
> eyes full of ejaculant, hands on their balls
> even those vowed celibate among them
> steal furtive glances and massage their cocks

(M6:3856–8)

The boy concludes that when the Sufi convent behaves like this, there is no hope for him among the ordinary worldly folk, who make little pretense to piety and chastity! He explains that he cannot even stay in the women's quarters because, just as the wife of Pharaoh had made advances to Joseph, so too would he be attacked and then the menfolk of those women would blame him for molesting them, scream bloody murder and have him drawn and quartered.

The boy concludes that he has no respite either with men or with women (and this boy is ugly: how much worse in the case of a handsome one!). Rumi, the poet, takes the boy's side in this tale and means for the reader to sympathize with him, on the principle that reason would dictate freedom from harassment for every woman and every boy, but there is a shortage of reason to go around (M6:3861). A pile of bricks will not deter the devil, so long as temptation is involved. One has to be protected from temptation by the chin hairs of piety that come with divine grace.

Clearly, the cult of the ephebe lived on in medieval Iran and men fancied androgynous pre-pubescent boys, at least until they sprouted facial hair. Under normal circumstances, Muslim women were largely segregated from non-related men, and appeared in public only in a veil, so adolescent boys often became platonic and also libidinous objects of desire. This homoerotic environment, however, should not be equated with homosexual orientation. For one thing, amorous attention was from the dominant party, the phallocrat, towards the penetrated party, male or female. When a boy passed a certain age and grew facial hair, he himself became a member of the sexually dominant class and would no longer submit to penetration. Violation of these social norms led to scandal and legal prosecution.

Furthermore, the men attracted to androgynous boys (marked as effeminate by their hairlessness) also desired women, married and had children. In any case,

Rumi condemns such sexual exploitation, both on humanitarian grounds and because it contravenes the law of Islam. Sexual pleasure may be pursued and enjoyed, but only within the confines of marriage.

The suggestion that the relationship between Shams and Rumi was a physical and homosexual one entirely misunderstands the context. Rumi, as a forty-year-old man engaged in ascetic practices and teaching Islamic law, to say nothing of his obsession with following the example of the Prophet, would not have submitted to the penetration of the sixty-year-old Shams, who was, in any case, like Rumi, committed to following the Prophet and opposed to the worship of God through human beauty. Rumi did employ the symbolism of homoerotic, or more properly, androgynous love, in his poems addressed to Shams as the divine beloved, but this merely adopts an already 300-year-old convention of the poetry of praise in Persian literature.

THE SYMBOLISM OF WINE IN RUMI'S POEMS

The drinking of wine and other liquors is forbidden in Islam, though the wine convivium was a regular part of the ceremonials of the royal courts of Iran, including the Seljuks. Though Hanafi law does not necessarily forbid the drinking of date wine (*nabid*), religious scholars and men of piety would not partake of this or other spirits, at least not in public. The distilling, consumption and sale of wine was not forbidden in the Islamic domains, however, to Christians, Zoroastrians and Jews. Wine taverns (*kharâbât*, literally "ruins") outside of major towns made not only drink, but also music, dancing girls and prostitutes available. Although the existence of such places offended the moral sensibilities of the ulama and tempted some Muslims to sin, governments frequently tolerated and even taxed them. The Ayyubids levied such a tax in Syria prior to 1215, when it was temporarily canceled by al-ʿÂdel, only to be reinstated and then canceled once again by al-Javâd in 1237. The Mamluk sultan Baybars canceled the wine and entertainment tax once again in 1266, but in 1281 an office was very briefly established in Damascus to collect such a tax until the objections of the ulama forced it to close. In about 1299, however, Kipchak, Ghâzân Khân's governor in Damascus, allowed the wine taverns (*hânât*) to operate once again. Once he left, Ibn Taymiya closed them right back down, breaking wine vessels and admonishing the owners. Ibn Kathîr tells us that one of the taverns in Damascus made as much as 1,000 dirhams per day (Zia 33, 185).

While Muslims, particularly the ulama (who were supposed to set the moral example for the community), were not supposed to partake, many Muslims would frequent the *kharâbât* (so the poets tell us), where they might carouse and indulge in sexually licentious behavior. To visit such an institution was, therefore, reprehensible in itself and the people who worked there socially unacceptable. Yet we find Shams al-Din of Tabriz commenting on the sinful of society and the wine taverns:

> Let's go out there a while to the *kharâbât*. God created those little women. Whether good or bad, let's look upon them. Let's go, as well, to the churches and look upon them. No one can bear to do this work of mine. What I do is not an appropriate course to follow by way of imitation. (Maq 302)

> I like pagans because they do not claim to be friendly. They say, "Yes, we are infidels, enemies." So let us teach them friendship, instruct them in unity. But he who claims to be a friend, yet is not, is fraught with danger. If anyone looks upon these *kharâbât* with the eye of pity, he will see that it is forbidden and deserving of punishment and retribution, but his eyes will fill with tears of pity and he will say, "O God, grant salvation from sin for them and for me and for all Muslims."
> Now, if you can maintain your belief in your shaykh with equanimity whether you see him in the *kharâbât* sitting and breaking bread with a *kharâbâti*, or see him in prayer, this is a great thing. If you lack this strength, when you see him in the *kharâbât*, say, "I do not understand the mystery of this. Only he knows and God." If you see him in prayer, say, "Yes, I know this, it is good." It would also be good, if you lack the strength, to regard the shaykh when in the *kharâbât* exactly as he were praying at the Kaaba or in paradise. (Maq 298–9)

Some Sufis, particularly the Malâmatis, did, indeed, drink wine. Even those who did not, however, used wine as a symbol of divine or mystical intoxication. As opposed to those ulama and ascetics who worshiped God out of fear, calculating their sins and good deeds, keeping account of the laws and exhortations which they observed as against those which they contravened or neglected, wine represented the dizzying effect of loving God with abandon, not out of fear of hell or hope of heaven, but because the worshiper wished to merge with the divine. It represents the *mysterium tremendum*, the sense of God's presence in the mind and heart of the worshiper, as opposed to the knowledge of God's law which the conventional ulama made the object of their religious studies. Likewise, the poetry of the Sufis rejects rationality (*caql*) for love (*ceshq*), the mode of fervent devotion. In the language of poetry, the excessive devotion of the true lover of God might lead to charges of heresy (*kofr*), but this true love is to be preferred to conventional faith (*imân*).

These are, however, poetic tropes. Though poetic trope and personal practice overlap in the case of some poets (Hâfez, for example), it is extremely difficult to conceive of Rumi drinking. Although he may have demonstrated greater compassion or tolerance for those who drank than did many of the ulama – as Shams urges in the passages above – Rumi's poetry certainly intends this symbolic meaning of wine, which Persian poets like Sanâ°i and cAttâr, and Arab poets like Ibn al-Fârid, had firmly established.

Several passages in the *Masnavi* refer to the unhealthy and undesired effects of earthly intoxication. The drunk young man will stumble in the road like an old infirm man. The symbolic wine, which comes from the covenant with God (K7:171), does not bring intoxication only for a night, like earthly wine (M4:2095–100). Rumi elsewhere tells his audience that they possess intelligence and should not veil it by lust. Lust acts like wine and cannabis, which a wise man would never touch. Again, however, Rumi shows that this real wine of drunkenness he mentions has a symbolic value. All carnality shuts our eyes and ears. It is not only wine that brings on intoxication, for Satan did not drink, but was drunk with pride (M4:3611–15).

8

The Poems

PERSIAN POETRY

Jalâl al-Din Rumi was not a professional poet, like Saᶜdi in his own age, or the majority of Persian poets writing in the two centuries prior to him. Even at the pre-Islamic courts of the Sasanians, Iranian poet–jongleurs had composed lyrical songs and poems for the rulers, and following the example set by Abu Nuwâs at the court of Hârun al-Rashid and al-Mutanabbî (whose poems we know Rumi enjoyed) at the court of Sayf al-Dowle, most Persian poets sought their fame at court or, in the case of epic or romance bards, like Ferdowsi and Nezâmi, dedicated their poems after composition to a local potentate, who might reward them monetarily and help publicize the poem. Professional poets usually composed for a sultan or prince or for high-ranking members of the military, in return for which they received state patronage – a stipend from the court and/or a direct reward for specific poems. Panegyric poetry in praise of the various rulers abounds, as such poets would offer a ceremonial ode, or *qaside*, on state occasions, commemorations, royal wine convivia and other festivals.

Alongside of such professional poetry, there existed a popular poetic tradition, usually in the form of quatrains, often composed and performed (i.e., sung) by unlearned or even illiterate poets in a specific meter of its own, which would circulate mouth to mouth. Such were the poems of ᶜOmar Khayyâm or of Bâbâ Tâher of Hamadân or Abu Saᶜid-e Abi al-Khayr.

About a hundred years before the birth of Rumi, Sanâᵓi (d. 1121) carved out a niche for a new kind of poetry with an alternative source of patronage – religious didactic poetry recited in gatherings of religious scholars, preachers and canon lawyers, specifically those with an inclination to ethical and metaphysical speculation. A half century prior to Sanâ⁾i, Nâser Khosrow had already dedicated himself to the composition of sectarian religious poems, but as an Ismaili, he lived more or less as a missionary, with the support of his religious community, whose temporal and spiritual leader was based in Egypt. With the establishment of regular devotional assemblages and mystical orders, combined with the collapse of the great Perso-Turkish empires like the Ghaznavids and Seljuks, religious and mystical themes began to dominate Persian poetry.

Rumi belongs to this non-professional class of poets, whose living depended not on panegyric and flattery of the sultan or other potentates, but on the expression of religious truth. Even in the Friday sermon at the mosque a preacher (khatib) would have to choose his words carefully so as to admonish the ruler without blatantly insulting him. In the realm of the khâneqâh, however, ethical and mystical poetry could address an audience of religious scholars and did not even have to discuss politics (though poets often did of course make veiled political commentary in the stories they told in verse).

Sultan Valad explains the difference between professional poetry and the poetry of saints at great length (SVE 53–5). When professional poets compose poetry, they use their thoughts and imagination to show off their own talents and to sculpt exaggerated lies out of words. When the saints compose poetry, they express the essence of the Koran, because they have effaced their own ego in the divine and move according to God's will. The saints, then, write poetry to the greater glory of God, not to the greater glory of themselves. Professional poets suppose that the poetry of the saints is no different from their own, but the breeze blowing over a garden brings fragrance whereas the same breeze blowing over a refuse heap brings ordure. If you have any sense of smell, you can tell the difference!

Just in case we remain in doubt about which poets belong in which category, Sultan Valad later returns to the theme of worldly versus spiritual verse. He says (SVE 211–12) that if you like to read the divâns of poets like Anvari and Zahir-e Fâryâbi, you are a man of this world, ruled by water and clay. If, on the other hand, you gravitate towards the divâns of Sanâ⁾i and ⁽Attâr, it means you are a man of heart, one of the saints. Even better for you if read the divân of Rumi, who was the pith, epitome and cream of the thought of Sanâ⁾i and ⁽Attâr.

Rumi himself says that when he first began to compose poetry, he felt himself impelled by some great purpose (dâ⁽ie⁾i bud ⁽azim ke mowjeb-e goftan bud). We may assume this refers primarily to the lyrical poetry of the ghazals, because Rumi goes on to say that this compulsion to poetry had ebbed to a great degree in his later life (Discourse 54, Fih 199). Afzal Iqbal (IqL xi) dates this period of "lyrical activity ... devoted to music, dance and poetry" from approximately 1245 to 1261, from the arrival of Shams to the beginning of the Masnavi.

RUMI'S TELLTALE SIGNATURE

The collection of lyrical poems attributed to Jalâl al-Din Rumi is usually known as the *Divân-e Shams-e Tabrizi*, or "collected works of Shams-e Tabrizi." There is no doubt, however, that Rumi authored the bulk of the poems in the published editions (though many spurious poems have found their way into the manuscript tradition). The genre conventions of the Persian ghazal call for the poet to adopt a poetic persona and to invoke that persona by name, usually toward the end of each poem, in the *takhallos*. Persian poets typically spoke in a public, not a personal voice, and adhered to established conventions. As such, the poetic persona, though associated of course with a recognizable style and the particular characteristic themes of a given poet, presented the audience with a kind of stage image or character, and not necessarily the private life of the individual poet. Therefore, the ghazal poet rarely used his given name (e.g., Mohammad) or his patronym (e.g., Abu al-Qâsem – father of Qâsem), but typically a name derived from a patron (e.g., Saʿdi), or one which touted his profession, accomplishments, social station, etc. (e.g., ʿAttâr – an apothecary; Hâfez – one who has memorized the Koran), or with an aspiration or spiritual quality (e.g., Sanâʾi – one of light). With this *nom de plume* (*takhallos*) the poet would, in effect, sign his poems, a signature he would weave into the text, usually as an apostrophe to his persona, by way of consoling himself, summing up his situation, or urging action on his audience. For example, Hâfez writes in the last line of a particularly anguished and plaintive ghazal:

> Hâfez, hush!
>> None knows the mysterious ways of God;
>>> who are you asking to answer your question:
>>> what has become of our generation?

As we have seen, Rumi was referred to among his own circle, and later on throughout the Muslim world, as "Our leader" or "My leader" – Mowlânâ or Mowlavi. He did not use this title to refer to himself, however. In his ghazals he used two signatures, either *Khâmush* (Silence!) or Shams-e Tabrizi. In the poems in which it appears, *Khâmush* usually calls for an end to the complaint of existential or ontological pain experienced in the absence of the object of love. This word effectively remonstrates with the poetic persona, pointing out the paradox of being unable to express in words the *mysterium tremendum* experienced in the presence of this numinous beloved. The poem then ends in an address to a personified silence, an embodiment of the *via negativa*; the signature also acts as a command to the reader or the mystic desirous of revealing the mysteries of mystical love: Silence! It is not through words but experience that the truth is known.

"Shams-e Tabrizi," the second and more common signature in Rumi's ghazals, suggests that Rumi has adopted the persona of Shams-e Tabrizi by way of union with his spirit. For this reason, the collection of Rumi's lyrical poems is known as the *Divân-e Shams-e Tabrizi*, which, according to authorial convention, would tend to suggest that the author of the poems is Shams of Tabriz, as in the *Divân-e Sanâ'i* or *Divân-e Hâfez* – the collected works of Sanâ'i or Hâfez. But we can also understand by it "the collected Shams-e Tabrizi poems." At least one very antique manuscript, copied out probably within the first quarter century after Rumi's death, felt the need to clarify this issue with the comment "The Divân of Mowlâna Jalâl al-Din, who uses the name Shams-e Tabrizi in some of the ghazals." Whether or not Rumi himself chose this as the name of his collection of lyrics, it reflects his identification with the divine beloved, overwhelmingly manifested in the person of Shams-e Tabriz, who brought about his spiritual metamorphosis and gave voice to his mystical longing. Not every poem evokes the memory or presence of Shams al-Din, however; we also find some poems addressed to Salâh al-Din Zarkub or Hosâm al-Din, or to the circle of Sufi disciples – the amoretti (*'oshshâq*), or would-be lovers of God.

In the poems with this signature, Shams-e Tabriz is typically invoked or addressed as a divine teacher or beloved, a persona independent of the speaker of the poem, whom we assume to be the voice of Rumi or the spiritual seeker. But the appeal to Shams-e Din is rhetorical – there can be no cure for the pain and suffering the speaker feels, no solution in this plane of existence for our distance and separation from our heavenly beloved. Of course, Shams is here a kind of imagined ghost writer, speaking through the lips of Rumi. Some question about the true author of the poems arose as a result of this pen name, but if any doubt remained, by 1936 Ghulam Dastgir of Hyderabad had written a series of nine articles in *Ma'ârif* establishing that the *Divân* was written by Rumi (IqL 135).

METRICS

Rumi occasionally expresses frustration with the constraints of meter, famously remarking in verse (D 38): All this ta-dum-da-dum ta-dum-da-dum just kills me! (see also "Studies of Rumi's Poetics" in chapter 13). But Rumi is an extremely rhythmic poet and an overview of the metrical system he worked with will probably do more good than harm.

Classical Persian poetry, following the model of Arabic, conforms to a quantitative metrics, based on the alternation of syllables of long and short duration in regular patterns. As in classical Latin or Greek verse, the listener theoretically experiences the difference between long and short syllables as a matter of time and not, as in English, of stress. Persian vowels *u*, *i* and *â* count long, as do the diphthongs *ay* and *ow*; the vowels *o*, *e* and *a* count short. Poets can call upon a fair number of elisions and metrical licenses to get the syllables to count out right (for example an *e* at the end of a word can count long or short), but basically, open syllables with a long vowel count as long (e.g., *Ru-mi* consists of two long syllables), whereas open syllables with a short vowel count as short (e.g., the first syllable in *gha-zal* counts as short). The word for God, *khodâ*, counts as a short followed by a long syllable (*kho* short and *dâ* long).

In syllables closed by a consonant, however, a short vowel makes the syllable long and a long vowel makes the syllable count metrically as a long followed by a short syllable. For example, the three syllables Mo-ham-mad count as short-long-long, whereas the two-syllable word "Ja-lâl" counts for metrical purposes as short-long-short. Likewise, words which end in a consonant cluster (-st, -rg, -ng, -nd, etc.) count an extra short vowel at the end; the words "Shams" and "Rum" would each count metrically as a long followed by a short syllable.

There is a wide variety of meters to choose from, often associated with a particular mood. A line or stich (*bayt* = tent) of Persian poetry consists of two hemistichs (*mesrâ^c* = flaps), visually separated by a space on the page and usually also by a syntactic break, or caesura. The meter (*bahr* = ocean) is made up of a certain number of feet (*owtâd* = poles) of three to four syllables (though some variations exist). For example, the *motaqâreb* meter of the *Shâh nâme* repeats the foot ˘ – – (traditionally described as *fa^culun* = ta dum dum) four times in each hemistich, with the very last syllable elided (catalexis):

˘ – -| ˘ – – -| ˘ – – -| ˘ –-||
ta-vâ-nâ bo-vad har ke dâ-nâ bo-vad

˘ – –| ˘ – -|˘ – -| ˘ – –
ze dâ-nesh de-le pir bor-nâ bo-vad

He who has knowledge possesses power
knowledge gives an old heart a new flower

In this example, each line of the Persian therefore contains twenty-two syllables, in contradistinction to the more common syllable counts of ten (pentameter) or eight (tetrameter) in a line of English verse.

Most of the possible feet in Persian metrics, however, consist of four syllables. To make up the *ramal* meter, the meter of Rumi's *Masnavi*, the common *fa^celâtun* foot – ˘ – – is repeated six times in the course of the line, but the last foot of each hemistich loses the last syllable, giving two full feet of – ˘ – – followed by a catalectic foot of – ˘ – to make up one hemistich, with two identical hemistichs giving a full line. The first line of the *Masnavi* runs as follows:

– ˘ – – | – ˘ – -| – ˘ – ||
besh-no(w) in nay chon she-kâ-yat mi-ko-nad

– ˘ –-| – ˘ – -| – ˘ –
az jo-dâ^ʾi-hâ he-kâ-yat mi-ko-nad

Listen to this reed flute as it complains
telling tales of heart-wrench, separation

This line of Rumi's *Masnavi* contains twenty-two syllables. By comparison, Dante or Petrarch's hendecasyllabics contain eleven syllables each, the French alexandrine extends to twelve and the common meter of English, the pentameter, measures in at ten. Therefore, two lines of Dante's *Divine Comedy* would contain the same number of syllables as this one line of the *Masnavi*; two lines of Milton's *Paradise Lost* would measure up two syllables short of it; and two lines of Racine's *Bérénice* would overrun it by two syllables. Therefore, in order to roughly match the length of the *Masnavi*'s 26,000 lines syllable for syllable, we would need more than 52,000 lines of English heroic couplets. Put another way, the hemistich (*mesrâ^c* or half line) of the average Persian poem roughly corresponds to a full line of English verse.

The poet may choose, depending upon the mood he wishes to create, a dimeter (uncommon), trimeter, tetrameter or pentameter length of line, but must observe a consistent length of line throughout the poem. While some Persian lines are shorter than the example of the *Masnavi*, others actually contain many more than twenty-two syllables per line. The following line in tetrameter *hazaj* from one of the ghazals of the *Divân-e Shams* runs to sixteen syllables per hemistich or thirty-two syllables per line, repeating the pattern ˘ - - - eight times in one line:

> ˘ -   - - | ˘ -   - - | ˘ - - -| ˘ - - -
> *delâ nazd-e kasi benshin ke u az del khabar dârad*

> ˘ - - - | ˘ - - -| ˘ - - -| ˘ - - -
> *be-zir-e ân derakhti row ke u gol-hâ-ye tar dârad*

> Heart! sit only at the feet of one who knows his hearts
>   Choose the shade beneath a tree where all the blossoms are

In addition to these simple meters, some composite meters alternate two dissimilar feet within one line. The *khafif* meter, for example, juxtaposes the - ˘ - - foot with the foot ˘ - - ˘ -, followed by a catalectic version of the first foot, ˘ - - which may also be replaced with - - as in the poem:

> - ˘ - -|˘ - - ˘ -| ˘   ˘   -||
> *ah che bi-ran-go bi-ne-shân ke ma-nam*

> - ˘ -   -| ˘ - - ˘ -| ˘   ˘   -
> *kay be-bi-nam ma-râ cho-nân ke ma-nam*

> Ahh, how colorless, unmanifest I am!
>   will I ever see me just the way I am?

RHYME AND REFRAIN

All medieval Persian poetry observes rhyme; there is no equivalent of blank verse. The rhyme scheme is furthermore determined by the genre of poem. Romance and epic invariably use the *masnavi*, or couplet form, in which the two hemistichs of a given line rhyme with one another, as indicated by the rhyming words in bold below (the underlined words will be explained momentarily):

*serr-e man az nâle-ye man **dur** <u>nist</u>*
*lik cheshm o gush râ ân **nur** <u>nist</u>*

*tan ze jân o jân ze tan **mastur** <u>nist</u>*
*lik kas râ did-e jân **dastur** <u>nist</u>*

*âtash ast in bâng-e nây o <u>nist</u> **bâd***
*har ke in âtash nadârad <u>nist</u> **bâd***

*âtash-e ʿeshq ast k-andar **nay** <u>fetâd</u>*
*jushesh-e ʿeshq-ast k-andar **may** <u>fetâd</u>*

My secret's soon divulged by my complaint
 but eyes and ears lack light, cannot discern it

Body from soul, soul from body aren't concealed
 but no one has the sight so sharp to see it

The stuff that fills the reed flute's fire, not wind
 Let who lacks such fire blow away like sand

What courses through the reed is love's own fire
 what bubbles in the wine is love's ferment

The ghazal and *qaside*, on the other hand, do not require rhyme at the end of each hemistich except in the first line. In all subsequent lines the rhyme is observed at the end of the line only, as in the first three lines of this poem, comparing the beloved to the firmament and the lovers or worshipers to the stars passing through the astrological houses:

beraftim ay ʿaqiq-e lâ makâni   *ze shahr-e to to bâyad ke bemâni*
safar kardim chun estâregân-e mâ   *ze to ham suye to ke âsemâni*
yeki surat ravad digar biâyad   *be mehmân khâne-at zirâ ke jâni*

we left, gem beyond dimension,
 your city, you must stay behind
we traveled like the stars
 from you to you, for you are sky
one face goes another takes its place
 as guest in your house, for you are life

Many poems repeat a refrain (*radif*) immediately after the rhyme word in each line; in the opening lines from Rumi's *Masnavi*, above, the refrain words, not strictly speaking considered part of the rhyme, are underlined. In the following three lines from one of Rumi's ghazals addressed to Salâh al-Din, the rhyme words are likewise highlighted in bold and the three-syllable refrain is underlined:

*motrebâ asrâr-e **mâ** <u>râ bâz gu</u>*   *qesse-hâ-ye jânfa**zâ** <u>râ bâz gu</u>*
mâ dahân bar baste-im emruz az u   *to hadis-e delgo**shâ** <u>râ bâz gu</u>*

        ❧ ❧ ❧

chon Salâh al-Din salâh-e jân-e mâst   *ân salâh-e jân-**hâ** <u>râ bâz gu</u>*

Tell my secrets, singer! Recount, reveal!
   stories to quicken souls, recount, reveal!
Today we all stand tongue-tied by his hands
   those heart releasing tales, recount, reveal!
Salâh al-Din's our spirit's common weal –
   what's welfare for our souls? recount, reveal!

Rumi makes full use of the rhyme richness of Persian; he frequently uses internal rhyme so that the rhyme word will occur two, three or even four times as often as prosody requires in a given line. He also tends to choose the more fluid meters and employ them rhythmically, as one would expect for poetry extemporaneously composed to a turning dance. The use of refrains in many of the ghazals also contributes to the highly cadenced and song-like rhythm.

One translator of Persian poetry has remarked that of English poets, Thomas Traherne most closely resembles Rumi. Though Traherne often gleefully celebrates the wonder of creation, to my ear his poems do not seem anywhere near as ecstatic or sonorously riveting. Perhaps some of the poems of Algernon Charles Swinburne ("Hertha," "The Triumph of Time," the prelude to "Tristram of Lyonesse," "Before the Beginning of Years," etc.) treat themes similar to Rumi's in a near approximation of the musical intensity of the metrics of many of Rumi's ghazals, though the dense sonorities, counterpoint and striking imagery of Gerard Manley Hopkins (e.g., "The Habit of Perfection," "The Blessed Virgin Compared to the Air we Breathe," "Pied Beauty," "As Kingfishers Catch Fire," etc.) also come to my mind, except that the juxtapositions and locutions of Rumi are more immediately apprehended for the most part. To the extent that Rumi's poems are difficult, this is because they assume a certain theological and mystical context, the allusions of which were not always transparent to late medieval readers of Persian, as the many commentaries show, much less to a modern Persian reader not trained in the traditional Islamic sciences, and more still to a Western reader who has not read up on Rumi's theology. There seems to me also a certain affinity with Walt Whitman, metrically as well as in the innovativeness of imagery and directness of expression.

The stories of the *Masnavi* can, of course, be enjoyed as stories, with little or no context. However, since the narrative poems depend more on events and allegory than upon language or verse to convey their message, and because most readers of modern poetry have little interest in reading long verse narratives, few portions of the *Masnavi* have been included here. An attempt has been made at the lyrical opening song of the reed flute and a few random stories appear as well. For the most part, though, I see little advantage in putting the *Masnavi* into verse form. Those who want the in-depth meaning of the *Masnavi* should read Nicholson's line-by-line translation and commentary. Those who just want to taste the flavor of the tales can read the prose retellings of Arberry and Nicholson.

As for the lyric poems, the sense and imagery generally speak directly and do not need a great deal of mediation. However, there are some allusions which will escape the non-Islamicist reader; most of these are explained in the notes. Some of the obvious references to verses of the Koran are given parenthetically, alongside the text. Serious readers will want to look up these allusions in the Koran. Be forewarned that not all English versions of the Koran follow exactly the same numbering convention; if you cannot find the reference, you may have to hunt around in the vicinity for the relevant section or use another translation.

FIFTY POEMS

Poem 1   *Che dânestam ke in sowdâ marâ z-in sân konad majnun*
D 1855 Meter: ˇ - - - ˇ - - - ˇ - - - ˇ - - - (*hazaj*)

> How could I know melancholia
>   would make me so crazy,
> make of my heart a hell
>   of my two eyes raging rivers?
> How could I know a torrent would
>   snatch me out of nowhere away,
> Toss me like a ship upon a sea of blood,
> that waves would crack that ship's ribs board by board,
>   tear with endless pitch and yaw each plank
> that a leviathan would rear its head,
>   gulp down that ocean's water,
>   that such an endless ocean could dry up like a desert,
> that the sea-quenching serpent could then split that desert
> could jerk me of a sudden, like Korah, with the hand of wrath
>   deep in to a pit?
>
> When these transmutations came about
> not desert, not sea remained in sight
> How should I know how it all happened
>   since how is drowned in the Howless?
>
> What a multiplicity of how could I knows!
>   but I don't know
>   for to counter
>   the sea rushing in my mouth
>   I swallowed a froth of opium

Notes

Korah (*Qârun*), sometimes identified with the Greek Croesus or the Biblical Korah, is in the Koran a man made arrogant by his exceeding wealth. He refused to listen to warnings that his worldly wealth would not profit him in the hereafter, and was eventually swallowed by the earth (K28:76–81). The staving of the ship's planks alludes to the story of Moses and Khezr, as detailed in the section "Sufi Bohemians" in the introduction to this book. We may conclude that, since Sultan Valad compares the relationship of Shams to Rumi to that of Khezr and Moses, this poem describes Rumi's experience of crisis after the disappearance of Shams. "The Howless" (*bi-chun*) is an epithet of God. He cannot be (because we cannot understand) and should not be (because it is an impertinence) asked to explain the logic of His doings. *Afyun* means opium (from the Greek *opion*), but was sometimes applied to theriaca or treacle in medieval Islamic manuals of medicine. It was used as an antidote to poisoning and to dementia, and apparently also to drowning (see Nafisi's notes, Sep 329–33). Between the drug's stupefying effect and the water rushing in his mouth, the poet falls silent.

Poem 2 *Ay rastakhiz-e nâgahân vay rahmat-e bi-montahâ*
D 1 Meter: - - ᴗ - - - ᴗ - - - ᴗ - - - ᴗ - (*rajaz*)

Sudden resurrection! Endless Mercy!
Blazing fire in the thickets of thought!
Today you came laughing
unlocking dungeons
came to the meek
like God's grace and bounty

You are antechamber to the sun
you are hope's prerequisite
you are sought
seeker
terminus
principia
You pulse in every chest
adorn every idea
excite desires
then permit their realization

Spirit-spiring, irreplaceable
delight of action
   and cognition
      (all the rest is pretext, fraud)
the former, illness
the latter, cure
     we're jaundiced by that fraud
     heart-set to slay an innocent
     Drunk, now on angel eyes   [K44:54]
       now on plain bread and soup
     Taste this intoxication,
     drop your ratiocination
     savor these delectables,
     drop the debatables
      a little bread and greens
     should not entail so much trouble

You implement a multichrome design
cast it like a net
white over Rome
black in Abyssinia
even in the midst of war,
you concoct a wondrous work
that no one's ever seen before!
 Boxing spirit's ear in secret
 dodging all others with excuses
 Shouting the depths of "Lord release me!"
 By God, my monarch, what a joy!

Silence! I am so frenetic,
I embraced knowledge in a rush
put down the paper,
 snap the pen,
the Sâqi enters: Cheers!

Notes

This is the first poem in Rumi's *Divân* as it is currently arranged, and so he
begins with a resurrection in the first line. "Angel eyes" alludes to the famous
beauties in the symbolic paradise of the Koran, who will consort with the
faithful (also K52:20, 56:22). The everyday quality portrayed by the soup and
bread in this poem, and the joking way that the poet receives the rebuke of
having his spirit's ears boxed, make the poem seem quite situational – almost as
if Shams had come unexpectedly when the poet and his companions were at

table. As Sâqi, or cup-bearer, he would represent the source of mystical inebriation and the rejection or short-circuiting of rationalist modes of discourse.

Poem 3   *Ân shekl bin v-ân shive bin v-ân qadd o khadd o dast o pâ*
D 5 Meter: - - ‿ - - - ‿ - - - ‿ - - - ‿ - (*rajaz*)

Look at that face
　　those manners
　　that frame
　　those cheeks
　　those arms and legs
　　That complexion
　　that strength
　　that shining orb
　　　filling out that shirt

Shall I compare to cypress? meadows?
　　　　　　to tulips? jessamine?
　　　　　　to the candle or the candelabra?
　　　　　　or to the rose dancing in the breeze?

O Love come like an agiary, assuming form and hue
Robbing the caravan of hearts along the highway
　　Good sir! Give us some respite.

In my flame and fire I pass the night to dawn
How blessed my victory at "The Sun in the zenith"　　　[K93:1]
I spin around his bright orb,
　　greet him without lips
throw myself down to earth
　　before he calls out "Come get it!"

Rose garden and paradise on earth you are
the eye and the light of the world you are
and also searing pain of the world
when your steps turn to cruelty
I come to pledge my life
you say
　　　　　Don't bother me, go!
I bow and obey and withdraw
you say
　　　　　Come here, you fool!

His image joins company with fiery lovers
    May your face
    never for a moment
    leave our sight!

Heart, patience!
Why so distracted from your focus
Do you ever steal an hour of sleep,
of a morning? in the evening?
The heart replies

      His beauteous face
      those two bewitching narcissi
      his brow of hyacinth
        rubies sweet to taste

Love,
  everywhere blessed by fair name and good repute
last night I christened you anew:
    Pain Incurable
You,
  the splendor of my being
  the mover of my spheres
    send flour, my dear, as grist
      to keep the mill from grinding to a halt and spinning free

No more will I speak,
say this line and that's enough:
  My being melts in this desire
    Befriend us, Our God!

Notes

Agiary is the word Anglo-Indian Zoroastrians use for fire-temple (Persian: *âtash-kade*). Zoroastrians do not worship fire, but revere it as the symbol of the beneficent force in the cosmos. As such, Rumi here makes a sophisticated reference to the divine beloved having taken on human form, a form that becomes the focus of worship of the faithful. The beauty of this godly youth overpowers the beholder and steals away his heart, just as a bandit might swoop down and plunder a caravan carrying goods from one town to another. The persona of the poem appeals to this godly incarnation for respite.

    "Good sir" (*fatâ*) means a young man (perhaps even a member of the *fotovvat* orders) and connotes a young warrior, a knight who, though holding to a code of chivalry, also has the power to plunder. The Sun "in the zenith" (*Shams al-zohâ*) of course alludes to the name of Shams in tandem with a verse of the Koran. "Come get it" (*salâ*) is usually a call to begin eating. The beloved's eyes are compared to the narcissus (or daffodil), and the lips to rubies; the brow, because curled and perfumed, resembles the hyacinth. The reference to the mill spinning suggests the poem was performed to the *samâ'*.

Poem 4   *Yâr marâ ghâr marâ 'eshq-e jegar khwâr marâ*
D 37 Meter: - ˇ ˇ - - ˇ ˇ - - ˇ ˇ - - ˇ ˇ - (*sari'*)

> I have this friend
> I have this cave   [K9:40]
> I am gutted by love
> you are that friend
> you are that cave
>   my lord, don't cast me off
>
> you are Noah you are numen
> you are conqueror you are conquest
> you are the breast laid open   [K94:1]
>   I stand at the door of mysteries
>
> you are light
> you are the final trumpet
> you are fortune, God-confirmed
> you're the bird of Mount Sinai
>   I the wounded captive in your beak
>
> a drop you are
> the sea you are
> grace you are
> wrath you are
> sugar, poison you are you are
>   do not afflict me any longer!
> You are the solar sign
> the house of Venus
> the paradise of hope
>   let me in, my Friend
> You are daylight
> you are fasting
> you are the wages of our begging
> You are water you are jug
>   let this lover drink!
> You are bait
> you are the trap
> You are wine
> you are the cup

you are cooked
you are raw
    Please do not leave me raw!

If this flesh would stop its spinning
    my heart would not be robbed so dizzy
you left town
    so I would not prattle on incessantly

Notes

The story of the friend in the cave comes in the Koran, and refers to Mohammad's flight out of Mecca with Abu Bakr as his soul companion. Chased by the Meccans who were intent on killing them, the two hid in a cave. A spider is said to have spun a web over the entrance of the cave, making it appear as though no one had entered the cave for some time. "The breast laid open" from K94:1 refers in the first instance to revelation sent down by God when Mohammad was in trying circumstances, which served to confirm him and make his breast swell or dilate (with joy). However, the biographical tradition preserves a story about the opening up of Mohammad's chest by an angel so that his heart could be removed, washed pure and replaced. From the last line we may conclude that the poet composed or intended this poem to be recited while turning in *samâ*. It apparently dates to the time of Shams' temporary absence or permanent departure.

Poem 5   *Ay sakht gerefte jâdovi râ*
D 116 Meter: - - ◡ ◡ - ◡ - ◡ - - (*hazaj akhrab maqbuz*)

I call upon you
        who practice ceaseless sorcery
        who make a lion a gazelle
        whose magic conjures double vision
        who makes our hands to rub our eyes
        who makes the sour citron
            change its colors
            to ripen into sweeter plums
Your magic makes the lamb a wolf
        makes a wheatspike barley corn
Your magic makes imagination's scroll unfold
        into proclamations of immortality

341

Touched by your sorcery
   even the wayward pagan's beard
      billows in the breeze of wisdom
Your sorcery's made a sophist of me
   you who with your marshaled truculence
      Moslemize humanity, Turkify all Hinduality

In the heat of battle you transform
the mammoth tusky elephant into a gnat
Then let them join in even combat,
destiny against divine decree
till one emerges true

Enough of sophistry:
   Hold your peace!
   Unleash the tongue of meaning

Notes

The raids which conquered India in the name of Muslim rulers were carried out mostly by the Turkish dynasty of the Ghaznavids. Turks earned the reputation as brave fighters, first as slaves, in which capacity they formed the royal guard of the caliph; then as the rulers of eastern Iran, under the Ghaznavids and Seljuks. The beloved is not infrequently compared to a young Turkish warrior-prince who slays suitors right and left with his haughty charms. On the other hand, the work of sorcery is generally considered a shamanistic, pagan, and non-Islamic activity. The "tongue of meaning" in the last line refers to the true inner meaning, as opposed to the superficial understanding. The word for meaning is *maʿnavi*, which also came to designate the *Masnavi* of Rumi – the couplets of true meaning. Divine decree (*qazâ*) and destiny (*taqdir*) are terms reflecting a theological crux in Islam, a problem dealt with in the *Masnavi* (see chapter 9, below).

Poem 6   *Del cho dâne mâ mesâl-e âsiâ*
D 181 Meter: - ˇ - - - ˇ - - - ˇ - (*ramal*)

The heart like grain
us like a mill
   how can the mill
   know why it turns?
Flesh, like the stone
water, our thoughts
Stone says: It knows
   the course, Water.

and Water says:
> Ask the miller;
> he sends water
> cascading down.

Miller tells you:
> Chewer of bread
> if not for this
> how bake, how eat?

And on and on
the cycle goes

Silence! Ask God
for He'll tell you.

Notes

Not surprisingly, Aflâki (Af 370–1) places the performance of this poem at a
mill. Whether this is really the case or not, the metaphor of spinning must
allude to the practice of turning in *samâ'*. I have attempted to render this poem
into the metrical constraint of four-syllable lines.

Poem 7   *Goftâ ke kist bar dar goftam kamin gholâmat*
D 436 Meter: - - ᵕ - ᵕ - - - - ᵕ - ᵕ - - (*mozâre'*)

And who	He asked	is at the door?
I said	The humblest of your servants	
	State your business! he demanded	
My lord	I said	to greet you.
How long	He asked	will you keep knocking?
I said	Until you answer	
He asked	How long will you ferment?	
I said	Until the Resurrection	
	I laid claim to love and swore many oaths	
	I boasted of bravery and dominion	
He warned	The Judge will call for you to prove your claims	
I said	My tears come freely forth, eye-witnesses	
	I submit the pallor of my face as evidence	
He said	Your evidence is inadmissible	
	your witnesses both blurred and tainted	
I said	Upon your majestic justice! They testify	
	both fair and true	

He said	Who came here with you?
I replied	O King, just the image I carry of you.
He asked	Who summoned you here?
I answered	The fragrance in your chalice
He demanded	State your purpose
Friendship	I responded and fidelity
He asked	What is it that you want from me?
I said	Your universal grace
He countered	There is a place more pleasant. Name it!
I replied	The Royal Palace
And what	He queried did you see there?
I said	A million blessings
And why	He asked is it now desolate?
I said	For fear of robbers.
And who	He asked is a robber?
I said	The robber is reproach
He said	And where can one take refuge?
In continence	I replied and piety
He asked	And what is continence
I said	The way to safety and salvation
He asked	And which way lies calamity?
	In the pathway of my love to you
	And how will you manage there?
	By being steadfast ...
Silence!	For if I tell you of his attributes
	you will lose yourself
	and find yourself
	homeless
completely without prospects	

Notes

"The fragrance in your chalice." Foruzânfar's text gives *jân-at*, which slightly violates the rhyme. Arberry amends it to *jâm-at* (MPR 1:178), which is the reading I have adopted, because the royal court is associated with ritual wine banquets and jewel-encrusted, even magic goblets. However, Rumi was not above such licenses and in many ways "the fragrance of your soul" sounds more powerful. The poem relates a symbolic encounter or dream image, which the poet then cuts off in the final line (he tells himself to be silent), for fear that the truth of what he has seen is too overpowering to hear.

Poem 8   *Har nafas âvâz-e ʿeshq mi-rasad az chap o râst*
D 463 Meter - ⌣ ⌣ -   - ⌣ ⌣ -   - ⌣ ⌣ -   ⌣̱ ⌣ -   (*monsareh*)

With each new breath the sound of love
surrounds us all from right and left
Now up we go, head heavenward
who wants to come and see the sights?
We've been before in heaven's realm,
The angels there our constant friends,
we'll go again
for we were born
all in that town.

We are ourselves above the skies
a greater host than angels there;
why should we not exceed their rank
since our abode is Majesty?
The purest pearl
does not belong
in earthly dust.

What brought you down? What place is this?
Pack up!
By fortune blessed to give our lives,
the caravan will guide our steps:
   Our pride in life, the Chosen One
   By His bright orb the moon was split
   (it would not turn its gaze away)
   And so luck smiled upon the moon
     the lowly moon that begs its light!
   The wind's sweet scent drips from his locks
   His image shines with brilliant rays
   from his bright face, reflecting from
   "And the sun in its zenith"   [K 93:1]
See how my heart with every beat
reveals the moon cleft clear in two
    why do you turn your sight down from such a sight?

Like water birds, man's born within
the sea of soul
How could he nest within the mire,
that ocean bird?
and we are all pearls in that sea,
afloat on it,
or else why wave on wave would surge
all through our hearts?
Over our boat just like a wave
broke "Am I not"   [K7:172]
Our ship's ribs staved the boat will sink
our time has come for reunion,
to meet with God.

Notes

It appears this poem may commemorate the night ascent of Mohammad into heaven (*meʿrâj*) or his birth (*mowled*). One of the miracles related of Mohammad is that he cleft the moon asunder. The Chosen One (Mostafâ) is an epithet of Mohammad. For the "sun in its zenith" see the note to poem 3. "Am I not your Lord?" is the question God poses to the children of Adam at the primordial covenant of man with God, to which everyone replied enthusiastically in the affirmative. The tale Aflâki tells in connection with this poem (Af 266–8), about Saʿdi of Shiraz asking for a new poem of Rumi's and sending it to the ruler, is completely apocryphal. There is no indication that Saʿdi, a contemporary of Rumi, had any familiarity with Rumi's poems. On the other hand, it is not impossible that Rumi quoted from or recited this poem as he lay dying (Af 966–7).

Poem 9   *Nowbat-e vasl o leqâ-st nowbat-e hashr o baqâ-st*
D 464 Meter: - ˇ ˇ - - ˇ ˇ - - ˇ ˇ - - ˇ - (*monsareh*)

And now it's time
        for love's union
        for God's vision
        for resurrection, everlasting life
      Time for grace, for blessing
        for surging pure oceans of purity
        the sea foams white, casts its treasures:

Fortunate dawn, morn of the light of God!
Whose face? What image? King or prince?
What ancient sage is this?
All these are only veils
fervid ardor burns these veils away
You have the mind's eye to taste him
You writhe for it in your head
but you are all of two minds
  an earthly head of clay
  and one celestial, pure
All these celestial heads
lay scattered in the dust
to show you that another mind's afoot
At root, essential mind is hidden
and only branches dangle to our eyes
Know that beyond this universe
another endless world awaits
  Seal up the skin, my host,
  no vintage can convey us there
  The jug of apprehension's bottlenecked in those straits
The Sun of Truth shone from Tabriz
      and I told him:
      Your light touches all
      and yet remains apart

Poem 10 *Bâr-e degar zarre-vâr raqs konân âmadim*
D 1720 Meter: - ◡ ◡ - - ◡ - (◡) - ◡ ◡ - - ◡ - (*monsareh*)

Once more we come like dust adance in air
  From beyond the skies of love, aturn
On the field of love like polo balls we roll
  skittering to the side, coming to the fore

Love reduces one to need – if that's your lot
  it suits you – not us, who come from the beyond
This gathering's in your honor and the guests
  have all arrived. But not for bread alone
  we come here; pour out the firewater!
As you course through our veins, made wretched by
  our wounds for you, thank God we come quick to life!

Shams of Truth this love of yours thirsts for my blood
    I head straight to it, blade and shroud in hand!
Tabriz aboil your salt alone can simmer!
    We – pride of all the earth in caring for you –
    have come to help you stir the age up.

Poem 11   *Row sar beneh bebâlin tanhâ marâ rahâ kon*
D 2039 Meter: - - ˘ - ˘ - - - - ˘ - ˘ - - (*mozâre͑*)

Go lay your head on your pillow, let me be alone
    leave me laid waste to wander the night, afflicted
Me and the waves of grief, alone, dusk to dawn
    Come be kind, if you will; go and be cruel, if you want.
Leave me, run, fast, or you'll fall likewise in affliction
    Choose the more wholesome path and leave harm's way
Me and the puddle of my eyes, huddled in sorrow's corner
    turning mill after mill after mill with my tears

Impudent, brazen, he murders me, stony his heart
none dare demand money to atone my blood
The monarch of handsome faces is under no duty to be true
    Sallow-faced lover, be patient, be true
    It is a pain cured only by dying
        I cannot tell you how to treat this pain

Last night I dreamt I saw an old man in the street of love
    he beckoned me with his hand, "Come this way, to me"
If a dragon blocks the path, love works like an emerald
    The glittering of the emerald will repulse the dragon

            Enough! I am senseless,
            If your skills can match the task
            Tell the dates of Bu ͑Ali
            and box the ears of Bu ͑Alâ

Notes

Aflâki (Af 589–90) relates that Rumi, still rhyming to the very end, composed this poem on his deathbed. Sultan Valad, very distraught, would not leave his side, but badly needed rest, so Rumi assured him that he felt well and encouraged Sultan Valad to go and lie down. He then began to say this poem, which Hosâm al-Din Chelebi wrote down. This has all the traces of a story made up to fit the poem. Far more likely, the poem dates from the period of Rumi's inconsolable grief after the final disappearance of Shams, though we see already a glimmer of catharsis in the vision of the old man. In ancient folklore, an emerald was believed to repulse dragons because its glittery green blinded them or deceived them into seeing another dragon. Bu ʿAli is taken as a reference to Abu ʿAli Ibn Sinâ (Avicenna), representing the wise philosopher type, where Bu ʿAlâ is taken as a reference to Abu ʿAlâ al-Maʿarri, a materialist philosopher. Both represent the limits of rationalist discourse for Rumi.

Poem 12   *Z-avval-e bâmdâd sar masti*
D 3153 Meter: ˘ ˘ - - ˘ - ˘ - - - (*khafif*)

> Top of the morning, you're already smashed –
>   yes you are, you tied your turban crooked!
> I swear to God, all night last night till dawn
>   you were drinking – pure wine, undiluted;
> It's plain in your eyes, your cheeks, your color
>   the sort you are – wouldn't put it past you.
> Give the tipplers some of what you tasted
>   O Guardian of all created blessings
>
> Today the lion prowls around for prey
>   the vale and mountain tremble at the thought
> From him you'll not escape by running!
>   submit like head-bowed lover and you're saved.
> You will live on in blissful safety
>   once you are joined to his eternal realm
>
> Run away from all this talk, run sixty leagues,
>   you're at sixes and sevens in talk's trap

Notes

Poem 12 and poem 13 show how Rumi reused themes and lines in various poems on different occasions. D 3153 and D 3154 both begin with the same line and use the same theme, but develop in different ways.

Poem 13   *Z-avval-e bâmdâd sar masti*
D 3154 Meter: ˘ ˘ - - ˘ - ˘ - - - (*khafif*)

> Top of the morning, you're already smashed
>   oh yes you are! you tied your turban crooked.
> Today your eyes look shot, all glazed over
>   I think you drank a hundred proof last night
> Light of our lives and light of our hearts!
>   Salutations to you! How are you feeling?

You imbibed and traveled to the heavens
   got yourself sotted and broke all bonds
      The face of reason always freezes hearts,
        The face of love turns all heads giddy
You got sotted, started wrestling lions
   wine-suckled, rode bareback on a lion's neck
Like an old shaykh the aged wine guided you
   Go now, freed from the ancient spinning wheel.

Sâqi, you hold truth and justice on your side
   refusing worship to all things but wine
You've borne away our reason,
but this time carry us away
like we'll never go again

Notes

The Sâqi is the cupbearer, the one who pours out the wine. Frequently conceived as an androgyne in Persian ghazal poetry, s/he befriends the poet in his woes and sometimes imparts ancient wisdom. Wine and the cupbearer were associated with the royal traditions of ancient Iran and with Zoroastrianism, and so represent a kind of pagan wisdom that is at once blasphemous to orthodoxy and releases the poet to see new horizons.

Poem 14   *Morde bodam zende shodam gerye bodam khande shodam*
D 1393 Meter: - ˇ ˇ - - ˇ ˇ - - ˇ ˇ - - ˇ ˇ - (*sari^c*)

I was dead, came back to life
I wept, began to laugh
Love's force came over me
Fortune smiled on me forever
My eye has seen its fill
my spirit feels no fear
I have a lion's gall
I'm luminous as Venus!
        You are not mad, he said
        You are not fit for this home
I went mad, was bound by chains

        You are not drunk, he said
        You don't belong among us, go
I went and got drunk, stuffed with joy

        You are not slain, he said
        You are not buried in joy
Before his vivifying face I fell down, dead

You are too clever by half, he said
drunk with doubt and fantasy
I got deceived, stunned, cut off from all

You glow like a candle, he said
the focus of our common adoration
I'm not together
I'm no candle
I'm dispersed like wisps of smoke

You're a shaykh and guide, he said
Go ahead and lead the way
I'm no shaykh
am not ahead
I am slave to your command

You have wings and feathers, he said
I need not give you means of flight
In yearning for his wings and feathers
I am clipped and plucked

New-found fortune told me:
Do not go away, do not take offense
for I am coming towards you
out of grace and kindness
Old love said to me:
Do not leave my side
Alright, I won't, I said
I've become grounded, abiding

You are the source of the rays of the sun
I am the shade beneath the willow tree
The radiant spirit touched and cleft my heart,
opened it, my heart. It spun a fresh silk,
my heart, made me enemy to these rags
In bliss the soul's form boasted on at dawn:
I was slave and bondsmen
I've become king and lord!
Paper I touch to write you cries sweet thanks
for it feels your endless sugar in me.
Base earth gives thanks for heaven's bowl inverted
that light rains through its turning apertures
Heaven's wheel thanks angels, king, dominion –
through His gifts and grace I'm brightness, bounty!
God's gnostic gives his thanks for eminence:
"a star above the seven spheres, I shine"

351

I was Venus, I am the moon
   I become celestial wheel
        with countless levels
I was Joseph, and now I engender Josephs

You've made me, brightest moon!
   Gaze into me and in yourself
for the traces of your smile
   have turned me to a field of laughing blossoms

Like a chess game
Be in motion
silent but expressive
For in castling with the world King
   how regal and auspicious
      I have become!

Notes

Joseph, of course, refers to the Biblical and Koranic Joseph, cast by his brothers into a well because he had received from his father a colored cloak, a token that he was his father's pride and joy. He is the ideal object of beauty in the Koran, who rebuffs unchaste advances from the Pharaoh's wife. The scent of Joseph's shirt and Joseph in the well are common motifs in Persian poetry.

Poem 15   *Bâz âmadam bâz âmadam az pish-e ân yâr âmadam*
D 1390 Meter: - - ˇ - - - - ˇ - - - ˇ - - - - - (*rajaz*)

Here I come again,
again I come from the Friend
Look at me, look at me,
I've come to look after you
I come in joy, rejoiced,
I come freed from all

   Several thousand years went by
   before I found the words:
I ascend, ascend
I dwelt up there, am heading there

Let me go again, again,
    I am at a loss here:
I was a divine bird
    see now how worldly mired I am
    I didn't see the trap
    and suddenly
        came up caught in it

I am pure light, my son,
not just a fistful of clay
The shell is not me
I came as the royal pearl within

Look at me
        not with outward eye
        but with inward heart;
Follow me there and see
        how unencumbered we become

I am
        above the four mothers
and I am
        above the seven fathers
I am
        the lodestar jewel
        come from the ore
            to be revealed

My beloved struts through the bazaar
        discerning, quick
to buy me out
or else what business
could I have at all
to be on the market
        – I come in search of him.

Shams-e Tabriz
        Won't you search me out,
        comb the earth, end to end?
            for I have criss-crossed
                    heart-sore
                and soul-sick
                through the sands
                of effacement

Notes

The "four mothers" alludes to the four constituent elements of antiquity: water, earth, fire and air. The "seven fathers" alludes to the seven stages or levels into which it was traditionally believed the heavens of the firmament were divided.

Poem 16   *Ayâ yâri ke dar to nâ-padid-am*
D 1507 Meter: ⌣ - - - ⌣ - - - ⌣ - - (*hazaj*)

> O Friend!
>> you who are invisible within me!
>>> I dreamt I saw you in wondrous forms.
>>>> Like the ladies of Egypt in their love for Joseph
>>>>> I cut citrons, lost control and cut my hand
>>>>>> Where has that moon gone?
>>>>>> Where those eyes of last night?
>>>>>> Where those ears that really heard me?
>>>>>>> Nowhere to be found:
>>>>>>>> not you
>>>>>>>> not me
>>>>>>>> not that moment
>>>>>>>> not those teeth that nipped my lips
>>>>>>> I am a silo brimming with melancholia
>>>>>>> for I reaped melancholy
>>>>>>>> after melancholy
>>>>>>>>> from that tillage
>>>>>>> You calm the hearts of the melancholic
>>>>>>> You are my Zu al-Nun, my Jonayd, my Bâyazid!

Notes

Zu (Dhû) al-Nun, Jonayd and Bâyazid were famous Sufis, often referred to as exemplary models of various aspects of the mystical path.

Poem 17   *Nagoftam-at marow ânjâ ke âshnâ-t manam*
D 1725 Meter: ⌣ - ⌣ - ⌣ ⌣ - - ⌣ - ⌣ - ⌣ ⌣ - (*mojtass*)

> Didn't I tell you:
>> "Don't go over there, for I am the one who knows you;
>> In this mirage of annihilation,
>> I am your source of life;
>> and if in anger for a million years
>>> you run from me, in the end you will return to me
>>>> for I am your destination."

Didn't I tell you:
   "Don't be content with the outer scheme
             and semblance of the world,
  for I am the architect
    of your pavilion of contentment."
Didn't I tell you:
   "I am the sea and you are just a fish in me;
  don't go on the dry and sandy beach
    for I am your liquid purity."
Didn't I tell you:
   "Don't step into a trap just like a bird.
  Come to me, for I am your wings and feathers
   and your power of flight."
Didn't I tell you:
   "They will rob you and leave you cold,
   for I am your hearth and fire."
Didn't I tell you:
   "They will fill you with ugly attributes
  so that you will lose your way to me,
    your fountain of sanctity."
Didn't I tell you:
   "Don't say how or from which quarter
    your affairs will be arranged;
      I create you out of nowhere and of nothing.
   If you are the lamp of hearts,
     know which way leads homeward.
  And if you have the qualities of a lord,
     know that I
        am
       your
     Overlord."

Poem 18   *Ah che bi rang o bi neshân ke manam*
D 1759 Meter: - ⌣ - - ⌣ - ⌣ - ⌣ ⌣ - (*khafif*)

Oh, how colorless
  and formless
       I am!
When will I ever see
  the am that I am?

You said:
 The secrets that you know, bring forth, put out, talk up!

Where is up
  or forth
 within this middle
   that I am?
When will my soul be still?
  It moves when motionless,
   the anima I am.
My sea has drowned within itself;
  what a strange and shoreless sea
    I am!

Not in this world
not in the next
  should you seek me out;
  both this and that have vanished
  in the world I am.
Like non-existence
  nothing profits me
  and nothing harms;
what a wondrous useless-harmless thing
   I am!

I said
  Friend, you are just like me!
He said
  How can you speak of likeness to
 the obviousness I am?
I said
  That's it, that's what you are!
He said
  Silence! No tongue has ever uttered
   what I am.
I said
  Since no tongue has given voice to you,
   Here I am! your unutterable exposition.
  In annihilation
   I became
    inconstant
   like the moon
  Now here I am! your sure-footed, footless runner.

A call arose
> Why do you run?
>> Look to see how manifestly hidden
>>> that I am
When I saw Shams-e Tabriz
> I became.
Now what a wondrous treasure-mine
and sea of pearls I am!

Poem 19   *Har ke az halqe-ye mâ jâ-ye degar bogrizad*
D 794 Meter: - ‿ - - ‿‿ - - ‿‿ - - ‿‿ - *(ramal makhbun)*

Whoever leaves our circle for another place
> might as well relinquish sense of sight and sound
A lover licks his liver's blood, lion-like;
> what lion-heart would shrink from love and guts?
Hearts suck up cruelty from heart-throbs like cubes of sugar;
> did you ever see a parrot turn from sugar?
It's a small gnat that turns at every headwind
> Only stealthy thieves scatter in moonlight.

Any head that the Lord strikes dumb or scrambles
> drops its place in heaven and heads for hellfire.
And he who fathoms death leaps to welcome death
> rushes for the robe, crown and realm eternal.
Fate decrees that so-and-so will die abroad
> and fear of the reaper spurs him from his home
Enough of stalking such unbecoming prey!
> for the night and its phantoms flee from the dawn.

Notes

The beloved is frequently compared to moonlight, so it is only thieves who would run from the presence of the beloved. "Fear of the reaper spurs him" alludes to a famous hadith: When God wants to seize one of His servants from a certain place on earth, He makes it necessary for that servant to go there. Rumi tells a tale about this in the *Masnavi*.

Poem 20   *Be man negar be do rokhsâr-e zaʿfarâni-ye man*
D 2077 Meter: ⌣ - ⌣ - ⌣ ⌣ - - ⌣ - ⌣ - ⌣ ⌣ - (*mojtass*)

Look at me –
these two cheeks
saffron-stained,
the worldly
multi-hued
signs of me,
and my soul,
ancient, wise,
set within
this, my frame –
    may my youth
    be as dust
    at its feet –
Look sharp now,
through my eyes –
    Do not let
    my seeming
    heartsomeness
    steal away
    with your heart.
These, my lips,
and once kissed
by their fate,
crunched out words
so sweet that
sugar blanched.
Ears will hear
the surface
of my words,
unpierced by
my soulful
thundering ...

What fires rage
in this world
from my breath,
forevers
bubble up
immortal
from my words,
evanesced?
Gazing on
Shams, the sun
    and the pride
    of Tabriz,
what was it
I saw that
set all these,
    my meanings,
in motion?

358

Poem 21 *Âb-e hayât-e ʿeshq râ dar rag-e mâ ravâne kon*
D 1821 Meter: - ◡ ◡ - ◡ - ◡ - - - ◡ - ◡ - ◡ - (*rajaz*)

Infuse our veins with love's aqua vitae
show us dark nocturne reflections
of the morning's draught
Father of fresh joys, course quick through our veins!
Like the magic grail
brim up both worlds, reveal the heavens
You who stalk my wits
who live by firing arrows
pinch my heartfeathers taut on to your string
raise your arms and take my life as target

    If reason's watchman blocks your path and plan
    Strategize, devise excuse, escape him
       Does the proverb go that piebalds know no generosity?
       talk tales of piebald grace and all believe
    The stars have played you like a pawn –
    made you march about, checkmated you
    Choose a knight, storm the castle, charge the king
    Get up, set your cap askance, avoid all traps
    Kiss the cheeks of spirit, comb the locks of joy
    Climb the heavens, get acquainted with the angels
    Reach the court of righteousness
       and bow in service to its threshold

Once his dreamy image makes your heart its haunt
Dwell phantomlike in heart and mind:
you'll see two tubs,
one full of fire and one of gold
choose the fire and plunge your hand right in
Be like him who spoke with God:
    Do not covet the golden tub
Take the fire into your mouth
turn the land into a tongue of fire
Tame the feral lions
make enemies your intimates
Call the foe's blood Magian wine
Come, Sâqi!
    We call on you to ward away dualities
    Put one strong shot in my palm
    and unite all multiplicities in one

It's true, this home, our world,
extends in six directions
yet just one point will orient us
since that focal point of adoration
has no homeland,
build your nest in nothingness
Time's a relicker, wearing all things out
for immortality don't look to it.
Everlasting life's above, beyond time's span
You are what's winnowed: the wheat
the body's so much straw
    unless you're an ass
    you don't munch on straw
    pick the meat and kernel

      The word is out
      why knock on the door?
      Knock down the door
        by your spirit
      set out for the psyche

Notes

Magian wine: see the note about Zoroastrianism in poem 13.

Poem 22   *Motreb-e mahtâb-ru ânche shenidi begu*
D 2245 Meter: - ˇ - - ˇ - - ˇ - - ˇ - (*monsareh*)

      Musician, bright of mien!
Tell us, what was it that you heard?
      Here you are among friends and you can
Tell us everything you saw.
      Our king and crown
      our realm of joy!
      Within the sanctum
      of the one who animates us
Tell us, what did you come across?
      The languid drunken eyes
      of one whose company God keeps?
      Last night in his bed of roses,
      what was it that you picked?
Tell us!

You slipped through my clutches
I lost hold of my tipsy heart
You who have seen it all
which one
tell us, did you choose?

The seasons come and go
but your festival
goes on and on forever
How in the world
did you escape unaided
from heaven's inexorable turning wheel?
Tell us!

I sank, sugar,
In the soul's fields of cane
Tell us if you tasted of its sweets
Wine pulls me left
heart pulls me right
What a pleasant pushing–pulling!
Tell us what repelled or pulled you?

You brim the goblet up with wine
disturb the peace, inciting riot
Tell us, how did you get the key to tavern doors?
Ferment of our tavern
radiance of our prayers
you who strip naked our desires,
tell us!

The moon in the sky
darkens, debased by clouds
You, orb untouched, beyond the clouds
tell us!

May your shade forever shelter us,
may your moon always beam bright,
may the wheel of heaven heed your wishes;
Tell us what has made you bolt and shy away?

Love asked
how did you fall for me in love last night?
I said
Don't beat around the question *how*,
what tapestry is this you've woven?
Tell us!

I was cautious
ascetic, a man at war with sin
My wholesome happiness!
why like a bird do you fly away
tell us

Poem 23   The Reed's Song
Beshnow in nay chun shekâyat mikonad
ME 1:1–34 Meter: - ˘ - - - ˘ - - - ˘ - (*ramal*)

Listen
as this reed
pipes its plaint
unfolds its tale
of separations:
Cut from my reedy bed,
my crying
ever since
makes men and women
weep
I like to keep my breast
carved with loss
to convey
the pain of longing –
Once severed
from the root,
thirst for union
with the source
endures
I raise my plaint
in any kind of crowd
in front of both
the blessed and the bad
For what they think they hear me say, they love me –
None gaze in me my secrets to discern
My secret is not separate from my cry
But ears and eyes lack light to see it.

Not soul from flesh
nor flesh from soul are veiled,
yet none is granted leave to see the soul.
Fire, not breath, makes music through that pipe –
    Let all who lack that fire be blown away.
It is love's fire that inspires the reed
    It's love's ferment that bubbles in the wine
The reed, soother to all sundered lovers –
its piercing modes reveal our hidden pain:
    (What's like the reed, both poison and physic,
    Soothing as it pines and yearns away?)
The reed tells the tale of a blood-stained quest
singing legends of love's mad obsessions

Only the swooning know such awareness
only the ear can comprehend the tongue

    In our sadness time slides listlessly by
    the days searing inside us as they pass.

But so what if the days may slip away?
so long as you, Uniquely Pure, abide.

    Within this sea drown all who drink but fish
    If lived by bread alone, the day seems long
    No raw soul ever kens the cooked one's state
    So let talk of it be brief; go in peace.

    Break off your chains
    My son, be free!
    How long enslaved
    by silver, gold?
    Pour the ocean
    in a pitcher,
    can it hold more
    than one day's store?
    The jug, like a greedy eye,
    never gets its fill
    only the contented oyster holds the pearl

The one run ragged by love and haggard
gets purged of all his faults and greeds
Welcome, Love!
sweet salutary suffering
and healer of our maladies!

cure of our pride
of our conceits,
Our Plato
Our Galen!
By Love
our earthly flesh
   borne to heaven
our mountains
   made supple
     moved to dance

Love moved Mount Sinai, my love,
and it made Moses swoon.   [K7:143]

Let me just touch those harmonious lips
and I, reed-like, will tell what may be told

A man may know a myriad of songs
but cut from those who know his tongue, he's dumb.
Once the rose wilts and the garden fades
the nightingale will no more sing his tune.

The Beloved is everything – the lover, a veil
The Beloved's alive – the lover carrion.
Unsuccored by Love, the poor lover is
a plucked bird
Without the Beloved's
surrounding illumination
how perceive what's ahead
and what's gone by?

Love commands these words appear;
if no mirror reflects them
in whom lies the fault?
The dross obscures your face
and makes your mirror
unable to reflect

Poem 24 *In khâne ke payvaste dar u bâng-e chaghâna-st*
D 332 Meter: - - ◡ ◡ - - ◡ ◡ - - ◡ ◡ - - (*hazaj akhrab makfuf*)

This house where the lute strings constantly strum –
   ask its lord
to whom does this house belong?
If this is the house of the Kaaba

364

how can it be so full of icons?
If this house is a Magian fane
how can the light of God be shining here?
There's a treasure in this house
too great for galaxies to hold

"House" and "lord"
are just a play, divertimento
Don't touch the House –
    this house is talisman
Don't speak to the lord –
    he's drunk all night

Musk and fragrance, the dust and thistles of this house
Verse and melody, the cries arising from this house
To sum up
he who gains entry to this house is
Sultan of the earth
Solomon of the age
My lord, kindly look down here
from your perch upon the parapet
for those soft cheeks
are touched by
constant fortune's kiss
By your life!
all else but the vision of your face –
                even ownership of earth –
to me is so much hocus pocus

The rose bower, baffled
wonders: what petals, what blossoms, these?
The birds, bewitched
twitter: what bait, what trap is this?

This is the lord of the sphere:
    an orb like the Moon or Venus
and this is the house of love:
    boundless, uncontained

Like a mirror to the soul
your visage fills the heart
the heart, like the comb
tangles in your tress

In the presence of Joseph –
    there where the ladies cut their hands
meet me, love
for my soul's somewhere in that space
All the house is drunk:
none knows what gives
nor wares who comes and goes

    Well, don't sit there on the doorstep –
    it's an omen that invites an ill
    come, quickly, in the house
        He who stands at thresholds
        darkens doorsteps

    God's drunkards, though a multitude
    are no more than one
    while the passion-drunk
    are dualist, trinitarian

    Charge into the lion's thicket
    unafraid of mauling
        for fearful thoughts
        are a sissy's plague
    Love and mercy –
    and not mauling
    await you there
        But standing outside the door
        your suppositions
        bar you like a bolt

Don't set fire to this thicket
be silent, heart!
hold your tongue
for your tongue
is a lick of flame.

Poem 25   *Ay bokhâri râ to jân pendâshte*
D 2382 Meter: - ˘ - -   - ˘ - -   - ˘ - (*ramal*)

    You who
    supposed steam
    to be spirit
    mistook gold druck
    for mine lode

You who
sink in the earth like Korah
believing earth to be sky
You who
looked on puppet plays of demons
and mistook them for humans
You from whom
for loathsomeness
love recoils
though you suppose
yourself involved
You
eyes teared
with pagan soot
imagining soot
shining light
You
like a worm
squirming
in lust's filth
supposing
lovers act the same.
Lust drunkenness – the curse's mark,
You who
confuse the Traceless
with a common mark
You
rotted amid words and sounds
You who
suppose God tongueless, dumb
The moon beams down
on your blind lunacy
You who
imagine the moon eclipsed

    All I have said
  I address to myself,
       you who
have assumed
like all the others

Notes

As a preacher and respected teacher, Rumi could easily lull his audience into thinking that he was giving them directives. In the end of this poem, though, he fools them by directing his words at himself.

Poem 26 *Zahi levâ va ʿalam lâ elâha ella llâh*
D 2407 Meter: ⏑ - ⏑ - ⏑ ⏑ - - ⏑ - ⏑ - ⏑⏑ - (*mojtass*)

What a banner, what a standard: There is no God but God!
raised on the pinnacle of pre-existence: There is no God but God!
How the King, like Moses, raises dust
from the sea of being and the void! There is no God but God!
The quality of purity's
a product of humility
that he showed Him in pre-eternity
There is no God but God!

One wrong from him bests a billion rights
What wondrous, pleasant tyranny!
There is no God but God!

Every spot he casts his glance
a million Eden-gardens grow
There is no God but God!

One fine day from sorrow's sea
I'll reach the shore
by waves of grace and bounty buoyed
There is no God but God!

Any one you see in sorrow's grip
has caught no scent
of spirit from my King
There is no God but God!

Since no collyrium can clear my eyes
of the King of Tabriz
What wondrous loss and lamentation: There is no God but God!
My heart and soul surge with the shout:
"Are you not?"
The King hears a thousand voices: Yes! There is no God but God!

The paradise of grace
the greatness of the prince
   Shams al-Din
What a wondrous cure of suffering: There is no God but God!
My heart circles
like an intimate
around Tabriz,
the sanctum sanctorum of   There is no God but God!
How pleasant would it be to say:
   Who is it at the door?
and hear him say: It's me.   There is no God but God!

Notes

"There is no God but God" is, of course, one of the most common phrases heard in an Islamic context; it is repeated five times a day from the minaret in the call to prayers. It is also used by many Sufis as a *zekr*, a mantra to concentrate their meditation.

Poem 27   *Ay Yusof-e khwosh nâm-e mâ khwosh mi-ravi bar bâm-e mâ*
D 4 Meter: - - ˘ - - - ˘ - - - ˘ - - - ˘ - (*rajaz*)

O Joseph (sweet the name!)
   is that you walking sweetly overhead
      along the roof?

Shatterer of my chalice
   Destroyer of my traps
      my light, my trumpet
         my victorious fortune!
           Stir up my ferment
              that my grapes may wine.

Thief of my heart and
   my highest aspiration
      where I turn to worship
         object of my adoration
           my friend, my defrauder
              seducer of my drunken heart!
                Don't kick the legs out from under me
                  Take my turban as my earnest

My heart got stuck in mud
up to its ankles
But I'd trade my life,
not just my heart
how the lovesick heart does burn!
So much for it,
so much for me!

Poem 28   *Man gholâm-e qamar-am ghayr-e qamar hich magu*
D 2219 Meter: - ‿ - -　‿ ‿ - -　‿ ‿ - -　‿ ‿ - (*ramal makhbun*)

I serve that orb in heaven,
say no word but Orb!
speak to me of nothing
but sweetness and light
Not of bother, but of treasure
and if you cannot find the words
don't bother.

Yesterday a craze came over me
Love saw, came up to me:
Here I am,
don't shout,
don't rip your shirt,
hush, shh!
I spoke:
Love, I'm scared of that other thing
There is no other thing, say nothing!
I will whisper secrets in your ear
you just nod in asseveration
speak in semaphore

A nova, a celestial love
burst bright above the heartpath
so exquisite the quest of heart,
it cannot be expressed
I asked:
Heart, what orb is this?
heart intimated:
beyond fathom
be quiet, forget!
Is this the face of man or angel?
Beyond men and angels
hush!

What is it!? Tell me, I'm in a whirl
        Whirl on, keep quiet!
        You sit within this room
        whose walls reflect
        mere forms and suppositions
        Get up, go out, move on,
        keep quiet!
I said:
Heart, befather me,
for doesn't this match God's description?
        Yes, my son, it does,
        but do not tell.

Notes

I have used "orb" throughout these translations to render what is literally "moon" (*mâh, qamar*). This is the shining visage of the beloved, beside which all other thoughts and images pale. Unfortunately, in English "moon face" does not have a very happy connotation.

Poem 29   Moses Rebukes the Shepherd, God Rebukes Moses
Did Musâ yek shobâni râ be râh
ME 2:1724–64 Meter: - ˘ - - - ˘ - - - ˘ - (*ramal*)

Moses saw a shepherd on the road
who kept crying out: O God, O Lord
    Where do I find you, that I might serve –
    sew your moccasins, and comb your hair
    wash your clothes for you, and kill your lice
    bring milk for you, O Lord Majestic!
    Kiss your little hands and rub your feet
    and at bed time sweep your place to sleep!
    May my goats all be your sacrifice,
    in whose name I call my hoes and hies

Hearing shepherd voice his silly hopes
    "Who's that you're talking with?" posed Moses
"With the One who fashioned us" said he
"Made the earth and heavens come to be"
    "Whoa," said Moses, "Wretched is your state!
    What Islam or blasphemy is that?
    Total nonsense, what delusions, false!
    Stuff and stop your mouth with cotton coarse!

You fill the world with stench of blaspheme
and tear faith's silken garb to tatters.
Fit for you are boots and moccasins,
but seemly for the Sun? Are such things?!
If you do not bite your lip and tongue,
flames will fill the world, all creatures singe"

Though no flames fell, why this blackish soot?
Spirits dark as coal and damned our souls?
Certain as you are that God is Judge,
How can you buy impudence and mud?
Unwise friendship is an enmity
God on high such service does not need
You speak like this with aunt and uncle –
God's grandeur needs no ease and comfort
Only sucklings – growing boys – drink milk
Only bare feet are for slippers fit.
You will say, but what of this, God's word:
   My servant is Me and I am him
   I fell ill you did not visit me
   It offended me and not just him
Even for such servants as they say:
   through Me he hears and sees
it's nonsense!
Don't speak rudely with the men of God
it dulls your heart, turns your pages black
If you call some man by "Fâteme"
though men and women are one specie
though this man's a calm one and serene
he'll try to slit your throat

To a woman "Fâteme" is praise
to a man this cuts him like a knife
Hand and foot in our respect may fit
It's – respecting God's transcendence – spit!
He's "He neither gives birth nor was born"   [K112:3]
He creates both mother and her son
We speak of birth for forms corporal
birth flows through our world material
formed of composition and decay
contingent on a Primal Mover.

372

Said the shepherd – Moses, you sewed shut
  my mouth and my soul scorched with regret
His cloak he rent, a hot sigh unleashed
his head into the desert bowed and left

Revelation came from God to Moses:
  You've torn My servant from My presence
  Were you sent in order to unite
  or to distinguish and divide?
  Avoid if you can separation
  "More hateful still to Me, estrangement"
  I to all their qualities assign
  and give a form to their expression
  What to some is praise, to you is blame
  What's honey to his taste, your poison
  Above pure/impure I'm sanctified
  far above all suave- and boorish-ness
  I command My servants worship Me
  not for My profit, but to bless them:
  Hindus praise Me in the Hindu tongue
  Sindis praise Me in the Sindi tongue
  I'm not made pure by their remembrance
  but pure, full of pearls, do they become
  We've no regard for words or language
  We look for spirit and behavior
  We see the heart and if that's humble
  ignore the words used, brash or mumbled

Notes

This passage occurs in Nicholson's edition at M2:1720–59. The story continues with God further reproaching Moses and Moses then chasing into the desert after the shepherd. He tells the shepherd that God has granted him permission to praise him in whatever way his heart desires: the rites and modes of praise are not important. It becomes evident, however, that the shepherd's suffering on account of the rebuke of Moses has elevated him to the next plane of spiritual development. This story was not new to Rumi; he probably adapted it from one of the versions appearing in *'Eqd al-farid, Sharh-e Nahj al-balâghe, 'Oyun al-akhbâr, Helyat al-owliâ* or elsewhere.

The phrases indented, "My servant is Me ...," etc., are taken from a hadith, or saying ascribed to the Prophet Mohammad. On the Day of Resurrection God will say to his servants, I was ill and you did not come to visit Me. The servant will reply, "But You have no body, how could I visit You?" God will answer that visiting people who are sick is in effect a visitation of God.

The phrase "More hateful to me is estrangement" is also a hadith. Fâteme is an Arabic name for girls, and the name of Mohammad's daughter. Each line of the English version here measures nine syllables.

Poem 30   Solomon Speaking the Language of the Birds
Chun Solaymân râ sarâparde zadand
ME1:1210–42 Meter: ‑ ˘ ‑ ‑ ‑ ˘ ‑ ‑ ‑ ˘ ‑ (*ramal*)

When Solomon's royal pavilion was pitched   [K27:15ff., 27:20]
all fowl came before him out of respect
They found he spoke their tongue and understood
One by one with zeal each hastened to his feet
Each bird departed from him all atwitter –
simpatico, a confidant and brother

Sharing the same tongue makes for ties and bonds
Talk with strangers feels like you're gagged and bound
Turk and Hindu might share good conversation
where two Turks might sense alienation.
The talk of intimates, then, is special,
Better be like-minded than like-worded
Beyond all speech, use of signs and gesture,
the heart knows many modes for meanings' transfer

Each bird told its secret arts and knowledge
boasting for Solomon of its powers
The turn came for the Hoopoe to explain
its talents, crafts and industries and thoughts
It said, "Shall I reveal a minor art
my king – keeping 'brevity is best' in mind?"
The king said, "Tell me what that art would be."
"When I soar over all, I downward gaze
from on those heights with sharp eyes, sure of sight;
On the ground I see water in the wells –
where it is, how deep and of what color,
why it springs up, whether from soil or stone.
O Solomon, keep this always in mind
as your armies march and camp in fields afar."
Then Solomon replied, "My good true friend,
in wastelands where deep water's wanting
perhaps you'll locate water for the army,
and quench your fellows' thirst along the way."

The Raven heard, came forward, full of envy
and said to Solomon, "His words deceive.
Talk before the king's a breach of etiquette,
especially false and foundless boasting.
Had he the constant power of sight he claims
How did he overlook the buried trap?
How did this trap, then, take him captive?
Why unfulfilled he sits inside a cage?"

Then Solomon demanded of the Hoopoe,
"At my first taste of wine poured from your hands
is it fitting that dregs should fill my mouth?
Why do you feign from milk inebriation;
in our presence, lie about your powers?"
He said, "O King, I'm but a naked beggar,
I beg, for God's sake, please don't heed my foe!
If the claims I make may seem invalid
I submit my neck to you, behead me.
  The crow denies divine decree, so he's
  a heretic, though his intellect's immense.
I do see traps from in the air, unless
divine decree cloaks my sight and reason.
In the face of God's decree, knowledge fades;
shadows blacken the moon, eclipse the sun.
  Such does divine decree become deployed:
  It's God's decree the crow deny decree.

Notes

The story occurs in Nicholson's edition at M1:1202–33.

Poem 31   The Parrot and the Oil
Bud baqqâl-i vo vay râ tuti²i
ME1: 248–66 Meter: - ˘ - - - ˘ - - - ˘ - (*ramal*)

Once there was this grocer with his parrot;
This parrot, green and sweet-of-speech, could talk.
It stayed at the shop, kept watch at the door,
trading with customers witty banter.
In human converse he was eloquent,
and in parrot twitter he was expert.

One day, startled, he fluttered cross the shop,
the bottles of rose oil overturning.
His master came from home to open shop
and sat down as an owner will, at leisure.
Finding the shop oiled and his garb soiled,
he smote the parrot's head, spilling feathers.

For several days the bird withheld from speech
and the grocer from regret let out a sigh.
He plucked his beard hairs, calling out "Alas!
I've lost my lucky sun behind the fog.
Better that the hand I raised had broken
than have it smite that sweet-tongued parrot's head!"
He gave alms awhile to every dervish
in hopes his bird might rediscover speech.

After three days and nights of misery
sitting at the shop perplexed, forlorn,
showing the bird all kinds of baubles,
perchance to coax him back again to words,
there passed a mendicant in sack-cloth dressed
feet unshod, head shaven shiny of its hair.
The parrot opened up its mouth again
and called out like a heckler to this dervish:
"So what made you, Baldy, join the hairless?
Been busy overturning bottles of oil?"
At this assumption all burst out in laughter –
    the bird supposed the pious monk like him!

    Don't suppose the pure your mirror image,
    Though it's true ewe and you may sound the same;
    The whole world's gone astray for just this reason:
        So few can recognize the saints of God.
    Folks compare their own selves to the prophets,
    and take God's saints for mortals, just like them.

Notes

The story occurs in Nicholson's edition at M1:247–65.

Poem 32   *Delâ nazd-e kasi benshin ke u az del khabar dârad*
D 563 Meter: ˘ - - - ˘ - - - ˘ - - - ˘ - - - (*hazaj*)

Heart,
sit at the foot of one who knows his hearts
rest beneath the tree whose boughs bud fresh
Don't wander all around the market of perfumes
sit in the stall of him who has a stash of sugar
You'll be fleeced by every seller –
without a scale to take their measure
you'll mistake the gilded slug for golden tender
They'll make you sit inside the shop
sweetly promising "Just one moment, please"
Don't sit there waiting,
there's another door goes out the back
Don't wait with bowl in hand for every pot to boil
what stews in every pot is not the same.
Not every cane-cut pen drips with sugar
not every under has above
not every eye's possessed of vision
not every sea conceals a pearl

Sing your little heart out, nightingale
for your famed intoxicated lamentation
echoes and transmutes the stony hills and granite boulders
If your head cannot contain you – lose it
you can't pass through the needle's eye a knotty thread
The awakened heart's a lamp
cloak it from contrary airs beneath your mantle
for the windy air will do it harm.
Pass beyond the winds and reach the spring
become a secret confidant, welling with emotion
   and then like a green tree you will swell with sap
   and come to fruition as it courses through your heart

Poem 33   *Andak andak jamᶜ-e mastân miresand*
D 819 Meter: - ˘ - - - ˘ - - - ˘ - (*ramal*)

Here a few, there a few
the drunkards all show up
the worshipers of wine
one by one turn up

along the way, heartmelters
all along they flow and flirt
smooth and pink-cheeked boys
arriving from the rose bowers
Little by little
in the world's egress–regress
beings come and nothings go
pockets all loaded up
like mines with gold
they come to visit those of empty-hand

You gaunt and battle-wearied of love's pastures!
Here come the hale and fattened up reserves
The pure of soul like beams of sun
shine from up above on earthly ones
Blessed the garden as it bears
fresh fruits in winter
for all the Marys
   Kindness their origin
   and to kindness they return
   coming from rose bower to
   to a bower of rose

Notes

The poem conjures up an initiatory ritual of some sort, fasting or serving in the Mevlevi kitchen perhaps. The initiates would typically be young adolescent boys, who are thus cast in a role similar to that of the Hellenistic ephebe.

Poem 34   *Suye atfâl bi-âmad be-karam mâdar-e ruze*
D 2375 Meter: - ⌣ - -   ⌣ ⌣ - -   ⌣ ⌣ - -   ⌣ ⌣ - - (*ramal makhbun*)

The Mother of fasting
comes to her children
bearing gifts
Don't let slip your hold
my child, from the hem
of the châdor of fasting
Look into her gentle face
drink her succulent milk
Make your homeland here
Sit down right here
at the door of fasting

See how the contented hand
becomes verdant before God!
See the Eden of the soul
drenched with the daffodils of fasting!

Why so carefree and smiling, Rosebud
when you're drenched in blood?
Could you be
the Isaac of God's Abraham
delighted by the dagger of fasting?

Why so in love with bread?
see the world baked afresh
Take the wheat of spirit
Watch out for the harvest of fasting

Notes

Châdor, literally "tent," is the cloth with which women in Iran cover their hair and bodies when in the presence of men to whom they are not related by blood or marriage.

Poem 35 *Bar band dahân az nân k-âmad shekar-e ruze*
D 2307 Meter: - - ᴗ ᴗ - - - - - - ᴗ ᴗ - - - - (*hazaj akhrab sâlem*)

Close your mouth to bread
for here comes the sugar of the fast
You've seen the arts of eating,
now look to the art of the fast
That king will crown your head
with two hundred realms
Hurry up and buckle on
the belt of the fast

Fly up from the dungeon world
to the heights
Acquire a God's-eye view
with the eyes of the fast
You majestic silver
all this while in a vat
the fire will serve you
in the sparks of the fast
Fasting is the moisture in the Zamzam well
It entered Jesus of Mary
and he reached the peak

of the fourth heaven
in the journey of the fast
The wings of birds
are strengthened by the seeds they eat
the wings of the angels fly with fasting

If the fast is hard,
yet it has a hundred charms
It has a certain sweetness,
the low blood sugar of the fast

The true fast is a mistress
veiled in her châdor,
don't look at the black cloth
but find the fast beneath it
It makes your neck narrow
It makes you safe from death
Thirty days you flail
upside down and downside up
within this sea
until you reach, my master
the pearl of the fast
With all his schemes and tricks and guile
Satan's every arrow breaks
upon the shield of the fast
Fasting tells of its own charge and feint better
so close the doors of speech
and open them to the door of the fast

You are, Shams al-Haqq of Tabriz,
both patience and abstinence
you pour out sugar on days of festival
as well as the grappling of fasting

Notes

Zamzam is the well in the sacred precincts of the Kaaba in Mecca, said to have been dug by Abraham. Pilgrims consider the water blessed and possessed of curative powers. For *châdor*, see the note to poem 34.

Poem 36 *Khonak ân dam ke neshinim dar ivân man o to*
D 2214 Meter: ⏑ ⏑ – – ⏑ ⏑ – – ⏑ ⏑ – – ⏑ ⏑ – (*ramal makhbun*)

> Bliss –
> the instant
> spent seated
> on the terrace,
> me next to you
> two forms and
> two faces
> with just one soul,
> me and you
>
> The chatter of birds
> the garden's murmur
> flowing
> like a fountain of youth
> as we stroll
> through roses,
> me and you
> The stars of the firmament, bent low to look over us
> Let's eclipse them, shine like the moon,
> me and you
>
> Me and you join,
> beyond Me
> beyond You
> in joy
> happy, released from delire and delusion
> Me and you, laughing like this,
> reach dimensions where celestial birds suck sugary cubes
> Magical! me and you, here,
> in our corner of earth,
> but wafting on airs of Iraq and Khorasan,
> me and you
> In one form here on earth
> in other forms in paradise,
> eternal, sunk in fields of sugar,
> me and you

Notes

The airs of Iraq and Khorasan may allude to musical modes, which might accompany the recitation of the poem. At the same time, Iraq might refer to

Tabriz, the city of Shams, situated in the west of Iran, in a province of the country known as Iranian Iraq, while Rumi came from the northeast of greater Iran, the province of Khorasan.

Poem 37   *Dar havâ-yat biqarâr-am ruz o shab*
D 302 Meter: - ˘ - - - ˘ - - - ˘ - (*ramal*)

> Night and day
> buffeted by fantasies of you
> head planted at your pedestal
> night and day
> Day and night
> I'll keep this up
> until I drive
> the night and day
> to love distraction
>
> lovers put down earnest
> heart and soul
> I make payments day and night
> with heart and soul
> your love plays me
> like a tune
> day and night
> sometimes harpstring, sometimes lyre
> you work me over
> with your plectrum
> day and night
> my high quivering notes
> scale the skies
> you poured out libations
> for all mankind forty-fold
> from that ferment
> I'm sotted night and day
> You drive a train of choke-reined lovers
> I walk in those chains
> Smashed, pulling your weight
> I stagger like a burdened camel
> day and night
>
> Unless I break fast with your sugar
> I'll keep hungry day and night
> until the judgment

My fortune will celebrate a festival
when I break fast at bounty's table
day and night
but the festival befalls us
only once in every year
I'm feted
with your full face
each new moon
night and day

Life of the night
pulse of the day
you animator
me anticipation
night and day
all anticipation
counting hours
day and night
until the tryst day
and the night you promised

He sowed such warmth
in my thirsty soul
I rain down tears
from my cloudy eyes
night and day

Notes

Drive the night and day to distraction: To make them like Majnun, the famous
lover of Layli, who pines away in his love for her, singing poems in the desert
night and day to his friends the animals (his name literally means "possessed,"
but he is proverbial for lovesickness).

Poem 38   *Cho âftâb bar âmad ze qaʿr-e âb-e siâh*
D 2408 Meter: ⌣ - ⌣ -   ⌣ ⌣ - -   ⌣ - ⌣ - <u>⌣ ⌣</u> - *(mojtass)*

Once the sun came out
     from the pit
   of a black well
in each and every beam
   you hear the call:
There is no God but God.
Not sunbeams but soulsun

383

stealing the bright garb
and halo from the sun
When the heart's orb
emerges Adam-like
from clay and water
a hundred suns like Joseph
sink into the well

Lift a head from the dust,
you're not less than an ant
Give tidings to the ants   [K27:18–19]
of fields and crops
Ignorant of our luscious hyacinth
the ant contents itself with rotted grain
Tell the ant:
it's spring, you have hands and feet
why not wend your way from graves to meadows?

Forget those ants of Solomon,
Rend the garments of desire!
For God's sake don't depress me
with such metaphors.
But the tailor cuts the cloth
to fit the customer
my garment's long
but then the customer is short
Bring me one of standing
and we'll cut a cloth so long
that the thread that holds the moon will snap

I'll keep silence from now on
for in my silence
Truth and error separate
just like wheat from chaff

Poem 39   *Ay qowm-e be hajj rafte kojâ'id, kojâ'id*
D 648 Meter: - - ˇ ˇ - - ˇ ˇ - - ˇ ˇ - - (*hazaj akhrab makfuf*)

Pilgrims on the way! where are you?
Here is the beloved, here!
Your beloved lives next door
wall to wall
why do you wander
round and round the desert?

If you look into the face of Love
and not just at its superficial form
You yourselves become the house of God
and are its lords

Ten times
you trod the trek unto that house
For once
come into this house
climb onto this roof
That sweet house of sanctity –
you have described its features in detail
But give me now some indication
of the features of its Lord
If you have seen that garden,
where is your bouquet of souvenirs?
If you are from God's sea,
where is your mother pearl of soul?

And yet, may all your troubles
bring you treasure
What pity that your treasures
lie buried in your selves

Notes

The poem is cast as an apostrophe to Muslims on the long road to the ritual pilgrimage (*hajj*) in Mecca and Medina. In Mecca, the pilgrims circumambulate the Kaaba, a square structure which used to house the idols of the Arabian tribes before Islam, but now is called the "house of God."

Poem 40   *Hilat rahâ kon ʿâsheqâ divâne show divâne show*
D 2131 Meter: - - ˘ - - - ˘ - - - - ˘ - - - - (*rajaz*)

Let go all your scheming, lover
let yourself go mad
go mad
just step into the heart of fire
make yourself a moth
a moth
Turn yourself into a stranger
raze your house down to the ground
then come stand here under one roof
beneath the same roof
and live among the lovers.

Scrape your breast, like a plate,
clean of envy, with cascades of water
then fill up like a chalice,
        like a chalice
with the wine of love
Metamorphose purely into soul
make yourself worthy of the Soulmate
If you're going to see the drunkards
        walk tipsy
        with inebriation
Like a model
your earring pendant dangles
brushing intimate against your cheek
incline that cheek and ear
        to the Mother Pearl
        that Precious Pearl
As your spirit rises in the air
from the sweetness of our tale
efface yourself
and like the lovers be a legend
        legendary
The Night of the Grave is what you are
The Night of Power is what you must become
For the power dwelling in all spirits
        be a nest
        make a home
Your thoughts go traipsing off
and drag you in their wake
With decision cut off all speculation
        be a leader
        stand in front
Desire clings, and lust, like locks upon our heart
become a key and turn like a tumbler
        like a tumbler

With light the Chosen One caressed
that moaning pillar
are you less than that piece of wood?
        cry out
        be empathetic
Though Solomon has told you:
  Listen to the language of the birds

like a trap the birds fly from you
               nestle them
               and be their nest
If that gorgeous idol shows her face
fill up with her like a mirror
if she lets her silky hair down
               become her comb
               and brush her
How long two-headed like a rook?
how long a peon like a pawn?
how long go crooked like a queen?
               be a master of the game
               and mate
Thankfully you've given love
many gifts and wealth
put away your money, give yourself
               be gratitude
               be grateful
For a while you were matter
for a while you were animal
for a while you were soul
               become the soulmate
               meet your soul
How long pace on the roof and vineyard?
Fly, my ratiocinating soul, into the house
Abandon all this rationalizing talk
               Don't wag the jaw
               don't jabber on

Notes

The Night of Power alludes to Surat al-Qadr of the Koran (K97:1–5), traditionally believed to be the night when Revelation came to the Prophet and commemorated in the last week of Ramadan. The Koran says that the angels and the spirit of God descend to bless every endeavor on this night. The Chosen One is Mostafâ, one of the epithets of Mohammad. According to tradition, he used to lean upon a tree trunk in the mosque at Medina as he preached. When a pulpit was constructed, this pillar cried out and is therefore known as the Moaning Pillar (*oston-e hannâne*, literally "the compassionate pillar"), which, even though inanimate, longed to be in the presence of the Prophet. God bestowed on Solomon, the heir of David, the bounty of understanding the speech of birds (*manteq al-tayr*) (K27:16ff.).

Poem 41 *Sibaki nim sorkh o nimi zard*
D 968 Meter: - ⌄ - - ⌄ - ⌄ - ⌣ ⌣ - (*khafif*)

A little apple
half red, half yellow
recalls a tale
of rose and saffron:

    sunder lover from beloved
       cuteness goes with the latter
          pain falls to the former
    Love reveals
    two contrary colors
    in one severance
    on the cheeks of each:
          yellow clashes on kissable cheeks
          red and hale feel cold to lovers' cheeks
When the babe begins to flirt
don't fight it, lover, humor her.

I'm like the thorn, my lord like the rose
Though the two are in reality one
He is the sun and I, then, the shade
From him eternity's heat, from me the cold
    When Goliath came to battle Saul: [K2:247–51]
    "David, measure the chainmail well!"   [K34:11]
The body bears the heart
but the heart rules the body
    just as woman gives birth to man
but within the heart
another heart is hidden
like a rider in a cloud of dust
       (the knight kicks up the dust
        it's him that makes it dance)
It's not like chess
    where you ponder your next move
Be reliant, like in backgammon:
    pray and cast your dice

The heart of the sun
is Shams of Tabriz
    all fruits of the heart
    bask in his warmth and grow

Notes

The lover's complexion should be sallow, for he suffers in his love; the object of his love, however, has a carefree attitude, for he/she can do without the lover. Therefore her cheeks are red and hale; it cannot be otherwise. This suffering of the lover, though, has an ultimate benefit and the lover should submit to it. The next few lines ("I'm like the thorn ... chainmail well") are in Arabic. The quotation from the Koran refers to the story of Saul (Tâlut) and David's battle against Goliath (Jâlut). The Koran says that God instructed David how to make his armor so that he would have victory. Since Saul won his victory by virtue of David, but grew jealous as a result (cf. the Hebrew Bible, 1 Samuel 17), this passage seems to continue the commentary on the unity of lover and beloved, despite their apparent duality. The poem would seem to date from the period after Shams' final disappearance, when Rumi comes to realize that Shams has become part of his own psyche. The reference to reliance, is of course reliance on God. The image is somewhat humorous, though, because of the incongruity of a pious Muslim gambling.

Poem 42   *Man bi-khwod o to bi-khwod mâ râ ki barad khâne*
D 2309 Meter: - - ˇ ˇ - - - - - ˇ ˇ - - - (*hazaj akhrab sâlem*)

> I'm out of my senses and you are smashed —
> who will see us home? I've told you so many times:
>> don't drink so much
>> just two glasses
>> maybe three
> I don't see a single sober soul in town
> each more demented and fermented than the next
>
> Soul of life!
>> come to the ruins
>> and taste the spice of life
>> what savor can the spirit know
>> without the converse of the soul's delight?
>> How can the heart rejoice
>> parted from the one who pumps it?
>
> In every corner lies a drunk
> and on the handle of a goblet
> and here's the Server who affirms our existence
> with her royal chalice.

Your sustenance: in the tavern
your income and expenses: wine
Never trust a sober soul
with a single drop of sustenance

Go on, play your lute
you drunken gypsy!
Who's more sotted, you or I?
I know my magic holds no spell
cast before a drunkard such as you!

> I left my house, a drunk came up to me
> his every look was pregnant
> with a hundred roses, garden bowers
> Like a ship without an anchor
> he wobbled left and bobbled right
> every wise and careful scholar
> nearly died on seeing him

> I asked him: Where are you from?
> He mocked me, saying: My dear
> I'm half from Turkestan
> I'm half from Central Asia
> I'm half clay and water
> I'm half heart and spirit
> half seashore, half precious pearl
> I said: Then, be my companion
> for we are kith and kin!
> He replied: I do not know my kin from strangers

I am heartlorn and unturbaned
hungover in the tavern
My breast swells heavy with a weight of words –
shall I get them off my chest, or no?

> When you walk with cripples
> you have to learn to limp
> I gave you this advice before
> from the sagest source
> have you ignored it?
> What a good little sot you are
> are you denser than a stick of wood?
> For in the end the Moaning Pillar cried:

Sun of Truth from Tabriz!
Now that you have stirred
such ravishing revolt in motion
why do you avoid us?

Notes

"Your sustenance: in the tavern" – the word Rumi uses is *vaqf*, the charitable
endowment set up in perpetuity to fund a mosque or college of law or Sufi
lodge. So, the persona here addressed has a permanent paid position in the
tavern, a place of ill repute in society, except that among the Sufis it is a symbol
of the mystic understanding of religion. The wise and careful scholars nearly die,
either because they pity his condition, or because they fall in love with him, or
both. Central Asia is actually Farghâne, a then Persian-speaking province on the
frontiers of the Jaxartes (Syr Daryâ). For "the Moaning Pillar" see the notes to
poem 40.

ROBÂ^C IS

Poem 43   Quatrain
DR 1022 (1035)

I met last night in stealth with Wisdom's elder
begged him to divulge in full life's secret
This he softly, softly whispered in my ear:
It must be seen, it can't be told, keep quiet!

Poem 44   Quatrain
DR 1891 (1716)

I once was an ascete – you made me sing
made me riot of the party – drunk with wine
You found me on a prayer rug – dignified
made me taunt and toy for children on my block

Poem 45   Quatrain
DR 1021 (993)

Don't be more than others – So I urge my heart
Salve their wounds with balm – not by rubbing salt
If you would have no other do you harm
Bite no back – do no bad deed – keep no bad thought

Poem 46   Quatrain
DR 11

> The moon waxes brighter with rhythmic lauds
> and shows the road of truth to those astray
> Morning, noon and night – make it your rosary
> That old saying – There is no God but God

Poem 47   Quatrain
DR 1789 (1652)

> You've filled my life with joy like sacks of sugar
> preserved me like a petaled rose, in sugar
> And now today I'm seized by peals of laughter –
>   what joyous sounds you sprinkled in my mouth!

Poem 48   Quatrain
DR 1048 (1042)

> Essence: poverty all else: attribute
> Good health: poverty all else: disease
> All the world is vanity, vexation
> Poverty from the world: our goal and treasure

Poem 49   Quatrain
DR 31 (46)

> Our charger speeds from chaos spurred by love
> Our evening always rosy with reunion's wine
> Till morn of Final Day our lips not once unmoist
> With such wines as our creed to us does not forbid

Poem 50   Quatrain
DR 35

> My embrace emptied of you and ever since
> None has ever heard my sobbing cease
> My heart, my soul, my eye, not one forgets
> For the sake of God! Keep me in remembrance

Notes

The quatrain, or the *robâ'i*, is a topical genre, with the last line functioning almost like the punchline in a joke, though the subject matter can be serious or humorous. As an epigrammatic form, I felt they should be constrained by some metrical form. Poem 43 and poem 50 both use the word for silence (*khamush/khâmush*) which often occurs in Rumi's ghazals as a kind of reminder or realization that the mystical truths cannot be told. "Rhythmic lauds" in poem 46 is *zekr*, the mantra used as part of personal and congregational worship by Sufis to focus the breath and attention. "Chaos" in poem 49 is the primordial nothingness (*ʿadam*) from which God brought creation into being. The *robâʿis* of Rumi given here are numbered according to the Kolliyât-e Divân-e Shams-e Tabrizi printed by Nashr-e Rabiʿ (Tehran, 1374/1995). This contains 1995 *robâʿis*. The corresponding number of each *robâʿi* as it appears in the first folio edition of Foruzânfar's text (University of Tehran, 1342/1963), which contains 1983 *robâʿis*, is given in parenthesis.

The Teachings

We now turn our attention to the main teachings of Rumi and the concepts that shaped his thought. Commentators have been writing on this topic for over six centuries now and modern scholars like Nicholson and Foruzânfar devoted the major part of their considerable scholarship to this endeavor. A detailed discussion of the topic is beyond the scope of this volume; readers wishing to pursue the matter further should refer to the works discussed in the section on scholarship, beginning in English with Annemarie Schimmel's *The Triumphal Sun* (1980), Alessandro Bausani's *Persia Religiosa: From Zarathustra to Bahâʾuʾllâh* (English translation forthcoming) and especially William Chittick's *The Sufi Path of Love* (1983). Of course, the reader should also consult the Discourses (*Fihe mâ fih*), readily available in the two English translations of Arberry and Thackston. Naturally the serious student of Rumi's thought will also want to read the *Masnavi* slowly from start to finish with a commentary, Nicholson's being the best available in English, letting the book sink in over time. However, inasmuch as a proper appreciation of Rumi's thought might easily take years to acquire, I have attempted in what follows to sketch a few of the main themes by way of background to enhance the reading of his poems.

THE QUESTION OF FORM AND CONTENT

Rumi does not present a philosophical system per se, and the poetic and discursive nature of his oeuvre makes it difficult to abstract a systematic theology. Most scholars remarking upon this point (and they nearly all do) consider it a serious fault, or at least a major annoyance. Anyone wishing to categorize or describe the general features of Rumi's thought will soon come to sympathize with this observation, but it ignores an obvious point. Rumi could have written a more traditional and systematic exposition of his ideas had he wished to do so; he had read the Hadith manuals, the classical manuals of Sufism, and was certainly conversant with other theological, ethical and legal treatises composed in the style of "systematic" medieval works of this nature, such as Ghazzâli's *Ehyâ ʿolum al-din* ("The Vivification of the Religious Sciences"). Yet Rumi quite consciously decided to present his ideas in discursive fashion, through anecdotes and mostly in verse, because of the rhetorical and heuristic effect this produced. While Rumi's immediate models in terms of generic structure are ʿAttâr and Sanâʾi, he also imitates (if not consciously, then by having internalized its narrative patterns) the literary style of the Koran. By the end of Book 3 of the *Masnavi* a certain jealous critic had raised a stink about the style of Rumi's magnum opus:

> I'm not upset by this, though such a kick
> might break the back of a simple-hearted mind

> (M3:4228)

Rumi describes the man as an ass raising his head from the stable and braying like an old woman:

> "This work" (he means the *Masnavi*) "is lousy,
> the story of the prophet, nothing new!
> Lacking discussion of secrets on high
> towards which the saints gallop their steeds apace,
> from stations of ascesis to effacement,
> step by step, upward to the tryst with God
> lacking definition, explanation
> of the mystic's flight, each stage and station."

> (M3:4233—6)

In response Rumi says that when the Book of God came down, the infidels caviled at it as well, dismissing it as legends and myths, lacking in depth and imagination, which even little children could understand – just a list of dos and don'ts and the stories of Joseph and his curly locks, of Jacob and Zolaykhâ and their troubles. This critic, perhaps a Sufi of the school of Ibn ʿArabi who assumed that a primer of Sufism ought to contain theosophical speculation and details about the stages along the way of the spiritual path (as earlier Sufi manuals did), complains that the *Masnavi* can be easily understood by all and expresses preference for an exposition that would confound the intellect. In reply, Rumi quotes God's response, spoken through Mohammad, to the objections raised against the Koran:

> He said, "If it appears so easy to you,
> then produce one sura of equal ease;
> Let men and genies and the skilled of pen
> bring forth just one verse as easy as this"

> (M3:4241–3)

This similarity has not been lost upon all commentators; already Jâmi called the *Masnavi* the Koran in Persian language. Indeed, S.H. Nasr describes an unpublished study by Hâdi Hâ°eri which argues that almost 6,000 lines, or about one-fourth of the *Masnavi*, consist of direct translations or paraphrases of the Koran (Che 183). Rumi clearly intends the *Masnavi* as an elaborate though somewhat disguised commentary on the Koran and the theological discourse which Muslim thinkers and gnostics developed on that scriptural basis.

We ought to recall at this point that Rumi came from a family of preachers and that he addressed himself to the wider lay public, not exclusively to the academia, or ulama of his day, among whom we may include the judges (*qozât*), jurisconsults (*foqahâ*), exegetes (*mofasserun*), Hadith scholars (*mohadessun*), legal theorists, philosophers (*motakallemin*), theosophizers (like Ibn ʿArabi or Sadr al-Din of Konya) and so forth. The occasional traveling scholar or dignitary may have attended Rumi's lectures, and before the advent of Shams, perhaps many of his students wished to learn Islamic law from him, teach *feqh* and issue fatwas. However, we do not hear of any jurists who went on to become noted scholars after having trained and studied with Bahâ al-Din or Jalâl al-Din in law, hadith, legal theory (*osul al-feqh*) or scholastic theology, from which we might conclude that the name of the Valad family did not have a wide cachet among legal scholars, at least not outside of Konya or the other cities nearby. The truly ambitious or gifted pupils of *feqh* would have been drawn to Aleppo, Damascus or even Baghdad, where they could study with world-famous scholars in the historically prestigious colleges.

In the early centuries of Islam, lectures and sermons, as well as more advanced classes, would be held on a regular basis at every mosque, with several popular teachers holding forth to their respective circle of students and disciples at one and the same time in the various corners of any given mosque. Other venues included the Nezâmiye and other colleges established in the eleventh century in many cities, as well as the smaller, privately owned Sufi lodges and hospices that began to spring up. Classes on law and theology were organized on sectarian lines according to the four Sunni schools and the Shiite, or Jaʿfari school, and one's affiliation would to some extent determine which teachers' lectures to attend. Ideally, a student coming to a city to study would spend the first two months visiting a number of potential teachers and seeking the counsel of others before deciding on one to work with; once having committed to a given subject and a given teacher, it was disrespectful to leave him before the course of studies had been completed (Zar 29–30).

This refers to the formal classes of the teachers. But most teachers also gave public lectures and broad-minded students made a point of attending the public lectures of as many different teachers as possible, especially visiting scholars, representing various schools of thought. Visitors from out of town would also come to hear the most popular and famous lecturers the area offered, for the Prophet had enjoined Muslims to seek knowledge even unto China. Knowledge of one's religious obligations – including the laws of prayer, fasting, alms and pilgrimage – was incumbent upon every Muslim, man or woman, to the extent that their social station or profession required. Those involved in commerce, for example, or any other profession, needed to know the applicable religious laws. Besides, the believers needed training in the life of the spirit in order properly to orient their lives to God (Zar 21–2). Therefore, religious lectures were attended even by those not formally pursuing the study of *feqh* and for them, the fame of the school or the teacher might be less important than the teacher's ability as an orator or reputation for piety. Popular preachers and ethically or mystically minded teachers might operate outside the traditional institutions of learning, holding forth in Sufi lodges rather than mosques or established colleges, and their approach to the inner meaning of scripture, the creed and worship, rather than the outward and legal forms, probably had far greater appeal to the lay public. In general (but not always!) sectarian concerns were de-emphasized or transcended in this milieu, especially if the speaker enjoyed a reputation for saintliness and could attract an ecumenical and socially diverse audience.

ʿAlâ al-Din Kay Qobâd attracted a number of scholars and teachers to Konya, an area that had not previously been a center of Islamic learning, creating a Persian-speaking cultural environment hospitable to an ethical and mystical vision of Islam. Bahâ al-Din obviously found the situation congenial and chose to settle there. A school was apparently built for him, so he and Rumi benefited from a kind of state patronage. Rumi spent some time studying in Damascus, an old center of Islamic learning still populated or frequented by some of the most famous scholars of Islam. He could have chosen to remain there and participate in its primarily Arabic cultural environment, attempting to secure a position in one of the major colleges, had he entertained ambitions to become a world-renowned authority in one of the traditional subjects – exegesis, *feqh, kalâm*, or even philosophy. That he chose to remain in Konya after the death of Borhân al-Din must reflect a level of comfort and contentment with his life there, his circle of followers and the wider audience he addressed, which we must assume was not primarily one of aspiring lawyers, philosophers or theoreticians.

The princes and other men of state who frequented the lectures of both Bahâ al-Din and his son, though not by any means uneducated, typically had not followed a course of study in the Islamic sciences like law or Hadith. They, of course, had some familiarity with the Koran and the basic rituals and requirements of Islam, but their training and tutoring tended more to belles-lettres: poetry, the "mirror for princes" literature, the letters and epistles of statecraft and government administration. Although the Seljuk dynasty was founded by men who spoke Persian only imperfectly and read it not at all, by the reign of Sanjar at the very latest, the Seljuks were very well acculturated to the Persian traditions of the royal court, statecraft, and literature. The Seljuks of Anatolia, such as ʿAlâ al-Din Kay Qobâd, strove to replicate and promote that cultural environment in Asia Minor, apparently as a matter of personal interest. Above and beyond a ruler's own personal predilection for the life of the mind, of course, patronage of religious learning helped to create a pious public image for the ruler, to foster respect for law and order and the collection of taxes, and to coopt the ulama into cooperation with the government.

Aside from the members of the ruling elite, we may surmise from remarks and names given by Aflâki and Sepahsâlâr that the audience in attendance at the lectures of Bahâ al-Din and his son in Konya consisted, in the main, of ordinary townsfolk from Konya and the surrounding villages, tradesmen like Salâh al-Din the Goldsmith, merchants, and so forth, many of whom were either uneducated or incompletely tutored in the traditional religious sciences. It was a religious duty to attend the mosque or *madrase*, listen to sermons and learn which behaviors God had enjoined on the faithful, which behaviors were praiseworthy, which ones were permissible, which were discouraged and which were forbidden. Though attending sermons at a mosque, college or Sufi lodge was expected pious behavior, people were free, of course, to choose the preacher or teacher whom they liked best. In larger towns, like Konya, sectarian concerns (Hanafis would normally attend a Hanafi sermon, etc.), family connections, physical proximity, the language (Arabic, Persian or Turkish) and the social prestige of the speaker, mosque or school undoubtedly played an important role in determining which sermon people chose to attend. But again, the world of religious scholarship in general, specifically Sufism, and in particular Rumi, tried to transcend parochial concerns. As Rumi says in his Discourses (Fih 23): "Though the shaykhs are varied to outward appearance, and differ with respect to conditions, deeds, their spiritual states, and their words, their object is one thing: the search for truth."

Then, as now, however, people undoubtedly gravitated toward the best orators and the most engaging speakers. If a preacher succeeded by argumentation, pious example or mere reputation in convincing members of his audience to dedicate their lives to study, asceticism, prayer or the mystical life, they might eventually reorder their lives, even in some cases forsaking their other activities, to enter a period of discipleship or companionship (*sohbat*) with their teacher. Some regular members of Rumi's audience evidently considered themselves disciples and adepts, while others undoubtedly came out of curiosity, a sense of piety, or from social obligation or recreation. Only those who maintained close companionship with him, however, would have been privy to his private classes and discourses.

Rumi's public message focuses on general questions of belief, behavior and spiritual orientation as befitted his audience, his own temperament and his family background as a preacher. One has the feeling reading the *Masnavi* that

Rumi considers doctrinal points of secondary importance to his principal goal of touching the heart of his listener and helping transform him or her into a lover of God, the Prophet and the Perfect Man.

Hence, I would argue that there is a heuristic method in what others have seen as the organizational madness of the *Masnavi*, a compendium of practical instruction that seeks to communicate its message to a wider audience, one disinclined to sit through dry abstract lectures on doctrine and theology, in an area which was not yet fully deepened in Islam. Rumi brings to bear a not inconsiderable erudition in his lectures, but wears it lightly, illustrating his points with entertaining, instructive and memorable tales, drawing together disparate themes and sources in rhizomic fashion, keeping the listener rooted to the theme without the listener even realizing where the argument is leading until it arrives. His teachings are carefully tailored to his audience, and would not have been formed this way had his audience been strictly scholars or theosophists. As Rumi himself puts it in his Discourses (Fih 22):

> These words are for the person who needs words in order to comprehend. There is no need for words with the one who can comprehend without words. After all, the heavens and the earths are a discourse for the one who comprehends it, born as they are from the utterance "Be and it is." What need has a man who can hear a soft voice for shouting and yelling?

The *Masnavi* is a kind of Koran commentary, but not in the conventional verse-by-verse manner; it concentrates on the spiritual message of scripture, as reflected through the discourses of theology, law and Sufism. It describes a path for the purification and sanctification of the soul that leads the soul back home to its heavenly abode. The all-consuming problem of human existence for Rumi stems from the painful experience of imperfection and unfulfillment caused by alienation from our potential, or more precisely, from our essential source. This problem is intractable to logic and reasoning and can only be solved phenomenologically and heuristically.

We have earlier discussed some of the works Rumi read and the gnostic thinkers with whom he was in contact. To understand Rumi's teachings properly, not only do we need to take his audience into consideration and the ways in which it may have shaped Rumi's mode of expression and the ideas he felt it important to communicate, but we also need to compare his teachings with his sources; only in this way can we discover which ideas he simply borrows, what he has synthesized, and what originated with him. Nicholson, Foruzânfar and other commentators point to earlier sources for specific stories, verses and quotations. The Afghan scholar Mahbub-e Serâj has contributed a study of Bahâ al-Din's influence on Rumi, *Mowlânâ-ye Balkh va pedar-ash: taʾsir-e Maʿâref bar Masnavi-ye Maʿnavi* (Kabul, da Jawaizo aw Kitabo da Khparawulo Mudiriyat, 1340/1961) and Abdul Hakim Khalifa has made a preliminary effort to situate Rumi's ideas in the context of Islamic scholastic and legal theology. Movahhed for the first time has given detailed specifics of some of the ideas Rumi derives from Shams. However, we still lack a systematic comparative study of these questions (aspiring Rumi scholars take note!).

REASON VERSUS SPIRIT

> Light up a fire of love within your soul
> Burn up these thoughts and words from head to toe!
>
> (M2:1763)

Though undoubtedly aware of the Islamic discourse on Greek philosophical concepts, Rumi does not address himself directly to this question. Indeed, he asks in the *Masnavi*:

> How much of all this wisdom of the Greeks?
> Don't forget to read the faithfuls' wisdom!

Rumi is not opposed to rational philosophy, but he perceives its limitation and inability to solve the important ontological problems of existence or to facilitate the process of human perfection. By rationalism, not only the philosophic tradition but also the practices of scholastic theology, religious jurisprudence and grammar are intended; anything, in short, which fills us with pride and leads us away from spiritual truth, kindness and humility.

The intellectual quest, however fine it may be, cannot compare to the spiritual quest. The intellect and the senses perceive cause and effect, whereas the spirit perceives wonders upon wonders; one may possess the former and yet totally lack the latter. But when one possesses that wondrous spirit and can see the truth, the principles of logic, like the staff of a blind man, become unnecessary (M1:1500–1509). Indeed, reliance upon reason can become a barrier to our growth and development:

> Far-sighted reason – I have tested it
> Henceforth I'll make myself demented!
>
> (M2:2332)

Logic, like the blind man's staff, simply props him up and allows him to grope inch by inch ahead. Without the prophets and the spiritual axis – the *qotb*, or saint of the age – to lead them, the world would remain devoid of true life, for the blind can neither plant and harvest nor build and trade on their own:

> Had He not showed you mercy and favor
> Your wooden deductions would snap in two;
> Who gave them their staff of analogies
> and proofs? One Manifest and Seeing!
> When that staff turns to an instrument
> of war and hate, shatter it, my blind one!
>
> (M1:2135–7)

Indeed, our logic, misemployed, leads us into the blindness of pride, and can cause us to rebel against simple but more spiritual truths, as in the story of the philosophical logician who, passing by a Koran school and hearing the teacher's explanation of a particular verse, subjected it to wilting ridicule with a blast of logic. Even though his remarks may have been reasonable, his motivations were to confound the faith of the hearers and belittle the spiritual truth of the Koran; consequently, he was struck blind that night in a dream (M2:1633ff.).

> He gave the staff to assist you forward
> but you raise it in anger against Him!
> Cabal of the blind! What is this you do?
> Turn toward a seeing eye for guidance!
> Take hold the hem of Him who gave the staff;
> Look what's befallen man's rebellious sins!

(M1:2138–40)

Without the humility of obedience and the deference of love, logic can prove a devious guide, like Ahriman, the evil force of Zoroastrian cosmology:

> The individuated intellect
> denies love, though it feigns intimacy.
> Knowing and clever, yet it is not naught.
> An angel not as naught is Ahriman.
> It can act as aid in our words and deeds
> But when it comes to being, it is naught
> For it would not willingly be as naught

(M1:1982–5)

Though logicians may stare at spiritual proofs in front of their face, they cannot perceive them clearly if they lack spiritual insight, for "the sun is the proof of the sun!" Logic is thus unable to save their souls, just as all the proud knowledge of the grammarian proved useless when his boat sank in a storm; unlike the unlettered boatman, whom he had humiliated, the grammarian lacked the salvific knowledge of how to swim (M1:2835). Instead of learning self-effacement, which would have taught him to float, he called everyone an ass and perished flailing in the sea.

> You may be the most learned of the age;
> And when the age, the world, come to an end?

(M1:2845)

Elsewhere, in the Discourses (Fih 157–8), Rumi returns to this topos of the dichotomy between prescriptive and pedantic grammatical knowledge and the pragmatic and experiential knowledge of the gnostic. A gnostic sits next to a grammarian, who lectures that all language is confined to one of three categories: nouns, verbs or particles. The gnostic feigns extreme distress and mocks him with this remark, "My life's work, my quest and effort of twenty years, all is in vain, for I have struggled in the hope that there is something beyond language; you have deflated my hopes."

In the *Masnavi* (M3:1380–85) Rumi gives the parable of a man slapped on the base of the neck. The assailant asks the smarting victim to reflect, before taking revenge, whether the sound of the smack was caused by the former's hand or the latter's neck. The victim replies that the pain is too great for him to consider such matters. Those in pain do not incline to such matters, those without suffering should ponder the matter. This illustrates that the man who is at pains to know God and live according to His desire and command must grapple with pragmatic and immediate cares that prevent him from worrying over abstract philosophical and theological concerns.

Not only do abstract and abstruse knowledge waylay our intellect and logic, but the morality of our motivations in acquiring it are suspect. Rumi rejects the stiff legalism and disputation (*nazar*) of the jurisconsults, urging us not to seek knowledge in this manner or for the purpose of self-aggrandizement or to obtain a teaching position (*mansab-e ta'lim*), for these are forms of lust. If by this means we were able to attain to truth, God would have had no reason to send us prophets (M4:3315–18), but God is the All-Sufficing and teaches us whatever we need to know without the intermediary of a book or teacher (M4:3519).

Early on, scholars tended to claim that Rumi "holds that intellect, as opposed to love, is of the devil [cleverness is from Satan and love from Adam]; he scorns book learning and tradition learning" or that Rumi speaks "in the language of emotion and imagination rather than in that of the intellect."[1] But this division is too facile. Rumi speaks of two different kinds of intellect, one of which can be acquired from books and teachers and preserved on the tablet of your memory. But true intellect comes from the Preserved Tablet (*lowh-e mahfuz*) of heaven, mentioned in the Koran, which can only come to a person by the grace of God (M4:1960ff.). Usually Rumi describes the difference in the established philosophical terminology of individual and universal reason. Our partial intellect can only see so far as our grave – our death on this plane (M4:3311), but for Rumi, Universal Intellect, *'aql-e koll*, is a creation of God or a positive force of the spiritual world. In most people, however, it is blocked by the dross of ego; even if the veil of self is as thin as an eyelid, it will blind us to the reality of things as they are. As a result, most of us possess only partial or individual reason, *'aql-e jozvi*. Our individual reasons can be trained by acquiring knowledge and this accounts for the differences in worldly intelligence, but we all stand in need of the Universal Intellect, which is possessed by the perfect intelligence, *kamel al-'aql*, in the person of a prophet or a saint, the cosmic man on earth, endowed with insight:

> Hidden within you is a partial reason
> In this world seek one of perfect reason;
> through him your partial joins the universal

(M1:1052–3)

This partial, worldly intelligence, if not guided by spiritual intelligence, leads us astray. It is therefore the spiritually undirected or misdirected use of the intellect that Rumi specifically condemns:

> Partial reason gives reason a bad name
> Base desire holds us back from our desires

(M5:463)

The post upon which Mohammad used to lean in the mosque at Medina cried out in lamentation in his absence, according to a hadith much loved by Sufis. You cannot hear the moaning of this post through the sense of reason, but through the faculty of spirit:

> The philosoph winds up through doubt, conjecture
> in denial. Bash your head against the wall!
> Water's wisdom, the words of dust and mud –
> these only hearts that feel can understand
> The philosophe who doubts Muhammad's post
> remains a stranger to the sense of saints

(M1:3278–80)

Of all the modes of knowing and subjects of study – theology, jurisprudence, grammar – it is the knowledge of spiritual poverty (*faqr*), the Sufi's way of learning God, that teaches us the most (M1:2830–34). Those who go beyond grammar (*nahv*) and *feqh* set these aside only to take up effacement (*mahv*) and *faqr*, the hearts of such as these reflect the emanations of the eight paradises from all eternity to all eternity and receive the blessing of God's vision (M3:3496–8). In humbling yourself, you find the justice of jurisprudence and the meaning of grammar and the coherence of syntax (M1:2847).

> Reason drives a camel, the camel's you,
> dragged this way and that, like it or not.
> The saints are reason's reason; in their tow
> plods an endless caravan – man's reason.

(M1:2498–9)

If reason and knowledge cannot on their own discover truth, Rumi speaks of meta-knowledges or modes of spiritual certainty. Knowledge (*'elm*) stands in an intermediate position, better than supposition (*zann*) but less than certainty (*yaqin*); knowledge longs for certainty and certainty longs for the vision of God (M3:4120). Rumi does not offer us a rigidly constructed epistemology, but in a gloss on Sura 102 of the Koran, he alludes to at least two types or levels of knowledge (M3:4125–6). There is, above commonplace knowledge, a certain knowledge (*'elm al-yaqin*):

> The husk and form of knowledge left behind
> For Certain Knowledge they unfurl a banner

(M1:3493)

Beyond that comes certainty itself (*'ayn al-yaqin*), in which a vision of the spiritual world is granted:

> By words you know for sure that fire exists?
>   Don't alight at a certain stage – seek fire!
>   The cooked, alone, knows Certainty itself
> If certainty you want, jump in the fire

(M2:860–61)

This certainty, the certainty of spiritual experience and gnosis, corresponds to Rumi's epitome of his own spiritual journey:

> Three short phrases tell the story of my life:
> I was raw, I got cooked, I burned

SPIRITUAL ORIENTATION

Following the doctrine of the Sufis, Rumi teaches that man's purpose is to achieve a proper spiritual orientation. This can come about through love and devotion to God, and by guidance at the hand of a spiritual master, not through reason or skill:

> You attain to knowledge by argument
> you attain a craft or skill by practice
> if spiritual poverty's what you want,
>   it's won by companionship, not hand or tongue
> The knowledge of it passes soul to soul
> not by way of talk or reams of notes
> Though the signs lie in the seeker's heart
> still, the seeker cannot yet ken the signs
> until his heart becomes exposed to light
> then God reveals: "Did We not expose" [K94:1]
> for We have exposed the chambers of your breast
> and placed the exposition in your heart

(M5:1062–5)

The practice of the way of spiritual poverty may fit within the conventional frameworks of religious piety, but not the path of love. Love will put one beyond the bounds of conventional expectations and pretensions to piety (DR 314 or 226):

> The lovers' gatherings make a different scene
> wine's love brings on distinctive ebriation
> the knowledge learned in school's one kind of thing,
> trafficking in love is quite another

And yet, the true lover of truth reveals himself whatever mode of discourse he chooses:

> A man in love, no matter what he says
> the smell of love wafts love-ward from his mouth

He speaks of jurisprudence, what emerges?
    from mystic poverty, a sweet effulgence.
He blasphemes, the scent of faith arises.
He offers doubts, no doubt we grow more sure

(M1:2880–83)

INNER MEANING

Like Sanâ²i and the other Sufis before him, Rumi held that the true meaning or significance (*ma'ni*) of things and words and religious praxis must be discovered and revealed beyond the outward surface or *zâher*. In philosophical and mystical discourse, particularly in a Shiite context, *zâher* is often contrasted with *bâten* in the respective senses of exoteric and esoteric, but *ma'ni* does not so strongly suggest allegorical and abstruse symbolic interpretation as does the word *bâten*; rather, *ma'ni* suggests the real experiential comprehension achieved through self-discipline and purity, not through easy or superficial or worldly understanding. Rumi continually urges his readers to discard the husk and taste the inner fruit of religion:

What is skin but multi-colored words
reflections upon a colorless pool
Words are like rinds and meanings the kernels
Words are like forms and meanings their spirits
The skin a faulty meaning can conceal
or jealously guard good meaning from view

(M1:1096–8)

The conflicts among men stem from names
Trace back the meaning and achieve accord

(M2:3680)

Though Muslims were encouraged to read the Koran in the medieval period, widespread illiteracy, as well as ignorance of Arabic among the Turkish- and Persian-speaking laity, often made this impractical or impossible for most people. This fact, combined with the general tendency to orthopraxy in Middle Eastern societies, meant that imitation of authorities played a large part in matters of ritual, worship and so forth. Islamic law calls for imitation of the legal decrees of those legal scholars recognized among the wisest of the age. Indeed, Rumi believes in the need for a spiritual guide, and advises that one should not cut oneself off from one's spiritual community until the truth has been realized within one, like a pearl formed in its shell. But if one imitates a guide out of selfish desire, it will deprive one of illumination (M2:568–9).

Although one must follow the true spiritual guide (see below), a spiritual orientation sometimes entails a rejection of dogmatic imitation (*taqlid*) and conformity, which can hamstring our intellect and mislead us (M1:2567). Rumi

405

tells the story of a Sufi traveler invited to dine and dance with a group of impoverished and caddish dervishes, who decide to sell his donkey while distracting him. They begin to dance and the Sufi, carried away by emotion, joins with them as they sing over and over again, "the donkey's gone." The Sufi's servant comes to inform him of the theft of his donkey, but concludes from the song that his master knew and did not care. When the distraught Sufi discovers what has happened, he explains:

> They were all saying it so mirthfully
> I too was spurred by joy to join with them
> Imitation of them brought me ruin
> A thousand curses on my imitation!
> and to think, an imitation of such bums!
>
> (M2:562–4)

The love of God, after all, transcends form and creed, ritual and dogma; as Rumi's God puts it:

> I have given everyone a character
> I have given each a terminology
>
> (M2:1754)
>
> ⁂
>
> Hindus praise me in the terms of India
> and the Sindis praise in terms from Sind
> I am not made pure by their magnificats
> It is they who become pure and precious
> We do not look to language or to words
> We look inside to find intent and rapture
>
> (M2:1757–9)
>
> ⁂
>
> Every prophet, every saint has his path
> but as they return to God, all are one
>
> (M1:3086)
>
> Love's folk live beyond religious borders
> The community and creed of lovers: God
>
> (M2:1770)

Rumi explains in Discourse 36 that just as God is the root of all being and creation secondary branches, so too love is at the root of the outward aspect of the things we see in this world. Love gives rise to a multiplicity of forms, but these are secondary and non-essential (Fih 139). This allows Rumi to adopt a very constructive ecumenical attitude toward various creeds. It is tempting to compare the Muslim poet Rumi's attitude to that of the Christian poet Dante; as Nicholson observed in 1914, Dante "falls far below the level of charity and tolerance" advocated and practiced by Rumi.[2]

OUTWARD OBSERVANCES

This ecumenical attitude does not mean, however, that one may dispense with the outward observances of religion. The saints do not fail to pray, to fast, to perform alms, to go on pilgrimage and so forth. The faithful Muslim worships through these obligatory observances, but the performance of such obligations does not confer a spiritual orientation:

> An ape can mimic man in all he does
> Supposing there's no difference in the deeds
> Malicious men can never comprehend:
> Some men are moved by His command to act,
> some (may dust pile on their heads!) by malice
> Hypocrites may pray beside the pious
> prompted not by abject need, but malice.
> In prayer and fasting, pilgrimage and alms
> both hypocrite and faithful win and lose:
> To the faithful in the end goes victory
> to the hypocrite, the ultimate defeat
> Though both are players in a single game
> They're continents apart in character.
> Each proceeds his own station to assume,
> moves on his designation to acquire.
> Call him believer, his soul rejoices
> Call him hypocrite, he's filled with fire

(M1:283–90)

This also means that, though it is only the refraction of truth's light into the human plane of existence that brings about religious differences, these differences are important to us on this plane. Thus Rumi sees sectarian claims as a danger, with various groups misleading us. Though Rumi does not choose to put this in terms of heresy, he does worry that we may be diverted and detoured from the direct path to truth by people crooked or deficient in love:

> Make only drunks and lovers your companions
> don't tie your heart strings to unworthy folk.
> Each faction tries to make you follow it:
> the crows to ruins, the parrots to sugar

(DR 630)

One observes the outward form with the *qâzis* and the men of literal legalism, while at the same time realizing that not all who observe this are sincere. We must strive to find the inner truth of these outward observances (M4:2175–8).

KORAN AND PROPHETS, OUR GUIDE

Contrary to his contemporary portrayal in the West as an apostle of non-denominational spirituality in which individuals can pursue the development of their soul outside the established religious traditions, particularly Islam, Rumi insists on the primacy of the Koran and the prophets as spiritual guides to mankind:

> Flee to God's Koran, take refuge in it;
> there with the spirits of the prophets merge.
> The book contains the acts of the prophets
> those fish of the pure sea of Majesty.
> If you read the Book without acceptance,
> what profit in meeting saints and prophets?
> When you accept the stories as you read
> the bird of your soul will feel encaged.
> A bird imprisoned in the cage must seek
> release, or failing that is ignorant.
> The only souls to have escaped the cage
> are the prophets, mankind's befitting guides.
> we hear them from beyond sing melodies
> of faith, "Here is your path, this way release."
> This is how we escape confining cage
> no recourse for this cage but by this path.
>
> (M1:1537–44)

The mission of the prophets is to connect people, to connect the parts to the whole (M1:2813).

SAINTS, SHAYKHS AND DISCIPLESHIP

The powers of the saints (*vali*, plural *owliâ*) are of an order just below those of the prophets, and they speak as in a veil with the voice of God (M1:1934–6). Like Esrâfil, the angel of resurrection, they possess the power to bring the dead back to life (M1:1930).

The saints even possess the power to alter destiny, as though altering the course of an arrow that has been fired. They can act as intermediaries to the hand of God and thereby sever the relationship between cause and effect, as well as blotting out from men's memories what has been said (M1:1669ff.).

There are many false shaykhs who pretend to be saints (*abdâl*) and repeat the outward terms and so forth, but have no scent or trace of God. Since it takes a long time for a man's conscience to reveal its depths and truths, a disciple (*morid*) may go through his spiritual apprenticeship to a shaykh before the latter's true character becomes clear. Even so, very occasionally, a very sincere seeker may obtain to spiritual insight through a false teacher (M1:2264–87). Also quite rarely, a traveler on the path may reach his goal without any *pir*, or master, to guide him, but only because the hearts of the *pirs* aid and succor him on the spiritual plane (M1:2974ff.).

But a disciple must not attempt to imitate the saint in all his deeds, for the disciple is not yet ripe and may find it injurious to him. The saint may drink a poison and produce a result like an antidote, whereas the same potion would make his student (*tâleb*) mad (M1:2603).

Some dervishes truly thirst for God, whereas others practice poverty in search of something besides God. One can draw a portrait of sorrow without the feeling of sorrow. Don't throw bread to the picture of a dog (M1:2752ff.).

The spiritual quest is filled with dangers and you need to choose a *pir* to guide and lead you, or else you will stray and come to perdition (M1:2943). Once a *pir* has accepted to guide you, you must submit to his authority, as Moses did to Khezr, even if his instructions confound you (M1:2969–73). If one is not oriented to the truth and does not heed his source of spiritual guidance, whether it be God or a great teacher, he is lost, as Rumi tells Salâh al-Din in one ghazal (D 484):

> All that distances you from the Friend is bad
> All that turns your face from him, though good, is bad

THE SPIRITUAL *AXIS MUNDI*

There must always be present in the world certain saints (*vali*), men beloved of God, around whom the spiritual realm revolves. To this saint the people must turn, regarding him as the Noah who pilots the Ark through the flood of worldly folk (M6:2225).

> So, in every age, a saint arises –
>   till the Day of Resurrection, ceaseless tests!
>   whoso has good character is saved
>   whoso has a heart like glass is broken
> That saint is the living steadfast Imam
> whether descended from ʿOmar or ʿAli.
> It is he, O seeker, Mahdi and Guide
> Whether seated before you or hid from sight.
>
> (M2:815–19)

The lesser saints descend from this king of saints, ranked according to a hierarchy:

> He is like light and wisdom is his Gabriel
> The lesser saints but lamps lit up by him.
> The one who's less than these lamps is our flame.
> Light emanates in grades as per a scheme,
> for seven hundred veils obscure Truth's light
> and all these veils of light stack up in tiers
> Behind each veil there stands a certain folk –
> these veils – rank after rank, till the Imam!
> Those at the bottom tier, in the weakness
> of their eyes, cannot bear the light above
> and the next tier through the weakness of their sight
> cannot stand the light of the tier above.
>
> (M2:819–24)

The power of the special saints (*abdâl*) closest to his rank derive from God and their bodies are composed, not of flesh and food, but of light. As such they exceed the angels and the spirit in station (M3:7–8).

Elsewhere, Rumi refers to this living saint or Imam as the spiritual *axis mundi*, or *qotb* (plural: *aqtâb*). The *qotb* is self-sufficient in spiritual matters and spins around himself, though the entire heavens turn about him (M5:2345). The *qotb*, like a lion, hunts down souls and the prey he slays becomes the food for others. Therefore, we must strive to please the *qotb* so that he will be strengthened and able to hunt well. When he is ill and unable to hunt, the rest of the people go without spiritual nourishment (M5:2340–41). The disciples of the *qotb* hunt like the fox, and should turn their prey over to the lion – *qotb* – so that all bodily weakness in the person around whom the spiritual world revolves may be warded off (M5:2346–50).

One such saint must always be present in the world. We may conclude that Shams and then Salâh al-Din and then Hosâm al-Din, or perhaps Rumi himself as mirrored through the latter two, functioned as the *axis mundi* of Rumi's spiritual world. At one point in the *Masnavi*, Rumi gives a longish list of the prophets and saints who have held this position, beginning with Adam, who designated Seth. After Seth came Noah, who passed his radiant spirit to Abraham, who in turn passed it to Ishmael and from there to David and Solomon, Jacob and Joseph, and finally Moses, Jesus and Mohammad (M2:910–21). Emerging from the prophets, one comes to the rightly guided caliphs, Abu Bakr, ᶜOmar, ᶜOsmân and ᶜAli (M2:922–5). From there we come to the realm of the Sufis, Jonayd, Bâyazid, Maᶜruf-e Karkhi, Ebrâhim-e Adham, Shaqiq-e Balkhi (M2:925–30).

But these saints are not always known in their own age to outward eyes; God jealously guards their identity from vulgar eyes:

> A hundred thousand hidden monarchs
> raise their proud heads up in the realm beyond
> Their names concealed – He is a jealous God!
> Not every beggar should pronounce their names!
>
> (M2:931–2)

Who then knows their names? One whose spirit has been emptied of deceit and does not pry and will not divulge sacred secrets:

> So that you do not tell the sultan's secret
> and pour out sweet sugar in front of flies
> that ear will drink in glory's mystery
> which, like the lily, has a tongue that's dumb
>
> (M3:20–21)

FATALISM, FREE WILL, DIVINE DECREE

The Koran emphasizes over and over again the omnipotence of God. The question whether man, in view of this divine omnipotence, possesses the freedom to act of his own accord or not is one of the most contentious issues in Islamic theology. Indeed, the Koran holds man responsible for his actions, promising blissful reward for righteousness and the torments of hell to the wicked, yet often speaks of God hardening the heart of His servants, thus seeming to transfer responsibility for their actions to Himself. Early on, two opposing schools of thought arose and crystallized around this issue, with first the Jabriyya, and later the Asharites, holding to determinism (*jabr*, or compulsion), the idea that no human deed, indeed, not even the falling of a leaf from a tree, can occur except at God's command. On the other hand, the Qadariyya, and subsequently the Mutazilites, held that man is a free agent and bears responsibility to choose the proper course of action. When posed the question why man should be punished or rewarded for deeds that God compelled him to commit, the Asharites replied that man becomes deserving of God's predetermined decree through a process of acquisition, or *kasb*, a not entirely convincing argument, but one upheld by Ghazzâli.

Rumi would have been thoroughly educated in the intricacies of such debates as a Hanafi preacher and religious scholar. He addresses the question frequently in different contexts in his *Masnavi* and generally avoids the extreme and dogmatic positions on the matter, preferring to illustrate, by means of juxtaposed stories, various situations involving the free will of the protagonist and various others involving the intervention or predetermination of God. By allowing the proponents of each position to speak for themselves, Rumi remains above the fray while nevertheless providing the reader with cogent briefs for both sides.

In one story of the *Masnavi* about a lion terrorizing the animals in a certain valley (M1:900ff.), the lion is encouraged not to chase after prey but to trust in God and accept whatever game fate might decree for him. In reply, the lion alludes to the famous hadith of the Prophet, "Tie your camel, then trust in God" (M1:912–13) and pleads that a person must first exert himself before relying upon God (M1:947). Rumi first allows the animals to argue for fatalistic acceptance of whatever occurs as God's decree, and we initially sympathize with this view, as illustrated in the story about a man who attempts to flee from the Angel of Death by having Solomon magically transport him to India, only to find that India is the appointed place of his demise (M1:956–70).

Eventually, though, Rumi undermines this doctrine of predestination: God has set a ladder before our feet which we have a responsibility to climb if we wish to reach the roof; since God has given us legs, we cannot pretend to be lame. A master hands his slave a shovel and the slave, without a word, knows what to do. So, too, we must seek to read God's implicit signs (M1:930ff.) and use our abilities in the effort to be thankful for his blessings; believing in predestination (*jabr*) amounts to a denial of those blessings (M1:938).

The doctrine of predestination, or *jabr*, commonly occurs in tandem with its opposite, free will, or *ekhtiâr*, both in the tradition of scholastic theology and in Rumi's *Masnavi* (e.g., 1:1468). The word *jabr* literally means "to reset broken bones" (the same Arabic root gives us the word "algebra" in European languages, or the process of righting broken equations), but as Rumi argues, strict belief in predestination is akin to putting a cast on an unbroken leg (M1:1071–2). As Rumi also points out, the same root (*j–b–r*) gives rise to the attribute of God, *al-jabbâr*, the Almighty, which the Koran invokes not to confirm that we have no free will, but to affirm our abjectness (M1:617).

> Our abjectness proves our indigence,
> our sense of shame proves that we have free will
> Were our wills not free, why then these feelings
> of guilt, regret, embarrassment and shame?
>
> (M1:618–19)

Those who assert, in effect, that our will is bound up like a broken leg, cripple the Koran's teaching about man's responsibility for his actions:

> Your passions guide your reading of Koran
> How base and crooked you make the Sunni creed!
>
> (M1:1081)

Rumi then strikes a parable to describe the Asharite theologians and the false analogical reasoning they employ (*ra'y*) to interpret (*ta'vil*) the Koran and justify their fatalistic doctrine of *jabr*; it is as if a fly sitting on a piece of straw in a puddle of donkey piss imagines itself on a ship in the sea:

> False exegetes, like flies, are full of it:
> their fancies – mule piss; their thoughts – all scuzz.
> Could flies but leave *ta'vil* and *ra'y* behind,
> Fortune would turn them into phoenixes!
>
> (M1:1088–9)

To Rumi it is clear that man does possess free will, for did he not choose to act virtuously, he would not deserve the reward it entails:

> Free will endows our worship with its savor
> for otherwise, the heavens turn, compelled
> revolving rewardless and unpunished.
> On Judgment Day free will's the skill that's judged!
>
> (M3:3287–8)

On the other hand, Rumi does admit the intervention of the divine in the world, or *qazâ*, a process by which God decrees that certain things come to be and in consequence of which our normal powers may be extended or suspended. On some occasions, God's decree supplements our own powers and gives us victory:

> Read commentaries on the Koran's verse:
> God said, "It was not you who shot your shot"   [K8:17]
> We fire but cannot make the arrows fly,
> We are the bow and God the arrow's flight.
>
> (M1:615–16)

On other occasions, God's decree – *qazâ* – may make us temporarily blind, crippling our reason and making us unable to distinguish head from toe for a while, before returning our powers (M1:2440). For example, a hoopoe bird, whose sight is so sharp that he can see water hidden in the earth from high in the sky, nevertheless flew into captivity because of God's decree; *qazâ* had made a concealed trap imperceptible to him:

> I see the trap from way up in the air
> Unless *qazâ* my eye of reason cloaks.
> *qazâ* arrives and knowledge goes to sleep,
> the moon goes black and covers up the sun.
>
> (M1:1231–2)

Likewise, it was *qazâ* that prevented Adam, who knew the beginning and end of all creatures, from understanding the inevitable consequences of his violation of God's prohibition in Eden. *Qazâ* made Adam suppose that this injunction was susceptible of conjecture or interpretation, *ta'vil*, the false exegesis of the theologians (M1:1250–51).

While God's decree is unavoidable, man at the same time elects and deserves what God decrees for him. Ultimately, man has free will and is responsible for his actions:

> See both: the act of God and our own act.
> That we act ourselves is most apparent!
> You doubt that creatures freely choose to act?
> Then never ask someone, "Why did you do that?"
> God's creation brings our acts to being;
> Our deeds – of handiwork divine the trace
>
> (M1:1480–83)

Most of us are unable to fathom the paradox that two principles which seem logically to contradict one another may nevertheless both be true at one and the same time (M1:1483ff.). Rumi holds that only saintly ones with spiritual insight can comprehend this mystery of free will and divine decree (M1:1466). If our spiritual ears and eyes are pure enough, we perceive God's inspiration (*vahy*) and choose the right course (M1:1461), which is also the course that God has destined for us. Both predestination and free will exist simultaneously, and as a proverbial saying undoubtedly known to Rumi phrased it, "Belief lies between predestination and free will."

Rumi illustrates the paradox by contrasting the response of Adam and Satan to the expulsion from Eden, emphasizing the virtue of man's humility in accepting responsibility for his actions: Satan could truly say that he fell because God seduced him, but this would conceal his own culpability; Adam can say that he has wronged himself, but he is also cognizant that it was God's decree.

> Said Satan: "Since by You I was seduced ..." [K7:16]
>   Base demon, hiding his part in the deed!
> Said Adam: "We've done wrong unto ourselves." [K7:23]
>   So Adam blamed himself (not blind, like us,
>   to God's hand in the deed, but of respect,
>   God's role in sin concealed) his fruit enjoyed:
> God asked Adam after his repentance:
>   Did I not bring this trial and sin to you?
>   Was this fate not by My divine decree?
>   Why hide this at the time of your atoning?
> Said Adam: Fearing disrespect to You.
> Said God: For this I've given you reward.
>
>   (M1:1488–93)

UNITY OF BEING

For Rumi, the creation is a multichrome and multiform manifestation of the single resplendent whiteness that is God. The creation is the explosion of this primal colorlessness into form and aspect, thereby producing the illusion of individuation, separation, distinction and opposition. Rumi explains that everyone views existence through a glass of a particular color, seeing truth refracted in a different hue, depending on his vantage point. One looks through a blue glass and sees blue, another through a red glass and sees red. Only the prophet, the true Imam, or exemplar, can look above the prism and discern the real and unrefracted whiteness of the light (the heading prior to M1:2365). Elsewhere he speaks of the unichromity of Jesus, whose purity could merge a myriad-colored coat into simple unrefracted light (M1:500–501). Mortal existence is lived out, however, below this plane, in the refracted rays of this light, and this gives rise to bewildering mysteries. How did color appear from colorlessness, and to what aim? Do apparent opposites really contend, or is it all illusion? (M1:2470ff.).

Using the Persian royal game of polo as a metaphor, Rumi postulates that the Koranic decree of God, "Be and it was," has smacked us into motion like a stick and ball and we are now rolling through both space and meta-space (*makân o lâ makân*). Smacked forward into the visible spectrum of creation, we are tinged with attributes that bring us into conflict and opposition:

Once colorlessness fell into color's grasp
A Moses came in conflict with a Moses.
But regain again your lessness-color
and Moses will with Pharaoh be at peace

(M1:2467–8)

❧ ❧ ❧

The shoe, sound man, put on the other foot:
Pharaoh's rebellion arose from Moses!

(M1:2481)

This discussion echoes with the debate over free will and predestination. If Lucifer (Iblis) rebelled against God, did not God decree that rebellion? If Pharaoh oppressed Moses and the Jews, did not God harden his heart? Are not Satan and Pharaoh equally the servants of God, serving His purpose at His command, though they are condemned as evil? Rumi expounds this doctrine of evil's hypostatized servitude to God with respect to Pharaoh (M1:2447ff.) and the proud archangel, Iblis (M2:2617ff.).

Beyond the dualisms of obedience and rebellion, faith and unbelief, good and evil, all of which are produced by the multiplicities brought into being in creation, there is but one singleness, and in this Rumi sees the meaning of the Islamic doctrine of *towhid* – divine unity. Of the designations "hypocrite" and "faithful" Rumi tells us that, though they are separated here on earth, they flow from the same meta-source:

A word's vileness does not reside in letters
If the sea tastes bitter do not blame the cup
The letters are the cup, the meaning, water;
Sea signifies: "With Him the Mother Book"
The sea of bitterness, the sea of sweetness:
Between them in this world "a wall uncrossed"   [K55:19–20]
Know that both seas flow from one origin
Cross both of them until you reach the source.

(M1:295–98)

If you remain entranced by the outward forms, your worship is idolatry. One loves the essence of a thing and not just its outward forms, for the outward forms are secondary. Indeed, love gives rise to a multiplicity of forms, all contingent, just as God's creation is contingent (Discourse 36, Fih 139). Likewise, the pilgrim at Mecca must not be concerned with the skin color of the man beside him; whether he be Arab, Turk or Indian, dark or light, his intention is the same color as your own (M1:2893–6).

Indeed, the fixation on a creedal form or a particular religious form becomes itself a failure to perceive the inner meaning, the central standpoint of oneness from which the multiplicity of signs radiates outward. When one looks at the glass of the lamp rather than the light radiating from it, it gives rise to duality and love of the lamp, whereas if one fixes one's gaze on the light, it can be seen emanating from different lamps in various shapes and sizes:

> Mind of the universe! Point of view
> makes all the difference we see between
> the believer, the Zoroast, the Jew
>
> (M3:1258)

Were it not so difficult to look beyond ourselves and focus on the end, the religions would never have come into conflict (M1:492). One must try to learn to live with this dilemma and know when to look to the light and when to the lamp. To say "I am the Truth" as Hallâj did is a mercy, an intuition of the truth of unity, albeit one that you have to sacrifice your Self in order to see; whereas to say "I am lord," as Pharaoh did, insistently foregrounds the lamp over the light and makes us accursed (M2:2522–3).

> Many the believers, but their faith is One
> One in soul, though many are their bodies
>
> (M4:408)

> * * *

> I speak of plural souls in name alone –
> One soul becomes one hundred in their frames;
> Just as God's single sun in heaven
> shines on earth and lights a hundred walls
> But all these beams of light return to one
> if you remove the walls that block the sun
> The walls of houses do not stand forever
> and believers, then, will be as but one soul
>
> (M4:415–18)

EVOLUTION OF SPIRIT

Rumi sees all creation, within both the physical and the metaphysical worlds, as a great upward spiral of metamorphoses. God grants the earth a throat to suck in moisture and grow verdure. God then gives the animals a mouth to consume these herbs. The animal, thus fattened, makes its way to the plate of man. Man expels it from his body and it turns to earth again, which eats up the lifeless body of man in the grave:

> I saw all atoms with their mouths agape
> Tell all they devour and the tale won't end!
>
> (M3:22–6)

But all things draw sustenance from God (M3:40) and one must strive to dull the spirit's appetite for bodily thoughts (M3:42–3). Since this is a dog-eat-dog world, only those who find everlasting life in God survive and are saved (M3:30). The minerals in the soil climb the food chain to become plants, the plants become animals, the animals man, man spirit:

I died to mineral, joined the realm of plants
I died to vegetable, joined animal
I died in the animal realm, became man
So why fear? When has dying made me less?
In turn again I'll die from human form
only to sprout an angel's head and wings
and then from angel-form I will ebb away
For "All things perish but the face of God"   [K28:88]
And once I'm sacrificed from angel form
I'm what imagination can't contain.
So let me be naught! Naughtness, like an organ,
sings to me: "We verily return to Him"   [K2:151]
Know that death – the community's agreed –
is like the fount of life in darkness hid

(M3:3901–7)

Rumi brings up this theme repeatedly (e.g., M4:3637ff.) and attributes the
motion of all particles upward through the cycle of forms to the powerful
attraction of love:

It's waves of love that make the heavens turn
Without that love the universe would freeze:
  no mineral absorbed by vegetable
  no growing thing consumed by animal
  no sacrifice of anima for Him
  Who inspired Mary with His pregnant breath
  Like ice, all of them unmoved, frozen stiff
  No vibrant molecules in swarms of motion
Lovers of perfection, every atom
turns sapling-like to face the sun and grow
Their haste to shed their fleshly form for soul
sings out an orison of praise to God

(M5:3853–9)

DIE BEFORE YOU DIE

As such, the seeker of God must die to self before he can shine with the divine
light. Dying to self, or even slaying the self, which is known by Sufis as the
greater jihad, includes learning to accede to God's will, putting out the fires of
ego, training the carnal self and concupiscent soul. When these veils of self are
lifted, the divine light of the soul shines through; when burnished of all its rust,
the mirror of the soul perfectly reflects the attributes of God.

The seeker of the Court of God's like this:
When God appears, the seeker fades away
Yes, this encounter brings eternal life
but before undying life effacement comes

How could shadows be seekers of the light?
When the light shines, the shadows disappear.
How could reason live when sacrificed to Him?
"All but His face shall perish from the earth"   [K28:88]
Being and nothing fade before His face;
What a miracle, to be in nothingness!
In these precincts wisdom and logic fail
and at this point, the pen is split in two

(M3:4658–63)

In the Discourses, Rumi explains it this way (Fih 24–5):

In His presence there is no room for two egos (*do anâ*). You say "ego," and He
"ego"? Either you die in His presence, or He will die in your presence, so that no
duality may remain. Yet it is impossible that He should die, either in the universe
or in the mind, for "He is the living, who does not die." He has grace in such
measure that, were it possible, He would die for you to remove the duality. But
since His death is impossible, you die so that He may become manifest in you
and the duality be lifted.

THE IMPORTANCE OF KORAN

Sahl al-Tostari (d. 896) claimed, as did Christian exegetes with respect to the Bible,
that every verse of the Koran had four senses, and Sufis appealed to a (probably
spurious) hadith in support of this principle. One of the headings of the *Masnavi*
alludes to another similar hadith which posits an exterior, interior and inner interior
meaning, up to seven layers of meaning. In the passage which comes under this
rubric (M3:4244–9), Rumi tells us that the words of the Koran have an outward
significance, but the interior meaning beneath that is awesome, overwhelming. And
beneath that interior meaning lies yet a third layer of meaning, in which all human
reason becomes lost. And further beyond that, the fourth layer of scripture's
meaning remains impenetrable to all but God, the Peerless and Incomparable.

My son, don't read Koran for outward sense!
    A demon looks on man and just sees clay
The outward Koran is like man's body:
    its features visible, its soul concealed
A man's own kith and kin may never know
    his soul a hair's breadth in a hundred years

(M3:4247–9)

We must read the Koran, but we must read it with insight in order to find the
remedy to our own psychic ills, as Rumi succinctly reminds us near the very end
of the *Masnavi*:

The whole Koran's a commentary on
sins of souls. Read the Book with open eyes!

(M6:4862)

Elsewhere Rumi quotes Sanâ⁾i on the failure of the literal-minded to apprehend the meaning of the Koran:

> How well the sage of Ghazna did express
> the spiritual likeness of those in veils
> who see only words in Koranic text
>   (small wonder from a people gone astray!):
> "The blind eye feels only the heat when struck
> by the enlightening rays of the sun"

(M3:4229–31)

This fate can be avoided by opening the heart and inscribing it with the meaning of the text of scripture:

> Tend within to opening of your heart
> or stand accused: "Do ye not see?"

[K51:21]
(M5:1072)

As Rumi tells us toward the end of Book 5 of the *Masnavi* (M5:3128–9), one should only find the meaning of the Koran by interrogating the text of the Koran, and beyond that, one may see its meaning reflected in the person who has burned away his self, who has been immolated upon the Book until his essential spirit is become Koran.

> When you possess the attributes of Glory
> pass like Abraham through fires of fleshly ills
> and the flames will feel cool and safe to you

(M3:9–10)

Having laid the groundwork for self-transformation, one then must pray for the descent of God's aid and blessing, that a new vista, a window onto the transcendent, might open to our soul:

> As I enter the solitude of prayer
> I put these matters to Him, for He knows
>   That's my prayer-time habit, to turn and talk
>   That's why it's said: "My heart delights in prayer"
> Through pureness a window opens in my soul
> God's message comes immediate to me
> Through my window the Book, the rain and light
> all pour into my room from gleaming source
>   Hell's the room in which there is no window
> To open windows, that's religion's goal

(M3:2400–404)

PART IV

RUMI AND THE MEVLEVIS IN

THE MUSLIM WORLD

10

The Mevlevi Order

Following what was by then a well-established custom, the disciples and descendants of Rumi formed a confraternity, or Sufi order, committed to following the worship practices, the spiritual discipline and the teachings traced back to Jalâl al-Din Rumi. This brotherhood (which has also included female disciples), named after "My Master," Mowlavi, is called the Mevlevi order (Mevlevi being the Turkish pronunciation of Mowlavi, though one also finds the Arabicized form Mawlawî/Mawlawiyya in many reference works). In more common parlance, however, the adherents of the Mevlevi order are known as the whirling dervishes or dancing dervishes, after the distinctive practice of meditative turning.

Some have argued that a proto-order probably already existed during the lifetime of Rumi himself (Jamal Elias, in OxE; Tahsin Yazıcı, in *EI²*). Early disciples most likely emulated the example of Rumi, Salâh al-Din and Hosâm al-Din in matters of worship; more likely than not the praxis of *samâ*ᶜ, the sending of disciples to the kitchen, and perhaps even the form of the turban, took ritual shape on the basis of oral memories of what Rumi or Shams had said or done on various occasions.

Although sizeable audiences attended Rumi's lectures and his fame had apparently spread beyond Konya during his lifetime, it seems unlikely that he directed a large coterie of disciples in any systematic fashion. Gölpınarlı argues that to view Rumi as the head of a Sufi order, or even the shaykh of a single Sufi lodge, would be an anachronism (GM 366–7). Rumi lived in a college and earned his living by teaching there. At first he preached and issued judicial opinions, or fatwas, but after encountering Shams he stopped teaching as he no longer wished to direct students in the conventional manner, and referred them instead to Salâh al-Din and subsequently to Hosâm al-Din. Nevertheless, Rumi continued to give counsel, deliver speeches and sermons, issue fatwas, meet with officials and intercede with the authorities on behalf of his friends and disciples.

Rumi did not, however, enjoin or observe the rituals typical of most Sufi orders, such as the bestowing of ceremonial cloaks, specifying periods of ascetic exercises, and so forth. On one occasion Aflâki does refer to Rumi cutting off the hair of an individual as a ritual way of confirming his discipleship (Af 391). However, this passage reflects a dream that Amir Ahmad Pâyporti had prior to meeting Rumi, and therefore tells us more about the common rituals of Sufi induction than the particular practice of Rumi. Gölpınarlı does allude to a passage in one of the manuscripts of the *Manâqeb al-'ârefin* that speaks of trimming a few hairs of the head, beard and mustache as a sign of entering the path of gnostic love, but this passage apparently does not appear in Yazıcı's critical edition (GM 367 n. 1). Since the Qalandars practiced the shearing and shaving of all hair, the passage mentioned by Gölpınarlı may simply reflect the practice of other orders; in any case, since it involves the cutting off of only a few hairs of the head, mustache and beard, we may classify this as a symbolic nod to common Sufi practice, rather than as a full-blown ritual.

We may tentatively conclude that Rumi functioned in his own, sui generis, sphere, somewhere between the established communities of the mosque, the *madrase* and the *khâneqâh*. He thus shared something, but not everything, with the worlds of the jurists and religious scholars, where he began preaching; the theologians or philosophers, whose topics and techniques of argumentation he borrowed while not fully sharing their presumptions; and the formalized Sufi orders, which his community of disciples increasingly came to resemble in successive generations.

We have seen that Aflâki portrays Rumi as not especially fond of receiving princes and other guests (e.g. Af 100, 256). But Tâj al-Din Mo'tazz Khorâsâni, the son of the chief *qâzi* of Jalâl al-Din Khwârazmshâh, was Rumi's favorite among the government officials who came to see him. Tâj al-Din had originally been sent to Anatolia by the Mongols to collect tribute/taxes from the Seljuks. Having received a chilly reception from 'Ezz al-Din Kay Kâus II, he went to Rokn al-Din Qelij Arslân IV, where he was warmly received by Mo'in al-Din Parvâne and put in charge of the government's financial concerns in Kastamonu and Ankara; under his direction the area enjoyed peace and prosperity. He died in Erzincan in 1278 (Mak 254–5). Aflâki describes him as one of Rumi's close disciples, and this seems likely, for Rumi wrote several letters to him asking for assistance, mostly on behalf of Hosâm al-Din and his children. Rumi used to refer to Tâj al-Din as "compatriot" (on account of their shared origins in Khorasan), "true seeker," and "profferer of the water of life" (Af 239).

Tâj al-Din erected several schools, Sufi lodges, hospices and hospitals in various places (Af 239). He supposedly asked Rumi to allow him to construct a hall (*dâr al-ʿoshshâqi*) for his Sufi followers (Af 241). Aflâki, citing a ghazal (D 1712) which he claims contains Rumi's reply, tells us that Rumi refused this request. According to Aflâki (242), Rumi felt that such material structures reflected a worldliness that at least contrasted, if it did not conflict, with the example of the Prophet.

Tâj al-Din, however, did not easily take no for an answer; he tried to send money to Rumi through an intermediary and, when this failed, appealed to Sultan Valad to intercede with Rumi on his behalf. Finally, Sultan Valad gave him the go ahead and some rooms were built for the disciples next to the ʿÂmere school where Rumi taught (Af 242), including a gathering hall (*jamâʿat khâne*, GM 86). Gölpınarlı (GM 87) believes that the hall functioned primarily as a room for reading and reciting. Rumi, for example, sometimes sat there alone engrossed in books and meditation (Af 97, 125) and at other times held classes there (Af 255). Some of the reports relayed by Aflâki reveal that the hall was also used for general social purposes: food was served there during the time of Ulu ʿÂref Chelebi (Af 922) and women would sit there with their babies (Af 830).

This same Tâj al-Din eventually secured a Sufi lodge for Hosâm al-Din (Af 242), who handled most of the contributions given to Rumi, as we have seen. It would appear that Hosâm al-Din may have already appointed some individuals during his lifetime to head up a fledgling network of Rumi disciples in various places. ʿAlâ al-Din of Amasya, for example, appears to have been associated with Hosâm al-Din before his formal association with Sultan Valad began (Af 877; Sep 154).

It is, however, Sultan Valad who claims to have regularized the positions of deputy (*nâyeb*) and successor (*khalife*) in the Mevlevi order. One of the individuals Sultan Valad appointed to head up a Mevlevi lodge outside Konya was Shaykh Solaymân Torkamâni, the son of Shaykh Hosayn Mevlevi. The charter for a pious endowment (*vaqf*) written out in the fall of 1297 indicates that Shaykh Solaymân established a Mevlevi lodge in the east of Kırşehir (Qirshahr) with a sizeable income. The document specifies that the shaykh of the lodge had to know the Mevlevi terminology and wear Mevlevi clothes, in addition to being a pious and well-mannered person (GM 62). This language suggests that the symbols of Mevlevi allegiance were already established, but that formal rituals (*samâʿ*, the initiation period, etc.) were as yet either not well defined or not obligatory, being left to the discretion of the shaykh at each individual lodge. It appears that Shaykh Solaymân predeceased Sultan Valad by two years, in 1310 (GM 63). In Erzincan, Sultan Valad established Hosâm al-Din Hosayn as the Mevlevi authority (Sep 154; GM 63).

But it was primarily in Konya, where the Valad family had been installed at the invitation of ʿAlâ al-Din Kay Qobâd, that Sultan Valad, with state patronage, established the Mevlevi order. When the Mevlevis expanded beyond Konya, they attempted to secure similar patronage arrangements from the aristocracy and/or local governors, and build their lodges with pious endowments (*vaqf*). When Rumi's grandson, ʿĀref Chelebi, forayed the frontiers outside Konya between 1312 and 1319 to promote the order, Aflâki tells us that he approached petty princes and local rulers, such as the Germiyanid ruler, Mehmed Beg, "Champion of the Faith," who built a mosque in Bergi in 1312 after conquering the town.

After the collapse of Seljuk power in Anatolia, the order named for Rumi maintained aristocratic ties and elite connections within the Sunni milieu, in contradistinction to the rural and often popular origins of other orders. Though some branches of the Mevlevis were later attracted to the Kızılbâş and Shiism, and eventually appealed to a more popular audience of Bektâshis, the main branch of the Mevlevis attracted the patronage and attention of the Ottoman sultans, particularly Murad II (1421–44 and 1446–51), Bâyezid II (1481–1512), Selim I (1512–20) and Murad III (1574–95). Murad II established a Mevlevi lodge as far north as Edirne, near the modern border with Bulgaria. Eventually, fourteen large Mevlevi lodges, or *tekke*s (from Persian *takiye*), were established in the cities of the Ottoman empire, with a further seventy-six minor lodges in provincial towns. State patronage actually kept the Mevlevis, whose shaykhs often wielded considerable power and influence, subordinate to the government, though the suspicions of sultans and other officials were sometimes aroused, in particular because the governors of Konya required the support and cooperation of the Mevlevis to enforce their rule there. The Grand Chelebi in Konya, the descendant of Rumi appointed to head the order, chose the shaykhs of each Mevlevi *tekke*, subject to the approval of an Islamic official, the Shaykh al-Islam, and the Ottoman sultan.

The Mevlevi lodges came to function as a kind of art academy or cultural center, as well as places for the practice of Mevlevi rituals. Once the study of Persian had been forbidden in the schools in Turkey, the Mevlevi lodges, which maintained this tradition in their Dâr al-Masnavis, or *Masnavi* Halls, became centers of literary study. In such an atmosphere, the great commentaries on the *Masnavi*, like those of Rosukhi Esmâʿil Dede of Ankara (d. 1631) and Sari ʿAbd Allâh (d. 1660) were written, usually under the influence of Ibn ʿArabi's doctrines. While the aristocratic and sophisticated aura of the Mevlevi order in the seventeenth through nineteenth centuries is clear, we should not assume that it has always been so; in the earliest period the Mevlevis had more popular roots in the mercantile classes (V. Holbrook, in LLM, 107). Even in the nineteenth century, Hâj Maʿsumʿali Shâh (1853–?), a Nimatullahi Sufi from Shiraz, wrote in his "Pathways to Mystic Truth" (*Tarâ'eq al-haqâ'eq*) that the Mevlevi order was by that time common in Anatolia, Syria, Egypt, the islands around Asia Minor and even in Iraq. It was popular, he says, with young and old alike, with aristocrats, scholars and the untutored, as well as palace officials and the sultan.[1]

THE SHRINE IN KONYA

Gölpınarlı (GM 87) believes Rumi did not personally favor building a dome or any other imposing structure over his father's resting place. To support this view, he adduces two lines from the *Masnavi* (M3:133–4) in which Rumi talks of the insignificance of mausoleums, domes and parapets as signs of spiritual grandeur in the eyes of the people of meaning. Of course, this statement of general principle does not necessarily lead to Gölpınarlı's specific conclusion; one may not need visible evidences of grandeur to perceive the *mysterium tremendum*, but it does not axiomatically follow that one must therefore reject such symbols on principle. On the other hand, Aflâki's report (Af 408–9) that Rumi had willed his disciples to build a large dome over his tomb, one that could be seen from a great distance, almost certainly reflects the wishes of Rumi's disciples, including Sultan Valad, rather than anything that Rumi himself said. Most likely this report is a later fabrication circulated to justify the disciples' actions and to encourage pilgrims to visit the shrine, especially because, as we have seen, other reports conveyed by Aflâki show Rumi opposed to receiving money from Tâj al-Din to expand the school.

In any case, the shrine in Konya marking his grave or *torbat* (Turkish *türbe*), supposedly constructed on the site of a garden owned by ʿAlâ al-Din Kay Qobâd which Rumi had frequented while alive, became a center of pilgrimage maintained by the pious endowments and donations of princes and Mevlevi followers. Within a few generations after his death, Qâzi Najm al-Din-e Tashti remarked (Af 597) that all graves (*gur khâne*) used to be called *torbe* (literally "earth" or "dust," but with the connotation of a respected, even sacred spot or shrine), but that now, when one heared the word *torbe*, one assumed it to refer to the resting place (*marqad*) of Mowlânâ. Konya is situated in south-central Anatolia, 107 kilometers to the east of Karaman, 262 kilometers southwest of Ankara and 657 kilometers south of Istanbul. The shrine of Rumi stands on the east edge of town on a street named for Rumi (Mevlânâ Caddesi), just off the main road to Adana. Just to the west stands the Sultan Selim mosque, built in the sixteenth century. Rumi's shrine was transformed into the Konya Mevlânâ Museum after the closing of the dervish lodges in 1925. Under this name, it continues to open its doors to tourists and pilgrims today. In 1999 the museum was opened to visitors for a modest admission charge (one million Turkish lira) every day from 9:30 to 12:00 and 1:30 to 5:00PM, and again in the evening on Thursdays.

The museum offers a number of displays, including a few miniatures depicting Rumi and many manuscripts. Here one may see manuscript copies of the *Masnavi*, including one dating to 1278 (which the Turkish government has published in a handsome facsimile); manuscripts of the *Divân-e kabir* (*Divân-e Shams*); of various *Masnavi* commentaries in Persian and Turkish; of the Koran; and of various Ottoman and Persian poets. Also on display is a huge *tasbih* (rosary) of 990 beads. The libraries of Mehmet Önder and of Abdülbaki Gölpınarlı are also housed in a separate part of the compound, along with a display of china and pottery. The Konya Chamber of Commerce maintains a web site where a number of photographs from the interior of the shrine can be viewed, at www.kto.org.tr/mevlana/resim.htm, and the exterior of the shrine can be seen in a few pictures on the web site at www.ege.edu.tr/Turkiye/si/Konya.html.

Visitors step through the main entrance of the compound, past the cells where the dervishes formerly lived, now converted into offices. They then enter into a paved marble courtyard with a fountain for ablutions covered by a marble canopy on colonettes. Next to this is a rose garden. To the right of the courtyard is the kitchen, in which wax models of Mevlevi dervishes in various poses have been placed. A little marble pool in front of the kitchen is called the *howz-e ʿors*, the wedding pool, wedding being the term used to describe the death anniversary of members of the order. Formerly, whenever the death anniversary of Rumi fell in the summer (according to the Islamic lunar calendar), it would be observed around this pool. Carpets would be spread and a ceremony would be held. If the anniversary fell in winter, as it always does now since the conversion to the solar calendar, the *samâ*ᶜ ceremonies would be observed inside the *samâ*ᶜ hall (Tfz 62). Also in this courtyard, just to the right of the entrance to the main building, one sees a free-standing memorial to the famous Ottoman architect Sinan Pâshâ (d. 1573).

The main structure in the shrine complex consisted of a mausoleum, a mosque and a *samâ*ᶜ hall. The mausoleum, extending along the length of the right side of the building, contains memorial cenotaphs for about three dozen members of Rumi's family and close associates. The bodies are actually interred in an underground crypt, and not within the sarcophagi, some of which have been moved around since the shrine became a museum in the 1920s (GB 236 n. 1). The various funerary inscriptions indicate that a number of women are buried here, including Rumi's second wife, Kerrâ Khâtun, who died late on Thursday, 13 Ramadan 691 (August 28, 1292) and Rumi's daughter by her, Maleke Khâtun, who died on 18 Shaᶜbân 703 (March 26, 1304; but GB 238 gives the date as 705/1306). The inscription on a black- and green-tiled sarcophagus tells us that a certain Jalâle Khâtun, a granddaughter of the King of Clerics, Bahâ al-Din, died in Muharram 681 (April 1282) and was buried here. Another Maleke Khâtun, this one the daughter of the Qâzi Tâj al-Din, also has a sarcophagus of black and green tile with an embossed inscription, indicating that she died on the night of Wednesday, 16 Jumâdi II 730 (April 6, 1330). There are at least seven other female Mevlevis buried here.

A number of the male members of the Mevlevi order who lived from the seventeenth through the nineteenth century, some of them Grand Chelebis (such as Bustân Chelebi and Hamdam Saᶜid Chelebi), were also laid to rest here. The Grand Chelebi ʿAbd al-Vâhed Chelebi was buried here as late as 1907.

More importantly, the cenotaph of Hosâm al-Din Chelebi stands to the fore, nearby those of Rumi's wife and daughter. In the center stands a marble cenotaph for Rumi; at his side is Sultan Valad. Both cenotaphs are covered with a gold-embroidered brocade stitched with Koranic verses, weighing twenty pounds and donated by Sultan ʿAbd al-Hamid in the nineteenth century. The silver railing around the tomb was donated by Hasan Pâshâ in 1599.

Behind them and slightly to their left, at the back of the room underneath the conical dome covered on the outside in green tile (hence the name, Yeşil Kubbe, the Green Dome), is the wooden carved cenotaph of Bahâ al-Din, perhaps originally designed for Rumi, and dating to the thirteenth century. In the same row, just to the left of Bahâ al-Din is the cenotaph for Salâh al-Din Zarkub. To the left of Salâh al-Din and one row forward are the grave markers of Ulu ʿÂref Chelebi (1272–1320), ʿÂbed Chelebi (d. 1338), and Salâh al-Din Zâhed Chelebi (1287–1334), the sons of Sultan Valad. Further to the left and in the same row with Bahâ al-Din is the resting place of Karim al-Din Bektamor (d. 1291), the shaykh of Sultan Valad. The second marker to the right of Bahâ al-Din is for ʿAlâ al-Din, the supposedly estranged son of Rumi (d. 1262). In all there are over fifty cenotaphs, not all of them identified.

The left-hand side of the shrine structure houses a small mosque at the front and a *samâ*ᶜ hall at the back. The *samâ*ᶜ *khâne* or audition hall dates from the era of Süleyman the Magnificent and is more or less square in shape, with an area at the back for visitors to watch from, the men at the bottom and the women on the balcony above. To the left was the musicians' gallery (*motreb khâne*), in front of which the Grand Chelebi would sit as *pust-neshin* to lead the ceremonies, with the *Masnavi* reciter and other dignitaries to his left. Toward the front, in the middle of the shrine, is a smallish mosque. The building is roofed by a number of smaller domes, in addition to the conical green faience dome.

The *samâ*ᶜ hall and the mosque now host a display of illuminated manuscripts from the Mevlevi shrine's library. The library included, of course, dozens of complete and partial copies of the *Masnavi*, dictionaries of the *Masnavi*, commentaries in Persian, and so forth. A few date from the Seljuk period, such as a manuscript of the *Masnavi* dated to 1278. Other manuscripts date to the fourteenth century, including a copy of the *Masnavi* from 1371 and a copy of Rumi's *Divân-e kabir*, as well as a copy of Sultan Valad's *Divân* from 1332. Abdülbâki Gölpınarlı has edited the catalog of manuscripts kept in the Mevlânâ Museum, consisting of the library maintained for the Mevlevi dervishes at Rumi's shrine. This catalog, *Mevlânâ Müzesi: Yazmalar Kataloğu* (Ankara: Türk Tarih Kurumu, 1967–94), contains a wide variety of the standard medieval Arabic works on Koran, Hadith, Islamic law, etc., a number of Persian poetry volumes and mystical treatises, as well as works related to members of the Mevlevi order.

The modern secular state of Turkey maintained an ambivalent attitude toward its Islamic past even up to the commemoration of the 700th anniversary of Rumi's death in 1973, which also corresponded to the 50th anniversary of the founding of the Republic of Turkey by Mustafa Kemal Atatürk (1881–1938). In a lavishly illustrated commemorative volume published by the Turkish Tourism Office, *Turkey, Fiftieth Anniversary of the Republic* (Ankara: Ajans Turk), all aspects of Turkey are celebrated, but only very little information on Konya and a brief mention of the Mevlevis can be found. Nevertheless, on December 17, 1954, the Turkish government held a ceremonial gathering in Konya to commemorate the anniversary of Rumi's death, to which a number of Europeans, including Annemarie Schimmel and Hellmut Ritter, were invited (RiM 249). Mevlevi dancers from all over the country were also invited to turn.

The visitors seen on a recent visit to the Mevlânâ Museum in Konya were mostly Turkish Muslims, preponderantly women, most of them wearing headscarves and observing the Islamic dress code. They revere Rumi as a saint and worker of miracles, even though most of them have never read the *Masnavi* or the *Divân*, even in Turkish translation (the Turks, of course, can no longer read Persian without studying it in university as a foreign language). Nevertheless, they believe in Rumi's powers and come here on pilgrimage to read from the Koran and pray, asking for health, wealth, children and the things one typically asks for at a saint's tomb. Small crowds of European tourists also show up at the museum, which is the mainstay of the Konya tourist industry, out of curiosity, usually with no knowledge of Rumi's works. There are, however, guided tours in English and German to provide a mishmash of fact and fiction by way of information, though a handful of Westerners also come as pilgrims, knowing Rumi and having read his works. As a calligraphic verse hanging in the entry cubicle reads:

> ka'bat al-'oshshâq bâshad in maqâm
> har ke nâqes âmad injâ shod tamâm

> This shrine is the Kaaba of the lovers:
> All who come here lacking find completion

In 1955 the Turkish government invited a delegation of ten Iranian writers to Turkey for a three-week cultural visit, which included Konya. On the plane to Turkey, the Iranian poet Sarmad, moved to tears by the prospect of visiting Rumi's shrine, extemporaneously composed a *masnavi* which he then recited at Rumi's mausoleum:

> The scent of love arrives from Konya's dust
> How welcome is that precious Konya's dust!
>
>   ✷ ✷ ✷
>
> A guest has come to call, arise and greet
> one cut from your same bed, a kindred reed.[2]

In the courtyard of the museum/shrine, one can purchase postcards, pamphlets, books and tapes, including histories of Rumi and the Mevlevis, versions of his poems and descriptions about this and other related sites, mostly in Turkish. A number of books about the shrine at Konya were written by the museum curator, Mehmet Önder, whose works are discussed at some length below, in chapter 13. Mention can be made here of one of his early reports on the school and house at the shrine, *Mevlana'nın Konyadaki evi ve medresesi* (Konya: Yenikitap Basımevi, 1956). An English version of one of Önder's guides has been published as *Konya: The Residence of Great Mevlâna, The Moslem Mystic And a Guide for the Ancient Art and Museums in the City* (Istanbul: Keskin Colour Ltd. Co. Printing House, 1970).

A CHRONOLOGY OF THE MEVLEVIS AFTER RUMI

c. 1274 Followers disagree over succession. Sultan Valad affirms Hosâm al-Din as head of the disciples

1277 Death of Mozaffar al-Din Amir Chelebi, son of Rumi by Kerrâ Khâtun (October 5)

c. 1284 Death of Chelebi Hosâm al-Din (October 30)
Sultan Valad takes over active stewardship of Rumi's disciples. Begins to appoint deputies in other cities and begins to give structure to the Mevlevis

1291 Sultan Valad composes his *Ebtedâ nâme* (*Valad nâme*) (from March 4 to June 4)

1292 Death of Karim al-Din Bektamor, the shaykh of Sultan Valad (November 1292/ Dhu al-hijja 691)

1292 Death of Kerrâ Khâtun, Rumi's second wife (August 28)

1304 Death of Maleke Khâtun, Rumi's daughter by Kerrâ Khâtun (March 26)

1312 Death of Sultan Valad

c. 1318 Sepahsâlâr composing his "Treatise"
Aflâki begins collecting "Acts of the Gnostics"

1320 Death of Ulu ʿÂref Chelebi, son of Sultan Valad

1338 Death of Amir ʿAbed Chelebi, son of Sultan Valad

1342 Death of Vâjed Chelebi, son of Sultan Valad

1350 Death of Amir ʿÂlem Chelebi, son of Ulu ʿÂref

c. 1353 Aflâki completes final recension of "Acts"

1360 Death of Aflâki (June 15)

1368 Death of Amir ʿÂdel Chelebi, son of Ulu ʿÂref

1395 Death of Amir ʿÂlem Chelebi II, son of Amir ʿÂbed

1421 Death of ʿÂref Chelebi II, son of Amir ʿÂdel

1460 Death of Pir ʿÂdel Chelebi II, son of Amir ʿÂlem

1509 Death of Jamâl al-Din Chelebi, son of Pir ʿÂdel

1544 Shâhedi composes his *Golshan-e asrâr* about famous Mevlevis of his era

c. 1545 Death of Divâne Mohammad Chelebi, Mevlevi shaykh at Karahisar who introduced Shiite rituals into the order

1546 Death of Yusof Sinechâk, Mevlevi shaykh in Istanbul

1561 Death of Khosrow Chelebi, grandson of Jamâl al-Din

1591 Death of Farrokh Chelebi, son of Khosrow Chelebi

1597 Founding of the Mevlevi lodge at Yenikapı by Kamâl Ahmad Dede

1630 Death of Bustân Chelebi, son of Farrokh Chelebi

1638 Death of Abu Bakr Chelebi, son of Farrokh Chelebi

1642 Death of ʿÂref Chelebi III, son of Valad Chelebi
1666 Death of Hosayn Chelebi, grandson of Farrokh Chelebi
1679 Death of ʿAbd al-Halim Chelebi, son of ʿAbd al-Rahmân
1705 Death of Bustân Chelebi II, son of ʿAbd al-Halim
1711 Death of Sadr al-Din Chelebi, son of Bustân Chelebi
1735 Death of Shaykh Sâqeb Mohammad Dede, author of a chronicle of the later Mevlevi order
1746 Death of Mohammad ʿÂref Chelebi, son of ʿAbd al-Rahmân
1785 Death of Abu Bakr Chelebi II, son of Mohammad ʿÂref
1797 Death of Asrâr Mohammad Dede, author of a *vita* of the Mevlevi poets
1815 Death of Hâj Mohammad Chelebi, son of Esmâʿil Chelebi
1858 Death of Saʿid Hamdam Chelebi, son of Hâj Mohammad
1866 Publication of Sharifzâde Sayyed Mohammad Fâzel Pâshâ's history of the Mevlevi order
1881 Death of Sadr al-Din Chelebi II, son of Hamdam
      Death of Fakhr al-Din Chelebi, son of Hamdam
1887 Death of Mostafâ Safvat Chelebi, son of Hamdam
1907 Death of ʿAbd al-Vâhed Chelebi, son of Hamdam
      ʿAbd al-Halim, son of ʿAbd al-Vâhed, becomes Grand Chelebi
1909 Bahâ al-Din Valad Chelebi becomes head of Mevlevis after ʿAbd al-Halim is deposed as Chelebi
1919 Bahâ al-Din is deposed and ʿAbd al-Halim is restored
1920 Death of ʿÂmel Chelebi, son of Yaʿqub Chelebi
1925 Turkish law requires Mevlevi order to cease operation
?   Death of ʿAbd al-Halim Chelebi, son of ʿAbd al-Vâhed
?   Death of Bahâ al-Din Valad Chelebi, son of Mostafâ Najib
1943 Death of Mohammad Bâqer Chelebi, son of ʿAbd al-Halim
?   Death of Shams al-Vâhed Chelebi II, son of ʿAbd al-Vâhed
               ✱ ✱ ✱
1975 Süleyman (Loras) Dede visits North America
1979 Jelaluddin Loras, son of Süleyman Dede, in North America to propagate Mevlevi practice
1985 Death of Süleyman Dede, January 19
1990 Kabir Helminski initiated as Mevlevi shaykh
1996 Death of Dr. Celâleddin Celebi (Jalâl al-Din Chelebi)
1996– Faruk Hemdem Celebi (Fâruq Hamdam Chelebi) as current Chelebi of the Mevlevi order

THE FORMATION OF THE ORDER

THE FIRST GENERATION OF DEVOTEES AND DISCIPLES AT THE SHRINE

We know the names of many individuals who served or lived at the shrine of Rumi. In 1291, Sultan Valad (SVE 396) mentions a certain **Serâj al-Din-e Masnavi-khwân**, whose occupation, as his nickname indicates, was to recite the *Masnavi* aloud. Serâj must surely have been blessed with a good voice and an excellent knowledge of the text to be chosen to perform such a service for the disciples. Sultan Valad tells us that one night in a dream he saw Chelebi Hosâm al-Din on the grave of Rumi, holding a copy of the *Masnavi* and reciting from it in a loud and passionate voice. Hosâm al-Din turned to Serâj al-Din and told him, "From now on I want you to recite this *Masnavi* just as I am reciting." We can imagine the authority this dream alone might have conferred upon Serâj al-Din and his particular style of recitation, but Sultan Valad goes on to praise him as one of his choice disciples (SVE 397). Sultan Valad describes him as righteous and ascetic, devout from his youth, but not a dry ascetic like some, rather one endowed with gnostic understanding, who was also a lover of saints and a follower of the path of spiritual poverty. Aflâki refers to him as his teacher (*ostâd*, Af 272), includes him among the saints (*vali*, e.g., Af 162, 222), and indicates that he would recite the *Masnavi* in the shrine (Af 739).

Sultan Valad's comments tell us that Serâj al-Din was no longer a youth in 1291, and Aflâki, who mentions him sixteen times, usually speaks of him as deceased. Aflâki (739) refers to him as the *Masnavi* reciter of the shrine, probably an official position or function for which he received a stipend. From the reports given by Aflâki (e.g., Af 162), Serâj had spent a good deal of time in the presence of Rumi and had been in Hosâm al-Din's inner circle. Saʿid Nafisi (Sep 380) speculates that the Mowlânâ Serâj al-Din Pâpivarti (?) described by Sepahsâlâr (Sep 154) as one of the close disciples of Rumi may be none other than Serâj al-Din the *Masnavi* cantor, and that he may have been from Sivas. If correct, this would mean that both Aflâki and Sepahsâlâr place Serâj al-Din with Rumi, at least during Hosâm al-Din's tenure, but perhaps not before 1258, since Serâj is nowhere associated with the name of Salâh al-Din.

It is to this Serâj al-Din that we owe the following story, relayed to us by Aflâki (739–41):

> One day, his holiness the successor of God among his people and the wayfarer on the path of truth, Hosâm al-Haqq va al-Din, may God sanctify his precious spirit, discovered that some of the disciples were with great enthusiasm and devotion closely reading the *Elâhi nâme* of the Sage [i.e., the *Hadiqe* of Sanâʾi] and the *Manteq al-tayr* of Farid al-Din ʿAttâr and also his *Mosibat nâme*. They derived great joy from the mysteries contained therein and marveled at their wondrous meanings. He then sought an opportunity (for opportunity is as fleeting as the clouds), and finding Rumi one night all on his own, bowed his head and said, "So many *divân*s of ghazals have been written and the lights of those mysteries have illumined shore and sea throughout the east and west. But by the grace of God, all the speeches of these orators fail to match the grandeur of your words. It would be a great mercy and blessing if a book like the *Elâhi nâme* of the Sage, or one in the meter of the *Manteq al-tayr* remained behind among the people of the world as a memento to comfort the souls of those suffering the pains of gnostic love. This servant of yours wishes that the friends of bright aspect, from all directions, will turn their heads toward your noble face and occupy themselves with nothing else. The rest of it is up to the bounty and favor of the master."

Rumi immediately produced a notebook from his blessed turban which explains the mysteries both generally and specifically. He then handed Chelebi Hosâm al-Din a paper on which the first eighteen lines of the *Masnavi*, from "Listen to this reed as it complains, telling tales of separation" up to "The raw one cannot ken the mind of one who's cooked, so let's be brief and get on with the point" were written in the meter *ramal-e mosaddas-e mahzuf.*

Still on the authority of Serâj al-Din, Aflâki goes on to tell us that Rumi had already been inspired by God with these verses and the idea to compose such a book before Hosâm al-Din approached him (Af 741).

Other disciples mentioned in Aflâki include Kamâl al-Din Tabrizi, the chief of the servants of the shrine (Af 427); Shaykh Bahâ al-Din Khayyât, the tailor, who served in the shrine (Af 933); Bahâ al-Din Bahri, a very learned man who served as the imam at the shrine (Af 442) and used to sit in the presence of Rumi to record his words as a kind of secretary or *kâteb-e asrâr* (Af 188). Akhi Amir Ahmad (Pâyporti), who lived in Bayburt, had wanted to travel to Konya and declare himself a disciple while Rumi was still alive, but as he was still young at that time, his parents did not allow it. When Sultan Valad traveled to Bayburt, Akhi Amir Ahmad became his disciple and subsequently the disciple of Ulu ᶜÂref (Af 390–92). On the other hand, Aflâki mentions that a singer, a certain Kamâl-e Qavvâl, performed for Rumi and asked for pay in return. He later went blind (Af 454), the implication being that he should have exercised his craft in the spirit of discipleship rather than demanding pecuniary reward.

THE CHELEBIS: THE FIRST GENERATIONS

The stewardship of the Mevlevi order became the hereditary responsibility of the descendants of Rumi all the way down to the present day, with only minor interruptions. During the first generation after Rumi, the descendants of Sultan Valad were called "Valadi" and those disciples who had been in the presence of Rumi were called "Mowlavi." Eventually, however, all those who formally entered the Mevlevi order at the permission of a shaykh came to be known as "Mowlavi." A title meaning "sir" or "master," "Chelebi," was first applied to Hosâm al-Din, though he has no part in the blood line of Rumi's grandsons. By the end of Sultan Valad's life, the title Chelebi had come to refer to Rumi's descendants in the line of Sultan Valad, and the title Grand Chelebi was reserved for the head shaykh of the Mevlevi order, presiding at Konya. Of course, other dervish orders, including the Bektâshis, also employed the title Chelebi, but without the specific meaning it held within Mevlevi circles.

ULU ᶜÂREF CHELEBI

Ulu ᶜÂref Chelebi (June 7, 1272–February 5, 1320) was born after sunset on Monday June 7, 1272 to Sultan Valad and Fâteme Khâtun. His maternal grandfather, Shaykh Salâh al-Din, had died some fourteen years earlier, but his paternal grandfather, Jalâl al-Din Rumi, who lived until his grandson was a year and a half old, must have often cradled the little boy in his arms. Sepahsâlâr (Sep 152) tells us that upon Ulu ᶜÂref's birth Rumi wrapped the boy in his wide sleeve and ordered that a *samâ*ᶜ be held in celebration. Aflâki (Af 828) tells us this went on for three days and nights, and gives further details. Rumi had been quite solicitous of Fâteme Khâtun's health during her pregnancy because she had lost many prior infants between the ages of six months and one year (Af 825–6). Hearing the good news of a healthy baby son, Rumi rushed into the birthing room and strewed gold coins on Fâteme Khâtun (Af 827).

Rumi told Sultan Valad that he saw the light of seven saints in the child: Bahâ al-Din, Borhân al-Din, Shams al-Din, Salâh al-Din, Hosâm al-Din, himself and that of Valad. "In truth, this ᶜÂref of ours combines the light of all the spiritual *axis mundi*s." Rumi then christened him Jalâl al-Din Faridun, a combination of his own title and the first name of the child's other grandfather, Salâh al-Din. Aflâki quotes a ghazal for Ulu ᶜÂref with the refrain "Faridun," which he ascribes to Rumi (Af 829). However, this poem does not appear in most copies of Rumi's *Divân* and is more likely a composition of Sultan Valad (GM 92 n. 2). In any case, Rumi instructed that, just as his own father had called Jalâl al-Din Mohammad not by his name but by the title Khodâvandgâr (Master), so Sultan Valad should call the child by the title Amir ᶜÂref, "Gnostic Prince" (Af 828). The Turkish equivalent for Amir, meaning "prince" or "commander," was Ulu, and it appears that people commonly referred to him either as Ulu ᶜÂref or simply as Chelebi.

Aflâki tells us a number of remarkable tales designed to showcase the spiritual prowess of the little babe, though they seem much inflated with hagiographical devotion. For example, as a six-month-old child, Ulu ᶜÂref began repeating the word "Allâh" (Af 830), the preferred *zekr* of the Valad family. Likewise, he did not suckle for three days after the death of Rumi, but when his mother finally gave him the breast, the light of saintship glowed so brightly around him that she became a disciple of her own child (Af 831–2).

Rumi played with the little child and made him laugh, explaining that the Prophet had set the example of cheering the hearts of little children (Af 833). On another occasion, when Ulu ᶜÂref was seven months old and his throat had swollen such that the doctors were unable to cure him and all feared he might die, Rumi drew seven vertical and seven horizontal lines on the affected area as a talisman and cured him. The companions interpreted this to mean he would live seven years or perhaps seventy, but eventually when he died in his forty-ninth year, it became clear that Rumi had promised seven times seven years (Af 836–7). The child was quite handsome (Af 834) and reminded Sultan Valad of the mannerisms of his father (Af 838). Likewise, Rumi reportedly saw himself in the child and when holding him did not wish to give him back to his father

(Af 901). Hosâm al-Din, too, enjoyed playing with him and longed to train the child himself in mystical states (Af 912).

Sultan Valad called his child "the shaykh of spirits" and would read Rumi's poems to him (Af 958). Sultan Valad thought that no one like him had set forth into the world (Af 900). He was also a favorite of his paternal step-grandmother Kerrâ Khâtun, and his paternal aunt, Maleke Khâtun (Af 911). Sultan Valad had the child educated by one of the close disciples of Rumi, Salâh al-Din of Malatya, who had such an impressive command of Arabic that he was known as Sibawayh the Second, and was probably a *faqih*, or jurisprudential scholar (Sep 383). By the age of six he was studying Koran with this Salâh al-Din (Af 837). As Tahsin Yazıcı points out ("Çelebi, ᶜĀref," *EIr*), he must also have had some literary training, but he grew up "rather spoiled" by all the attention and respect shown to him by the Mevlevis.

When the child grew older, Sultan Valad pressured him to marry so that the leadership of the Mevlevi order would continue in the line of Rumi's descendants. Ulu ᶜĀref preferred to remain single, but finally consented (Af 842–3) and wed Dowlat Khâtun, the daughter of Amir Qaysar Tabrizi. Two male children were born of this union; Aflâki (843) tells us the older was named Amir ᶜÂlem by Sultan Valad and the younger was named Amir ᶜÂdel by Mozaffar al-Din (though this could not have been Rumi's other son, who died in 1272). Ulu ᶜĀref also sired a girl, Maleke Khâtun, but Gölpınarlı (GM 94) believes Ulu ᶜĀref may have died before her birth.

Ulu ᶜĀref and his Temper

Marriage was not the only subject over which father and son differed. Sultan Valad preferred for Ulu ᶜĀref to act as his disciple and to repeat his teachings, but Ulu ᶜĀref insisted on speaking on behalf of Rumi (Af 910–11). On another occasion we find Ulu ᶜĀref making up after a quarrel with his father by playing a musical instrument and reciting poems (Af 955–7).

Once Ulu ᶜĀref saw a man in Sivas with exceedingly long dirty fingernails and toenails, chattering much nonsense while playing with stones. The people had gathered around him listening reverently and giving him gifts of food and sweets; the people called him Khwâje Erzurum and thought him a holy man. Ulu ᶜĀref went up and slapped him three times, knocking him down on his face, telling him to go take up a trade. This caused a commotion among the people and Ulu ᶜĀref was detained, but with the support of the troops of the local governor, ᶜArab Nuyân, and the help of ruffians of Konya and Kayseri, he was released and proceeded on to Tokat (Af 852–5). Khwâje Erzurum died a week later and upon Ulu ᶜĀref's return many of the Khwâje's former partisans supposedly pledged their allegiance to Ulu ᶜĀref. Aflâki (856) tells us that when Ulu ᶜĀref returned home to Konya, Sultan Valad congratulated him for rebuking this man.

On a trip through Marand in Iranian Azerbayjan, probably sometime before 1295, Ulu ʿÂref quarreled once again, this time with a certain Shaykh Jamâl al-Din-e Eshâq of Marand. This ascetic Sufi was much revered in the area and would compose poetry, sometimes answering poems of Rumi and claiming "I am the manifestation of the Master Rumi." This Shaykh Eshâq did in the presence of Ulu ʿÂref, not realizing that he was Rumi's grandson, and received a slap for his presumption. "You're no match even for the dogs in his alley, how dare you forge such a boastful lie." More wrestling and slapping ensued and the townspeople rushed to Shaykh Eshâq's defense. Ulu ʿÂref was saved from their midst and set off for Tabriz. However, three days later this same shaykh, overcome by a mystical state, supposedly fell off the roof while whirling in ecstasy and died. Upon Ulu ʿÂref's return from Tabriz, most of the people of Marand became his disciples (Af 849–51).

Ulu ʿÂref traveled widely, although he kept house near the shrine of Rumi, probably in the area known as the Circle of Chelebi. During most of his travels Aflâki accompanied him, recording his words and deeds, so that we have a first-hand source for some of his adventures, however biased and miracle-mongering it may be. It was Ulu ʿÂref who encouraged Aflâki to write his chronicle. Unfortunately, however, Aflâki is concerned only with anecdotal fragments, not with historical details or chronicling the course or purpose of Ulu ʿÂref's journeys. Ulu ʿÂref apparently undertook these journeys partly out of the pleasure of tourism (*tafarroj*) and partly in conjunction with the efforts to expand and consolidate the Mevlevi order. We find him in Sivas, performing *samâ'* and checking in on the lodge (*zâvie*) of the Mevlevi disciples there (Af 852). He also traveled in all directions throughout Anatolia, to Lârende, Niğde, Aksaray, Sivas, Tokat, Amasya, Denizli, Menteshe, Akşehir, Beyşehir, Karahisar, Antakya, Erzinjan, Bayburt, Erzurum, and to western Iran, including Marand and Tabriz (GM 97). Ulu ʿÂref visited Sivas, Tokat and Tabriz while his father was still alive, apparently after 1295, when Ghâzân Khân assumed the Ilkhanid throne (GM 98).

His Contact with Rulers

In the course of his journeys Ulu ʿÂref had contact with various powerful men and women. Gaykhâtu (Kayghâtu), a brother of the Ilkhanid ruler Arghun, entered Konya in 1290 at the head of an army. When Arghun died in May 1291, Gaykhâtu made a bid for the throne, during which he sacked the areas of Eregli, the city of Lârende, Denizli and the Menteshe area, and struck fear into the hearts of the citizens of Konya from November 1291 to February 1292 (CaT 298). In Erzurum this Gaykhâtu had a wife named Pâshâ Khâtun, who not only considered Ulu ʿÂref her shaykh but was also in love with him, at least according to Aflâki's source. She detained Ulu ʿÂref there, probably on his return from Tabriz, despite his father's letters calling him to return to Konya. When she died Ulu ʿÂref was greatly affected; he attended the commemorations at her graveside held one week after and then forty days after her death and composed a quatrain on each of these occasions before returning to Konya (Af 889–91).

A subsequent Ilkhanid ruler, Ghâzân Khân (r. 1295–1304), after hearing a report of Ulu ʿÂref's spiritual powers, expressed the desire to meet him, but Ulu ʿÂref demurred, promising instead to pray for the sultan from afar. This only increased Ghâzân's insistence to meet him. Eventually Ghâzân's wife, Iltormesh Khâtun, arranged for a large *samâ* gathering and invited Ulu ʿÂref. He came to her tent and after reading from the Koran and reciting some ghazals, he performed the *samâ* (Af 846–7). Both Iltormesh and Ghâzân fell under his spell. Aflâki (848) tells us that Ghâzân Khân would ask the poets and mystics who attended his court, such as Qotb al-Din Shirâzi (d. 1311), Homâm-e Tabrizi (d. 1314) and Rashid al-Din (d. 1318), to talk about Rumi and his verses. Ghâzân even had some lines of Rumi about converting the Tatars, which Ghâzân believed applied to him, sewed with gold thread into one of his royal robes (Af 838–9). Likewise, the Mevlevi influence on Ghâzân resulted in the appointment of ʿAlâ al-Din b. Farâmarz Kay Qobâd III in 1297 as the governor of Anatolia, based in Konya. The grateful ʿAlâ al-Din dutifully honored Sultan Valad and Ulu ʿÂref (Af 839).

The successor of Ghâzân Khân, Oljâytu (Öljeytü, r. 1314–17), had become a Muslim like Ghâzân, but preferred the Shiite creed. He forbade the mention of the Sunni companions of the Prophet in the Friday prayers of Anatolia and wanted to dig up the body of Abu Bakr and remove it from the precincts of the Prophet's grave (Af 858). Sultan Valad wanted to send Ulu ʿÂref to Soltâniye, the Mongol capital situated to the west of Zanjân in Iran, to try to dissuade Oljâytu from this course of action. Ulu ʿÂref was about to set out when his father died, causing a delay in this mission until 1315, according to Aflâki (859). He stopped in Bayburt to see Akhi Amir Ahmad Pâyporti (Pâyporti meaning from Bayburt), one of the Mevlevi shaykhs, in the month of Ramadan (November 1315). According to the dates which Aflâki gives (Af 860), Ulu ʿÂref tarried there (or along the way, in Kayseri and Sivas) at least until the advent of the ʿId al-fitr in A.H. 716 (December 1316). After reaching Ahlat on Lake Van he received word on the 1st of Dhu al-qaʿda (January 15, 1317) that Oljâytu had died (Af 860). He proceeded to Soltâniye anyway, where he arrived on February 21, 1317. He stayed in Soltâniye for about a year and held the *samâ* ceremony (T. Yazıcı, *EIr*), which disturbed the viziers and other notables, who were still in mourning (Af 861).

In Menteshe, Ulu ʿÂref attracted the attention of the local governor, Masʿud Beg, who held a *samâ* session in his honor. Masʿud Beg gave Ulu ʿÂref a number of valuable gifts and became a disciple along with Shojâʿ al-Din Urkhân (d. c. 1329), Masʿud Beg's son (Af 852). Another Shojâʿ al-Din, Inânch Beg, the Amir of Denizli, also held a feast in honor of Ulu ʿÂref (Af 864). Likewise,

Ulu ʿÂref met with the Germiyanid prince Yaʿqub Beg, who, accompanied by his daughter, paid him much respect in Kütâhya (Af 947). This Yaʿqub Beg eventually left all his agricultural lands in a pious endowment (*vaqf*) to Ulu ʿÂref (GM 138). Once Ulu ʿÂref found it necessary to write to Amir Badr al-Din Ebrâhim Beg (r. 1315–34) about the return of a marble pool which had been sent as a gift from Kütâhya for the *khâneqâh* at the shrine of Rumi in Konya and confiscated through subterfuge by Jalâl-e Kuchek (Af 906–7). In short, there were few local rulers in Anatolia with whom Ulu ʿÂref did not have some kind of contact or dealings (see GM 104 for a more complete list).

His Ties with Mevlevi Lodges and Other Sufis

Not all Ulu ʿÂref's journeys were undertaken to visit kings and governors. As head of the Mevlevi community in Konya, he would visit the Mevlevi hospices in other cities. While in Soltâniye in 1317 Ulu ʿÂref visited the lodge of Shaykh Sohrâb-e Mevlevi (Af 896). In Amasya he met with the deputy appointed by Hosâm al-Din, ʿAlâ al-Din Âmasivi, and held a *samâʿ* session attended by all the Mevlevi companions, complete with readings from the Koran, the *Masnavi* and ghazals. Ulu ʿÂref obviously felt that ʿAlâ al-Din was too independent and derided his lowly spiritual station in front of his disciples, telling him that though he read the *Masnavi*, he understood nothing of it. Eventually ʿAlâ al-Din's lodge caught fire a couple of times and most of his disciples came over to Ulu ʿÂref (at least in the telling of Aflâki, 877–9).

His appearance in Bayburt (Pâyport) apparently led to the conversion of many men and women, though certainly not the entire population, male and female, as Aflâki (Af 390) would have us believe. In Denizli, he appointed Mowlânâ Kamâl al-Din, Mowlânâ Mohyi al-Din and Tâj al-Din the *Masnavi* reciter to administer the Mevlevi affairs. In Tokat, he had a female disciple, ʿÂrefe-ye Khwoshleqâ of Konya, who won over many converts. In Karaman Akhi Mohammad Beg was appointed and it was probably he who established the tombs for Rumi's mother, wife and brother there (GM 118).

He did not confine his association with mystics only to the Mevlevis. While in Soltâniye Ulu ʿÂref visited the shrine of Barâq Bâbâ ("hairless dog"), an ecstatic wandering dervish from Tokat who had won the favor of Oljâytu and managed to gather a following. His host at the Barâqi shrine, Hayrân Amirji, later paid a return visit to Konya (Af 860). Ulu ʿÂref also performed the *samâʿ* with non-Mevlevis, such as the Akhi Ahmad Shâh Qazzâz in Tabriz (Af 894), and associated with Refâʿi and other Sufis (GM 114–16).[3]

Several accounts in Aflâki suggest that Ulu ʿÂref used to drink and Gölpınarlı speculates that he may have been an alcoholic (GM 107–13). Several stories also suggest that women fell easily in love with him (GM 113–14). This may in part have to do with his closeness to Malâmati strains of Sufism, and his association with the likes of Barâq Bâbâ and his successor Hayrân Amirji.

In his sixteenth-century Turkish chronicle *Menâkıb-i Hvoca-i cihân ve netîce-i cân*, Vâhedi vehemently denounces the socially deviant dervishes of Barâq Bâbâ's ilk, and describes a group called the Shams-e Tabrizis who shave their heads and faces, walk barefoot and wear felt cloaks and caps of black and white. Supposedly, in addition to playing music and chanting, they also drank wine. No other source mentions this group and, given Vâhedi's polemical purposes (he praises the law-abiding Mevlevis), one wonders to what extent we may rely upon this information. But Ahmet Karamustafa argues on this basis in *God's Unruly Friends* (Salt Lake City: University of Utah Press, 1994) that the Mevlevi order has always harbored "two conflicting modes of spirituality," the arm of Sultan Valad, which conforms to the laws of Islam, and the "social deviants," who believed that their ecstatic experiences placed them beyond the pale of the law. Karamustafa believes that Ulu ʿÂref Chelebi represents this antinomian strain of Mevlevi practice, who took as their exemplar Shams-e Tabrizi (Karamustafa, 81–2).

Ulu ʿÂref's disciple, Aflâki, does not however depict Shams al-Din as a particularly antinomian figure. This trend seems more likely due to the influence of other Sufi orders and wandering dervishes, such as Barâq Bâbâ, with whom Ulu ʿÂref associated, and in later years, with the Horufi, Qalandari and Shiite influences of Divâne Mohammad (see below).

The Death of Ulu ʿÂref Chelebi

Ulu ʿÂref died, according to Sepahsâlâr (Sep 152) and Aflâki (Af 971), on Tuesday, 24 Dhu al-hijja 719, corresponding to February 5, 1320. He is buried on the upper left side of the shrine of Rumi, just before the grave of Shaykh Karim al-Din, but there is no inscription on his sarcophagus (GM 123).

Aflâki liberally sprinkles samples of Ulu ʿÂref's quatrains throughout the text. One manuscript of the *Manâqeb al-ʿârefin* in the Mevlevi lodge in Yenikapı includes a selection of 82 ghazals and 80 *robâ'i*s, all in Persian, ascribed to him. Most of these are poems in imitation of or response to poems of Rumi (GM 123), but far inferior to their exemplars. F.N. Uzluk published a collection of Ulu ʿÂref's quatrains in Turkish and Persian as *Ulu Ârif Çelebiʾnin rübaileri* (Istanbul: Kurtulmuş, 1949).

SHAMS AL-DIN AMIR ʿÂBED CHELEBI

Before he died Amir ʿÂref appointed his half-brother, **Shams al-Din Amir ʿÂbed Chelebi**, to succeed him as the head of the Mevlevi order (Af 975). Sultan Valad had composed a few lines in honor of Amir ʿÂbed (GM 129), though he was apparently born after the death of Rumi and never enjoyed the favor of his grandfather's presence. Like Ulu ʿÂref, Amir ʿÂbed is described by Aflâki as a Qalandari Sufi, one who does not observe the laws outwardly (Af 976), and also a rather quarrelsome fellow (GM 130). Aflâki knew and served Amir ʿÂbed personally, but does not seem closely attached to him. Sepahsâlâr (Sep 153) hardly seems to know him and passes over him quickly, preferring to speak of his half-brothers, Amir Zâhed and Hosâm al-Din Vâhed, the "greatest of the spiritual axes," who have followed the ways of their grandfather. Even Aflâki, who apparently accompanied him at times, gives comparatively little information about ʿÂbed Chelebi.

He lived during the reign of the Ilkhanid Abu Saʿid Bahâdor Khân (r. 1316–35), who actually entrusted most of the affairs in Anatolia to Timurtâsh (executed 1327). Timurtâsh wrested control of Konya from the Karamanids in 1320 and eventually proclaimed himself to be a sort of *mahdi* to both Sunnis and Shiites (CaT 302). Amir ʿÂbed Chelebi, unlike most of the notables in town, rarely attended this strict and zealous man's gatherings, though Gölpınarlı attributes the displeasure of Timurtâsh with Amir ʿÂbed Chelebi principally to his drinking (GM 131). In any case, Artanâ (Eretna), one of Timurtâsh's former lieutenants, appointed Amir ʿÂbed to act as his political emissary to the Uch (?) territory. Amir ʿÂbed did not want the position, which required him to leave Konya, but felt compelled to accept it (Af 978). He returned to Konya sometime after 1327 (GM 132) and eventually died, according to Aflâki (Af 992) on 5 Muharram 739, corresponding to July 24, 1338.

In the sixteenth century the founders of the early Mevlevi order, at least up to this point, were recognizable by name outside Konya. Hosayn Karbalâʾi mentions the "noble chain" (*selsele-ye sharife*) of the spiritual leaders of the order, going back to Bahâ al-Din, Borhân al-Din, Shams al-Din and forward through Salâh al-Din, Hosâm al-Din, Sultan Valad, Chelebi ʿÂref and Amir ʿÂbed Chelebi.

The famous traveler **Ibn Battûta** (1304–69 or 1377) went through Konya in about 1332, describing it as a great city with beautiful buildings, very wide streets, plenty of water, rivers, gardens and fruits (Bat 293). He remarks that Konya's bazaars were well organized, with each guild located in a different place. He himself stayed with Qâzi Ibn Qalamshâh in the latter's lodge (*zâvie*) while in Konya. This *qâzi*, whose spiritual lineage supposedly reached to ʿAli, evidently headed an Akhi or *fotovvat* order, as had Hosâm al-Din, and had a large gathering of students or disciples who wore distinctive pants (*sarâvil*). This at least tells us that the Mevlevis had not cornered the market for mysticism in Konya; other orders and lodges continued to operate at this time, this one perhaps geared to the artisan classes.

Apparently a Mâleki jurist with a leaning to Sufism, Ibn Battûta therefore had some familiarity with this particular milieu. Unfortunately, though, his chronicle was not written down during his travels, but was turned into narrative form sometime between the years 1354 and 1357, a few years after his return to Fez. If he did take any notes during his travels, those pertaining to the years prior to 1345 (including, therefore, his visit to Konya) were lost during a pirate attack, so Ibn Battûta apparently dictated his account of Konya from memory. His travelog does not follow his itinerary in journal format, giving instead a composite description of all the places he visited, some of them more than once, as he criss-crossed back and forth on his various journeys. Ibn Battûta felt insecure about his style as a writer and therefore dictated his recollections to an editor, Ibn Juzayy, who implies that he often did not follow Ibn Battûta's account verbatim. There are many errors of fact, as we might expect of a writer going through unfamiliar lands where foreign languages were spoken (Ibn Battûta's command of Persian and Turkish is doubtful), and he sometimes admits that he cannot remember the names of people or places. In some places, Ibn Juzayy has apparently relied upon earlier travelogs or geographical works, such as the *Rihla* of Ibn Jubayr. Some later authors, such as Ibn Khaldûn, expressed the opinion that Ibn Battûta had greatly exaggerated his account.

One of the principal facts about Konya which Ibn Battûta tells us (Bat 294) is the existence of the *torbe*, or shrine, of "the Shaykh, the Righteous Imam, Jalâl al-Din, known as Mowlânâ, who was of great station." He mentions the existence of a group "in the land of Rum" who trace themselves to this master and are known by his name – the Jalâliye. Ibn Battûta provides a theoretical justification for this nomenclature, explaining that the order's name derives from the first name of its founder, as in the case of the Ahmadiye (known today as the Refâ°iye) in Iraq and the Haydariye in Khorasan. Taking into account the twenty-year remove at which the book was written down and the possible problems that Ibn Battûta, as an Arabic speaker, may have had in understanding his Persian and Turkish interlocutors, the accuracy of his memory on this score is highly doubtful. The existence of manuscripts of the *Masnavi* and other works from prior to and near the time of Ibn Battûta's visit signed by individuals known as "al-Mowlavi" proves that at least some of the followers of Rumi were already known by the moniker Mowlavi (Mevlevi in Turkish pronunciation), by this time. One passage of the "Acts" of Aflâki (Af 958) also speaks of the hospice of the Mevlevis (*zâvie-ye Mevleviân*) in a passage pertaining to the reign of Ulu °Âref Chelebi, which would date the usage of this term to 1320 or earlier, or, in any case, even if the term "Mevlevi" is used here anachronistically, prior to 1353 when Aflâki completed his work. Ibn Battûta's account does confirm that the Mevlevis functioned in the 1330s like other Sufi orders; they were well known not only in Konya, but apparently also in other parts of Anatolia, though Ibn Battûta does not describe meeting them elsewhere.

Ibn Battûta tells of a large hospice built on the shrine, open to all who come and go. He gives no details, however, about who heads the order, what they believe, or how many disciples frequent the shrine. He tells a story which he takes from unidentified sources, introduced by "it is said that" (*yudhkaru annahu*). This leaves one with the impression that he may not have paid a personal visit to the shrine; if he did, he does not seem to recall much about it.

It is clear from his remarks, however, that the poetry of Rumi enjoyed no small reputation in Konya for its profundity. Ibn Battûta tells us that the people in the region hold in high esteem a book of his composed in "rhymed Persian couplets which cannot be understood," relying upon its word, teaching it and reciting it in their hospices on Thursday evenings" (Bat 294). It is worth remarking that Ibn Battûta does not remark upon the poetry of Rumi's contemporary, ʿErâqi, or the disciples of Sadr al-Din Qonavi. He does, however, mention the grave of Faqih Ahmad, said to be the teacher of Jalâl al-Din. This Faqih Ahmad is also mentioned several times in Aflâki's *Manâqeb*, where he is described as a disciple of Bahâ al-Din, though he evidently enjoyed his own reputation for piety. When he died in 1221, the young Rumi supposedly read the prayer for the dead at his graveside (Af 420).[4]

AFTER ʿABED CHELEBI

Hosâm al-Din Vâjed Chelebi, another son of Sultan Valad and the half-brother of ʿAbed Chelebi, assumed the stewardship of the order for the next four years, until he died in early February 1342 (end of Shaʿbân 742). Aflâki gives only six lines about this figure, and we may assume that the writer either barely knew him or did not greatly care for him (Af 992). Next in line of succession was a son of Ulu ʿAref, **Bahâ al-Din Amir ʿAlem Chelebi**. Sultan Valad gave him the name Amir ʿAlem, along with the title "Prince" (*Shâhzâde*, Af 843), so we may conclude Amir ʿAlem was born prior to 1312. Amir ʿAlem headed the Mevlevi community for the next eight years in name only, for he spent most of the time far from Konya (Af 992–3). Whether he was involved in spreading and strengthening the order in far-away locales we cannot know, but Gölpınarlı points out that since the Mevlevi shrine contains no gravestone to mark his resting place, he probably died abroad. Quite likely he accompanied his father, Ulu ʿAref, on his many journeys, choosing or being asked to stay somewhere (GM 132). Already while he was away, the Mevlevis in Konya apparently relied upon his brother, **Amir ʿAdel Chelebi**, to act as head of the order (Af 993). Amir ʿAdel, Ulu ʿAref's younger son, was likewise named by Sultan Valad, who called him Mozaffar al-Din (Af 843). Again, we may conclude that he was born prior to 1312, while Sultan Valad was alive. Gölpınarlı gives two different dates for his death, 1368 (GM 199) and 1383 (GM 133).

Amir ʿAlem II, son of ʿAbed Chelebi, became head shaykh of the Mevlevis after the death of Amir ʿAdel Chelebi in 1368. Sâqeb Dede tells us that the people of Konya used to ask this Amir ʿAlem II to name their newborn children. When he died in 1395 **ʿÂref Chelebi II**, son of Amir ʿAdel, replaced him as head of the Mevlevi order and presided over the whirling dervishes during the reign of Tamerlane. Amir ʿAlem II, like his grandfather Ulu ʿÂref, traveled quite a bit before passing away in 1421 (GM 134). At this point, a son of Amir ʿAlem II by the name of **Pir ʿAdel Chelebi II** took over the leadership of the Mevlevi community. It was supposedly during the stewardship of Pir ʿÂdel Chelebi II that the Mevlevi ceremonies began to assume a ritual form, after adopting certain Naqshbandi influences (GM 134–5). After this, while the order remained centered at the shrine in Konya, the influence of the Istanbul lodges took on greater weight as the politics of Anatolia shifted to the Ottoman empire.

THE LATER HISTORY OF THE MEVLEVIS

THE SOURCES

The information we have about the sons and grandsons of Sultan Valad come mostly from Aflâki who completed his *Manâqeb* in 1353 (GM 174). Aflâki died in 1360 and we have no contemporary chronicles for the tenure of subsequent generations of the Chelebis and other Mevlevi shaykhs. Aflâki provides us extremely scant information about Vâjed, ʿÂlem and ʿÂdel Chelebi and even these reflect late additions to the text. We do find a good deal of first-hand information about some important figures in Mevlevi history in **Shâhedi**'s "Garden of Secrets," *Golshan-e asrâr,* a Persian verse autobiography written in 1544, when the author was at an advanced age. Unfortunately, because it includes mention of Mevlevis drinking and using opium, from about the seventeenth century it has effectively been on an unofficial index of prohibited books among the Mevlevi dervishes. Manuscripts of it are therefore quite rare (GM 174).

The next known history of the Mevlevis was written by **Sâqeb Mostafâ Dede** (Sakıb Dede), the Mevlevi shaykh of the lodge in Kütahya, who died in 1735. This takes up the history of the Konya Chelebis where Aflâki leaves off, and adds two further sections, one about the shaykhs of the regional lodges and one about the famous individual Mevlevi dervishes (GM 25). The work was published in Cairo in a volume of 645 pages as *Safine-ye nafise-ye Mevleviân* (Cairo: Wahbiya, 1283/1866). It seems to rely upon oral lore current among the Mevlevis. Given the late nature of this source, one cannot put a great deal of faith in it for at least the fourteenth through sixteenth centuries; it is full of historical errors and Gölpınarlı (GM 133–4) gives examples of Sâqeb Dede's confusion of historical personages from the fourteenth century. Yet it is the only source that provides a chronicle of the whole period (GM 26).

A number of supplementary works also exist, including the lives of the Mevlevi poets compiled by **Esrâr Mohammad Dede** (Asrâr Dede, 1748–96), himself a member of the Mevlevi order and a poet. Esrâr Dede entered the Galata Mevlevi lodge in Istanbul at a young age and in the 1790s, under Shaykh Ghâleb, became the Master of the Cauldron at the Galata lodge, responsible for the initiation of novices committed to the *chelle* of 1,001 days' service in the kitchen, which they spent mostly in seclusion and fasting. Any educated Ottoman of this period would of course have studied Persian and Arabic, in addition to his native Turkish. But the remarkable Esrâr Dede also acquired Latin and Italian and published a Turkish–Italian dictionary, in addition to composing ghazals of his own in Turkish (OLP 257–8) under the influence of Rumi's *Divân*. At the urging of **Shaykh Ghâleb Es^cad Dede** (Şeyh Gâlib Es^cad Dede, 1757–99, on whom see the section "Ottoman Lands" in chapter 11), who also came from a family of Mevlevis, Esrâr Dede determined to bring the work of Sâqeb Dede up to date and to provide a selection of the poems of famous Mevlevi poets. Unfortunately, he includes some non-Mevlevi poets and is generally as unreliable as Sâqeb (GM 26).

An abridged version of Esrâr Dede's work has been published by ^cAli Anvar as *Samâ^c khâne-ye adab* (Istanbul: ^cÂlam, 1309/1891). A few decades before this, **Sharifzâde Sayyed Mohammad Fâzel Pâshâ** (d. 1882) composed a work about the history of the Mevlevi order entitled *Sharh-e haqâyeq-e azkâr-e Mowlânâ* (Istanbul: Mahram Efendi-ye Bosnavi, 1866). Somewhat later, **Mehmed Ziyâ Ihtifâlçi** (1865–1927) authored a history of the Mevlevi lodge of Yenikapı (Istanbul: Kervan, 1976), founded in 1597 by Kamâl Ahmad Dede (d. 1617) (see GM 23–28).

These, and a few other sources, form the basis for **Abdülbaki Gölpınarlı**'s wonderful history of the Mevlevis after Rumi, upon which the current chapter draws heavily for its information. This constitutes the second volume to Gölpınarlı's biography of Rumi and focuses on Sultan Valad, the history of the Chelebis, the history of the various Mevlevi lodges, and their rituals, clothes and music. The book was published in Turkish as *Mevlânâ'dan sonra Mevlevîlik* (Istanbul: Inkılap, 1953; 2nd ed. 1983). A Persian translation was done by Towfiq Sobhâni as *Mowlaviye ba^cd az Mowlânâ* (Tehran: Kayhân, 1987). Ayten Lermioğlu provides a brief but well researched introduction to the major figures of the early Mevlevi order and some of the later followers in his *Hz. Mevlâna ve Yakınlari* (Istanbul: Redhouse Yayınevi, 1969).

Another useful source for the history and rituals of the Mevlevis comes from an Iranian invited to Konya as part of a cultural exchange between Iran and Turkey, **Abu al-Qâsem Tafazzoli**. His book on the rituals of the Mevlevis, *Samâ^c-e darvishân dar torbat-e Mowlânâ* (Tehran: Mo'allef, 1370/1991), borrows heavily from Gölpınarlı, but adds some of his own observations as a practicing Mevlevi shaykh. Two works in English, *The Whirling Dervishes* by **Ira Shems Friedlander** (New York: Macmillan, 1975; Albany; NY: SUNY Press, 1992) and *Mevlana Celaleddin Rumi and the Whirling Dervishes* by **Talat Sait Halman** and **Metin And** (Istanbul: Dost, 1983; 2nd ed., 1992) provide very useful and engaging introductions to the Mevlevis and their ceremonies.

SHIITE INFLUENCES ON THE MEVLEVIS

The father of Ebrâhim Dede **Shâhedi** (1470–1550), the chronicler mentioned above, studied in Iran and assumed the shaykh-ship of a hospice in Moğla, where Shâhedi was born. The father died when Shâhedi was only ten, and he became an apprentice silk merchant for a while. Eventually, he went to pursue an education in a *madrase* in Istanbul, but left his studies disgusted with the worldliness of the profession. In fact, it drove him to drink. Back in Moğla, he became a follower of Shaykh Badr al-Din. He became a Mevlevi disciple at the age of twenty-four through his attraction to Pâshâ Chelebi, a descendant of Rumi (but not one of the Konya Chelebis). Shâhedi accompanied a Mevlevi dervish to the lodge at Lazkiye, near Konya, where he entered the order and became tutor to Pâshâ Chelebi's son, though he could not completely repent of drinking raki. At some later point he composed a commemorative poem for the accession to the throne of an Ottoman prince in Manisa, which led to the prince dedicating many charitable trusts to the Mevlevis (Holbrook, in LLM, 111, 115–18). Besides his autobiographical chronicle, Shâhedi authored a number of other works in Persian and Turkish (see chapter 11).

Shâhedi met **Divâne Mohammad Chelebi** (Mehmed Çelebi, d. after 1545) in Kütahya and became his dedicated disciple. This "madman" Mohammad Chelebi, a descendant of Sultan Valad through his daughter Motahhare, was an important Turkish poet who apparently combined Shiite, Horufi and Qalandari beliefs with his Mevlevi practices (GM 137–61, LLM 118). He visited Ibn ʿArabi's tomb and also visited the Bektâshi lodge in Karaman and took a number of the Bektâshi dervishes with him to the Shiite shrines in Najaf and Karbala, and from there proceeded to Imam Rezâ's shrine in Mashhad (GM 147). According to Sâqeb Dede, Divâne Mohammad was given two banners, a big pot and some dishes from the Imam's shrine (*âstân-e qods-e Razavi*). He brought these pots and dishes, which are identified by inscriptions as part of the endowment of the Imam Rezâ's shrine, to Konya. They were used to cook a special rice pudding, *shoʿle zard*, each year in the month of Ramadan (GM 154). It was thus through Divâne Mohammad Chelebi that the influence of Shiism first permeated the Mevlevi order.

On other journeys, Divâne Mohammad would wander the hills and valleys, sometimes with disheveled hair and sometimes with hair and face, including eyebrows, shaved, wearing only a long smock open at the chest (Turkish *tennure*), a Qalandar's cloak, and occasionally a Mevlevi hat and sometimes a twelve-pointed crown/headgear (*tâj*) belonging to Shams-e Tabrizi (Tfz 71–4). In short, he was a very antinomian figure who smoked opium and even drank in the mosque and tossed wine on the walls out of his Malâmati beliefs (GM 148, 156–7). He traveled extensively and supposedly founded the Mevlevi lodges in Aleppo, Burdur, Egridir, Egypt, Algeria, Midilli and other places (GM 161). He also freed Ebrâhim Golshani from jail in Egypt (GM 148).

Divâne Mohammad composed a number of poems in Turkish, a collection of which Gölpınarlı presents (GM 567–96). One of these poems explains the Mevlevi principles of turning, and has been translated into French by Marijan

Molé in "La Danse extatique en Islam," *Les Dances sacrées* (Paris: du Seuil, 1963, 248–51) and into English in E. de Vitray-Meyerovitch's *Rumi and Sufism* (Sausalito, CA: Post-Apollo, 1987, 49–51). When Divâne Mohammad died, Shâhedi converted the Sufi lodge of Sayyed Kamâl in Moğla, where his own father had been shaykh, to a Mevlevi lodge. Shâhedi died in 1550 in Karahisar and was buried next to Divâne Mohammad Chelebi, who had died a few years earlier (GM 178).

Senân al-Din **Yusof-e Sinechâk** (d. 1546) was another disciple of Divâne Mohammad Chelebi, and like him a Shiite. He became the Mevlevi shaykh at the lodge in Yenice in Macedonia, where he was born. When Sinechâk objected to an attempt by the mayor of the city to confiscate the Mevlevi property, a dead body was tossed into the courtyard of the lodge and Sinechâk realized he had better leave town (GM 165). He traveled for an extended period, becoming a disciple of Ebrâhim Golshani (d. 1533) in Egypt for a while, then going on to Jerusalem where he stayed for some while in the Mevlevi hospice. From there he made a pilgrimage to the graves of the Twelver Shiite Imams, including Karbala and Mashhad (GM 166). On his return he went to Konya, where he became the head of the Mevlevi order. When he finally settled down, it was in Istanbul, where he died in 1546 in the Sütlüce retreat. His as yet unpublished Persian poetry betrays Horufi and Shiite influence on his thought (Yazıcı, "Dede Yūsof Sīnačāk," *EIr*).

On 10 Muharram A.H. 954 (March 2, 1547), the first Ashura following Sinechâk's death, his students and a few other Mevlevis traveled to his grave in the Ja῾farâbâd cemetery with money collected from the nobles of Istanbul. There they performed the Mevlevi *samâ῾* and proceeded to observe the Shiite ritual mourning ceremonies for Imam Hosayn, including flagellating themselves with razors (*qamme-zani*) to bleed on the martyred Imam's behalf (GM 165). After the sixteenth century, however, we no longer read of Mevlevi *samâ῾* sessions held outside the lodges (Tfz 73–4).

Sinechâk authored two popular works for Mevlevi disciples: an abridgement of Sultan Valad's *Rabâb nâme* and an abridgement of Rumi's *Masnavi*. The latter work, the *Jazire-ye Masnavi*, a selection of 366 lines from the *Masnavi* compiled in 1571, proved a popular work. A number of commentaries in Turkish were devoted to Sinechâk's epitome by authors such as the Malâmati dervish ῾Abd Allâh of Bosnia (d. 1644); the Mevlevi Shaykh of Syria, **῾Elmi Dede Baghdâdi** (d. 1661); and the Mevlevi shaykh of the Galata lodge, **Ghâleb Es῾ad Dede** (d. 1799). A further selection of forty lines from this work was made by Ebrâhim Jevri (d. c. 1655), who interspersed each line with five lines of his own commentary; this was published as part of *Shahr-e entekhâb* (Istanbul: ῾Âmere, 1269/1852).

Sinechâk's own poems show him to be under the influence of Ibn ῾Arabi's theosophy of the unity of being. Not only this, he appears to sympathize with the Horufi belief in transmigration of souls (GM 167, 596–605). He likewise seems to have inspired a number of his students and companions to write poetry (GM 167–8).

POPULAR DEVOTION

In Islamic countries the Koran has often been used for prognostication (*estekhâre*) or as a kind of horoscope before undertaking journeys, important transactions, making decisions or in case of illness. After declaring the intention to take an omen, one opens the book at random and reads a verse, the tone or content of which reveals what action should or should not be undertaken. Iranians commonly use the *Divân* of Hâfez, nicknamed the Tongue of the Unseen, to take omens (*fâl*), but among the Mevlevis, the *Masnavi* and the *Divân-e Shams* served this popular purpose.

In the Chester Beatty manuscript of the *Divân* a marginal note indicates that in 1585 a certain Darvish Ghonche ("Blossom"), who had a pupil nicknamed Banafshe ("Violet"), fell ill in Egypt in the house of a certain Mohyi. The Mevlevis there came to visit him and after a bit of conversation, they decided to take an omen for everyone present from the "*Divân* of his holiness, our great master," beginning with the ailing Darvish Ghonche (D viii): "We opened the book and this page came up. All of us cried out and even Darvish Ghonche, weak as he was, got up and began to turn in *samâ*ᶜ. After beginning to sweat, he was healed." Why? Because the book opened up to a verse containing mention of both blossoms (*ghonche*) and violets (*banafshe*): a splendid omen, indeed.

THE CHELEBIS THROUGH THE SIXTEENTH AND SEVENTEENTH CENTURIES

By the 1500s the great-grandchildren of Sultan Valad had passed on and handed on the order to the next generation. Pir ᶜÂdel Chelebi II's son, **Jamâl al-Din Chelebi**, took over the order in 1460 and remained in charge for sixty-two years, until 1509. In 1466 the Ottomans captured Konya and from then on the Chelebis and the Mevlevis lived under Ottoman rule up until the establishment of the Turkish Republic after the First World War. Jamâl al-Din Chelebi apparently maintained friendly relations with the Ottoman sultan Bâyezid II (r. 1481–1512), who paid for Mowlavi ᶜAbd al-Rahman to undertake repairs and refurbishments to Rumi's shrine in Konya and also provided expensive brocade to lay over the sepulchers (GM 200). This is in keeping with Bâyezid's general policy of providing centers to the various dervish orders (LDL 6).

This policy made an impression. Writing in 1487 Dowlatshâh reports that the Mevlevi convent and lodge in Konya was one of the most impressive Sufi centers. Rumi's shrine was a center of pilgrimage, bright and decked out with many carpets, always featuring a lavish spread. Dowlatshâh is aware that the sultans of Anatolia had ensured its upkeep with a plethora of pious endowments (Dow 222).

Sultan Selim I (r. 1512–20) and Sultan Süleyman (r. 1520–66) reigned during the tenure of **Khosrow Chelebi**, the grandson of Jamâl al-Din. Sultan Selim provided for a number of pious endowments for the Mevlevis and provided a plumbing system for the shrine. Sultan Süleyman had a *samâ͑ khâne*, or performance hall, and a mosque built for the Mevlevis. He also erected the marble sarcophagus on Rumi's resting place, at which point the earlier wooden sarcophagus was moved over the grave of his father, Bahâ al-Din Valad (GM 201). As a result of Ottoman patronage the Mevlevis, in particular Khosrow Chelebi, enjoyed a period of luxury.

When Khosrow died in 1561, his son **Farrokh Chelebi** assumed his place and the Karatay school in which Rumi used to teach was added to the Grand Chelebi's properties. Subsequently the Grand Chelebis would teach here, receiving a salary in addition to the stipend that the pious endowments of the Mevlevi estates provided for them. Sultan Murad III (r. 1574–95) further enhanced the complex at Konya and established a Mevlevi lodge in Edirne (GM 202–3; Godfrey Goodwin, in LDL, 62). The lavish lifestyle of Farrokh Chelebi led to the depletion of a large portion of the revenues of the Mevlevi endowments and the dispersion of the Chelebis to other endowed properties around Karahisar. In the end, the other members of the Chelebi family successfully petitioned the state to curtail Farrokh's powers for a period of eighteen years. However, he apparently remained in charge of the order, if not of its purse strings, until his death in 1591.

This did not, however, adversely affect the Ottoman sultans' favorable attitude toward Rumi. Sultan Ahmed I (r. 1603–17) composed a poem in Turkish indicating that having read the *Masnavi* of Rumi, he wore its gem-like meaning like an earring. Sultan Ahmed apparently participated in the *samâ͑* and encouraged others to follow Rumi, the sultan of the realm of meaning. **Bustân Chelebi**, who acted as Grand Chelebi from 1591 to 1630, journeyed to Istanbul to receive the favors of Ahmed I, who apparently had seen Bustân in a dream and therefore accorded him great respect (GM 204). Unlike his father, Bustân supposedly spent a great deal of money on the poor and on the spread and upkeep of the order. He expanded the lodge in Syria and appointed Qertâl Dede to head it, had the Mevlevi lodge in Yenikapı built for Shaykh Kamâl Ahmad Dede (d. 1601), and the one in Gallipoli for Shaykh Aghâzâde Mohammad Dede (d. 1653). Rosukhi Ankaravi, the commentator, wrote a poem in praise of Bustân, who, it appears was greatly loved. During his reign the order expanded a great deal, in part due to the popularity of the Mevlevi *samâ͑* rituals which had by this time taken shape, and the Chelebis dispersed by Farrokh Chelebi's wasteful ways were able to return to Konya (GM 205–6).

With **Abu Bakr Chelebi**, the son of Farrokh Chelebi, and head of the Mevlevi order from 1630, the good relations with the Ottoman sultans were interrupted. Supposedly because of his efforts to stop Murad IV from storming about the shrine of Rumi in a demeaning and disrespectful way, but most probably on account of a more complicated dispute, Abu Bakr Chelebi was exiled to Istanbul, where he remained until his death in 1638 (GM 206–14). He probably brought with him from Konya the copy of Rumi's letters which are now housed in the Mevlevi lodge at Yenikapı (Mak 11).

At this point the stewardship of the Mevlevis transferred to **Âref Chelebi III** from Karahisar, who was descended from Rumi on his mother's side, but was otherwise unrelated to Abu Bakr Chelebi, thus constituting the first breach in the dynastic descent of the Grand Shaykh-ship of the Mevlevis (GM 213). He led the community for four years until his death in 1642, at which time the position of Grand Chelebi reverted to a grandson of Farrokh Chelebi, **Hosayn Chelebi**. Once again, the sources point to a dispute over his tenure (GM 214–15).

When Hosayn Chelebi died in 1666, **ʿAbd al-Halim Chelebi** next took the helm of the Mevlevis until his death in 1679. During his tenure some religious scholars successfully suppressed the *samâ^c* ceremonies of the various dervish lodges for a time. Next in line came **Bustan Chelebi II**, or Black Chelebi (Kara Bustân), on account of his dark complexion. During his reign, in 1685, permission for the *samâ^c* was once again granted (GM 215–18). However, owing to complaints alleging the Chelebi's non-payment of taxes, Bustân II was eventually summoned to join the army by Sultan Süleyman II. This did not quiet the matter, however; as a result of the continuing complaints of his opponents, the stipend and paid teaching position of the Chelebis were rescinded and Bustân II was exiled to Cyprus. His nephew **Jalâl Chelebi** took his place at the head of the order, but it took only eighteen days for him to prove ineffective and for Sadr al-Din Chelebi to take his place. After only forty days in Cyprus, however, Bustân Chelebi II received a pardon and returned to Konya (GM 218–19).

Ironically, an earthquake managed to repair the crack in the Chelebis' relationship with the Ottoman government. When the dome over Rumi's shrine in Konya was damaged, Sultan Mustafâ II ordered that the structure be fixed at taxpayers' expense. These repairs were completed in 1698 (GM 220).

THE MEVLEVIS IN THE EIGHTEENTH AND NINETEENTH CENTURIES

Sadr al-Din Chelebi, the son of Bustân II, assumed the leadership of the Mevlevi community on his father's death in 1705. Once again the Grand Chelebi found himself at odds with the government, this time over the use of felt or silk for ceremonial skullcaps. Sadr al-Din was summoned to Istanbul but fell ill on the way and, turning back to Konya, died in 1711 (GM 220).

Sâqeb Dede's history comes to an end about this time and, though he provides a great deal of misinformation on matters to which he was not an eyewitness, he at least provides us with some legendary accounts. We have no other general narrative of the Mevlevis for subsequent years. Gölpınarlı succeeds in pasting together a wealth of information from documentary and other written sources, and it is certain that with the Ottoman archives, the private archives of the Mevlevi lodges, and the accounts of foreign travelers and contemporary observers, it will be possible to give a reasonably accurate documentation of the history of the Mevlevis in the eighteenth through the twentieth centuries.

One document shows us that after the death of Abu Bakr Chelebi II, a dispute over who would become the next Grand Chelebi ensued, with as many as thirty or forty members of the Chelebi clan claiming the right. On Sunday May 22, 1785 a tribunal consisting of the Ottoman Sadr-e Aᶜzam, Shâhin ᶜAli Pâshâ (d. 1789) and several *qâzi*s convened in Istanbul in the presence of the competing claimants. The *Masnavi* reciter of Konya was rejected on the grounds that he was too wealthy. The Mevlevi Shaykh of Karaman was rejected on the grounds that he was too politically independent. Both of them then weighed in for **Hâj Mohammad Efendi**, the son of Esmâᶜil, who was appointed the next Chelebi. Those who opposed him were sent into exile (GM 221).

Mohammad Chelebi had the good fortune to lead the Mevlevi order during the reign of Sultan Selim III (r. 1789–1807), a staunch patron and supporter of the Mevlevis. He nevertheless opposed the sultan's reforms and sought to hang on to the revenues of the Mevlevi endowments, which did eventually win concessions for the Mevlevis (GM 222–6). By this point in time, the Istanbul Mevlevi lodges actually wielded more influence than the Konya lodge, owing to their proximity to the Ottoman capital and the intellectual currents of the day.

When Mohammad Chelebi died, his son, **Saᶜid Hamdam Chelebi** took over on March 18, 1815. Three weeks later he went to Istanbul to see the Sadr-e Aᶜzam, the Ottoman vizier, who bestowed a number of fine fur robes on the Chelebis along with a sum of money. After about a month, Hamdam Chelebi proceeded to Üsküdar with a number of Mevlevi shaykhs and dervishes in tow (GM 226). When the Ottomans went to war with Russia, Saᶜid Hamdam left Sâleh Dede, the Shaykh of Bursa, in charge of the Mevlevis and headed a symbolic contingent of nine dervishes to fight in the army. A further number of Mevlevi dervishes from Karahisar and Bursa also joined the army (GM 227).

Şerif Mardin argues (OxM) that after the Ottoman ulama began to discourage the teaching of Persian in the Turkish *madrases*, the Mevlevis might have fallen under suspicion of supporting the enemy Safavids in Iran. From the seventeenth century onward, however, the Mevlevis were influential in Ottoman court and palace circles. During the nineteenth century, the Grand Chelebi of the Mevlevi order would act as the "girder of the sword" at the enthronement ceremony of each new Ottoman sultan. Sultan Selim III (r. 1789–1807) felt a strong attraction to the Mevlevis and even composed one of the musical accompaniments for the Mevlevi rituals, *suz-e delârâ*, which Shaykh ᶜAbd al-Bâqi Nâser Dede (1765–1821) notated in 1794 (Walter Feldman, in LDL, 189). The

Mevlevis likewise enjoyed the favor of Sultans ʿAbd al-Majid (r. 1839–61) and ʿAbd al-Hamid II (r. 1876–1909); Sultan ʿAbd al-ʿAziz (r. 1861–76) was himself even a practicing member of the Mevlevi order, though after he visited Western Europe he came to admire the French model of public education over traditional Islamic ones. Nevertheless, official Ottoman support for the Mevlevis continued even under Mehmed V (r. 1909–18), though some Mevlevis appear to have supported the Young Turks in their 1908 uprising.

The Ottomans were not equally fond of all the dervish orders. In 1826, under the military reforms of Mahmud II (r. 1808–39), the Janissaries and the Bektâshis were suppressed and many of their public and military functions were transferred either to the Mevlevis or the Naqshbandis (Raymond Lifchez, in LDL, 7). The pious endowments (*owqâf*, Turkish *evkaf*) which provided the maintenance and upkeep for many of the *tekkes*, schools and other properties, also came under assault during the reign of Sultan Mahmud II and the subsequent Tanzimat reforms. Other reforms included the substitution of the fez for the turban as part of a more modern and egalitarian dress code. The sense that the dervishes constituted a kind of "parasitic class" (J.R. Barnes, in LDL, 40–41), with their lucrative endowments draining the public treasury, would later lead to the abolition of all the Sufi orders under Atatürk in 1925.

Hamdam Chelebi, perhaps in response to this kind of resentment, established a public library out of the books that had previously been in the private collection of the Chelebis (GM 228). After the death of Hamdam Chelebi in 1858, his son **Mahmud Sadr al-Din Chelebi II** officially assumed his place on April 12, 1859. When the latter died in 1881, the Chelebis sent a telegram requesting that the Shaykh al-Islam appoint his older brother, **Ebrâhim Fakhr al-Din**, the acting Mevlevi shaykh in Magnesia, as Grand Chelebi. But Ebrâhim died after only one year and his brother, **Mostafâ Safvat** next assumed the position of Grand Chelebi until his death in 1887. **ʿAbd al-Vâhed Chelebi**, another son of Hamdam, and a staunch Alavi, succeeded him. ʿAbd al-Vâhed won a reputation as "the father of the poor" for his generosity in almsgiving; he visited the poorhouses incognito every month to make a financial contribution. A painting of a *samâʿ* ceremony at the Galata lodge held on July 24, 1888 and attended by several high-ranking Mevlevi shaykhs, as well as some government officials, gives us a portrait of ʿAbd al-Vâhed Chelebi (reproduced in black and white in LDL 277).

By this point the Mevlevis had become heavily involved in Turkish politics. **Mohammad Reshâd**, the brother of ʿAbd al-Hamid II, was a member of the Mevlevi lodge in the Galata quarter of Istanbul. In 1896 the Committee of Union and Progress staged an attempted coup to replace ʿAbd al-Hamid with Mohammad Reshâd as sultan. The Mevlevis in Galata had acted as a conduit for correspondence between the Committee of Union and Progress, an arm of the Young Turks, and Mohammad Reshâd. The Mevlevi lodge at Yenikapı also distributed leaflets of the Committee of Union and Progress. In 1899 the Mevlevi shaykh in Izmir, Reshâd Efendi, allied with the Young Turks and was arrested and exiled for his pains. Around 1901 the Mevlevi dervish Tâhir Dede tried to continue publishing the banned journal *Resimli Gazete*, an organ of the Young Turks. Another Mevlevi shaykh, Mehmed Efendi, was exiled along with his associates among the Young Turks to Angora (Ankara). In 1908 the Grand Chelebi, fearing for his life, went so far as to request asylum from the British vice-consul in Konya.[5]

At last the revolt of the Young Turks succeeded in 1908 in compelling Sultan ʿAbd al-Hamid II to recognize once again the suspended constitution. By December 17, 1908 the Turkish Parliament had begun to meet and eventually, on April 26, 1909 ʿAbd al-Hamid was deposed. His brother, Mohammad Reshâd V, a member of the Mevlevi lodge in Galata, was installed as sultan of the constitutional monarchy.

Returning now to the succession of the Chelebis within the Mevlevi order, ʿAbd al-Vâhed died in 1907 and was succeeded by his son, **ʿAbd al-Halim Chelebi II**. After only a few years, however, ʿAbd al-Halim was deposed, according to Gölpınarlı because of his personal lifestyle. He was replaced in 1909 by **Mohammad Bahâ al-Din Valad Chelebi**, reputedly a descendant of Rumi only on his mother's side of the family, though he was at pains to prove otherwise (GM 228–9). Bahâ al-Din Valad Chelebi had supported the Committee of Union and Progress and would later lead a contingent of Mevlevis to Syria during the First World War, which achieved very little other than the illness and death of a number of Mevlevi shaykhs. With the defeat of the Ottomans in the First World War and the death of Mohammad Reshâd V (r. 1909–18), Bahâ al-Din Valad Chelebi was removed as head of the Mevlevis and ʿAbd al-Halim was once again reinstated as the Grand Chelebi (GM 230) on June 3, 1919 (GM 233).

The political instability of the period is reflected in the uncertain circumstances of the stewardship of the Mevlevi order, though disputes over the control of the pious endowments controlled by the Mevlevis also played a part (GM 323–4). The draft of a letter written by ʿAbd al-Halim and apparently addressed to the British powers expresses disapproval of the participation of the Mevlevis in the war effort, explaining that the Mevlevis should not involve themselves in racial and religious disputes, but should focus instead on social and intellectual service to the world (GM 232). ʿAbd al-Halim's letter also denounces the Committee of Union and Progress and explains that though he cooperated with the Young Turks for about six months, he soon realized they were headed in the wrong direction. ʿAbd al-Halim also complains that he had been deposed without any religious or legal justification, and argues that he had the support of the people of Konya (GM 232–3). The newspapers announced his restoration as Grand Chelebi in the late spring of 1919.

ʿÂmel Chelebi, the son of Yaʿqub Chelebi, was slated to take over the office in 1920, but he died in that same year and ʿAbd al-Halim retained his position as Grand Chelebi, only to be deposed once again in 1925 in favor of Bahâ al-Din Valad. Both ʿAbd al-Halim and Bahâ al-Din were elected to the Ottoman Parliament for a time, but Turkey was declared a republic shortly thereafter and the dervish orders were closed down in 1925. The function of the Grand Chelebi lapsed at this point, though the office was transferred to Syria for a time, before being banished from there. A number of Mevlevis have since exercised a kind of charismatic influence in Konya or Istanbul, though the hierarchical structure of the Mevlevis has naturally broken down since the dervish orders were banned from functioning. The leading figures of the latter half of this century include especially Süleyman Loras Dede (d. 1985), Celâleddin Çelebi (d. 1996), Huseyin Top (*post-neşin*), Nail Kesova (Galata shaykh) and the current shaykh in Konya, Faruk Hemdem Çelebi.

THE DIFFUSION OF THE MEVLEVIYE AND ITS RELATION TO OTHER ORDERS

Rumi's popularity spread throughout the Persian- and Turkish-speaking worlds not through institutional structures, but by virtue of his poetry. The Mevlevi order did not spread as widely as several important Sufi orders, remaining confined for the most part to Ottoman territory. Though official patronage could prove extremely beneficial to a Sufi order by attracting influential disciples and by aiding in the acquisition of property and/or endowments, it also brought on certain limitations. Jamal Elias (OxE) attributes the relative failure of the Mevlevi order to attract formal converts and to establish centers outside the Ottoman domains to its reputation as an ally of the Ottoman state. Once the Safavids established power in Iran in the sixteenth century, having relied primarily upon the Sufi milieu for their support, the Mevlevis would have been tainted by their association with the Ottoman court. This, coupled with Rumi's Sunnism, would probably have led the Safavids, with their zealous Shiism, to view Mevlevi activity with suspicion. This does not, however, satisfactorily account for why the Mevlevi order did not spread eastward to Iran or India during the fourteenth and fifteenth centuries, before becoming closely associated with the Ottoman court.

Mevlevi cells were established in areas conquered by the Ottomans, such as Greece, Bosnia and other parts of the Balkans. Mevlevi lodges were even established in Tripoli and Jerusalem, though in the Levant the Mevlevis took firm root only in Damascus, where Rumi had studied and where Shams had initially gone into hiding, and in nearby Homs and Beirut.

As late as the 1920s, in the course of remarks about the Bektâshi order in Bulgaria, S.W. Zwemer remarked that the Mevlevis were active in the region, too ("Islam in South Eastern Europe," *The Moslem World* 17 [1927]: 331–58).

However, according to Nathalie Clayer, *Mystique, état et sociéte: Les Halvetis dans l'aire balkanique de la fin du XVe siècle à nos jours* (Leiden: Brill, 1994), the Mevlevis never had widespread influence in the Balkans (p. 35). The branch of the Khalvati (Halveti) order that formed around Ebrâhim Golshani (Ibrahim Gülşeni) became influential in Istanbul, southern Greece and Crete (p. 96). The Khalvati order of Sufis occupied an intermediate stratum between the eccentricities of the Refâᶜiye order, the heterodoxies of the Bektâshis and the elitism of the Mevlevis. Golshani came to Diyarbakir from Tabriz after the Safavids took power and was eventually summoned to Istanbul by the Ottoman sultan Süleyman. There he wrote a work called *Maᶜnavi* on the model of Rumi's *Masnavi*, which he submitted, after obtaining verification that it included nothing heretical, to the Shaykh al-Islam, Kemâlpâshâzâde. Thus, although the Mevlevis did not actively spread as widely as some of the other orders, most of the Ottoman orders were in any case indebted to Rumi in one fashion or another.

Evliya Çelebi (1614–82), who gathered statistics on the buildings in Istanbul in 1635 at the request of Sultan Mehmed IV, counted over 550 *tekkes* (some of them must have been quite rudimentary) with a total of 6,000 dervish cells (Lifchez, in LDL, 89). According to the statistical surveys of Klaus Kreiser, there were between 2,000 and 3,000 *tekkes* throughout Anatolia and Rumelia in the nineteenth century, with 300 *tekkes* in Istanbul, the majority of which were continuously occupied. In the 1870 census 1,826 Istanbuli men – perhaps one percent of the adult male population – registered as living in a cell (*hücrenişin*) in one of the various dervish lodges. The numbers break down as follows, indicating that the Mevlevis were the second-largest order in Istanbul: 525 Naqshbandis, 300 Mevlevis, 199 Sonbolis and 173 Qâderis. As many as 60,000 Istanbul men were affiliated with an order, but did not live in a lodge. The Mevlevi lodges at Bâb-e jadid (139 residents) and Galata (85 residents) ranked as the two largest residential lodges in Istanbul (LDL 49, 51–2). Between 1820 and 1920, according to membership statistics for the *tekkes* of Istanbul, there were only about two thousand official members of Sufi orders, representing about three percent of the Muslim population of the city. Of these, thirty percent were Naqshbandi, twenty percent Mevlevi, eleven percent Sonboli, seven percent Refâᶜi and five percent Khalvati. This would give an average of approximately four hundred permanently active Mevlevis in Istanbul during this period.

Likewise, in southern Europe the Mevlevis have disappeared, except for in Yugoslavia. The last mention of the Mevlevi order in Albania dates to 1907. In Bosnia-Hercegovina there was a Mevlevi *tekke* in the Bebasa quarter of Sarajevo (Tekija na Bendbâshi) which fell into disuse around the year 1924 and was eventually demolished in 1959. In Yugoslavia, Mevlevi centers were reported after the Ottomans in Skoplje, Štip, Bitolj and Veles, but by 1939 only one was mentioned in Macedonia. Ismail, the last Mevlevi Shaykh of Peć, went to

Turkey after 1941 and Hakki, the last Mevlevi Shaykh of Skoplje, emigrated to Turkey in 1954. Though the Mevlevis were no longer active in Greece, Foruzânfar mentions that there was still a *khâneqâh* on Cyprus practicing Rumi's method of *samâ^c* at about this time.[6]

In seventeenth-century Palestine and Syria, the Mevlevis were functioning robustly enough to deserve a 41-page monograph of their own, written by ^cAbd al-Ghanî b. Ismâ^cîl al-Nâbûlusî (1641–1731) and published as *Kitâb al-^cuqûd al-lu^?lu^?iyya fî tarîq al-sâda al-Mawlawiyya* (Damascus: al-Taraqqî, 1932; 2nd printing). Mevlevi centers operated in Aleppo, Tripoli, Lattakia, Antioch, Homs, Damascus and Jerusalem.

As early as 1516 Sultan Selim visited Shaykh Akhfashzâde of the Mevlevi center (*zâvie*) in Jerusalem, which was apparently built on the site of the Crusader's Church of St. Agnes. The Mevlevi center included a mosque, *madrase* and kitchen. By 1586 a "*khâneqâh*" was built above the mosque by Khodâverdi Abu Saffayn, in which the Jerusalem Mevlevis performed the *samâ^c*. Nâbûlusî visited this Mevlevi "*tekke*" in 1690. He observed the turning ceremony from the seat of honor and afterwards went to the coffee house. Much impressed with the experience and the architecture and decor of the center, he composed a *qaside* to commemorate the experience.

Evliya Çelebi mentions this same Mevlevi mosque in the old city of Jerusalem, in the Ottoman neighborhood near the Damascus gate. The *sijill* records reveal that the Mevlevi community here was relatively prosperous in the seventeenth century. The Ottoman governor Mohammad Pâshâ dedicated an orchard to the Mevlevis as a *vaqf*, appointing Ahmad Efendi, the Mevlevi shaykh in Jerusalem, as trustee. In 1688 the Mevlevis of Jerusalem had an income of over 2,000 qorush from their endowments of shops and houses.

The shaykh of the Mevlevis in Jerusalem was usually appointed from Tripoli in Lebanon. The Jerusalem center was renovated in 1725 and a substantial trust still funded the property in 1843 when Shaykh Mohammad headed the community. The Jerusalem Mevlevis continued to perform the *samâ^c* in this particular center through May of 1967, but Israeli troops occupied the neighborhood in June of that year in the course of the Six Day War. The shaykh of the Jerusalem Mevlevis at the time, ^cÂdel b. Ahmad, left the city for good and the community remained without a leader. Mevlevi activity in Jerusalem soon lapsed, though the Mevlevi mosque still stands and the attached Mevlevi *madrase* now functions as a school.[7]

The Damascus Mevlevi *tekke* continued to function until circa 1965, when its elder shaykh, Fâ^?eq, passed away.[8] Indeed, after the closure of the dervish centers in Turkey in 1925, the Grand Chelebi of the Mevlevis, **Mohammad Bâqer Chelebi**, the son of ^cAbd al-Halim, came to Aleppo and established authority over the Mevlevi lodges outside Turkey. The government of Syria accused him of spying or acting as a Turkish agent and deported him in 1937.

His brother, **Solaymân Vâhed Chelebi**, headed the Syrian Mevlevis after this. When Mohammad Bâqer died in Istanbul in 1943, the new Syrian government did not affirm Solaymân Vâhed and his position as head of the order was officially decommissioned in 1944 (GM 234).

Professor Heshmat Moayyad of the University of Chicago visited the lodges of the Mevlevis in Syria in 1993. He mentions that the lodge in Damascus, across from the railroad station, now functions like a small mosque. Moayyad found the shaykh, or *morshed*, of the Mevlevis, a descendant of Rumi, sitting outside the building selling wares and trinkets. When queried, the shaykh expressed pessimism about the small number of Mevlevis left in Damascus and the possibility that they might once again become active. In Aleppo the Mevlevi lodge, situated on a crowded street near the Traveler's Hotel (Fondoq al-sayyâhin), also functions today like a small mosque. In the graveyard adjacent to the building about ten or fifteen Mevlevi shaykhs lie buried, their headstones all featuring a sculpted Mevlevi dervish hat.[9] The small circle of Syrian Mevlevis keep a low profile and seem very circumspect about allowing access to outsiders, perhaps in view of political considerations.

Not all Muslims had a favorable view of the Mevlevis, even in modern times. We have seen how many of the ulama in medieval times opposed *samâ'*, and many continue to do so today, feeling that the practices of the Sufis are indecorous and undignified. The Egyptian thinker **Muhammad Rashîd Ridâ** (1865–1935), a political firebrand but a religious conservative, describes an invitation he received from Mevlevis in Cairo to attend the *samâ'* ceremony at their *khâneqâh* after Friday prayers. Ridâ tells us that these meetings began each year in the spring and that an area was dedicated for spectators. As Ridâ explains, the dervishes walked in clad in tunics white as snow and resembling brides' dresses, while their shaykh assumed the place of honor. They whirled to the nay, their robes billowing out in circles, equidistant from one another. Without encroaching on each other's space, they stretched their arms out and crooked their necks, passing one by one before the shaykh and bowing to him. When Ridâ asked what was going on, he was told it was the ritual prayer of the Mevlevi order, founded by Rumi, author of the *Masnavi*. An enraged Ridâ could not control himself and stood up to make a scene. He shouted out in the middle of the *samâ'* hall that the act of dancing was forbidden and he denounced all those who would practice it by reciting the verse from the Koran (K6:70): "They have made their religion into a plaything and a joke." He stood up, commanded everyone to leave, asked God to pardon them, and stormed out. He admits that, though a few people followed him out, the majority stayed behind to participate in the ceremony despite his outburst.[10]

The Mevlevis did not have active centers outside Cairo in the nineteenth century. Twenty-one Mevlevis were invited to participate in the commemoration of Muhammad 'Alî's birthday in December of 1870, and Hasan Efendi, the shaykh of the Mevlevi *tekke*, was considered the order's representative. However, the government apparently perceived the Mevlevi *tekke* as a sui generis institution and not an order native to Egypt, since the Mevlevis were not included on the Governor of Cairo's list of officially recognized and approved orders.

Perhaps the modernist and rationalist attitude toward religion in Cairo contributed to the lapse of the Mevlevi order in Egypt. In 1898, the first year of its publication, Ridâ's *al-Manâr* published an article criticizing the commercialization of Muslim religious performances in front of Europeans. Undoubtedly, Europeans familiar with the Mevlevis of Istanbul were also coming to watch the Whirling Dervishes at their *tekke* on Suyûfiyya Street in Cairo.[11]

The Mevlevis never found a foothold in Central Asia and though many Sufi orders continued to function in the Soviet Union despite the government's hostility, the Mevlevi order was not among them.[12]

THE MEVLEVI LODGES

The Mevlevis operated vital and vibrant dervish centers in several Ottoman cities. The Mevlevis generally built their lodges on the outskirts of town, though often, as the population grew, they would find themselves incorporated into the expanding neighborhoods of the city. A larger lodge typically consisted of complex of gardens, a residence for the shaykh and his family, a hall for the performance of the *samâ*, a small mosque and a cemetery. The compound of the Mevlevi lodge also included small cells for the dervishes to live in, a library, a kitchen and dining room, a cistern and toilets. The shaykhs, musicians and dervishes were laid to rest in the cemeteries, their graves usually marked by tall tombstones, almost the height of a person, engraved with an inscription in Turkish and topped by a stone carving of the traditional Mevlevi headdress.

The door entering on to the *samâ* hall faced the *qeble*, and around the hall a section, sometimes a balcony, was included from which visitors could view the turning ceremony. The hall usually included a pulpit and an area where the musicians sat. The Mevlevis made their *samâ* halls in an oval shape, with an imaginary line down the middle, at the center of which was the pole (*noqte-ye qotb*), symbolizing the center of the universe. At the end of each turning ceremony the *Masnavi* was recited and explained; since the vast majority of Mevlevis were native Turkish speakers, the Mevlevi lodges would typically offer Persian classes so that the disciples could better understand the teachings of Rumi (GM 413–15).[13]

According to Gölpınarlı (GM 405–6), Mevlevi centers were of two kinds. Of the larger "thresholds" (*âstâne*), where the 1,001-day initiation period would take place, there were fourteen; the shrine in Konya was the primary threshold, followed by those in Karahisar, Manisa (Magnesia) and Aleppo. A further four (out of five) Mevlevi lodges in Istanbul functioned as *âstâne*s, with the others in Bursa, Eskişehir, Gallipoli, Kastamonu, Kütahya, Cairo and Rumelia. The other type of lodge was called a "retreat" (*zâvie*), of which there were seventy-six, not including the retreats in smaller villages. Both *âstânes* and *zâvies* had their own shaykhs, but the shaykhs of the retreats held a lower position in the hierarchy than the shaykhs of the *âstânes*. Retreats were located throughout Anatolia and also in Mecca and Medina in the Arabian peninsula; Baghdad and Mosul in Iraq; Tabriz in Iran; Lattakia, Homs and Hama in Syria; Cyprus; as well as Edirne, Salonika and Belgrade in Europe. The most important of all the *zâvie*, however, was the one in **Karaman** (Lârende), where the tomb of Rumi's mother is nicely kept up, along with several other sarcophagi (GM 406). D. Ali Gulcan has gathered together material about the Mevlevi lodge in Karaman and its history in his *Karaman Mevlevihanesi, Mevlevilik ve Karamanlı Mevlevı velileri* (Konya: Mader-i Mevlânâ Camii Koruma, 1977).

Although dervish lodges were theoretically endowed by a pious charitable trust (*vaqf*) in perpetuity, it would not infrequently happen that operating expenses or other income was usurped. Sometimes the lodges of one order would be transferred to the control of a rival order due to misappropriation of funds or some other factor. For example, a *vaqf* document dating from the time of Mehmet the Conqueror (d. 1451) establishes a pious trust for the retreat (*zâvie*) of the Qalandarkhâne in Istanbul, a church which had been converted to a mosque. This document specifies that the *samâ^c* should be performed and the *Masnavi* taught here after the Friday prayers. However, it would appear that this retreat lost the character of a Mevlevi lodge shortly thereafter (GM 407–8). In 1847 the Istanbul Mevlevi lodges depended upon farm rents and real estate receipts from villages in Anatolia and Thrace, as well as revenues from public baths. Some of the Istanbul lodges also received food rations from the endowments at the Süleymaniye and Lâleli mosques; others received fixed amounts from customs and poll taxes. Several government agencies also supplied food to the Galata lodge; after 1847 the various remittances from tax, custom and rent monies were replaced with direct salaries from the government treasury to the shaykhs and *tekkes*. The Mevlevi lodges in Istanbul were receiving around 12,000 to 13,000 kuruş per year at this time (Klaus Kreiser, in LDL, 52–3).

Divâne Mohammad Chelebi apparently established the **Galata**, or Pera lodge in 1491, named after the neighborhood in which it was built (Kule-Qâpusi). This was the first specifically Mevlevi lodge in Istanbul (GM 408), apparently constructed on the site of the Byzantine monastery of St. Theodore (LDL 101). Safâ^ɔi Dede of Sinop (d. 1533) was the shaykh of this lodge at one time, but not long afterward the Khalvati order took it over until ^cAbdi Dede (d. 1631) appealed to the authorities to have it returned to the Mevlevis. Subsequently Esmâ^cil Ankaravi (d. 1631), the famous commentator on the *Masnavi*, took over as the shaykh of this lodge and was buried here (GM 408). When Evliya Çelebi visited the lodge, it had one hundred rooms for dervishes, no sight of which remain in the present compound.

The Galata lodge burned in a fire in 1766, but Sultan Mostafâ III made restorations, as did Sultan Selim III, Mahmud II and ʿAbd al-Majid I (the latter after another fire in 1855), as the inscriptions show. The current structure dates to the time of Kudretullah Dede, who acted as the shaykh in Galata from 1818 to 1871. He is buried in the cemetery within the compound of the Galata lodge, an area known as Khâmushân (the Silent Ones), where dozens of Mevlevis from the nineteenth century lie buried, though the burial ground is now much smaller than it once was. A mausoleum built near the entrance of the compound in 1818 houses seven wooden sarcophagi marking the resting place of other famous members of this lodge, especially the poets Shaykh Ghâleb (Şeyh Gâlib, d. 1799) and Esrâr Dede (d. 1796). Formerly there were several more structures on the property, including a library, a residence for the shaykh, a dormitory for the dervishes and so forth. The Pera area of Galata in Istanbul was quite popular with Western travelers in the nineteenth century, and many of them have left accounts of their visits to the Galata Mevlevi lodge.

The Galata lodge, off Galip Dede Caddesi in the Beyoğlu quarter of Istanbul, a few blocks to the east of the Galata tower, now functions as the **Museum of Ottoman Literature (Divan Edebiyatı Müzesi)**. It houses a number of musical instruments used in the Mevlevi performances (kudum, novbe, nay, etc.), a few nineteenth-century European paintings of the *samâʿ* ceremony, and some manuscript copies of the *Masnavi* (including one dated 1466 in the hand of ʿAli Hâfez, and one dated 1478 in the hand of Mohammad b. Yusof al-Din Jamshâh). The ample gardens to the right and behind the *samâʿ* hall must once have afforded a wonderful atmosphere for reading and meditation; unfortunately, the Turkish government does not currently provide funds for a gardener and consequently (as of May 1999) the shrubs and weeds have taken over. A *samâʿ* session is held on the last Sunday of every month.[14]

An important Mevlevi dervish in the early part of this century, **Tahir Olgun al-Mevlevi** (1877–1951), wrote a booklet on the **Yenikapı** lodge and its leaders, *Yenikapı mevlevihanesi postnişini şeyh Celaleddin merhum efendi*, published in Istanbul. A. Atilla Şentürk has written a biography of Tahir Olgun as *Tahirʾul-Mevlevi: hayatı ve eserleri* (Çemberlitaş, Istanbul: Nehir, 1991). Tahir al-Mevlevi composed a number of poems in Turkish which have been edited by Cemal Kurnaz and Gülgün Erisen as *Çilehane mektupları: Tahiruʾl-Mevleviʾnin Mevlevi ailesi hatırat ve tahassusatını havi olarak Ahmed Remzi Dedeʾye mektuplar* (Ankara: Akçağ, 1995). Mâlquch Mohammad Beg founded the Yenikapı lodge in 1597. Aghâzâde Mohammad Dede, the founder of the Mevlevi lodge in Gallipoli, was appointed shaykh at Yenikapı. Sultan Selim III restored the lodge in 1804 (GM 411), but it burned to the ground in the last quarter of the twentieth century. Sultan-zâde Noʿmân Dede Beg, who had for four years been the shaykh at Galata, was replaced in 1790, at which time he moved to Üsküdar (Scutari), where he built the last Mevlevi retreat (considered a *zâvie*, not an *âstâne*) in Istanbul, which also functioned as a hospice for Mevlevis traveling to Istanbul from Anatolia and vice versa (GM 411–12).

MEVLEVI RITUALS

Sultan Valad may have given structure to the Mevlevi order, but not until the time of his grandson, Pir ʿÂdel Chelebi (d. 1460), did the orders' rituals assume their basic shape (Yazıcı, *EI²*). Since then, however, the only significant change we know of in Mevlevi praxis occurred during the reign of Selim III (1789–1807), which mostly affected the circumstances, locale and frequency of the performance of *samâᶜ* (OxE). Of course, as a result of the secularizing reforms of Atatürk, the dervish lodges were closed down in 1925 and the tradition was effectively brought to an end, though the Turkish government now allows the turning ceremony to continue in the guise of a folk dance.

Gölpınarlı, who visited the Galata lodge as an initiate before the closure of the *tekkes* in 1925, has written at length about the rituals of the Mevlevis in *Mevlânâ'dan sonra Mevlevîlik* (GM). Celaleddin Çelebi, descendant of Rumi and Grand Shaykh of the Mevlevis before his death in 1996, describes the Mevlevi rituals as practiced in the 1990s in his *Hz. Mevlânâ'da ilim, gel çağrıları* (Konya: Il Kültür Müdürlügü). The books of Shems Friedlander; Metin And and Talat Halman; and Abu al-Qâsem Tafazzoli all describe the ceremonies at great length, while both Yazıcı in the *Encyclopaedia of Islam* and Elias in the *Oxford Encyclopedia of the Modern Islamic World* give concise accounts. For this reason we shall not go into extensive description of the modern *samâᶜ* ceremony here.

SAMÂᶜ

The practice of *samâᶜ*, including the hiring of musicians and the composition of poems, dates to the lifetime of Rumi. We may presume that the poems used in *samâᶜ* were primarily ghazals, but Rumi or Hosâm al-Din must also have recited the *Masnavi* to the disciples. The reading of the *Masnavi* in the Mevlevi hospices on Thursdays was an established ritual by the time Ibn Battûta came to Konya in the early 1330s. Tahsin Yazıcı (*EI²*) feels that Salâh al-Din Zarkub was training individuals in the ways of *samâᶜ* and concludes that this major ritual therefore descends for the most part from Rumi.

The later *samâᶜ* ceremony would be held on the wood floor of the audience or turning hall (Persian *samâᶜ khâne*; modern Turkish, *semahane*). The typical performance floor, as in the Galata lodge, was semicircular or even octagonal in shape, though in the shrine in Konya the turning hall has a boxier feel. The dome overhead, along with the cosmic symbolism with which the ceremony was invested, heightened the impression of circularity. Various eighteenth- and nineteenth-century drawings and paintings by European visitors to Istanbul capture the visual impression of the ceremony (see chapters 13 and 15). The turning hall had chambers along the outside edge to accommodate onlookers. Women could also attend, but came in through a separate entrance and usually sat above the men, in the second-floor gallery. The turning hall also featured a separate seating area for musicians, a separate area for disciples and an elevated box seat for the sultan.

One dervish, called the Meydâncı, officiates at the ceremony, placing the skin on which the shaykh will sit at the opposite end of the room from the *qeble*, or direction of prayer, marked in the Mevlevi lodges, and in mosques, by a decorated alcove, the *mehrâb*. After calling for prayer to be sounded, the shaykh enters, followed by the dervishes, called *samâ'-zan* (Turkish, *semazen*). After the prayers, the *semazen*s gather around their shaykh to listen to hymns and readings from *Masnavi*, accompanied by music. The shaykh then recites the prayer of the skin, or *post-duası*. Then come salutations to a simple beat with the participants walking up in a circle, their arms folded under their cloaks, to the skin. They bow to the person in front and behind themselves and the shaykh takes his seat on the skin. The *semazen* then begin to twirl their bodies counterclockwise, pivoting on the left foot. There are four sections, or *salâm*, to a full turning ceremony, all accompanied by music.

The dervishes extend their arms, holding one hand toward heaven and the other toward the earth, symbolizing man's situation as a spiritual creature in the physical plane, and pivot on the left foot. The orbit of the dervishes is said to resemble the celestial music of the spheres. The ceremony has been often described and photographed (see, e.g., Friedlander, *The Whirling Dervishes*), and also filmed (see, e.g., Fehmi Gerceker, *Tolerance*). A picture is worth a thousand words and readers desirous of knowing more should watch the elaborate ceremony (see "The Music of the Mevlevis" and "Rumio on Video" in chapter 15). However, the following description by an Iranian historian, Khân Malek Sâsâni, who went to Istanbul as the Iranian chargé d'affaires from 1918 to 1923, is not without interest. In his memoirs *Yâdbud-hâ-ye sefârat-e Estânbul* (2nd printing, Tehran: Bâbak, 1354/1975, 166–72), he describes a visit to the official Mevlevi ceremonies at the Galata lodge in Istanbul (Tfz 77–85):

> On the 'Id al-adhâ holy day I went to the *â'in-e sharif* ceremonies at the Mevlevi lodge in Istanbul. At that time the elder Chelebi ['Abd al-Halim Chelebi], the descendant of Mowlânâ, was in Istanbul and the ceremonies were performed in his presence. Before the ceremonies began, when the Chelebi realized that I was a representative of Iran, he showed me honor and hosted me and we entered the *samâ'* auditorium together. He sat at one side of the round hall on a platform covered with a black skin. One by one the dervishes, with black cloaks and long white sleeveless shirts called *tennure*, entered the hall and sat on their knees facing the Chelebi. One of them stood up and began to recite this ghazal of Rumi aloud: *In khâne ke payvaste dar ân chang o chaghâne ast* ... [see poem 24 in chapter 8].

Then two nay players began to play, one with soft, high notes and the other replying with loud, low notes. At this time, the leaders of the order ... came in, and behind them some dervishes with ceremonial clothes got up and came up to where the Chelebi was seated to pay their respects. Then, one by one, they began to walk all around the hall in single file. The Mevlevis call these three circlings the stages of the soul (*maqâmât-e ruh*) ...

Then the Chelebi went to the head of the circle of disciples ... took two or three steps forward toward the skin-covered platform where the Elder of the Order was seated, and offered greetings. Then he turned around to the dervishes coming behind him, and politely greeted them. He circled around the hall with them three times and sat down. He gave them permission to dance and one by one, the dervishes ... shed their cloaks and stepped on to the floor. After bowing to the covered platform on the ground that represents the place of Mowlânâ, they raised their hands as if they wanted to fly, the right palm facing skyward and the left palm facing down, as if to accept blessings from heaven and bestow them on the people of earth. They began to circle. The white unsplit *tennure*, lifted by the wind as they spun, would open like an overturned tulip ... The singers began to recite [a poem by Rumi] to the accompaniment of instruments and drum ...

After a quarter of an hour they stopped to catch their breath and walked around the hall once. There were ten musicians. Like the narrator of a Shiite passion play (*ta'zie*), one person would call out for the musicians the required mode of each piece. For example, "The second salutation in (the mode) Isfahan" [followed by poems]; "The third salutation in Nahâvand" [followed by poems]; "The fourth salutation in Do-gâh" [followed by poems, including the first two lines from poem 39 and the first line of poem 14 in chapter 8] ...

After each round they rested for a quarter of an hour by walking around the hall and then they began to dance again. At the end of each song, there was a fast musical passage with tambourine and drum. The musical instruments with which they play the maqâms and melodies of Iran and recite are six: nay, setâr, kamânche, tabl, sanj-e kuchek, daff.

INITIATION

The dervish lodges, though not exactly like monasteries, were a primarily masculine milieu. Typically, one became a novice as an adolescent boy and application could be made only by recommendation of an older initiate. Supplicants under the age of eighteen could only live in the *tekke* after producing written permission from their parents. But there were two levels of affiliation with the Mevlevi order. An initiate could live in the *tekke* and go through the rigorous three-year discipline of a *chelle*, for which he earned the designation of Dede. This long period of apprenticeship is a distinctive feature of Mevlevi practice; during this time the novice learns the *Masnavi* and the turning ceremony.

Alternatively, an initiate could become a non-resident member of the lodge, a *muhip* (*mohebb*). A *muhip* did not need to complete the three-year *chelle* and could live a normal family life in his home. But a *dede*, a member resident in the lodge, should not take a wife, since women could not live in the *tekke*. However, Mevlevi women were allowed to observe the public *samâ*[c] ceremony on Thursday nights and some of them might even perform their own turning ritual in street clothes in another room (Friedlander, *The Whirling Dervishes*, 109).

If admitted by the shaykh, a novice would come to the *tekke* on an appointed day wearing the distinctive conical cap (*sikke*). He would kiss the shaykh's hand and sit to his left, both facing the *qeble*. The shaykh would announce that they would read a prayer of repentance. Taking the *sikke* of the applicant in both hands, he would read the Sura of Sincerity (*Ikhlâs*, K114) from the Koran, blowing three times on the *sikke*. The shaykh then held the *sikke* toward the *qeble*, kissed it three times and placed it on the candidate's head, explaining that in so doing, he was acting on behalf of Mowlânâ. The shaykh then raised the supplicant to his feet, kissed him and took him to a *dede* in the kitchen to be educated and trained.

Sometime before the nineteenth century the clothes of the Mevlevis had taken on ritual significance. They wore felt hats around which the shaykhs wound a turban. When the novice completed his 1,001 days of initiation, the shaykh would bestow a cloak (*kesve*) on him and award him with a cell in the *tekke*. Their praxis, according to Ma[c]sum[c]ali Shâh, included *zekr*, meditation, restraint of the heart, morning litanies (*owrâd*) and *samâ*[c] (Saf 3/1: 456).

To visit a shaykh or *dede* at one of the Mevlevi lodges, Gölpınarlı indicates that one would give a token gift to the gatekeeper on the street, enter through the portal and stand before the shaykh's residence. The gatekeeper would relay the request for an audience and, when beckoned forward, he would pause at the threshold to ask for permission by calling out *Destur*? If the Shaykh replied in the affirmative with *Hu*, the visitor would step into the room with his right foot, remove his shoes, and then use the ritual Mevlevi greeting (*niâz*), which consisted of touching the right big toe to the left big toe and bowing with the fingers of the right hand spread over the heart. At this point, the visitor would say, "I begin with the name of God," and grasping the hand of the shaykh, both would bow and kiss the other's hand at the same time. They would probably drink coffee while they talked (Lifchez, in LDL, 112).

REPUBLICAN REPRESSION AND MEVLEVI RESURGENCE

The Republic of Turkey, formed in October 1923 under Atatürk, abolished the caliphate in March of 1924, sending Sultan [c]Abd al-Majid into exile in Switzerland. A month later the Shari[c]a courts were closed, the wearing of Islamic dress was banned, women were unveiled, polygamy was suspended, and the Gregorian calendar was adopted. Turkey's clocks were set to the Greenwich mean, the metric system was adopted, the Arabic script was abandoned and the Latin script was adapted to Turkish.

On December 13, 1925, Law 677, proposed by Atatürk and titled the "Suspension of pious foundations and religious titles, the banning of mystical societies and displays of dervishes and the suspension of Sufi hospices and hostels," was ratified by the parliament (cited in Tfz 87–91):

Article 1: All of the Sufi hospices in the Republic of Turkey, whether pious endowments, personal property of shaykhs, or by whatever other arrangements founded, will be closed and the right of ownership suspended. Those which are being used as mosques may continue in their present form. All religious titles – Shaykh, dervish, disciple, Dede, Chelebi, Sayyed, Bâbâ, Naqib, Caliph, fortune-teller, sorcerer, healer, prayer-writer for helping people acquire their desires, and all manner of occupations of this sort, as well as the wearing of dervish garments, are forbidden. The graves of sultans and the shrines of dervishes are closed and the occupation of shrine custodian is voided. All persons who reopen closed-down Sufi hospices, hostels or shrines, or those people who use mystical titles to attract followers or serve them, will be sentenced to at least three months in prison and a fine of 50 lira.

Article 2: This law will take effect immediately.

Article 3: The government will be responsible to implement the law.

At the end of his memoirs, Khân Malek Sâsâni writes (Tfz 85):

But with the edict of 4 September 1925 all of these customs – which led thousands of people to read the poems of Mowlânâ in Persian and play Persian melodies and to look towards Iran – were suspended. All of the *tekkes* were closed and the pious endowments of the Mevlevi hospices were expropriated and the spiritual influence of Iran which had extended from Crete to Hungary and from the city of Tayyebe to Tarâkia and Anatolia, was all brought to an end and erased. And no one in Iran realized it or said a word or wrote about it. As if nothing at all had ever happened!

Two years later, in the winter of 1927, Atatürk made an exception in the case of the Mevlevis, and allowed the shrine of Rumi in Konya to reopen as a museum, the Mevlânâ Müzesi, the funds for which were provided by the Ministry of Vaqfs. Sadettin Heper, who had been in charge of the drummers (*kudumzenbâshi*) at the Yenikapı Mevlevi *tekke* in Istanbul when it was closed down in 1925, approached the mayor of Konya in 1953 and prevailed upon him to permit the *samâ^c* ceremony to be publicly performed. This was under the stipulation that the ceremony be construed as a celebration of a great Turkish poet rather than a religious ritual, though Heper insisted that the Koran had to be recited. In December 1953 the first authorized Mevlevi *samâ^c* in almost three decades was performed in the cinema in Konya, with only three musicians and two people turning in street clothes. The ceremony took place again in 1954, and in 1955 the Tourist Association of Konya advertised the event, which now included the Sultan Veled Walk and the wearing of *tennures* and *sikkes*. By the following year, two ceremonies took place, one in Konya and the other in Ankara (Friedlander, *The Whirling Dervishes*, 106–13).

UNESCO declared 1973 the Year of Rumi in honor of the 700th anniversary of his passing. The Turkish government held an "International Mevlânâ Seminar" in Ankara from 15 to 17 December, at which point the gathering adjourned to Konya, where the *samâ^c* was performed in the gymnasium of Konya's high school, a site chosen by the government in preference to the shrine, to ensure that the turning ceremony be perceived as a cultural or even athletic event, rather than a sacred one. Two shaykhs sat on the skin of honor, Salmân Tuzun, the Istanbul shaykh, and Süleymân Lorâs Dede, the Konya shaykh (Tfz 101–3).

The Turkish government's relaxation of restrictions on the performance of *samâ^c* helped to reinvigorate the Mevlevi order and contributed to its spread around the world. Today about 50,000 people attend the week-long December commemoration of Rumi's death, including both Turks and tourists. Official Turkish government statistics indicate that in 1985 some 477,290 Turks and 100,105 foreigners visited the tomb, and that number increases with every passing year (Tfz 9–10).

11

Rumi in the Muslim World

> The mystic *Masnavi* of our Rumi:
>   Koran incarnate in the Persian tongue!
> How can I describe him and his majesty?
>   Not prophet, but revealer of a Book.
>
>   Jâmi

Rumi's impact on Sufism and Islam in Iran and countries where Persian was formerly spoken, read or written is impossible to measure and difficult to overstate. As Arberry points out in *Rumi, Poet and Mystic*, "every Sufi after him capable of reading Persian has acknowledged his unchallenged leadership." Schimmel's statement that "it would be difficult to find any literary and mystical work composed between Istanbul and Bengal which contains no allusion to Rumi's thought or quotation from his verse" (ScB 5) exuberantly overstates the case, but the fact that such a remark can be made even hyperbolically, or the fact that some mendicant dervishes in Sind are said to have disposed of all their books with the exception of the Koran, the *Masnavi* of Rumi and the *Divân* of Hâfez, testify to the penetration of the legendary influence of Rumi throughout Islamic culture, especially in Turkey, Iran and the Indian subcontinent.[1]

RUMI IN LITERATURE

Though the language of the Koran and Islamic legal scholarship was Arabic, the predominantly Turkic rulers of Muslim India preferred Persian as the language of sophisticated expression at court. The Moghul emperors and other local dynasties in the Indian subcontinent patronized Persian to such an extent that many of the best Persian poets left Iran during the sixteenth and seventeenth centuries and brought into being a new style of Persian poetry, known as the "Indian style" (*sabk-e Hendi*) in Delhi. A vast number of copies of the major works of classical Persian were copied out in India during this period, some of them in proto-critical editions, with the copyist consulting multiple manuscripts. Indian readers of Persian had a particular affinity for mystical works, and many commentators offered companion volumes to explain the grammatical as well as the symbolic meaning of Persian texts, especially Hâfez' *Divân* and Rumi's *Masnavi*. This was also true at the Ottoman court where, though Turkish was the native language, Persian was a major literary language.

IRAN AND INDIA

The Sufi orders found India congenial ground, both for its theosophical speculation and for its popular worship of saints. In fact, it was through the popular devotion of the Sufi orders that large numbers of the populace in India became attracted to Islam. The poet–saint of Panipat, **Bu ʿAli Qalandar** (d. 1327), is said to have visited Konya and met Rumi; this seems somewhat unlikely, but Qalandar's Persian *masnavi*s are said to betray the influence of Rumi. Within a couple generations after Rumi, **Sharaf al-Din Maneri** (1263– 1351), who lived near Patna in India, is already quoting from the *Masnavi* of "Mowlânâ Rumi" in his *Hundred Letters* (New York: Paulist Press, 1980, 322), spiritual meditations which he wrote in 1347. India gave birth to at least one major order, the Cheshtis, and both this order, and a branch of the Naqshbandis, also very active in India, though not tracing their spiritual heritage through Rumi, nevertheless held him in great veneration.

We have already seen that Rumi's disciples recited the *Masnavi* in weekly public ceremonies in Konya when Ibn Battûta came through town in the 1330s, and Sultan Valad promoted the poetry of Rumi in Anatolia, both by writing similar verse of his own and by fostering the spread of an order dedicated to Rumi. Meanwhile, in Iran, ʿAlâ al-Dowle Semnâni (1261–1336) speaks of "Mowlânâ Rumi" in the collection of his lectures, *Resâle-ye eqbâlie*, saying that he never heard the words of Rumi without experiencing joy. Though Kamâl-e Khojandi (d. c. 1401) and Shâh Neʿmat Allâh Vali (c. 1330–1431) do mention Rumi, it does not appear that fourteenth-century poets like Hâfez or Khwâju knew Rumi's poems (ME 1:lxxxi). This changed in the fifteenth century, however, with Kamâl al-Din Khwârazmi's *Masnavi* commentary (see below), and Shâh Qâsem Anvâr's (1356–1434) praise of Rumi. Shâh Dâʿi of Shiraz (fl. 1460) also quoted Rumi in his *ʿEshq nâme* and wrote a gloss on the *Masnavi* (ME 1:lxxxi).

Jâmi (d. 1492), perhaps the most respected and influential Persian poet of his era, made Rumi a household word by praising him in the 1470s in terms that almost make him into a prophet (see the rubric at the beginning of this chapter). To Jâmi is attributed the saying that the Spiritual *Masnavi* of Mowlavi is the Koran in Persian tongue, though this is also attributed to Shaykh Bahâ'i in different form. In his "Salâmân and Absâl," translated by FitzGerald, Jâmi quotes Rumi in such a way that we may infer that Rumi's *Masnavi* provided the inspiration for the work. Referring to the remarkable aptness of two lines from the *"Masnavi* of the Master" – in which Rumi wonders how he can continue to rhyme and versify when the source of his equilibrium had perished – Jâmi explains that his poem is an effort eloquently to praise God, his heart's desire. As a Naqshbandi Sufi, Jâmi made Rumi quite popular with this order.

Even the Shiites revered Rumi, as shown by the short *masnavi Nân va halvâ* of **Shaykh Bahâ al-Din ʿÂmeli** (Shaykh Bahâ'i, 1547–1621), widely read in India by Sunnis and Shiites alike, which forms a kind of introduction to Rumi's spiritual couplets. Shaykh Bahâ'i follows Rumi's meter in this poem, as also in a longer *masnavi* called the *Tuti nâme,* which elaborates on the parrot parables which Rumi tells in his *Masnavi* (M1:247ff. and 1547ff.). An earlier poet and author who displayed strong affinities for Shiism (he even wrote an impassioned account of the martyrdom of Hosayn, though he did not consider himself a sectarian Shiite), **Mollâ Hosayn Vâʿez-e Kâshefi** (d. 1504), composed *Lobb-e lobâb-e Masnavi-ye Mowlânâ-ye Rum,* a verse précis of the *Masnavi,* which has been published in the Noʿmâni Kotobkhâne in Kabul, an indication of the continuing popularity of the *Masnavi* in Afghanistan. The Shiite scholar Shushtari (d. 1691) in his "Gatherings of the Faithful" (*Majâles al-moʾmenin*) even considers Rumi to be among the true Shiites, as reported by **Mirzâ Mohammad Bâqer Khwânsâri** (1811–95) in his *Rowzat al-jannât* (Beirut: Dâr al-Islâmiyya, 1991, 8:63), an encyclopedia of famous religious scholars, which includes Rumi, and describes the *Masnavi* as a book "esteemed by scholars and the common folk, whether Shiite or not." One suspects that the Safavid government, with its forceful encouragement of Shiism as the state and even national religion of Iran, created an impetus among men of letters to salvage the long tradition of Sunni Persian poetry and philosophy by appropriating it as Shiite. A study of the manuscript tradition may demonstrate that the explicitly Shiite poems wrongly attributed to Rumi date from the sixteenth or seventeenth centuries, by which point the Mevlevi order itself had come under the influence of Shiism through Yusof Sinechâk, who himself traveled from Istanbul across Iran to Mashhad (See chapter 10). Otherwise, zealous Shiites in Iran have sometimes attacked the *Masnavi* as a Sunni work with a polemical bias; even in the twentieth century, Shiites in Mashhad would sometimes destroy copies of the *Masnavi.* Given the popularity and appeal of Rumi's poetry, appropriating him as a Shiite author presented a far more palatable solution to this sectarian dilemma. A new study of Rumi's impression of Shiism by the pen of Qodrat Sowlati, *Moʿarrefi az tashayyoʿ dar Masnavi-ye maʿnavi* ([Tehran]: Abrun, 1998), perhaps addresses some of these questions.

Meanwhile, at the court of the Sunni Moghuls, the eclectic and very open-minded Emperor **Akbar** (r. 1556–1605) issued a decree indicating that when government employees were not at work, they should occupy their time reading ethical works like those of Ghazzâli and Nasir al-Din Tusi, as well as the *Masnavi* of Rumi, to keep them from temptation and avarice in the administration of affairs of state. Schimmel mentions "an Indian historian" writing even earlier, shortly before 1500, who says that as far east as Bengal the *Masnavi* was even being recited by Hindu Brahmins (ScW 32). The Sufi Sarkhwosh supposedly encountered one Hindu ascetic near Ajmit and upon asking why he did not convert to Islam, the Hindu recited a line from the *Masnavi*:

> Once the colorless became enmeshed in colors
> A Moses came into conflict with a Moses

> (M1:2467)

By this he meant that the apparent contradiction in their beliefs disappeared if one looked beyond the phenomenal world to the metaphysical plane.

Though Aurangzeb (r. 1658–1705) reversed Akbar's trend of religious tolerance and reasserted a stricter orthodoxy toward the end of the Moghul empire, even Aurangzeb could not resist the beauty of Rumi and is said to have been moved to tears by the *Masnavi*.[2]

In the eighteenth century, **Shâh Vali Allâh** (1702–63), a Naqshbandi Sufi poet from Delhi, adapted the story of the elephant in the dark in his *Hojjat Allâh al-bâleghe*, written about 1741. The mystic poet and musician **Shâh ʿAbd al-Latif of Bhit** (1689–1752) composed one poem with a repeating line explicitly invoking Rumi, his beliefs and his quest for God and beauty. ʿAbd al-Latif also reflects the influence of Rumi in his Sindi work, *Shâh jô risâlô*. The Urdu poet **Mir Dard of Delhi** (1721–85) quotes Rumi frequently in his *ʿElm al-ketâb*.[3]

A nineteenth-century work, the "Tablet of Salmân" (*Lowh-e Salmân*) by **Baha'u'lláh** (1817–92), the prophet-founder of the Baha'i religion, quotes and comments upon this same verse about colorlessness caught captive in the world of colors.[4] An Iranian nobleman exiled from Iran to Baghdad for his religious beliefs, Baha'u'lláh frequently incorporated quotations of Rumi into his works of the 1850s and early 1860s, such as *Haft vâdi* ("The Seven Valleys"), which Baha'is regard as divine revelation. Summoned by the Ottoman authorities to Istanbul, where he arrived in August 1863, Baha'u'lláh perhaps observed Mevlevi rituals for the first time. Further exiled to Adrianople (Edirne), Baha'u'lláh resided in the Morâdiye quarter near the Mevlevi lodge during the last week of December 1863, and at least one member of his entourage was in contact with the Mevlevis there. A Canadian Baha'i woman, Marion Jack, painted a picture of this Mevlevi lodge when she made a pilgrimage to Edirne in 1933. While in Istanbul in the autumn of 1863, Baha'u'lláh composed his "Blessed Masnavi"

(*Masnavi-ye mobârak*), perhaps in response to the Mevlevis' devotion to Rumi's *Masnavi*.

The modern Iranian poet **Mehdi Akhavân-e Sâles** (d. 1991) promoted an Iranian national consciousness in his poems and essays that harked back to pre-Islamic Zoroastrian traditions and myths. Akhavân seems to allude to Rumi's verse on the colorless world in his famous poem, "Winter" (*Zemestân*, 1956), where it seems to argue for political non-alignment and the transcendence of the black-and-white dichotomies of ideology:

> I'm neither from Rum, nor from Abyssinia
> I am that very colorless colorlessness

OTTOMAN LANDS

Within a quarter century of the death of Rumi, at the same time that Sultan Valad was supervising the spread of the Mevlevi order, Seljuk power began to wane and the star of ʿOsmân, the eponymous founder of the Ottoman empire, began to rise. By the end of the fourteenth century, the Ottomans controlled all of Anatolia and a large part of the Balkans. **Khalil Pâshâ** (1570–1629), the Ottoman Grand Falconer and commander of the feared royal guards, the Janissaries, though himself an adherent of the Jelveti order of dervishes, stopped in Konya at the tomb of Rumi in 1607 while on his way to Aleppo to put down a Syrian revolt. According to the *Ghazâ nâme*, this little pilgrimage moved the whole army to tears and Khalil penned a number of verses inspired by Rumi. In his travelog, Evliya Çelebi mentions that **Malek Ahmed Pâshâ** (1588–1662), an ethnic Abkhazian who held a number of governorships and eventually became deputy Grand Vizier of the Ottomans, had several thousand verses of Rumi's *Masnavi* (as well as ʿAttâr's *Pand nâme*) at his recall.[5]

Of course, it was mostly in literature that the influence of Rumi was felt. It goes without saying that the descendants of Rumi and the adherents of the Mevlevi order studied Rumi's works on a regular basis with devotional attachment, but it was not only Mevlevis who looked to Rumi's poetic models. Although a folk poet and not a Mevlevi, **Yunus Emre** (1238–1320) was well versed in Rumi's poetry. He participated in at least one Mevlevi *samâ* ceremony and explicitly expressed his indebtedness to Rumi's spiritual example in one line (GB 402), though he considered himself a disciple of Tâbdeq Bâbâ (GB 400; *EI*²). Even Turkish Sufis who did not read Rumi directly may have imbibed Rumi's ideas at second-hand through the influential Emre, whose *Divân* was published by Gölpınarlı (Istanbul: Ahmet Halit, 1943). **Ommi Kemâl**, a fifteenth-century poet associated with the Safavid order in Ardabil before it turned to politics and Shiism, compiled a Turkish *divân* that reflects the influence of Rumi; Kemâl must have read Rumi's story of the boiling chickpeas from the *Masnavi* (M4:232–5), as it forms the basis and inspiration for one of his poems (William Hickman, in LDL, 204). Likewise, **Muini** (Mo‘ini), another fifteenth-century poet, translated the first book of Rumi's *Masnavi* into Ottoman Turkish as *Mesnevi-i murâdiyye*, romanized and edited by Kemal Yavuz (Ankara: Kültür ve Turizm Bakanlığı, 1982).

Mevlevi poets were instrumental in the formation of the courtly *divân* poetry of the Ottomans, composed in Turkish on the models of Persian ghazals, both in terms of content and in terms of prosody (GM 530–35). Gölpınarlı considers many of the most famous and influential Ottoman poets, including Nef‘i (1572?–1635), Nâbi (1642–1712) and Nedim (d. 1730) as Mevlevis (GM 533–4), though this may not have been their primary identity or affiliation. Because Ottoman *divân* poetry flourished primarily in an aristocratic milieu under court patronage, and because the Mevlevi order developed close ties with the Ottoman sultans and the aristocracy, most Turkish ghazal poets would have been quite familiar with Rumi. On the other hand, Mevlevi biographers have been too quick to count famous poets among their number. Gölpınarlı, for example, argues that though Esrâr Dede, in his work on the lives of the Mevlevi poets, claims **‘Osmân Ruhi** (d. 1605) as a Mevlevi, placing him at the Galata lodge in Istanbul for a time and later at the shrine of Rumi in Konya, in reality Ruhi was a soldier and more likely a Horufi than a Mevlevi (OLP 244–5; GM 26).

Shâhedi (d. 1550), whom we met earlier as an influential sixteenth-century propagator of the Mevlevi order (chapter 10), himself composed poems, though less than four dozen of these have survived. Some of these he wrote in Turkish and others in Persian, though Gölpınarlı thought his Persian verse exceedingly poor (GM 183–4). Though not an influential poet in Turkish, he had a better command of Turkish verse, both quantitative and metrical. He followed the meter of Rumi's *Masnavi* in his own short *masnavi* of 1536, "Unity's Bower," *Gülşen-i vahdet*, though he seems here more under the influence of ‘Attâr and Shabestari than Rumi (Victoria Holbrook, in LLM, 110). He also composed an Arabic treatise, "Shâhedian Visions," *Moshâhedât-e Shâhediye*, in which his shaykh slays him in order that he may ascend into the Mevlevi Realm of the Imaginal World, where he meets with Rumi, who places a crown upon his head (Holbrook, in LLM, 112–13). In 1515 Shâhedi had compiled an important though quite small Persian–Turkish dictionary in verse (!), "The Souvenir" (*Tohfe*), which remained popular for some while (Holbrook, in LLM, 109).

A number of respected poets were, however, clearly committed Mevlevis. **Neshâti** (d. 1674) of Edirne was initiated under Ağazâde Mehmed Dede, shaykh of the Mevlevi lodges in Gallipoli and later in Istanbul (Beşiktaş). When his master died in 1652, Neshâti went to Konya but eventually became the shaykh of the Mevlevi lodge in Edirne. He was a proponent of the Indian style of Persian poetry, which he helped introduce into Turkish, and he reflected Rumi's thought in his own verse. As head of a Mevlevi lodge, he did not need courtly patronage to support his poetry, but he nevertheless won the admiration of many professional poets (OLP 172). Mahmut Kaplan has edited his poems as *Neşâti divânı* (Izmir: Akademi, 1996).

Shaykh Ghâleb (Şeyh Mehmed Es^cad Galib, 1757–99) came from a Mevlevi family – his father Mostafâ Rashid (d. 1801) was an adept of the Yenikapı lodge, but also had leanings to Malâmati Sufism, as his tombstone reveals (GM 375). Though educated at home by his father and Mevlevi tutors – he supposedly learned Persian through reading Shâhedi's *Tohfe* with his father (Holbrook, in LLM, 109) – he chose to follow the other part of his father's legacy, as a poet and bureaucrat associated with the Ottoman Imperial Council. Ghâleb did not like the decadent lifestyle of the court poets, but he worked for the government for a time. A precocious poet, he had already compiled a *divân* of his own lyric poetry by the age of twenty-four and in the following year he composed his 2,100-line verse romance *Hüsn ü aşk* (Istanbul: Altın, 1968), which incorporated Mevlevi theosophy and solidified an enduring reputation for Ghâleb.[6]

In 1783 Ghâleb abandoned the civil service to return to his Mevlevi roots, but avoided the Mevlevi lodge his father and grandfather had frequented. Instead, he went to Rumi's shrine in Konya to initiate the 1,001-day period of seclusion (*chelle*), but did return to Istanbul and the Yenikapı lodge to complete his period as a novice.

In 1791 Ghâleb became the shaykh of the Mevlevi lodge in Galata, where he developed a close relationship with the Ottoman sultan Selim III. As we have seen, Selim III was himself a poet and a member of the Mevlevi order, and composed music for the *samâ^c* ceremony. He frequented the Mevlevi lodge in Galata, which, under his patronage, became the center of intellectual activity in Istanbul; Selim III's sister, Princess Beyhân, also became a friend of Ghâleb. Shaykh Ghâleb promoted the reforms of Selim III in his later poetry, until his premature death from tuberculosis at the age of forty-two (OLP 258–60).

Gölpınarlı wrote on Shaykh Ghâleb (Istanbul: Varlık, 1953) and published his poetry, but more recently Muhsin Kalkışım has edited Ghâleb's poetry as *Şeyh Gâlib Dîvânı* (Ankara: Akçağ, 1994). We have already encountered Shaykh Ghâleb's friend, **Esrâr Dede** (1748–96), who compiled a biography of the Mevlevi poets, in the previous chapter. Esrâr Dede, a poet like his spiritual guide Ghâleb, also died far too young, a circumstance which Ghâleb lamented in a beautiful elegy (see OLP 258 for a translation of the opening lines).

Solaymân (Süleymân) Nahifi (d. 1739), a scribe and fine calligrapher affiliated at various times with the Mevlevi, Khalvati and Hamzavi orders, made a brilliant translation of the *Masnavi* into Turkish, preserving much of the meter and phrasing of the original. It was published at the Bulâq Press in Cairo in 1852 (reprint, Istanbul: Sönmez). The fact that no complete Turkish translation of the *Masnavi* was attempted before Nahifi indicates the extent to which native Turkish speakers continued to read Rumi in the original Persian. In fact, even in the twentieth century, a form of Persian was still used by the descendants of the last Mevlevi shaykhs in Istanbul for certain topics of conversation (Holbrook, in LLM, 100).

Mevlevi poets continued their association with the Ottoman court in the nineteenth century. **Keçecizâde Izzet Mollâ** (1786–1829) came from a family of jurists with Mevlevi connections. His father was exiled and died when Izzet was only thirteen, and Izzet, though also trained in Islamic law, gave himself over to drink and debauchery. Hâlet Efendi, a powerful government official and Mevlevi member, took Izzet under his wing; under his influence, Izzet took up the theme of Mevlevi theosophy in the poem *Gülşen-i aşk*, probably with an eye to Shaykh Ghâleb's *Hüsn ü aşk*. After the execution of Hâlet Efendi, Izzet became the chief *qâzi* of Galata, but was exiled to Keshân as punishment for satirizing the Grand Vizier in verse. He composed a narrative poem on suffering here (*Mihnet-keshân*) and then apologized to the sultan in a *qaside*. This earned him a pardon, but as a result of his vocal opposition to the 1828 war against Russia, he was exiled again, this time to Sivas, where he soon died.

The last Mevlevi poet to make a name in Turkish poetry, **Yenişehirli Avni** (1826–83), read the *Masnavi* with Abd al-Rahmân Sâmi Pâshâ and eventually translated it into Turkish verse (GM 190). In addition to a command of Persian poetry, Avni knew Greek and Arabic, as well as some French. He came from his native Larissa to Istanbul in 1854, where he attended the Mevlevi lodges. He married the daughter of Huseyin Nezif, the shaykh of the Beşiktaş lodge, before becoming the secretary to the Ottoman governor of Baghdad in about 1860. In addition to mysticism, Avni was rather given to spirits (OLP 265). M. Kayahan Özgül provides a selection of his works and an introduction to his life in *Yenişehirli Avnî* (Ankara: Kültür Bakanlığı, 1990).

Nahifi's translation of the *Masnavi*, mentioned above, did not meet with the approval of Khayri Beg (d. 1890), who both criticized and set out to improve upon it. Unfortunately the result, published in 1890, was quite horrible (GM 190). The number of translations done in the nineteenth century which include the forged "Book 7" of the *Masnavi* show how widely the Mevlevis and others in Turkish lands had come to accept this as part of Rumi's work; the Bulâq Press in Egypt published Farrokh Efendi's (d. 1840) translation of this forged appendix along with Nahifi's translation of the authentic *Masnavi* in 1869. **Fayz Allâh Rahimi** (d. 1924) compiled a selection of fifty-five of the stories in the *Masnavi* in Turkish as *Golzâr-e haqiqat* (Istanbul: Maktab-e Tayyebe-ye ʿAskariye, 1908–9?). **Feyzullah Sacit Ülkü** did a verse translation into Turkish (Istanbul: Türkiye Yayınevi, 1945). **Gölpınarlı**, who discusses the history of Turkish translations of the *Masnavi* (GM 190–92), himself translated the *Masnavi* into prose along with his commentary, which appeared in six volumes in 1974, but was revised before his death, as *Mesnevi: tercemesi ve şerhi* (Istanbul: Inkılap ve Aka, 1981–4). *Mevlâna Şiiri Antolojisi* collects a number of poems written in Turkish in praise of Rumi from the twelfth through the twentieth century.

Rumi's influence on the Muslim world has by no means been confined to poets and scholars in Asia and Asia Minor. In the former Yugoslavia, at least two Turkish-language poets refer to Rumi and his thought in their works: Avni Egullu and Zeynel Beksaç. **Fejzulah Hadžibajrić** (d. 1990) kept alive the tradition of the Dâr al-Masnavi, or *Masnavi* College, and composed the most recent *Masnavi* commentary in a western language (T. Zarcone, "Tasawwuf," in *EI²*).

HISTORY OF COMMENTARIES ON THE *MASNAVI*

MEDIEVAL AND PRE-MODERN COMMENTARIES

Commentaries on the *Masnavi* have been composed in Persian, Turkish, Arabic and Urdu throughout the medieval and pre-modern period. There was even an institute in Baghdad, the Dâr al-Masnavi, principally devoted to the study of Rumi's *Masnavi* (MRC 307–8), along the lines of the Hadith and Koran institutes. The earliest exegetes wrote in Persian, and although most educated Turkish and Urdu speakers through the nineteenth century could also read Persian, it stands to reason that those for whom Persian was a second or third language required more assistance in understanding the import of Rumi's Persian than a native Persian-speaker would. Furthermore, the Mevlevi order operated primarily in Turkish-speaking lands and Rumi's popularity in India even outstripped his popularity in Iran, so that study of Rumi in Anatolia and India, and explications of the *Masnavi* in Turkish and Urdu, became more prevalent and assumed a greater importance than the ones in Persian. Finally, the major presses in the Islamic world in the nineteenth century were located in Istanbul, Lucknow and Cairo; printed editions of texts were usually undertaken in those cities, rather than in Iran.

Although the following history of pre-modern scholarship on Rumi generally groups the works by language, it should be remembered that Turkish and Urdu authors would often have had recourse to the Persian commentaries, so that the commentary traditions should not necessarily be considered as separate and distinct. However, just as most modern Italian readers will read primarily in Italian and most British or American readers will read in English, and so forth, the tradition of Rumi exegesis tended to develop with slightly different emphases in the different discourse communities, whether linguistic or philosophical. Furthermore, the commentaries tended to form around particular theosophical discourses, specifically that of Ibn ʿArabi, and these schools naturally project Rumi's ideas through the lens of their own doctrines. The following discussion of the commentary tradition is drawn from library catalogs, the introductions to some of the works mentioned, the preface to the seventh volume (Books 1 and 2: Commentary) of Nicholson's *The Mathnawi of*

Jalálu᾽ddín Rúmí (xi–xiii), the preface to Foruzânfar's edition of the *Masnavi* and Gölpınarlı's discussion in his work on the Mevlevis (GM 184–93). As Nicholson says (xii), though one cannot afford to ignore the "immense and bewildering mass of exegetical materials" on the *Masnavi*, the greater part of it yields bitter fruit and does not repay the time and effort it takes to wade through.

In 1320 **Ahmad Rumi**, a contemporary of Sultan Valad's son, Ulu ᶜAref Chelebi, composed a non-traditional Koran commentary of sorts, inspired by Rumi's *Masnavi*. This work, "The Fine Points of Spiritual Truths," *Daqâyeq al-haqâyeq*, edited by Mohammad Rezâ Jalâli Naᵓini and Mohammad Shirvâni and published by the Iranian government's Conseil Supérieur de la Culture et des Arts (Showrâ-ye ᶜÂli-ye Farhang va Honar, 1354/1975), features eighty chapters each beginning with a verse of the Koran or a hadith from the Prophet, which is then explained and pointed with an appropriate though rather poorly versified tale. Each discussion then concludes with a relevant quotation from Rumi's *Masnavi*, which would appear to be the motivating inspiration of the work. Composed just eight years after the death of Sultan Valad, it can apparently be considered the first commentary on the *Masnavi* and doubtless represents the very first effort to rearrange its contents in a systematic exposition of Rumi's philosophy, an endeavor that almost all Western scholars of Rumi over the last two hundred years have also chosen to pursue.

Khwâje Abu al-Vafâ Khwârazmi, a Sufi of the fifteenth century (d. 1432), had a great interest in the works of Rumi. He transferred this interest to his students and disciples, in particular **Kamâl al-Din Hosayn b. Hasan Khwârazmi** (d. 1437), an important metaphysical thinker and Kobravi Sufi who composed his first *Masnavi* commentary in verse in the *motaqâreb* meter: "Treasuries of Spiritual Truths in the Mysteries of the Fine Points," *Konuz al-haqâᵓeq fi romuz al-daqâᵓeq*, the title of which alludes to Ahmad Rumi's work. He then proceeded, at the request of his friends and disciples, to do a prose commentary, the first book of which he dedicated to Zahir al-Din Ebrâhim Sultan, a grandson of Tamerlane, upon its completion in 1430. Kamâl al-Din Khwârazmi persevered in this task and by the end of 1432 he had finished Book 2 and part of Book 3 (up to the story of the death of Belâl), though he apparently did not make any further progress. This commentary, "Gems of Mystery and Roses of Light," *Javâher al-asrâr va zavâher al-anvâr*, available in a multi-volume edition by Javâd Shariᶜati (Isfahan: Mashᶜal-e Esfahân, 1981?), features biographical notices of ten great Sufi predecessors of Rumi and a glossary of the gnostic terms current amongst them. It also includes copious quotations from the *Divân-e Shams* in order to explain ideas in the *Masnavi*.

A few years later Nezâm al-Din Mahmud of Shiraz produced a gloss, *Hâshie-ye Dâᶜi*. But important work was done outside of Iran, too. In India,

ʿAbd al-Latif al-ʿAbbâsi (d. c. 1639) diligently compiled as many as eighty manuscripts to prepare his proto-critical edition of the *Masnavi*, "The Definitive Copy" (*Noskhe-ye nâsekhe*). The great virtue of his subsequent commentary, "The Subtleties of Meaning," *Lataʾef al-maʿnavi*, and the accompanying dictionary of the text, *Lataʾef al-loghât*, is the relative authenticity of the *Masnavi* text he used as a basis. In 1673 **Mowlavi Mohammad Rezâ** of Lahore explained the difficult verses of the *Masnavi* in his "Reza's Revelations," *Mokâshafât-e Razavi*, an edition of which was lithographed in Lucknow in 1877 and has recently been published in Tehran in an edition by Kurosh Mansuri. **Mowlavi Vali Mohammad of Akbarâbâd**, who thought Rezâ's revelations hardly illuminating, harshly attacked it along with other earlier commentaries in his plainly titled "*Masnavi* Commentary" of 1728, *Sharh-e Masnavi*. ʿAbd al-ʿAli Mohammad b. Nezâm al-Din **Bahr al-ʿOlum** (1731–1810), nicknamed "the Ocean of Knowledge," wrote a commentary in Persian which was eventually lithographed in Lucknow in 1876 and again in Bombay the following year. A committed adherent of the pantheism of the *vahdat al-vojud* school of Sufism who also wrote a commentary on Ibn ʿArabi's *Fusûs al-hikam*, Bahr al-ʿOlum interprets the *Masnavi* through this lens.

"The Treasures of Gnosis and the Secrets of Faith," from the pen of Mohammad **Sâleh Qazvini Rowghani** (d. 1705), a Shiite who lived in Mashhad, confines itself to explaining the difficult verses of the *Masnavi*. The author used the Konya manuscript of 1278 (A.H. 677) for his text of the *Masnavi*; only the commentary of Book 4 survives in a unique autograph manuscript discovered in Qazvin, and published by Ahmad Mojâhed as *Konuz al-erfân va romuz al-iqân* (Tehran: Rowzane, 1374/1995). **Khwâje Ayyub**, writing in 1708, managed to make it through all six books of the *Masnavi*, proceeding line by line, defining the difficult words and glossing the meaning. His judicious quotation and evaluation of the views of previous commentators make his Persian "Hidden Mysteries" one of the most useful medieval commentaries. Mohammad Javâd Shariʿat has recently published a two-volume edition of this text as *Asrâr al-ghoyub* (Tehran: Asâtir, 1377/1998).

In the nineteenth century, on the pretext of explaining some of the abstruse passages of the *Masnavi*, one of Iran's great philosophers, **Mollâ Hâdi Sabzevâri** (1798–1873), offered an analysis of Rumi from the point of view of his own Divine Sophia (*Hekmat-e Elâhi*) school of thought. He gives grammatical explanations for confusing passages, but explicitly turns the exegesis of the *Masnavi* into a philosophical exegesis of the Koran. Sabzevâri completed the volume, *Sharh-e asrâr-e Masnavi*, in 1858 and dedicated it to a Qajar prince, Sultan Morâd. His work has been published in the 1970s in Tehran (by Sanâʾi) and again in selections as *Sharh-e Masnavi*, edited by Mostafâ Borujerdi (Tehran: Vezârat-e Farhang va Ershâd-e Eslâmi, 1374/1995). As described by John Cooper ("Rûmî and Hikmat" in LCP, 431):

It is not a work which lends itself readily to translation; the text is technical, highly condensed, often elliptical and the commentary frequently seems to ask for more clarification than the poetry. It gives the impression of being the record of sessions during which Rumi's poem was read, with pauses every now and then, to explain difficulties.

Cooper (LCP 422) also points out that **Mollâ Sadrâ** (d. 1641), the mentor of Sabzevâri, quoted the *Masnavi* frequently in his *Se asl* ("Three Principles").

By the sixteenth and seventeenth centuries, the majority of Mevlevi dervishes would have been culturally or even ethnically Turk. Though Persian remained an important language of the court and of culture, Turkish had become the official language in the Ottoman domains and it therefore comes as no surprise that the great commentaries of this period were written in Turkish. The first translation to Turkish of the *Masnavi* came as early as the first half of the fifteenth century, during the reign of Sultan Morâd II, according to Hasibe Mazioğlu (ScT 476 n. 9). But the commentary industry did not get really underway until the sixteenth century. Mostafâ **Soruri** Mosleh al-Din (d. 1562), a Turkish poet who also wrote commentaries on the *Divân* of Hâfez and the *Golestân* of Sa‘di, produced a six-volume *Masnavi* commentary, never published. These were the results of the classes Soruri used to teach on the *Masnavi* in Istanbul at sunset (GM 185–6). **Sudi** (d. 1597) is more famous for his commentary on Hâfez, but also wrote a *Masnavi* commentary, also never published. The commentary of **Sham‘i** (d. after 1601), however, proved very popular. He began writing as a free man in February of 1587, but was imprisoned by Sultan Morâd III after the fourth book was completed. Sultan Morâd summoned him on October 23, 1591 and instructed him to complete his commentary. Sham‘i completed Book 5 in October of 1593, but when Sultan Morâd died, did not feel the need to complete his work immediately. He began Book 6 seven years later in 1601 in the name of Mehmet III. Gölpınarlı believes his drinking and profligate ways may be responsible for the many mistakes in the commentary (GM 186–7).

In the seventeenth century, Mohammad Sha‘bânzâde compiled a Turkish dictionary of the *Masnavi* called *Mozher al-eshkâl*, dedicated to Hosayn Pâshâ Ohrili (d. 1622). But perhaps the greatest of the Turkish commentaries is that of **Rosukhi Esmâ‘il Dede Anqaravi** (Rüsuhî Ismâîl Ankaravî, d. 1631), the Mevlevi shaykh of the Galata lodge. This seven-volume work, called "The Opener of the Verses," *Fâteh al-abyât* (Egypt: Hedeviye, 1873) or simply "Anqaravi's *Masnavi* Commentary," *Mesnevi-i şerif şerhi* (Istanbul: ‘Âmere, 1872), includes a Turkish translation of each line of Rumi's Persian, as well as a commentary; Nicholson (M xii) remarked that this work proved more helpful to him than any other in preparing his English commentary. However, Anqaravi unfortunately chose an error-riddled exemplar of the *Masnavi* text as the basis of his commentary and included the forged "Book 7" as if it were Rumi's. He probably also never saw works that would have assisted his understanding of Rumi's true doctrines, such as the *Maqâlât-e Shams*, and instead relied upon the theosophy of Ibn ʿArabi. All of this upset the other Mevlevi shaykhs, who wanted to prevent him from distributing his commentary. Despite all these problems, Gölpınarlı feels it is probably the best commentary – which, however, tells us more about the poor state of the commentary tradition than the excellence of Anqaravi's commentary (GM 187). Foruzânfar, on the other hand, found this commentary so absurd that he questioned Anqaravi's command of Persian (FB 161).

Changi Yusof Dede b. Ahmad al-Mowlavi, shaykh of the Mevlevi lodge in the small village of Beşiktaş on the Bosphorus, produced an Arabic commentary for Syrian disciples there who could not comfortably read Turkish. Foruzânfar (*Sharh-e Masnavi* 1:xiii) and Schimmel (ScT 373) thought Yūsof Dede lived in the nineteenth century, but Gölpınarlı (GM 187–8) places his death in 1669. Entitled "The Sure Path for Students of the *Masnavi*," *al-Manhaj al-qawî li tullâb al-Mathnawî* (Cairo: Wahbiya, 1289/1872, first published in 1219/1804) it derives mainly from Rosukhi Anqaravi's commentary, condensing and translating it to Arabic, though Foruzânfar did not think highly of the quality of the prose. It also aims to please members of the Kobravi order, by throwing in quotations from Najm al-Din Kobrâ's Koran commentary. Because it provides the meaning of each line in Arabic before interpreting it, the *Manhaj* effectively contains an Arabic translation of the *Masnavi* as well as a commentary.

Anqaravi's was the first commentary to influence the Western perception of Rumi, when Joseph von Hammer-Purgstall published a study of it as *Bericht über den zu Kairo im Jahre D.H. 1251 (1835) in sechs Foliobänden erschienenen türkischen Commentar des Mesnewi Dschelaleddin Rumi's* (Vienna: Akademie der Wissenschaften, 1851). In an interesting twist, Anqaravi's Turkish commentary has been translated into Persian by ʿEsmat Sattârzâde as *Sharh-e kabir-e Anqaravi* (Tehran: Mihan, 1969–) so Persian readers can better understand Rumi.

It will be noted that seventeenth- and eighteenth-century Ottomans vied with one another in feats of exegesis, striving to create ever more detailed commentaries on the *Masnavi*. So, we find the Malâmati dervish, **Sâri ʿAbd Allâh Efendi** (1586–1660) analyzing Rumi from the point of view of the theosophy of Ibn ʿArabi in a commentary called "Brilliant Gems of the Masnavi," *Javâher-e bavâher-e Masnavi*. Though he only covered Book 1 of the *Masnavi*, he managed to fill five volumes and 2,500 pages in so doing, adding in his introduction rather fanciful information about the life of Mowlânâ.

Two centuries later, once printing presses had been established in Turkey, this manuscript was published at the ʿAmere Press in Istanbul in 1870–72 as *Mesnevi-i şerif*. A decade earlier the same press had published the rather grandiosely titled "Spirit of the Masnavi," *Ruh al-Masnavi*, a two-volume commentary covering only the first 738 lines of the *Masnavi* by **Ismâil Hakkı** of **Bursa** (1653–1725). Ismâil Hakki was a Jelveti Sufi but, wishing to memorialize his name, decided to write a commentary on the *Masnavi* of Rumi. Another non-Mevlevi, **Shaykh Morâd Bokhâri** (d. 1848) of the Naqshbandi order, founded a Dâr al-Masnavi in Istanbul; he began a commentary on the work in September 1839 and by the evening of April 25, 1845 was at work on Book 6.

TWENTIETH-CENTURY TRENDS

Gölpınarlı (GM 193) points out that most *Masnavi* commentaries were written to make a name for the author and had more to do with their own thoughts and speculations than with anything found in Rumi's text (it is small comfort to remark that the academy has changed very little since those days). So many individuals have devoted so much time to the text of the *Masnavi*. However, not everyone has time to read all six books and a further six books of commentary on the text itself. Modern commentators at least tend to focus on Rumi and often condense and select rather than expanding and interpolating. The great Persian scholar Ahmed Ateş, for example, chooses just the first eighteen lines of the *Masnavi* and explains them in just thirteen pages in "Mesnevi'nin onsekiz beytinin mânası" from *Fuad Köprülü Armağanı* (Istanbul: Osman Yalçın Matbaası, 1953; 37–50).

This long tradition of writing glosses or commentaries in the medieval style continued in several journals published in Istanbul in the nineteenth century (e.g., *Muhibbân, Hikmet, Jaride-ye Sufi, Tasavvof, Mahfel*) and persisted until well into the twentieth century. In Turkey, not only Mevlevis but dervishes from other orders and statesmen tried their hand at explaining Rumi's *Masnavi*. **ʿÂbedin Pâshâ** b. Ahmed (1843–1906), the Ottoman governor of Angora (Ankara), provides a Turkish translation as well as commentary in the six volumes of his *Tercüme ve şerh-i Mesnevi-i şerif* (Istanbul: Mahmud Bey, 1887; reprinted 1909). Ahmet ʿAvni Konuk (1873–1938), in addition to translating Rumi's Discourses into Turkish and composing a musical interlude for the Mevlevi ceremony, published a six-volume commentary in traditional style. Even after the Second World War, such conventional commentaries were still being produced, as the "Lessons on the Masnavi" by **Tâhir Olgun al-Mevlevi** (1877–1951), who taught the *Masnavi* at the Süleymaniye mosque, shows (GM 189). Three volumes were eventually published in fascicle form in Istanbul (ʿÂmere, 1949–50; reprinted in Konya: Selam, 1963), but this took him only through Book 1. Zarcone ("Tasawwuf," *EI²*) notes that the entire work was published in Istanbul in 1963, running to fourteen volumes. As late as 1973, the *Şerhli Mesnevi-yi şerif* of Kanan Rifai appeared in Istanbul.

In the Indian subcontinent, Mohammad Yusof ʿAli Shâh Cheshti Nezâmi Golshanâbâdi provided the Persian text of the *Masnavi* with Urdu verse translation and interlinear commentary in six volumes as *Pirâhan-e Yusofi* (lithographed at Lucknow in 1889 and in Kanpur in 1897; reprinted Lucknow: Naval Kishor, 1918). ʿAbd al-Majid Khân of Pilibhit, who also wrote a commentary on the Persian poet ʿOrfi of Shirâz, gave the world a second Urdu commentary with his multi-volume "Gnostic Garden," *Bustân-e maʿrefat* (Lucknow: Naval Kishor, 1927).

In Iran large line-by-line commentaries were still appearing in the middle of this century. **Musâ Nasri** matched the six books of the *Masnavi* with the six volumes of his *Nasr va sharh-e Masnavi* (Tehran: Kolâle-ye Khâvar, 1948–51). **Mohammad Taqi Jaʿfari** penned an even larger eight-volume commentary in the 1970s, *Tafsir va naqd va tahlil-e Masnavi* (Tehran: Sahâmi 1970–), based upon the Ramazâni text.

RECENT SCHOLARLY COMMENTARIES

Abdülbâki Gölpınarlı and **Mohammad Esteʿlâmi** have both produced commentaries with their critical editions of the text of the *Masnavi*, the former in Turkish, the latter in Persian. **ʿAbd al-Hosayn Zarrinkub** has contributed perhaps the most interesting scholarly approach to the understanding of the *Masnavi* in his two complementary works, "The Secret of the Reed," *Serr-e nay* (Tehran: ʿElmi, 1985), and "The Ocean in a Jug," *Bahr dar kuze* (Tehran: ʿElmi, 1987). In 1998 the most recent commentary, the six volumes of **Karim Zamâni-Jaʿfari**'s *Sharh-e jâmʿe-ye Masnavi-ye maʿnavi* (Tehran: Ettelâʿât, 1372–7), begun in 1993, was completed. Any future readers consumed with a desire to explicate Rumi will need to work from these, and from **Sâdeq Gowharin**'s seven-volume dictionary (1958–75) of the words and expressions of the *Masnavi*. The commentary which **Badiʿ al-Zamân Foruzânfar** left incomplete at his death is also indispensable for the earlier parts of the *Masnavi*. For the publication details of these and other modern scholarly works on Rumi, see chapter 13.

ABRIDGEMENTS

The selection and abridgement of the *Masnavi* began at least as early as the fifteenth century with the works of Jâmi and has a venerable history. Indeed, **Yusof Sinechâk** (d. 1546, see chapter 10) composed the first one sometime between 1495 and 1498, "An Island in the Masnavi," *Cezîre-i Mesnevî*. He chose 60 lines from each of the 6 books and wove them together in a seemingly seamless text of 360 lines. Sinechâk's work inspired a number of tertiary works in Turkish, commentaries upon his *Cezîre*, especially among Mevlevis also associated the Malâmati order (Holbrook, in LLM, 110). Thirty years later, in 1530, the Mevlevi activist **Shâhedi** completed his *Golshan-e towhid* (Istanbul: Tıbbiye, 1298/1881). This selects 600 lines of Rumi's *Masnavi* and adds 3,000 more lines of verse commentary by Shâhedi in Persian to explain in abridged form what transpires in between the lines of Rumi he has selected (GM 179–80).

Sabuhi Ahmad Dede (d. 1647), the shaykh of the Mevlevi lodge in Yenikapı, produced his "Selections from the *Masnavi*," *Ekhtiârât-e Masnavi*, in 1617. Sometimes abridgements were packaged as part of an anthology of favorite poets, as can be seen in one two-volume manuscript in the Konya Museum, which includes excerpts from the *Masnavi* along with poems of ʿErâqi, Amir Khosrow, Shabestari and others.

Foruzânfar presented a choice annotated selection of stories from the *Masnavi* as *Kholâse-ye Masnavi* (Tehran: Bânk-e Melli, 1942). So also did the writer Jamâlzâde (see below, "Rumi as Exponent of Human Liberation"). The opening lines of the *Masnavi*, the "reed's song," provide the pre-text for the brief commentary of Karim Zamâni Jaʿfari, *Nay nâme: dar tafâsir-e Masnavi-ye maʿnavi* (Tehran: Ettelâʿât, 1989). **Mohammad-ʿAli Eslâmi-Nodushan** provides a very large selection of the *Masnavi* along with commentary in his *Bâgh-e sabz-e ʿeshq* (Tehran: Yazdân, 1998). **Mahdokht Bânu Homâʾi** has selected the first and second books of the *Masnavi* and published them with brief commentary in Persian and English translation in her *Serr-e delbarân dar hadis-e digarân* (Boston: Pârs, 1998). Some selections from the ghazals have also been printed with an introduction and notes in Mohammad-Rezâ Shafiʿi-Kadkani's *Gozide-ye ghazaliyât-e Shams* (Tehran: Ketâb-hâ-ye Jibi (Sahâmi), 1352/1973).

RUMI IN MODERN MUSLIM LITERATURE AND THOUGHT

Shebli Noʿmâni (1857–1916), the great Indian scholar of Persian literature, was a modernist Muslim very much attracted to Rumi, as was Iqbal after him. Noʿmâni was known to maintain contact with Naqshbandi Sufis and when he visited Istanbul in 1893, he may very well have met Mevlevis. He wrote the first biography of Rumi in any language, *Savâneh-e Mowlânâ Rum* (Lahore: Naval Kishor, 1909), which went through several editions (2nd ed., Amritsar: Electric Press, 1938; 3rd ed., Sayyed Emtiâz ʿAli Tâj, President of the Progress of Literature Circle, Lahore). It was also translated into Persian as *Savâneh-e Mowlavi Rumi* by Sayyed M.T. Fakhr-e Dâʿi Gilâni (1953). Noʿmâni was very fond of Rumi's theory of evolution, in which he saw certain similarities to Hindu philosophy and even the doctrines of metempsychosis. He compared Rumi's theory of evolution to Darwinian evolution (as Iqbal would later compare it to Bergson's *évolution creatrice*), though the ethical evolution of soul distinguishes it from animal evolution. Noʿmâni found Rumi's teachings in harmony with other nineteenth-century scientific discoveries in physics and biology, but essentially viewed Rumi in the tradition of Islamic scholastic theology, though his theology was not systematic like Ghazzâli's, nor did Rumi condemn any religion as wholly false.[7]

MUHAMMAD IQBAL

Muhammad Iqbal (1873–1938), born in Siyalkot in the Punjab to a family of the Brahmin caste that had converted to Islam three hundred years earlier, lived in Lahore, India (Pakistan since partition). Iqbal stands out as perhaps the Muslim world's greatest poet and thinker of this century. Educated in England, he wrote a dissertation on the development of metaphysics in Persia and returned to Lahore, where he taught philosophy and English literature, eventually taking up the practice of law and political activism on behalf of Indian independence and the Muslim League.

Drawing upon both Islamic and Western philosophy, Iqbal sought to reconstruct traditional Islam in a modern form. He wrote and spoke in Urdu, Persian and English, composing a number of lyric poems in Urdu and several important philosophical poems in Persian. Iqbal, like all educated Muslims in the subcontinent, learned the *Masnavi* of Rumi at an early age and not infrequently quoted lines from it to punctuate points he wished to make, both in conversation and in his written works, such as *The Reconstruction of Religious Thought in Islam*. Likewise, Iqbal was sometimes asked to comment on the meaning of various verses of Rumi. The quotation of these verses sometimes moved the sensitive Iqbal to tears.[8]

Iqbal wrote of Rumi as a pantheist in his *Metaphysics of Persia* (1908), an idea he apparently received through Hegel and Western philosophy. In his first poetic work, *Asrâr-e khodi*, written in 1915 (see R.A. Nicholson's translation, *The Secrets of the Self* (*Asrar-i-Khudi*) [London: Macmillan, 1920; revised ed. Lahore: Sh.M. Ashraf, 1940; frequent reprints]), Iqbal critiqued Hâfez and the bombastic mystification into which the gnostic and philosophical tradition of Islam, under the influence of Hellenism, had sunk. After about 1911, however, he came to see Rumi as an advocate of the praxis of divine love and self-transcendence, with which Iqbal himself could identify. Rumi appears to him in *Secrets of the Self* and urges him to sing, becoming his guide, just as Shams had earlier played the role of Khezr for Rumi and urged him to sing. This appears to have been a real vision of Rumi, not a metaphor or literary apostrophe. As Iqbal phrases it, "The master of Rum transmuted my earth to gold/And set my ashes aflame" (See *Secrets of the Self*, 9–11). From this point onward, Iqbal saw himself as a disciple of Rumi in many ways. Iqbal regarded the *Masnavi* as the second most important book, after the Koran, and advised Muslim intellectuals to read it. He also had a hand in instigating ʿAbd al-Majid Daryâbâdi's edition of *Fihe mâ fih*, which appeared in 1922.

Iqbal's Urdu poem of 1923, *Payâm-e mashreq* ("Message of the East"), combines his love for Rumi with his love for Goethe, and replies to the latter's *West-östliche Divân*, in which Rumi outshines Goethe, who had failed to understand Rumi's spiritual discovery. Rumi appears again and again as Iqbal's spiritual guide. In *Bâl-e Jebril*, "Gabriel's Wing," Iqbal poses questions in Urdu, juxtaposed with the answers from the Persian of Rumi's *Masnavi*. As Schimmel notes in her study of Iqbal, *Gabriel's Wing* (Leiden: Brill, 1963, 357), Iqbal wrote his *masnavis* in the same meter as Rumi's poem, so that he could seamlessly include quotations from Rumi.

But the work of Iqbal which most concerns us here is his long Persian poem of 1932, *Jâvid nâme*, "The Book of Eternity," named after his son, Jâvid. This is a *masnavi* inset with ghazals, at least one of which is borrowed from Rumi's *Divân*. The *Jâvid nâme* takes Dante's *Paradiso* as its paradigm (though Iqbal was probably also conscious of a number of other Persian and Arabic models). On his journey through heaven, Iqbal is led not by Beatrice, but by Jalâl al-Din Rumi, who guides him from earth through the spheres of the moon, Mercury (where he meets Zoroaster, Buddha, Christ, Mohammad and the Bâbi heroine Tâhirih), Venus, Mars, Jupiter, Saturn, the space beyond (where he encounters Nietzsche) and finally to paradise. Here the mysticism of Rumi merges with Hegelian dialectic and the thought of Bergson, to clear a path for the Muslim community to follow into heaven. Iqbal found Rumi's concept of man and the soul congenial to his own view of human destiny. In contradistinction to other gnostic systems, which seemed to deprive man of responsibility or effort, Rumi emphasized the need to strive for perfection and the stages of spiritual evolution. This activism is what distinguished Rumi from the more decadent kinds of fatalistic mysticism and thought Iqbal had earlier decried. Hermann Hesse referred to Iqbal's "Book of Eternity" as a combination of Vedanta, Koranic ethics, Islamic mysticism and Western philosophy. It was, in an allusion of course to Goethe, an *Öst-westliche Divan* ("Eastern-Occidental *Divân*").

The *Jâvid nâme*, with Rumi cast as celestial guide, has been translated into Italian by Alessandro Bausani as *Il Poema celeste* (Rome: Instituto italiano per il Medio ed Estremo Oriente, 1952; [Bari]: Leonardo da Vinci editrice, 1965); into German by Annemarie Schimmel as *Buch Der Ewigkeit* (Munich: Max Hueber, 1957; the comments by Hesse are to be found in the foreword, p. v); and into English as *Javidnâma* by A.J. Arberry (UNESCO Collection of Representative Works, Pakistan Series [London: Allen & Unwin, 1966]). But it is primarily in the Islam of the subcontinent that Iqbal's impact is felt; revered as one of the founding fathers of the state of Pakistan, his works remain highly regarded in Muslim circles in that country and in India. In 1933 Mohammad Nâder Shah, the ruler of Afghanistan, invited Iqbal to help form that country's system of higher education, so his influence extends to other areas as well.

Iqbal has himself been called the "Rumi of the Age" in a book by Khwâja A. ᶜErfâni (Tehran, 1953). A memorial for Iqbal was erected in the garden of the Mevlevi compound in Konya by the city government there (ScB 22). Iqbal also inspired a large number of publications on Rumi in Pakistan, including, for example, a translation of the *Masnavi* into Punjabi verse by Maulvi Mohammad Shah Din Qureishi (*Masnavi Sharif* [Lahore, 1939?]). Sayyed Mohammad Akram (1932–) published a study of the influence of Rumi's style on Iqbal, *Eqbâl dar râh-i Mowlavi: sharh-e hâl va âsâr va sabk-e ashᶜâr va afkâr-e Eqbâl* (2nd ed., Lahore: Iqbal Akadmi Pakistan, 1982), and Vazir al-Hasan ᶜÂbedi contributed an investigation into the *Masnavi* as a source for Iqbal's ideas, on the occasion of the 100th anniversary of his birth: *Iqbal ke shi'ri ma'akhaz Masnavi Rumi* (Lahore: Majles-e Taraqqi-ye Adab/Iqbal Academy, 1977).

PAKISTAN

Despite the towering presence of Iqbal in national consciousness and Islamic thought, Rumi continues to hold the interest of Pakistani authors in his own right. The late **Fazlur Rahman** (1919–88), a modernist Muslim thinker who studied in England and taught at the University of Chicago, told me in the spring of 1984 that he had learned Persian at his father's knee through the *Masnavi* of Rumi, memorizing large passages from it. He recited several passages by heart in his sweetly lilting South Asian accent. Though Rahman felt little sympathy for Sufism, the *Masnavi*, which he described as a work of "surpassing beauty" (see his *Islam* [2nd ed., Chicago: University of Chicago Press, 1979], 164) always retained a place in his heart. Rahman quoted and at some level believed Rumi's doctrine that the form of worship for Hindus is excellent for Hindus (*Islam*, 155).

Numerous authors have carried on the *Masnavi* commentary tradition in Urdu. The Sunni scholar **Fayz Ahmad Ovaysi** (1932?–), author of a number of works on sectarian subjects – including a critique of Shiite beliefs, a synopsis of the Deoband school of Wahhabis, a brief on the proper Sunni devotional attitude toward the Prophet, as well as a commentary on the Koran – presents an Urdu translation in the course of his two-volume commentary, *Sedâ-ye navi* (Bahawalpur: Ovaysie Rezvie, 1976–79). Earlier, **Mohammad Nazir 'Arshi**, a clinical doctor who also wrote on the practice of medicine in Pakistan, had somehow managed to find the time between treating patients to contribute his own seventeen-volume exegesis of the *Masnavi* under the title *Meftâh al-'olum* (Lahore: Quraishi, 1925; reprint: Shaikh Ghulam 'Ali, 1977). **Mohammad 'Abd al-Majid Yazdâni** expended his efforts in a different task: making a concise selection of the poem for those who do not have time to read thousands of pages in exposition and explication of the meanings of the *Masnavi*. He titled his 200-page abridgement, which provides the poetry in Persian and a brief commentary in Urdu, "The Words of Rumi, or a Selection of the Masnavi, Which is the Koran in Persian Tongue," *Gofte-ye Rumi* (Lahore: Mo'in al-adab, 1976).

It is not only the poetry of Rumi that attracts Urdu readers. **Mohammad Riâz** has made a one-volume annotated collection of Rumi's letters and discourses available to Urdu readers as *Maktubât va khotbât-e Rumi* (Lahore: Iqbal Academy of Pakistan, 1988). Pakistani readers have even provided a market for publications on Rumi in languages other than Urdu. For example, a Pakistani lawyer, Masud al-Hasan, has written dozens of books on subjects as diverse as modern law, the Koran, Islamic history, Muslim women, Iqbal, and a guidebook to Lahore. In addition, he culled and translated his own selections from the *Masnavi* into English as *Stories from Rumi* (Karachi and Lahore: Ferozsons, 1977?).

A new biography of Rumi in Urdu has recently replaced No͑mâni's *Savâneh*, now somewhat out of date: **Muhammad Riyâz Qadri**'s *Manâqeb-e Rumi: Maulana Rum ki ruhani aur batini zindagi ki ek jhalak* (Rawalpindi: Ziyâiye, 1997). Meanwhile, **Ghulamu Muhammadu Shahvani**'s "Treasury of Knowledge" makes the ideas of the *Masnavi* available in Sindi (͑*Ilmi khazano*, 1965–).

INDIA

Nor have India's Muslims ignored Rumi in recent years. A facsimile of a *Masnavi* manuscript dated 1691 and written out by the hand of Ustâd ͑Abd al-Karim was published in 1933, apparently in Hyderabad, as *The Mathnawi of Jalal-ud-Din Rumi*, edited by G. Yazdâni (1885–1962) with an introduction in English and Urdu. A facsimile reprint of **Talammoz Hosayn**'s voluminous *Mer͗ât al-Masnavi*, presented as a mirror for the stories and anecdotes of the *Masnavi*, appeared under the title *A͗ine-ye qesas va hekam-e Masnavi* (Hyderabad: Nashriât-i Mâ, 1361/1982). Mirzâ Nezâm Shâh Labib translated various didactic stories from the *Masnavi* into Urdu in 1945 as *Hekâyat-e Rumi* (Delhi: Anjoman-e Taraqqi-ye Urdu, 1945). Shamus-ud-Din Hairat Kamili (1890–1968), a classical music master and scholar, translated the first book of the *Masnavi* into Kashmiri.

The Urdu poet and philosopher **Nushur Vahidi** (1912–83) also came under Rumi's spell. He distilled the essence of Book 1 of the *Masnavi* into "The Claret of India, The Wine of Rum," a large collection of Urdu ghazals, quatrains and other poems: *Sahbâ-yi Hind aur Badah-yi Rum* (2nd ed., Lucknow and New Delhi: Jami͑ah, 1989). Zakir Hussain (1897–1969), a Muslim associate of Gandhi and president of India from 1967 to 1969, also used to quote one line in particular from Rumi's *Masnavi*.[9]

Sufism and Bhakti: Mawlânâ Rûm and Śrî Râmakrishna by **Imadulhasan Azad Faruqi** (New Delhi: Abhinav, 1984) details the growth of Sufism and Bhakti systems and then compares the concept of Sufi love (͑*eshq*) with the concept of Bhakti in the lives of Rumi and Ramakrishna (1836–86), concluding with love as a way to God. Faruqi completed this study as his dissertation for the degree of Master of Literature at the Department of Religious Studies in the Punjabi University of Patiala. Although it examines both the Western and Hindu sources on Rumi and Indian Sufism, it is more interesting for its combination of subject matter than its results. At the Department of Indian Philosophy and Religion at Benaras Hindu University, **Rasih Güven**, a Turk, wrote a dissertation entitled *The Absolutism of Sankaracarya as Compared with Mawlana Jalalu͗ddin Rumi's School of Thought* (Ankara: Net Offset, 1957; reprinted 1991).

With Rumi's example of tolerance, the experience of Hindu–Muslim ecumenicism under Emperor Akbar, and the unific teachings of Kabir or Gandhi, it should come as no surprise that some non-Muslim authors in India have also devoted their attention to Rumi. In the nineteenth century, the Radha

Swami doctrine of Swami Maharaj (Shiv Dayal Sâheb, or Tulsi Ram, 1818–78) incorporated quotations from Rumi and the *Masnavi*, as did Swami Rama Tiratha (1873–1906) and, in the twentieth century, Bhagawan Das.[10]

Jagadisacandra Vacaspati wrote a biography of Rumi in Hindi, *Maulana Ruma aura unka kavya* (Calcutta: Hindi Pustaka Ejensi, 1922). The poet **Vinoda Candra Pandeya** (1932–), who has rendered both Kabir and Sanskrit religious literature into Hindi, recently translated the entire *Masnavi*, following the text of Nicholson's edition, as *Jalalauddina Rumi krta Masanavi* (New Delhi: Siddhartha, 1996). In the east of India, **Girish Chandra Sen** made the major ideas of Islam available to Bengali speakers in a series of books about Mohammad (1917), Ghazzâli and ʿAttâr, as well as one on Ramakrishna. In 1914 he published a study of ʿAttâr's *Manteq al-tayr* and Rumi's *Masnavi* as *Tattvaratnamala: arthat tattvasastrasambandhiya racanabali: Parasya pustaka Mantekottayara o Masnabi Maulabi Roma haite sankalita* (Calcutta: Mangalagañja Misana). He was later to publish a Bengali translation of the Koran (1936).

In 1960 **Harendrachandra Paul**, a Bengali, wrote his dissertation (in English) on Rumi at the University of Calcutta in 1960, which he published in 1985 as *Jalalud-Din Rumi and His Tasawwuf* (Calcutta: Sobharani Paul). A second volume appeared as *The Epilogue* (Calcutta: M.I.G. Housing Estate, 1988). Despite what the title insinuates, at over seven hundred pages, *The Epilogue* was hardly an afterthought to the first volume. These studies focus on Mevlevi history and belief, and the psychology of Sufism. **M.G. Gupta**, also writing in English, published a translation and commentary of the first 4,500 lines of the Masnavi as *Maulana Rum's Masnawi* (Agra: MG Publishers, 1990).

THE ARAB WORLD

Unlike the Turks, the Arabs did not produce volume after volume of translation and commentary on Rumi. Yusof b. Ahmad al-Mowlavi's *Manhaj al-qawî* supplies a prose translation of each line of the *Masnavi*, and this remained for some time the only, or the only well-known, Arabic version of the poem. ʿAbd al-Wahhâb ʿAzzâm did some selections from Rumi in Arabic as *Fusûl min al-Mathnawî* (Cairo, 1946). ʿAbd al-ʿAzîz Sâhib al-Jawâhir provides the Persian text of the *Masnavi* with an interlinear Arabic translation in his *Jawâhir al-athâr fî tarjamat Mathnawî Mawlânâ Khwudâvandgâr* (University of Tehran, 1957). The Syrian Ministry of Culture and Guidance of the People published a huge selection of Hâfez, Saʿdi and Rumi in the Arabic translations of **Muhammad al-Furâtî** (1880–1978) as *Rawâ'iʿ al-shiʿr al-fârisî* (Damascus: Wizârat al-Thaqâfah al-Qawmî, 1963), and this includes some selections from the *Masnavi* in Arabic verse (pp. 3–71). **Muhammad Hasan al-Aʿzamî** teamed up with **al-Sawî ʿAlî Shalân** for translations of five representative poets of Islam – Saʿdi, ʿAttâr, Hâli, Muhammad Iqbal and Rumi – as *al-Aʿlâm al-khamsa li* *al-shᶜir al-Islâmî* (Beirut: ᶜIzz al-Dîn, 1982). Another complete Arabic translation and commentary on the *Masnavi* came from the pen of **Ibrâhîm al-Dasûqî Shitâ** in six volumes beginning in 1992 (Cairo: al-Zahrâ) and completed in 1996 (Cairo: al-Majlis al-Aᶜlâ li al-Thaqâfa). Shitâ (d. 1999) also wrote about Iranian literature and Sufism, translated Sanâ᾽i's *Hadiqat al-haqiqe* and compiled a Persian–Arabic dictionary, and therefore has an excellent background to carry out this project. **Al-Sayyid Muhammad Jamâl al-Hâshimî** produced a selection in Arabic of the stories of the *Masnavi* as *Hikâyât wa-ᶜibâr min al-Mathnawî* (Beirut: Dâr al-Haqq, 1995). **Rajâ ᶜAbd al-Munᶜim Jabr** published a comparative study of the influence of Rumi, Dante and Shakespeare in world literature, *Fî al-adab al-muqaran* (Cairo: al-Shabâb, 1988).

AFGHANISTAN

Since Balkh, Rumi's supposed city of birth, is situated in Afghanistan, right on the border with Tajikistan, Afghans and Tâjiks consider Rumi a countryman and a source of patriotic pride. In a series of *masnavi*s, the poet of Patna, Mirzâ ᶜAbd al-Qâder **Bidel** (1665–1722, pronounced Bêdil by Afghans), developed his own mystical philosophy that differs from Rumi's, and yet also owes something to it. Along with Rumi, Bidel remains the most beloved classical Persian poet in Afghanistan.

The editor of Bidel's massive *Divân*, **Khalil Allâh Khalili** (1907–87), himself the most celebrated modern poet in Afghanistan, also came under the sway of Rumi. Khalili wrote poems in praise of Rumi called "From Balkh to Konya" (Kabul: Ministry of Information and Culture, 1346/1967). In a work titled "Song of the Reed," *Nay nâme* (Kabul: Ministry of Information and Culture, 1973), Khalili presents two poems of Jâmi and Yaᶜqub Charkhi (d. 1448) written under Rumi's inspiration. Khalili prefaced the work, published during UNESCO's Year of Rumi to commemorate the 700th anniversary of his death, with a long introduction about Rumi's life. A selection of Khalili's Persian quatrains, also reflecting the influence of Rumi, have twice been made available in English translation, first in Baghdad as *Rubaᶜiyat* (1975, Persian text with Arabic and English translations), and then in London at Idries Shah's Octagon Press: *Quatrains of Khalilulla Khalili* (1981; 2nd ed. 1987).

The great Afghan scholar ᶜAbd al-Hayy Habibi (1910–) edited a metrical commentary on two verses of the *Masnavi* by the nineteenth-century Afghan, **Mehrdel Khân Mashreqi of Qandahar** (1797–1855). Like Khalili's work, this too was published in 1973 in Kabul. Afghanistan had already commemorated the 700th anniversary of Rumi's death, which took place according to the Islamic lunar calendar in 1953 (A.H. 1372); that year saw the publication of a commemorative article in Afghanistan by Ahmad ᶜAli Kohzâd: "Mowlânâ Jalâl al-Din of Balkh," emphasizing Rumi's Afghan origins, and a small commemorative booklet, *Goldaste-ye ᶜeshq* (A Bouquet of Love), printed in Kabul.

RUMI AS EXPONENT OF HUMAN LIBERATION IN REVOLUTIONARY IRAN

The people and government of Turkey recognize Rumi as an apostle of tolerance, as evident from the comments of two recent Turkish ministers of culture in the introductions to Nevit Ergin's translations of Rumi's *Divân*, published with funding from the Turkish government, and in the Fehmi Gerceker film, *Tolerance: Dedicated to Mawlânâ Jalâl al-Din*. Though Rumi remained a committed Muslim, his mysticism holds as a basic premise that God and Truth transcend sectarian, historical and cultural differences, and his mode of religious life stressed a sense of joy and love for the divine and its many effulgences in the human plane, in contrast to the legalistic strictures of many Muslim preachers and scholars, while his method of preaching involved encouragement by anecdotes and poetry, in contrast to dire threats and compulsion. The Ministry of Culture and Islamic Guidance in Iran seems to have undertaken to promote the Turks' view of Rumi, while at the same time of course strengthening cultural and religious ties between the two countries; in 1990 it compiled and published a series of Turkish scholars' writings on Rumi together with the articles of some Persian colleagues in *Mowlânâ az didgâh-e Torkân va Irâniân*.

The Koran teaches that Abraham and Moses and the lesser prophets, as well as Jesus, were all sent by God, and that the followers of Judaism and Christianity are all People of the Book, that is the divine Book, successive chapters of which were revealed as God's guidance to humanity. Though the Koran urges the rooting out of polytheism and idol-worship, and is somewhat ambiguous about the pre-Islamic religious traditions of Iran, most Muslims came to include Zoroastrians as People of the Book, and in India, certainly by the Moghul period, many Muslims had in practice recognized the hand of God in the Hindu tradition, though originally Hindus and Buddhists had been considered idol-worshipers. Rumi, if the accounts of his funeral procession are basically accurate (and there is no compelling reason to discount them), won the respect and admiration of the Jewish and Christian communities during his lifetime and had perhaps even attracted some converts to his open-minded vision of Islam. Certainly his presence and example in Konya must have militated against any pre-existing tendencies toward sectarian hostility in the region. It is reported that in the seventeenth century, a time when as yet few Muslims were reading or referring directly to the text of the Bible, a Mevlevi from Konya, ʿAssâr Dede, studied the Christian and Jewish scriptures.[11]

IRANIAN PHILOSOPHERS AND THEOLOGIANS

Meanwhile, in Iran, Rumi has inspired philosophers and theologians, as well as political activists, with a vision of a tolerant society. Shiite scholarship of the last few centuries has often tended to focus in minute detail on matters of Islamic law, with ayatollahs compiling manuals called "Clarification of Questions" (*Resâle-ye towzih al-masâ'el*) as guides for lay people, giving their collected fatwas on various issues. A famous example would be Ayatollah Khomeini's 5,000-plus pages of his *Towzih al-masâ'el* (1964, with numerous subsequent editions and reprints), translated into English in 1984 as *A Clarification of Questions* (but it should be noted that Khomeini also wrote mystical poetry in his student days!).

For Iranians disenchanted with the legalistic and prescriptive interpretations of Islam found in the writings of many ayatollahs, or those opposed to the often invasive imposition of a puritanical understanding of Islamic morality by the authorities or by vigilante groups on behalf of the Islamic Republic of Iran, Rumi offers an alternative vision of Islamic piety, one characterized by an expansive view of the relationship between man and God, tolerance for the beliefs and spiritual station of others, and a concentration on the inner meaning of spirituality, rather than the outward forms and rituals of worship. After the death of Mohammad Rezâ Shâh, his son, who for some years after the 1979 Revolution comported himself as monarch-in-exile of Iran, called upon the Iranian people in a videotaped message to adhere to the true Islam, the Islam of spirituality (*Eslâm-e ma'navi*) and kindness. Without explicitly mentioning him, these words perhaps conjured up for some listeners the example of Rumi's tolerance and his "Couplets of Spirituality," *Masnavi-ye ma'navi*.

Islamic thinkers in Iran, of course, look primarily to the sayings of the Imams 'Ali (d. 661), Hosayn (d. 680) and Ja'far al-Sâdeq (d. 765), as well as to early Shiite history, for models of the just society. Ali Shariati (d. 1977), a sociologist trained in France and much influenced by Frantz Fanon's theories of anti-colonial struggle, espoused a kind of Islamic socialism as an indigenous Iranian response to Western colonialism and cultural imperialism. Though Shariati, one of the foremost intellectual architects of the Iranian Revolution of 1979, did not concern himself with mystical Islam, he does quote from Rumi in at least one article, "Art Awaiting the Saviour" (*News and Views* 1, 132). Also promoting an activist vision of Islam that would lead to social equality, Ayatollah Mortezâ Motahhari (assassinated May 1979) played an important role in the theorizing that led to the revolution. In his "Divine Justice," or *'Adl-e elâhi* (Tehran: Sahâmi, 1352/1973, 62) Motahhari quotes Rumi to the effect that justice means putting something in its proper place, whereas assigning things to the wrong place constitutes an injustice; for example justice consists in giving water to trees and injustice consists in watering thorns.

Most Islamic thinkers, however, have looked to Rumi's *Masnavi* for insight into theological questions such as free will and predestination. For example, **Jalâl al-Din Homâ'i** (1900–1980) wrote a short treatise upon the philosophical implications of Rumi's views on free will for the later Isfahan school of Mollâ

Sadrâ (*Do resâle dar falsafe-ye Eslâmi*, Tehran: Anjoman-e Shâhenshâhi-ye Falsafe-ye Eslâmi [Royal Philosophical Society of Iran], 2536/1978). Though such works properly belong to the history of modern scholarship or Muslim theology, because of the current political situation in Iran, we may also consider them as ideological statements. For example, not long after the Iranian Revolution and the closing of the universities in Iran, Rahim Nezhâd-Salim published a book provocatively entitled "The Limits of Human Freedom," enticing the reader with the promise of a political treatise, until we come to the subtitle, "According to Rumi," and the sub-subtitle "Free Will and Predestination," *Hodud-e âzâdi-ye ensân az didgâh-e Mowlavi (jabr o ekhtiâr)* (Tehran: Tahuri, 1985), at which point it becomes clear that this is a historical study of the attempts to resolve an old theological crux, beginning with the rationalist approaches of the Mutazilites, Avicenna, Ghazzâli, Fakhr al-Din Râzi, Nasir al-Din Tusi and leading to the more experiential approach of the Sufis, culminating in the views of Rumi. One must wonder, however, if the author or publisher has had some concealed motive in marketing such a book with this title.

Turning from the philosophy of the human soul to the psychology of spiritual development, Homâ'i, in his introduction to Rumi (*Mowlavi che miguyad*), wrote that no product of the human mind was as original, salutary and eternal as the *Masnavi*. Mohammad Jaᶜfar Mosaffâ, writing in the 1980s, explores Rumi's *Masnavi* as a key for self-realization, albeit under the guidance of a spiritual master: *Bâ pir-i: kârbord-e Masnavi dar khwod-shenâsi* (Mashhad: Mahdi). Ravân Farhâdi contributes a short treatise on the meaning of love in Rumi's works, *Maᶜni-ye ᶜeshq nazd-e Mowlânâ* (Tehran: Asâtir, 1372/1993). In an article titled "The Concept of Knowledge in Rûmî's Mathnawî," Mohammad Esteᶜlâmi remarks upon the ability of Rumi and his *Masnavi* to act as "a guide and master" for modern man in his quest for peace and spiritual satisfaction (LCP 401).

Thus, Esteᶜlâmi's labors to produce a new critical edition of the *Masnavi* were motivated by spiritual as well as scholarly concerns. Indeed, the Islamic Revolution Publishing and Educational Organization has also seen to it that Rumi's philosophy remains a part of the curriculum in the Islamic Republic; it published an annotated selection, with vocabulary, from *Fihe mâ fih* in 1987 primarily for high school and college students.

RUMI AND CREATIVE WRITING

Surprisingly, Rumi also appears as an influence on the thinking of secular Iranian writers of a political bent. **Sayyed Mohammad-ᶜAli Jamâlzâde** (1892–1997), though the son of a progressive cleric, remained a secular thinker critical of religious hypocrisy. Jamâlzâde's collection *Once Upon a Time* (*Yeki bud, yeki nabud*, Berlin, 1921; English translation by H. Moayyad and P. Sprachman,

Bibliotheca Persica, New York: SUNY Press, 1985) marks the beginning of a truly modernist Persian prose literature, for which he has been hailed as the father of the modern Persian short story. In his "Cry of the Reed" (*Bâng-e nây*, Tehran: Book Society of Persia, 1958), Jamâlzâde praises the storytelling ability and technique of Rumi in the *Masnavi* and provides a wonderful selection of tales for the Persian general reader, which served to introduce a generation of younger Westernizing Iranian readers to the delights of the classical heritage of Rumi (apparently it also helped inspire Arberry's collection, *Tales from the Masnavi*, described in chapter 13, below).

A progressive Iranian nationalist, **Hosayn Kâzemzâde Irânshahr** (1884–1962), who wrote about happiness, the progress of civilization and the history of his country, also turned his attention to the opening lines of the *Masnavi*, on which he wrote a commentary, *Tafsir-i maʿnavi bar dibâche-ye Masnavi*. **Rezâ Barâheni** (1935–), a translator, author and pioneering critic and chronicler of Iran's modern literature, was imprisoned and tortured in 1973 after helping to found the Iranian Writers' Committee against Censorship. International pressure from PEN and Amnesty International helped secure his release and Barâheni then went to the United States, where he forged relationships with American writers and intellectuals at the University of Iowa's International Writing Program and various other universities, playing an instrumental role in conveying the anti-Shah message of Iranian students to the American public. His poems and creative writings in English have not stood the test of time well, though the American authors E.L. Doctorow and John Leonard spoke highly of his work at the time. Though a political writer, Barâheni points to Rumi in an interview for *Contemporary Authors* as the primary influence on him as a poet. It was only after reading Rumi that he came to know "the meaning of poetry." Barâheni collaborated with the well-known translator Willis Barnstone on some ghazals of Rumi, and an example of their efforts, "Caring for My Lover" (477–78), appears in the anthology *World Poetry*, edited by K. Washburn and J. Major (New York: Norton, 1998).

Mahmud Eʿtemâdzâde, better known as **Beh Âzin** (1915–), born in Rasht, studied in France and returned to Iran, where, after stints in the Iranian navy and at the Ministry of Education, he made his career as an author, playwright and translator from Persian to French. His collections of short stories, spanning four decades, often deal with themes of class struggle and reflect his Marxist politics. Beh Âzin became a Communist Party activist, for which he was rewarded with periods of imprisonment under the governments of both the Shah and the Islamic Republic, an experience commemorated in two books, "Guest of these Gentlemen" (*Mehmân-e in âqâyân*, 1970) and "The Other Side of the Wall: A Statement on Freedom" (*An su-ye divâr: goftâr dar âzâdi*, 1977).[12] More recently, Beh Âzin's "On the Shores of the *Masnavi*," *Bar daryâ-kenâr-e Masnavi* ([Tehran]: Nashr-e Jâmi, 1991), has dipped into the ocean of Rumi in search of a political solution.

Rumi's ghazals continue to inspire poets in Iran. **A. Behdâd** has recently composed a small book of twenty poems, "Poems of the Sun," *Divân-e khworshid* ([Tehran]: Sanâ'i, 1998), written in imitation of ghazals in Rumi's *Divân-e Shams.*

ABDOL KARIM SOROUSH

Hosayn Dabbâgh, known by his nom de plume, **Abdol Karim Soroush** (ʿAbd al-Karim Sorush, 1945–), has become one of the most controversial figures in Iranian politics over the last decade. His speeches given in Iran and abroad argue for a pluralistic civil society. Since both the social conditions of individuals and their understanding of the revealed word differ, the imposition of a particular religious ideology can only flatten and distort the full range of religious truth. Thus, though not opposed to the ideals of the Revolution, Soroush favors an Islamic democracy. As such, he rejects Khomeini's theory of government, *velâyat-e faqih*, according to which the scholars of religious law undertake political rule in the name of the Hidden Imam until such time as he returns to the world to establish divine justice. Upon this theory rests the authority and legitimacy of the Islamic Republic of Iran, and since 1980, criticism of it has been considered beyond the pale. Although a committed Muslim, Soroush argues for separation of church and state on the grounds that it prevents the two fundamental spheres of society – religion and politics – from corrupting one another.

Were it not for Soroush's earlier credentials as a revolutionary activist (he had a role in the closing and restructuring of Iranian universities on ideological foundations, but resigned from his post on the Committee for Cultural Revolution in 1987), he surely would have been imprisoned or assassinated for statements made in his public lectures. As it is, conservative activists, many of them from the ranks of Hezbollah, have disrupted his lectures, sometimes attacking Soroush physically. In 1996, after complaining in an open letter about the failure of the civil authorities to protect him (the offices of the magazine which published his letter, *Kiân*, were attacked), he stopped lecturing in public and decided to go abroad.

Soroush was not educated in a traditional religious seminary, but developed close ties to Shariati and Motahhari, the two major theorists of Islam as a political force for social change. After completing his study of pharmacology in Iran, Soroush went to England to study the history and philosophy of science. At the height of the revolution against the Shah, he returned to Iran and eventually established a program in the history and philosophy of science at the University of Tehran. In addition to works on Islamic philosophy, prayer and Shiite religious figures (such as Imam ʿAli), Soroush has written many books on ideology and democracy, as well as translations of Western works on the philosophy of science.

His book on the dynamic nature of the world (*Nehâd-e nâ-ârâm-e jahân*) draws upon the ideas of Mollâ Sadrâ and the Isfahan school (as did the book by

Homâ²i, mentioned above, on Rumi's treatment of free will) to argue that the nature of being is not static and that human knowledge is ever-evolving. In the mid-1980s Iranian television broadcast a series of lectures by Soroush on Rumi, which proved very popular. In 1994 Soroush published "The Story of the Spiritual Masters," *Qesse-ye arbâb-e ma'refat* (Tehran: Me'râj, 1994), a work which appeals specifically to the example of Mohammad Iqbal and his ideas about the revivification of the Islamic sciences and reassertion of the native intellectual and cultural tradition as against unthinking submission to Western culture.

In this work on the Iranian masters of spirituality, Soroush poses the question: to which vision of Islam should we return? He formulates his answer by focusing on Mohammad Ghazzâli, Fayz-e Kâshâni, Rumi, Hâfez and the intellectual architect of a socialist and activist brand of Shiite Islam, Dr. 'Ali Shariati, whose teachings and lectures played a large role in giving shape to the intellectual and revolutionary vision of Islam that now informs the ruling ideology in Iran. Soroush examines the attitude of the great spiritual teachers and renovators of Islam toward religious law and the people who practice it. He points out that Rumi, like Ghazzâli, did not object to the ulama in principle, but unlike Ghazzâli, Rumi's mysticism was fiery and all-consuming; Rumi's implicit critique of the legalistic vision of Islam went further than Ghazzâli's careful objections or his partial permissiveness toward *samâ'* and other frowned-upon activities. "The Story of the Spiritual Masters" prominently features historical critiques of Islamic legal scholarship (*feqh*) and, by extension, the conceptual foundations of the Islamic Republic and its imposition of an Islamic cultural revolution.

Soroush has laced "The Story of the Spiritual Masters" with quotations from Rumi and, with evident love for the poet, holds Rumi above Ghazzâli and Hâfez as representative of the truest form of Islamic spirituality. Soroush even tries to prove this point by quoting approving remarks of Ayatollah Khomeini about Rumi, pointing out that Khomeini quoted Rumi upon the death of Ayatollah Motahhari. Soroush also claims (376–7) that while he was visiting the shrine of Rumi (he gave a paper comparing Hâfez and Rumi at the National Rumi Congress in Konya in 1988), he heard it related from a knowledgeable source that Imam Khomeini had wished to visit the shrine of Rumi while he was exiled to Bursa, in Turkey. This would only be allowed, however, by the secular Turkish state if he removed his clerical garb and made the journey in civilian clothes. Khomeini refused to accept these conditions, but according to this unnamed source, later regretted not having visited the shrine.

By the fall of 1996, Soroush had published his own edition of Rumi's *Masnavi*, based upon the earliest surviving manuscript. This particular manuscript has been made available in a facsimile edition by Nasrollah Pourjavady and was used as the basis for the editions of Gölpınarlı and Este'lâmi, so Soroush's *Masnavi* is unlikely to become the scholarly standard. It does demonstrate, however, the importance of Rumi as an intellectual source and cultural icon for the proponents of pluralistic and self-aware Islam, as opposed to those who would impose the values of an ideological and legalistic Islam on society. Like Motahhari and Shariati, Soroush is also interested in the question of justice, which he considers from the perspective of the *Masnavi* in a 26-page pamphlet entitled *Non-Causal Theory of Justice in Rumi's Work* (Binghamton, NY: Global Publications, 1992).

A few months prior to the May 1997 presidential elections in which Mohammad Khâtami emerged victorious, Soroush toured North America giving lectures on Rumi, many of them on university campuses. In March 1997, I attended his talk at the University of Chicago, sponsored by the Muslim Students' Association, in the course of which Soroush delineated three major modes of knowing God, an observation already made in the medieval period by Muslims: (1) the project of religious legal scholarship, which attempts to understand and approach God through discovery, codification and adherence to his outward laws; (2) the rationalist effort to understand God through logical philosophy; and (3) the passionate individual and experiential approach to God, exemplified by the Sufism of Rumi and characterized by tolerance. Soroush read many lines from Rumi, though he seemed to rush pro forma through the written text of his lecture, becoming animated only during the question-and-answer session, during which he demonstrated a facile wit and commanding stage presence. Elsewhere on his tour in the United States, he angrily defended Rumi from the critiques of Iranian intellectuals such as Ahmad Kasravi and Ahmad Shâmlu.

Soroush returned to Iran in April 1997, where he has been attacked periodically at public appearances, notably in November 1997 at Amir Kabir University. He was also dismissed from his positions at the University of Tehran. But he remains popular with many Iranian Islamist youth, including many of the supporters of President Khâtami. In March of 1998, Soroush participated in a conference, "Civil Society in Contemporary Iran," held at the University of London School of Oriental and African Studies in England.[13]

RUMI AS BRIDGE TO RAPPROCHEMENT?

Sufism has also played an oblique role in bridging, through cultural means, the political differences between Iran and the U.S. In addition to the positive image created in the minds of many Americans by Iranian practitioners of the Sufi Path (Nimatullahis and Shah Maghsoudis, for example), in at least one recent Iranian film by the noted director **Daryush Mehrjui**, an oblique connection is made between Sufism and America. Mehrjui studied at UCLA's film school and was featured on American television in a 1997 episode of Ted Koppel's *Nightline* and in a 1998 segment of *60 Minutes* by reporter Christiane Amanpour. For the script of his film *Pari* (1995), Mehrjui very loosely adapted J.D. Salinger's novella *Franny and Zooey* (1961) to an Iranian context. The lead actress, Niki

Karimi, plays a student who falls ill at college because of the involuntary Sufi visions she keeps having. Here, Sufism, though not specifically Rumi, becomes a means of escape, or hope of escape, from a constrictive and depressing situation to a space of personal freedom and psychological healing. Unfortunately, Salinger's attorneys have curmudgeonly taken legal action to prevent the film from being shown in the U.S.

Meanwhile, two animated shorts based on stories from the *Masnavi* have been filmed in Iran in the last decade or so. The first retells the story of the parrot and the merchant who travels to India, *Tuti va bâzargân*, directed by **Manuchehr Ahmadi** for an Iranian television series (1987, 15 minutes). The other, produced by the Committee for the Intellectual Development of Children and Youth, features the story of the parrot and the grocer (see poem 31 in chapter 8) in *Tuti va baqqâl* (1991, 32 minutes), directed by ʿAbd Allâh ʿAli-morâd, with a screenplay by **Ebrâhim Foruzesh** and music by Kâmbiz Rowshanravân. Contemporary performances of Persian traditional music also seem to hint at a desire for greater tolerance and religious understanding in the many popular renditions of Rumi's poems (see chapter 15).

In 1985 an Iranian national at the University of Massachusetts completed his degree in education with "A Comparative Study and Critique of Philosophical and Educational Essentialism," which draws upon Plato, Aristotle, Rumi and Mollâ Sadrâ to unify Western and Iranian theories of education. Even the Islamic Republic of Iran tries to bask in the glow of Rumi; through a government agency, the Council for the Promotion of Persian Language and Literature in North America, it sponsored an international conference in June of 1997 titled "Rumi: Poet of the Heart, Light of the Mind," though "ambassador of tolerance" would have been just as apt, insofar as the conference was held at Columbia University in New York City in the heart of the Great Satan, but not very far from the United Nations. And Rumi was one of the topics raised by **Barry Rosen**, former press attaché at the American Embassy in Tehran who was taken hostage along with fifty-one other Americans in November 1979, in a meeting arranged in July 1998 with one of his captors, **Abbas Abdi**, a revolutionary student follower of Ayatollah Khomeini. Rosen was initially reluctant to meet his former captor but finally agreed, in hopes of improving American–Iranian relations.

What would Rumi make of all this? In the sixth line of the *Masnavi* the reed flute complains that it is loved for what people suppose its melody to say, though no one actually delves within to comprehend the truth of the mysteries it reveals:

> *har kasi az zann-e khwod shod yâr-e man*
> *az darun-e man najost asrâr-e man*

> All befriend me hearing what they want to hear
> none seek those secrets that I bear within

496

PART V

RUMI IN THE WEST,

RUMI AROUND THE WORLD

12

Rumi Moves into Western Consciousness

EUROPEAN IMPRESSIONS OF THE MEVLEVIS

Few European travelers or diplomats have demonstrated extensive exposure to or concern with the Mevlevis. Occasional remarks on dervishes can be found here and there, but most European diplomats were concerned with the "heathen Turks" as potential enemies, or potential allies; beyond political matters, their interests extended to court life and harem intrigues, and, by the nineteenth century, to local costume and customs. The remarks of independent travelers, on the other hand, often present a mishmash of fact and imaginative fantasy born of observation, along with a great deal of misinformation or simple misimpressions left to them by guides. A prime example of such misguided travelogs can be found in R.P. Lister, *A Muezzin from the Tower of Darkness Cries* (New York: Harcourt Brace, 1967).

The earliest "travelog" is perhaps that of Georgius de Hungaria (c. 1422–1502) who, while a sixteen-year-old student in Mühlbach, fell captive to the Turks and was hauled off to Ottoman lands in slavery, leaving him with an apocalyptic outlook on life well after his release in 1458. After about five years of captivity, he came to doubt his Christian beliefs and began to study Islam intensively, especially the Sufi orders. His book on the circumstances, mores and craftiness of the Turks, *Tractatus de Moribus, Condicionibus et Nequicia Turcorum*, published in 1481 (ed. Reinhard Klockow, Cologne: Böhlau, 1993), explains that after learning the prayers of the "Turkish sect" (*secta Turcorum*) and partaking in dervish ceremonies for about six or seven months, his faith in Christianity and Catholic doctrine was restored, so that he condemns all he saw and heard of Turkish beliefs as "diabolic illusions" (302–3). Georgius relates his experience among the dervishes ("deruishler") in their "tekye" and gives a detailed description of the Mevlevi "czamach" (his Latin rendering of *samâ᷇*). Though he does not identify Rumi or the Mevlevis by name, we recognize them from the characteristic description of their dignified whirling:

> qui fit quadam tocius corporis regulata et bene modificata agitatione cum honestis et dignis et ualde decentibus omnium membrorum motibus, secundum modulationem mensure instrumenti musici ad hoc conuenienter aptate et in fine per modum vertigines quodam motu velocissimo circulari[t] et rotatione uel reuolutione, in quo tota uis ipsius ludi consistit.

> who sway their entire body in a regular and well-measured manner, with a decorous, dignified, and very chaste movement of their limbs, matching the rhythmic modulations of the musical instruments, creating finally a whirl of dizzying velocity, a rotation and revolution, in which the power of these performances consist.

Georgius also speaks of the sermons given by the dervishes and the lines of verse recited by them (he quotes two Turkish poems, apparently by Yunus Emre), which he feels are closer in sensibility to the Christian than the "Turkish" religion. These men of religion seem so pious in all their doings that they appear more angelic than human, though he adds, lest his Christian brethren think him a touch too sympathetic, that Satan manifests himself as an angel of light (*Tractatus de moribus*, 275ff., 412–15). One hundred and fifty years later, Du Loir reported to France on the internal politics of the Ottomans in a series of letters. In the course of these letters, published as *Les voyages du sieur Du Loir* (Paris, 1654), he describes the scene at a Mevlevi ceremony (149ff.). This dance of the dervishes continued to mesmerize European onlookers, as we shall see in chapter 13.

The Danish author and collector of fairy and folk tales, **Hans Christian Andersen**, visited Turkey in his travels through southern Europe, as described in his *En Digters Bazar* (1842; English version: *A Poet's Bazaar*, New York, 1871). Andersen witnessed the turning ceremony of the "Mewlewis" of Pera, which he notes usually occurs on Thursdays and Fridays. After removing his boots, he entered the cloister, where he remarks upon the beautiful view and the civil treatment afforded to him by the Turks, who made room for him from a better vantage point. Andersen described the dance, which lasted an hour, as a sort of ballet, almost graceful, especially in comparison to the howling dervishes he had seen in Scutari (Üsküdar). The dance was intended to represent the course of the planets, with two dervishes standing in the center of the circle turning on a fixed spot while the rest of the dervishes circled around these two. Andersen found the "sleepy music" rather monotonous and described the dancers at the end as "pale as death"; the whole spectacle had for him the character of silent insanity. But Andersen drew some sketches of the dervishes which circulated later in England.[1]

John Porter Brown, the secretary and dragoman of the American legation to the Ottoman empire, apparently spent much of the time at his post in Constantinople reading Persian, Arabic and Turkish manuscripts and visiting Dervish lodges, where he made many "liberal and intelligent, sincere and most faithful friends." Brown read a number of classical works on the topic of the dervish orders, but relied also on first-hand information provided him by practicing dervishes, in particular a Qâderi dervish, who appears to have provided information that is at times inaccurate, legendary, or self-promotional. Nevertheless, the resulting book, *The Dervishes; or Oriental Spiritualism* (London: Trübner, 1868), is quite good. He views the Mevlevis' music as a means to calm the senses (15) and states that the Istanbul Mevlevis perform *esme-jalil* on Fridays and Sundays, a *zekr* session in the *samâ^c* hall, during which the word God (Allâh) is repeatedly chanted (55–6). No other order does this particular *zekr* (201). Every dervish *tekke* has a particular day of the week set aside for its exercises, which allows the members of various different orders to participate in each others' ceremonies. The Mevlevi ritual turning is the hardest, though, and cannot be performed spontaneously, but must first be learned. Anyone who knows how to turn, however, can simply borrow the traditional tall Mevlevi cap (*sikke*) and the wide-skirted tunic (*tennure*) with the Mevlevi vest (*destegül*) (198–9). His detailed description of the *samâ^c* ceremony sounds very much like what we see performed today. He mentions that if any of the dancers are overcome by the performance and fall, they will withdraw (200). The *samâ^c-zan* offers a prayer to the sultan "with a long series of titles" at the end of the ceremony (200).

Brown says that non-Muslim foreigners are allowed to watch from one part of the gallery or from a small apartment, where they must stand (201). A proper Mevlevi *tekke* has eighteen chambers, the dervishes always say eighteen vows, and each occupant of these chambers receives eighteen piasters per day. The neophyte disciple serves in the kitchen for 1,001 days and his room is Chelle Hojresi. Brown seems to credit the stories of Rumi's power of levitation into heaven and attributes the whirling rite to this – the music kept him from disappearing entirely into the sky (202). Of the *Masnavi* itself – "the Methnevee Shereef" – he opines that it is "too mystical to permit of a close translation" (202).

He remarks that none of the Mevlevis are allowed to beg, but often will bestow water to the thirsty in the street (205). Brown mentions a treatise by a recently deceased learned shaykh of the Mevlevis that explains the Mevlevis' view of spiritual existence (205). The work reproduces a number of drawings, including, on the title page, "The Mevlevee Sheiky of Pera, Constantinople, who has his hand on three large books."

John P. Durbin, an American concerned with the state of Christianity in the Holy Land, reports upon his travels in his two-volume *Observations in the East* (New York: Carlton & Phillips, 1845; 10th ed., 1854). In Constantinople, the same John Brown of the American legation arranged for Durbin and his party to visit three mosques (201) and probably also for their visits with the Mevlevi Shaykh of Pera. Durbin contrasts the two most interesting sects of dervishes in Constantinople, the "Howling Dervishes" of Scutari and the "Dancing Dervishes" of Pera. Of the howling Refā^ci dervishes, he tells us, "No pen could describe these wild and frantic exhibitions," and describes what he calls instruments of torture on the walls (230).

By contrast, he formed a very favorable impression of the Mevlevis (231–2):

> The dancing Dervishes have their monastery and humble mosque in Pera. At one o'clock we went, slippers in hand, as shoes must be left at the door, but found that we were too early. Our company consisted of seven or eight, among whom were Mr. and Mrs. W., of Liverpool, who had been of our party in visiting mosques. We did not know how far the company of a lady might embarrass the request, yet we ventured to send a messenger to the chief of the Dervishes, asking permission to pay him a visit. It was granted; and leaving our shoes at the door, we ascended to a plain, uncarpeted ante-room, through which we passed into a small, well-furnished saloon, with divans on three sides. In one corner, as the honourable place, sat a small, mild-looking man, with green turban and green gown. He did not rise when we entered, but put his hand to his breast, then to his forehead, beckoned us to be seated, and then ordered coffees and pipes. His demeanour was exceedingly agreeable and dignified, exhibiting intelligence and sweetness of temper. The esteem in which he was held was apparent from the visits paid him by distinguished persons while we sat. A little sylph-like creature, about four years old, came in, leaped on the divan, fell on her knees before the venerable [232] man, and, perfectly motionless, received his silent benediction in three warm, full respirations in her beautiful face, when her melting eyes looked into his beaming with benignity, and then she flitted across the room and disappeared with her attendant, who had stood at the door. She had been sent by her mother for the good man's blessing. Not a word was spoken in the room during this brief but impressive incident.
>
> At length we were conducted to the mosque [rather, this must have been the *samâ^c* hall], and seats were brought for us. The central parts of the floor were enclosed by a low railing, outside of which, under the galleries, stood the spectators. The common form of prayer was first performed, the chief leading; then all arranged themselves at nearly equal distances in a circle within the railings; and, dropping their outer garments where they stood, they walked slowly round to the chief, made him each a profound bow, and then twirled away to his right, spinning around on their feet until their long skirts filled with air, and spread out like an inverted funnel. They continued to whirl round on their feet with steady yet dizzying velocity, at the same time circulating slowly around the enclosed space, holding their arms aloft and the palms of their hands upward. In two minutes they were in motion, and notwithstanding their eyes shut, they never came in collision with each other, and a man walked among them the whole time. There were fifteen whirling at once in a circle of twenty-five or thirty

feet in diameter. There was nothing violent in their movements, but the impression was that of calmness and strength; yet it was very exhausting, as the swollen veins of their necks and their flushed countenances sufficiently testified. All were silent during the exercises.

The facing page (233) provides a drawing of one such dancing dervish with his eyes closed in meditation.

Obviously, the presence of Europeans and European women caused no objections, and perhaps even enhanced the reputation of the dervish lodge in question. Mevlevi women were allowed, in any case, to attend the turning ceremonies and sit in separate quarters in the gallery. As early as 1836, Julia Pardoe had visited the "chapel of the Turning Dervishes" in Istanbul, as she recounts in *The City of the Sultan* (London: Henry Colburn, 1837; pp. 41–2):

> I paid two visits to the convent of Turning, or as they are commonly called in Europe, Dancing Dervishes, which is situated opposite the Petit Champs Des Morts, descending towards Galata. The court of the Tekie is entered by a handsomely ornamented gate and having passed it, you have the cemetery of the brethren on your left hand, and the gable of the main building on your right. As you arrive in front of the convent, the court widens, and in the midst stands a magnificent tree of great antiquity, carefully railed in; while you have on one side the elegant mausoleum in which repose the superiors of the order; and on the other the fountain of white marble, roofed in like an oratory, and enclosed on all its six sides from the weather, where the Dervishes perform their ablutions ere they enter the chapel ...
>
> The chapel is an octagonal building of moderate size, neatly painted in fresco. The centre of the floor is railed off, and the enclosure is sacred to the brotherhood; while the outer circle, covered with Indian matting, is appropriated to visitors. A deep gallery runs round six sides of the building, and beneath it, on your left hand as you enter, you remark the lattices through which the Turkish women witness the service. A narrow mat surrounds the circle within the railing and upon this the brethren kneel during the prayers; while the centre of the floor is so highly polished by the perpetual friction that it resembles a mirror and the boards are united by nails with heads as large as a shilling to prevent accidents to feet of the Dervishes during their evolutions ...
>
> Above the seat of the superior, the name of the founder of the Tekie is written in gold on a black ground in immense characters. This seat consists of a small carpet, above which is spread a crimson rug, and on this the worthy principal was squatted when we entered, in an ample cloak of Spanish brown.
>
> One by one the Dervishes entered the chapel, bowing profoundly at the little gate of the enclosure, took their places on the mat and bending down, reverently kissed the ground; and then, folding their arms meekly on their breasts, remained buried in prayer, with their eyes closed and their bodies swaying slowly to and fro. They were all enveloped in wide cloaks of dark coloured cloth with pendant sleeves; and wore their genlafs, which they retained during the whole of the service.

There was a deep stillness, broken only by the breath of prayer or the melancholy wailing of the muffled instruments, which seemed to send forth their voice of sadness from behind a cloud in subdued sorrowing, like the melodious plaint of angels over fallen mortality – the concentrated and pious self-forgetfulness of the community, who never once cast their eyes over the crowds that thronged their chapel.

Immediately after passing with a solemn reverence, twice performed, the place of the High Priest, who remained standing, the Dervishes spread their arms and commenced their revolving motion; the palm of the right hand being held upwards, and that of the left downwards. Their under dresses consisted of a jacket and petticoat of dark coloured cloth, that descended to their feet; the higher order of brethren being clad in green, and the others in brown, or a sort of yellowish gray; about their waists they wore girdles, edged with red, to which the right side of the jacket was closely fastened, while the left hung loose; their petticoats were of immense width and laid in large plaits, beneath the girdle, and, as the wearers swung around, formed a bell-like appearance; these latter garments are worn only during the ceremony, and are exchanged in summer for white ones of lighter material.

The number of those who were "on duty," was nine; seven of them being men and the remaining two, mere boys, the youngest certainly not more than ten years old ... So true and unerring were their motions that, although the space which they occupied was somewhat circumscribed, they never once gained upon each other and for five minutes they continued twirling round and round, as though impelled by machinery, their pale passionless countenances perfectly immobile, their heads slightly declined towards the right shoulder, and their inflated garments creating a cold, sharp air in the chapel from the rapidity of their action. At the termination of that period, the name of the Prophet occurred in the chant, which had been unintermitted in the gallery; and, as they simultaneously paused, and, folding their hands upon their breasts, bent down in reverence at the sound, their ample garments wound about them at the sudden check.

This and other European accounts of the Mevlevi lodge in Galata made it something of a tourist landmark. John Murray's *Handbook for Travellers in Constantinople, Brûsa and the Troad* (London, 1893) described the Galata lodge as a curious attraction and the entire surrounding area became something of a European quarter, with a famous French restaurant nearby, and a German school on the adjoining property to the south (LDL, 104, 102).

Seventy years after Miss Pardoe, another European lady visited this lodge. **Lucy M.J. Garnett** records in her *Turkish Life in Town and Country* (Putnam, 1904) that the Mevlevis were still "the most popular, one might almost say the most fashionable of all the orders" (180). She says that members of each Dervish order greet their brethren with specific salutations, different from the typical Muslim salutation, *Salâm* (peace). The Mevlevis greeted one another in Turkey with the salutation *Eshk olsoun* which she renders as "Let it be love" (187–8), whereas most other dervishes said simply *Yâ hu*, "O He [God]!" Garnett also relates, on the basis of a personal conversation with the two wives of the Mevlevi Shaykh of Magnesia that Mevlevi shaykhs tended to remain monogamous, taking a second wife only if the first wife failed to bear an heir.

On a visit to Konya in the spring of 1913, **F.W. Hasluck**, who had been working in Greece and other parts of the Near East as an archaeologist since 1899, became interested in the Mevlevis and Rumi's associations with Christians, particularly at the Church of St. Chariton. Hasluck determined to undertake a comparative study of the folklore of Christianity and Islam in Asia Minor and when his *Christianity and Islam under the Sultans* (Oxford: Clarendon, 1929) appeared posthumously, it demonstrated the survival of folk practice and belief in Asia Minor and perhaps helped ameliorate some of the hostile Euro-Christian view of the "heathen" Turks and their strange ways.

Nor did French travelers ignore the Mevlevis. **Clément Huart**, who would later translate the "Acts" of Aflâki, spent some time in Konya with the Mevlevis in the late 1800s, a trip he describes in *Konia, la ville des derviches tourneurs: souvenirs d'un voyage en Asie mineure* (Paris: Ernest Leroux, 1897). One of Huart's readers was **Maurice Barrès** (1862–1923), an anti-Dreyfusard politician and novelist much attracted to mysticism. Barrès journeyed through Lebanon, Syria and Turkey during 1914, where he encountered the Mevlevis and learned of Rumi, as he recounts in his travelog, "An Inquiry into the Countries of the Levant," which could not be published until after the First World War: *Une enquête aux pays du Levant* (Paris: Plon-Nourrit, 1923; reprinted in *L'Oeuvre de Maurice Barrès*, ed. Philippe Barrès, vol. 11, Paris: Club de l'Honnête Homme, 1967). Though a man of government affairs, Barrès was also attracted to questions of religion and ethics, and went on to form a Paris society, The Club of the Honest Man. Barrès recounts that while favorably disposed to the *danseurs mystiques*, he at first objected to sharing his automobile with an old and unkempt Mevlevi dervish outside the Taurus mountians (*L'Oeuvre*, 11:375). Barrès also met with the head of the Mevlevi order in Konya, identified only as Chelebi (391ff., 413ff.), but who must be either Bahâ al-Din or ʿAbd al-Halim. This Chelebi does not seem deeply grounded in knowledge of the manuscript sources of the order, insofar as he attributes a book titled *Manhaj al-foqarâ*, containing the rules of the Mevlevi order, to Rumi (393) and calls Shams al-Din an illumined, though uneducated (*ignorant*, 392; *illettré*, 398) teacher. The dance, in particular, of the Mevlevi devotees attracted Barrès, and when he asked Chelebi for an explanation of its significance, he was told, "Jalâl al-Din thought that there are many paths to reach God, but the quickest is the dance" (416). Barrès also understood the Chelebi to say that, while not the person of God, the Mevlevi shaykh represents God on earth to the Mevlevis. It is in this capacity that the Mevlevi shaykh authorizes the disciples to dance. The first dance is knowledge, the second is seeing with the eyes, the third that of total understanding (418). Barrès was shown the supposed grave of Shams in Konya, marked only by a decorative sun, but with no inscription (424). The encounter proved one of the most interesting in Barrès' life (394) and left a lasting impression, for he continued to meditate upon and mention Rumi in his notebooks (published as *Mes Cahiers*) until the end of his life.

Grace Ellison, who had already written two books about Turkish women, was the first Englishwoman to visit Turkey after the establishment of the Turkish Republic. She met with the Grand Chelebi in Konya at his invitation in 1923, so it would appear that ʿAbd al-Halim had indeed determined to cultivate relationships with foreign authors. In the account of her sojourn, *An Englishwoman in Angora* (New York: Dutton, 1923), she confesses a fascination with the "weird rhythm" of the Mevlevi dancers, whose swirling skirts seem to her like "gigantic mauve and brown poppies on the polished floor" (281).

A number of travelers from Czarist Russia who visited Istanbul also provide us with eye-witness accounts of Mevlevi ceremonies. These include a report from S.N., a Russian diplomat, covering the months June to October 1861, which describes the visit of ʿAbd al-ʿAziz to the Mevlevi *tekke* in Pera shortly after his coronation as sultan ("Kontantinopol'skie pis'ma [1861–6], *Russki Vestnik*). The Russian poet and correspondent Nikolai Vail'evich Berg (1824–84) witnessed a Mevlevi turning ceremony in the fall of 1860. He compares this to a ceremony of the Refâʿis in his article "Dervishi-vertuny i dervishi-zavyvateli" (*Kaledioskop* 24 [1861]: 189–91). Other Russian observers include a professor of church history at the Kharkov Ecclesiastical Academy, Amfian Stepanovish Levedev (1833–1910), who describes his 1873 visit to a Mevlevi lodge in Constantinople ("Iz putevykh vospominanii," *Pravoslavnyi Sobesednik* (1882) 1:138–50, 2:353–70); and A.F. Morokin, a correspondent for the newspaper *Rusʾ*, who describes a Mevlevi ceremony around the turn of the century in a monograph about his trip to the Crimea and Constantinople, *Poezdka v Krym i Konstantinopol* (Moscow, 1901; 2nd ed., 1907).[2]

RUMI IN NINETEENTH-CENTURY WESTERN THOUGHT AND THEOLOGY

HERESIARCH OF PANTHEISM OR ANTIDOTE TO EPICURIANISM?

When works on the doctrines of the Sufis and translations of portions of the *Masnavi* began to appear in the nineteenth century, leading European scholars and philosophers concluded that Rumi had taught a kind of pantheism. In 1821 an introduction to Sufism appeared, published in Latin and therefore addressing a specifically clerical or pan-European scholarly audience. The author, a German Protestant minister who would later become an influential nineteenth-century theologian, **Friedrich August Deofidus** (later F.A.G.) **Tholuck** (1799–1877), styled his book "The Pantheistic Theosophy of the Persians," *Ssufismus sive* *theosophia persarum pantheistica* (Berlin: Duemmleri, 1821). In this study, and in his later German anthology *Blüthensammlung aus der morgenländischen Mystik* (Berlin: Duemmleri, 1825), which provides excerpts from the writings of a number of Sufis, Tholuck characterized Rumi as a proponent of a Manichaean vision of creation, in which the material world held the human soul in captivity. Under the rubric "Deus est qui in mortalium precibus se ipse veneratur, se ipse adorat" (In the prayers of mortals, it is God who venerates and worships Himself), Tholuck quotes from the third book of the *Masnavi*. He expresses surprise at the dangerous idea quoted by Rumi that every prayer is said to be itself the answer to that prayer.

If this perceived tendency toward pantheism disturbed Tholuck, it enthused **Georg Wilhelm Friedrich Hegel** (1770–1831), the great dialectician and philosopher of history. Hegel became aware of Rumi both through Tholuck and through the translations of Rückert (see "Rumi in German," in chapter 14). Hegel admired Rückert's adaptations of Rumi so much that he reproduced two of them in the discussion of pantheism in his "Encyclopedia of the Philosophical Sciences in Outline" (*Enzyklopädie der philosophischen Wissenschaften im Grundrisse*, 1827). Here Hegel remarks upon Rumi's view of the soul's unity, with the One taking the form of love. Indeed, it has been argued that Rumi's teachings influenced the development of Hegel's dialectic of history; during the 1970s, when Marxist and Islamicist revolutionary rhetoric began to coalesce in Iran, a member of the Iranian Communist Party even called Rumi "the Hegel of the East."[3]

Rumi, though no longer understood today as an exponent of pantheism per se, was still viewed this way at the turn of the century, as evident in Hermann Ethé's (1844–1917) study of Persian literature, "Neupersische Litteratur" (in Wilhelm Geiger's *Grundriss der iranischen Philologie*, Strasburg: Trubner, 1896–1904). Ethé says that Rumi is not only the greatest mystical poet of Islam, but even the world's greatest pantheistic poet. Though Ethé's scholarly comment betrays an admiration for this God-infused cosmology, many men of the cloth in Europe found Sufi pantheism alarming and warned their congregations not to fall victim to its blasphemous seductions. Professor and Reverend W.R. Inge (1860–1954), for example, harshly criticized Sufism (and Ralph Waldo Emerson) for having bruited about the message of pantheistic mysticism in the West. Instead, he offered a more salubrious form of occidental spirituality at Oxford in his 1899 Brampton Lectures, published as *Christian Mysticism*, which does not mention Rumi at all.

Some ministers found the craze for ʿOmar Khayyâm, which swept England and America in the 1870s and lasted well into the 1920s, far more dangerous. Though some erroneously read Khayyâm's poems in a Sufi spirit, most recognized them as expressions of a philosophical hedonism and agnostic or even atheological bent of mind; the fact that churchgoing folk were forming clubs and societies around the reading and appreciation of Khayyám's poetry spurred the clergy to action. Whatever the dangers of alien and non-Christian modes of spirituality may have been, at least, as spiritual modes, they shared the assumption of God, which an increasing number of Westerners, as a result of higher criticism or secular philosophies, alarmingly did not. If Persian poetry appealed to Western audiences, as it clearly did, why not replace the epicurean and despairing Khayyám with Rumi, for whom the universe was theosemic, everything a sign pointing toward God? A Scottish clergyman and theologian, **William Hastie** (1842–1903), author of works like *The Theology of the Reformed Church* and *Outlines of Pastoral Theology for Young Ministers and Students*, therefore set out to give the public Rumi as an antidote to Khayyám, an objective he makes explicit in the introduction to his *The Festival of Spring from the Divan of Jelaleddin* (Glasgow: MacLehose, 1903), with English translations he did on the basis of Rückert's German.

By the first half of the twentieth century, theologians and scholars of religion in Europe had become acquainted with Rumi and held a generally favorable opinion. **Christian Karl Josias von Bunsen** (1791–1860), Prussian ambassador to the Vatican, was in the first place a linguist and liberal theologian. Bunsen numbered Schleiermacher, Max Müller and Thomas Arnold (father of Matthew) among his friends, and Florence Nightingale looked to him for edification on points of religion and metaphysics. Bunsen, an advocate of the idea that all languages came from one original source, had learned Arabic and Persian from the French orientalist Silvestre de Sacy (1758–1838). Bunsen read Rumi's *Masnavi*, probably introducing the subject of Rumi's metaphysics in conversation with his friends, thus creating a favorable opinion of him among intellectual religious liberals. Friedrich Rückert perhaps first learned of Rumi from Bunsen in Vienna between 1817 and 1818.[4] Volume 17 (October 1905–September 1906) of the journal *Expository Times (Christian Literature)* carried an article (452ff.) by the orientalist **Claud Field** (1863–1941, son of John Field, a British soldier and evangelist in India), which introduces Rumi as a poet in need of a translator like FitzGerald so that Englishmen might become familiar with him.

RUMI, ECUMENICISM AND COMPARATIVE RELIGION

Martin Buber (1878–1965) included a few quotations from Rumi in an anthology of ecstatic expressions of man's relationship to God, *Ekstatische Konfessionen*, (Jena, 1909). Otto Weinreich, a historian of religion, reviewing this book in 1910, quotes a story by Rumi; a number of other German theologians and scholars of religion seem to have shared his admiration for Rumi. Schimmel (ScT 394–5) sees the influence of Rumi in the teachings of the Jewish philosopher **Constantin Brunner** (d. 1934) about the need for a spiritual leader to guide the masses. **K.V. Zettersteen** (1866–1953) provided a Swedish translation of the passage (introduced to European readers by Tholuck) from Book 3 of the *Masnavi* in which Khezr tells the doubt-struck worshiper that his calling out to God is itself an answer to his prayer. **Nathan Söderblom** (1866–1931), one of the founders of the modern discipline of history of religions, included this passage in his anthology of religious texts, *Främmande religionsurkunder* (Stockholm, 1908). Through Söderblom and Nicholson, the Christian thinker **Friedrich Heiler** took up this teaching of Rumi about prayer (from the *Masnavi*, M3:189) in his book on the history and psychology of prayer, *Das Gebet* (5th ed., Munich, 1923, p. 225), currently available in English as *Prayer* (Oxford: Oneworld). Still interested several decades later, Heiler repeatedly quotes Rumi (via Schimmel's German translations) in his study of the phenomenology of religion, *Erscheinungsformen und Wesen der Religion* (Stuttgart: T.W. Kohlhammer, 1961). Heiler appeals to the authority of Rumi's spiritual teachings in this work almost as often as he refers to Eckhart or St. Francis of Assisi. Not surprisingly, the Romanian scholar of religious and mystical systems of thought **Mircea Eliade** devotes a section of his *History of Religious Ideas* (Chicago: University of Chicago Press, 1985; French original, 1983) to Rumi, whose "passionate ardor and poetic power" Eliade describes as "unequalled" (3:147).

An Iranian student at the University of Heidelberg, Germany, Manutschehr Aschtiani (1930–), produced a comparative study of the relationship between God, man and the world in German and Iranian mysticism, specifically comparing Rumi and Eckhart for his 1971 dissertation, *Der dialektische Vorgang in der mystischen "Unio-Lehre" Eckharts und Maulanas und seine Vermittlung durch ihre Sprache*. Lynn Bauman has taken up Rumi's method of expressing his vision in the *Masnavi* in her dissertation "The Hermeneutics of Mystical Discourse," accepted at the University of Texas, Arlington, in 1990. Straddling the line between mysticism, psychology and education, Delores Liston completed her dissertation in 1994 at the University of North Carolina at Greensboro on "Joy: A Phenomenological and Aesthetic View," drawing for its philosophy of joy on Buddhism, Hinduism and Martins Buber and Heidegger; and for its aesthetics on Plato, Rilke and Rumi.

Outside the academy, a number of modern advocates of the Perennial Philosophy, such as René Guénon (1886–1951), Titus Burckhardt (1908–84) and Frithjof Schuon (1907–98), have introduced Western readers to the intricacies of Sufi thought in a comparativist context; all of them are, of course, familiar to some extent with Rumi, though they draw more heavily from the theoretical expositions of Ibn ʿArabi in their writings. This perennialist theosophy, whether derived from Eastern works in translation or through modern Western practitioners, has contributed to the spirit of ecumenicism and interreligious dialogue now commonly promoted among Western theologians like Wilfred Cantwell Smith and Hans Küng. It was Guénon, a Frenchman who adopted Islam and eventually settled in Cairo, who played the leading role (along with the great Hallâj scholar, Louis Massignon) in introducing Sufi ideas to intellectuals and people of faith in the West. One of Guénon's friends, **Ananda Coomaraswamy** (1877–1947), born in Sri Lanka (Ceylon), educated in England, and resident in the United States for the last thirty years of his life, called Rumi and Meister Eckhart the two piers of the bridge of understanding that will finally span Western and Eastern civilization.[5]

The call for a greater spirit of ecumenicism and interfaith dialogue is joined by S.H. Nasr from the vantage point of an Iranian Muslim, who argues the case on the basis of Rumi's verse in his *Need for a Sacred Science* (Albany, NY: SUNY Press, 1993). Professors of comparative religion like **Geoffrey Parrinder** include Rumi in their studies (*Mysticism in the World Religions*, London: Sheldon, 1976) and the philosopher of religion **John Hick** begins a chapter titled "The Pluralistic Hypothesis" in his *An Interpretation of Religion: Human Responses to the Transcendent* (New Haven: Yale University Press, 1989) under Rumi's rubric: "The Lamps are different but the Light is the same." **Aldous Huxley** (1894–1963), now remembered mostly for his novel *Brave New World*, was once equally influential for his espousal of Eastern beliefs, specifically those of Ramakrishna. His *Perennial Philosophy* (New York and London: Harper & Brothers, 1946), a compendium of sayings culled from more than a hundred religious thinkers around the world, quotes Rumi, whom Huxley knew through Whinfield's translation of the *Masnavi*, fifteen times, with only Eckhart, St. John of the Cross, François de Sales, Chuang Tzu, Christ and Buddha appearing as frequently.

The ecumenical spirit of Rumi fused with the catholic spirit of Christianity in the small book *The Persian Sufis* (London: Allen & Unwin, 1964) by the Dominican friar **Cyprian Rice**. Rice studied with R.A. Nicholson (see "Editions and Studies of Rumi" in chapter 13, below) and deeply admired him. Having caught something of Nicholson's enthusiasm for Rumi, Rice wished to introduce him to Catholic audiences, expressing the hope that Persian Sufism, and in particular Rumi, would "make possible a welding of religious thought between East and West, a vital oecumenical commingling and understanding" (10). Rice did at least succeed in receiving a Nihil Obstat from the Vatican for the book. Also from the Catholic tradition, **Karen Armstrong**, a former nun turned author on interfaith works, includes a brief outline of the life of Rumi in her best-seller, *A History of God* (New York: Knopf, 1994).

In the Protestant tradition, an American from Louisiana, **Roy Carroll DeLamotte** (1917–?), obtained a bachelor's degree in divinity at Emory University, becoming an ordained minister of the United Methodist Church. He went on to teach religion and philosophy at Paine College in Augusta, Georgia after completing his Ph.D. in world religions at Yale University in 1953, where he did his dissertation on "The Characteristics of Mystical Experience Revealed by the Figures of Speech in the Mathnawi of Jalalu'ddin Rumi." This study was published nearly thirty years later under the title *Jalaluddin Rumi: Songbird of*

Sufism (Lanham, MD: University Press of America, 1980), after DeLamotte had published two novels with Doubleday in the 1960s under the pseudonym Gregory Wilson.

DeLamotte describes himself as a student of unitive mysticism, especially the communication of this experience in symbolic form. Following Nicholson, he condemns Rumi's *Masnavi* for being "inexcusably verbose" and for the tangents and interruptions by means of which it intrudes upon the narrative, yet he obviously loves its vision. As set out in his introduction, DeLamotte aims to discuss the relationship of Rumi's mystical experience to his figures of speech and to categorize the ideas of the poem in a logical and compact manner. He proceeds on the basis of Nicholson's translation and commentary, though he does imply a knowledge of Persian and Arabic.

DeLamotte's study of Rumi must have distinguished him among Methodist ministers, though it is not at all surprising to find Rumi the topic of discussion in a Unitarian Universalist worship service. In a sermon on December 17, 1995, the anniversary of Rumi's death, the Reverend Samuel Trumbore delivered a sermon titled "Seeking the Beloved," in which he quoted a ghazal of Rumi as translated by Daniel Liebert and a hymn based on another Rumi poem and set to music by Reverend Lynn Ungar.

Rumi has also provided devotional inspiration to Catholics, as evidenced in an article by Peggy Rosenthal ("Until I call Him by His Name," *America*, 176 [May 3, 1997]: 19), who keeps the translation of Rumi by Star and Shiva near her kitchen table. Rumi has even been imagined in conversation with various icons of Catholic theology and spirituality, including Thomas Aquinas, St. John of the Cross and Jacopone da Todi.[6]

Three decades earlier, **Dag Hammarskjöld** (1905–61), United Nations Secretary-General and winner of the Nobel Peace Prize for his work in the Middle East, quoted Rumi ("The lovers of God have no religion but God alone") as an icon of world-embracing tolerance in his widely translated work, *Markings* (*Vagmarken*, Stockholm, 1963; English, New York: Knopf, 1964). Taking up this interreligious and international spirit, the British actress **Vanessa Redgrave** has narrated a thirty-minute film by a Turkish director, **Fehmi Gerceker**, called *Tolerance: Dedicated to Mawlânâ Jalâl al-Din Rumi* (Landmark Films, 1995), inspired by Rumi and the Mevlevis. Gerceker views Rumi as one of the earliest advocates of interreligious dialogue and ecumenicism, an "apostle of tolerance," who taught "acceptance, urging human beings to respect each other's faiths, orientations, and religious ideals."

SUFISM AND PSYCHOLOGY: RUMI AS RORSHACH

Although Carl Jung invokes the name of Rumi once in his *Mysterium Coniunctionis* (volumes 10 and 11 of his *Psychologische Abhandlungen*, Zurich: Rascher, 1955–6), he does so only through a very secondary source and does not seem to have read Rumi directly. Joseph Campbell shows more than a passing acquaintance with Rumi in a note to his *Hero With a Thousand Faces* (Bollingen Series 17, Princeton: Princeton University Press, 1968), describing Rumi as an advocate of tolerance. The Jungian therapist **Helen Luke** (1904–95) spent the last months of her life, between October and January 1994, discovering Rumi for the first time. She had intended to make a story adapted from Rumi's *Masnavi* about the monster in the well who devours all who enter it the centerpiece of the introduction for her book *The Way of Woman: Awakening the Perennial Feminine* (New York: Doubleday, 1995; see the introduction by Barbara Mowat), but died before completing it.

Perhaps Luke had come to know of Rumi by way of the Iranian psychoanalyst **Abdol Reza Arasteh** (1927–92). Arasteh came to the United States in 1951, obtained his doctorate and returned to the University of Tehran as an associate professor of psychology. He returned to the U.S. a few years later to take up a position in oriental studies at Princeton, after which he conducted research on higher consciousness with Erich Fromm from 1960 to 1962. Arasteh subsequently directed multi-disciplinary research at the Psychiatric Institute of Washington, and also spent extended periods in India (Allahabad University), Japan (Kagawa and Komazawa universities) and Iran (University of Tehran) as visiting professor and as consultant to the United Nations and Gandhi Peace Foundation, acting as ambassador for the message of Rumi.

As a result of his collaboration with Fromm, Arasteh published *Rumi, the Persian: Rebirth in Creativity and Love* (Lahore: Sh. Muhammad Ashraf, 1963 and 1965; New York: Orientalia Art, 1970; Boston: Routledge & Kegan Paul, 1974). **Erich Fromm**, author of the best-selling *Art of Loving* and many other works such as *Escape from Freedom* and *Ye Shall be as Gods* encouraging liberation of the human psyche from patterns of thought that hinder self-actualization, contributed the preface to *Rumi, the Persian*, in which he compares Rumi to Eckhart, except that he finds Rumi sometimes bolder in his means of expression and "less fettered by traditionalism" (viii–ix). Fromm characterizes Rumi's teachings as urging the mystic to go beyond the union with God and aim for a transcendent union with life (ix). Not only does Fromm praise Rumi as a precursor of the ideas of Renaissance humanism and the concept of religious tolerance as found in Erasmus or Nicholas de Cusa, he also admires Rumi's anticipation of Ficino's explanation of love "as the fundamental creative force." Indeed, Fromm sees Rumi as a precursor of his own understanding of the human psyche, who discussed not only the instincts and the power of reason that controls them, but also the role of "the unconscious and cosmic consciousness." For Fromm, Rumi was already addressing "the problems of freedom, of certainty, of authority" (ix). Arasteh dedicates several pages of *Rumi, the Persian* to a comparison of the close relationship he sees between the thought of Fromm and Rumi (177–87).

More recently, another Iranian, Ali Shariat Kashani, has completed his doctoral thesis at the University of Paris 7 in clinical psychology, using Rumi's poetry as a prod to the social construction of identity: *La Quête d'identité en poésie mystique persane: approche psychologique sur la base de l'oeuvre de Djalaloddin Rumi* (Villeneuve d'Ascq: Presses Universitaires du Septentrion, 1997).

UNCHURCHED SPIRITUALITY: TURNING TO RUMI

The influence of Rumi on modes of thinking in the West, though, makes itself felt not so much in the churches and not so much in the academy or in quasi-scientific approaches to the mind, as in the popular movements and spiritual practices imported from points east and designated generally as New Age spirituality. Perhaps the earliest of these to promote Rumi in any fashion was "The Fourth Way" of **George Ivanovitch Gurdjieff** (c. 1872–1949), who taught an amalgam of esoteric Christian and Sufi beliefs, beginning in Tiflis in 1919 with his Institute for the Harmonious Development of Man, which was moved to France in 1922 as a result of the Russian Revolution. Gurdjieff claimed to have been initiated into something called the Sarmoun Brotherhood, a Sufi order in a remote and inaccessible part of Afghanistan. This Sarmoun Brotherhood is known only through the claims of Gurdjieff and the followers of Idries Shah (see below), who speak of having met members of the Sufi order who had trained Gurdjieff in Afghanistan. Gurdjieff does refer to the stories of the wise idiot Mullah Nasruddin in the introduction of *Meetings with Remarkable Men* (New York: Dutton; London: Routledge & Kegan Paul, 1963; frequent reprints), where he also claims to speak Persian, though the transliterated examples given in English are unintelligible (perhaps Gurdjieff's "Persian" represents another Iranian dialect or language, like Ossetic; alternatively his transliteration may be corrupt, or he may have simply misremembered or made it up).

Whatever the circumstances of Gurdjieff's encounter with Sufism, he taught his followers to perform a complex meditative dance, theatrical performances of which brought Gurdjieff considerable attention in Paris and the U.S. in 1923. Features of this ritual dance, as documented in Peter Brook's film adaptation of *Meetings with Remarkable Men* (Remar Productions, 1978), bear strong resemblance to the turning of the Mevlevis and also to the movements of the ritual prayers of Islam. Indeed, in a lecture he gave in Paris on Christmas Day 1923, Gurdjieff admitted that he was familiar with the praxis of various Sufi orders, including the Mevlevis. "Rafael Le Fort" (probably a pseudonym for Idries Shah), who novelistically traces the sources of Gurdjieff in *The Teachers of Gurdjieff* (London: Gollancz, 1966), winds up studying the *Masnavi* in both English (probably Nicholson's translation) and Persian in Jerusalem, while trying to track down Gurdjieff's masters, and discovers in the process that Rumi was one of Gurdjieff's inspirations (71–85); later on, he learns in Tabriz that Gurdjieff studied the *samâ^c* of the Mevlevis, though Gurdjieff was actually a Naqshbandi (107).[7]

Gurdjieff and his leading disciple, P.D. Ouspensky (who, however, left Gurdjieff in 1924), therefore helped spread the devotional dance of the Mevlevis to a Western audience, whether or not that audience was conscious of its origins. Some of those attracted to Gurdjieff include Frank Lloyd Wright, the Jungian psychologist Maurice Noll, authors Katherine Mansfield, Christopher Isherwood and Aldous Huxley, as well as the editor of the journal *New Age*, Alfred Orage. Although it was discouraged for Gurdjieff's followers to talk in theological language, Sophia Grigorievena Ouspensky, known as Madame Ouspensky (though it is doubtful she was ever legally married to Mr. Ouspensky; she remained with Gurdjieff even after P.D. Ouspensky left), used to hold readings on the weekend from religious sources such as the *Philokalia*, Buddhist scriptures and Rumi's *Masnavi* at Lyne Place, a house in Surrey, England, where by 1938 about a hundred people were gathering on Sundays. One of Gurdjieff's students, Professor **Kenneth Walker** (1882–1966), recalls that "the fascinating collection of stories" of the *Masnavi* used to make the Gurdjieffites laugh at their own weaknesses, since they were "almost identical with those displayed by the absurd characters portrayed in the book." In a later book, *Diagnosis of Man* (Baltimore and London: Jonathan Cape, 1942; revised ed.: Penguin, 1962), Walker quoted the story of the elephant in the dark, which he had learned via Sanâ$^{\circ}$i and Rumi.[8]

Another member of the Gurdjieff entourage, **J.G. Bennett**, continued to seek out other teachers. Bennett's spiritual thirst led him to Catholicism, Maharishi Mahesh Yogi and Sufism, which he encountered in a trip to Turkey, Syria, Iraq and Iran in 1953. Among the Sufis he met during this journey were a rather unconventional Mevlevi dervish, Farhad Dede, and a Naqshbandi dervish, Emin Chikou. In subsequent years he also met Hasan Shushud (a Turkish Sufi master who taught the path of Absolute Liberation, Itlak Yolu), the Mevlevi Shaykh Süleyman Dede, and Idries Shah. These encounters turned Bennett's espousal of Gurdjieff's Fourth Way into a kind of non-Islamic Sufism of the True Way. Eventually Bennett turned over his center and his disciples to the care of Idries Shah in 1966.

One of the two hundred or so disciples Bennett initiated into the Fourth Way in the 1940s and 1950s was **John Wilkinson**. Wilkinson, who still gives seminars based on the teachings he learned from Bennett, also claims initiation into the Mevlevi order, though this remains for him a secondary affiliation. Another apostle from the East, Merwan Sheriar Irani, known as **Meher Baba** (1894–1969), was born to a Zoroastrian family in Poona, India. Irani was initiated into the spiritual life through contact with a Sufi woman, "Babajan," in 1913, after which he undertook his own spiritual mission in 1921, gathering a number of disciples through his work. He eventually established a colony in Meherabad, near Ahmednagar, India, performing charitable acts, such as administering a hospital. Though Baba took a vow of silence in 1925 which he observed until the end of his life (he communicated with his followers by means of an alphabet board and hand gestures), he was very fond of Persian Sufi poets and encouraged his followers to translate Rumi and especially Hâfez. His doctrines include many sayings that sound very much like Rumi, such as "We must die to self in order to live in God. Thus death is life."

Meher Baba came to the U.S. in 1931. His followers have a retreat in Myrtle Beach, South Carolina, which Baba visited several times, though the main concentration of the "Lovers of Meher Baba" now live in Australia. One of those Australian disciples, poet and playwright **Francis Brabazon** (1907–84), published a large number of works inspired by Baba, including the long narrative poem *Stay with God: A Statement in Illusion on Reality* (Woombye, Queensland: Edwards & Shaw for Garuda Books, 1959; reprinted Melbourne: New Humanity Books, 1990), which incorporates a biography of Meher Baba and expounds upon his teachings. Among the "avatars of God," Brabazon includes Siva, Rama, Krishna, Abraham, Zoroaster, Buddha, Jesus, Mohammad and Meher Baba. But in every age, he says, there exist five Perfect Masters and Rumi figures in the poem (28–9) as one of the Perfect Masters for his own age, who became "glorious/Light of God" after first writing "books of the-ol-ogy" containing "words without wisdom." But Rumi left "all this bookmaking, this darkening of counsel" after he "started tagging around with his new friend," Shams-e Tabriz, "a Roadsman debonair and dusty." Brabazon explains in the note on Rumi (158) that loyalty and obedience to a master is necessary for all aspirants, though the idea is difficult for Westerners to accept. Elsewhere (84), Brabazon quotes Baba quoting Rumi, to the effect that a single moment spent with a saint is equal to a hundred years of prayer and penance. As Meher Baba pointed out, Rumi was here speaking only of the saints, from which we can but imagine the exalted state of the Perfect Master (See also "Rumi as Muse" in chapter 14, below).

The prolific **Idries Shah** (1924–96) was born to a Scottish mother and Afghan father in Simla, India, but came to England as a teenager. His father, Sirdar Ikbal, and brother, Omar Ali Shah, have both undertaken translations of Persian literature in their own right, but Idries is the most famous scion of the household, which traces its descent back to the Prophet Mohammad. Initiated into the Naqshbandi order in Afghanistan, Shah came to London in the 1960s and sought out the remnants of Gurdjieff's following, notably J.G. Bennett, attempting to convince them that Gurdjieff had borrowed most of his ideas from Sufism. Shah has ever since energetically promoted Sufism to a Western audience in a number of books which he and his disciples authored. Presenting Sufism to westerners as a method of self-realization – "learning how to learn" as the title of one of his books describes it – rather than as a mystical system, Shah's impact has been enormous. He has won the admiration of a number of writers, poets and journalists, his home and center have been fashionable hangouts for high society, and the BBC produced a documentary, *Dreamwalkers*, about Shah and Sufism for British television in 1970.

Shah, as a non-denominational and non-traditional Sufi, promotes neither any specific order nor a belief in Islam to his followers. As one of the more transcendent Sufi figures, Rumi appeals to all orders; to quote from him does not therefore suggest a particular affiliation or creed, but a kind of quintessential Sufi wisdom. Coming from the subcontinent, Shah would have been far more familiar with Persian than with Arab Sufism, and, as mentioned earlier, South Asian Muslims hold Rumi in particular esteem. Of course, by the 1960s Rumi also enjoyed the advantage in Britain of name recognition, thanks to the labors of Nicholson and Arberry.

It therefore comes as no surprise that Shah relies upon the stories of Rumi more than those of any other Sufi. In keeping with his vision of Sufism as a version of the Perennial Philosophy recast as a training of the mind, Shah does not insist on the importance of names, dates and particularities in introducing Sufism to a Western audience. He nevertheless does introduce a number of Sufi poets by name, providing a biography of each in *The Sufis* (New York: Doubleday, 1964 and numerous reprints), with its introduction by the English poet Robert Graves. A biographical sketch of Rumi appears in that work, and a handful of translations from the *Divân-e Shams* are to be found in Shah's *The Way of the Sufi* (London: Jonathan Cape, 1968; frequent reprints), which was awarded a prize by UNESCO and favorably reviewed in the *New York Times*. Stories from the *Masnavi* are told in several of Shah's works, including *Tales of the Dervishes: Teaching Stories of the Sufi Masters over the Past Thousand Years* (London: Jonathan Cape, 1967), *The Elephant in the Dark* (London: Octagon, 1974), and *The Dermis Probe* (London: Jonathan Cape, 1970) (an allusion to feeling the skin of the elephant in the dark), all reprinted numerous times. *The Caravan of Dreams* (London: Octagon, 1968) contains a couple of pages of aphorisms and maxims under the legend "Meditations of Rumi."

Shah also promoted Aflâki's miraculous tales from the life of Rumi, publishing two versions: first a reprint of J.W. Redhouse's translation *Legends of the Sufis* (See chapter 14, below) with a foreword by Shah (London: Theosophical Publishing House, 1976), and then *The Hundred Tales of Wisdom: Life, Teachings and Miracles of Jalaludin Rumi from Aflaki's "Munaqib," Together with Certain Important Stories from Rumi's Works* (London: Octagon, 1978), presenting Shah's own translations from the Persian of Aflâki (including sundry lines from Rumi's ghazals which appear in Aflâki's anecdotes), interspersed with a few tales from the *Masnavi*.

Though Shah acted as the patron of the Cambridge Poetry Festival in 1975, his interest in Rumi lies not so much in its literariness but in the ideas, most particularly the teaching stories and their psychological effect upon the reader/listener. Shah usually retells Rumi's *Masnavi* stories in the capacity of storyteller and teacher rather than as a translator. *The Way of the Sufis* does incorporate some conventional translations of the ghazals, in somewhat more modern language than that of Nicholson, but not in a noticeably "poetic" style.

Shah's books have been translated into twelve languages and have sold about fifteen million copies worldwide to a wide cross section of libraries, students of Sufism, curiosity seekers and the general public. Shah was taken to task by some for distorting the message of Sufism, specifically by excising its Islamic content and foisting an ungrounded and undisciplined substitute for real spirituality on unsuspecting Westerners.

Such was the essence of the critique of **Seyyed Hossein Nasr** (1933–), an Iranian-born and U.S.-educated philosopher of Islam, who has helped make Islam known in the West. In a review of Shah's *The Sufis* in the journal *Islamic Studies* (December 1964), Nasr accuses him of divorcing Sufism from Islam and turning it into a kind of esotericism and pseudo-spiritualism (531–33). In his *Sufi Essays* (Albany, NY: SUNY Press, 1972), Nasr alludes to Shah when he speaks of the "occultist tinge" given to Sufism "completely divorced from Islam" in Western circles, specifically in England (15). Nasr held university positions in Iran from 1958 through 1975, but tainted by his association with the government of the overthrown Shah of Iran, Nasr has lived in the U.S. since the 1979 Revolution. Nasr has written scholarly essays and studies of a number of philosophical and mystical thinkers of Islam for Western audiences, as well as books for young Muslims living in the West. In part to counter Shah's Sufism, and in part so that Iran might not go without a publication in English commemorating the 700th anniversary of Rumi's death, Nasr wrote a small book on Rumi himself, *Jalal al-Din Rumi: Supreme Persian Poet and Sage* (Tehran: High Council of Culture and the Arts, 1974).

Whatever the merit of these criticisms, Shah's promotion of Sufism in the English-speaking world during the 1960s, a time when many young Westerners turned to Eastern philosophy and religion (particularly Hinduism and Buddhism, and only to a lesser extent to Sufism), played an important role in the later canonization of Rumi as one of the patron saints of New Age spirituality during the 1980s and 1990s. Octagon, the press Shah established in London, keeps his works and other works about Sufism in print and can be accessed via the web at www.clearlight.com/~sufi/index.shtml.

The whirling dervishes have attracted the attention of French scholars and travelers for over a century and their sacred dance continues to captivate French-speaking audiences today. **Michel Random** (1933–) became attracted to Gurdjieff in the early 1960s and went on to write several books about Japan and the martial arts. He published in Tunisia *Mawlana Djalal-ud-Din, Rumi: le soufisme et la danse* (Tunis: Sud-Editions, 1980), including photographs, an

introduction by the modern mystic Titus Burckhardt, and an afterword by
Maurice Bejart, the ballet choreographer and theater director.

The Mevlevi whirling had earlier influenced the Dances of Universal Peace
by the Western Sufi teacher and Zen master **Samuel L. Lewis** (1896–1971),
known jocularly as Sufi Sam, more seriously as Murshid Sam, who lies buried in
a shrine at the Lama Foundation in San Cristobal, New Mexico. Lewis learned
his mysticism in San Francisco from Rabia Martin (d. 1947), who had become a
disciple of Inayat Khan prior to the First World War. Lewis traveled through
Asia and Africa, returning in 1966 to form his own Sufi group in San Francisco.
Pir Vilayat Khan visited Lewis in San Francisco in 1968 and 1969 and taught
him the Mevlevi dance tradition, which he combined with other dance
techniques learned from Ruth St. Denis (1880–1968). Lewis offered to take the
role of Shams to Khan's Rumi, according to Lewis' successor, Pir-o-Murshid
Moineddin, head of the Sufi Islamia Ruhaniat Society, formed in 1977 by some
students of Hazrat Vilayat Khan (see below) unhappy with his regulations.[9]

Beginning in the late 1960s, Murshid Sam began using a cycle of over five
hundred dances, collectively referred to as the **Dances of Universal Peace**, to
promote peace through the arts. These dances are kept alive by devotees in many
countries who perform them in schools, prisons, and at ecumenical events. In
1973 the International Network for the Dances of Universal Peace (see
www.teleport.com/~indup for their website) published a booklet in Seattle, *The
Whirling Ecstasy*, featuring selections in English of Clément Huart's French
translation of Aflâki.

After a stint with the singing group The Springfields, Englishman **(Tim)
Reshad Feild** (1934–) undertook a spiritual journey as a result of his wife's
illness, which during the 1960s and 1970s led him through America and the
East, including a stay in a Zen monastery in Japan. In 1962 Feild met the head
of the Sufi order in the West, Pir Vilayat Khan, and in 1969 he ran into Bulent
Rauf, a Turkish devotee of Ibn ʿArabi with connections to the Mevlevi order, in
the shop of a London antiques dealer. Rauf introduced Feild to the shaykh of
the Mevlevi order, Süleyman Dede, who initiated Feild as a Mevlevi in Los
Angeles in 1976, supposedly designating him as a shaykh. It was also through
Feild that Kabir Helminski (see below) was first introduced to the Mevlevis.

Feild relates his journey to Turkey in *The Last Barrier: A Journey through the
World of Sufi Teaching* (New York: Harper & Row, 1976) and reveals in the
course of *The Invisible Way* (San Francisco: Harper & Row, 1979), a novel about
his visit to Konya, that his spiritual teacher was a Turkish whirling dervish. Feild
presents himself, however, as the founder of the Living School, which though
based upon "the essence of the knowledge of the Sufi Tradition" is not an Islamic
Sufism, but a kind of Perennial Philosophy. Feild describes himself as an
independent teacher and esoteric healer. He founded the Institute for Conscious
Life in 1976, which has evolved into the Mevlana Foundation. Feild now acts as

"spiritual adviser" to the Mevlana Foundation in Boulder, Colorado, and to the Turning Society in British Vancouver, where he now lives. He has made a video of himself and his students performing the *samâ* on the anniversary of Rumi's death, *Turning Toward the Morning of Your Life*.[10]

By 1976 the youth movement in the West had accepted, often rather too readily, Eastern spirituality and its supposed anti-materialist, anti-capitalist *Weltanschauung*. The Maharishi Mahesh Yogi had temporarily won John Lennon, Mia Farrow, Donovan Leitch and other celebrities to Transcendental Meditation. George Harrison had helped popularize both Ravi Shankar and the Krishna Consciousness movement, and the books of gurus from Ram Das to Satya Sai Baba and J. Krishnamurti filled up the shelves in the chain bookstores of America, while classes on various forms of Yoga proliferated. All this troubled Ravi Shankar, who warned, "You cannot just brush the surface of a culture and pretend you have found an answer."[11]

Although Sufism did not attract quite such intense attention as did Hindu- and Buddhist-based systems of Bhakti or Vedanta, it did interest some, particularly after the commemoration of the 700th anniversary of Rumi's death and the promotion of the "Whirling Dervishes" as a tourist attraction. A number of Westerners began to practice "Sufi dance," sometimes combined with odd behavior that led some in the San Francisco Bay Area to speak of the "goofy Sufis." Some ephemeral publications inspired by Rumi, such as Duncan McNaughton's (1942–) *Rumi is Buried at Konya* (Bolinas, CA: D. McNaughton, 1973) and James Moores' *Whirling Dervishes* (London: International Rumi Committee, 1974), appeared around this time.

The popularity of Sufism has perhaps now eclipsed the Indophilic spirituality of the 1960s. The New Age journal *Gnosis* set a new sales record with its Winter 1994 issue (vol. 30) dedicated to Sufism, including articles by Mevlevis Kabir Helminski and Camille Helminski, and the Mevlevi affiliate Refik Algan. Idries Shah, who had been promoting Sufism for more than a decade in London, was already fretting in the 1970s about the superficial understanding of Sufism and "dervish dancing" spreading among certain individuals. His preface to the reprint of Redhouse's translation of Aflâki explains that the miraculous stories it recounts should not necessarily be taken literally, but were used by Sufi teachers to gauge the psycho-spiritual reactions of the listener. Shah also admits, however, what is closer to the truth – that unsophisticated followers of the Mevlevis from a very early period believed literally in the miraculous anecdote and/or used it as a tool of literary propaganda to magnify the importance of their master. That Westerners got a watered-down and distorted version of Sufism, then, is no wonder. Already in 1656, Katip Chelebi (1609–57), in a work critical of the Muslim system of education, had warned that practicing Sufis in Turkey were applying Rumi's whirling in an ungrounded fashion. By way of example, he accused the Khalvatis of having completely forgotten the purpose of *samâ*.[12]

The Sufi movement is now represented in the West by a number of different orders, almost all of which acknowledge the spiritual greatness of Rumi, even if they do not follow his discipline. Before Idries Shah, **Hazrat Inayat Khan** (1882–1927) of India lived a good portion of his life in the West, spreading his ideas about spiritual education and psychology. Inayat Khan talked about Rumi and the allegory of the hollow reed as early as 1923; he gives a commentary on the opening lines of the *Masnavi* in *Sufi Mysticism* (London: Barrie & Jenkins, for the Sufi Movement, 1973, p. 141), which appears as volume 10 in Khan's "Orange Book" series, *The Sufi Message*. Hazrat Inayat Khan founded the Sufi Order of the West, now the Sufi Order International (see www.sufiorder.org), leadership of which has passed on to his son, **Pir Vilayat Inayat Khan** (1916–). Among the other publications of the Sufi Order is *Toward the One* (New York: Harper Colophon, 1974), a book based upon the lectures of Pir Vilayat given in Arizona, California, New York and France from 1970 to 1973 and apparently designed to attract maturing flower children with its illustrations, photos and wise quotes from various Sufi and Hindu mystics. This also includes some quotes from Rumi and several pictures of the Whirling Dervishes. Coleman Barks and Pir Vilayat teamed up for the volume *The Hand of Poetry*, featuring Barks' "translations" of five Persian poets, including Rumi, along with Inayat Khan's commentary.

Despite Rumi's close association with the Mevlevis, rival orders like the Nimatollahis, the various branches of the Naqshbandis and the International Association of Sufism, which holds ecumenical conferences on Sufism in the West, not infrequently appeal to Rumi and hold him in reverence. The Rifāᶜi–Maᶜrufi Order of America, for example, co-sponsored the "Rumi Festival," at the University of North Carolina in September 1998 to mark the birth of Rumi. The Shahmaghsoudis or M.T.O. (Maktab-e Tariqe-ye Ovaysi) International, founded by Shah Maghsoud Angha (b. 1945), has actively cultivated a Western audience, establishing several centers throughout the U.S. and Europe from their base in California and on the Internet. Shah Maghsoud has published several books in English, including translations of his own poetry and essays on Sufi thought. Like most Sufis in the West, he incorporates Rumi in his teachings. He also makes implicit claims for his own poems by publishing them alongside classic Persian bards like Khayyâm, Hâfez and Rumi in *Selections: Poems from Khayam, Rumi, Hafez, Shah Maghsoud* (San Rafael, CA: International Association Of Sufism, 1991). In 1983 Nahid Angha, the daughter of Shah Maghsoud, helped co-found the International Association of Sufism, which gathers adherents of the different orders and teachers together for the annual International Sufi Symposium.

MODERN MEVLEVIS

Although restricted by law in Turkey from promoting itself as a living spiritual practice, the Mevlevi order does enjoy the freedom to do so in the United States.

While the Mevlevi order has been comparatively slow to establish its presence in the West, a small number of Americans now consider themselves adepts of or affiliated with the Mevlevis. When funds were raised for the Mevlevi Shaykh in Konya, **Süleyman Loras Hayati Dede** (d. 1985), to visit the U.S. in 1976, he found a ready-made audience for the practice of meditative dance among the disciples of Samuel Lewis on the West Coast. Those who came to the Music Camp in Mendocino were not only receptive to but enthusiastic about the Mevlevi practice of *samâ*, or turning. The women who met him were pleasantly surprised by the respect Süleyman Dede showed them, since they were aware that the Mevlevi tradition had become, like most Sufi orders, quite male oriented. At a retreat named Hurkalya in San Anselmo, California, Western women performed the turning dance they had learned from Murshid Sam as they sang the Quaker spiritual "'Tis a Gift to be Simple." A group from California visited him again at his home in Konya in 1979.

Süleyman Dede was one of the last Mevlevis to follow the traditional initiation (*chelle*) of 1,001 days of service in the kitchen. In fact, Süleyman Dede entered a Mevlevi *tekke* at the age of eighteen and served in the kitchen, not for three, but for twenty-three years, at which time he was formally accorded the rank of Dede and given a cell in which to live in the *tekke*. As noted above ("Mevlevi Ritual" in chapter 10), married men were traditionally not allowed to live in the Mevlevi lodges, but an exception was made in the case of Süleyman Dede, and his wife and children were also allowed to reside with him, though this was after the lodges ceased functioning as such by legal decree. Nevertheless, Süleyman Dede was permitted to feed the poor from the Mevlevi kitchen.

In 1978 the son of Süleyman Dede, **Jelaluddin Loras**, who had studied with Helveti and Mevlevi dervishes in Turkey, came to New York and affiliated for a while with Pir Vilayat Khan. He then made his way to Mendocino where he connected with members of the Islamia Ruhaniat Society and began teaching them a form of Mevlevi turning in the early 1980s. Eventually he formed the **Mevlevi Order of America** in conjunction with some of the former devotees of Samuel Lewis in northern California, such as Mariam Baker. Loras now divides his residence between Hawaii and Konya, making frequent visits to his circles of disciples in Los Angeles and the San Francisco Bay area; Eugene and Portland, Oregon; Seattle, Washington; and Vancouver, Canada. He also tours with his disciples to lecture and present the turning ceremony to the American public.

Loras gives his disciples Sufi names and encourages them to study the *Masnavi* daily. He recommends Nicholson's meticulous translation for this purpose, though his disciples also derive inspiration from the more accessible versions of Barks. They learn the opening Sura of the Koran in Arabic and are often exposed to Islamic principles, but the Mevlevi Order of America does not require conversion to Islam. They do not require any change in religious affiliation and focus not on divisive issues of doctrine, but on forging communal bonds by concentrating on spiritual psychology and sharing in the fellowship of *zekr* and turning. The primary practice revolves, of course, around the turning ceremony. The Mevlevi Order of America offers an annual nine-month sequence of night classes to train adepts to become *semazens*. A network of disciples appointed by Loras teach these classes; an adept cannot turn before an audience before having successfully trained to become a *semazen*.

The Mevlevi Order of America has its own publication, *The Lovers of Mevlana*, edited by Mariam Baker and a web site, www.hayatided.org/index.html. In 1998 Loras led a pilgrimage of American Mevlevis to Turkey, where they performed turning ceremonies not only in the Galata Mevlevi lodge in Istanbul, but also in the *samâ^c* hall of the Mevlânâ Museum in Konya. Although Loras had been allowed to perform a turning ceremony in the courtyard of the shrine complex one day in 1994 after the museum had closed, the museum officials and Turkish authorities seem very nervous about the *samâ^c* hall being used for its original purpose. In any case, twenty-two American Mevlevis, including fourteen women, were allowed to turn in the *samâ^c* hall, even though Turkish Mevlevis have not been allowed to use the hall for purely meditative turning in decades. Loras will direct the Hayati Dede Institute of Sacred Studies, a kind of modern-day Dâr al-Masnavi, with classes on *Masnavi*, calligraphy, poetry and Koran. Two-week courses are scheduled to take place in a retreat (*zâvie*) in Konya constructed for this purpose.[13]

Shaykh **Kabir Edmund Helminski** was initiated as a Mevlevi dervish by Süleyman Dede in 1980 and studied under him for five years, visiting him annually in Konya until his death in 1985. Helminski was eventually recognized as a Mevlevi shaykh in 1990 by **Celâleddin Çelebi**. After completing several years of service, Helminski received his formal designation (*ijazet*) from the Chelebi, who appointed Helminski the representative of the Mevlevi order in North America. Just before his death in 1996, Celaleddin had established the International Mevlevi Foundation to act as an umbrella organization to coordinate the efforts of Mevlevis in different countries. The International Mevlevi Foundation, now headed by Faruk Hemdem Çelebi, Celâleddin's son, met in June 1996 in Bodrum, Turkey with representatives of the Mevlevi order from Austria, Chile, England, Germany, Iran, Switzerland and Turkey in attendance.

Although the position of Grand Chelebi no longer exists as a formal designation, Faruk Hemdem Çelebi has generally been recognized as the highest authority among the Mevlevis since Celâleddin Çelebi's death. Only he can authorize someone to act as shaykh, wear its insignia and guide disciples. Five individuals have officially been designated as shaykhs of the Mevlevi order and view themselves as operating under the authority of Faruk Hemdem: Hüseyin Top and Nail Kesova in Istanbul, Andaç Arbaş in Ankara, Abu al-Qâsem Tafazzoli in Tehran and Kabir Helminski in California. These shaykhs operate more-or-less independently, but must adhere to the values and traditions of the Mevlevi order, as handed down orally from shaykh to shaykh.

Helminski has written a primer for spiritual thinking and practice, *Living Presence: A Sufi Way to Mindfulness and the Essential Self* (New York: Jeremy Tarcher, 1992). Helminski's own spiritual trek began with a Jesuit education under Reverend Martin D'Arcy (1888–1976), after which he studied Zen Buddhism with Suzuki Roshi. He also lived at the Lama Foundation while Sam Lewis and Ram Das (1913–) were there, and associated with various Gurdjieff students (vii). This book presents the Perennial Philosophy abstracted from all of these practices, without many Mevlevi specifics, though the chapter rubrics and one full ghazal (61–2) do come from Rumi.

Kabir, and his wife of twenty-five years, Camille, direct the **Threshold Society**, probably the most visibly active Mevlevi enterprise in the world. Indeed, Brattleboro, Vermont, the location of the Threshold Society's meeting center and office, was declared "New Konya" in a 1994 conference on "Mevlana and Human Rights" held in the old Konya. The Threshold Society operated out of top-floor offices and a turning hall on Main Street in Brattleboro for most of the 1990s, but moved to Aptos, California, near Santa Cruz, in 1999.[14] In addition to the Brattleboro Center and the new Mevlevi Center in Aptos, the Threshold Society has *zekr* and study circles in San Diego, Portland, Washington state and the District of Columbia, as well as in Canada (Montreal, London and Toronto), Santiago, Chile and Mexico City. It also holds occasional classes and spiritual retreats and maintains a very informative web site (www.sufism.org). About 3,000 people are on the mailing list for the Threshold Society's quarterly newsletter, *Eye of the Heart*.

Though the Mevlevi teachings obviously draw their inspiration from Islam, the Threshold Society does not require conversion to Islam in order for an individual to become a Mevlevi dervish. It encourages, but does not make obligatory, the five ritual prayers of Islam. It does enjoin the practice of private *zekr*, recommending at least a half hour of prayers and remembrance of God every morning. The aims of the Society include encouraging and facilitating "the direct personal experience of God," the sharing of "principles of spiritual development," achieving a "contemporary expression of the classical Sufi path," fostering a "true partnership of man and woman," and recognizing "the unity and interdependence of all human beings and all life."

Kabir Helminski explains that the way of Rumi opens to all humanity "the essence of the Prophetic tradition, the core of the Judaeo-Christian–Islamic heritage," affording entry to the "primordial religion of humanity" which Rumi describes as the Religion of Love. The Threshold Society therefore serves "a broad function beyond any Sufi order or religious belief," while at the same time providing for formal initiation of individuals desiring to follow specifically Mevlevi praxis. The Threshold Society has also formed an ethics committee and formulated a statement on the parameters and responsibilities of the master–disciple relationship. It has been active in Christian–Muslim dialogue, helping to organize the conference "Two Sacred Paths" with the episcopal archdiocese of Washington at Washington's National Cathedral in November 1998. Kabir Helminski also spoke at a congressional hearing of the Human Rights Caucus on the persecution of Muslims around the world.

The Threshold Society works in close cooperation with the Mevlana Culture and Art Foundation of Istanbul and Ankara (directed by Hakan Talu and Serhat Sarpel), which the Turkish government permits to represent the Mevlevi order, but only as a cultural, not a religious, institution. The Threshold Society aims to "make a tangible contribution to our culture through service, art, music and literature." Toward that end, it has published forty books, most of them original titles on Sufism, spiritual psychology or other mystical traditions, including translations and works by American Sufi teachers and scholars. Because the imprint's distributor recently went bankrupt, the backlist of Threshold Books has been sold to Shambhala Books. Among the titles published by the Threshold Society are Wheeler Thackston's translation of Rumi's Discourses (*Signs of the Unseen*), and a forthcoming translation of a Mevlevi liturgical book (*Mevlevi Wird*). The Threshold Society has also sponsored three American tours of the Whirling Dervishes from Turkey.

Another activity of the Threshold Society has been to create, particularly through the efforts of Camille Helminski, a space for women in traditional Mevlevi praxis. She has written a number of articles about the history of women in Sufism and encouraged the practice of turning by women. Celâleddin Çelebi, as shaykh of the Mevlevi order in Konya, was asked to formulate an official position on the matter. In order to do so, he asked the American disciples who practiced gender-integrated turning to write to him about their experiences. In a letter dated November 11, 1991, Celâleddin formally granted permission for male and female Mevlevis to turn together, not only in private but occasionally also in public *samâ‘* sessions. Faruk Hemdem Çelebi has allowed this practice to continue.[15]

SUFISM IN THE MAINSTREAM

The influence of Sufism in the West now extends far beyond all the orders and their teachers. Phanes Press, which offers a number of titles on Hermetic occultism, early Christian spirituality and other topics of esoteric religion, has published a superb collection of translations in a modern free-verse idiom, *The Drunken Universe: An Anthology of Persian Sufi Poetry* (Grand Rapids, MI, 1987) by Persian scholars Peter Lamborn Wilson and Nasrollah Pourjavady. The one poem (D 2172) by Rumi featured in *The Drunken Universe* comes across as fresh, sincere and full of feeling, although instead of "wash yourself/with yourself," rendering the phrase as "wash yourself of self" would more closely convey the sense of *az khwod*. In a later work, *Sacred Drift* (1993), from another publisher historically associated with a particular style of life and school of writing, City Lights Books of San Francisco, Wilson presents some playful versions of Rumi in the context of a discussion about the "nomadosophy" of mystical and heretical Islam, focused on the themes of Khezr, the flying carpet and other travel motifs.

The internationally known novelist **Doris Lessing** (1919–), born in Iran to British parents, learned of Sufism through Idries Shah's *The Sufis*, which she read in 1964 and later described as "the most surprising book I had read" and "the definitive book for our time." In the obituary she wrote for Shah in the London *Daily Telegraph*, Lessing considered Shah her teacher, as well as a "good friend," "the wittiest person I expect ever to meet." She wrote the preface for Shah's 1996 book *Learning How to Learn*, and often refers to Shah and his influence on her beliefs. She occasionally incorporates Sufi stories and themes in her fiction and it has even been argued that Sufistic beliefs and concepts inform many passages of her novels and stories.[16] In any case, Lessing is quite familiar with Rumi and prefaces the fourth part of *The Four-Gated City* (New York: Knopf, 1969) with an extended quotation from the *Masnavi*.

The prolific science fiction author **Philip K. Dick** (1928–82) was prone to mystical experiences of his own, which led to a lifelong interest in Indian and Iranian religions and philosophies, which he sometimes incorporated into his novels (*Eye in the Sky* is about a Babi planet and Zoroastrianism features in some of his other stories). We can be sure Dick was acquainted with Rumi, as he describes himself as a pantheistic monist and attributes a brief quote to Rumi in *The Shifting Realities of Philip K. Dick: Selected Literary and Philosophical Writings* (ed. L. Sutin, New York: Pantheon, 1995). Sufi ideas also turn up in the works of other science fiction writers, such as Frank Herbert's *Dune* and Lessing's *Shikasta*.

Science fiction readers do not normally take the Sufism they encounter as seriously as do New Age readers, who now have several shelves of titles to choose from in bookstores and libraries, many of which invoke Rumi. In 1986 **Jack Kornfield**, an American who trained as a Buddhist monk and then became a psychologist, began giving talks to the Spiritual Emergency Network, a group of psychologists and spiritual counselors who approach symptoms usually considered indicative of mental illness rather as poorly understood but "powerful spiritual transitions" the subjects are undergoing. These talks resulted in a book, *A Path With Heart: A Guide Through the Perils and Promises of Spiritual Life* (New York: Bantam, 1993), which, though primarily Buddhist in orientation, includes several quotes from Coleman Barks' versions of Rumi. Michael W. Fox in *The Boundless Circle* (Wheaton, IL: Quest Books, 1996) labors under the mis-impression that Rumi and Sufism teach reincarnation (258), a conclusion he leaps to on the basis of Rumi's dictum about man proceeding from mineral to vegetable to human state. Sam Keen, author of the best-selling *Fire in the Belly*, quotes Rumi in *Hymns to an Unknown God* (New York: Bantam, 1994), while Khephra Burns and Susan Taylor draw upon Aldous Huxley, Helminski and Chittick for the quotations of Rumi they include in *Confirmation: The Spiritual Wisdom that has Shaped Our Lives* (New York: Anchor Books, 1997). **Stephen Mitchell**, "translator" of Rilke and the Bible, also weighed in with *The Enlightened Heart: An Anthology of Sacred Poetry* (New York: Harper & Row, 1989 and 1993), which provides selections from forty-eight poets in about 170 pages. The Rumi versions of Coleman Barks figure quite prominently in this mix. R.A. Herrera includes a chapter on Rumi by Schimmel along with a number of other figures in his *Mystics of the Book: Themes, Topics, and Typologies* (New York: Lang, 1993).

Between the 1930s and 1970s, with the promotion of Rumi by Gurdjieff's circle, by Meher Baba and by Idries Shah, Rumi's fame began to grow among Westerners attracted to non-traditional modes of spirituality. With the renewed freedom granted to the Mevlevi dervishes in Turkey to perform their "folk" dance, the commemoration of the 700th anniversary of his death took on international proportions and led to the rediscovery and reprinting of the scholarly works by Redhouse, Nicholson and Arberry. At the same time, a couple of intriguing works for a more popular audience appeared, attracting greater attention to the Mevlevis. **Ira Shems Friedlander**'s *The Whirling Dervishes (Being an account of the Sufi order known as the Mevlevis and its founder the poet and mystic Mevlana Jalaluʾddin Rumi)* recounts popular and legendary anecdotes of Rumi's life, reflecting the information purveyed to tourists in Konya, and gives details about the history of the order, the legal restrictions imposed by the Republic of Turkey and the practice of *samâʿ*, including an informative section on Mevlevi music by Nezih Uzel. Originally published in 1975 (New York: Macmillan) on the heels of the seventh centenary of Rumi's death, it has proved of enduring interest. The SUNY series on Islam, edited by Seyyed Hossein Nasr, has reprinted the volume with a foreword from Annemarie Schimmel (Albany NY: SUNY Press, 1992).

Talat Sait Halman and **Metin And** had earlier teamed up for the excellent *Mevlana Celaleddin Rumi and the Whirling Dervishes: Sufi Philosophy, Whirling Rituals, Poems of Ecstasy, Miniature Paintings* (Istanbul: Dost, 1983; 2nd ed., 1992); unfortunately, it does not seem to have gained a distributor in the West and is therefore only available to visitors in Turkey or in research libraries. It includes many photographs, miniatures from the *Savâqeb al-manâqeb*, an article by Halman introducing Rumi's thought ("Love is All: Mevlana's Poetry and Philosophy"), and one by And ("Sema: The Spiritual Concert of the Mevlevis"). Though aimed at a more popular audience, this attractive book provides Halman's very beautiful translations of some of the poems of Rumi and a wealth of interesting and mostly accurate information.

Today more than ever the word "Sufism" conjures up the image of a turning Mevlevi dervish, now an icon of Islamic spirituality and the cultural and musical heritage of Turkey. The cover of the recent reprint of J. Spencer Trimingham's *The Sufi Orders in Islam* (Oxford: Oxford University Press, 1998) features a photograph of Mevlevis in a whirl of white. Another book by Denise Breton and Christopher Largent, *Love, Soul and Freedom: Dancing with Rumi on the Mystic Path* (Center City: Hazelden, 1998) offers Rumi as a modern non-parochial world mystic. In *Publishers Weekly* Bob Summer notes the brisk market for books on Sufism in America ("Clear Some Shelf Space for Sufism," January 9, 1995, 33–5), giving a sales figure of 50,000 copies for Coleman Barks and John Moyne's *Open Secret*. By 1998, three years after its publication, *The Essential Rumi* by Barks had sold over 110,000 copies! Any publisher would rejoice to sell this many copies of a book of modern American poetry, but if we take into account the dozen other Rumi volumes by Barks and the dozen-odd versions of Rumi by other authors, the laurel of best-selling poet in America with which Summer in *Publishers Weekly* and then Alexandra Marks in *The Christian Science Monitor* crowned Rumi is probably no exaggeration, even if the ultimate authority for the assertion is Coleman Barks himself.

As early as the mid-1970s, Rumi had become an acknowledged saint of New Age consciousness and the human potential movement for at least a certain segment of Western readers. The popularly canonized Rumi, in the guise not so much of a practicing Muslim mystic but rather as a saintly non-denominational theosophist, was able to transcend the barriers of time and culture. However, the available translations in English did not conform to modern taste; the perceived demand for new versions was soon filled by poets like Bly and Barks (see chapter 14, below). Before turning to the translations, however, we should first consider the history of Rumi scholarship, which is intimately intertwined both with the history of Rumi's thought and the history of his poetry in the West.

13

A History of Rumi Scholarship

Barthélémy d'Herbelot (1625–95) set Western study of the Middle East on a solid footing with a voluminous encyclopedic dictionary in the best tradition of the French philosophes. His *Bibliothèque orientale* (Paris: Compagnie des Librairies, 1697) constitutes a "universal dictionary" of the "Orient," a compendium of 8,600 entries chock full of information on the people, history, traditions, legends, religions, politics, government, laws, customs, wars, revolutions, poetry, etc. of the Middle East. The *Bibliothèque orientale* proved the standard reference work throughout the eighteenth and into the nineteenth century. Among the Persian poets, Saˁdi, Ferdowsi, Anvari, Rudaki and Hâfez rate longish entries, but d'Herbelot devotes no separate entry to Rumi, mentioning him only under the rubric of the "Maulavi" or the Mevlevi order, famous for their flute music and their dancing. D'Herbelot refers to the fact that the members of the Mevlevi order regularly read a book called the *Masnavi* by "Gemaleddin al-Balkhi" (who is, of course, Jalâl al-Din al-Balkhi, i.e., Rumi), and mentions the existence of Persian and Turkish commentaries on the book, including the one by Mevlevi Anqaravi.

In Great Britain, the academic establishment formally began to promote the study of Arabic in 1632 when Cambridge University inaugurated a chair of Arabic with an endowment from London businessman, and later Lord Mayor, Thomas Adams. A chair at Oxford followed soon after, endowed by Archbishop Laud and first occupied by Edward Pococke (1604–91) in 1636. The scholarly endeavors of the earliest occupants of these chairs centered primarily around Arabic and Hebrew, such that we find Professor Simon Ockley (1678–1720) at Cambridge confessing in 1716 his weakness in Persian: "How often have I endeavoured to perfect myself in that easy and delicate language; but my malignant and envious stars have still combined to frustrate my attempts" (AOE 43).

But **Sir William Jones** (1746–94), often credited with the "discovery" of the existence of the structural and lexical relations between the Indo-European languages, catapulted Persian to the forefront of British oriental studies with his translations from Persian in the 1770s, stirring up admiration all over Europe for the beauty of Persian poetry (See chapter 14). After accepting a post in Calcutta, where he desired to perfect his knowledge of "oriental" languages, Jones found "so much Arabic or Persian to read, that all my leisure in a morning, is hardly sufficient for a thousandth part of the reading" he wished to accomplish. Among the Persian works listed in Jones' notebook under "Order of Persian Reading," Rumi's *Masnavi* appears in the eighth position. In a letter written to Richard Johnson on March 8, 1787(?), Jones indicates he will soon have leisure to read the "Mesnavi" and asks to borrow Johnson's copy. This copy of the *Masnavi*, or some other copy which later passed into Jones' possession, has the following notes written in the margin:

> So extraordinary a book as the Mesnavi was never, perhaps, composed by man. It abounds with beauties, and blemishes, equally great; with gross obscenity, and pure ethicks; with exquisite strains of poetry, and flat puerilities; with wit, and pleasantry, mixed with dull jests; with ridicule on all established religions, and a vein of sublime piety; it is like a wild country in a fine climate overspread with rich flowers, and with the odour of beasts. I know of no writer, to whom the Maulavi can justly be compared, except Chaucer or Shakespeare.[1]

In *A Catalogue of the Most Valuable Books in the Persian Language*, Jones mentions the existence of at least two copies of the *Masnavi* known to him in Europe, one in the Oxford library and one in private hands. *The Works of Sir William Jones* (London, 1807) introduces the *Masnavi* as follows:

> A poetical work called Mesnavi, upon several subjects, of religion, history, morality, and politicks; composed by Geláleddîn, surnamed Rúmi – this poem is greatly admired in Persian, and it really deserves admiration. (5:324–5)

Jones' *Grammar of the Persian Language* (1771) became the principal text for students of the language in England. **Edward FitzGerald** (1809–83), who was reading this grammar in the winter of 1853–1854, found it so delightful and full of poetic taste that he admitted to "a sort of Love for it." Jones' grammar included a brief mention of "the Mesnavi of the excellent Geláleddîn" and in later editions, edited by the Rev. Samuel Lee (9th ed., London, 1828), one finds a quotation of the first line of the "Mathnavî" of "Mawlawi Rúm," as a prosodic example, along with a summary translation (probably added by Lee):

> Hear from the reed when it tells a tale;
> And of separations it laments.

By the middle of the nineteenth century, though Hâfez' *Divân* in England and Saᶜdi's *Golestân* in British India enjoyed far greater fame, students of Persian had also begun reading parts of Rumi's *Masnavi*. **Edward Byles Cowell** (1826–1903), a brewer's son from Ipswich who proved a brilliant linguist in school, had learned Persian by the tender age of sixteen through Major W.B. Hockley of the Indian army, upon whom Edward FitzGerald would also call for help with the language. Though Cowell went on to become Professor of Sanskrit at Cambridge, he maintained an active interest in Persian and was, in fact, responsible for the course of instruction in that language. Cowell recommended the *Masnavi* to his students, setting it as part of the examinations for the linguistic genius **Edward Henry Palmer** (1840–83) in 1867 (AOE 127–8). Palmer eventually included a few of the Rumi *études* he had done in preparation for his exams in *Song of the Reed and Other Pieces* (London: Trübner, 1877).

In order to obtain a post in India, the British army now required an examination in Persian, and we find many British officers and colonial administrators stationed in India or other parts of the empire pursuing the study and translation of Persian languages – Colonel Wilberforce Clark, Major J. Stephenson, Dame Gertrude Bell. E.G. Browne, the most celebrated scholar of Persian literature, likewise studied the *Masnavi* of Rumi and the *Divân* of Hâfez in preparation for his Language Tripos exam in the summer of 1884. Cowell had collected at least two manuscripts of Rumi's *Divân*, which were later made available to Browne and Nicholson for their researches (for Cowell and Palmer, see also "Rumi in the English Speaking World" in chapter 14).

EDITIONS AND STUDIES OF RUMI

Edward Granville Browne (1862–1926), Professor of Persian at Cambridge University, displayed a remarkable interest in the metaphysical thought of the Iranians, initially sparked by the description of the Bâbi movement in the Comte de Gobineau's *Les Religions et les philosophies dans l'Asie centrale* (1865). Besides his sympathetic enthusiasm for the Bâbi and Bahá'í religions and for the Persian Constitutional Revolution of 1906–11, Browne is best known for his four-volume magnum opus, *A Literary History of Persia* (Cambridge: Cambridge University Press, 1902, 1906, 1920, 1924), which provides extensive extracts in translation of Persian poetry and prose, and though somewhat dated, remains even today the best available continuous narrative of the intellectual history of Iran in English. Browne calls Rumi "without doubt the most eminent Sufi poet whom Persia has produced, while his mystical Mathnawí deserves to rank amongst the great poems of all time" (BLH 2:515). Browne's outline history of Rumi's life has the particulars generally correct, though he believed Shams to have been killed in a riot in Konya along with Rumi's elder son. Browne wished to believe Aflâki, who wrote only forty-five years after Rumi's death at the instruction of the latter's grandson, but he nevertheless recognized that Aflâki records much that is "quite incredible" and his account is "marred by not a few anachronisms and other inconsistencies" (BLH 2:519).

Browne provides a translation of the prose preface to Book 1 of the *Masnavi*, which Rumi described as "the roots of the roots of the roots of religion," and also his own verse rendering, in high Victorian style, of the story of the Jewish vizier from the *Masnavi* (BLH 2:519–20). Ultimately, however, Browne's cultivation of the career of Reynold Alleyne Nicholson, who must be regarded, along with Badiᶜ al-Zamân Foruzânfar, as the century's greatest scholar of Rumi, proved of far more importance than Browne's own researches in this regard. In the introduction to his edition of the *Masnavi*, Nicholson credits Browne with suggesting, though not in so many words, that he undertake the project of editing and translating Rumi, by reading with him and helping him to appreciate the "Persian Koran."

REYNOLD ALLEYNE NICHOLSON

Unlike many a flamboyant British orientalist with passions tending to politics and exploration, **R.A. Nicholson** (1868–1945) came from a family of academics (his grandfather, a follower of Swedenborg, was a Biblical scholar) and greatly preferred, when not golfing, to sit in his study with his books. In all his years of study of Persian and Arabic, Nicholson never once visited the Middle East and he never learned to speak the languages whose literatures were the object of his study, though he could read and interpret them better than most native speakers. After losing interest in his first field, classics, Nicholson turned to Arabic and Persian, passing the Indian Languages Tripos in 1892, becoming a Fellow of Trinity College, Cambridge, and eventually lecturer in Persian, a position he held from 1902 until the death of E.G. Browne in 1926, at which point Nicholson became Sir Thomas Adams Professor of Arabic (1926–33).

Throughout a distinguished career of scholarly publication, Nicholson's many studies and translations of Persian and Arabic poetry, and of the manuals and doctrines of Sufism, demonstrated the great extent to which Islamic philosophy was indebted to Neoplatonism. Nicholson's correspondence with Sir Muhammad Iqbal, the future exponent of the state of Pakistan, who had studied for a brief time at Cambridge, helped in some way to shape Iqbal's thinking and thereby contributed to the development of modern Islamic philosophy.

Nicholson's first and greatest love, not surprising in view of his contemplative temperament, however, was Jalâl al-Din Rumi. At the age of thirty, Nicholson published his *Selected Poems from the Dívâni Shamsi Tabríz* (Cambridge: Cambridge University Press, 1898), which provided the first text-critical edition of a collection of poems by Rumi, along with facing English translation, introduction and extensive notes. This volume, reissued in 1952 and made available in paperback in 1977, continues to aid students of Persian literature and of Sufism wishing to read Rumi in the original. It must, however, be used with great caution, since Foruzânfar's critical edition of the *Divân* (see below) rejects seven of the fifty poems Nicholson found attributed to Rumi in the manuscript tradition as unauthentic. Any publishers contemplating reprints of this work should add a notice to the effect that these poems (i.e., numbers IV, VIII, XII, XVII, XXXI, XXXIII and XLIV) are no longer thought to come from the pen of Rumi.

Although Nicholson's verse translations from Persian and Arabic have not aged particularly well, many in Edwardian England, including his teacher Browne, considered them quite beautiful. Nicholson's prose translations, however, are not so dated as his verse, and in a 1924 article in the Centenary Supplement to the *Journal of the Royal Asiatic Society,* Nicholson first introduced the West to the Discourses of Rumi, *Fihe mâ fih* (available heretofore only in manuscript, since the Persian text had not yet been published at that time). He later published brief specimens of the work in translation, suggesting to his student, A.J. Arberry, the idea of providing a full translation.

Nicholson's greatest work, though, was his edition, translation and commentary on Rumi's *Masnavi.* For Nicholson, the *Masnavi*

> exhibits more fully than the *Díwán-i Shams-i Tabríz,* the marvellous range of Jalálu'ddín's poetic genius. His Odes reach the utmost heights of which a poetry inspired by vision and rapture is capable, and these alone would have made him the unchallenged laureate of Mysticism. But they move in a world remote from ordinary experience, open to none but "the unveiled," whereas the Mathnawí is chiefly concerned with problems and speculations bearing on the conduct, use, and meaning of Life. (AOE 221)

Oddly enough, Nicholson could not at all appreciate the style and language of the Koran, and early on in his studies, he likewise spoke of the teachings of Jalâl al-Din Rumi as "allegorical, rambling, tedious, often obscure," in comparison to the "systematic, precise and lucid" nature of Ghazzâli's thought.[2]

Even so, Nicholson found Rumi more profound than Ghazzâli, and far preferable to the Koran, though the *Masnavi* was written in explanation of the esoteric meaning of the Koran:

> This vast rambling discourse provides instruction and entertainment for all seekers. Few would care to read it through; but everyone can find in it something to suit his taste, from abstruse and recondite theories of mystical philosophy to anecdotes of a certain kind, which are told in the plainest terms possible. (AOE 221–2)

Not contented simply to work from the available printed editions of the *Masnavi* and the existing Turkish commentaries, Nicholson set about editing the more than 25,000 lines of the poem from a variety of medieval and early modern manuscripts. Nicholson spared no pains in this task; after deciding to translate the obscene lines into Latin, he studied Juvenal and Persius in order to perfect an authentic ribald poetic idiom in Latin (AOE 223). The task consumed eight volumes and fifteen years, from 1925 to 1940, and it also sapped the power of sight from Nicholson's eyes. But the result was an excellent critical edition of the Persian text, and a full translation, supplemented by extensive notes and commentary intended to facilitate the scholarly study of the text, particularly the theosophy of Rumi. The notes include references to earlier Sufi doctrines and poets, giving specific relevant background information to help with the understanding of Rumi's allusions.

Before this scholarly project was completed, Nicholson condensed the results of his labors on the *Masnavi* into a collection of under two hundred pages intended for a popular audience. The *Tales of Mystic Meaning, Being Selections from the Mathnawi of Jalal-ud-Din Rumi* (London: Chapman & Hall; New York: Frederick Stokes, 1931) presented fifty-one of the choicest stories with an introduction in which Nicholson explained something of the ramifications of the *Masnavi* and the nature of Rumi's teachings.

Nicholson had intended to produce an authoritative account of Rumi's life, but did not live to fulfill this expectation. He did compile a selection of poems "illustrating Sufi doctrine and experience as depicted by the greatest of Iranian mystical poets, Jalâluʾl-Dîn Rûmî," which appeared posthumously, edited by Nicholson's erstwhile student, A.J. Arberry (see below), as *Rumi: Poet and Mystic* (London: Allen & Unwin, 1950). Unwin reprinted this volume a half dozen times through the 1970s and Oneworld has made the book available since 1995. It has continued to inspire several generations of readers with its perspicacious translations (see chapter 14, below).

Nicholson's dedication of his life's work to Rumi sparked the interest of many other scholars and amateurs, and his Persian edition of the text of the *Masnavi* remains the most widely read and referenced text of the poem not only in the West, but also in India and in Iran itself, though scholars will now want to refer to the more accurate editions of Esteʿlâmi and Gölpınarlı. Despite the proliferation of newer *Masnavi* commentaries in Iran and Turkey, Nicholson's commentary has recently been translated to Persian by Hasan Lâhuti with an introduction by Jalâl al-Din Ashtiâni (Tehran: ʿElmi va Farhangi, 1995). It remains useful because most writers and translators have taken their quotations from the *Masnavi* following the numbering of Nicholson's edition of the text.

When Nicholson died, Badiʿ al-Zamân Foruzânfar, who perhaps later surpassed Nicholson as this century's most prolific Rumi scholar, composed a long elegy in Persian verse to pay him homage.

ARTHUR JOHN ARBERRY

Born into a poor and puritanical Christian family, **A.J. Arberry** (1905–69) lost his faith largely as a result of reading George Bernard Shaw. Transformed by his encounter with Islamic mysticism, however, Arberry resumed actively practicing Christianity, with the realization, no doubt learned from Rumi, that "Jew, Muslim, Hindu, Buddhist, Parsi – all sorts and conditions of men" were and are illuminated by God, "the One Universal," whose light, as the Koran states, is neither of East nor West (MPR 2:xiii–xiv). Arberry met and began studying with Nicholson at Cambridge in 1927, after completing the examinations in classics; reflecting over his career toward the end of his life, Arberry described his encounter with Nicholson as the turning point of his life. Arberry went on to obtain his doctorate in 1936 and after stints teaching classics in Cairo, as a librarian in the India Office and as Professor of Persian at the University of London, he returned to Cambridge to assume the Sir Thomas Adams Chair of Arabic after the death of Nicholson, a position he held until his death in 1969.

Translator of the Koran and many works from Persian and Arabic, as well as an editor of manuscripts, the prolific Arberry also authored general introductions to Sufism and Middle Eastern literature, as well as two histories of British orientalists. Extensive as had been his teacher, Nicholson's, work on Rumi, Arberry did manage to find some solid ground of his own to cover, contributing to our understanding of Rumi over the course of his career with a number of scholarly translations. First, taking a cue from the popularity of FitzGerald's translation of Khayyâm, Arberry culled a selection from the quatrains found in the *Divân-e Shams* (though not all of these can be considered genuine compositions of Rumi), and put them into English verse as *The Rubaʿiyat of Jalal ul-Din Rumi* (London: Emery Walker, 1949). He next translated the important collection of Rumi's lectures, *Fihe mâ fih*, as *Discourses of Rumi* (London: John Murray, 1961; several reprints).

Arberry was hoping, toward the end of his life, to publish a complete study of the life, writings and teachings of Rumi, including "an extended analysis of the contents, pattern and doctrine of the Masnavi" (ATM 18). He did not live to complete this task, but he did make several further contributions to the spread of knowledge about Rumi, all of which remain quite important.

As a work for the general public, Arberry prepared two hundred of the stories told by Rumi as *Tales from the Masnavi* and *More Tales from the Masnavi* (London: Allen & Unwin, 1961 and 1963, respectively), the first of which includes an introductory sketch about the background and nature of Rumi's magnum opus. Arberry described his method as "putting the original verse-couplets into rhythmical prose," to which spare notes were added. One of the stories presented in the first volume, "The Jewish King and the Christian," occasioned unfavorable comment from post-Holocaust readers, who considered the story anti-Semitic, and found it shocking either that the mystic Rumi would have composed it, or that Arberry would retell it. Arberry admits in the introduction to the second volume that he had not anticipated such criticism and apologizes for failing to take such sensitivities into account. He explains that

Rumi, who accepted wholeheartedly the Jewish prophets, did not mean any disrespect to Judaism, per se, but that he often criticized the failings of believers – Christians and Muslims, as well as Jews – to live up to the dictates of their respective religions. He goes on to point out that Rumi viewed all acts, good and evil, as part of God's purpose, appearing evil only in relation to our limited view of existence. With this apologia, Arberry pointed out that another such story, "The Devotion of Bilal," was appearing in the second volume, but posed the question: "To a man of such all-embracing charity, how can so base a motive as anti-Semitism be imputed?"

Arberry had hoped to continue work on the *Masnavi* with a third book in this series, reflecting the view, already espoused by Nicholson, that the tales were what held an audience's attention, and reading through the whole work tended to confuse the reader because of its desultoriness. After presenting the two hundred most interesting tales, Arberry hoped to present translations from "the didactic passages which intersperse, and very frequently interrupt these tales." A methodical arrangement of such passages would make Rumi's "theological and mystical doctrine self-explanatory" and the role that the tales play in "illustrating that somewhat complex and abstruse doctrine" would become clear. Arberry did not, however, manage to bring this plan to completion; instead, he next presented an extended selection of Bahâ al-Din Valad's discourses, which he included in a book of source texts called *Aspects of Islamic Civilization as Depicted in the Original Texts* (New York: A.S. Barnes; London: Allen & Unwin, 1964; several reprints). No full translation into English of Bahâ al-Din's *Maʿâref* has as yet been attempted, though the present author has the project in mind.

In 1963, **Ehsan Yarshater**, then Professor of Persian at Columbia University and editor of the Persian Heritage series (and now editor of the remarkable *Encyclopaedia Iranica*), determined to make further selections of the *Divân-e Shams* available to English readers. Yarshater, remarking that Rumi's collection of ghazals contains "some of the most inspiring poems written in the Persian language," unsurpassed in "sheer depth and exuberance of feeling," noted that the *Divân* had nevertheless remained largely untranslated into English, with the exception of the fifty poems published by Nicholson more than sixty years earlier. Yarshater therefore invited Arberry, whom he considered the "outstanding choice" because of his knowledge of Persian literature, his extensive experience in translating and his "personal affinities with the mystical thought of the poet," to undertake this "most difficult task" (MPR 2:vii).

We may consider the two resulting volumes, *Mystical Poems of Rūmī* (London: Allen & Unwin; Chicago: University of Chicago Press, 1968; reprint 1972) and *Mystical Poems of Rūmī, 2* (Chicago: University of Chicago Press, 1979; reprint, 1991), which provide literal lineated prose versions of four hundred ghazals, as Arberry's most important contribution to the dissemination of the poetry and thought of Rumi in the West. Though he did not live to see the publication of the second volume, the manuscript of which was annotated and prepared for publication by Professor Hasan Javadi (one of my own teachers at Berkeley), Arberry has exercised an enduring influence on the current generation of translators; both those who know and those who do not know Persian rely, at least in part, upon his literal renderings of the poems from the *Divân-e Shams* for the meaning of what Rumi wrote.

Arberry was a public intellectual, well known in the Anglo-American world. When he died in 1969, obituary articles appeared in the *Times Literary Supplement* (August 29), *Books Abroad* (Summer 1969), the *Spectator* (October 2), the *New York Times Book Review* (October 5) and the *Christian Century* (December 3). For more on his translations, see chapter 14.

STUDIES OF RUMI'S PHILOSOPHY

Though the teachings of Rumi were handed down from generation to generation within the Mevlevi order in the Ottoman domains until the closure of the dervish lodges under Atatürk, the method of transmission from shaykh to disciple naturally focused on the implementation of Rumi's teachings in the individual and personal experience of the adepts, not on a systematic understanding of Rumi as a philosophical thinker. In India and the Arab world, as we have seen, many commentaries have been written on the *Masnavi*, but most of these proceed verse by verse with the object of explicating the meaning, and interpreting it in terms of Ibn ᶜArabi's theosophy. Few of the medieval commentaries make the attempt to codify and systematize Rumi's teachings.

The effort to expound the teachings of Rumi in terms of modern scholarly methodology can be said to have begun in the work of the great Indian scholar of Persian literature **Shebli Noᶜmâni** (1857–1916). In addition to his history of Persian literature, Shebli wrote a study of Rumi's life published in 1909 as *Savâneh-e Mowlânâ Rum* (see chapter 11), in which he made a brief effort to group the contents of the *Masnavi* under various philosophical and religious categories. Nicholson likewise had made a preliminary effort in this direction by collecting disparate verses of Rumi under philosophical headings in his *Selected Poems from the Dīvān* in 1898. As we have seen, the Muslim philosopher Muhammad Iqbal had also adumbrated the teachings of Rumi in modern form in a number of his poems, but rather than set forth the basic teachings of Rumi, Iqbal utilized them to expound his own philosophy.

Khalifa ᶜAbdul Hakim, an Indian Muslim who obtained his doctorate at the University of Heidelberg in Germany, inspired in part, no doubt, by Iqbal's interest in Rumi, wrote as his dissertation in 1925 *The Metaphysics of Rumi*, which was published in book form in English in 1933. At that time, neither Nicholson's critical edition of the *Masnavi* nor Foruzânfar's edition of the *Divân-e Shams* was as yet available and Dr. ᶜAbdul Hakim was therefore compelled to rely upon the text of faulty nineteenth-century lithographed editions of Rumi's poems. Furthermore, he did not provide translations of most of the verses quoted. After the publication of Nicholson's critical edition and translation of the *Masnavi*, ʿAbdul Hakim wished to prepare a second edition of his book quoting the Persian text as it appears in Nicholson's edition, followed by Nicholson's translation. He died before this task could be completed, but Bashir Ahmad Dar undertook this labor and a posthumous second edition of Hakim's *The Metaphysics of Rumi: A Critical and Historical Sketch* was published by the Institute of Islamic Culture in Lahore, Pakistan, in 1959.

The Metaphysics of Rumi attempts to trace the history of certain concepts in the Koran and early Sufism before coming to Rumi's particular formulation of the problem. ʿAbdul Hakim sees Rumi as an eclectic Islamic thinker, in whose work is reflected the "Semitic monotheism" of the Koran; Platonic, Peripatetic, Pythagorean and Neoplatonic philosophy; scholastic theology; Avicenna's epistemology; Ghazzâli's prophetology and Ibn ʿArabi's Monism. In short, Rumi's *Masnavi* provides "an unsystematic epitome of all the philosophical and theological thoughts developed in Islam" (KAH 9). As such, ʿAbdul Hakim is conscious that a systematic theology of Rumi would require several volumes to unravel the various strains of thought and the method in which Rumi weaves them together. He has something more modest in mind, and chooses to focus on "the problem of Personality, divine and human," the "central problem" with which Rumi grapples (KAH 3). The chapter rubrics of the book, however, provide a list of Rumi's major concerns as identified by ʿAbdul Hakim: The Nature of the Soul, The Problem of Creation, Evolution, Love, Freedom of the Will, The Ideal Man, The Survival of Personality, God and Sufi Pantheism. Dr. ʿAbdul Hakim finds the attempt to distill the essence of Rumi's thought a laborious task requiring "a good deal of patience." He repeatedly expresses irritation at Rumi (as did Hakim's teacher, Nicholson), for not having organized his teachings in systematic linear fashion (KAH 3, 7, 9, etc.). In his frustration, Hakim calls him "an awfully boring teacher" and a "painfully unsystematic writer" in contrast, for example, to Ghazzâli, who is "systematic, precise and lucid," though seldom able to match Rumi in passion or profundity. Though a relatively short work, *The Metaphysics of Rumi* laid the groundwork for later studies of Rumi's theology.

Afzal Iqbal (1919–94) was born in Lahore, attended the Government College there and then the University of the Punjab. After the partition of India, he became a Pakistani citizen and served between 1950 and 1979 in the Ministry of Foreign Affairs as part of Pakistan's legations to Iran and a number of other countries. Afzal Iqbal translated Camus into Urdu and published two volumes of his own Urdu poetry, but when he was invited to lecture to audiences at universities around the world, it was in his capacity as author of works in English. These included such topics as the history of the Khilafat movement and modern Islam, the formation of Pakistan, Islamic history and culture, and, of course, Rumi. His study of Rumi, *The Life and Thought of Maulana Jalaluddin Rumi*, building upon Hakim's foray into the intellectual sources of Rumi, set forth Rumi's ideas in a more organized and comprehensive way. This work, the first attempt at a book-length biography of Rumi in English, has proved quite influential through its many revisions and reprintings, and in the form of Turkish, Urdu and Persian translations. *The Life and Thought* was first published in 1956 (Lahore: Bazm-i Iqbal) and a revised edition, incorporating the suggestions of "learned critics in Asia and Europe" (viii), appeared in 1964 with a foreword by A.J. Arberry. For the third edition, which would have appeared in 1973 to mark the 700th anniversary of Rumi's death were it not delayed by labor disputes, Iqbal thoroughly revised everything but the first chapter and gave the effort a slightly different name, *The Life and Work of Muhammad Jalal-ud-Din Rumi* (Lahore: Institute of Islamic Culture, 1974 and 1978). This was followed by further editions (5th ed., London: Octagon, 1983; 6th ed., Islamabad: Pakistan National Council of Arts, 1991) and a Persian translation (Tehran: Nashr-e Markaz, 1375/1996).

Iqbal set out to supplement the "outstanding work" of "Professor Farozan Far" (sic), which, however failed to provide much of the cultural context "so necessary for investing a personality with any degree of tangibility" (ix). Acknowledging the translations of Redhouse, Whinfield, Wilson and Nicholson, Iqbal points out that they provide little in the way of information about the poet's life. Iqbal expresses disappointment over Nicholson's posthumous *Rumi: Poet and Mystic*, because Nicholson was supposed to have left behind copious biographical materials on the poet. Afzal draws instead upon Shebli's Urdu biography, but points out that Shebli did not have access to *Fihe mâ fih* or to Shams' *Maqâlât*. Beyond all the scholarly justifications for the work, however, a personal devotion to Rumi as a spiritual teacher who "helped me solve many a vexed problem of my life" (2) motivated Afzal Iqbal, who undoubtedly looked upon Rumi through the eyes of his modern compatriot and namesake, Muhammad Iqbal. Afzal asked Foruzânfar's help in obtaining an illustration of Rumi, for he had never seen any portrait of the Master and longed to know what he looked like. Afzal Iqbal eventually received a copy of a portrait of Rumi done in the sixteenth century, which he treated as if it were an authentic likeness, subjecting it to a physiological analysis reminiscent of craniology and Victorian character studies (1).

Afzal Iqbal's study seeks to "reconstruct the atmosphere – political, social, economic and literary" of Rumi's time, and proceeds from there to periodize Rumi's life into the formative and student years of 1207 to 1244, followed by the encounter with Shams and the resulting revolution he produced within Rumi, from 1245 to 1261. In subsequent chapters, Iqbal discusses the *Divân* as the product of a lyrical period brought about by this revolution, and the

Masnavi as a product of the years from 1261 to 1273. He then turns his attention to chapters on the message of the *Masnavi* and "The Poet as Thinker." The final chapter helpfully renders the Latin passages from Nicholson's translation of the *Mathnawi* into English, affording modern readers with no training in classics an understanding of the naughty vignettes from the *Masnavi*.

Afzal Iqbal later published a study called *The Impact of Maulana Jalaluddin Rumi on Islamic Culture* (Tehran: Regional Cultural Institute, 1975; Persian translation, 1985), and is the author of *Reflections on Rumi* and a volume of Urdu verse, both in press.

ANNEMARIE SCHIMMEL

Annemarie Schimmel (1922–), who has spent most of her life reading and living with Islamic and particularly Sufi texts from the perspective of a believer and an academic, introduces the thought of Rumi in several works, both German and English, notably *The Triumphal Sun: A Study of the Works of Jalâloddin Rumi* (London: Fine Books, 1978; London: East–West Publications, 1980; 2nd ed., Albany, NY: SUNY Press, 1993) and *I am Wind, You are Fire: The Life and Work of Rumi* (Boston, MA: Shambhala, 1992). Her wide reading in the sources of Indian Islam and Sufism gives her an expansive perspective on what Rumi has meant in the Muslim world, a theme she treats often, including but not limited to a chapter from *The Triumphal Sun* and also in her essay "Mawlânâ Rûmî: Yesterday, Today and Tomorrow" (Poe 5–27). Her study *Friedrich Rückert: Lebensbild und Einführung in sein Werk* (Freiburg im Breisgau: Herder, 1987) details Rumi's influence on German Romanticism. Beyond this, her intimate familiarity with Rumi comes from repeated reading of his poems over a long period of time, beginning with her translations of his poetry in 1948 and her study of his imagery in *Die Bildersprache Dschelâladdin Rumis* (vol. 2 of *Beiträge zur Sprach- und Kulturgeschichte des Orients*; Walldorf-Hessen: Verlag für Orientkunde Dr. H. Vorandran, 1949). She has translated not only the poems, but also the "Discourses" (*Fîhe mâ fîh*) into German, which appeared as *Von Allem und vom Einen* (Munich: Diederichs, 1988).

Schimmel's commitment to Rumiology is longstanding. She was the first European to address the gathering of members of parliament at the commemoration of the anniversary of Rumi's birth on December 17, 1954 in Konya (RiM 249). As an introduction to the sense of Rumi's work, her books are an excellent choice, particularly *The Triumphal Sun* and, for a more general public, *I am Wind You are Fire*, which the title page insists is not a translation of her German work by the same title, *"Ich bin Wind und du bist Feuer"; Rumi, Leben und Werk des Mystikers* (Munich: Diederichs, 1991).

Schimmel provides a long investigation into Rumi's theology in her *Triumphal Sun* (ScT 225–336) which provides copious citations from Koran, Hadith and the prose and poetry of Rumi. Her grounding of Rumi in the specifics of the Islamic tradition is quite useful, especially as a corrective to portrayals of Rumi as a non-denominational mystic. However, one sometimes gets the sense that Schimmel seizes on a wide variety of different statements or allusions and presents them as representations of fixed or elaborated doctrines, whereas often in the particular context in which Rumi employs them they seem to be passing allusions to symbols, beliefs and debates within the Islamic tradition, rather than arguments or considered positions on the issues raised. Indeed, as a preacher, Rumi tends to employ such allusions to rhetorical effort to embroider his ethical points.

Nevertheless, Schimmel, like ʿAbdul Hakim before her, tries to isolate several important issues that Rumi elaborates in an original or consistent manner, including the station of man, Revelation and the role of the prophets, the progression of matter and spirit through the world of existence, the nature of love and the function of prayer. Schimmel marshals a great deal of evidence, displaying long years of reading in Rumi, but not infrequently makes errors of citation, fudges matters or is too quick to credit the reports of Aflâki. Despite such problems, though, Schimmel has provided us with extremely useful resources in her *Triumphal Sun* and creative yet learned ways of approaching Rumi.

Full as she is of insight and information, for those trying to track down references or establish historical facts, Schimmel is unfortunately not always precise in her citations. She is a voracious reader of primary texts from Muslim India as well as from Iran and Turkey, and she admirably assimilates and internalizes the information in the text, but her reading of secondary materials in Persian is not extensive, and she sometimes fails adequately to incorporate Western scholarship, as well. For example, in more than one of her books, Schimmel refers to Foruzânfar as the editor of Sepahsâlâr's *Resâle*, though the Tehran edition of 1325/1946–7 which Schimmel cites in her bibliography was undertaken by Saʿid Nafisi (1895–1966), rather than Foruzânfar, as the title page of the book clearly states. To carp at such oversights may seem petty and contentious, but other scholars rely upon Schimmel's *Triumphal Sun,* her *Mystical Dimensions of Islam* (1975) and her *As Through a Veil* (1982) as bibliographical references for Rumi, so her errors are widely replicated (e.g., Fatemeh Keshavarz in *Reading Mystical Lyric*). Unfortunately, this is not the only problem in her citations.[3] To be fair, *Triumphal Sun* includes a huge number of items in its bibliography and provides extremely useful information in an easily accessible form; but the reader should be forewarned to doublecheck Schimmel's references.

RUMI IN GERMAN SCHOLARSHIP

Among German scholars who have devoted their attention to Sufism, the systematic and exacting standards of Hellmut Ritter, Fritz Meier, Richard

Gramlich and J.C. Bürgel are truly admirable. Consider, for example, the Swiss scholar **Fritz Meier**'s (1912–98) work on Bahâ al-Din Valad, *Bahâ²-i Walad: Grundzüge seines Lebens und seiner Mystik* (Leiden: Brill, 1989), running to over 450 pages. Meier has done more than any other single person in the West to clarify the biographical details and theology of Rumi's father and, thereby, Rumi himself. Meier's thorough and precise study provides an amazing mine of carefully researched and carefully considered information, as well as a wealth of insightful analysis about Rumi's family and their area of operations.

Meier's 1976 work, *Abū Saʿīd-i Abū al-Hayr: Wirklichkeit und Legende* (Tehran and Liège: Bibliothèque Pahlavi, 1976), although it deals with a Sufi who lived two centuries before Rumi and Shams-e Tabrizi, nevertheless includes extensive references to the *Maqâlât-e Shams* wherever it is pertinent to various Sufi concepts. By contrast, Schimmel, who published her large book about Rumi (*The Triumphal Sun*) two years later in 1978, did not even bother to consult the *Maqâlât* of Shams, contenting herself with citation of the portions mentioned by Gölpınarlı in his biography of Rumi! What's more, Meier includes numerous references and even translates passages from the "Treatise" of Sepahsâlâr. He also published studies of the "dervish dance" ("Der Derwischtanz: Versuch eines Überblicks," *Asiatische Studien* 8 [1954]: 107–36) and the ceremonies commemorating the 700th anniversary of Rumi's death ("Zum 700. Todestag Mawlânâs, des Vaters der Tanzenden Derwische," *Asiatische Studien* [1974]).

Much of Meier's research is predicated upon the efforts of **Hellmut Ritter** (1892–1971), who uncovered in Istanbul the manuscripts of the *Masnavi* that Nicholson had used in making his critical edition. Ritter began publishing a series of articles about Rumi in the journal of the German Oriental Society, *Zeitschrift der Deutschen Morgenländenischen Gesellschaft*, including a study of the sources of Rumi's mysticism ("Die Flötenmystik Ĝalâladdîn Rumis und ihre Quellen," no. 92, 1932) and a study of the eighteen opening lines of the *Masnavi* ("Das Pröomium des Maṯnawî-i Mawlawî," no. 93,1 [1933]: 169–96). In subsequent years, he followed these up with articles about the history of Rumi and his circle in *Der Islam* ("Maulânâ Ĝalâluddîn Rûmî" und sein Kreis: Philologika XI," no. 26, [1942]: 116–58 and 221–49), which laid the groundwork for his article "Djalâl al-Dîn Rûmî" in the *Encyclopaedia of Islam* and his article on Rumi in the Turkish *Islâm Ansiklopedisi*. Ritter also wrote an important review article of newer works on Rumi and the Mevlevi order ("Neue Literatur über Maulânâ Ĝalâluddin Rûmî" und seinen Orden," *Oriens* 13–14 [1960–61]: 342–54), and two articles about *samâʿ*: "Der Reigen der 'Tanzende Derwische,'" *Zeitschr. für Vergleichende Musikwissenschaft* 1 ([1933]: 28–40), and the ceremonies commemorating Rumi's death anniversary in Konya, "Die Mevlânafeier in Konya vom 11.17. Dezember 1960" (*Oriens* 15 [1962]). Ritter's amazing study of ʿAttâr, "The Sea of Soul," *Das Meer der Seele:*

Welt, Mensche und Gott in den Geschichten des Farîduddîn ʿAttâr (Leiden: Brill, 1955; reprinted 1978 and soon to be available in English translation), provides excellent and even indispensable background to the study of Rumi's thought.

RUMI IN FRENCH SCHOLARSHIP

A French translation and commentary on the *Masnavi* was prepared at the end of the eighteenth century, but never published (see chapter 14). Had it been available for study, perhaps the Baron Bernard Carra de Vaux (b. 1867) would not have found the structure of the *Masnavi* so disconcerting:

> The composition of the Ma<u>th</u>nawí is, it must be granted, very disjointed; the stories follow one another in no order, the examples suggest reflections which in their turn suggest others so that the narrative is often interrupted by long digressions; but this want of order seems to be a result of the lyrical inspiration, which carries the poet along as if by leaps and bounds, and if the reader yields to it, the effect is by no means displeasing. It would be fatiguing to read the book right through, but if one opens this immense poem by chance and reads a few pages, one cannot fail to be deeply impressed.

In addition to the article on Rumi for the first edition of the *Encyclopaedia of Islam* (s.v. Djalál al-Dín Rúmí), where the passage above appears, Carra de Vaux devoted several pages (291–306) to Rumi in his study of the mystical philosopher al-Ghazzâli, *Gazali* (Paris: Alcan, 1902; reprint, Amsterdam: Philo, 1974). In France, however, undoubtedly because no translation of the poems of Rumi captured the imagination of the French-speaking public as it had in Germany, French interest in Sufism turned to other subjects, such as Mansur al-Hallâj, to whom Louis Massignon devoted his intense spiritual and scholarly interest. Massignon in his *Essai sur les origines du lexique technique de la mystique musulmane* (Paris: J. Vrin, 1928; now available in English translation) and the Jesuit Paul Nwyia in his *Exégèse coranique et langage mystique* (Beirut: Dar El-Maschreq Éditeurs, 1970) both devoted minute attention to the vocabulary of Sufism. These studies provide important background information for the Sufi terminology Rumi uses, even though they do not specifically address Rumi.

If French scholars did not join the Rumi bandwagon early on, the whirling dervishes nevertheless proved an abiding interest of French travelers to the Middle East. **Clément Huart** (1854–1926), author of many literary, historical and geographical studies on the Middle East, as well as translations of Persian and Arabic works, discussed Konya, "the city of the whirling dervishes," at length in his *Konia, la ville des derviches tourneurs: souvenirs d'un voyage en Asie mineure* (Paris: Ernest Leroux, 1897). A quarter century later he revisited the subject with his two-volume translation of Aflâki's hagiography of whirling dervish saints, *Les Saints des derviches tourneurs* (Paris: Ernest Leroux, 1918–22). This proved an important source for later writers on Rumi, though it unfortunately accorded an undeserved authority to Aflâki as a historical source;

furthermore, subsequent scholars have pointed to many errors in Huart's translation.

One of Huart's readers was **Maurice Barrès** (1862–1923), whom we have already met (see chapter 12 above) as one of those Western travelers deeply impressed by the Mevlevis and their turning ceremony. Perhaps the philosopher **Henri Bergson** (d. 1941) read about Rumi in the work of Barrès, for the father of modern Iranian literature, Mohammad-ʿAli Jamâlzâde, who lived much of his life in Europe, claims that Bergson used to say in his lectures at the Sorbonne that Rumi's *Masnavi* was one of the most important books that mankind had yet produced ("Mowlânâ va Masnavi," in *Yâd nâme-ye Mowlavi*, ed. ʿAli-Akbar Moshir-Salimi [Tehran: UNESCO–Iran Commission, 1337/1958] 17). **Raymond Renefer** (1879–1957), an artist and illustrator, who had earlier illustrated one of the books of Maurice Barrès, almost certainly learned of Rumi through Barrès. Renefer, writing shortly after the war under the pseudonym Myriam Harry, penned a biography of Rumi as mystic dancer and poet, *Djelaleddine Roumi, poète et danseur mystique* (Paris: Flammarion, 1947). A Turk studying in Paris, I. Teymourtache, wrote his thesis in 1952 on Rumi, "Le Mysticisme de Djalâl-od-Dîn Rûmî," an important study including many translations, which unfortunately did not find a publisher; however, it did provide the basis, along with A.H. Tchélébi's translations of Rumi's quatrains (see chapter 14, below), for the lead article by Pierre Robin, "Djelal-eddin El Roumi, poète et danseur mystique" (Harry's book evidently provided the name), in the August 1955 issue of the cultural journal *Cahiers du Sud*. Two decades later, a commemorative booklet for the 700th anniversary of Rumi's death was published in French by the Iranian scholar Zabih Allâh Safâ as *Djalâl al-Din Mawlavi: grand penseur et poète* (Tehran: Conseil Supérieur de la Culture et des Arts, 1974).

The dance of the dervishes has never ceased to fascinate the French; Marijan Molé has provided an excellent extended study of the sacred dance of the Mevlevi dervishes in his article "La Danse extatique en Islam" in the compendium *Les Danses sacrées* (Paris: Éditions du Sevil, 1963, 4:145–280). Oddly, however, the prolific and imaginative **Henri Corbin**, whose works innovatively and in considerable depth treat the cosmological and esoteric doctrines of Iranian Islam, in particular those of Shehâb al-Din Sohravardi (d. 1191), a near contemporary of Bahâ al-Din Valad, was not much attracted to Rumi, orienting himself rather to the Illuminationist (*eshrâqi*) theosophers and to Ibn ʿArabi. His four-volume work on Iranian Islam (*En Islam iranien*, 1971) and his "Man of Light in Iranian Sufism" (*L'Homme de lumière dans le soufisme iranien*, 1971) devote precious little attention to Rumi, though he does see the influence of Rumi's *Masnavi* – specifically the story about the Holy Spirit appearing to Maryam (M3:3769) – on Mir Dâmâd (d. 1631?), a philosopher of the Isfahan school who apotheosizes Mary as a feminine archetype of mystical union. Corbin's musings on the "Sophianic Feminine" have, however, inspired at least one brief comparative study of the imagery of Rumi and Ibn ʿArabi in English by R.W.J. Austin (LCP 233–45), and two books: Sachiko Murata's *The Tao of Islam: A Sourcebook on Gender Relationships in Islamic Thought* (Albany, NY: SUNY Press, 1992), which provides some quotations from Rumi about the *feminina divina*; and Annemarie Schimmel's *My Soul is a Woman: The Feminine in Islam* (New York: Continuum, 1997), which provides extracts from stories in Rumi's *Masnavi* concerning women and their qualities.

In 1948 René Patris had published a "garland from Iran," *La Guirlande de l'Iran* (Paris: Flammarion), featuring adaptations of Persian poems along with twenty-five Persian miniatures; it includes Ferdowsi, Nezâmi, Khayyâm, Saʿdi and Hâfez, but ignores Rumi altogether. Henri Massé's *Anthologie persane* (Paris: Payot, 1950) does not ignore Rumi, but devotes only eleven pages to him, consisting of block prose translations from the *Divân* and the *Masnavi*. The French public did not enjoy easy access to Rumi in translation until the 1970s, and only after this did Rumi himself receive sustained and detailed attention from French scholars, thanks to **Eva de Vitray-Meyerovitch**. De Vitray-Meyerovitch, a Rumi disciple, began her scholarly career with a number of translations of the modern Pakistani thinker Muhammad Iqbal, starting with his *Reconstruction of Religious Thought in Islam* (*Reconstruire la pensée religieuse de l'Islam*, Paris: Maisonneuve, 1955), followed by the *Payâm-e Mashriq: message de l'Orient* (Paris: Les Belles Lettres, 1956), in conjunction with M. Achena, and finally the work in which Rumi guides Iqbal through the heavens, the *Jâvid nâme* (*Djâvid-Nâma: le livre de l'éternité*, Paris: Albin Michel, 1962), which she translated in collaboration with M. Mokri.

Iqbal guided de Vitray-Meyerovitch's attention to Rumi, and she next set to work on two studies of his life and two translations of his works. In 1972 her study on mysticism and poetry in Islam, specifically Rumi and the Mevlevis, which originated as her *thèse des lettres* at the University of Paris, completed amidst the student upheavals of May 1968, appeared under the title *Mystique et poésie en Islam: Djalâl-od-Dîn Rûmî et l'ordre des derviches tourneurs* (Paris: Desclée de Brouwer, 4th ed., 1982). Then came *Rûmî et le soufisme* (Paris: du Seuil, 1977), published in the series "Spiritual Masters" and aimed at a wider thinking public; it has been translated to English by Simone Fattal as *Rûmî and Sufism* (Sausalito, CA: Post Apollo, 1987). This includes black-and-white photographs of Mevlevi dervishes and architectural sites associated with Rumi and presents a traditional sketch of his life, primarily on the basis of Aflâki's hagiography, and an outline of the development of the Mevlevi order. The bulk of the book is devoted to a general description of Sufism, weaving in quotations from the classical manuals of Sufism and from the poems of Rumi. The translations follow the text rather closely, in the fashion of Nicholson or Arberry, but read more poetically.

De Vitray-Meyerovitch has proven herself a devoted and indefatigable translator of the works of Rumi. Her translations include *Odes mystiques: Dîvân-e Shams-e Tabrîzî par Mawlânâ Djalâl-od-Dîn Rûmî* (Paris: Klincksieck, 1973; published as part of the Persian series in UNESCO's "Collection d'oeuvres représentatives"), a selection of poems from the *Divân-e Shams*, translated in collaboration with Mohammad Mokri, a Kurdish scholar who has written in French on the mythology of light and fire in Zoroastrianism and compiled a Persian ornithological dictionary. She then made Rumi's Discourses available to the French public as *Le Livre du dedans: Fîhi-mâ-fîhi Djalâl-ud-Dîn Rûmî* (Paris: Sindbad, 1976), though her translation of the title as "the book of the interior" is in error – it means rather "in it what is in it," a miscellany or collected fragments. She also produced the first selection of Rumi's letters in any European language, *Lettres: Djalâl-od-Dîn Rûmî* (Paris: J. Renard, 1990). In the meantime, she had taken up the cause of Sultan Valad, providing the first European-language renderings of his work, first his "Discourses," *Maître et disciple: Kitâb al-Maʿârif Sultân Valad* (Paris: Sindbad, 1982), and then his *Valad nâme* or *Ebtedâ nâme*, rendered in French as *La Parole secrète: l'enseignement du maître soufi Rumi* in collaboration with Djamchid Mortazavi (Paris: Le Rocher, 1988). Working again with Mortazavi, de Vitray-Meyerovitch produced a full translation of the *Masnavi* as *Mathnawi: la quête de l'absolu* ([Monaco]: du Rocher, 1990).

A member of the prestigious Centre National de la Recherche Scientifique (CNRS), de Vitray-Meyerovitch has also taught Islamic philosophy at the universities of al-Azhar and Ayn Shams in Cairo. Through her, some of the luminaries of contemporary French critical theory have come to know of Rumi. For example, in 1973–4, after a trip to China, the Lacanian theorist **Julia Kristeva** sponsored a seminar at the University of Paris 7 on the aesthetics and semiotics of translating "oriental" languages, in which de Vitray-Meyerovitch participated (see her "La 'Poétique' de l'Islam" in *La Traversée des signes*, ed. J. Kristeva [Paris: du Seuil, 1975, part of Philippe Sollers' series Tel Quel], 195–222). In the course of discussions, Kristeva expressed interest in Rumi's interpretation of dreams (212), in possible similarities between Rumi's teaching methods in the master–disciple relationship and Western schools of psychoanalysis (210), and finally in the semiotics of the dance (214ff.). **Gilbert Rouget**, chair of the Department of Ethnomuiscology at the Musée de l'Homme in Paris and director of research at CNRS, also relied upon de Vitray-Meyerovitch's studies, as well as those of Marijan Molé, in his study of the relations between music and possession, *Music and Trance* (French, 1980; English translation 1985). **Mircea Eliade**, one of the towering figures of comparative religion (see "Rumi, Ecumenicism and Comparative Religion," in chapter 12), also based his understanding of Rumi on de Vitray-Meyerovitch's studies and translations.

RUMI IN ROME

In 1974, a scholarly conference was held in Rome to commemorate the 700th anniversary of Rumi's death. Attended by the remarkable Persian scholar **Alessandro Bausani** (1921–88), the proceedings were published as *Nel centenario del poeta mistico persiano Galal-ad-Din Rumi* (Rome: Accademia nazionale dei Lincei, 1975). An amazingly prolific and polyglot scholar, Bausani had included a lengthy section on Rumi's theosophy in his groundbreaking study on the history of religious ideas in Iran, *Persia religiosa: da Zaratushtra a Bahâ'u'llâh* (Milan: Il Saggiatore, 1959). Bausani summarized the matter for his portion of the *Encyclopaedia of Islam* article ("Djalāl al-Dīn Rūmī") on Rumi's thought. Previously, **Martine Mario Moreno** had collected a sample of only five Rumi poems in Italian translation in his anthology of Arabo-Persian mystic poetry, *Antologia della mistica Arabo-Persiana* (Bari: G. Laterza, 1951 63–89). But Bausani added some wonderful Italian samples of Rumi in his *Persia religiosa*, as well as in his history of Persian literature, *La letterature persiana* (Florence: Sansoni, 1968) and finally in a separate volume dedicated to Rumi, entitled *Gialal ad-Din Rumi: Poesie mistiche* (Milan: B.U.R., 1980), which contains fifty ghazals and twelve quatrains. Subsequent to this, **Gabriele Mandel** devoted a portion of her *Il Sufismo, vertice della piramide esoterica* (Milan: Sugar Co, 1977) to Rumi. The basic facts of Rumi's life and poetry had been discussed for the first time in Italian in the wonderful compendium of the University of Turin professor **Italo Pizzi**, *Storia della poesia persiana* (1894), which provides five passages from the *Masnavi* and six poems from the *Divân* in Italian translation. But on the whole, Rumi is not as well known in Italy as in France, Germany or in English-speaking countries.

THE STUDY OF RUMI IN TURKEY

As we have seen in chapter 10, many Turkish authors have written commentaries on the *Masnavi*. The pre-modern Turkish commentaries percolated through to Europe and formed the early basis for Western scholarship on Rumi. For example, in 1851 von Hammer-Purgstall, who had already published a number of translations of Rumi, published a lengthy series of articles in the "Philosophical–Historical Journal of the Viennese Scientific Academy" reviewing a six-volume Turkish commentary on the *Masnavi* which had been published in Cairo in 1835. Nicholson relied extensively on Anqaravi's commentary, which in large part explains why he thought Rumi under the spell of Ibn ʿArabi.

Istanbul, along with Bombay, was one of the first places in the Islamic world to publish books consistently in languages using the Arabic script. Several commentaries on the *Masnavi* and other works related to Rumi or the Mevlevi order, both old and new, were published by the ʿÂmere printing press in Istanbul during the nineteenth century. These include *Hall-e tahqiqât* (1852), containing Turkish translations of the *Masnavi* by Ibrahim Çevri (d. 1655) and Yusof Sinechâk (d. 1546), and the eighteenth-century commentaries of Ismâil Hakkı of Bursa (*Ruh ül-mesnevi*, 1870), and the above-mentioned Anqaravi's *Şerh-e şerif* (1872) on the *Masnavi*.

At about this time, other Turks began to apply the rudiments of modern scholarly methodology in brief monographs, such as Imamzade Salih Sami in his 22-page pamphlet on Rumi and Shams, *Mevlânâ Celâleddin Rumi ve Şemseddin Tebrizi* (ʿÂlem Matbaası, 1312/1894–5). Another short pamphlet about Rumi and Shams appeared in Armenian, just before the genocide: *Arewelki khorhurdneren* (K. Polis: Tpagrutiwn O. Arzuman, 1912), by Harutiwn Mrmerean (1860–1926). We have already had occasion to mention the works of the Mevlevi scholar Tahir Olgun, who wrote about the Yenikapı Mevlevi lodge and its shaykh, or *post-nişin*. His "Mirror on to Mowlânâ," *Mirat-i hazret-i Mevlana* (Istanbul: Cemal Efendi, 1315/1897) provided interested readers with a thirty-page study of the matter. Twenty years later, Osman Behcet provided a slightly longer study of the life and thought of Rumi in his *Mevlana Celaleddin Rumi, hayatı, mesleği* (Istanbul: Evkaf, 1336/1918).

TURKISH LOCAL AND NATIONAL PRIDE

Although it is written in French, Turkish nationalism nevertheless displays itself in the small monograph about so-called "Turkish" philosophers, by the professor of philosophy Mustafa Rahmi, *Conception sur la vie de quelques philosophes turcs: Gazali, Celaleddin, Younus Emre, Kinalioğlu Ali Efendi* (Izmir: Bilgi, 1933), which appropriates the Persian-speaking Ghazzâli and Rumi, who were culturally, and probably also ethnically, Iranian. Similarly, some Turkish authors (Uzluk, Sevengil) have argued that the word *samâ^c* comes not from Arabic, but from a Turkish word meaning either "shaman" or "turning and singing." Of course, the fact that earlier Sufi authors writing in Arabic used the word *samâ^c* in this sense, deriving it from the perfectly common Arabic root to hear (s-m-^{c}), means that we can easily dismiss this argument, though Turkish tribal traditions have doubtless added to the flavor of Sufi *samâ^c* as practiced in Anatolia and Central Asia. Rasıh Güven (QMF 81) even tries to derive the word *samâ^c* from a Sanskrit term used in yoga. A touch of Ockham's Razor would suffice to slice these arguments to pieces.

Beginning in the 1950s **Mehmet Önder** set to work on a series of books on Turkish museums, Atatürk and other subjects pertaining to the national and cultural history of Turkey. Önder acted as the director of the Mevlânâ Museum for some time and produced a number of pamphlets related to it. These include *Mevlâna: hayatı, şahsiyeti, eserleri, türbesi* (Konya: Yeni Kitap, 1952), about Rumi and his shrine, expanded a few years later from twenty-nine to sixty-two pages as *Mevlâna ve türbesi* ([Istanbul]: s.n., 1957), including a section about

Rumi's thought and other additions. Önder wrote one pamphlet on the sarcophagus of Rumi (Konya, 1958), a guide to the Mevlânâ Museum, *Mevlana müzesi rehberi* (Istanbul: Millî Eğitim, 1962), from which derived his English-language versions of guide books for foreign tourists, *The Mevlana Museum: Mevlana Museum and the Ottoman Mausoleums Nearby* (n.p.: Ajans-Türk,1960) and *Mevlana and the Mevlana Museum* (Istanbul: Aksit Culture and Tourism, 1985). An earlier book, *Mevlânâ şehri Konya* (Konya: Yeni Kitap, 1962; Ankara: Güven Matbaası, 1971), provides a history of Konya, the city of Rumi, an epitome of which was translated into English by Ertuğrul Uçkun as *Konya: The Residence of the Great Mevlana, the Moslem Mystic, and a Guide for the Ancient Art and Museums in the City* (Istanbul: Keskin Colour Ltd. Co. Printing House, n.d.).

Over the years Önder has provided Turkish readers with a number of anthologies of Rumi's work in translation, including a compilation of stories taken from the *Masnavi* and an anthology of poems inspired by Rumi in Turkish. These are *Mevlana Mesnevi'den Hikayeler* and *Mevlana şiirleri antolojisi*, both published in Ankara by Türkiye Iş Bankası in 1970 and 1973, respectively.

Mevlana Jelaleddin Rumi (Ankara: Ministry of Culture, 1990), a translation by P.M. Butler of a Turkish work by Mehmet Önder of the same name (1986), was printed by a typesetter with an imperfect knowledge of English, as the many mistakes reflect. The book lists in its bibliography several scholarly works, such as Gölpınarlı's biography, Schimmel's *Triumphal Sun*, de Vitray-Meyerovitch's *Mystique et poésie*, Afzal Iqbal's *Life and Thought of Rumi*, and it relies upon Nicholson and Arberry for English translations of the *Divân* and Discourses. However, it is almost certainly based primarily on Gölpınarlı, to whom it does great disservice. This rather unsophisticated work has two principal goals – to assist tourists who want to know something more about Rumi than can be gleaned from the museum brochures, and to aggrandize Turkish culture. The book likes to tell colorful stories, and for that reason basically repeats much of Aflâki, though it does at least question the idea that Shams was murdered. It drops the names of several Western works (probably once again for the benefit of tourists), such as those by Myriam Harry and Barrès, without, however, integrating them into the narrative. It does, however, present several color reproductions, notably an imagined portrait of Rumi and a painting in the Topkapı Museum library of Mevlevi dervishes dancing. It also features several passages of poetry rendered into bland but decipherable English.

This book betrays either willful ignorance or craven servility to the patron for which it was composed, the Turkish Ministry of Culture. In the introduction, Önder refers to Rumi as "the great Turkish mystic" and "a great Turkish intellectual." He then turns Rumi into a Turkish prophet, calling Mevlâna "the eternal gift of the Turkish people to all humanity" (210). In fact, there is no reference to the minor detail that the language spoken by Bahâ al-Din was Persian or that ʿAttâr wrote his *Asrâr nâme* in Persian, nor do we learn that Rumi composed the *Masnavi* in Persian until page 138, three pages after learning that the prose prefaces to each book are in Arabic (but then Önder [101] even insinuates that the Koran is in Turkish!). Throughout Önder deliberately leaves us to assume that Rumi's other works are in Turkish, and indeed, when he can no longer contain his misplaced patriotism, bursts out with the utterly ludicrous statement that "There is no doubt that Mevlâna's mother tongue was Turkish," since Balkh, from which he migrated with his father, was the cultural centre of Turkestan and Khorasan, "both regions of predominantly Turkish population" (207). Though Önder begrudgingly allows that Rumi was probably taught Arabic and Persian at a very early stage in his education (208), he insists that Rumi spoke Turkish throughout his life (whether the Kipchak or Oguz dialect, Önder cannot tell), not only with his family, but also "when addressing the people and in his sermons." Rumi chose to write "most of his works in Persian and some in Arabic" only because it was the convention of the day (208). Önder's "evidence" for this insupportable, unbearable nonsense consists of the assertion that Rumi uses an Anatolian Persian dialect (whatever that might be, it would still not be Turkish, which is from an altogether different language family), and that his *Divân* and *Masnavi* are interspersed with a "particularly high percentage" of couplets and passages in Turkish. This is a very creative use of statistics, since a couple of dozen at most of the 35,000 lines of the *Divân-e Shams* are in Turkish, and almost all of these lines occur in poems that are predominantly in Persian.

The quarrel between Persian and Turkish literature extends back to the sixteenth century. Mir ʿAli Shir Navâ'i of Herat (1441–1501), the patron of the poet Jâmi, expressed the opinion that Turkish was a far more subtle, supple and poetic language than either Arabic or Persian (but especially Persian) in his "Judgement Between the Two Languages," *Mohâkamât al-loghatayn* (trans. Robert Devereux, Leiden: Brill, 1966). But then, the abilities of Navâ'i in composing poetry in his native Chaghatai Turkish far exceeded his minor talents in Persian verse, which he wrote under the sobriquet Fâni; such was the judgment of Bâbur, and we might well concur. In any case, we can forgive the linguistic chauvinism of poets and authors who believe their language to be the best since Babel, but Önder must surely know that Rumi wrote and spoke Persian. Therefore, we can only surmise that his cultural jingoism represents a conscious effort to rob Rumi of his Persian and Iranian heritage, and claim him for Turkish literature, ethnicity and nationalism.

Talat Sait Halman has judiciously summarized the uses to which Rumi had been put by Turks up to 1975 in his "The Turk in Mawlânâ/Mawlânâ in Turkey" (Che 217–54). And how would Rumi respond to all this nationalist posturing?

A language shared brings kinship and a bond
but talk with folk of unlike mind's a chain:
    Often Turk and Hindu can communicate
    whereas two Turks may meet and feel estranged
The lingo the like-minded share is best!
Better a common heart than common tongue.

(M1:1205–7)

Önder also describes his accidental discovery of a trapdoor at the base of the wooden sarcophagus/cenotaph in the memorial of Shams-e Tabrizi, a pyramid-shaped "stucered stucture" (sic) in classic Seljuk style. Önder cleaned away the rubble and soil blocking the steps, under which he found a cellar cut out of stone in Seljuk style, which he says was covered with "Khorassan plaster." Gölpınarlı, whom he had called to look at it, arrived a few days later and promptly proclaimed that this was the grave of Shams (105–6); this theory was used as evidence for the belief that Shams was murdered by Rumi's disciples, but as we have seen (see "Murder Most Foul?" in chapter 4, above), this scenario is extremely unlikely.

Other Turkish scholars, like Talat Halman and Mikâil Bayram (Konya), have discussed such matters rationally and criticized Önder's gullibility and negligence. For example, Önder claimed that Rumi's own handwriting appears on the margins of a manuscript of Shams-e Tabrizi's *Maqâlât* indicating the date of death for Borhân al-Din. He also maintained that a certain carpet in the Konya Museum belonged to the Seljuk era and was given to Rumi by Sultan Kay Qobâd, whereas this carpet actually dates to the sixteenth century (Bay 150). But the information provided to most tourists in Konya is tainted by Önder and is uncritically repeated in some Western sources, mostly popular, particularly those by writers not versed in Persian.

This is not to deny the utility of some of Önder's work. He edited commemorative volumes on the occasion of the 700th anniversary of Rumi's death: *Mevlâna: hayatı, eserleri (700. ölüm yıldönümüne armağan)* (Istanbul: Tercüman, 1973) and the proceedings of a seminar *Bildiriler: Mevlâna'nın 700. ölüm yıldönümü dolayısile uluslararası Mevlana semineri* (Ankara: Türkiye Iş Bankası, 1974). But the book for which Önder will be most remembered, undertaken with Ismet Binark and Nejat Sefercioglu, is a large bibliography in two volumes (Basmalar and Yazmalar) of works by and about Rumi, *Mevlâna bibliyografyası* (Ankara: Türkiye Iş Bankası, 1973 and 1975). To this, Erdogan Erol and Fevzi Gunuc have added a supplement mentioning 57 additional books and 1,000 articles, *Basın hayatı'nın 40. yılında Mehmet Önder bibliyografyası, 1944–1984* (Ankara: Güven, 1984).

Ibrahim Hakkı Konyalı wrote a large history of his native Konya, *Konya Tarihi* (Konya: Yeni Kitap, 1964), which includes a very long section on the Mevlevi shrine, or Mevlâna Türbesi. Not only Konya, but also Karaman, where

550

Rumi's mother is buried, and Galata, where the Mevlevi lodge was an important nineteenth-century cultural center, have generated local interest in Rumi and his order. For an example of this genre of study, see **D. Ali Gülcan**'s work on the Mevlevi lodge in Karaman, *Karaman Mevlevihanesi, Mevlevilik ve Karamanlı Mevlevi velileri* (Mader-i Mevlana Camii Koruma, 1977?).

Turkish scholars have gathered for frequent national and international academic congresses on Rumi (**Millî Mevlâna Kongresi**) at the Seljuk University in Konya, founded in 1975. National Rumi congresses were held here in May of 1985 and 1986 and April of 1988; the proceedings of all three have been published by the Seljuk University Press, comprising mostly shorter articles on the history of various Mevlevi figures and the architectural monuments. An international congress was held at the same venue in 1987 which, though it continued to draw mostly Turkish scholars, also attracted several European scholars of note. The opening remarks by Halil Cin noted that the United Nations had declared 1986 the Year of Peace and suggested that the Rumi congresses be seen in that light; he announced an award, the "Selçuk University Mevlana Universal Love Award," to be granted to those who produce original research on Rumi. A 1991 conference in Ankara devoted attention to the Mevlevi lodges and their pious foundations, "Türk Vakıf Medeniyetinde Hz. Mevlânâ ve Mevlevîhânelerin Yeri Semineri," proceedings in *IX. Vakıf Haftası Kitabı* (Ankara: Vakıflar Genel Müdürlüğü Yayınlari, 1992).

GENTLEMEN AND SCHOLARS

Tahsin Yazıcı's marvelous critical edition of the *Manâqeb* of Aflâki, with its careful collation of manuscripts and scholarly annotations, has been referred to ubiquitously in this book; mention has also been made of his Turkish translation of this work. He has also contributed several articles for the *Encyclopaedia Iranica*, including concise summaries of various Mevlevi figures (e.g., Ebrâhim Dede, Divâne Chelebi, Yusof Sinechâk, etc.).

The 1992 study, *The Essence of Rumi's Masnevi* (Konya: Misket), by **Erkan Türkmen**, the chair of the Department of Eastern Languages and Literatures at the Seljuk University in Konya, organizes the ideas of the *Masnavi* and presents the essence of the commentary tradition's observations, whether Turkish, Ottoman Turkish, Urdu, Persian or English. He relies upon Meier's dating against Gölpınarlı, and provides a very useful reconstruction of the history of Rumi's family, incorporating information from Turkish sources. Türkmen has also written a few articles on Rumi, which have been collected in *Rumi as a True Lover of God* (Istanbul: Baltac Tourism, 1988; reprinted 1990). Türkmen has established himself, along with **Mikâil Bayram**, whose works are discussed elsewhere in this volume, among the current generation of Turkish experts on Rumi and successors to the mantle of Gölpınarlı.

ABDÜLBÂKI GÖLPINARLI

Gölpınarlı's father, Ahmad Medhat Effendi, or Ahmad Âgâh, was a newspaper reporter. **Abdülbâki Gölpınarlı** (1900–1982) was born on January 12, 1900 in Istanbul. He studied the traditional Islamic sciences (he was a Sunni), attending the Mevlevi lodge in Galata in his youth. One of this teachers was Shaykh Hosayn Fakhr al-Din, the shaykh of the Bahârie Mevlevi lodge; a picture of an adolescent Gölpınarlı dressed in Mevlevi garb survives. Gölpınarlı graduated from college in 1930 and taught in various high schools while he finished his doctorate in literature at the University of Ankara. He taught Turkish and Persian literature at Ankara before transferring to the University of Istanbul. Gölpınarlı took early retirement in 1949 and lived in the Üsküdar neighborhood, but would receive visitors on Tuesdays at the Süleymâniye library in Istanbul, where he worked among a pile of books, compiling catalogs of the manuscripts held there. He also cataloged the manuscripts at the Mevlânâ Museum in Konya.

Gölpınarlı was a man of medium height and completely white hair in his later years, who carried around a black briefcase almost everywhere he went. A witty man with a good sense of humor, he had a fabulous memory, even recalling the catalog numbers of manuscripts he had consulted long ago. He knew many Iranian scholars and would speak with them in Persian. When asked by Towfiq Sobhâni to write an autobiographical note, Gölpınarlı simply quoted a variant of Rumi's line:

> My life's yield
> but three words:
> I burned, I
> burned, I burned.

Ali Alparslan has written a biography of this great scholar, *Abdülbâki Gölpınarlı* (Ankara: Kültür Bakanlığı, 1996), which includes a number of Gölpınarlı's original poems (18–37).

As an author Gölpınarlı produced book-length studies of Malâmati Sufism (1931), Yunus Emre (1936) and Mohammad and the Hadith (1957), among others. As a textual scholar, he also produced a number of editions of classical texts, including the *Divân*s of Emre (1948), Fozuli (1950), Nedim (1951), etc. Gölpınarlı also translated many works from Persian to Turkish, including Hâfez (*Divân*, 1944), ʿAttâr (*Manteq al-tayr*, 1944–5; *Elâhi nâme*, 1947), and Shabestari (*Golshan-e râz*, 1944).

Of course, he devoted the bulk of his translation efforts from Persian to Turkish to the works of Rumi, beginning with the six volumes of the *Masnavi* (1941–6). He followed this with selections from the quatrains (1945) and selections from the *Divân-e Shams* (*Gül-deste*, 1955). Then came a full translation of the lyric poems (*Divân-e kebir*) with notes and commentary, begun in 1957 and completed in 1974. He also brought out a Turkish version of Sultan Valad's *Ebtedâ nâme* (1976). Nor did he ignore Rumi's prose, churning out Turkish versions of the Discourses (1959), the letters (1963), and the "Seven Sermons" (1965).

Gölpınarlı furthermore contributed to our knowledge of Rumi in several works of original scholarship, beginning with a biography of Rumi, *Mevlânâ Celâleddin: hayatı, felsefesi, eserleri, eserlerinden seçmeler* (Istanbul: Inkılap Kitabevi, 1951; 2nd revised ed. 1959). Next came a large book on the history of the Mevlevi order, *Mevlana'dan sonra Mevlevîlik* (Istanbul: Inkılap, 1953), followed by another about the customs and principles of the Mevlevi order, *Mevlevî: âdâb ve erkânı* (Istanbul: Inkılap ve Aka, 1963). After all these translations and critical studies, Gölpınarlı obviously had a deep understanding of Rumi and his works, which he displays in his six-volume *Masnavi* commentary, *Mesnevi şerhi* (Istanbul: Başbakanlık Kültür, 1973–4). Gölpınarlı constantly revised his works and republished them, so those wishing to know his final views on a topic should take care to read the third edition of his biography of Rumi. A revised edition of his commentary and translation of the *Masnavi* began to appear the year before he died as *Mesnevi: tercemesi ve şerhi* (Istanbul: Inkılap ve Aka, 1981–84) in six volumes. Towfiq Sobhâni has rendered this and a number of Gölpınarlı's other Turkish works on Rumi into Persian, so that Iranian scholars now have ready access to his conclusions.

THE STUDY OF RUMI IN ARABIC

The Mevlevi lodges in Damascus and Jerusalem functioned until recently, though interest in Jalâl al-Din Rumi in the Arab world owes more perhaps to his fame in the West as a distinguished representative of Islamic belief and praxis. We have already looked at the translations of Rumi into Arabic (chapter 11). In addition, a few scholars writing in Arabic have produced studies of the life and poetry of "Mawlânâ Jalâl al-Dîn al-Rûmî." These include a short monograph of that name by Abû al-Hasan ʿAlî Nadwî (Cairo: al-Mukhtâr al-Islâmî, 1974), and another by Mustafâ Ghâlib (Beirut: ʿIzz al-Dîn, 1982). A much longer work by ʿInâyat Allâh Iblâgh al-Afghânî (a scholar based in Cairo with a family background in Afghanistan) analyzes Rumi's intermediary position between the Sufis and the theologically oriented ulama: *Jalâl al-Dîn al-Rûmî bayna al-sûfiyyah wa ʿulamâ al-kalâm* (Cairo: al-Dâr al-Misriyyah al-Lubnâniyyah, 1987).

Muhammad ʿAbd al-Salâm Kafâfî, a professor in the universities of Cairo and Beirut, has devoted the most attention to Rumi with his long book on the life and poetry of Rumi, *Jalâl al-Dîn al-Rûmî fî hayâtih wa shʿirih* (Beirut: Dâr al-Nahdah al-ʿArabiyyah, 1971), and his earlier translation to Arabic of Book 1 of the *Masnavi* with commentary, *Mathnawî Jalâl al-Dîn al-Rûmî* (Sayda: al-Maktabah al-ʿAsriyyah, 1965)

THE STUDY OF RUMI IN PERSIAN

Given that Rumi wrote in Persian, it is not surprising that Iranian scholars have written a mass of important works of philological and philosophical analysis. The first Iranian whose work on Rumi can be said to be in some way informed by scholarly methodologies was **Rezâ Qoli Khân Hedâyat**, who about 120 years ago produced an edition of the *Divân-e Shams* at Tabriz with a historical introduction, utilized by Nicholson and others (see chapter 7, above).

For several decades after this editions and studies of Rumi appeared only in India or Turkey, until a scholar and cleric from Isfahan, **Jalâl al-Din Homâ'i** (1900–1980), produced his edition of Sultan Valad's *Valad nâme* (Tehran: Eqbâl, 1937) on the history of Bahâ al-Din and Jalâl al-Din. Homâ'i, who from an early age had devoted his attention to Rumi, added a very substantial and excellent introduction which provides us with a critical history of Rumi and his family. His daughter, Mahdokht Bânu Homâ'i, has recently seen a revised printing of this work through the press as *Valad nâme* (Tehran: Homâ, 1376/ 1997). She also produced a translation of selected passages of the *Masnavi* with commentary (see "Abridgements" in chapter 11).

The elder Homâ'i, a prolific and detail-minded scholar with a sharp and original seminary-trained intellect, wrote on grammar, rhetoric, poetry, theology and philosophy. He also edited a number of classical texts and composed verse of his own. Subsequent to the essential groundwork of editing Sultan Valad's history, Homâ'i contributed two other books on Rumi: a substantial study of Rumi's philosophy and theology, *Mowlavi nâme: Mowlavi che miguyad* (Tehran: Agâh, 1977), and an analysis of one of the *Masnavi*'s stories, *Tafsir-e Masnavi-ye Mowlavi: dâstân-e qal'e-ye zât al-sovar yâ diz-e hushrobâ* (Tehran: University of Tehran Press, 1970). Homâ'i also composed a 400-page manuscript on the life of Rumi, which remains unpublished, though parts of it have appeared in the commemorative volume *Yâdnâme-ye Mowlavi* and in a preface to an edition of the *Divân-e Shams*.

BADIC AL-ZAMÂN FORUZÂNFAR

As his name suggests, **Badi^c al-Zamân Foruzânfar** (1900–1970) was the "wonder of his age." He had the habit of reading through every book he got his hands on before he could bring himself to put it down. Foruzânfar frequented book stalls and stores and, like Erasmus, preferred to spend his money on reading material rather than food or clothes. His memory was nearly photographic and he never needed to refer to notes in his lectures, even when citing page numbers or reciting longer passages from poems or philosophy texts (his students would sometimes check the page number of sources he mentioned to try to catch him out, but rarely found any errors). Foruzânfar would recite poems in an expressive and emotional tone, the verse of Rumi often bringing tears to his eyes, a moisture which he would soon transfer to the eyes of his students with the cadences and intonation of his recitation.

Foruzânfar recalls that he heard (and memorized) his first ghazal of Rumi in 1920, learning from his teacher, Adib-e Nayshâburi, the famous ghazal beginning (D 441):

> Let me see your face,
>   for I long for the roses
> Let me taste your parted lips
>   for I long for endless sugar

Though an enthusiast for the Persian poetry of the tenth through twelfth centuries, Adib-e Nayshâburi, himself a well-known poet, felt disdain for and knew little about anything written from the Mongol invasions onward. For this reason he taught his pupils only this one poem of Rumi. The Hedâyat and Lucknow editions of the *Divân-e Shams* were not in circulation among Shiite seminary students in Mashhad in those days since Rumi, a Sunni author, was not considered a suitable subject of study for future Shiite theologians. Foruzânfar had no further access to Rumi until he received the gift of a cashmere shawl from a Qajar official, Qavvâm al-Saltane, in exchange for a panegyric Foruzânfar had composed for him. The shawl was quickly sold and a copy of Hedâyat's biography of the poets, *Majmaᶜ al-fosahâ*, was purchased with the proceeds. Hedâyat included a good selection of ghazals from Rumi in his treatment of the life of Shams-e Tabriz, and these Foruzânfar devoured and memorized while at home in his village in the spring of 1921. Upon returning to Mashhad, he recited them for his teacher and asked for help in understanding difficult passages.

Unable to find an edition of the *Divân*, he had to wait until 1924, when he went to Tehran, to learn more Rumi. There he met a certain Sufi who had copied out a selection of poems from Rumi and others in a notebook which he used to carry about with him, reciting aloud from it with great emotion whenever the opportunity presented itself. Foruzânfar spent the summers with this Sufi, chanting Rumi most days from seven in the morning until five in the afternoon. He also came into contact with another poet, Adib-e Pishâvari, who was extremely fond of Rumi.

Finally, Foruzânfar found a copy of the *Divân-e Shams* selling for 25 rials. In order to buy it he sold the fine winter cloak of lamb's wool his mother had sent to replace what had been stolen from him by Turkmen highwaymen. He spent six months reading this in 1933–4, marking all the poems that did not, in his opinion, conform to the mystical ethos of Jalâl al-Din Mowlavi. It was at this point that he decided to write a biography of Rumi. After critically reading through the edition once more in the winter of 1934–5, Foruzânfar came to the conclusion that the Lucknow printing of the *Divân-e Shams* was fatally flawed.

Many poems of other poets had found their way in to this collection, as he demonstrated in his biography of Rumi, published in the following year (see below). Subsequently, Foruzânfar obtained two partial manuscripts of the *Divân* from the early sixteenth century, on the basis of which he began the second volume of his study of Rumi.

His mother's death intervened in September 1936, followed by the death of a number of the teachers and scholars who had encouraged Foruzânfar's work, and he was forced to turn his attention to other subjects for a while, notably lexicography. Foruzânfar's first study, a history of the poets of the early centuries of Persian literature, *Sokhan va sokhanvarân* (1929–33), had introduced the early Persian poets, their patrons, dates, etc., in a modern systematic fashion for the first time. Although Persian men of letters had been producing lives of the poets for centuries, these usually consisted of a few dates and names, some mostly legendary anecdotes and biographical information extracted (often erroneously) from their poems.

For his doctoral dissertation, Foruzânfar produced the first systematic literary biography in Persian that was fully informed by modern scholarly principles. This was an investigation into the life and circumstances of Rumi, published in 1936 as *Resâle dar ahvâl va zendegâni-ye Mowlânâ Jalâl al-Din Mohammad*, which Zarrinkub describes as the best dissertation ever written in Iran. A revised edition appeared in 1954 and was until recently the most important source for the life of Rumi. It was translated into Turkish by Feridun Nafiz Uzluk and informed the work of many Turkish authors, including Gölpınarlı.

Because several important sources, such as the *Ma'âref* of Bahâ al-Din and the *Fihe mâ fih* of Rumi had never been published, Foruzânfar referred to whatever manuscript sources he could obtain, and introduced these prose texts to the public for the first time. For the text of the ghazals, he had to refer to the inaccurate Lucknow edition of the *Divân* and the uncritical edition of the *Masnavi* by 'Alâ al-Dowle. Although now dated, Foruzânfar's biography remains an important and still useful source for the history of Rumi.

In 1940 the Ministry of Culture asked that a selection of the *Masnavi* be prepared for Iranian students. Foruzânfar responded two years later with a copiously annotated collection of twenty-three episodes chosen from Books 1 and 2 (*Kholâse-ye Masnavi*, Tehran: University of Tehran Press, 1943). In the introduction Foruzânfar defends the great mystical poets and thinkers from the harsh criticism of Sufism that had been leveled by some modernists (such as Shebli No'mâni and Ahmad Kasravi), pointing out that the deep metaphysical ideas of the *Masnavi* should not be confused with the sometimes shallow practices of popular Sufism. The work also provides bibliographical notes on some of the medieval commentaries which he consulted in preparation of his notes.

Foruzânfar eventually undertook his own commentary on the *Masnavi*, but did not complete more than three volumes of this before his death (*Sharh-e Masnavi-ye sharif,* Tehran: University of Tehran Press, 1967–9). Zarrinkub, who has written two *Masnavi* commentaries of his own, feels that no other exegete can hold a candle to Foruzânfar, whose knowledge of Rumi was so vast that when he put down his pen, the final word had been said. Professor As^cad ^cAli of the University of Damascus recounts that Foruzânfar had an impressive knowledge of the works of Arab poets and that when an Arabic line was recited to him, he could provide the rest of the poem from memory. Foruzânfar even corrected the Arabs' pronunciation of Rumi's favorite word, *'ishq*, which in Syrian colloquial would become *'ushq*.[4]

Foruzânfar's biography of Rumi was translated into Turkish as *Mevlana Celaleddin* by Feridun Nafiz Uzluk (Istanbul: Millî Eğitim, 1990), thus affording Turkish readers a second opinion to the biographical work of Gölpınarlı.

RUMI REFERENCE TOOLS

We owe a great debt to **Sâdeq Gowharin** (d. 1995) for his philological study of Rumi, a seven-volume dictionary of the words and expressions appearing in the *Masnavi*, an indispensable reference tool for the mystical and symbolic allusions embedded in Rumi's terminology: *Farhang-e loghât va ta^cbirât-e Masnavi* (Tehran: University of Tehran Press, 1958–75). Gowharin also edited other Sufi texts (e.g., ^cAttâr's "Conference of the Birds"), and therefore has a solid background to carry out this work; he illustrates the usage of each word with several lines of verse as exemplar, and his dictionary of the *Masnavi* also serves as a partial cross-reference to the text.

A concordance of the *Masnavi* in four volumes by **Mohammad Taqi Ja^cfari** under the title "From Sea to Sea," *Az daryâ be daryâ* (Tehran: Vezârat-e Ershâd-e Eslâmi, 1985–6) and **Mohammad Javâd Shari^cat**'s *Kashf al-abyât-e Masnavi-e Nikolson* (Isfahan: Kamâl, 1984), a line-by-line index of Nicholson's edition of the *Masnavi*, are the tools to use for locating particular verses of the text. Foruzânfar's dictionary of the hadith appearing in the *Masnavi, Ahâdis-e Masnavi* (Tehran: University of Tehran Press, 1955; reprint Tehran: Amir Kabir, 1968), gives background and sources for the prophetic traditions alluded to in the *Masnavi*. **^cAli-Rezâ Mansur Mo^ɔayyad** in his *Ersâl al-masal dar Masnavi* (Tehran: Sorush, 1986) has isolated a number of Persian proverbs coined in the text. **Mahdokht Purkhâleqi Chatrudi** has given us a concise dictionary of the prophets, Sufi terms and other allusions found in the stories of the *Masnavi*, as *Farhang-e qesse-hâ-ye payâmbarân* (Mashhad: Âstân-e Qods-e Razavi, 1992), which gives useful background information; Western readers wishing to understand the *Masnavi* more deeply would benefit from a translation of this work. For the stories of the prophets and the mystical allusions appearing in the ghazals of Rumi, readers can refer to **Taqi Purnâmdâriân**'s *Dâstân-e* *payâmbarân dar Kolliyât-e Shams* (Tehran: Motâle^cât va Tahqiqât-e Farhangi, 1985), a very useful commentary and guide to the lyric poems.

Before the above-mentioned bibliography of Önder appeared, **Mândânâ Sadiq Behzâd** had compiled a ninety-page compilation of books by and about Rumi in various languages. Her work was published by the Center for Library Services of the Institute for Scientific and Educational Research and Planning as *Ketâb nâme-ye Mowlavi* (Tehran, 1351/1973).

^CABD AL-HOSAYN ZARRINKUB

Zarrinkub (1922 –), as prolific as his interests are wide ranging, has penned major studies on the history of Islam, the development of Sufism, the life of Ghazzâli, the principles of literary criticism, the aesthetics of modern Persian poetry, and studies of the classical authors. On Rumi, he has written three major works, two of them innovative and insightful *Masnavi* commentaries: "The Secret of the Reed," *Serr-e nay* (Tehran: ^cElmi, 1985), and the two volumes explaining and annotating selected passages, "The Ocean in a Jug," *Bahr dar kuze* (Tehran: ^cElmi, 1987, reprints). Anyone with a serious interest in the *Masnavi* will want to become familiar with these two original works.

These works proved somewhat intimidating for general readers, however, and many individuals wrote, phoned and otherwise urged Zarrinkub to undertake a book on Rumi written in non-scholarly language without distracting scholarly apparatus (ZrP 9–12). Zarrinkub obliged with a biography called "Step by Step to the Meeting with God," *Pelle pelle tâ molâqât-e Khodâ* (Tehran: ^cElmi, 1994). Zarrinkub presents an image of Rumi as perceived by his devoted spiritual followers, but filtered through a psychological lens that takes the hagiographer's cultural circumstances into account and discounts the obviously impossible (ZrP 13). Of course, Zarrinkub has a vast knowledge at his disposal and draws upon the works of Rumi, Bahâ al-Din, Borhân al-Din, Sultan Valad, Shams and others.

The great virtue of this work is that it creates a readable historical novel of Rumi's life, extrapolating from fact and legend, with an admixture of psycho-biography, to portray a full and accessible picture of the man. Indeed, Zarrinkub's "Step by Step to the Meeting with God" would make for a good film script. The Iranian public devoured this book by a noted professor and contemporary thinker; it appeared in 1994 and went through eight reprintings within one year. Of course, since it includes only partial footnotes and one cannot always distinguish the legendary or the merely speculative from the factual, a rigorous scholarly biography is still needed.

MOHAMMAD-^CALI MOVAHHED

Movahhed worked for the Iranian National Oil Company, in which capacity he has written about mineral rights (1973) and other legal aspects of the oil industry in Iran (1978), as well as the United Arab Emirates' claim of sovereignty over the disputed islands of Tonb and Abu Musa in the Persian Gulf (1994). He has also translated several works into Persian, including an Arthur Koestler novel (1982), the travelog of Ibn Battûta from Arabic (1991), and a 1979 book on conversion to Islam and the poll tax (1996).

His abiding interest, however, has been and remains Shams of Tabriz and his relation to Rumi. Some twenty years ago, Movahhed first published a 457-page annotated edition of the *Maqâlât-e Shams-e Tabrizi* (Tehran: Dâneshgâh-e San°ati-ye Aryâmehr [Aryamehr Polytechnic University], 2536/1977). Even with Movahhed's engineering background, a polytechnic university must have seemed an unlikely publisher for a work of medieval mysticism (diversifying university press editors, please take note)! For Movahhed, the painstaking labor of collating numerous manuscripts to produce the much larger edition of the *Maqâlât* in 1990 was born of love: it made him feel a participant in the encounter between Rumi and Shams. Movahhed also drew inspiration from the example of the great Iranian philologist and literary scholar Mojtabâ Minovi, who had been preparing an edition of the *Masnavi* when he died. Movahhed cites the encouragement and assistance given to him by an associate of Minovi, °Ali-Rezâ Haydari (Maq 65–6).

After completing his edition of the *Maqâlât*, Movahhed turned his attention to teasing out from it a history of the life of Shams. The resulting book, *Shams-e Tabrizi* (Tehran: Tarh-e Now, 1996), synthesizes the information in the *Maqâlât* and gives an excellent summary and outline of the life of Shams. Chapter 4 on Shams in the present book owes a heavy debt to these two works of Movahhed.

MOHAMMAD ESTE°LÂMI

Este°lâmi, an Iranian scholar who has taught at McGill University in Canada and at the University of California, Berkeley, offers a new critical edition of the *Masnavi* in a text which improves upon Nicholson's edition. This includes an extensive introduction with one of the best summaries of Rumi's life in Persian, and a commentary at the end of each one of the six volumes: *Masnavi-ye Jalâl al-Din Mohammad-e Balkhi* (Tehran: Zavvâr, 1981; reprints 1990, 1993, 1996).

RUMI'S RELIGIOUS THOUGHT

In the last half of the twentieth century our understanding of Rumi and his teachings has grown far more sophisticated, a development due in large part to the publication of critical editions of his works, through which readers have come more directly into contact with Rumi's own thinking without the mediation of the Ibn °Arabi-influenced tradition of exegesis.

As Nicholson's edition of the *Masnavi* appeared between 1925 and 1933, Hellmut Ritter began uncovering further manuscripts in Istanbul, with the help of Gölpınarlı, that shed further light on the text and on Rumi and his circle. The publication of Foruzânfar's edition of *Fihe mâ fih* (1951) and Arberry's English

559

translation of 1961, Foruzânfar's further critical editions of the *Maʿâref* of Bahâ al-Din (1955 and 1959) and Borhân al-Din (1961), Yazıcı's critical edition of Aflâki (1959), and the critical edition of the *Divân* (1957–67) provided a basis for a clearer understanding of Rumi's teachings. Bausani's extensive section on Rumi's thought in his *Persia religiosa* in 1959 has been discussed above.

In 1975 Chelkowski's *The Scholar and the Saint* brought together a number of lectures and essays on al-Biruni and Rumi, including the one by **Parviz Morewedge**, "Philosophical Interpretation of Rumi's Mystical Poetry: Light, the Mediator and the Way" (Che 187–216). Schimmel's study of Rumi's prophetology in the third chapter of her *Triumphal Sun* (1993) made a huge step forward, supplemented by her later article "Yusuf in Mawlana Rumi's Poetry" (LLM 45–60). Schimmel's student John Renard wrote his dissertation on Rumi's prophetology as "Flight of the Royal Falcons" at Harvard in 1978; it has since appeared as *All the King's Falcons: Rumi on Prophets and Revelation* (Albany, NY: SUNY Press, 1994), including a useful index of *Masnavi* passages on the various prophets. **William Chittick** made extensive use of Rumi's poetry, which he quotes copiously in his own translation in *The Sufi Path of Love: The Spiritual Teachings of Rumi* (Albany, NY: SUNY Press, 1983), an important advance in our knowledge of Rumi's theosophy, conveniently organized into topics by an expert on Ibn ʿArabi. Chittick's later article on "Rumi and wahdat al-wujud" (Poe) draws on that expertise to discount Ibn ʿArabi's supposed influence on Rumi (on which see chapter 9, above). In a 1987 conference on Rumi at UCLA, **Hamid Dabashi** presented a paper later published under the title "Rumi and the Problems of Theodicy: Moral Imagination and Narrative Discourse in a story of the Masnavi" (Poe), which touches on Rumi's teachings and his poetics.

STUDIES OF RUMI'S POETICS

After Nicholson's selected annotated translations from the *Divân*, perhaps the first extended study of a poem by Rumi appeared in **Hans Heinrich Schaeder**'s 1925 article on the concept of the Perfect Man, "Die islamische Lehre vom vollkommenen Menschen ..." (*Zeitschrift der Deutschen Morgenländischen Gesellschaft* 79:168–92), which analyzes Rumi's imagery of the cup and cup-bearer, particularly in the poem D 2395. **Gustav Richter** (1906–39) pursued oriental studies at Breslau University. He published literary studies of the medieval Islamic "Mirror for Princes" genre (Leipzig, 1932) and the style of the Koran (Leipzig, 1940). Prior to that, his three lectures on the stylistics of Rumi's poems had been published as *Persiens Mystiker Dschelalad-Din Rumi: eine Stildeutung in drei Vortägen* (Breslau, 1933). Richter shows how the *Masnavi* follows the paradigm of the Koran in integrating stories, parables, ethical exhortations and didactic philosophy, which may at first glance seem randomly digressive, but when regarded more deeply, resolve into an intricate pattern, like a Persian carpet. This monograph, despite winning a certain degree of praise

(Arberry described it as "illuminating" and Bausani called it very interesting and important, though full of over-involute and sometimes obscure reasoning), does not seem to have dispelled the impression, repeated by Arberry in 1961, that the *Masnavi* is "even at repeated reading a disconcertingly diffuse and confused composition." But as Foruzânfar points out again in the introduction to his commentary (*Sharh-e Masnavi*, 1:ii):

> The *Masnavi* is not divided into chapters and sections like other books; it has a style similar to the noble Koran, in which spiritual insights, articles of belief, the laws and principles of faith, and exhortations are set forth and mixed together according to divine wisdom. Like the Book of Creation, it has no particular order.

Early in her career Annemarie **Schimmel**, under the influence of Ritter's study of imagery in Nezâmi, wrote her *Die Bildersprache Dschelaladdin Rumis* (Walldorf-Hessen: Verlag für Orientkunde, 1949), a subject to which she returned in English in part 2 of her *Triumphal Sun*. Her Index of Concepts and Technical Terms in that volume provides those curious about particular tropes and images in the works of Rumi with an excellent place to begin. In a more recent study, Schimmel links the imagery in Rumi's poems to the seasonal variations in Konya (Che 255–73).

Robert Rehder, who has also grappled with the difficulties of style and structure in Hâfez, takes on Rumi in "The Style of Jalâl al-Din Rûmî" (Che 275–85). **J.C. Bürgel** tries to describe the organizing principle of Rumi's lyrical poems in his article "Ecstasy and Order: Two Structural Principles in the Ghazal Poetry of Jalâl al-Din Rumi" (LLM 61–74) and in another article, "'Speech is a Ship and Meaning the Sea': Some Formal Aspects of the Ghazal Poetry of Rumi" (Poe). **Amin Banani** also weighs in on the achievement of Rumi in his "Rumi as Poet" (Poe). **James Roy King** attempts to solve the riddle of Rumi's digressiveness in his "Narrative Disjunction and Conjunction in Rumi's Mathnawi," *Journal of Narrative Technique* 19, 3 (1989): 276–85.

In Iran, the venerable literary critic and Iranian senator, ʿ**Ali Dashti** (1895–?), gave his analysis of Rumi's poems in *Sayri dar divân-e Shams* (Tehran: Ibn Sinâ, 1958; frequent reprints). Writing in English, **Gholam Hosein Yousofi** discusses Rumi's narrative technique in "Mowlavi as a Storyteller" (Che 287–306). **Mehdi Borhâni** in *Talkhand: Tanz dar dâstân-ha-ye Masnavi* (Tehran: Kandu, 1994) provides a useful rundown of Rumi's use of satire in the stories of the *Masnavi*. Rumi's poetics of silence, along with the surrealism and symbolism in his ghazals, was the focus of **Sayyed Hosayn Fâtemi**'s study, *Tasvir-gari dar ghazaliyât-e Shams* (Tehran: Amir Kabir, 1985).

More recently **Fatemeh Keshavarz** urges readers to engage anew with the medieval Near Eastern lyric and with the poems of Rumi, by "observing the poems in action" (ix) in her book *Reading Mystical Lyric: The Case of Jalal al-Din Rumi* (Columbia, SC: University of South Carolina Press, 1998), which appeared as part of the University of South Carolina series, Studies in Comparative Religion. The series editor, Frederick Denny, remarks in the preface that "in this day of global fundamentalisms and stress between Islam and the West, people on all sides nevertheless find common ground in the poems of Jalâl al-Din Rumi." Keshavarz attacks the idea that Rumi's poems were written reluctantly and discusses the importance of paradox as a literary device in his oeuvre. She applies Western studies of metaphysical poetry and the poetics of silence, bringing Kierkegaard and Heidegger into the equation. Those inclined to postmodern discourse may find this study thought-provoking.

Sirus Shamisâ points out in his study of the Persian ghazal, *Sayr-e ghazal dar she'r-e fârsi* (Tehran: Ferdowsi, 1983, 95–104), that Rumi composed poems extemporaneously, in response to personal events, not in a studied poetic fashion, but in an almost trance-like state of *samâ'*:

> *To mapendâr ke man she'r be-khwod miguyam*
> *tâ ke bidâr-am o hoshyâr yek dam nazanam*

> Do not suppose I sing these poems of myself
> so long as I am awake and conscious
> I do not breathe a word!

This produces a new stylistics, one in which rules of prosody and diction are violated and new, non-conventional metaphors spring out:

> Here, say something new
> to refresh this world and that,
> release the limitless world from
> all its limitations

> (from D 546)

This gives his poems an ecstatic quality not found in some of the more recherché verse of professional poets. It may also in part explain why, as Afzal Iqbal remarks (IqL 157), unlike many of the ghazals of Hâfez, Rumi's "are the expression of a sustained emotion, and are marked by a unity of theme."

Even so, Rumi chafes under the constraints of form, unable to bring his translogical experience into the yoke of words, as he says in his *Masnavi* (M1:1727–30):

> My mind is on rhymes and my heartsome one says:
> Think about nothing but seeing me!
> Sit back and relax, my rhyming Rumi –
> You're fortune's rhyme, as far as I can see.
> What are words that you rack your brains for them?
> – Nothing but thorns on a trellis of vines!
> Words, sound and speech I throw them down to talk
> with you without these getting in the way!

and again in this ghazal (D 48):

I'm free of these stichs and sonnets
    my king and monarch of eternity!
dum-ta-ta-dum dum-ta-ta-dum dum-ta-ta-dum has killed me!
    May a flood wash over my rhymes and sophistry:
        nothing but skin and rind,
            fit for the pith of professional poets

It is therefore somewhat ironic that Rumi, along with the later poet Sâ'eb, left behind the largest oeuvre of ghazals of any Persian poet. Rumi also used more meters than any other poet – forty-eight in all – though the bulk of the poems follow one of the more danceable rhythms like *hazaj* and *rajaz* (Shamisâ, *Sayr-e ghazal*, 97). This activity of composing in rhyme and verse was a daily routine for him, and the poems frequently allude to the performance occasion, as in the final line of this ghazal (D 772):

We need a couple more lines yet
    You make them – it's sweeter coming from you
since the clouds of your mind
    make verdant my heart and breast

SCHOLARLY ENTHUSIASMS: RUMI TESTIMONIALS

Sometimes the process of collating manuscripts or working with the words of a given poet for many years can dull one's sense of appreciation. But familiarity did not breed contempt for Rumi, quite the contrary. Sir Muhammad Iqbal wrote that "the world of today needs a Rumi to create an attitude of hope, and to kindle the fire of enthusiasm for life." E.G. Browne called Rumi "without doubt the most eminent Sufi poet whom Persia has produced, while his mystical *Mathnawí* deserves to rank amongst the great poems of all time." E. Denison Ross wrote in *The Persians* (Oxford: Clarendon, 1931) that the *Masnavi* is "one of the most remarkable works in the literature of the world" (132). More recently, William Chittick has said that "One does not have to appreciate poetry to realize that Rumi is one of the greatest spiritual teachers who ever lived" (www.directnet.com/books/rumiintro.html). And Nicholson, on completing his masterly edition and translation of the *Masnavi* remarked:

Familiarity does not always breed disillusion. Today the words I applied to the author of the *Mathnawí* thirty-five years ago, "the greatest mystical poet of any age," seem to me no more than just. Where else shall we find such a panorama of universal existence unrolling itself through Time into Eternity?

As Foruzânfar put it at the UNESCO festival commemorating Rumi:

Though the world and civilization have made great progress, there are still many things in ethics and philosophy in the *Masnavi* that mankind hasn't yet understood ... He's not just a poet – Rumi's poems are the continuation of the heavenly books and divine truths.[5]

563

14

Translations, Transpositions, Renditions, Versions and Inspirations

IN THE BEGINNING

Early European translations of Persian literature made Rumi's contemporary, Saʿdi (d. 1292), whose humanist ethos was seen to share in the spirit of the Enlightenment, a figure of admiration for thinkers like Voltaire and Emerson. But the first Persian poet truly to find a home in the European imagination was Hâfez (d. 1390), felicitously presented to the English public by **Sir William Jones** (1746–94). Jones had picked up Arabic and Persian during his year at Oxford, reading Saʿdi in Persian with the aid of the Latin translation of George Gentius (1618–87) and the lexicon of Franziscek Meninski (1623–98), before leaving college at age nineteen to accept a position as private tutor to Lord Althorp, Earl Spencer.[1]

At the end of his interpretive translation of "A Persian song of Hafiz," Jones beseeched that his "simple lay" might "go boldly forth," and indeed it did, inspiring a virtual cottage industry of Hâfez translations. By 1801, there were no less than five different collections of Hâfez by various English translators, but Rumi remained as yet virtually unknown in Britain. "Oriental" Jones became one of the twenty members of Samuel Johnson's famous "Club" in 1773 and president in 1780; here he associated every other Friday with luminaries like Richard Sheridan, Edward Gibbon and Adam Smith. Jones was thus a well-known literary figure in England, as well as a judge, scholar of languages (he is credited with having discovered the family relationship between the Indo-European languages) and founder of the Royal Asiatic Society of Bengal in 1784. His renditions of Persian poems received high praise from Goethe in the latter's *West-östlicher Divan*, warranted mention in the notes of poets like Robert

Southey and Thomas Moore and turned up in allusions by Shelley and Tennyson (AOE 82). Through Jones, Persian lyrical poetry made an enormous impact on nineteenth-century English letters.

Jones gave a lecture to the Asiatic Society in December 1791 "On the Mystical Poetry of the Persians and Hindus," which included the opening lines of Rumi's *Masnavi*, the first rendering of Rumi into English, and perhaps the first translation of him into any European vernacular language. Though it never received as much notice as his Hâfez, Jones' quotation from Rumi did eventually make it to the printed page in his *Asiatick Researches* of 1794:

> Hear, how yon reed in sadly pleasing tales
> Departed bliss and present woe bewails!
> "With me, from native banks untimely torn,
> Love-warbling youths and soft-ey'd virgins mourn
> O! Let the heart, by fatal absence rent,
> Feel what I sing, and bleed when I lament"[2]

PARLEZ-VOUS RUMI?

Shortly thereafter an Austrian diplomat, **Jacques van Wallenbourg** (1763–1806), was posted to Istanbul in the capacity of Turkish translator. Apparently, however, he fancied Persian poetry better than diplomatic translation and, evidently impressed by the spirituality of the Mevlevis he encountered, began working on the *Masnavi*. He edited the Persian text of the poem and completed what was reputed to be a scrupulously faithful French translation, with prose paraphrases in places where servile faithfulness would have produced unidiomatic results. Unfortunately, his labors perished in a fire in Pera in 1799 before they could be published and preserved to posterity. But for this accident, Rumi's influence in France and the rest of early nineteenth-century Europe might perhaps have rivaled that of Hâfez. As it was, the French public did not see Rumi in print until an 1857 magazine article by F. Baudry, which introduced the story of Moses and the Shepherd from the *Masnavi* ("Moïse et le Chevrier", *Magasin Pittoresque*, 242).

For the lyrical poems, French readers had to wait almost a hundred years for **Assâf Hâlet Tchélébi**'s (1907–58) translations of Rumi's quatrains, done directly from the 1894 edition of the *Rubâ'iyât* printed by Valad Chelebi Efendi, descendant of Rumi and head of the Mevlevi order after 1909. This edition of 1,646 quatrains appeared in the Istanbul-based Persian-language journal *Akhtar*. Tchélébi, himself a Surrealistic Turkish poet (Asaf Hâlet Çelebi in Turkish spelling), chose 276 quatrains which he felt especially appropriate to introduce to French readers and published them in French translation as *Roubâ'yat* (Paris: Librarie d'Amérique et d'Orient, 1950). The same author also wrote on the life and personality of Rumi and the place of the Mevlevi order in Turkish culture: *Mevlânâ ve Mevlevîlik* (Istanbul: Nurgök, 1957).

As for the ghazals, Pierre Robin offered fourteen of them, done into French from Nicholson's English versions, in an article in *Cahiers du Sud* (41, August 1955); a recent hefty volume in the Connaissance de l'Orient series, *Le Livre de Chams de Tabriz: cent poèmes* (Paris: Gallimard, 1993), offers one hundred more in collaborative translations by Mahin Tajadod, Nahal Tajadod and Jean-Claude Carrière, with annotations and an introduction. But Rumi had already become widely available to French readers in the 1970s through the many translations of de Vitray-Meyerovitch (see "Rumi in French Scholarship" in chapter 13, above).

RUMI IN GERMAN

Rumi first captured the imagination of the Western public in the German-speaking world. **Joseph von Hammer-Purgstall** (1774–1856), an Austrian diplomat who returned to Vienna in 1807 from the Near East, began publishing a journal of oriental studies, the *Fundgruben des Orients*, from 1809 to 1814. Hammer-Purgstall encouraged Valentin Freiherr von Hussard to translate a little something by and about Rumi for this journal. After having turned his attention to Hâfez in 1812, Hammer-Purgstall wrote an influential history of Persian literature, *Geschichte der schönen Redekünste Persiens* (Vienna, 1818), which presented the German public with seventy passages from Rumi's *Masnavi* and the *Divân-e Shams* (173–95). Unlike many later readers in England, who were to conceive of Hâfez and even Khayyâm as Sufi poets, Hammer-Purgstall perceived the difference between Rumi's mystical focus and Hâfez' human concerns. As Hammer-Purgstall saw it, though the lyricism of poets like Hâfez had indeed allowed them to see above the sun and moon, Rumi had soared on the wings of spirituality above Time and Space and into the pre-eternal Beyond. Rumi was the "greatest mystic poet of the Orient, the oracle of the Sufis" and his *Masnavi* was "the handbook of all the Sufis."

Inspired by the Persian poetry which he read in Hammer-Purgstall's books, the famous philosopher-poet **Johann Wolfgang von Goethe** (1749–1832) composed his *West-östlicher Divan* ("Poems East and West," 1819), German adaptations of the spirit of the Persian poets. But Rumi did not much impress Goethe, who found Hâfez much more to his liking; Goethe permits Rumi only a couple of verses in his West–Eastern dialogue and, in the extensive notes to the poem, dismisses Rumi's theology as a not very cohesive patchwork of tales, legends, vignettes and anecdotes teaching a kind of Pantheism.

Despite Goethe's dismissal, **Friedrich Rückert** (1788–1866), who had already published a number of German sonnets, came under the spell of Rumi and studied Persian with Hammer-Purgstall in Vienna, producing in 1819 a small but exquisite number of German poems, *Ghaselen*, which, though not exactly translations, were based upon the content and form of poems in the *Divân-e Shams*. Forty-two of these poems were published in his *Taschenbuch für Damen* (Tübingen: Cotta, 1821), reprinted in a facsimile edition of 150 copies as *Mystische Ghaselen nach Dschelaleddin Rumi der Perser* (Hamburg: Lerchenfeld, 1927) and again in *Östliche Rosen* (Leipzig, 1822), a volume which elicited Goethe's praise in a review in *Kunst und Altertum.*

As poetic achievements, Rückert's translations far surpassed Hammer-Purgstall's efforts, which the Persian scholar Hermann Ethé would later describe as almost repellent in their lack of poetic form and sensibility. Rückert's poems, on the other hand, won the admiration of philosophers like Hegel and musicians like Franz Schubert and Richard Strauss, who, along with many other composers, set Rückert's poems to music. Rückert, who had gone on to become Professor of Oriental Philology at the universities of Erlangen and Berlin, produced a further collection of ghazals in 1836, consisting of adaptations in the style of Rumi, based upon the earlier translations of his teacher Hammer-Purgstall and Rückert's own poetry. Hammer-Purgstall likewise engaged in similar adaptations of Rumi, creating a long *masnavi* of his own inspired by Rumi and Islamic symbolism.[3] In 1851 Hammer-Purgstall also contributed a very insightful study of the *Masnavi* based on a Turkish commentary of the poem that had appeared in print in Cairo in 1835 (see chapter 11).

Among later translators inspired by Rückert (and by Goethe) we may number the poet **August Graf von Platen** (1796–1835), who began teaching himself Persian in August 1820. A few weeks later, he went to see Rückert in Ebern and in the following year, 1821, published his own collection of *Ghaselen.* Platen was particularly concerned as a poet with matters of form and genre; it is perhaps indicative of how congenial he found the ghazal form that while he composed only eighty sonnets, he wrote over 150 *ghaselen.* Thus, Rumi, along with Hâfez, inspired the creation of a new German verse-form.[4]

Those specifically attracted to Rumi's ghazals included the Austrian orientalist **Vincenz von Rosenzweig-Schwannau**, who published seventy-five poems culled from "the Divân of the greatest mystical poet of the Persians, Jalâl al-Din Rumi" including Persian text, notes and a German translation, as *Auswahl aus den Divanen des grössten mystischen Dichters Persiens, Mewlana Dschelaleddin Rumi* (Vienna: Mechitaristen-Congregations-Buchhandlung, 1838). Though Rosenzweig-Schwannau created quite attractive and musical translations, Nicholson chided him for his many editorial blunders and mistaken interpretations.

Almost ninety years later, **Hanns Meinke** (1884–1974), who had published several volumes of poetry with titles like "A Child in a Great Garden and the Magic of Merlin," created new versions of Rumi's ghazals on the basis of Rückert and other German translations. In 1926 he published just 490 copies of a 31-page booklet entitled *Chymische Hochzeit Merlins und Rumis; sufische Ghaselen aus dem Diwan-i Schems-i Tabrizi Dschelal-Ed-Din-Rumis* (Chemnitz: W. Adam), though Schimmel recalls that he also distributed to his friends handwritten and illuminated copies of the poems, which she describes as "faithful to Rumi in their frenzied love and absolute surrender" (ScT 395). The literary critic and poet **Ernst Bertram** (1884–1957) offered versions of Persian poems based upon earlier German translations in his *Persische Spruchgedichte* (Leipzig: Insel, 1944; 2nd ed., Wiesbaden, 1949), which Schimmel (ScT 395) describes as successful in Germanizing the "dark harmonies of some of Rumi's verses." Bertram served as Professor of German Literature in Cologne from 1922 until the end of the Second World War. He wrote studies of the poets Hofmannsthal (1907) and Stefan George (1908), of Nietzsche's mythology (1918), of the novels of Adalbert Stifter, and of Shakespeare (1951), in addition to several books of his own poetry. Though he had privately protested against the 1933 Nazi burnings of the books of Thomas Mann and Friedrich Gundolf, he was dismissed from his position along with other academics as part of the Allied program of denazification.

At the beginning of her scholarly career, **Annemarie Schimmel** (1922–), who has discussed the influence of Rumi on German literature in several books and articles, published *Lied der Rohrflöte* ("Song of the Reed Flute," 1948), containing her own ghazals and quatrains "in the spirit of Rumi." Near the end of his life, a Turko-Swiss architect and Zurich city planner named **Ernst Egli** (1893–1974) published "Dervish Dances," *Derwisch-Tanze* (Meilen: Magica-Verlag, 1973), a small collection of German verse inspired by the poems of Rumi. The Swiss scholar **Johann Christoph Bürgel**, whose work includes several academic articles on the poetics of Rumi, published a collection of Rumi's ghazals and quatrains, including commentary, in very attractive rhyming German verse under the titles "Light and Whirling," *Licht und Reigen* (Bern and Frankfurt: Herbert Long, Peter Long, 1974, part of the Masterpieces of Persian Literature in the Persian Heritage series), and "Visions from the Heart: One Hundred Quatrains," *Dschalaluddin Rumi: Traumbild des Herzens: Hundert Vierzeiler* (Zurich: Manesse, 1993). **Cyrus Atabay** (1929–96), an Iranian-born aristocrat who lived most of his life outside Iran and wrote his own poetry in German, added to these yet another new translation from the *Divân*, "The Sun from Tabriz," *Die Sonne von Tabriz: Gedichte, Aufzeichnungen und Reden* (Dusseldorf: Eremiten, 1988), a small, limited edition punctuated with essays and graphic designs from artist Winfred Gaul (1928–). **Gunther G. Wolf** has produced a German translation of Nicholson's *Selected Poems* from the *Divân-e Shams* as "Flames of Love," *Flammen der Liebe* (Heidelberg, 1988) in the Pure Lyric series of Hermes Press.

But the nineteenth-century versions continue to inspire, as can be seen in the 1912 Stuttgart edition of Rückert and Hammer-Purgstall's Rumi, *Ghaselen der Dschelâl-eddin Rumi,* with artwork by the poet and unique illustrator **Karl Thylmann** (1888–1916), and in a reissue of Rückert's "Ghasels" under the title "The Sea of the Heart Flows in a Thousand Ways," *Das Meer des Herzens geht in tausend Wogen* (Frankfurt: Dağyeli, 1988). The Austrian Academy of Sciences, with support from the cultural attaché of the Islamic Republic of Iran, has recently published another collection of Rumi's "mystical lovesongs" in parallel Persian and German columns. This goes under the equally romantic rubric "Never is One who Loves Alone," and showcases the efforts of two Austrian Persianists, reprinting the work of Rosenzweig-Schwannau and introducing the previously unpublished translations of **Uto von Melzer** (1881–1961), who taught at Graz. These translations have been collated and revised by Monika Hutterstrasser and edited by Nosratollah Rastegar in *Nie ist wer liebt allein: mystische Liebeslieder aus dem Diwan-i şams von Maulana Galaluddin Rumi* (Graz: Leykam, 1994).

While the lyricism of Persian poetry most captivated German poets and readers, the narrative verse of the *Masnavi* has not gone wholly ignored. A German diplomat named **Georg Rosen** (1820–91) devoted his attention to the *Masnavi*, putting about a third of Book 1 (vv. 1–1371) into rhymed German verse. He excused himself for presenting only about five percent of the whole on the grounds that few people would care to devote a considerable part of their lives to translating the whole text, parts of which Rosen esteemed of unequal aesthetic merit. Compared to other early translators of the *Masnavi*, Rosen did not feel himself constrained to observe the structure of the original closely, but he does convey the meaning rather accurately. His translation of "The Masnavi or Couplets of Rumi," *Mesnevi oder Doppelverse des Scheich Mevlânâ Dschalâladdân Rûmî*, first published in a limited edition (Leipzig: Vogel, 1849), was subsequently reprinted in 1913 along with an introduction by his son, **Friedrich Rosen** (1865–1935), who carried on his father's profession of diplomat and orientalist and composed, among other things, a grammar of Persian for German-speakers. **Walter von der Porten** (b. 1880) offered his own quite free German adaptations of selections "From the Book of the Reed Pipe" in *Aus dem Rohrflötenbuch des Scheich Dschelal ed-Din Rumi* (Hallerau: J. Hegner, 1930). More recently, **Gisela Wendt** published selected tales from the *Masnavi* in German translation under the title *Die Flucht nach Hindustan und andere Geschichten aus dem Mathnawi Dschalaluddin Rumi* (Amsterdam: Castrum Peregrini, 1989), adding to her earlier volume of Rumi's quatrains with the same publisher: *Dschalaluddin Rumi Vierzeiler* (1981). The indefatigable Annemarie Schimmel has also turned a selection of stories from the *Masnavi* into elegant German verse as *Das Mathnawi: Ausgewählte Geschichten* (Basel: Sphinx, 1994).

RUMI IN THE ENGLISH-SPEAKING WORLD

THE NINETEENTH CENTURY

Persian lyric poetry was transported on the wings of German Romanticism directly to the New World, where it materialized in transcendental form in the

1840s. **Ralph Waldo Emerson** (1803–82) encountered Persian literature initially in the German translations of Hammer-Purgstall, Goethe and Rückert, and began introducing it, along with the literature and thought of India, to the American intellectuals. In addition to paving the way for the innovations of the American poets Walt Whitman and Emily Dickinson, Emerson helped to shape an American interest in non-European thought and poetry. In a journal entry of 1847, Emerson shows how totally his transcendental vision naturalized foreign strains of thought with the remark that "a good scholar will find Aristophanes and Hafiz and Rabelais full of American history" (*The Journal and Miscellaneous Notebooks*, 10:35).

Born in Boston to a Unitarian minister, Emerson had enrolled in Harvard College at the precocious age of fourteen, and went on to complete divinity school. He was ordained as a minister in 1829 but, overcome with doubts about Christianity, he resigned in 1832. He then launched a career as a public lecturer and founded the Transcendentalist Club, which promoted a philosophy identifying nature and man as similar manifestations of the divine. As editor of the most influential cultural journal of America, *The Dial*, his fame also spread to Europe, and when he traveled there, he met English literary luminaries like Coleridge, Wordsworth and Carlyle. Emerson would also become one of the most prominent of America's abolitionists.

In 1846 Emerson acquired a copy of Hammer-Purgstall's translations of Hâfez, and subsequently of his *Geschichte der schönen Redekünste Persiens*. Emerson particularly liked Hâfez, and also Sa°di (he wrote the preface for a translation of Sa°di published in 1865), but he also translated snippets from Anvari, Nezâmi, Ibn Yamin and the other poets he had read in Hammer-Purgstall. Emerson's verse translations follow Hammer-Purgstall closely and therefore follow the Persian rather closely, as well. In his *May Day* (1867) Emerson included a poem attributed by Hammer-Purgstall to Rumi, but which Emerson mistakenly transcribed under the name Helâli. In a manuscript not published until after his death, Emerson did a couple of lines from Rumi, again without attribution, as "The Soul"[5]:

> I am the falcon of the spirit world,
>   Escaped out of the highest heaven
> Who out of desire of the hunt,
>   Am fallen into earthly form
> Of the Mount Kaf am I the Simorg,
>   Whom the net of Being holds imprisoned
> Of Paradise am I the Peacock,
>   Who has escaped from his nest.

Though Emerson's own poetry initially won favorable comment, critical taste began to turn away from it in the 1880s. Yet many of his Hâfez translations still read favorably in comparison with subsequent renditions.

In 1856 **Edward Byles Cowell** (1826–1903; see "History of Scholarship" in chapter 13) provided his good friend **Edward FitzGerald** (1809–83) with the Persian manuscript and the expert assistance that led to *The Rubâʿiyât of ʿOmar Khayyâm*, perhaps the most successful translation, except for the King James Bible, in the history of English literature. Cowell, who disapproved of Khayyâm on religious grounds, was temperamentally more inclined to Rumi, whom he also introduced to FitzGerald. FitzGerald wrote to Cowell in January of 1848 indicating that he had very much liked a paper Cowell wrote for the *People's Journal* (4:355–8) on the "Mesnaví," but admits to not quite following the latter part of the Mosaic legend discussed there and wonders if Cowell had not left something out. Again in March of 1851 in a letter to Mrs. Cowell, FitzGerald admits to some confusion over Cowell's rendition of the story of the Greek and Chinese painters, wondering whether the Greek wall had reflected the Chinese painting "or the face of Nature, as a camera obscura does?"

Over the course of their almost thirty years of correspondence, FitzGerald repeatedly coaxed and urged Cowell to translate the *Masnavi*, mentioning the subject on at least eighteen separate occasions. Though FitzGerald was intimately familiar with Saʿdi and Jâmi, he admitted in 1857 to knowing little of "Jeláleddín," and did not have a high impression of the artistry of his poetry, which he knew in German translation as well as from Cowell. FitzGerald nevertheless recognized the importance of the *Masnavi* and told Cowell in December of 1861:

> What I do only comes up as a Bubble to the Surface and breaks: whereas you, with exact Scholarship, might make a lasting impression of such an Author. So I say of Jeláluddín, whom you need not edit in Persian, perhaps, unless in selections, which would be very good work: but you should certainly translate for us some such selections.

Again in December of 1862 he wrote to Cowell, now busy with Sanskrit works:

> You will one Day again take up Persian as Child's Play; but I still wish you would do the Mesnaví as I wanted you to do it – an Abstract of it – which I feel sure would interest a large Body of English Readers. It seems to me you might soon accomplish this by bestowing half an hour a Day on it. This is surely the Persian Work we most want in English.

Realizing by 1870 that Cowell would probably never have the leisure for "the one Persian Book perhaps most worth translating, and hitherto untranslated," FitzGerald says:

> you should really do the Mesnavi: but I suppose you will not. It should be done by somebody. Twenty years ago I might have tried my hand under your guidance; but that is all over now.

He nevertheless continued gently to prod Cowell into providing an abridged translation of the *Masnavi*. Cowell, however, did not approve of abridgements and the entire *Masnavi* was just too demanding a task. FitzGerald wrote to him on February 11, 1875:

> But for these Eyes, I think I should have made a shot at reading the Mesnavi, which, I persist in saying, you should translate, and condense, for us ... But I shall not alter your Opinion.[6]

In the end neither FitzGerald nor Cowell found time for Rumi, but another scholar, **Sir James William Redhouse** (1811–92), did. Best known for his work as a lexicographer of Ottoman Turkish, Redhouse had however sometimes worked with Persian, translating, for example, Nâser al-Din Shah's European travelog. Redhouse probably became attracted to Rumi through the influence of the Mevlevis in Turkey and, at the age of seventy, he published the first extended portion of the *Masnavi* in English: Book 1 of the six books of Rumi's magnum opus. In Redhouse's day, titles more aptly described the contents of a book than they usually do today, and his gave a fairly full indication: *The Mesnevi of Mevlânâ (our Lord) Jelâlu-ʾd-Dîn, Muhammed, er-Rûmî. Book the first. Together with some account of the life and acts of the Author, of his ancestors, and of his descendants; illustrated by a selection of characteristic anecdotes, as collected by their historian, Mevlânâ Shemsu-ʾd-Dîn Ahmed, el Eflâkî, el-ʿArifî* (London: Trubner, 1881). The introduction (135 pages), consisting of long excerpts from Aflâki's hagiography, proved perhaps even more influential than the text of the poem (290 pages), as it canonized the use of Aflâki in Western scholarship as a historical source for biographical information about Rumi.

This abridged **translation of Aflâki** has been revised several times as *Legends of the Sufis: Selected Anecdotes from the Work Entitled The Acts of the Adepts (Menaqibu larifin)* by "Shemsu-d-din Ahmed El Eflaki." Editions appeared through Kingston (London, 1965), and after that through the Theosophical Publishing House (1976), including a preface by the modern Sufi teacher Idries Shah. Shah, following on Redhouse's example, would later provide a new selection from Aflâki in his own translation as *The Hundred Tales of Wisdom: Life, Teachings, and Miracles of Jalaludin Rumi from Aflaki's Munaqib, together with certain important stories from Rumi's Works* (London: Octagon, 1978). This has not displaced Redhouse, however, whose *Legends of the Sufis* was recently made available in Spanish as *Leyendas de los sufíes: historias de la vida y enseñanzas de Rumi* (Madrid: EDAF, 1997). It should be noted that Redhouse wrote before the adoption of a uniform system for transliteration of the Arabic/Persian script; this, combined with the fact that as an Ottomanist he often followed the Turkish pronunciation of Persian names, makes many of his spellings inconsistent with modern usage.

As to Redhouse's rendering of the *Masnavi* itself, despite his self-professed lack of ability to versify, he found it necessary to put the poem in traditional rhyme and meter. If a rhythmic equivalent of tone-deafness exists, Redhouse was afflicted. This makes for frustrating reading and Redhouse's grasp of Persian mystical poetry did not always prove equal to the task of faithfully rendering the meaning. But his was the first continuous translation of any of the books of the *Masnavi*, and it helped create an interest in the poem.

Thirty years later, one of Redhouse's readers, **Charles Edward Wilson** (b. 1858), first of Cambridge and then Professor of Persian at the University of London, determined to make more of the *Masnavi* available to English readers. C.E. Wilson's *The Maṣnavî, by Jalâlu'd-Dīn Rûmî. Book II (translated for the first time from the Persian into prose, with a commentary)* appeared in London in Probsthain's Oriental series in 1910, the first volume a translation and the second a commentary, rectifying the problems of Redhouse by putting the Persian into straightforward and pleasant enough lineated English prose. Nicholson, while working on his own translation, consulted Wilson, whom he complimented as a "trustworthy predecessor" with "sound" and "carefully executed" principles, even though Nicholson found it necessary to correct the "occasional strange lapses of judgement and errors of fact" that marred the work. Though Nicholson's own translation and commentary, completed on the basis of his superior critical edition of the Persian text, supersedes Wilson's, Wilson nevertheless remains a reliable guide to Book 2. A Pakistani reprint appeared shortly after the 700th commemoration of Rumi's death (Karachi: Indus, 1976).

Until recently, most English readers of the *Masnavi* first encountered the work in E.H. Whinfield's excellent abridgement. **Edward Henry Whinfield** (1836–1922) was well versed in Persian mystical poetry, having previously translated Shabestari's verse epitome of Sufi teaching, *Golshan-e râz* ("The Garden of Mystery"), in 1880; he also collaborated with the great Persian scholar Mirzâ Mohammad Qazvini on an edition and translation of Jâmi's study of Sufism, *Lavâ'eh*, in the introduction to which Whinfield expounds upon the Greek influence on Sufism.

Whinfield rightly observed that Rumi's mysticism is "experimental" rather than "doctrinal." His 330-page abridged translation presents a tasteful and representative selection of about 3,500 of the approximately 25,500 lines of the *Masnavi*, though he inadvertently includes some scribal interpolations which appear in the uncritical edition of the Persian text he consulted but are not from Rumi. Whinfield renders the selections in lineated prose, corresponding to the lines of the original poem, interspersed with passages of paraphrase in paragraph form, all of which remain clear and readable. It was originally published in 1887 in London by Trubner as *Masnaví-i Ma'naví, the Spiritual Couplets of Maulâná Jalâlu-'d-Dín Muhammad i Rúmí*, with a second edition appearing in 1898; reprints include an Octagon Press edition in 1973 on the 700th anniversary of Rumi's death, to which Idries Shah added a preface for the 1979 edition (reprint 1994). As recently as 1996, Whinfield's *Masnavi* was reprinted in Tehran as part of the Persian Heritage series for English-speakers in Iran. In North America, however, Whinfield's work is most widely known as a Dutton paperback, under the title *Teachings of Rumi: The Masnavi of Maulana Jalalu'd-Din Muhammad i Rumi* (New York, 1973, 1975, etc.).

This was not the first time that Dutton had published Rumi; a year prior to the appearance of Wilson's Book 2 of the *Masnavi*, **F(rederick) Hadland Davis** published *The Persian Mystics: Jalalu'd-Din Rumi* (London: John Murray, 1907 and 1912; and New York: Dutton, 1908 and 1909), a small book in the influential Wisdom of the East series, the aim of which was to create goodwill and understanding between East and West and to revive "the true spirit of Charity" amongst men, irrespective of race or creed. Davis, who wrote elsewhere on Japan and Lafcadio Hearn, gives a sensible introduction to the life and works of Rumi in tandem with selections from both the *Divân-e Shams* (in the translations of Nicholson and William Hastie) and the *Masnavi* (in Whinfield's translation). The Islamic-oriented Kazi Publications in Chicago, which has reprinted a large number of older works on Sufism, made this available once again in 1985 and Sh. Muhammad Ashraf publishers in Lahore, Pakistan has also reprinted the work.

The Festival of Spring from The Díván of Jeláleddín (Glasgow: MacLehose & Sons, 1903), a delightful selection of Rumi's poems "rendered in English Gazels" after the German versions of Rückert by **William Hastie**, a minister and Professor of Divinity at the University of Glasgow, has been mentioned earlier ("Rumi in Nineteenth-Century Western Thought and Theology," in chapter 12). Bound in an elegant leather volume, these translations were offered to the Christian public as a mystical antidote to Khayyâm's hedonism. Though it did nothing to undercut the popularity of Khayyâm, it did introduce Rumi's ghazals to a general audience for the first time in English. Though clearly a product of an earlier poetic style and sensibility, modern readers will nevertheless find these versions quite charming and accessible. Indeed, those partial to verse will find that no other English translations of Rumi's (actually Rückert's) ghazals can best Hastie, who here and there even manages successfully to mimic the verse features of the Persian, as in the refrain to "The Beloved All in All." This collection deserves reprinting.

ANTHOLOGIES

The original pantheon of Persian poets, as viewed from the West, included Hâfez, Sa'di, Ferdowsi, and Jâmi. By the last quarter of the nineteenth century, with Edward FitzGerald's astonishingly successful translation of Khayyâm following upon Jones, Goethe and Emerson's earlier fascination for Hâfez, Persian poetry enjoyed a highly favorable reputation in the West. If not exactly a household world, Rumi now began to edge his way into the canon; although he stood far behind Khayyâm and Hâfez, and even to the back of Sa'di and Ferdowsi, he attained high enough rank to win a place in a number of anthologies that found their way on to the shelves of thinking readers in the Anglo-American world.

Perhaps the first was **Louisa Stuart Costello**'s *The Rose Garden of Persia* (London: Longman, Brown, Green & Longmans, 1845). Between illuminated frontispieces and decorated pages, Costello interspersed a wealth of biographical information and intelligent commentary based on the European scholarship of the day. The paramount purpose of the book, though, was the poetry selections, which she grouped by author and translated into respectable rhyme and verse. She quotes William Jones on the superiority of Rumi to Hâfez: "There is a depth and solemnity in his works unequalled by any poet of this class; exen [sic] Hafiz must be considered inferior to him" (105). She also cites a Persian critic to the effect that the "Moolah of Rûm" understood the workings of love more wisely than Hâfez. Nevertheless, Costello relied upon the existing body of translations and scholarship then available in Europe for her information and, as a result, could only devote three pages to Rumi, two of them consumed by description. She provides just one poem, which appears quite Anglicized (106):

> "Tell me, gentle traveller, thou
>   Who hast wandered far and wide,
> Seen the sweetest roses blow,
>   And the brightest rivers glide;
> Say, of all thine eyes have seen,
> Which the fairest land has been?"
>
> "Lady, shall I tell thee where,
> Nature seems most blest and fair,
> Far above all climes beside? –
> 'Tis where those we love abide:
> And that little spot is best,
> Which the loved one's foot hath pressed."

The opening lines of the *Masnavi* had earlier inspired the title for the anthology, *The Song of the Reed and Other Pieces* (London: Trubner, 1877). These English verse renderings of Persian poetry by the Cambridge professor and explorer **Edward Henry Palmer** (1840–82) are quite charming and melodious, Palmer having already published in his youth a "merrie, metrical and monastical romaunce" called "Ye Hole in Ye Walle" (1860). In addition to Palmer's verse rendering of the *Masnavi*'s prologue, which Browne describes as "rather freely translated," but "graceful and thoroughly imbued with the spirit of the poem" (BLH 2:521), Palmer's anthology also includes four stories from the beginning of Book 1 of the *Masnavi*, along with translations of Hâfez, Anvari, Khayyâm and Ferdowsi, and what Browne called "original verses of less value." Palmer's *Song of the Reed* opens thus:

List to the reed, that now with gentle strains
Of separation from its home complains.

Down where the waring rushes grow
   I murmured with the passing blast,
And ever in my notes of woe
   There live the echoes of the past.

My breast is pierced with sorrow's dart,
   That I my piercing wail may raise;
Ah me! the lone and widowed heart
   Must ever weep for bye-gone days.

The Scotsman **Samuel Robinson** (1794–1884) so admired the translations of William Jones that he set out to learn Persian himself, and by 1823 had presented a paper to the Manchester Literary and Philosophical Society about Ferdowsi. Though he felt his command of Persian inadequate to the task, bolstered by a careful reading of the works of other scholars, Robinson printed his own translations of a number of different Persian poets in English prose: Jâmi in 1872, Nezâmi in 1873, Hâfez in 1875, Saʿdi in 1876 and, finally, Rumi in 1882. After receiving some favorable notice in the newspapers and the encouragement of W.A. Clouston, who had printed a similar volume of Arabic poetry, Robinson collected all his translations into one large volume (664 pages), *Persian Poetry for English Readers, being specimens of six of the greatest classical poets of Persia: Ferdusi, Nizami, Sadi, Jelal-ad-Din Rumi, Hafiz, and Jami, with biographical notices and notes* (Glasgow: M'Laren, 1883), and had three hundred copies printed for private circulation.

Though Robinson did include Rumi as the last member of his pantheon of Persian poets, he devoted far less space to Rumi (pp. 367–82) than to any of the other poets. Robinson prefaces each work with a biographical and critical sketch, and in the case of Rumi, draws upon Ousley's *Lives of the Persian Poets* for a quite sober account of Rumi's life; so sober, in fact, that it omits any mention of Shams al-Din. Robinson presents three selections from the *Masnavi*, including "The Merchant and the Parrot," "The Lovers" and the prologue. The rather awkward mix of poetic diction and not particularly felicitous syntax results from his aim of closely following the Persian. It does have the advantage of transparent clarity, though, as seen in the prologue:

List how that reed is telling its story; how it is bewailing
   the pangs of separation.
Whilst they are cutting me away from the reed-bed, men and
   maidens are regretting my fluting.
My bosom is torn to pieces with the anguish of parting, in my
   efforts to express the yearnings of affection.
Every one who liveth banished from his own family will long
   for the day which will see them re-united.

Although not originally distributed widely in the West because of its limited print run and private circulation, an international committee of scholars selected Robinson's translation (along with several other books on Iranian culture) for reprinting in the Pahlavi Commemorative Reprint series, sponsored by the Royal Government of Iran to commemorate the fiftieth anniversary of the coronation of Rezâ Shah and the founding of the Pahlavi dynasty. This facsimile reprint (prepared from the copy contained in the library of the University of Chicago) was published in an edition of one thousand copies in Tehran in the spring of 1976, making Robinson's translations somewhat more generally available.

Nathan Haskell Dole (1852–1935), litterateur and publisher in Boston, can claim credit for a huge number of editions of American authors and poets, as well as translations of major figures of world literature. With the assistance of Belle Walker (who went on six years later to write a book about card games!), Dole put together two volumes of Persian poetry as *Flowers from Persian Poets* (New York: Thomas Crowell, 1901), which presented selections from numerous poets, including the *Masnavi* translations of Whinfield. **Charles Dudley Warner**'s monumental and critically acclaimed project, *The Library of the World's Best Literature: Ancient and Modern* (New York: Peale, 1896, and frequent reprints), features several Persian poets introduced by **A.V.W. Jackson** (1862–1937), Professor of Indo-Iranian languages at Columbia University. Volume 32 includes Rumi, represented by a few selections from the *Masnavi* in the translations of Redhouse, Robinson, and Wilson, to which Jackson added a sample of his own.

But even as late as 1900, Rumi did not make the cut for the Columbia professor Richard Gottheil's two-volume collection of *Persian and Japanese Literature* (New York and London: Colonial Press, 1900). Though Rumi did figure in the anthologies of scholars like Browne, Nicholson and Arberry, as late as mid-century we find Major **J.C.E. Bowen**, representing the last of the British colonial officers in India or the Middle East to try his hand at Persian verse, laboring outside Tehran to produce an anthology, *Poems from the Persian* (London: Blackwell, 1948; reprinted 1950, 1964), featuring short snippets of poems in English meter and verse. These do not succeed in shaking off the Romantic and Victorian atmosphere of his predecessors, but more importantly from our point of view, Bowen entirely excluded Rumi from the twelve classical poets of Persia he presents!

By this time, however, Rumi had begun to transcend the character role of "oriental" poet and had stepped on to the stage of world poetry. An adaptation of a Rumi poem by William R. Alger appeared in the anthology *The World's Best Poetry* (New York: Bigelow & Smith, 1904, 4:405–6), edited by Washington Gladden, under the rubric "Death: Immortality: Heaven." **Mark Van Doren**'s *Anthology of World Poetry* (New York: Literary Guild of America, 1928) – an influential volume for several generations of Americans – introduces a number of Persian poets, with Rumi represented by Nicholson's translation from the *Divân-e Shams*, "A Beauty that All Night Long ...".

TWENTIETH-CENTURY RUMI

J. (Jamsetji or Jamshedji) E. Saklatwalla, an English-speaking Parsi in Bombay, published several books in the 1920s and 1930s about important Iranian figures, such as the first Iranian convert to Islam, Salmân-e Fârsi. His favorite subject, however, was ʿOmar Khayyâm, whose vogue was still at its apogee in Europe and America (where Khayyâm became the patron saint of bootleggers during the era of Prohibition). Saklatwalla's interest in Persian poetry evidently centered in the epigrammatic genre, specifically the quatrain (*robâ'i* or *do-bayti*), for in addition to his works on Khayyâm, he published a small book just before the Second World War called *The Rubaiyat-i-Baba Tahir Uryan Hamadani: A Lament* (Bombay, 1939). The book contains sixty-two quatrains of Bâbâ Tâher of Hamadan, a folk poet of the eleventh century, but hidden within its pages one also finds sixty-two lines from Rumi's *Divân-e Shams*, with Persian text and English translation.

Though we have already discussed Professor **Reynold A. Nicholson** (1868–1945) in chapter 13, it should be noted that the two small volumes he presented to the wider public as an epitome of his researches on Rumi include some renderings in verse. Nicholson described himself as "Don, dervish and dull bookworm too" in *The Don and the Dervish* (London: Dent, 1911), a volume containing original verse of his own along with poems from (or more properly, inspired by) Hâfez. Though not widely distributed, this collection was quite favorably received. Nicholson's teacher, Browne, spoke extremely highly of Nicholson's verse renderings of Eastern poetry, deploring the fact that the drudge work of "editing, proof-correcting, attending futile meetings and restating ascertained facts for a public apparently insatiably greedy of Encyclopaedias" kept Nicholson from producing more. The present writer cannot, unfortunately, concur with Browne's enthusiastic opinion; Nicholson's verse translations, which reflect a Victorian sensibility, were already in his own day rather out of touch with the revolution of literary modernism and today sound quite dated and sentimental. The few samples translated by Browne himself, in his *Literary History*, surpass the verse renderings of Nicholson.

Nicholson's *Rumi, Poet and Mystic* (1950, still available through Oneworld) begins with a verse "Prelude" which Nicholson wrote for his own pleasure and included as a dedicatory overture to the book because it "brings together some of Rumi's characteristic ideas in a simple and compendious form." The great majority of the selections Nicholson chose for this book come, not surprisingly, from the *Masnavi*, but include as well a few samples from the *Divân-e Shams* or from the Discourses (*Fihe mâ fih*). Several of the poems Nicholson rendered in rhymed verse, such as "The Song of the Reed" (the opening lines of the *Masnavi*), "Remembered Music," "Love the Hierophant," etc. Still others ("Divine Beauty," "The Truth Within Us," "The True Sufi,", etc.) he put in blank verse, though the majority appear in a prose that observes the original Persian line-breaks and remains as faithful as possible in English to the original Persian syntax.

In his earlier *Tales of Mystic Meaning* (NiT, 1931) most of the fifty-one stories from the *Masnavi* appear as they had in his multi-volume scholarly version of the *Masnavi*, but Nicholson admits to minor pruning and trimming of the longer stories and other slight modifications. He also presents two of the stories in verse: "The Man who Flew to Hindustan" (III) in blank verse, and "The Paladin of Qazwin" (XIII) in rhyme. The charms of the latter translation in comparison with all the other lineated prose versions clearly show the importance of poetic form to the *Masnavi*. Contrary to what many translators have assumed, one cannot simply extract the narrative and the teachings from the *Masnavi* and re-order them in prose in some more linear and systematic fashion; this destroys the effect of the original, which requires a discursive attention and all the lulling rhythms and punctuating rhymes which shape the exposition into aphoristic and memorable form.

Nicholson's successor, **A.J. Arberry** (1905–69), in addition to possessing eminent credentials as a philologist of both Arabic and Persian (see chapter 13), desired to share his enthusiasm for Persian poetry with a wider audience. To that end, Arberry put his indefatigable talents to prolific use as a translator, producing many works on individual poets (Rumi, Khayyâm, etc.) and Sufis, as well as compiling anthologies of Islamic literature to introduce the reading public to a wide range of Muslim authors. The impulse to anthologize necessarily entails a need to choose and select, and Arberry, like Matthew Arnold before him, viewed his task as public intellectual to pick the best of oriental poetry and provide a sampling of available translators. In his anthology of verse translations of Persian poetry, *The Rubáiyát of Omar Khayyám and other Persian Poems* which appeared in the Everyman's Library series (London: Dent, 1954; frequent reprints), Arberry selects Sir William Jones' version to represent the opening lines of the *Masnavi*, and indeed, Jones' rendering, though the very first attempt in English, seems to me the most poetically successful. This volume also reprises a number of Arberry's versions of the quatrains of Rumi and three of Nicholson's rhymed and versified renditions, as well as one ghazal from Arberry himself.

Arberry's versions of the quatrains from the *Rubâiyât of Jalal ul-Din Rumi* turn out in English as octuplet lines, usually with four pairs of rhymes (as opposed to the four lines and three or four mono-rhymed words of the original Persian). Metrically, these poems do not flow mellifluously and tend to sound rather trite. Arberry, we can conclude, did not attempt to translate as a poet, but as a scholar faithful to the presence of rhyme and meter in the originals. Even though clear and faithful, Arberry's verse translations of the quatrains will probably not please readers with an ear for modern metrics, to say nothing of free verse partisans. Though most of these translations are no more than fifty years old, they already had a rather old-fashioned cast to them when composed and will sound outmoded to most readers. Even his prose style sometimes seems oblivious of or even consciously resistant to the critical and stylistic currents that revolutionized the literary world in his youth (Imagism, Surrealism, Futurism, Cubism), though to be fair, Arberry sometimes consciously chose an archaizing style to simulate the classical register of a text, as in the case of *The Koran Interpreted* (1953).

On the other hand, Arberry's prose in *Tales from the Masnavi* and *More Tales from the Masnavi* remains quite accessible and provides a more literary and readerly text than Nicholson's complete and academic version. While one wishes Arberry had not extracted the connective tissue between stories, he merely followed other translators in assuming the meat of the *Masnavi* to reside in its entertaining anecdotes.

By the time of his two volumes of *The Mystical Poems of Rumi*, Arberry had abandoned the effort at versifying and adopted Nicholson's method of didactic translations. As Arberry himself explains, he intended these versions primarily for non-specialist readers and therefore made the renderings "as literal as possible, with a minimal concession to readability" (MPR 1:5). The flavor of Arberry's literal versions vis-à-vis his verse renditions can be gauged from the two different translations he offered of Rumi's poem (D 2214) beginning *Khonak ân dam ke neshinim dar ivân man o to*, appearing respectively in his *Mystical Poems* (2:64) and in his *Classical Persian Literature* (London: Allen & Unwin, 1958, 220–21). Interested readers can compare the two versions of Arberry with that of Nicholson (NiD, 153). Note that Arberry follows Nicholson rather closely in his literal version, except that he uses the Foruzânfar edition of the Persian text, which differs somewhat from Nicholson's own Persian text.

Arberry carefully selected the ghazals translated in *Mystical Poems* as representative of the range of theme and thought, and of the various levels of complexity, found in the *Divân-e Shams*. The first volume of *Mystical Poems* presents 200 poems chosen from the first half (poems 1–1,620) of Foruzânfar's critical edition of the Persian text of Rumi's *Divân*; the second volume, prepared for publication only after Arberry's death, contains 200 further poems gleaned from the second half (poems 1,621–3,229). Though Arberry's literal cribs lack any artistry of language whatsoever, they have ironically (or perhaps this was what Arberry intended all along) inspired and invited a multitude of English-to-English "translations." Most of the popular modern versions of Rumi by American poets, poetasters, spiritualists and poseurs are obliged to Arberry and Nicholson for the meaning of the original.

RUMI AMONG THE POETS

As early as 1907, F. Hadland Davis thought he had detected currents of Sufism in the poems of Thomas Lake Harris and in Stephen Phillip's "Mapressa." Davis also points to "The Turning Dervish" by the Symbolist poet **Arthur Symons** (1865–1945). Symons visited Constantinople in September 1902, where he undoubtedly witnessed a Mevlevi ceremony; his poem commemorating the event appeared in the *Saturday Review* (no. 94) in December 1902 and was reprinted a couple of months later in *Living Age* (no. 236, February 21, 1903), before making its way into *A Book of Twenty Songs* (London: Dent, 1905) and *The Fool of the World* (London: Heinemann, 1906). "The Turning Dervish" imagines the experience of the Mevlevi dancer growing dizzy until his senses focus on a transcendent point and he drowns in love "and am in God." Whether or not Symons had seen Nicholson's 1898 collection from the *Divân-e Shams* is unclear, though it was not unusual for late Victorian poets to have an acquaintance with translations of Rumi, in view of the vogue for *poetica Persiana* created by FitzGerald's Khayyâm.

J.E. FLECKER

James Elroy Flecker (1884–1915) knew the poems not only in translation, but in the original. In May of 1908, Flecker left Oxford for Cambridge, where he studied under the great Persianist Edward G. Browne. Having received a scholarship from the British Foreign Office, and inspired by the recent successes of the constitutionalism of the Young Turk movement, he chose Ottoman Turkey as his future theater of operations. Though an erratic student, Flecker learned Russian, Persian and Turkish once he decided truly to apply himself. Unfortunately, tuberculosis cut short his diplomatic career before it really began, but his training, and the time he spent in Constantinople, Beirut and Damascus, led Flecker to use "oriental" themes in his own poetry.

A friend of Rupert Brooke and admirer of Yeats, Flecker would later be identified as one of the circle of "Georgian" poets published in the influential anthologies of that name. Reacting against the poetic models of nineteenth-century England, Flecker favored the Parnassian poetry of France; his own career reflects the transitional period from the Victorian style to modernism. By the time he learned of Rumi, whom he read with his professor and adviser at Cambridge, E.G. Browne, Flecker had already published two books of verse – *The Best Man* (1906) and *The Bridge of Fire* (1907). Browne almost certainly assigned him Nicholson's 1898 volume, *Selected Poems from the Diváni Shams*, with the Persian text of the poems and facing translations. Under Rumi's influence (but noticeably affected by FitzGerald's Khayyâm, as well), Flecker composed a pseudo-translation of a ghazal in December 1908, which he titled "The Lover of Jalaluᵓddin," published posthumously in J.C. Squire's edition of

Flecker's *Collected Poems* (New York: Knopf, 1927). Flecker paid close attention to the metrical and formal aspects of the Persian; several of his English poems even borrow the verse forms of Persian, such as "a ghazel" entitled "Yasmin," another called "War Song of the Saracens," and the *tarji᷾ band* (refrain-poem) "Saadabad," which appeared in *The Golden Journey to Samarkand* (London: Max Goschen, 1913). Flecker also did a prose translation of parts of Sa᷾di's *Golestân*, though he is most remembered for the Middle Eastern settings and thematics of his later work, especially the posthumously published play, *Hassan* (London: Heinemann; New York: Knopf, 1922), which, set to the music of Delius, had a successful run on the London stage in 1923.[7]

COLIN GARBETT

Colin Campbell Garbett, born to British parents in India in 1881, pursued a career in government; after graduating from Cambridge, he held several important positions in Britain's Indian Civil Service in the Punjab (1904–41), as well as a stint as secretary to the High Commissioner of Iraq (1919–22). After Indian independence, Garbett moved to the Traansvaal, South Africa, where he taught as a classics master (1951–2). In addition to his own memoirs, a book about government administration in the Punjab (1910), and a history of Christ Church in Simla, India (1944), Garbett translated a number of Rumi's poems as *Sun of Tabriz (A Lyrical Introduction to Higher Metaphysics)* (Cape Town, South Africa: Beerman, 1956). This came with lavish illustrations by Sylvia Baxter, to whom he evidently dedicated the book. The volume does not seem to have found its way to many readers in England or America and so has not had a wider impact, but it did go through two separate editions in May and December of 1956. The book describes itself on the title page as "selected poems of J.a.l.a.l.u-᾽d-d.i.n. R.u.mi.": one wonders what purpose all the periods separating the letters of the author's name serve. They are mirrored, however, in the truckload full of diploma and degree abbreviations following Garbett's name (i.e., K.C.I.E., C.S.I., C.M.G., O.St.J., M.A., LL.B., F.R.G.S., F.R.S.A.).

Sun of Tabriz appeared in an irregular size-format, with the text only on the recto side, and the facing left-hand side of the page reserved for notes and commentary. The borders of the poems are decorated with occult-looking drawings ("glyphs"), and interspersed between the pages are color illustrations by Baxter featuring a poet sitting with his wine glass or his female beloved, or with the imago of the *divina feminina* piercing the clouds. Though Sylvia Baxter explains the meaning of these illustrations in a series of notes, they seem to have been rendered with the text of Hâfez or Khayyâm, rather than Rumi, in mind. Indeed, the whole work seems pitched to an imagined audience of now spiritually minded former devotees of the ᷾Omar Khayyâm craze. Garbett's introduction brings in the metaphysical kitchen sink, including references to Kahlil Gibran, Browning, Emerson, Juan de la Cruz, the doctrines of reincarnation and karma, the Qabalah, Rosicrucians, Spiritualists and Radhaswamis. All in all, Garbett speaks of Rumi as a Theosophist might speak of Madame Blavatsky's teachers.

A Lt. Colonel Gifford, whose qualifications stem from his former post as "Adviser in Languages to the Government of British-India," explains in a foreword to *Sun of Tabriz* that it takes sincerity and courage to essay a metrical translation of Rumi in English, because the translator must maintain a "gossamer touch" to avoid turning it all into doggerel. What did the reviewers conclude? Laurence Lockhart described Garbett's translations as "readable and poetic," and what's more, "imbued with the true mystical spirit" (*Royal Central Asian Journal* 44 [April 1957]: 164–5), though Peter Avery was less sanguine in his "Jalal ud-Din Rumi and Shams-i-Tabrizi with certain Problems in Translation" (*Muslim World* 46, 3 [July 1956]: 250–52).

Although the cover page claims translation credit for Garbett, all twenty-four of the poems rendered here are to be found in more literal versions in Nicholson's *Selected Poems from the Divân-i Shams*, so the word "translation" has already acquired its elastic meaning of taking prosy explanatory English versions and dressing them up in a poetic idiom. Garbett claims that the symbol of human love in Rumi represents "three separate experiences" and suggests that the translator's job involves indicating "which is the subject of the particular poem," which he insinuates Nicholson has failed to do (xi). In case the reader might doubt this, Garbett provides two of his poems in "literal translations in free style" in an appendix so that the reader "may appreciate the effort that has been made to be 'faithful.'" Unfortunately, this reader has been unable to acquire a taste for Garbett's rhymes and metrics; for poems written in the 1950s, they appear as stylistic anachronisms and though they possess a palpable sense of rhythm, they seem to lilt along like something from Kipling rather than Rumi. Still, Garbett's book marks Rumi's transition from a subject for scholarship and discussions about pantheism to a patron saint for New Age spirituality and popular poetry.

NAZIM HIKMET

The first true free verse poet to discover Rumi and draw upon him for inspiration was a Turk, **Nazim Hikmet** (1902–63), a Marxist and social-realist poet influential in the creation of the modern poetic idiom in Turkish. In Book 2 of his *Human Landscapes*, there is a fictitious poet called Jelal, and in Book 1 we find reference to the silky-smooth face of the beloved in Persian miniatures, a beloved for whom the shaykh's flute sings. These constitute possible though not necessarily explicit allusions to Rumi. In a poem called "Rubaiyat" published about 1947, Hikmet does, however, begin with explicit reference to Rumi and to a specific quatrain, Rumi's best in Hikmet's estimation. The poem proceeds to play with the metaphysical implications of the absence of the beloved, in Hikmet's case a woman, before moving on to ʿOmar Khayyâm.

Of course, the scholar Gölpınarlı produced a large selection of Rumi's poems in a faithful Turkish translation a few years later (*Divân-i kebir: gül-deste*, 1955), but this did not reach an audience beyond Turkey. Hikmet, on the other hand, is one of the few non-European poets of the twentieth century whose works have won an international audience, partly because of the beauty of his poetry and possibly also because of his Communist affiliations. The Soviet Persian scholar Radii Fish, author of a biography of Rumi (See "Rumi Around the World", p. 612), translated Hikmet into Russian, and this led to a few Soviet composers doing musical settings of Hikmet's poems. Ali Yunus provided a small book of Hikmet in English as early as 1954 (*Poems by Nazim Hikmet*, New York: Masses & Mainstream). *The American Poetry Review* featured Hikmet in 1974, and Copper Beech published a limited edition of translations in the following year, supposedly including Hikmet's Rumi-inspired "Rubaiyat," though I have been unable to track down a copy to verify this. However, the well-known Iraqi modernist poet ʿAbd al-Wahhâb al-Bayyâtî did write a poem dedicated to Hikmet, borrowing from the trope of the *Masnavi*'s lamenting flute. Thus Hikmet's poem can be seen as part of the international, and even the English, translation history of Rumi.

ROBERT DUNCAN

Rumi also found a friend in a gifted American modernist poet, **Robert Edward Duncan** (1919–88). Born in Oakland, California, Duncan studied medieval society under Ernst Kantorowicz (1895–1963), a towering figure in the study of the culture of the European Middle Ages at the University of California, Berkeley, in the 1930s and 1940s, and then went on to become one of the founding members of the Black Mountain poetry school. Though not himself one of the circle of Beat Poets, Duncan's poems helped shape the emerging American poetry scene of the 1950s and 1960s. His poems have been repeatedly anthologized, his work has been the subject of book-length studies, and his influence on the free verse movement in the United States is crucial. Lawrence Ferlinghetti eulogized him as having "had the finest ear this side of Dante."

Duncan had a strong interest in the occult, reincarnation and Hindu and Christian mysticism. He was the lifelong gay lover of the painter Jesse Collins, to whom he dedicated an eleven-page poem, "Circulations of the Song (After Jalâl al-Din Rumi)." Duncan probably encountered Rumi through the San Francisco Sufi movement of Rabia Martin, reinvigorated in the 1960s by Samuel Lewis and Pir Vilayat Khan, and the publicity surrounding the 700th anniversary of Rumi's death in 1973. Duncan could have drawn upon the works of Idries Shah, or the scholarly work of Nicholson and Arberry for his knowledge of Rumi's poems. He may even have read Hikmet's "Rubaiyat," insofar as Copper Beech was an influential poetry publisher. In any case, by February 1976 Duncan was including a version of his Rumi-inspired

"Circulations of the Song" in his public readings in Seattle and Kansas. That summer, sections of the poem were published in a review by David Quarles in *The Advocate*. The full text appeared in 1977 in the prominent literary journal *Partisan Review* (44, 1: 87–98), and once again in 1983 in the journal *Temenos* (no. 4, 77–86). Duncan then published the poem in a prominent place – as the final envoy – in his book *Ground Work: Before the War* (New York: New Directions, 1984), which also includes meditations on the metaphysical poets and études on Dante.

Duncan was quite particular about the format in which his poems were published, the line-breaks and spacings meticulously signifying stage directions for how he wished them to be recited. Though not a translation of a specific poem by Rumi, "Circulations of the Song" demonstrates a remarkable familiarity with or intuition about the spirit, pacing and style of Rumi's ghazals. To my taste, this is the closest and most satisfying approximation in the English language of the experience of reading Rumi's ghazals in the original Persian.

Whether or not **Ghulam Muhammad Fayez** knew Duncan's work, he was by this time thinking about the mystic images shared in common by Rumi and American poets. His 1978 dissertation at the University of Arizona was titled "Mystic Ideas and Images in Jalal al-Din Rumi and Walt Whitman." Another graduate student, **Sabrina Caine**, definitely did know Duncan's work. Her dissertation at the State University of New York, "Eros and the Visionaries: A Depth Psychological Approach," an examination of the relationship between art and erotic vision, introduced Rumi to a comparative literature audience, juxtaposed with Blake, Yeats, D.H. Lawrence and Duncan. **Edmund White** (1940–), author of *The Gay Joy of Sex* and numerous novels, recollects in a 1994 self-interview (see *Review of Contemporary Fiction*, 1996) that he embedded a prose "sestina" based upon a poem of Rumi in his 1978 novel *Nocturnes for the King of Naples* (New York: St. Martin's Press). There is no explicit reference to Rumi in the novel, but perhaps White, unless he has misremembered the influence, alludes to a passage (63–4) which employs rhyme and echoes with the main theme of the *Divân-e Shams*. If so, this would constitute a second imitation of a poem by Rumi in the 1970s by a gay author.

DANIEL LIEBERT

Perhaps inspired by Duncan, an otherwise unknown author by the name of **Daniel Liebert** produced what may be the first book-length collection of Rumi in modern free verse: *Rumi: Fragments, Ecstacies*, "published" by Source Books and "produced" by Sunstone Press from post-office boxes in Cedar Hill, Missouri and Santa Fe, New Mexico, respectively. This slender volume (45 pages) is printed in a non-traditional format with pages 11 inches long by 5½ inches wide, stapled in a slightly thicker textured paper binding with folded flaps – all typical bibliographic indicators of poetry or a work of inspirational character. Liebert, credited as translator, evidently draws inspiration from Rumi as a spiritual teacher, describing in the brief preface (5) how Rumi saw in the face of Shams al-Din "the image of the timeless Beloved" and was transformed by the process into one "bewildered with love, shattered, magnificent, angelic." Liebert calls Rumi "deiform" and "awesome" in terms of his humility, but describes his message as a simple one – "your helplessness and need are the Way." Liebert devotes great care and obvious talent to making the poems read as poetry, though, rather than didactic modern verse or mushy New Age platitudes. His images and phrasing often startle with their crispness and though not following traditional meters, his stanzas exude a haiku-like quality and create a musicality of phrasing and patterning based on syllable count.

Liebert presents twenty-four poems under the rubric "Fragments. Ecstacies" with only numbers for titles. He does not specify the source of each poem, though most of these evidently present lyrics from the *Divân-e Shams*. Following these we find, under the rubric "Lectures," some aphoristic sentences on the blindness and pride of reason and intellect. Though in prose, these and the brief story from the *Masnavi* about the Queen of Sheba and Solomon nevertheless possess a freshness of expression. The last section, "The Key: Rumi's Essential Teaching," presents some short meditations on various topics, in a prose that makes them new and exciting, though the passages have been encountered before in Nicholson. The collection closes with a final selection of free verse, titled "No Longer Drunk, But the Wine Itself," a medley of poems treating the theme of mystical inebriation.

Liebert's translations read as coherent and compelling English poems, and though he is not above dropping out lines or smoothing over an image, he subtly preserves an Islamic flavor to the poems, some of which still possess an occasional strangeness that would mark them as translations even for readers unaware of the source. But Liebert is confident enough about the flow of the poems in English to dispense with notes and commentary, providing only a two-paragraph introduction to the poet and his meeting with Shams, which seems to be the captivating fact about his life for Liebert. And, in the result, we sense much of the music, fervor and spirit of Rumi's Persian.

Though we cannot be sure in the case of Liebert that he worked directly from the Persian (my efforts to locate the author proved fruitless), we know that **David Martin** (1944–) did. Martin, who had earlier directed the Shiva Poetry Theater in Chicago and published his own poems in a number of literary journals, spent the years 1975–7 at the Iranian Cultural Research Institute in Tehran. He subsequently published translations of the modern Iranian poets Forugh Farrokhzâd and Sohrâb Sepehri. Before turning his attention to the modernist poets, he had tried his hand at some of the classical Persian poets. In *Comitatus* (15, 1984), a journal of medieval and renaissance studies published at

UCLA, Martin published translations of three Persian poets, Khâqâni, Sa ͨ di and Rumi. His translations of Rumi jettison the scholarly lineation and attempt to construct a unified whole out of the poems, but the diction and dramatic effects reflect to my ear a somewhat quaint and old-fashioned sensibility, as if the translator were reading the poems through the lens of eighteenth- and nineteenth-century English translations of the Persian in high Romantic or Victorian style.

ROBERT BLY

Whether or not poems published in an academic journal like *Comitatus* found a wider audience among practicing poets, Duncan's imitation of Rumi, if not Liebert's or Martin's, was almost certainly known to **Robert Ellwood Bly** (1926–), one of America's best-known living poets. Bly established his reputation in the 1960s with several books of poetry of a politically activist and anti-war cast. Throughout the 1960s and 1970s, in addition to publishing twenty books of his own poetry, winning a number of fellowships and awards, directing his own poetry press, editing several anthologies and promoting his own theory of composition ("Leaping Poetry"), Bly has been an active "translator," turning English prose summaries or old-fashioned verse translations of a wide variety of poets (e.g., Neruda, Mandelstam, Basho, Lorca, Jimenez, Tranströmer, Rilke, etc.) into a modern American idiom. Bly presents his program of translation in *The Eight Stages of Translation* (Boston, MA: Rowan Tree Press, 1983; 2nd ed., St. Paul, MN: Ally Press, and Boston, MA: Rowan Tree, c. 1986), which appeared at about the time he was completing his own versions of Rumi. He rejected what he saw as Anglo-American poetry's distorting concern with form, meter and technique and has preferred to privilege the content of poetry.

Unlike most modern American poets, who also hold faculty positions in colleges or universities, Bly remains (despite his Harvard education) a deliberately non-academic poet, choosing to live in rural Minnesota, as his farmer father did before him. His poetic theory, diction and imagery reflect his concerns with consciousness, nature and the visionary life. Bly's wide-ranging spiritual interests are reflected in many of the poets he chooses for translation. Early in the 1970s, Bly read the fifteenth-century mystic and proponent of Hindu–Muslim unity Kabir, in English versions by Rabindranath Tagore and Evelyn Underhill, done in turn from a Bengali translation. Bly felt the English renderings awful, but deeply appreciated their spirit and determined to do his own versions of them in the voice of contemporary American spirituality. This resulted first in the publication of several small pamphlets of Kabir poems, and eventually led to *The Kabir Book: Forty-four of the Ecstatic Poems of Kabir* (Boston: Beacon Press, 1977). Kabir himself likely read Rumi, and it therefore comes as no surprise that Bly found his way to Rumi (and after that, to Mirabai), as well.

In the 1980s, feeling that American culture stymies and distorts the male psyche, Bly spearheaded a movement to help men re-envision a healthy and authentic mode of masculinity. Through his book *Iron John: A Book about Men* (Reading, MA: Addison-Wesley, 1990; frequent reprints) and the weekend retreats for male healing he has led throughout the 1980s with Michael Meade and James Hillman, Bly has attracted a wider audience to poetry, which otherwise survives among a rather small niche market in the United States. In view of his calling to help heal the American male psyche, one may surmise that Bly's interest in Rumi was not confined to the text of the poems, but also encompassed the legendary relationship between Rumi and Shams and the way it exemplifies the spiritual nurturing that a strong male role-model can provide.

Bly published a slender book (44 pages) of versions of Rumi that he did with Coleman Barks as *Night and Sleep* (Cambridge, MA: Yellow Moon, 1981), with illustrations by Rita Shumaker. Two years later he came out with a pamphlet of sixteen pages containing his own Rumi poems, *When Grapes Turn to Wine* (Cambridge, MA: Firefly, 1983; reprint Yellow Moon, 1986). Bly recited these poems in public on several occasions, and has even attended a scholarly conference in Washington D.C. for this purpose. In December 1994, Bly appeared along with the dancer "Zuleikha" in New York City to commemorate the 750th anniversary of Shams' meeting with Rumi.

More importantly, Bly introduced his friend Coleman Barks to Rumi and urged that Barks do similar "translations" from the scholarly versions of Nicholson and Arberry. Bly has collaborated with Barks at recitations of their versions of Rumi, including a cassette recording, *Poems of Rumi* (Berkeley, CA: Audio Literature, 1989), with musical accompaniment. Neither Bly nor Barks strive to create meter or thick sound patterning in their versions of Rumi, but their instinct to evoke the song-like qualities of Rumi's poems with instrumental accompaniment to create ambience goes some way towards compensating for this. Instead of choosing culturally appropriate Iranian or Turkish music, however, Bly and Barks opted for Indian sitar, tabla, flute and percussion, presumably because they themselves, or the New Age audience to which such poems appealed, have associated the sitar with Eastern spirituality at least since George Harrison took up the instrument in the 1960s. I personally find Bly's voice on this tape irritating and his recitation style incongruous to the tone and tenor of Rumi's poems, though he has many partisans.

Bly has generously promoted Barks' Rumi translations, featuring them in such anthologies as *The Soul is Here for its Own Joy: Sacred Poems from Many Cultures* (Hopewell, NJ: Ecco Press, 1995) and *The Rag and Bone Shop of the Heart: Poems for Men* (New York: HarperCollins, 1992), which Bly edited in conjunction with James Hillman and Michael Meade. The former book includes thirty-two "translations" of Rumi, some credited to Barks and some to Bly, though Bly omits to mention here that people like Arberry and Nicholson actually made it possible for him to understand the content of Rumi's original. Bly gives the impression of an accomplished polyglot, claiming at the end of the introduction that all translations are his own, "unless otherwise noted" (xv). However, further investigation not infrequently suggests that he lacks the linguistic competence to read and understand in their original languages the poems he "translates." In the credits, of course, where Bly lists the source of previously published material, the names of linguistically competent translators may be found, but he does not make a habit of noting the specific provenance of individual poems.

For example, in the case of Rumi, Bly knows the content of the poems he himself translates either through Nicholson or Arberry; in the case of Hâfez, Bly apparently has access to the meaning of the Persian through Leonard Lewisohn or other scholars; in the case of Kabir, through Tagore and others; in the case of Mirabai, Jane Hirshfield first made it possible for Bly to understand the Rajasthani. On the other hand, Bly unfailingly credits his friend Coleman Barks, even though some of the poems he credits exclusively to Barks were actually "translated" with the help of John Moyne. *The Rag and Bone Shop* includes ten Rumi poems – one from Bly himself and the others all from Barks – and appropriates Rumi for Bly's project of reclaiming masculinity by calling Rumi "one of the great preserves of wildness" (4). It would appear that, just as Shams al-Din transformed Rumi's life and gave him a poetic voice, Bly has likewise nurtured and transformed Barks's career as poet.

COLEMAN BARKS

Coleman Bryan Barks (1937–) grew up in Chattanooga, Tennessee and studied at the University of California, Berkeley, and the University of North Carolina at Chapel Hill, where he received a Ph.D. in 1968, after writing his dissertation on the short novels of Joseph Conrad. He secured a teaching position at a university (he has recently retired from the University of Georgia), published three collections of his own poetry (*The Juice*, 1971; *New Words*, 1976 and *We're Laughing at the Damage*, 1977) and worked his way into anthologies of regional and new poets through the 1970s. Then, in 1976 Robert Bly showed him the scholarly versions of Rumi's poems by Arberry and Nicholson and told Barks, "These poems need to be released from their cages." Barks feels that these poems transformed his life. He worked with Bly on the *Night and Sleep* volume, published his own collection of Rumi poems, *Open Secret* (Putney, VT: Threshold Books, 1984), and visited Konya in 1984 on a kind of spiritual pilgrimage during which, in observance of Ramadan, he fasted.

Barks works "pretty much every morning" from "literal, scholarly transcriptions" of the poems which he receives from John Moyne, or from the existing translations of the nineteenth and twentieth centuries, and turns these into "valid poems in American English."[8] The scholarly translations certainly include those of Nicholson and Arberry, who are obviously not given credit on the cover of the book. However, **John Abel Moyne** (born Javâd Moᶜin), a professor emeritus of linguistics at the City University of New York, does receive front-cover billing on some of Barks's books. Moyne has published several volumes on computational and psycholinguistics, artificial intelligence, as well as a number of computer programs. In addition to machine languages, Moyne knows at least one natural language besides English – his native Persian – and he analyzed verbal constructions in Persian for his 1970 Ph.D. dissertation.

It is difficult to estimate the accuracy of the cribs Moyne supplies to Barks, since Moyne does not publish anything of his own on Persian poetry, preferring to stand in Barks's shadow. Barks may delete or modify what Moyne provides him in the process of poetifying the English; on the other hand, a deep understanding of the Persian of Rumi, with its thirteenth-century poetic conventions and religious allusions, requires something beyond a linguist's concern with language. This question may be answered by the slim monograph Moyne recently published, *Rumi and the Sufi Tradition* (Binghamton, NY: Global Publications [SSIPS], 1998), which I have not yet seen.

Barks holds some terminological misconceptions, such as the idea that "Dervish means doorway, an open space through which something can happen, so a dervish is a surrendered person." Though Barks does not mention a source, he may have acquired this erroneous notion from John Brown's 1867 book *The Dervishes* (49). Rather, the word dervish (Persian *darvish*) stems from an Avestan word meaning "poor" and came to connote, in the Islamic period, a mendicant practicing the path of poverty. Likewise, Barks's contention that a "Sufi" is an "openhearted person"[9] is rather reductive. Barks also labors under some misconceptions about the original text of Rumi, such as the observation that "there are some odes that have numbers like No. 3748 on them."[10] In reality, all the poems in modern editions of the *Divân-e Shams* are numbered, though these numbers were not assigned by Rumi. Rumi's ghazals, once collected, were organized in the conventional late medieval fashion, in alphabetical order based upon the last letter of the poem, to which are assigned sequential numbers in modern editions. Unfortunately, none of the printed editions contain ode no. 3748; the number of "odes" – ghazals and *qasides* and *tarjiᶜ bands* – does not exceed 3,500 in the largest printed collection. A trifling point, perhaps, but this imprecision is indicative of the degree to which Barks is handicapped by his lack of Persian. If Barks ever discussed such matters with Moyne, Moyne does not seem to have corrected Barks or coached him very carefully.

Questions of accuracy and authorship aside, however, Barks is, indeed, quite accomplished at making poems in a modern American idiom that appeals to a wide audience. The sales figures of Barks's Rumi constitute incontrovertible proof of this, along with the fact that large crowds attend his delightful Rumi recitations. Barks criss-crosses the country to give readings, usually in small theaters, poetry revivals, on college campuses and in Sufi gatherings, most often accompanied by an ensemble of jazz or New Age musicians providing ambience. Barks argues, like Bly – his mentor in such matters – that the musical rendition of poetry is the typical performance mode in most indigenous cultures. This doctrine may not apply to most English poets since the Enlightenment, but it is most appropriate in the case of Rumi. Barks commands ticket prices of nearly $30 on some occasions and recites for free on others; his deep voice and genial stage presence make his Rumi readings an engaging experience.

Barks has a disciple's devotional attitude toward Rumi and some awareness of the Mevlevi traditions about Rumi, which he shares, along with some Mulla Nasr al-Din stories, in between the poems. He is aware that the prosody of Rumi's Persian verse creates a rhythmic and perhaps even trance-like attention in the listener, but chooses to translate into free verse to avoid making the poems sound "contrived" to a modern reader. Barks feels that Rumi would have wanted his poems to resonate in translation with the culture of the target language. Because of his lived experience with Rumi, Barks has some insights that scholars sometimes do not notice or neglect to emphasize; in awe at the sheer volume of Rumi's poems, for example, Barks estimates that Rumi composed twelve to fourteen poems a day for the last dozen years of his life. For Barks, Rumi is not only a poet, but also a great spiritual teacher, who "can see what each soul needs at any particular moment."

Barks's translations assume the language and feel of a certain idiom of contemporary American poetry – free verse aiming for the rhythms and virtues of simple speech and breathing (a technical term in the vocabulary of Charles Olson), in which sound effects or technical artifice are downplayed. Formal technique and crafted language do not appear to concern him greatly as a poet; in teaching at least one creative writing course at the University of Georgia, Barks required no books and encouraged his students to write freely, intensely and imaginatively, leaving them to find their own subject matter and form.

Barks's versions of Rumi do not rearrange the order of the lines or create "impressions" or emotional summaries in English of the original meaning (as, for example, Daniel Ladinsky claims to do in the case of Hâfez). Barks does, however, frequently leave out material that might seem repetitious to an American audience not experiencing the poem in the metrical rhymes of the Persian. Furthermore, Barks often seems at times to have imprecisely or even incorrectly apprehended the meaning of the original. At other times he fudges culturally or religiously specific details. When Barks works on his own, his Rumi is a translation of English to English; only when he works with John Moyne can we speak of translations from Persian to English. Whether re-Englishing Arberry and Nicholson or working from scratch, Barks/Moyne do distort, as comparison of their versions with more faithful translations will show.[11] Though Barks may round off the edges, his versions remain translations and not adaptations or imitations, insofar as they follow the structure of the original poems.

The versions of Bly and Barks also have the virtue of presenting Rumi's poems as structural wholes rather than as discrete lines. The Persian critical tradition often reductively analyzed ghazals as concatenations of individual, metrically identical lines strung together on the thread of rhyme, with no overarching thematic or poetic structure. Translators, especially scholars, have often been unable to see beyond this superficial view of the ghazal. Since most translators of Persian poetry (with the notable exception of Dick Davis) no longer put their English versions in rhyme and meter, this aural thread remains untied in English and, unless the translator finds some other organizing structural principle, the whole does indeed seem to unravel into individual lines in poems of a non-linear, non-narrative nature.

On the other hand, Bly and Barks tend to present Rumi as a guru rather calmly dispensing words of wisdom capable of resolving, panacea-like, all our ontological ailments. This effect is created in their writing not only by simple diction and plain sentences, but by the tendency to resolve paradoxes, and in the breathy knowing pauses and placid demeanors of their recitation style. In reality, Rumi, especially in the *Divân*, is a poet of overpowering longing, trying to grope through his acute and shattering sense of loss – loss of Shams and alienation in the material world from the spiritual source – to achieve catharsis, usually in some kind of silent, sagacious suffering. Rumi's Persian ghazals, spontaneous, excited, full of sonorous, urgent sound play and rhythm, constantly toy with unresolved paradoxes, and do not impress the reader with a sense of serene wisdom calmly dispensed, but with frenetic search and longing to understand. Bly and Barks's view of Rumi corresponds more closely to the tenor of the narrator of the *Masnavi* than to the poet of the ghazals.

This view of Rumi as sage leads Barks and Bly to teleport the poems of Rumi out of their cultural and Islamic context into the inspirational discourse of non-parochial spirituality, all of which makes for a Rumi who shares the social assumptions of a modern American audience. For example, in his rendition of the chickpea story from the *Masnavi*, Barks introduces a sexual twist, and in another poem speaks of "sexual love," where the concept is wholly alien to the original. These wrinkles presumably aim to make Rumi more palatable to us, but tend instead to distort the poet and the person. Nevertheless, at his best, Barks provides accessible contemporary versions, filtered through the lens of a New Age and particularly American idiom, of a wide selection from the poetic corpus Rumi left behind. Barks's versions have found a wide popular audience for Rumi in late twentieth-century postmodern America, a feat achieved for no Persian poet since Edward FitzGerald's Khayyâm 150 years ago. Without Coleman Barks, the demand for the book you currently hold in your hands would be slight.

Though the public has loved his versions of Rumi, the American poetry world has shown little appreciation for the Rumi poems of Bly and Barks. Although the first collection by Barks and Moyne, *Open Secret*, garnered appreciative blurbs from William Stafford and was named the best poetry translation for 1984 by the *Bloomsbury Review,* one does not find Barks and his Rumi poems in contemporary American poetry collections, except in the anthologies for which Bly has functioned as editor, or popular anthologies of poetry for lovers or for wedding ceremonies. Barks had won a few awards for his own poems before turning to Rumi; the poetry world now seems either to begrudge him his popular success or to dismiss him for his lack of attention to the formal and technical qualities of concern to some other poets.

Barks's Rumi series includes *The Illuminated Rumi* (New York: Broadway Books, 1997), a coffee-table book of 128 pages with translations and commentary provided by Barks, and "illuminations" (read: angels and other spiritually oriented New Age illustrations) provided by Michael Green, who has also illustrated other Eastern religious books like *Zen and the Art of Macintosh.* The illustrations are primarily what's on offer in this volume; those desiring a serious sample of Barks's work on Rumi are instead advised to try *The Essential Rumi* (New York: Harper, 1995; paperback, 1996). Although the cover design of *The Essential Rumi* is inexplicably based upon a Portuguese rather than a Persian carpet, at least the book culls a representative selection of Barks's Rumi poems from a number of his smaller books (see below). *The Essential Rumi* is essentially a blockbuster poetry volume, having sold 110,000 copies according to a report in the *Los Angeles Times* (Mary Rourke, "The Mysterious Hold of a 13th Century Mystic," June 18, 1998, E1).

Barks originally published his work with Threshold Books, the publishing arm of the Mevlevi order in the U.S., but after establishing a successful market for Rumi, he was able to create his own imprint, Maypop Books, based in Athens, Georgia (Maypop's web page is mirrored through www.ccnet.com/ ~rudra/maypop.htm). Many performances of Barks's Rumi poems are also available on cassette (see "Reciting Rumi," in chapter 15). Throughout the mid-1980s, Barks produced nearly one collection per year on average, most of them between 80 and 100 pages and selling for under US$10 in 1997.

Among these titles are *Open Secret: Versions of Rumi*, translated with John Moyne (Brattleboro, VT: Threshold Books, 1984; now available through Shambhala, Boston, MA), which presents a selection of "odes" and quatrains from the *Divân* and passages from the *Masnavi*, along with an introduction. It won a Pushcart Writer's Choice Award, and though such awards tend to reflect the allegiances of style and school between writers and judges, judging from the sale of over 50,000 copies, the book succeeded with readers in a way few poetry publishers would dare to dream of. *Unseen Rain: Quatrains of Rumi*, again with Moyne (Threshold, 1986), contains 150 of the quatrains attributed to Rumi.

We Are Three (Athens, GA: Maypop, 1987) offers further selections from the *Divân* and the *Masnavi*. *These Branching Moments* (Providence, RI: Copper Beech, 1987), from one of the publishers carrying the titles of Robert Bly, presents forty poems from the *Divân-e Shams*. *This Longing* (Threshold, 1988) presents more "poems" and "teaching stories" from the *Masnavi*, along with some letters of "Jelaluddin Rumi." *Delicious Laughter* (Maypop, 1989) features "rambunctious teaching stories and other more lyric sections from the *Mathnawi*," while *Like This* (Maypop, 1990) offers forty-three further ghazals from the *Divân*. Next came *Feeling the Shoulder of the Lion* (Threshold, 1991) with yet more selections from the *Masnavi*, and *One-Handed Basket Weaving* (Maypop, 1991; reprinted Berkeley: Quelquefois, 1993), a topical selection of twenty passages from the *Masnavi* on the theme of work. We return to the short form of the *robâ'i* in *Birdsong* (Maypop, 1993), which offers fifty-three quatrains, followed by *Say I Am You: Poetry Interspersed with Stories of Rumi and Shams*, once again with John Moyne (Maypop, 1994), the third collection combining selections from both the *Divân* and the *Masnavi*. It also features some stories of Shams-e Tabrizi.

Barks has gone on to write about and "translate" a number of other mystic poets, including Lalla of Kashmir, the sixth Dalai Lama of Tibet, and Joe Miller of San Francisco. He also expanded his repertoire of Persian poems to include reworkings of earlier English versions of Sanâ'i, 'Attâr and Hâfez, in *The Hand of Poetry, Five Mystic Poets of Persia* (New Lebanon, NY: Omega, 1993), aimed at an American Sufi audience.

Barks has spread the fame of Rumi from California to the New York Island and from the Redwood Forest to the Gulf Stream waters, even if Rumi has had to become a naturalized American in the process.

HOW DO YOU SAY "TRANSLATION" IN ANOTHER LANGUAGE?

Because of the artistic and popular success of Rückert's German adaptations of Rumi, many early translators such as Emerson and Hastie rendered their Rumi from German to English. In the British empire, however, as long as the Union Jack still fluttered over parts of India, Persian was not such an exotic language to learn and many army officers, diplomats and adventurers wound up with a decent or even excellent command of it. This led to the next wave of translations, which was followed by the era of scholars like Nicholson and Arberry, whose translations, although accurate and academic, lack all modern aesthetic sensibility. Enter the professional and established poets, like Barks and Bly, who chisel poems in their own voice out of literal versions or scholarly cribs in their own language.

The idea that poets can "translate" without knowing the source language seems to have originated with Ezra Pound and his circle; Pound took Ernest Fenellosa's scholarly translations of Li Po's Chinese poems and Japanese Noh plays and worked them into a startlingly new kind of English poem.

Interestingly, Fenellosa had started off as a disciple of Ralph Waldo Emerson, who had done so many English versions of Persian and Sanskrit working from German translations. Emerson may not have known the original languages, but he was nevertheless translating them second-hand, turning German versions of Persian poems into English and making a number of Persian authors available in English for the first time. Pound, however, took the English notes and literal versions of Fenellosa and made them anew in English as Imagist poems; they served a purpose in Pound's aesthetic agenda, and this purpose stood above questions of accuracy in translation for Pound. Pound, of course, had studied comparative literature and understood several European languages, living and dead; he spoke and wrote fluently in Italian, could translate directly from Provençal and French; he even learned to write in Chinese characters. Pound did not believe in making metrical translations; rather he strove to recreate an overall sense of the music of the poem in English. Likewise, he did not hesitate to alter the meaning or translate freely where this served his purpose.[12]

John Dryden (1631–1700), in the preface to his translation of Ovid's *Epistles* (1680), identified this style of translation as imitation:

> where the translator (if now he has not lost that name) assumes the liberty, not only to vary from the words and sense, but to forsake them both as he sees occasion, and taking only some general hints from the original, to run division on the groundwork, as he pleases.

One may describe FitzGerald's Khayyâm as just that, though FitzGerald had read and understood the Persian original. Dryden did not approve of this method of translation, though he equally disapproved of what he dubbed "metaphrase," a slavish copying of the original word by word, a strategy which frequently resulted in unidiomatic English. Dryden preferred paraphrase, in which the translator renders the overall sense of the original sentence by sentence, without necessarily following the original verbatim.

Robert Lowell, who followed a practice similar to Pound in recreating Latin or other poems in English, referred to his versions of foreign-language poems as "imitations." Pound himself sometimes called his translations "transmogrifications." Translators who are accomplished poets in their own right often find it difficult to contain their poetic personas when reworking the poems of other minds in other languages. Whether because of the translator's prior fame or because of the more readerly quality of such imitations, they typically prove more successful than the efforts of philologists and literary scholars (Sir William Jones is a notable exception to this rule). Of course, the resulting imitations are hybrids, containing the genes of the original poet and also of the translator. As Dryden put it, "imitation ... is the most advantageous way for a translator to shew himself, but the greatest wrong which can be done to the memory and reputation of the dead."

Already in the classical period, the Latin authors had isolated adaptation, paraphrase and metaphrase as differing strategies of translation. Until very recently, however, imitation or adaptation assumed the translator's competence in the foreign language he worked from. Over the last several decades, however, American free verse poets seem to have jettisoned the category of imitation and now treat all reworkings of a poem originally from another language as if they were "translations," even where the "translator" knows nothing of the original language. Not translations of the original, and not second-hand translations of German or other European-language versions of the original, they are intra-lingual English-to-English "translations," paraphrases in a recognizable poetic idiom of literal cribs of a foreign-language poem. The theoretical justification for doing this, if any is needed, comes from Pound's dictum to "make it new." Such "translations" do just that, taking an old, literal English and making it new. In this way, the adaptor can market his own muse under the brand name of a foreign poet of established reputation.

Adapting the work of foreign poets, receiving inspiration from them, and creating works somehow modeled on or influenced by them certainly constitutes a vital part of any healthy literary tradition. One may sculpt an English poem from the raw clay of a literal prose crib – and it does take a certain skill to do this successfully. It is unlikely, however, that the "average" English-speaker would use the word "translation" to describe the process of rewording a prose English text into a "poetic" English text, where the person doing the rewording lacks knowledge of the foreign-language original. The fact that people like Barks resort to a linguist like Moyne to assist them reflects an understanding or an anxiety that the act of translation is dependent on having a first-hand experience of the poem in the original. A good translation operates on a series of checks and balances, an equilibrium between the systole and diastole of the source language and the target language. A writer who does not know the language of the original text functions without the constraints of sensitivity to the original language, the nuances of what it says and how it says it, the pauses, the phrasing, the sonorities. Unfortunately, many of those claiming credit as "translators" of Rumi have bleached the word of any signification.

William Stanley Merwin (1927–), an established American poet in his own right and prolific "translator" of poetry, participated with several other poets in a project to translate the ghazals of the Urdu poet Ghâlib. Merwin explains that he did multiple versions of each poem and has continued to revise them. I have been told that Merwin also published a free "translation" of a poem by Rumi in an American literary journal in the early to mid-1980s, but I have not succeeded in tracking it down. In any case, the idea of doing multiple renditions of a given poem speaks to the anxiety about what exactly constitutes translation. Is it understanding an aesthetic artifact in one language and culture and transferring its essence to an aesthetic artifact in another language and culture? Or can it be understanding an explanation of an aesthetic artifact from another language and culture and turning that into an aesthetic artifact in your own language?

JASCHA KESSLER

New York City-born writer, critic and Emeritus Professor of English and Modern Literature at UCLA, **Jascha Frederick Kessler** (1929–), has won several awards and fellowships and acted as a literary critic in magazines, newspapers and on Los Angeles radio. In addition to three books of his own poetry and several works of fiction, Kessler has also edited *American Poems: A Contemporary Collection* (1964) and worked on a wide range of collaborative translation projects, mostly from Eastern European poets, but including the Persian modernist poet Forugh Farrokhzâd, whose poems he translated with fellow UCLA professor **Amin Banani** as *Bride of Acacias* (Delmar, NY: Caravan, 1983). Before turning to modern Persian poetry, Kessler had been a lecturer for the U.S. Department of State in Iran in 1974, where he evidently encountered Rumi. He does, therefore, have some understanding of the culture and country of Iran, but he nevertheless turned to Banani, a professor of Persian literature, when he wanted to begin translating parts of Rumi's *Masnavi* in about 1976.

Kessler and Banani replicated the free verse of Farrokhzâd in English free verse, but preserved the traditional verse qualities of the original in their English versions of Rumi. Kessler believes in distinguishing between translation and adaptation, as he explains in an article titled "Translating Exotic Poetry: A Gordian Knot," which appeared in *Translation East and West: A Cross-Cultural Approach*, edited by C. Moore and L. Lower (Honolulu: College of Languages, Linguistics and Literature, University of Hawaii, 1992). Kessler expresses impatience with adaptations, which he describes as "wax flowers," at best a kind of vanity for the translating poet, an irresponsible and frivolous business (181). This does not mean, however, that all translators need necessarily possess a native or even full grasp of the source language (180); one might collaborate with someone who does have a firm grasp of the original language and literary tradition. This may even help the translators fulfill the dual responsibility of keeping faith with the original while at the same time making a reasonable contribution to the target language's poetic tradition (184).

Kessler and Banani provide an example of their collaborative effort in the *Translation East and West* volume (183–4), and Kessler has also privately provided me with further samples. These feature rhyme and meter, approaching the poems as metrical units consisting of a series of more-or-less self-contained lines, a format often used to translate the ghazal. Kessler muses (184) that Rumi might have written like Auden had he lived today and spoken English (I would have chosen either Langston Hughes or Jorie Graham as more or less contemporary models), and wonders whether one can closely approach the poet separated by a cavernous cultural divide and a time gap of 900 years (sic; the time gap between us and Rumi's poetic output of the 1240s–1270s is, of course, only about 750 years).

JONATHAN STAR

According to the jacket blurbs on his books, **Jonathan Star** graduated from Harvard, where he studied "Eastern religion and architecture." He has published translations of the *Tao te Ching* and original writings of a spiritual character. He has also studied with various Zen and Yogi masters. Like Kessler and Banani or Barks and Moyne, Star initially teamed up with an Iranian and native Persian-speaker, Shahram Shiva, for his first Rumi book, *A Garden Beyond Paradise: The Mystical Poetry of Rumi* (New York: Bantam, 1992). After that, however, Star and Shiva went their separate ways, but from the subsequent solo effort of each of them, it is clear that Star's contribution lay in the English phrasing and Shiva's in the literal meanings. For his own collection, *Rumi: In the Arms of the Beloved* (New York: Tarcher/Putnam, 1997), Star gives himself credit as translator, though he admits that all the quatrains are based upon "literal translations" by Shiva, and the longer poems are all taken from English versions by Arberry, Nicholson, Schimmel, Chittick, Ergin or Barks. Though Star implies by citing it in his bibliography that he has used Foruzânfar's edition of the *Divân*, he only cites volume 8 of that work (which does contain the quatrains, but none of the other poems Star has "translated"). Star repeats the mistakes made by Shiva, as well as adding many interpretive miscues of his own. Clearly, Star does not know Persian; he has performed his "translation" to transform English texts from one form to another.

Star intends to give us the source of each of the poems he has done, but unfortunately, due either to inattentiveness or to working at second-hand, he confuses the numbering of the two different editions of Rumi's quatrains used by Shiva, with the result that his numbering of the *robâ'iyât* (pp. 206–7) is frequently incorrect. He also wrongly includes one *robâ'i* by Khayyâm (169), which he inexplicably lists as poem 7 in Rumi's *robâ'iyât!* Had this poem even belonged to Rumi in the first place, it would have come as 1393 in Foruzânfar's numbering, because of its rhyme scheme, not as number 7. Perhaps the notes of Shiva misled him or Star misinterpreted them (Shiva indicates in *Garden Beyond Paradise* that he has included some quatrains which are traditionally attributed to Rumi, but do not appear in Foruzânfar's text). In any case, this particular poem is quite at odds with Rumi's *Weltanschauung*, and one is greatly surprised to find it sneaking its way in to this volume. Star also wrongly interprets some of the quatrains he renders (46, 92), and plays rather freely with others (e.g., 105, 106, 157).

All caviling aside, however, Star's re-renderings flow easily and clearly and are not devoid of their own appeal. As for the book which Star and Shiva produced together, *A Garden Beyond Paradise*, it contains 160 quatrains and 31 "odes."

Most of the translations in this volume were done collaboratively, though Star was already translating a few "odes" by himself on the basis of Nicholson and Arberry. Shiva, on the other hand, reads the poems in the original and provides the basic meaning of what Rumi said. The translations tend to be rather free, omitting and adding where it suits. As for the style, they strove to create a "terse, cadent" English sculpted into a form that would give "some sense of the repetitive and breathless urgency so characteristic of Rumi's original." This objective of making the poems "sound like Rumi, feel like Rumi" and capture his spirit distinguishes their effort from that of Barks, though both Barks/Bly/Moyne and Star/Shiva share the view of Rumi as "poet–saint." Star/Shiva distinguish their work from Arberry and Nicholson, on the other hand, with the observation that though the scholarly versions were "diligent and precise" they made "minimal concession to readability" (xxiii–xxv).

A chart (xxiv) helpfully plots the rhyme scheme of Rumi's quatrain and "ode" (ghazal), but unfortunately inverts the place of the recurring rhyme. Persian is written right to left and perhaps this accounts for the transposition – rather than AA AB AC, it should read AA BA CA. Furthermore, the last line of the ghazal must conform with the rhyme in the rest of the poem, so the rhyme scheme for last line should read EA, not EE. Despite these problems, this book provides a readable selection of Rumi in English which does not simplify and tame his language as much as do Barks and Bly.

SHAHRAM SHIVA

The Iranian-born New Yorker Shahram Shiva "comes from a long line of Persian poets" and has worked as a clothing designer, artist and photographer. His *Rending the Veil: Literal and Poetic Translations of Rumi* (Prescott, AZ: Hohm Press, 1995) presents a selection of Rumi's quatrains in a format designed to function both as a "reading guide" and a translation (xvi). Shiva has selected 252 of Rumi's *robâ'is*, emphasizing those with unique imagery (xxiii). He culls the poems from two different printings – the University of Tehran and the Amir Kabir – of Foruzânfar's critical edition of the *Divân-e Shams*. *Rending the Veil* presents the text of each poem in large, calligraphic Persian script, followed by a transliteration so that those unable to read Persian can hear the sounds of the original. There follows a verbatim rendering of the Persian and then an idiomatic "semi-poetic" translation (xxiii). This is a very helpful procedure for students of Persian and will, I hope, encourage lovers of Rumi to acquire Persian.

Unfortunately, however, the literal renderings in this volume show many errors of understanding, some of which produce embarrassing howlers. For example, in one poem (85) Shiva reads *do kun* (two derrières), instead of the correct *do kown* (two planes of existence – either this world and the hereafter, or the physical and spiritual planes). In order to avoid indecency, Shiva translates as

599

if the text read *do kuh* (two mountains)! Elsewhere, he mistakenly reads *pârsâ'i* as "Persian blood" (58), when it actually means "celibacy" or "continence," and translates *migu* (go on talking) as "don't speak" (24). There are numerous smaller errors, especially in the transliteration, though these will merely affect the pronunciation, not the meaning. This must be said, since Shiva implies that his versions have a superior insight into the poems, by virtue of his direct access to the Persian (xxii).

Shiva maintains a very useful web site dedicated to Rumi (www.rumi.net) where one may see samples of his translations and of Rumi's quatrains. He gives Rumi concerts and workshops for a living, samples of which can be seen on cable television in New York City. He also leads nine-day tours to Konya for $2,700 round trip from New York and will teach people in minutes how to do the dervish turning comfortably with his "Four-Step Method," which he developed in consultation with a whirling Persian master named Javâd. Shiva's *Hush Don't Say Anything to God: Passionate Poems of Rumi* was scheduled to appear in the fall of 1999 through Jain publications.

JAMES COWAN

A kind of modern-day explorer, **James G. Cowan** (1942–) lives as an art teacher among the Kukatja aborigines in the Tanami Desert in northwest Australia. He has written a number of books about tribalism and aboriginal religion, such as his memoir and travelog *Two Men Dreaming* (1995), and a work of historical fiction, *A Mapmaker's Dream: The Meditations of Fra Mauro* (1996). Cowan's interest in non-Western spirituality impelled him to explore Konya (among other places), where he visited the sites associated with Jalâl al-Din Rumi and gathered quite a bit of information. Indeed, Cowan displays more familiarity with Shams al-Din Tabrizi, paraphrasing a story from the *Maqâlât*, than most of the other writers who have treated the topic, and he sketches in some interesting impressionistic details of Rumi's life. Much of this material he must have gleaned from Schimmel, Türkmen, Önder and other Rumi books available in English in Turkey.

Unfortunately, Cowan lacks the contextual background properly to evaluate his sources, and the lengthy introduction to his *Rumi's Divan of Shems of Tabriz: A New Interpretation* (Element Books, 1997) therefore gives a mishmash of fact and fiction, along with his own interpretations which, though colorful, present a sometimes fanciful and distorted picture of Islamic philosophy, the background of Shams, etc.[13] Cowan betrays the mistakes of an autodidact, such as the mixing of various transliterations (representing mostly Turkish, but occasionally Arabic and Persian pronunciation, obviously taken from the various sources Cowan quoted) as if they were all the same language (e.g., Bahauddin, Hujjat-ul-Islam, Alaodin, Shems-i-Tabriz, Ebubekir, Mathnawi, parindah, medrese, sobhet), reserving one accent mark only for Mevlana Jaláluddin Rumi; indeed, the first edition of the book, *Where Two Oceans Meet: Selection of Odes from the "Divan of Shems of Tabriz"* (Shaftesbury, UK and Rockport, MA: Element, 1992) indicated that Cowan had translated the poems from Arabic! Although Cowan includes some footnotes and a bibliography (the latter including works by Nietzsche, Van Gogh, Marcelo Ficino, Kazantzakis, Arthurs Miller and Rimbaud, and Dietrich Fischer-Dieskau!), he obscures his sources in the text and weaves them in with his own assured assertions, creating the illusion of expertise. With this lector's caveat, Cowan's introductory essay can nevertheless prove quite entertaining and stimulating reading.

The "New Interpretation" of the title refers to the fact that Cowan has taken Nicholson's 1898 collection of fifty poems from the *Divân-e Shams* and reworked them into "modern verse structures," replacing the Victorian diction and rectifying Nicholson's decision to make a "literal translation at the expense of the text's inherent verbal dexterity and beauty" (41). Cowan claims to have broken down the odes "into their original beyts, or couplets" as a conscious decision to make the line of thought in the poems "less diffuse." Of course, Nicholson had already translated line by line, so Cowan's remarks apparently refer to the decision to lineate the poems on the page as separate couplets, a practice which in fact exacerbates the disconnectedness he observes between the various lines. His aesthetic sees the emotions of a poem coming from cadence, while the intellectual appreciation comes from the words. He has therefore tried to "compress Rumi's discursiveness" to match word and rhythm perfectly. I must confess, however, my inability to discern any pattern in Cowan's metrics.

RE-PACKAGING RUMI

Robert Van de Weyer (1950–) spent the late 1980s and early 1990s producing edition after edition of inspirational poetry, including volumes on John Donne, Blake, a Christmas treasury for families, and a book of prayers. He currently produces (or "edits") a series called "Philosophers of the Spirit," which straddles the market between classic literature and New Age spirituality. This slim series (each volume is about ninety pages long) "introduces the modern reader to the wisdom of the great philosophers in an easily readable form," aiming to inform while it inspires. Earlier volumes included such thinkers and mystics as Spinoza, Pascal, Chuang Tzu, Kierkegaard, Eckhart, Hildegard von Bingen, etc., and now we have, with a bright colorful cover, *Rumi in a Nutshell* (London, Auckland and Sydney: Hodder & Stoughton, 1998). The back cover blurb, which indicates that Rumi "lived in Persia and Afghanistan in the 13th century," fudges matters quite a bit – Afghanistan did not exist, and anyway the cities where Rumi lived as a boy are actually in Tajikistan and Central Asia today, though he lived most of his life in Turkey. Nevertheless, the introduction to Rumi's life and the general comments about Sufism and the Koran provide fairly accurate and thoughtful points for consideration. The text itself consists of prose paragraphs from the *Masnavi*, the bulk of which constitute the spiritual teachings of Rumi; only a short section of "parables" at the end of the book give the extended stories that make the reading of the *Masnavi* so enjoyable. Van de Weyer relies upon Nicholson, Arberry and Chittick for these selections.

A Cambridge-educated economist, **Krish Khosla**, has invested his emotional capital in Rumi, whom he has studied in India for the past thirty years. Khosla does not appear to have picked up Persian as part of that study, since his *Rumi Speaks Through Sufi Tales* (Chicago: Kazi, 1996) was apparently done on the basis of Nicholson's full translation of the *Masnavi*. Nicholson's prose is, of course, consciously academic; Khosla's prose is clear, but with a rather old-fashioned ring. Khosla has also published *Rumi's Sufism* (Kazi, 1996).

DEEPAK CHOPRA

According to the official web page hosted for him by his publisher (www.randomhouse.com/Chopra) **Deepak Chopra** is a "leading, internationally recognized motivational speaker," who directs the Sharp Institute for Human Potential and Mind/Body Medicine in San Diego and serves as educational director of the Chopra Center for Well Being (est. August 1996) in La Jolla, California. Author of the best-seller *Ageless Body, Timeless Mind* (New York: Harmony Books, 1993), Chopra styles himself as a spiritual health guru combining Western medicine and the techniques of Ayurvedic yoga, in which capacity he has appeared frequently on public television in the United States.

Chopra recently jumped on the Rumi bandwagon with *Love Poems of Rumi* (Harmony, 1998). The idea for this sixty-page volume, which credits Chopra as editor, came to him in February 1996, while teaching a course called "Seduction of Spirit." At that time he met a certain Fereydoun Kia, who introduced Chopra to a "love song" of Rumi that Kia had translated into English. That very evening a woman from the course performed an "ecstatic dervish dance" as Chopra recited the poem in English and music was played to her movements. Ostensibly overwhelmed with emotion, Chopra said "Let's do a new translation of love poems by Rumi." Kia, described in the book as a "Farsi scholar," indicates in the acknowledgement that he had for quite some time been immersed in the poems of Rumi and "the task of relaying their spiritual message" to Chopra.

Unfortunately, either Fereydoun failed to convey or Deepak failed to heed that message. Although at least one poem ("Die! Die!," 37–8) recognizably follows the text of a ghazal by Rumi, these "new translations" are by and large not "direct" translations of the text, but adaptations, or "moods captured as certain phrases radiated from the original Farsi." As such, they have far more to do with Chopra's New Age garrulity (or guru-ality) than with Rumi's Shams-fired Muslim mysticism.

Chopra evidently did not spend much time learning about Rumi's life; not only does the book fail to introduce the reader to the name of Shams, it reflects confusion about the century in which Rumi lived. At the end of the introduction we read that Rumi's teachings "live on one thousand years after he walked on this earth," though poor Rumi has only been in the ground for 725 years. In addition to Kia's "mood" translations, Chopra includes the text of four poems from the collection *Bird Song* by Coleman Barks, who, in a gesture of mutual admiration, has contributed a testimonial blurb for the dust jacket.

The influence of Chopra, described by Robin Givhan in a recent *Washington Post* article (April 6, 1998, D1) as "popular culture's most irritating Zen doctor," has moved Rumi into the glamorous world of high fashion. Designer Donna Karan, describing herself as enamored of light, introduced her new fall fashions, inspired by none other than the love poems of Rumi. Her models sauntered down the runway accompanied by a soundtrack with readings from Deepak's versions of Rumi by such discerning mystics and literary connoisseurs as Madonna and Demi Moore. That soundtrack, however, is very pleasant to listen to; anyone interested in Chopra's versions of Rumi would be well advised to invest in the CD version, *A Gift of Love* (see "Reciting Rumi" in chapter 15).

AIMING FOR AUTHENTICITY

A modern spiritualist and author of several books on various mystic traditions of the world, **Andrew Harvey** (1952–) is a disciple of Mother Meera (1960–), whom he describes as "an incarnation of the Divine Mother on earth," whose work transcends religious or mystical traditions with unconditional Love to transform humanity, help it rediscover its spiritual roots and achieve harmony.[14] Harvey, who now lives in Paris, grew up in India and was inducted into the spiritual path by a Tibetan monk, as described in his book, *A Journey in Ladakh* (1983). He has produced a number of poetry and inspirational volumes and has promoted a mystical approach to religion in a number of other works, such as his anthology of *The Essential Mystics: The Soul's Journey into Truth* (New York: Harper, 1996) and *Son of Man: The Mystical Path to Christ* (New York: Tarcher, 1998). In addition to the *Divine Feminine* (1996), Harvey has an interest in gay spirituality, as attested by his *The Essential Gay Mystics* (Harper, 1997). Curiously, though Harvey misleadingly appropriates Hâfez, Sa^cdi, ^cErâqi and other Persian poets as gay or bisexual, he does not subject Rumi to the same treatment.

After Mother Meera came to him speaking words of wisdom, Harvey's interest in mystical modes came to focus on Rumi; he dedicates the *Way of Passion: A Celebration of Rumi* (Berkeley: Frog, 1994; reprinted London: Souvenir, 1995 and made into an audio book in that same year) to the rather unlikely duo of Mother Meera and Shams-e Tabriz. Harvey's first attempts to understand the metaworld of Rumi led to *Love's Fire: Re-creations of Rumi* (Ithaca, NY: Meeramma Publications, 1988) and *Speaking Flame* by Rumi, as "re-created" by Andrew Harvey (Meeramma, 1989). Five years later, after the publication of some of his Rumi poems in the *Partisan Review* (57, 1 [1990]: 113), he conceived *The Way of Passion* when "the sudden naked truth" revealed itself in the spring of 1993 during a series of lectures Harvey delivered at the California Institute of Integral Studies in San Francisco. Before presenting these lectures, conceived as a "Sufi celebration" and described by Harvey as "a dance around Rumi and that mystery of Love he lived and expressed so completely" (ix), Harvey grappled with the question of how to present Rumi to a modern American audience. He dreamed that an old man in a sunny mosque had instructed him to be "passionate and precise, drunken and perfectly sober." Harvey sees in Rumi, whom he compares to Ramakrishna, Sri Aurobindo, Teilhard de Chardin, and the Dalai Lama, among others, a modern spiritual guide out of the slough of our dying materialistic civilization. For Harvey, Rumi is a "doctor of souls" whose message can bring us to our spiritual senses and keep us from destroying the planet before it is too late (*Way of Passion*, 2).

The Society for the Study of Native Arts and Sciences sponsored a second book by Harvey, *Light upon Light: Inspirations from Rumi* (Berkeley: North Atlantic, 1996), with photographs by Eryk Hanut. This nonprofit society is an educational corporation seeking to "develop an educational and cross cultural perspective linking various scientific, social, and artistic fields." *Light upon Light* is meant to be read deliberatively and meditatively, or heard like a symphony (x–xi). The over-wide format of the book (9.5 inches long, 7 inches wide), somewhat smaller than a typical coffee-table book, and the page layout – passages of a page or less, usually accompanied by a facing photograph – suggest a medieval spiritual manual or daybook. It includes longer poems from the *Divân-e Shams* and the *Masnavi*, long prose passages from the Discourses, quatrains, and a few short passages from Rumi's letters, but most of the brief quotations peppering the text come from the *Divân* or the "Discourses" (xi).

As sources for his Rumi translations, Harvey relies upon the French versions of Eva de Vitray-Meyerovitch (*Light upon Light*, 247) and upon conversations with her in Paris. In addition, Harvey works with the popularized versions of Bly, Barks, Star and Shiva, as well as the scholarly versions of Whinfield, Nicholson, Arberry, Schimmel and Chittick. In short, he uses a variety of renderings in at least two different languages to help him approach the essence of Rumi (x). These do not, however, include the Persian originals of Rumi, so Harvey discreetly and accurately refers to his poems as re-creations or "trans-creations." Harvey's own versions nevertheless read very nicely for the most part, though he sometimes seems to simplify the narrative progression for the purpose of teaching a doctrine. Harvey projects an essentially mythical Rumi in the role of great Sufi and mystical teacher.

Harvey's adaptation of Rumi's quatrains, *Love's Glory: Re-creations of Rumi* (San Francisco and Berkeley: Balthazar and North Atlantic), also appeared in 1996. More recently, Harvey has expanded the scope of his interest in Sufism to other poets with his *Perfume of the Desert: Inspirations from Sufi Wisdom*

(Wheaton, IL: Quest Books, 1999). This book, working again with Eryk Hanut, of course includes Rumi, but not so prominently as before.

In all these books, Harvey demonstrates a working knowledge of Sufism and familiarity with a range of books about Rumi available in Western languages. Although he repeats hagiographical material as though it were factual, and generally avoids presenting Rumi within the context of Islam as a religious discipline or theological system, Harvey has contributed a useful guide to his life. More than that, he has made an appealing brief for Rumi as proponent of the Perennial Philosophy and transformer of psyches for a new age, delineating four stages of spiritual growth which he illustrates with quotations from Rumi.

KABIR AND CAMILLE HELMINSKI

Kabir Helminski (1947–), whom we met as Shaykh of the Mevlevi order in America (see chapter 12), has selected and edited *The Rumi Collection: An Anthology of Translations of Mevlâna Jalâluddin Rumi* (Brattleboro, VT: Threshold, 1998), which quite selflessly gathers samples of the Rumi renderings of nine different English translators and imitators. Newcomers to Rumi or those wishing to introduce him to a friend should begin with *The Rumi Collection*, as it will familiarize the reader with the style of the various translators and allow her to find the one(s) she likes best with minimal effort and expense. Helminski recognizes that poetic translation is inherently quite subjective since it aims to render the presence of a given poet's individuality in a perceptible way (xi). Though he obviously celebrates the multiple English versions of Rumi, he worries that the Western translations of Rumi have recreated him according to our own stereotypes of the spiritual rebel, the ecstatic mystic and the man of enlightened consciousness (xv). Translators may pursue different paths and emulate various facets of the original. For Helminski, the original rhythm and sonority of the poem and the transcendent tone are what he focuses upon in trying to recreate English versions of the poems, an objective which leads him to opt for Anglo-Saxon monosyllables over multisyllabic Latinate styles (xii).

Helminski does know some Persian. He begins his work of translation from the literal scholarly versions in English, and then cross-checks these directly with the original Persian. To my taste, Helminski's own versions come closer to the original than most of the others whose work he presents. Helminski translates into free verse with a fine sense of phrasing, pacing and authenticity. His own Rumi translations began with *Ruins of the Heart: Selected Lyric Poetry of Jelaluddin Rumi* (Putney, VT: Threshold, 1981), one of the earliest poetic Rumi translations. This volume of fifty-five pages has since been replaced by the longer *Love is a Stranger* (Threshold, 1993).

Since then, Kabir has collaborated with wife Camille (1951–) on *Rumi: Daylight. A Daybook of Spiritual Guidance* (Threshold, 1990) which provides 365 selections, one for each day of the year, from Books 1 and 2 of the *Masnavi*.

This format proved very popular and led the Helminskis to produce a second volume, *Jewels of Remembrance: A Daybook of Spiritual Guidance* (Threshold, 1996), which presents 365 selections from the last four books of the *Masnavi*. These latter selections are arranged to describe and guide a spiritual journey, but the selections are rearranged into the original order of the *Masnavi* on a web site (hcgl1.eng.ohio-state.edu/~hoz/mesnevi.html).

Kabir Helminski has also published an article, "I Will Make Myself Mad," in *Parabola* 23, 2 (Summer 1998): 9–14, which analyzes the ecstatic statements of Rumi and other Sufis as expressions, not of the emotions, but of the spiritual release that comes with detachment from Self. With *The Drop that Became the Sea* (Threshold, 1989), done with Refik Algan, Helminski turned his attention to translating the Turkish poet Yunus Emre. Camille Helminski has gone on to do a daybook of verses from the Koran, *The Light of Dawn* (Threshold, 1998) and has also worked with Refik Algan on the translation from Turkish of Ahmet Hilmi's *Awakened Dream*, the vision of an early nineteenth-century Turkish Sufi.

NADER KHALILI

Iran has produced many a fine architect and mathematician. **E. Nader Khalili**, an Iranian expatriate living in California since 1970, promotes a visionary new building technique of adobe and ceramic houses, an affordable "earth architecture" that produces ecologically harmonious structures. His "geltaftan" process fires clay or adobe structures from the inside with homemade torches, as one would a ceramic bowl. This practical and low-cost method has attracted some attention; he has been recognized with a number of awards and grants, has worked with the United Nations and even with NASA designing structures for a theoretical moon colony. His impassioned and poetic books have attracted notice in architectural magazines and the mayor of Hesperia hailed his designs as having the "potential of revolutionizing the housing industry." Khalili believes that every man and woman should be able to "heal and shelter themselves," and for this reason works with "the simplest of elements – earth, water, air and fire." Khalili has made a number of videos documenting the building technique of fired-earth schools in Iran, India and the U.S.

Khalili established the California Institute of Earth Art and Architecture (Cal-Earth) in 1986, inspired by Rumi, who believed elemental matter to consist of water, earth, wind and fire (as did all other medieval Persian poets, as well), yet saw love as the mortar holding the metaphysical universe together. Like the Turko-Swiss city-planner Ernst Egli before him, Khalili has tried his hand at reconstructing Rumi's poetry in another language. Though Khalili describes a dream he had of a conversation with Rumi as the proximate cause for his efforts over 1991–2 to translate some of the ghazals of Rumi, he must also have found the English-to-English versions of Bly and Barks dissatisfying. Burning Gate Press, which first published Khalili's three books on physical architecture, also published his *Rumi: Fountain of Fire* in paperback in 1994. Cal-Earth Press in Hesperia, California, Khalili's own endeavor, produced a second edition in 1996. This contains seventy-five poems from Rumi's *Divân-e Shams*, translated directly from the Persian text, with a note at the end of each poem indicating the number of the poem in the Persian edition.

Khalili's friend William Chittick, who provides a long informative blurb for *Fountain of Fire*, feels that most "poetic" English renditions appear pale and inaccurate in comparison with Rumi's Persian, and expresses pleasure at the results of Khalili's efforts. Khalili renders each verse (*bayt*) of Rumi in one or two stanzas of three to four short lines, usually between five to seven syllables, weaving a fine thread of narrative or argument through the various stanzas to make the poems read as structural wholes. This vision of the ghazals as organic whole is, of course, to be found in Bly and Barks before him, as is the attitude of reverence toward Rumi as great wise teacher. But Khalili's free verse Rumi has more natural verve to my ear than most of Barks' breathier, pause-punctuated stanzas or sentences.

The fact that Khalili worked directly from the Persian, rather than from existing translations, has not necessarily made his versions more accurate. He sometimes misreads the drama or the sense of the line, and purposely bleeds the poems of cultural and Islamic allusions. He excises all the lines containing mention of Shams-e Tabriz, which, of course, significantly alters the nature of the poetic persona we hear. This highlights something which may not be readily apparent to non-Persian readers; Rumi's poetry speaks through the idioms of medieval Persian poetry, relying upon allusions and conventions which may be lost upon the untrained modern reader of Persian, or may in some few cases even sound old-fashioned or retrograde. Though modern Persian-speakers in Iran, Afghanistan or Tajikistan can readily understand the grammar and much of the vocabulary of thirteenth-century Persian (unlike the case of English-speakers and thirteenth-century English), they may not understand all the assumptions behind the images and references in the poems. Just as a modern American may not understand all the nuances or allusions of Shakespeare or Spenser without some prior background in English literature, so, too, a modern Iranian reader not versed in medieval poetry may only vaguely understand many lines of medieval Persian poetry; indeed, specialists disagree over the exact meaning of many lines.

Khalili has effectively performed two translations with his Rumi poems: he has deliberately rounded off the obscure edges and unfamiliar contours to make the poems more immediate for a modern audience, and he has rendered the poems from the Persian language into English. With this caveat in mind, Khalili's Rumi is full of charm. It does not read like a translation, yet it manages to convey the spirit of some of Rumi's many moods in a viable modern idiom. In contrast to many other Rumi interpreters, Khalili understands and conveys that Rumi is not always a tranquil guru speaking from the peaks of enlightenment, but a pained and frenzied seeker. Khalili is said to be at work on a second volume of Rumi, containing versions of his quatrains or *robâ'is*.[15]

NEVIT ERGIN

Nevit Oguz Ergin, M.D., was born in Turkey in 1928, but lives and practices medicine in Valencia, California. He has worked with a nonprofit organization called the Society for Understanding Mevlana and with the Turkish Ministry of Culture. Ergin produced two small collections of translations of Mevlana Celaleddin Rumi (following the Turkish pronunciation), which are widely available in the United States: the first a selection of quatrains, *Crazy as we Are: Selected Rubais* (Prescott, AZ: Hohm, 1992), and the second a selection of ghazals, *Magnificent Ones* (Burdett, NY: Larson, 1993). Ergin's English gives fairly accurate English renderings of Gölpınarlı's Turkish translations, which are, in turn, accurate translations of the Persian. Though Ergin in these two collections tends (like many modern "translators") to relate to Rumi's poems more as spiritual quips than as poetry, his versions are clear and readable.

In the introduction to *Magnificent Ones*, Dr. Ergin provides a few autobiographical details, explaining that while he had practiced breathing exercises out of curiosity as a youth, his introduction to Rumi and Sufism did not come until his late twenties, when he met a Sufi author by the name of Hasan Lotfi Shushud (Şuşud) in 1956. Ergin read Rumi's *Divân* at that time and the reader is left to infer that he did so at least partly in Persian, though this seems quite unlikely. First, Ergin's education took place after Turkey had switched from the use of the Arabic to the Latin script, making Ottoman Turkish texts inscrutable to modern Turks who have not spent some time learning it. Persian is not only written in the Arabic script but comes from an entirely different language family, and though Turkish adopted a good deal of Persian vocabulary, a modern Turk must study Persian as a foreign language just as a modern English-speaker must study French as a foreign language. Given Dr. Ergin's pursuit of medicine, it seems unlikely he has spent the time necessary to acquire Persian well enough to understand Rumi in the original.

Second, Ergin recalls that Gölpınarlı's Turkish translations were not only "more easily available to buy" in Turkey, but also easier for him to read than "13th century colloquial Farsi works." While Rumi's Persian does indeed contain some colloquial Persian (and even the occasional Turkish and Greek), this characterization, along with Ergin's misspellings of Persian words and names (e.g., Risals, Fihi ma Jihi, Firuzenfar) and his misconceptions about the medieval Persian manuscript tradition, lead me to conclude that Ergin was unfamiliar or at most only cursorily acquainted with the Persian text of Rumi.

Rather, Ergin first read Rumi in the Turkish scholar Gölpınarlı's *Gül-Deste: Divân-i Kebir'den seçme Şiirlerin tercemeleri* (Istanbul: Remzi, 1955), an anthology of Rumi's ghazals in Turkish translation, which Ergin admits he did not begin fully to understand until the mid-1980s. By this time, Gölpınarlı's Turkish translation of the entire 44,000 verses of the *Divân-e Shams* had been published (*Divân-i kebir Tercemesi*, 1957–8), and Ergin claims to have compared this with the original Persian. Oddly, however, Ergin did not see fit to use the printed editions of the *Divan* which were readily available from Iran – in particular the text-critical edition of Foruzânfar – but claims to have used a single "handwritten Farsi edition" (i.e., a manuscript copy of the *Divân* in Persian, nos. 68–9 in the Mevlânâ Museum in Konya) by Osmon Oğlu Mevlevi Hosan. Having learned from Gölpınarlı that there are textual questions about the authenticity of some of the poems attributed to Rumi, Ergin has resolved them on the basis, not of the manuscript tradition, but of "the content of annihilation and spiritual abstraction that characterizes Mevlana and no one else" (*Magnificent Ones*, 7).

Nevertheless, Gölpınarlı is an excellent guide to Rumi and Ergin follows him in most particulars, giving a table of important dates in the life of Rumi in the introduction to *Crazy as we Are*, based upon the fourth edition of Gölpınarlı's biography of Rumi (iii). Ergin preserves throughout the Turkish spellings (e.g., Seljug, Necmeddin, Mevlana, Celaleddin, Gevher, Veled), though he seems aware from English-language works that these names are generally spelled differently in the West. There are many typographical errors pertaining to dates and names, as well as the erroneous claim that Rumi belonged to the Malâmati order and that he was about sixty years of age when he first met Shams (vi).

At the suggestion of the government of Turkey, the United Nations declared 1995 the Year of Tolerance in honor of Rumi. As part of this commemoration, the Republic of Turkey's Ministry of Culture determined to publish the entirety of Rumi's *Divân-e kabir* (i.e. *Divân-e Shams*) in Ergin's English translation. Appearing in handsomely bound, simulated-leather paperbacks, this comprised at least five volumes, following the traditional Mevlevi grouping of the *Divân* by meters. Echo Publications, an evidently itinerant publishing house affiliated with the Society for Understanding Mevlana, worked in conjunction with the Turkish Ministry of Culture to issue the following titles in Ergin's *Divân-e kebir* series, all appearing in 1995: *Meter 1: Bahr-i Recez* (Walla Walla, WA: Current Books); *Meter 2: Bahr-i Muzari-Ariz-* (Sun Valley, CA: Echo Publications); *Meter 3: Bahr-i Hezec-Ahrab-* (Lake Isabella, CA: Echo); *Meter 4: Bahr-i Muzari. Ahrab-i Mekfut* (Lake Isabella, CA: Echo); *Meters 5,6, 7a: Bahr-e Hafif, Rezec Makfuf, Muctez* (San Clemente, CA: Echo). The series continued to come out in 1996 through Kazi Publications in Chicago.

These books feature reproductions from pages of a copy of the *Divân* made in 1368, along with a preface setting out Gölpınarlı's argument rejecting the traditional date of Rumi's birth in 1207 (as discussed in chapter 7, above, this argument is unsound). Ergin appends some useful notes to his translations which, though rather plain, follow Gölpınarlı's Turkish translations of the text clearly and fairly accurately. In these later works, Ergin has, with the help of the Turkish government, abandoned the pretension of working directly from "colloquial Farsi," and admitted to working from Gölpınarlı. *Meter 1* comes with an introduction by Ercan Karakaş, Turkey's Minister of Culture in 1995, who says Rumi has "a matchless place in Turkish–Islamic literature and culture," and exemplifies the virtue of tolerance. The introduction to *Meter 2* from D. Fikri Saglar, the new Minister of Culture, reiterates the role of Rumi as apostle of tolerance and expresses the wish that people would read the poems and learn peace and tolerance from him.

All told, this collection features some 840 ghazals of Rumi in over 1,700 pages of text. Ergin planned to publish two or three additional meters per year from the *Divân* – which has 21 meters in all – every year (*Meter 4*, vi). This would require another fourteen years or so to complete, but Ergin's collective oeuvre is already the largest collection of Rumi's ghazals available in English (Arberry's two volumes of *Mystical Poems of Rumi* provide only 400 of the 3,200 or more lyrical poems). Recognizing that not everyone will want to acquire the entire *Divân* in English, Ergin has recently published a new selection from *Meter 2, The Glory of Absence* (Lake Isabella, CA: Echo, 1997).

RUMI TODAY AND TOMORROW

After the spate of English-to-English "translations" of Rumi in America, a sizeable translation from French to English by **Muriel Maufroy** came out as *Breathing Truth: Quotations from Jalaluddin Rumi* (London: Sanyar, 1997). An Afghan scholar of Persian literature, **Ravân Farhâdi**, who has done a brief study of the meaning of love in Rumi's poetry, *Maʿni-ye ʿeshq nazd-e Mowlânâ* (Tehran: Asâtir, 1993), is said to be at work on a new complete translation of the *Masnavi* with **Ibrahim Gamard**. Gamard learned Persian out of devotion to Rumi and, judging from the samples that have appeared on the Sunlight email list (see "The Web of Rumi" in chapter 15), the Gamard–Farhâdi translation, like the selections by Kabir and Camille Helminski, preserves more of the poetic quality of the work than Nicholson's parenthetic prose. A complete poetic translation of the poem will be warmly welcomed.

RUMI AS MUSE

WRITERS UNDER RUMI'S SPELL

The followers of Meher Baba hold Hâfez in particular esteem as a great mystic, but also leave room for Rumi and other Persian poets. We have already met the Australian playwright and dramatist **Francis Brabazon**. Active in the 1950s and 1960s, Brabazon became a devotee toward the end of Baba's life, composing a number of hymns and poems under his influence, such as *Journey with God* (1971), the greater half of which consists of the teachings of Meher Baba.

610

Brabazon's sequel to this work, *Stay with God: A Statement in Illusion on Reality* (Sydney: Garuda Books, 1959), is an extended metaphysical poem (166 pages) which features Rumi and Shams prominently among the mystics. The Meher Baba Foundation at Balmain, New South Wales, made a revised edition available in 1977 and New Humanity Books, also a Meher Baba imprint, made a third edition, complete with illustrations by John Parry, available in 1990 (see "Unchurched Spirituality," in chapter 12, above).

The Los Angeles-born poet **Robert Bringhurst** (1946–) served some while as a journalist in Beirut and in Israel during the 1960s and has edited Arabic poetry in translation. He now lives in British Columbia, where he has become part of the Canadian poetry scene, publishing several collections of poems and contributing to anthologies of Canadian literature. His *Pieces of Map, Pieces of Music* (Toronto: McClelland & Stewart, 1986; Port Townshend, WA: Copper Canyon, 1987), explicitly appeals to the example of Kabir and Rumi, but fails to match their expansive insight.

Herbert Mason (1932–), much influenced by the French Catholic scholar of Islamic mysticism Louis Massignon, wrote about the early Sufi Mansur al-Hallâj before turning his attention to Rumi. Not advertised as a translation, Mason's *A Legend of Alexander and The Merchant and the Parrot: Dramatic Poems* (Notre Dome: University of Notre Dame Press, 1986), bases the second of its two dramatic pieces, "The Merchant and the Parrot," upon a famous story from Book 1 of the *Masnavi*.

Regina Sara Ryan (1945–) was born in New York and became a Roman Catholic nun at the age of eighteen, but was released from her vows eight years later. She has since taught high school and community college, and after an extended pilgrimage to India, she authored with John Travis a popular manual for physical and spiritual health, *The Wellness Workbook* (1981, revised 1986). Her *In Praise of Rumi* (Prescott, AZ: Hohm, 1989) is rather coy about the identity of its author(s), encouraging the reader to infer they are poems by unknown Sufis; Ryan herself explicitly claims credit only for the introduction, and the advertising copy describes it as "a collaborative effort by numerous poets." I suppose, however, the poems must come from Ryan herself, or from "Yogi Ramsuratkar, my Shams," to whom she dedicates the book. Ryan explains that the same spirit found in the poems animated St. John of the Cross, St. Teresa, Julian of Norwich, Ibn ʿArabi and so forth, and warns the reader of the transformative power of Rumi's spirit; to praise Rumi befittingly, one must throw himself "at the Beggar's feet" (viii). Despite the mysterious airs of the introduction, the short poems prove very much in the spirit of Rumi. Indeed, the best of these poems inspired by and in the mode of Rumi recall the mood and tenor of the poems of the *Divân-e Shams* better than some of the English-to-English "translations." She has since done a similar volume, *In Praise of Japanese Love Poetry* (Hohm, 1994).

According to *Contemporary Authors* (Detroit: Gale), Scottish poet **James Dickie** (1934–), a Muslim convert and translator of Andalusian (Arabic) poetry, claims membership in something called the International Rumi Society. **Stephen Toth, Jr.** (1950–), a Rosicrucian and Actualist poet who published four books of poems in the 1970s, has cited Persian poets like Khayyâm, ʿAttâr and Rumi among his major influences. **James Edward Tolan**, who earned his Ph.D. at the University of Southwestern Louisiana in 1997 in American literature with a dissertation entitled "Another Gorgeous Mistake (Original Writing, Poetry, Love, Free Verse)," took inspiration from the unlikely combination of Sappho, Alan Dugan, Antonio Machado, Robert Creeley and Rumi (as refracted through the lens of modern American poets).

CHILDREN'S BOOKS

Though cast as an Indian tale and not as a story from Rumi (and indeed, the story is a Buddhist parable), the blind men and the elephant (see "Rumi-mania" in the introduction for a translation of Rumi's version) has featured in a number of children's stories, such as *The Blind Men and the Elephant*, retold by Karen Backstein and illustrated by Annie Mitra (New York: Scholastic, 1992). An earlier title by the same name, by J.G. Saxe, *The Blind Men and the Elephant* (New York: McGraw Hill, 1963; frequent reprints), however, takes the tale from Rumi. An English-born playwright, screenwriter and author of children's books, **Arthur Scholey** (1932–), has tackled the tales of Rumi's contemporary Saʿdi in his *Discontented Dervishes and Other Persian Tales*, illustrated by William Rushton (London: Deutsch, 1977; Dutton reprint, 1982), and is said to be at work on a book of Rumi's tales retold for children, tentatively titled "The Caliph's Reward." For her Bank Street College of Education thesis in 1994, **Kaela Lee** authored an illustrated children's book, "The Mouse and the Camel: a Fable Based on the Teaching Tale by Jalaluʾl-Din Rumi." **Liz Meg Rosenberg** included poems of Rumi in English translation in an anthology of "Earth-Shattering Poems" for young adult readers, twelve to thirteen years of age, which she compiled for her 1997 Ph.D. dissertation at the State University of New York, Binghamton. **Denys Johnson-Davies**, best known for his translations of modern Arabic literature, provides schoolchildren with an introduction to the life of Rumi and an assortment of his stories, accompanied by the illustrations of Laura De La Mare, in *Rumi: Poet and Sage*, a small book in the Heroes from the East series (London: Hood, 1997).

RUMI AROUND THE WORLD

Rumi is only now catching the wave in **Spanish**-speaking countries; perhaps the great Spanish Islamicists felt a natural kinship for Ibn ʿArabi and other Andalusian mystics and philosophers, and are only now turning to Rumi, because of his popularity. Rumi has made an appearance, however, in several

Spanish versions. Selections of the *Masnavi* first appeared in Mexico in the series "Clasicos de la literatura," published as *El Mathnavi de Jala Ud-Din Rumi y otros textos* (Mexico, D.F.: SEP/Trillas, 1982), translated, adapted and introduced by Oscar Zorilla with revisions by Maria Angeles Gonzalez. Following this, another selection appeared in Spain, in the Coleccion vision libre series, as *El Masnavi: las enseñanzas de Rumi* (Barcelona: Vision, 1984; reprint Barcelona: Edicomunicación, 1998). Selections of Rumi's *Divân* are also available in Carmen Liaño's translation, *Diwan de Shams de Tabriz* (Madrid: SUFI, 1995) in the Colección Generalife. Alberto Manzano's *Poemas sufíes* (Madrid: Hiperión, 1988; reprinted 1993) offer some further Spanish versions of Rumi.

Most of the Spanish editions of Rumi's poetry are, however, translated not from the Persian, but second-hand, from other European languages. Antonio López Ruiz translated *150 Cuentos Sufíes: extraídos del Matnawi* (Barcelona: Paidós, 1991), a French selection of the *Masnavi* which had been compiled by Ahmed Kudsi Erguner and Pierre Maniez in 1988. Esteve Serra's *El Canto del sol* (Palma de Mallorca: Olañeta, 1998) renders into Spanish de Vitray-Meyerovitch's *Le Chant du soleil* (Paris: Table Ronde, 1993); Juan Vivanco renders an Italian translation of the *Masnavi* into Spanish as *El Canto del derviche: parbolas de la sabiduría sufí* (Barcelona: Grijalbo, 1997); and Alfonso Colodrón makes Jonathan Star's English reworkings of Rumi, *In the Arms of the Beloved*, available in Spanish as *Rumi: en brazos del amado: antología de poemas místicos* (Madrid: Edaf, 1998).

In **Sweden** Axel Eric Hermelin translated Nicholson's entire English version of the *Masnavi* into Swedish in the four volumes of *Mesnavi Skrifven of DjalâliD-Din Rûmi* (Lund: Carlbloms, 1933–6). More recently, Ulla Olsson has continued the tradition of *Masnavi* scholarship in Sweden with *Vem ar hjalte?: Iranska traditioner i tidiga furstespeglar och Jalal al-Din Rumis Masnavi* (Institutionen for religonsvetenskap, Goteborgs Universitet, 1995).

In the **Czech Republic**, selections of the *Masnavi* have appeared in the scholarly versions of Jirí Becka with verse renderings by Josef Hirsal, as *Dzalaleddin Balchi Rumi* (Prague: Protis, 1995).

In **Poland**, under the influence of Rückert's German versions of Rumi, Tadeusz Micinski published versions of Rumi which the composer Szymanowski would incorporate into a symphony (see "Rumi as *Lieder*", p. 616). Micinski's work appeared in "Mevlana Dzelaleddin Rumi," *Chimera* T. IX z. 27 ([Warsaw, 1915]: 373–400) and *Dzelaleddin Rumi, Divan* (Warsaw/Krakow, 1921, 258–62). Antoni Lange, also working from German, compiled translations of a number of Persian poets, including Khayyâm, Ferdowsi, Khâqâni and Hâfez, as well as three pages of Rumi (pp. 263–6) in his *Dywan Wschodni. Wybor arcydziel literatury egipskiej, perskiej i indyskiej* (Warsaw/Krakow, 1921). Versions of Rumi were to be found even earlier, though, in Karol Mecherzynski's *Przeglad literatury lodoow wschodnich* (Krakow, 1851).

Imperial **Russia** shared a common border with Iran over which several skirmishes were fought during the nineteenth century. Since Russia, in agreement with the British, exercised a sphere of influence over the north of Iran, Russian scholars and diplomats during the Czarist period took an interest in Iranian philosophy and religion, as well as Persian poetry. In 1895 V. Zhukovsky included specimens of Persian verse in his study of Persian mysticism and human cognition, and just prior to the October Revolution, A. Krimsky made more selections available in his history of Persian literature and Sufi theosophy (*Istoriya Persii, eye literatura, teosophiya derveshisma*, Moscow, 1914–17), arguing that Persian Sufism represents a kind of simultaneous pantheism and deism. Possibly through these translations, the Christian mystic Semyon Ludigovich Frank (1877–1950) picked up some Sufi influences. But Leninist hostility to religion and mysticism, and to the Sufi orders which the Soviet state feared as potential causes of political instability, discouraged the development of Russian scholarship in this direction.

E.E. Bertels did carry out philologically oriented studies of Persian Sufism and poetry (*Sufiyskaya Literatura: Izbrannye Trudy III*, Moscow, 1965; a German translation was made by Hellmut Ritter), but Marietta Tigranovna Stepaniants has asserted that she, by virtue of a four-year stay in Toronto at McGill's Islamic Studies Institute, was the first Soviet scholar to escape the ideological orbit of Marxist-Leninism in her study of the philosophy of Sufism (*Filosofskie aspekty sufizma*, Moscow, 1987), now available in a revised English version as *Sufi Wisdom* (Albany, NY: SUNY Press, 1994). The Russian text included considerable source material in Russian translation, including original versions of Ibn ʿArabi, Muhammad Iqbal, and, of course, Rumi, to illustrate various points being made.

Despite Stepaniants' claim, Radii Fish had already penned a study of the life of Rumi in Russian. Fish had earlier taken an interest in the Marxist Turkish poet Nazim Hikmet and his Rumi biography, *Dzhalaliddin Rumi* (Moscow: Molodaia gvardiia, 1972), has won some attention. A revised edition of the work, *Dzhalaleddin Rumi* (Moscow: Izd-vo "Nauka," 1985; reprint 1987), provides the story of Rumi's life on the basis of original sources, but it contains few translations. An Uzbek translation of this work appeared in 1986, described as a historical–biographical novel, *Zhaloliddin Rumii* (Tashkent: Ghafu Ghulom nomidagi Adabiet va sanat, 1986). In the year before Stepaniants' study of Sufism appeared, a 270-page selection of poems from the *Masnavi* had been published in a Russian translation by Naum Grebnev with an extensive introduction on Sufism and Rumi by O.F. Akimushkin of the St. Petersburg Oriental Institute: *Poema o skrytom smysle: izbrannye pritchi Dzhalaladdin Rumi* (Moscow: Nauka, 1986). Indeed, a small selection of Rumi's poems had been published even earlier by Vladimir Derzhavin (1908–) as *Pritchi* (Moscow: Izd-vo "Khudozhestvennaia lit-ra," 1969).

But while Soviet scholars in Moscow and the Ukraine may have been newly rediscovering the virtues of Rumi, the Persian-speaking Tâjik scholars, who took pride in Rumi as virtually a national poet (Vakhsh, Bahâ al-Din's place of residence, is situated in modern Tajikistan), had never forgotten him. In **Tajikistan**, the stories of Rumi's *Masnavi* were presented in a guise acceptable to Marxists as popular poetry or storytelling in *Pritchi v "Masnavi"* (*Hekâyat-hâ-ye khalqi-ye Masnavi*) (Dushanbe: Nashriât-e Dowlati-ye Tâjikestân, 1963). Nodir Odilov subsequently published a study of a little more than a hundred pages in Dushanbe, the Tâjik capital, along with some illustrative passages of the poems in translation, as *Mirovozrenie Dzhalaliddina Rumi* (Dushanbe: Izdatelstvo Irfon, 1974).

In **Japan**, the great scholar of theoretical Sufism **Toshihiko Izutsu** (1914–) has written on the Koran, compared Sufism with Taoism and discussed Ibn ʿArabi's theosophy at length. He also translated Rumi's Discourses into Japanese from Foruzânfar's edition under the title *Rumi goroku*, which can be found as volume 11 in his collected works, *Izutsu Toshihiko chosakushu* (Tokyo: Chuo Koronsha, 1991–3).

In **Greece**, only a few studies and translations of Rumi have appeared. The first was a well-informed analysis containing some translations: Gregoriou D. Ziaka's *Apo to mystikismo tou kosmou tes Anatoles: Ho mystikos poietes Maulana Jalaladdin Rumi kai he didaskalia autou* (Thessalonica: Aristoteleion Panepistemion, 1973; 2nd ed., Ekdoseis P. Pournara, 1987). Ziaka also focused on Rumi in his *He ennoia tes eleutherias tes vouleseos kai tou kakou eis ton metagenesteron islamikon mystikismon* (Thessalonica, 1973). These apparently sparked the interest of Alexiou Taki, who subsequently published *Mia zontane didaskalia* (Athens: Ekdoseis Tesseris Epoches, 1989–). The Greek attraction to Rumi stems in part from the proximity of Turkey, in part because of Rumi's example of respectful and cordial Muslim–Christian interaction, and not least because Rumi composed a few lines in demotic Greek. Gregore Mpairaktare has addressed the last point in his *Oi Hellenikoi stichoi tou Roumi (13os aionas) poiete kai philosophou apo te Vaktriane tes Kentrikes Asias* (1996).

Rumi has also made the passage from Konya to **Israel**, but only via American translation. It seems incongruous, given Israel's relative proximity to Turkey and Iran, that Rumi should come to Hebrew via a German scholar writing in English. But Hanah Ginguld has lately made Schimmel's Rumi translations in *Look! This is Love* available to the Israeli New Age audience as *Habet! zo ahavah: ha-shirim shel Rumi* (Hod ha-Sharon: Astrolog, 1998).

The preceding account of the translation history of Rumi, though it does give an idea of the wealth of material in various languages by and about Rumi, does not exhaust the subject.

Rumi Mirrored in Multimedia

Commercial success in print often enables a literary work to cross over to other more popular media. This has, of course, been true for many years, with fairy tales being turned into ballets, folktales made into operas, and plays and novels into movies. With the recent explosion of multimedia formats this phenomenon has rapidly accelerated. European recording companies like Harmonia Mundi have intelligently presented traditional music from various cultures around the world for many years now, and over the last decade or two, the increasing popularity of "world music" has made recordings from Iran, Turkey and elsewhere available in American book, record and appliance superstores. Over the last five years, the World Wide Web has mesmerized computer users around the globe and led to the proliferation of web pages and sites dedicated to special interests.

Rumi has found his way on to records, CDs and cassettes, in a host of recordings, including Mevlevi *samâ* ceremonies, original compositions setting his poems to music, and recitations by various performers, impresarios, paraphrasers and Persian-speakers. A number of documentaries about the Whirling Dervishes have been made, and films inspired in one way or another by Rumi are now in the offing. A whole host of web pages also devote themselves in whole or in part to Rumi. The following gives some indication of the many modes in which Rumi has been morphed off the page and the multiple media in which Rumi has been imagined.

RUMI AS *LIEDER*: HIS POEMS SET TO MUSIC IN THE WEST

The poems of **Friedrich Rückert**, both the adaptations of Rumi and also his other German poems, inspired many a composer. Among the poems from

Rückert's "oriental rose garden" which had Rumi as their muse, we may note principally the following *lieder* and their composers:

"Wohl endet Tod des Lebens Not"
Carl Banck (1809–89), Op. 70, 16
Georg Göhler (1874–1954), c. 1930

"Die Schöpfung ist zur Ruh gegangen"
Georg Göhler, c. 1930
Richard Strauss, Op. 62

"Heim" (Gott geleite die armen traurigen Kranken heim)
Ferdinand Hiller (1811–85), Op. 165, 4 (choral work)
Hiller wrote a book about Goethe's musical life and must have been aware of other Persian poetry in German translation.

"Und dann nicht mehr" (Ich sah Sie nur ein Einzigmal)
Richard Strauss, Op. 87, 2
Anton M. Storch (1815–87)

"Kehr Ein bei Mir" (Du bist die Ruh)
Franz Schubert, D 776

"Lachen und Weinens Grund"
Franz Schubert, D 777

"Die ihr mit den Oden linde"
Robert Kahn (1865–1951), Op. 34, 1

"Ich bin die Seel' im all"
Josep Soler, Chamber music with percussion instruments, written for alto-soprano, vibraphone and guitar, following Rückert's translation (Frankfurt: Zimmermann, 1980).

The Polish composer **Karol Szymanowski** (1882–1937) set a translation of a poem from Rumi's *Divân-e Shams* to music in his Symphony no. 3, Opus 27. The text of "Song of the Night" (*Pies'n' o nocy*) came from a translation by Polish poet **Tadeusz Micinski** (1873–1918), done from the German of Rückert. The translation has a romantic cast to it, suggesting two lovers contemplating the majestic night and its astrological signs. It preserves the *radif*, or refrain, "tonight" (*emshab*) of Rumi's poem in Polish as *nocy tej*. The poem in question, *Makhosb ay yâr-e mehmândâr emshab* (D 296), might be rendered into English as follows:

> Do not sleep,
>   my hospitable friend, tonight
>   for you are spirit
>   and we are ill, tonight

banish sleep from inner eyes
    let mysteries appear, tonight
Though a giant planet, revolve around this moon,
    circling through the turning sky, tonight
In the constellations the prey of Altair
    glides by like the soul of the winged Ja'far

Polish God has given you to burnish
    separation's rust
        from the deep dark blue, tonight

Praise God, all creatures are asleep
    leaving me involved with my Creator
  What wakeful fortune, bright glory!
    I am conscious of a wakeful God, tonight!
      If my eyes had rested shut
      until the dawn, they were despised, tonight

Though the market place is empty, look!
    what commerce in the milky ways, tonight
Our night is day in the world of those stars
    and so they come out to view, tonight
The lion rushes on the bull
Mercury wears a turban on its crowns
    Saturn plants surreptitious seeds of tumult
    Jupiter showers golden coins

I sit silent, lips unmoved, yet
    many a thing I speak of
      without words
        tonight

"The winged Ja'far" alludes to the brother of 'Ali, who was killed holding the Muslim standard in a battle against the Byzantine army in 629. His epithet *tayyâr* is similar to the name of the star Altair (which took its Latin name from Arabic), and the poet, who lies awake pasturing the stars through the field of the night, imagines Ja'far-e Tayyâr flying past his cognate constellation, Altair.

Szymanowski began his symphony in the fall of 1914 and completed it in 1916. Originally scheduled for a performance in St. Petersburg on November 19, 1916, it had to be postponed and did not receive its premiere until five years later in London. Though he conceived it for orchestra and chorus, Szymanowski allowed performances with solo tenor or solo soprano and no doubt many concert-goers first met Rumi in this form in the years between the world wars. At least two recordings feature the third symphony: First, *Szymanowski, Symphony no. 3* (London 425 625–2, 1990; liner notes by Christopher Palmer) recorded in 1980 by the Detroit Symphony Orchestra, with Antal Dorati, conductor, and Ryszard Karczykonski, tenor; and second,

Szymanowski – Stabat Mater (EMI S55121 2, 1994; liner notes by Rubin Golding), recorded by the City of Birmingham Symphony Orchestra in 1993 with Jon Garrison as tenor and Simon Rattle conducting.

In 1973 the Turkish conductor **Ali Dogan Sinangil** (1934–) composed a musical setting for a Turkish translation of Rumi's poetry, called *Mevlana Oratorio*. Sinangil conducted a performance of his *Mevlana Oratorio* with the Istanbul State Opera and Ballet, selections of which appear on a recording of the same name (Lausanne: Gallo, 1995, CD-836). In Hungary, Esin Afsar produced a collection of Sufi songs in Turkish, *Yunus Emre & Mevlana* (Hungaroton Classic, 1994, HCD 31573).

The prolific Canadian artist and composer **R. Murray Schafer** has published the sheet music for his brief oratorio, *Divan i Shams i Tabriz for Orchestra, Seven Singers and Electronic Sounds. Part One: Lustro* (Toronto: Universal Edition, 1977). This fifty-one-page score lasts about twenty-three minutes in performance by a vocal septet. Two years later Schafer recorded his double LP album, *Loving: Music for the Morning of the World* (Waterloo, Ontario: Melbourne, 1979, SMLP 4035-6). *Loving*, a dramatic work in French and English for two actors and four singers, performed by Trulie MacLeod, Gilles Savard and Mary Lou Fallis, again features lyrics from Rumi. Schafer and his music are the subject of a book by Stephen Adams, *R. Murray Schafer* (Toronto: University of Toronto Press, 1983).

Gamelan music provides the setting for **Vincent McDermott**'s (1933–) composition "Sweet-Breathed Minstrel," a 1982 piece composed around a Rumi poem. **Stephen Dickman**'s (1943–) LP record of original songs with Arthur Weisberg and Phylis Bryn-Julson, *The Song of the Reed* (NY: Composers Recording, 1983), characterized as contemporary American music, includes two songs in English translation by Rumi, "Song of the Reed" (8:30) and "Love, the Hierophant" (9:43).

In 1986 **Ton de Leeuw** (1926–) composed an original sacred choral work with texts in Dutch and French translated from the works of four Sufis: Hallâj, Ibn ʿAbbâd, Ibn ʿAtâ Allâh and Rumi. The score of this work – *Transparence*, a fifteen-minute piece for mixed choir, trumpet, tuba, two horns and two trombones – was published in Amsterdam in 1993, but I know of no recordings.

A composer and professor of theory and composition at the School of Music at the University of Washington, **Diane Thome**, completed a composition in November of 1990 which features six lines from various poems in Kabir Helminski's translations of Rumi, *The Ruins of the Heart*. The lines of Rumi are alternately declaimed or sung in choral style by a soprano, Mary Henderson, and embedded in a musical setting with orchestra and synthesized natural and synthetic sounds. The piece, titled "The Ruins of the Heart," appears as volume 12 in the CDCM Computer Music Series, *Composers in the Computer Age I*

(Centaur Records 1992, CRC 2144) with the Cincinnati Philharmonic Orchestra and Gerhard Samuel, conductor.

Andrew List has composed chamber music for a number of poems by American poets, including Emily Dickinson and Walt Whitman. He chose three Rumi poems in translation as the setting for his *Oh My Beloved: Three Songs for Mezzo-soprano, Clarinet and Piano* (1995). A music theorist and composer at the University of Illinois, **Ben Johnston**, has created a piece called *Quietness* for texts of Rumi's poems in the translation of Moyne and Barks, as described in *Perspectives of New Music* 34, 1 (Winter 1996): 178–82. **Jonathan Harvey**, apparently a relative of the Rumi exponent Andrew Harvey, has used the latter's translations as the song for his 1996 musical setting for double choir, *How Could the Soul not Take Flight* (London: Faber, 1997).

Also in 1997, **Graeme Reyell** and keyboardist **Roger Mason** teamed up for an international production recorded in London, New York and Tel Aviv. The resulting cassette, *Vision II* (New York: Angel, 1997), contains original music and lyrics adapted from Rumi and sung in Persian and English. The same year saw the appearance of a CD entitled *The Loan* (Vancouver, British Columbia: Songlines, 1997) in the jazz/world music tradition by **Brad Shepik and the Commuters**. This collection, inspired by the musical traditions of Turkey, Iran, the Balkans and Africa, includes a short track called "Rumi," recorded in May of 1996. Mention has already been made of the group **Three Fish**, featuring Pearl Jam's bassist Jeff Ament, and its use of tales from the *Masnavi* (see "Rumi-mania" in the Introduction).

TURNING, TURNING WE COME OUT RIGHT: RUMI IN BALLET, MODERN DANCE AND OPERA

If the use of Rumi poems as librettos for all of these oratorios and *lieder* comes as a surprise, his influence on contemporary dance should not. As early as April 9, 1761, at a performance of **C.S. Fravart**'s *Soliman the Second*, European audiences were presented with a divertissement inspired by the whirling dervishes. On December 20, 1788 the ballet *Les Derviches*, based on a Mevlevi ritual, was performed at the Paris Théâtre des Grands Danseurs du Roi. At the Ballet Suédois the audience of November 13, 1920 was treated to the premiere of *Dervishes*, choreographed by Jean Borlin and composed by **Alexander Glazounov** (1865–1936), with a setting resembling a Mevlevi lodge designed by Mouveau. The pioneers of modern dance in America, **Ted Shawn** (1891–1972) and **Ruth St. Denis** (1880–1968), whose Denishawn company drew much of its inspiration from the Orient, incorporated Mevlevi turning. Even though musical scholars have ruled out the possibility that Beethoven's "Chorus of the Dervishes" from *Die Ruinen von Athen* (Op. 113) may reflect first-hand knowledge of Mevlevi music, the Mevlevis have nevertheless made an impression on the classical music tradition in the West.[1]

Samuel Lewis and his discovery of Mevlevi dance through Ruth St. Denis and Vilayat Khan has already been mentioned. The American review *Dance Magazine* has provided reviews of the performances of the Mevlevi members on tour by Alexandria Dionne (January 1997) and Doris Hering (May 1997). Trained in ballet, **Robin Becker** has performed with the Martha Graham Dance Company and taught with the American Ballet Theatre. She now directs her own dance company and has become very involved in the Omega Institute, an American Sufi order. She draws upon the teachings of Pir Inayat Khan and Emilie Conrad Da'oud in performing dances of "universal peace" and conducting meditative dance/breathing workshops on "the body as a sacred expression." Sufi dance naturally cannot ignore Rumi, whose influence is made explicit in a New York performance of Becker's "Dances of Rumi," filmed by Johannes Holub on the video recording, *Robin Becker and Company* (1994).

The famous director of the Ballet of the Twentieth Century, **Maurice Béjart**, has used the movements of Mevlevi turning in his own works and derives inspiration from Rumi's poetry. The Performance Group directed by **Richard Schechner** of New York University has likewise used Mevlevi whirling in workshops and performances.[2]

If some Muslim scholars felt uncomfortable with *samâ'*, even Rumi, an outspoken exponent of the dance, would have been shocked by *Rapture Rumi* with music composed by **Steven Flynn** and performed by Flynn and Armando Steven for the American belly dancer **Delilah**, who markets a number of instructional, meditational and exercise belly-dance videos, produced by Visionary Dance Productions in Seattle. Though there are no vocals, the advertising copy promises that "Hot rhythms and yearning melodies combine to make songs that speak of the desires of both body and soul." The fifty-two minutes of music on *Rapture Rumi* include one piece titled "Rumi and Shems."

The Byrr Hoffman Group, **Robert Wilson**'s (1941–) dance company, has used Mevlevi movements through the choreography of Andy Degroat in *Ka Mountain and Guardenia Terrace* (1972), which was set in the ruins of Persepolis, near Shiraz, Iran, and also in the fifth act of *The Life and Times of Joseph Stalin* (1973). A recent conceptual portfolio of Wilson's works (*Robert Wilson: RWWM*, ed. Sebastian Lohse and Vittorio Santoro [Zurich: Memory/ Cage Editions, 1997]) confirms his interest in Rumi with its photographs, original drawings, quotations and interviews.

Wilson teamed with **Philip Glass** (1937–), who had studied with Boulanger and later worked with the Indian musicians Ravi Shankar and Alla Rakha on a number of operas. Glass's minimalist opera *Einstein on the Beach* (1976) made him famous; he stuck with rather cerebral themes for *Satyagraha* (1980), a Gandhian opera with Sanskrit libretto, and *Akhnaten* (1984), based on the Hebrew Bible. His most recent project has been *Monsters of Grace* (version 1.0, 1998), with staging by Robert Wilson, including 70 millimeter film by Diana

Walczak and Jeff Kleiser which requires 3-D glasses, with digital technology by Silicon Graphics. The opera opens with simple music and blue light that fades to white, symbolizing the intersection of time and space. It features thirteen scenes, six of them staged live and the others generated by computer, presenting disparate images that form no particular narrative or story. The music incorporates electronic samplings of traditional Persian music and a quartet singing the texts of Coleman Barks' *Rumi*. This multimedia project received mixed reviews upon its debut in UCLA's Royce Hall (e.g., Mark Swed, *Los Angeles Times*, April 17, 1998, F1 and Bernard Holland, *New York Times*, April 17, 1998, E30), but as it was a work still in progress (billed as version 1.0), it may assume improved form as it travels to the multiple commissioners of the project around the U.S. and Europe.

THE MUSIC OF THE MEVLEVIS

Ismail Hakkı of Bursa (1653–1725), one of the Turkish commentators on the *Masnavi*, wrote a treatise called *Ketâb al-nejât* which provides details on the history of the musical performances of the Mevlevi order. In modern times, both **Talat Halman** and **Shems Friedlander** have described the musical and turning ceremony of the Mevlevis in English in some detail. These three works are all based on observation of later Mevlevi tradition, but Rumi himself certainly held music and dance in high esteem (See chapter 7). Ali Asani has studied Rumi's attitude in "Music and Dance in the Work of Mawlana Jalal al-Din Rumi," *Islamic Culture* 60, 2 (April 1986, 41–5).

The Mevlevi *samâ^c* begins with the *na^{c}at-e Mowlânâ*, an invocation of praise of the Prophet attributed to Rumi, for which a musical accompaniment was composed by **Buhurizâde Mustafa Itri** (1640–1712). This is typically followed by an instrumental improvisation (*taqsim*) on the nay, and after that by the "Cycle of Sultan Valad," during which the dervishes walk around the *samâ^c khâne* three times to the accompaniment of the rhythmical *pishrow* (*peşrev*). Another *taqsim* and then the four *salâm*s ensue. The performance ends with a further *peşrev* and a final nay *taqsim*, after which the dervishes retire and the Koran reciter chants a brief passage of scripture. After the Koran recitation, a prayer is then said before the shaykh, formerly intoned for the life and health of the Ottoman sultan and now for all humanity.

Besides the obvious reed flute, or nay, the other instruments include the kudum (*naqqâre*), a small double drum played with sticks. The kudum is made of copper covered with camel or sheepskin; two kudums of different tone are usually played at once. The rabâb, a two-stringed, bowed instrument, formerly made from a coconut shell covered by animal skin with two horsetail strings, is tuned to a five-note interval. In 1973 the violoncello was also introduced to Mevlevi performances. Among the composers of music for the Mevlevi *ayin-i şerif* ceremonies were **Ismail Dede Hamâmizâde** (1777–1845); a court composer, he is considered an important reformer of the Turkish musical tradition. In the previous century **Nayi ʿOsmân Dede**, who in 1672 became shaykh of the Galata Mevlevi lodge, had composed four great Mevlevi ceremonies (*râst, chârgâh, ʿoshshâq* and *hejâz*), which were written down in musical notation in 1936 and performed at the Konya ceremonies in December 1973. The Ottoman sultan **Selim III** (1761–1808) also composed a piece for the third *salâm* of one Mevlevi musical ceremony; this can be heard on the cassette *Sûz-i dil-ârâ âyın-i şerifi: Üçüncü Selim* (Konya: Kültür ve Turizm Dernegi, TS2240). The music reflects Turkish and not Iranian tradition, and is not quite as antique as sometimes represented. The current musical forms did not originate in the lifetime of Rumi and new compositions have been added well into the nineteenth century by figures like the head muezzin Rifat Bey (1820–c. 1895) and **Ahmet Avni Konuk** (1873–1938), whose *Ru-ye ʿErâq* was performed in Konya in 1964. This was recorded by Bernard Mauguin and issued as an LP album in UNESCO's series "Musical Anthology of the Orient" under the title *Turkish Music: Music of the Mevlevi* (Barenreiter Musicaphon, BM30 L2019), including detailed liner notes and photographs.[3]

The modern Mevlevi dervishes have worked with a number of companies wishing to record and distribute their music. The "Sheik ul Mevlevi" in Galata, **Nail Kesova**, appears with the **Galata Mevlevi Music and Sema Ensemble of Istanbul** on *The Music of Islam, vol. 9: Mawlawiyah Music of the Whirling Dervishes* and *vol. 14: Mystic Music through the Ages, Traditional Mevlevi Sufi Music* (Tucson: Celestial Harmonies, 1998). Shaykh Nail Kesova and Hafiz Kanı Karaca also appear on *Quran Recitation*, volume 10 of the same series (Celestial Harmonies, 1997).

Ahmet Ertegün, one of the Turkish brothers instrumental in the jazz recording industry in the United States, produced *Music of the Whirling Dervishes* for Atlantic Records in 1987 (Atlantic 82493-2). The performance, recorded on October 31, 1978, a year in which a Mevlevi ensemble had toured the United States, includes the *Naat-e Mevlana* as composed by Itri in the seventeenth century and recited by **Kanı Karaca**; *ayin*s sung by Hüseyin Top as the *ayinhan* or vocalist; *peşrev* composed by **Emin Effendi** (1884–1945); and *ayin-i şerif* composed by **Köçek Mustafa Dede** (seventeenth century). Liner notes are provided by Talat Sait Halman, former Turkish Minister of Culture, who wrote a book on Rumi and the Mevlevis with Metin And (1983). This recording was originally released as part of a double LP accompanying the 1987 "Age of Sultan Süleyman the Magnificent" exhibition, thus emphasizing the Mevlevis as a tourist attraction in the context of Turkey's imperial and artistic heritage.

"*Wherever You Turn is the Face of God*": *Mevlevi Ceremonial Music* (Waterlily Acoustics, 1995, WLA-ES-50-CD) features the **Mevlevi Ensemble of Turkey** directed by **Doğan Ergin** with Kanı Karaca and liner notes by Kabir Helminski and Dr. **Celâleddin Çelebi**, a twenty-first generation grandson in direct line of descent of Rumi, and head of the Mevlevi order. "Kavi" Alexander of California, a recording engineer, told Helminski, Shaykh of the Mevlevi order in America (see chapter 12, "Modern Mevlevis"), that in 1978 he had had a dream of Rumi, who told him to "record my music." Therefore, when the Mevlevi Ensemble toured the U.S. in 1994, including an appearance at the Cathedral of St. John the Divine in New York City, Alexander rigged up special equipment for an analog recording of the November 18, 1994 performance of the ceremony in Christ the King Chapel, St. Anthony's Seminary, an old Franciscan chapel in Santa Barbara, California. It begins with a *zekr* medley, a meditational chant of *Labbayk* ("Here I am"), the pilgrim's ritual cry to God, by Kanı Karaca. It then proceeds to a classical Mevlevi composition (*Ferahfezâ âyīn*) by Ismâil Dede Efendi, including Turkish lyrics by the thirteenth-century mystic poet **Yunus Emre**.

In the liner notes Celâleddin Çelebi details the parts of the ceremony and their meanings, and translations of the lyrics are provided, only a minority of which are from Rumi. In any case, the special recitation style and the heavy Turkish accent of the Mevlevis makes virtually any passage they perform from the original words of Rumi all but incomprehensible to modern Persian-speakers. The fame of the Mevlevi Ensemble is almost reaching folk-rock star proportions, and they fill not only intimate theaters like Merkin Hall in New York City, but larger venues on college campuses in the U.S. such as the Veterans Wadsworth Theater at UCLA and the Lisner Auditorium at George Washington University. At a 1997 performance crowds blocked the passageway in front of the Lisner auditorium hoping to get a scalped ticket outside (Sarah Kaufman, "Dervishes' Whirl of Difference," *Washington Post*, February 4, 1997, E1). Some observers feel uncomfortable about the propriety of holding the Mevlevi spiritual rituals in a secular venue and have given unfavorable reviews because of this (L.P. O'Neil, "Spin Control: The Dervishes' Solemn Whirl," *Washington Post*, September 29, 1998, D5). But visitors to Konya highly recommend the Mevlevi ceremonies of Rumi's death anniversary in December, the so-called *shab-e ʿarus*, or nuptial night of Rumi's return to the beloved arms of God.[4]

Helminski appears again, not on the liner notes of the Mevlevi Ensemble, but as a performer for *Garden Within the Flames: Songs of the Sufi Path* (Interworld Music, 1997), described as traditional Turkish devotional songs in the Illahi genre, often sung with texts of Rumi and Yunus Emre, rendered in contemporary manner and sung to the accompaniment of the saz, oud, bendir and nay. These are performed by the ensemble **Dost**, consisting of Kabir and Camille Helminski, Fred Stubbs and a chorus from the Threshold Society, the Mevlevi Center formerly in Brattleboro, Vermont, now in Aptos, California. Also on the same label is *Returning: The Music of the Whirling Dervishes* (Interworld CD-916) performed in 1995 by the Mevlevi dervishes under the direction of Doğan Ergin (who provides the *âyin* in Ferahnâk mode), with Kanı Karaca reciting the Koran.

The December festival of the Mevlevi dervishes of Syria was captured on a 7-inch phonograph record in the 1950s by **Deben Bhattacharya**, who provides the French liner notes to *Les Derviches tourneurs* (Paris: BAM, LD 384). In 1977 the Istanbul Sema Group, featuring Süleyman Erguner on nay and Nezih Uzel on bendir performed Mevlevi music; this recording has been issued on compact disc as *Mevlana: Music of the Whirling Dervishes* (Hollywood, CA: Hemisphere/ Metro Blue, 1993).

Shaykh Hamza Shakkûr and the Al-Kindî ensemble join together on the CD *Syrie: musique des derviches tourneurs de Damas* (France: Auvidis Records, 1994, Ethnic Series B6813), which includes chanting from the Koran and a number of Arabic poems in praise of the Prophet, *muwashshaha* and *qasidas*, performed in a recital (*nawba*) at the Grand Mosque of the Ummayads in Damascus on June 13, 1994. The Mevlevi order in Syria does not enjoy anything like the influence or prestige of the Mevlevis in Konya and Istanbul and we may assume that the performance here does not represent an unbroken tradition; quite likely it is influenced by the practice of other Sufi orders and the Alevis. But in the summer of 1996, the Mevlevi dervishes of Syria performed in Lucerne, Switzerland, in the annual International Musikfestwochen, dedicated that year to the theme of "The Healing Power of Music."

A six-volume recording of Mevlevi music appeared through Kent Records in Turkey as *Mevlana Mistik Türk Müziqi*. Even non-Mevlevi Turks have produced "Mevlevi" records. The Paris-based traditional Turkish musician **Kudsi Erguner** performed part of a Mevlevi ceremony at the Festival des Arts Traditionnels in Rennes, France in 1981 using non-Mevlevi performers. Instead, this performance featured an ensemble led by Muzaffereddin Ozak from the Halveti order at Nureddin Cerrahi's shrine; it was recorded and released as *Derviches tourneurs de Turquie: la cérémonie des Mevlevi* (France: Arion, 1991, ARN 64159), volume 2 of the Arion series "Musique soufi." The Necdet Yasar Ensemble performed a part of a Mevlevi *âyin* at the University of Maryland in April 1989; this can be heard on *Music of Turkey* (Chapel Hill, NC: Music of the World, 1992).

RECITING RUMI

The Rumi craze has received some radio play, as the subject of **Ellen Kushner**'s *Sound and Spirit*, a program airing on National Public Radio's affiliate, WGBH Boston (Program 233: week of August 11, 1997). Many of the translations and renditions of Rumi available in book form also appear on cassette, since busy American commuters, who spend numerous hours per week on the road, often find the time for "reading" only in the car. Furthermore, poetry recitation has come into vogue once again and Coleman Barks and Robert Bly have particularly emphasized the performance aspect of their translations of Rumi. Their success in the art of performing poetry has led many other translators and paraphrasers to imitate their Rumi repertoire.

Audio Literature in Berkeley, California, for example, has made **Andrew Harvey**'s commentary on Rumi in *The Way of Passion* available in a double cassette (1995), with music on nay and bandir by Steve Coughlin (who, in his affiliation with the Mevlevi order, uses the name Hazur Nawaz). **Qahira Qalbi**, a Sufi teacher who holds workshops at various retreats in the U.S., has produced her own cassette of Rumi translations, *Rumi: Readings From the Soul*, apparently from the versions of Barks, accompanied by flute and tabla.

Coleman Barks, however, holds justifiable pride of place among American Rumi reciters. Performances of most of his books have been recorded live or in the studio, and packaged and repackaged in various formats under various titles, selling for between $10 and $20 apiece. These include the cassette *Open Secret: Ancient Wisdom for Modern Living* (Emeryville, CA: Enhanced Audio Systems, 1987), with Barks and Dorothy Fadiman reading translations from Barks' books *Open Secret* and *We Are Three*, accompanied by Jan Keene (flute) and Shams Kairys (violin). The double cassette *Poems of Rumi, Translated and Spoken by Robert Bly and Coleman Barks* (South San Francisco, CA: Audio Literature, 1989) features the poems as read by the translators to the accompaniment of two musicians, David Whetstone on the sitar and Marcus Wise on the tabla, both of whom participated in Bly's recitation of his Kabir book in 1988. The Indian instrumentation was, of course, appropriate to the Kabir poems, but one wonders why Turkish or Persian music was not chosen for Rumi. The same musicians, along with others on flute, ceramic bowl and percussion, appear once again on the double cassette *Rumi: Voice of Longing* (Boulder, CO: Sounds True Audio, 1994), with Barks reciting.

Next, there is *Rumi: Poet of Divine Ecstasy* (San Francisco, CA: New Dimensions Foundation, 1991), a cassette featuring recitations and a conversation between Barks and Michael Toms about Rumi. *Like This*, a cassette of the book, features Barks reading his translations accompanied by some more ethnically relevant music, provided by Hamza el-Din on oud and tar, and Huzur Coughlin on nay. *I Want Burning: The Ecstatic World of Rumi, Hafiz, and Lalla*, based upon a printed work of the same title, features Coleman Barks and dancer Zuleikha in performance in Santa Fe with Pepe Mendoza on Andean flute and Shabda Owens on keyboard and tar (Boulder, CO: Sounds True Recordings, 1992, A197). The audio edition of the book *Hand of Poetry* by Barks and **Inayat Khan** features four separate cassettes or CDs, corresponding to the various poets treated. *Dust Particles in Sunlight: Poems of Rumi* contains the portion devoted to Rumi, featuring the recitation of Barks and Mary Sinclair, and a reading of Khan's commentaries by Lory Messina with musical accompaniment.

A Gift of Love (New York City: Tommy Boy Music, 1998), the CD package of Rumi readings put together by "Deepak and Friends," outdoes Barks at his own game. **Deepak Chopra** wraps his lavishly packaged CD not in the typical clear jewel case, but in a cardboard dust jacket. After sliding off the jacket, one finds an elaborate fold-out cover slightly reminiscent of the artwork on George Harrison's album *Material World* of the early 1970s. Nestled inside the cover one discovers a pouch containing a full-color booklet which features posed close-up photographs reminiscent of trendy perfume commercials. A recessed slot holds the hot-pink compact disc which, when removed, reveals a photograph of a henna-dyed pattern, in keeping with the Eastern Indian theme.

Adam Plack and Yaron Fuchs produced and arranged the music for *A Gift of Love*, which they composed in conjunction with Sussan Deyhim and Richard Horowitz. The soundtrack, a vaguely exotic but soothingly subdued jazz/New Age fusion, features an ensemble that draws upon a diversity of instruments, including guitars, keyboards, clarinet, bansuri, synthesized sounds, voice, tar, setar, nay, drums and percussions. The music, inspired by "the love poems of Rumi" (by which is intended the book of Chopra's "translations"), features a few purely instrumental pieces, such as the prelude, "Valentine to Rumi," but primarily functions as an attractive rhythmic background for the poems (samples can be heard at Chopra's web site, www.Chopra.com).

As in the print version of his book, *The Love Poems of Rumi*, Chopra includes four of Coleman Barks' translations on the CD, while the other thirty-two "poems" recited here are by Chopra, few of which bear any recognizable resemblance to specific poems of Rumi. The reciters include Chopra himself, of course, along with a number of Hollywood celebrities, such as Demi Moore, Martin Sheen, Goldie Hawn, Debra Winger, Madonna, and a few peace activists, like the Civil Rights hero Rosa Parks. The recitations are generally well done; anyone interested in what Deepak Chopra has done with "Rumi" would be well advised to buy the CD rather than read the book. Apparently, *A Gift of Love* was so successful that it is now sold at a higher price, piggybacked with a second companion CD featuring Chopra reading from his "Seven Laws of Love." Chopra's love gift also caught the attention of *The Advocate*, a Los Angeles-based periodical for the gay liberation movement (see "Soul Music," *The Advocate* 767 [September 1, 1998]: 54).

THE REAL, ORIGINAL RUMI: RENDITIONS OF THE POEMS IN PERSIAN

Even those who do not speak Persian would probably appreciate hearing Rumi's ghazals recited in the original language. There are two distinct traditions, the recitation of Persian poetry and the singing of poetic texts, both usually accompanied by music. Since the Iranian Revolution, **Farhang-e Farrahi** has produced a recording in Los Angeles of the recitation style. This offers his interpretation of a nice selection of Rumi poems, along with at least one poem attributed to Rumi in some of the pre-Foruzânfar editions of the *Divân*, but which is actually the work of another author (*Ânânke be sar dar talab-e Ka'be davidand*). **Koorosh Angali** recites the poems to the accompaniment of **Alan Kushan** on santur in a recent CD release, *Rumi I*, by X Dot 25 in Emeryville, California. But the definitive interpretation of Rumi is that of **Ahmad Shâmlu**, Iran's premier modernist poet of the 1960s and 1970s. Shâmlu has recited a number of classical poets, and his choice of poems, as well as his expressive and dramatic voice, reveals the inner meaning of the poems in a new light. Shâmlu has twice recorded his recitations of Rumi, once in the 1970s and again more recently, with exquisitely matched musical selections. Though his voice has aged and lost some of its strength, both the new poems he adds and the subtle differences in approach to his earlier renditions make both tapes thoroughly enjoyable and illuminating.

The Iranian Revolution of 1979 initially produced a climate inhospitable for musical performances; the war with Iraq, combined with over-zealous piety, curtailed musical expression to the performance of anthems and military marches. The thriving commercial pop music industry in Iran was banned as decadent and hegemonically Western; pre-Revolution popular music was not publicly performed or broadcast in Iran until 1998, and then only very sparingly (as in the film *Snowman*, which was banned for some time). Many singers went into exile, mostly in Los Angeles, where they continue to produce new pop songs. Most performers of traditional Iranian art music remained in Iran, however, and after Mohammad Khâtami became Culture Minister in the 1980s, concerts and recordings of traditional music with male vocalists were allowed back on the air. The singing of poetic texts by Rumi is such an integral part of the traditional Persian music repertoire that even if we delimit the sample to recordings currently available on cassette or CD, it would be nearly impossible to list them all. The following select discography should, however, help guide those interested in hearing Rumi sung in Persian.

Persian musicians play improvisationally within the parameters of the *radif* system, twelve traditional modes or *dastgâh* (similar to the *maqâm* in Arabic and Turkish music), which are further divided into subscales of shorter suites and melodies (*gushe*). As with the north Indian raga, each Persian mode is associated with a particular mood and sometimes with a particular time of day. Lyrics consist usually of classical poetic texts, typically chosen from Hâfez, Sa'di or Rumi. The singer does not normally include all the lines of the poem, but selects at his discretion the best or most lyrical lines. The performance of one poem often segues into or even interlinks lines from poems by other poets, not necessarily in the same rhyme or meter, but ideally in the same mood or on the same theme. The principal styles of song are the unmetered *âvâz*, which includes ample opportunity for the artist to display his virtuosity by a kind of elongated chanted glissando recitative, and the measured, rhythmic *tasnif.*

Persian music was traditionally monophonic, with the singer accompanied by one wind or string instrument and perhaps one percussion instrument, which would echo or foreshadow the melodic line of the singer's voice. In this century, a trend toward ensemble playing has developed, but the ensembles do not usually play harmonically. Iranian instruments include a hammer dulcimer, the santur; various lutes or plucked string instruments, the tar and the setar (*târ* is a Persian word meaning string), and the tanbur; a bowed string instrument, the kamânche; the traditional drum, zarb (tombak), usually held in the lap and played with the fingers of both hands; and the tambourines, daff and dâyere.

Though Rumi himself played the rabâb and Sultan Valad composed a poem named after that string instrument, the instrument primarily associated with Rumi is the nay (ney), or reed flute, because of the opening lines of the *Masnavi*, told through the voice of a flute. The flute has been cut from its bed of reeds, and now laments for its source; because it is emptied of self, divine mysteries can flow through it and move the souls of its listeners. In Iran, the opening lines of the *Masnavi*, known as the *Nay nâme*, are frequently performed, and are associated with a specific traditional melody. The nay was originally a Persian folk instrument, and someone in the Valad family entourage quite possibly brought one to Anatolia, along with the traditional melodies of Khorasan. Arab and Turkish reed pipes, also known as "nay," are probably derived from the popular Persian instrument, though the Arabo-Turkic nay has an extra finger hole and two additional bands. Quite likely, the Mevlevi order in Anatolia was in large part responsible for the spread of the instrument.

If the instrument par excellence of Rumi and the Mevlevis is the reed pipe, the premier flutist in Iran in modern times is generally recognized as Hasan Kasâ'i, and after him, his pupil, **Mohammad Musavi** (1946–). An example of Musavi's technique in the mode Navâ can be heard in a recording made in Tehran in the spring of 1980 by the French scholar Jean During, who supplies the excellent liner notes for volume 4 of the series *Anthologie de la musique traditionnelle de l'Iran* (France: Ocora, 1981, LP 558 563), which features Mahmud Karimi chanting a number of poems, including the opening verses of the *Masnavi*.

Traditional Persian art music has historically been sung by men, but in the Pahlavi period a number of female divas such as **Khâtere Parvâne** established themselves, often with state patronage (from Radio–Television Iran or the Fine Arts Organization). Because the Islamic Republic of Iran regards the female singing voice as erogenous, woman are no longer permitted to sing in mixed gatherings in public, nor are recordings of female vocalists played on the radio. Before the Revolution, however, Parvâne recorded a few lines from the *Masnavi*, in the mode Shur:

ʿâsheqi paydâ-st az zâri-ye del
nist bimâri cho bimâri-ye del

Love presents its wretched symptoms in the heart
Heartsickness, what an incomparable illness!

This appeared originally on an LP record, *Classical Music of Iran*, released by Folkways in 1966, but reappeared on cassette in 1991 after the Smithsonian Institute acquired the label (Smithsonian Folkways C-SF 40039).

Another female vocalist, **Marzie**, though not trained as an art musician, performed with tarist Farhang-e Sharif and other instrumentalists in the 1970s for the Iranian radio program *Golhâ-ye rangârang* ("Colorful Bouquets;" e.g., program nos. 134, 286, etc.), which occasionally included portions of Rumi's poems along with other texts. Marzie has recently gone into exile and quite publicly become a supporter of the opposition Mojâhedin, an Iranian political party and paramilitary group attempting to overthrow the government of the Islamic Republic by force of arms from guerilla bases in Iraq.

Unlike the two songstresses mentioned above, **Parisâ** (Fâteme Vâʿezi), a student of Mahmud Karimi who won critical and popular acclaim at the Shiraz Fine Arts Festival in 1976, has shown a personal interest in the praxis of Sufism. Though excelling in particular at the ghazals of Hâfez, Parisâ recorded in the years prior to the Iranian Revolution a number of ghazals from the *Divân-e Shams*, notably *Ay Yusof-e khwosh nâm-e mâ* (poem 27 in chapter 8) in the scale Bayât-e Tork; she likewise performed the opening lines of the *Masnavi* accompanied by nay.

As a result of the ban on female public performance, Parisâ has unfortunately now lost a good deal of control of her voice, which she compensates for by shouting the notes, as can be heard on recordings made during the last three years, when she has been allowed to travel to Europe and the United States on concert tours. The 1995 CD by PlayaSound (Boulogne, France: PS65155) makes available her concert in the Royal Festival Hall, featuring an ensemble led by a female composer and kânunist, Malihe Saʿidi. This includes two *tasnifs* or rhythmic song settings of poems by Rumi, *Makon yâr* and *Bâz âmadam* ("I've come again," see poem 15 in chapter 8). The latter title, in the context of Parisâ's return to the concert stage, takes on a particular relevance. In April–May of 1998 she toured the United States with an instrumental ensemble, including the fabulous **Hossein Omoumi** on nay, performing Rumi's *Masnavi* in a prominent place in the program. Omoumi's warm low vocals and innovative technique on the nay are particularly suited to performance of the *Masnavi*.

By far the best Iranian traditional vocalist is **Mohammad Rezâ Shajariân**, whose singing career was launched with his first-place showing in an international Koran recitation contest in the 1960s. His warm and steady voice, even in the lowest registers, coupled with the beauty of his *tahrir* (improvisational free-form modulation of the voice) and his precise ear for timing and phrasing of lyrics, has enchanted Iranian listeners for three decades, though his voice now shows the signs of age. Shajariân has recorded numerous pieces of Rumi and has toured Europe and the United States on several occasions. Shajariân's recordings of ghazals from the *Divân-e Shams* include the cassette *Mâhur* (1985) with Parviz Meshkâtiân on setar and Mohammad Mousavi on nay, featuring the poem *Dar havâ-yat* (poem 37 in chapter 8). Working with the Symphonic Orchestra of Tehran, Shajariân recorded a warmly melodious if rather subdued rendition of the poem *Ay Yusof-e khwosh nâm-e mâ* (poem 27 in chapter 8), composed by Parviz Meshkâtiân and arranged by Kâmbiz Rowshanravân, available on the cassette *Dud-e ʿud* ("The Incense of Sandalwood/The Sound of the Oud") from the 1980s.

The Kurdish singer **Shahrâm Nâzeri** (1950–) from Kermanshah in western Iran lacks Shajariân's range in the low register and his control at high volume. However, Nâzeri performs Rumi in attractive and crowd-pleasing formats that have captured the affection of youth and other Iranians not previously partial to traditional Iranian music, in a way that the more obscure and difficult scales and modes sometimes chosen by Shajariân have not. Indeed, Nâzeri's performances have even attracted the attention of Western fans of international music, as the *Christian Science Monitor*'s review of Nâzeri's performance at the World Sacred Music Festival in Fez, Morocco, demonstrates (Jonathan Curiel, "Iran's Pavarotti," June 11, 1997).

Although the octocentennial of Rumi's birth will not occur until 2007 according to the solar calendar, it has already occurred according to the Islamic lunar calendar. Under the Islamic calendar, the 800th anniversary of the birth of Rumi fell on 6 Rabiʿ al-avval of 1404, corresponding to December 11, 1983. In commemoration, Nâzeri teamed up with **Jalâl Zulfonoun** on setar for a cassette recording that proved immensely popular in Iran, *Gol-e sad barg* ("The Hundred-Petaled Rose") in the mode Bayât-e Tork (Bayât-e Zand suite). It includes a passage from the *Masnavi* and several of the ghazals of the *Divân-e Shams*, including: *Del-e man rây-e to dârad* (D 759); *Andak andak* (poem 33 in chapter 8); *Che dânestam* (poem 1 in chapter 8); and *Delâ nazd-e kasi benshin* (poem 32 in chapter 8). The cassette is available in the United States from Caltex Records (C458).

About the same time, a cassette was released in the U.S. of the *robâʿiyât*, or quatrains of Rumi, entitled *Songs of Rumi*, sung by Sharam Nazare (sic) (New Lebanon, NY: Sacred Spirit Music), with an unidentified ensemble providing accompaniment. Nâzeri also sings the poem *Hin sokhan-e tâze begu* (D 546) in the mode segâh, with Dâryush Pirniâkân on tar, in an Iranian recording entitled *Sokhan-e tâze*.

Les maîtres de la musique traditionnelle, volume 3 of Radio France's Iran series (Ocora C560026, 1992), records a November 1988 performance of Nâzeri with

Daryush Talâ°i on setar and Bizhan Kâmkâr on zarb and daff at the Théâtre de la Ville in Paris. This CD, distributed by Harmonia Mundi, includes liner notes by Jacques Dupont and an interview with Nâzeri. The program featured a rendition of part of the *Masnavi* in the Afshâri mode, along with selections from other poets, like Hâfez. Portions of this program, including the *Masnavi* passage, were released in Iran on cassette as *Konserti Digar 39 (Mâhur)* in 1993. *Daff va nay*, a cassette distributed by the Iranian Ministry of Culture and Islamic Guidance in 1991, featured two poems of Rumi performed by Nâzeri in Kurdish style with Bizhan Kâmkâr on daff and Mohammad °Ali Kâyâni-nezhâd on nay.

In the fall of 1989, santurist **Farâmarz Pâyvar** (1933–) led an ensemble of master musicians of Iran, including °Ali-Asghar Bahâri (1905–) on kamânche, Jalil-e Shahnâz (1921–) on tar, Mohammad Esmâ°ili (1934–) on zarb and Mohammad Mousavi (1946–) on nay. Together they performed a program in the mode Abu °Atâ°, including Nâzeri singing selections from Rumi's *Masnavi* (*Har ke u az hamzabâni*) and ghazals (*Bâ man sanamâ*), among other poems. *Âtash dar Nayestân* (Caltex Records 2079 CD), a 1991 recording featuring Nâzeri as vocalist accompanied by the setar ensemble of Jalâl Zulfonoun, includes a composition by Zulfonoun for the poem *Yâr marâ* (poem 4 in chapter 8).

Nâzeri toured the U.S. and Europe with the Shams Tanbur Players Ensemble in the early 1990s, featuring mystical music in Kurdish style. A tape and video of the compositions by Kaykhosrow Purnâzeri includes the poems *Row sar be-neh be-bâlin* (poem 11 in chapter 8), *Hilat rahâ kon* (poem 40 in chapter 8) and part of the ghazal beginning *Man* (*mast o to divâne*) (poem 42 in chapter 8). Also with the Shams Tanbur Players, Nâzeri performed the poem *Motreb-e mahtâb-ru* (poem 22 in chapter 8) on the tape *Mahtâbru* from the mid-1990s, also available on the *Mystified* CD from Kereshmeh Records (QTCD-1001). With the °Âref and Shaydâ ensembles, Nâzeri sings *Morde bodam* (poem 14 in chapter 8), available on the CD *Shurangiz* (Caltex 2042).

The tar and setar player **Mohammad Rezâ Lotfi** provides some poems of Rumi and Hâfez on *Mystery of Love* (Kereshmeh Records KCD 109), with liner notes from Robert Bly and Lotfi. The oud player and singer **°Abd al-Vahhâb-e Shahidi** comes from a somewhat older generation that does not practice the lengthened *tahrir* – virtuosic modulation and glissando of the voice so favored by Shajariân and Nâzeri. Shahidi has recorded Rumi's poem *Bi to be sar nemishavad* (D 553) in the mode Shur, accompanied by Farâmarz Pâyvar and his ensemble. In this performance, a rendition of the first few lines of the *Masnavi* precedes the ghazal in question. Originally released in Iran, the tape and CD were reissued in California after the Iranian Revolution by Soundex Enterprises, Inc. (Cassette: ARCT-209). A translation of this ghazal follows:

I manage fine with no others around;
I cannot manage without you
   My heart bears your brand,
   it won't wander away from you
   Reason's eye blurs with your wine
   heaven's wheel spins under your thumb
   Pleasure's nose follows your lead
I cannot manage without you
   Psyche ferments at your mention
   The heart drinks nectar from your hand
   and reason lets out with the roar:
I cannot manage without you
   My potion and intoxication,
   my flowering time, my garden bloom,
   my sleep, my peace
I cannot manage without you
   My pomp, my presence, dominion, wealth!
   You are my crystal water and
I cannot manage without you
   You alternate between
   being true and being cruel
   You're mine – where are you off to?
I cannot manage without you
   They offer heart, you snatch it
   they vow, repent, you break it
   All this and more you do
I cannot manage without you
   If only the world were inverted
   We could live without you –
     there where Eden's garden is Gehenna
I cannot manage without you
   If you're head, I stand pat, your foot
   If you're palm, I'm in hand, your flag
   If you go, I'm undone, a nothing
I cannot manage without you
   You've charmed me from my sleep
   you've washed me clear away
   You've cut me off from all
I cannot manage without you
   If you will not be my partner
   my affairs are all ashambles!
   My counselor, my consoler –
I cannot manage without you
   Living lacks joy without you
   dying lacks joy without you

How can I clear my mind of care for you?
I cannot manage without you
    Whatever I say, my source,
    reveals my strengths and faults
    So please, be gracious!
    and repeat with me:
I cannot manage without you.

In Afghanistan the recording industry and the state-sponsored radio and television programming were not as well developed and organized in the 1970s as in Iran. As a consequence, traditional Afghan musicians were typically understood or presented in the West as folk music performers. Iranian listeners did not particularly care for Afghan pronunciation of Persian, though the Afghan pronunciation is linguistically more conservative and therefore closer to the medieval pronunciation of Rumi, and most young Afghans, at least prior to the Soviet invasion and the inhuman strictures of the Taliban, preferred to listen to pop music. Nevertheless, **Mohammad Sadiq Fetrat Nâshenâs** achieved some reputation as a traditional singer who sometimes included the poems of Rumi in his repertoire. The United Nations High Commission for Refugees recorded a rendition by Nâshenâs in Peshawar, Pakistan, of a poem attributed to Rumi, *Man ân ruz budam ke asmâ nabud* ("I was there on the day before things were named").

In Pakistan, **Qawwâli**s (singers of Sufi songs and poems) of various Sufi orders sometimes perform poetic texts by Rumi, though texts attributed to Rumi are more common than texts actually by him. Among the Nizamuddin Auliya order, the Qawwâlis usually sing two verses of the *Masnavi* and then continue with another verse of Amir Khosrow or some other poet in the same rhyme and meter. The Qawwâlis associate one particular melody, not with the Hindustani musical tradition, but with what they believe to be the original tune of the *Masnavi*. The sheet music and a CD recording of part of a performance of this song (*Moflesânim âmade dar ku-ye to*) have been published.[5] **Nusrat Fâteh ꜥAli Khân** has also recorded a poem traditionally ascribed to Rumi, "Munâjât of Rumi"; however, this does not appear in Foruzânfar's edition of the *Divân*.

In Iran, Rumi's roots as a culture icon run very deep and poetry – even medieval poetry – is so much a part of Persian consciousness that singers have performed the poems of Rumi in pop style to good effect. For example, the female vocalist **Giti** recorded an artistically successful pop song with lyrics by Rumi (*Pir man-am, javân man-am*) in a vintage 1970s album named after Mowlânâ. A second song on the album features a poem widely but wrongly attributed to Rumi. The text of this incorrectly attributed poem appears in the 1957 Amir Kabir edition of Rumi's poems, *Kolliyât-e Shams-e Tabrizi* (no. 903, pp. 382–3). Even though it is not an authentic composition of Rumi himself, it does represent the philosophy of the Mevlevis; because the poem itself is quite beautiful, and because one has to admire and encourage the inclusion of mystical poetry in pop songs, a translation follows:

Har lahze be-shekl-i ân bot-e ͨayyâr bar âmad

Moment to moment, new in form
That ravishing idol appears
  steals the heart and disappears
minute by minute, in new garb
  now young, cheeks smooth, at times in beard
At times into a clod of clay descends
  diving and delving for meaning
At times into a pot of shaped adobe
  and goes to Eden, ascending
Not abrogation, transmigration,
  in truth, that gorgeous heartnapper
becomes sword, slayer of the age
  glinting again and again, forever
He spent a term on earth, came down
as Jesus from the sky, spread joy
  returned again, reciting glory
Once he came as Noah, drowned
the world in prayer, embarked the Ark
Once he came as Abraham, the Friend
emerging from the heart of fire
  turning all the flames to flowers
Once as Joseph, lumen of the world,
sent his coat from Egypt, giving sight
  as light coursed through the eyes of Jacob
He came to shepherd, with white hand
made his staff slough off wooden skin,
  assume snakeform; held back foam waves
He came as Sâleh, called mankind   [an Arabian Prophet
               named in the Koran]

to heedfulness, came from the hills
  as she camel, manifest
The intellect – trained, wise, perfect
swooned, sweetly buzzed by drink, and high
on the mountain top appeared,
an elder more giddy than youth
He came as Job, both ache and cure,
patient in the face of worms   [Kermân ?]
heart burning with the cry: beware
  His eyes full of the light of life
In the belly of the whale at sea
  he came as Jonah; purified
  he came as Moses, sought to see

climbed to the summit of Sinai
he came as Jesus, in the cradle
gave witness to the holy ghost
filled the palm with snakes
     animated by his miracle
He crooked his finger, split the moon
     hailing with the beloved's eyes

Out the door he goes, once again
by spirit sent, comes back
     adored by seraphs, lord of hosts
      In envy Satan shouts denials
He carves a block of wood, tunes it
     harmony and canon of the world
with two hundred fretting strings,
     weeping with panged and plaintive heart

It was him, I swear to God,
who came and went from age to age,
the final time in Arab form
     came in possession of the earth
He it was, in truth, who said
in a voice from God: "I am Truth"
     From the gallows hung not Mansur   [i.e., Hallâj]
     as you wrongly thought, but him

This moment he is hid, seek him
if you can see with inner eye
     That's how all these words came to be –
     expressed before the eyes through him –
He's not uttered any blasphemy
do not deny him; deniers
are heretics, infernal, damned.
He was Tabriz, also the sun
of meaning, in gardens of light
In mystery's ferment He appeared
and became manifest in love.

Los Angeles-based Persian pop star **Amir Ârâm** even brought Rumi to the dance floor with an early 1980s album that included one song based on quatrains from Khayyâm, and another on Rumi's ghazal *Morde bodam* (poem 14 in chapter 8).

The cassette *Bakht-e bidâr* ("Smiling Fortune") by **Turaj Zâhedi**, a singer and composer who frequently works with film soundtracks, appeared in about 1995 on the Avâ-ye Chang label, and contained two *tasnifs* based on Rumi poems. One of these, *Z-ân azali nur ke parvarde-and* (D 993), Zâhedi dedicates to the musician who helped launch his career, Feridun Shahbâziân.

RUMIO ON VIDEO

Love's Confusing Joy (David Grubin Productions and Public Affairs Television/ WNET, 1995) was filmed at a Barks poetry reading in New Jersey and includes an interview with **Bill Moyers**. This program was shown on public television throughout the United States as part of the *Language of Life* series and the interview appears in Bill Moyers' book of the same name.

Tolerance: Dedicated to Mawlana Jalal al-Din Rumi, a film by **Fehmi Gerceker**, scripted by **Talat Halman** and narrated by **Vanessa Redgrave**, with the music of Kudsi Erguner, and the *samâᶜ* performance of the Galata Mevlevi Ensemble, has been mentioned already. This half-hour film provides an excellent introduction to Rumi and the Mevlevis and a number of modern artists or thinkers who champion them. A number of documentaries about the Turkish Whirling Dervishes have also been made. The commemoration of the 700th anniversary of Rumi's death was filmed in Turkey by Dianna Cilento as *Turning* (1973). Giraard Vericruysse followed with *Whirling Dervishes* (1978), a short glimpse of the *samâᶜ* ceremony during Süleyman Dede's lifetime. A few decades later Penny Ward's production of *The Whirling Dervishes of Turkey* (NY: World Music Institute, 1997) features a much longer *samâᶜ* ceremony with Celâleddin Çelebi presiding and Kabir Helminski reading from Rumi. The North American members of the Mevlevi Order of America also perform the turn; they have produced a short video of the turning ceremony held in Seattle under the direction of Jelaluddin Loras on December 17, 1995 to commemorate the night of Rumi's passing, *Semá of Peace* (1995).

American actress **Debra Winger** (1955–) has also gotten in on the act of narrating Rumi videos with *Rumi: Poet of the Heart* (San Anselmo, CA: Magnolia Films, 1998). Written, produced and directed by Haydn Reiss, this hour-long film was funded by the Friends of Poetry and the Witter Bynner Foundation for Poetry. *Poet of the Heart* features an outline of Rumi's life, along with interviews and readings by Coleman Barks and Robert Bly, guru Deepak Chopra and religion scholar Huston Smith. Hamza El Din and Jai Uttal provide musical ambience.

Born in 1966 to Iranian parents living in Washington, D.C., Khashyar Darvish of Wakan films, a PBS production company, has won awards for his documentary *Black Hawk Waltz: Tales of a Rocky Mountain Town*. He has written a script for a film about Persians in America with the working title *Farewell to Rumi*. Darvish also has a script for a documentary biography of Rumi's life and is actively looking for a financial backer to begin filming.[6]

The Californian video artist **Bill Viola** (1951–) has from the 1970s quoted Rumi frequently in his journals, notes, interviews and books, integrating them into his own work and philosophy, although he does not reveal the sources of the translations he uses. No mere decoration for Viola, Rumi's poetry is central to his ideas of perception, as documented in *Reasons for Knocking at an Empty House* (Cambridge, MA: MIT Press, 1995), Viola's writings from 1973–4, the year of the international Rumi commemoration. The video *Outside the Lines*, produced by Bill Ferguson as part of the series *Persistence of Vision* (Los Angeles: Voyager, 1989), also provides background on Viola's work.

Viola's installations, a kind of conceptual art centered in some way on video, have won critical acclaim throughout Europe and America. Viola was chosen as the American contributor to the forty-sixth Venice Biennale in 1996 and his five-part installation *Bill Viola: Buried Secrets*, which was later on view for the American public in Arizona and Boston, featured a video of ten faces, all with gagged mouths, talking about their lives. One may perhaps understand the piece, which Viola attributes to the inspiration of Rumi, as a rather weird interpretation of Rumi's poetics of silence (Charles Gandee, "Life After Venice," *Vogue* 186 [April 1996]: 166).

THE WEB OF RUMI: RUMI ON THE INTERNET

The information on personal web pages is not necessarily accurate and one should use information gleaned from non-authoritative sources with care. Nevertheless, the Web provides access to many images, sounds and much information not easily obtained elsewhere. Rumi's popularity in the West comes at a time when the personal computer and the Internet are attractive media of communication, and many web sites have incorporated their creators' love for Rumi in some way. The following list provides some of the more interesting web sites associated with Rumi. Note, however, that the changing nature of the World Wide Web makes many web sites ephemeral; though the sites and addresses given below were current as of August 1998, there is no guarantee that they will still exist when you try to access them. Some of the sites mentioned below are linked to the companion website for this book.

http://www.webcom.com/threshld/
The Threshold Society in Vermont, representative of the Mevlevi order in North America. An extensive site with a wealth of information and publications devoted to the Mevlevi order, including photographs of the Mevlevi shrine in Konya, photos of the recent shaykhs of the order, excerpts from the *Maqâlât* of Shams, schedules of the retreats and other programs of the order, an article on women Sufis by Camille Helminski, etc.

http://turkey.org/f_tourism.htm
A site hosted by the Turkish Ministry of Culture in Turkish and in English, follow the links for "Who is Who" and "Mevlana." This presents Rumi and the associated Mevlevi sites and festivals from the perspective of Turkish tourism.

http://www.onelist.com/subscribe.cgi/sunlight
A moderated email list providing daily translations of Rumi in English
from a wide variety of translators.

http://www.stud.ifi.uio.no/~shaziam/rumi2.html
Provided a different Rumi translation by Nader Khalili each
time you accessed the site. Now apparently defunct, but the reader can
nevertheless see a sample of this site where cyber-surfers could for some
time find free translations of Rumi on the Web.

http://www.zbnet.com/rumi/
A tribute page for Rumi with rhyming translations by Shahriar Shariari and
Persian text of about sixty ghazals, a few passages from the *Masnavi*, some
original verse inspired by Rumi, modern paintings in Persian miniature
style and many Rumi links. Those who prefer rhymed verse may find these
versions attractive.

http://www.rassouli.com/rumi.htm
Freydoon Rassouli's paintings in modern Iranian style inspired by various
Persian poets. On this page one can view (and purchase) five inspired by
Rumi.

http://www.Rumi.net
Shahram Shiva's Rumi site, which includes information on
Shiva's performances, Shiva himself, and the tours Shiva leads to Konya for
$2,700.

Tariqas email discussion list at majordomo@world.std.com
An unmoderated discussion list for individuals with an interest in Sufism
and the Perennial Philosophy; discussion often focuses on Rumi and Sufi
teachers in the West.

Alt.Fan.Jalaludin Rumi
A now dormant usenet forum that used to feature discussion of Rumi.

http://www.geocities.com/Broadway/6700/Mevlana.htm
Nevit's comprehensive links to Rumi sites, with a Turkish emphasis.

http://www.armory.com/~thrace/sufi
A site established by N. Tsolak with a biographical profile of Rumi and a
collection of his poems from various translators.

http://www.turknet.com/music/index.html
A site with some samples of Mevlevi music hosted by Türknet, a Turkish
tourism consortium.

http://www.kto.org.tr/mevlana/resim.htm
http://www.ege.edu.tr/Turkiye/si/Konya.html
Two sites, the first hosted by the Konya Chamber of Commerce and the second by Ege University in Izmir, with photographs from Konya associated with Rumi and the Mevlevis.

http://www.chattanooga.net/baylor/academic/english/studentwork/rumi/
rumi.html
A very interesting site created by students at Baylor High School in Chattanooga, Tennessee, the alma mater of Coleman Barks. It contains essays, artwork, poetry and other creations reacting to Barks' translation of Rumi; this moving site illustrates the power of Barks to communicate with and inspire an audience of young Americans through the poems of Rumi.

http://hcgl1.eng.ohio-state.edu/~hoz/sufism/dervis.html
http://www.naqshbandi.net/haqqani/Sufi/saints/Sayiddina_Rumi.html
Both give explanations and images of Mevlevi *samâ^c* ceremonies.

http://www.lumen.org/issue_contents/contents30.html
Winter 1994 issue (no. 30) of *Gnosis* has articles about Sufism in the West with Kabir Helminski, Camille Helminski and an interview with Refik Algan, described as a partial devotee of the Mevlevis (pp. 34–9).

DESIGNER DERVISHES: RUMI AND THE MEVLEVIS IN PAINTING

Persian and Turkish miniatures from the fifteenth through the eighteenth centuries representing the scenes from Aflâki's *Acts of the Gnostics* abound, especially in illustrated manuscript editions of *Savâqeb al-manâqeb* (an abridgement of Aflâki's work) and its Turkish translations. The British Library has several miniatures depicting Rumi, as detailed by Norah Titley, *Miniatures from Persian Manuscripts* (London: British Museum, 1977; 11, 15 and 189). The mythical meeting of Rumi and ʿAttâr is imagined in a copy of Jâmi's *Nafahât al-ons* illustrated with seventeen miniatures and made for the emperor Akbar in Agra in 1603. In a *Divân* of Hâfez made in Kashmir in the eighteenth century, the thirty-fourth of thirty-six miniatures depicts Rumi with Hâfez, in an anachronistic, or rather a mythical, scene. A copy of the *Majâles al-ʿoshshâq* ("Gatherings of the Mystic Lovers") with seventy-nine miniatures made circa 1560 in Shiraz shows Sadr al-Din of Konya paying homage to Rumi outside the shop of Salâh al-Din Zarkub. The British Museum's collection also houses three miniatures of Rumi in eighteenth-century Moghul manuscripts.

Simple paintings and sketches of the figure of Rumi, not properly miniatures, circulated in calligraphy and sketch albums, and also as individual portraits. Of course, all of these portraits, which present Rumi in various guises

and at various ages, are the product of artists' imagination, as we have no indication that Rumi or Shams or any other early member of the order ever sat for a portrait, though Mevlevi dervishes and shaykhs did pose for live portraits and photographs in the nineteenth century. Some miniatures have been reproduced in various Islamic art books, mostly in poor quality black and white, though here and there one can see the original miniature on display, such as an illustration in the Topkapı Museum in Istanbul taken from a copy of the *Jâme^c*
al-seyar painted in Baghdad in the late sixteenth or early seventeenth century, which depicts the first meeting of Shams and Rumi. A work devoted to the reproduction of all known miniatures and sketches of Rumi and the Mevlevis would make a fine publication.

Şahabettin Uzlik has published a work of this sort in Turkish, *Mevlevilikte Resim Resimde Mevleviler* (Ankara: Türk Tarih Kurumu, 1957), which outlines the cosmological importance of the concept of image and drawing (*naqsh*) in Rumi's poetry and traces the history of representations of Rumi and the Mevlevis. It presents a number of illustrations (unfortunately not in the highest quality reproductions) including portraits of Rumi and Shams, scenes of Rumi reading with Shams, early modern miniatures featuring Mevlevi dervishes, a drawing by Ustâd ʿAli Rezâ of a Mevlevi nay player done in 1896, drawings of a Mevlevi shaykh from the same period, drawings by Hüsnü Yusuf Bey of Mevlevi performances and lodges, the *samâ^c* ceremony at the Galata lodge, early modern miniatures of Mevlevis and figures from the early history of the order, etc.

Uzlik also gives sporadic information about European paintings depicting the Mevlevis, including a painting by **Francis Smith** from 1769 of the Galata Mevlevi ceremony, titled *Danses réligeuses des derviches tourneurs dans leur Mevlahané à Pára*. There is also a drawing by the botanist **Tournefort** (d. 1708?) called *A Dance of Dervices* with three figures. **Jan Baptiste van Mour** (d. 1737), who did numerous drawings of Istanbul and Turkey in the early 1700s, shows the crowded interior of a circular and apparently domed building with several stories of large windows and natural light pouring down upon what are clearly meant to be Mevlevi dervishes. In this work from circa 1707, some of the dervishes are involved in *samâ^c*, but look rather as if they are playing at airplanes. Some stand in a trance-like state (*hâl*), others just stand around, and one lies prostrate. Other European artists who took Mevlevis as subjects include Hilair, who made a drawing of a shaykh and his dervishes; **Fausto Zonaro** and his drawing of a nay player; Hubert, Bauer and Sinety with their drawings; and **Amadeo Preziosi** (1816–82), whose 1857 canvas depicts a scene of somewhat wilder abandon than we now associate with Mevlevi dervishes. Preziosi's Istanbul work is printed in an album of color lithographs called *Stamboul: Recollections of Eastern Life*, published in 1858, further editions of which appeared in 1861, 1863 and 1883 (LDL 280). Many drawings of Mevlevi costumes also appear in English books from the early 1800s, etc.

A few Europeans, such as the Swede Guillaume Berggren (d. 1920), established photography studios in Istanbul in the second half of the nineteenth century. The photographs wound up in postcards and souvenir albums. Since the Europeans knew the Mevlevis – the dancing dervishes – best among all the dervishes, a preponderance of the photos from this period depicting "dervishes" feature specifically Mevlevi dervishes. Such photos were usually posed in groups in the studio, and the Mevlevis, though standing still for the camera, would raise their arms above their head in imitation of the *samâ*. In her article "Dervish Images," Nancy Micklewright reproduces one such photo by Berggren (LDL 271), and a portrait of a Mevlevi shaykh in Bursa (LDL 272).

Rachel Milstein's *Miniature Painting in Ottoman Baghdad* (Costa Mesa, CA: Mazda, 1989) gives fine reproductions, both color and black and white, of a number of miniatures produced by the Mevlevi workshop in Baghdad in the sixteenth century, which included famed Mevlevi calligraphers like **Nosayra Dede** and **Qusi** (ʿAbd al-Bâqi al-Mowlavi). Illustrated manuscripts produced by or for the Mevlevis of Baghdad during this period include a copy of Jâmi's lives of the Sufis, *Nafahât al-ons*, dated 1593; a copy of Aflâki's *Manâqeb*, dedicated to Sultan Mehmed III; a copy of the abridgement of that work, *Savâqeb*, dated 1599; a copy of the *Masnavi*, dated 1603; and a copy of the *Jâmeʿ al-seyar* dedicated to the vizier Hasan Pâshâ.

Mehmet Önder in *Mevlâna Jelaleddin Rûmî* (trans. P.M. Butler [Ankara: Ministry of Culture, 1990]) reproduces some Turkish manuscript miniatures, including one belonging to the Topkapı Museum library (1479), showing Rumi dancing in Salâh al-Din Zarkub's shop (241). In another miniature, Rumi stands with both arms raised up at head level, almost in the position of prayer, with long sleeves drooping downward, in front of a group of turbaned notables who are evidently agitated about his dancing. There is also a portrait of Bahâ al-Din Valad with a pepper beard, seated alone (239), and another with Rumi and his family and a few disciples, all of whom wear the characteristic tall, rounded hat. Only Rumi has a turban at the base of his hat, whereas other Mevlevis are depicted outside their homes wearing turbans and no hats. A woman also appears in this miniature, somewhat disheveled (238). Another miniature shows Rumi accepting a plate of food from a turbaned notable on behalf of the disciples at his back, while another notable kneels and kisses the hem of Rumi's skirt (242). In the depictions of Mevlevi disciples, a few have full black beards, but most are fuzzless youth, indicating their status as young novices.

A volume as important for its artwork as for its translations is the *Divan-E-Shams* of "Jalaluddin Mohammad Rumi" (New York: Vincent Fitzgerald, 1996). Between the white muslin-covered boards which protect the fifty-five leaves, some of which fold out to reveal their artwork, the eye encounters not only selected translations of the *Divân* by **Zahra Partovi**, but also original etchings, lithographs, silkscreens, collages and glass sculptures by fifteen artists. Rumi also provides a somewhat incongruent frame for a small album of modern photographs – *Heartwood: Meditations on Southern Oaks* (Boston, MA: Bullfinch Press, 1998) sets a meditative tone for each of **William Guion**'s black-and-white photos of tree landscapes by their juxtaposition with four or five lines of Rumi's verse on facing pages, excerpted from the Barks/Moyne translations, on facing pages. This slender volume will probably wind up on many a coffee table to calm and inspire.

Nor could one forget the adorable little ceramic kitsch figurines made in Turkey and sold to tourists for about $30 that depict Mevlevi dervishes, specifically the *semazen* (*samâᶜ-zan*) and the *kudümzen*. The film *The Sufi Way* by comparative religions scholar Huston Smith even opens with an extended scene of a little set of Mevlevi figurines twirling round and round and round.

Epilogue: The Fruit of Translation

The choice of what poems to translate, whether to use verse or free forms, whether or not to annotate, all affect the outcome, as does the translator's knowledge of the original language, her understanding of the poet's milieu and the mental images and assumptions about the poet and his message she carries around with her.

I do not think poems from a different time, place and *Weltanschauung* should be flavored in translation just to make them more palatable to modern Western sensibility. Imitation and adaptation of poems from a foreign language is a time-honored and often inspiring activity, which frequently enriches the poetic tradition. To my mind, however, *translations* should aim to preserve the cultural assumptions, imagery and complexity of the original. Readers do not always benefit in the long run from having the contours of a foreign text reduced to denominators and assumptions held in common with their own cultural framework; while this makes foreign texts accessible, it also tends to distort them. I think most serious readers of Rumi would prefer to have difficulties and obscurities in his poetry made comprehensible through context and commentary, rather than by smoothing them away in translation. This process expands the reader's horizons, rather than delimiting the author's vista.

Among the modern "translations" of Rumi in English, many are actually adaptations, as the "translators" have had no access to the original text. The typical reader for these kind of adaptive translations is perhaps someone impressed with Rumi's reputation as a spiritual teacher, someone who wants to relate Rumi's insights to his or her own postmodern situation in a consumer society. The work of Coleman Barks and Robert Bly has spoken most successfully to these readers. Personally, I prefer Jonathan Star's renditions among this category. But the single most successful imitation of Rumi, to my mind, is that of Robert Duncan, who makes no pretension to translation, but most successfully captures the experience of reading Rumi in the original.

Nader Khalili works from the original Persian and succeeds in distilling the spirit of Rumi's ghazals into a very accessible form. I think that Daniel Liebert has also successfully recreated the Persian reader's experience of Rumi's ghazals. Nevit Ergin, by committing himself to translate the entire corpus of the *Divân* (working from Turkish, not the original Persian), perhaps promises to afford English readers their most comprehensive look at the lyrical Rumi.

Most of these poetic versions fail to take account of the Islamic context of Rumi's teachings, either because the translators do not have a deep understanding of the spiritual and intellectual matrix which made Rumi's poems possible, or because they are not interested in the specifics of his spirituality, but rather in their portability and general applicability. Still others have translated primarily as a vehicle to get to the intellectual core of Rumi's philosophy, categorize his ideas and make them more transparent and intelligible. Chittick, Arberry, Nicholson and many others have tackled this task and produced books that help us understand Rumi's ideas more systematically. Indispensable as these are, this does Rumi the preacher and poet an injustice, as he did not intend to create a systematic theology, but rather used the ghazal as a means for metamorphosis and emotional catharsis and the *Masnavi* as a heuristic means of inspiring and transforming others.

Mystical experience, to the extent that it is meta-rational and beyond cognition, perhaps resides more in the form of expression than is the case with other genres. The mere abstraction of the content of a mystical or gnostic poem therefore cannot hope to explain to the reader the phenomenon the poet wishes to communicate. This is, in any case, true for all good lyrical poetry – a simple restatement of the meaning or the ideas in a poem can never constitute a translation. The explanatory and prosaic versions of the poems from the *Divân-e Shams*, then, such as Arberry has produced, can never do justice to the poems and this has led a handful of poets to rework his scholarly cribs. Some translations, the English versions of Schimmel, for example, straddle the ground somewhere between scholarly and poetic versions (her German versions are more successful as literary translations than her English).

Selections from the *Masnavi* have been available now for well over a century and Whinfield's compilation has much to recommend it. Nicholson and Arberry's artistic prose renditions of some of the tales from the *Masnavi* are still delightful to read, though removing the stories from the pattern of the text tends to distort it. Nicholson's complete rendering of the *Masnavi* has the virtue of reproducing the warp and woof of the text along with a very full commentary (which now needs to be revised in light of subsequent scholarship); however, the parenthetic and heady prose (not to mention the use of Latin for the naughty bits) takes most of the joy out of reading it. A new version of the entire text of the *Masnavi*, perhaps in blank or even rhyming verse, along with an up-to-date scholarly commentary is needed.

We began this book with the aim of holding up a candle to illumine the mammoth elephant – the object of devotion, of scholarly study, emblem of religious tolerance, of political liberation – which Rumi and the Mevlevis have become. Not just to describe, but to record the significance of Rumi for a wide range of audiences across the world and through the ages. It is hoped that what you have read will aid and enhance the future study and enjoyment of the remarkable man and poet born nearly eight hundred years ago. Whatever version of the poems or particular approach or methodology – scholarly, popular, spiritual – the reader prefers, by knowing what others have thought, and felt, interpreted, and translated, a more complete picture of the Rumi phenomenon will emerge.

In Book 2 of the *Masnavi* Rumi tells a story most germane to questions of translation and language. Nothing else could sum up our discussion of the opposing views and approaches of the various translators, scholars and readers of Rumi more appropriately (M2:3681–92):

> A man gave four companions one dirham
> The first said I will get *Angur* with it
> The second, who was Arab, answered, No!
> I want *'Enab*, and not *Angur*, you rogue!
> The third, a Turk, in Turkish chimed: It's mine!
> I do not want your *'Enab*, but *Ozom*
> A Greek, the fourth, called out: Put a stop to
> all this nonsense! It's *Estâfil* I want.
>
> > Ignorant of the secret of these names
> > through discord they were led to wrangling
> > Long on ignorance, of understanding shorn,
> > each punched, in knuckleheadedness, the other

Rumi is himself the "master of mysteries, precious polyglot" who, were he present among us, could have brought the various translations into accord with the observation that we are all asking for the same thing in a different language:

> Then he would have said: I can fulfill
> all four of your desires with one dirham
> If you entrust me wholly with your hearts
> your one dirham will work for all of you
> One dirham can provide for four desires
> Four foes, united, can become as one
> The words of each of you bring trouble, strife
> My words will bring the four of you accord
> So you be quiet, then –
> > "Hold ye your tongues!"   [K7:203]
> > > Let me
> > > become your tongue
> > > in conversation

Maps

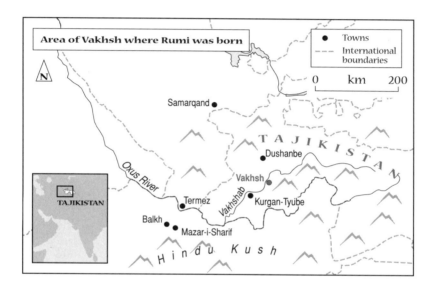

Area of Vakhsh where Rumi was born

Towns
International boundaries

0   km   200

Samarqand

TAJIKISTAN

Dushanbe

Vakhsh

Oxus River

Vakhshab

Termez   Kurgan-Tyube

Balkh
Mazar-i-Sharif

Hindu Kush

TAJIKISTAN

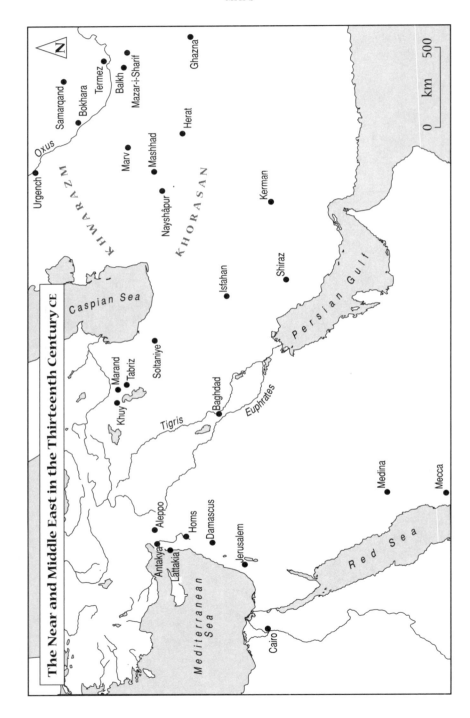

The Near and Middle East in the Thirteenth Century CE

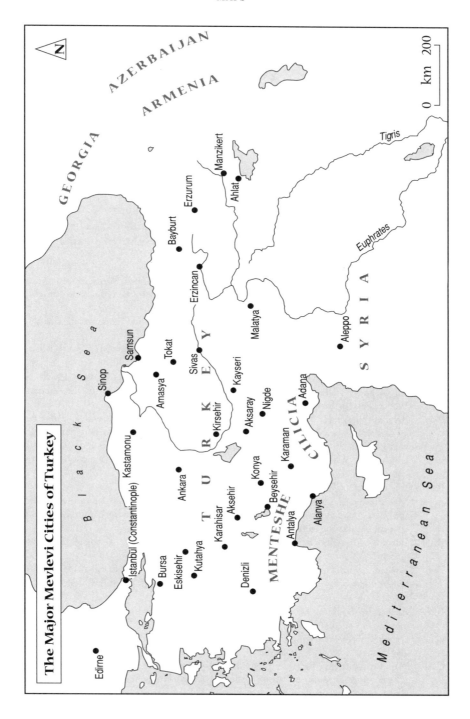

The Major Mevlevi Cities of Turkey

References

ABBREVIATIONS FOR FREQUENTLY CITED SOURCES

In an effort to keep notes to a minimum, most of the references in the book are given in parentheses in the body of the text. The following two- or three-letter codes indicate the source, followed by the page number(s). This is not a comprehensive listing of the sources used; bibliographic annotations occur throughout the narrative of the text.

Af   Shams al-Din Ahmad al-Aflâki, *Manâqeb al-ʿârefin*, ed. Tahsin Yazıcı, 2 vols. (Ankara: Türk Tarih Kurumu Basımevi, 1959). Reference is made to the offset reprint (Tehran: Donyâ-ye Ketâb, 1983).

Akh   Mohammad Javâd Mashkur, ed., *Akhbâr-e Salâjeqe-ye Rum* (Tehran: Ketâbforushi-ye Tehrân, 1350/1971).

AOE   A.J. Arberry, *Oriental Essays: Portraits of Seven Scholars* (London: George Allen & Unwin, 1960; reprinted Richmond, Surrey: Curzon Press, 1997).

ATM   A.J. Arberry, *Tales from the Masnavi* (London: George Allen & Unwin, 1961).

AMT   A.J. Arberry, *More Tales from the Masnavi*. UNESCO Collection of Representative Works: Persian Series (London: George Allen & Unwin, 1963).

Bah   Bahâ al-Din Valad, *Maʿâref: majmuʿe-ye mavâʿez va sokhanân-e Soltân al-ʿolamâ Bahâ al-Din Mohammad b. Hosayn Khatibi-ye Balkhi*, ed. Badiʿ al-Zamân Foruzânfar, 2 vols. (Tehran: Edâre-ye Koll-e Entebâʿât-e Vezârat-e Farhang, 1955 and 1959). A 2nd edition was published in Tehran in 1973, but reference has been made to the two-volume first edition.

Bat   Ibn Battûta, *Rihlat Ibn Battûta* (Beirut: Dâr Bayrut, 1985).

Bay   Mikâil Bayram, "Sayyed Borhân al-Din Mohaqqeq Termezi dar talâtom-e havâdes-e siâsi," in *Mowlânâ az didgâh-e Torkân va Irâniân* (Tehran: Ministry of Culture and Islamic Guidance, 1990), 149–58.

BLH   Edward Granville Browne, *A Literary History of Persia*, 4 vols. (Cambridge: Cambridge University Press, 1902–24).

Bor   Borhân al-Din Mohaqqeq, *Maʿâref: majmuʿe-ye mavâʿez va kalemât-e Sayyed Borhân al-Din Mohaqqeq-e Termedi*, ed. Badiʿ al-Zamân Foruzânfar (Tehran: Edâre-ye Koll-e Negâresh-e Vezârat-e Farhang, 1961).

BPR   Alessandro Bausani, *Persia religiosa: da Zaratustra a Bahâʾuʾllâh* (Milan: Saggiatore, 1959).

CaT   Claude Cahen, *Pre-Ottoman Turkey: A General Survey of the Material and Spiritual Culture and History, c. 1071–1330*, trans. J. Jones-Williams (New York: Taplinger, 1968).

CBa   William Chittick, "Rumi and Wahdat al-Wujûd," in *Poetry and Mysticism in Islam: The Heritage of Rumi*, ed. Amin Banani, Richard Hovannisian and Georges Sabagh (New York: Cambridge University Press, 1994).

Che   Peter Chelkowski, ed., *The Scholar and the Saint: Studies in Commemoration of Abu ʾl-Rayhan al-Bīrūnī and Jalal al-Din al-Rūmī* (New York: Hagop Kevorkian Center for Near Eastern Studies and New York University Press, 1975).

CSP   William Chittick, *The Sufi Path of Love: The Spiritual Teachings of Rumi* (Albany, NY: State University of New York Press, 1983).

D   *Divân-e Shams-e Tabrizi.* Following the edition of Badiᶜ al-Zamân Foruzânfar, *Kolliyât-e Shams yâ Divân-e Kabir*, 10 vols. (Tehran: University of Tehran Press, 1957–67; reprinted in a smaller format in the early 1960s. Amir Kabir reprinted the entire series in nine volumes, 2535/1977). D followed by a number indicates the number of the ghazal, while D followed by R or T and then a number indicates the number of the *robâᶜi* or *tarjiᶜ band.*

Dow   Dowlatshâh-e Samarqandi, *Tazkerat al-shoᶜarâ*, ed. Mohammad ᶜAbbâsi (Tehran: Bârâni, 1337/1958).

*EI*²   *Encyclopaedia of Islam*, 2nd edition (Leiden: E.J. Brill, 1960–).

EIr   *Encyclopaedia Iranica*, ed. Ehsan Yarshater (London: Routledge & Kegan Paul, 1982–).

FA   Badiᶜ al-Zamân Foruzânfar, *Sharh-e ahvâl va naqd va tahlil-e âsâr-e Shaykh Farid al-Din Mohammad-e ᶜAttâr-e Nayshâburi* (Tehran: Tehran University Press, 1339–40/1960–61). Reprint Ketâbforushi-ye Dehkhodâ, 1975.

FB   Badiᶜ al-Zamân Foruzânfar, *Resâle-ye tahqiq dar ahvâl va zendegi-ye Mowlânâ Jalâl al-Din Mohammad mashhur be Mowlavi*, revised 2nd edition (Tehran: Zavvâr, 1954). The first edition was published in 1937.

Fih   Rumi, *Fihe mâ fih az goftâr-e Mowlânâ Jalâl al-Din Mohammad mashhur be Mowlavi*, ed. Badiᶜ al-Zamân Foruzânfar, 5th printing (Tehran: Amir Kabir, 1983). First published 1951.

FMQ   Badiᶜ al-Zamân Foruzânfar, *Maʾâkhez-e qesas va tamsilât-e Masnavi* (Tehran: Majles, 1954).

GB   Abdülbâki Gölpınarlı, *Mevlâna Celâleddin: hayatı, felsefesi, eserleri, eserlerinden seçmeler* (Istanbul: Inkılap, 1951). Revised editions appeared in 1952, 1959 and 1985. Reference is made in these pages to the Persian translation by Towfiq Sobhâni, *Mowlânâ Jalâl al-Din* (Tehran: Institute for Humanities and Cultural Studies, 1996).

GM   Abdülbâki Gölpınarlı, *Mevlânâʾdan sonra Mevlevîlik* (Istanbul: Inkılap Kitabevi, 1953; 2nd edition 1983). Reference is made in these pages to the Persian translation of the 2nd edition of Gölpınarlı's work: *Mevlevi baᶜd az Mowlânâ*, trans. Towfiq Sobhâni (Tehran: Kayhân, 1988).

Hum   R. Stephen Humphries, *From Saladin to the Mongols: The Ayyubids of Damascus, 1193–1260* (Albany, NY: State University of New York Press, 1977).

IqL   Afzal Iqbal, *The Life and Work of Muhammad Jalal-ud-Din Rumi*, 6th edition (Lahore: Pakistan National Council, 1991). First published as *The Life and Thought of Maulana Jalal-ud-Din Rumi* (Bazm-i-Iqbal, 1956), with a revised edition in 1964 and a third revised edition in 1974 (Lahore: Institute of Islamic Culture).

IS   Seyyed Hossein Nasr, ed., *Islamic Spirituality: Manifestations* (New York: Crossroad, 1991). Includes articles by Muhammad Isa Waley on Najm al-Din Kobrâ (80–104) and by William Chittick on Rumi and the Mawlawiyyah (105–26), which are cited here.

JNO   ᶜAbd al-Rahmân Jâmi, *Nafahât al-ons men hazarât al-qods*, ed. Mehdi Towhidipur (Tehran: Mahmudi, 1336/1958). Reprinted 1996 (Tehran: ᶜElmi).

K   Koran (Qurʾân). Translations are the author's. Note that the numbering of the verses in certain translations (e.g., Marmaduke Pickthall) differ from the standard numbering accepted by most Muslims and scholars.

KAH   Khalifa Abdul Hakim, *The Metaphysics of Rumi: A Critical and Historical Sketch*, 2nd edition (Lahore: The Institute of Islamic Culture, 1959). First published 1933.

LCP   Leonard Lewisohn, ed., *Classical Persian Sufism: From its Origins to Rumi* (London: Khaniqahi Nimatullahi Publications, 1993). Reprinted as *The Heritage of Sufism, Volume 1* (Oxford: Oneworld, 1999).

LDL   Raymond Lifchez, ed., *The Dervish Lodge: Architecture, Art, and Sufism in Ottoman Turkey* (Berkeley: University of California Press, 1992).

LeS   Guy LeStrange, *The Lands of the Eastern Caliphate* (London: Frank Cass, 1905; reprint 1966).

LLM   Leonard Lewisohn, ed., *The Legacy of Mediaeval Persian Sufism* (London: Khaniqahi Nimatullahi Publications, 1992). Reprinted as *The Heritage of Sufism, Volume 2* (Oxford: Oneworld, 1999).

M   Rumi, *Masnavi-ye ma'navi*, ed. R.A. Nicholson as *The Mathnawí of Jalálu'ddín Rúmí*, E.J.W. Gibb Memorial, new series (London: Luzac & Co., 1925, 1929, 1933). A one-volume edition was subsequently issued in Iran (Tehran: Amir Kabir, 1957); reference is made in these pages to the 8th printing of the Amir Kabir edition, 1982.

Mak   Rumi, *Maktubât-e Mowlânâ Jalâl al-Din Rumi*, ed. Towfiq Sobhâni (Tehran: Markaz-e Nashr-e Dâneshgâhi, 1992).

Maq   Shams al-Din Tabrizi, *Maqâlât-e Shams-e Tabrizi*, ed. Mohammad-'Ali Movahhed (Tehran: Sahâmi, Enteshârât-e Khwârazmi, 1990). This is a two-volume edition; the first volume was originally published separately (Tehran: Dâneshgâh-e San'ati, 1977).

MAS   Fritz Meier, *Abū Sa'īd-i Abū al-Hayr: Wirklichkeit und Legende* (Tehran and Liège: Bibliothèque Pahlavi, 1976).

ME   Rumi, *Masnavi*, ed. Mohammad Este'lâmi, 7 vols. (Tehran: Zavvâr, 1987). 2nd edition 1990.

Mei   Fritz Meier, *Bahâ'-i Walad: Grundzüge seines Lebens und seiner Mystik* (Leiden: E.J. Brill, 1989, in *Acta Iranica*'s troisième série, Textes et Mémoires, vol. 14).

Mov   Mohammad-'Ali Movahhed, *Shams-e Tabrizi* (Tehran: Tarh-e Now, 1996).

MPR1   A.J. Arberry, *Mystical Poems of Rūmī* (Chicago: University of Chicago Press, 1968).

MPR2   A.J. Arberry, *Mystical Poems of Rūmī, 2: Second Selection* (Chicago: University of Chicago Press, 1979).

MRC   George Makdisi, *The Rise of Colleges* (Edinburgh: Edinburgh University Press, 1981).

NiD   R.A. Nicholson, ed. and trans., *Selected Poems from the Dīvāni Shamsi Tabrīz* (Cambridge: Cambridge University Press, 1898). Reprinted 1952 and 1977.

NiM   R.A. Nicholson, "Mysticism," in *The Legacy of Islam*, ed. Thomas Arnold (Oxford: Clarendon Press, 1931).

NiT   R.A. Nicholson, *Tales of Mystic Meaning, Being Selections from the Mathnawi of Jalal-ud-Din Rumi* (London: Chapman & Hall; New York: Frederick Stokes, 1931).

OLP   Walter Andrews, Najaat Black and Mehmet Kalpaklı, eds., *Ottoman Lyric Poetry* (Austin: University of Texas Press, 1997).

Owh   *Manâqeb-e Owhad al-Din Hâmed b. Abi al-Fakhr-e Kermâni*, ed. Badi' al-Zamân Foruzânfar (Tehran: Bongâh-e Tarjome va Nashr-e Ketâb, 1347/1969).

OxE   Jamal Elias, "Mawlawiyya," in *Oxford Encyclopedia of the Modern Islamic World*, ed. John L. Esposito, 4 vols. (New York: Oxford University Press, 1995).

OxM   Şerif Mardin, "Mevlevi," in *Oxford Encyclopedia of the Modern Islamic World*, ed. John L. Esposito, 4 vols. (New York: Oxford University Press, 1995).

Poe   Amin Banani, Richard Hovannisian and Georges Sabagh, eds., *Poetry and Mysticism in Islam: The Heritage of Rumi* (New York: Cambridge University Press, 1994).

QMF   S.H. Qasemi, ed., *The Maulavi Flute* (New Delhi: New Age International, 1997).

RaJ   Hâfez Hosayn Karbalâ²i-ye Tabrizi, *Rowzat al-jenân va jannât al-janân*, ed. Ja^cfar Soltân al-Qorrâ²i, 2 vols. (Tehran: Bongâh-e Tarjome va Nashr-e Ketâb, 1965–70).

RiM   Hellmut Ritter, "Die Mevlânafeiern in Konya vom 11–17 Dezember 1960," *Oriens* 15 (1962): 249–70.

RiN   Hellmut Ritter, "Neue Literatur über Maulânâ Celâluddîn Rûmî und seinen Orden," *Oriens* 13–14 (1960–61): 342 et. seq.

Saf   Zabih Allâh Safâ, *Târikh-e adabiyât dar Irân*, 4th printing (Tehran: Ferdows, 1987).

ScB   Annemarie Schimmel, "Mawlânâ Rûmî: Yesterday, Today, and Tomorrow," in *Poetry and Mysticism in Islam: The Heritage of Rumi*, ed. Amin Banani, Richard Hovannisian and Georges Sabagh (New York: Cambridge University Press, 1994).

ScP   Annemarie Schimmel, *Pain and Grace* (Leiden: E.J. Brill, 1976).

ScT   Annemarie Schimmel, *The Triumphal Sun: A Study of the Works of Jalâloddin Rumi*. Bibliotheca Persica, Persian Studies Series (Albany, NY: State University of New York Press, 1993). Previous editions appeared in London, East–West Publications, 1980 and Fine Books, 1978. Reference in these pages is made to the revised 1993 edition.

ScW   Annemarie Schimmel, *I am Wind, You are Fire: The Life and Work of Rumi* (Boston, MA and London: Shambhala, 1992).

Sep   Faridun b. Ahmad Sepahsâlâr, *Resâle-ye Sepahsâlâr*, ed. by Sa^cid Nafisi (Tehran: Eqbâl, 1325/1947); reprinted as *Zendeginâme-ye Mowlânâ Jalâl al-Din Mowlavi* in 1983.

SVE   Sultan Valad, *Ebtedâ nâme*, as it is commonly called by Turkish scholars, or *Valad nâme*, as it is usually known in Iran. *Masnavi-ye Valadi, enshâ²e Bahâ² al-Din b. Mowlânâ Jalâl al-Din Mohammad b. Hosayn-e Balkhi, mashhur be Mowlavi*, ed. Jalâl al-Din Homâ²i (Tehran: Eqbâl, 1316/1937).

Tfz   Abu al-Qâsem Tafazzoli, *Samâ^c-e darvishân dar torbat-e Mowlânâ* (Tehran: Mo²allef, 1370/1991).

TrS   J. Spencer Trimingham, *The Sufi Orders in Islam*, 2nd edition (Oxford: Oxford University Press, 1998). 1st edition, 1971 (Oxford: Clarendon Press).

Tür   Erkan Türkmen, *The Essence of Rumi's Masnevi* (Konya: Seljuk University Press, 1992).

Zar   Borhân al-Din al-Zarnūjī, *Ta^clīm al-Muta^callim: Ṭarīq at-Ta^callum; Instruction of the Student: The Method of Learning*, trans. G.E. Von Grunebaum and Theodora Abel (New York: King's Crown Press, 1947).

Zia   Nicola Ziadeh, *Urban Life in Syria Under the Early Mamluks* (Beirut: Faculty of Arts and Sciences, American University of Beirut, 1953; reprint, Westport, CT: Greenwood Press, 1970).

ZrJ   ^cAbd al-Hosayn Zarrinkub, *Jostoju dar tasavvof* (Tehran: Amir Kabir, 1369/1990). First published 1978.

ZrP   ^cAbd al-Hosayn Zarrinkub, *Pele-pele tâ molâqât-e Khodâ: darbâre-ye zendegi, andishe va soluk-e Mowlânâ Jalâl al-Din Rumi* (Tehran: Enteshârât-e ^cElmi, 1373/1994).

Notes

INTRODUCTION

1. Specifically in the Pali Udâna, part of the Tripitaka, probably compiled in the second century B.C. Sanâ'i may have learned this parable from Ghazzâli, who quotes a version of it in his "Vivication of the Religious Sciences." Rumi was apparently aware of both versions, which give slightly different versions of the circumstances, but he follows Sanâ'i in much of the wording of the verse. See Fritz Meier, "Nature in the Monism of Islam" in *Spirit and Nature: Papers from the Eranos Yearbooks* (New York: Pantheon Books, Bollingen Series, 1954), 166–70. See Hadiqat al-haqiqat va Shari'at al-tariqat, ed. M.T. Modarres-e Razavi (Tehran: University of Tehran 1359/1981).

2. See W. Heffening (for Joseph Schacht), "Hanafiyya," and also Wilferd Madelung, "al-Mâturīdī" and "Mâturīdiyya," in *EI²*.

3. For a fuller description of the medieval *madrase* system, interested readers may consult George Makdisi, *The Rise of Colleges* (Edinburgh: Edinburgh University Press, 1981); J. Pedersen (and G. Makdisi), "Madrasa," in *EI²*; Carl Petry, *The Civilian Elite of Cairo in the Later Middle Ages* (Princeton: Princeton University Press, 1981); Jonathan Berkey, *The Transmission of Knowledge in Medieval Cairo: A Social History of Islamic Education* (Princeton: Princeton University Press, 1992) and Michael Chamberlain, *Knowledge and Social Practice in Medieval Damascus, 1190–1350* (Cambridge: Cambridge University Press, 1994).

4. Foruzânfar gives the form of the word as *mashâqqi* (Owh 2) in the text, but reads *mashshâqi* in the glossary (Owh 301). Though in some periods this may refer to a letter-writing or teaching of penmanship, here it apparently refers to construction work. According to what Aflâki and Shams al-Din say, Movahhed (Mov 69–70) concludes that the word means heavy construction labor, and not simply plastering or painting, as Foruzânfar glosses it.

5. The names of some Arabic authors and their works have been transliterated according to Persian pronunciation, for the sake of consistency with the transliteration system used in this work. Readers will encounter the conventional spellings of these names in other works as Kalâbâdhî's *Kitâb al-ta'arruf li madhhab al-tasawwuf, Qût al-qulûb, Kitâb al-luma'* of al-Sulamî, *al-Risâla* of al-Qushayrî, *Hilyat al-awliâ* of Abû Nu'aym Isfahânî, etc. My apologies to Arabists for the odd sensation this must create, but I trust they will nevertheless recognize the names.

6. See *The Doctrine of the Sûfîs* (trans. A.J. Arberry, 1935, several reprints); *The Kashf al-Mahjub* (trans. R.A. Nicholson, 1911 and frequently reprinted), *The Alchemy of Happiness* by Ghazzâli (available in several different translations); *Ruzbihan Baqli* by Carl Ernst (London: Curzon, 1996); *Early Islamic Mysticism* (trans. Michael Sells, New York: Paulist Press, 1996); *Mystical Dimensions of Islam* by Annemarie Schimmel

(Chapel Hill: University of North Carolina Press, 1975); as well as a host of other works.

7. For more information about this concept, see the translation of Jili's work by Titus Burckhardt, *Universal Man* (Sherborne: Beshara, 1983).

8. *Divân-e Sanâʾi*, ed. Modarres-e Razavi, 2nd ed. (Tehran: Sanâʾi, 1983), 1074 (for the Persian text of the poem), 34ff. (Koran interpretation), and 164, line 12 (*zekr* and *samâʿ*).

9. For the transmission history of Persian robâʿi's and ghazals see Fritz Meier, *Die schöne Mahsati: ein beitrag zur Geschichte des persischen Vierzeilers* (Wiesbaden: Franz Steiner, 1963), esp. 1–2 and 20–21. See also Franklin D. Lewis, "Reading, Writing and Recitation: Sanâʾi and the Origins of the Persian Ghazal" (Ph.D. Dissertation, University of Chicago, 1995), esp. 225–52. See also the view of M. Amin Riâhi in his edition of Râzi's Mersâd al-ʿebâd (Tehran: ʿElmi va Farhangi, 1377/1998), 67–68.

10. Interested readers may consult Fritz Meier's *Abū Saʿī d-i Abūʾl-Hayr: Wirklichkeit und Legende* (Tehran and Liège: Acta Iranica, 1976); Hellmut Ritter, "Philologika XV," *Oriens* 12 (1959): 1–88; and J.T.P. de Bruijn, "The Qalandariyyāt in Mystical Poetry" (LDL, 75–86). Ahmet Karamustafa describes the Qalandars of Anatolia during Rumi's time and in subsequent centuries in his *God's Unruly Friends* (Salt Lake City: University of Utah Press, 1994).

CHAPTER 1

1. Philologika XI: "Maulānā Ǧalāladdīn Rūmī und sein Kreis," *Der Islam* 26 (1942): 140–44.

2. In A.J. Arberry, ed. and trans. *Aspects of Islamic Civilization* (Ann Arbor, University of Michigan Press, 1967), 227–55.

3. Hellmut Ritter, "Djalâl al-Din Rumi," in *EI²* and Hamid Algar, "Bahâ al-Din Mohammad Walad," in *EIr.*

4. Concerning Balkh, see C.E. Bosworth, "Balk̲ (ii.)" in *EIr* and W. Barthold, *An Historical Geography of Iran*, trans. Svat Soucek, ed. C.E. Bosworth (Princeton: Princeton University Press, 1984), 6ff.

5. Foruzânfar's introduction to the *Maʿâref* (lâm/ze–lâm/he) shows that sermons 129, 151, 180, 192, 221, 227, 255, 265 and 261 all stem from the time Bahâ al-Din spent in Vakhsh. The dates of these sermons can be surmised on the basis of internal evidence, and Meier (Mei 15–35) builds upon this. Although Meier identified Vakhsh as the domicile of Bahâ al-Din as early as 1976 in *Abu Saʿīd-i Abū al-Hayr* (Leiden: Brill), this point has not yet sunk in with most Western scholars. Neither have Afghanis, who like to claim Rumi as a native son, nor Tâjiks, who could take legitimate pride in their compatriot and perhaps try to excavate the Islamic settlement in Vakhsh, taken notice of the likelihood that Rumi came from Vakhsh.

6. The name given to this "stone bridge" varied, depending on the language of the geographer or mapmaker describing it. It has been called Qantere al-hejâre, Pol-e sangin and Tâsh küpruk in Arabic, Persian and Turkish, respectively.

7. MRC 217–18 and J. Pedersen, "Khatib," in *EI²*. Cf. Carl Petry, *The Civilian Elite of Cairo in the Later Medieval Ages* (Princeton: Princeton University Press, 1981), 260–61.

8. On Baghdad, see *EI²* and Guy Le Strange, *Baghdad During the Abbasid Caliphate* (Oxford: Clarendon, 1900; reprinted London: Curzon/New York: Barnes & Noble, 1972), 100, 266–70, 278, 296–300.

9. Azmi Avcioglu, "Karamandʾda mader-i Mevlânâ câmi ve türbesi" *Konya dergisi* 5,35: 2088.

10. In addition to the Hanafi *madrases*, Aleppo had twenty Shâfeᶜi *madrases*, with a further eight *madrases* between the Hanbalis and Mâlekis. Aleppo was also home to six Hadith institutes, Dâr al-hadith. Beyond the thirty-four Hanafi *madrases*, Damascus had thirty-five for the Shâfeᶜis, eight for the Hanbalis and seven *madrases* with instruction in more than one school of law. By the end of the fifteenth century, Noᶜaymi counted forty-nine Hanafi schools in Damascus, three of them jointly teaching Hanafi and Shâfeᶜi law (Zia 248 n. 11).

11. See Hermann Landolt's English introduction to *Marmuzât-e asadi dar mazmurât-e Dâvudi*, ed. Mohammad-Rezâ Shafiᶜi-Kadkani (Tehran: McGill University Institute of Islamic Studies, 1973) and pages 4–5 of the text. Compare also Mei 41–2.

12. Two studies have shed a great deal of light on the interaction of Byzantine Christianity, the Greek-speaking inhabitants of Anatolia, and their Turco-Persian Muslim rulers. F.W. Hasluck provided an excellent foundation for this discussion with the two volumes of his *Christianity and Islam under the Sultans* (Oxford: Clarendon, 1929). Two subsequent books by Speros Vryonis, Jr., *The Decline of Medieval Hellenism in Asia Minor and the Process of Islamization from the Eleventh through the Fifteenth Century* (Berkeley: University of California Press, 1971) and a collection of his articles reprinted as *Studies on Byzantium, Seljuks, and Ottomans* (Malibu, CA: Undena, 1981) made great strides forward. Claude Cahen's *Pre-Ottoman Turkey*, trans. J. Jones-Williams (New York: Taplinger, 1968) also provides useful background information.

13. On the Seljuks, see John E. Woods, "The Seljuqs of Anatolia," *Encyclopaedia Britannica Online* (www.eb.com); also "Djalâl al-Dîn Khwârazmshâh," "Ghurids," "Kaykâus," "Kayḳobâd," "Kaykhusraw," by various authors, all in *EI²*; Mohammad Javâd Mashkur in his introduction to *Akhbâr-e Salâjuqe-ye Rum* (Akh), which contains an abridgement of Ibn-e Bibi; the full text of Ibn-e Bibi's chronicle is published as *El-Evâmirüʾl-ʿAlâʾiyye fîʾl-umûriʾl-ʿAlâʾiyye*, ed. Adnan Sadik Erzi (Ankara: Türk Tarih Kurumu, 1956); Mehmed Fuad Köprülü, *The Seljuks of Anatolia*, trans. Gary Leiser (Salt Lake City: University of Utah Press, 1992) and *A History of the Seljuks: Ibrahim Kafesoğlu's Interpretations and the Resulting Controversy*, trans. Gary Leiser (Carbondale: Southern Illinois University Press, 1988).

14. Mahbub-e Serâj, *Mowlânâ-ye Balkhi va pedar-ash: taʾsir-e Maʿâref bar Masnavi-ye Maʿnavi* (Kabul, 1340/1961), 42–50. Cited in Mei 6.

15. Hellmut Ritter, *Der Islam* 26 (1942): 140, 226, and *Oriens* 8 (1955): 359–61.

16. Alessandro Bausani, "Theism and Pantheism in Rumi," *Iranian Studies* 1 (1968): 10–12, 18.

17. Readers doubting the exaggerated and mythical nature of the Sufi hagiographies should consult the acts of Abu Saᶜid Ibn Abi al-Khayr as described in Mohammad b. al-Monavvar's *Asrâr al-towhid*, translated by Bernard O'Kane as *The Secrets of God's Mystical Oneness* (Costa Mesa, CA: Mazda/Bibliotheca Persica, 1992); or ᶜAttâr's *Tazkerat al-owliâ*, available in the translation and abridgement of A.J. Arberry, *Muslim Saints and Mystics* (London: Routledge & Kegan Paul, 1966).

18. See A. Gölpınarlı's Turkish translation of the *Ibtidâ nâme* (Konya: Konya Turizm Dernegi, 1976), 237n.

19. Dominique Sourdel, "Réflexions sur la diffusion de la madrasa en orient du XIe au XIIIe siècle," *Revue des études islamiques* 44 (1976): 174; and J. Sourdel-Thomine, "al-Harawī al-Mawsilī," *EI²*.

20. For information on educational institutions in Nayshâpur, see Richard Bulliet, *The Patricians of Nayshâbur* (Cambridge, MA: Harvard University Press, 1972), 249–55. For colleges in Iran generally, see Hosayn Soltânzâde, *Târikh-e madâres-e Irân: az ᶜahd-e bâstân tâ taʾsis-e Dâr al-Fonun* (Tehran: Âgâh, 1364/1985).

CHAPTER 2

1. Yâqût b. ʿAbd Allâh al-Hamawî, *Muʿjam al-buldân*, 5 vols. (Beirut: Dâr Sâdir, 1955–7), 2:285.
2. Mohammad b. Mohammad b. Sasrâ, *A Chronicle of Damascus 1389–1397*, trans. and ed. William Brinner (Berkeley: University of California Press, 1963), 1:65, 177. Note that there is also a Moqaddamiye Madrase in Aleppo, established in a converted church in 1124. This *madrase*, with an inscription from 1168 still stands, about 250 meters to the southwest of the Halâviye Madrase, near the Antioch Gate in the thirteenth-century exterior wall of Aleppo. It is entirely possible that Aflâki has confused the Moqaddamiye Madrase of Damascus with the one in Aleppo.

CHAPTER 3

1. John Woods, "Anatolia" (History of the Seljuks) *Encyclopaedia Britannica Online* (www.eb.com).
2. Jalâl al Din Rumi, *Majâles-e Sabʿe (Haft Khatâbe)*. ed. Towfiq Sobhâni (Tehran: Kayhân, 1365/1986; reprinted 1372/1993), Sermon 6, 107–11.
3. The mythical winged beast on which Mohammad ascended on his journey through the heavens.

CHAPTER 4

1. Aloys Sprenger, *A Catalogue of the Arabic, Persian and Hindustany Manuscripts of the Libraries of the King of Oudh* (Calcutta: J. Thomas, 1854), 490.
2. *Tabaqât al-Shâfiʿiyya*, ed. Kamâl Yûsuf al-Hût (Beirut: Dâr al-Kutub al-ʿIlmiyya, 1987), 1:240–41.
3. E.g. al-Esnavi, *Tabaqât al-Shafiʿiyya*, 2:232; Mov 89.
4. Omid Safi also accepts the thesis that Shaykh Mohammad is none other than Ibn ʿArabi in a forthcoming paper, "Did the Two Oceans Meet? Connections and Disconnections between Ibn al-ʿArabî and Rûmî," in *Journal of Muhyiddin Ibn ʿArabi Society.*
5. In his biography of Rumi, Foruzânfar twice refers to the *al-Kavâkeb al-moziʾe* by Mohyi al-Din ʿAbd al-Qâder, giving this name in the heading where he discusses the source (FB 57, 59). This *lapsus calami* should read *al-Javâher al-moziʾe fi tabaqât al-Hanafiye*, as it does in the rest of the book (e.g., FB 3 n. 1, 189, etc.; perhaps the confusion stems from the citation in Shebli Noʿmâni's *Savâneh*, 9). The author is Mohyi al-Din ʿAbd al-Qâder Ibn Abi al-Vafâ al-Qorayshi. Movahhed (Mov 199), following Foruzânfar's mistake, cites it as *Kavâkeb* and assumes it would be the oldest source claiming that Shams had been killed. But it is likely that Ibn Abi al-Vafâ wrote his encyclopedia as a mature scholar, in which case his version of the murder of Shams almost certainly postdates Aflâki's.
6. Aflâki relates an account (Af 155) that tells of Rumi writing a letter of intercession to Moʿin al-Din Parvâne for someone accused of murder who had taken refuge in the home of one of Rumi's disciples. The Parvâne replied that a case of murder was not something that he could have an influence over, to which Rumi replied that a person who slays another is considered the son of the Angel of Death, suggesting that the killer works on behalf of divine decree. This answer pleased the Parvâne, who helped get the victim's family to consent to a charge of manslaughter and accept a payment of blood money, so that the killer could be freed.

If this anecdote has any basis in fact, which seems questionable, it certainly does not pertain to Shams al-Din, who disappeared in 1247 or 1248, before the Mongols appointed Mo'in al-Din as Rokn al-Din's representative (1256) and well before he came to power in Konya (1261). Prior to that, Mo'in al-Din would have been a military commander in Tokat. Besides, Aflâki's account implies that the killer on the run in this case was an unknown individual and not someone associated with Rumi or his family. Another anecdote related by Aflâki describes Rumi writing to 'Alam al-Din Qaysar on behalf of a preacher very devoted to Rumi who had punched someone who spoke ill of Rumi, killing him, and fled to Rumi's home in Konya. He was eventually released upon payment of 40,000 dirhams as blood money to the relatives (Af 459). Quite likely the account which attributes this incident to the Parvâne does so incorrectly; 'Alam al-Din acted as a governor under Kay Khosrow III (r. 1264–82) and again cannot have had anything to do with the death of Shams.

These anecdotes do show, however, what we already knew by common sense: murder and manslaughter could not simply be ignored in Seljuk Konya, even by the powerful. If these anecdotes have any basis in fact, they prove that cases of murder could not be hushed up. The whole town of Konya would have found out about the case in question because it involved the mediation of the de facto ruler of the Seljuk empire, the family of the victim, the family or friends of the accused, and at least one judge (though not mentioned in the tale, a judge would have had to be involved in finalizing the blood money payment). It strains credulity to the breaking point to imagine that such a thing could have been kept a secret.

7. See "Damascus" in *EI²* and William Brinner's annotations and maps in his translation of Muhammad b. Sasrâ's *A Chronicle of Damascus, 1389–1397* (Berkeley: University of California Press, 1963).

8. Farhad Daftary, *The Ismailis: Their History and Doctrines* (Cambridge: Cambridge University Press, 1990), 415.

9. Fasih-e Khavâfi, *Mojmal-e Fasihi*, ed. Mahmud Farrokh, 2 vols. (Mashhad, 1339–40/ 1960–61), 2:380; cited Mov 208.

10. Khavâfi, *Mojmal* 2:343; cited Mov 208.

11. Mohammad Amin-Riâhi, "Manâr-e Shams-e Tabriz dar Khuy va Qâzi Rokn al-Din Khu'i, mamduh-e Khâqâni," *Yaghma* 11,1 (Farvardin 1337/April–May 1979): 5–11.

12. Mohammad Amin-Riâhi, *Târikh-e Khuy* (Tehran: Tus, 1372/1993), 94.

CHAPTER 5

1. For more general information on these brotherhoods, see Claude Cahen and F. Taeschner, "Futuwwa" and Taeschner, "Akhi" and "Akhi Ewrân" in *EI²*.

2. Mikâil Bayram, *Ahi Evren ve Ahi Teşkilâtı'nın Kuruluşu* (Konya: M. Bayram, 1991) and *Fatma Bacı ve Baciyân-ı Rûm* (Konya: M. Bayram, 1994). For the life of Akhi Evren and his activities in Konya, as well as the attitude of Rumi, Hosâm al-Din and the Mevlevis toward him, see especially *Ahi Evren*, 80–96. The comment about the allusions to Ahi Evren in the *Masnavi* were made by Bayram in an interview with the author (May 15, 1999).

3. See *Divanı Sultan Veled*, ed. F. Nafiz Uzluk (Ankara: Uzluk Basımevi, 1941), 1.

4. E.J.W. Gibb, *History of Ottoman Poetry* (London: Luzac & Co., 1900–1909), 1:141–63.

5. Mecdut Mansuroğlu prepared an edition that attempts to do that by presenting the Turkish poems in Latin transcription along with facsimiles of the manuscript in Persian script: *Sultan Veled'in Türkçe Manzumeleri* (Istanbul: Pulhan Matbaasi, 1958). One of Sultan Valad's descendants, Qestamuni Mab'uni Velet Chelebi (1869–?), had earlier

collected these Turkish poems and an edition appeared in Ottoman Turkish as *Divân-e Torki-ye Soltân Valad (qoddesa serroho)*, edited by Kalb‘ali Mo‘allem Raf‘at (1876–1953) at the ‘Amere Press in Istanbul in 1922 (A.H. 1341). This 132-page text was reprinted in 1925 (A.H. 1343). Recently, M.S. Fomkin has produced a Russian study of these Turkish-language poems as *Sultan Veled i ego tiurkskaia poeziia* (Moscow: "Nauka," Izdatelskaia firma "Vostochnaia lit-ra," 1994). Meanwhile, the Greek verses from the *Rabâb nâme*, along with some extracts from the Greek poems in the *Divân*, are presented by P. Burguière and R. Mantran in "Quelques vers grecs du XIIIe siècle," *Byzantion* 22 (1952): 63–80.

CHAPTER 6

1. Khvâjeh Sadid al-Din Mohammad Ghaznavi, *The Colossal Elephant and his Spiritual Feats (Shaykh Ahmad-e Jâm)*, trans. Heshmat Moayyad and Franklin Lewis (forthcoming).

2. Reproductions of these miniatures can be seen in *Mevlana Celaleddin Rumi and the Whirling Dervishes* (Istanbul: Dost Yayinlari, 1983) by Talat Sait Halman and Metin And; in Rachel Milstein's *Miniature Painting in Ottoman Baghdad* (Costa Mesa, CA: Mazda, 1990); and in A. Süheyl Ünver's *Sevakıb-ı menakıb: Mevlânâ'dan hatıralar* (Istanbul: Organon, 1973).

3. Mohammad Taqi Bahâr, *Sabk Shenâsi*, 3 vols. (Tehran: Amir Kabir, 1370/1991), 3: 185.

CHAPTER 7

1. See John Woods, "Anatolia" (History of the Seljuks), *Encyclopaedia Britannica Online* (www.eb.com); Carole Hillenbrand, "Mu‘in al-Din Parvâne," in *El²*; Mak 289–99 on Parvâne.

2. See, e.g., Manuchehr Saduqi-Sohâ, "Elteqâ-ye do daryâ," *Kayhân-e andishe* 61, pp. 3–10; Sayyed Hasan Amin, "Molâqât-e Mowlânâ bâ Ebn-e ‘Arabi," *Kayhân-e andishe* 69, pp. 145–9; Sayyed Hasan Amin, "Payvand-e Mowlânâ-ye Rumi bâ Ebn-e ‘Arabi," *Iran Shenasi* 9, 3 (Fall 1997): 465–79.

3. *Yâd nâme-ye Mowlavi*, ed. ‘Ali-Akbar Moshir-Salimi (Tehran: UNESCO–Iran Commission, 1337/1958), 141, 148.

4. An online description of the Chester Beatty Collection of Islamic MSS may be seen at www.cbl.ie/coislm.htm.

5. Franklin D. Lewis, "Reading Writing and Recitation: Sanâ’i and the Origins of the Persian Ghazal," (Ph.D. dissertation, University of Chicago, 1995), 225–52.

6. See R.A. Nicholson, *The Mathnawí of Jalálu’ddín Rúmí*, vol. 1 (London: Luzac & Co., 1925), English introduction, 11.

7. Nicholson, *Mathnawí*, 1:12.

8. R.A. Nicholson, *The Mathnawí of Jalálu’ddín Rúmí*, vol. 5 (London: Luzac & Co., 1933), xviii.

9. R.A. Nicholson, *The Mathnawí of Jalálu’ddín Rúmí*, vol. 3 (London: Luzac & Co., 1929), xv–xviii.

10. Nicholson, *Mathnawí*, 5: xvi.

11. *The Mathnawí of Jalálu’ddín Rúmí, edited from the oldest manuscripts available; with critical notes, translation, and commentary* (London: Luzac & Co.). Volume 1: Persian Text, Books 1–2 (1925); Volume 2: English Translation (1926); Volume 3: Persian Text, Books 3–4 (1929); Volume 4: English Translation (1930); Volume 5: Persian Text,

Books 5–6 (1933); Volume 6: English Translation (1934); Volume 7: Commentary, Books 1–2 (1937); Volume 8: Commentary, Books 3–6 (1940).

12. Nicholson, *Mathnawi*, 1: 18–19.

13. See *A Sufi Rule for Novices*, trans and ed. Menahem Milson (Cambridge, MA: Harvard University Press, 1975).

14. Faqih Ahmad is mentioned several times by Aflâki (e.g., Af 39–40). He was apparently a disciple of Bahâ al-Din and became a wandering hermit. For a poem ascribed to Ahmad-e Faqih, see *Charkh nâme* in Fevziye Abdullah Tansel, *Turk-Islam edebiyati: Türkçe Dinî Metinler*, vol. 2 (Ankara: Üniversitesi Basımevi, 1971), 5–7.

15. *Rashf al-nasâʾeh al-imâniye*, ed. Najib Mâyel Haravi (Tehran: Bonyâd, 1986), 13–14.

16. These occur at Bah 1:10, 11, 108, 129, 208, 223, 225, 238, 259, 267, 276, 331, 332, 347, 360, 403; and Bah 2:19, 77, 95.

17. First, Şerefeddin Yaltkaya's article, "Mevlâna da Türkçe kelimelar ve Türkçe siirler" in *Turkiyat Mecmuasi* (1934): 112–68; and then Mecdut Mansuroğlu's "Celaluddin Rumi's Turkish verse," in *Ural-altaische Jahrbücher* 24 (1952): 106–15. Hosayn Mohammadzâde Saddiq reconstructs several of Rumi's Turkish poems in his *Sayr-i dar ashʿâr-e Torki-ye maktab-e Mevleviye* (Tehran: Qoqnus, 1990), and critiques Foruzânfar for having distorted these lines beyond recognition in his edition of the *Divân-e Shams*.

18. P. Burguière and R. Mantran, "Quelques vers grecs du XIII siècle en caractères arabs," *Byzantion* 22 (1952): 63–79.

19. Gölpınarlı, "Mawlânâ, Şams-i Tabrîzî ile altmış iki yaşında Buluştu," *Şarkıyat Mecmuası* 3 (1959): 156–61. Cited in Mov 127ff. Cf. the earlier GM 97.

20. See ScT 12. Schimmel does not, however, cite either Waley or Gölpınarlı's *Şarkiyat Mecmuası* article in this regard and may be working only from Gölpınarlı's earlier partial argument in GM 97. Jan Rypka, *History of Iranian Literature* (Dordrecht: D. Reidel, 1968), 244 n. 76.

21. Waley, "'Free Once More': Notes on the Chronology of Jalal Ad-din Rumi's Life," in *Mevlâna ve ya ama Sevinici*, ed. F. Halici (Konya: Konya Turizm Dernegi, 1978).

CHAPTER 9

1. R.A. Nicholson, *The Idea of Personality in Sufism* (Cambridge: Cambridge University Press, 1923), 51; E.H. Whinfield, *Masnavi i Maʾnavi*, 2nd ed. (London: K. Paul, Trench, Trubner & Co., 1898), xxxv.

2. R.A. Nicholson, *Mystics of Islam* (London: G. Bell & Sons, 1914; reprinted Routledge & Kegan Paul, 1979; Arkana, 1989), 100.

CHAPTER 10

1. *Tarâʾeq al-haqâʾeq* (Tehran, 1318/1900) 2:140–41; cited in Saf 3/1:456. The critical edition in three volumes by Mohammad Jaʿfar Mahjub (Tehran: Sanâʾi) in the 1970s has replaced the previous edition cited by Safâ, but I did not have access to it.

2. Tafazzoli included this and other poems Sarmad composed on this journey to Turkey in the collection *Naghme-ye kamâl*; cited in Taf 3–4 n. 1.

3. Lütfi Kaleli's *Alevi, Sünni inancinda Mevlana, Yunus ve Hacı Bektaş gerçegi* (Istanbul: Alev, 1993) studies the cross-fertilization of various Sufi groups in Anatolia, specifically, Rumi, Yunus Emre (1241–32) and Hâji Bektâsh (1210–71).

4. On Ibn Battûta, see Charles Beckingham, "Ebn Battûta," in *EIr*. The evaluation of Ibn Battûta as a source comes from Ross E. Dunn, *The Adventures of Ibn Battuta* (Berkeley:

University of California Press, 1986), 310–16. The Hakluyt Society has made the entire narrative available in a four-volume English translation by H.A.R. Gibb.

5. M. Şükrü Hanioğlu, *The Young Turks in Opposition* (Oxford: Oxford University Press, 1995), 54–5, 85, 251.

6. Klaus Kreiser, "Notes sur le présent et le passé des ordres mystique en Turquie," 55; Alexandre Popovic, "Sud-Est Europeén," 77 and Fred de Jong, "Machreq Arabe," 214, all in *Les Ordres mystiques dans L'Islam*, ed. Alexandre Popovic and Gilles Veinstein (Paris: L'École des Hautes Études en Sciences Sociales, 1986).

7. Nasra Hassan, "One Hundred Steps to Mevlana," *Eye of the Heart* 3,1 (May 1999): 9–13; Dror Ze'evi, *An Ottoman Century: The District of Jerusalem in the 1600s* (Albany, NY: SUNY Press, 1996), 69.

8. Fred de Jong, "Machreq Arabe," p. 214 in *Les Ordres mystiques dans L'Islam*; B. Foruzânfar, "She'r-e Mowlavi," in *Yâd nâme-ye Mowlavi*, ed. 'Ali-Akbar Moshir-Salimi (Tehran: UNESCO–Iran Commission, 1337/1958), 147; and an article by Mohammad Javâd Mashkur and Hasan-e Gharavi-ye Esfahâni about the Mevlevis in Damascus, "Sufiân-e Mowlavi dar Dameshq," in *Honar va mardom* 151 (1354/1975).

9. Heshmat Moayyad, "Safar nâme-ye Shâm," *Iran Shenasi* 6, 1 (Spring 1994), 4.

10. From Rida's *al-Manâr wa al-Azhâr* (Cairo: Matba'at al-Manâr, 1934), 171–2, cited in Albert Hourani, *Arabic Thought in the Liberal Age* (Cambridge: Cambridge University Press, 1983), 225.

11. F. de Jong, *Turuq and Turuq-Linked Institutions in Nineteenth Century Egypt* (Leiden: Brill, 1978), 65–77, 80, 84 n. 263, 170 n. 177.

12. Alexandre Bennigsen and S. Enders Wimbush, *Mystics and Commissars: Sufism in the Soviet Union* (Berkeley: University of California Press, 1985).

13. A number of local histories, mostly in Turkish, have reconstructed the development of these important centers. These include *Türk Vakıf medeniyetinde Hz. Mevlânâ ve mevlevihanelerin yeri semineri* (Ankara: Vakıflar Genel Müdürlüğü yayınları, 1992), which gives information on the endowed properties of the Mevlevis in Turkey; Irfan Ünver Nasrattinoğlu's study of Divâne Chelebi and the Mevlevis in Karahisar, *Mevlana'nın torunu Sultan Divani ve Afyonkarahisar Mevlevi dergahı* (Ankara: MN Ofset, 1990); and Ahmet Suheyl Ünver's article about the establishment of the Mevlevi order in Salonika, Greece, "Selânik Mevlevîhanesi 1913–15," *Mevlânâ Yıllığı* (Konya: Turizm Derneği, 30–33).

14. See Raymond Lifchez, "Lodges of Istanbul," in LDL, 73–129, esp. 101–13 on the Mevlevi lodges, which include many drawings and plans, including the Galata Mevlevi lodge. See also the article "Galata Mevlevihanesi" by Aslı Kayabal in *Sky Life*, the magazine of the Turkish Airlines (no. 158, July 1996). This article is available online at: www.access.ch/tuerkei/GRUPE/skylife/Galata.htm; one may also check the display at www.kultur.gov.tr/b-a-divan.html. Can Keramteli's *Galata Mevlevihanesi, Divan Edebiyatı Müzesi* ([Istanbul]: Touring and Automobile Club of Turkey, 1977) offers many photographs of the beautiful *samâ'* hall with its chandelier and two-story observation balcony.

CHAPTER 11

1. For studies of the influence of Rumi on the literature of the Muslim world, one should consult the numerous articles and books of Schimmel, especially ScT and ScP, *Mevlâna Celâlettin Rumi'nin Şark ve Garp'ta tesirleri* (Ankara: Gutenberg Matbaası, 1963), and her *Gabriel's Wing: A Study into the Religious Ideas of Sir Muhammad Iqbal* (Leiden: Brill, 1963). See also Afzal Iqbal, *The Impact of Mowlânâ Jalâluddin Rumi on Islamic*

Culture (Tehran: RCD Cultural Institute, 1974), and Shojâ^c al-Din Shafâ, "Naqsh-e Mowlavi dar adabiyât-e jahân," in *Yâd nâme-ye Mowlavi*, ed. ^cAli-Akbar Moshir-Salimi (Tehran: UNESCO–Iran Commission, 1337/1958), 104–9.

2. Schimmel, *Gabriel's Wing*, 355.
3. Refer to Saiyid Athar Abbas Rizvi, *Shah Wali Allah and his Times* (Canberra, Australia: Marifat Publishing House, 1980); N.A. Baloch, *Maulana Jalaluddin Rumi's Influence on Shah Abdul Latif* (International Mevlana Seminar, Ankara, 1973); and Schimmel's *Pain and Grace* (Leiden: Brill, 1976) for these and other examples.
4. For more on this commentary, see Juan Cole's discussion at http://h-net2.msu.edu/ -bahai/notes/vol3/rumi.htm.
5. *The Intimate Life of an Ottoman Statesman*, trans. Robert Dankoff (Albany, NY: SUNY Press, 1991), 279.
6. Readers interested in this work – "Beauty and Love" – and its intertexuality with Rumi's *Masnavi* should consult Victoria Holbrook's study, *The Unreadable Shores of Love* (Austin: University of Texas Press, 1994; esp. pp. 32–50).
7. Aziz Ahmad, *Islamic Modernism in India and Pakistan, 1857–1964* (Oxford: Oxford University Press, 1967), 176–7.
8. See the various essays in *Iqbal: Poet-Philosopher of Pakistan*, ed. Hafeez Malik (New York: Columbia University Press, 1971) and Schimmel, *Gabriel's Wing*, 353–62.
9. Rajmohan Gandhi, *Eight Lives: A Study of the Hindu–Muslim Encounter* (Albany, NY: SUNY Press, 1986), 295.
10. S.A.H. Abidi, "Maulânâ Jalâl-ud-din Rumi, his Times and Relevance to Indian Thought," in *The Maulavi Flute*, ed. S.H. Qasemi (New Delhi: New Age International, 1997), 219–25.
11. Eva de Vitray-Meyerovitch, *Mystique et poésie en Islam*, 61, cited by Rachel Milstein, *Miniature Painting in Ottoman Baghdad* (Costa Mesa, CA: Mazda, 1990), 3.
12. For a biography of Beh Âzin and a translation of one of his stories, see Heshmat Moayyad, ed., *Stories From Iran: A Chicago Anthology* (Washington, D.C.: Mage, 1992), 87ff.
13. On Soroush, see Afshin Matin-Asgari, "'Abdolkarim Sorush and the Secularization of Islamic Thought in Iran," *Journal of Iranian Studies* 30, 1–2 (Winter/Spring, 1997): 95–115. See also the article by Scott MacLeod in *Time* magazine 149, 25 (June 23, 1997); the web site affiliated with Soroush and his supporters: www.seraj.org and www.iranian.com/Feb97/Editor/Letters/Houston.html.

CHAPTER 12

1. Jes Asmussen, "Hans Christian Andersen and Jalâlu'd-Din Rumi's Whirling Dervishes," *Temenos* 16 (1980): 5–9.
2. This information comes from Theofanis Stavrou and Peter Weisensel, *Russian Travelers to the Christian East: From the Twelfth to the Twentieth Centuries*, (Columbus, OH: Slavica Publishers, 1985), 327, 333–4, 387, 748.
3. R. Kodve-Khorb, "Maulawis Mystik und seine Dialektik," in *Trudi XXV mezhdunarodni Kongressa Vostokovedov* (Moscow, 1963), 2:362–4 and Ehsân Tabari (under the pseudonym Emâmi), *Mowlânâ Jalâl al-Din: Hegel-e sharq ast* (Tehran: Nashriât-e Beh-pish, n.d.).
4. Florence Nightingale, *Suggestions for Thought*, ed. M. Calabria and J. Macrae (Philadelphia: University of Pennsylvania Press, 1994), xxiii–xxxv, and Hartmut Bobzin, "Christian Carl Josias von Bunsen und sein Beitrag zum Studium Orientalischer Sprachen," in *Universeller Geist und guter Europäer: Christian Carl Josias von Bunsen*, ed. H.R. Ruppel (Kohrbach: Bing, 1991), 81–102.

5. Coomaraswamy, "Understanding and Reunion: An Oriental Perspective," in *The Asian Legacy and American Life*, ed. Arthur Christy (New York: Greenwood, 1968; originally published 1942), 229.

6. For the text of Trumbore's sermon, see the web site: www.cyberstreet.com/trumbore/sermons/s5c3.htm. For Aquinas and Rumi, see John Renard's "The Dominican and the Dervish: A Christian–Muslim Dialog That Might Have Been between Aquinas and Rumi," *Journal of Ecumenical Studies* 26 (Spring 1992); for John of the Cross and Rumi, the 1992 honors thesis by Hafez Nasr at the College of William and Mary; and finally Chohre Rassekh, *Mystical Poetry of Jalaloddin Rumi and Jacopone da Todi: A Comparison* (Ottawa: National Library of Canada, 1989).

7. Gurdjieff, "The Echo of the Champs-Elysées" I, 37, part 2, as cited by Idries Shah. See "Omar M. Burke," *Among the Dervishes*, 2nd ed. (London: Octagon, 1993); something called the "Sarmoun Society of North America" maintains a web site at members.tripod.com/~Sarmoun/index.html.

8. See Walker, *A Study of Gurdjieff's Teaching* (London: Jonathan Cape, 1957), 195; and James Webb, *The Harmonious Circle* (New York: Putnam, 1980), 410.

9. "Murshid Sam, an American Original," *Caravanserai: the Journal of the International Sufi Movement*, 19 (Spring 1996): 28–33. See also Murshid Sam's autobiographical *Sufi Vision and Initiation*, ed. Neil Douglas-Klotz, a.k.a. Murshid Saadi Shakur (San Francisco: Prophecy Publications, 1986) and his *The Jerusalem Trilogy: Song of the Prophets* (Novato, CA: Prophecy Pressworks, 1975), which includes his poems. My account also draws upon J. Gordon Melton, *Encyclopedia of American Religions*, 6th ed. (Detroit: Gale Research, 1999), and information provided by some former students of Lewis and posted to the Tariqas mailing list April 17–19, 1998.

10. For a history of Sufism in the West, see the detailed study by Andrew Rawlinson in *Diskus* 1,1 (1993): 45–83, and the web site at www.unimarburg.de/fb11/religionswissenschaft/journal/diskus/rawlinson.html, upon which the account given here of Bennett, Feild and Pir Vilayat Khan draws heavily. See also Carl Ernst, *Shambhala Guide to Sufism* (Boston, MA: Shambhala, 1997).

11. From the liner notes to the LP-album *Raga*, the soundtrack for the movie of the same name (Apple Records SWAO3384, 1971).

12. *The Balance of Truth*, trans. G.L. Lewis (London: Allen & Unwin, 1957), 43ff.

13. The information on the Mevlevi Order of America comes from conversations with some of the followers of Jelaluddin Loras and from the *Lovers of Mevlana* journal, including Fatima Lassar, "Like a Kindly Grandfather," 3, 2 (Summer 1998): 17 and Michael Bielas, "Shrine of Divine Lovers," 3,1 (Spring 1998): 11–13.

14. Email: mevlana@cruzio.com; fax: 831–465–1057.

15. This information comes from several articles in the Threshold Society's journal, *Eye of the Heart*; from personal correspondence with Kabir Helminski; as well as from *Contemporary Authors*, and Melton, *Encyclopedia of American Religions*. See also the article "Sufi Faith Gains a Foothold in Vermont's Green Hills," in the *Washington Post*, January 19, 1997.

16. See Müge Galin, *Between East and West: Sufism in the Novels of Doris Lessing* (Albany, NY: SUNY Press, 1997) and Shadia Fahim, *Doris Lessing and Sufi Equilibirum: The Evolving Form of the Novel* (New York: St. Martin's Press, 1994).

CHAPTER 13

1. *The Letters of Sir William Jones*, ed. Garland Cannon (Oxford: Clarendon, 1970), 632, 735. The title is given as "Mesnair," though this may possibly result from a misreading of Jones' handwriting.

2. *The Idea of Personality in Sufism* (Cambridge: Cambridge University Press, 1923), 51–2.

3. For example, Schimmel gives contrary information in *Triumphal Sun*'s citations of Kovde-Khorb, ScT 391 and 480.

4. The biographical information on Foruzânfar is taken from volume 1 of his introduction to the *Kolliyât-e Shams* and from a series of commemorative articles in *Kelk* 73–5 (March–June 1996) written by his students and colleagues, especially Hosayn Khatibi (203–5) and ʿAbd al-Hosayn Zarrinkub (210ff.). The story of Foruzânfar's correction of a Syrian professor's pronunciation of Arabic comes from Heshmat Moayyad's "Safar nâme-ye Shâm," *Iran Shenasi* 6, 1 (Fall 1994): 10–11.

5. Some of these quotations are given in Arberry's foreword (pp. v–vi) to Afzal Iqbal's *The Life and Thought of Maulana Jalal-ud-Din Rumi* in 1956. For Foruzânfar, see his "Sheʿr-e Mowlavi," in *Yâdnâme-ye Mowlavi*, ed. ʿAli-Akbar Moshir-Salimi (Tehran: UNESCO–Iran Commission, 1337/1958), 151, 152.

CHAPTER 14

1. Lord Teignmouth, *Memoirs of the Life, Writings, and Correspondence, of Sir William Jones* (Philadelphia: W.M. Poyntell, 1805), 34–5. Gentius' edition and translation of Saʿdi was published in 1651 as *Musladini Sadi Rosarium politicum, sive, Amoenum sortis humanae theatrum: de Persico in Latinum versum.*

2. *The Collected Works of Sir William Jones*, ed. Garland Cannon, 13 vols. (New York: New York University Press, 1993), 4: 230–31.

3. See Schimmel, *Triumphal Sun* (ScT 388–92) for an outline of the history of German translations of Rumi. Schimmel, who edited the collected works of Rückert in two volumes (*Ausgewählte Werke*, 1987), has analyzed them as well in her *Orientalische Dichtung in der Übersetzung Friedrich Rückerts* (Bremen: Schünemann, 1963). She has also contributed an article, "Ein unbekanntes Werk Joseph von Hammer-Purgstalls" ("An Unknown Work of Hammer-Purgstall") in *Die Welt des Islams*, n.s. 15, 1974). Note, however, Hartmut Bobzin's corrections of the dates and details given by Schimmel in his "Platen und Rückert im Gespräch über Hafis," in *August Graf von Platen: Leben, Werk, Wirkung*, ed. H. Bobzin and G. Och, 104–21 (Paderborn: Ferdinand Schöningh, 1998).

4. See Hulya Naciye Unlu, "Form, Gehalt und Symbolik des orientalischen Ghasels in der deutschen Dichtung" (Ph.D. dissertation, University of Michigan, 1989). See also Ursula Wertheim, *Von Tasso zu Hafis* (Berlin: Rütten & Loening, 1965) and Bobzin, "Platen und Rückert," 108–9.

5. Emerson; *Collected Poems and Translations* (Library of America, 1994), 495.

6. *Letters of Edward FitzGerald*, ed. Alfred and Annabelle Terhune (Princeton: Princeton University Press, 1980), 1:594; 2:25, 50, 122, 135, 157, 172, 261, 15, 465, 569, 571; 3:20, 78, 262, 321, 404, 406, 477, 551, 667.

7. Flecker, *Collected Poems*, 87. See also John Sherwood, *No Golden Journey* (London: Heinemann, 1973) for details of Flecker's life and career, esp. 78–100 and 186.

8. Bill Moyers, *The Language of Life: A Festival of Poets* (New York: Doubleday, 1995), 46.

9. Moyers, *The Language of Life*, 43.

10. Moyers, *The Language of Life*, 45.

11. See the comparison of one Barks/Moyne poem from *Open Secret* with a literal translation by Dick Davis in Müge Galin, *Between East and West* (Albany, NY: SUNY Press, 1997), 46–9. Comparison may also be made between some of the versions in this present volume with those of Barks/Moyne.

12. K.K. Ruthven, *A Guide to Ezra Pound's Personae (1926)* (Berkeley: University of California Press, 1969) and Ronald Bush, "Pound and Li Po: What Becomes a Man," in *Ezra Pound Among the Poets*, ed. George Bornstein, pp. 35–62 (Chicago: University of Chicago Press, 1985).

13. The book appears in the series "Element Classics of Spirituality," published simultaneously in Brisbane, Australia; Shaftesbury, England; and Rockport, Massachusetts. Element Classics produced editions of the Bhagavad Gita, the Dhammapada, the Tao Te Ching, Pilgrim's Progress and The Cloud of Unknowing along with Cowan's Rumi in 1997.

14. See Mother Meera's web page: mothermeera.com/home.html for more information.

15. Samples of Khalili's translation of Rumi can be found on the Web at www.directnet. com/books/rumipoem.html. Khalili's biographical information: www.calearth.org/booksand.htm. Chittick's evaluation at: www.directnet.com/books/rumiintro.html.

CHAPTER 15

1. Talat Sait Halman and Metin And, *Mevlana Celaleddin Rumi and the Whirling Dervishes: Sufi Philosophy, Whirling Rituals, Poems of Ecstasy, Miniature Paintings* (Istanbul: Dost, 1983; 2nd ed. 1992), 73; Wolfgang Sieber, "Musikalischer Exotismus bei Ludwig van Beethoven," in *Gedenkschrift Hermann Beck*, ed. Hermann Dechant and W. Sieber, pp. 133–42 (Laaber: Laaber Verlag, 1982); Heinz-Peter Seidel, "Studien zum Usul Devir kebir in den Peşrev der Mevlevi," *Mitteilungen der Deutschen Gesellschaft für Musik des Orients* 11 (1972–3): 8–69; Kamae Miller, ed., *Wisdom Comes Dancing: Selected Writings of Ruth St. Denis on Dance, Spirituality and the Body* (Seattle: PeaceWorks, 1997).

2. Halman and And, *Mevlana Celaleddin Rumi*, 74–5.

3. Nezih Uzel in Ira Shems Friedlander, *The Whirling Dervishes* (New York: Macmillan, 1975; Albany, NY: SUNY Press, 1992), 127–41, Halman and And, *Mevlana Celaleddin Rumi* and the liner notes from the CDs below provide descriptive accounts of the ceremony. See also the description on the Threshold Society website: www.webcom. com/threshld. For scholarly discussion, in addition to the works in French, especially that of Marijan Molé, a number of articles in German by Hellmut Ritter, Fritz Meier, K. Reinhard and H.P. Seidel provide analysis of the Mevlevi musical and dance tradition. In Turkish, there is *Hz. Mevlânâ ve Mevlevi âyînleri* (Çemberlitaş, Istanbul, Milliyetciler Dernegi, 1969) and two compilations of music titled *Mevlevi ayinleri*, the first edited by Rauf Yekta (Istanbul, 1923–39) and the second by Sadettin Heper (Konya: Konya Turzim Dernegi, 1974 and 1979); and also *Sermu'ezzin Rifat Bey'in ferahnâk Mevlevi ayini*, ed. Bulent Aksoy (Beşiktaş, Istanbul: Pan, 1992).

4. Christina Damyer, "Touching Heaven with Turkey's Whirling Dervishes," *San Francisco Chronicle* (June 3, 1990, T6); Carla Hunt, "Turkey's Dervishes to Whirl in December," *Travel Weekly* (November 19, 1997 [1956, 72], E7); Sherry Marker, "A Whirl Through Istanbul, *New York Times*, Late Edition (August 16, 1998, Sec. 5, 6).

5. Regula Qureshi, *Sufi Music of India and Pakistan* (Chicago: University of Chicago Press, 1995, 27–9, and track 6 on the accompanying CD).

6. See www.wakan.com.

Index

[handwritten margin note: Fattal, S. 544]

McNaughton, D
519